THE
MICHELIN

GREAT BRITAIN | IRELAND

THE MICHELIN GUIDE'S COMMITMENTS
EXPERIENCED IN QUALITY!

Whether they are in Japan, the USA, China or Europe, our inspectors apply the same criteria to judge the quality of each and every hotel and restaurant that they visit. The Michelin guide commands a worldwide reputation thanks to the commitments we make to our readers – and we reiterate these below:

Anonymous inspections

Our inspectors make regular and anonymous visits to hotels and restaurants to gauge the quality of products and services offered to an ordinary customer. They settle their own bill and may then introduce themselves and ask for more information about the establishment. Our readers' comments are also a valuable source of information, which we can follow up with a visit of our own.

Independence

To remain totally objective for our readers, the selection is made with complete independence. Entry into the guide is free. All decisions are discussed with the Editor and our highest awards are considered at a European level.

Our famous one ✿, two ✿✿ and three ✿✿✿ stars identify establishments serving the highest quality cuisine – taking into account the quality of ingredients, the mastery of techniques and flavours, the levels of creativity and, of course, consistency.

Selection and choice

The guide offers a selection of the best hotels and restaurants in every category of comfort and price. This is only possible because all the inspectors rigorously apply the same methods.

✿✿✿ THREE MICHELIN STARS
Exceptional cuisine, worth a special journey!
Our highest award is given for the superlative cooking of chefs
at the peak of their profession. The ingredients are exemplary,
the cooking is elevated to an art form and their dishes are often
destined to become classics.

✿✿ TWO MICHELIN STARS
Excellent cooking, worth a detour!
The personality and talent of the chef and their team is evident
in the expertly crafted dishes, which are refined, inspired and
sometimes original.

✿ ONE MICHELIN STAR
High quality cooking, worth a stop!
Using top quality ingredients, dishes with distinct flavours are
carefully prepared to a consistently high standard.

😊 BIB GOURMAND
Good quality, good value cooking.
'Bibs' are awarded for simple yet skilful cooking for under £28
or €40.

Annual updates
All the practical information, classifications and awards
are revised and updated every year to give the most
reliable information possible.

Consistency
The criteria for the classifications are the same in every
country covered by the MICHELIN guide.

The sole intention
of Michelin is to make
your travels safe
and enjoyable.

Follow our
anonymous inspectors:
@MichelinGuideUK

Patricia Niven

4

DEAR READER

We are delighted to present the 2017 edition of the *Michelin* guide to Great Britain and Ireland – a guide to the best places to eat and stay in England, Wales, Scotland, Northern Ireland and the Republic of Ireland.

● The guide caters for every type of visitor, from business traveller to families on holiday, and lists the best establishments across all categories of comfort and price – from lively bistros and intimate townhouses to celebrated restaurants and luxurious hotels. So, whether you're visiting for work or pleasure, you'll find something that's right for you.

● All of the establishments in the guide have been selected by our team of famous Michelin inspectors, who are the eyes and ears of our readers. They always pay their own bills and their anonymity is key to ensuring that they receive the same treatment as any other guest. Each year, they search for new establishments to add – and only the best make it through! The 'best of the best' are then recognised with awards.

● Our famous one ✿, two ✿✿ and three ✿✿✿ stars identify establishments serving the highest quality cuisine – taking into account the quality of ingredients, the mastery of techniques and flavours, the levels of creativity and, of course, consistency. Stars are not our only awards; look out too for the Bib Gourmands ⓐ, which highlight restaurants offering good quality, good value cooking.

● Michelin Travel Partner is committed to remaining at the forefront of the culinary world and to meeting the needs of our readers. Please don't hesitate to contact us – we'd love to hear your opinions on the establishments listed within these pages, as well as those you feel could be of interest for future editions.

● We hope you enjoy your dining and hotel experiences – happy travelling with the 2017 edition of the Michelin guide!

CONTENTS

Introduction

The MICHELIN guide's commitments 2

Dear reader 4

A culinary History 8

Seek and select: how to use this guide 12

2017... New awards in this year's guide 14

Map of Starred establishments 16

Map of Bib Gourmand establishments 18

Restaurants & Hotels   20

GREAT BRITAIN

Great Britain & Ireland map 22

● London 24
   Stars and Bib Gourmands 28
   London Index 30
   Maps 170

● England 214
   Maps 216
   Stars and Bib Gourmands 242
   Our Top Picks 246

● Scotland 642
   Maps 644
   Stars and Bib Gourmands 652
   Our Top Picks 653

● Wales 746
   Maps 748
   Stars and Bib Gourmands 750
   Our Top Picks 751

House of Tides

IRELAND

● **Northern Ireland** **790**
   Maps 792
   Stars and Bib Gourmands 794
   Our Top Picks 795

● **Republic of Ireland** **812**
   Maps 814
   Stars and Bib Gourmands 818
   Our Top Picks 819

Index of towns   **916**

Index of maps   **934**

Town plan key   **935**

A CULINARY HISTORY

Britain hasn't always been known for its vibrant culinary scene – indeed, the food of the 'masses' started out dull and dreary, with meals driven by need rather than desire. So how did we get to where we are today? Well, it took quite a few centuries...

There's no place like Rome

The Romans kick-started things with their prolific road building, opening up the country and allowing goods to be transported more easily, country-wide. The Vikings brought with them new smoking and drying techniques for preserving fish, and the Saxons, who were excellent farmers, cultivated a wide variety of herbs – used not only for flavouring but to bulk-out stews. They also made butter, cheese and mead (a drink made from fermented honey); with the lack of sugar to sweeten things, honey was very important, and bees were kept in every village. The Normans introduced saffron, nutmeg, pepper, ginger and sugar – ingredients used in the likes of plum pudding, hot cross buns and Christmas cake. They also encouraged the drinking of wine. Meat was a luxury reserved for those with money, so the poor were left with bread, cheese and eggs as their staple diet.

The Middle Ages saw the wealthy eating beef, mutton, pork and venison, along with a great variety of birds, including blackbirds, greenfinches, herons and swans; and when the church decreed that meat couldn't be eaten on certain days, they turned to fish. Breakfast was eaten in private; lunch and dinner, in the great hall; and on special occasions they held huge feasts and banquets with lavish spectacles, musicians

Manchester House

Joanna Wnuk/Zoonar GmbH RM/age Fotostock

and entertainment. The poor, meanwhile, were stuck with their simple, monotonous fare: for lunch, cheese and coarse, dark bread made from barley or rye; and in the evening, pottage, a type of stew made by boiling grain, vegetables and, on occasion, some rabbit – if they could catch one.

Sugar and spice...

Things really began to take off in Tudor times, with spices being brought back from the Far East, and sugar from the Caribbean. Potatoes and turkeys were introduced from north America; the latter were bred almost exclusively in Norfolk, then driven to London in flocks of 500 or more and fattened up for several days before being sold. The poor baked bread, salted meat, preserved vegetables, made pickles and conserves, and even brewed their own beer. As the water was so dirty, the children drank milk, the adults drank ale, cider or perry, and the rich drank wine.

Little changed until the rise of the British Empire, when new drinks such as tea, coffee and chocolate appeared, and coffee houses started to spring up – places where professionals could meet to read the news-paper and 'talk shop'. More herbs and spices were brought back, this time from India, and exotic fruits such as bananas and pineapples came onto the scene. Despite improvements in farming, the poor continued to eat bread, butter, cheese, potatoes and bacon; butcher's meat remained a luxury.

Import–ant times

Advancements continued to pick up pace in Victorian times. The advent of the railways and steamships made it possible to import cheap grain from North America, and refrigeration units allowed meat to be brought in from Argentina and Australia. The first fish and chip shops opened in the 1860s and the first convenience food in tins and jars went on sale. The price of sugar also began to drop and sweets such as peanut brittle, liquorice allsorts and chocolate bars came into being.

In the early 20C, the cost of food fell dramatically: in 1914 it accounted for up to 60% of a working class family's income and by 1937, just 35%. Then, as things were beginning to look up, the war intervened and staple food items such as meat, sugar, butter, eggs and tea were rationed until long after the war had ended.

The late 20C saw a surge in technological and scientific advancements, and the creation of affordable fridges, freezers and microwave ovens meant that food could be stored for longer and cooked more easily. In an increasingly time-pressured world, convenience and time-saving became key, increasing the popularity of the 'ready meal' and takeaway outlets.

As immigration increased, so too did the number of restaurants serving cuisine from different nations. What started as a handful of Indian and Chinese restaurants, has now moved on in the 21C to cover everything from Thai to Turkish, Jamaican to Japanese.

Not only has the range of dining establishments increased but, with the opening up of European borders and the ease of travel and transport, many supermarkets have also started to stock a range of foreign products, from pierogi to paneer.

The British Aisles

Supermarkets may now offer an endless choice of products but at the same time, an increased interest in health and wellbeing has sparked a trend for using seasonal ingredients from small, local producers – with a focus on reducing food miles. With increasing concerns about the origins of produce and the methods used in mass-production, many people are now turning back to the traditional 'farmers' market' or opting for 'organic' alternatives, where the consumer can trace the product back to its source or be assured of a natural, ethical or sustainable production method.

This can be seen in a true British institution – the pub. Take the traditional Sunday roast, one of the country's favourite meals; some chewy meat and microwaved veg won't cut it anymore – consumers now want to see top quality seasonal ingredients on their plate, sourced from the nearby farmer or the local allotment, and freshly prepared in the kitchen. And chefs are rising to the challenge: exploring new ways of using British ingredients, and reviving and reinventing traditional regional recipes.

In the past Britain may have lagged behind its European neighbours, due, in part, to its having a largely industrial economy. But what is in no doubt today, is that it's certainly making up for lost time. It may not have such a clear culinary identity as say, France or Italy, but it now offers greater choice and diversity by providing chefs with the freedom and confidence to take inspiration from wherever they wish and bring together flavours from across the globe.

SEEK AND SELECT...
HOW TO USE THIS GUIDE

HOTELS

Hotels are classified by categories of comfort, from 🏨🏨🏨 to 🏠.

Red: Our most delightful places.

🏨 🏨 Other accommodation (guesthouses, farmhouses and private homes).

Within each category, establishments are listed in order of preference.

RESTAURANTS

Restaurants are classified by categories of comfort, from XxXxX to X.

Red: Our most delightful places.

🍺 🍺 Pubs serving good food.

Within each category, establishments are listed in order of preference.

Stars

Michelin stars are awarded to establishments serving cuisine, of whatever style, which is of the highest quality. The cuisine is judged on the quality of ingredients, the skill in their preparation, the combination of flavours, the levels of creativity, the value for money and the consistency of culinary standards.

❀❀❀ **Exceptional** cuisine, worth a special journey!

❀❀ **Excellent** cooking, worth a detour!

❀ **High quality** cooking, worth a stop!

Bib Gourmand

❀ Good quality, good value cooking.

Locating the establishment

Location and coordinates on the town plan, with main sights.

Key words

Each entry comes with two keywords, making it quick and easy to identify the type of establishment and/or the food that it serves.

ENGLAND

BEAULIEU
Hampshire - Pop. 726 - Brockenhurst - ⬛
◻ London 55 mi - Coventry 88 mi - Ips⬛

🏨🏨 **Manor of Roses**
ROMANTIC • STYLISH With its ch⬛ this charming 18C inn has a timel⬛ marry antique furniture with moc⬛ lised. The wicker-furnished conse⬛
18 rooms – †£62/ £120 ††£62⬛
Town plan: D1-a – *Palace Ln* ⬛S⬛
❀ Scott's –See restaurant listing

🏨🏨 **Wentworth**
FRIENDLY • COSY Ivy-clad Victo⬛ the bedrooms; some are traditi⬛ bright and modern. 19C restaura⬛
28 rooms – † £61/106 ††£61/⬛
Town plan: D1-c – *35 Charles St* ⬛
www.wentworth.com – *Closed Ja⬛*

XXX **Scott's**
❀ FRENCH • CLASSIC This elegant⬛ 18C inn; head to the terrace for ⬛ and efficient, and only top quality⬛ dishes. Cooking has a classical ba⬛
→Spiced scallops with cauliflow⬛ Roast duck breast, smoked bacc⬛ soufflé with Sichuan spiced choc⬛
Menu £30/50 (dinner only) – ⬛
Town plan: D1-a – *Palace Ln* ⬛S⬛
www.Scotts.com – *Closed Decem⬛*

XX **Sea Grill** ⓝ
❀ MEATS AND GRILLS • BISTRO S⬛ lage, this laid-back bar-restauran⬛ classic. The eggs are from their ⬛ nearby farms.
Menu £28 (weekday dinner)
Town plan: D1-c – *12 Robert St* ⬛
www.seagrill.co.uk – *Closed Dece⬛*

map n°6-B2
Leicester 74 mi – Norwich 61 mi

rquet floors and old wood panelling, Traditional country house bedrooms and service is discreet and persona- errace overlook the lovely gardens.
£11
01590 612 324 – www.roses.com

A carved wooden staircase leads to aid mahogany furniture, others are nporary furnishings.
– 3 suites
020 7491 2622 –

is found at the heart of an alluring the lovely gardens. Service is polite sed in the refined, precisely prepared ern touches.
pple, coriander and cumin velouté. d creamed potatoes. Seville orange m.
/61
1590 612 324 (booking essential) – ary

arge red-brick inn in a delightful vil- ct spot for a pint and a home-cooked and meats are free range and from

5/72
020 7491 2622 –

Facilities & services

	Particularly interesting wine list
	Notable cocktail list
	Restaurant or pub with bedrooms
	Peaceful establishment
	Great view
	Lift (elevator) • Wheelchair access
	Air conditioning (in all or part of the establishment)
	Outside dining available
	Open for breakfast • Small plates
	Restaurant offering vegetarian menus
	Restaurant offering lower priced theatre menus
	Special facilities for children
	No dogs allowed
	Wellness centre
	Sauna • Exercise room
	Swimming pool: outdoor or indoor
	Garden or park • Tennis court
	Golf course
	Conference room
	Private dining room
	Car park • Garage
	Credit cards not accepted
	Nearest Underground station (London)

N New establishment in the guide

Prices

- Prices are given in £ sterling, and in € euros for the Republic of Ireland.
- All accommodation prices include both service and V.A.T. Restaurant prices include V.A.T. and service is also included when an **s** appears after the prices.

Restaurants		**Hotels**	
Menu £13/28	Fixed price menu. Lowest/highest price.	† £50/90 †† £100/120	Lowest/highest price for single and double room.
Carte £20/35	À la carte menu. Lowest/highest price.	†† £100/120	Bed & breakfast rate.
s	Service included.	£5	Breakfast price where not included in rate.

2017...
NEW AWARDS IN THIS YEAR'S GUIDE

STARS... ✿

✿✿✿

England	Bray	**Fat Duck**

✿✿

England	Darlington/Summerhouse	**Raby Hunt**

✿

London	Camden/Bloomsbury	**The Ninth**
	Hackney/London Fields	**Ellory**
	Hackney/London Fields	**Pidgin**
	Kensington and Chelsea/Chelsea	**Five Fields**
	Lambeth/Clapham Common	**Trinity**
	Westminster/Belgravia	**Céleste**
	Westminster/Mayfair	**Veeraswamy**
	Westminster/St James's	**Ritz Restaurant**
England	Burchett's Green	**Crown**
	Egham	**Tudor Room**
	Grasmere	**Forest Side**
	Hampton in Arden	**Peel's**
	Ilfracombe	**Thomas Carr @ The Olive Room**
	Kingham	**The Wild Rabbit**
	Windermere/Bowness-on-Windermere	**Gilpin Hotel & Lake House**
Wales	Anglesey (Isle of)/Menai Bridge	**Sosban & The Old Butchers**
	Penarth	**James Sommerin**
Republic of Ireland	Dublin/Blackrock	**Heron & Grey**

14

A complete list of Stars and Bib Gourmands 2017 are at the beginning of each region.

... AND BIB GOURMANDS

London

Camden/Bloomsbury	**Barbary**
Ealing	**Charlotte's W5**
Hackney/Hackney	**Legs**
Islington/Canonbury	**Primeur**
Islington/Islington	**Bellanger**
Lambeth/Clapham Common	**Upstairs (at Trinity)**
Southwark/Southwark	**Padella**
Tower Hamlets/Bethnal Green	**Marksman**
Tower Hamlets/Bethnal Green	**Paradise Garage**
Tower Hamlets/Spitalfields	**Gunpowder**
Westminster/Regent's Park	**Foley's**
Westminster/Regent's Park	**Newman Arms**
Westminster/Soho	**Bao**
Westminster/Soho	**Hoppers**
Westminster/Strand and Covent Garden	**Vico**

England

Butlers Cross	**Russell Arms**
Dummer	**Sun Inn**
Great Malvern/Welland	**The Inn at Welland**
Manchester	**El Gato Negro**
Old Alresford	**Pulpo Negro**
Ripley	**Anchor**
St Tudy	**St Tudy Inn**

Scotland

Edinburgh	**The Scran & Scallie**

Northern Ireland

Moira	**Wine & Brine**

15

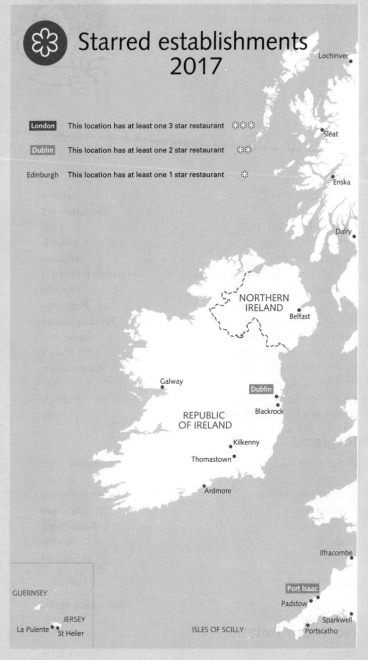

Starred establishments 2017

London   This location has at least one 3 star restaurant ✿✿✿

Dublin   This location has at least one 2 star restaurant ✿✿

Edinburgh   This location has at least one 1 star restaurant ✿

Lochinver

Sleat

Eriska

Dalry

NORTHERN IRELAND

Belfast

Galway

Dublin

Blackrock

REPUBLIC OF IRELAND

Kilkenny

Thomastown

Ardmore

Ilfracombe

Port Isaac

Padstow

Sparkwell

Portscatho

GUERNSEY

JERSEY

La Pulente · St Helier

ISLES OF SCILLY

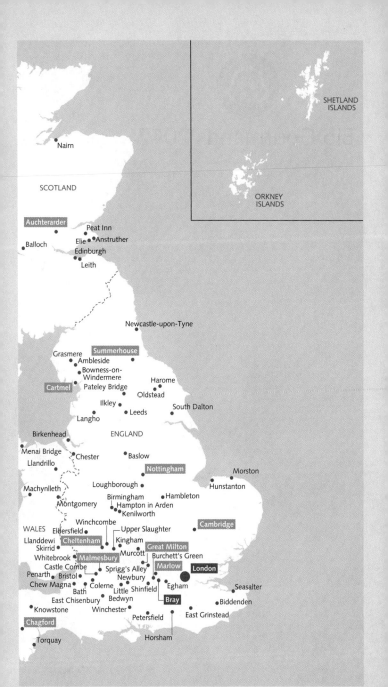

SHETLAND
ISLANDS

ORKNEY
ISLANDS

Nairn

SCOTLAND

Auchterarder
Peat Inn
Balloch
Elie • Anstruther
Edinburgh
Leith

Newcastle-upon-Tyne

Grasmere
Summerhouse
Ambleside
Bowness-on-
Windermere
Harome
Cartmel
Pateley Bridge
Oldstead
Ilkley
Leeds
South Dalton
Langho

Birkenhead
ENGLAND
Menai Bridge
Llandrillo
Chester
Baslow

Morston
Nottingham

Machynlleth
Loughborough
Hunstanton
Hambleton
Birmingham
Montgomery
Hampton in Arden
Kenilworth

WALES
Winchcombe
Cambridge
Eldersfield
Upper Slaughter
Llanddewi
Cheltenham
Kingham
Great Milton
Skirrid
Murcott
Burchett's Green
Whitebrook
Malmesbury
Marlow
Castle Combe
Sprigg's Alley
London
Penarth
Bristol
Newbury
Chew Magna
Colerne
Shinfield
Egham
Bath
Little
Seasalter
East Chisenbury
Bedwyn
Bray
Knowstone
Winchester
Biddenden
Chagford
Petersfield
East Grinstead

Torquay
Horsham

17

Bib Gourmands 2017

- This location has at least one Bib Gourmand establishment

Kilberry

NORTHERN
IRELAND

Holywood
Belfast
Lisbane

Moira

Carrickmacross

REPUBLIC
OF IRELAND

Dublin
Clontarf

Lisdoonvarna

Clonegall

Adare

Cashel

Dingle

Killorglin

Fennor

Duncannon

Kinsale

GUERNSEY

JERSEY

Beaumont

St Tudy

Padstow
Tavistock

Halsetown
St. Ives

Newlyn
Porthleven

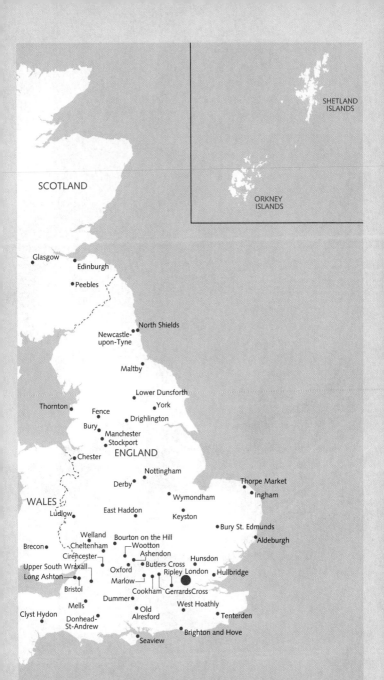

SHETLAND
ISLANDS

ORKNEY
ISLANDS

SCOTLAND

Glasgow
Edinburgh
Peebles

North Shields
Newcastle-
upon-Tyne

Maltby

Lower Dunsforth
Thornton
Fence • York
Bury Drighlington
Manchester
Stockport
Chester ENGLAND

Nottingham
Derby
Thorpe Market
Ingham
Wymondham
WALES
Ludlow East Haddon
Keyston
Bury St. Edmunds
Brecon Welland Bourton on the Hill Aldeburgh
Cheltenham Wootton
Cirencester Ashendon Hunsdon
Upper South Wraxall Oxford Butlers Cross
Long Ashton Marlow Ripley London Hullbridge
Bristol Cookham GerrardsCross
Mells Dummer West Hoathly
Clyst Hydon Donhead- Old Tenterden
St-Andrew Alresford
Brighton and Hove
Seaview

19

Alasdair Thomson/iStock

GREAT BRITAIN

Great Britain & Ireland

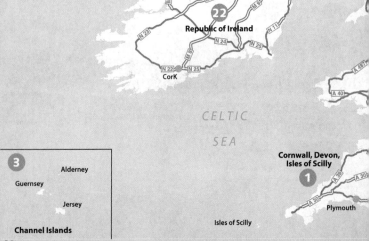

17 Highland & The Islands

ATLANTIC

OCEAN

20 Northern Ireland — Belfast

21 Republic of Ireland

IRISH SEA

Dublin

22 Republic of Ireland

CorK

CELTIC SEA

Cornwall, Devon, Isles of Scilly

1

Plymouth

3 Alderney

Guernsey

Jersey

Channel Islands

Isles of Scilly

18 Shetland & Orkney

Shetland Islands

Orkney Islands

NORTH SEA

Aberdeen

16
Central Scotland

Dundee

Edinburgh

Glasgow

Borders,
Edinburgh & Glasgow
15

14
Northumberland,
Durham

Newcastle-upon-Tyne

Sunderland

Middlesbrough

12
Cumbria

13
Yorkshire

Leeds

Blackpool
11
Bradford
Kingston
upon Hull

Cheshire,Lancashire,
Isle of Man
Liverpool
Manchester

9

Birkenhead
Sheffield
Stoke-
on-Trent

Derbyshire,Leicestershire,
Northamptonshire,
Rutland,Lincolnshire,
Nottinghamshire

19
Nottingham

Norwich

Wales
Wolverhampton
Leicester

8

10
Birmingham

Norfolk,Suffolk,
Cambridgeshire

Herefordshire,
Worcestershire,
Shropshire,Staffordshire,
Warwickshire
Coventry

Ipswich

Northampton

Bedfordshire,
Hertfordshire,Essex

6
Oxfordshire,
Buckinghamshire
Reading

Cardiff
Bristol

7

LONDON
Southend-
on-Sea

Somerset, Dorset,
Gloucestershire,
Wiltshire

2
Southampton

Portsmouth

East Sussex,
Kent

Bournemouth
Brighton

5

Hampshire,
Isle of Wight,
Surrey, West Sussex

4

FRANCE

23

LONDON

London is one of the most cosmopolitan, dynamic, fashionable and cultured cities on earth, home not only to such iconic images as Big Ben, Tower Bridge and bear skinned guards, but also Bengali markets, speedboat rides through the Docklands and stunning views of the city atop the very best of 21C architecture. From Roman settlement to banking centre to capital of a 19C empire, the city's pulse has never missed a beat; it's no surprise that a dazzling array of theatres, restaurants, museums, markets and art galleries populate its streets.

The city is one of the food capitals of the world, where you can eat everything from Turkish to Thai and Polish to Peruvian; diners here are an eclectic, well-travelled bunch who gladly welcome all-comers and every style of cuisine. Visit one of the many food markets like Borough or Brixton to witness the capital's wonderfully varied produce, or pop into a pop-up to get a taste of the latest trends. If it's traditional British you're after, try one of the many pubs in the capital; this was, after all, where the gastropub movement began.

- Michelin Road map n° 504
- Michelin Green Guide: London

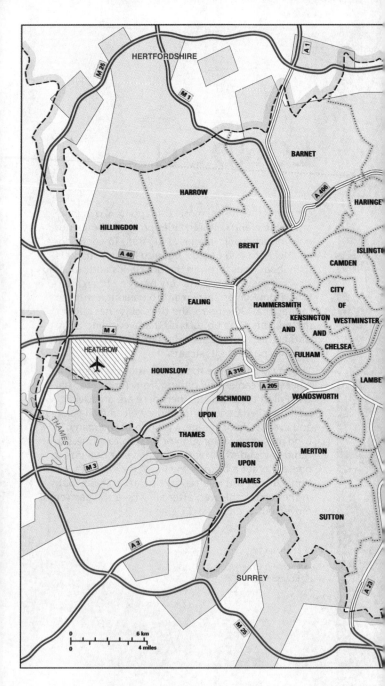

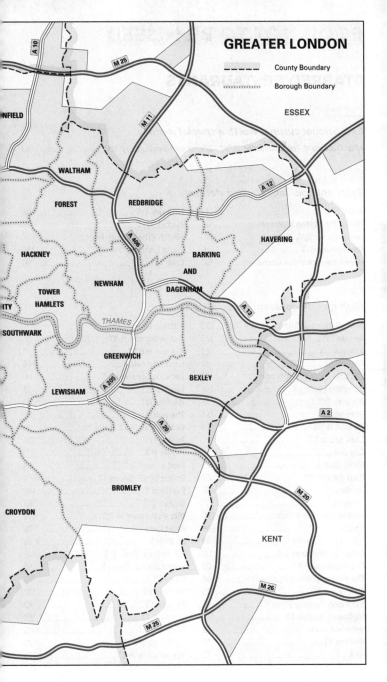

GREATER LONDON

- - - - County Boundary
.... Borough Boundary

ESSEX

ENFIELD

M 25

A 10

M 11

WALTHAM

FOREST

REDBRIDGE

A 406

HAVERING

A 12

HACKNEY

NEWHAM

BARKING

AND

DAGENHAM

TOWER

HAMLETS

ITY

THAMES

A 13

SOUTHWARK

GREENWICH

LEWISHAM

A 205

BEXLEY

A 20

A 2

BROMLEY

M 20

CROYDON

KENT

M 26

M 25

27

FOOD NOT TO BE MISSED

STARRED RESTAURANTS

❀ ❀ ❀

Exceptional cuisine, worth a special journey!

Alain Ducasse at The Dorchester XxXxX   129

Gordon Ramsay XxxX   89

❀ ❀

Excellent cooking, worth a detour!

Araki XX   134

Dinner by Heston Blumenthal XxX   127

Le Gavroche XxxX   130

Greenhouse XxX   131

Hélène Darroze at The Connaught XxxX   130

Ledbury XxX   96

Marcus XxxX   125

Sketch (The Lecture Room and Library) XxxX   130

Umu XxX   131

❀

High quality cooking, worth a stop!

Alyn Williams at The Westbury XxxX   130

Amaya XxX   126

Ametsa XxX   126

Angler XX   84

L'Atelier de Joël Robuchon X   163

Barrafina (Soho) X   156

Benares XxX   132

Bonhams XX   134

Céleste N XxxX   125

Chez Bruce XX   122

City Social XxX   62

Clove Club X   73

Club Gascon XX   62

Dabbous X   56

Ellory N X   71

Fera at Claridge's XxxX   130

Five Fields N XxX   89

Galvin La Chapelle XxX   118

Galvin at Windows XxX   131

The Glasshouse XX   107

The Goring (Dining Room) XxX   166

Gymkhana XX   135

Hakkasan Hanway Place XX   55

Hakkasan Mayfair XX   135

Harwood Arms 🍴   76

Hedone XX   79

HKK XX   72

Kai XxX   132

Kitchen Table at Bubbledogs XX   55

Kitchen W8 XX   94

Lima Fitzrovia X   146

Locanda Locatelli XxX   141

Lyle's X   73

Murano XxX   131

The Ninth N X   56

Outlaw's at The Capital XX   90

Pétrus XxX   126

Pidgin N X   71

Pied à Terre XxX   55

Pollen Street Social XX   134

Portland X   146

Quilon XxX   167

Ritz Restaurant N XxXxX   149

River Café XX   76

St John X   82

Seven Park Place XxX   149

Social Eating House X   155

Story XX   110

Tamarind XxX   132

Texture XX   142

Trinity N XX   101

Trishna X   145

La Trompette XX   79

Veeraswamy N XX   135

Yauatcha Soho XX   154

Five Fields

BIB GOURMAND 🐷

Good food, good value cooking

L'Amorosa X	77	Hereford Road X	123
Anchor and Hope 🍺	116	Honey and Co X	56
A. Wong X	168	Hoppers N X	158
Azou X	77	Indian Essence XX	53
Bao N X	160	José X	112
Barbary N X	57	Kateh X	123
Barnyard X	57	Legs N X	70
Barrica X	56	Market X	58
Bellanger N XX	86	Marksman N 🍺	117
Bistro Union X	101	Morito (Finsbury) X	84
Blixen X	118	Newman Arms N 🍺	148
Brasserie Zédel XX	154	Opera Tavern X	165
Brawn X	116	Padella N X	115
Cafe Spice Namaste XX	120	Palomar X	157
Canton Arms 🍺	103	Paradise Garage N X	117
Charlotte's W5 N X	67	Picture Fitzrovia X	146
Comptoir Gascon X	83	Polpetto X	156
Copita X	156	Primeur N X	81
Dehesa X	156	Provender X	105
Drapers Arms 🍺	87	St John Bread and Wine X	118
Elliot's X	115	Salt Yard X	56
Empress 🍺	74	Taberna do Mercado X	119
Foley's N X	146	Trullo X	81
Grain Store X	100	Upstairs (at Trinity) N X	101
Great Queen Street X	59	Vico N X	165
Gunpowder N X	119	Yipin China X	86

ALPHABETICAL LIST OF RESTAURANTS

100 Wardour St XX	154
10 Greek Street X	157
28°-50° Fetter Lane X	66
34 XxX	133
45 Jermyn St XX	151
500 X	81

A

L'Absinthe X	60
A Cena XX	109
Alain Ducasse at The Dorchester XxXxX ✿✿✿	129
Albert's Table XX	66
Al Duca XX	151
The Alfred Tennyson 🍴	126
Almeida XX	86
Alyn Williams at The Westbury XxxX ✿	130
Amaranto XxX	134
Amaya XxX ✿	126
Ametsa XxX ✿	126
L'Amorosa X☺	77
Anchor and Hope 🍴☺	116
Andina X	73
Angelus XX	123
Angler XX ✿	84
Anglesea Arms 🍴	77
Anglo X	59
L'Anima XxX	72
L'Anima Café XX	73
Antico X	112
Antidote X	158
Aqua Shard XX	111
Arabica Bar and Kitchen X	115
Araki XX ✿✿	134
Archipelago XX	144
Artusi X	113
L'Atelier de Joël Robuchon X ✿	163
Au Lac X	85
L'Autre Pied XX	143
Avenue XX	151
A. Wong X☺	168
Azou X☺	77

B

Babur XX	103
Babylon XX	95
Balcon XX	150
Balthazar XX	163
Baltic XX	114
Bandol X	92
Bao X☺	160
Baozi Inn X	160
Barbary X☺	57
Barbecoa XX	64
Bar Boulud XX	127
Barnyard X☺	57
Barrafina (Adelaide St) X	163
Barrafina (Drury Ln) X	164
Barrafina (Soho) X ✿	156
Barrica X☺	56
Barshu X	160
Beagle X	70
Beast XX	144
Beef and Brew X	59
Beijing Dumpling X	160
Bellanger XX☺	86
Benares XxX ✿	132
Bentley's XX	137
Bernardi's XX	142
Berners Tavern XX	143
Bibendum XxX	90
Bibigo X	159
Bibo X	121
Bingham Restaurant XX	108
Bird of Smithfield X	65
Bistro Aix X	78
Bistro Union X☺	101
Bistrotheque X	117
Blanchette X	157
Blixen X☺	118
Bluebird XX	91
Blue Elephant XX	75
Blueprint Café X	111
Bob Bob Ricard XX	154
Bocca di Lupo X	157
Boisdale of Canary Wharf XX	118
Bo Lang X	92
Bombay Brasserie XxxX	98

Bone Daddies 𝖃 159
Bonhams 𝖃𝖃 ⊛ 134
Bonnie Gull 𝖃 147
Boqueria (Battersea) 𝖃 121
Boqueria (Brixton) 𝖃 101
Le Boudin Blanc 𝖃 139
Boulestin 𝖃𝖃 150
Boundary 𝖃𝖃𝖃 72
Brackenbury 𝖃 77
Bradley's 𝖃𝖃 60
Brasserie Gustave 𝖃𝖃 91
Brasserie Vacherin 𝖃 116
Brasserie Zédel 𝖃𝖃 ⊛ 154
Brawn 𝖃 ⊛ 116
Bread Street Kitchen 𝖃𝖃 62
Brown Dog 🍴 106
Brumus 𝖃𝖃 152
Builders Arms 🍴 93
Bull and Last 🍴 58
Butlers Wharf Chop House 𝖃 112

C

Cafe Murano (St James's) 𝖃𝖃 151
Cafe Murano
   (Strand and Covent Garden) 𝖃𝖃 163
Cafe Spice Namaste 𝖃𝖃 ⊛ 120
Cambio de Tercio 𝖃𝖃 98
Canonbury Kitchen 𝖃 81
Cantina Del Ponte 𝖃 111
Canton Arms 🍴 ⊛ 103
Capote y Toros 𝖃 99
Le Caprice 𝖃𝖃 150
Caravan 𝖃 85
Casse Croûte 𝖃 112
Cây Tre 𝖃 159
Céleste 𝖃𝖃𝖃𝖃 ⊛ 125
Ceviche Old St 𝖃 85
Ceviche Soho 𝖃 159
Chada 𝖃𝖃 120
The Chancery 𝖃𝖃 63
Chapter One 𝖃𝖃𝖃 53
Chapters 𝖃𝖃 103
Charlotte's Bistro 𝖃𝖃 79
Charlotte's W5 𝖃 ⊛ 67
Charlotte's Place 𝖃 67
Chez Bruce 𝖃𝖃 ⊛ 122
Chicken Shop 𝖃 59
Chiltern Firehouse 𝖃𝖃 143

China Tang 𝖃𝖃𝖃 133
Chiswell Street Dining Rooms 𝖃𝖃 64
Chop Shop 𝖃 152
Chucs Bar and Grill 𝖃𝖃 139
Chutney Mary 𝖃𝖃𝖃 149
Cigala 𝖃 57
Cigalon 𝖃𝖃 64
The Cinnamon Club 𝖃𝖃𝖃 167
Cinnamon Culture 𝖃𝖃 53
Cinnamon Kitchen 𝖃𝖃 63
Cinnamon Soho 𝖃 158
City Social 𝖃𝖃𝖃 ⊛ 62
Clarke's 𝖃𝖃 94
Claude's Kitchen 𝖃 75
Clerkenwell Kitchen 𝖃 85
Clos Maggiore 𝖃𝖃 162
Clove Club 𝖃 ⊛ 73
Club Gascon 𝖃𝖃 ⊛ 62
Colbert 𝖃𝖃 92
Le Colombier 𝖃𝖃 91
Colony Grill Room 𝖃𝖃 135
Comptoir Gascon 𝖃 ⊛ 83
Copita 𝖃 ⊛ 156
Copita del Mercado 𝖃 119
Corner Room 𝖃 117
Corrigan's Mayfair 𝖃𝖃𝖃 133
Coya 𝖃𝖃 137
Craft London 𝖃 68
Cross Keys 🍴 93
Crown 🍴 109
Cut 𝖃𝖃𝖃 133

D

Dabbous 𝖃 ⊛ 56
Dairy 𝖃 102
Dean Street
   Townhouse Restaurant 𝖃𝖃 154
Dehesa 𝖃 ⊛ 156
Delaunay 𝖃𝖃𝖃 161
Les Deux Salons 𝖃𝖃 163
Dickie Fitz 𝖃𝖃 144
Dinings 𝖃 147
Dinner by Heston Blumenthal 𝖃𝖃𝖃 ⊛ ⊛ .. 127
Dishoom 𝖃 165
Dock Kitchen 𝖃 96
Donostia 𝖃 147
Drakes Tabanco 𝖃 57
Drapers Arms 🍴 ⊛ 87

Duck and Rice X 158
Duck and Waffle XX 64
Duke of Sussex ᵗᴰ 66
Dysart Petersham XX 108

E

Ealing Park Tavern ᵗᴰ 67
Earl Spencer ᵗᴰ 121
Electric Diner X 97
Elliot's X ⓐ 115
Ellory X ⊛ 71
Ember Yard X 156
Empress ᵗᴰ ⓐ 74
Enoteca Turi XX 168
L'Etranger XX 98
Eyre Brothers XX 72

F

Fellow ᵗᴰ 100
Fenchurch XX 63
Fera at Claridge's XXXX ⊛ 130
Fifteen London X 70
Fischer's XX 145
Fish Market X 65
Five Fields XXX ⊛ 89
Flat Three XX 96
Flesh and Buns X 58
Foley's X ⓐ 146
Foxlow (Clerkenwell) X 83
Foxlow (Stoke Newington) X 74
Franco's XX 151
Frenchie X 164
The French Table XX 100
Friends XX 78
The Frog X 119

G

Galley X 86
Galvin Bistrot de Luxe XX 143
Galvin La Chapelle XXX ⊛ 118
Galvin at Windows XXX ⊛ 131
Garnier XX 93
Garrison ᵗᴰ 113
Gauthier - Soho XXX 153
Le Gavroche XXXX ⊛ ⊛ 130
Gilbert Scott XX 100
The Glasshouse XX ⊛ 107

Good Earth XX 92
Goodman Mayfair XX 138
Gordon Ramsay XXXX ⊛ ⊛ ⊛ 89
The Goring (Dining Room) XXX ⊛ 166
Grain Store X ⓐ 100
Grand Imperial XXX 167
Granger and Co. Clerkenwell X 83
Granger and Co. King's Cross X 100
Granger and Co. Notting Hill X 97
Great Queen Street X ⓐ 59
Greenhouse XXX ⊛ ⊛ 131
The Grill XXX 133
Gunpowder X ⓐ 119
Gymkhana XX ⊛ 135

H

Hakkasan Hanway Place XX ⊛ 55
Hakkasan Mayfair XX ⊛ 135
Ham Yard XX 154
Hana X 121
Haozhan X 157
Harwood Arms ᵗᴰ ⊛ 76
Hawksmoor (City of London) X 65
Hawksmoor (Knightsbridge) XX 91
Hawksmoor (Mayfair) XX 135
Hawksmoor (Spitalfields) X 119
Hawksmoor
    (Strand and Covent Garden) X 164
Hazara XX 54
Heddon Street Kitchen XX 136
Hedone XX ⊛ 79
Hélène Darroze at The
    Connaught XXXX ⊛ ⊛ 130
Herbert's X 52
Hereford Road X ⓐ 123
High Road Brasserie X 80
Hill and Szrok X 71
Hix (Soho) XX 155
Hix Mayfair XXX 134
Hix Oyster and Chop House X 83
HKK XX ⊛ 72
Honey and Co X ⓐ 56
Hoppers X ⓐ 158
Hush XX 138

I

Iberica Marylebone XX 145
il trillo XX 92

Imperial China 🍴🍴🍴 154
Indian Essence 🍴🍴 🍸 53
Indian Zilla 🍴🍴 106
Indian Zing 🍴🍴 76
Ivy Chelsea Garden 🍴🍴 90
Ivy Market Grill 🍴🍴 163
The Ivy 🍴🍴🍴 162

Kitchen Table at Bubbledogs 🍴🍴 ✿ 55
Kitchen W8 🍴🍴 ✿ 94
Kitty Fisher's 🍴 139
Koji 🍴 75
Kouzu 🍴 169
Koya Bar 🍴 160
Kurobuta Marble Arch 🍴 124

J

Jidori 🍴 69
Jinjuu 🍴 158
José 🍴 🍸 112
José Pizarro 🍴 65
J. Sheekey 🍴🍴 162
J. Sheekey Oyster Bar 🍴 164
Jugged Hare 🍺 66

K

Kai 🍴🍴🍴 ✿ 132
Karnavar 🍴 66
Kateh 🍴 🍸 123
Keeper's House 🍴🍴 138
Kennington Tandoori 🍴🍴 102
Kensington Place 🍴 95
Kenza 🍴🍴 64
Kerbisher and Malt 🍴 67
Kiku 🍴🍴 139
King's Head 🍺 109
Kiraku 🍴 67

L

Lady Ottoline 🍺 58
Lamberts 🍴 120
Lardo 🍴 71
Latium 🍴🍴 143
Launceston Place 🍴🍴🍴 94
Ledbury 🍴🍴🍴 ✿✿ 96
Legs 🍴 🍸 70
Les 110 de Taillevent 🍴🍴 145
Light House 🍴 104
Light on the Common 🍴 104
Lima Fitzrovia 🍴 ✿ 146
Lima Floral 🍴 164
Linnea 🍴🍴 107
Little Social 🍴 139
Lobos 🍴 116
Lobster Pot 🍴 102
Locanda Locatelli 🍴🍴🍴 ✿ 141
London House 🍴🍴 120
Luc's Brasserie 🍴🍴 64
Lurra 🍴🍴 142

Michelin

Lutyens XxX 62
Lyle's X☺ 73

M

Mac and Wild X 147
The Magazine XX 127
Magdalen XX 111
Malabar XX 95
Manchurian Legends X 160
The Manor X 102
Manuka Kitchen X 75
Marcus XxxX ✿✿ 125
Margaux X 99
Marianne XX 123
Market X☺ 58
Market Cafe X 71
Marksman ⫓☺ 117
Masala Grill XX 91
MASH XX 155
Massimo XX 168
Matsuba X 108
Matsuri XX 150
Mayfair Chippy X 140
May the Fifteenth X 102
Maze XX 136
Maze Grill Mayfair XX 138
Maze Grill Park Walk XX 91
Mazi X 96
Medlar XX 90
Mele e Pere X 157
Merchants Tavern XX 72
Michael Nadra XX 79
Michael Nadra Primrose Hill XX 60
Milos XxX 150
Min Jiang XxX 94
The Modern Pantry Clerkenwell X 85
The Modern Pantry
  Finsbury Square XX 84
Momo XX 136
Mon Plaisir XX 55
Morito (Finsbury) X☺ 84
Morito (Hoxton) X 71
Moro X 84
Mr Todiwala's Kitchen XX 78
Murano XxX✿ 131

N

Nanban X 101
Newman Arms ⫓☺ 148

New St Grill XX 63
The Ninth X☺ 56
Noble Rot X 57
Nobu XX 138
Nobu Berkeley St XX 137
Nopi X 156
Northall XxX 167

O

Oblix XX 111
Odette's XX 60
Ognisko XX 99
Oklava X 74
Oldroyd X 86
Oliver Maki X 158
Olivo X 169
Olivocarne X 169
Olivomare X 169
Olympic Café + Dining Room X 106
One-O-One XxX 90
One Sixty X 60
Opera Tavern X☺ 165
Opso X 147
The Orange ⫓ 169
Orrery XxX 142
Osteria Dell' Angolo XX 168
Ostuni X 52
Ottolenghi (Islington) X 86
Ottolenghi (Spitalfields) X 119
Ours XX 98
Outlaw's at The Capital XX☺ 90
Oxo Tower XxX 114
Oxo Tower Brasserie X 115

P

Padella X☺ 115
Painted Heron XX 91
Palmerston ⫓ 113
Palomar X☺ 157
Paradise by way of Kensal Green ⫓... 52
Paradise Garage X☺ 117
Park Chinois XxX 132
Parlour ⫓ 52
Paternoster Chop House X 65
Percy and Founders XX 144
Petersham Nurseries Café X 108
La Petite Maison XX 137
Pétrus XxX☺ 126
Peyote X 139

Pharmacy 2 XX 103
Picture Fitzrovia X ⊛ 146
Picture Marylebone X............................. 147
Pidgin X ⊛ 71
Pied à Terre XXX ⊛ 55
Pig and Butcher ⅼ⊡ 87
Piquet XX 142
Pizarro X.. 112
Plateau XX... 118
Plum Valley XX 155
Pollen Street Social XX ⊛ 134
Polpetto X ⊛ 156
Polpo at Ape and Bird X 57
Polpo Covent Garden X 165
Polpo Smithfield X 83
Polpo Soho X 157
Le Pont de la Tour XXX 110
Portland X ⊛... 146
Portman ⅼ⊡.. 148
Portrait X.. 152
Primeur X ⊛... 81
Princess of Shoreditch ⅼ⊡...................... 74
Princess Victoria ⅼ⊡................................. 77
Provender X ⊛.. 105
The Providores XX..................................... 145

Q
Quaglino's XX 151
Quality Chop House X............................. 84

Quilon XXX ⊛ 167
Quo Vadis XXX 153

R
Rabbit X... 92
Rabot 1745 XX 114
Red Fort XXX 153
Refuel XX 155
Rétro Bistrot XX 108
Retsina X 54
Rex Whistler XX 168
Rib Room XXX 90
The Richmond X 69
Riding House Café X................................. 146
Ritz Restaurant XXXXX ⊛ 149
Riva X 106
Rivea XX 127
River Café XX ⊛ 76
Rivington Grill XX 73
Roast XX 114
Roka (Aldwych) XX.................................... 162
Roka (Bloomsbury) XX 55
Roka (Mayfair) XX 136
Rosa's Soho X 159
Rosita X 121
Rotorino X.. 69
Roux at the Landau XXX 142
Roux at Parliament Square XXX 167
Royal China XX 145

Gymkhana

Royal China Club ✗✗ 143
Rules ✗✗ 162

S

Sager + Wilde ✗ 117
St John ✗ ✿ 82
St John Bread and Wine ✗ ⊕ 118
St John Maltby ✗ 113
St John's Tavern 🍴 81
Sake No Hana ✗✗ 150
Salt and Honey ✗ 124
Salt Yard ✗ ⊕ 56
Santini ✗✗✗ 167
Sardine ✗ 70
Sartoria ✗✗✗ 133
Sauterelle ✗✗ 63
Scott's ✗✗✗ 132
Seven Park Place ✗✗✗ ✿ 149
Sexy Fish ✗✗ 137
Shayona ✗ 52
The Shed ✗ 95
Shikumen (Ealing) ✗ 67
Shikumen (Hammersmith) ✗✗ 77
Shoryu ✗ 152
Simply Thai ✗ 109
Sinabro ✗ 120
Six Portland Road ✗ 96
sixtyone ✗✗ 144

Sketch (The Lecture Room
    and Library) ✗✗✗ ✿ ✿ 130
Sketch (The Gallery) ✗✗ 136
Skylon ✗✗✗ 103
Smokehouse 🍴 80
Smokehouse 🍴 82
Social Eating House ✗ ✿ 155
Social Wine and Tapas ✗ 146
Soif ✗ 121
Som Saa ✗ 120
Sonny's Kitchen ✗ 106
Sosharu ✗✗ 82
Spring ✗✗ 162
Spuntino ✗ 158
The Square ✗✗✗✗ 131
Story ✗✗ ✿ 110
Swagat ✗ 108

T

Taberna do Mercado ✗ ⊕ 119
Takahashi ✗ 104
Talli Joe ✗ 58
Tamarind ✗✗✗ ✿ 132
Tandis ✗ 54
Tapas Brindisa ✗ 115
Tate Modern (Restaurant) ✗ 114
Tendido Cero ✗ 99
Tendido Cuatro ✗ 75

Yauatcha

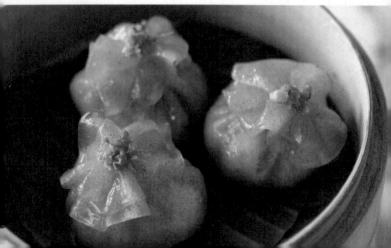

Terroirs X 165
Texture XX ✿ 142
Theo Randall XX 136
Thomas Cubitt 🍴 169
Toa Kitchen XX 123
Tokimeitē XX 138
Tommy Tucker 🍴 76
Tonkotsu X 161
Tramshed X 73
Tredwell's X 164
Trinity XX ✿ 101
Trishna X ✿ 145
La Trompette XX ✿ 79
Trullo X ⊛ 81
Typing Room XX 116

U

Umu XXX ✿ ✿ 131
UNI XX 168
Union Street Café XX 114
Upstairs at The Guildford Arms X 68
Upstairs (at Trinity) X ⊛ 101

V

Le Vacherin XX 66
Vanilla Black XX 63
Vasco and Piero's Pavilion XX 155
Veeraswamy XX ✿ 135
Vico X ⊛ 165
Victoria 🍴 107
Viet Grill X 74
Village East X 111
Vinoteca X 147
Vintage Salt X 87

Vivat Bacchus X 65
Vivat Bacchus London Bridge X 112

W

The Wallace XX 144
Well 🍴 85
White Onion X 104
Wild Honey XX 137
The Wolseley XXX 150
The Woodford XX 105
Wormwood X 97
Wright Brothers X 115

X

Xian XX 53
XO XX 54

Y

Yashin XX 95
Yashin Ocean House XX 99
Yauatcha City XX 62
Yauatcha Soho XX ✿ 154
Yipin China X ⊛ 86
York and Albany XX 58

Z

Zafferano XXX 126
Zaika XX 95
Zayane X 97
Zelman Meats X 159
Zoilo X 148
Zuma XX 128
Zumbura X 102

PARTICULARLY PLEASANT RESTAURANTS

XxXxX

Alain Ducasse at The Dorchester 129

Ritz Restaurant 149

XxXX

Fera at Claridge's 130
Hélène Darroze at The Connaught 130
Marcus 125

Sketch (The Lecture Room
and Library) 130

XxX

Bibendum 90
Boundary 72
Cut 133
Delaunay 161
Dinner by Heston Blumenthal 127
Galvin La Chapelle 118

The Goring (Dining Room) 166
Greenhouse 131
Park Chinois 132
Pétrus 126
Quo Vadis 153
Scott's 132

XX

Angelus 123
Angler 84
Araki 134
Bar Boulud 127
Clos Maggiore 162
Colony Grill Room 135
Gilbert Scott 100
Hawksmoor (Mayfair) 135

HKK 72
J. Sheekey 162
Momo 136
Outlaw's at The Capital 90
River Café 76
Rules 162
Sketch (The Gallery) 136
Spring 162

X

L'Atelier de Joël Robuchon 163
Blixen 118
Le Boudin Blanc 139
Dehesa 156
J. Sheekey Oyster Bar 164

Little Social 139
Nopi 156
Petersham Nurseries Café 108
Quality Chop House 84

RESTAURANTS CLASSIFIED ACCORDING TO TYPE

Argentinian

Zoilo 𝕏 148

Asian

Bao 𝕏 ⊛ 160
Bone Daddies 𝕏 159
Flesh and Buns 𝕏 58
Jinjuu 𝕏 158
XO 𝕏𝕏 54

Austrian

Fischer's 𝕏𝕏 145

Basque

Donostia 𝕏 147
Lurra 𝕏𝕏 142

Chinese

A. Wong 𝕏 ⊛ 168
Baozi Inn 𝕏 160
Barshu 𝕏 160
Beijing Dumpling 𝕏 160
Bo Lang 𝕏 92
China Tang 𝕏𝕏𝕏 133
Duck and Rice 𝕏 158
Good Earth 𝕏𝕏 92

Grand Imperial 𝕏𝕏𝕏 167
Hakkasan Hanway Place 𝕏𝕏 ❀ 55
Hakkasan Mayfair 𝕏𝕏 ❀ 135
Haozhan 𝕏 157
HKK 𝕏𝕏 ❀ 72
Imperial China 𝕏𝕏𝕏 154
Kai 𝕏𝕏𝕏 ❀ 132
Manchurian Legends 𝕏 160
Min Jiang 𝕏𝕏𝕏 94
Park Chinois 𝕏𝕏𝕏 132
Plum Valley 𝕏𝕏 155
Royal China 𝕏𝕏 145
Royal China Club 𝕏𝕏 143
Shikumen (Ealing) 𝕏 67
Shikumen (Hammersmith) 𝕏𝕏 77
Toa Kitchen 𝕏𝕏 123
Xian 𝕏𝕏 53
Yauatcha City 𝕏𝕏 62
Yauatcha Soho 𝕏𝕏 ❀ 154
Yipin China 𝕏 ⊛ 86

Classic cuisine

Ritz Restaurant 𝕏𝕏𝕏𝕏𝕏 ❀ 149

Creative

Ametsa 𝕏𝕏 ❀ 126
Archipelago 𝕏𝕏 144
Corner Room 𝕏 117

Michelin

L'Etranger XX 98
Flat Three XX 96
   Greenhouse XxX ❀❀ 131
   Pied à Terre XxX ❀ 55
   Pollen Street Social XX ❀ 134
   The Providores XX 145
   Texture XX ❀ 142

Creative British

Anglo X 59
Dairy X 102
Fera at Claridge's XxX ❀ 130
The Manor X 102

Creative French

Céleste XxX ❀ 125

Fish and chips

Kerbisher and Malt X 67
Vintage Salt X 87

French

L'Absinthe X 60
Alain Ducasse
   at The Dorchester XxXxX ❀❀❀ 129
Angelus XX 123
L'Atelier de Joël Robuchon X ❀ 163
Balcon XX 150
Balthazar XX 163
Bar Boulud XX 127
Bellanger XX ⊜ 86
Bibendum XxX 90
Bistro Aix X 78
Bistrotheque X 117
Blanchette X 157
Le Boudin Blanc X 139

Boulestin XX 150
Boundary XxX 72
Brasserie Gustave XX 91
Brasserie Vacherin X 116
Brasserie Zédel XX ⊜ 154
Casse Croûte X 112
Chez Bruce XX ❀ 122
Cigalon XX 64
Clos Maggiore XX 162
Club Gascon XX ❀ 62
Colbert XX 92
Le Colombier XX 91
Comptoir Gascon X ⊜ 83
Les Deux Salons XX 163
Galvin Bistrot de Luxe XX 143
Galvin La Chapelle XxX ❀ 118
Garnier XX 93
Gauthier - Soho XxX 153
Le Gavroche XxXX ❀❀ 130
Gordon Ramsay XxXX ❀❀❀ 89
The Grill XxX 133
High Road Brasserie X 80
Les 110 de Taillevent XX 145
Little Social X 139
Lobster Pot X 102
Luc's Brasserie XX 64
Marianne XX 123
Mon Plaisir XX 55
La Petite Maison XX 137
Pétrus XxX ❀ 126
Piquet XX 142
Le Pont de la Tour XxX 110
Provender X ⊜ 105
Rétro Bistrot XX 108
Roux at the Landau XxX 142
Sauterelle XX 63
Six Portland Road X 96
Sketch (The Lecture Room
   and Library) XxXX ❀❀ 130

Araki

Soif 🕽 121
The Square 🕽🕽🕽🕽 131
Le Vacherin 🕽🕽 66

Greek

Mazi 🕽 96
Opso 🕽 147
Retsina 🕽 54

Indian

Amaya 🕽🕽🕽 ⊕ 126
Babur 🕽🕽 103
Benares 🕽🕽🕽 ⊕ 132
Bombay Brasserie 🕽🕽🕽🕽 98
Cafe Spice Namaste 🕽🕽 ⊕ 120
Chutney Mary 🕽🕽🕽 149
The Cinnamon Club 🕽🕽🕽 167
Cinnamon Culture 🕽🕽 53
Cinnamon Kitchen 🕽🕽 63
Cinnamon Soho 🕽 158
Dishoom 🕽 165
Gunpowder 🕽 ⊕ 119
Gymkhana 🕽🕽 ⊕ 135
Hazara 🕽🕽 54
Indian Essence 🕽🕽 ⊕ 53
Indian Zilla 🕽🕽 106
Indian Zing 🕽🕽 76
Karnavar 🕽 66
Kennington Tandoori 🕽🕽 102
Malabar 🕽🕽 95
Masala Grill 🕽🕽 91
Mr Todiwala's Kitchen 🕽🕽 78
Painted Heron 🕽🕽 91
Quilon 🕽🕽🕽 ⊕ 167
Red Fort 🕽🕽🕽 153
Shayona 🕽 52
Swagat 🕽 108
Talli Joe 🕽 58
Tamarind 🕽🕽🕽 ⊕ 132
Trishna 🕽 ⊕ 145
Veeraswamy 🕽🕽 ⊕ 135
Zaika 🕽🕽 95
Zumbura 🕽 102

Italian

500 🕽 81
A Cena 🕽🕽 109
Al Duca 🕽🕽 151
Amaranto 🕽🕽🕽 134

L'Amorosa 🕽 ⊕ 77
L'Anima 🕽🕽 72
L'Anima Café 🕽🕽 73
Antico 🕽 112
Artusi 🕽 113
Bernardi's 🕽🕽 142
Bibo 🕽 121
Bocca di Lupo 🕽 157
Cafe Murano (St James's) 🕽🕽 151
Cafe Murano
    (Strand and Covent Garden) 🕽🕽 163
Canonbury Kitchen 🕽 81
Cantina Del Ponte 🕽 111
Chucs Bar and Grill 🕽🕽 139
Enoteca Turi 🕽🕽 168
Franco's 🕽🕽 151
il trillo 🕽🕽 92
Lardo 🕽 71
Latium 🕽🕽 143
Locanda Locatelli 🕽🕽🕽 ⊕ 141
Massimo 🕽🕽 168
Mele e Pere 🕽 157
Murano 🕽🕽🕽 ⊕ 131
Olivo 🕽 169
Olivocarne 🕽 169
Osteria Dell' Angolo 🕽🕽 168
Ostuni 🕽 52
Padella 🕽 ⊕ 115
Polpetto 🕽 ⊕ 156
Polpo at Ape and Bird 🕽 57
Polpo Covent Garden 🕽 165
Polpo Smithfield 🕽 83
Polpo Soho 🕽 157
Riva 🕽 106
River Café 🕽🕽 ⊕ 76
Rotorino 🕽 69
Santini 🕽🕽🕽 167
Sartoria 🕽🕽🕽 133
Spring 🕽🕽 162
Theo Randall 🕽🕽 136
Trullo 🕽 ⊕ 81
Union Street Café 🕽🕽 114
Vasco and Piero's Pavilion 🕽🕽 155
Vico 🕽 ⊕ 165
Zafferano 🕽🕽🕽 126

Japanese

Araki 🕽🕽 ⊕ ⊕ 134
Dinings 🕽 147
Jidori 🕽 69

Kiku XX 139
Kiraku X 67
Koji X 75
Kouzu X 169
Koya Bar X 160
Kurobuta Marble Arch X 124
Matsuba X 108
Matsuri XX 150
Nanban X 101
Nobu XX 138
Nobu Berkeley St XX 137
Oliver Maki X 158
Roka (Aldwych) XX 162
Roka (Bloomsbury) XX 55
Roka (Mayfair) XX 136
Sake No Hana XX 150
Shoryu X 152
Soshiaru XX 82
Takahashi X 104
Tokimeitē XX 138
Tonkotsu X 161
Umu XxX✿✿ 131
UNI XX 168
Yashin XX 95
Yashin Ocean House XX 99
Zuma XX 128

Korean

Bibigo X 159
Hana X 121

Lebanese

Kenza XX 64

Meats and grills

34 XxX 133
Barbecoa XX 64
Beast XX 144
Beef and Brew X 59
Chicken Shop X 59
Chop Shop X 152
Cut XxX 133
Electric Diner X 97
Foxlow (Clerkenwell) X 83
Goodman Mayfair XX 138
Hawksmoor (City of London) X 65
Hawksmoor (Knightsbridge) XX 91
Hawksmoor (Mayfair) XX 135

Hawksmoor (Spitalfields) X 119
Hawksmoor
  (Strand and Covent Garden) X 164
Hill and Szrok X 71
MASH XX 155
Maze Grill Mayfair XX 138
Maze Grill Park Walk XX 91
New St Grill XX 63
Oblix XX 111
Rib Room XxX 90
Tramshed X 73
Vivat Bacchus X 65
Vivat Bacchus London Bridge X 112
Zelman Meats X 159

Mediterranean cuisine

Blixen X⊕ 118
Brackenbury X 77
Dehesa X⊕ 156
Dock Kitchen X 96
Duke of Sussex ▮⊃ 66
Earl Spencer ▮⊃ 121
Ember Yard X 156
Empress ▮⊃⊕ 74
The French Table XX 100
Garrison ▮⊃ 113
Kateh X⊕ 123
Light House X 104
Margaux X 99
Market Cafe X 71
May the Fifteenth X 102
Moro X 84
The Ninth X✿ 56
Nopi X 156
Opera Tavern X⊕ 165
The Orange ▮⊃ 169
Ottolenghi (Islington) X 86
Ottolenghi (Spitalfields) X 119
Palmerston ▮⊃ 113
Pizarro X 112
Rivea XX 127
Rosita X 121
Sager + Wilde X 117
Salt Yard X⊕ 56
Sardine X 70
Social Wine and Tapas X 146
Sonny's Kitchen X 106
Terroirs X 165
Wormwood X 97

Barrafina

Mexican

Peyote ✕ 139

Modern British

45 Jermyn St ✕✕ 151
The Alfred Tennyson ⌐◌ 126
Almeida ✕✕ 86
Anchor and Hope ⌐◌⏣ 116
Anglesea Arms ⌐◌ 77
Berners Tavern ✕✕ 143
Bistro Union ✕⏣ 101
Bluebird ✕✕ 91
Brown Dog ⌐◌ 106
Chiswell Street Dining Rooms ✕✕ 64
Corrigan's Mayfair ✕✕✕ 133
Craft London ✕ 68
Dean Street Townhouse
    Restaurant ✕✕ 154
Drapers Arms ⌐◌⏣ 87
Ealing Park Tavern ⌐◌ 67
Ellory ✕✿ 71
Fifteen London ✕ 70
Great Queen Street ✕⏣ 59
Harwood Arms ⌐◌✿ 76
Keeper's House ✕✕ 138
Legs ✕⏣ 70
Linnea ✕✕ 107
London House ✕✕ 120
Lyle's ✕✿ 73
Magdalen ✕✕ 111
Market ✕⏣ 58
Newman Arms ⌐◌⏣ 148
Oldroyd ✕ 86

Olympic Café + Dining Room ✕ 106
Paradise by way of Kensal Green ⌐◌ 52
Parlour ⌐◌ 52
Pharmacy 2 ✕✕ 103
Picture Fitzrovia ✕⏣ 146
Picture Marylebone ✕ 147
Pidgin ✕✿ 71
Rabbit ✕ 92
Refuel ✕✕ 155
Roast ✕✕ 114
The Shed ✕ 95
sixtyone ✕✕ 144
Tate Modern (Restaurant) ✕ 114
Tredwell's ✕ 164
La Trompette ✕✕✿ 79
Upstairs at The Guildford Arms ✕ 68
Upstairs (at Trinity) ✕⏣ 101
Victoria ⌐◌ 107
The Wallace ✕✕ 144
Well ⌐◌ 85
The Woodford ✕✕ 105

Modern cuisine

100 Wardour St ✕✕ 154
10 Greek Street ✕ 157
28°-50° Fetter Lane ✕ 66
Albert's Table ✕✕ 66
Alyn Williams
    at The Westbury ✕✕✕✿ 130
Antidote ✕ 158
Aqua Shard ✕✕ 111
L'Autre Pied ✕✕ 143
Avenue ✕✕ 151
Babylon ✕✕ 95

Bingham Restaurant XX	108
Blueprint Café X	111
Bob Bob Ricard XX	154
Bonhams XX ✿	134
Bradley's XX	60
Brawn X ㋐	116
Bread Street Kitchen XX	62
Brumus XX	152
Le Caprice XX	150
The Chancery XX	63
Chapter One XxX	53
Chapters XX	103
Charlotte's Bistro XX	79
Charlotte's W5 X ㋐	67
Charlotte's Place X	67
City Social XxX ✿	62
Clarke's XX	94
Claude's Kitchen X	75
Clerkenwell Kitchen X	85
Clove Club X ✿	73
Cross Keys ㏌	93
Dabbous X ✿	56
Delaunay XxX	161
Dickie Fitz XX	144
Duck and Waffle XX	64
Dysart Petersham XX	108
Elliot's X ㋐	115
Fellow ㏌	100
Fenchurch XX	63
Five Fields XxX ✿	89
Frenchie X	164
The Frog X	119
Galvin at Windows XxX ✿	131
The Glasshouse XX ✿	107
Grain Store X ㋐	100
Granger and Co. Clerkenwell X	83
Granger and Co. King's Cross X	100
Granger and Co. Notting Hill X	97
Ham Yard XX	154
Heddon Street Kitchen XX	136
Hedone XX ✿	79
Hélène Darroze at The Connaught XxxX ✿ ✿	130
Herbert's X	52
Hush XX	138
King's Head ㏌	109
Kitchen Table at Bubbledogs XX ✿	55
Kitchen W8 XX ✿	94
Kitty Fisher's X	139
Launceston Place XxX	94
Ledbury XxX ✿ ✿	96
Lutyens XxX	62
The Magazine XX	127
Manuka Kitchen X	75
Marcus XxxX ✿ ✿	125
Maze XX	136
Medlar XX	90
Michael Nadra XX	79
Michael Nadra Primrose Hill XX	60
Odette's XX	60
Orrery XxX	142
Ours XX	98
Oxo Tower XxX	114
Oxo Tower Brasserie X	115
Percy and Founders XX	144
Petersham Nurseries Café X	108
Plateau XX	118
Portland X ✿	146
Portman ㏌	148
Portrait X	152
Primeur X ㋐	81
Quaglino's XX	151
Rabot 1745 XX	114
Riding House Café X	146
Roux at Parliament Square XxX	167
St John's Tavern ㏌	81

Trishna

Salt and Honey X 124
Seven Park Place XxX ⊛ 149
Sinabro X 120
Sketch (The Gallery) XX 136
Skylon XxX 103
Smokehouse 🗗 82
Social Eating House X ⊛ 155
Story XX ⊛ 110
Thomas Cubitt 🗗 169
Trinity XX ⊛ 101
Typing Room XX 116
Village East X 111
Vinoteca X 147
White Onion X 104
Wild Honey XX 137
The Wolseley XxX 150
York and Albany XX 58

Moroccan

Momo XX 136
Zayane X 97

North African

Azou X ⊛ 77

North American

One Sixty X 60
Spuntino X 158

Peruvian

Andina X 73
Ceviche Old St X 85
Ceviche Soho X 159
Coya XX 137
Lima Fitzrovia X ⊛ 146
Lima Floral X 164

Polish

Ognisko XX 99

Portuguese

Taberna do Mercado X ⊛ 119

Provençal

Bandol X 92

Scottish

Mac and Wild X 147

Seafood

Angler XX ⊛ 84
Bentley's XX 137
Bonnie Gull X 147
Fish Market X 65
Galley X 86
J. Sheekey XX 162
J. Sheekey Oyster Bar X 164
Kensington Place X 95
Milos XxX 150
Olivomare X 169
One-O-One XxX 90
Outlaw's at The Capital XX ⊛ 90
The Richmond X 69
Scott's XxX 132
Sexy Fish XX 137
Wright Brothers X 115

South Indian

Hoppers X ⊛ 158

Spanish

Barrafina (Adelaide St) X 163
Barrafina (Drury Ln) X 164
Barrafina (Soho) X ⊛ 156
Barrica X ⊛ 56
Boqueria (Battersea) X 121
Boqueria (Brixton) X 101
Cambio de Tercio XX 98
Capote y Toros X 99
Cigala X 57
Copita X ⊛ 156
Copita del Mercado X 119
Drakes Tabanco X 57
Eyre Brothers XX 72
Iberica Marylebone XX 145
José X ⊛ 112
José Pizarro X 65
Lobos X 116
Morito (Finsbury) X ⊛ 84
Morito (Hoxton) X 71
Tapas Brindisa X 115
Tendido Cero X 99
Tendido Cuatro X 75

Thai

Blue Elephant XX	75
Chada XX	120
Rosa's Soho X	159
Simply Thai X	109
Som Saa X	120

Traditional British

Barnyard X⊕	57
Beagle X	70
Bird of Smithfield X	65
Boisdale of Canary Wharf XX	118
Builders Arms ⫶⊡	93
Bull and Last ⫶⊡	58
Butlers Wharf Chop House X	112
Canton Arms ⫶⊡⊕	103
Colony Grill Room XX	135
Crown ⫶⊡	109
Dinner	
by Heston Blumenthal XXX ✿✿	127
Foxlow (Stoke Newington) X	74
Friends XX	78
Gilbert Scott XX	100
The Goring (Dining Room) XXX ✿	166
Hereford Road X⊕	123
Hix (Soho) XX	155
Hix Mayfair XXX	134
Hix Oyster and Chop House X	83
Ivy Chelsea Garden XX	90
Ivy Market Grill XX	163
The Ivy XxX	162
Jugged Hare ⫶⊡	66
Lady Ottoline ⫶⊡	58
Lamberts X	120
Light on the Common X	104
Marksman ⫶⊡⊕	117
Mayfair Chippy X	140
Merchants Tavern XX	72
Noble Rot X	57
Northall XxX	167
Paradise Garage X⊕	117

Paternoster Chop House X	65
Pig and Butcher ⫶⊡	87
Princess of Shoreditch ⫶⊡	74
Princess Victoria ⫶⊡	77
Quality Chop House X	84
Quo Vadis XXX	153
Rex Whistler XX	168
Rivington Grill XX	73
Rules XX	162
St John X✿	82
St John Bread and Wine X⊕	118
St John Maltby X	113
Smokehouse ⫶⊡	80
Tommy Tucker ⫶⊡	76

Turkish

Oklava X	74

Vegetarian

Vanilla Black XX	63

Vietnamese

Au Lac X	85
Cây Tre X	159
Viet Grill X	74

World cuisine

Arabica Bar and Kitchen X	115
Baltic XX	114
Barbary X⊕	57
Caravan X	85
Chiltern Firehouse XX	143
Foley's X⊕	146
Honey and Co X⊕	56
The Modern Pantry Clerkenwell X	85
The Modern Pantry	
Finsbury Square XX	84
Palomar X⊕	157
Tandis X	54

Restaurants with outside dining

The Alfred Tennyson 🍴 126
Amaranto XXX 134
Anchor and Hope 🍴🌸 116
Angler XX❄❀ 84
Anglesea Arms 🍴 77
Antidote X 158
A. Wong X🌸 168
Barnyard X🌸 57
Barrafina (Drury Ln) X 164
Barrica X 56
Beagle X 70
Bibo X 121
Bingham Restaurant XX 108
Bistro Union X🌸 101
Blue Elephant XX 75
Boisdale of Canary Wharf XX 118
Boqueria (Battersea) X 121
Le Boudin Blanc X 139
Boulestin XX 150
Boundary XXX 72
Brackenbury X 77
Brasserie Vacherin X 116
Brown Dog 🍴 106
Bull and Last 🍴 58
Butlers Wharf Chop House X 112
Cantina Del Ponte X 111
Le Caprice XX 150

Chapters XX 103
Charlotte's W5 X🌸 67
Charlotte's Place X 67
Chiltern Firehouse XX 143
Chucs Bar and Grill XX 139
Cigala X 57
Cinnamon Culture XX 53
Cinnamon Kitchen XX 63
Cinnamon Soho X 158
Clerkenwell Kitchen X 85
Copita del Mercado X 119
Crown 🍴 109
Dean Street
   Townhouse Restaurant XX 154
Dehesa X🌸 156
Dickie Fitz XX 144
Dishoom X 165
Dock Kitchen X 96
Drapers Arms 🍴🌸 87
Duke of Sussex 🍴 66
Dysart Petersham XX 108
Ealing Park Tavern 🍴 67
Earl Spencer 🍴 121
Ellory X❄ 71
Empress 🍴🌸 74
Fish Market X 65
Foxlow (Stoke Newington) X 74
The Frog X 119

Gymkhana

Galvin Bistrot de Luxe XX 143
Galvin La Chapelle XxX ✿ 118
Grain Store X ⊕ 100
Granger and Co. King's Cross X 100
Ham Yard XX 154
Hazara XX 54
Heddon Street Kitchen XX 136
Herbert's X 52
Hereford Road X ⊕ 123
High Road Brasserie X 80
Hill and Szrok X 71
Hix Oyster and Chop House X 83
Hush XX 138
il trillo XX 92
Indian Zing XX 76
Ivy Chelsea Garden XX 90
Ivy Market Grill XX 163
José Pizarro X 65
J. Sheekey XX 162
King's Head ⑩ 109
Kurobuta Marble Arch X 124
Lady Ottoline ⑩ 58
Lardo X 71
Ledbury XxX ✿ ✿ 96
Light on the Common X 104
London House XX 120
Lurra XX 142
The Magazine XX 127
Market Cafe X 71
Marksman ⑩ ⊕ 117
May the Fifteenth X 102
Mazi X 96
Medlar XX 90
Michael Nadra Primrose Hill XX 60
The Modern Pantry Clerkenwell X 85
Momo XX 136
Morito (Finsbury) X ⊕ 84
Moro X 84
New St Grill XX 63
Odette's XX 60
Ognisko XX 99
Olivomare X 169
One Sixty X 60
Opso X 147

Orrery XxX 142
Ostuni X 52
Oxo Tower XxX 114
Oxo Tower Brasserie X 115
Painted Heron XX 91
Paradise Garage X ⊕ 117
Parlour ⑩ 52
Paternoster Chop House X 65
Percy and Founders XX 144
Petersham Nurseries Café X 108
La Petite Maison XX 137
Pig and Butcher ⑩ 87
Plateau XX 118
Polpo Smithfield X 83
Le Pont de la Tour XxX 110
Princess of Shoreditch ⑩ 74
Princess Victoria ⑩ 77
Provender X ⊕ 105
Rabot 1745 XX 114
The Richmond X 69
Ritz Restaurant XxXxX ✿ 149
River Café XX ✿ 76
Roka (Bloomsbury) XX 55
Roka (Mayfair) XX 136
Sager + Wilde X 117
St John's Tavern ⑩ 81
Santini XxX 167
Sartoria XxX 133
Smokehouse ⑩ 80
Smokehouse ⑩ 82
Taberna do Mercado X ⊕ 119
Tandis X 54
Tredwell's X 164
Trinity XX ✿ 101
La Trompette XX ✿ 79
Victoria ⑩ 107
Vivat Bacchus London Bridge X 112
Well ⑩ 85
Yashin Ocean House XX 99
Yauatcha City X 62
York and Albany XX 58
Zafferano XxX 126

ALPHABETICAL LIST OF HOTELS

45 Park Lane 🏨 129

A

Ace Hotel 🏨 72
Andaz Liverpool Street 🏨 61
Artist Residence 🏨 166

B

Baglioni 🏨 94
Batty Langley's 🏨 118
Beaufort 🏨 89
The Beaumont 🏨 129
Belgraves 🏨 125
Berkeley 🏨 124
Bermondsey Square 🏨 110
Bingham 🏨 107
Blakes 🏨 97
Brown's 🏨 129
Bulgari 🏨 127

C

Café Royal 🏨 153
The Capital 🏨 88
Charlotte Street 🏨 140
Chesterfield 🏨 129
Chiltern Firehouse 🏨 140
Claridge's 🏨 128
Connaught 🏨 128
Corinthia 🏨 165
Covent Garden 🏨 55

D

Dean Street Townhouse 🏨 153
Dorchester 🏨 128
Dorset Square 🏨 141
Draycott 🏨 88
Dukes 🏨 149
Durrants 🏨 141

E

Egerton House 🏨 88
The Exhibitionist 🏨 98

F

Four Seasons (Canary Wharf) 🏨 117
Four Seasons (Mayfair) 🏨 128

G

The Gore 🏨 98
Goring 🏨 166
Great Northern H. London 🏨 100

H

Halkin 🏨 125
Ham Yard 🏨 152
Haymarket 🏨 148
Hazlitt's 🏨 153
High Road House 🏨 79
Hilton London Bankside 🏨 113
Hilton London Heathrow
    Airport Terminal 5 🏨 78
Hotel du Vin 🏨 104
The Hoxton (Holborn) 🏨 59
The Hoxton (Shoreditch) 🏨 70

J

Jumeirah Carlton Tower 🏨 88

K

K + K George 🏨 93
Knightsbridge 🏨 89

L

The Lanesborough 🏨 124
Langham 🏨 140
The Levin 🏨 89
The London Edition 🏨 140
London Marriott H. County Hall 🏨 .. 103
Lord Milner 🏨 166

M

Malmaison 🏨 82
Mandarin Oriental Hyde Park 🏨 127
Marble Arch by Montcalm 🏨 141
M by Montcalm 🏨 70
The Milestone 🏨 94
Mondrian London 🏨 113

Montcalm London City
at The Brewery 61

N

No.11 Cadogan Gardens 89
Number Sixteen 98
No. Ten Manchester Street 141

O

One Aldwych 161

P

The Pelham 97
Petersham 107
The Portobello 96

R

Ritz 148
The Rookery 82
Rosewood London 59
Royal Garden 93

S

St James' Court 166
St James's Hotel and Club 149

St Martins Lane 161
St Pancras Renaissance 99
Sanderson 140
Savoy 161
Shangri-La 110
Sofitel 78
Sofitel London St James 148
Soho 152
South Place 83
Stafford 149
Sumner 141

T

Threadneedles 61
Town Hall 116
Twenty Nevern Square 93

W

Waldorf Hilton 161
The Wellesley 125
Westbury 129

Z

Zetter 84
Zetter Townhouse Marylebone 141

Clove Club

PARTICULARLY PLEASANT HOTELS

🏨

Berkeley	124
Claridge's	128
Connaught	128
Corinthia	165
Dorchester	128
Four Seasons (Mayfair)	128
Mandarin Oriental Hyde Park	127
Ritz	148
Savoy	161

🏨

45 Park Lane	129
The Beaumont	129
Bulgari	127
Café Royal	153
Goring	166
Ham Yard	152
The Lanesborough	124
One Aldwych	161
Soho	152

🏨

Blakes	97
The Capital	88
Charlotte Street	140
Chiltern Firehouse	140
Covent Garden	55
Dukes	149
Halkin	125
The Milestone	94
South Place	83
Stafford	149
Town Hall	116

🏨

Batty Langley's	118
Egerton House	88
Knightsbridge	89
The Levin	89
Number Sixteen	98
Zetter Townhouse Marylebone	141

Boroughs and areas

Greater London is divided, for administrative purposes, into 32 boroughs plus **the City:** these sub-divide naturally into minor areas, usually grouped around former villages or quarters, which often maintain a distinctive character.

BRENT

Church End

✗ Shayona   AC ⏹ P

INDIAN · FAMILY Opposite the striking Swaminarayan Temple is this simple, sattvic restaurant: it's vegetarian and 'pure' so avoids onion or garlic. Expect curries from the north, dosas from the south and Mumbai street food. No alcohol so try a lassi.

Menu £10 (weekday lunch) – Carte £13/20

Town plan: 2C3-a - 54-62 Meadow Garth ⊠ NW10 8HD – ⊖ Stonebridge Park – ☎ 020 8965 3365 – www.shayonarestaurants.com – Closed 19-20 October and 25 December

Kensal Green

🍴 Paradise by way of Kensal Green   🍸 AC ⇔

MODERN BRITISH · PUB Less a pub, more a veritable fun palace. Music, comedy and film nights happen upstairs; the bar and restaurant are wonderfully quirky; staff are contagiously enthusiastic and the European themed food is prepared with genuine care.

Carte £26/45

Town plan: 16L4-x - 19 Kilburn Ln ⊠ W10 4AE – ⊖ Kensal Green. – ☎ 020 8969 0098 – www.theparadise.co.uk – dinner only and lunch Saturday and Sunday

🍴 Parlour   🍸 🏠 🖳

MODERN BRITISH · PUB A fun, warmly run and slightly quirky neighbourhood hangout. The menu is a wonderfully unabashed mix of tradition, originality and reinvention. Don't miss the cow pie which even Dan, however Desperate, would struggle to finish.

Menu £15 (weekday lunch) – Carte £20/40

Town plan: 16L4-r - 5 Regent St ⊠ NW10 5LG – ⊖ Kensal Green – ☎ 020 8969 2184 – www.parlourkensal.com – Closed 1 week August, 10 days Christmas-New Year and Monday

Queen's Park

✗ Ostuni   🏠 AC

ITALIAN · NEIGHBOURHOOD The cuisine of Puglia, the red hot heel in Italy's boot, is celebrated at this rustic local restaurant. Don't miss the olives, creamy burrata, fava bean purée, the sausages and bombette, or the orecchiette – the ear-shaped pasta.

Carte £16/40

Town plan: 10M3-b - 43-45 Lonsdale Rd ⊠ NW6 6RA – ⊖ Queen's Park – ☎ 020 7624 8035 – www.ostuniristorante.co.uk – Closed 25 December

BROMLEY

Keston

✗ Herbert's   🏠 ♿ AC 🖳

MODERN CUISINE · FASHIONABLE A neat, contemporary restaurant in shades of grey, occupying a pleasant spot overlooking the Common. The European cooking is modern but the combinations of ingredients are reassuringly familiar.

Carte £20/47

Town plan: 8G6-x - 6 Commonside ⊠ BR2 6BP – ☎ 01689 855501 – www.thisisherberts.co.uk – Closed Sunday dinner and Monday

Farnborough

XxX Chapter One 🍽 AC ♿ P

MODERN CUISINE · FRIENDLY Long-standing restaurant with many regulars, its stylish bar leading into an elegant, modern dining room. Wide-ranging menus offer keenly priced, carefully prepared modern European dishes; cooking is light and delicate, mixing classic and modern flavours. Assured service.

Menu £20/40

Town plan: 8G6-c - Farnborough Common, Locksbottom ⊠ BR6 8NF
– ℰ01689 854848 – www.chapteronerestaurant.co.uk – Closed 2-4 January

Orpington

XX Xian AC

CHINESE · NEIGHBOURHOOD Stylish, modern dining room with banquette seating, bamboo matting on the walls and six super lithographs of the famous Terracotta Warriors of Xian. Appealing menu offers flavoursome, authentic Chinese dishes, with something for everyone.

Menu £10 (weekday lunch) – Carte £18/32

Town plan: 8G6-a - 324 High St. ⊠ BR6 0NG – ℰ01689 871881
– Closed 2 weeks May, 1 week October, 25-26 December, Sunday lunch and Monday

Petts Wood

XX Indian Essence ♿ AC

🐶 INDIAN · NEIGHBOURHOOD Atul Kochhar of Benares is one of the owners of this smart and contemporary Indian restaurant. Everything is made in-house, from the masala paste to the kulfi; dishes are vibrant and flavoursome and the prices are good.

Menu £19/25 (weekdays) – Carte £25/34

Town plan: 8G5-e - 176-178 Petts Wood Rd ⊠ BR5 1LG – ℰ01689 838700
– www.indianessence.co.uk

Sundridge Park

XX Cinnamon Culture 🍴 I♡

INDIAN · NEIGHBOURHOOD Former Victorian pub transmogrified into a smart Indian restaurant where the cooking is undertaken with care. A plethora of menus include tasting and vegetarian options, as well as a monthly menu focusing on one region.

Menu £21 (weekday lunch) – Carte £24/39

Town plan: 8G5-z - 46 Plaistow Ln ⊠ BR1 3PA – ℰ020 8289 0322
– www.cinnamonculture.com – Closed 26 December and Monday

CAMDEN

Belsize Park

XX XO

ASIAN · NEIGHBOURHOOD Busy bar behind which is a slick and stylish dining room. Vibrant atmosphere; popular with all the good-looking locals. Japanese, Korean, Thai and Chinese cooking; dishes are best shared.

Menu £ 10 (lunch) – Carte £ 22/51

Town plan: 11N2-a - *29 Belsize Ln* ⊠ *NW3 5AS* – ⊖ *Belsize Park*
- *☏ 020 7433 0888 – www.rickerrestaurants.com/xo – Closed 25-26 December and 1 January*

XX Hazara

INDIAN · NEIGHBOURHOOD At this keenly run, modern Indian restaurant, the adventurous diner will find specialities from all regions. Game and fish stand out – the owner goes personally to Smithfield and Billingsgate to ensure the quality of the produce.

Carte £ 19/33

Town plan: 11N2-n - *44 Belsize Ln* ⊠ *NW3 5AR* – ⊖ *Belsize Park*
- *☏ 020 7423 1147 – www.hazararestaurant.com*
- *dinner only and lunch Saturday-Sunday*
- *Closed 25-26 December and 1 January*

X Retsina

GREEK · RUSTIC Family-run restaurant whose unapologetically traditional menu offers all the Greek classics but the charcoal grill makes souvla, kebabs and cutlets the best choices. Simple, bright and airy room with a friendly atmosphere.

Carte £ 24/34

Town plan: 11N2-n - *48-50 Belsize Ln* ⊠ *NW3 5AR*
- ⊖ *Belsize Park* – *☏ 020 7431 5855*
- *www.retsina.squarespace.com*
- *Closed 25-26 December, 1 January, Monday lunch and bank holidays*

X Tandis

WORLD CUISINE · NEIGHBOURHOOD Persian and Middle Eastern food whose appeal stretches way beyond the Iranian diaspora. The specialities are the substantial and invigorating khoresh stew and the succulent kababs; end with Persian sorbet with rosewater.

Carte £ 16/26

Town plan: 11P2-x - *73 Haverstock Hill* ⊠ *NW3 4SL* – ⊖ *Chalk Farm*
- *☏ 020 7586 8079 – www.tandisrestaurant.com*
- *Closed 25 December*

Bloomsbury

🏠 Covent Garden

LUXURY · DESIGN Popular with those of a theatrical bent. Boldly designed, stylish bedrooms, with technology discreetly concealed. Boasts a very comfortable first floor oak-panelled drawing room with its own honesty bar. Easy-going menu in Brasserie Max.

59 rooms – 🛏£ 230/300 🛏🛏£ 300/370 – ☐ £ 20

Town plan: 31AP2-x - 10 Monmouth St ⊠ WC2H 9HB – ⊖ Covent Garden
- 𝒞 020 7806 1000 - www.firmdalehotels.com

🍴🍴🍴 Pied à Terre
⏱

CREATIVE · ELEGANT For over 25 years, David Moore's restaurant has stood apart in Charlotte Street, confident in its abilities and in the loyalty of its regulars. Subtle decorative changes keep it looking fresh and vibrant, while Andrew McFadden delivers refined, creative, flavoursome cooking.
→ Scallop ceviche with cucumber, balsamic and dill. Fallow deer with black pearl curry, smoked bacon and beetroot. Pineapple with kaffir lime and coriander.
Menu £ 38/80

Town plan: 31AN1-a - 34 Charlotte St ⊠ W1T 2NH – ⊖ Goodge Street
- 𝒞 020 7636 1178 (booking essential) - www.pied-a-terre.co.uk - Closed last week December-5 January, Saturday lunch, Sunday and bank holidays

🍴🍴 Hakkasan Hanway Place
⏱

CHINESE · TRENDY There are now Hakkasans all over the world but this was the original. It has the sensual looks, air of exclusivity and glamorous atmosphere synonymous with the 'brand'. The exquisite Cantonese dishes are prepared with care and consistency by the large kitchen team; lunch dim sum is a highlight.
→ Dim sum platter. Roasted duck with black truffle sauce. Jivara bomb.
Menu £ 38/128 - Carte £ 32/94

Town plan: 31AP2-y - 8 Hanway Pl. ⊠ W1T 1HD – ⊖ Tottenham Court Road
- 𝒞 020 7927 7000 - www.hakkasan.com - Closed 24-25 December

🍴🍴 Kitchen Table at Bubbledogs (James Knappett)
⏱

MODERN CUISINE · FASHIONABLE Fight through the crowds enjoying a curious mix of hotdogs and champagne and head for the curtain – behind it is a counter for 19 diners. Chef-owner James prepares a no-choice menu of around 12 dishes. The produce is exemplary; the cooking has a clever creative edge; and the dishes have real depth.
→ Truffle-roasted Jersey Royals with bacon and crème fraîche. Cornish lobster with chilli, wild garlic and coral foam. Gooseberry and yoghurt parfait with almonds.
Menu £ 88 - tasting menu only

Town plan: 31AN1-g - 70 Charlotte St ⊠ W1T 4QG – ⊖ Goodge Street
- 𝒞 020 7637 7770 (booking essential) - www.kitchentablelondon.co.uk - dinner only - Closed 1-14 January, 17 August-2 September, 23-27 December, Sunday and Monday

🍴🍴 Mon Plaisir

FRENCH · FAMILY This proud French institution opened in the 1940s. Enjoy satisfyingly authentic classics in any of the four contrasting rooms, full of Gallic charm; apparently the bar was salvaged from a Lyonnais brothel.
Menu £ 16/24 - Carte £ 32/46

Town plan: 31AQ2-g - 19-21 Monmouth St. ⊠ WC2H 9DD – ⊖ Covent Garden
- 𝒞 020 7836 7243 - www.monplaisir.co.uk - Closed 25-26 December, Easter Sunday-Monday and Sunday

🍴🍴 Roka

JAPANESE · FASHIONABLE Bright, atmospheric interior of teak and oak; bustling and trendy feel. Contemporary touches added to Japanese dishes; try specialities from the on-view Robata grill. Capable and chatty service.
Carte £ 40/70

Town plan: 31AN1-k - 37 Charlotte St ⊠ W1T 1RR – ⊖ Goodge Street
- 𝒞 020 7580 6464 - www.rokarestaurant.com - Closed 25 December

X Dabbous (Ollie Dabbous) 🏆 AC
☸

MODERN CUISINE · DESIGN Still one of the most popular spots in town – the kitchen adopts the 'less is more' approach and the food comes with an elegantly restrained finesse and a bewitching purity. Most have the 7-course menu with its stimulating and sublime combinations of ingredients. The ersatz-industrial room has a simple elegance.

→ Peas with mint. Braised turbot with lemon verbena. Cherry blossom tea-soaked barley flour sponge with Tahitian vanilla cream.

Menu £ 28/59

Town plan: 31AN1-r - 39 Whitfield St ⊠ W1T 2SF
– ⊖ Goodge Street – ℰ 020 7323 1544 (booking essential) – www.dabbous.co.uk
– Closed 10 days Christmas-New Year, Easter and Sunday

X The Ninth 🆕 (Jun Tanaka) AC
☸

MEDITERRANEAN CUISINE · BRASSERIE Jun Tanaka's first restaurant – the ninth in which he has worked – is this neighbourhood spot with a lively downstairs and more intimate first floor. Cooking uses classical French techniques with a spotlight on the Med; dishes look appealing but the focus is firmly on flavour. Vegetables are a highlight.

→ Smoked duck breast, caramelised chicory and walnuts. Charcoal-roasted celeriac with smoked almonds and wild garlic. Caramelised lemon tart with fromage frais.

Menu £ 21 (weekday lunch) – Carte £ 28/47

Town plan: 31AN1-j - 22 Charlotte St ⊠ W1T 2NB
– ⊖ Goodge Street – ℰ 020 3019 0880 – www.theninthlondon.com
– Closed Christmas-New Year, Sunday and bank holidays

X Salt Yard 🕃 AC 🍷
🍴

MEDITERRANEAN CUISINE · TAPAS BAR Ground floor bar and buzzy basement restaurant specialising in good value plates of tasty Italian and Spanish dishes, ideal for sharing; charcuterie a speciality. Super wine list.

Carte £ 17/28

Town plan: 31AN1-d - 54 Goodge St. ⊠ W1T 4NA – ⊖ Goodge Street
– ℰ 020 7637 0657 – www.saltyard.co.uk – Closed 25 and dinner 24 and 31 December, 1 January

X Honey & Co AC 🗔 🍴
🍴

WORLD CUISINE · SIMPLE The husband and wife team at this sweet little café were both Ottolenghi head chefs so expect cooking full of freshness and colour. Influences stretch beyond Israel to the wider Middle East. Open from 8am; packed at night.

Menu £ 30 – Carte £ 25/31

Town plan: 18Q4-c - 25a Warren St ⊠ W1T 5LZ
– ⊖ Warren Street – ℰ 020 7388 6175 (booking essential)
– www.honeyandco.co.uk
– Closed 25-26 December and Sunday

X Barrica 🍸 AC 🍷
🍴

SPANISH · TAPAS BAR All the staff at this lively little tapas bar are Spanish, so perhaps it's national pride that makes them run it with a passion lacking in many of their competitors. When it comes to the food authenticity is high on the agenda.

Carte £ 19/36

Town plan: 31AN1-x - 62 Goodge St ⊠ W1T 4NE
– ⊖ Goodge Street – ℰ 020 7436 9448 (booking essential)
– www.barrica.co.uk
– Closed 25-26 December, 1 January, Sunday and bank holidays

X **Barbary** N   AC 🍴

🌐 **WORLD CUISINE · TAPAS BAR** A sultry, atmospheric restaurant from the team behind Palomar: a tiny place with 24 non-bookable seats squeezed around a horseshoe-shaped, zinc-topped counter. The menu of small sharing plates lists dishes from the former Barbary Coast. Service is keen, as are the prices.

Carte £ 22/37

Town plan: 31AQ2-k - *16 Neal's Yard* ⊠ *WC2H 9DP* – ⊖ *Covent Garden (bookings not accepted) – www.thebarbary.co.uk – Closed 25-26 December and Monday*

X **Drakes Tabanco**   AC 🍴

SPANISH · SIMPLE Taking advantage of our newfound fondness for fino is this simple tabanco, from the people behind nearby Barrica and Copita. The small, Andalusian-inspired tapas menu uses imported produce from Spain alongside British ingredients.

Carte £ 22/34

Town plan: 31AN1-t - *3 Windmill St* ⊠ *W1T 2HY* – ⊖ *Goodge Street – ℰ 020 7637 9388 – www.drakestabanco.com – Closed Sunday and bank holidays*

X **Cigala**   🕸 🍷 🎍 AC 🍴 ♿

SPANISH · NEIGHBOURHOOD Longstanding Spanish restaurant, with a lively and convivial atmosphere, friendly and helpful service and an appealing and extensive menu of classics. The dried hams are a must and it's well worth waiting the 30 minutes for a paella.

Menu £ 24 (weekdays) – Carte £ 26/39

Town plan: 32AR1-a - *54 Lamb's Conduit St.* ⊠ *WC1N 3LW* – ⊖ *Russell Square – ℰ 020 7405 1717 (booking essential) – www.cigala.co.uk – Closed 25-26 December, 1 January, Easter Sunday and Easter Monday*

X **Noble Rot** N   🕸 AC

TRADITIONAL BRITISH · RUSTIC A wine bar and restaurant from the people behind the wine magazine of the same name. Unfussy cooking comes with bold, gutsy flavours; expect fish from the Kent coast as well as classics like terrines, rillettes and home-cured meats.

Carte £ 30/43

Town plan: 18R4-r - *51 Lamb's Conduit St* ⊠ *WC1N 3NB* – ⊖ *Russell Square – ℰ 020 7242 8963 (booking advisable) – www.noblerot.co.uk – Closed 25-26 December and Sunday*

X **Barnyard**   🎍 AC

🌐 **TRADITIONAL BRITISH · RUSTIC** Dude food prepared with integrity draws the crowds to this fun little place co-owned by Ollie Dabbous. The food arrives all at once on enamel plates, and dishes are full of rustic, artery-hardening goodness yet are prepared with precision and care. Just be ready to queue, as it seats fewer than 50.

Menu £ 21 (lunch) – Carte £ 17/32

Town plan: 31AN1-b - *18 Charlotte St* ⊠ *W1T 2LZ* – ⊖ *Goodge Street – ℰ 020 7580 3842 (bookings not accepted) – www.barnyard-london.com – Closed 25-26 December*

X **Polpo at Ape & Bird**   🍴

ITALIAN · RUSTIC Even experienced restaurateurs have to sometimes have a rethink. When Russell Norman found his Ape & Bird pub wasn't working, he simply turned it into another Polpo. Expect the same style of small plates, just in a bigger place with a couple of bars.

Menu £ 25 – Carte £ 12/21

Town plan: 31AP2-q - *142 Shaftesbury Ave* ⊠ *WC2H 8HJ* – ⊖ *Leicester Square – ℰ 020 7836 3119 (bookings not accepted) – www.polpo.co.uk*

✗ Flesh & Buns

ASIAN · TRENDY A loud, fun basement next to the Donmar. There's plenty of Japanese dishes but star billing goes to the hirata bun – the soft Taiwanese-style steamed pillows of delight that sandwich your choice of meat or fish filling.
Menu £ 19 (lunch and early dinner) – Carte £ 21/47
Town plan: 31AQ2-q - *41 Earlham St* ✉ *WC2H 9LX* – ↔ *Leicester Square*
– ☎ *020 7632 9500 (booking advisable) – www.fleshandbuns.com – Closed 24-25 December*

✗ Talli Joe

INDIAN · FASHIONABLE Talli means 'tipsy' in Hindi and this lively place was inspired by India's dive bars. Cocktails and tapas-style small plates are the order of the day; some dishes are old family favourites of the chef, while others have a Western edge.
Carte £ 18/28
Town plan: 31AP2-r - *152-156 Shaftesbury Ave* ✉ *WC2H 8HL* – ↔ *Covent Garden*
– ☎ *020 7836 5400 – www.tallijoe.com – Closed 25-26 December, 1 January and Sunday*

░ Lady Ottoline

TRADITIONAL BRITISH · COSY A charming traditional feel and a keen sense of history have always defined this classic Victorian pub. Stout British dishes are served in the ground floor bar and the more sedate upstairs dining room.
Carte £ 26/43
Town plan: 32AR1-c - *11a Northington St* ✉ *WC1N 2JF* – ↔ *Chancery Lane.*
– ☎ *020 7831 0008 – www.theladyottoline.com – Closed bank holidays*

Camden Town

✗✗ York & Albany

MODERN CUISINE · INN This handsome 1820s John Nash coaching inn was rescued by Gordon Ramsay a few years ago after lying almost derelict. It's a moot point whether it's still an inn or more a restaurant; the food is sophisticated and the service is bright.
Menu £ 21 (weekday lunch) – Carte £ 30/49
9 rooms ⌂ – ♦£ 105/205 ♦♦£ 295/330
Town plan: 12Q3-s - *127-129 Parkway* ✉ *NW1 7PS* – ↔ *Camden Town*
– ☎ *020 7592 1227 – www.gordonramsayrestaurants.com/york-and-albany/*

✗ Market

MODERN BRITISH · NEIGHBOURHOOD Market fresh produce is used to create satisfying and refreshingly matter of fact British dishes, at excellent prices that entice plenty of passers-by. Appealing décor of exposed brick walls, old school chairs and zinc-topped tables.
Menu £ 12 (weekday lunch)/18 – Carte £ 28/35
Town plan: 12Q3-x - *43 Parkway* ✉ *NW1 7PN* – ↔ *Camden Town*
– ☎ *020 7267 9700 (booking essential) – www.marketrestaurant.co.uk – Closed 25 December-2 January, Sunday dinner and bank holidays*

Dartmouth Park

░ Bull & Last

TRADITIONAL BRITISH · NEIGHBOURHOOD A busy Victorian pub with plenty of charm and character; the upstairs is a little quieter. Cooking is muscular, satisfying and reflects the time of year; charcuterie is a speciality.
Carte £ 25/44
Town plan: 12Q1-a - *168 Highgate Rd* ✉ *NW5 1QS* – ↔ *Tufnell Park.*
– ☎ *020 7267 3641 (booking essential) – www.thebullandlast.co.uk – Closed 23-25 December*

Hatton Garden

✗ Anglo ⓝ

CREATIVE BRITISH · RUSTIC As its name suggests, British produce is the main-stay of the menu at this pared-down, personally run restaurant. Concise à la carte at lunch; 7 course tasting menu in the evening. Cooking is well-executed with assured, harmonious flavours.

Menu £ 45 (dinner) – Carte lunch £ 35/48

Town plan: 32AS1-o - *30 St Cross St* ⊠ *ECIN 8UH* – ⊖ *Farringdon*
– *𝒞 020 7430 1503 – www.anglorestaurant.com – Closed 22 December-17 January, Saturday lunch, Sunday and Monday*

Holborn

🏨 Rosewood London ⌂ ⓢⓟ 🈁 🛌 🔁 ⅙ 🅰🅲 💆 🚗

HISTORIC · ELEGANT A beautiful Edwardian building that was once the HQ of Pearl Assurance. The styling is very British and the bedrooms are uncluttered and smart. Cartoonist Gerald Scarfe's work adorns the walls of his eponymous bar. A classic brasserie with a menu of British favourites occupies the former banking hall.

306 rooms – 🛏£ 378/882 🛏🛏£ 378/882 – ⌸ £ 20 – 44 suites

Town plan: 32AR1-x - *252 High Holborn* ⊠ *WC1V 7EN* – ⊖ *Holborn*
– *𝒞 020 7781 8888 – www.rosewoodhotels.com/london*

🏠 The Hoxton ⌂ 🔁 ⅙ 🅰🅲 🌣 💆

TOWNHOUSE · CONTEMPORARY When the room categories are Shoebox, Snug, Cosy and Roomy, you know you're in a hip hotel. A great location and competitive rates plus a retro-style diner, a buzzy lobby and a 'Chicken Shop' in the basement.

174 rooms ⌸ – 🛏£ 69/299 🛏🛏£ 69/299

Town plan: 31AQ1-h - *199 - 206 High Holborn* ⊠ *WC1V 7BD* – ⊖ *Holborn*
– *𝒞 020 7661 3000 – www.thehoxton.com*

✗ Great Queen Street 🅰🅲
🕸

MODERN BRITISH · RUSTIC The menu is a model of British understatement and is dictated by the seasons; the cooking, confident and satisfying with laudable prices and generous portions. Lively atmosphere and enthusiastic service. Highlights include the shared dishes like the suet-crusted steak and ale pie for two.

Menu £ 22 (weekday lunch) – Carte £ 21/38

Town plan: 31AQ2-c - *32 Great Queen St* ⊠ *WC2B 5AA* – ⊖ *Holborn*
– *𝒞 020 7242 0622 (booking essential) – www.greatqueenstreetrestaurant.co.uk*
– *Closed Christmas-New Year, Sunday dinner and bank holidays*

Kentish Town

✗ Chicken Shop ⅙ 🅰🅲

MEATS AND GRILLS · RUSTIC Simply great chicken – marinated, steamed and finished over wood and charcoal – with a choice of sides and three desserts. It all happens in a noisy, mildly chaotic basement but it's great fun and good value. Be ready to queue.

Carte £ 16/21

Town plan: 12Q2-c - *79 Highgate Rd* ⊠ *NW5 1TL* – ⊖ *Kentish Town*
– *𝒞 020 3310 2020 (bookings not accepted) – www.chickenshop.com – dinner only and lunch Saturday-Sunday*

✗ Beef & Brew ⓝ 🅰🅲

MEATS AND GRILLS · SIMPLE The name says it all. A fun place that looks not unlike a butcher's shop. Prices are kept down by using lesser cuts of meat, like onglet or flat iron, and beers are from small artisan brewers. Don't miss the brisket jam nuggets.

Carte £ 18/27

Town plan: 12Q2-t - *323 Kentish Town Rd* ⊠ *NW5 2TJ* – ⊖ *Kentish Town*
– *𝒞 020 7998 1511 (bookings advisable at dinner) – www.beef-and-brew.co.uk*
– *Closed Monday lunch*

Primrose Hill

XX Odette's 🛱 AC 🕼 ⇔

MODERN CUISINE · NEIGHBOURHOOD A long-standing local favourite. Warm and inviting interior, with chatty yet organised service. Robust and quite elaborate cooking, with owner passionate about his Welsh roots. Good value lunch menu.

Menu £ 22 (weekday lunch) – Carte £ 31/48

Town plan: 11P3-b - *130 Regent's Park Rd.* ✉ *NW1 8XL* – ⊖ *Chalk Farm*
– 𝒞 *020 7586 8569* – *www.odettesprimrosehill.com* – *Closed 25 December-7 January and Monday except December*

XX Michael Nadra Primrose Hill 🍸 🛱 � AC 🕼

MODERN CUISINE · NEIGHBOURHOOD Michael Nadra went north for his second branch and took over this unusual, modern building. The menu resembles his Chiswick operation, which means flavours from the Med but also the odd Asian note. The bar offers over 20 martinis.

Menu £ 27/38

Town plan: 12Q3-m - *42 Gloucester Ave* ✉ *NW1 8JD* – ⊖ *Camden Town*
– 𝒞 *020 7722 2800* – *www.restaurant-michaelnadra.co.uk/primrose* – *Closed 24-28 December and 1 January*

X L'Absinthe 🕸 AC 🖳 ⇔

FRENCH · BISTRO A classic French bistro offering a great atmosphere, a roll-call of favourites from cassoulet to duck confit, and a terrific wine list where only corkage is charged on the retail price. Ask for a table on the ground floor.

Menu £ 10 (weekday lunch) – Carte £ 22/38

Town plan: 11P3-s - *40 Chalcot Rd* ✉ *NW1 8LS* – ⊖ *Chalk Farm*
– 𝒞 *020 7483 4848* – *www.labsinthe.co.uk* – *Closed 1 week Christmas and Monday dinner*

Swiss Cottage

XX Bradley's AC 🕼 🗟

MODERN CUISINE · NEIGHBOURHOOD A stalwart of the local dining scene and ideal for visitors to the nearby Hampstead Theatre. The thoughtfully compiled and competitively priced set menus of mostly classical cooking draw in plenty of regulars.

Menu £ 28 – Carte £ 33/43

Town plan: 11N2-e - *25 Winchester Rd.* ✉ *NW3 3NR* – ⊖ *Swiss Cottage*
– 𝒞 *020 7722 3457* – *www.bradleysnw3.co.uk* – *Closed Sunday dinner*

West Hampstead

X One Sixty 🛱 AC

NORTH AMERICAN · SIMPLE A fun, stripped back bar and restaurant, based on an American smokehouse. Meats are smoked in-house to a temperature of 160°F – hence the name. Eat with your fingers and explore the list of over 50 craft beers from around the world.

Carte £ 25/38

Town plan: 10M2-s - *291 West End Ln.* ✉ *NW6 1RD* – ⊖ *West Hampstead*
– 𝒞 *020 7794 9786* – *www.one-sixty.co.uk* – *dinner only and lunch Saturday-Sunday* – *Closed 25-30 December*

CITY OF LONDON

Hotels

🏨 Andaz Liverpool Street

BUSINESS · DESIGN A contemporary and stylish interior hides behind the classic Victorian façade. Bright and spacious bedrooms boast state-of-the-art facilities. Various dining options include a brasserie specialising in grilled meats, a compact Japanese restaurant and a traditional pub.

267 rooms – ♦£ 173/683 ♦♦£ 189/699 – ☲ £ 18 – 3 suites

Town plan: 34AX2-t - ✉ EC2M 7QN – ⊖ Liverpool Street – ℰ 020 7961 1234
– www.andaz.com

🏨 Threadneedles

BUSINESS · MODERN A converted bank, dating from 1856, with a smart, boutique feel and a stunning stalned-glass cupola in the lounge. Bedrooms are very stylish and individual, featuring Egyptian cotton sheets, iPod docks and thoughtful extras. Spacious bar and restaurant; a striking backdrop to the classical menu.

74 rooms – ♦£ 149/599 ♦♦£ 149/599 – ☲ £ 15

Town plan: 33AW2-y - 5 Threadneedle St. ✉ EC2R 8AY
– ⊖ Bank – ℰ 020 7657 8080
– www.hotelthreadneedles.co.uk

🏨 Montcalm London City at The Brewery

BUSINESS · CONTEMPORARY The majority of the contemporary rooms are in the original part of the Whitbread Brewery, built in 1714; ask for a quieter one overlooking the courtyard, or one of the 25 found in the 4 restored Georgian townhouses across the road.

235 rooms ☲ – ♦£ 147/400 ♦♦£ 187/500 – 7 suites

Town plan: 33AV1-r - 52 Chiswell St ✉ EC1Y 4SA
– ⊖ Barbican
– ℰ 020 7614 0100
– www.themontcalmlondoncity.co.uk

Chiswell Street Dining Rooms – See restaurant listing

Prices quoted after the symbol ♦ refer to the lowest rate for a single room in low season, followed by the highest rate in high season. The same principle applies to the symbol ♦♦ for a double room.

Restaurants

XXX City Social

MODERN CUISINE · ELEGANT Jason Atherton took over in 2014 and made the place bigger and better looking with a darker, moodier feel. The City views are as impressive as ever, especially from tables 10 & 15. The flexible menu is largely European and the cooking manages to be both refined and robust at the same time.

→ Yellowfin tuna tataki with cucumber salad and ponzu dressing. Braised Irish short-rib with celery, watercress and red wine sauce. Chocolate soufflé with orange ice cream.

Carte £ 43/72

Town plan: 33AW2-s - Tower 42 (24th floor), 25 Old Broad St ⊠ EC2N 1HQ
– ⊖ Liverpool Street – ℰ 020 7877 7703 – www.citysociallondon.com – Closed Sunday and bank holidays

XXX Lutyens

MODERN CUISINE · FASHIONABLE The unmistakable hand of Sir Terence Conran: timeless and understated good looks mixed with functionality, and an appealing Anglo-French menu with plenty of classics such as fruits de mer and game in season.

Menu £ 25/33 – Carte £ 30/62

Town plan: 32AT2-c - 85 Fleet St. ⊠ EC4Y 1AE – ⊖ Blackfriars
– ℰ 020 7583 8385 – www.lutyens-restaurant.com – Closed 1 week Christmas-New Year, Saturday, Sunday and bank holidays

XX Club Gascon (Pascal Aussignac)

FRENCH · INTIMATE The gastronomy of Gascony and France's southwest are the starting points but the assured and intensely flavoured cooking also pushes at the boundaries. Marble and huge floral displays create suitably atmospheric surroundings.

→ Foie gras terrine with caviar and an oceanic crisp. Lamb with vermouth sauce, mussels and crisp sweetbreads. Scrambled Brillat-Savarin cheese with truffled honey and pistachio.

Menu £ 35/68 – Carte £ 37/58

Town plan: 33AU1-z - 57 West Smithfield ⊠ EC1A 9DS – ⊖ Barbican
– ℰ 020 7600 6144 (booking essential) – www.clubgascon.com – Closed Christmas-New Year, Monday lunch, Saturday, Sunday and bank holidays

XX Yauatcha City

CHINESE · FASHIONABLE A more corporate version of the stylish Soho original, with a couple of bars and a terrace at both ends. All the dim sum greatest hits are on the menu but the chefs have some work to match the high standard found in Broadwick Street.

Menu £ 29 (weekday lunch) – Carte £ 24/56

Town plan: 34AX1-w - Broadgate Circle ⊠ EC2M 2QS – ⊖ Liverpool Street
– ℰ 020 3817 9880 – www.yauatcha.com – Closed 24 December-3 January and bank holidays

XX Bread Street Kitchen

MODERN CUISINE · TRENDY Gordon Ramsay's take on NY loft-style dining comes with a large bar, thumping music, an open kitchen and enough zinc ducting to kit out a small industrial estate. For the food, think modern bistro dishes with an element of refinement.

Carte £ 32/57

Town plan: 33AV2-e - 10 Bread St ⊠ EC4M 9AJ – ⊖ St Paul's
– ℰ 020 3030 4050 (booking advisable) – www.breadstreetkitchen.com

LONDON ENGLAND

XX **Vanilla Black** 🅰🅘

VEGETARIAN · INTIMATE A vegetarian restaurant where real thought has gone into the creation of dishes, which deliver an array of interesting texture and flavour contrasts. Modern techniques are subtly incorporated and while there are some original combinations, they are well judged.

Menu £ 27/42

Town plan: 32AS2-e - *17-18 Tooks Ct.* ⊠ *EC4A 1LB* – ⊖ *Chancery Lane* – 𝒞 *020 7242 2622 (booking essential)* – *www.vanillablack.co.uk* – *Closed 2 weeks Christmas and bank holidays*

XX **New St Grill** 🕸🍷🏠🅑🅐

MEATS AND GRILLS · FRIENDLY D&D converted an 18C warehouse to satisfy our increasing appetite for red meat. They use Black Angus beef: grass-fed British, aged for 28 days, or corn-fed American, aged for 40 days. Start with a drink in the Old Bengal Bar.

Menu £ 27 (lunch and early dinner) – Carte £ 35/69

Town plan: 34AX2-n - *16a New St* ⊠ *EC2M 4TR* – ⊖ *Liverpool Street* – 𝒞 *020 3503 0785* – *www.newstreetgrill.com* – *Closed 25 December-3 January except dinner 31 December*

XX **Sauterelle** 🍷🅑🅘⇔

FRENCH · DESIGN Impressive location on the mezzanine floor of The Royal Exchange; ask for a table overlooking the Grand Café which was the original trading floor. A largely French-inspired contemporary menu makes good use of luxury ingredients.

Menu £ 25 – Carte £ 32/44

Town plan: 33AW2-a - *The Royal Exchange* ⊠ *EC3V 3LR* – ⊖ *Bank* – 𝒞 *020 7618 2483* – *www.royalexchange-grandcafe.co.uk* – *Closed Christmas, Easter, Saturday, Sunday and bank holidays*

XX **The Chancery** 🅐⇔

MODERN CUISINE · CHIC An elegant restaurant that's so close to the law courts you'll assume your fellow diners are barristers, jurors or the recently acquitted. The menu is appealingly concise; dishes come with a classical backbone and bold flavours.

Menu £ 40/68

Town plan: 32AS2-a - *9 Cursitor St* ⊠ *EC4A 1LL* – ⊖ *Chancery Lane* – 𝒞 *020 7831 4000* – *www.thechancery.co.uk* – *Closed 23 December-4 January, Saturday lunch, Sunday and bank holidays*

XX **Fenchurch** 🍷≤🅑🅐⇔

MODERN CUISINE · DESIGN Arrive at the 'Walkie Talkie' early so you can first wander round the Sky Garden and take in the views. The smartly dressed restaurant is housed in a glass box within the atrium. Dishes are largely British; flavour combinations are complementary and ingredients top drawer.

Menu £ 32 (weekday lunch) – Carte £ 44/73

Town plan: 34AX3-a - *Level 37, 20 Fenchurch St* ⊠ *EC3M 3BY* – ⊖ *Monument* – 𝒞 *0333 772 0020 (booking advisable)* – *www.skygarden.london* – *Closed Sunday dinner*

XX **Cinnamon Kitchen** 🍷🏠🅑🅐🐾⇔

INDIAN · TRENDY Sister to The Cinnamon Club. Contemporary Indian cooking, with punchy flavours and arresting presentation. Sprightly service in large, modern surroundings. Watch the action from the Tandoor Bar.

Menu £ 20 (lunch and early dinner) – Carte £ 24/51

Town plan: 34AX1-2-e - *9 Devonshire Sq* ⊠ *EC2M 4YL* – ⊖ *Liverpool Street* – 𝒞 *020 7626 5000* – *www.cinnamon-kitchen.com* – *Closed Saturday lunch, Sunday and bank holidays*

XX Kenza

🏆 🅰🅒 ⇔

LEBANESE · EXOTIC DÉCOR Exotic basement restaurant, with lamps, carvings, pumping music and nightly belly dancing. Lebanese and Moroccan cooking are the menu influences and the food is authentic and accurate.

Menu £ 30/50 – Carte £ 29/43

Town plan: 34AX2-c - *10 Devonshire Sq.* ✉ *EC2M 4YP –* ⊖ *Liverpool Street – ℰ 020 7929 5533 – www.kenza-restaurant.com – Closed 24-25 December, Saturday lunch and bank holidays*

XX Cigalon

🅰🅒 ⇔

FRENCH · INTIMATE Pays homage to the food and wine of Provence, in an appropriately bright space that was a once an auction house. All the classics are here, from bouillabaisse to pieds et paquets. Busy bar in the cellar.

Menu £ 27/35 – Carte £ 31/37

Town plan: 32AS2-x - *115 Chancery Ln* ✉ *WC2A 1PP –* ⊖ *Chancery Lane – ℰ 020 7242 8373 – www.cigalon.co.uk – Closed Christmas and New Year, Saturday, Sunday and bank holidays*

XX Luc's Brasserie

FRENCH · BRASSERIE A classic French brasserie looking down on the Victorian splendour of Leadenhall Market and run with impressive efficiency. The menu has all the French favourites you'll ever need, along with steaks in all sizes and chops aplenty.

Menu £ 18 (lunch) – Carte £ 26/71

Town plan: 34AX2-v - *17-22 Leadenhall Mkt* ✉ *EC3V 1LR –* ⊖ *Bank – ℰ 020 7621 0666 (booking essential) – www.lucsbrasserie.com – lunch only and dinner Tuesday-Thursday – Closed Christmas, New Year, Saturday, Sunday and bank holidays*

XX Barbecoa

🏆 🅰🅒

MEATS AND GRILLS · DESIGN Set up by Jamie Oliver, to show us what barbecuing is all about. The prime meats, butchered in-house, are just great; go for the pulled pork shoulder with cornbread on the side. By dessert you may be willing to share.

Menu £ 27 (weekday lunch) – Carte £ 33/64

Town plan: 33AV2-v - *20 New Change Passage* ✉ *EC4M 9AG –* ⊖ *St Paul's – ℰ 020 3005 8555 (booking essential) – www.barbecoa.com – Closed 25-26 December and 1 January*

XX Chiswell Street Dining Rooms

🏆 ♿ 🅰🅒 🐾

MODERN BRITISH · BRASSERIE A Martin brothers' restaurant in a corner of the old Whitbread Brewery. The cocktail bar comes alive at night. They make good use of British produce, especially fish from nearby Billingsgate.

Menu £ 38 – Carte £ 31/57

Town plan: 33AV1-r - *Montcalm London City hotel, 56 Chiswell St* ✉ *EC1Y 4SA –* ⊖ *Barbican – ℰ 020 7614 0177 – www.chiswellstreetdining.com – Closed 25-26 December, 1 January, Saturday and Sunday*

XX Duck & Waffle

🏆 ≤ ♿ 🅰🅒 🖵 📋 ⇔

MODERN CUISINE · TRENDY The UK's highest restaurant, on the 40th floor of Heron Tower. The menu is varied and offal is done well – try the crispy pig's ears. It's open 24 hours a day and offers breakfast, lunch and dinner, as well as brunch at weekends.

Carte £ 30/65

Town plan: 34AX2-a - *Heron Tower (40th floor), 110 Bishopsgate* ✉ *EC2N 4AY –* ⊖ *Liverpool Street – ℰ 020 3640 7310 (booking essential) – www.duckandwaffle.com*

✗ Bird of Smithfield 🍷 AC ▯ ⇔

TRADITIONAL BRITISH · DESIGN Feels like a private members' club but without the smugness. Five floors of fun include a cocktail bar, lounge, rooftop terrace and small, friendly restaurant. The appealing British menu makes good use of the country's larder.

Menu £18 (lunch and early dinner) – Carte £26/46

Town plan: 33AU1-s - 26 Smithfield St ⊠ EC1A 9LB – ⊖ Farringdon
– ℰ 020 7559 5100 (booking essential) – www.birdofsmithfield.com – Closed Christmas, New Year, Sunday and bank holidays

✗ Hawksmoor 🐝 🍷 AC ▯ ⇔

MEATS AND GRILLS · TRADITIONAL DÉCOR Fast and furious, busy and boisterous, this handsome room is the backdrop for another testosterone filled celebration of the serious business of beef eating. Nicely aged and rested Longhorn steaks take centre-stage.

Menu £28 (lunch and early dinner) – Carte £23/71

Town plan: 33AV2-a - 10-12 Basinghall St ⊠ EC2V 5BQ – ⊖ Bank
– ℰ 020 7397 8120 (booking essential) – www.thehawksmoor.com – Closed 24 December-2 January, Saturday, Sunday and bank holidays

✗ José Pizarro 🏠 🕭 AC 🍽

SPANISH · TAPAS BAR The eponymous chef's third operation is a good fit here: it's well run, flexible and fairly priced – and that includes the wine list. The Spanish menu is nicely balanced, with the fish and seafood dishes being the standouts.

Carte £24/31

Town plan: 34AX1-p - 36 Broadgate Circle ⊠ EC2M 1QS
– ⊖ Liverpool Street – ℰ 020 7256 5333 – www.josepizarro.com
– Closed Sunday

✗ Fish Market 🏠 🕭 AC

SEAFOOD · FRIENDLY How to get to the seaside from Liverpool Street? Simply step into this bright fish restaurant, in an old warehouse of the East India Company, and you'll almost hear the seagulls. The menu is lengthy and the cooking style classic.

Menu £20 – Carte £27/39

Town plan: 34AX2-f - 16b New St ⊠ EC2M 4TR – ⊖ Liverpool Street
– ℰ 020 3503 0790 (booking advisable) – www.fishmarket-restaurant.co.uk
– Closed 25-26 December, 1 January, Sunday dinner and bank holidays

✗ Vivat Bacchus 🐝 AC ⇔

MEATS AND GRILLS · WINE BAR Wine is the star at this bustling City spot: from 4 cellars come 500 labels and 15,000 bottles. The menu complements the wine: steaks, charcuterie, sharing platters and South African specialities feature along with great cheeses.

Carte £20/45

Town plan: 32AT1-c - 47 Farringdon St ⊠ EC4A 4LL – ⊖ Farringdon
– ℰ 020 7353 2648 – www.vivatbacchus.co.uk – Closed Christmas-New Year, Sunday and bank holidays

✗ Paternoster Chop House 🏠 AC

TRADITIONAL BRITISH · BRASSERIE Appropriately British menu in a restaurant lying in the shadow of St Paul's Cathedral. Large, open room with full-length windows; busy bar attached. Kitchen uses thoughtfully sourced produce.

Menu £20 (lunch and early dinner) – Carte £28/49

Town plan: 33AU2-x - Warwick Ct., Paternoster Sq. ⊠ EC4M 7DX – ⊖ St Paul's
– ℰ 020 7029 9400 – www.paternosterchophouse.co.uk – Closed 26-30 December, 1 January, lunch Saturday and dinner Sunday

✗ 28°-50° Fetter Lane   🕸 AC ⇔

MODERN CUISINE · WINE BAR From the owner of Texture comes this cellar wine bar and informal restaurant. The terrific wine list is thoughtfully compiled and the grills, cheeses, charcuterie and European dishes are designed to allow the wines to shine.

Menu £ 20 (weekday lunch) – Carte £ 26/51

Town plan: 32AS2-s - *140 Fetter Ln* ⊠ *EC4A 1BT* – ⊖ *Temple* – ℰ *020 7242 8877*
– *www.2850.co.uk* – *Closed Saturday, Sunday and bank holidays*

🍺 Jugged Hare   AC 🖫 🕸 ⇔

TRADITIONAL BRITISH · PUB Vegetarians may feel ill at ease – and not just because of the taxidermy. The atmospheric dining room, with its open kitchen down one side, specialises in stout British dishes, with meats from the rotisserie a highlight.

Carte £ 30/60

Town plan: 33AV1-x - *42 Chiswell St* ⊠ *EC1Y 4SA* – ⊖ *Barbican*.
– ℰ *020 7614 0134 (booking essential)* – *www.thejuggedhare.com* – *Closed 25-26 December*

CROYDON
South Croydon

✗✗ Albert's Table   ♿ AC

MODERN CUISINE · NEIGHBOURHOOD Named after the chef-owner's grandfather, this restaurant has a loyal local following. Gutsy, full-flavoured dishes use the best ingredients from Surrey, Sussex and Kent. Portions are generous and combinations rooted in the classics.

Menu £ 24 (weekdays) – Carte £ 32/48

Town plan: 7E6-x - *49b South End* ⊠ *CR0 1BF* – ℰ *020 8680 2010*
– *www.albertstable.co.uk* – *Closed Sunday dinner and Monday*

✗ Karnavar 🆕   ♿ AC 🍷

INDIAN · NEIGHBOURHOOD This simple neighbourhood restaurant is passionately run and service is helpful and friendly; take their advice and try some of the Karnavar Signature dishes. Cooking – from all over India – is tasty and authentic with a modern twist.

Menu £ 10 (weekday lunch) – Carte £ 20/37

Town plan: 7E6-r - *62 South End* ⊠ *CR0 1DP* – ℰ *020 8686 2436*
– *www.karnavar.com* – *Closed 2-3 January and Monday lunch except bank holidays*

EALING
Acton Green

✗✗ Le Vacherin   AC

FRENCH · BRASSERIE Authentic feel to this comfortable brasserie, with its brown leather banquette seating, mirrors and belle époque prints. French classics from snails to duck confit; beef is a speciality.

Menu £ 28 – Carte £ 29/53

Town plan: 6C4-f - *76-77 South Par* ⊠ *W4 5LF* – ⊖ *Chiswick Park*
– ℰ *020 8742 2121* – *www.levacherin.com* – *Closed Monday lunch*

🍺 Duke of Sussex   🍴

MEDITERRANEAN CUISINE · PUB Bustling Victorian pub, whose striking dining room was once a variety theatre complete with proscenium arch. Stick to the Spanish dishes; stews and cured meats are the specialities. BYO on Mondays.

Carte £ 23/35

Town plan: 6C4-f - *75 South Par* ⊠ *W4 5LF* – ⊖ *Chiswick Park*.
– ℰ *020 8742 8801* – *www.realpubs.co.uk*

Ealing

� Charlotte's W5   🍷 🛜 ♿ AC 🖥 🍽

MODERN CUISINE · NEIGHBOURHOOD It's all about flexibility at this converted stable block – you can come for a drink, a snack or a full meal. Every dish is available in a choice of three sizes and every bottle of wine is offered by the glass or carafe. The charming service team add to the buzz.

Carte £ 24/34

Town plan: 1B3-c - *Dickens Yard, Longfield Ave* ✉ *W5 2BF* – ⊖ *Ealing Broadway*
- ℰ *020 3771 8722* – *www.charlottes.co.uk*

X Charlotte's Place   🛜

MODERN CUISINE · BISTRO Warmly run neighbourhood restaurant opposite the Common; divided between bright ground floor room and cosier downstairs. Menu is an appealing mix of British and Mediterranean influences.

Menu £ 20/42

Town plan: 2C3-c - *16 St Matthew's Rd* ✉ *W5 3JT* – ⊖ *Ealing Common*
- ℰ *020 8567 7541* – *www.charlottes.co.uk* – *Closed 26 December and 1 January*

X Kiraku   AC 🍽 ⇔

JAPANESE · FRIENDLY The name of this cute little Japanese restaurant means 'relax and enjoy' - easy with such charming service. Extensive menu includes zensai, skewers, noodles, rice dishes and assorted sushi; ask if you want them in a particular order.

Carte £ 13/38

Town plan: 2C3-v *8 Station Par, Uxbridge Rd.* ✉ *W5 3LD* – ⊖ *Ealing Common*
- ℰ *020 8992 2848* – *www.kiraku.co.uk* – *Closed Christmas-New Year and Monday*

X Shikumen   AC 🍽 ⇔

CHINESE · BRASSERIE Sister to the restaurant of the same name in Shepherd's Bush: this branch serves dim sum only – four choices are about right but if you're feeling hungry do order a rice bowl. Well-spaced tables and a dark, moody atmosphere.

Carte £ 18/28

Town plan: 2C3-s - *26-42 Bond St* ✉ *W5 5AA* – ⊖ *Ealing Broadway*
- ℰ *020 8567 2770* – *www.shikumen.co.uk*

X Kerbisher & Malt   ♿ AC

FISH AND CHIPS · SIMPLE The fish and chip shop reinvented... fresh, sustainably sourced fish is cooked to order in rapeseed oil; chips are made from British spuds and fried separately; and packaging is biodegradable. There's another branch in Hammersmith.

Carte approx. £ 16

Town plan: 2C3-m - *53 New Broadway* ✉ *W5 5AH* – ⊖ *Ealing Broadway*
- ℰ *020 8840 4418* – *www.kerbisher.co.uk*

South Ealing

🍺 Ealing Park Tavern   🛜

MODERN BRITISH · TRENDY An impressive Arts and Crafts property, dating from 1886 and brought up to date thanks to a splendid refurbishment from the Martin Brothers. Cooking is robust yet with a refined edge. The pub also boasts its own brewery at the back.

Menu £ 19 (lunch and early dinner) – Carte £ 33/57

Town plan: 6C4-e - *222 South Ealing Rd* ✉ *W5 4RL Ealing* – ⊖ *South Ealing*
- ℰ *020 8758 1879* – *www.ealingparktavern.com*

Good quality cooking at a great price?
Look out for the Bib Gourmand 🏮.

GREENWICH

✗ Craft London   ♟ �&. A/C

MODERN BRITISH · DESIGN Chef Stevie Parle has created a striking space beside the O2 that includes a coffee shop, a cocktail bar, and a restaurant championing seasonal British produce. They do their own curing and smoking, and roast their own coffee.

Menu £ 35/55 – Carte £ 31/49

Town plan: 7F4-f - *Peninsula Sq* ⊠ *SE10 0SQ* – ⊖ *North Greenwich*
– 𝒞 020 8465 5910 – www.craft-london.co.uk – dinner only and Saturday lunch
– Closed Christmas-New Year, Sunday and Monday

✗ Upstairs at The Guildford Arms ⓝ

MODERN BRITISH · NEIGHBOURHOOD Upstairs at this handsome corner pub, Simon Wills is creating accomplished dishes which showcase the finest produce that his home county, Kent, has to offer. Portions are equivalent to a generous starter, so 3 or 4 will more than satisfy.

Carte £ 29/33

Town plan: 7F4-u - *55 Guildford Grove* ⊠ *SE10 8JY* – ⊖ *Greenwich (DLR)*
– 𝒞 020 8691 6293 – www.theguildfordarms.co.uk – dinner only – Closed
25-26 December and Sunday-Tuesday

HACKNEY

Dalston

✗ Rotorino   AC ▤

ITALIAN · SIMPLE You'll immediately warm to this stylish yet down to earth Italian. The staff are very welcoming and knowledgeable and the delicious Southern Italian specialities like caponata and gnudi are great value. Ask for one of the booths.

Menu £ 19 (early dinner) **s** – Carte £ 22/36

Town plan: 14U3-w - *434 Kingsland Rd ✉ E8 4AA*
- ⊖ *Dalston Junction*
- ℰ *020 7249 9081 – www.rotorino.com*
- *dinner only and Sunday lunch – Closed 23 December-2 January*

✗ The Richmond   🏠 AC

SEAFOOD · FASHIONABLE This was once a pub but where the bar was is now a counter where you're more likely to see someone shucking oysters, because seafood and excellent raw fish lie at the core of this operation. It's run by the team behind Elliot's.

Carte £ 21/35

Town plan: 14U3-n - *316 Queensbridge Rd ✉ E8 3NH*
- ⊖ *Dalston Junction – ℰ 020 7241 1638 (booking essential)*
- *www.therichmondhackney.com*
- *Closed 25-26 December*

✗ Jidori 🅝   🍽 ♿ ▤

JAPANESE · BISTRO A sweet, unadorned yakitori-style restaurant serving succulent skewers of chicken, cooked on a charcoal-fired Kama-Asa Shoten grill imported from Japan. Charming staff and a good selection of cocktails, sake and craft beers.

Carte £ 17/28

Town plan: 14U2-y - *89 Kingsland High St ✉ E2 8BP – ⊖ Dalston Kingsland*
- *ℰ 020 7686 5634 (bookings not accepted) – www.jidori.co.uk*
- *dinner only and lunch Wednesday-Friday*
- *Closed 25-26 December, 1 January and Sunday*

Don't expect guesthouses 🏠 to provide the same level of service as a hotel. They are often characterised by a warm welcome and décor which reflects the owner's personality. Those shown in red 🏠 are particularly charming.

Hackney

✗ Legs

MODERN BRITISH · NEIGHBOURHOOD An urban, no-frills bistro with a lively atmosphere, charming staff and food which is bursting with freshness and flavour. Lunch offers some interesting sandwiches, while dinner means a daily changing selection of small plates for sharing. The wine list focuses on organic wines from small producers.

Carte £ 25/35

Town plan: 14V2-s - *120 Morning Ln* ⊠ *E9 6LH* – ⊖ *Hackney Central – 𝒞 020 3441 8765 – www.legsrestaurant.com – dinner only – Closed Sunday-Tuesday*

Hoxton

🏨 M by Montcalm

BUSINESS · DESIGN Contemporary hotel with a smart spa and a relaxed restaurant, set within a striking modern building. Appropriately for a hotel in Tech City, you can control the bedroom lighting, music, etc. from the bedside iPad.

269 rooms – ✚£ 136/330 ✚✚£ 180/400

Town plan: 19T4-m - *151-157 City Rd* ⊠ *EC1V 1JH* – ⊖ *Old Street – 𝒞 020 3837 3000 – www.mbymontcalm.co.uk*

🏨 The Hoxton

BUSINESS · PERSONALISED Industrial-style urban lodge with a rakish, relaxed air, youthful clientele and even younger staff. Bedrooms are compact but have some nice touches; choose a 'concept' room for something different. Open-plan restaurant with American menu and great cocktails.

210 rooms � – ✚£ 69/299 ✚✚£ 69/299

Town plan: 19T4-x - *81 Great Eastern St.* ⊠ *EC2A 3HU* – ⊖ *Old Street – 𝒞 020 7550 1000 – www.thehoxton.com*

✗ Fifteen London

MODERN BRITISH · NEIGHBOURHOOD Trainees at Jamie Oliver's charitable restaurant learn about cooking seasonal British food – dishes that have personality and are all about flavour. The same menu is served in the ground floor restaurant and the livelier cellar.

Carte £ 24/50

Town plan: 19T4-c - *15 Westland Pl* ⊠ *N1 7LP* – ⊖ *Old Street – 𝒞 020 3375 1515 (booking essential) – www.fifteen.net – Closed 25-26 December and 1 January*

✗ Beagle

TRADITIONAL BRITISH · RUSTIC Occupying three vast converted railway arches: one houses the bar; one the dining room; and the third is the kitchen. The British menu, with touches of Italian, changes twice a day and its contents are determined by the seasons.

Menu £ 19 (weekday lunch) – Carte £ 21/36

Town plan: 20U4-a - *397-400 Geffrye St* ⊠ *E2 8HZ* – ⊖ *Hoxton – 𝒞 020 7613 2967 – www.beaglelondon.co.uk – Closed Sunday dinner*

✗ Sardine 🆕

MEDITERRANEAN CUISINE · FASHIONABLE A compact restaurant with a communal table at the heart of proceedings. The food comes from Southern Europe, particularly France, and dishes are rustic, unfussy and very tasty; try the lamb à la ficelle, cooked over an open fire.

Town plan: 19T4-r - *Parasol Art Gallery, 15 Micawber St* ⊠ *N1 7TB* – ⊖ *Old Street – 𝒞 020 7490 0144 – www.sardine.london – Closed Christmas-New Year and Monday*

X **Morito** N   ⚓ AC 🍽

SPANISH · SIMPLE Sam and Sam Clark's second Morito has all the utilitarianism of its older sister but much more space. Small plates draw their influences from Spain, North Africa and the Eastern Mediterranean, including the chef's homeland, Crete.

Carte £ 25/40

Town plan: 14U3-o - 195 Hackney Rd ⊠ E2 8JL – ⊖ Hoxton – ☏ 020 7613 0754 – www.moritohackneyroad.co.uk – Closed Christmas, Monday lunch and bank holidays

London Fields

X **Ellory** N (Matthew Young)   🍴 & 🍽
£3

MODERN BRITISH · SIMPLE An unpretentious, stripped back restaurant on the ground floor of Netil House; a collaboration between chef Matthew Young and sommelier Jack Lewens. The menu changes daily and the simply described, modern dishes are original, attractive, perfectly balanced and rich in flavour.

→ White asparagus, seaweed and trout roe. Turbot with lardo and artichoke. Rhubarb with cow's curd ice cream and tarragon.

Carte £ 27/36

Town plan: 14V3-e - Netil House, 1 Westgate St ⊠ E8 3RL – ⊖ London Fields – ☏ 020 3095 9455 – www.ellorylondon.com – dinner only and lunch Friday-Sunday – Closed 23 December-3 January, Sunday dinner and Monday

X **Pidgin** N   ☕
£3

MODERN BRITISH · NEIGHBOURHOOD Owners James and Sam previously ran a supper club before opening this delightful little place with its eleven closely packed tables. The no-choice four course menu changes weekly, as does the wine list, and the modern British dishes are easy on the eye, thoughtfully conceived and full of flavour.

→ Fried chicken with caviar, buttermilk and walnut. Cauliflower, juniper, pine and brown butter. Jasmine rice ice cream with apricot and elderflower.

Menu £ 37 – tasting menu only

Town plan: 14V2-d - 52 Wilton Way ⊠ E8 1BG – ⊖ Hackney Central – ☏ 020 7254 8311 (booking essential) – www.pidginlondon.com – dinner only and lunch Saturday and Sunday – Closed Monday

X **Lardo**   🍴 & AC 🖥 🍽

ITALIAN · BISTRO A delightful Italian eatery with a big open kitchen and a faux industrial look; housed in the striking 1930s Arthaus building. Daily menu of tasty small plates; try the succulent home-cured meats and the terrific pizzas.

Carte £ 15/34

Town plan: 14V2-h - 197-205 Richmond Rd ⊠ E8 3NJ – ⊖ Hackney Central – ☏ 020 8985 2683 – www.lardo.co.uk – Closed 21 December-2 January

X **Hill & Szrok**   🍴

MEATS AND GRILLS · NEIGHBOURHOOD Butcher's shop by day; restaurant by night, with a central marble-topped table, counters around the edge and a friendly, lively feel. Daily blackboard menu of top quality meats, including steaks aged for a minimum of 60 days. No bookings.

Carte £ 17/34

Town plan: 14V3-z - 60 Broadway Market ⊠ E8 4QJ – ⊖ Bethnal Green – ☏ 020 7254 8805 (bookings not accepted) – www.hillandszrok.co.uk – dinner only and Sunday lunch – Closed 23 December-3 January

X **Market Cafe**   ☕ 🍴 🍽

MEDITERRANEAN CUISINE · NEIGHBOURHOOD This former pub by the canal appeals to local hipsters with its retro looks, youthful service team and Italian-influenced menu. Cooking is fresh and generous and uses some produce from the local market; homemade pasta a feature.

Carte £ 16/34

Town plan: 14V3-m - 2 Broadway Mkt ⊠ E8 4QG – ⊖ Bethnal Green – ☏ 020 7249 9070 – www.market-cafe.co.uk – Closed 25 December

Shoreditch

🏠 Ace Hotel

BUSINESS · MINIMALIST What better location for this achingly trendy hotel than hipster-central itself – Shoreditch. Locals are welcomed in, the lobby has a DJ, urban-chic rooms have day-beds if you want friends over and the minibars offer everything from Curly Wurlys to champagne. British favourites in the stylish brasserie.

258 rooms – 👤£ 129/600 👤👤£ 129/600 – ☕£ 10 – 3 suites
Town plan: 20U4-p - *100 Shoreditch High St* ✉ *E1 6JQ*
– ⊖ *Shoreditch High Street* *–* ☎ *020 7613 9800* *– www.acehotel.com*

XXX Boundary

FRENCH · DESIGN Sir Terence Conran took a warehouse and created a 'caff' with a bakery and shop and this stylish, good-looking French restaurant serving plenty of cross-Channel classics. There's also a Mediterranean restaurant on the roof. Bedrooms are comfy and individual.

Menu £ 29 (dinner) – Carte £ 29/67

17 rooms – 👤£ 190/600 👤👤£ 190/600 – ☕£ 12 – 5 suites
Town plan: 20U4-b - *2-4 Boundary St* ✉ *E2 7DD* *–* ⊖ *Shoreditch High Street*
– ☎ *020 7729 1051* *– www.theboundary.co.uk – Closed Sunday dinner*

XXX L'Anima

ITALIAN · FASHIONABLE Very handsome room, with limestone and leather creating a stylish, glamorous environment. Appealing menu is a mix of Italian classics and less familiar dishes, with the emphasis firmly on flavour. Service is smooth and personable.

Menu £ 35/40 – Carte £ 35/72

Town plan: 34AX1-a - *1 Snowden St, Broadgate West* ✉ *EC2A 2DQ*
– ⊖ *Liverpool Street* *–* ☎ *020 7422 7000 (booking essential)* *– www.lanima.co.uk*
– Closed 25-26 December, Saturday lunch, Sunday and bank holidays

XX HKK

☸ **CHINESE · ELEGANT** Cantonese has always been considered the finest of the Chinese cuisines and here at HKK it is given an extra degree of refinement. Expect classic flavour combinations delivered in a modern way. The room is elegant and graceful; the service smooth and assured.

→ HKK chicken and truffle soup. Cherry wood roast Peking duck. Green apple parfait with cardamom cake and crispy apple noodle.

Menu £ 35/88 – Carte lunch £ 28/65

Town plan: 34AX1-h - *88 Worship St* ✉ *EC2A 2BE* *–* ⊖ *Liverpool Street*
– ☎ *020 3535 1888* *– www.hkklondon.com – Closed 25 December and Sunday*

XX Merchants Tavern

TRADITIONAL BRITISH · BRASSERIE The 'pub' part – a Victorian warehouse – gives way to a large restaurant with the booths being the prized seats. The cooking is founded on the sublime pleasures of seasonal British cooking, in reassuringly familiar combinations.

Menu £ 18 (lunch) – Carte £ 31/53

Town plan: 20U4-t - *36 Charlotte Rd* ✉ *EC2A 3PG* *–* ⊖ *Old Street*
– ☎ *020 7060 5335* *– www.merchantstavern.co.uk – Closed 25-26 December and 1 January*

XX Eyre Brothers

SPANISH · ELEGANT Sleek, confidently run and celebrating all things Iberian, as well as drawing on the brothers' memories of their childhood in Mozambique. Delicious hams; terrific meats cooked over lumpwood charcoal. If in a larger group, pre-order paella or a whole suckling pig. Tapas is served in the bar.

Carte £ 25/45

Town plan: 19T4-k - *70 Leonard St* ✉ *EC2A 4QX* *–* ⊖ *Old Street*
– ☎ *020 7613 5346* *– www.eyrebrothers.co.uk – Closed*
24 December-4 January, Sunday dinner and bank holidays

PRACTISE THE ART
of FINE FOOD.

Live in Italian

XX L'Anima Café

ITALIAN • BRASSERIE A baby sister to L'Anima around the corner but more than a mere café: this is a big, bright restaurant with a busy bar and deli. The fairly priced menu includes plenty of pizza and pasta dishes. A DJ plays on Thursdays and Fridays.

Carte £ 22/40

Town plan: 34AX1-h - *10 Appold St ✉ EC2A 2AP - ⊖ Liverpool Street - ✆ 020 7422 7080 - www.lanimacafe.co.uk - Closed Saturday lunch and Sunday*

XX Rivington Grill

TRADITIONAL BRITISH • BISTRO A well-run buzzy restaurant in a converted red-brick warehouse; popular with the local community of artists. Very appealing seasonal British menu, with plenty of comforting classics. Keenly priced wine list – and over 100 gins.

Carte £ 21/41

Town plan: 20U4-e - *28-30 Rivington St ✉ EC2A 3DZ - ⊖ Old Street - ✆ 020 7729 7053 - www.rivingtonshoreditch.co.uk - Closed 25-26 December*

X Clove Club (Isaac McHale)

✿

MODERN CUISINE • TRENDY The smart, blue-tiled open kitchen takes centre stage in this sparse room at Shoreditch Town Hall. Set menus showcase expertly sourced produce in dishes that are full of originality, verve and flair – but where flavours are expertly judged and complementary; seafood is a highlight.

→ Raw Orkney scallop, hazelnut, clementine and Périgord truffle. Dry-aged Challans duck in three servings. Warm blood orange, sheep's milk yoghurt mousse and fennel granité.

Menu £ 65/95 – Carte lunch £ 37/56

Town plan: 20U4-c - *380 Old St ✉ EC1V 9LT - ⊖ Old Street - ✆ 020 7729 6496 (bookings advisable at dinner) - www.thecloveclub.com - Closed 2 weeks Christmas-New Year, August bank holiday, Monday lunch and Sunday*

X Lyle's (James Lowe)

✿

MODERN BRITISH • SIMPLE The young chef-owner is an acolyte of Fergus Henderson and delivers similarly unadulterated flavours from seasonal British produce, albeit from a set menu at dinner. This pared-down approach extends to a room that's high on functionality, but considerable warmth comes from the keen young service team.

→ Gloucester Old Spot, chicory and apple mustard. Dover sole with rape greens and whey butter. Concorde pear with oats.

Menu £ 49 (dinner) – Carte lunch £ 26/36

Town plan: 20U4-s - *Tea Building, 56 Shoreditch High St ✉ E1 6JJ - ⊖ Shoreditch High Street - ✆ 020 3011 5911 - www.lyleslondon.com - Closed Sunday and bank holidays*

X Andina

PERUVIAN • SIMPLE Andina may be smaller and slightly more chaotic that its sister Ceviche, but this friendly picantería with live music is equally popular. The Peruvian specialities include great salads and skewers, and ceviche that packs a punch.

Menu £ 9 (lunch) – Carte £ 17/33

Town plan: 20U4-w - *1 Redchurch St ✉ E2 7DJ - ⊖ Shoreditch High Street - ✆ 020 7920 6499 (booking essential) - www.andinalondon.com*

X Tramshed

MEATS AND GRILLS • BRASSERIE A 1905 Grade II warehouse is home to Mark Hix's cavernous brasserie. The Damien Hirst cow and cockerel in formaldehyde give a clue to the menu – it's all about chicken and beef. Swainson House Farm chickens and Glenarm steaks are accurately cooked and delicious.

Carte £ 18/66

Town plan: 20U4-d - *32 Rivington St ✉ EC2A 3LX - ⊖ Old Street - ✆ 020 7749 0478 - www.chickenandsteak.co.uk - Closed 25 December*

✗ Oklava ❶   🅰🄲

TURKISH · BISTRO An oklava is a traditional Turkish rolling pin used to make pastries and pides, both of which appear on the menu; for the chef is a Turkish Cypriot and cooks her 'small plate' interpretations of classic dishes from these countries.

Carte £ 24/38

Town plan: 20U2-r - *74 Luke St ⊠ EC2A 4PY –* ⊖ *Old Street –* ✆ *020 7729 3032 (booking essential) – www.oklava.co.uk – Closed Sunday dinner and bank holidays*

✗ Viet Grill   🅰🄲

VIETNAMESE · FRIENDLY Owned by the team behind Cây Tre which means that service is charming and helpful and the Vietnamese food is fresh and authentic. Larger parties should consider ordering one of their 'feast' menus, which require 48 hours' notice.

Carte £ 20/35

Town plan: 20U4-v - *58 Kingsland Rd ⊠ E2 8DP –* ⊖ *Hoxton –* ✆ *020 7739 6686 (booking essential) – www.vietgrill.co.uk – Closed 24-26 December*

🍺 Princess of Shoreditch   🕸 🏠

TRADITIONAL BRITISH · PUB There has been a pub on this corner site since 1742 but it is doubtful many of the previous incarnations were as busy or as pleasant as the Princess is today. The best dishes are those with a rustic edge, such as goose rillettes or chicken pie.

Carte £ 27/38

Town plan: 19T4-a - *76-78 Paul St ⊠ EC2A 4NE –* ⊖ *Old Street – ✆ 020 7729 9270 (booking essential) – www.theprincessofshoreditch.com – Closed 24-26 December*

Stoke Newington

✗ Foxlow   🏠 🅰🄲

TRADITIONAL BRITISH · FAMILY Foxlow is the less bellicose brand from the people behind the Hawksmoor steakhouses. Here it's all about families and the local neighbourhood. The menu is safe and appealing but it would be churlish to avoid the steaks.

Menu £ 18 (weekdays) – Carte £ 25/42

Town plan: 14U1-s - *71-73 Church St ⊠ N16 OAS –* ⊖ *Canonbury – ✆ 020 7481 6377 – www.foxlow.co.uk – Closed 24 December-1 January*

South Hackney

🍺 Empress   🏠
🐾

MEDITERRANEAN CUISINE · PUB Food is at the centre of proceedings at this neighbourhood pub: the menu is short, simple and pleasingly seasonal and dishes demonstrate the kitchen's confidence and ability. Prices are kept in check and Sunday lunch is a languid affair.

Carte £ 25/33

Town plan: 3F3-d - *130 Lauriston Rd, Victoria Park ⊠ E9 7LH –* ⊖ *Homerton. – ✆ 020 8533 5123 – www.empresse9.co.uk – Closed 25-26 December and Monday lunch except bank holidays*

HAMMERSMITH and FULHAM

Fulham

✗✗ Blue Elephant   🏠 A/C

THAI · EXOTIC DÉCOR Relocated from Fulham Road to these swankier and appropriately exotic premises, spread over two floors and with two great riverside terraces. The menu traverses Thailand; curries are a strength.

Carte £ 34/51

Town plan: 23N8-x - *The Boulevard, Imperial Wharf ⊠ SW6 2UB*
- *⊖ Imperial Wharf – 𝒞 020 7751 3111 (booking advisable)*
- *www.blueelephant.com*
- *dinner only and Sunday lunch*
- *Closed 25-26 December, 1 January and Monday*

✗ Tendido Cuatro   A/C 🍴

SPANISH · NEIGHBOURHOOD Along with tapas, the speciality is paella. Designed for a hungry two, they vary from seafood to quail and chorizo; vegetarian to cuttlefish ink. Vivid colours used with abandon deck out the busy room.

Menu £ 30 (lunch and early dinner) – Carte £ 21/44

Town plan: 22M8-x - *108-110 New Kings Rd ⊠ SW6 4LY – ⊖ Parsons Green*
- *𝒞 020 7371 5147 – www.cambiodetercio.co.uk*
- *Closed 2 weeks Christmas*

✗ Koji   A/C 🍴

JAPANESE · WINE BAR After nearly 30 years, Mark Barnett retired his Mao Tai Chinese restaurant and in its place opened this fun, contemporary wine bar serving Japanese food. The menu mixes the modern with the classic, and the Nobu influences are obvious.

Carte £ 31/54

Town plan: 22NZH-e - *58 New King's Rd ⊠ SW6 4LS – ⊖ Parsons Green*
- *𝒞 020 7731 2520 – www.koji.restaurant*
- *Closed 24-26 December and Monday*

✗ Manuka Kitchen   A/C 🍴

MODERN CUISINE · RUSTIC The two young owners run their simple little restaurant with great enthusiasm and their prices are keen. Like the magical Manuka honey, the chef is from New Zealand; his menu is varied and his food is wholesome and full of flavour.

Carte £ 23/35

Town plan: 22M8-k - *510 Fulham Rd ⊠ SW6 5NJ*
- *⊖ Fulham Broadway – 𝒞 020 7736 7588 – www.manukakitchen.com*
- *Closed 25-26 December, Sunday dinner and Monday lunch*

✗ Claude's Kitchen

MODERN CUISINE · BISTRO Two operations in one converted pub: 'Amuse Bouche' is a well-priced champagne bar; upstairs is an intimate dining room with a weekly changing menu. The cooking is colourful and fresh, with the odd challenging flavour combination.

Carte £ 27/38

Town plan: 22M8-a - *51 Parsons Green Ln ⊠ SW6 4JA – ⊖ Parsons Green.*
– ℰ 020 7371 8517 (booking essential) – www.amusebouchelondon.com – dinner only – Closed Sunday

▯☐ Harwood Arms

MODERN BRITISH · PUB Its reputation may have spread like wildfire but this remains a proper, down-to-earth pub that just happens to serve really good food. The cooking is very seasonal, proudly British, full of flavour and doesn't seem out of place in this environment. Service is suitably relaxed and friendly.

→ Wye Valley asparagus on toast with Cornish crab, watercress and pressed egg. Haunch of Berkshire fallow deer with wild garlic, beetroot and smoked bone marrow. Vanilla custard tart with date and sticky toffee ice cream.

Menu £ 36 (weekday lunch)/43

Town plan: 22M7-a - *Walham Grove ⊠ SW6 1QP – ⊖ Fulham Broadway.*
– ℰ 020 7386 1847 (booking essential) – www.harwoodarms.com
– Closed 24-27 December, 1 January and Monday lunch except bank holidays

▯☐ Tommy Tucker

TRADITIONAL BRITISH · PUB The old Pelican pub was revamped by the owners of nearby Claude's Kitchen. It's bright and open plan, with an unstructured menu divided under headings of 'meat', 'fish' and 'fruit and veg'. The cooking is rustic and satisfying.

Carte £ 19/35

Town plan: 22M8-s - *22 Waterford Rd ⊠ SW6 2DR – ⊖ Fulham Broadway.*
– ℰ 020 7736 1023 – www.thetommytucker.com
– Closed 25 December

Be sure to read the section 'How to use this guide'.
It explains our symbols, classifications and abbreviations
and will help you make a more informed choice.

Hammersmith

✗✗ River Café (Ruth Rogers)

ITALIAN · FASHIONABLE It's all about the natural Italian flavours of the superlative ingredients. The on-view kitchen with its wood-fired oven dominates the stylish riverside room; the contagiously effervescent atmosphere is helped along by very charming service.

→ Chargrilled squid with red chilli and rocket. Wood-roasted veal chop with salsa verde and slow-cooked peas. Chocolate Nemesis.

Carte £ 60/82

Town plan: 21K7-c - *Thames Wharf, Rainville Rd ⊠ W6 9HA – ⊖ Barons Court*
– ℰ 020 7386 4200 (booking essential) – www.rivercafe.co.uk – Closed Christmas-New Year, Sunday dinner and bank holidays

✗✗ Indian Zing

INDIAN · NEIGHBOURHOOD Chef-owner Manoj Vasaikar seeks inspiration from across India. His cooking balances the traditional with the more contemporary and delivers many layers of flavour – the lamb dishes and breads are particularly good. The restaurant is always busy yet service remains courteous and unhurried.

Menu £ 12/15 – Carte £ 20/43

Town plan: 21K7-a - *236 King St. ⊠ W6 0RF – ⊖ Ravenscourt Park*
– ℰ 020 8748 5959 – www.indianzing.co.uk

X L'Amorosa

ITALIAN · NEIGHBOURHOOD Former Zafferano head chef Andy Needham has created a warm and sunny Italian restaurant – one that we'd all like to have in our high street. The quality of the produce shines through and homemade pasta dishes are a highlight.

Menu £ 16 (weekday lunch) – Carte £ 25/36

Town plan: 21K7-s - *278 King St* ⊠ *W6 0SP* – ⊖ *Ravenscourt Park* – *✆ 020 8563 0300* – *www.lamorosa.co.uk* – *Closed 1 week August, 1 week Christmas, Sunday dinner, Monday and bank holidays*

X Azou   AC

NORTH AFRICAN · NEIGHBOURHOOD Silks, lanterns and rugs add to the atmosphere of this personally run, North African restaurant. Most come for the excellent tajines with triple steamed couscous. Much is designed for sharing.

Carte £ 20/38

Town plan: 21J7-u - *375 King St* ⊠ *W6 9NJ* – ⊖ *Stamford Brook* – *✆ 020 8563 7266 (booking essential)* – *www.azou.co.uk* – *dinner only* – *Closed 1 January and 25 December*

X Brackenbury   🏠

MEDITERRANEAN CUISINE · NEIGHBOURHOOD A much loved neighbourhood restaurant given a new lease of life. The kitchen looks to Italy, France and the Med for inspiration and doesn't waste time on presentation; dishes feel instinctive and flavours marry well.

Menu £ 16 (weekday lunch) – Carte £ 27/42

Town plan: 15K6-c - *129 - 131 Brackenbury Rd* ⊠ *W6 0BQ* – ⊖ *Ravenscourt Park* – *✆ 020 8741 4928* – *www.brackenburyrestaurant.co.uk* – *Closed Christmas, New Year, Easter, August bank holiday, Sunday and Monday*

🏠 Anglesea Arms   🏠

MODERN BRITISH · NEIGHBOURHOOD One of the daddies of the gastropub movement. The seasonal menu gives the impression it's written by a Brit who occasionally holidays on the Med – along with hardy dishes are some that display a pleasing lightness of touch.

Carte £ 22/34

Town plan: 15K6-e - *35 Wingate Rd* ⊠ *W6 0UR* – ⊖ *Ravenscourt Park* – *✆ 020 8749 1291* – *www.angleseaarmspub.co.uk* – *Closed 24-26 December*

Shepherd's Bush

XX Shikumen   ⅊ AC

CHINESE · INTIMATE Impressive homemade dim sum at lunch and excellent Peking duck are the standouts at this unexpectedly sleek Cantonese restaurant in an otherwise undistinguished part of Shepherd's Bush.

Carte £ 22/48

Town plan: 15K6-s - *58 Shepherd's Bush Grn* ⊠ *W12 8QE* – ⊖ *Shepherd's Bush* – *✆ 020 8749 9978* – *www.shikumen.co.uk* – *Closed Christmas*

🏠 Princess Victoria   🍸 🏠 AC P

TRADITIONAL BRITISH · PUB Magnificent Victorian gin palace, with original plasterwork. The kitchen knows its butchery; pork board, homemade sausages and terrines all feature. Excellent wine list, with over 350 bottles.

Menu £ 13 (weekday lunch) – Carte £ 23/47

Town plan: 15J5-a - *217 Uxbridge Rd* ⊠ *W12 9DH* – ⊖ *Shepherd's Bush.* – *✆ 020 8749 5886* – *www.princessvictoria.co.uk* – *Closed 24-27 December*

HARINGEY

Crouch End

✗ Bistro Aix   🆎 ⇔

FRENCH · BISTRO Dressers, cabinets and contemporary artwork lend an authentic Gallic edge to this bustling bistro, a favourite with many of the locals. Traditionally prepared French classics are the highlights of an extensive menu.

Menu £ 18 – Carte £ 25/49

Town plan: 3E2-v - *54 Topsfield Par, Tottenham Ln* ⊠ *N8 8PT* – ⊖ *Crouch Hill* – 𝒞 *020 8340 6346 – www.bistroaix.co.uk – dinner only and lunch Saturday-Sunday – Closed 24, 26 December and 1 January*

HARROW

Pinner

✗✗ Friends   🆎

TRADITIONAL BRITISH · COSY This characterful, low-beamed restaurant has been proudly and personally run for over 20 years – and has a history stretching back over 500 more. Cooking is classical and carefully done, and the service is well-paced and friendly.

Menu £ 18 (weekday lunch)/23 – Carte £ 29/45

Town plan: 1B2-a - *11 High St* ⊠ *HA5 5PJ* – ⊖ *Pinner* – 𝒞 *020 8866 0286* – *www.friendsrestaurant.co.uk – Closed 25-26 December, 26-27 May, Sunday dinner, Monday and bank holidays*

HEATHROW AIRPORT

🏨 Sofitel   ⑂ ⑱ 🕸 ⅃₅ ⊡ & 🆎 ⅏ 🔥 🚗

BUSINESS · CONTEMPORARY Smart and well-run contemporary hotel, designed around a series of atriums, with direct access to T5. Crisply decorated, comfortable bedrooms with luxurious bathrooms. Choice of restaurant: international or classic French cuisine.

605 rooms ⌑ – ♦£ 169/350 ♦♦£ 169/450 – 27 suites

Town plan: 5A4-a - *Terminal 5, Heathrow Airport* ⊠ *TW6 2GD* – ⊖ *Heathrow Terminal 5* – 𝒞 *020 8757 7777 – www.sofitelheathrow.com*

🏨 Hilton London Heathrow Airport   ⑂ ⇦ ⑱ 🕸 ⅃₅ ⊡ & 🆎 ⅏ 🔥

BUSINESS · MODERN A feeling of light and space pervades this modern, 🅿 corporate hotel. Soundproofed rooms are fitted to a good standard; the spa offers wide-ranging treatments. Open-plan Gallery for British comfort food.

350 rooms – ♦£ 129/289 ♦♦£ 129/289 – ⌑ £ 22 – 4 suites

Terminal 5, Poyle Rd, Colnbrook ⊠ *SL3 0FF – West : 2.5 mi by A 3113* – 𝒞 *01753 686860 – www.hilton.com/heathrowt5*

Mr Todiwala's Kitchen – See restaurant listing

✗✗ Mr Todiwala's Kitchen   🆎 🅿

INDIAN · FRIENDLY Secreted within the Hilton is Cyrus Todiwala's appealingly stylish, fresh-looking restaurant. The choice ranges from street food to tandoor dishes, Goan classics to Parsee specialities; order the 'Kitchen menu' for the full experience.

Carte £ 32/60

Hilton London Heathrow Airport Terminal 5 Hotel, Poyle Rd, Colnbrook ⊠ *SL3 0FF – West : 2.5 mi by A 3113* – 𝒞 *01753 766482* – *www.hilton.com/heathrowterminal5 – dinner only – Closed Christmas and Sunday*

HOUNSLOW

Chiswick

High Road House

TOWNHOUSE • MINIMALIST Cool, sleek hotel and club, the latter a slick place to lounge around or play games. Light, bright bedrooms with crisp linen. A carefully appointed, fairly-priced destination.

14 rooms - †£ 140/265 ††£ 140/265 - £ 22

Town plan: 21J7-e - *162 Chiswick High Rd ✉ W4 1PR - ⊖ Turnham Green - ✆ 020 8742 1717 - www.highroadhouse.co.uk*

High Road Brasserie - See restaurant listing

La Trompette

MODERN BRITISH • NEIGHBOURHOOD Chez Bruce's sister is a delightful neighbourhood restaurant that's now a little roomier. The service is charming and the food terrific. Dishes at lunch are quite simple but great value; the cooking at dinner is a tad more elaborate.

→ Raw scallops with pickled cucumber, kohlrabi and English wasabi. Shoulder of suckling pig, creamed potato, white sprouting broccoli, chilli and garlic. Rhubarb crumble soufflé with rhubarb ripple ice cream.

Menu £ 30 (lunch and early dinner)/50

Town plan: 21J7-y - *5-7 Devonshire Rd ✉ W4 2EU - ⊖ Turnham Green - ✆ 020 8747 1836 (booking essential) - www.latrompette.co.uk - Closed 24-26 December and 1 January*

Hedone (Mikael Jonsson)

MODERN CUISINE • DESIGN Mikael Jonsson, former lawyer turned chef, is not one for complacency so his restaurant continues to evolve. The content of his surprise menus is governed entirely by what ingredients are in their prime - and it is this passion for produce which underpins the superlative and very flavoursome cooking.

→ Warm Devon crab with velvet crab consommé, hazelnut mayonnaise and Granny Smith apple. Squab pigeon with chard, olive and coffee-powdered carrots, pigeon jus. Vanilla millefeuille with aged balsamic vinegar.

Menu £ 45/125 - surprise menu only

Town plan: 6C4-g - *301-303 Chiswick High Rd ✉ W4 4HH - ⊖ Chiswick Park - ✆ 020 8747 0377 (booking essential) - www.hedonerestaurant.com - dinner only and lunch Friday-Saturday - Closed 2 weeks summer, 2 weeks Christmas-New Year, Sunday and Monday*

Michael Nadra

MODERN CUISINE • NEIGHBOURHOOD Half way down a residential side street is this intimate little place where the closely set tables add to the bonhomie. Dishes are modern, colourful and quite elaborate in their make-up; it's worth going for the sensibly priced set menu and the chosen wines.

Menu £ 27/38

Town plan: 21J7-z - *6-8 Elliott Rd ✉ W4 1PE - ⊖ Turnham Green - ✆ 020 8742 0766 - www.restaurant-michaelnadra.co.uk - Closed 24-27 December, 1 January and Sunday dinner*

Charlotte's Bistro

MODERN CUISINE • NEIGHBOURHOOD A pleasant, unpretentious bistro; run by a friendly team, with a well-priced menu of flavoursome, well prepared dishes of largely European provenance. Little sister to Charlotte's Place in Ealing.

Carte £ 25/38

Town plan: 21J7-a - *6 Turnham Green Terr ✉ W4 1QP - ⊖ Turnham Green - ✆ 020 8742 3590 (booking advisable) - www.charlottes.co.uk*

✗ High Road Brasserie   🏠 ♿ AC

FRENCH · FASHIONABLE Authentic brasserie, with mirrors, panelling and art deco lighting. Despite the high volume of customers, the classic dishes are prepared with care and staff cope well with being busy.

Carte £ 20/36

Town plan: 21J7-e - *High Road House Hotel, 162 Chiswick High Rd.* ✉ *W4 1PR*
– ⊖ *Turnham Green –* ☎ *020 8742 7474 (booking essential)*
– www.highroadhouse.co.uk

🍴 Smokehouse   🛋 🏠

TRADITIONAL BRITISH · NEIGHBOURHOOD A sizeable pub with a delightful rear garden is the site of the second Smokehouse. The Belted Galloway burgers with pulled pork fly out of the kitchen but the winning dish is the short rib Bourguignon with creamy mash.

Carte £ 28/34

Town plan: 6C4-s - *12 Sutton Ln North* ✉ *W4 4LD –* ⊖ *Chiswick Park.*
– ☎ *020 3819 6066 – www.smokehousechiswick.co.uk – Dinner only and lunch Friday to Sunday*

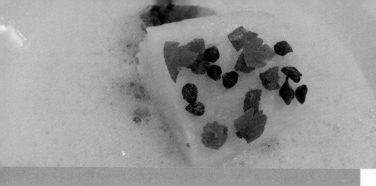

ISLINGTON

Archway

✗ 500

ITALIAN · FRIENDLY Small, fun and well-priced Italian that's always busy. Good pastas and bread; the veal chop and rabbit are specialities. The passion of the ebullient owner and keen chef are evident.

Carte £ 22/31

Town plan: 12R1-y - 782 Holloway Rd ⊠ N19 3JH – ⊖ Archway
– ℰ 020 7272 3406 (booking essential) – www.500restaurant.co.uk – dinner only and lunch Friday-Sunday – Closed 2 weeks summer and 2 weeks Christmas-New Year

🍴 St John's Tavern

MODERN CUISINE · PUB A Junction Road landmark with friendly service and a great selection of artisan beers. Tapas is served in the front bar; head to the vast, hugely appealing rear dining room for well-crafted British and Mediterranean dishes.

Carte £ 18/36

Town plan: 12Q1-s - 91 Junction Rd ⊠ N19 5QU – ⊖ Archway. – ℰ 020 7272 1587 (booking advisable) – www.stjohnstavern.com – Closed 25-26 December, 1 January and Monday lunch

Canonbury

✗ Trullo

ITALIAN · NEIGHBOURHOOD While the ground floor has kept its well-worn, homely feel, the basement has an all-American look, with exposed brick, industrial ducting and red banquettes. Rustic, well-priced dishes include house specialities cooked on the charcoal grill and great pasta, hand-rolled before each service.

Carte £ 22/38

Town plan: 13S2-t - 300-302 St Paul's Rd ⊠ N1 2LH – ⊖ Highbury & Islington – ℰ 020 7226 2733 (booking essential) – www.trullorestaurant.com – Closed Christmas-New Year and Sunday dinner

✗ Primeur

MODERN CUISINE · SIMPLE A relaxed neighbourhood restaurant whose concertina doors fold back to reveal a quirky interior with counter seating around the edges and a huge communal table. Plates are small and designed for sharing; understated but packed with flavour – simplicity is key, allowing the ingredients to really shine.

Carte £ 20/31

Town plan: 13T2-p - 116 Petherton Rd ⊠ N5 2RT – ⊖ Canonbury
– ℰ 020 7226 5271 – www.primeurn5.co.uk – Closed Christmas, Monday, dinner Sunday and lunch Tuesday-Thursday

⚔ Canonbury Kitchen   AC

ITALIAN · NEIGHBOURHOOD A bright, local Italian with seating for just 40; exposed brick walls and painted floorboards add to the fresh feel. The kitchen keeps things simple and the menu pricing is prudent.

Menu £ 12 – Carte £ 26/36

Town plan: 13S3-c - 19 Canonbury Ln ⊠ N1 2AS – ⊖ Highbury & Islington – ℰ 020 7226 9791 – www.canonburykitchen.com – dinner only and lunch Saturday-Sunday – Closed Sunday dinner

🕽️ Smokehouse   🏠 &

MODERN CUISINE · PUB You can smell the oak chips in the smoker as you approach this warm, modern pub. Meat is the mainstay – the peppered ox cheeks are a firm favourite – but whilst flavours are gutsy, the smoking and barbecuing is never overpowering.

Carte £ 28/34

Town plan: 13T3-h - 63-69 Canonbury Rd ⊠ N1 2DG – ⊖ Highbury & Islington. – ℰ 020 7354 1144 (booking advisable) – www.smokehouseislington.co.uk – dinner only and lunch Saturday-Sunday – Closed 24-26 December

Clerkenwell

🏨 Malmaison   ⚘ 🖃 & AC ⚓ ♨

TOWNHOUSE · MODERN Striking early 20C red-brick building overlooking a pleasant square. Stylish, comfy public areas. Bedrooms in vivid, bold colours, with plenty of extra touches. Modern brasserie with international menu; grilled meats a highlight.

97 rooms – ♥£ 150/350 ♥♥£ 150/420 – ☖ £ 15

Town plan: 33AU1-q - 18-21 Charterhouse Sq ⊠ EC1M 6AH – ⊖ Barbican – ℰ 020 7012 3700 – www.malmaison.com

🏠 The Rookery   AC ♨

TOWNHOUSE · PERSONALISED A row of charmingly restored 18C houses which remain true to their roots courtesy of wood panelling, flagstone flooring, open fires and antique furnishings. Highly individual bedrooms have feature beds and Victorian bathrooms.

33 rooms – ♥£ 195/225 ♥♥£ 265/650 – ☖ £ 12

Town plan: 33AU1-p - 12 Peters Ln, Cowcross St ⊠ EC1M 6DS – ⊖ Farringdon – ℰ 020 7336 0931 – www.rookeryhotel.com

⚔⚔ Sosharu 🅽   AC

JAPANESE · FASHIONABLE The seventh London restaurant from Jason Atherton and the first serving Japanese food is this bustling operation with a chic, understated style. Six small plates with a large rice pot or a 'classic' between two will do nicely.

Menu £ 20/30 – Carte £ 29/52

Town plan: 32AT1-s - 63 Clerkenwell Rd ⊠ EC1M 5RR – ⊖ Farringdon – ℰ 020 3805 2304 – www.sosharulondon.com – Closed bank holidays except Good Friday and Sunday

⚔ St John   AC ⇦

❀

TRADITIONAL BRITISH · MINIMALIST A glorious celebration of British fare and a champion of 'nose to tail' eating. Utilitarian surroundings and a refreshing lack of ceremony ensure the food is the focus; it's appealingly simple, full of flavour and very satisfying.

➔ Roast bone marrow and parsley salad. Pheasant and trotter pie. Ginger loaf and butterscotch sauce.

Carte £ 28/49

Town plan: 33AU1-k - 26 St John St ⊠ EC1M 4AY – ⊖ Farringdon – ℰ 020 7251 0848 (booking essential) – www.stjohnrestaurant.com – Closed Christmas-New Year, Saturday lunch, Sunday dinner and bank holidays

✗ Comptoir Gascon

FRENCH · BISTRO Buzzy restaurant; sister to Club Gascon. Rustic and satisfying specialities from the SW of France include wine, bread, cheese and plenty of duck, with cassoulet and duck rillettes perennial favourites and the duck burger popular at lunch. Great value set 3 course menu. Produce on display to take home.

Menu £ 15 (weekday lunch) – Carte £ 21/34

Town plan: 32AT1-a - *61-63 Charterhouse St.* ✉ *EC1M 6HJ* – ⊖ *Farringdon*
– ✆ *020 7608 0851 (booking essential)* – *www.comptoirgascon.com*
– *Closed Christmas-New Year, Sunday, Monday and bank holidays*

✗ Polpo Smithfield

ITALIAN · FRIENDLY For his third Venetian-style bacaro, Russell Norman converted an old meat market storage facility; it has an elegantly battered feel. Head first for the Negroni bar downstairs; then over-order tasty, uncomplicated and very satisfying dishes to share. Bookings only taken up to 5.30pm.

Carte £ 20/30

Town plan: 33AU1-u - *3 Cowcross St* ✉ *EC1M 6DR* – ⊖ *Farringdon.*
– ✆ *020 7250 0034* – *www.polpo.co.uk* – *Closed Christmas, New Year and Sunday dinner*

✗ Granger & Co. Clerkenwell

MODERN CUISINE · FAMILY Aussie food writer and restaurateur Bill Granger's 2nd London branch is a stylish affair. His food is inspired by his travels, with the best dishes being those enlivened with the flavours of SE Asia; his breakfasts are also renowned.

Carte £ 19/40

Town plan: 19S4-y - *50 Sekforde St* ✉ *EC1R 0HA* – ⊖ *Farringdon*
– ✆ *020 7251 9032* – *www.grangerandco.com* – *Closed Sunday dinner*

✗ Foxlow

MEATS AND GRILLS · NEIGHBOURHOOD From the clever Hawksmoor people comes this fun and funky place where the staff ensure everyone's having a good time. There are steaks available but plenty of other choices with influences from Italy, Asia and the Middle East.

Menu £ 18 (weekdays) – Carte £ 22/41

Town plan: 33AU1-b - *69-73 St John St* ✉ *EC1M 4AN* – ⊖ *Farringdon*
– ✆ *020 7680 2700* – *www.foxlow.co.uk* – *Closed 24 December-1 January, Sunday dinner and bank holidays*

✗ Hix Oyster and Chop House

TRADITIONAL BRITISH · BISTRO Appropriately utilitarian surroundings put the focus on seasonal and often underused British ingredients. Cooking is satisfying and unfussy, with plenty of oysters and aged beef served on the bone.

Menu £ 10 (weekday lunch) – Carte £ 20/58

Town plan: 33AU1-e - *36-37 Greenhill Rents* ✉ *EC1M 6BN* – ⊖ *Farringdon*
– ✆ *020 7017 1930* – *www.hixoysterandchophouse.co.uk* – *Closed 25-29 December, Saturday lunch and bank holidays*

Finsbury

🏨 South Place

BUSINESS · DESIGN Restaurant group D&D's first venture into the hotel business is a stylish affair; unsurprising as its interior was designed by Conran & Partners. Bedrooms are a treat for those with an eye for aesthetics and no detail has been forgotten. The ground floor hosts 3 South Place, a bustling bar and grill.

80 rooms - �£ 185/350 ♦♦£ 185/350 – ☕ £ 17 – 1 suite

Town plan: 33AW1-v - *3 South Pl* ✉ *EC2M 2AF* – ⊖ *Moorgate*
– ✆ *020 3503 0000* – *www.southplacehotel.com*
❀ **Angler** – See restaurant listing

⌂ Zetter

TOWNHOUSE · MODERN A trendy and discreet converted 19C warehouse with well-equipped bedrooms that come with pleasant touches, such as Penguin paperbacks. The more idiosyncratic Zetter Townhouse across the square is used as an overflow.

59 rooms – ♦£150/498 ♦♦£150/498 – ☟£14

Town plan: 19S4-s - St John's Sq, 86-88 Clerkenwell Rd. ✉ EC1M 5RJ
– ⊖ Farringdon – ℰ 020 7324 4444 – www.thezetter.com

✗✗ Angler

SEAFOOD · ELEGANT Built into the eaves of D&D's South Place hotel, but this 7th floor room feels very much like a stand-alone entity and is bright, elegant and intimate. Fish is the mainstay of the menu; its quality is supreme and the kitchen has a light, yet assured touch.

→ Yellowfin tuna tartare, lime, chilli and avocado. Roast fillet of John Dory with langoustines, mushrooms, truffle and pumpkin. Chocolate fondant with pistachio ice cream.

Menu £35 – Carte £42/66

Town plan: 33AW1-v - South Place Hotel, 3 South Pl ✉ EC2M 2AF – ⊖ Moorgate
– ℰ 020 3215 1260 (booking advisable) – www.anglerrestaurant.com – Closed 26-30 December, Saturday lunch and Sunday

✗✗ The Modern Pantry Finsbury Square ⓝ

WORLD CUISINE · BRASSERIE Spacious, elegant dining room on the ground floor of the imposing Alphabeta Building, with a lively bar counter for 'global tapas' and sherry liveners. Extensive menu of internationally influenced dishes; puddings are a highlight.

Menu £23 (weekday lunch) – Carte £31/47

Town plan: 33AW1-m - 14 Finsbury Sq ✉ EC2A 1AH – ⊖ Moorgate
– ℰ 020 3696 6565 – www.themodernpantry.co.uk – Closed 25 December and Sunday dinner

✗ Quality Chop House

TRADITIONAL BRITISH · COSY In the hands of owners who respect its history, this 'progressive working class caterer' does a fine job of championing gutsy British grub; game is best but steaks from the butcher next door are also worth ordering. The terrific little wine list has lots of gems. The Grade II listed room, with its trademark booths, has been an eating house since 1869.

Menu £15 (weekday lunch) – Carte £24/44

Town plan: 19S4-h - 92-94 Farringdon Rd ✉ EC1R 3EA – ⊖ Farringdon
– ℰ 020 7278 1452 (booking advisable) – www.thequalitychophouse.com – Closed Sunday dinner and bank holidays

✗ Moro

MEDITERRANEAN CUISINE · FRIENDLY It's the stuff of dreams - pack up your worldly goods, drive through Spain, Portugal, Morocco and the Sahara, and then back in London, open a restaurant and share your love of Moorish cuisine. The wood-fired oven and chargrill fill the air with wonderful aromas and food is vibrant and colourful.

Carte £31/43

Town plan: 19S4-m - 34-36 Exmouth Mkt ✉ EC1R 4QE – ⊖ Farringdon
– ℰ 020 7833 8336 (booking essential) – www.moro.co.uk – Closed dinner 24 December-2 January, Sunday dinner and bank holidays

✗ Morito

SPANISH · TAPAS BAR From the owners of next door Moro comes this authentic and appealingly down to earth little tapas bar. Seven or eight dishes between two should suffice but over-ordering is easy and won't break the bank.

Carte £14/29

Town plan: 19S4-b - 32 Exmouth Mkt ✉ EC1R 4QE – ⊖ Farringdon
– ℰ 020 7278 7007 – www.morito.co.uk – Closed 24 December-2 January, Sunday dinner and bank holidays

✗ Ceviche Old St ❶ 🍷 AC 🎐

PERUVIAN · BRASSERIE Sister to the Soho original is this buzzy Peruvian restaurant in the former Alexandra Trust Dining Rooms, built by tea magnate Sir Thomas Lipton. Start with ceviche and a pisco sour; dishes are easy to eat, vibrant and full of flavour.

Menu £12 (weekday lunch) – Carte £17/32

Town plan: 19T4-s - *2 Baldwin St* ✉ *EC1V 9NU* – ⊖ *Old Street*
– ✆ *020 3327 9463* – *www.cevicheuk.com*

✗ The Modern Pantry Clerkenwell 🛋 AC 🎐 🍽

WORLD CUISINE · DESIGN Fusion cooking that uses complementary flavours to create vibrant, zesty dishes. The simple, crisp ground floor of this Georgian building has the buzz; upstairs is more intimate. Clued-up service.

Carte £26/37

Town plan: 19S4-k - *47-48 St John's Sq.* ✉ *EC1V 4JJ* – ⊖ *Farringdon*
– ✆ *020 7553 9210 (booking advisable)* – *www.themodernpantry.co.uk*
– *Closed August bank holiday and 25-26 December*

✗ Caravan 🎐 🍽

WORLD CUISINE · TRENDY A discernible Antipodean vibe pervades this casual eatery, from the laid-back charm of the service to the kitchen's confident combining of unusual flavours. Cooking is influenced by owner's travels – hence the name.

Carte £26/35

Town plan: 19S4-c - *11-13 Exmouth Market* ✉ *EC1R 4QD* – ⊖ *Farringdon*
– ✆ *020 7833 8115 (booking advisable)* – *www.caravanrestaurants.co.uk*
– *Closed 25, 26 and 31 December, 1 January*

✗ Clerkenwell Kitchen 🛋 🎐

MODERN CUISINE · FRIENDLY The owner of this simple, friendly, tucked away eatery worked with Hugh Fearnley-Whittingstall and is committed to sustainability. Daily changing, well-sourced produce; fresh, flavoursome cooking.

Carte £15/28

Town plan: 19S4-v - *27-31 Clerkenwell Cl* ✉ *EC1R 0AT* – ⊖ *Farringdon*
– ✆ *020 7101 9959 (booking advisable)* – *www.theclerkenwellkitchen.co.uk* – *lunch only* – *Closed Christmas-New Year, Saturday, Sunday and bank holidays*

🍺 Well 🛋

MODERN BRITISH · PUB This well-supported neighbourhood pub has an intimate basement with sofas and bright artwork and a ground floor dining room packed with wonky tables. Seasonal dishes are carefully cooked and full of flavour.

Carte £26/41

Town plan: 19S4-x - *180 St John St* ✉ *EC1R 4JY* – ⊖ *Farringdon.*
– ✆ *020 7251 9363* – *www.downthewell.com*
– *Closed 25-26 December*

Highbury

✗ Au Lac AC

VIETNAMESE · FRIENDLY Sweet, long-standing Vietnamese restaurant run by two brothers. New dishes are regularly added to the already lengthy but authentic and keenly priced menu, whose dishes exhibit plenty of fresh and lively flavours.

Carte £12/24

Town plan: 13T1-b - *82 Highbury Park* ✉ *N5 2XE* – ⊖ *Arsenal* – ✆ *020 7704 9187*
– *www.aulac.co.uk*
– *dinner only and lunch Thursday-Friday*
– *Closed 24-26 December, 1-2 January and 1 week early August*

Islington

XX Bellanger ⓝ   🏛 📶 🖥 🎧 ⇄

🏠 **FRENCH · BRASSERIE** All-day brasserie, with the sumptuous style of an authentic grand café, modelled on those opened in Paris by the Alsatians at the turn of the century. Regional French and Alsatian-inspired fare is served from breakfast until late.

Carte £ 21/43

Town plan: 13S3-d - 9 Islington Grn ⊠ N1 2XH – ⊖ Angel – ℰ 020 7226 2555 (bookings advisable at dinner) – www.bellanger.co.uk – Closed 25 December

XX Almeida   🏛 📶 🍸 ⇄

MODERN BRITISH · BRASSERIE Opposite the award-winning theatre of the same name is this smoothly run, sophisticated restaurant. The kitchen uses European and British influences to create confident and at times innovative dishes which allow the main ingredient to shine.

Menu £ 19 (lunch and early dinner) – Carte £ 30/67

Town plan: 13S3-r - 30 Almeida St. ⊠ N1 1AD – ⊖ Angel – ℰ 020 7354 4777 – www.almeida-restaurant.com – Closed 26 December, 1 January, Sunday dinner and Monday lunch

X Yipin China   📶 ⇄

🏠 **CHINESE · SIMPLE** The menu at this modest little place features Hunanese, Cantonese and Sichuanese specialities, but it is the spicy, chilli-based dishes from Hunan province – which use techniques like smoking and curing – that really stand out.

Carte £ 19/42

Town plan: 13S3-b - 70-72 Liverpool Rd ⊠ N1 0QD – ⊖ Angel – ℰ 020 7354 3388 – www.yipinchina.co.uk – Closed 25 December

X Ottolenghi   📶 🖥 🍽 🎧

MEDITERRANEAN CUISINE · FASHIONABLE Two communal tables form the centrepiece of this coolly decorated deli/restaurant. The frequently changing menu offers fresh, vibrant flavours from the Med, North Africa and Middle East; three dishes each is about right.

Carte £ 23/45

Town plan: 13S3-k - 287 Upper St. ⊠ N1 2TZ – ⊖ Highbury & Islington – ℰ 020 7288 1454 (booking essential) – www.ottolenghi.co.uk – Closed 25-26 December, and dinner Sunday and bank holidays

X Galley ⓝ   🍸 📶 🍽

SEAFOOD · BRASSERIE A smart, colourful seafood restaurant with a brasserie feel; there's a bar at the front and a few prized booths, but the best seats in the house are at the kitchen counter. The hot or cold seafood platters are great to share.

Menu £ 18/28 – Carte £ 30/57

Town plan: 13S3-a - 105-106 Upper St ⊠ N1 1QN – ⊖ Highbury and Islington – ℰ 020 3670 0740 – www.galleylondon.co.uk – Closed 25 December and 1 January

X Oldroyd ⓝ   🍽

MODERN BRITISH · INTIMATE The eponymous Oldroyd is Tom, who left his role with the Polpo group to open this busy little bistro. It's all about small plates – ingredients are largely British, influences are from within Europe and dishes are very easy to eat.

Menu £ 15 (weekday lunch) – Carte £ 21/32

Town plan: 13S3-w - 344 Upper St ⊠ N1 0PD – ⊖ Angel – ℰ 020 8617 9010 – www.oldroydlondon.com – Closed 25-26 December

X Vintage Salt

FISH AND CHIPS · RUSTIC Not exactly your average chippy – there are cocktails, weekend brunches and starters like crab on toast. Butties are fun for a quick snack but most come for Camden Hells battered fish. They also do takeaway and delivery.

Carte £ 16/33

Town plan: 13S3-s - *189 Upper St* ⊠ *N1 1RQ* – ⊖ *Highbury and Islington* – *☎ 020 3227 0979 (booking essential at dinner) – www.vintagesalt.co.uk – Closed 25-27 December and lunch Monday-Friday*

Drapers Arms

MODERN BRITISH · NEIGHBOURHOOD Anyone unfamiliar with Britain's bounteous larder should get along to this down-to-earth Georgian pub to enjoy ingredients like lamb's tongues, smoked eel, blade steak and rabbit in dishes that are satisfying, gutsy and affordable.

Carte £ 23/32

Town plan: 13S3-x - *44 Barnsbury St* ⊠ *N1 1ER* – ⊖ *Highbury & Islington.* – *☎ 020 7619 0348 (bookings advisable at dinner) – www.thedrapersarms.com – Closed 25-26 December*

Pig and Butcher

TRADITIONAL BRITISH · PUB Dating from the mid-19C, when cattle drovers taking livestock to Smithfield Market would stop for a swift one, and now fully restored. There's a strong British element to the daily menu; meat is butchered and smoked in-house.

Carte £ 28/44

Town plan: 13S3-e - *80 Liverpool Rd* ⊠ *N1 0QD* – ⊖ *Angel.* – *☎ 020 7226 8304 (booking advisable) – www.thepigandbutcher.co.uk – dinner only and lunch Friday-Sunday – Closed 25-27 December*

KENSINGTON and CHELSEA
(ROYAL BOROUGH OF)

Chelsea

Jumeirah Carlton Tower

BUSINESS · MODERN Imposing international hotel overlooking a leafy square and just yards from all the swanky boutiques. Well-equipped rooftop health club has great views. Generously proportioned bedrooms boast every conceivable facility.

207 rooms – †£ 350/835 ††£ 350/835 – ☑ £ 32 – 57 suites

Town plan: **37AJ6-r** - Cadogan Pl ⊠ SW1X 9PY
- ⊖ Knightsbridge – ℰ 020 7235 1234
- www.jumeirah.com/jct

Rib Room – See restaurant listing

The Capital

LUXURY · CLASSIC This fine, thoroughly British hotel has been under the same private ownership for over 40 years. Known for its discreet atmosphere, conscientious and attentive service and immaculately kept bedrooms courtesy of different designers.

49 rooms – †£ 250/355 ††£ 295/550 – ☑ £ 17 – 1 suite

Town plan: **37AJ5-a** - 22-24 Basil St. ⊠ SW3 1AT
- ⊖ Knightsbridge – ℰ 020 7589 5171
- www.capitalhotel.co.uk

❀ **Outlaw's at The Capital** – See restaurant listing

Draycott

TOWNHOUSE · PERSONALISED Charming 19C house with elegant sitting room overlooking tranquil garden for afternoon tea. Bedrooms are individually decorated in a country house style and are named after writers or actors.

35 rooms – †£ 192/199 ††£ 378/558 – ☑ £ 22

Town plan: **37AJ7-c** - 26 Cadogan Gdns ⊠ SW3 2RP – ⊖ Sloane Square
- ℰ 020 7730 6466 – www.draycotthotel.com

Egerton House

TOWNHOUSE · CLASSIC Compact but comfortable townhouse in a very good location, well-maintained throughout and owned by the Red Carnation group. High levels of personal service make the hotel stand out.

28 rooms – †£ 295/425 ††£ 295/425 – ☑ £ 29

Town plan: **37AH6-e** - 17-19 Egerton Terr ⊠ SW3 2BX
- ⊖ South Kensington – ℰ 020 7589 2412
- www.egertonhousehotel.com

Knightsbridge ☑ AC ✷

LUXURY · PERSONALISED Charming and attractively furnished townhouse in a Victorian terrace, with a very stylish, discreet feel. Every bedroom is immaculately appointed and has a style all of its own; fine detailing throughout.

44 rooms – ♦£ 215/275 ♦♦£ 235/445 – ☲ £ 14

Town plan: 37AH6-s - *10 Beaufort Gdns* ☒ *SW3 1PT* – ⊖ *Knightsbridge* – ℰ *020 7584 6300* – www.knightsbridgehotel.com

The Levin ✿ ☑ AC

TOWNHOUSE · CLASSIC Little sister to The Capital next door. Impressive façade, contemporary interior and comfortable bedrooms in a subtle art deco style, with marvellous champagne mini bars. Simple dishes served all day down in basement restaurant Le Metro.

12 rooms ☲ – ♦£ 248/382 ♦♦£ 255/389

Town plan: 37AJ5-c - *28 Basil St.* ☒ *SW3 1AS* – ⊖ *Knightsbridge* – ℰ *020 7589 6286* – www.thelevinhotel.co.uk

No.11 Cadogan Gardens ✿ ⅏ ᒪ♨ ☑ AC ✷

TOWNHOUSE · PERSONALISED Townhouse hotel fashioned out of four red-brick houses and exuberantly dressed in bold colours and furnishings. Theatrically decorated bedrooms vary in size from cosy to spacious. Intimate basement Italian restaurant with accomplished and ambitious cooking.

56 rooms – ♦£ 250/370 ♦♦£ 250/370 – ☲ £ 18 – 7 suites

Town plan: 37AJ7-n - *11 Cadogan Gdns* ☒ *SW3 2RJ* – ⊖ *Sloane Square* – ℰ *020 7730 7000* – www.11cadogangardens.com

Beaufort ☑ AC ✷

TRADITIONAL · CLASSIC A vast collection of English floral watercolours adorn this 19C townhouse, set in a useful location. Modern and co-ordinated rooms. Tariff includes all drinks and afternoon tea.

29 rooms – ♦£ 180/228 ♦♦£ 250/456 – ☲ £ 16

Town plan: 37AH6-n - *33 Beaufort Gdns* ☒ *SW3 1PP* – ⊖ *Knightsbridge* – ℰ *020 7584 5252* – www.thebeaufort.co.uk

✖✖✖✖ Gordon Ramsay ✿✿✿ AC ᛁ♡

✿✿✿ FRENCH · ELEGANT Gordon Ramsay's flagship restaurant is a model of composure and professionalism. The service is discreet and highly polished, yet also warm and reassuring. The cooking bridges both classical and modern schools and is executed with considerable poise, a lightness of touch and remarkable attention to detail.

→ Ravioli of lobster with langoustine, salmon, oxalis and wood sorrel. Dover sole with razor clams, young peas and lemon beurre noisette. Lemonade parfait with honey, bergamot and sheep's milk yoghurt.

Menu £ 65/110

Town plan: 37AJ8-c - *68-69 Royal Hospital Rd.* ☒ *SW3 4HP* – ⊖ *Sloane Square* – ℰ *020 7352 4441 (booking essential)* – www.gordonramsayrestaurants.com – *Closed 21-28 December, Saturday and Sunday*

✖✖✖ Five Fields (Taylor Bonnyman) ✿✿ ᗒ AC ⇔

✿ MODERN CUISINE · NEIGHBOURHOOD A formally run yet intimate restaurant, with a discreet atmosphere and a warm, comfortable feel. Modern dishes are skilfully conceived, quite elaborate constructions; attractively presented and packed with flavour. Produce is top-notch and often comes from the restaurant's own kitchen garden in East Sussex.

→ Veal sweetbread with carrot, apple and tamarind. Herdwick mutton with green olive, anchovy and baby gem. Ginger, rhubarb and vanilla.

Menu £ 60

Town plan: 37AJ7-s - *8-9 Blacklands Terr* ☒ *SW3 2SP* – ⊖ *Sloane Square* – ℰ *020 7838 1082 (booking essential)* – www.fivefieldsrestaurant.com – *dinner only – Closed Christmas-mid January, first 2 weeks August, Saturday-Sunday and bank holidays*

XXX Bibendum ⚜ AC 🍸

FRENCH · DESIGN Located on the 1st floor of a London landmark – Michelin's former HQ, dating from 1911. French food comes with a British accent and there's fresh seafood served in the oyster bar below. It's maintained a loyal following for over 20 years.

Menu £ 34 (weekdays) – Carte £ 27/63

Town plan: 37AH7-s - ⊠ SW3 6RD – ⊖ South Kensington – ℰ 020 7581 5817
– www.bibendum.co.uk – Closed dinner 24 December, 25-26 December and
1 January

XXX Rib Room 🍸 AC ⇄ 🚗

MEATS AND GRILLS · ELEGANT Rib of Aberdeen Angus, steaks and other classic British dishes attract a prosperous, international crowd; few of whom appear to have a beef with the prices at this swish veteran.

Menu £ 28 (weekday lunch) – Carte £ 50/120

Town plan: 37AJ6-r - Jumeirah Carlton Tower Hotel, ⊠ SW1X 9PY
– ⊖ Knightsbridge – ℰ 020 7858 7250 – www.theribroom.co.uk

XXX One-O-One AC

SEAFOOD · INTIMATE Smart ground floor restaurant; it might be lacking a little in atmosphere but the seafood is good. Much of the excellent produce is from Brittany and Norway; don't miss the King crab legs which are the stars of the show.

Menu £ 20 (lunch and early dinner) – Carte £ 43/106

Town plan: 37AJ5-t - Park Tower Knightsbridge Hotel, 101 Knightsbridge
⊠ SW1X 7RN – ⊖ Knightsbridge – ℰ 020 7290 7101
– www.oneoonerestaurant.com

XX Outlaw's at The Capital ⚜ 🍸 AC 🍸 ⇄
✿

SEAFOOD · INTIMATE An elegant yet informal restaurant in a personally run hotel. The seasonal menus are all about sustainable seafood, with fish shipped up from Cornwall on a daily basis. The original modern cooking is delicately flavoured and ingredient-led, with the spotlight on the freshness of the produce.
→ Cured monkfish with fennel, parsley and lemon. Hake with mussels, cider and clotted cream sauce. Passion fruit tart and sorbet with white chocolate and pistachio.

Menu £ 29/55

Town plan: 37AJ5-a - The Capital Hotel, 22-24 Basil St. ⊠ SW3 1AT
– ⊖ Knightsbridge – ℰ 020 7591 1202 (booking essential)
– www.capitalhotel.co.uk – Closed Sunday and Easter Monday

XX Medlar ⚜ 🍴 AC ⇄

MODERN CUISINE · NEIGHBOURHOOD A charming, comfortable and very popular restaurant with a real neighbourhood feel, from two alumni of Chez Bruce. The service is engaging and unobtrusive; the kitchen uses good ingredients in dishes that deliver distinct flavours in classic combinations.

Menu £ 28/46

Town plan: 23N7-x - 438 King's Rd ⊠ SW10 0LJ – ⊖ South Kensington
– ℰ 020 7349 1900 – www.medlarrestaurant.co.uk – Closed 24-26 December and
1 January

XX Ivy Chelsea Garden 🆕 🍸 🍴 & AC 🔲

TRADITIONAL BRITISH · FASHIONABLE A sophisticated restaurant with a lively atmosphere; start with a cocktail, then head down to the orangery or out to the garden. The menu covers all bases; from breakfast through to lunch, afternoon tea and dinner, with brunch at weekends.

Carte £ 26/68

Town plan: 37AH8-c - 197 King's Rd ⊠ SW3 5ED – ⊖ South Kensington
– ℰ 020 3301 0300 (booking essential) – www.theivychelseagarden.com

XX Masala Grill 🍷 🗚 ⇔

INDIAN · EXOTIC DÉCOR When the owners moved Chutney Mary to St James's after 25 years they wisely installed another Indian restaurant in her place. It's still awash with colour and vitality but is less expensive and more varied in its influences.

Carte £ 24/39

Town plan: 23N8-v - *535 King's Rd* ✉ *SW10 0SZ* – ⊖ *Fulham Broadway*
- *𝒞 020 7351 7788 – www.masalagrill.co – dinner only and Sunday lunch*

XX Le Colombier ⇔

FRENCH · NEIGHBOURHOOD Proudly Gallic corner restaurant in an affluent residential area. Attractive enclosed terrace. Bright and cheerful surroundings and service; traditional French cooking.

Menu £ 20 (lunch) – Carte £ 34/61

Town plan: 37AG7-e - *145 Dovehouse St.* ✉ *SW3 6LB* – ⊖ *South Kensington*
- *𝒞 020 7351 1155 – www.le-colombier-restaurant.co.uk*

XX Painted Heron 🏠 🗚

INDIAN · NEIGHBOURHOOD Smart, well-supported and quite formally run Indian restaurant. Nooks and crannies create an intimate atmosphere; and there's a heated cigar terrace. Fish and game dishes are the highlights of the contemporary cooking.

Menu £ 15 (lunch) – Carte £ 26/42

Town plan: 23N7-d - *112 Cheyne Walk* ✉ *SW10 0DJ* – ⊖ *Fulham Broadway*
- *𝒞 020 7351 5232 – www.thepaintedheron.com – Closed lunch 1 January*

XX Bluebird 🍷 🗚 🐾 ⇔

MODERN BRITISH · DESIGN Not just for a night out with friends – with a foodstore, cellar, bakery, café and courtyard there's enough here for a day out too. Big menu to match the big room: everything from British classics to steaks, salads and shellfish.

Menu £ 20 (lunch and early dinner) – Carte £ 27/87

Town plan: 36AF8-n - *350 King's Rd.* ✉ *SW3 5UU* – ⊖ *South Kensington*
- *𝒞 020 7559 1000 – www.bluebird-restaurant.co.uk*

XX Hawksmoor 🍷 🗚

MEATS AND GRILLS · BRASSERIE The Hawksmoor people turned to rarefied Knightsbridge for their 5th London branch. Steaks are still the star of the show but here there's also plenty of seafood. Art deco elegance and friendly service compensate for the basement site.

Menu £ 28 (weekday lunch) – Carte £ 26/94

Town plan: 37AH6-r - *3 Yeoman's Row* ✉ *SW3 2AL* – ⊖ *South Kensington*
- *𝒞 020 7590 9290 – www.thehawksmoor.com – Closed 24-26 December and 1 January*

XX Maze Grill Park Walk 🗚

MEATS AND GRILLS · FASHIONABLE The site of Aubergine, where it all started for Gordon Ramsay, now specialises in steaks. Dry-aged in-house, the meats are cooked on a fierce bit of kit called a Montague grill. There's another Maze Grill close by in Royal Hospital Road.

Carte £ 24/80

Town plan: 36AF8-x - *11 Park Walk* ✉ *SW10 0AJ* – ⊖ *South Kensington*
- *𝒞 020 7255 9299 – www.gordonramsayrestaurants.com/maze-grill-park-walk/*

XX Brasserie Gustave 🗚 ⇔

FRENCH · BRASSERIE All the traditional French favourites are here, from snails to boeuf Bourguignon and rum baba, all prepared in a way to make Escoffier proud. Studded leather seating and art deco style posters complete the classic brasserie look.

Menu £ 20/28 – Carte £ 32/69

Town plan: 37AG7-v - *4 Sydney St* ✉ *SW3 6PP* – ⊖ *South Kensington*
- *𝒞 020 7352 1712 – www.brasserie-gustave.com*
- *Closed 24-30 December*

XX il trillo   🕸 🏠 AC

ITALIAN · FRIENDLY The Bertuccelli family have been making wine and running a restaurant in the Tuscan Hills for over 30 years. Two of the brothers now run this smart local which showcases the produce and wine from their region. Delightful courtyard.

Carte £ 33/55

Town plan: 36AE8-s - *4 Hollywood Rd* ✉ *SW10 9HY* – ⊖ *Earl's Court*
– *✆ 020 3602 1759 – www.iltrillo.net – dinner only and lunch Saturday-Sunday*
– *Closed 10 days August and 1 week Christmas*

XX Colbert   🍷 AC 🖳

FRENCH · BRASSERIE With its posters, chessboard tiles and red leather seats, Colbert bears more than a passing resemblance to a Parisian pavement café. It's an all-day, every day operation with French classics from croque monsieur to steak Diane.

Carte £ 23/54

Town plan: 38AK7-t - *50-52 Sloane Sq* ✉ *SW1W 8AX* – ⊖ *Sloane Square*
– *✆ 020 7730 2804 (booking advisable) – www.colbertchelsea.com – Closed 25 December*

XX Good Earth   AC 🕪

CHINESE · ELEGANT The menu might appear predictable but this long-standing Chinese has always proved a reliable choice in this area. Although there's no particular geographical bias, the cooking is carefully executed and dishes are authentic.

Carte £ 26/51

Town plan: 37AH6-h - *233 Brompton Rd.* ✉ *SW3 2EP* – ⊖ *Knightsbridge*
– *✆ 020 7584 3658 – www.goodearthgroup.co.uk*
– *Closed 23-31 December*

X Bandol 🆕   🕸 AC 🍽

PROVENÇAL · DESIGN Stylishly dressed restaurant with a 100 year old olive tree evoking memories of sunny days spent on the French Riviera. Sharing plates take centre stage on the Provençal and Niçoise inspired menu; seafood is a highlight.

Menu £ 20 (weekday lunch) – Carte £ 29/52

Town plan: 36AE8-b - *6 Hollywood Rd* ✉ *SW10 9HY* – ⊖ *Earl's Court*
– *✆ 020 7351 1322 – www.barbandol.co.uk – Closed 24-26 December and 1 January*

X Bo Lang   🍷 AC

CHINESE · TRENDY It's all about dim sum at this diminutive Hakkasan wannabe. The kitchen has a deft touch but stick to the more traditional combinations; come with friends for the cocktails and to mitigate the effects of some ambitious pricing.

Menu £ 22 (weekday lunch) – Carte £ 25/48

Town plan: 37AH7-a - *100 Draycott Ave* ✉ *SW3 3AD*
– ⊖ *South Kensington* – *✆ 020 7823 7887*
– *www.bolangrestaurant.com*

X Rabbit   🍷 🍽

MODERN BRITISH · RUSTIC The Gladwin brothers have followed the success of The Shed with another similarly rustic and warmly run restaurant. Share satisfying, robustly flavoured plates; game is a real highlight, particularly the rabbit dishes.

Menu £ 14 (weekday lunch)/37 – Carte £ 22/31

Town plan: 37AH7-r - *172 King's Rd* ✉ *SW3 4UP* – ⊖ *Sloane Square*
– *✆ 020 3750 0172 – www.rabbit-restaurant.com*
– *Closed 22 December-2 January*

Cross Keys

MODERN CUISINE • PUB Chelsea's oldest pub, dating from 1708, reopened in 2015 having been saved from property developers. The place has genuine character and warmth. The style of cooking is largely contemporary, although there are also dishes for traditionalists.

Carte £ 29/44

Town plan: 23N7-r - *1 Lawrence St ✉ SW3 5NB - ⊖ Sloane Square. - ✆ 020 7351 0686 - www.thecrosskeyschelsea.co.uk - Closed 24 December dinner and 25 December*

Builders Arms

TRADITIONAL BRITISH • PUB Smart looking and busy pub for the Chelsea set; drinkers are welcomed as much as diners. Cooking reveals the effort put into sourcing decent ingredients; rib of beef for two is a favourite. Thoughtfully compiled wine list.

Carte £ 23/42

Town plan: 37AH7-x - *13 Britten St ✉ SW3 3TY - ⊖ South Kensington. - ✆ 020 7349 9040 (bookings not accepted) - www.geronimo-inns.co.uk*

Earl's Court

K + K George

BUSINESS • MODERN In contrast to its period façade, this hotel's interior is stylish, colourful and contemporary. The hotel is on a quiet street, yet close to the Tube and has a large rear garden where you can enjoy breakfast in summer. Comfortable bar/lounge and a spacious restaurant serving a wide-ranging menu.

154 rooms - †£ 119/330 ††£ 119/350 - ☕ £ 18

Town plan: 35AC7-s - *1-15 Templeton Pl ✉ SW5 9NB - ⊖ Earl's Court - ✆ 020 7598 8700 - www.kkhotels.com*

Twenty Nevern Square

TOWNHOUSE • PERSONALISED Privately owned townhouse overlooking an attractive Victorian garden square. It's decorated with original pieces of hand-carved Indonesian furniture; breakfast in a bright conservatory. Some bedrooms have their own terrace.

20 rooms ☕ - †£ 99/249 ††£ 119/299

Town plan: 35AC7-u - *20 Nevern Sq. ✉ SW5 9PD - ⊖ Earl's Court - ✆ 020 7565 9555 - www.twentynevernsquare.co.uk*

Garnier

FRENCH • NEIGHBOURHOOD A wall of mirrors, rows of simply dressed tables and imperturbable service lend an authentic feel to this Gallic brasserie. The extensive menu of comforting French classics is such a good read, you'll find it hard to choose.

Menu £ 18/22 - Carte £ 34/55

Town plan: 36AD7-a - *314 Earl's Court Rd ✉ SW5 9QB - ⊖ Earl's Court - ✆ 020 7370 4536 - www.garnier-restaurant-london.co.uk - Closed Monday and Tuesday*

Kensington

Royal Garden

BUSINESS • MODERN A tall, modern hotel with many of its rooms enjoying enviable views over the adjacent Kensington Gardens. All the modern amenities and services, with well-drilled staff. Bright, spacious Park Terrace offers an international menu as well as afternoon tea for which you're accompanied by a pianist.

394 rooms - †£ 190/440 ††£ 240/490 - ☕ £ 21 - 17 suites

Town plan: 36AD5-c - *2-24 Kensington High St ✉ W8 4PT - ⊖ High Street Kensington - ✆ 020 7937 8000 - www.royalgardenhotel.co.uk*

Min Jiang - See restaurant listing

🏨 The Milestone 　　　　　　　　🐾 🌿 🕭 ⬆ 🄰🄲

LUXURY · PERSONALISED Elegant and enthusiastically run hotel with decorative Victorian façade and a very British feel. Charming oak-panelled sitting room is popular for afternoon tea; snug bar in former stables. Meticulously decorated bedrooms offer period detail. Ambitious cooking in discreet Cheneston's restaurant.

62 rooms 🍽 - 🛏£ 348/480 🛏🛏£ 400/1000 – 6 suites

Town plan: 36AE5-u - *1-2 Kensington Ct* ✉ W8 5DL – ⊖ High Street Kensington – ✆ 020 7917 1000 – www.milestonehotel.com

🏨 Baglioni 　　　　　　　　　　🐾 🕭 ⬆ 🄰🄲 🎎

LUXURY · PERSONALISED Opposite Kensington Palace and no escaping the fact that this is an Italian owned hotel. The interior is bold and ornate and comes with a certain swagger. Stylish bedrooms have a masculine feel and boast impressive facilities.

67 rooms – 🛏£ 315/425 🛏🛏£ 315/425 – 🍽£ 26 – 15 suites

Town plan: 36AE5-e - *60 Hyde Park Gate* ✉ SW7 5BB
– ⊖ High Street Kensington – ✆ 020 7937 8886 – www.baglionihotels.com

🍴 Min Jiang 　　　　　　　　　　🍷 ≤ 🄰🄲 ⇦

CHINESE · ELEGANT The cooking at this stylish 10th floor Chinese restaurant covers all provinces, but Cantonese and Sichuanese dominate. Wood-fired Beijing duck is a speciality. The room's good looks compete with the great views of Kensington Gardens.

Menu £ 40/80 – Carte £ 30/98

Town plan: 36AD5-c - *Royal Garden Hotel, 2-24 Kensington High St (10th Floor)* ✉ W8 4PT – ⊖ High Street Kensington – ✆ 020 7361 1988 – www.minjiang.co.uk

🍴 Launceston Place 　　　　　　　　　　🄰🄲 ⇦

MODERN CUISINE · NEIGHBOURHOOD Few restaurants engender a greater sense of local customer loyalty and proprietorial pride than longstanding Launceston Place. It's formally run but not so much that it impinges on customers' enjoyment. The cooking has a classical French base yet is unafraid to try new things.

Menu £ 30/55

Town plan: 36AE5-a - *1a Launceston Pl* ✉ W8 5RL – ⊖ Gloucester Road
– ✆ 020 7937 6912 *(bookings advisable at dinner)*
– www.launcestonplace-restaurant.co.uk – Closed 25-30 December, 1 January, Tuesday lunch and Monday

🍴 Kitchen W8 　　　　　　　　　　🄰🄲

🍀 MODERN CUISINE · NEIGHBOURHOOD A joint venture between Rebecca Mascarenhas and Philip Howard. Not as informal as the name suggests but still refreshingly free of pomp. The cooking has depth and personality and prices are quite restrained considering the quality of the produce and the kitchen's skill.
➜ Salad of veal with charred asparagus, peas and truffle pesto. Fillet of Cornish turbot with St Austell Bay mussels, mousserons, onions and parsley. Passion fruit cream with cured pineapple, lime and mango.

Menu £ 25 (lunch and early dinner) – Carte £ 35/53

Town plan: 35AC5-a - *11-13 Abingdon Rd* ✉ W8 6AH – ⊖ High Street Kensington – ✆ 020 7937 0120 – www.kitchenw8.com – Closed 24-26 December and bank holidays

🍴 Clarke's 　　　　　　　　　　🕭 🄰🄲 🖥 ⇦

MODERN CUISINE · NEIGHBOURHOOD Forever popular restaurant that has enjoyed a loyal local following for over 30 years. Sally Clarke uses the freshest seasonal ingredients and her cooking has a famed lightness of touch.

Menu £ 27/39 – Carte £ 41/55

Town plan: 27AC4-c - *124 Kensington Church St* ✉ W8 4BH
– ⊖ Notting Hill Gate – ✆ 020 7221 9225 *(booking advisable)*
– www.sallyclarke.com – Closed 2 weeks August, Christmas-New Year, Sunday and bank holidays

XX Babylon

MODERN CUISINE · FASHIONABLE Found on the 7th floor and affording great views of the city skyline and an amazing 1.5 acres of rooftop garden. Stylish modern décor in keeping with the contemporary, British cooking.

Menu £ 28 (lunch) – Carte £ 42/58

Town plan: 36AD5-n - *The Roof Gardens, 99 Kensington High St* ✉ *W8 5SA – (entrance on Derry St)* – ⊖ *High Street Kensington* – ✆ *020 7368 3993 – www.roofgardens.virgin.com – Closed 24-30 December, 1-2 January and Sunday dinner*

XX Zaika

INDIAN · EXOTIC DÉCOR The cooking focuses on the North of India and the influences of Mughal and Nawabi, so expect rich and fragrantly spiced dishes. The softly-lit room makes good use of its former life as a bank, with its wood-panelling and ornate ceiling.

Menu £ 22 (lunch) – Carte £ 28/67

Town plan: 36AD5-r - *1 Kensington High St.* ✉ *W8 5NP – ⊖ High Street Kensington – ✆ 020 7795 6533 – www.zaikaofkensington.com – Closed 25-26 December, 1 January and Monday lunch*

XX Yashin

JAPANESE · DESIGN Ask for a counter seat to watch the chefs prepare the sushi; choose 8, 11 or 15 pieces, to be served together. The quality of fish is clear; tiny garnishes and the odd bit of searing add originality.

Carte £ 38/89

Town plan: 35AC5-c - *1A Argyll Rd.* ✉ *W8 7DB – ⊖ High Street Kensington – ✆ 020 7938 1536 (booking essential) – www.yashinsushi.com – Closed 24-25 and 31 December, 1 January*

XX Malabar

INDIAN · NEIGHBOURHOOD Opened in 1983 in a residential Notting Hill street, but keeps up its appearance, remaining fresh and good-looking. Balanced menu of carefully prepared and sensibly priced Indian dishes. Buffet lunch on Sunday.

Carte £ 15/39 **s**

Town plan: 27AC3-e - *27 Uxbridge St.* ✉ *W8 7TQ – ⊖ Notting Hill Gate – ✆ 020 7727 8800 – www.malabar-restaurant.co.uk – dinner only and lunch Saturday-Sunday – Closed 1 week Christmas*

X Kensington Place

SEAFOOD · NEIGHBOURHOOD 2017 marks the 30th birthday of this iconic brasserie which helped change London's dining scene forever. Fish is the focus of the fairly priced menu which mixes classics like prawn cocktail and fish pie with more modern dishes.

Menu £ 20 (lunch and early dinner) – Carte £ 28/47

Town plan: 27AC3-z - *201-209 Kensington Church St.* ✉ *W8 7LX – ⊖ Notting Hill Gate – ✆ 020 7727 3184 – www.kensingtonplace-restaurant.co.uk – Closed Sunday dinner, Monday lunch and bank holidays*

X The Shed

MODERN BRITISH · RUSTIC It's more than just a shed but does have a higgledy-piggledy charm and a healthy dose of the outdoors. One brother cooks, one manages and the third runs the farm which supplies the produce for the earthy, satisfying dishes.

Carte £ 18/30

Town plan: 27AC3-s - *122 Palace Gardens Terr* ✉ *W8 4RT – ⊖ Notting Hill Gate – ✆ 020 7229 4024 – www.theshed-restaurant.com – Closed Monday lunch and Sunday*

✗ Mazi   🏡 🍴

GREEK · FRIENDLY It's all about sharing at this simple, bright Greek restaurant where traditional recipes are given a modern twist to create vibrant, colourful and fresh tasting dishes. The garden terrace at the back is a charming spot in summer.

Menu £ 13 (weekday lunch) – Carte £ 28/54

Town plan: 27AC3-a - 12-14 Hillgate St ⊠ W8 7SR – ⊖ Notting Hill Gate
– ℰ 020 7229 3794 – www.mazi.co.uk – Closed 24-26 December and 1-2 January

North Kensington

🏠 The Portobello   ⊕ 🍽

TOWNHOUSE · PERSONALISED An attractive Victorian townhouse in an elegant terrace. Original and theatrical décor. Circular beds, half-testers, Victorian baths: no two bedrooms are the same.

21 rooms ⌖ – 🛉£ 175 🛉🛉£ 195/395

Town plan: 27AB2-n - 22 Stanley Gdns. ⊠ W11 2NG – ⊖ Notting Hill Gate
– ℰ 020 7727 2777 – www.portobellohotel.com

✗✗✗ Ledbury (Brett Graham)   🕸 🏡 AC
😋 😋 **MODERN CUISINE · NEIGHBOURHOOD** Brett Graham's husbandry skills and close relationship with his suppliers ensure the quality of the produce shines through and flavour combinations linger long in the memory. This smart yet un-showy restaurant comes with smooth and engaging service. Only a tasting menu is served at dinner on weekends.

→ White beetroot baked in clay with English caviar and smoked & dried eel. Berkshire muntjac with smoked bone marrow, quince and vegetables. Brown sugar tart with stem ginger ice cream.

Menu £ 50/95

Town plan: 27AB2-c - 127 Ledbury Rd. ⊠ W11 2AQ – ⊖ Notting Hill Gate
– ℰ 020 7792 9090 – www.theledbury.com – Closed 25-26 December, August bank holiday and lunch Monday-Tuesday

✗✗ Flat Three   AC 🎛
CREATIVE · DESIGN Basement restaurant blending the cuisines of Scandinavia, Korea and Japan. Not everything works but there's certainly ambition. They make their own soy and miso and serve more foraged ingredients than you'll find in Ray Mears' pocket.

Menu £ 33 (early dinner) – Carte £ 31/77

Town plan: 27AA4-k - 120-122 Holland Park Ave ⊠ W11 4UA – ⊖ Holland Park
– ℰ 020 7792 8987 – www.flatthree.london – dinner only and lunch
Friday-Saturday – Closed 26 December-6 January, 15-26 August, Sunday and Monday

✗ Six Portland Road 🆕   AC
FRENCH · NEIGHBOURHOOD An intimate and personally run neighbourhood restaurant owned by Oli Barker, previously of Terroirs. The menu changes frequently and has a strong French accent; dishes are reassuringly recognisable, skilfully constructed and very tasty.

Carte £ 27/56

Town plan: 27AA4-n - 6 Portland Rd ⊠ W11 4LA – ⊖ Holland Park
– ℰ 020 7229 3130 – www.sixportlandroad.com – Closed Christmas-New Year, last 2 weeks August, Monday and Sunday dinner

✗ Dock Kitchen   🏡 ⅋ 🎛
MEDITERRANEAN CUISINE · DESIGN What started as a 'pop-up' became a permanent feature in this open-plan former Victorian goods yard. The chef's peregrinations inform his cooking, which relies on simple, natural flavours.

Carte £ 23/38

Town plan: 16L4-k - Portobello Dock, 342-344 Ladbroke Grove ⊠ W10 5BU
– ⊖ Ladbroke Grove – ℰ 020 8962 1610 – www.dockkitchen.co.uk
– Closed Christmas, Sunday dinner and bank holidays

Granger and Co. Notting Hill

MODERN CUISINE • FRIENDLY When Bill Granger moved from sunny Sydney to cool Notting Hill he opened a local restaurant too. He's brought with him that delightful 'matey' service that only Aussies do, his breakfast time ricotta hotcakes and a fresh, zesty menu.

Carte £ 23/43

Town plan: 27AC2-x - *175 Westbourne Grove ✉ W11 2SB - ⊖ Bayswater - ☎ 020 7229 9111 (bookings not accepted) - www.grangerandco.com - Closed August bank holiday weekend and 25-26 December*

Wormwood

MEDITERRANEAN CUISINE • NEIGHBOURHOOD The look is New England with a Moorish edge and it's named after the primary herb in absinthe; throw in North African dominated Mediterranean food with a creative edge and you have a restaurant doing something a little different.

Carte £ 26/39

Town plan: 27AB1-w - *16 All Saints Rd ✉ W11 1HH - ⊖ Westbourne Park - ☎ 020 7854 1808 - www.wormwoodnottinghill.com - Closed 28 August-3 September 24-28 December, 1-2 January, Monday lunch and Sunday*

Zayane (N)

MOROCCAN • NEIGHBOURHOOD An intimate neighbourhood restaurant owned by Casablanca-born Meryem Mortell and evoking the sights and scents of North Africa. Carefully conceived dishes have authentic Moroccan flavours but are cooked with modern techniques.

Carte £ 27/36

Town plan: 16L4-z - *91 Golborne Rd ✉ W10 5NL - ⊖ Westbourne Park - ☎ 020 8960 1137 - www.zayanerestaurant.com*

Electric Diner

MEATS AND GRILLS • RUSTIC Next to the iconic Electric Cinema is this loud, brash and fun all-day operation with an all-encompassing menu; the flavours are as big as the portions. The long counter and red leather booths add to the authentic diner feel.

Carte £ 17/34

Town plan: 27AB2-e - *191 Portobello Rd ✉ W11 2ED - ⊖ Ladbroke Grove - ☎ 020 7908 9696 - www.electricdiner.com - Closed 30-31 August and 25 December*

South Kensington

Blakes

LUXURY • DESIGN Behind the Victorian façade is one of London's first 'boutique' hotels. Dramatic, bold and eclectic décor, with oriental influences and antiques from around the world. Mediterranean-influenced cooking in the spacious restaurant.

45 rooms - †£ 220/270 ††£ 330/600 - ☕ £ 16 - 8 suites

Town plan: 36AF7-n - *33 Rowland Gdns ✉ SW7 3PF - ⊖ Gloucester Road - ☎ 020 7370 6701 - www.blakeshotels.com*

The Pelham

LUXURY • ELEGANT Great location if you're in town for museum visiting. It's a mix of English country house and city townhouse, with a panelled sitting room and library with honesty bar. Sweet and intimate basement restaurant with Mediterranean menu.

51 rooms - †£ 180/335 ††£ 260/480 - ☕ £ 18 - 1 suite

Town plan: 37AG6-z - *15 Cromwell Pl ✉ SW7 2LA - ⊖ South Kensington - ☎ 020 7589 8288 - www.pelhamhotel.co.uk*

🏠 Number Sixteen

TOWNHOUSE · ELEGANT Elegant and delightfully furnished 19C townhouses in smart neighbourhood. Discreet entrance, comfortable sitting room, charming breakfast terrace and pretty little garden at the back. Bedrooms in an English country house style.

41 rooms – ♦£ 150/190 ♦♦£ 235/340 – ☑ £ 14

Town plan: 36AF7-d - *16 Sumner Pl.* ✉ *SW7 3EG* – ⊖ *South Kensington* – ☏ *020 7589 5232* – *www.firmdalehotels.co.uk*

🏠 The Exhibitionist

TOWNHOUSE · ELEGANT A funky, design-led boutique hotel fashioned out of several 18C townhouses. The modern artwork changes every few months and the bedrooms are individually furnished – several have their own roof terrace.

37 rooms – ♦£ 199/239 ♦♦£ 229/319 – ☑ £ 16 – 2 suites

Town plan: 36AF6-b - *8-10 Queensberry Pl* ✉ *SW7 2EA* – ⊖ *South Kensington* – ☏ *020 7915 0000* – *www.theexhibitionisthotel.com*

🏠 The Gore

TOWNHOUSE · CLASSIC Idiosyncratic, hip Victorian house close to the Royal Albert Hall, whose charming lobby is covered with pictures and prints. Individually styled bedrooms have plenty of character and fun bathrooms. Bright and casual bistro.

50 rooms – ♦£ 275/650 ♦♦£ 275/650 – ☑ £ 15

Town plan: 36AF5-n - *190 Queen's Gate* ✉ *SW7 5EX* – ⊖ *Gloucester Road* – ☏ *020 7584 6601* – *www.gorehotel.com*

𝕏𝕏𝕏𝕏 Bombay Brasserie

INDIAN · EXOTIC DÉCOR Plush new look for this well-run, well-known and comfortable Indian restaurant; very smart bar and conservatory with a show kitchen. More creative dishes now sit alongside the more traditional.

Menu £ 25 (weekday lunch) – Carte £ 34/47

Town plan: 36AE6-y - *Courtfield Rd.* ✉ *SW7 4QH* – ⊖ *Gloucester Road* – ☏ *020 7370 4040 (bookings advisable at dinner)* – *www.bombayb.co.uk* – *Closed 25 December*

𝕏𝕏 Ours 🆕

MODERN CUISINE · FASHIONABLE The latest chapter in Tom Sellers' story is this immense restaurant featuring trees, a living plant wall of 1,200 flower pots and a mezzanine level bar-lounge. Modern menu of seasonal, ingredient-led dishes with a fresh, light style.

Menu £ 45/55 – Carte £ 30/69

Town plan: 37AH6-o - *264 Brompton Rd* ✉ *SW3 2AS* – ⊖ *South Kensington* – ☏ *020 7100 2200 (booking advisable)* – *www.restaurant-ours.com* – *Closed 24-28 December*

𝕏𝕏 L'Etranger

CREATIVE · NEIGHBOURHOOD Eclectic menu mixes French dishes with techniques and flavours from Japanese cooking. Impressive wine and sake lists. Moody and atmospheric room; ask for a corner table.

Menu £ 25 (weekdays)/45 – Carte £ 29/61

Town plan: 36AE6-c - *36 Gloucester Rd.* ✉ *SW7 4QT* – ⊖ *Gloucester Road* – ☏ *020 7584 1118 (booking essential)* – *www.etranger.co.uk*

𝕏𝕏 Cambio de Tercio

SPANISH · COSY A long-standing, ever-improving Spanish restaurant. Start with small dishes like the excellent El Bulli inspired omelette, then have the popular Pluma Iberica. There are super sherries and a wine list to prove there is life beyond Rioja.

Menu £ 45/55 – Carte £ 30/66 **s**

Town plan: 36AE7-a - *163 Old Brompton Rd.* ✉ *SW5 0LJ* – ⊖ *Gloucester Road* – ☏ *020 7244 8970* – *www.cambiodetercio.co.uk* – *Closed 2 weeks December and 2 weeks August*

XX Yashin Ocean House

JAPANESE · CHIC The USP of this chic Japanese restaurant is 'head to tail' eating although, as there's nothing for carnivores, 'fin to scale' would be more precise. Stick with specialities like the whole dry-aged sea bream for the full umami hit.

Carte £ 20/86

Town plan: 36AF7-y - 117-119 Old Brompton Rd ⊠ SW7 3RN
– ⊖ Gloucester Road – ℰ 020 7373 3990 – www.yashinocean.com – Closed Christmas

XX Ognisko

POLISH · BISTRO Ognisko Polskie Club was founded in 1940 in this magnificent townhouse – its restaurant is now open to the public. The gloriously traditional Polish menu celebrates cooking that is without pretence and truly from the heart.

Menu £ 22 (lunch and early dinner) – Carte £ 27/37

Town plan: 37AG5-r - 55 Prince's Gate, Exhibition Rd ⊠ SW7 2PN
– ⊖ South Kensington – ℰ 020 7589 0101 – www.ogniskorestaurant.co.uk
– Closed 24-26 December and 1 January

X Tendido Cero

SPANISH · TAPAS BAR It's all about the vibe here at Abel Lusa's tapas bar, just across the road from his Cambio de Tercio restaurant. Colourful surroundings, well-drilled service and a menu of favourites all contribute to the fun and lively atmosphere.

Menu £ 35 (dinner) – Carte £ 21/51

Town plan: 36AE7-e - 174 Old Brompton Rd. ⊠ SW5 0LJ – ⊖ Gloucester Road
– ℰ 020 7370 3685 – www.cambiodetercio.co.uk – Closed 2 weeks Christmas-New Year

X Capote y Toros

SPANISH · TAPAS BAR Expect to queue at this compact and vividly coloured spot which celebrates sherry, tapas, ham... and bullfighting. Sherry is the star; those as yet unmoved by this most underappreciated of wines will be dazzled by the variety.

Menu £ 30 – Carte £ 20/51

Town plan: 36AE7-v - 157 Old Brompton Road ⊠ SW5 0LJ – ⊖ Gloucester Road
– ℰ 020 7373 0567 – www.cambiodetercio.co.uk – dinner only – Closed 2 weeks Christmas, Sunday and Monday

X Margaux

MEDITERRANEAN CUISINE · TRENDY Spain and Italy are the primary influences at this modern bistro. There are classics aplenty alongside more unusual dishes. The wine list provides a good choice of varietals and the ersatz industrial look is downtown Manhattan.

Menu £ 15 (weekday lunch) – Carte £ 30/52

Town plan: 36AE7-m - 152 Old Brompton Rd ⊠ SW5 0BE – ⊖ Gloucester Road
– ℰ 020 7373 5753 – www.barmargaux.co.uk – Closed 24-26 December and 1 January

KING'S CROSS ST PANCRAS

St Pancras Renaissance

BUSINESS · ELEGANT This restored Gothic jewel was built in 1873 as the Midland Grand hotel and reopened in 2011 under the Marriott brand. A former taxi rank is now a spacious lobby and all-day dining in the old booking office. Luxury suites in Chambers wing; Barlow wing bedrooms are a little more functional.

245 rooms – †£ 250/400 ††£ 400/450 – ☐ £ 18 – 10 suites

Town plan: 18R4-d - Euston Rd ⊠ NW1 2AR – ⊖ King's Cross St Pancras
– ℰ 020 7841 3540 – www.stpancraslondon.com

Gilbert Scott – See restaurant listing

🏠 Great Northern H. London ☆ ⬆ ⬇ & A/C ✗

HISTORIC BUILDING · CONTEMPORARY Built as a railway hotel in 1854; reborn as a stylish townhouse. Connected to King's Cross' western concourse and just metres from Eurostar check-in. Bespoke furniture in each of the modern bedrooms, and a pantry on each floor.

91 rooms – 🛏£ 249/299 🛏🛏£ 249/299 – ☕ £ 25 – 1 suite

Town plan: 12R3-n - *Pancras Rd* ✉ *N1C 4TB* – ⊖ *King's Cross St Pancras*
– ☎ *020 3388 0818* - *www.gnhlondon.com*

XX Gilbert Scott 🍷 & A/C 🖥

TRADITIONAL BRITISH · BRASSERIE Run under the aegis of Marcus Wareing and named after the architect of this Gothic masterpiece, the restaurant has the look of a Grand Salon but the buzz of a brasserie. It celebrates the UK's many regional and historic specialities.

Menu £ 21 (lunch) – Carte £ 28/61

Town plan: 18R4-d - *St Pancras Renaissance Hotel, Euston Rd* ✉ *NW1 2AR*
– ⊖ *King's Cross St Pancras* – ☎ *020 7278 3888* – *www.thegilbertscott.co.uk*

X Grain Store 🍷 🏠 & A/C ⏰

🐸

MODERN CUISINE · RUSTIC Big, buzzy 'canteen' from Bruno Loubet and the Zetter hotel people. Eclectic, clever dishes – influenced by Bruno's experiences around the world - are packed with interesting flavours and textures; vegetables often take the lead role.

Carte £ 15/35

Town plan: 12R3-s - *Granary Sq, 1-3 Stable St* ✉ *N1C 4AB*
– ⊖ *King's Cross St Pancras* – ☎ *020 7324 4466* - *www.grainstore.com*
– *Closed 24-25 December, 1 January and Sunday dinner*

X Granger & Co. King's Cross ⓝ 🍷 🏠 & A/C 🖥 🍴

MODERN CUISINE · FRIENDLY The third London outpost for Aussie chef Bill Granger is a bright, buzzing place serving small plates, barbecue dishes, and bowls and grains, with plenty of South East Asian flavours. Dishes are vibrant, fresh and uplifting.

Carte £ 22/30

Town plan: 12R3-c - *Stanley Building, 7 Pancras Sq.* ✉ *N1C 4AG*
– ⊖ *King's Cross St Pancras* – ☎ *020 3058 2567* – *www.grangerandco.com*
– *Closed 25-26 December*

🍴 Fellow A/C ⬌

MODERN CUISINE · RUSTIC Anonymous façade but moody and atmospheric inside, with a cool cocktail bar. The lean menu of European dishes uses well-sourced ingredients. Fish from Cornish day boats is a highlight; cheeses are British and puds worth a flutter.

Carte £ 24/37

Town plan: 12R3-x - *24 York Way* ✉ *N1 9AA* – ⊖ *King's Cross St Pancras.*
– ☎ *020 7833 4395* – *www.thefellow.co.uk* – *Closed 25-27 December*

KINGSTON UPON THAMES

Surbiton

XX The French Table A/C ⬌

MEDITERRANEAN CUISINE · NEIGHBOURHOOD Husband and wife run this lively local: he cooks and she runs the show, assisted by her team of friendly staff. Expect zesty and satisfying French-Mediterranean cooking, as well as great bread, as they also run the bakery next door.

Menu £ 25/42

Town plan: 6C5-a - *85 Maple Rd* ✉ *KT6 4AW* – ☎ *020 8399 2365*
– *www.thefrenchtable.co.uk* – *Closed Sunday and Monday*

LAMBETH

Brixton

✗ Boqueria   🍴 ⇌

SPANISH · TAPAS BAR Contemporary tapas bar, named after Barcelona's famous food market. Sit at the counter rather than in the unremarkable dining room. Highlights include the assorted cured hams and an excellent Crema Catalana.

Carte £ 11/19

Town plan: 24R9-x - *192 Acre Ln.* ⊠ *SW2 5UL* – ⊖ *Clapham North*
– 𝒞 020 7733 4408 – www.boqueriatapas.com – dinner only and lunch Saturday-Sunday – Closed 25 December

✗ Nanban ⓝ   AC

JAPANESE · SIMPLE A ramen-bar-cum-izakaya, tucked away at the back of Brixton market and owned by former MasterChef winner, Tim Anderson. Food is fresh and full of flavour; the spicy, super-crispy chicken karaage will have you coming back for more.

Carte £ 13/25

Town plan: 25S9-n - *426 Coldharbour Ln* ⊠ *SW9 8LF* – ⊖ *Brixton*
– 𝒞 020 7346 0098 – www.nanban.co.uk
– Closed Monday lunch

Good quality cooking at a great price?
Look out for the Bib Gourmand ⊛.

Clapham Common

✗✗ Trinity   ❀ ⌂ AC
❀❀

MODERN CUISINE · FASHIONABLE The cooking at this longstanding, bright and warmly run neighbourhood restaurant is less elaborate than it once was – and is all the better for it. The focus remains on the primary ingredient which is given space to shine.

→ Crispy pig's trotters, sauce gribiche and crackling. Fillet of sea bass with roast onions, fennel, shrimps and basil. Salted caramel custard tart.

Menu £ 30 (weekday lunch) – Carte £ 37/52

Town plan: 24Q9-a - *4 The Polygon* ⊠ *SW4 0JG* – ⊖ *Clapham Common*
– 𝒞 020 7622 1199 – www.trinityrestaurant.co.uk
– Closed 24-30 December and 1-2 January

✗ Bistro Union   ⌂ AC 🍴
❀

MODERN BRITISH · NEIGHBOURHOOD The little sister to Trinity restaurant is fun and affordable, with a welcoming feel and sweet staff. The menu is appealingly flexible, whether you're here for brunch or a full dinner; eschew starters in favour of their great 'snacks'.

Menu £ 26 (weekday dinner) – Carte £ 22/40

Town plan: 7E4-s - *40 Abbeville Rd* ⊠ *SW4 9NG* – ⊖ *Clapham South*
– 𝒞 020 7042 6400 (booking advisable) – www.bistrounion.co.uk – Closed 24-27 December

✗ Upstairs (at Trinity) ⓝ   ❀ AC
❀

MODERN BRITISH · FASHIONABLE The open-plan kitchen is the focus of this more relaxed room upstairs from Trinity. It's all about sharing the visually appealing, flavoursome and reasonably priced plates, which bring a hint of the Mediterranean with them.

Carte £ 20/36

Town plan: 24Q9-a - *4 The Polygon* ⊠ *SW4 0JG* – ⊖ *Clapham Common*
– 𝒞 020 7622 1199 – www.trinityrestaurant.co.uk – dinner only – Closed 24-30 December, 1-2 January, Sunday and Monday

X **The Manor**

CREATIVE BRITISH · NEIGHBOURHOOD Fans of The Dairy will like The Manor – they share ownership and menu formats and have similar cuisine styles. With its distressed looks and young, informed service, it certainly captures the zeitgeist. The innovative cooking uses modern techniques and bursts with flavour.

Menu £ 25 (weekday lunch) – Carte £ 20/30

Town plan: 24Q9-b - 148 Clapham Manor St ⊠ SW4 6BX – ⊖ Clapham Common – ℰ 020 7720 4662 – www.themanorclapham.co.uk – Closed 21-27 December, 1 January, Sunday dinner, Tuesday lunch and Monday

X **Dairy**

CREATIVE BRITISH · RUSTIC The higgledy-piggledy, homemade look of this fun, lively restaurant adds to its charm. What you don't expect is such innovative cooking. The earthy, easy-to-eat food is driven by seasonality – some produce is grown on the roof. You can also try their pintxos bar next door.

Menu £ 25 (weekday lunch) – Carte £ 22/28

Town plan: 24Q9-d - 15 The Pavement ⊠ SW4 0HY – ⊖ Clapham Common – ℰ 020 7622 4165 (booking essential at dinner) – www.the-dairy.co.uk – Closed Christmas, Sunday dinner, Monday and Tuesday lunch

X **May the Fifteenth**

MEDITERRANEAN CUISINE · RUSTIC Formerly Abbeville Kitchen – the chef took over this bistro and christened it after the date he signed the forms. The food remains as was: gutsy and wholesome, with fair prices and plenty of choice.

Menu £ 20 (weekday lunch) – Carte £ 23/38

Town plan: 7E4-a - 47 Abbeville Rd ⊠ SW4 9JX – ⊖ Clapham South – ℰ 020 8772 1110 (bookings advisable at dinner) – www.abbevillekitchen.com – dinner only and lunch Friday-Sunday – Closed 24-26 and 31 December and 1 January

X **Zumbura**

INDIAN · NEIGHBOURHOOD Going from running a furniture business to opening a restaurant seems to be working for the three friends behind this modern Indian. It's all about small plates, which are fresh tasting, subtly spiced and surprisingly light.

Carte £ 13/28

Town plan: 24Q9-z - 36a Old Town ⊠ SW4 0LB – ⊖ Clapham Common – ℰ 020 7720 7902 – www.zumbura.com – dinner only – Closed 25 December and 1 January

Kennington

XX **Kennington Tandoori**

INDIAN · NEIGHBOURHOOD Kowsar Hoque runs this contemporary Indian restaurant with great pride and his eagerness and professionalism filters through to his staff. The food is prepared with equal care – try the seasonal specialities and the excellent breads.

Menu £ 33 – Carte £ 20/35

Town plan: 40AS8-a - 313 Kennington Rd ⊠ SE11 4QE – ⊖ Kennington – ℰ 020 7735 9247 (booking advisable) – www.kenningtontandoori.com – Closed 25-26 December

X **Lobster Pot**

FRENCH · TRADITIONAL DÉCOR Family-run, with exuberant décor of fish tanks, portholes and even the sound of seagulls. Classic seafood menu with fruits de mer, plenty of oysters and daily specials. Good crêpes too.

Carte £ 41/85

Town plan: 40AT7-e - 3 Kennington Ln. ⊠ SE11 4RG – ⊖ Kennington – ℰ 020 7582 5556 – www.lobsterpotrestaurant.co.uk – Closed 25 December-2 January, Sunday and Monday

Southbank

🏨 London Marriott H. County Hall

BUSINESS · MODERN Occupying the historic County Hall building on the banks of the River Thames. Bedrooms are spacious, stylish and modern; many enjoy river and Parliament outlooks. Impressive leisure facilities. World famous views too from wood-panelled Gillray's, which specialises in steaks.

200 rooms – †£ 420/600 ††£ 600/900 – ☕ £ 22 – 5 suites

Town plan: **40AR5-a** - *Westminster Bridge Rd* ✉ *SE1 7PB* – ⊖ *Westminster* – ✆ *020 7928 5200* – *www.marriott.co.uk/lonch*

XXX Skylon

MODERN CUISINE · DESIGN Ask for a window table here at the Royal Festival Hall. Informal grill-style operation on one side, a more formal and expensive restaurant on the other, with a busy cocktail bar in the middle.

Menu £ 20/28 – Carte £ 27/38

Town plan: **32AR4-a** - *1 Southbank Centre, Belvedere Rd* ✉ *SE1 8XX* – ⊖ *Waterloo* – ✆ *020 7654 7800* – *www.skylon-restaurant.co.uk* – *Closed 25 December*

Stockwell

🍺 Canton Arms

TRADITIONAL BRITISH · PUB An appreciative crowd of all ages come for the earthy, robust and seasonal British dishes which suit the relaxed environment of this pub so well. Staff are attentive and knowledgeable.

Carte £ 19/35

Town plan: **24R8-a** - ✉ *SW8 1XP* – ⊖ *Stockwell.* – ✆ *020 7582 8710 (bookings not accepted)* – *www.cantonarms.com* – *Closed Christmas-New Year, Monday lunch, Sunday dinner and bank holidays*

Vauxhall

XX Pharmacy 2 🅽

MODERN BRITISH · DESIGN Pharmacy was the place to be in the '90s and in 2016 Damien Hirst revived the name for the restaurant in his Newport Street Gallery. The medicinally-themed decoration is familiar yet more vivid. For the food he has paired up with Mark Hix – the best dishes are the more British ones.

Carte £ 27/55

Town plan: **24R7-v** - *Newport Street Gallery, Newport St* ✉ *SE11 6AJ* – ⊖ *Vauxhall* – ✆ *020 3141 9333* – *www.pharmacyrestaurant.com* – *Closed Christmas, Sunday dinner and Monday*

LEWISHAM

Blackheath

XX Chapters

MODERN CUISINE · BRASSERIE A classic, bustling brasserie that keeps the locals happy, by being open all day and offering everything from Mediterranean-influenced main courses to meats cooked over charcoal. There's also a kids' menu and wines by the pichet.

Menu £ 18 (weekdays) – Carte £ 23/33

Town plan: **7F4-c** - *43-45 Montpelier Vale* ✉ *SE3 0TJ* – ✆ *020 8333 2666* – *www.chaptersblackheath.com* – *Closed 2-3 January*

Forest Hill

XX Babur

INDIAN · NEIGHBOURHOOD Good looks and innovative cooking make this passionately run and long-established Indian restaurant stand out. Influences from the south and north west feature most and seafood is a highlight - look out for the 'Treasures of the Sea' menu.

Menu £ 31/37 – Carte £ 27/36

Town plan: **7F4-s** - *119 Brockley Rise* ✉ *SE23 1JP* – ⊖ *Honor Oak Park* – ✆ *020 8291 2400* – *www.babur.info* – *Closed 26 December*

MERTON
Wimbledon

Hotel du Vin

BUSINESS · CONTEMPORARY A charming part-Georgian house surrounded by over 30 acres of parkland. Dine in the light and airy Orangery or in the restaurant overlooking an Italian sunken garden; French-influenced menus offer something for everyone. Bedrooms are comfortable and well-equipped; ask for one with views of the park.

48 rooms ⌨ – ♦£145/220 ♦♦£155/230 – 2 suites

Town plan: 6C5-x - *Cannizaro House, West Side, Wimbledon Common*
✉ *SW19 4UE* – ☏ *0330 024 0706* – *www.hotelduvin.com*

White Onion ⓝ

MODERN CUISINE · BISTRO A relaxed bistro deluxe with a handsome marble-topped bar and an attentive young team. Flavoursome classic French cooking has clever modern touches. Great value set lunch and a terrific selection of wine by the glass and carafe.

Menu £20 (lunch) – Carte £29/48

Town plan: 6D5-w - *67 High St* ✉ *SW19 5EE* – ⊖ *Wimbledon*
– ☏ 020 8947 8278 – www.thewhiteonion.co.uk
– Closed first 2 weeks August, 25 December-5 January, Monday, lunch Tuesday-Wednesday and Sunday dinner

Light House

MEDITERRANEAN CUISINE · NEIGHBOURHOOD A neighbourhood favourite offering Mediterranean cooking in smart, comfortable surroundings. The food is wholesome and confident, with plenty of bold flavours; Italian dishes and puddings are the highlights and staff are calm and cheery.

Menu £16/25 – Carte £27/41

Town plan: 6D5-u *x- 75-77 Ridgway* ✉ *SW19 4ST* – ⊖ *Wimbledon*
– ☏ 020 8944 6338 – www.lighthousewimbledon.com
– Closed 25-26 December, 1 January and Sunday dinner

Takahashi ⓝ

JAPANESE · FRIENDLY The eponymous chef-owner of this sweet spot is a Nobu alumnus and his wife runs the service with a personal touch. Mediterranean ingredients bring a creative edge to the pure, delicately flavoured dishes. Sushi and sashimi are a highlight.

Menu £22/37 – Carte £19/60

Town plan: 6D5-s - *228 Merton Rd* ✉ *SW19 1EQ* – ⊖ *South Wimbledon*
– ☏ 020 8540 3041 (booking essential) – www.takahashi-restaurant.co.uk
– dinner only and lunch Saturday-Sunday
– Closed Monday and Tuesday

Light on the Common ⓝ

TRADITIONAL BRITISH · NEIGHBOURHOOD All-day neighbourhood restaurant offering an extensive menu to take you through from breakfast until dinner. Staff are helpful and friendly and the setting bright and modern; ask for a seat in the conservatory at the back.

Menu £23 (weekday dinner) – Carte £24/40

Town plan: 6D5-c - *48 High St* ✉ *SW19 5AX* – ⊖ *Wimbledon*
– ☏ 020 8946 3031 – www.lightwimbledon.co.uk
– Closed 25 December and Sunday dinner

An important business lunch or dinner with friends?
The symbol ⇔ indicates restaurants with private rooms.

LONDON ENGLAND

104

REDBRIDGE
Wanstead

✗ Provender   🏠 AC 🖳

FRENCH · BISTRO A modern, busy and bustling neighbourhood bistro courtesy of experienced restaurateur Max Renzland. The well-priced French cooking is pleasingly rustic and satisfying, with great charcuterie, appealing salads and well-timed grills.

Menu £ 13 (weekdays) – Carte £ 20/46

Town plan: 4G2-x - *17 High St* ✉ *E11 2AA* – ⊖ *Snaresbrook* – *☎ 020 8530 3050* – *www.provenderlondon.co.uk*

South Woodford

✗✗ The Woodford 🅽   🍸 ⇲

MODERN BRITISH · FASHIONABLE A former nightclub with a glitzy cocktail bar. Like the décor, the cooking is eye-catching and modern with the odd playful note; dishes demonstrate the kitchen's understanding of classical French techniques and desserts are a highlight.

Menu £ 24 (weekday lunch) – Carte £ 36/64

Town plan: 4G2-w - *159 High Rd* ✉ *E18 2PA* – ⊖ *South Woodford* – *☎ 020 8504 5952* – *www.thewoodford-e18.com* – *Closed Monday and Tuesday*

RICHMOND-UPON-THAMES

Barnes

✕✕ Indian Zilla   AC I℣ ⇦

INDIAN · NEIGHBOURHOOD Bright, contemporary restaurant with attentive, friendly service. Modern menu includes a few classics; the authentic, fully-flavoured dishes display a lightness of touch.

Carte £ 20/43

Town plan: 21K8-k - *2-3 Rocks Ln.* ✉ *SW13 0DB* – 𝒞 *020 8878 3989*
– *www.indianzilla.co.uk* – *dinner only and Sunday lunch* – *Closed 25 December*

✕ Sonny's Kitchen   AC ⇦

MEDITERRANEAN CUISINE · NEIGHBOURHOOD A longstanding and much-loved neighbourhood spot with a bright, relaxed feel and some striking art on the walls; co-owned by Barnes residents Rebecca Mascarenhas and Phil Howard. Menus are all-encompassing and portions generous.

Menu £ 20 (weekday lunch) – Carte £ 26/38

Town plan: 21K8-x - *94 Church Rd* ✉ *SW13 0DQ* – 𝒞 *020 8748 0393*
– *www.sonnyskitchen.co.uk* – *Closed 25-26 December, 1 January and bank holiday Mondays*

✕ Riva   AC

ITALIAN · NEIGHBOURHOOD A restaurant built on customer loyalty; the regulars are showered with attention from the eponymous owner. Gutsy, no-nonsense dishes, full of flavour. Interesting all-Italian wine list.

Carte £ 33/52

Town plan: 21K8-a - *169 Church Rd.* ✉ *SW13 9HR* – 𝒞 *020 8748 0434* – *Closed 2 weeks August, Easter, Christmas-New Year, bank holidays and Saturday lunch*

✕ Olympic Café + Dining Room   ⅙ AC ⤶

MODERN BRITISH · BRASSERIE An all-day brasserie housed in what was once the world's greatest recording studio – artists like the Stones and Led Zeppelin recorded seminal albums here. No 'Goat's Head Soup', instead an appealing selection of British comfort food.

Carte £ 22/57

Town plan: 21J8-s - *117-123 Church Rd* ✉ *SW13 9HL* – 𝒞 *020 8912 5161 (bookings advisable at dinner)* – *www.olympiccinema.co.uk* – *Closed 25 December*

🍺 Brown Dog   🏡

MODERN BRITISH · PUB Concealed in a maze of residential streets is this homely, relaxed pub with a lived-in feel. The balanced menu offers traditional and flavoursome fare like venison pie or haddock fishcake; all done 'properly'.

Carte £ 23/42

Town plan: 21J8-9-b - *28 Cross St* ✉ *SW13 0AP* – ⊖ *Barnes Bridge (Rail).*
– 𝒞 *020 8392 2200* – *www.thebrowndog.co.uk* – *Closed 25 December*

East Sheen

🏚 Victoria   ⇦ 🏡 🖵 P

MODERN BRITISH · PUB A proper local, with a lived-in feel, especially in the bars; if you're here to eat head for the conservatory, which overlooks a terrace. The appealing menu offers a good range of dishes and comes with a distinct Mediterranean slant, with Middle Eastern influences never far away.

Carte £ 26/44

7 rooms 🖵 – †£ 95/125 ††£ 95/135

Town plan: 6C4-h - 10 West Temple Sheen ⊠ SW14 7RT
– ⊖ Mortlake (Rail). – ℰ 020 8876 4238
– www.thevictoria.net

Kew

✗✗ The Glasshouse   🎗 🗚

🕸 MODERN CUISINE · FASHIONABLE The Glasshouse is the very model of a modern neighbourhood restaurant and sits in the heart of lovely, villagey Kew. Food is confident yet unshowy – much like the locals – and comes with distinct Mediterranean flavours along with the occasional Asian hint. Service comes with the eagerness of youth.
→ Duck breast with foie gras parfait, balsamic and beetroot. Loin of lamb with braised shoulder, boulangère potatoes and pea & wild garlic emulsion. Warm custard brioche with roasted apples and tarte Tatin ice cream.

Menu £ 30 (weekday lunch)/50

Town plan: 6C4-z - 14 Station Par. ⊠ TW9 3PZ – ⊖ Kew Gardens
– ℰ 020 8940 6777 – www.glasshouserestaurant.co.uk – Closed 24-26 December and 1 January

✗✗ Linnea   🗚

MODERN BRITISH · NEIGHBOURHOOD The chef-owner of this pared down yet elegant room is from Sweden – Linnea is his country's national flower. The monthly menu offers modern, unfussy dishes with Scandinavian techniques of pickling, curing and air-drying in evidence.

Menu £ 20/28

Town plan: 6C4-u - 12 Kew Grn. ⊠ TW9 3BH – ⊖ Kew Gardens
– ℰ 020 8940 5696 – www.linneakew.co.uk – Closed Christmas, Sunday dinner and Monday

Richmond

🏨 Petersham   🎗 ≤ 🛏 🖵 ᬒ 🎶 🧳 P

HISTORIC · CLASSIC Extended over the years, a fine example of Victorian Gothic architecture, with Portland stone and self-supporting staircase. The most comfortable bedrooms overlook the Thames. Formal restaurant in which to enjoy a mix of classic and modern cooking; ask for a window table for terrific park and river views.

58 rooms 🖵 – †£ 110/145 ††£ 157/220 – 1 suite

Town plan: 6C4-j - Nightingale Ln ⊠ TW10 6UZ – ⊖ Richmond
– ℰ 020 8940 7471 – www.petershamhotel.co.uk
– Closed 25-26 December

🏨 Bingham   🛏 🗚 🎶 🧳 P

TOWNHOUSE · MODERN A pair of conjoined and restored Georgian townhouses; a short walk from Richmond centre. Ask for a room overlooking the river and garden. Contemporary bedrooms, some with four-posters.

15 rooms – †£ 129/325 ††£ 149/365 – 🖵 £ 17

Town plan: 6C4-c - 61-63 Petersham Rd. ⊠ TW10 6UT – ⊖ Richmond
– ℰ 020 8940 0902 – www.thebingham.co.uk
Bingham Restaurant – See restaurant listing

✗✗ Bingham Restaurant

MODERN CUISINE · DESIGN Its riverside setting adds to the charm of this comfortable and enthusiastically run hotel restaurant. The various menus provide plenty of choice; the cooking is a blend of the modern and the classical and dishes are nicely balanced.

Carte £ 25/55

Town plan: 6C4-c - *Bingham Hotel, 61-63 Petersham Rd.* ✉ *TW10 6UT – ⊖ Richmond – ✆ 020 8940 0902 – www.thebingham.co.uk – Closed Sunday dinner*

✗✗ Dysart Petersham

MODERN CUISINE · INTIMATE A pub built in the 1900s as part of the Arts and Crafts movement but now run as quite a formal restaurant. The kitchen uses top-notch ingredients and adds subtle Asian tones to a classical base. Occasional music recital suppers.

Menu £ 28 (weekdays) – Carte £ 37/50

Town plan: 6C4-d - *135 Petersham Rd* ✉ *TW10 7AA – ✆ 020 8940 8005 (booking advisable) – www.thedysartpetersham.co.uk – Closed Sunday dinner and Monday*

✗ Petersham Nurseries Café

MODERN CUISINE · RUSTIC On a summer's day there can be few more delightful spots for lunch, whether that's on the terrace or in the greenhouse. The kitchen uses the freshest seasonal produce in unfussy, flavoursome dishes that have a subtle Italian accent.

Carte £ 28/52

Town plan: 6C4-k - *Church Ln (off Petersham Rd)* ✉ *TW10 7AG – ✆ 020 8940 5230 (booking essential) – www.petershamnurseries.com – lunch only – Closed 24-27 December and Monday*

✗ Matsuba

JAPANESE · DESIGN Family-run Japanese restaurant with just 11 tables; understated but well-kept appearance. Extensive menu offers wide range of Japanese dishes, along with bulgogi, a Korean barbecue dish.

Menu £ 39 – Carte £ 22/42

Town plan: 6C4-n - *10 Red Lion St* ✉ *TW9 1RW – ⊖ Richmond – ✆ 020 8605 3513 – www.matsuba-restaurant.com – Closed 25-26 December, 1 January and Sunday*

✗ Swagat

INDIAN · BISTRO A very likeable little Indian restaurant, run by two friends who met while training with Oberoi hotels in India. One partner organises the warm service; the other prepares dishes with a pleasing degree of lightness and subtlety.

Menu £ 30 – Carte £ 20/35

Town plan: 6C4-b - *86 Hill Rise* ✉ *TW10 6UB – ⊖ Richmond – ✆ 020 8940 7557 (booking essential) – www.swagatindiancuisine.co.uk – dinner only – Closed 25 December*

Teddington

✗✗ Rétro Bistrot

FRENCH · BISTRO Gallic charm is in abundance at this bistro deluxe, with its exposed brick walls, comfy banquettes and art for sale. Classic French dishes are prepared with innate skill; the set menu is great value and desserts are a highlight.

Menu £ 11/23 – Carte £ 28/55

Town plan: 5B5-n - *114-116 High St* ✉ *TW11 8JB – ⊖ Teddington (Rail) – ✆ 020 8977 2239 – www.retrobistrot.co.uk – Closed Sunday dinner and Monday*

X **Simply Thai**   &. [AC]

THAI · NEIGHBOURHOOD Simple Thai restaurant offering a huge array of dishes. Cooking is adjusted for Western tastes but makes commendable use of British ingredients; the signature dishes are a good bet. Come on a Sunday for good value street food.

Carte £ 21/31

Town plan: 5B5-x - *196 Kingston Rd.* ✉ *TW11 9JD* – ⊖ *Hampton Wick (Rail)* – *℘ 020 8943 9747* – *www.simplythai-restaurant.co.uk* – *dinner only* – *Closed 25-26 December*

🍴 **King's Head**   🍴 &. P

MODERN CUISINE · NEIGHBOURHOOD Britain has its pubs and France its brasseries; The King's Head does its bit for the entente cordiale by combining both. Have a drink in the front bar, then enjoy rustic classics in the rear brasserie.

Menu £ 10 (weekday lunch) – Carte £ 23/40

Town plan: 5B5-c - *123 High St* ✉ *TW11 8HG* – ⊖ *Teddington (Rail).* – *℘ 020 3166 2900* – *www.whitebrasserie.com*

Twickenham

XX **A Cena**   [AC]

ITALIAN · NEIGHBOURHOOD The menu at this bigger-than-you-first-think restaurant covers all parts of Italy but there's more of a northern bias in winter; pasta is a highlight. The owners may not be Italian but you can't fault their passion and enthusiasm.

Menu £ 10 (weekday lunch) – Carte £ 21/40

Town plan: 6C4-p - *418 Richmond Rd.* ✉ *TW1 2EB* – ⊖ *Richmond* – *℘ 020 8288 0108* – *www.acena.co.uk* – *Closed 2 weeks August, Sunday dinner, Monday lunch and bank holidays*

🍴 **Crown**   🍴 &. ⇔ P

TRADITIONAL BRITISH · PUB Relaxed, stylish pub with parquet floors and feature fireplaces; sit in the airy, elegant rear restaurant, with its high vaulted ceiling and garden view. Global, bound-to-please menus offer fresh, tasty, amply-sized dishes.

Carte £ 21/40

Town plan: 5B4-c - *174 Richmond Rd, St Margarets* ✉ *TW1 2NH* – ⊖ *St Margarets (Rail).* – *℘ 020 8892 5896* – *www.crowntwickenham.co.uk* – *Closed 26 December*

SOUTHWARK

Bermondsey

🏨 Shangri-La   ⩗ ⋖ 🖼 ⅃ₐ 🖵 🖵 & AC 🚫 🛎 🚗

LUXURY · ELEGANT When your hotel occupies floors 34-52 of The Shard, you know it's going to have the wow factor. The pool is London's highest and north-facing bedrooms have the best views. An East-meets-West theme includes the restaurant's menu and afternoon tea when you have a choice of traditional English or Asian.

202 rooms – 🛏£ 350/575 🛏🛏£ 350/575 – ⬜£ 32 – 17 suites

Town plan: 33AW4-s - *The Shard, 31 St Thomas St* ✉ *SE1 9QU*
– ⊖ *London Bridge* – ✆ *020 7234 8000 – www.shangri-la.com/london*

🏨 Bermondsey Square   🖵 & AC 🛎

BUSINESS · MODERN Cleverly designed hotel in a regenerated square, with subtle '60s influences and a hip feel. Relaxed public areas; well-equipped bedrooms include stylish loft suites.

90 rooms – 🛏£ 99/239 🛏🛏£ 99/239 – ⬜£ 11

Town plan: 42AX6-n - *Bermondsey Sq, Tower Bridge Rd* ✉ *SE1 3UN*
– ⊖ *London Bridge* – ✆ *020 7378 2450 – www.bermondseysquarehotel.co.uk*

XXX Le Pont de la Tour   🕸 🍷 ⋖ 🏠 & 🖐

FRENCH · ELEGANT Few restaurants can beat the setting, especially when you're on the terrace with its breathtaking views of Tower Bridge. For its 25th birthday it got a top-to-toe refurbishment, resulting in a warmer looking room in which to enjoy the French-influenced cooking.

Menu £ 20/32 – Carte £ 34/67

Town plan: 34AY4-c - *36d Shad Thames, Butlers Wharf* ✉ *SE1 2YE*
– ⊖ *London Bridge* – ✆ *020 7403 8403 – www.lepontdelatour.co.uk – Closed
1 January*

XX Story (Tom Sellers)   & AC
❀

MODERN CUISINE · DESIGN Tom Sellers offers a 6 or 10 course lunch and a 12 course dinner menu; serving just 12 tables in what used to be a public toilet and now looks like a Nordic eco-lodge. Modern techniques and a light touch result in food with a back-to-nature feel and strong earthy flavours. Dishes are colourful, playful and easy to eat.

→ Heritage potato cake with shallots. Scallops with ash-roasted cucumber and dill. Chocolate and lovage.

Menu £ 39 (weekday lunch)/100

Town plan: 42AY5-s - *199 Tooley St* ✉ *SE1 2JX* – ⊖ *London Bridge*
– ✆ *020 7183 2117 (booking essential) – www.restaurantstory.co.uk – Closed
2 weeks Christmas-New Year, Easter, Sunday, Monday lunch and bank holidays*

✕✕ Magdalen

MODERN BRITISH · NEIGHBOURHOOD The clever sourcing and confident British cooking will leave you satisfied. Add genial service, an affordable lunch menu and a food-friendly wine list and you have the favourite restaurant of many.

Menu £ 17 (lunch) – Carte £ 29/50

Town plan: 34AX4-b - *152 Tooley St.* ✉ *SE1 2TU* – ⊖ *London Bridge*
- 𝒞 *020 7403 1342* – *www.magdalenrestaurant.co.uk* – *Closed Sunday, Saturday lunch and bank holidays*

✕✕ Oblix

MEATS AND GRILLS · TRENDY A New York grill restaurant on the 32nd floor of The Shard; window tables for two are highly prized. Meats and fish from the rotisserie, grill and Josper oven are the stars of the show; brunch in the lounge bar at weekends.

Menu £ 32 (lunch) – Carte £ 29/156

Town plan: 33AW4-e - *Level 32, The Shard, 31 St Thomas St.* ✉ *SE1 9RY*
- ⊖ *London Bridge* – 𝒞 *020 7268 6700*
- *www.oblixrestaurant.com*

✕✕ Aqua Shard

MODERN CUISINE · FASHIONABLE The Shard's most accessible restaurant covers all bases by serving breakfast, brunch, lunch, afternoon tea and dinner. If you don't mind queuing, you can even come just for a drink. The contemporary cooking makes good use of British ingredients and comes with a degree of finesse in flavour and looks.

Menu £ 36 (weekday lunch)/48 – Carte £ 39/79

Town plan: 33AW4-e - *Level 31, The Shard, 31 St Thomas St,* ✉ *SE1 9RY*
- ⊖ *London Bridge* – 𝒞 *020 3011 1256* – *www.aquashard.co.uk*
- *Closed 25 December*

✕ Blueprint Café

MODERN CUISINE · BRASSERIE Retractable, floor to ceiling windows make the most of the river views from this bright restaurant overlooking the Thames. Cooking is light, seasonally pertinent and easy to eat and the set menus come with appealing price tags.

Menu £ 25 (weekday lunch) – Carte £ 27/47

Town plan: 34AY4-u - *28 Shad Thames, Butlers Wharf* ✉ *SE1 2YD*
- ⊖ *London Bridge* – 𝒞 *020 7378 7031* – *www.blueprintcafe.co.uk*
- *Closed 1 January and Sunday dinner*

✕ Village East

MODERN CUISINE · TRENDY Counter dining is the focus in the main room; those celebrating can tuck themselves away in a separate bar. Cooking mixes contemporary dishes with Mediterranean-inspired plates; the confit turkey leg is the house speciality.

Carte £ 27/45

Town plan: 42AX5-a - *171-173 Bermondsey St* ✉ *SE1 3UW* – ⊖ *London Bridge*
- 𝒞 *020 7357 6082* – *www.villageeast.co.uk*
- *Closed 24-26 December*

✕ Cantina Del Ponte

ITALIAN · RUSTIC This Italian stalwart offers an appealing mix of classic dishes and reliable favourites from a sensibly priced menu, in pleasant faux-rustic surroundings. Its pleasant terrace takes advantage of its riverside setting.

Menu £ 16/23 – Carte £ 28/49

Town plan: 34AY4-c - *36c Shad Thames, Butlers Wharf* ✉ *SE1 2YE*
- ⊖ *London Bridge* – 𝒞 *020 7403 5403* – *www.cantina.co.uk*
- *Closed 25 December*

✗ Butlers Wharf Chop House   ⪦ ⌂ AC

TRADITIONAL BRITISH · BRASSERIE Grab a table on the terrace in summer and dine in the shadow of Tower Bridge. Rustic feel to the interior; noisy and fun. The menu focuses on traditional English ingredients and dishes; grilled meats a speciality.

Carte £ 25/60

Town plan: 34AY4-n - *36e Shad Thames, Butlers Wharf* ✉ *SE1 2YE*
– ⊖ London Bridge – ✆ 020 7403 3403 – www.chophouse-restaurant.co.uk
– Closed 1 January

✗ Vivat Bacchus London Bridge   器 ⌂

MEATS AND GRILLS · WINE BAR Wines from the South African owners' home-land feature strongly and are well-suited to the meat dishes – the strength here. Choose one of the sharing boards themed around various countries, like Italian hams or South African BBQ.

Carte £ 20/45

Town plan: 33AW4-n - *4 Hays Ln* ✉ *SE1 2HB* – ⊖ *London Bridge*
– ✆ 020 7234 0891 – www.vivatbacchus.co.uk – Closed Christmas-New Year, Sunday and bank holidays

✗ Pizarro   AC 盲 ⇔

MEDITERRANEAN CUISINE · NEIGHBOURHOOD José Pizarro has a refreshingly simple way of naming his establishments: after José, his tapas bar, comes Pizarro, a larger restaurant a few doors down. Go for the small plates, like prawns with piquillo peppers and jamón.

Menu £ 35 – Carte £ 25/45

Town plan: 42AX6-r - *194 Bermondsey St* ✉ *SE1 3UW* – ⊖ *Borough*
– ✆ 020 7378 9455 – www.josepizarro.com – Closed 24-28 December

✗ Antico   🍸 AC 🕸

ITALIAN · NEIGHBOURHOOD A former antiques warehouse, with a fun atmo-sphere. Straightforward Italian food has its focus on comfort; homemade pasta dishes are a highlight. The downstairs cocktail bar offers over 80 gins and their own brand of tonic water.

Menu £ 17 (lunch and early dinner) – Carte £ 25/36

Town plan: 42AX6-e - *214 Bermondsey St* ✉ *SE1 3TQ* – ⊖ *London Bridge*
– ✆ 020 7407 4682 – www.antico-london.co.uk
– Closed 24-26 December, 1 January and Monday

✗ Casse Croûte

FRENCH · BISTRO Squeeze into this tiny bistro and you'll find yourself trans-ported to rural France. A blackboard menu offers three choices for each course but new dishes are added as others run out. The cooking is rustic, authentic and heartening.

Carte £ 28/35

Town plan: 42AX5-t - *109 Bermondsey St* ✉ *SE1 3XB* – ⊖ *London Bridge*
– ✆ 020 7407 2140 (booking essential) – www.cassecroute.co.uk – Closed Sunday dinner

✗ José   ᕷ AC 盲
(😊)

SPANISH · MINIMALIST Standing up while eating tapas feels so right, especially at this snug, lively bar that packs 'em in like boquerones. The vibrant dishes are intensely flavoured; five per person should suffice; go for the daily fish dishes from the blackboard. There's a great list of sherries too.

Carte £ 12/28

Town plan: 42AX5-v - *104 Bermondsey St* ✉ *SE1 3UB* – ⊖ *London Bridge*
– ✆ 020 7403 4902 – www.josepizarro.com – Closed 24-26 December and Sunday dinner

X **St John Maltby** ⓝ

TRADITIONAL BRITISH · BISTRO An austere, industrial-style dining space, tucked under a railway arch in deepest Bermondsey. Cooking is tasty, satisfying and as British as John Bull and the earthy, original selection of wines are also available to take away.

Carte £ 31/35

Town plan: 20U6-s - *41 Ropewalk, Maltby St* ✉ *SE1 3PA* – ⊖ *London Bridge* – *℘ 020 7553 9844 (booking advisable) – www.stjohngroup.uk.com/maltby_street* – *dinner only and lunch Friday-Sunday – Closed Christmas, New Year and Sunday dinner-Tuesday*

🍺 **Garrison**   🅰🅲 ▯ ↔

MEDITERRANEAN CUISINE · PUB Known for its charming vintage look, booths and sweet-natured service, The Garrison boasts a warm, relaxed vibe. Open from breakfast until dinner, when a Mediterranean-led menu pulls in the crowd.

Menu £ 24/29 – Carte £ 26/38

Town plan: 42AX5-z - *99-101 Bermondsey St* ✉ *SE1 3XB* – ⊖ *London Bridge.* – *℘ 020 7089 9355 (booking essential at dinner) – www.thegarrison.co.uk* – *Closed 25-26 December*

East Dulwich

🍺 **Palmerston**   🎱 ↔

MEDITERRANEAN CUISINE · PUB A brightly run Victorian pub that has a comfortable, lived-in feel and lies at the heart of the local community. The cooking has a satisfying, gutsy edge with meat dishes, especially game, being the highlight.

Menu £ 15 (weekday lunch) – Carte £ 28/55

Town plan: 26U9-x - *91 Lordship Ln* ✉ *SE22 8EP* – ⊖ *East Dulwich (Rail).* – *℘ 020 8693 1629 – www.thepalmerston.co.uk – Closed 25-26 December and 1 January*

Peckham

X **Artusi**

ITALIAN · NEIGHBOURHOOD An enthusiastically run Italian restaurant which shows Peckham is on the rise. The kitchen displays clear respect for the seasonal ingredients, dishes are kept honest and the prices are more than fair.

Carte £ 19/35

Town plan: 26U9-a - *161 Bellenden Rd* ✉ *SE15 4DH* – ⊖ *Peckham Rye* – *℘ 020 3302 8200 (booking essential at dinner) – www.artusi.co.uk – Closed 2 weeks Christmas and bank holidays*

Southwark

🏨 **Mondrian London**   ⚡ ⟨ 🛋 ⓦⓘⓕⓘ 🎵 Ⅰѕ 🛗 ⟨ 🅰🅲 🛁 🚗

BUSINESS · DESIGN The former Sea Containers house now has slick, stylish look evoking the golden age of the transatlantic liner. Rooms come with a bright splash of colour; Suites have balconies and Superiors, a river view. Globally influenced small plates in smart restaurant, with meat and fish from the grill & clay oven.

359 rooms – 🛏£ 232 🛏🛏£ 319 – 🍴£ 16 – 5 suites

Town plan: 32AT3-x - *20 Upper Ground* ✉ *SE1 9PD* – ⊖ *Southwark* – *℘ 020 3747 1000 – www.mondrianlondon.com*

🏨 **Hilton London Bankside** ⓝ   ⚡ 🏊 Ⅰѕ 🛗 ⟨ 🅰🅲 🛁

BUSINESS · MODERN A sleek, design-led hotel with faux industrial touches; ideally situated for visiting the attractions of the South Bank. Spacious, contemporary bedrooms are furnished in a minimalist style. Impressive pool in the basement. OXBO serves a range of British dishes including meats from the Josper grill.

292 rooms – 🛏£ 230/260 🛏🛏£ 230/260 – 🍴£ 30 – 30 suites

Town plan: 33AU4-b - *2-8 Great Suffolk St* ✉ *SE1 0UG* – ⊖ *Southwark* – *℘ 020 3667 5600 – www.londonbankside.hilton.com*

✗✗✗ Oxo Tower

MODERN CUISINE · FASHIONABLE Set on top of an iconic converted factory and providing stunning views of the Thames and beyond. Stylish, minimalist interior with huge windows. Expect quite ambitious, mostly European, cuisine.

Menu £ 34 (lunch) – Carte £ 41/76

Town plan: **32AS3-a** - *Oxo Tower Wharf (8th floor), Barge House St* ✉ *SE1 9PH* – ⊖ *Southwark* – ℰ *020 7803 3888 – www.harveynichols.com – Closed 25 December*

Oxo Tower Brasserie – See restaurant listing

✗✗ Roast

MODERN BRITISH · FASHIONABLE Known for its British food and for promoting UK producers – not surprising considering the restaurant's in the heart of Borough Market. The 'dish of the day' is often a highlight; service is affable and there's live music at night.

Menu £ 30/38 – Carte £ 39/69

Town plan: **33AV4-e** - *The Floral Hall, Borough Mkt* ✉ *SE1 1TL* – ⊖ *London Bridge* – ℰ *020 3006 6111 (booking essential)* – *www.roast-restaurant.com – Closed 25-26 December and 1 January*

✗✗ Baltic

WORLD CUISINE · BRASSERIE A bright, buzzing restaurant with wooden trussed ceilings, skylights and sleek styling. The menu specialises in Eastern European food, from Poland, Russia, Bulgaria and even Siberia. Dumplings and meat dishes stand out – and the vodkas will warm the heart.

Menu £ 18 (weekday lunch)/25 – Carte £ 25/36

Town plan: **32AT4-e** - *74 Blackfriars Rd* ✉ *SE1 8HA* – ⊖ *Southwark* – ℰ *020 7928 1111 (bookings advisable at dinner) – www.balticrestaurant.co.uk* – *Closed 24-26 December and Monday lunch*

✗✗ Union Street Café

ITALIAN · TRENDY Occupying a former warehouse, this Gordon Ramsay restaurant has been busy since day one and comes with a New York feel, a faux industrial look and a basement bar. The Italian menu keeps things simple and stays true to the classics.

Menu £ 20 (weekday lunch) – Carte £ 39/47

Town plan: **33AU4-u** - *47-51 Great Suffolk Street* ✉ *SE1 0BS* – ⊖ *London Bridge* – ℰ *020 7592 7977 – www.gordonramsayrestaurants.com/union-street-cafe/*

✗✗ Rabot 1745

MODERN CUISINE · DESIGN Want something different? How about cocoa cuisine? Rabot 1745 is from the owners of Hotel Chocolat and is named after their estate in St Lucia. They take the naturally bitter, spicy flavours of the bean and use them subtly in classically based dishes. The chocolate mousse dessert is pretty good too!

Carte £ 26/42

Town plan: **33AW4-c** - *2-4 Bedal St, Borough Mkt* ✉ *SE1 9AL* – ⊖ *London Bridge* – ℰ *020 7378 8226 – www.rabot1745.com – Closed 25-30 December, Sunday and Monday*

✗ Tate Modern (Restaurant)

MODERN BRITISH · DESIGN A contemporary, faux-industrial style restaurant on the ninth floor of the striking Switch House extension. Modern menus champion British ingredients; desserts are a highlight and the wine list interesting and well-priced.

Carte £ 27/56

Town plan: **33AU3-s** - *Switch House (9th floor), Tate Modern, Bankside* ✉ *SE1 9TG* – ⊖ *Southwark* – ℰ *020 7401 5621 – www.tate.org.uk – lunch only and dinner Friday-Saturday – Closed 24-26 December*

✗ Elliot's

MODERN CUISINE · RUSTIC A lively, unpretentious café which sources its ingredients from Borough Market, in which it stands. The appealing menu is concise and the cooking is earthy, pleasingly uncomplicated and very satisfying. Try one of the sharing dishes.

Carte £ 19/31

Town plan: 33AV4-h - *12 Stoney St., Borough Market* ✉ *SE1 9AD*
- ⊖ *London Bridge* - ℰ *020 7403 7436 (booking advisable)*
- *www.elliotscafe.com* – *Closed Sunday and bank holidays*

✗ Oxo Tower Brasserie

MODERN CUISINE · DESIGN Less formal but more fun than the next-door restaurant. Open-plan kitchen produces modern, colourful and easy-to-eat dishes with influences from the Med. Great views too from the bar.

Menu £ 30 (lunch and early dinner) – Carte £ 27/49

Town plan: 32AS3-a - *Oxo Tower Wharf (8th floor), Barge House St* ✉ *SE1 9PH*
- ⊖ *Southwark* - ℰ *020 7803 3888* – *www.oxotowerrestaurant.com* – *Closed 25 December*

✗ Padella ⓝ

ITALIAN · BISTRO This lively little sister to Trullo offers a short, seasonal menu where hand-rolled pasta is the star of the show. Sauces and fillings are inspired by the owners' trips to Italy and prices are extremely pleasing to the pocket. Sit at the ground floor counter overlooking the open kitchen.

Carte £ 14/20

Town plan: 33AW4-d - *6 Southwark St, Borough Market* ✉ *SE1 1TQ*
- ⊖ *London Bridge (bookings not accepted)* – *www.padella.co* – *Closed 25-26 December, Sunday dinner and bank holidays*

✗ Tapas Brindisa

SPANISH · TAPAS BAR A blueprint for many of the tapas bars that subsequently sprung up over London. It has an infectious energy and the well-priced, robust dishes include Galician-style hake and black rice with squid; do try the hand-carved Ibérico hams.

Carte £ 20/32

Town plan: 33AV4-k - *18-20 Southwark St, Borough Market* ✉ *SE1 1TJ*
- ⊖ *London Bridge* - ℰ *020 7357 8880 (bookings not accepted)*
- *www.brindisatapaskitchens.com*

✗ Wright Brothers

SEAFOOD · COSY Originally an oyster wholesaler; now offers a wide range of oysters along with porter, as well as fruits de mer, daily specials and assorted pies. It fills quickly and an air of contentment reigns.

Carte £ 21/87

Town plan: 33AV4-m - *11 Stoney St., Borough Market* ✉ *SE1 9AD*
- ⊖ *London Bridge* - ℰ *020 7403 9554 (booking advisable)*
- *www.thewrightbrothers.co.uk* – *Closed bank holidays*

✗ Arabica Bar & Kitchen

WORLD CUISINE · RUSTIC The owner-chef once sold mezze in Borough Market so it's no surprise he opened his Levantine-inspired restaurant under a railway arch here. This fun, cavernous place serves sharing plates from Egypt, Syria, Iraq, Jordan and Lebanon.

Menu £ 17/25 – Carte £ 17/32

Town plan: 33AV4-s - *3 Rochester Walk, Borough Mkt* ✉ *SE1 9AF*
- ⊖ *London Bridge* - ℰ *020 3011 5151 (bookings advisable at dinner)*
- *www.arabicabarandkitchen.com* – *Closed 25-27 December and Sunday dinner*

X **Lobos** ⬛ 🅰️ 🍽️

SPANISH · TAPAS BAR A dimly lit, decidedly compact tapas bar under the railway arches – sit upstairs to enjoy the theatre of the open kitchen. Go for one of the speciality meat dishes like the leg of slow-roasted Castilian milk-fed lamb.

Carte £14/51

Town plan: 33AW4-a - 14 Borough High St ⊠ SE1 9QG – ⊖ London Bridge – ☎ 020 7407 5361 – www.lobostapas.co.uk – Closed 25-26 December and 1 January

🍴 **Anchor & Hope** ☕

😊 MODERN BRITISH · PUB As popular as ever thanks to its congenial feel and lived-in looks but mostly because of the appealingly seasonal menu and the gutsy, bold cooking that delivers on flavour. No reservations so be prepared to wait at the bar.

Menu £15 (weekday lunch) – Carte £18/34

Town plan: 32AT4-n - 36 The Cut ⊠ SE1 8LP – ⊖ Southwark. – ☎ 020 7928 9898 (bookings not accepted) – www.anchorandhopepub.co.uk – Closed Christmas-New Year, Sunday dinner, Monday lunch and bank holidays

SUTTON
Sutton

X **Brasserie Vacherin** 🍷 ☕ ♿ 🅰️ 🖥️ 📷

FRENCH · BRASSERIE Relaxed, modern French brasserie with tiled walls, art nouveau posters and deep red banquettes. Good value midweek set price menu and à la carte of French classics. Diligent service.

Menu £20 (lunch and early dinner) – Carte £26/36

Town plan: 6D6-x - 12 High St ⊠ SM1 1HN – ☎ 020 8722 0180 – www.brasserievacherin.co.uk

TOWER HAMLETS
Bethnal Green

🏨 **Town Hall** 🔲 💆 🔼 ♿ 🅰️ 🧖

LUXURY · DESIGN Grand Edwardian and Art Deco former council offices converted into a stylish, trendy hotel, whilst retaining many original features. Striking, individually decorated bedrooms come with retro furnishings and frequently changing art.

98 rooms 🛏️ – ♟️£162/429 ♟️♟️£186/452 – 57 suites

Town plan: 20V4-x - Town Hall Hotel, Patriot Sq ⊠ E2 9NF – ⊖ Bethnal Green – ☎ 020 7871 0460 – www.townhallhotel.com

Typing Room • Corner Room – See restaurant listing

XX **Typing Room** 🅰️

MODERN CUISINE · FASHIONABLE The room once home to the town hall's typing pool is now dominated by an open kitchen. Choose the 5 or 7 course menu to experience earthy and elaborate cooking that's heavily influenced by new Nordic cuisine. The tone and style of the service suit the place perfectly.

Menu £24/75

Town plan: 20V4-x - Town Hall Hotel, Patriot Sq ⊠ E2 9NF – ⊖ Bethnal Green – ☎ 020 7871 0461 – www.typingroom.com – Closed Sunday dinner and Monday

X **Brawn** 🍴 🅰️

😊 MODERN CUISINE · NEIGHBOURHOOD Unpretentious and simply kitted out with a great local atmosphere and polite, helpful service. The name captures the essence of the cooking perfectly: it is rustic, muscular and makes very good use of pork. Interesting wine list with a focus on natural and organic wines.

Carte £23/33

Town plan: 20U4-z - 49 Columbia Rd ⊠ E2 7RG – ⊖ Bethnal Green – ☎ 020 7729 5692 – www.brawn.co – Closed Christmas-New Year, Sunday dinner, Monday lunch and bank holidays

Paradise Garage

TRADITIONAL BRITISH • BISTRO This north-of-the-river sister to Clapham's Manor and Dairy is set under the railway arches in lively Bethnal Green and shares a menu format with its older siblings. The constantly evolving collection of small plates are British at heart and come with compelling contrasts in temperature, texture and flavour.

Menu £ 25 (weekday lunch) – Carte £ 25/36

Town plan: 20V4-a - *Arch 254, Paradise Row ✉ E2 9LE – ⊖ Bethnal Green – ✆ 020 7613 1502 – www.paradise254.com – Closed 2 weeks Christmas-New Year, Sunday dinner, Monday and lunch Tuesday*

Corner Room

CREATIVE • INTIMATE Hidden upstairs in the old town hall is this bright, intimate space – first have a drink in the little bar. The core ingredient of each dish is British and the assured cooking makes you feel you're getting a real taste of nature.

Menu £ 23 (lunch)/45 – Carte £ 20/29

Town plan: 20V4-x - *Town Hall Hotel, Patriot Sq ✉ E2 9NF – ⊖ Bethnal Green – ✆ 020 7871 0461 (bookings advisable at dinner) – www.cornerroom.co.uk*

Sager + Wilde

MEDITERRANEAN CUISINE • RUSTIC Friendly neighbourhood restaurant – a former wine bar – set underneath a railway arch. Tasty, well-priced, creative dishes have a Mediterranean heart and an eye-catching modern style, with some interesting combinations.

Menu £ 38

Town plan: 20V4-s - *250 Paradise Row ✉ E2 9LE – ⊖ Bethnal Green – ✆ 020 7613 0479 – www.sagerandwilde.com – dinner only and lunch Friday-Sunday – Closed Monday and Tuesday*

Bistrotheque

FRENCH • NEIGHBOURHOOD When the exterior is as irredeemably bleak as this, you just know it's going to be painfully cool inside. This bustling space in a converted sweatshop is great fun; its menu is French-bistro in style. Live music at weekend brunch.

Menu £ 23 (early dinner) – Carte £ 23/55

Town plan: 14V3-s - *23-27 Wadeson St ✉ E2 9DR – ⊖ Bethnal Green – ✆ 020 8983 7900 (booking advisable) – www.bistrotheque.com – dinner only and lunch Saturday-Sunday – Closed 24-26 December*

Marksman

TRADITIONAL BRITISH • FRIENDLY With its quirky, brown-tiled façade, this pub has long been a local landmark; the wood-panelled bar retains the feel of a traditional boozer, while the first floor dining room is more modern. Simply cooked, seasonal British dishes are wonderfully fresh, well-balanced and full of flavour.

Carte £ 19/35

Town plan: 20U3-m - *254 Hackney Rd ✉ E2 7SJ – ⊖ Hoxton. – ✆ 020 7739 7393 – www.marksmanpublichouse.com – Closed 25 December, 1 January, Sunday dinner and Monday*

Canary Wharf

Four Seasons

BUSINESS • MODERN Professionally run international hotel geared mainly to the local corporate market. The Premier rooms boast impressive views across the river. Spacious restaurant, with river-facing terrace and menu that covers all parts of Italy.

142 rooms – †£ 330/530 ††£ 350/550 – 14 suites

Town plan: 3F3-a - *Westferry Circus ✉ E14 8RS – ⊖ Canary Wharf – ✆ 020 7510 1999 – www.canaryriversideplaza.com*

✗✗ Plateau ♞ 🍴 AC 🔟 ⇆

MODERN CUISINE · DESIGN Being surrounded by tall glass buildings means you feel you're in Manhattan and the striking room has its own retro 1960s look. The Grill is for steaks from the Josper grill; the more formal restaurant for French-inspired dishes.

Menu £ 25 (weekdays) – Carte £ 31/61

Town plan: 3F3-n - *Canada Place (4th floor), Canada Square* ⊠ *E14 5ER* – ⊖ *Canary Wharf* – ℰ *020 7715 7100* – *www.plateau-restaurant.co.uk – Closed 25 -26 December, 1-2 January and Sunday*

✗✗ Boisdale of Canary Wharf ♞ 🍴 AC ⇆

TRADITIONAL BRITISH · FASHIONABLE It's the 1st floor for the relaxed, art deco inspired Oyster bar, with its crustacea, burgers and top quality steaks. The grander 2nd floor has a stage for live jazz (a charge is made) and offers plenty of dishes of a Scottish persuasion.

Carte £ 29/80

Town plan: 3F3-s - *Cabot Pl* ⊠ *E14 4QT* – ⊖ *Canary Wharf* – ℰ *020 7715 5818* *(booking advisable)* – *www.boisdale.co.uk – Closed bank holidays*

Spitalfields

🏠 Batty Langley's ♦ ዹ AC ⅏

TOWNHOUSE · ELEGANT It looks and feels like a Georgian house, thanks to the antique furniture and attention to detail, yet even the façade was rebuilt. The luxurious rooms come with flowing drapes, reproduction fireplaces and lovely bathrooms. An oasis of composed elegance.

29 rooms – 🛏£ 195/280 🛏🛏£ 280/1000 – ☲ £ 12 – 1 suite

Town plan: 34AY1-y - *12 Folgate St* ⊠ *E1 6BX* – ⊖ *Liverpool Street* – ℰ *020 7377 4390* – *www.battylangleys.com*

✗✗✗ Galvin La Chapelle 🍴 ዹ AC ⇆
🏵

FRENCH · FORMAL The Victorian splendour of St Botolph's Hall, with its vaulted ceiling, arched windows and marble pillars, lends itself perfectly to its role as a glamorous restaurant. The food is bourgeois French with a sophisticated edge and is bound to satisfy.

→ Home-cured Shetland salmon with fennel, avocado and ruby grapefruit. Tagine of Bresse pigeon with couscous and harissa sauce. Tarte Tatin with crème Normande.

Menu £ 29 (lunch and early dinner) – Carte £ 48/67

Town plan: 34AY1-v - *35 Spital Sq* ⊠ *E1 6DY* – ⊖ *Liverpool Street* – ℰ *020 7299 0400* – *www.galvinrestaurants.com – Closed dinner 25-26 December and 1 January*

✗ Blixen ♞ ዹ AC 🖵 ⇆
😊

MEDITERRANEAN CUISINE · DESIGN From the same stable as Riding House Café comes this charmingly run and good looking restaurant with lots of natural light. An appealing European menu offers carefully prepared, keenly priced dishes. You'll want to return for breakfast, or cocktails in the basement bar.

Menu £ 24 – Carte £ 16/37

Town plan: 34AY1-w - *65a Brushfield St* ⊠ *E1 6AA* – ⊖ *Liverpool Street* – ℰ *020 7101 0093* – *www.blixen.co.uk – Closed Sunday dinner*

✗ St John Bread and Wine AC 🖵 📑
😊

TRADITIONAL BRITISH · BISTRO Part-wine shop and local restaurant with a stripped back style. The highly seasonal and appealing menu changes twice a day; the cooking is British, uncomplicated and very satisfying. Try the less familiar dishes.

Carte £ 26/40

Town plan: 34AY1-a - *94-96 Commercial St* ⊠ *E1 6LZ* – ⊖ *Liverpool Street* – ℰ *020 7251 0848* – *www.stjohnbreadandwine.com – Closed 25-26 December and 1 January*

✗ Taberna do Mercado 🈁 🈁

PORTUGUESE · SIMPLE An appealingly modest little place from Nuno Mendes, serving small plates of Portuguese classics. You'll see staples elevated to a higher level: alheira, Bísaro pork and prawn rissois all deliver wonderful flavours. The wine list, staff, crockery and cutlery are all Portuguese too.

Menu £ 15 – Carte £ 16/32

Town plan: 34AY1-m - *Old Spitalfields Market, 107b Commercial St ⊠ E1 6BG – ⊖ Liverpool Street – ℰ 020 7375 0649 – www.tabernamercado.co.uk – Closed Christmas and Sunday dinner*

✗ Ottolenghi 🍽 🆎 🈁 🈁 🈂

MEDITERRANEAN CUISINE · DESIGN A cross between the original Islington shop and Nopi, their Soho restaurant. The room's bright white look reminds you that the food's all about freshness. Dishes are as flavoursome as they are colourful and sharing is encouraged.

Carte £ 26/67

Town plan: 34AY1-e - *50 Artillery Ln ⊠ E1 7LJ – ⊖ Liverpool Street – ℰ 020 7247 1999 (booking essential) – www.ottolenghi.co.uk – Closed dinner 24-27 and 31 December, 2 January, 2 and 30 May and Sunday dinner*

✗ Hawksmoor 🍽 🆎

MEATS AND GRILLS · RUSTIC Unremarkable surroundings in a modern building. Here it's not really about the starters or the puds – the star is the great British beef, hung for 35 days, which comes from Longhorn cattle in the heart of the Yorkshire Moors.

Menu £ 25 (weekdays)/28 – Carte £ 23/60

Town plan: 34AY1-s - *157a Commercial St ⊠ E1 6BJ – ⊖ Shoreditch High Street – ℰ 020 7426 4850 (booking essential) – www.thehawksmoor.com – Closed 24-26 December and Sunday dinner*

✗ Copita del Mercado 🈁 ⅙ 🆎 🈁

SPANISH · TAPAS BAR Petticoat Lane is the mercado in question and is the location of this more comfortable sister to the Soho original. The menu also differs by offering a little more originality; go for the daily specials. Gin is also a speciality.

Carte £ 17/51

Town plan: 34AY2-f - *60 Wentworth St ⊠ E1 7AL – ⊖ Aldgate East – ℰ 020 7426 0218 – www.copitadelmercado.com – Closed Christmas-New Year, Easter and Sunday*

✗ Gunpowder 🆕 ⅙ 🈁

INDIAN · SIMPLE A loud, buzzy restaurant with just ten tightly packed tables, serving vibrant small plates from across the Indian regions. The name is a reference to the chef's daily-made spice mix and his menu takes its influence from old family recipes. Standout dishes include deep-fried crab and crispy pork ribs.

Carte £ 20/30

Town plan: 34AY1-g - *11 White's Row ⊠ E1 7NF – ⊖ Liverpool Street – ℰ 020 7426 0542 (bookings not accepted) – www.gunpowderlondon.com – Closed Sunday*

✗ The Frog 🆕 🍽 🈁 🈁

MODERN CUISINE · NEIGHBOURHOOD Ambitious young chef Adam Caxton is making a splash with his restaurant, set in the old Truman brewery; the décor may be neutral but the menu offers small plates which are modern and creative, with playful elements and vibrant flavour and texture combinations. Craft beers and cocktails add to the fun.

Carte £ 24/36

Town plan: 34AY1-f - *2 Ely's Yard, Old Truman Brewery, Hanbury St. ⊠ E1 6QR – ⊖ Shoreditch High Street – ℰ 020 3813 9832 (booking essential) – www.thefrogrestaurant.com – Closed Sunday dinner and Monday*

✗ Som Saa 🅝   🍸 ♿ AC

THAI · RUSTIC Som Saa's success took it from pop-up to permanent restaurant, with a lively atmosphere and a rustic, industrial look. Menus showcase the diversity of Thai cuisine. 4 or 5 dishes between two are recommended – and do try a cocktail or two!

Carte £ 25/29

Town plan: 34AY1-t - *43a Commerical St* ✉ *E1 6BD* – ⊖ *Aldgate East*
– ✆ 020 7324 7790 (bookings advisable at dinner) – www.somsaa.com – Closed Christmas and dinner Sunday

Whitechapel

✗✗ Cafe Spice Namaste   AC 🍴♥

😊 INDIAN · NEIGHBOURHOOD Fresh, vibrant and fairly priced Indian cuisine from Cyrus Todiwala, served in a colourfully decorated room that was once a magistrate's court. Engaging service from an experienced team.

Menu £ 35 (weekdays) – Carte £ 25/40

Town plan: 34AZ3-z - *16 Prescot St.* ✉ *E1 8AZ* – ⊖ *Tower Hill* – ✆ *020 7488 9242*
– www.cafespice.co.uk – Closed Saturday lunch, Sunday and bank holidays

WANDSWORTH

Balham

✗ Lamberts   AC

TRADITIONAL BRITISH · NEIGHBOURHOOD Locals come for the relaxed surroundings, hospitable service and tasty, seasonal food. Sunday lunch is very popular. The enthusiasm of the eponymous owner has rubbed off on his team.

Carte £ 27/36

Town plan: 6D5-h - *2 Station Par, Balham High Rd.* ✉ *SW12 9AZ* – ⊖ *Balham*
– ✆ 020 8675 2233 – www.lambertsrestaurant.com – Closed 25-27 December, Sunday dinner and Monday

Battersea

✗✗ London House   🍸 🏵 ♿ AC

MODERN BRITISH · NEIGHBOURHOOD One doesn't always associate neighbourhood restaurants with Gordon Ramsay but London House is an appealing place. It's comfortable and well run and the classically-based dishes come with modern touches and ingredients that marry well.

Menu £ 20 (weekday lunch) – Carte £ 32/44

Town plan: 23N8-h - *7-9 Battersea Sq, Battersea Village* ✉ *SW11 3RA*
– ⊖ Clapham Junction – ✆ 020 7592 8545
– www.gordonramsayrestaurants.com/london-house/

✗✗ Chada   AC

THAI · FRIENDLY A much loved local Thai restaurant which opened back in 1986 and is still run with considerable charm by its owner. The extensive menu includes a selection of 'small eats' representing refined street food.

Carte £ 18/37

Town plan: 23P8-x - *208-210 Battersea Park Rd.* ✉ *SW11 4ND*
– ⊖ Clapham Junction – ✆ 020 7622 2209 – www.chadathai.com – dinner only
– Closed Sunday and bank holidays

✗ Sinabro   AC

MODERN CUISINE · NEIGHBOURHOOD The main room feels almost kitchen-like, courtesy of a wall of stainless steel; sit at the wooden counter – made by the chef-owner's father. Confidently prepared dishes rely largely on classic French flavours but are modern in style.

Menu £ 13 (weekday lunch) – Carte £ 29/44

Town plan: 23P9-r - *28 Battersea Rd* ✉ *SW11 1EE* – ⊖ *Clapham Junction*
– ✆ 020 3302 3120 – www.sinabro.co.uk – Closed 2 weeks mid-August, 25 December,1 January, Sunday and Monday

X **Soif**   &&&& AC

FRENCH · NEIGHBOURHOOD A busy bistro-cum-wine-shop with a great atmosphere. The satisfying French food takes regular excursions across the border into Italy and the thoughtfully compiled wine list includes plenty of 'natural' wines from artisan winemakers.

Carte £ 29/42

Town plan: 23P9-c - 27 Battersea Rise ⊠ SW11 1HG – ⊖ Clapham Junction – ☏ 020 7223 1112 (booking essential at dinner) – www.soif.co – Closed Christmas and New Year, Sunday dinner, Monday lunch and bank holidays

X **Boqueria**   ☎ AC 📖 ⟳

SPANISH · TAPAS BAR Occupying a converted bank and smarter than the first branch in Brixton but still delivering the true flavours of Spain. Try the dishes unique to here, like the classic Mallorcan dish Coca Mallorquina and the island sausage Sobrasada.

Carte £ 12/20

Town plan: 24Q8-a - 278 Queenstown Rd ⊠ SW8 4LT – ⊖ Clapham Junction – ☏ 020 7498 8247 – www.boqueriatapas.com – Closed 25 December

X **Rosita**   📖

MEDITERRANEAN CUISINE · FRIENDLY The owner's aunt lent her name to this fun sherry and tapas bar. Dishes include flavoursome meats and seafood cooked on the Josper grill. There is much sherry by the glass and suggested pairings with certain dishes.

Carte £ 11/23

Town plan: 6D4-g - 124 Northcote Rd ⊠ SW11 6QU – ⊖ Clapham Junction – ☏ 020 7998 9093 – www.rositasherry.net – Closed 25-26 December and lunch 1 January

X **Hana**   ⟳

KOREAN · SIMPLE A warm, sweet little Korean restaurant. Yang Yeum chicken and Pa Jeon pancake are popular starters; bibimbap rice dishes burst with flavour; seafood cooked on the barbeque is very good; and they do their own version of Bossam.

Carte £ 16/26

Town plan: 23P9-a - 60 Battersea Rise ⊠ SW11 1EG – ⊖ Clapham Junction – ☏ 020 7228 2496 – www.facebook.com/londonhana/ – Closed 24-26 December

Putney

X **Bibo**   ☎ AC

ITALIAN · BISTRO A fun neighbourhood Italian which comes with an appealing vibe, clued up service and well-priced food that's effortlessly easy to enjoy. Its name means 'to drink' and the Italian wine list is well worth exploring.

Menu £ 17/23 – Carte £ 26/36

Town plan: 22L9-b - 146 Upper Richmond Rd ⊠ SW15 2SW – ⊖ East Putney – ☏ 020 8780 0592 – www.biborestaurant.com – Closed 25-26 December, Monday lunch and bank holidays

Southfields

🍴 **Earl Spencer**   ☎

MEDITERRANEAN CUISINE · RUSTIC A handsome Edwardian pub with a bright, welcoming feel; a baseline lob away from the All England Tennis Club. Fervently seasonal cooking has a strong traditional base. The only irritant is that one has to order everything at the bar.

Carte £ 24/35

Town plan: 6D4-c - 260-262 Merton Rd ⊠ SW18 5JL – ⊖ Southfields. – ☏ 020 8870 9244 – www.theearlspencer.com – dinner only and lunch Friday to Sunday

Wandsworth

XX Chez Bruce (Bruce Poole)   😣 AC ⬦

FRENCH · BRASSERIE Flavoursome, uncomplicated French cooking with hints of the Mediterranean, prepared with innate skill; well-organised, personable service and an easy-going atmosphere - some of the reasons why Chez Bruce remains a favourite of so many.

→ Fishcake with moules marinière, poached egg and sprouting broccoli. Rump of veal with leek & bacon sausage, gnocchi, wild garlic and thyme. Cherry jelly with chocolate mousse and pistachio madeleine.

Menu £ 30/50

Town plan: 6D5-e - *2 Bellevue Rd ☒ SW17 7EG* – ⊖ *Tooting Bec*
– *℘ 020 8672 0114 (booking essential)* – *www.chezbruce.co.uk* – *Closed 24-26 December and 1 January*

WESTMINSTER (City of)

Bayswater and Maida Vale

✗✗ Angelus   🏄 A/C ⟷

FRENCH · BRASSERIE Hospitable owner has created an attractive French brasserie within a 19C former pub, with a warm and inclusive feel. Satisfying and honest French cooking uses seasonal British ingredients.

Menu £ 23 – Carte £ 40/61

Town plan: 29AG2-c - 4 Bathurst St ⊠ W2 2SD – ⊖ Lancaster Gate
– ☎ 020 7402 0083 – www.angelusrestaurant.co.uk
– Closed 24-25 December and 1 January

✗✗ Marianne   A/C 🕙

FRENCH · COSY The eponymous Marianne was a finalist on MasterChef. Her restaurant is a sweet little place with just 6 tables. Concise daily lunch menu and seasonal tasting menu; cooking is classically based but keeps things quite light.

Menu £ 35/85 – tasting menu only

Town plan: 27AC1-m - 104a Chepstow Rd ⊠ W2 5QS – ⊖ Westbourne Park
– ☎ 020 3675 7750 (booking essential)
– www.mariannerestaurant.com
– dinner only and lunch Friday-Sunday
– Closed 22 December-5 January , August bank holiday and Monday

✗✗ Toa Kitchen   A/C ⟷

CHINESE · FRIENDLY There's an overwhelming number of Chinese restaurants on Queensway so search out Toa Kitchen and head for the Chef's Specials for good, authentic Cantonese dishes. Service from owner Mr Fung and his team is also a cut above average.

Carte £ 14/25

Town plan: 28AD2-t - 100 Queensway ⊠ W2 3RR – ⊖ Bayswater
– ☎ 020 7792 9767 – www.toakitchen.com
– Closed 25 December

✗ Hereford Road   🏠 A/C
(😊)

TRADITIONAL BRITISH · NEIGHBOURHOOD Converted butcher's shop specialising in tasty British dishes without frills, using first-rate, seasonal ingredients; offal a highlight. Booths for six people are the prized seats. Friendly and relaxed feel.

Menu £ 14 (weekday lunch) – Carte £ 22/32

Town plan: 27AC2-s - 3 Hereford Rd ⊠ W2 4AB – ⊖ Bayswater
– ☎ 020 7727 1144 (booking essential) – www.herefordroad.org
– Closed 24 December-3 January and August bank holiday

✕ Kateh 🔊   A/C

MEDITERRANEAN CUISINE · NEIGHBOURHOOD Booking is imperative if you want to join the locals who have already discovered what a little jewel they have in the form of this buzzy, busy Persian restaurant. Authentic stews, expert chargrilling and lovely pastries and teas.

Carte £ 21/39

Town plan: 28AE1-a - *5 Warwick Pl* ⊠ *W9 2PX* – ⊖ *Warwick Avenue*
– ℰ 020 7289 3393 (booking essential) – www.katehrestaurant.co.uk – dinner only and lunch Friday-Sunday – Closed 25-26 December

✕ Salt & Honey ●   A/C

MODERN CUISINE · BISTRO A cosy neighbourhood restaurant in a residential area just north of Hyde Park. Well-priced, colourful, boldly flavoured dishes use the best British ingredients; expect Mediterranean and Middle Eastern flavours – and plenty of Manuka honey.

Menu £ 15 (weekday lunch) – Carte £ 24/38

Town plan: 29AG2-a - *28 Sussex Pl* ⊠ *W2 2TH* – ⊖ *Lancaster Gate*
– ℰ 020 7706 7900 (bookings advisable at dinner)
– www.saltandhoneybistro.com – Closed 25-26 December, 1 January and Monday

✕ Kurobuta Marble Arch   🍸 🏠   A/C 📖

JAPANESE · NEIGHBOURHOOD The Aussie owner-chef's fun Japanese restaurant was influenced by an izakaya. The robata grill provides the sticky BBQ pork belly for the pork buns; the black pepper soft shell crabs fly out of the kitchen; and the yuzu tart is good.

Carte £ 17/32

Town plan: 29AH2-m - *17-20 Kendal St* ⊠ *W2 2AW* – ⊖ *Marble Arch*
– ℰ 020 3475 4158 – www.kurobuta-london.com – Closed 25 December

---

Symbols shown in red 🏛️ ✕✕✕ indicate particularly charming establishments.

Belgravia

🏛️🏛️ Berkeley   🔲 🌐 ⋙ 🏋️ ⬆ A/C 🧖 🚗

GRAND LUXURY · ELEGANT A discreet and very comfortable hotel with an impressive rooftop pool and opulently decorated, immaculately kept bedrooms. Relax in the gilded, panelled Collins Room or have a drink in the ice cool Blue Bar.

210 rooms – ♦£ 540/750 ♦♦£ 600/870 – � £ 32 – 28 suites
Town plan: 38AK5-e - *Wilton Pl* ⊠ *SW1X 7RL* – ⊖ *Knightsbridge*
– ℰ 020 7235 6000 – www.the-berkeley.co.uk
❀❀ **Marcus** – See restaurant listing

🏛️🏛️ The Lanesborough ●   🏋️ ⬆ & A/C 🧖 🚗

GRAND LUXURY · ELEGANT A multi-million pound refurbishment has restored this hotel's Regency splendour; its elegant Georgian-style bedrooms offering bespoke furniture, beautiful fabrics, tablet technologies and 24 hour butler service. Opulent Céleste serves rich French cooking under its domed glass roof.

93 rooms – ♦£ 500/740 ♦♦£ 500/740 – � £ 38 – 30 suites
Town plan: 38AK5-c - *Hyde Park Corner* ⊠ *SW1X 7TA*
– ⊖ Hyde Park Corner – ℰ 020 7259 5599
– www.lanesborough.com
❀ **Céleste** – See restaurant listing

Halkin

LUXURY • ELEGANT Opened in 1991 as one of London's first boutique hotels and still looking sharp today. Thoughtfully conceived bedrooms with silk walls and marbled bathrooms; everything at the touch of a button. Abundant Armani-clad staff. Small, discreet bar.

41 rooms – †£ 300/420 ††£ 400/500 – ☕£ 30 – 6 suites

Town plan: 38AK5-b – *5 Halkin St ✉ SW1X 7DJ – ⊖ Hyde Park Corner – ✆ 020 7333 1000 – www.comohotels.com/thehalkin*

✿ **Ametsa** – See restaurant listing

The Wellesley

TOWNHOUSE • ART DÉCO Stylish, elegant townhouse inspired by the jazz age, on the site of the famous Pizza on the Park. Impressive cigar lounge and bar with a super selection of whiskies and cognacs. Smart bedrooms have full butler service; those facing Hyde Park the most prized. Modern Italian food in the discreet restaurant.

36 rooms – †£ 350/599 ††£ 350/599 – ☕£ 34 – 14 suites

Town plan: 38AK5-w – *11 Knightsbridge ✉ SW1X 7LY – ⊖ Hyde Park Corner – ✆ 020 7235 3535 – www.thewellesley.co.uk*

Belgraves

BUSINESS • MODERN US group Thompson's first UK venture is an elegant and stylish boutique-style hotel with a hint of bohemia. Uncluttered, decently proportioned bedrooms come with oak flooring and lovely marble bathrooms. Light, Mediterranean-influenced dishes served in Pont St restaurant.

85 rooms – †£ 359/599 ††£ 360/660 – ☕£ 20

Town plan: 38AK6-c – *20 Chesham Pl ✉ SW1X 8HQ – ⊖ Knightsbridge – ✆ 020 7858 0100 – www.thompsonhotels.com*

XXXX Marcus

✿✿ MODERN CUISINE • ELEGANT Marcus Wareing's flagship is elegant, stylish and eminently comfortable, with a relaxed feel and engaging staff who get the tone of the service just right. The menu is flexible and dishes come with a refreshing lack of complication; relying on excellent ingredients and accurate techniques to deliver well-defined flavours.

→ Salmon with langoustine, buttermilk and quince. Herdwick lamb with onion and anchovy. Pumpkin custard, maple syrup and passion fruit.

Menu £ 49/85

Town plan: 38AK5-e – *Berkeley Hotel, Wilton Pl ✉ SW1X 7RL – ⊖ Knightsbridge – ✆ 020 7235 1200 – www.marcus-wareing.com – Closed Sunday*

XXXX Céleste Ⓝ

✿ CREATIVE FRENCH • ELEGANT The Lanesborough Hotel's restaurant is dressed in opulent Regency clothes; its vast chandeliers, Wedgwood blue friezes and fluted columns giving it a luxurious, formal feel. Classic French cuisine is delivered in an original, modern style; the richness of the dishes reflects the opulence of the décor.

→ Pan-fried langoustine with wild grains and basil-infused broth. Pigeon, petits pois à la Française and potato soufflé. Guanaja chocolate with caramelised cashew nut praline and coffee bean ice cream.

Menu £ 29 (lunch) – Carte £ 42/88

Town plan: 38AK5-c – *The Lanesborough Hotel, Hyde Park Corner ✉ SW1X 7TA – ⊖ Hyde Park Corner – ✆ 020 7259 5599 – www.lanesborough.com*

LONDON ENGLAND

✕✕✕ Pétrus

❀ ⓑ AC ⓨ ⌂

❀ FRENCH · ELEGANT Gordon Ramsay's Belgravia restaurant is a sophisticated and elegant affair. The service is discreet and professional, and the cooking is rooted in classical techniques but isn't afraid of using influences from further afield. The superb wine list has Château Pétrus going back to 1924.

→ Seared Orkney scallop with braised kombu and bacon & egg sabayon. Rack of Herdwick lamb with pommes purée, artichoke and wild garlic. Coconut parfait with dark chocolate and lime.

Menu £ 38/95

Town plan: 38AK5-v - *1 Kinnerton St* ✉ *SW1X 8EA* – ⊖ *Knightsbridge*
– 𝒞 020 7592 1609 – www.gordonramsay.com/petrus – Closed 21-27 December, 1 January and Sunday

✕✕✕ Ametsa

AC

❀ CREATIVE · ELEGANT Whilst the father and daughter team from the celebrated Arzak restaurant in San Sebastián are behind it, Ametsa has its own style. Most ingredients are sourced from within the British Isles but the flavours, combinations and colours are typically Basque and the dishes are wonderfully vibrant.

→ Scallops 'at home'. Beef fillet with green tomato. Orange French toast and spinach.

Menu £ 28/110 – Carte £ 58/85

Town plan: 38AK5-b - *Halkin Hotel, 5 Halkin St* ✉ *SW1X 7DJ*
– ⊖ Hyde Park Corner – 𝒞 020 7333 1234 – www.comohotels.com/thehalkin
– Closed 24-26 December, lunch 31 December, Sunday and lunch Monday

✕✕✕ Amaya

🏆 AC 🍽 ⓨ ⌂

❀ INDIAN · DESIGN Order a selection of small dishes from the tawa griddle, tandoor or sigri grill and finish with a curry or biryani. Dishes like lamb chops are aromatic and satisfying and the cooking is skilled and consistent. This busy Indian restaurant is bright, colourful and lively; ask for a table by the open kitchen.

→ Flash-grilled rock oysters with coconut and ginger. Slow-roasted leg of baby lamb, cumin and garam masala. 'Passion in chocolate'.

Menu £ 24 (weekday lunch) – Carte £ 34/70

Town plan: 37AJ5-k - *Halkin Arcade, 19 Motcomb St* ✉ *SW1X 8JT*
– ⊖ Knightsbridge – 𝒞 020 7823 1166 – www.amaya.biz

✕✕✕ Zafferano

🏠 AC ⌂

ITALIAN · FASHIONABLE The immaculately coiffured regulars continue to support this ever-expanding, long-standing and capably run Italian restaurant. They come for the reassuringly familiar, if rather steeply priced dishes from all parts of Italy.

Carte £ 36/79

Town plan: 37AJ5-f - *15 Lowndes St* ✉ *SW1X 9EY* – ⊖ *Knightsbridge*
– 𝒞 020 7235 5800 (booking essential) – www.zafferanorestaurant.co.uk – Closed 25 December

🍴 The Alfred Tennyson

🏠 ⌂

MODERN BRITISH · PUB A cosy, enthusiastically run pub with a busy first-come-first-served ground floor and a more formal upstairs dining room. Classic dishes have light, modern touches; expect smoked mackerel, duck and venison alongside steaks, burgers and pies.

Carte £ 29/50

Town plan: 38AK5-d - *10 Motcomb St* ✉ *SW1X 8LA* – ⊖ *Knightsbridge.*
– 𝒞 020 7730 6074 (booking advisable) – www.thealfredtennyson.co.uk – Closed 25 December

Hyde Park and Knightsbridge

🏨 Mandarin Oriental Hyde Park ⟨ 🗎 🕲 🕸 ♨ 🗐 🕭 🗛 ❄ 🏊

GRAND LUXURY · CLASSIC The Rosebery, a salon for afternoon tea, is the newest addition to this celebrated hotel which dates from 1889. The luxurious spa now includes a pool; the service is as strong as ever; and the bedrooms, many of which have views of Hyde Park, are spacious and comfortable.

194 rooms – 🛏£ 600/1020 🛏🛏£ 600/1020 – 🍽£ 26 – 25 suites

Town plan: 37AJ5-x – 66 Knightsbridge ✉ SW1X 7LA – ⊖ Knightsbridge
– ✆ 020 7235 2000 – www.mandarinoriental.com/london

❀❀ **Dinner by Heston Blumenthal • Bar Boulud** – See restaurant listing

🏨 Bulgari 🗎 🕲 ♨ 🗐 🕭 🗛 🏊

LUXURY · ELEGANT Impeccably tailored hotel making stunning use of materials like silver, mahogany, silk and marble. Luxurious bedrooms with sensual curves, sumptuous bathrooms and a great spa – and there is substance behind the style. Down a sweeping staircase to the Alain Ducasse restaurant.

85 rooms – 🛏£ 560/790 🛏🛏£ 560/790 – 🍽£ 34 – 23 suites

Town plan: 37AH5-k – 171 Knightsbridge ✉ SW7 1DW – ⊖ Knightsbridge
– ✆ 020 7151 1010 – www.bulgarihotels.com/london

Rivea – See restaurant listing

🍴🍴🍴 Dinner by Heston Blumenthal 🕸 🗛 ⟷

❀❀ TRADITIONAL BRITISH · DESIGN Don't come expecting 'molecular gastronomy' – this is all about respect for, and a wonderful renewal of, British food, with just a little playfulness thrown in. Each one of the meticulously crafted and deceptively simple looking dishes comes with a date relating to its historical provenance.
➜ Mandarin, chicken liver parfait and grilled bread (c.1500). Roast Iberico pork chop with spelt, ham hock and sauce Robert (c.1820). Tipsy cake with spit-roast pineapple (c.1810).

Menu £ 40 (weekday lunch) – Carte £ 58/121

Town plan: 37AJ5-x – Mandarin Oriental Hyde Park Hotel, 66 Knightsbridge,
✉ SW1X 7LA – ⊖ Knightsbridge – ✆ 020 7201 3833 – www.dinnerbyheston.com
– Closed 17-31 October

🍴🍴 Bar Boulud 🕭 🗛 ⟷

FRENCH · BRASSERIE Daniel Boulud's London outpost is fashionable, fun and frantic. His hometown is Lyon but he built his considerable reputation in New York, so charcuterie, sausages and burgers are the highlights.

Menu £ 19 (weekday lunch) – Carte £ 26/57

Town plan: 37AJ5-x – 66 Knightsbridge ✉ SW1X 7LA – ⊖ Knightsbridge
– ✆ 020 7235 2000 – www.mandarinoriental.com/london

🍴🍴 Rivea 🕸 🕭 🗛 🍷 ⟷

MEDITERRANEAN CUISINE · DESIGN Elegant basement restaurant where blues and whites make reference to warmer climes – and also to its sister in St Tropez. Precise, unfussy cooking focuses on the French and Italian Riviera, with an interesting range of vibrant small plates.

Menu £ 26 (lunch) – Carte £ 39/49

Town plan: 37AH5-k – Bulgari Hotel, 171 Knightsbridge ✉ SW7 1DW
– ⊖ Knightsbridge – ✆ 020 7151 1025 – www.rivealondon.com

🍴🍴 The Magazine 🍽 🏠 🕭 🗛 🖵

MODERN CUISINE · DESIGN Designed by the late Zaha Hadid, the Serpentine Sackler Gallery comprises a restored 1805 gunpowder store and a modern tensile extension. The Magazine is a bright open space with an easy-to-eat menu of dishes whose influences are largely from within Europe.

Menu £ 24 – Carte £ 26/40

Town plan: 29AG4-t – Serpentine Sackler Gallery, West Carriage Dr, Kensington
Gardens ✉ W2 2AR – ⊖ Lancaster Gate
– ✆ 020 7298 7552 – www.magazine-restaurant.co.uk
– lunch only – Closed Monday

✗✗ Zuma 🍷 AC

JAPANESE · FASHIONABLE Now a global brand but this was the original. The glamorous clientele come for the striking surroundings, bustling atmosphere and easy-to-share food. Go for the more modern dishes and those cooked on the robata grill.

Carte £ 30/80

Town plan: 37AH5-m 5 Raphael St ✉ SW7 1DL – ⊖ Knightsbridge
– ℰ 020 7584 1010 (booking essential) – www.zumarestaurant.com – Closed 25 December

Mayfair

⛒⛒⛒⛒ Dorchester 🕙 🄥 ℔ 🔁 ⅆ AC 🆒 🆔 🚗

GRAND LUXURY · CLASSIC One of the capital's iconic properties offering every possible facility and exemplary levels of service. The striking marbled and pillared promenade provides an elegant backdrop for afternoon tea. Bedrooms are eminently comfortable; some overlook Hyde Park. The Grill is for all things British; Alain Ducasse waves Le Tricolore; China Tang celebrates the cuisine of the Orient.

250 rooms – ╫£ 325/925 ╫╫£ 355/995 – ☷ £ 35 – 51 suites
Town plan: 30AK4-a - Park Ln ✉ W1K 1QA – ⊖ Hyde Park Corner
– ℰ 020 7629 8888 – www.dorchestercollection.com

❀❀❀ **Alain Ducasse at The Dorchester • The Grill • China Tang** – See restaurant listing

⛒⛒⛒⛒ Claridge's 🄥 ℔ 🔁 ⅆ AC 🆔

GRAND LUXURY · CLASSIC Claridge's has a long, illustrious history dating back to 1812 and this iconic and very British hotel has been a favourite of the royal family over generations. Its most striking decorative feature is its art deco. The hotel also moves with the times.

197 rooms – ╫£ 480/1140 ╫╫£ 480/1140 – ☷ £ 34 – 62 suites
Town plan: 30AL2-c - Brook St ✉ W1K 4HR – ⊖ Bond Street – ℰ 020 7629 8860
– www.claridges.co.uk

❀ **Fera at Claridges** – See restaurant listing

⛒⛒⛒⛒ Connaught 🄥 🖥 🕙 ℔ 🔁 AC 🆒 🆔

GRAND LUXURY · CLASSIC One of London's most famous hotels; restored and renovated but still retaining an elegant British feel. All the luxurious bedrooms come with large marble bathrooms and butler service. There's a choice of two stylish bars and Espelette is an all-day venue for classic French and British dishes.

121 rooms – ╫£ 540/990 ╫╫£ 630/1110 – 25 suites
Town plan: 30AL3-e - Carlos Pl. ✉ W1K 2AL
– ⊖ Bond Street – ℰ 020 7499 7070
– www.the-connaught.co.uk

❀❀ **Hélène Darroze at The Connaught** – See restaurant listing

⛒⛒⛒⛒ Four Seasons 🕙 🄥 ℔ 🔁 ⅆ AC 🆔 🚗

GRAND LUXURY · MODERN Reopened in 2011 after a huge refurbishment project and has raised the bar for luxury hotels. Striking lobby sets the scene; sumptuous bedrooms have a rich, contemporary look and boast every conceivable comfort. Great views from the stunning rooftop spa.

193 rooms – ╫£ 330/630 ╫╫£ 330/630 – ☷ £ 30 – 33 suites
Town plan: 30AL4-v - Hamilton Pl, Park Ln ✉ W1J 7DR – ⊖ Hyde Park Corner
– ℰ 020 7499 0888 – www.fourseasons.com/london

Amaranto – See restaurant listing

The Beaumont

LUXURY · ART DÉCO From a 1926 former garage, restaurateurs Chris Corbin and Jeremy King fashioned their first hotel; art deco inspired, it's stunning, stylish and exudes understated luxury. The attention to detail is exemplary, from the undeniably masculine bedrooms to the lively, cool cocktail bar and busy brasserie.

73 rooms – †£ 435/585 ††£ 435/585 – 10 suites

Town plan: 30AK2-x - Brown Hart Gdns ⊠ W1K 6TF – ⊖ Bond Street
– ℰ 020 7499 1001 – www.thebeaumont.com

Colony Grill Room – See restaurant listing

45 Park Lane

LUXURY · MODERN It was the original site of the Playboy Club and has been a car showroom but now 45 Park Lane has been reborn as The Dorchester's sister hotel. The bedrooms, all with views over Hyde Park, are wonderfully sensual and the marble bathrooms are beautiful.

46 rooms – †£ 495/695 ††£ 495/695 – ☲ £ 21 – 10 suites

Town plan: 30AK4-r - 45 Park Ln ⊠ W1K 1PN – ⊖ Hyde Park Corner
– ℰ 020 7493 4545 – www.45parklane.com

Cut – See restaurant listing

Westbury

BUSINESS · MODERN As stylish now as when it opened in the 1950s. Smart, comfortable bedrooms with terrific art deco inspired suites. Elegant, iconic Polo bar and bright, fresh sushi bar. All the designer brands outside the front door.

246 rooms ☲ – †£ 263/599 ††£ 263/599 – 13 suites

Town plan: 30AM3-z - Bond St ⊠ W1S 2YF – ⊖ Bond Street – ℰ 020 7629 7755
– www.westburymayfair.com

❀ Alyn Williams at The Westbury – See restaurant listing

Brown's

LUXURY · CLASSIC Opened in 1837 by James Brown, Lord Byron's butler. This urbane and very British hotel with an illustrious past offers a swish bar with Terence Donovan prints, bedrooms in neutral hues and a classic English sitting room for afternoon tea.

117 rooms – †£ 420/905 ††£ 420/950 – ☲ £ 35 – 28 suites

Town plan: 30AM3-d - 33 Albemarle St ⊠ W1S 4BP – ⊖ Green Park
– ℰ 020 7493 6020 – www.roccofortehotels.com

Hix Mayfair – See restaurant listing

Chesterfield

TOWNHOUSE · CLASSIC An assuredly English feel to this Georgian house. Discreet lobby leads to a clubby bar and wood panelled library. Individually decorated bedrooms, with some antique pieces. Intimate and pretty restaurant.

107 rooms ☲ – †£ 195/390 ††£ 220/510 – 4 suites

Town plan: 30AL3-f - 35 Charles St ⊠ W1J 5EB – ⊖ Green Park
– ℰ 020 7491 2622 – www.chesterfieldmayfair.com

Alain Ducasse at The Dorchester

❀❀❀ **FRENCH · ELEGANT** Elegance, luxury and attention to detail are the hallmarks of Alain Ducasse's London outpost, where the atmosphere is warm and relaxed. The kitchen uses the best seasonal produce, whether British or French, to create visually striking, refined modern dishes. The 'Table Lumière' with its shimmering curtain affords an opulent, semi-private dining experience.

→ Dorset crab, celeriac and caviar. Simmered halibut with winkles, cockles and razor clams marinière. 'Baba like in Monte Carlo'.

Menu £ 60/95

Town plan: 30AK4-a - Dorchester Hotel, Park Ln ⊠ W1K 1QA
– ⊖ Hyde Park Corner – ℰ 020 7629 8866 (booking essential)
– www.alainducasse-dorchester.com – Closed 3 weeks August, first week January, 26-30 December, Easter, Saturday lunch, Sunday and Monday

WESTMINSTER (City of)

LONDON ENGLAND

XXXX Sketch (The Lecture Room & Library) ⊕ AC ⑩

🕄🕄 **FRENCH · LUXURY** Mourad Mazouz and Pierre Gagnaire's 18C funhouse is awash with colour, energy and vim and the luxurious 'Lecture Room & Library' provides the ideal setting for the sophisticated French cooking. Relax and enjoy artfully presented, elaborate dishes that provide many varieties of flavours and textures.
→ Pike soufflé with watercress poached trout and frogs legs. Organic rack of pork with sage, mango vinegar and seasonal fruit. Pierre Gagnaire's 'grand dessert'.
Menu £ 35/120 – Carte £ 112/140

Town plan: 30AM2-h - 9 Conduit St (1st floor) ⊠ W1S 2XG – ⊖ Oxford Circus – ℰ 020 7659 4500 (booking essential) – www.sketch.london – Closed 24 -lunch 31 December, last 2 weeks August, Saturday lunch, Sunday and Monday

XXXX Hélène Darroze at The Connaught ⊕ AC ⇔

🕄🕄 **MODERN CUISINE · LUXURY** From a Solitaire board of 13 marbles, each bearing the name of an ingredient, you choose 5, 7 or 9 (courses); this highlights the quality of produce used. The cooking is lighter these days yet still with the occasional unexpected flavour. The warm service ensures the wood-panelled room never feels too formal.
→ Scallop, tandoori spices, carrot, citrus and coriander. Pigeon with beetroot and foie gras. Savarin Armagnac, rhubarb and ginger.
Menu £ 52/92

Town plan: 30AL3-e - Connaught Hotel, Carlos Pl. ⊠ W1K 2AL – ⊖ Bond Street – ℰ 020 7107 8880 (booking essential) – www.the-connaught.co.uk

XXXX Le Gavroche (Michel Roux Jnr) ⊕ AC ⇔

🕄🕄 **FRENCH · INTIMATE** Classical, rich and indulgent French cuisine is the draw at Michel Roux's renowned London institution. The large, smart basement room has a clubby, masculine feel; service is formal and structured but also has charm.
→ Mousseline de homard au champagne et caviar. Côte de veau rôtie, morilles et ail sauvage. Omelette Rothschild.
Menu £ 57/128 – Carte £ 67/165

Town plan: 30AK3-c - 43 Upper Brook St ⊠ W1K 7QR – ⊖ Marble Arch – ℰ 020 7408 0881 (booking essential) – www.le-gavroche.co.uk – Closed Christmas-January, Saturday lunch, Sunday, Monday and bank holidays

XXXX Fera at Claridges ⊕ & AC ⑩ ⇔

🕄 **CREATIVE BRITISH · ELEGANT** Earth-father, forager supreme and gastronomic alchemist Simon Rogan brings his wonderfully natural, unforced style of cooking to the capital. The deftly balanced and cleverly textured dishes deliver multi-dimensional layers of flavours and the grand room has been transformed into a thing of beauty.
→ Rose veal tartare with oyster and kohlrabi. Turbot in pine oil, Jerusalem artichoke, oyster mushroom and spring herbs. Meadowsweet cake, celeriac, apple and burnt honey.
Menu £ 39/110 – Carte £ 53/85

Town plan: 30AL2-c - Claridge's Hotel, Brook St ⊠ W1K 4HR – ⊖ Bond Street – ℰ 020 7107 8888 (booking advisable) – www.feraatclaridges.co.uk

XXXX Alyn Williams at The Westbury ⊕ & AC ⑩ ⇔

🕄 **MODERN CUISINE · DESIGN** Confident, cheery service ensures the atmosphere never strays into terminal seriousness; rosewood panelling and a striking wine display add warmth. The cooking is creative and even playful, but however elaborately constructed the dish, the combinations of flavours and textures always work.
→ Poached foie gras with smoked eel, dulse and mushroom broth. Herdwick lamb with sweetbread kofta, pickled aubergine, feta and cucumber. Caramelised Arctic roll, coffee and vanilla custard millefeuille.
Menu £ 30/65

Town plan: 30AM3-z - Westbury Hotel, 37 Conduit St ⊠ W1S 2YF – ⊖ Bond Street – ℰ 020 7183 6426 – www.alynwilliams.com – Closed first 2 weeks January, last 2 weeks August, Sunday and Monday

130

XxxX The Square

FRENCH · ELEGANT It was all change in 2016 when Philip Howard stepped down as chef after 25 years. This smart and sophisticated restaurant also changed hands and now belongs to Marlon Abela, whose group includes The Greenhouse.

Menu £ 40/95

Town plan: 30AM3-v - 6-10 Bruton St. ⊠ W1J 6PU – ⊖ Green Park
– ℰ 020 7495 7100 – www.squarerestaurant.com – Closed 24-26 December and Sunday lunch

XxX Greenhouse

CREATIVE · FASHIONABLE Chef Arnaud Bignon's cooking is confident, balanced and innovative and uses the best from Europe's larder; his dishes exude an exhilarating freshness. The breadth and depth of the wine list is astounding. This is a discreet, sleek and contemporary restaurant with well-judged service.
→ Orkney scallop with sea urchin, fennel and clementine. Monkfish with onion, banana, kaffir lime and dukkah. Mananka chocolate with kumquat and coriander.

Menu £ 40/95

Town plan: 30AL3-m - 27a Hay's Mews ⊠ W1J 5NY – ⊖ Hyde Park Corner
– ℰ 020 7499 3331 – www.greenhouserestaurant.co.uk – Closed Saturday lunch, Sunday and bank holidays

XxX Umu

JAPANESE · FASHIONABLE Stylish, discreet interior using natural materials, with central sushi bar. Extensive choice of Japanese dishes; choose one of the seasonal kaiseki menus for the full experience. Over 160 different labels of sake.
→ Cornish line caught squid with Exmoor caviar. Grade 11 Japanese Wagyu smoked à la minute. Caramel custard with fuki.

Menu £ 35/155 – Carte £ 57/158

Town plan: 30AL3-k - 14-16 Bruton Pl. ⊠ W1J 6LX – ⊖ Bond Street
– ℰ 020 7499 8881 – www.umurestaurant.com – Closed Christmas, New Year, Saturday lunch, Sunday and bank holidays

XxX Murano (Angela Hartnett)

ITALIAN · FASHIONABLE Angela Hartnett's Italian influenced cooking exhibits an appealing lightness of touch, with assured combinations of flavours, borne out of confidence in the ingredients. This is a stylish, elegant room run by a well-organised, professional and friendly team who put their customers at ease.
→ Crab tortellini & bisque with cucumber, turnip and spring onion. Smoked pigeon with orange purée, fennel, pine nuts and pancetta. Pistachio soufflé with hot chocolate sauce.

Menu £ 33/65

Town plan: 30AL4-b - 20 Queen St ⊠ W1J 5PP – ⊖ Green Park
– ℰ 020 7495 1127 – www.muranolondon.com – Closed Christmas and Sunday

XxX Galvin at Windows

MODERN CUISINE · FRIENDLY The cleverly laid out room makes the most of the spectacular views across London from the 28th floor. Relaxed service takes the edge off the somewhat corporate atmosphere. The bold cooking uses superb ingredients and the classically based food comes with a pleasing degree of flair and innovation.
→ French asparagus with organic egg and a praline & chickpea tuile. Roast fillet of halibut with pommes purée, shiitake mushrooms, prawn & dashi broth. Nougat parfait with banana, muscovado meringues and black pepper ice cream.

Menu £ 33/70

Town plan: 30AL4-e - London Hilton Hotel, 22 Park Ln (28th floor) ⊠ W1K 1BE
– ⊖ Hyde Park Corner – ℰ 020 7208 4021 – www.galvinatwindows.com
– Closed Saturday lunch and Sunday dinner

131

XXX Benares (Atul Kochhar)   🕸 AC 🌱 ⬦
❀
INDIAN · CHIC No Indian restaurant in London enjoys a more commanding location or expansive interior. Atul Kochhar's influences are many and varied; his spicing is deft and he makes excellent use of British ingredients like Scottish scallops and New Forest venison. The Chef's Table has a window into the kitchen.
→ Pan-seared scallops, broccoli couscous and cauliflower purée. Old Delhi style tandoori chicken, makhani sauce and spring salad. Dark chocolate mousse, passion fruit and hot chocolate sauce.

Menu £ 35 (lunch and early dinner) – Carte £ 50/91

Town plan: 30AL3-q - *12a Berkeley Square House, Berkeley Sq.* ✉ *W1J 6BS*
– ⊖ *Green Park –* ✆ *020 7629 8886 – www.benaresrestaurant.com – Closed 25 December, 1 January and Sunday lunch*

XXX Tamarind   AC 🌱
❀
INDIAN · CHIC Makes the best use of its basement location through smoked mirrors, gilded columns and a somewhat exclusive feel. The appealing northern Indian food is mostly traditionally based; kebabs and curries are the specialities, the tandoor is used to good effect and don't miss the carefully judged vegetable dishes.
→ Spiced chickpeas with wheat crisps, yoghurt and tamarind chutney. Lamb simmered with shallots and pickling spices. Cardamom flavoured hung yoghurt.

Menu £ 22/75 – Carte £ 36/69

Town plan: 30AL4-h - *20 Queen St.* ✉ *W1J 5PR –* ⊖ *Green Park*
– ✆ *020 7629 3561 – www.tamarindrestaurant.com – Closed 25-26 December, 1 January and Saturday lunch*

XXX Kai   🕸 AC 🌱 ⬦
❀
CHINESE · INTIMATE There are a few classics on the menu but Chef Alex Chow's strengths are his modern creations and re-workings of Chinese recipes. His dishes have real depth, use superb produce and are wonderfully balanced. The interior is unashamedly glitzy and the service team anticipate their customers' needs well.
→ Halibut with ginger, spring onions and soy. Kagoshima Wagyu with 7 spice salt and rice balls. Durian and vanilla soufflé with salted caramel.

Carte £ 39/136

Town plan: 30AK3-n - *65 South Audley St* ✉ *W1K 2QU –* ⊖ *Hyde Park Corner*
– ✆ *020 7493 8988 (booking essential) – www.kaimayfair.co.uk – Closed 25-26 December and 1 January*

XXX Park Chinois 🆕   🍸 AC ⬦
CHINESE · EXOTIC DÉCOR Old fashioned glamour, strikingly rich surroundings, live music and Chinese food combine to great effect at this sumptuously decorated restaurant spread over two floors and created by Alan Yau – one of the UK's most influential restaurateurs.

Carte £ 40/107

Town plan: 30AM3-f - *17 Berkeley St* ✉ *W1J 8EA –* ⊖ *Green Park*
– ✆ *020 3327 8888 (booking essential) – www.parkchinois.com*

XXX Scott's   AC 🌱 ⬦
SEAFOOD · FASHIONABLE Proof that a restaurant can have a long, proud history and still be fashionable, glamorous and relevant. It has a terrific clubby atmosphere and if you're in a two then the counter is a great spot. The choice of prime quality fish and shellfish is impressive.

Carte £ 37/57

Town plan: 30AK3-h - *20 Mount St* ✉ *W1K 2HE –* ⊖ *Bond Street*
– ✆ *020 7495 7309 – www.scotts-restaurant.com – Closed 25-26 December*

Symbols shown in red 🏠 XXX indicate particularly charming establishments.

XxX Cut   🖰 AC

MEATS AND GRILLS · DESIGN The first European venture from Wolfgang Puck, the US-based Austrian celebrity chef, is this very slick, stylish and sexy room where glamorous people come to eat meat. The not-inexpensive steaks are cooked over hardwood and charcoal and finished off in a broiler.

Menu £ 29 (weekday lunch) – Carte £ 51/176

Town plan: 30AK4-r – *45 Park Lane Hotel, 45 Park Ln ✉ W1K 1PN*
– ⊖ Hyde Park Corner – ✆ 020 7493 4545 (booking essential) – www.45parklane.com

XxX 34   🖫 AC ⇔

MEATS AND GRILLS · BRASSERIE A wonderful mix of art deco styling and Edwardian warmth makes it feel like a glamorous brasserie. A parrilla grill is used for fish, game and beef – choose from Scottish dry-aged, US prime, organic Argentinian and Australian Wagyu.

Menu £ 28 (weekday lunch) – Carte £ 34/60

Town plan: 30AK3-b – *34 Grosvenor Sq (entrance on South Audley St)*
✉ W1K 2HD – ⊖ Marble Arch – ✆ 020 3350 3434 – www.34-restaurant.co.uk
– Closed 25-26 December, dinner 24 December and lunch 1 January

XxX The Grill   🎇 🖰 AC 🖵

FRENCH · ELEGANT The re-launched Grill is relaxed yet formal, with an open kitchen and a striking, hand-blown Murano glass chandelier as its centrepiece. Grill favourites sit alongside modern day classics on the menu; sharing dishes are a good choice, as are the speciality soufflés. Service is smooth and highly professional.

Menu £ 39 (weekday lunch) – Carte £ 43/89

Town plan: 30AK4-a *Dorchester Hotel, Park Ln ✉ W1S 2XG*
– ⊖ Hyde Park Corner – ✆ 020 7659 4500 (booking advisable)
– www.dorchestercollection.com

XxX Corrigan's Mayfair   🖰 AC ⇔

MODERN BRITISH · ELEGANT Richard Corrigan's flagship celebrates British and Irish cooking, with game a speciality. The room is comfortable, clubby and quite glamorous and feels as though it has been around for years.

Menu £ 25 (weekday lunch) – Carte £ 32/79

Town plan: 30AK3-a – *28 Upper Grosvenor St. ✉ W1K 7EH – ⊖ Marble Arch*
– ✆ 020 7499 9943 – www.corrigansmayfair.com – Closed 25-30 December,
Saturday lunch and bank holidays

XxX Sartoria   🌤 🖰 AC ⇔

ITALIAN · CHIC A longstanding feature on Savile Row but now looking much more dapper. Francesco Mazzei, formerly of L'Anima, hooked up with D&D to take the reins and the place now feels more energised. There are hints of Calabria but the menu covers all Italian regions and keeps things fairly classical.

Menu £ 27 (weekday lunch) – Carte £ 26/58

Town plan: 30AM3-c *20 Savile Row ✉ W1S 3PR – ⊖ Oxford Circus*
– ✆ 020 7534 7000 – www.sartoria-restaurant.co.uk – Closed
25-26 December, Saturday lunch, Sunday and bank holidays

XxX China Tang   🖫 🖰 AC ⇔

CHINESE · FASHIONABLE Sir David Tang's atmospheric, art deco-inspired Chinese restaurant, downstairs at The Dorchester, is always abuzz with activity. Be sure to see the terrific bar, before sharing the traditional Cantonese specialities.

Menu £ 30 (lunch) – Carte £ 28/79

Town plan: 30AK3-e *Dorchester Hotel, Park Ln ✉ W1K 1QA*
– ⊖ Hyde Park Corner – ✆ 020 7629 9988 – www.chinatanglondon.co.uk – Closed
24-25 December

LONDON ENGLAND

133

LONDON ENGLAND

✗✗✗ Amaranto · 🍽 🏡 & 🅰🄲 ⇔ 🚗

ITALIAN · FASHIONABLE It's all about flexibility here, as the Italian-influenced menu is served in the stylish bar, in the comfortable lounge, on the great terrace or in the restaurant, which is decorated in the vivid colours of the amaranth plant.

Carte £ 28/68

Town plan: 30AL4-v - *Four Seasons Hotel, Hamilton Pl, Park Ln* ✉ *W1J 7DR*
– ⊖ *Hyde Park Corner* – 𝒞 *020 7319 5206*
– *www.fourseasons.com/london/dining*

✗✗✗ Hix Mayfair · & 🅰🄲 🍴

TRADITIONAL BRITISH · TRADITIONAL DÉCOR This wood-panelled dining room is lightened with the work of current British artists. Mark Hix's well-sourced menu of British classics will appeal to the hunter-gatherer in every man.

Menu £ 28 (dinner) – Carte £ 33/65

Town plan: 30AM3-d *Brown's Hotel, 33 Albemarle St* ✉ *W1S 4BP*
– ⊖ *Green Park* – 𝒞 *020 7518 4004*
– *www.hixmayfair.com*

✗✗ Araki (Mitsuhiro Araki) · 🅰🄲 ⇔
£3£3 JAPANESE · INTIMATE Mitsuhiro Araki is one of Japan's great Sushi Masters who closed his Tokyo restaurant to relocate to London because he wanted a fresh challenge. From one of 10 seats at his beautiful cypress counter, watch him deftly prepare Edomae sushi using European seafood. It's very expensive but the different cuts of tuna are stunning and the rice, grown by his father-in-law back in Japan, is also excellent.

→ Sake-steamed abalone with grilled scallop. Tuna tartare with truffle and wasabi. Welsh eel sushi

Menu £ 300 – tasting menu only

Town plan: 30AM3-e - *12 New Burlington St* ✉ *W1S 3BF* – ⊖ *Oxford Circus*
– 𝒞 *020 7287 2481 (booking essential)* – *www.the-araki.com* – *dinner only*
– *Closed 27 July-31 August, Christmas- first week January and Monday*

✗✗ Pollen Street Social (Jason Atherton) · 🕸 🍽 🅰🄲 🍴 ⇔
£3 CREATIVE · FASHIONABLE The restaurant where it all started for Jason Atherton when he went solo. Top quality British produce lies at the heart of the menu and the innovative dishes are prepared with great care and no little skill. The room has plenty of buzz, helped along by the 'dessert bar' and views of the kitchen pass.

→ Crab salad with apple, coriander, black garlic, lemon purée and brown crab on toast. Loin and braised neck of lamb with roast artichoke, Merguez sausage, curds & whey. Bitter chocolate pavé with olive biscuit and chocolate ice cream.

Menu £ 32 (lunch) – Carte £ 60/70

Town plan: 30AM2-c - *8-10 Pollen St* ✉ *W1S 1NQ*
– ⊖ *Oxford Circus* – 𝒞 *020 7290 7600 (booking essential)*
– *www.pollenstreetsocial.com* – *Closed Sunday and bank holidays*

✗✗ Bonhams · 🕸 & 🅰🄲
£3 MODERN CUISINE · MINIMALIST Established in 1793, Bonhams is now one of the world's largest fine art and antique auctioneers. Its restaurant is bright, modern and professionally run. Dishes are elegant and delicate and there is real clarity to the flavours. The wine list has also been very thoughtfully compiled.

→ Pertuis asparagus with soft-boiled egg, confit lemon and trout eggs. Roast Cornish brill with cauliflower couscous and curried mussels. Floating island with sour cherry purée, pistachio anglaise and bitter chocolate sorbet.

Menu £ 60 (dinner) – Carte £ 38/68

Town plan: 30AL2-n *101 New Bond St* ✉ *W1S 1SR* – *(lower ground floor)* – *For dinner entrance via Haunch of Venison Yard off Brook St* – ⊖ *Bond Street*
– 𝒞 *020 7468 5868 (booking advisable)* – *www.bonhams.com* – *Closed 2 weeks August, 24 December-2 January, Saturday-Sunday, dinner Monday-Tuesday and bank holidays*

XX Gymkhana

INDIAN · INTIMATE If you enjoy Trishna then you'll love Karam Sethi's Gymkhana – that's if you can get a table. Inspired by Colonial India's gymkhana clubs, the interior is full of wonderful detail and plenty of wry touches; ask to sit downstairs. The North Indian dishes have a wonderful richness and depth of flavour.

→ Kid goat methi keema, salli and pao. Wild muntjac biryani, pomegranate and mint raita. Cardamom and strawberry kheer.

Menu £ 25 (lunch and early dinner)/80 – Carte £ 25/61

Town plan: 30AM3-a - 42 Albemarle St ⊠ W1S 4JH – ⊖ Green Park
– ☏ 020 3011 5900 (booking essential) – www.gymkhanalondon.com – Closed
1-3 January, 25-27 December and Sunday

XX Hakkasan Mayfair

CHINESE · MINIMALIST Less a copy, more a sister to the original; a sister who's just as fun but lives in a nicer part of town. This one has a funky, more casual ground floor to go with the downstairs dining room. You can expect the same extensive choice of top quality, modern Cantonese cuisine; dim sum is a highlight.

→ Jasmine tea-smoked organic pork ribs. Roast silver cod with champagne and honey. Jivara bomb.

Menu £ 38 (lunch and early dinner) – Carte £ 34/101

Town plan: 30AL3-a - 17 Bruton St ⊠ W1J 6QB – ⊖ Green Park
– ☏ 020 7907 1888 (booking essential) – www.hakkasan.com – Closed
24-25 December

XX Veeraswamy

INDIAN · DESIGN It may have opened in 1926 but this celebrated Indian restaurant just keeps getting better and better! The classic dishes from across the country are prepared with considerable care by a very professional kitchen. The room is awash with colour and it's run with great charm and enormous pride.

→ Wild tiger prawns, coriander, mint and chilli. Pistachio and almond crusted lamb chops. Caramelised banana kulfi.

Menu £ 30 (lunch and early dinner) – Carte £ 40/55

Town plan: 31AN3-t - Victory House, 99 Regent St ⊠ W1B 4RS – Entrance on Swallow St. – ⊖ Piccadilly Circus – ☏ 020 7734 1401 – www.veeraswamy.com

XX Colony Grill Room

TRADITIONAL BRITISH · BRASSERIE Based on 1920s London and New York grill restaurants, The Beaumont's Colony Grill comes with leather booths, striking age-of-speed art deco murals and clever lighting. By making the room and style of service so defiantly old fashioned, Chris Corbin and Jeremy King have created somewhere effortlessly chic.

Carte £ 27/79

Town plan: 30AK2-x - The Beaumont Hotel, Brown Hart Gdns. ⊠ W1K 6TF
– ⊖ Bond Street – ☏ 020 7499 9499 (booking essential)
– www.colonygrillroom.com

XX Hawksmoor

MEATS AND GRILLS · FASHIONABLE The best of the Hawksmoors is large, boisterous and has an appealing art deco feel. Expect top quality, 35-day aged Longhorn beef but also great seafood, much of which is charcoal grilled. The delightful staff are well organised.

Menu £ 28 (lunch and early dinner) – Carte £ 23/59

Town plan: 30AN3-m - 5a Air St ⊠ W1J 0AD – ⊖ Piccadilly Circus
– ☏ 020 7406 3980 (booking advisable) – www.thehawksmoor.com – Closed
24-26 December

XX Momo 🛱 AK

MOROCCAN · EXOTIC DÉCOR An authentic Moroccan atmosphere comes courtesy of the antiques, kilim rugs, Berber artwork, bright fabrics and lanterns – you'll feel you're eating near the souk. Go for the classic dishes: zaalouk, briouats, pigeon pastilla, and tagines with mountains of fluffy couscous.

Menu £ 20 (weekday lunch) – Carte £ 28/51

Town plan: 30AM3-n - *25 Heddon St.* ⊠ *W1B 4BH* – ⊖ *Oxford Circus*
– *☎ 020 7434 4040* – *www.momoresto.com* – *Closed 25 December and 1 January*

XX Sketch (The Gallery) 🍸 AK

MODERN CUISINE · TRENDY The striking 'Gallery' has a smart look from India Mahdavi and artwork from David Shrigley. At dinner the room transmogrifies from art gallery to fashionable restaurant, with a menu that mixes the classic, the modern and the esoteric.

Carte £ 37/80

Town plan: 30AM2-h - *9 Conduit St* ⊠ *W1S 2XG* – ⊖ *Oxford Circus*
– *☎ 020 7659 4500 (booking essential)* – *www.sketch.london* – *dinner only*
– *Closed 25 December*

XX Heddon Street Kitchen 🍸 🛱 ও AK 🖵 ⇆

MODERN CUISINE · BRASSERIE Gordon Ramsay's follow up to Bread Street is spread over two floors and is all about all-day dining: breakfast covers all tastes, there's weekend brunch, and an à la carte offering an appealing range of European dishes executed with palpable care.

Menu £ 27 (lunch and early dinner) – Carte £ 30/53

Town plan: 30AM3-y - *3-9 Heddon St* ⊠ *W1B 4BE* – ⊖ *Oxford Circus*
– *☎ 020 7592 1212* – *www.gordonramsayrestaurants.com/heddon-street-kitchen/*
– *Closed 25 December*

XX Roka 🍸 🛱 AK

JAPANESE · ELEGANT London's third Roka ventures into the rarefied surroundings of Mayfair and the restaurant's seductive looks are a good fit. All the favourites from their modern Japanese repertoire are here, with the robata grill taking centre stage.

Carte £ 24/116

Town plan: 31AN1-k - *30 North Audley St* ⊠ *W1K 6HP* – ⊖ *Bond Street*
– *☎ 020 7305 5644* – *www.rokarestaurant.com* – *Closed Christmas-New Year*

XX Theo Randall 🍸 AK 🕥 🕏 ⇆

ITALIAN · CLASSIC DÉCOR A lighter, less formal look to the room was unveiled in 2016 to celebrate Theo's 10 years at the InterContinental. The lack of windows and the corporate nature of the hotel have never helped but at least there is now greater synergy between the room and the rustic Italian fare, made with prime ingredients.

Menu £ 27/33 – Carte £ 40/65

Town plan: 30AL4-k - *InterContinental London Park Lane, 1 Hamilton Pl, Park Ln* ⊠ *W1J 7QY* – ⊖ *Hyde Park Corner* – *☎ 020 7318 8747* – *www.theorandall.com*
– *Closed Christmas, Easter, Saturday lunch, Sunday dinner and bank holidays*

XX Maze 🐴 🍸 ও AK ⇆

MODERN CUISINE · FASHIONABLE This Gordon Ramsay restaurant still offers a glamorous night out, thanks to its great cocktails, effervescent atmosphere and small plates of Asian influenced food. Three or four dishes per person is about the going rate.

Menu £ 30 (weekday lunch) – Carte £ 44/76

Town plan: 30AK2-z - *10-13 Grosvenor Sq* ⊠ *W1K 6JP* – ⊖ *Bond Street*
– *☎ 020 7107 0000* – *www.gordonramsayrestaurants.com/maze/*

XX Nobu Berkeley St 🍸 AC 🍲

JAPANESE · FASHIONABLE This branch of the glamorous chain is more of a party animal than its elder sibling at The Metropolitan. Start with cocktails then head upstairs for Japanese food with South American influences; try dishes from the wood-fired oven.

Menu £ 40 (lunch) – Carte £ 30/92

Town plan: 30AM3-b - *15 Berkeley St. ⊠ W1J 8DY –* ⊖ *Green Park – ℰ 020 7290 9222 (booking essential) – www.noburestaurants.com – Closed 25 December and Sunday lunch except December*

XX Sexy Fish 🆕 🍸 AC

SEAFOOD · DESIGN Everyone will have an opinion about the name but what's indisputable is that this is a very good looking restaurant, with works by Frank Gehry and Damien Hirst, and a stunning ceiling by Michael Roberts. The fish comes with various Asian influences but don't ignore the meat dishes like the beef rib skewers.

Carte £ 33/90

Town plan: 30AL3-w - *Berkeley Sq. ⊠ W1J 6BR –* ⊖ *Green Park – ℰ 020 3764 2000 – www.sexyfish.com – Closed 25 December*

XX Bentley's AC ⇔

SEAFOOD · TRADITIONAL DÉCOR In 2016 this seafood institution celebrated its centenary. It comes in two parts: upstairs is the more formal and smartly dressed Grill, with seafood classics and grilled meats; on the ground floor is the Oyster Bar which is more fun and does a good fish pie.

Menu £ 25 (weekday lunch) – Carte £ 33/76

Town plan: 31AN3-c - *11-15 Swallow St. ⊠ W1B 4DG –* ⊖ *Piccadilly Circus – ℰ 020 7734 4756 – www.bentleys.org – Closed 25 December, 1 January, Saturday lunch and Sunday*

XX Coya 🍸 AC 📋 ⇔

PERUVIAN · FRIENDLY A lively, loud and enthusiastically run basement restaurant that celebrates all things Peruvian, from the people behind Zuma and Roka. Try their ceviche and their skewers, as well as their Pisco Sours in the fun bar.

Menu £ 21 (weekday lunch) – Carte £ 33/57

Town plan: 30AL4-d - *118 Piccadilly ⊠ W1J 7NW –* ⊖ *Hyde Park Corner – ℰ 020 7042 7118 (booking advisable) – www.coyarestaurant.com – Closed 24-26 December and 1 January*

XX Wild Honey AC 🕸

MODERN CUISINE · DESIGN Elegant wood panelling and ornate plasterwork may say 'classic Mayfair institution' but the personable service team keep the atmosphere enjoyably easy-going. The kitchen uses quality British ingredients and a French base but is not afraid of the occasional international flavour.

Menu £ 30/35 (weekdays) – Carte £ 39/60

Town plan: 30AM2-w - *12 St George St. ⊠ W1S 2FB –* ⊖ *Oxford Circus – ℰ 020 7758 9160 – www.wildhoneyrestaurant.co.uk – Closed 25-26 December, 1 January and Sunday*

XX La Petite Maison 🍽 AC

FRENCH · BISTRO A little piece of southern France and Ligurian Italy in Mayfair. The slickly run sister to the Nice original has a buzzy, glamorous feel, with prices to match. Just reading the menus of Mediterranean dishes will improve your tan.

Carte £ 30/70 **s**

Town plan: 30AL2-m *54 Brooks Mews ⊠ W1K 4EG –* ⊖ *Bond Street – ℰ 020 7495 4774 (booking essential) – www.lpmlondon.co.uk – Closed Christmas-New Year*

XX Keeper's House

MODERN BRITISH · INTIMATE Built in 1860 and fully restored, this house is part of the Royal Academy. Two intimate dining rooms are lined with green baize and hung with architectural casts. The emphasis is on seasonality, freshness and contrasts in textures.

Menu £ 21 (lunch)/26 – Carte £ 27/44

Town plan: 30AM3-x - *Royal Academy of Arts, Burlington House, Piccadilly* ⊠ *W1J 0BD* – ⊖ *Green Park* – *ℰ 020 7300 5881* – *www.keepershouse.org.uk* – *Closed 25-26 December and Sunday*

XX Maze Grill Mayfair

MEATS AND GRILLS · FASHIONABLE Next door to Maze and specialising in steaks cooked on the Josper grill. Expect a good range of aged meat, including Aberdeen Angus (28 days), Dedham Vale (31), USDA Prime (36) and Wagyu 9th Grade (49), served on wooden boards.

Menu £ 27 (lunch) – Carte £ 29/88

Town plan: 30AK2-a - *London Marriott Hotel Grosvenor Square, 10-13 Grosvenor Sq* ⊠ *W1K 6JP* – ⊖ *Bond Street* – *ℰ 020 7495 2211* – *www.gordonramsayrestaurants.com*

XX Goodman Mayfair

MEATS AND GRILLS · BRASSERIE A worthy attempt at recreating a New York steakhouse; all leather and wood and macho swagger. Beef is dry or wet aged in-house and comes with a choice of four sauces; rib-eye the speciality.

Carte £ 28/103

Town plan: 30AM2-e - *26 Maddox St* ⊠ *W1S 1QH* – ⊖ *Oxford Circus* – *ℰ 020 7499 3776 (booking essential)* – *www.goodmanrestaurants.com* – *Closed Sunday and bank holidays*

XX Tokimeitē 🆕

JAPANESE · CHIC Yoshihiro Murata, one of Japan's most celebrated chefs, teamed up with the Zen-Noh group to open this good looking, intimate restaurant on two floors. Their aim is to promote Wagyu beef in Europe, so it's understandably the star of the show.

Carte £ 28/136

Town plan: 30AM3-k - *23 Conduit St* ⊠ *W1S 2XS* – ⊖ *Oxford Circus* – *ℰ 020 3826 4411* – *www.tokimeite.com* – *Closed 25 December and Sunday dinner*

XX Hush

MODERN CUISINE · FASHIONABLE If there's warmth in the air then tables on the large courtyard terrace are the first to go. The ground floor serves brasserie classics prepared with care; there's a stylish cocktail bar upstairs, along with smart private dining rooms.

Carte £ 28/61

Town plan: 30AL2-v - *8 Lancashire Ct., Brook St.* ⊠ *W1S 1EY* – ⊖ *Bond Street* – *ℰ 020 7659 1500 (booking essential)* – *www.hush.co.uk* – *Closed 25 December and 1 January*

XX Nobu

JAPANESE · FASHIONABLE Nobu restaurants are now all over the world but this was Europe's first and opened in 1997. It retains a certain exclusivity and is buzzy and fun. The menu is an innovative blend of Japanese cuisine with South American influences.

Menu £ 30 – Carte £ 24/73

Town plan: 30AL4-c - *Metropolitan Hotel, 19 Old Park Ln* ⊠ *W1Y 1LB* – ⊖ *Hyde Park Corner* – *ℰ 020 7447 4747 (booking essential)* – *www.noburestaurants.com*

XX **Kiku**   🔥 AC ⇔

JAPANESE · NEIGHBOURHOOD For over 35 years this earnestly run, authentically styled, family owned restaurant has been providing every style of Japanese cuisine to its homesick Japanese customers, from shabu shabu to sukiyaki, yakitori to teriyaki.

Menu £ 24 (weekday lunch) – Carte £ 23/78

Town plan: 30AL4-g - *17 Half Moon St.* ⊠ *W1J 7BE* – ⊖ *Green Park*
– ☎ 020 7499 4208 – www.kikurestaurant.co.uk – Closed 25-27 December,
1 January and lunch Sunday and bank holidays

XX **Chucs Bar and Grill**   🍴 AC 🔲

ITALIAN · ELEGANT Like the shop to which it's attached, Chucs caters for those who summer on the Riviera and are not afraid of showing it. It's decked out like a yacht and the concise but not inexpensive menu offers classic Mediterranean dishes.

Carte £ 38/59

Town plan: 30AM3-r - *30b Dover St.* ⊠ *W1S 4NB* – ⊖ *Green Park*
– ☎ 020 3763 2013 (booking essential) – www.chucsrestaurant.com – Closed
25-26 and dinner 24 and 31 December, 1 January and bank holidays

X **Le Boudin Blanc**   🍴 AC 🔲 ⇔

FRENCH · RUSTIC Appealing, lively French bistro in Shepherd Market, spread over two floors. Satisfying French classics and country cooking are the draws, along with authentic Gallic service. Good value lunch menu.

Menu £ 15 (lunch and early dinner) – Carte £ 28/53

Town plan: 30AL4-q - *5 Trebeck St* ⊠ *W1J 7LT* – ⊖ *Green Park*
– ☎ 020 7499 3292 – www.boudinblanc.co.uk – Closed 24-26 December and
1 January

X **Little Social**   🍷 & AC 🍴 ⇔

FRENCH · BISTRO Jason Atherton's lively French bistro, opposite his Pollen Street Social restaurant, has a clubby feel and an appealing, deliberately worn look. Service is breezy and capable and the food is mostly classic with the odd modern twist.

Menu £ 25 (weekday lunch) – Carte £ 33/58

Town plan: 30AM2-r - *5 Pollen St* ⊠ *W1S 1NE* – ⊖ *Oxford Circus*
– ☎ 020 7870 3730 (booking essential) – www.littlesocial.co.uk – Closed Sunday
and bank holidays

X **Kitty Fisher's**

MODERN CUISINE · BISTRO Warm, intimate and unpretentious restaurant – the star of the show is the wood grill which gives the dishes added depth. Named after an 18C courtesan, presumably in honour of the profession for which Shepherd Market was once known.

Menu £ 30 (weekday lunch) – Carte £ 33/54

Town plan: 30AL4-s - *10 Shepherd Mkt* ⊠ *W1J 7QF* – ⊖ *Green Park*
– ☎ 020 3302 1661 (booking essential) – www.kittyfishers.com – Closed Christmas,
New Year, Easter, Sunday and bank holidays

X **Peyote**   & AC 🍽 ⇔

MEXICAN · TRENDY From the people behind Zuma and Roka comes a 'refined interpretation of Mexican cuisine' at this fun, glamorous spot. There's an exhilarating freshness to the well-judged dishes; don't miss the great guacamole or the cactus salad.

Menu £ 24 (weekdays) – Carte £ 30/60

Town plan: 30AM3-m - *13 Cork St* ⊠ *W1S 3NS* – ⊖ *Green Park*
– ☎ 020 7409 1300 (booking essential) – www.peyoterestaurant.com – Closed
Saturday lunch and Sunday

Mayfair Chippy

AC ⇔

TRADITIONAL BRITISH · VINTAGE There are chippies, and there is the Mayfair Chippy. Here you can get cocktails, wine, oysters, starters and dessert but, most significantly, the 'Mayfair Classic' – fried cod or haddock with chips, tartar sauce, mushy peas and curry sauce.

Carte £ 20/35

Town plan: 30AK2-e - 14 North Audley St ⊠ W1K 6WE – ⊖ Marble Arch – ℰ 020 7741 2233 – www.eatbrit.com – Closed 25 December and 1 January

Regent's Park and Marylebone

The London Edition

La ⊡ AC ⌖ ⍟

BUSINESS · DESIGN Formerly Berners, a classic Edwardian hotel, strikingly reborn through a partnership between Ian Schrager and Marriott – the former's influence most apparent in the stylish lobby and bar. Slick, understated rooms; the best ones have balconies.

173 rooms – †£ 250/500 ††£ 250/500 – ⊇ £ 26 – 9 suites

Town plan: 31AN2-b - 10 Berners St ⊠ W1T 3NP – ⊖ Tottenham Court Road – ℰ 020 7781 0000 – www.editionhotels.com/london

Berners Tavern – See restaurant listing

Langham

⬛ ⓢ ⍟ La ⊡ & AC ⍟

LUXURY · ELEGANT Was one of Europe's first purpose-built grand hotels when it opened in 1865. Now back to its best, with its famous Palm Court for afternoon tea, its stylish Artesian bar and bedrooms that are not without personality and elegance.

380 rooms – †£ 360/960 ††£ 360/960 – ⊇ £ 32 – 24 suites

Town plan: 30AM1-n - 1c Portland Pl, Regent St ⊠ W1B 1JA – ⊖ Oxford Circus – ℰ 020 7636 1000 – www.langhamhotels.com

Roux at The Landau – See restaurant listing

Chiltern Firehouse

⊡ & AC

TOWNHOUSE · GRAND LUXURY From Chateau Marmont in LA to The Mercer in New York, André Balazs' hotels are effortlessly cool. For his London entrance, he sympathetically restored and extended a Gothic Victorian fire station. The style comes with an easy elegance; it's an oasis of calm and hardly feels like a hotel at all.

26 rooms – †£ 495/1020 ††£ 495/1020 – ⊇ £ 25 – 16 suites

Town plan: 30AK1-a - 1 Chiltern St ⊠ W1U 7PA – ⊖ Baker Street – ℰ 020 7073 7676 – www.chilternfirehouse.com

Chiltern Firehouse – See restaurant listing

Charlotte Street

⍟ La ⊡ AC ⌖ ⍟

LUXURY · CONTEMPORARY Stylish interior designed with a charming, understated English feel. Impeccably kept and individually decorated bedrooms. Popular in-house screening room. Colourful restaurant whose terrace spills onto Charlotte Street; grilled meats a highlight.

52 rooms – †£ 225/470 ††£ 225/470 – ⊇ £ 15 – 4 suites

Town plan: 31AN1-e - 15 Charlotte St ⊠ W1T 1RJ – ⊖ Goodge Street – ℰ 020 7806 2000 – www.charlottestreethotel.co.uk

Sanderson

⍟ ⓢ La ⊡ AC

LUXURY · MINIMALIST Originally designed by Philippe Starck and his influence is still evident. The Purple Bar is dark and moody; the Long Bar is bright and stylish. Bedrooms are crisply decorated and come complete with all mod cons.

150 rooms – †£ 234/538 ††£ 234/538 – ⊇ £ 18

Town plan: 31AN1-c - 50 Berners St ⊠ W1T 3NG – ⊖ Oxford Circus – ℰ 020 7300 1400 – www.morganshotelgroup.com

Zetter Townhouse Marylebone 🅝

TOWNHOUSE · ELEGANT A stylish Georgian townhouse, with a sumptuously decorated lounge and cocktail bar and beautifully appointed bedrooms; the best features a roll-top bath on its rootop terrace. Friendly, professional staff and impressive eco credentials.

24 rooms – ♦£ 290/480 ♦♦£ 290/480 – ☲ £ 14

Town plan: 29AJ2-a - 28-30 Seymour St ⊠ W1H 7JB – ⊖ Marble Arch
– ℰ 020 7324 4544 – www.thezettertownhouse.com

Durrants

TRADITIONAL · CLASSIC Traditional, privately owned hotel with friendly, long-standing staff. Bedrooms are now brighter in style but still retain a certain English character. Clubby dining room for mix of British classics and lighter, European dishes.

92 rooms – ♦£ 195 ♦♦£ 250/350 – ☲ £ 20 – 4 suites

Town plan: 30AK1-e - 26-32 George St ⊠ W1H 5BJ – ⊖ Bond Street
– ℰ 020 7935 8131 – www.durrantshotel.co.uk

Dorset Square

TOWNHOUSE · CONTEMPORARY Having reacquired this Regency townhouse, Firmdale refurbished it fully before reopening it in 2012. It has a contemporary yet intimate feel and visiting MCC members will appreciate the cricketing theme, which even extends to the cocktails in their sweet little basement brasserie.

38 rooms – ♦£ 165/200 ♦♦£ 205/245 – ☲ £ 13

Town plan: 17P4-s - 39-40 Dorset Sq ⊠ NW1 6QN – ⊖ Marylebone
– ℰ 020 7723 7874 – www.dorsetsquarehotel.co.uk

Marble Arch by Montcalm

TOWNHOUSE · CONTEMPORARY Bedrooms at this 5-storey Georgian town-house come with the same high standards of stylish, contemporary design as its parent hotel opposite, the Montcalm, but are just a little more compact.

42 rooms – ♦£ 253/374 ♦♦£ 263/374 – ☲ £ 20

Town plan: 29AJ2-a - 31 Great Cumberland Pl ⊠ W1H 7TA – ⊖ Marble Arch
– ℰ 020 7258 0777 – www.themarblearch.co.uk

No. Ten Manchester Street

TOWNHOUSE · MODERN Converted Edwardian house in an appealing, central location. A discreet entrance leads into a little lounge and an Italian-themed bistro; the semi-enclosed cigar bar is also a feature. Neat, well-kept bedrooms.

44 rooms – ♦£ 165/385 ♦♦£ 165/385 – ☲ £ 17 – 9 suites

Town plan: 30AK1-v - 10 Manchester St ⊠ W1U 4DG – ⊖ Baker Street
– ℰ 020 7317 5900 – www.tenmanchesterstreethotel.com

Sumner

TOWNHOUSE · PERSONALISED Two Georgian terrace houses in central location. Comfy, stylish sitting room; basement breakfast room. Largest bedrooms, 101 and 201, benefit from having full-length windows.

19 rooms ☲ – ♦£ 160/300 ♦♦£ 160/300

Town plan: 29AJ2-c - 54 Upper Berkeley St ⊠ W1H 7QR – ⊖ Marble Arch
– ℰ 020 7723 2244 – www.thesumner.com

Locanda Locatelli (Giorgio Locatelli)

ITALIAN · FASHIONABLE Giorgio Locatelli's Italian restaurant may be into its second decade but still looks as dapper as ever. The service is smooth and the room was designed with conviviality in mind. The hugely appealing menu covers all regions; unfussy presentation and superb ingredients allow natural flavours to shine.
➜ Pan-fried scallops with celeriac purée and saffron vinaigrette. Cornish red mullet wrapped in Parma ham with fennel and tomato sauce. Gorgonzola panna cotta, chocolate crumble, pear foam and honey ice cream.

Carte £ 37/63

Town plan: 29AJ2-r - 8 Seymour St. ⊠ W1H 7JZ – ⊖ Marble Arch – ℰ 020 7935 9088
– www.locandalocatelli.com – Closed 25-26 December and 1 January

XXX Roux at The Landau   🗚 ⇔

FRENCH · ELEGANT Grand, oval-shaped hotel restaurant run under the aegis of the Roux organisation. Classical, French-influenced cooking is the order of the day, but a lighter style of cuisine using the occasional twist is also emerging.

Menu £ 39 – Carte £ 43/79

Town plan: 30AM1-n - *Langham Hotel, 1c Portland Pl., Regent St. ⊠ W1B 1JA – ⊖ Oxford Circus – ℰ 020 7636 1000 – www.rouxatthelandau.com – Closed Saturday lunch and Sunday*

XXX Orrery   🍴 🗚 ⇔

MODERN CUISINE · NEIGHBOURHOOD These are actually converted stables from the 19C but, such is the elegance and style of the building, you'd never know. Featured is elaborate, modern European cooking; dishes are strong on presentation and come with the occasional twist.

Menu £ 30/55

Town plan: 18Q4-a - *55 Marylebone High St ⊠ W1U 5RB – ⊖ Regent's Park – ℰ 020 7616 8000 (booking essential) – www.orrery-restaurant.co.uk*

XX Texture (Agnar Sverrisson)   🕸 🗚 ⇔
🕸

CREATIVE · DESIGN Technically skilled but light and invigorating cooking from an Icelandic chef-owner, who uses ingredients from his homeland. Bright restaurant with high ceiling and popular adjoining champagne bar. Pleasant service from keen staff, ready with a smile.

→ Norwegian King crab with coconut, ginger, lime leaf and lemongrass. Black Angus rib-eye with ox cheek, horseradish and olive oil béarnaise. Icelandic skyr with vanilla ice cream, rye breadcrumbs and Yorkshire rhubarb.

Menu £ 29/85 – Carte £ 50/84

Town plan: 30AK2-p - *34 Portman St ⊠ W1H 7BY – ⊖ Marble Arch – ℰ 020 7224 0028 – www.texture-restaurant.co.uk – Closed first 2 weeks August, 1 week Easter, Christmas-New Year, Sunday and Monday*

XX Piquet 🄽   🍸 ⅋ 🗚 🐾 ⇔

FRENCH · BISTRO Smoothly run, elegantly dressed basement bistro deluxe. Classic French dishes are made using the finest Kentish produce; portions are generous and pack a flavoursome punch. Cocktails and small plates in the Fir Room upstairs.

Menu £ 24 – Carte £ 29/59

Town plan: 31AN2-v - *92-94 Newman St ⊠ W1T 3EZ – ⊖ Tottenham Court Rd – ℰ 020 3826 4500 – www.piquet-restaurant.co.uk – Closed 25-26 December, 1-2 January and Sunday dinner*

XX Lurra 🄽   🍴 🗚 🎐

BASQUE · DESIGN Its name means 'land' in Basque and reflects their use of the freshest produce, cooked over a charcoal grill. Choose tasty nibbles or sharing plates like 14 year old Galician beef, whole grilled turbot or slow-cooked shoulder of lamb.

Carte £ 25/65

Town plan: 29AJ2-c - *9 Seymour Pl ⊠ W1H 5BA – ⊖ Marble Arch – ℰ 020 7724 4545 – www.lurra.co.uk – Closed Monday lunch and Sunday dinner*

XX Bernardi's 🄽   🍸 🗚 🔲 ⇔

ITALIAN · NEIGHBOURHOOD A modern neighbourhood Italian: chic yet relaxed and with a friendly atmosphere. Pop in for breakfast, brunch, lunch, dinner or cicchetti and cocktails; everything is homemade and dishes are vibrantly flavoured, with a lightness of touch.

Menu £ 18 (weekday lunch) – Carte £ 30/42

Town plan: 29AJ2-x - *62 Seymour St ⊠ W1H 5BN – ⊖ Marble Arch – ℰ 020 3826 7940 – www.bernardis.co.uk*

✗✗ L'Autre Pied ⒶⒸ ⒾⓋ

MODERN CUISINE · DESIGN This sibling of Pied à Terre in Charlotte Street has a more relaxed feel and a real sense of neighbourhood; ask for a table by the window to better enjoy the local 'village' feel. The European-influenced food is modern without being unfamiliar.

Menu £ 29/50

Town plan: 30AK1-d - *5-7 Blandford St.* ✉ *W1U 3DB* – ⊖ *Bond Street*
– ✆ *020 7486 9696* – *www.lautrepied.co.uk* – *Closed 4 days Christmas, 1 January and Sunday dinner*

✗✗ Latium ⒶⒸ

ITALIAN · NEIGHBOURHOOD An Italian stalwart with warm, welcoming service, a contemporary look and a loyal following. The menu focuses on Lazio but travels the length of Italy for inspiration; 'fatto a casa' is their motto and fresh pasta, their speciality.

Menu £ 21 (weekdays) – Carte £ 28/42

Town plan: 31AN1-n - *21 Berners St.* ✉ *W1T 3LP* – ⊖ *Oxford Circus*
– ✆ *020 7323 9123* – *www.latiumrestaurant.com* – *Closed 25-26 December, 1 January and lunch Saturday-Sunday*

✗✗ Berners Tavern ♿ ⒶⒸ 🖵 ⇔

MODERN BRITISH · BRASSERIE What was once a hotel ballroom is now a very glamorous restaurant, with every inch of wall filled with gilt-framed pictures. Jason Atherton has put together an appealing, accessible menu and the cooking is satisfying and assured.

Menu £ 25 (lunch) – Carte £ 34/67

Town plan: 31AN2-b - *The London Edition Hotel, 10 Berners St* ✉ *W1T 3NP*
– ⊖ *Tottenham Court Road* – ✆ *020 7908 7979*
– *www.bernerstavern.com*

✗✗ Royal China Club ⒶⒸ ⒾⓋ

CHINESE · ELEGANT 'The Club' is the glittering bauble in the Royal China chain but along with the luxurious feel of the room comes an appealing sense of calm. Their lunchtime dim sum is very good; at dinner try their more unusual Cantonese dishes.

Carte £ 32/70

Town plan: 30AK1-c - *40-42 Baker St* ✉ *W1U 7AJ* – ⊖ *Baker Street*
– ✆ *020 7486 3898* – *www.royalchinagroup.co.uk* – *Closed 25-27 December*

✗✗ Galvin Bistrot de Luxe 🌂 ♿ ⒶⒸ 🍷 ⇔

FRENCH · BISTRO Firmly established modern Gallic bistro with ceiling fans, globe lights and wood-panelled walls. Satisfying and precisely cooked classic French dishes from the Galvin brothers. The elegant basement cocktail bar adds to the comfy feel.

Menu £ 22/24 (weekdays) – Carte £ 33/55

Town plan: 30AK1-f - *66 Baker St.* ✉ *W1U 7DJ* – ⊖ *Baker Street*
– ✆ *020 7935 4007* – *www.galvinrestaurants.com* – *Closed dinner 24 December-26 December and 1 January*

✗✗ Chiltern Firehouse 🌂 ⒶⒸ 🖵 ⇔

WORLD CUISINE · FASHIONABLE How appropriate – one of the hottest tickets in town is a converted fire station. The room positively bursts with energy but what makes this celebrity hangout unusual is that the food is rather good. Nuno Mendes' menu is full of vibrant North and South American dishes that are big on flavour.

Carte £ 37/65

Town plan: 30AK1-a - *Chiltern Firehouse Hotel, 1 Chiltern St* ✉ *W1U 7PA*
– ⊖ *Baker Street* – ✆ *020 7073 7676* – *www.chilternfirehouse.com*

XX The Wallace

MODERN BRITISH · FRIENDLY Large glass-roofed courtyard on the ground floor of Hertford House, home to the splendid Wallace Collection. Menu of Modern British dishes, with plenty to please vegetarians. The ambience is sedate and service is smooth and unruffled.

Menu £ 23 – Carte £ 31/48

Town plan: 30AK1-2-k - Hertford House, Manchester Sq ⊠ W1U 3BN
– ⊖ Bond Street – ℰ 020 7563 9505
– www.peytonandbyrne.co.uk/the-wallace-restaurant/index.html – lunch only and dinner Friday-Saturday – Closed 24-26 December

XX Beast   🕭 AC

MEATS AND GRILLS · ELEGANT An underground banquet hall with three exceedingly long tables set for communal dining. The main event is a perfectly cooked hunk of rib-eye steak and a large platter of succulent warm King crab. Bring a big appetite and a fat wallet.

Carte £ 60/100

Town plan: 30AL2-d - 3 Chapel Pl ⊠ W1G 0BG – ⊖ Bond Street
– ℰ 020 7495 1816 – www.beastrestaurant.co.uk – Closed Sunday, lunch Monday-Wednesday and bank holidays

XX sixtyone   🕭 AC ⇔

MODERN BRITISH · ELEGANT A joint venture between chef Arnaud Stevens and Searcy's, in a space leased from the Montcalm hotel. The light-filled room is stylish and slick with an eye-catching ceiling display. British cooking is modern and at times quite playful.

Menu £ 25 (lunch and early dinner) – Carte £ 33/84

Town plan: 29AJ2-q - Montcalm Hotel, 61 Upper Berkeley St ⊠ W1H 7TW
– ⊖ Marble Arch – ℰ 020 7958 3222 – www.montcalm.co.uk – Closed Sunday and Monday

XX Dickie Fitz 🆕   🍴 🏠 🕭 AC 🔲

MODERN CUISINE · FRIENDLY A light and airy restaurant with soft yellow banquettes and a striking glass-panelled, art deco inspired staircase. Cooking is full of flavour and originality, with a subtle mix of Australian, Pacific and Asian influences.

Carte £ 25/46

Town plan: 31AN1-s - 48 Newman St ⊠ W1T 1QQ – ⊖ Goodge Street
– ℰ 020 3667 1445 – www.dickiefitz.co.uk – Closed Sunday dinner and bank holiday Monday

XX Percy & Founders   🍴 🏠 🕭 AC 🔲 ⇔

MODERN CUISINE · BRASSERIE Where Middlesex hospital once stood is now a residential development that includes this all-day operation. It's a mix between a smart pub and a modern brasserie and the kitchen brings quite a refined touch to the seasonal menu.

Carte £ 25/49

Town plan: 31AN1-f - 1 Pearson Sq, (off Mortimer St) ⊠ W1T 3BF
– ⊖ Goodge Street – ℰ 020 3761 0200 – www.percyandfounders.co.uk

XX Archipelago   AC

CREATIVE · EXOTIC DÉCOR Eccentric decoration that makes you feel you're in a bazaar. The exotic menu reads like an inventory at an omnivore's safari park; it could include crocodile, zebra and wildebeest.

Carte £ 32/46

Town plan: 30AM1-e - 53 Cleveland St ⊠ W1T 4JJ – ⊖ Goodge Street
– ℰ 020 7637 9611 – www.archipelago-restaurant.co.uk – Closed 24-28 December, Saturday lunch, Sunday and bank holidays

Bookatable
by Michelin

Discover Restaurants You Love

Bookatable by Michelin is Europe's leading restaurant reservations website: helping millions of diners make bookings at restaurants they love. Discover **gastro pubs** and **high street favourites**, **Michelin star restaurants** and hot-off-the-press deals, and make free, instantly confirmed bookings.

www.bookatable.co.uk

A service of

XX Fischer's   🅰 ⬚

AUSTRIAN · BRASSERIE An Austrian café and konditorei that summons the spirit of old Vienna, from the owners of The Wolseley et al. Open all day; breakfast is a highlight – the viennoiserie are great. Schnitzels are also good; upgrade to a Holstein.

Carte £ 29/47

Town plan: 30AK1-b - *50 Marylebone High St ⊠ W1U 5HN* – ⊖ *Baker Street*
– *℘ 020 7466 5501 – www.fischers.co.uk*
– *Closed 24-25 December and 1 January*

XX The Providores   🅰 🏮

CREATIVE · TRENDY Packed ground floor for tapas; upstairs for innovative fusion cooking, with spices and ingredients from around the world, including Australasia. Starter-sized dishes at dinner allow for greater choice.

Menu £ 34 (dinner) – Carte £ 35/49

Town plan: 30AK1-y - *109 Marylebone High St. ⊠ W1U 4RX* – ⊖ *Bond Street*
– *℘ 020 7935 6175 – www.theprovidores.co.uk*
– *Closed 25-26 December*

XX Iberica Marylebone   🅰 🏮 ⬚

SPANISH · FAMILY Some prefer the intimacy of upstairs, others the bustle of the ground floor with its bar and deli. Along with an impressive array of Iberico hams are colourful dishes to share, such as glossy black rice with cuttlefish and prawns.

Menu £ 22 (weekday dinner) – Carte £ 14/46

Town plan: 18Q4-x - *195 Great Portland St ⊠ W1W 5PS*
– ⊖ *Great Portland Street* – *℘ 020 7636 8650 – www.ibericarestaurants.com*
– *Closed 24-26 December, Sunday dinner and bank holidays*

XX Les 110 de Taillevent 🅝   🕸 🅰

FRENCH · ELEGANT Ornate high ceilings and deep green banquettes create an elegant look for this brasserie deluxe. Dishes are firmly in the French vein and they offer 110 wines by the glass: 4 different pairings for each dish, in 4 different price brackets.

Menu £ 30 – Carte £ 35/67

Town plan: 30AL2-f - *16 Cavendish Sq ⊠ W1G 9DD* – ⊖ *Oxford Circus*
– *℘ 020 3141 6016 – www.les-110-taillevent-london.com/ – Closed 7-29 August,
25 December and 1 January*

XX Royal China   🅰 🕃

CHINESE · EXOTIC DÉCOR Barbequed meats, assorted soups and stir-fries attract plenty of large groups to this smart and always bustling Cantonese restaurant. Over 40 different types of dim sum served during the day.

Menu £ 30 (lunch)/38 – Carte £ 20/74

Town plan: 30AK1-h - *24-26 Baker St ⊠ W1U 7AB* – ⊖ *Baker Street*
– *℘ 020 7487 4688 – www.royalchinagroup.co.uk*

X Trishna (Karam Sethi)   🅰 🕃 ⬚
🕸

INDIAN · NEIGHBOURHOOD Double-fronted, modern Indian restaurant dressed in an elegant, understated style. The coast of southwest India provides the influences and the food is balanced, satisfying and executed with care – the tasting menus provide a good all-round experience.
→ Aloo shakarkandi chaat. Bream with green chilli, coriander and smoked tomato kachumber. Kheer with cardamom, fig, raisin and pistachio.

Menu £ 35 (lunch) – Carte £ 26/46

Town plan: 30AK1-r *15-17 Blandford St. ⊠ W1U 3DG* – ⊖ *Baker Street*
– *℘ 020 7935 5624 – www.trishnalondon.com – Closed 25-27 December and
1-3 January*

Portland
⊗⊗ 🅰🅲 ♿

🎗 MODERN CUISINE · INTIMATE A no-frills, pared-down restaurant that exudes honesty. One look at the menu and you know you'll eat well: it twists and turns on a daily basis and the combinations just sound right together. Dishes are crisp and unfussy but with depth and real understanding – quite something for such a young team.

→ Celeriac and grain risotto, scorched cod cheek and nettle sauce. Cornish monkfish with courgette, preserved lemon and almond. Steamed chocolate & ale cake, beer caramel and barley ice cream.

Carte £ 35/52

Town plan: 30AM1-p – 113 Great Portland St ⊠ W1W 6QQ
– ⊖ Great Portland Street – ℰ 020 7436 3261 (booking essential)
– www.portlandrestaurant.co.uk – Closed Sunday

Lima Fitzrovia
🍸 🅰🅲 ⊛

🎗 PERUVIAN · NEIGHBOURHOOD Lima Fitzrovia is one of those restaurants that just makes you feel good about life – and that's even without the Pisco Sours. The Peruvian food at this informal, fun place is the ideal antidote to times of austerity: it's full of punchy, invigorating flavours and fantastically vivid colours.

→ Braised octopus with purple corn and Botija olives. Beef with yellow potato purée and cow's milk. Dulce de leche ice cream with bee pollen.

Menu £ 25 (lunch and early dinner) – Carte £ 41/53

Town plan: 31AN1-h – 31 Rathbone Pl ⊠ W1T 1JH – ⊖ Goodge Street
– ℰ 020 3002 2640 – www.limalondongroup.com/fitzrovia – Closed Monday
lunch and bank holidays

Social Wine & Tapas
⊗⊗ 🅰🅲 🍴

MEDITERRANEAN CUISINE · NEIGHBOURHOOD Another from the Jason Atherton stable, and the name says it all. Urban styling, with wines on display; sit in the moodily lit basement. A mix of Spanish and Mediterranean dishes, with some Atherton classics too; desserts are a highlight.

Menu £ 20 (lunch) – Carte £ 15/36

Town plan: 30AK2-t – 39 James St ⊠ W1U 1DL – ⊖ Bond Street
– ℰ 020 7993 3257 (bookings not accepted) – www.socialwineandtapas.com
– Closed bank holidays

Picture Fitzrovia
🍸 🅰🅲 🍴

🍇 MODERN BRITISH · SIMPLE An ex Arbutus and Wild Honey triumvirate have created this cool, great-value restaurant. The look may be a little stark but the delightful staff add warmth. The small plates are vibrant and colourful, and the flavours are assured.

Menu £ 45 – Carte £ 24/37

Town plan: 30AM1-t – 110 Great Portland St. ⊠ W1W 6PQ – ⊖ Oxford Circus
– ℰ 020 7637 7892 – www.picturerestaurant.co.uk – Closed Sunday and bank
holidays

Foley's 🆕
🍸 🅰🅲 🍴

🍇 WORLD CUISINE · NEIGHBOURHOOD Cosy up in one of the ground floor booths or head downstairs to the engine room of this lively, well-run restaurant, with its busy open kitchen and counter seating, and its barrel-vaulted caves for six. Vibrant, original small plates reflect the international spice trail; 3 or 4 dishes will suffice.

Carte £ 23/30

Town plan: 30AM1-f - 23 Foley St ⊠ W1W 6DU – ⊖ Goodge Street
– ℰ 020 3137 1302 (booking advisable) – www.foleysrestaurant.co.uk – Closed
Sunday

Riding House Café
🍸 🅰🅲 🔌 🍴 ♿

MODERN CUISINE · RUSTIC It's less a café, more a large, quirkily designed, all-day New York style brasserie and cocktail bar. The small plates have more zing than the main courses. The 'unbookable' side of the restaurant is the more fun part.

Carte £ 23/41

Town plan: 30AM1-k - 43-51 Great Titchfield St ⊠ W1W 7PQ – ⊖ Oxford Circus
– ℰ 020 7927 0840 – www.ridinghousecafe.co.uk – Closed 25-26 December

✗ Mac & Wild 🅽   [AC]

SCOTTISH · FRIENDLY The owner of this 'Highland restaurant' is the son of an Ardgay butcher – it is all about their wild venison and top quality game and seafood from Scotland. Don't miss the 'wee plates' like the deliriously addictive haggis pops. There's also a choice of over 100 whiskies.

Carte £ 23/50

Town plan: 30AM1-a - 65 Great Tichfield St ⊠ W1W 7PS – ⊖ Oxford Circus – ℰ 020 7637 0510 – www.macandwild.com – Closed Sunday dinner

✗ Opso   🍷 🍴 ⬩ 🖥 🗄 ⬩

GREEK · NEIGHBOURHOOD A modern Greek restaurant which has proved a good fit for the neighbourhood – and not just because it's around the corner from the Hellenic Centre. It serves small sharing plates that mix the modern with the traditional.

Menu £ 15 (weekday lunch) – Carte £ 17/45

Town plan: 30AK1-s 10 Paddington St ⊠ W1U 5QL – ⊖ Baker Street – ℰ 020 7487 5088 – www.opso.co.uk – Closed 23 December-3 January and Sunday dinner

✗ Donostia   🖥

BASQUE · TAPAS BAR The two young owners were inspired by the food of San Sebastiàn to open this pintxos and tapas bar. Sit at the counter for Basque classics like cod with pil-pil sauce, chorizo from the native Kintoa pig and slow-cooked pig's cheeks.

Carte £ 10/37

Town plan: 29AJ2-s 10 Seymour Pl ⊠ W1H 7ND – ⊖ Marble Arch – ℰ 020 3620 1845 – www.donostia.co.uk – Closed Christmas, Easter and Monday lunch

✗ Vinoteca   🕸 [AC]

MODERN CUISINE · WINE BAR Follows the formula of the original: great fun, great wines, gutsy and wholesome food, enthusiastic staff and almost certainly a wait for a table. Influences from sunnier parts of Europe, along with some British dishes.

Menu £ 16 (weekday lunch) – Carte £ 21/36

Town plan: 29AJ2-v - 15 Seymour Pl. ⊠ W1H 5BD – ⊖ Marble Arch – ℰ 020 7724 7288 (booking advisable) – www.vinoteca.co.uk – Closed Christmas, bank holidays and Sunday dinner

✗ Bonnie Gull

SEAFOOD · SIMPLE Sweet Bonnie Gull calls itself a 'seafood shack' – a reference perhaps to its modest beginnings as a pop-up. Start with an order from the raw bar then go for a classic like Cullen skink, a whole Devon cock crab or fish and chips.

Carte £ 22/44

Town plan: 30AM1-b - 21a Foley St ⊠ W1W 6DS – ⊖ Goodge Street – ℰ 020 7436 0921 (booking essential) – www.bonniegull.com – Closed 25 December-2 January

✗ Picture Maylebone 🅽   🍷 🍴 [AC]

MODERN BRITISH · DESIGN After the box office success of the first Picture comes this follow-up. The owners clearly understand what makes a good neighbourhood restaurant – they offer a flexible, well-priced menu, a loyalty scheme and BYO Mondays.

Menu £ 22 (lunch) – Carte £ 27/37

Town plan: 30AL1-m - 19 New Cavendish St ⊠ W1G 9TZ – ⊖ Bond Street – ℰ 020 7935 0058 – www.picturerestaurant.co.uk – Closed Sunday and bank holidays

✗ Dinings

JAPANESE · COSY It's hard not to be charmed by this sweet little Japanese place, with its ground floor counter and basement tables. Its strengths lie with the more creative, contemporary dishes; sharing is recommended but prices can be steep.

Carte £ 24/57

Town plan: 29AH1-c - 22 Harcourt St. ⊠ W1H 4HH – ⊖ Edgware Road – ℰ 020 7723 0666 (booking essential) – www.dinings.co.uk – Closed Christmas

Zoilo

ARGENTINIAN • FRIENDLY It's all about sharing so plonk yourself at the counter and discover Argentina's regional specialities. Typical dishes include braised pig head croquettes or grilled scallops with pork belly, and there's an appealing all-Argentinian wine list.

Menu £10 (weekdays) – Carte £20/46

Town plan: 30AK2-z - *9 Duke St.* ✉ *W1U 3EG* – ⊖ *Bond Street* – ✆ *020 7486 9699* – *www.zoilo.co.uk*

Newman Arms Ⓝ

MODERN BRITISH • FRIENDLY A charming Georgian pub with a quaint wood-panelled upstairs dining room – ask to sit at one of the window tables. The menu may be short but every ingredient is super-fresh; often arriving from the sea or field within 24 hours. Cornish beef and lamb are the stars – along with the fish from the day boats.

Menu £15 (weekday lunch) – Carte £26/39

Town plan: 31AN1-s - *23 Rathbone St* ✉ *W1T 1NG* – ⊖ *Goodge St* – ✆ *020 3643 6285* – *www.newmanarmspub.com* – *Closed 24-26 December and bank holidays*

Portman

MODERN CUISINE • PUB The condemned on their way to Tyburn Tree gallows would take their last drink here. Now it's an urbane pub with a formal upstairs dining room. The ground floor is more fun for enjoying the down-to-earth menu.

Carte £25/48

Town plan: 29AJ2-n - *51 Upper Berkeley St* ✉ *W1H 7QW* – ⊖ *Marble Arch.* – ✆ *020 7723 8996* – *www.theportmanmarylebone.com*

St James's

Ritz

GRAND LUXURY • CLASSIC World famous hotel, opened in 1906 as a fine example of Louis XVI architecture and decoration. Elegant Palm Court famed for its afternoon tea. Many of the lavishly appointed and luxurious rooms and suites overlook the park.

136 rooms – †£355/875 ††£430/1130 – ☕£35 – 24 suites

Town plan: 30AM4-c - *150 Piccadilly* ✉ *W1J 9BR* – ⊖ *Green Park* – ✆ *020 7493 8181* – *www.theritzlondon.com*

✿ **Ritz Restaurant** – See restaurant listing

Haymarket

LUXURY • PERSONALISED Smart and spacious hotel in John Nash Regency building, with a stylish blend of modern and antique furnishings. Large, comfortable bedrooms in soothing colours. Impressive basement pool is often used for private parties.

50 rooms – †£230/320 ††£230/1395 – ☕£15 – 3 suites

Town plan: 31AP3-x - *1 Suffolk Pl.* ✉ *SW1Y 4HX* – ⊖ *Piccadilly Circus* – ✆ *020 7470 4000* – *www.haymarkethotel.com*

Brumus – See restaurant listing

Sofitel London St James

LUXURY • ELEGANT Great location for this international hotel in a Grade II former bank. The triple-glazed bedrooms are immaculately kept; the spa is one of the best around. The bar is inspired by Coco Chanel; the lounge by an English rose garden.

183 rooms – †£240/400 ††£240/400 – ☕£25 – 18 suites

Town plan: 31AP3-a - *6 Waterloo Pl.* ✉ *SW1Y 4AN* – ⊖ *Piccadilly Circus* – ✆ *020 7747 2200* – *www.sofitelstjames.com*

Balcon – See restaurant listing

🏠 Dukes   ✿ ⌚ 🛏 ⬆ 🅰🄲 🔱

TRADITIONAL · CLASSIC The wonderfully located Dukes has been steadily updating its image over the last few years, despite being over a century old. Bedrooms are now fresh and uncluttered and the atmosphere less starchy. The basement restaurant offers a modern menu, with dishes that are original in look and elaborate in construction.

90 rooms – ♦£ 346/440 ♦♦£ 400/490 – ⌚£ 24 – 6 suites

Town plan: 30AM4-f - *35 St James's Pl.* ✉ *SW1A 1NY* – ⊖ *Green Park*
- ✆ *020 7491 4840* – *www.dukeshotel.com*

🏠 Stafford   ✿ ⌚ 🛏 ⬆ 🅰🄲 🔱

TOWNHOUSE · GRAND LUXURY Styles itself as a 'country house in the city'; its bedrooms are divided between the main house, converted 18C stables and a more modern mews. Legendary American bar a highlight; traditional British food served in the restaurant.

104 rooms – ♦£ 350/535 ♦♦£ 350/535 – ⌚£ 25 – 15 suites

Town plan: 30AM4-u - *16-18 St James's Pl.* ✉ *SW1A 1NJ* – ⊖ *Green Park*
- ✆ *020 7493 0111* – *www.thestaffordlondon.com*

🏠 St James's Hotel and Club   ⌚ ⬆ 🅰🄲 ✗ 🔱

BUSINESS · MODERN 1890s house, formerly a private club, in a wonderfully central yet quiet location. Modern, boutique-style interior with over 300 European works of art from the '20s to the '50s. Fine finish to the compact but well-equipped bedrooms.

60 rooms – ♦£ 265/550 ♦♦£ 265/550 – ⌚£ 23 – 10 suites

Town plan: 30AM4-k - *7-8 Park Pl.* ✉ *SW1A 1LS* – ⊖ *Green Park*
- ✆ *020 7316 1600* – *www.stjameshotelandclub.com*

  ✸ **Seven Park Place** – See restaurant listing

🍴🍴 Ritz Restaurant   🪑 🅰🄲 🕙

✸ **CLASSIC CUISINE · LUXURY** Thanks to the lavishness of its Louis XVI decoration, there is nowhere grander than The Ritz. The classic cuisine uses extravagant ingredients along with subtle contemporary elements to lift dishes to new heights while still respecting their heritage. The formal service is now more youthful and enthusiastic.

➔ Langoustine with broad beans and mint. Loin of lamb with pommes Anna and shallot & herb crust. Custard tart with poached rhubarb and ginger ice cream.

Menu £ 49 (weekday lunch) – Carte £ 72/103

Town plan: 30AM4-c - *Ritz Hotel, 150 Piccadilly* ✉ *W1J 9BR* – ⊖ *Green Park*
- ✆ *020 7300 2370* – *www.theritzlondon.com*

🍴🍴 Seven Park Place   🅰🄲 ⬅

✸ **MODERN CUISINE · COSY** William Drabble's cooking is all about the quality of the produce, much of which comes from the Lake District, and his confident cooking allows natural flavours to shine. This diminutive restaurant is concealed within the hotel and divided into two; ask for the warmer, gilded back room.

➔ Poached native lobster tail with asparagus and champagne hollandaise. Griddled fillet of sea bass with salt-baked celeriac, apple and truffle. Victoria pineapple confit with vanilla and coconut sorbet.

Menu £ 32 (weekday lunch)/63

Town plan: 30AM4-k - *St James's Hotel and Club, 7-8 Park Pl* ✉ *SW1A 1LS*
- ⊖ *Green Park* – ✆ *020 7316 1615 (booking essential)*
- *www.stjameshotelandclub.com* – *Closed Sunday and Monday*

🍴🍴 Chutney Mary   🍸 🅰🄲 🕙 ⬅

INDIAN · ELEGANT After 25 years in Chelsea, one of London's pioneering Indian restaurants is now establishing itself in a more central position. Spicing is understated; classics are done well; and some regional dishes have been subtly updated.

Menu £ 30 (weekday lunch) – Carte £ 35/60

Town plan: 30AM4-c - *73 St James's St* ✉ *SW1A 1PH* – ⊖ *Green Park*
- ✆ *020 7629 6688* – *www.chutneymary.com* – *Closed Sunday*

XxX The Wolseley   🅰️ 🔲 🎧 ⟷

MODERN CUISINE · FASHIONABLE This feels like a grand and glamorous European coffee house, with its pillars and high vaulted ceiling. Appealing menus offer everything from caviar to a hot-dog. It's open from early until late and boasts a large celebrity following.

Carte £ 22/68

Town plan: 30AM3-q - *160 Piccadilly* ✉ *W1J 9EB* – ⊖ *Green Park*
– 𝒞 020 7499 6996 (booking essential) – www.thewolseley.com – Closed dinner 24 December

XxX Milos Ⓝ   🍹 🦽 🅰️ ⟷

SEAFOOD · ELEGANT London's branch of this international group of Greek seafood estiatorios makes the most of the grand listed building it occupies. Choose from the impressive display of fish flown in daily from Greek waters – and prepare for a sizeable bill.

Menu £ 29/49 – Carte £ 58/130

Town plan: 31AP3-k - *1 Regent St* ✉ *SW1Y 4NR* – ⊖ *Piccadilly Circus*
– 𝒞 020 7839 2080 – www.milos.ca – Closed 25 December and Sunday

XX Balcon   🅰️ 🔲

FRENCH · BRASSERIE A former banking hall with vast chandeliers and a grand brasserie look. It's open from breakfast onwards and the menu features French classics like snails and cassoulet; try the charcuterie from Wales and France.

Menu £ 20 (lunch) – Carte £ 25/45

Town plan: 31AP3-a - *Sofitel London St James Hotel, 8 Pall Mall.* ✉ *SW1Y 4AN*
– ⊖ Piccadilly Circus – 𝒞 020 7389 7820 – www.thebalconlondon.com

XX Matsuri   🅰️ ⟷

JAPANESE · CLASSIC DÉCOR One of London's longest standing traditional Japanese restaurants. Teppanyaki is their speciality; the top-notch ingredients include American Black Angus and Japanese beef. A sushi counter is also available.

Carte £ 30/169

Town plan: 31AN4-w - *15 Bury St.* ✉ *SW1Y 6AL* – ⊖ *Green Park*
– 𝒞 020 7839 1101 – www.matsuri-restaurant.com – Closed 25 December and 1 January

XX Le Caprice   🍸 🅰️ 🎧 🍵

MODERN CUISINE · FASHIONABLE For over 35 years Le Caprice's effortlessly sophisticated atmosphere and surroundings have attracted a confident and urbane clientele. The kitchen is well-practised and capable and there's something for everyone on their catch-all menu.

Menu £ 20 (weekday lunch) – Carte £ 32/65

Town plan: 30AM4-h - *Arlington House, Arlington St.* ✉ *SW1A 1RJ*
– ⊖ Green Park – 𝒞 020 7629 2239 – www.le-caprice.co.uk – Closed 24-26 December

XX Sake No Hana   🍹 🅰️

JAPANESE · MINIMALIST A modern Japanese restaurant within a Grade II listed '60s edifice – and proof that you can occasionally find good food at the end of an escalator. As with the great cocktails, the menu is best enjoyed when shared with a group.

Menu £ 31 – Carte £ 22/69

Town plan: 30AM4-n - *23 St James's* ✉ *SW1A 1HA* – ⊖ *Green Park*
– 𝒞 020 7925 8988 – www.sakenohana.com – Closed 25 December and Sunday

XX Boulestin   🍹 🍸 🔲 🍵 ⟷

FRENCH · ELEGANT Nearly a century after Xavier Marcel Boulestin opened his eponymous restaurant showcasing 'Simple French Cooking for English Homes', his spirit has been resurrected at this elegant brasserie, with its lovely courtyard terrace.

Menu £ 25 – Carte £ 33/60

Town plan: 31AN4-s - ✉ *SW1A 1EF* – ⊖ *Green Park* – 𝒞 020 7930 2030
– www.boulestin.com – Closed Sunday and bank holidays

XX Cafe Murano   AC 🍷 ⇔

ITALIAN · FASHIONABLE Angela Hartnett and her chef have created an appealing and flexible menu of delicious North Italian delicacies – the lunch menu is very good value. It's certainly no ordinary café and its popularity means pre-booking is essential.

Menu £ 19 (weekdays)/23 – Carte £ 25/64

Town plan: 30AM4-m - *33 St. James's St* ⊠ *SW1A 1HD* – ⊖ *Green Park*
– ℰ 020 3371 5559 (booking essential) – www.cafemurano.co.uk – Closed Sunday dinner

XX 45 Jermyn St 🄽   🕸 🍷 AC 🖵

MODERN BRITISH · BRASSERIE What was Fortnum & Mason's Fountain restaurant for 60 years is now a bright, contemporary brasserie. The sodas, coupes and floats pay tribute to its past and cooking has a strong British element. Prices can be steep but, in contrast, the well-chosen wine list has very restrained mark-ups.

Carte £ 26/66

Town plan: 31AN3-f - *45 Jermyn St.* ⊠ *SW1 6DN St James's* – ⊖ *Piccadilly Circus*
– ℰ 020 7205 4545 – www.45jermynst.com – Closed 25-26 December

XX Franco's   AC 🖵 🕾

ITALIAN · TRADITIONAL DÉCOR Open from breakfast until late, with a café at the front leading into a smart, clubby restaurant. The menu covers all parts of Italy and includes a popular grill section and plenty of classics.

Menu £ 26 – Carte £ 30/60

Town plan: 30AM3-i - *61 Jermyn St* ⊠ *SW1Y 6LX* – ⊖ *Green Park*
– ℰ 020 7499 2211 (booking essential) – www.francoslondon.com – Closed Sunday and bank holidays

XX Avenue   🕸 🍷 ὀ AC 🖵 🕾 ⇔

MODERN CUISINE · ELEGANT Avenue has gone all American, with a smart look from Russell Sage and a contemporary menu inspired by what's cooking in Manhattan. Wine is also made more of a feature; and, of course, the cocktails at the long, lively bar are great.

Menu £ 25 (weekdays) – Carte dinner £ 32/49

Town plan: 31AN4-y - *7-9 St James's St.* ⊠ *SW1A 1EE* – ⊖ *Green Park*
– ℰ 020 7321 2111 – www.avenue-restaurant.co.uk – Closed Sunday dinner and bank holidays

XX Al Duca   AC 🖵 🕾

ITALIAN · FRIENDLY Cooking which focuses on flavour continues to draw in the regulars at this warm and spirited Italian restaurant. Prices are keen when one considers the central location and service is brisk and confident.

Menu £ 17/30

Town plan: 31AN3-r - *4-5 Duke of York St* ⊠ *SW1Y 6LA* – ⊖ *Piccadilly Circus*
– ℰ 020 7839 3090 – www.alduca-restaurant.co.uk – Closed Easter, 25-26 December, 1 January, Sunday and bank holidays

XX Quaglino's   AC 🕾 ⇔

MODERN CUISINE · DESIGN An updated look, a new bar and live music have added sultriness and energy to this vast, glamorous and colourful restaurant. The kitchen specialises in contemporary brasserie-style food.

Menu £ 20 (weekdays)/30 – Carte £ 36/66

Town plan: 30AM4-j - *16 Bury St* ⊠ *SW1Y 6AJ* – ⊖ *Green Park*
– ℰ 020 7930 6767 – www.quaglinos-restaurant.co.uk – Closed Easter Monday and Sunday dinner

XX Brumus

MODERN CUISINE · FASHIONABLE Pre-theatre dining is an altogether less frenzied activity when you can actually see the theatre from your table. This is a
modern, elegant space with switched-on staff. Stick to the good value set menu
or the 'dish of the day'.

Menu £ 20 – Carte £ 25/61

Town plan: 31AP3-x – Haymarket Hotel, 1 Suffolk Pl ✉ SW1Y 4HX
– ⊖ Piccadilly Circus – ✆ 020 7470 4000 – www.haymarkethotel.com

X Portrait

MODERN CUISINE · DESIGN Set on the top floor of National Portrait Gallery with
rooftop local landmark views: a charming spot to dine or enjoy breakfast or afternoon tea. Carefully prepared modern European dishes; good value pre-theatre
and weekend set menus.

Menu £ 27 – Carte £ 34/49

Town plan: 31AP3-n – National Portrait Gallery (3rd floor), St Martin's Pl.
✉ WC2H 0HE – ⊖ Charing Cross – ✆ 020 7312 2490 (booking essential)
– www.npg.org.uk/portraitrestaurant – lunch only and dinner Thursday-Saturday
– Closed 24-26 December

X Chop Shop

MEATS AND GRILLS · SIMPLE Spread over two floors and with an ersatz industrial look, this lively spot could be in Manhattan's Meatpacking district. Start with
a cocktail, then order 'jars', 'crocks' or 'planks' of mousses, meatballs and
cheeses; then it's the main event – great steaks and chops.

Menu £ 19/35 – Carte £ 24/41

Town plan: 31AP3-c – 66 Haymarket ✉ SW1Y 4RF – ⊖ Piccadilly Circus
– ✆ 020 7842 8501 – www.chopshopuk.com

X Shoryu

JAPANESE · SIMPLE Owned by the Japan Centre opposite and specialising in
Hakata tonkotsu ramen. The base is a milky broth made from pork bones to
which is added hosomen noodles, egg and assorted toppings. Its restorative
powers are worth queuing for. There are a two larger branches in Soho.

Carte £ 20/40

Town plan: 31AN3-s – 9 Regent St. ✉ SW1Y 4LR – ⊖ Piccadilly Circus (bookings
not accepted) – www.shoryuramen.com – Closed 25 December and 1 January

Soho

Soho

LUXURY · PERSONALISED Stylish and fashionable hotel that mirrors the vibrancy of the neighbourhood. Boasts two screening rooms, a comfortable drawing room and up-to-the-minute bedrooms; some vivid, others more muted but all
with hi-tech extras.

96 rooms – †£ 235/340 ††£ 285/540 – ⊇ £ 14 – 7 suites

Town plan: 31AN2-n – 4 Richmond Mews ✉ W1D 3DH
– ⊖ Tottenham Court Road – ✆ 020 7559 3000 – www.sohohotel.com

Refuel – See restaurant listing

Ham Yard

LUXURY · ELEGANT Opened in 2014, this stylish hotel from the Firmdale group
is set around a courtyard – a haven of tranquillity in the West End. Each of the
rooms is different but all are supremely comfortable. There's also a great roof
terrace, a theatre, a fully stocked library and bar... and even a bowling alley.

91 rooms – †£ 260/380 ††£ 260/380 – ⊇ £ 14 – 2 suites

Town plan: 31AN3-p – 1 Ham Yard, ✉ W1D 7DT – ⊖ Piccadilly Circus
– ✆ 020 3642 2000 – www.firmdalehotels.com

Ham Yard – See restaurant listing

🏨 Café Royal ☆ ▣ ⑨ ⋔ ㎙ ☰ ♿ AC ℀ 🏊

GRAND LUXURY · HISTORIC One of the most famous names of the London social scene for the last 150 years is now a luxury hotel. The bedrooms are beautiful, elegant and discreet and the wining and dining options many and varied
– they include the gloriously rococo Oscar Wilde bar, once home to the iconic
Grill Room.

160 rooms – ♦£ 330/500 ♦♦£ 330/600 – ☲ £ 32 – 16 suites

Town plan: 31AN3-r - 68 Regent St ⊠ W1B 4DY – ⊖ Piccadilly Circus
– ℰ 020 7406 3333 – www.hotelcaferoyal.com

🏨 Dean Street Townhouse ⬍ AC ℀

TOWNHOUSE · CLASSIC In the heart of Soho and where bedrooms range from
tiny to bigger; the latter have roll-top baths in the room. All are well designed
and come with a good range of extras. Cosy ground floor lounge.

39 rooms – ♦£ 300/450 ♦♦£ 300/550 – ☲ £ 15

Town plan: 31AP2-t - 69-71 Dean St. ⊠ W1D 3SE – ⊖ Piccadilly Circus
– ℰ 020 7434 1775 – www.deanstreettownhouse.com

Dean Street Townhouse Restaurant – See restaurant listing

🏨 Hazlitt's AC ℀

TOWNHOUSE · HISTORIC Dating from 1718, the former house of essayist and
critic William Hazlitt still welcomes many a writer today in its role as a charming
townhouse hotel. It has plenty of character and is warmly run. No restaurant so
breakfast in bed really is the only option – and who is going to object to that?

30 rooms – ♦£ 210/235 ♦♦£ 300/650 – ☲ £ 12

Town plan: 31AP2-u - 6 Frith St ⊠ W1D 3JA – ⊖ Tottenham Court Road
– ℰ 020 7434 1771 – www.hazlittshotel.com

🍴🍴🍴 Quo Vadis AC ▭ 🍷 ⇔

TRADITIONAL BRITISH · FASHIONABLE Owned by the Hart brothers, this Soho
institution dates from the 1920s and is as stylish and handsome as ever. The
menu reads like a selection of all your favourite British dishes – game is always
a highlight. At the end of 2016 it is giving up space to accommodate Barrafina.

Menu £ 20 – Carte £ 33/48

Town plan: 31AP2-v - 26-29 Dean St ⊠ W1D 3LL – ⊖ Tottenham Court Road
– ℰ 020 7437 9585 – www.quovadissoho.co.uk – Closed 25-26 December,
1 January and bank holidays

🍴🍴🍴 Gauthier - Soho AC ﹗♡ ⇔

FRENCH · INTIMATE Detached from the rowdier elements of Soho is this charming Georgian townhouse, with dining spread over three floors. Alex Gauthier offers assorted menus of his classically based cooking, with vegetarians particularly
well looked after.

Menu £ 18 (lunch)/75

Town plan: 31AP2-k - 21 Romilly St ⊠ W1D 5AF – ⊖ Leicester Square
– ℰ 020 7494 3111 – www.gauthiersoho.co.uk – Closed Monday lunch, Sunday and
bank holidays except Good Friday

🍴🍴🍴 Red Fort 🍸 AC 🍷

INDIAN · EXOTIC DÉCOR A smart, stylish and professionally run Indian restaurant that has been a feature in Soho since 1983. Cooking is based on the Mughal
Court and uses much UK produce such as Welsh lamb; look out for more unusual
choices like rabbit.

Menu £ 15/59 – Carte £ 32/65

Town plan: 31AP2-z - 77 Dean St. ⊠ W1D 3SH – ⊖ Tottenham Court Road
– ℰ 020 7437 2525 (bookings advisable at dinner) – www.redfort.co.uk – Closed
Sunday

XXX Imperial China 🛎️ ⟷

CHINESE · ELEGANT Sharp service and comfortable surroundings are not the only things that set this restaurant apart: the Cantonese cooking exudes freshness and vitality, whether that's the steamed dumplings or the XO minced pork with fine beans.

Menu £ 20/36 – Carte £ 16/96

Town plan: 31AP3-e - *White Bear Yard, 25a Lisle St* ⊠ *WC2H 7BA*
– ⊖ *Leicester Square* – ℰ *020 7734 3388 (booking advisable)*
– *www.imperialchina-london.com* – *Closed 25 December*

XX Yauatcha Soho 🍷 🛎️ 📋
⭐

CHINESE · DESIGN Refined, delicate and delicious dim sum; ideal for sharing in a group. It's over 10 years old yet the surroundings are still as slick and stylish as ever: choose the lighter, brighter ground floor or the darker, more atmospheric basement.
→ Scallop shui mai. Kung pao chicken with cashew nut. Chocolate 'pebble'.

Menu £ 29 (weekday lunch) – Carte £ 18/61

Town plan: 31AN2-k - *15 Broadwick St* ⊠ *W1F 0DL* – ⊖ *Tottenham Court Road*
– ℰ *020 7494 8888* – *www.yauatcha.com* – *Closed 25 December*

XX Brasserie Zédel 🍷 🛎️
😊

FRENCH · BRASSERIE A grand French brasserie, which is all about inclusivity and accessibility, in a bustling subterranean space restored to its original art deco glory. Expect a roll-call of classic French dishes and some very competitive prices.

Menu £ 13/20 – Carte £ 19/41

Town plan: 31AN3-q - *20 Sherwood St* ⊠ *W1F 7ED* – ⊖ *Piccadilly Circus*
– ℰ *020 7734 4888 (booking advisable)* – *www.brasseriezedel.com* – *Closed 24-25 December and 1 January*

XX Bob Bob Ricard 🍷 🛎️

MODERN CUISINE · VINTAGE Everyone needs a little glamour now and again and this place provides it. The room may be quite small but it sees itself as a grand salon – ask for a booth. The menu is all-encompassing – oysters and caviar to pies and burgers.

Carte £ 32/87

Town plan: 31AN2-s - *1 Upper James St* ⊠ *W1F 9DF* – ⊖ *Oxford Circus*
– ℰ *020 3145 1000* – *www.bobbobricard.com*

XX 100 Wardour St 🆕 🍷 🛎️ 🍸 ⟷

MODERN CUISINE · CONTEMPORARY DÉCOR D&D have reinvented the space formerly occupied by Floridita and the original Marquee Club. At night, head downstairs for cocktails, live music and a modern menu with Japanese and South American influences. In the daytime stay on the ground floor for an all-day menu, a bar and a pop-in/plug-in lounge.

Menu £ 30 (weekday dinner) – Carte £ 17/57

Town plan: 31AN2-v - *100 Wardour St* ⊠ *W1F 0TN* – ⊖ *Tottenham Court Road*
– ℰ *020 7314 4000* – *www.100wardourst.com* – *Closed 25-26 December*

XX Ham Yard 🍷 🏡 ⅾ 🛎️ 🍸

MODERN CUISINE · BRASSERIE An exuberantly decorated restaurant; start with a cocktail – the bitters and syrups are homemade with herbs from the hotel's roof garden. The menu moves with the seasons and the kitchen has the confidence to keep dishes simple.

Menu £ 20 (dinner) – Carte £ 28/46

Town plan: 31AN3-p - *Ham Yard Hotel, 1 Ham Yard,* ⊠ *W1D 7DT*
– ⊖ *Piccadilly Circus* – ℰ *020 3642 1007* – *www.firmdalehotels.com*

XX Dean Street Townhouse Restaurant 🏡 🛎️ 🍸 📶 🍸

MODERN BRITISH · BRASSERIE A Georgian house that's home to a fashionable bar and restaurant which is busy from breakfast onwards. Appealingly classic British food includes some retro dishes and satisfying puddings.

Menu £ 29 – Carte £ 29/44

Town plan: 31AP2-t *Dean Street Townhouse Hotel, 69-71 Dean St.* ⊠ *W1D 3SE*
– ⊖ *Piccadilly Circus* – ℰ *020 7434 1775 (booking essential)*
– *www.deanstreettownhouse.com*

✗✗ Vasco and Piero's Pavilion   [AC] ⇔

ITALIAN · FRIENDLY Regulars and tourists have been flocking to this institution for over 40 years; its longevity is down to a twice daily changing menu of Umbrian-influenced dishes rather than the matter-of-fact service or simple decoration.

Menu £18 (lunch and early dinner) – Carte £25/55

Town plan: 31AN2-b - 15 Poland St ⊠ W1F 8QE – ⊖ Oxford Circus
– ℰ020 7437 8774 (booking essential at lunch) – www.vascosfood.com – Closed Saturday lunch, Sunday and bank holidays

✗✗ Plum Valley   ⇔

CHINESE · DESIGN Its striking black façade makes this modern Chinese restaurant easy to spot in Chinatown. Mostly Cantonese cooking, with occasional forays into Vietnam and Thailand; dim sum is the strength.

Menu £38 – Carte £19/37

Town plan: 31AP3-i - 20 Gerrard St. ⊠ W1D 6JQ – ⊖ Leicester Square
– ℰ020 7494 4366 – Closed 23-24 December

✗✗ Refuel   🍷 & [AC]

MODERN BRITISH · FASHIONABLE At the heart of the cool Soho hotel is their aptly named bar and restaurant. With a menu to suit all moods and wallets, from Dover sole to burgers, and a cocktail list to lift all spirits, it's a fun and bustling spot.

Menu £21/25 – Carte £31/54

Town plan: 31AN2-n - Soho Hotel, 4 Richmond Mews ⊠ W1D 3DH
– ⊖ Tottenham Court Road – ℰ020 7559 3007 – www.sohohotel.com

✗✗ Hix   🍷 [AC] 🕙 🐾 ⇔

TRADITIONAL BRITISH · FASHIONABLE The exterior may hint at exclusivity but inside this big restaurant the atmosphere is fun, noisy and sociable. The room comes decorated with the works of eminent British artists. Expect classic British dishes and ingredients.

Menu £20 (weekday lunch) – Carte £27/65

Town plan: 31AN3-l - 66-70 Brewer St. ⊠ W1F 9UP – ⊖ Piccadilly Circus
– ℰ020 7292 3518 – www.hixsoho.co.uk
– Closed 25-26 December

✗✗ MASH   🎋 🍷 [AC] 🐾 ⇔

MEATS AND GRILLS · BRASSERIE A team from Copenhagen raised the old Titanic and restored the art deco to create this striking 'Modern American Steak House', offering Danish, Nebraskan and Uruguayan beef. A great bar and slick service add to the grown up feel.

Menu £25 – Carte £30/94

Town plan: 31AN3-i - 77 Brewer St ⊠ W1F 9ZN – ⊖ Piccadilly Circus
– ℰ020 7734 2608 – www.mashsteak.co.uk – Closed 24-26 December and Sunday lunch

✗ Social Eating House   🍷 [AC]
❀

MODERN CUISINE · FASHIONABLE There's a something of a Brooklyn vibe to this Jason Atherton restaurant, with its bare brick and raw plastered walls and its speakeasy bar upstairs. It's great fun, very busy and gloriously unstuffy; the menu is an eminently good read, with the best dishes being the simplest ones.
→ Smoked Lincolnshire eel with salt & vinegar potatoes, macadamia and rock samphire. Rack of Herdwick lamb with confit neck, peas and sheep's ricotta. Chocolate crémeux with salted caramel, mascarpone and almond biscotti.

Menu £21 (lunch and early dinner) – Carte £39/57

Town plan: 31AN2-t - 58 Poland St ⊠ W1F 7NR – ⊖ Oxford Circus
– ℰ020 7993 3251 (booking advisable) – www.socialeatinghouse.com – Closed Christmas, Sunday and bank holidays

LONDON ENGLAND

❌ Barrafina   🔠 🍴

SPANISH · TAPAS BAR Be prepared to queue for gaps at the counter at this terrific tapas bar. Wonderfully fresh ingredients allow their natural flavours to shine; the seafood is particularly good. At the end of 2016 it will be rehoused within Quo Vadis, a street away.

→ Pimientos de padrón. Octopus with capers. Créma Catalana.

Carte £ 15/34

Town plan: 31AP2-c - *54 Frith St.* ✉ *W1D 3SL* – ⊖ *Tottenham Court Road*
– ℰ 020 7440 1456 (bookings not accepted) – www.barrafina.co.uk – Closed bank holidays

❌ Dehesa   🐝 🏡 🔠 🍴 ⇔

MEDITERRANEAN CUISINE · TAPAS BAR Repeats the success of its sister restaurant, Salt Yard, by offering flavoursome and appealingly priced Spanish and Italian tapas. Busy, friendly atmosphere in appealing corner location. Terrific drinks list too.

Carte £ 14/36

Town plan: 30AM2-i - *25 Ganton St* ✉ *W1F 9BP* – ⊖ *Oxford Circus*
– ℰ 020 7494 4170 – www.dehesa.co.uk – Closed 25 December

❌ Nopi   🍷 ♿ 🔠 🖵 🍴 🕸

MEDITERRANEAN CUISINE · DESIGN The bright, clean look of Yotam Ottolenghi's charmingly run all-day restaurant matches the fresh, invigorating food. The sharing plates take in the Mediterranean, the Middle East and Asia and the veggie dishes stand out.

Carte £ 34/48

Town plan: 31AN3-g - *21-22 Warwick St.* ✉ *W1B 5NE* – ⊖ *Piccadilly Circus*
– ℰ 020 7494 9584 – www.nopi-restaurant.com
– Closed 25-26 December

❌ Ember Yard   🍷 🔠 🍴 ⇔

MEDITERRANEAN CUISINE · TAPAS BAR Those familiar with the Salt Yard Group will recognise the Spanish and Italian themed menus – but their 4th fun outlet comes with a focus on cooking over charcoal or wood. There's even a seductive smokiness to some of the cocktails.

Carte £ 20/33

Town plan: 31AN2-e - *60 Berwick St* ✉ *W1F 8DX* – ⊖ *Oxford Circus*
– ℰ 020 7439 8057 (booking advisable) – www.emberyard.co.uk – Closed 25-26 December and 1 January

❌ Polpetto   🔠 🍴

ITALIAN · SIMPLE Re-opened by Russell Norman in bigger premises. The style of food is the perfect match for this relaxed environment: the small, seasonally inspired Italian dishes are uncomplicated, appealingly priced and deliver great flavours.

Carte £ 12/18

Town plan: 31AN2-u - *11 Berwick St* ✉ *W1F 0PL* – ⊖ *Tottenham Court Road*
– ℰ 020 7439 8627 – www.polpetto.co.uk
– Closed Sunday

❌ Copita   🔠 🍴

SPANISH · TAPAS BAR Perch on one of the high stools or stay standing and get stuck into the daily menu of small, colourful and tasty dishes. Staff add to the atmosphere and everything on the Spanish wine list comes by the glass or copita.

Carte £ 15/30

Town plan: 31AN2-h - *27 D'Arblay St* ✉ *W1F 8EP* – ⊖ *Oxford Circus*
– ℰ 020 7287 7797 (bookings not accepted) – www.copita.co.uk – Closed Sunday and bank holidays

X **Palomar**   🕭 🗚 🎬

WORLD CUISINE · TRENDY A hip slice of modern-day Jerusalem in the heart of theatreland, with a zinc kitchen counter running back to an intimate, wood-panelled dining room. Like the atmosphere, the contemporary Middle Eastern cooking is fresh and vibrant.
Carte £ 23/42

Town plan: 31AP3-s - *34 Rupert St ⊠ W1D 6DN* – ⊖ *Piccadilly Circus* – ☏ *020 7439 8777 (booking advisable)* – *www.thepalomar.co.uk* – *Closed 25-26 December and Sunday dinner*

X **Mele e Pere**   🍽 🗚 🎬

ITALIAN · FRIENDLY Head downstairs – the 'apples and pears'? – to a vaulted room in the style of a homely Italian kitchen, with an appealing Vermouth bar. The owner-chef has worked in some decent London kitchens but hails from Verona so expect gutsy Italian dishes.
Menu £ 23 (dinner) – Carte £ 23/43

Town plan: 31AN3-h *46 Brewer St ⊠ W1F 9TF* – ⊖ *Piccadilly Circus* – ☏ *020 7096 2096* – *www.meleepere.co.uk* – *Closed 25-26 December and 1 January*

X **Blanchette**   🗚 🎬 ⇔

FRENCH · SIMPLE Run by three frères, Blanchette takes French bistro food and gives it the 'small plates' treatment. It's named after their mother – the ox cheek Bourguignon is her recipe. Tiles and exposed brick add to the rustic look.
Menu £ 20 – Carte £ 14/22

Town plan: 31AN2-g - *9 D'Arblay St ⊠ W1F 8DR* – ⊖ *Oxford Circus* – ☏ *020 7439 8100 (booking essential)* – *www.blanchettesoho.co.uk*

X **Bocca di Lupo**   🗚 🎬 ⇔

ITALIAN · TAPAS BAR Atmosphere, food and service are all best when sitting at the marble counter, watching the chefs at work. Specialities from across Italy come in large or small sizes and are full of flavour and vitality. Try also their gelato shop opposite.
Carte £ 15/58

Town plan: 31AN3-e - *12 Archer St ⊠ W1D 7BB* – ⊖ *Piccadilly Circus* – ☏ *020 7734 2223 (booking essential)* – *www.boccadilupo.com* – *Closed 25 December and 1 January*

X **Polpo Soho**   🍽 🗚 🎬 ⇔

ITALIAN · TAPAS BAR A fun and lively Venetian bacaro, with a stripped-down, faux-industrial look. The small plates, from arancini and prosciutto to fritto misto and Cotechino sausage, are so well priced that waiting for a table is worth it.
Menu £ 25 – Carte £ 12/21

Town plan: 31AN2-g - ⊠ *W1F 9SB* – ⊖ *Oxford Circus* – ☏ *020 7734 4479* – *www.polpo.co.uk*

X **10 Greek Street**   🏵 🗚 🎬 ⇔

MODERN CUISINE · BISTRO With just 28 seats and a dozen at the counter, the challenge is getting a table at this modishly sparse-looking bistro (no bookings taken at dinner). The chef-owner's blackboard menu comes with Anglo, Med and Middle Eastern elements.
Carte £ 29/67

Town plan: 31AP2-e - *10 Greek St ⊠ W1D 4DH* – ⊖ *Tottenham Court Road* – ☏ *020 7734 4677* – *www.10greekstreet.com* – *Closed Christmas, Easter and Sunday*

X **Haozhan**   🗚

CHINESE · DESIGN Interesting fusion-style dishes, with mostly Cantonese but other Asian influences too. Specialities like jasmine ribs or wasabi prawns reveal a freshness that marks this place out from the plethora of Chinatown mediocrity.
Menu £ 14 – Carte £ 15/43

Town plan: 31AP3-u - *8 Gerrard St ⊠ W1D 5PJ* – ⊖ *Leicester Square* – ☏ *020 7434 3838* – *www.haozhan.co.uk* – *Closed 24-25 December*

✗ Cinnamon Soho ☕ 🏠 AC 🍴 🕸

INDIAN · FRIENDLY Younger and more fun than its sister the Cinnamon Club. Has a great selection of classic and more modern Indian dishes like Rogan Josh shepherd's pie. High Chai in the afternoon and a pre-theatre menu that's a steal.

Carte £ 16/33

Town plan: 31AN2-3-a - *5 Kingly St* ☒ *W1B 5PF* – ⊖ *Oxford Circus*
– ℰ 020 7437 1664 – www.cinnamonsoho.com – Closed 1 January

✗ Duck & Rice AC

CHINESE · INTIMATE Alan Yau is one of our most innovative restaurateurs and once again he's created something different – a modern pub with a Chinese kitchen. Beer is the thing on the ground floor; upstairs is for Chinese favourites and comforting classics.

Carte approx. £ 38

Town plan: 31AN2-w - *90 Berwick St* ☒ *W1F 0QB* – ⊖ *Tottenham Court Road*
– ℰ 020 3327 7888 – www.theduckandrice.com

✗ Antidote 🐝 🏠

MODERN CUISINE · INTIMATE Plates of cheese and charcuterie are the draw in the ground floor wine bar. Upstairs in the dining room you'll find menus focusing on prime, seasonal ingredients accompanied by a wine list specialising in organic and biodynamic wines.

Carte £ 30/41

Town plan: 31AN2-j *12A Newburgh St* ☒ *W1F 7RR* – ⊖ *Oxford Circus*
– ℰ 020 7287 8488 (booking advisable) – www.antidotewinebar.com – Closed Sunday

✗ Jinjuu ☕ AC

ASIAN · DESIGN American-born celebrity chef Judy Joo's first London restaurant is a celebration of her Korean heritage. The vibrant dishes, whether Bibimbap bowls or Ssam platters, burst with flavour and are as enjoyable as the fun surroundings.

Menu £ 15 (weekday lunch)/42 – Carte £ 26/86

Town plan: 31AN2-d - *15 Kingly St* ☒ *W1B 5PS* – ⊖ *Oxford Circus*
– ℰ 020 8181 8887 – www.jinjuu.com – Closed 25 December

✗ Hoppers 🆕 ☕ AC 🍴

🐸 SOUTH INDIAN · SIMPLE Street food inspired by the flavours of Tamil Nadu and Sri Lanka features at this fun little spot from the Sethi family (Trishna, Gymkhana). Hoppers are bowl-shaped pancakes made from fermented rice and coconut – ideal with a creamy kari. The 'short eats' are great too, as are the prices, so expect a queue.

Carte £ 13/27

Town plan: 31AP2-z - *49 Frith St* ☒ *W1D 4SG* – ⊖ *Tottenham Court Road*
– ℰ 020 3011 1021 (bookings not accepted) – www.hopperslondon.com – Closed 1-3 January and 24-31 December.

✗ Oliver Maki 🆕 AC

JAPANESE · MINIMALIST A small, eagerly run corner restaurant from a group with branches in Kuwait and Bahrain. The modern Japanese food has a more pronounced fusion element than similar types of place – not everything works but the confident kitchen uses good produce.

Carte £ 38/56

Town plan: 31AP2-a - *33 Dean St* ☒ *W1D 4PW* – ⊖ *Leicester Square*
– ℰ 020 7734 0408 – www.olivermaki.co.uk

✗ Spuntino AC 🍴

NORTH AMERICAN · RUSTIC Influenced by Downtown New York, with its no-booking policy and industrial look. Sit at the counter and order classics like mac 'n' cheese or mini burgers. The staff, who look like they could fix your car, really add to the fun.

Carte £ 14/22

Town plan: 31AN3-j - *61 Rupert St.* ☒ *W1D 7PW* – ⊖ *Piccadilly Circus (bookings not accepted) – www.spuntino.co.uk – Closed dinner 24 December, 25-26, 31 December and 1 January*

X **Bibigo** 🍷 🅰🅲 📋 ⇷

KOREAN · FRIENDLY The enthusiastically run Bibigo represents Korea's largest food company's first foray into the UK market. Watch the kitchen send out dishes such as kimchi, Bossam (simmered pork belly) and hot stone galbi (chargrilled short ribs).

Menu £13 – Carte £20/29

Town plan: 31AN2-x - *58-59 Great Marlborough St ⊠ W1F 7JY*
- ⊖ *Oxford Circus*
- ✆ *020 7042 5225 – www.bibigouk.com*

X **Zelman Meats** 🅽

MEATS AND GRILLS · RUSTIC Those clever Goodman people noticed a lack of affordable steakhouses and so opened this fun, semi-industrial space. They serve three cuts of beef: sliced picanha (from the rump), chateaubriand, and a wonderfully smoky short rib.

Carte £35/49

Town plan: 31AN2-y - *2 St Anne's Ct ⊠ W1F 0AZ* – ⊖ *Tottenham Court Rd*
- ✆ *020 7437 0566 – www.zelmanmeats.com – Closed bank holidays, dinner Sunday and lunch Monday*

X **Ceviche Soho** 🍷 🅰🅲 📋

PERUVIAN · FRIENDLY Based on a Lima Pisco bar, Ceviche is as loud as it is fun. First try the deliriously addictive drinks based on the Peruvian spirit Pisco, and then share some thinly sliced sea bass or octopus, along with anticuchos skewers.

Carte £16/27

Town plan: 31AP2-w - *17 Frith St ⊠ W1D 4RG* – ⊖ *Tottenham Court Road*
- ✆ *020 7292 2040 (booking essential) – www.cevicheuk.com/soho*

X **Cây Tre** 🅰🅲 🍽

VIETNAMESE · MINIMALIST Bright, sleek and bustling surroundings where Vietnamese standouts include Cha La Lot (spicy ground pork wrapped in betel leaves), slow-cooked Mekong catfish with a well-judged sweet and spicy sauce, and 6 versions of Pho (noodle soup).

Menu £15 (lunch)/23 – Carte £19/30

Town plan: 31AP2-m - *42-43 Dean St ⊠ W1D 4PZ* – ⊖ *Tottenham Court Road*
- ✆ *020 7317 9118 (booking advisable) – www.caytresoho.co.uk*

X **Rosa's Soho**

THAI · SIMPLE The worn-in, pared down look of this authentic Thai café adds to its intimate feel. Signature dishes include warm minced chicken salad and a sweet pumpkin red curry. Tom Yam soup comes with a lovely balance of sweet, sour and spice.

Menu £20 – Carte £19/25

Town plan: 31AP2-j - *48 Dean St ⊠ W1D 5BF* – ⊖ *Leicester Square*
- ✆ *020 7494 1638 (booking advisable) – www.rosasthaicafe.com*
- *Closed 25-26 December*

X **Bone Daddies** 🅰🅲

ASIAN · FASHIONABLE Maybe ramen is the new rock 'n' roll. The charismatic Aussie chef-owner feels that combinations are endless when it comes to these comforting bowls. Be ready to queue then share a table. It's a fun place, run by a hospitable bunch.

Carte £16/24

Town plan: 31AN2-y - *31 Peter St ⊠ W1F 0AR* – ⊖ *Piccadilly Circus*
- ✆ *020 7287 8581 (bookings not accepted) – www.bonedaddies.com – Closed 25 December*

X **Barshu** `AC` ⬦

CHINESE · **EXOTIC DÉCOR** The fiery and authentic flavours of China's Sichuan province are the draw here; help is at hand as the menu has pictures. It's decorated with carved wood and lanterns; downstairs is better for groups.

Carte £ 27/69

Town plan: 31AP2-g - *28 Frith St.* ✉ *W1D 5LF* – ⊖ *Leicester Square* – ✆ *020 7287 8822 (booking advisable)* – *www.barshurestaurant.co.uk* – *Closed 24-25 December*

X **Baozi Inn** ⌗

CHINESE · **RUSTIC** Buzzy, busy little place that's great for a quick bite, especially if you like pork buns, steaming bowls of noodles, a hit of Sichuan fire and plenty of beer or tea. You'll leave feeling surprisingly energised and rejuvenated.

Carte £ 15/22

Town plan: 31AP3-r - *25-26 Newport Court* ✉ *WC2H 7JS* – ⊖ *Leicester Square* – ✆ *020 7287 6877 (bookings not accepted)* – *Closed 24-25 December*

X **Manchurian Legends** `AC`

CHINESE · **SIMPLE** Try specialities from a less familiar region of China: Dongbei, the 'north east'. As winters there are long, stews and BBQ dishes are popular, as are pickled ingredients and chilli heat. Further warmth comes from the sweet natured staff.

Menu £ 16/25 – Carte £ 20/38

Town plan: 31AP3-z - *16 Lisle St* ✉ *WC2H 7BE* – ⊖ *Leicester Square* – ✆ *020 7287 6606* – *www.manchurianlegends.com* – *Closed Christmas*

X **Bao** `AC`

⊛ ASIAN · **SIMPLE** There are some things in life worth queueing for – and that includes the delicious eponymous buns here at this simple, great value Taiwanese operation. The classic bao and the confit pork bao are standouts – along with 'small eats' like trotter nuggets. There's another Bao in Windmill St.

Carte £ 17/27

Town plan: 31AN2-f - *53 Lexington St* ✉ *W1F 9AS* – ⊖ *Tottenham Court Road* – ✆ *020 3019 2200 (bookings not accepted)* – *www.baolondon.com* – *Closed Sunday*

X **Koya Bar** ⌨ ▤

JAPANESE · **SIMPLE** A simple, sweet place serving authentic Udon noodles and small plates; they open early for breakfast. Counter seating means everyone has a view of the chefs; bookings aren't taken and there is often a queue, but the short wait is worth it.

Carte £ 10/23

Town plan: 31AP2-c - *50 Frith St* ✉ *W1D 4SQ* – ⊖ *Tottenham Court Road* – ✆ *020 7433 4463 (bookings not accepted)* – *www.koyabar.co.uk* – *Closed 24-25 December and 1 January*

X **Beijing Dumpling** `AC`

CHINESE · **NEIGHBOURHOOD** This relaxed little place serves freshly prepared dumplings of both Beijing and Shanghai styles. Although the range is not as comprehensive as the name suggests, they do stand out, especially varieties of the famed Siu Lung Bao.

Menu £ 18 – Carte £ 10/40

Town plan: 31AP3-e - *23 Lisle St.* ✉ *WC2H 7BA* – ⊖ *Leicester Square* – ✆ *020 7287 6888* – *Closed 24-25 December*

If you are looking for particularly charming accommodation, book a hotel shown in red: 🏨, 🏠...🏨🏨.

X Tonkotsu

JAPANESE • RUSTIC Some things are worth queuing for. Good ramen is all about the base stock: 18 hours goes into its preparation here to ensure the bowls of soup and wheat-based noodles reach a depth of flavour that seems to nourish one's very soul.

Carte £ 17/26

Town plan: 31AP2-q - *63 Dean St ✉ W1D 4QG - ⊖ Tottenham Court Road - ✆ 020 7437 0071 (bookings not accepted) - www.tonkotsu.co.uk*

Strand and Covent Garden

Savoy

GRAND LUXURY • ART DÉCO A legendary hotel; its luxurious bedrooms and stunning suites come in Edwardian or art deco styles. Have tea in the Thames Foyer, the hotel's heart, or drinks in the famous American Bar or the moodier Beaufort Bar. Along with the Savoy Grill is Kaspar's, an informal seafood bar and grill which replaced the River restaurant.

267 rooms - †£ 420/1500 ††£ 420/1500 - ☕£ 35 - 45 suites

Town plan: 31AQ3-s - *Strand ✉ WC2R 0EU - ⊖ Charing Cross - ✆ 020 7836 4343 - www.fairmont.com/savoy*

One Aldwych

GRAND LUXURY • MODERN Former 19C bank, now a stylish hotel with lots of artwork; the lobby changes its look seasonally and doubles as a bar. Stylish, contemporary bedrooms with the latest mod cons; the deluxe rooms and suites are particularly desirable. Impressive leisure facilities. Light, accessible menu at Indigo.

105 rooms - †£ 387/770 ††£ 387/770 - ☕£ 19 - 12 suites

Town plan: 32AR3-r - *1 Aldwych ✉ WC2B 4BZ - ⊖ Temple - ✆ 020 7300 1000 - www.onealdwych.com*

Waldorf Hilton

HISTORIC • ELEGANT Impressive curved and columned façade: an Edwardian landmark in a great location. Stylish, contemporary bedrooms in calming colours have superb bathrooms and all mod cons. Tea dances in the Grade II listed Palm Court Ballroom. Stylish 'Homage' is popular for afternoon tea and relaxed brasserie style dining.

298 rooms - †£ 219/599 ††£ 229/609 - ☕£ 22 - 12 suites

Town plan: 32AR2-s - *Aldwych ✉ WC2B 4DD - ⊖ Temple - ✆ 020 7836 2400 - www.hilton.co.uk/waldorf*

St Martins Lane

LUXURY • DESIGN The unmistakable hand of Philippe Starck is evident at this most contemporary of hotels. Unique and stylish, from the starkly modern lobby to the state-of-the-art bedrooms, which come in a blizzard of white.

206 rooms ☕ - †£ 199/500 ††£ 199/500 - 2 suites

Town plan: 31AP-AQ3-e - *45 St Martin's Ln ✉ WC2N 3HX - ⊖ Charing Cross - ✆ 020 7300 5500 - www.morganshotelgroup.com*

XXX Delaunay

MODERN CUISINE • ELEGANT The Delaunay was inspired by the grand cafés of Europe but, despite sharing the same buzz and celebrity clientele as its sibling The Wolseley, is not just a mere replica. The all-day menu is more mittel-European, with great schnitzels and wieners.

Carte £ 27/64

Town plan: 32AR2-x - *55 Aldwych ✉ WC2B 4BB - ⊖ Temple - ✆ 020 7499 8558 (booking essential) - www.thedelaunay.com - Closed dinner 24 December and 25 December*

XXX The Ivy

TRADITIONAL BRITISH · FASHIONABLE This landmark restaurant has had a facelift and while the glamorous clientele remain, it now has an oval bar as its focal point. The menu offers international dishes alongside the old favourites and personable staff anticipate your every need.

Menu £ 23 (weekday lunch) – Carte £ 30/65

Town plan: 31AP2-p - *9 West St* ✉ *WC2H 9NE* – ⊖ *Leicester Square*
– ℰ *020 7836 4751* – *www.the-ivy.co.uk*
– *Closed 25 December*

XX J Sheekey

SEAFOOD · FASHIONABLE Festooned with photographs of actors and linked to the theatrical world since opening in 1890. Wood panels and alcove tables add famed intimacy. Accomplished seafood cooking.

Menu £ 24 – Carte £ 33/69

Town plan: 31AP3-v - *28-32 St Martin's Ct,* ✉ *WC2N 4AL* – ⊖ *Leicester Square*
– ℰ *020 7240 2565 (booking essential)* – *www.j-sheekey.co.uk*
– *Closed 25-26 December*

XX Spring

ITALIAN · FASHIONABLE Spring occupies the 'new wing' of Somerset House that for many years was inhabited by the Inland Revenue. It's a bright, feminine space under the aegis of chef Skye Gyngell. Her cooking is Italian influenced and ingredient-led.

Menu £ 28 (lunch)/32 – Carte £ 40/67

Town plan: 32AR3-c - *New Wing, Somerset House, Strand* ✉ *WC2R 1LA*
– *Entrance on Lancaster Pl* – ⊖ *Temple* – ℰ *020 3011 0115 (booking advisable)*
– *www.springrestaurant.co.uk* – *Closed Sunday dinner*

XX Rules

TRADITIONAL BRITISH · TRADITIONAL DÉCOR London's oldest restaurant boasts a fine collection of antique cartoons, drawings and paintings. Tradition continues in the menu, specialising in game from its own estate.

Carte £ 36/71

Town plan: 31AQ3-n - *35 Maiden Ln* ✉ *WC2E 7LB* – ⊖ *Leicester Square*
– ℰ *020 7836 5314 (booking essential)* – *www.rules.co.uk* – *Closed
25-26 December*

XX Clos Maggiore

FRENCH · CLASSIC DÉCOR One of London's most romantic restaurants – but be sure to ask for the enchanting conservatory with its retractable roof. The sophisticated French cooking is joined by a wine list of great depth. Good value and very popular pre/post theatre menus.

Menu £ 23 (weekday lunch)/38 – Carte £ 37/66

Town plan: 31AQ3-a - *33 King St* ✉ *WC2E 8JD*
– ⊖ *Leicester Square*
– ℰ *020 7379 9696* – *www.closmaggiore.com*
– *Closed 24-25 December*

XX Roka

JAPANESE · FASHIONABLE This is the fourth and largest Roka in the group. It shares the same stylish look, efficient service and modern Japanese food, although there are some dishes unique to this branch. Consider the Tasting menu for a good all-around experience.

Menu £ 27 – Carte £ 32/58

Town plan: 32AR2-v - *71 Aldwych* ✉ *WC2B 4HN* – ⊖ *Temple* – ℰ *020 7294 7636*
– *www.rokarestaurant.com*
– *Closed 25 December*

XX Les Deux Salons

FRENCH · BISTRO Sir Terence Conran took over this handily-placed site in 2015 and injected a tidy sum into its redesign. On the ground floor is a café, a bistro serving all the French classics, a bar and an épicerie. Upstairs is a more formal restaurant.

Menu £ 17 (early dinner) – Carte £ 26/70

Town plan: 31AQ3-m - 40-42 William IV St ⊠ WC2N 4DD – ⊖ Charing Cross – ☏ 020 7420 2050 – www.lesdeuxsalons.co.uk – Closed 25-26 December and 1 January

XX Café Murano

ITALIAN · NEIGHBOURHOOD The second Café Murano is in the heart of Covent Garden, in a space much larger than the St James's original; head for the smart marble-topped counter at the back. Appealing menu of Northern Italian dishes cooked with care and respect.

Menu £ 17 – Carte £ 31/49

Town plan: 32AR3-o - 36 Tavistock St ⊠ WC2E 7PB – ⊖ Charing Cross – ☏ 020 7240 3654 – www.cafemurano.co.uk – Closed Sunday dinner

XX Ivy Market Grill

TRADITIONAL BRITISH · DESIGN Mere mortals can now experience a little of that Ivy glamour by eating here at the first of their diffusion line. Breakfast, a menu of largely British classics and afternoon tea keep it busy all day. There's another branch in Chelsea.

Menu £ 21 (early dinner) – Carte £ 25/54

Town plan: 31AQ3-z - 1 Henrietta St ⊠ WC2E 8PS – ⊖ Leicester Square – ☏ 020 3301 0200 – www.theivymarketgrill.com

XX Balthazar

FRENCH · BRASSERIE Those who know the original Balthazar in Manhattan's SoHo district will find the London version of this classic brasserie uncannily familiar in looks, vibe and food. The Franglais menu keeps it simple and the cocktails are great.

Menu £ 18 (weekday lunch) – Carte £ 27/56

Town plan: 31AQ2-t - 4-6 Russell St. ⊠ WC2B 5HZ – ⊖ Covent Garden – ☏ 020 3301 1155 (booking essential) – www.balthazarlondon.com – Closed 25 December

X L'Atelier de Joël Robuchon

☸

FRENCH · ELEGANT Creative, skilled and occasionally playful cooking; dishes may look delicate but pack a punch. Ground floor 'Atelier' comes with counter seating and chefs on view. More structured 'La Cuisine' upstairs and a cool bar above that.

→ Egg cocotte carbonara style with black truffle. Pyrenean milk-fed lamb cutlets with fresh thyme. Praline custard with hazelnut and white coffee ice cream.

Menu £ 38 (lunch and early dinner) – Carte £ 40/90

Town plan: 31AP2-n - 13-15 West St. ⊠ WC2H 9NE – ⊖ Leicester Square – ☏ 020 7010 8600 – www.joelrobuchon.co.uk – Closed 25-26 December,1 January and August bank holiday Monday

X Barrafina

SPANISH · TAPAS BAR The second Barrafina is not just brighter than the Soho original – it's bigger too, so you can wait inside with a drink for counter seats to become available. Try more unusual tapas like ortiguillas, frit Mallorquin or the succulent meats.

Carte £ 14/34

Town plan: 31AQ3-x - 10 Adelaide St ⊠ WC2N 4HZ – ⊖ Charing Cross – ☏ 020 7440 1456 (bookings not accepted) – www.barrafina.co.uk – Closed Christmas, New Year and bank holidays

X Barrafina ⓝ

SPANISH · TAPAS BAR The third of the Barrafinas is tucked away at the far end of Covent Garden; arrive early or prepare to queue. Fresh, vibrantly flavoured fish and shellfish dishes are a real highlight; tortillas y huevos also feature.

Carte £ 24/47

Town plan: 31AQ2-a - *43 Drury Ln* ⊠ *WC2B 5AJ* – ⊖ *Covent Garden* – *☎ 020 7440 1456 (bookings not accepted) – www.barrafina.co.uk – Closed bank holidays*

X J. Sheekey Oyster Bar

SEAFOOD · INTIMATE An addendum to J. Sheekey restaurant. Sit at the bar to watch the chefs prepare the same quality seafood as next door but at slightly lower prices; fish pie and fruits de mer are the popular choices. Open all day.

Carte £ 25/41

Town plan: 31AP3-v - *33-34 St Martin's Ct.* ⊠ *WC2 4AL* – ⊖ *Leicester Square* – *☎ 020 7240 2565 – www.j-sheekey.co.uk* – *Closed 25-26 December*

X Frenchie ⓝ

MODERN CUISINE · BISTRO A well-run modern-day bistro – younger sister to the Paris original, which shares the name given to chef-owner Greg Marchand when he was head chef at Fifteen. The adventurous, ambitious cooking is informed by his extensive travels.

Menu £ 28 (weekday lunch) – Carte £ 33/47

Town plan: 31AQ3-c - *16 Henrietta St* ⊠ *WC2E 8QH* – ⊖ *Covent Garden* – *☎ 020 7836 4422 (booking advisable) – www.frenchiecoventgarden.com* – *Closed 25-26 December and 1 January*

X Hawksmoor

MEATS AND GRILLS · RUSTIC Steaks from Longhorn cattle lovingly reared in North Yorkshire and dry-aged for at least 35 days are the stars of the show. Atmospheric, bustling basement restaurant in former brewery cellars.

Menu £ 25 (weekdays)/28 – Carte £ 22/60

Town plan: 31AQ2-f - *11 Langley St* ⊠ *WC2H 9JG* – ⊖ *Covent Garden* – *☎ 020 7420 9390 – www.thehawksmoor.com* – *Closed 24-26 December*

X Tredwell's

MODERN BRITISH · BRASSERIE A modern brasserie from Marcus Wareing, with an art deco feel. Cooking is best described as modern English; dishes show a degree of refinement, and a commendable amount of thought has gone into addressing allergen issues.

Menu £ 25 (lunch and early dinner) – Carte £ 26/51

Town plan: 31AP2-s - *4 Upper St Martin's Ln* ⊠ *WC2H 9EF* – ⊖ *Leicester Square* – *☎ 020 3764 0840 – www.tredwells.com – Closed 25-26 December, 1 January and Easter Monday*

X Lima Floral

PERUVIAN · FASHIONABLE This second Lima branch has a light and airy feel by day and a cosy, candlelit vibe in the evening; regional Peruvian dishes are served alongside the more popular causa and ceviche. Basement Pisco Bar for Peruvian tapas and Pisco sours.

Menu £ 18 (weekdays) – Carte £ 32/48

Town plan: 31AQ3-k - *14 Garrick St* ⊠ *WC2E 9BJ* – ⊖ *Leicester Square* – *☎ 020 7240 5778 – www.limalondongroup.com/floral – Closed 26-27 December, 2 January, bank holiday Mondays*

Vico

ITALIAN • BISTRO A relaxed modern-day trattoria with a fountain at its centre and an authentic Gelupo ice cream bar. Authentic Italian dishes are simply cooked, super-fresh and seasonal; generous of portion and vibrant in colour and flavour.

Carte £ 23/40

Town plan: 31AP2-b - *1 Cambridge Circus ✉ WC2H 8PA – ⊖ Leicester Square – ✆ 020 7379 0303 – www.eatvico.com – Closed 25 December and 1 January*

Opera Tavern

MEDITERRANEAN CUISINE • TAPAS BAR Shares the same appealing concept of small plates of Spanish and Italian delicacies as its sisters, Salt Yard and Dehesa. All done in a smartly converted old boozer which dates from 1879; ground floor bar and upstairs dining room.

Carte £ 14/25

Town plan: 31AQ2-y - *23 Catherine St. ✉ WC2B 5JS – ⊖ Covent Garden – ✆ 020 7836 3680 – www.operatavern.co.uk – Closed 25 December and 1 January*

Polpo Covent Garden

ITALIAN • SIMPLE First Soho, now Covent Garden gets a fun Venetian bacaro. The small plates are surprisingly filling, with delights such as pizzette of white anchovy vying with fennel and almond salad, fritto misto competing with spaghettini and meatballs.

Carte £ 12/21

Town plan: 31AQ3-p - *6 Maiden Ln. ✉ WC2E 7NA – ⊖ Leicester Square – ✆ 020 7836 8448 – www.polpo.co.uk – Closed 25-26 December*

Dishoom

INDIAN • EXOTIC A facsimile of a Bombay café, of the sort opened by Persian immigrants in the early 20C. Try baked roti rolls with chai, vada pav (Bombay's version of the chip butty), a curry or grilled meats. There's another branch in Shoreditch.

Carte £ 13/30

Town plan: 31AP2-j - *12 Upper St Martin's Ln ✉ WC2H 9FB – ⊖ Leicester Square – ✆ 020 7420 9320 (booking advisable) – www.dishoom.com – Closed 24 December dinner, 25-26 December and 1-2 January*

Terroirs

MEDITERRANEAN CUISINE • WINE BAR Flavoursome French cooking, with extra Italian and Spanish influences and a thoughtfully compiled wine list. Eat in the lively ground floor bistro/wine bar or in the more intimate cellar, where they also offer some sharing dishes like rib of beef for two.

Carte £ 24/37

Town plan: 31AQ3-h - *5 William IV St ✉ WC2N 4DW – ⊖ Charing Cross – ✆ 020 7036 0660 – www.terroirswinebar.com – Closed 25-26 December, 1 January, Sunday and bank holidays*

Victoria

Corinthia

GRAND LUXURY • ELEGANT The restored Victorian splendour of this grand, luxurious hotel cannot fail to impress. Tasteful and immaculately finished bedrooms are some of the largest in town; suites come with butlers. The stunning spa is over four floors.

294 rooms – †£ 342/1140 ††£ 342/1140 – ☕ £ 32 – 23 suites

Town plan: 31AQ4-x - *Whitehall Pl. ✉ SW1A 2BD – ⊖ Embankment – ✆ 020 7930 8181 – www.corinthia.com/london*

Northall • Massimo – See restaurant listing

🏨 Goring
🛏 🛗 AC 🚭 🧖

LUXURY · ELEGANT Under the stewardship of the founder's great grandson, this landmark hotel has been restored and renovated while maintaining its traditional atmosphere and pervading sense of Britishness. Expect first class service and immaculate, very comfortable bedrooms, many of which overlook the garden.

69 rooms 🛏 – ♦£ 335/615 ♦♦£ 380/710 – 8 suites

Town plan: 38AL6-a - *15 Beeston Pl* ⊠ *SW1W 0JW* – ⊖ *Victoria* - *☏ 020 7396 9000* - *www.thegoring.com*

⚜ **Dining Room at The Goring** – See restaurant listing

🏨 St James' Court
🏋 🧖 💆 🛗 ♿ AC 🚭 🧖

LUXURY · CLASSIC Built in 1897 as serviced accommodation for visiting aristocrats. Behind the impressive Edwardian façade lies an equally elegant interior. Quietest bedrooms overlook a courtyard. Relaxed, bright Bistro 51 comes with an international menu; Bank offers brasserie classics in a conservatory.

318 rooms – ♦£ 198/594 ♦♦£ 198/594 – 🛏£ 21 – 20 suites

Town plan: 39AN5-6-e - *45 Buckingham Gate* ⊠ *SW1E 6BS* – ⊖ *St James's Park* - *☏ 020 7834 6655* - *www.tajhotels.com/stjamescourt*

⚜ **Quilon** – See restaurant listing

🏠 Artist Residence
AC 🚭

TOWNHOUSE · PERSONALISED A converted pub made into a comfortable, quirky townhouse hotel, with stylish bedrooms featuring mini Smeg fridges, retro telephones, reclaimed furniture and pop art. Cool bar and sitting room beneath the busy Cambridge Street Cafe.

10 rooms – ♦£ 190/230 ♦♦£ 210/450 – 🛏£ 10

Town plan: 38AL7-r - *52 Cambridge St* ⊠ *SW1V 4QQ* – ⊖ *Victoria* - *☏ 020 7931 8946* - *www.artistresidencelondon.co.uk*

🏠 Lord Milner
🛗 AC 🚭

TOWNHOUSE · CLASSIC A four storey terraced house, with individually decorated bedrooms, three with four-poster beds and all with smart marble bathrooms. Garden Suite is the best room; it has its own patio. Breakfast served in your bedroom.

11 rooms – ♦£ 80/145 ♦♦£ 110/275 – 🛏£ 14

Town plan: 38AL6-k - *111 Ebury St* ⊠ *SW1W 9QU* – ⊖ *Victoria* – *☏ 020 7881 9880* - *www.lordmilner.com*

🍴 Dining Room at The Goring
⚜ 🛏 AC

⚜ **TRADITIONAL BRITISH · ELEGANT** A paean to all things British and the very model of discretion and decorum – the perfect spot for those who 'like things done properly' but without the stuffiness. The menu is an appealing mix of British classics and lighter, more modern dishes, all prepared with great skill and understanding.

→ Broth of Cornish squid, plaice and red prawn with roast garlic and saffron. Fallow deer with parsnip, mushroom duxelle, glazed faggot and pine nut. Caramel cream with sea buckthorn jelly, mandarin sorbet and fresh orange.

Menu £ 45/57

Town plan: 38AL6-a - *Goring Hotel, 15 Beeston Pl* ⊠ *SW1W 0JW* – ⊖ *Victoria* - *☏ 020 7396 9000* - *www.thegoring.com* - *Closed Saturday lunch*

Prices quoted after the symbol ♦ refer to the lowest rate for a single room in low season, followed by the highest rate in high season. The same principle applies to the symbol ♦♦ for a double room.

XxX Quilon

INDIAN · DESIGN A meal here will remind you how fresh, vibrant, colourful and healthy Indian food can be. Chef Sriram Aylur and his team focus on India's southwest coast, so the emphasis is on seafood and a lighter style of cooking. The room is stylish and comfortable and the service team, bright and enthusiastic.
→ Lotus stem and colocasia chop with mango and mint. Braised lamb shank with freshly ground herbs. Creamy vermicelli kheer with rose ice cream.

Menu £ 31/60 – Carte £ 34/67

Town plan: 39AN5-6-e - St James' Court Hotel, 41 Buckingham Gate
⊠ SW1E 6AF – ⊖ St James's Park – ℰ 020 7821 1899 – www.quilon.co.uk
– Closed 25 December

XxX Roux at Parliament Square

MODERN CUISINE · ELEGANT Light floods through the Georgian windows of this comfortable restaurant within the offices of the Royal Institute of Chartered Surveyors. Carefully crafted, elaborate and sophisticated cuisine, with some interesting flavour combinations.

Menu £ 35 (weekday lunch)/59

Town plan: 39AP5-x - Royal Institution of Chartered Surveyors, Parliament Sq.
⊠ SW1P 3AD – ⊖ Westminster – ℰ 020 7334 3737 (bookings advisable at lunch)
– www.rouxatparliamentsquare.co.uk – Closed Saturday, Sunday and bank holidays

XxX Northall

TRADITIONAL BRITISH · BISTRO The Corinthia Hotel's British restaurant champions our indigenous produce, and its menu is an appealing document. It occupies two rooms: head for the more modern one with its bar and booths, which is less formal than the other section.

Menu £ 24/75 – Carte £ 26/73

Town plan: 31AQ4-x - Corinthia Hotel, Whitehall Pl. ⊠ WC2N 5AE
– ⊖ Embankment – ℰ 020 7321 3100 – www.thenorthall.co.uk

XxX The Cinnamon Club

INDIAN · HISTORIC Tourists and locals, politicians and business types – this smart Indian restaurant housed in the listed former Westminster Library attracts all types. The fairly elaborate dishes arrive fully garnished and the spicing is quite subtle.

Menu £ 26 (lunch) – Carte £ 31/68

Town plan: 39AP6-c - 30-32 Great Smith St ⊠ SW1P 3BU – ⊖ St James's Park
– ℰ 020 7222 2555 – www.cinnamonclub.com – Closed bank holidays

XxX Santini

ITALIAN · FASHIONABLE Santini has looked after its many immaculately coiffured regulars for 30 years. The not inexpensive menu of classic Italian dishes is broadly Venetian in style; the daily specials, pasta dishes and desserts are the standout courses.

Carte £ 30/67

Town plan: 38AL6-v - 29 Ebury St ⊠ SW1W 0NZ – ⊖ Victoria
– ℰ 020 7730 4094 – www.santinirestaurant.com – Closed 23-26 December,
1 January and Easter

XxX Grand Imperial

CHINESE · ELEGANT Grand it most certainly is, as this elegant restaurant is in the Grosvenor Hotel's former ballroom. It specialises in Cantonese cuisine, particularly the version found in Hong Kong; steaming and frying are used to great effect.

Menu £ 30/60 – Carte £ 20/71

Town plan: 38AL6-u - Grosvenor Hotel, 101 Buckingham Palace Rd ⊠ SW1W 0SJ
– ⊖ Victoria – ℰ 020 7821 8898 – www.grandimperiallondon.com – Closed
25-26 December

✗✗ Massimo   🔥 AC ⟺

ITALIAN · ELEGANT Opulent, visually impressive room with an oyster bar on one side. On offer are traditional dishes true to the regions of Italy; fish and seafood dishes stand out. Impressive private dining room comes with its own chef.

Menu £ 30 – Carte £ 28/57

Town plan: 31AQ4-x - *Corinthia Hotel, 10 Northumberland Ave.* ✉ *WC2N 5AE – ⊖ Embankment – ℰ 020 7321 3156 – www.corinthia.com/london – Closed Sunday*

✗✗ Enoteca Turi ⓝ   🍃 AC

ITALIAN · NEIGHBOURHOOD In 2016 Putney's loss was Pimlico's gain when, after 25 years, Guiseppe and Pamela Turi had to find a new home for their Italian restaurant. They brought their warm hospitality and superb wine list with them, and the chef has introduced a broader range of influences from across the country.

Menu £ 26 (lunch) – Carte £ 32/54

Town plan: 38AK7-s - *87 Pimlico Rd* ✉ *SW1W 8PU – ⊖ Sloane Square – ℰ 020 7730 3663 – www.enotecaturi.com – Closed 25-26 December, 1 January, Sunday and bank holiday lunch*

✗✗ Osteria Dell' Angolo   AC ⟺

ITALIAN · NEIGHBOURHOOD At lunch, this Italian opposite the Home Office is full of bustle and men in suits; at dinner it's a little more relaxed. Staff are personable and the menu is reassuringly familiar; homemade pasta and seafood dishes are good.

Carte £ 32/45

Town plan: 39AP6-n - *47 Marsham St* ✉ *SW1P 3DR – ⊖ St James's Park – ℰ 020 3268 1077 (booking essential at lunch) – www.osteriadellangolo.co.uk – Closed 1-4 January, Easter, 24-28 December, Saturday lunch, Sunday and bank holidays*

✗✗ UNI ⓝ   AC

JAPANESE · DESIGN Sweet restaurant offering flavoursome Nikkei cuisine, fusing the flavours of Japan and Peru: Nobu without the paparazzi and the prices. Small, stylish and spread across three levels – sit at a table, at the counter or in a cosy cellar alcove.

Carte £ 27/75

Town plan: 38AL6-c - *18a Ebury St* ✉ *SW1W 0LU – ⊖ Victoria – ℰ 020 7730 9267 – www.restaurantuni.com*

✗✗ Rex Whistler   🍃 🔥 AC

TRADITIONAL BRITISH · CLASSIC DÉCOR The £ 45million renovation of Tate Britain included a freshening up of its restaurant and restoration of Whistler's mural, 'The Expedition in Pursuit of Rare Meats', which envelops the room. The monthly menu is stoutly British and the remarkably priced wine list has an unrivalled 'half bottle' selection.

Menu £ 31

Town plan: 39AP7-w - *Tate Britain, Millbank* ✉ *SW1P 4RG – ⊖ Pimlico – ℰ 020 7887 8825 – www.tate.org.uk – lunch only – Closed 24-26 December*

✗ A. Wong   🌿 AC 🍽

🅐 **CHINESE · FRIENDLY** A modern Chinese restaurant with a buzzy ground floor and a sexy basement. Menus are continually evolving and the cooking is light, fresh and well-balanced, with lunchtime dim sum the star of the show. Service is keen, as are the prices.

Menu £ 14 (weekday lunch) – Carte £ 22/33

Town plan: 38AM7-w - *70 Wilton Rd* ✉ *SW1V 1DE – ⊖ Victoria – ℰ 020 7828 8931 (booking essential) – www.awong.co.uk – Closed 23 December-4 January, Sunday and Monday lunch*

Kouzu 🍷 AC

JAPANESE · DESIGN Occupying two floors of an attractive 19C Grade II building is this modern Japanese restaurant. Those who know Zuma or Nobu will not only recognise the style of the food but will also find the stylish surroundings familiar.
Menu £ 20 (lunch)/85 – Carte £ 27/111
Town plan: 38AL6-v - *21 Grosvenor Gdns* ⊠ *SW1 0BD –* ⊖ *Victoria*
*– ℰ 020 7730 7043 – www.kouzu.co.uk – Closed 24-25 December, 1 January,
Saturday lunch and Sunday*

Olivocarne 🍷 AC

ITALIAN · FASHIONABLE Just when you thought Mauro Sanno had this part of town sewn up he opens another restaurant. This one focuses on meat dishes, along with a selection of satisfying Sardinian specialities and is smarter and larger than his others.
Menu £ 25 (weekday lunch) – Carte £ 30/54
Town plan: 38AK7-d - *61 Elizabeth St* ⊠ *SW1W 9PP –* ⊖ *Sloane Square*
– ℰ 020 7730 7997 – www.olivorestaurants.com

Olivo AC

ITALIAN · NEIGHBOURHOOD Carefully prepared, authentic Sardinian specialities are the highlight at this popular Italian restaurant. Simply decorated in blues and yellows, with an atmosphere of bonhomie.
Menu £ 25 (weekday lunch) – Carte £ 31/46
Town plan: 38AL6-z - *21 Eccleston St* ⊠ *SW1W 9LX –* ⊖ *Victoria*
*– ℰ 020 7730 2505 (booking essential) – www.olivorestaurants.com – Closed
lunch Saturday-Sunday and bank holidays*

Olivomare 🍴 AC

SEAFOOD · DESIGN Expect understated and stylish piscatorial decoration and seafood with a Sardinian base. Fortnightly changing menu, with high quality produce, much of which is available in the deli next door.
Carte £ 33/44
Town plan: 38AL6-b - *10 Lower Belgrave St* ⊠ *SW1W 0LJ –* ⊖ *Victoria*
– ℰ 020 7730 9022 – www.olivorestaurants.com – Closed bank holidays

Thomas Cubitt

MODERN CUISINE · PUB A pub of two halves: choose the busy ground floor bar with its accessible menu or upstairs for more ambitious, quite elaborate cooking with courteous service and a less frenetic environment.
Carte £ 29/44
Town plan: 38AK6-e - ⊠ *SW1W 9PA –* ⊖ *Sloane Square. – ℰ 020 7730 6060
(booking essential) – www.thethomascubitt.co.uk*

The Orange

MEDITERRANEAN CUISINE · FRIENDLY The old Orange Brewery is as charming a pub as its stucco-fronted façade suggests. Try the fun bar or book a table in the more sedate upstairs room. The menu has a Mediterranean bias; spelt or wheat-based pizzas are a speciality. Bedrooms are stylish and comfortable.
Carte £ 28/40
4 rooms ⊈ – ∤£ 210 ∤∤£ 250
Town plan: 38AK7-k - *37 Pimlico Rd* ⊠ *SW1W 8NE –* ⊖ *Sloane Square.
– ℰ 020 7881 9844 – www.theorange.co.uk*

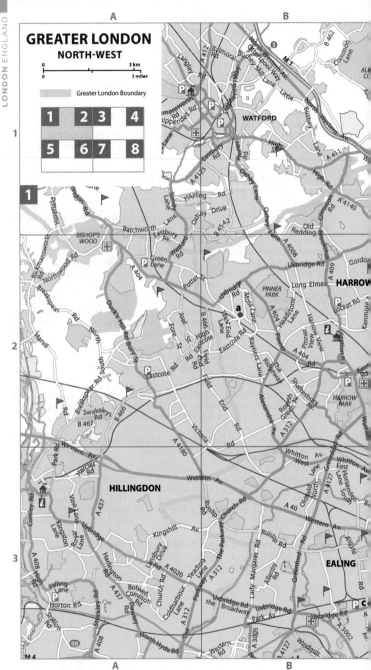

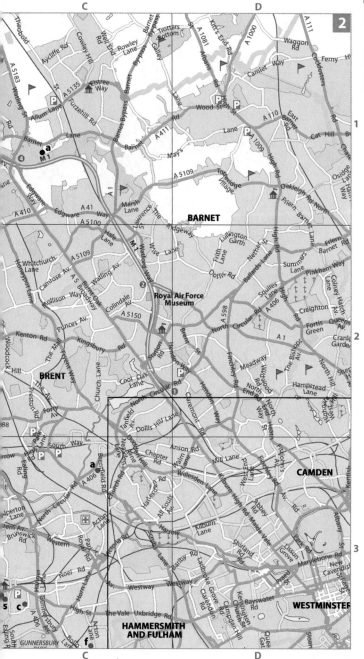

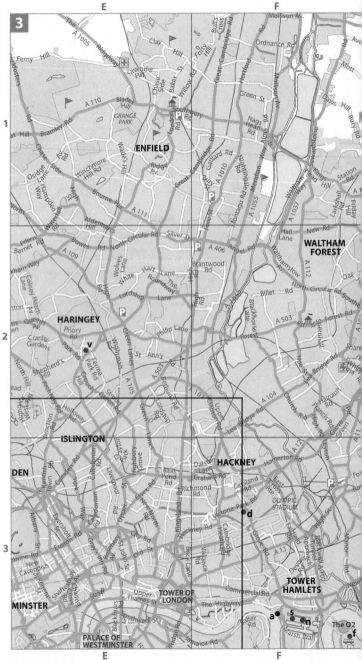

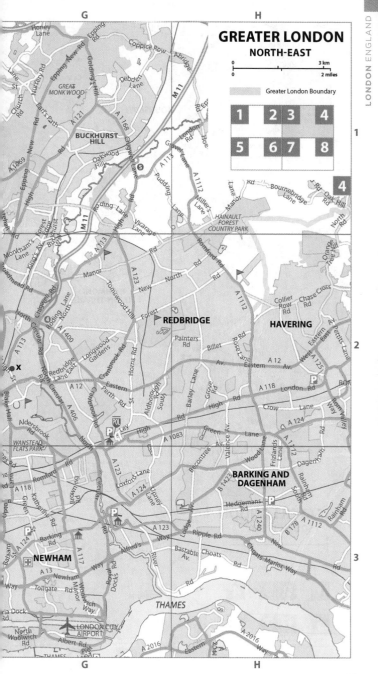

GREATER LONDON
NORTH-EAST

| 0 | | | 3 km |
| 0 | | 2 miles | |

Greater London Boundary

| 1 | 2 | 3 | 4 |
| 5 | 6 | 7 | 8 |

1

4

2

3

BUCKHURST HILL

HAINAULT FOREST COUNTRY PARK

REDBRIDGE

HAVERING

WANSTEAD FLATS PARK

BARKING AND DAGENHAM

NEWHAM

LONDON CITY AIRPORT

THAMES

G

H

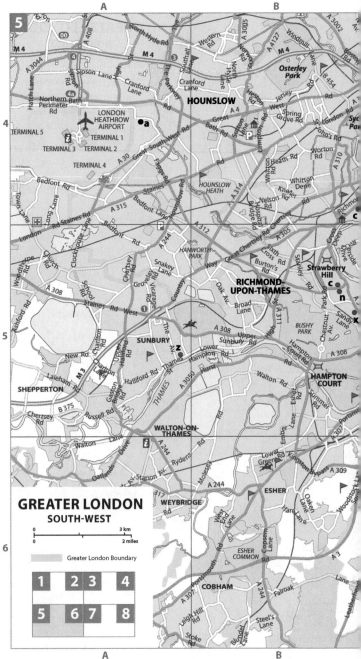

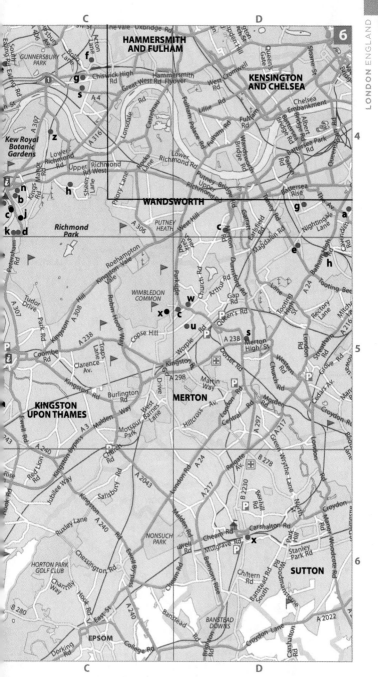

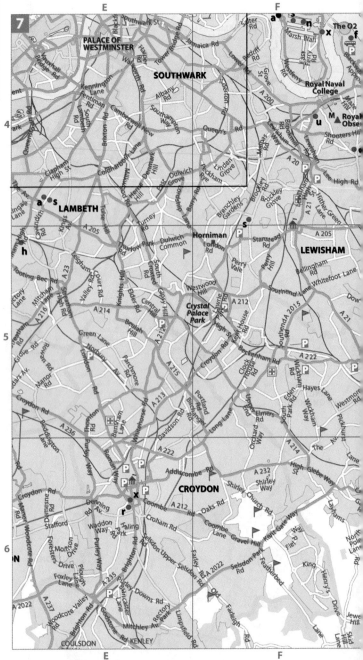

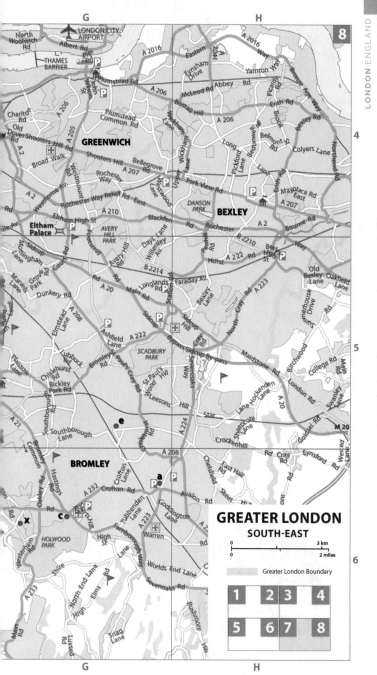

GREATER LONDON
SOUTH-EAST

0 — 3 km
0 — 2 miles

Greater London Boundary

| 1 | 2 | 3 | 4 |
| 5 | 6 | 7 | 8 |

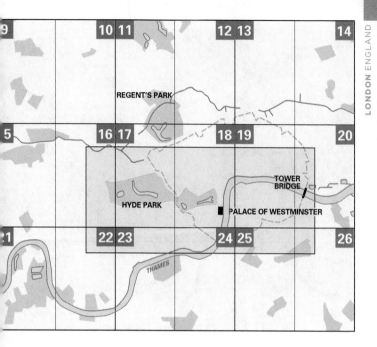

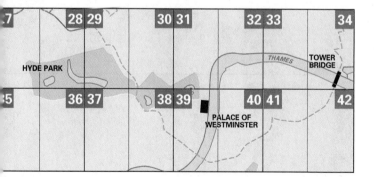

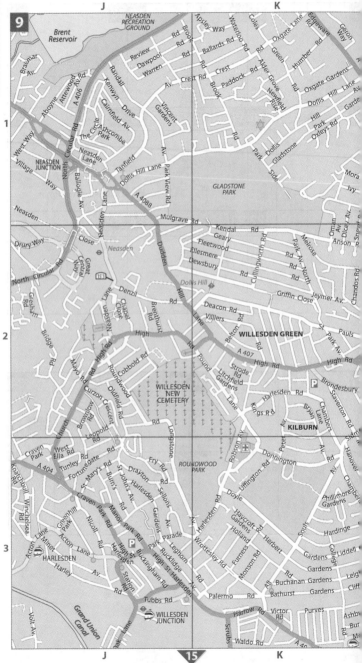

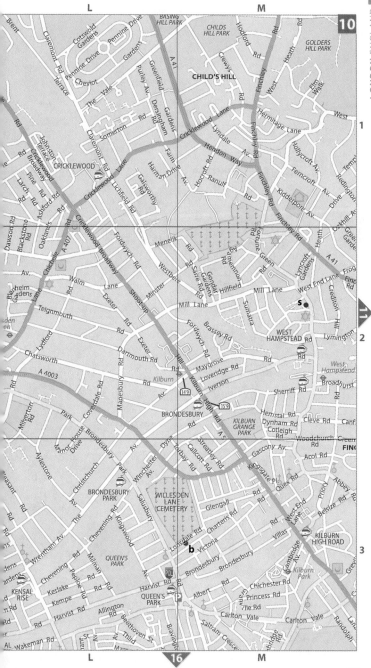

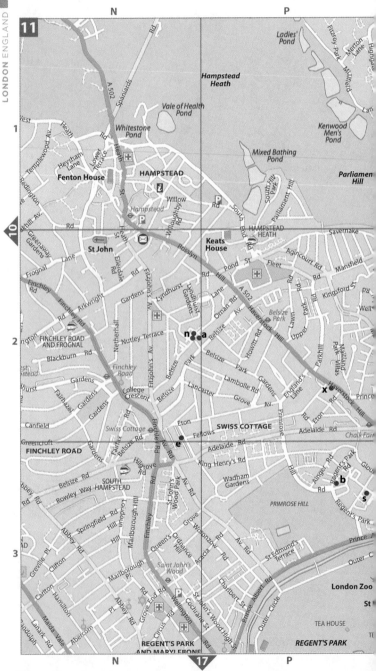

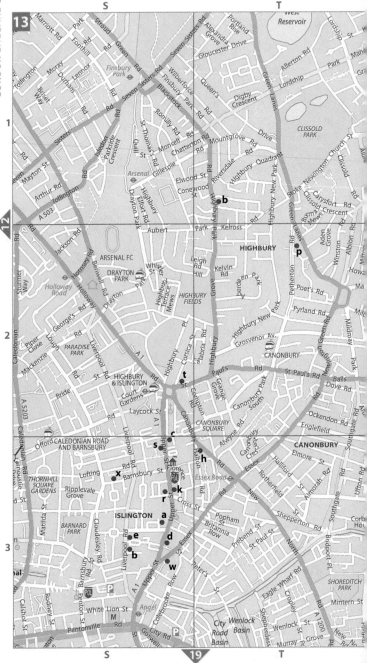

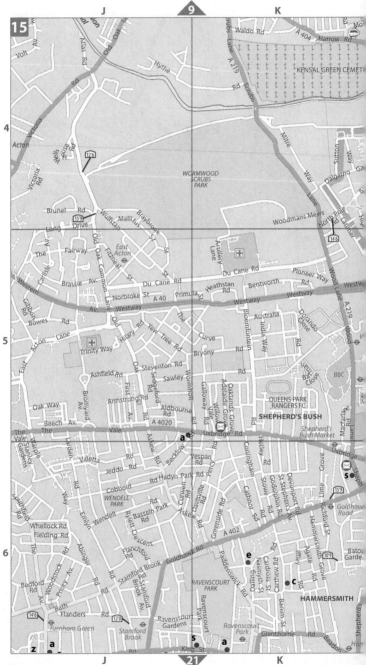

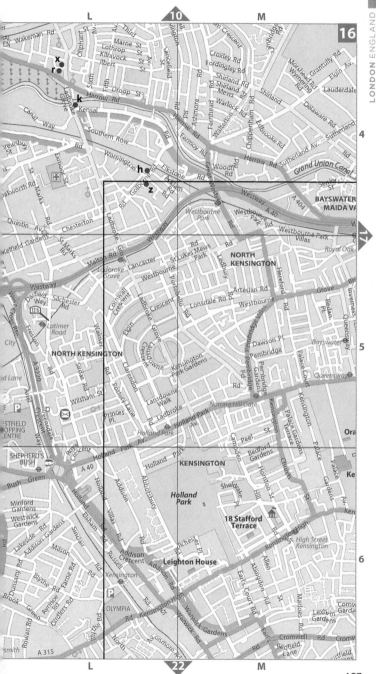

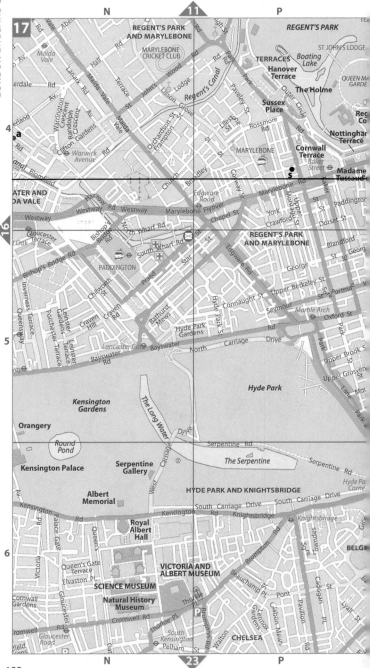

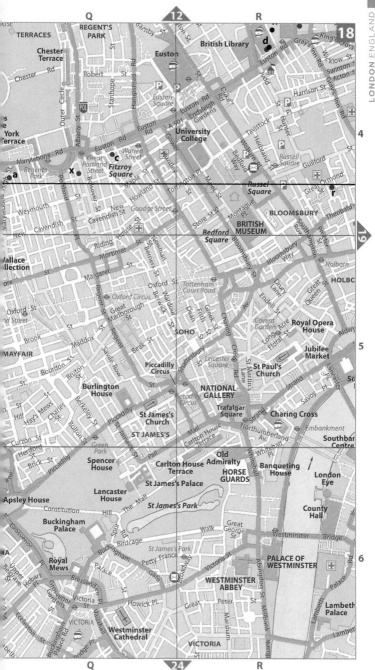

TERRACES
REGENT'S PARK
Chester Terrace
Chester Rd
York Terrace

Q

Barnby St
Euston
British Library

d

King's Cross
Gray's
cklow t
Swinton
Acton

Robert St
Stanhope St
Euston Square
Euston Rd
A-501 Euston Rd
Endsleigh Gardens
Dukes Rd
Harrison St

Outer Circle
Albany St

University College

Tavistock
Woburn
Hunter

Regent's Park
a

Marylebone Rd
Great Portland Street
Warren Street
c
x
Fitzroy Square

Gower St
Grafton Way
Bedford Way
Russell Square
Guilford

Maple St
Torrington Pl
Keppel St
Malet St
Montague Pl

Great Ormond
r

Weymouth St
New Cavendish St
Riding House St
Goodge Street

Store St
RUSSEL Square

BLOOMSBURY
Theobald's

Wallace Collection
ore

Mortimer St
Margaret St
Oxford Circus

Newman St
Berners St
Wardour St

Bedford Square
BRITISH MUSEUM
Bloomsbury Way

Southampton Row
Proctor St

Holborn
HOLBC

Oxford St
d Street

Great Marlborough St
Regent St
Bewick St
Dean St
Greek St
Frith St

Tottenham Court Road

Drury Lane
Endell St
Great Queen St

MAYFAIR

Maddox St
Brook St

Savile Row
Beak St

Shaftesbury Av
Charing Cross Rd

SOHO
Leicester Square

Covent Garden
Long Acre
Floral St
Royal Opera House
Aldwy

Bourdon St
Bruton St
Berkeley St

Piccadilly Circus
St Martin's Lane
St Paul's Church

Jubilee Market
Strand
So

Hay's Mews
Charles St
Bolton St

Burlington House
Piccadilly Circus

NATIONAL GALLERY
Trafalgar Square

Savoy Pl
Charing Cross

Hill
Curzon St

Piccadilly
St James's St

St James's Church
ST JAMES'S

Mall
Carlton House Terrace
Northumberland Av

Embankment
Southbar Centre

Hertford St
Brick St
Piccadilly
Green Park

Pall Mall
Old Admiralty
HORSE GUARDS

Whitehall
Banqueting House

London Eye

Apsley House

Spencer House
Lancaster House

Carlton House Terrace
St James's Palace

The Mall
St James's Park

County Hall

Constitution Hill
Buckingham Palace
St James's Park
Walk
Great George St
Westminster
Bridge

Grosvenor
Royal Mews

Birdcage Walk
Petty France
Broadway

WESTMINSTER ABBEY

PALACE OF WESTMINSTER

Lambeth Palace

Upper
Hobart Pl
Bressenden Pl
Buckingham Palace Rd
Victoria St

Victoria Pl
Howick Pl
Great Peter St
Marsham St
Abingdon St
Millbank

Lambeth

eth
Eccleston

Westminster Cathedral
VICTORIA

Q

R

12

24

189

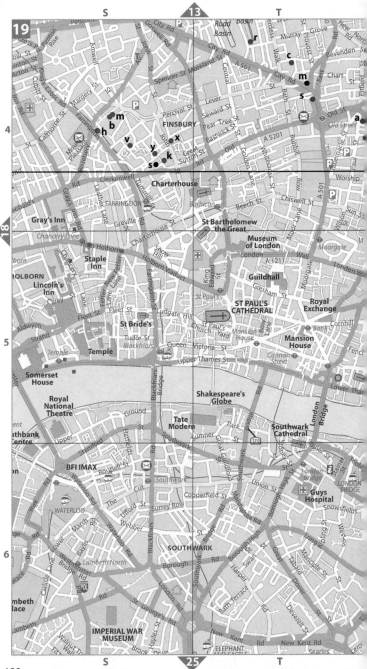

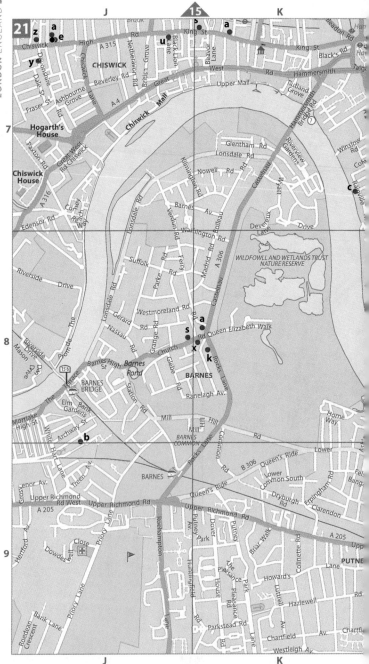

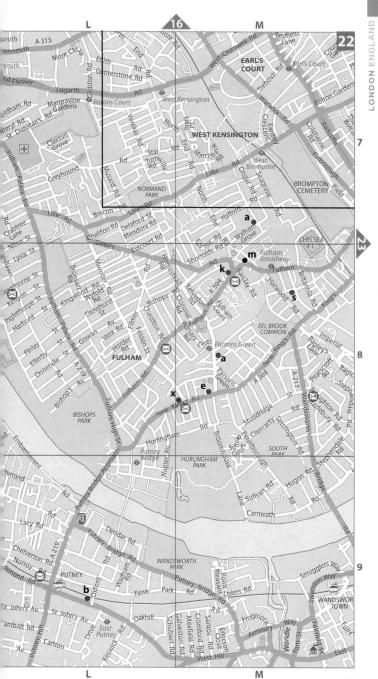

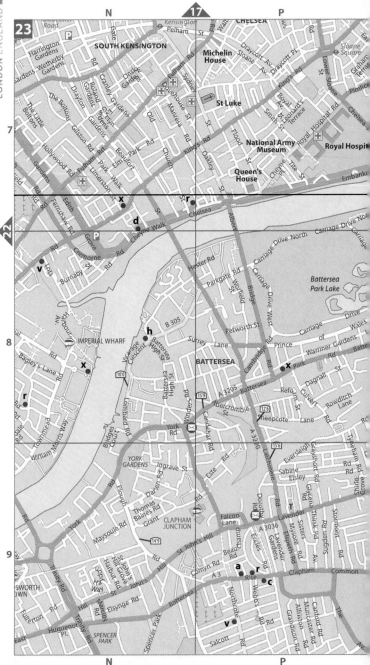

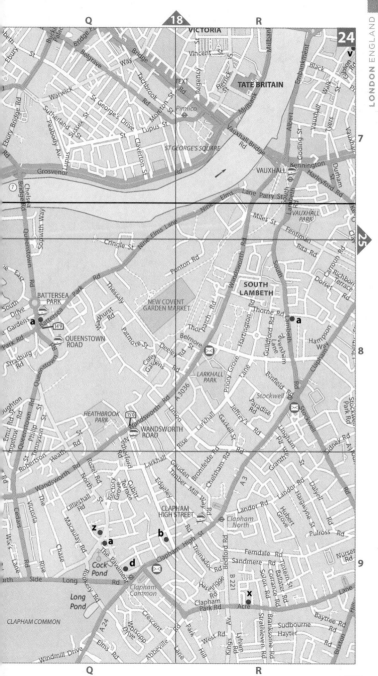

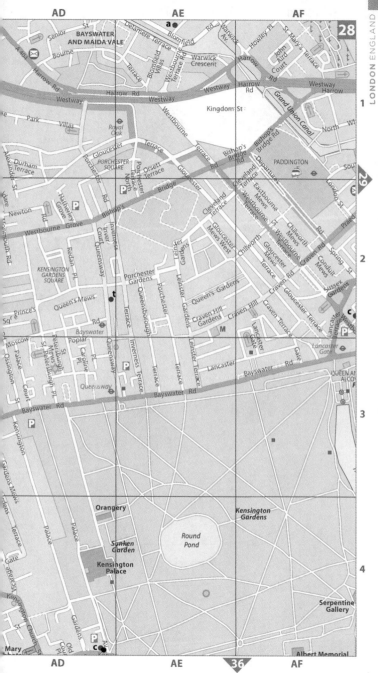

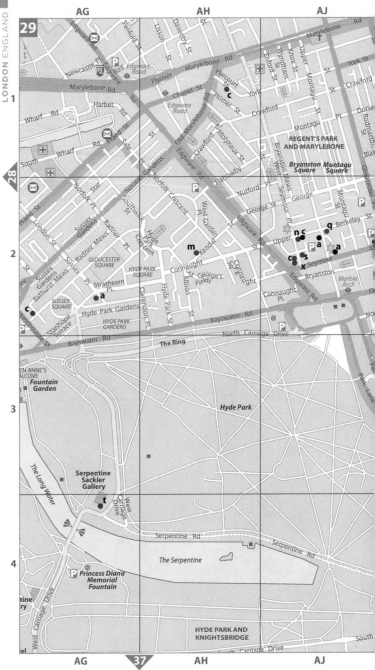

AK AL AM

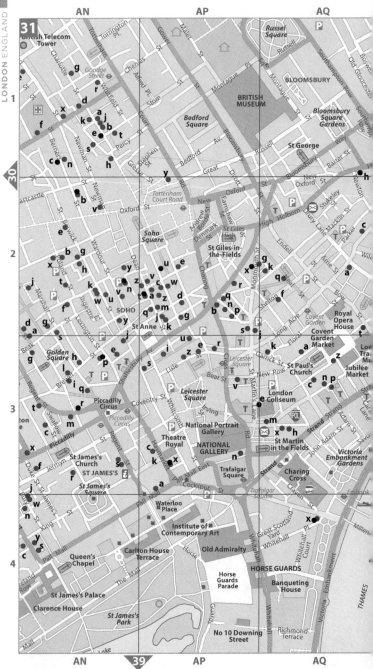

AN AP AQ

British Telecom Tower

Torrington Pl.

Gower

Malet

Russel Square

P

Chenies

Store

Montague Pl.

BLOOMSBURY

Bedford Square

BRITISH MUSEUM

Bloomsbury Square Gardens

St George

Bloomsbury Way

New Oxford St

Oxford St

Tottenham Court Road

St Giles High St

St Giles-in-the-Fields

High Holborn

Soho Square

Endell

Drury La

Covent Garden

Royal Opera House

SOHO

St Anne

Long Acre

Covent Garden Market

St Paul's Church

Jubilee Market

Golden Square

Leicester Square

St Martin's La

London Coliseum

Piccadilly Circus

National Portrait Gallery

NATIONAL GALLERY

St Martin in the Fields

Strand

Victoria Embankment Gardens

Theatre Royal

Trafalgar Square

Charing Cross

Piccadilly

St James's Church

ST JAMES'S

Pall Mall East

Cockspur

Trafalgar Square

St James's Square

Waterloo Place

Institute of Contemporary Art

Old Admiralty

HORSE GUARDS

Banqueting House

THAMES

Queen's Chapel

Carlton House Terrace

Horse Guards Parade

St James's Palace

Clarence House

St James's Park

No 10 Downing Street

Richmond Terrace

AN AP AQ

39

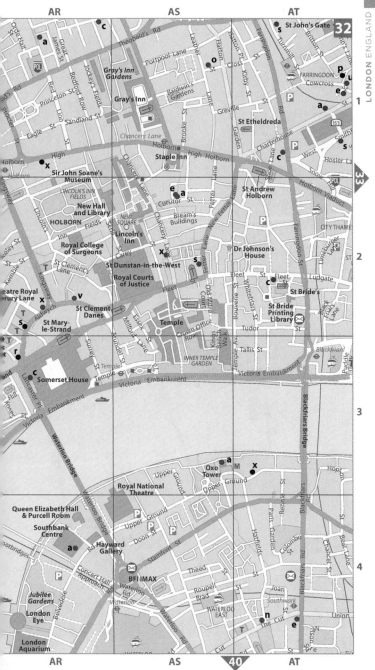

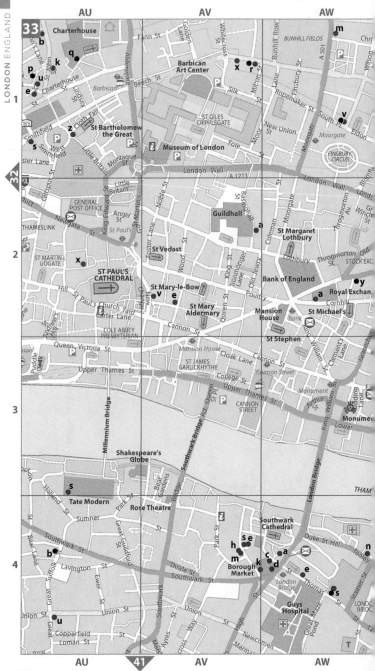

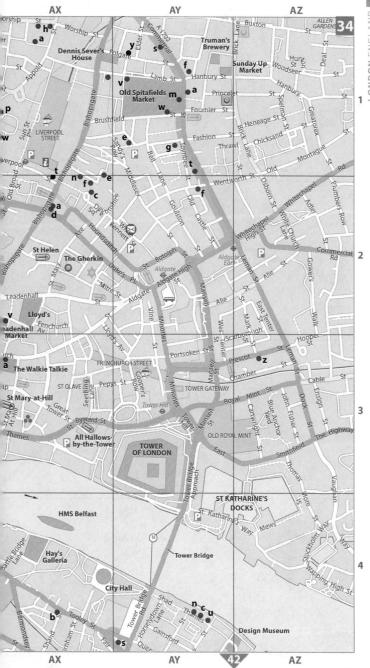

AX   AY   AZ

34

ALLEN GARDENS

Worship St
Worship St

Dennis Sever's House

Folgate St

Truman's Brewery

Sunday Up Market

Brick Lane

Buxton St

Commercial

Elder St

Lamb St

Hanbury St

Old Spitafields Market

Princelet St

Fournier St

Fashion St

Brushfield St

Heneage St

Chicksand

Thrawl St

Toynbee St

Bell Lane

Old Castle St

Wentworth St

Whitechapel High St

LIVERPOOL STREET

Bishopsgate

Old Broad St

St Helen

The Gherkin

Aldgate

Aldgate East

Leman St

Commercial Rd

Lloyd's

Leadenhall Market

Fenchurch Av

The Walkie Talkie

FRENCHURCH STREET

ST OLAVE

Pepys St

Cooper's

TOWER GATEWAY

Prescot St

St Mary-at-Hill

Great Tower St

Byward St

Tower Hill

OLD ROYAL MINT

The Highway

All Hallows-by-the-Tower

TOWER OF LONDON

Smithfield

HMS Belfast

ST KATHARINE'S DOCKS

Hay's Galleria

Tower Bridge

City Hall

Design Museum

Wapping High St

AX   AY   AZ

42

205

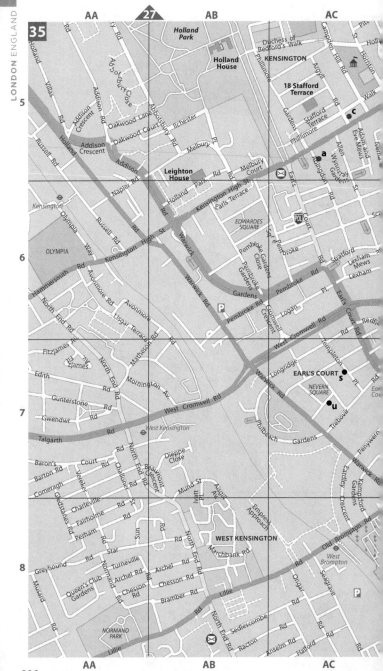

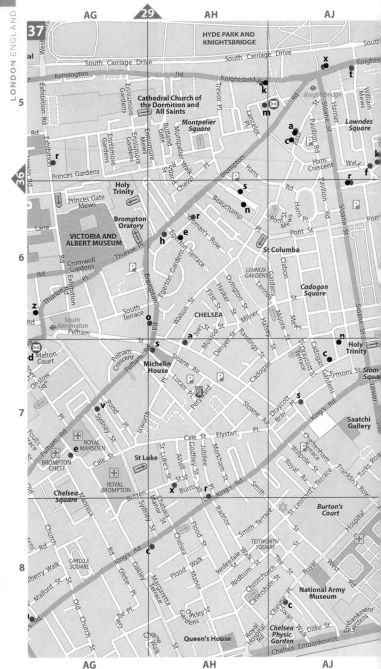

29

36

AG AH AJ

HYDE PARK AND
KNIGHTSBRIDGE

South Carriage Drive
South Carriage Drive

Kensington Rd

Exhibition Gardens
Ennismore Gardens
Ennismore Gardens
Ennismore Mews

Cathedral Church of
the Dormition and
All Saints

Montpelier
Square

Knightsbridge

Knightsbridge

x
t
Knights

William
Mews

Harriet

Sloane St

Pavilion Rd

Lowndes
Square

a
c

Hans
Crescent

Wal

k
f
r

Exhibition Rd

Exhibition Rd

r

Princes Gardens

Princes Gate
Mews

Holy
Trinity

Brompton
Oratory

VICTORIA AND
ALBERT MUSEUM

Cromwell
Gardens

Lane

Rutland Gate
Montpelier Walk
Montpelier Pl

Cheval Pl

Brompton Rd

Hans Rd

Hans Rd

Pavilion Rd

Pavilion Rd

P

P

Beauchamp Pl

s

n

Pont St

Pont St Mews

Pont Pl

St Columba

LENNOX
GARDENS

Clabon

Lennox Gardens

Cadogan
Square

Sloane St

r

h
e

Yeoman's Row
Egerton Terrace

Egerton Gardens

Thurloe Pl

Cromwell Rd

z

Thurloe Rd

Exhibition Rd

South Kensington

South
Terrace

Pelham

Walton St

Hasker St

First St

Ovington St

Milner St

Moore St

Halsey St

CHELSEA

Cadogan
Gardens

Draycott Pl

Draycott Terrace

Holy
Trinity

n

c

Symons St

Sloane
Square

Saatchi
Gallery

Lower

o

Brompton Rd

a

s

Sydney Pl

Ixworth Pl

Pond Pl

Pelham Crescent

Michelin
House

Sloane Av

Lucan Pl

Petyward

Cale St

d
Melton
Court

Onslow Sq

Foulis Terrace

Fulham Rd

Fulham Rd

v

e

ROYAL
MARSDEN

BROMPTON
CHEST

Cale St

St Luke's

Sydney St

ROYAL
BROMPTON

St Luke's St

Astell St

Godfrey St

Jubilee Pl

Markham St

Elystan Pl

Cadogan St

Blacklands Terrace

Draycott Av

Bray Pl

s

King's Rd

King's Rd

Cheltenham Terrace

Walpole St

Royal Av

St Leonard's Terrace

Franklin's Row

Turks Row

Burton's
Court

Chelsea
Square

Britten St

x
Burns

r

King's Rd

Radnor Walk

Smith Terrace

Smith St

TEDWORTH
SQUARE

Hospital

National Army
Museum

CARLYLE
SQUARE

Mulberry Walk

Mallord St

Old Church St

King's Rd

Oakley St

Glebe Pl

Margaretta Terrace

c

Chelsea Manor St

Flood St

Flood Walk

Chelsea Manor Gardens

Oakley Gardens

Cheyne Row

Redesdale St

Manor St

Redburn St

Christchurch St

Caversham St

Royal Hospital Rd

The Vale

West Rd

Royal Av

c

Chelsea
Physic
Garden

Cheyne Walk
Swan Walk
Dilke St

Chelsea Embankment

Embankment
Gardens

Queen's House

AG AH AJ

208

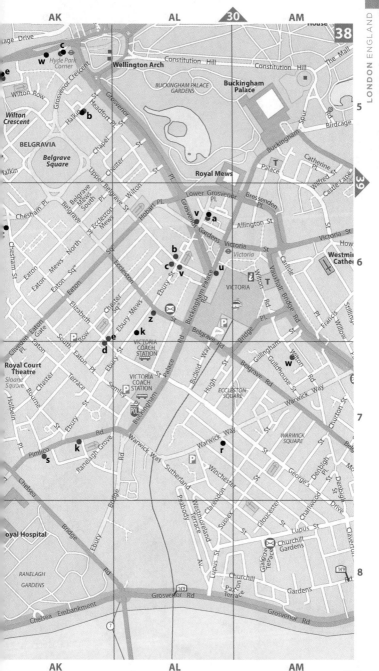

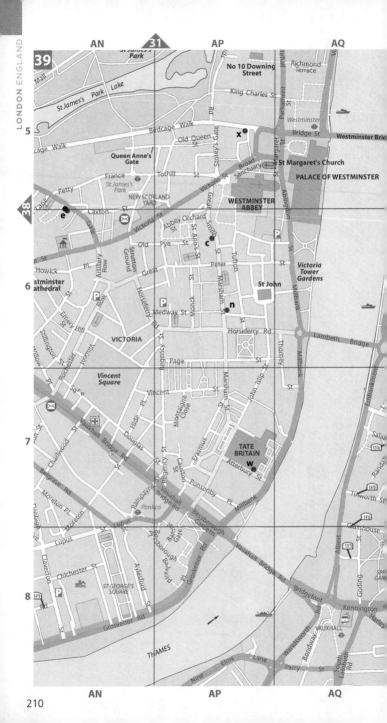

AN AP AQ

St James's Park

No 10 Downing Street
Richmond Terrace
Mall
King Charles St
St James's Park Lake
Whitehall
Westminster
Birdcage Walk
Bridge St
Westminster Brie
cage Walk
Old Queen St
Storey's Gate
x
5
Queen Anne's Gate
Broad Sanctuary
St Margaret's Church
France
St James's Park
Tothill St
Victoria St
Great Smith St
Margaret St
PALACE OF WESTMINSTER
Petty
Abingdon
NEW SCOTLAND YARD
WESTMINSTER ABBEY
Caxton
e
Victoria
St Ann's St
Abbey Orchard St
P
St
Old Pye St
c
Tufton St
Peter St
Howick Pl.
Strutton Ground
Great
Marsham St
St John
Victoria Tower Gardens
Artillery Row
Horseferry Rd
stminster athedral
6
P
Row
P
n
Emery Hill St
Stillington St
Medway St
Monck St
Horseferry Rd
Millbank
Lambeth Bridge
willow St
VICTORIA
Regency St
Thorney St
Vincent
Square
Page St
Marsham St
John Islip St
Rochester
Hide St
Vincent
Montaigne Close
Millbank St
Embankment
Sala
136
7
Douglas
Vauxhall Bridge Rd
Chadwick St
Erasmus St
Clayton St
TATE BRITAIN
Randa
Belgrave Rd
Moreton Pl.
Rampayne St
Regency St
Ponsonby Pl.
Atterbury St
w
149
Tinworth St
Moreton St
Vauxhall Bridge Rd
Bessborough St
Millbank
nabeigh
Lupus St
Pimlico
Bessborough Gardens
Grasshouse
Claverton St
Lupus St
Tachbrook St
Bessborough Pl.
Grosvenor Rd
Albert
133
Chichester St
Aylesford St
Vauxhall Bridge Rd
Bridgefoot
SPRI GAR
8
P
149
ST GEORGE'S SQUARE
Grosvenor Rd
Kennington
Harley
Wandsworth Rd
VAUXHALL
Bondway
Goding
THAMES
Nine Elms Lane
Parry St
South Lambeth Rd

AN AP AQ

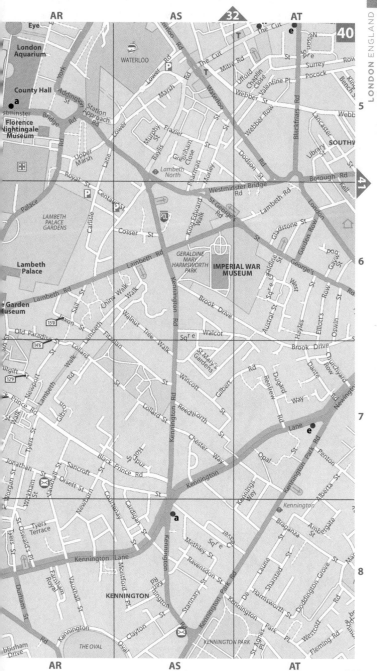

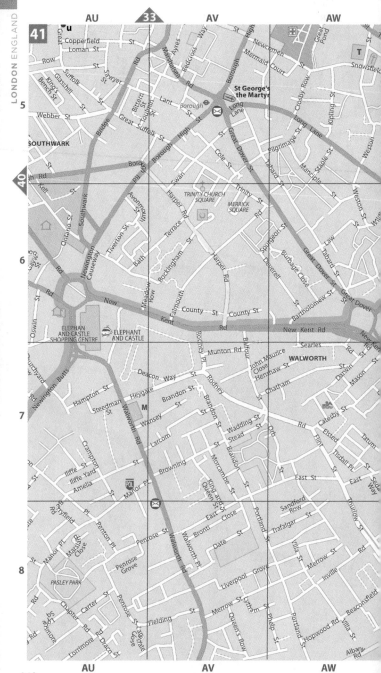

AU · AV · AW

SOUTHWARK

Copperfield St
Loman St
Row
Suffolk St
Glasshill St
King's Bench St
Webber St
Great Suffolk St
Bridge
Ayres St
Marshalsea Rd
Redcross Way
Borough
Lant St
Borough
Bittern St
Toulmin St
Sawyer St
Borough High St
Mermaid Court
Newcomen St
Great Pond
Snowsfield
St George's
the Martyr
Long Lane
Crosby Row
Kipling St
Long Lane
Weston St
Kent Rd
Ontario St
Southwark
Newington Causeway
Tiverton St
Avonmouth St
Harper Rd
Bath
Terrace
Rockingham St
Cole St
Great Dover St
Tabard St
Pilgrimage St
Manciple St
Stable St
Weston St
Law St
TRINITY CHURCH SQUARE
MERRICK SQUARE
Trinity St
Harper Rd
Spurgeon St
Deverell St
Great Dover St
Burbage Close
Bartholomew St
Great Dover St
New Kent Rd
Meadow Row
Falmouth Rd
County St
County St
New Kent Rd
New Kent Rd
ELEPHANT AND CASTLE SHOPPING CENTRE
ELEPHANT AND CASTLE
Oswin St
New Kent Rd
Rodney Pl
Munton Rd
Balfour St
Searles Rd
John Maurice Close
Henshaw St
WALWORTH
Deacon Way
Heygate St
Brandon St
Rodney Rd
Chatham St
Darwin St
Mason St
Newington Butts
Hampton St
Steedman St
Walworth Rd
Wansey St
Larcom St
Brandon St
Wadding St
Stead St
Orb St
Catesby St
Elsted St
Flint St
Tisdall Pl
Tatum St
Crampton St
Iliffe St
Iliffe Yard
Amelia St
Browning St
Manor Pl
Morecambe St
King and Queen St
East St
Brandon St
Rd
East St
East St
Sandford Row
Thurlow St
Sedan Way
Manor Pl
Penton Pl
Masters
Close
Penrose St
Bronti Pl
Date St
Portland St
Trafalgar St
Villa St
Merrow St
Inville Rd
PASLEY PARK
Penrose Grove
Penrose St
Stopford Rd
Walworth Rd
Liverpool Grove
Merrow St
Smyrk's Rd
Queen's Row
Phelp St
Fielding St
Portland St
Hopwood Rd
Villa St
Beaconsfield
Albany Rd
Chapter Rd
Carter St
Dale Rd
Larrimore Rd

AU · AV · AW

212

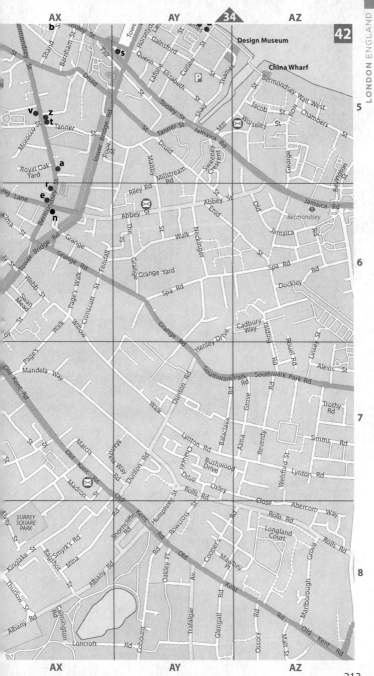

ENGLAND

A vision of England sweeps across historic buildings and rolling landscapes, but from the rugged splendour of Cornwall's cliffs to pounding Northumbrian shores, this image seeks parity with a newer picture of Albion: refined cities whose industrial past has been reshaped by a shiny, interactive reality. The country's bones and bumps are a reassuring constant: the windswept moors of the south west and the craggy peaks of the Pennines, the summery orchards of the Kentish Weald, the constancy of East Anglian skies and the mirrored calm of Cumbria's lakes.

Renewed interest in all things regional means restaurants are increasingly looking to serve dishes rooted in their locality. Think Melton Mowbray pie in Leicestershire or Lancashire hotpot in the north west – and what better place to eat cheese than where it was made? Seafood is an important part of the English diet: try shrimps from Morecambe Bay, oysters from Whitstable, crab from Cromer and fish from Brixham. Sunday pub roasts are another quintessential part of English life – and a trip to the South West wouldn't be complete without a cream tea.

- Michelin Road map n° 502, 503, 504 and 713
- Michelin Green Guide: Great Britain

FoodCollection/Photononstop

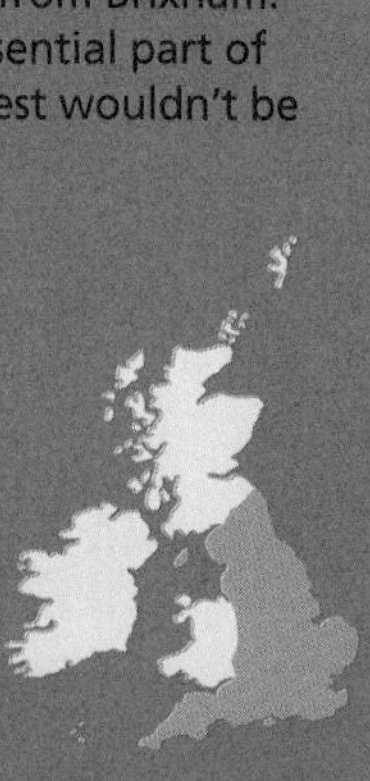

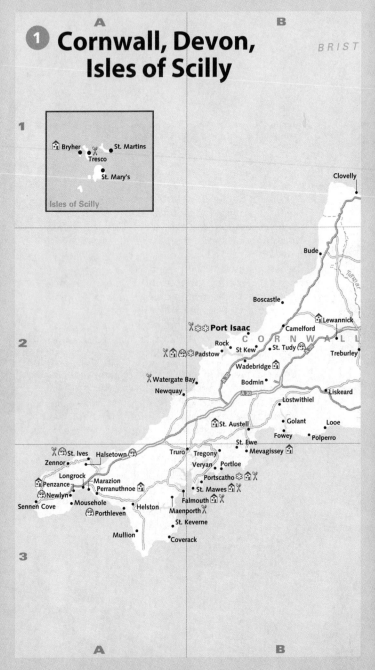

Cornwall, Devon, Isles of Scilly

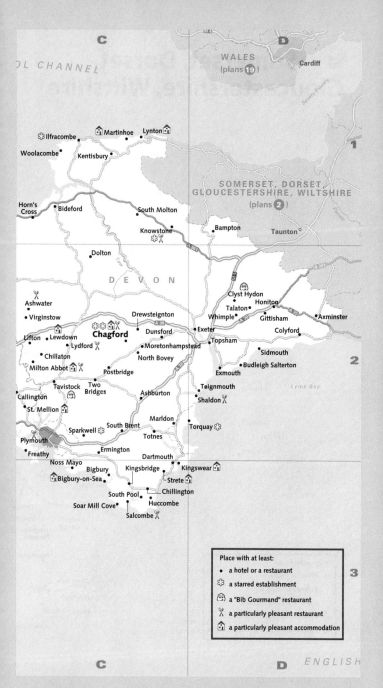

Place with at least:

- a hotel or a restaurant
- ❀ a starred establishment
- Ⓑ a "Bib Gourmand" restaurant
- ✕ a particularly pleasant restaurant
- ⌂ a particularly pleasant accommodation

217

Somerset, Dorset, Gloucestershire, Wiltshire

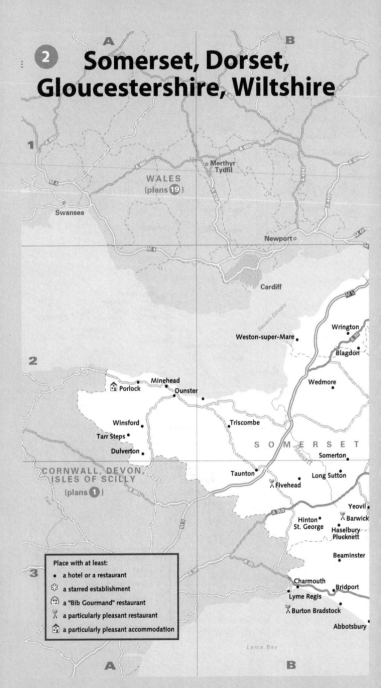

1

WALES
(plans **19**)

Merthyr Tydfil

Swansea

Newport o

Cardiff

Wrington

Weston-super-Mare

Blagdon

2

Minehead

Porlock

Wedmore

Dunster

Winsford

Triscombe

S O M E R S E T

Tarr Steps

Somerton

Dulverton

CORNWALL, DEVON,
ISLES OF SCILLY
(plans **1**)

Taunton

Long Sutton

Fivehead

Yeovil

Hinton
St. George

Barwick

Haselbury
Plucknett

Beaminster

Place with at least:

- a hotel or a restaurant
- ✿ a starred establishment
- ☺ a "Bib Gourmand" restaurant
- ✗ a particularly pleasant restaurant
- ⌂ a particularly pleasant accommodation

3

Charmouth

Bridport

Lyme Regis

Burton Bradstock

Abbotsbury

Lyme Bay

A   B

218

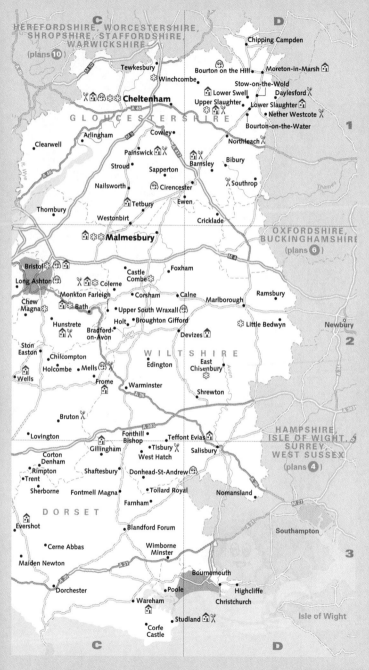

C **HEREFORDSHIRE, WORCESTERSHIRE, SHROPSHIRE, STAFFORDSHIRE, WARWICKSHIRE** (plans 10)

D

Chipping Campden

Tewkesbury

Bourton on the Hill ● Moreton-in-Marsh

Winchcombe

Stow-on-the-Wold

Cheltenham ● Lower Swell ● Daylesford

Upper Slaughter ● Lower Slaughter

G L O U C E S T E R S H I R E ● Nether Westcote

● Bourton-on-the-Water

Arlingham ● Cowley ● Northleach

Clearwell

Painswick ● Bibury

Stroud ● Sapperton ● Barnsley

Nailsworth ● Cirencester ● Southrop

Thornbury ● Tetbury ● Ewen

Westonbirt ● Cricklade

Malmesbury ●

OXFORDSHIRE, BUCKINGHAMSHIRE (plans 6)

Bristol ● Castle Combe ● Foxham

Long Ashton ● Colerne

Chew Magna ● Monkton Farleigh ● Corsham ● Calne ● Marlborough ● Ramsbury

Bath ● Upper South Wraxall

Hunstrete ● Holt ● Broughton Gifford

Ston Easton ● Bradford-on-Avon ● Devizes ● Little Bedwyn ● Newbury

W I L T S H I R E

Chilcompton ● Edington ● East Chisenbury

Holcombe ● Mells

Wells ● Frome ● Warminster ● Shrewton

Bruton

Lovington ● Fonthill Bishop ● Teffont Evias

HAMPSHIRE, ISLE OF WIGHT, SURREY, WEST SUSSEX (plans 4)

Corton Denham ● Gillingham ● Tisbury ● West Hatch ● Salisbury

Rimpton ● Shaftesbury ● Donhead-St-Andrew

Trent ● Fontmell Magna ● Tollard Royal ● Nomansland

Sherborne ● Farnham

D O R S E T

Evershot ● Blandford Forum ● Southampton

Cerne Abbas ● Wimborne Minster

Maiden Newton

Bournemouth

Dorchester ● Poole ● Highcliffe

Wareham ● Christchurch

Corfe Castle ● Studland ● Isle of Wight

C D

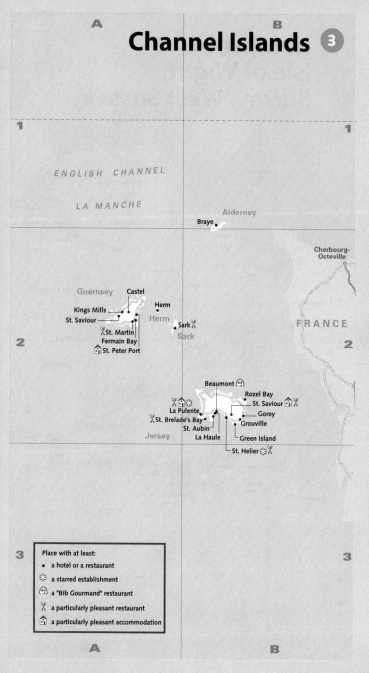

Channel Islands 3

ENGLISH CHANNEL

LA MANCHE

Alderney

Braye

Cherbourg-
Octeville

Guernsey   Castel
                        Herm
Kings Mills
St. Saviour   Herm
                        Sark
St. Martin
Fermain Bay   Sark
St. Peter Port

FRANCE

Beaumont
                    Rozel Bay
                        St. Saviour
La Pulente
St. Brelade's Bay   Gorey
St. Aubin   Grouville
La Haule   Green Island
Jersey
St. Helier

Place with at least:
- • a hotel or a restaurant
- ❀ a starred establishment
- ☺ a "Bib Gourmand" restaurant
- ✗ a particularly pleasant restaurant
- ⌂ a particularly pleasant accommodation

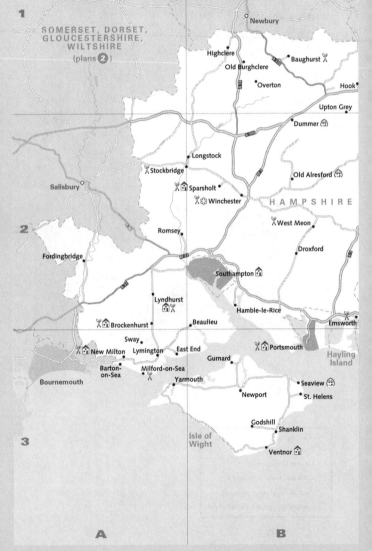

Reading

Newbury

SOMERSET, DORSET,
GLOUCESTERSHIRE,
WILTSHIRE
(plans 2)

Highclere
Old Burghclere
Baughurst ✗
Overton
Hook
Upton Grey
Dummer 🏠

Longstock
✗ Stockbridge
Old Alresford 🏠
✗ Sparsholt
✗ ✿ Winchester
HAMPSHIRE
Salisbury
Romsey
✗ West Meon
Droxford
Fordingbridge
Southampton 🏠
Lyndhurst
🏠✗
Hamble-le-Rice
Emsworth
✗ 🏠 Brockenhurst
Beaulieu
Sway
✗ 🏠 New Milton
Lymington
East End
✗ 🏠 Portsmouth
Hayling
Island
Barton-
on-Sea
Milford-on-Sea
✗
Gurnard
Yarmouth
Bournemouth
Seaview 🏠
Newport
St. Helens
Isle of
Wight
Godshill
Shanklin
Ventnor 🏠

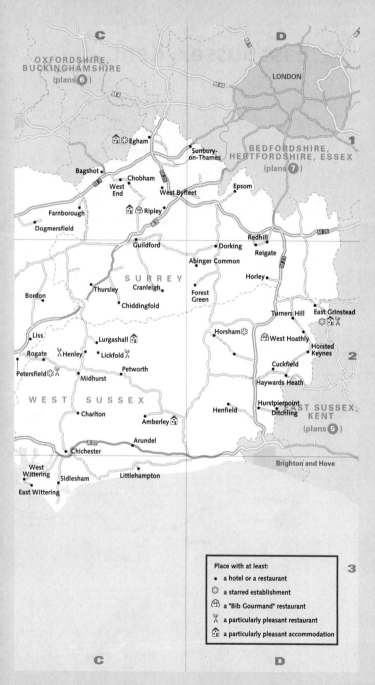

Place with at least:
- • a hotel or a restaurant
- ❀ a starred establishment
- ⓑ a "Bib Gourmand" restaurant
- ✕ a particularly pleasant restaurant
- ⌂ a particularly pleasant accommodation

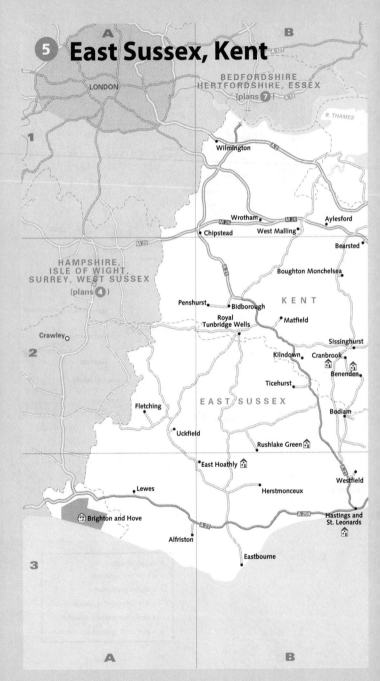

LONDON

BEDFORDSHIRE
HERTFORDSHIRE, ESSEX
(plans 7)

R. THAMES

Wilmington

HAMPSHIRE,
ISLE OF WIGHT,
SURREY, WEST SUSSEX
(plans 4)

Wrotham
Chipstead
West Malling
Aylesford
Bearsted

Boughton Monchelsea

KENT

Penshurst
Bidborough
Royal
Tunbridge Wells
Matfield

Sissinghurst
Kilndown
Cranbrook
Benenden

Crawley

EAST SUSSEX
Ticehurst
Bodiam

Fletching

Uckfield

Rushlake Green

East Hoathly

Westfield

Lewes
Herstmonceux

Brighton and Hove

Hastings and
St. Leonards

Alfriston

Eastbourne

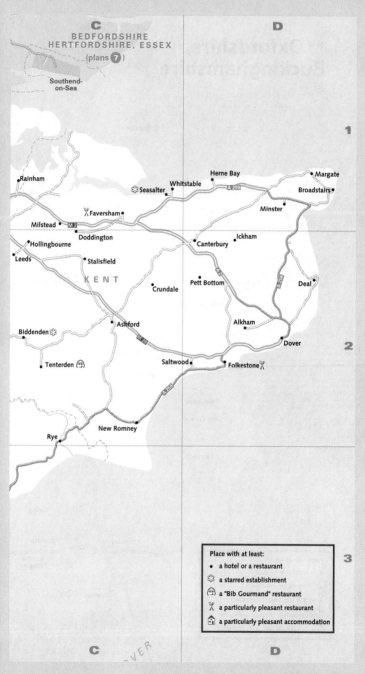

Southend-
on-Sea

1

Rainham

Herne Bay

Margate

✿ Seasalter Whitstable

Broadstairs •

Minster

✕ Faversham •

Milstead M 2

Doddington

Ickham

Hollingbourne

Canterbury

Leeds

Stalisfield

K E N T

Pett Bottom

Deal

Crundale

Biddenden ✿

Ashford

Alkham

M 20

Tenterden 🅐

Saltwood • Folkestone ✕

Dover

2

New Romney

Rye

3

Place with at least:
• a hotel or a restaurant
✿ a starred establishment
🅐 a "Bib Gourmand" restaurant
✕ a particularly pleasant restaurant
🏠 a particularly pleasant accommodation

C

D

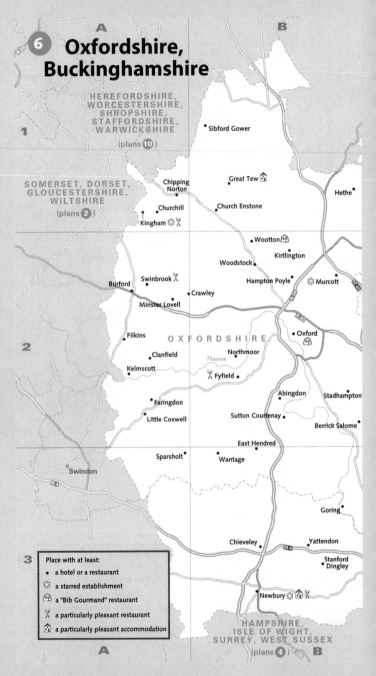

Oxfordshire, Buckinghamshire

A

B

HEREFORDSHIRE, WORCESTERSHIRE, SHROPSHIRE, STAFFORDSHIRE, WARWICKSHIRE
(plans 10)

1

SOMERSET, DORSET, GLOUCESTERSHIRE, WILTSHIRE
(plans 2)

Sibford Gower

Great Tew 🏠

Hethe

Chipping Norton

Church Enstone

Churchill

Kingham 🕸 ✗

Wootton 😊

Kirtlington

Woodstock

Hampton Poyle

🕸 Murcott

Burford

Swinbrook ✗

Crawley

Minster Lovell

OXFORDSHIRE

Oxford 😊

2

Filkins

Clanfield

Northmoor

Thames

Kelmscott

✗ Fyfield

Abingdon

Stadhampton

Faringdon

Little Coxwell

Sutton Courtenay

Berrick Salome

East Hendred

Sparsholt

Wantage

Swindon

Goring

Chieveley

Yattendon

Stanford Dingley

3

Newbury 🕸 🏠 ✗

Place with at least:
- • a hotel or a restaurant
- 🕸 a starred establishment
- 😊 a "Bib Gourmand" restaurant
- ✗ a particularly pleasant restaurant
- 🏠 a particularly pleasant accommodation

HAMPSHIRE, ISLE OF WIGHT, SURREY, WEST SUSSEX
(plans 4)

A

B

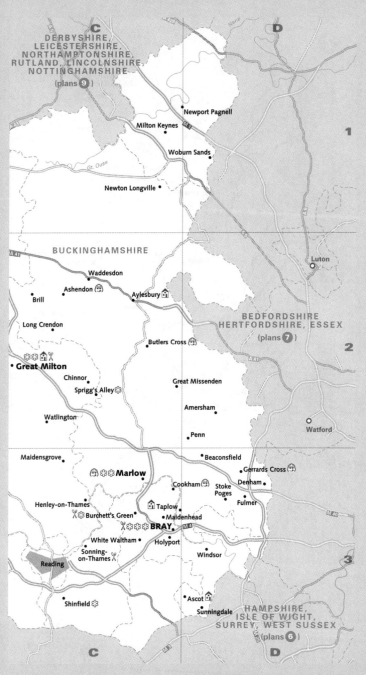

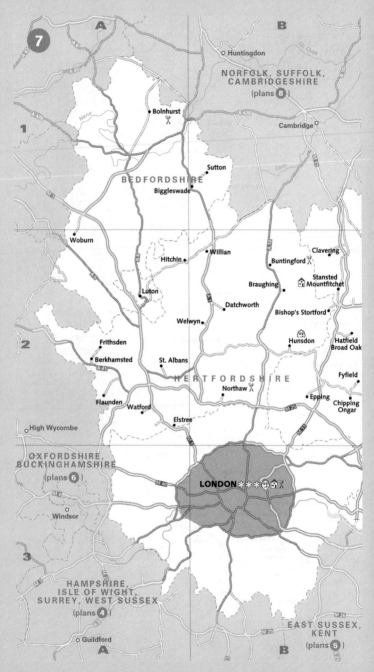

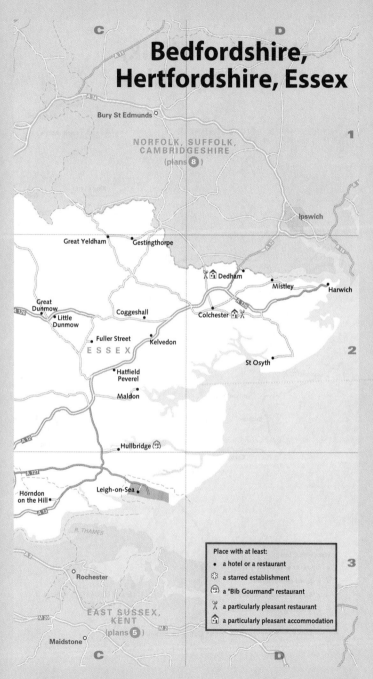

Bedfordshire,
Hertfordshire, Essex

Bury St Edmunds

NORFOLK, SUFFOLK,
CAMBRIDGESHIRE
(plans 8)

Ipswich

Great Yeldham • Gestingthorpe •

Dedham

Mistley • Harwich •

Great
Dunmow •
• Little
Dunmow

Coggeshall •

Colchester

E S S E X
• Fuller Street • Kelvedon

St Osyth

• Hatfield
Peverel

Maldon •

Hullbridge

Horndon
on the Hill •
Leigh-on-Sea •

R. THAMES

Rochester

EAST SUSSEX,
KENT
(plans 5)

Maidstone

Place with at least:
- • a hotel or a restaurant
- ❀ a starred establishment
- ☺ a "Bib Gourmand" restaurant
- ✗ a particularly pleasant restaurant
- 🏠 a particularly pleasant accommodation

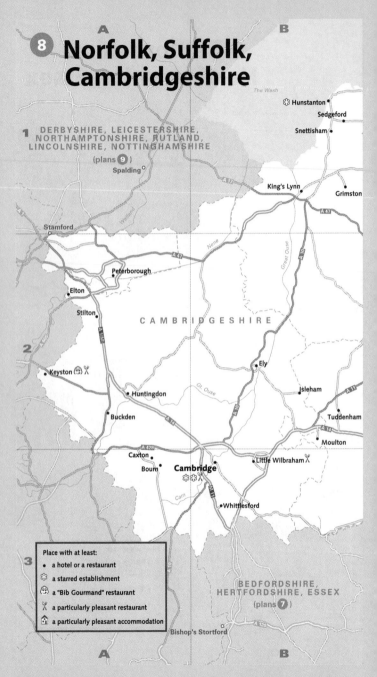

C

D

Brancaster
Staithe
Holkham   Wells-next-the-Sea
Titchwell   Blakeney   Sheringham
         Burnham   Morston ❄ 🏠 ✕   Cromer
         Market
Stanhoe   Holt
                                                        Thorpe Market 😊 ✕   1
Great Bircham
                    Thursford
                    Green
                              Itteringham   North Walsham
                                        Aylsham
                 Wellingham   Ingham 😊
                              Reepham

         N O R F O L K

                                                        Horning

Swaffham   Norwich   A 47   Bure

Watton   Yare

                 Attleborough

                                                                        2
                 Pulham Market   Bungay
Thetford
         North Lopham
                                                        Southwold
         ✕ Stanton   Walberswick
Bury   Darsham
St Edmunds 😊 ✕   Westleton

                 Earl Stonham
                              S U F F O L K   Snape
         ✕ 🏠
Lavenham   Bildeston   Ufford   Aldeburgh 😊
                                                    Orford 🏠
Long Melford   Woodbridge
         Hadleigh   Ipswich
                                              Ramsholt
         ✕ Stoke-by-Nayland   3
         Stratford St Mary

                                        ○ Harwich

         Colchester

C

D

231

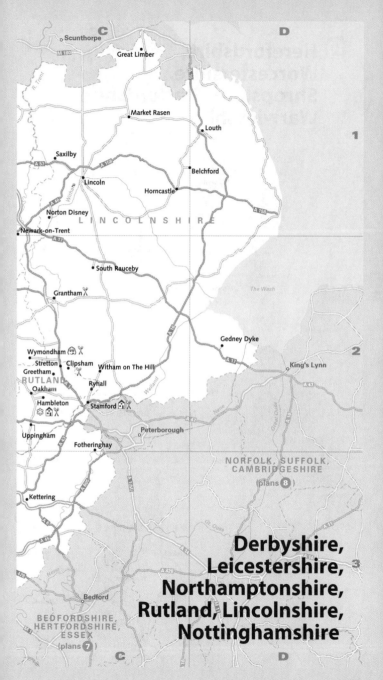

Derbyshire,
Leicestershire,
Northamptonshire,
Rutland, Lincolnshire,
Nottinghamshire

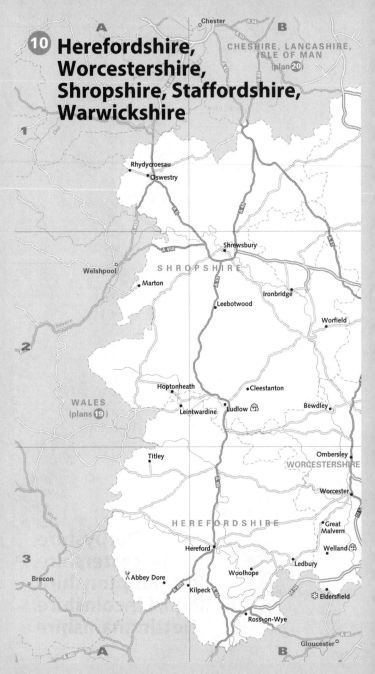

10 Herefordshire, Worcestershire, Shropshire, Staffordshire, Warwickshire

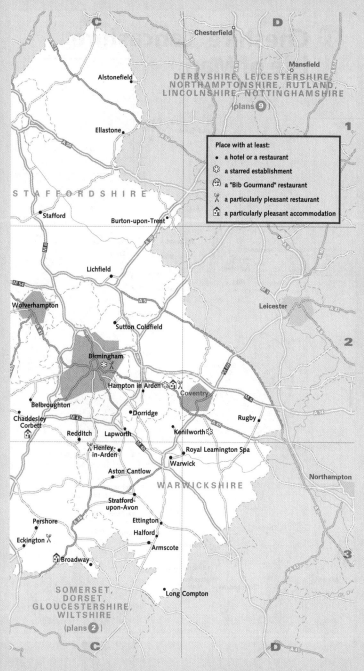

Chesterfield

Mansfield

DERBYSHIRE, LEICESTERSHIRE, NORTHAMPTONSHIRE, RUTLAND, LINCOLNSHIRE, NOTTINGHAMSHIRE
(plans 9)

Alstonefield

Ellastone

Place with at least:
- • a hotel or a restaurant
- ✿ a starred establishment
- 🐵 a "Bib Gourmand" restaurant
- 🏃 a particularly pleasant restaurant
- 🏠 a particularly pleasant accommodation

S T A F F O R D S H I R E

Stafford

Burton-upon-Trent

Lichfield

Leicester

Wolverhampton

Sutton Coldfield

Birmingham ✿🏃

Hampton in Arden ✿🏠🏃
Coventry

Belbroughton

Chaddesley Corbett 🏠

Redditch

Lapworth

Dorridge

Henley-in-Arden 🏃

Rugby

Kenilworth ✿

Royal Leamington Spa

Warwick

Aston Cantlow

Northampton

W A R W I C K S H I R E

Stratford-upon-Avon

Pershore

Eckington 🏃

Ettington

Halford

Armscote

Broadway 🏠

SOMERSET, DORSET, GLOUCESTERSHIRE, WILTSHIRE
(plans 2)

Long Compton

235

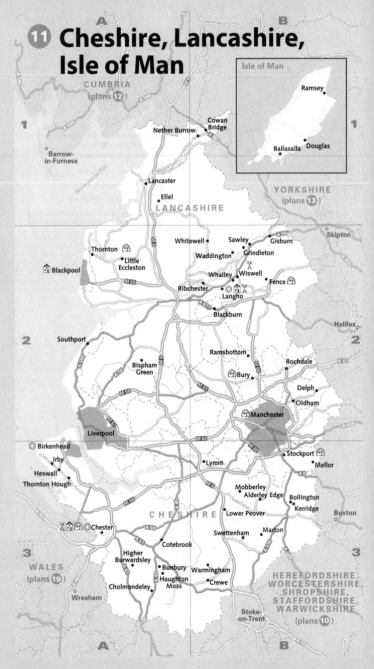

11 Cheshire, Lancashire, Isle of Man

Isle of Man

Ramsey

Ballasalla · Douglas

CUMBRIA (plans 12)

Barrow-in-Furness

Morecambe Bay

Nether Burrow · Cowan Bridge

Lancaster

Ellel

LANCASHIRE

YORKSHIRE (plans 13)

Skipton

Thornton

Little Eccleston

Blackpool

Whitewell · Sawley · Gisburn

Waddington · Grindleton

Whalley · Wiswell · Fence

Ribchester · Langho

Blackburn

Southport

Bispham Green

Ramsbottom

Rochdale

Halifax

Bury

Delph

Oldham

Manchester

Liverpool

Birkenhead

Irby

Heswall

Thornton Hough

Stockport

Mellor

Lymm

Mobberley · Alderley Edge · Bollington

Kerridge

Buxton

CHESHIRE

Lower Peover

Marton

Swettenham

Chester

Cotebrook

Higher Burwardsley

Bunbury

Warmingham

Haughton Moss

Crewe

WALES (plans 19)

Wrexham

Cholmondeley

Stoke-on-Trent

HEREFORDSHIRE, WORCESTERSHIRE, SHROPSHIRE, STAFFORDSHIRE, WARWICKSHIRE (plans 10)

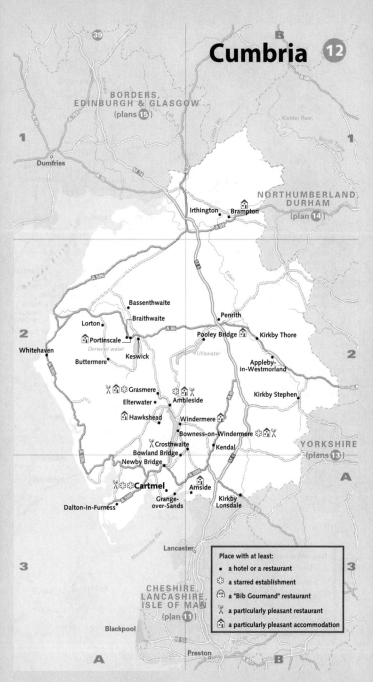

Cumbria 12

BORDERS, EDINBURGH & GLASGOW (plans 15)

Dumfries

NORTHUMBERLAND DURHAM (plan 14)

Irthington • Brampton

Whitehaven

Bassenthwaite •
Lorton • Braithwaite
Portinscale
Derwent water
Buttermere • Keswick

Penrith •
Pooley Bridge • Kirkby Thore
Ullswater
Appleby-in-Westmorland

Grasmere
Elterwater • Ambleside
Hawkshead
Windermere
Bowness-on-Windermere
Crosthwaite
Bowland Bridge
Newby Bridge
Cartmel
Dalton-in-Furness
Grange-over-Sands
Arnside

Kirkby Stephen

Kendal

YORKSHIRE (plans 13)

Kirkby Lonsdale

Lancaster

CHESHIRE, LANCASHIRE ISLE OF MAN (plan 11)

Blackpool

Preston

Place with at least:
- • a hotel or a restaurant
- ✿ a starred establishment
- ⊕ a "Bib Gourmand" restaurant
- ✗ a particularly pleasant restaurant
- ⌂ a particularly pleasant accommodation

237

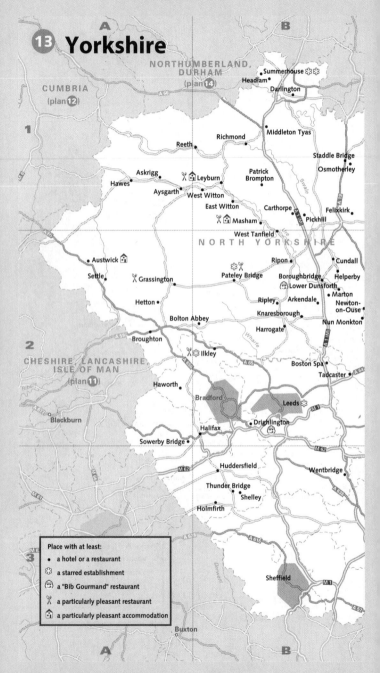

13 Yorkshire

NORTHUMBERLAND, DURHAM (plan 14)

CUMBRIA (plan 12)

Summerhouse 🏵️🏵️
Headlam •
• Darlington

Reeth • Richmond • • Middleton Tyas

Askrigg • ✂️🏠 Leyburn
Hawes • Aysgarth
West Witton
East Witton • ✂️🏠 Masham
West Tanfield •

Patrick Brompton •

Staddle Bridge •
Osmotherley •

Carthorpe •
Pickhill •
Felixkirk •

NORTH YORKSHIRE

Austwick 🏠
Settle •
✂️ Grassington •
Hetton •
Bolton Abbey •
Broughton •

🏵️✂️ Pateley Bridge
Ripon •
Boroughbridge •
🏠 Lower Dunsforth
Ripley • Arkendale •
Knaresborough •
Harrogate
Wharfe

Cundall •
Helperby •
Marton •
Newton-on-Ouse •
Nun Monkton •

CHESHIRE, LANCASHIRE, ISLE OF MAN (plan 11)

✂️🏵️ Ilkley
Haworth •
Bradford
Halifax •
Drighlington 🏠
Sowerby Bridge •

Boston Spa •
Leeds 🏵️
Tadcaster •

Blackburn •

Huddersfield •
Thunder Bridge •
Shelley •
Holmfirth •

Wentbridge •

Sheffield

Buxton

Place with at least:

- • a hotel or a restaurant
- 🏵️ a starred establishment
- 🏠 a "Bib Gourmand" restaurant
- ✂️ a particularly pleasant restaurant
- 🏠 a particularly pleasant accommodation

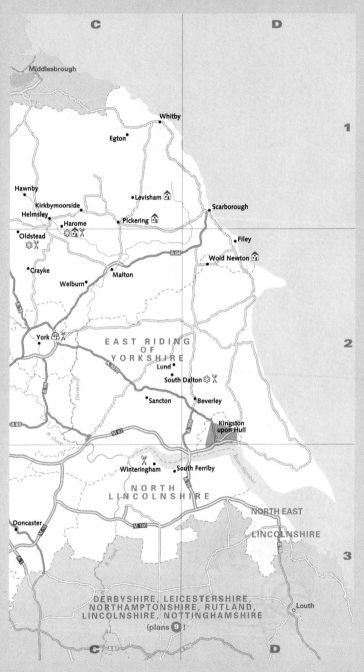

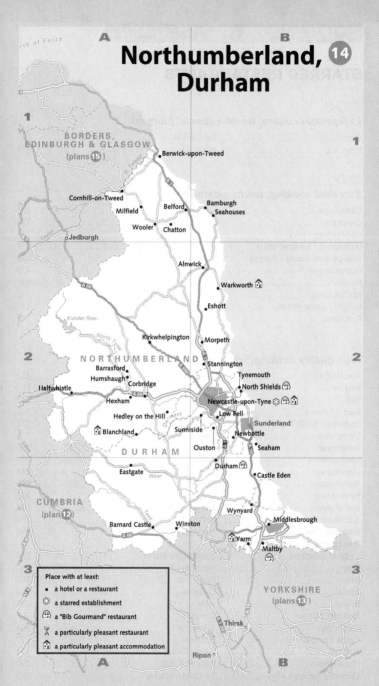

Northumberland, Durham

Place with at least:
- a hotel or a restaurant
- ✿ a starred establishment
- ☺ a "Bib Gourmand" restaurant
- ✗ a particularly pleasant restaurant
- ⌂ a particularly pleasant accommodation

STARRED RESTAURANTS

✿✿✿
Exceptional cuisine, worth a special journey!

Bray	Fat Duck **N**	299
Bray	Waterside Inn	299

✿✿
Excellent cooking, worth a detour!

Cambridge	Midsummer House	322
Chagford	Gidleigh Park	328
Cheltenham	Le Champignon Sauvage	343
Darlington / Summerhouse	Raby Hunt **N**	368
Grange-over-Sands / Cartmel	L' Enclume	402
Malmesbury	The Dining Room	477
Marlow	Hand and Flowers	487
Nottingham	Restaurant Sat Bains	510
Oxford / Great Milton	Belmond Le Manoir aux Quat' Saisons	522
Port Isaac	Restaurant Nathan Outlaw	537

✿
High quality cooking, worth a stop!

Ambleside	The Samling	252
Baslow	Fischer's at Baslow Hall	263
Bath	Bath Priory	267
Bath / Colerne	Restaurant Hywel Jones by Lucknam Park	269
Beverley / South Dalton	Pipe and Glass Inn	275
Biddenden	West House	276
Birkenhead	Fraiche	278
Birmingham	Adam's	280
Birmingham	Carters of Moseley	284
Birmingham	Purnell's	280
Birmingham	Simpsons	280
Birmingham	Turners @ 69	284
Blackburn / Langho	Northcote	286
Blakeney / Morston	Morston Hall	288
Bourton-on-the-Water / Upper Slaughter	Lords of the Manor	296
Bray	Hinds Head	300
Bray	Royal Oak	300
Bristol	Casamia	308
Bristol	wilks	309
Burchett's Green	Crown **N**	317
Cambridge	Alimentum	324
Castle Combe	Bybrook	327
Chester	Simon Radley at Chester Grosvenor	348
Chew Magna	Pony and Trap	350
Chinnor / Sprigg's Alley	Sir Charles Napier	353

Michelin

East Chisenbury	Red Lion Freehouse	380
East Grinstead	Gravetye Manor	381
Egham	Tudor Room **N**	384
Eldersfield	Butchers Arms	384
Grasmere	Forest Side **N**	403
Hampton in Arden	Peel's **N**	409
Helmsley / Harome	Star Inn	418
Horsham	Restaurant Tristan	429
Hunstanton	The Neptune	432
Ilfracombe	Thomas Carr @ The Olive Room **N**	434
Ilkley	Box Tree	434
Jersey / La Pulente	Ocean	335
Jersey / St Helier	Bohemia	337
Jersey / St Helier	Ormer by Shaun Rankin	337
Kenilworth	Cross at Kenilworth	438
Kingham	The Wild Rabbit **N**	442
Knowstone	Masons Arms	447
Leeds (West Yorkshire)	The Man Behind the Curtain	451
Loughborough	John's House	467
Marlborough / Little Bedwyn	Harrow at Little Bedwyn	486
Murcott	Nut Tree	497
Newbury	Woodspeen	500
Newcastle upon Tyne	House of Tides	502
Oakham / Hambleton	Hambleton Hall	513
Oldstead	Black Swan	515
Padstow	Paul Ainsworth at No.6	523
Pateley Bridge	Yorke Arms	525
Petersfield	JSW	530
Port Isaac	Outlaw's Fish Kitchen	537
Portscatho	Driftwood	539
Reading / Shinfield	L'Ortolan	541
Sparkwell	Treby Arms	576
Torquay	The Elephant	597
Whitstable / Seasalter	The Sportsman	617
Winchcombe	5 North St	621
Winchester	Black Rat	623
Windermere / Bowness-on-Windermere	Gilpin Hotel and Lake House **N**	627

BIB GOURMANDS 🏵
Good quality, good value cooking

Aldeburgh	Lighthouse	249
Ashendon	The Hundred of Ashendon	256
Blackpool / Thornton	Twelve	287
Boroughbridge / Lower Dunsforth	The Dunsforth	292
Brighton and Hove	64°	305
Brighton and Hove	Chilli Pickle	304
Bristol	No Man's Grace	310
Bristol / Long Ashton	Bird in Hand	311
Bury	Waggon	319
Bury St Edmunds	Pea Porridge	319
Butlers Cross	Russell Arms **N**	320
Cheltenham	The Tavern	345
Chester	Joseph Benjamin	349
Cirencester	Made by Bob	358
Clyst Hydon	Five Bells Inn	361
Cookham	White Oak	362
Derby	Ibérico World Tapas	373
Donhead St Andrew	The Forester	375
Drighlington	Prashad	377
Dummer	Sun Inn **N**	378
East Haddon	Red Lion	381
Fence	White Swan	394
Gerrards Cross	Three Oaks	400
Great Malvern / Welland	The Inn at Welland **N**	405
Hullbridge	Anchor	431
Hunsdon	Fox and Hounds	431
Ingham	Ingham Swan	435
Jersey / Beaumont	Mark Jordan at the Beach	334
Keyston	Pheasant	441
Ludlow	Green Café	471
Maltby	Chadwicks Inn	477
Manchester	El Gato Negro **N**	483
Marlow	The Coach	487
Mells	Talbot Inn	490
Moreton-in-Marsh / Bourton on the Hill	Horse and Groom	495
Newcastle upon Tyne	Broad Chare	503
Newlyn	Tolcarne Inn	503
North Shields	River Cafe on the Tyne	506
Nottingham	Ibérico World Tapas	511
Old Alresford	Pulpo Negro **N**	514

Oxford	Magdalen Arms	521
Oxford	Oli's Thai	520
Padstow	Rick Stein's Café	524
Porthleven	Kota	537
Porthleven	Square	538
Ripley (Surrey)	Anchor	545
St Ives	Black Rock	555
St Ives / Halsetown	Halsetown Inn	557
St Tudy	St Tudy Inn N	559
Stockport	brassicagrill	581
Tavistock	Cornish Arms	591
Tenterden	Swan Wine Kitchen	592
Thorpe Market	Gunton Arms	594
Upper South Wraxall	Longs Arms	603
West Hoathly	Cat Inn	612
Wight (Isle of) / Seaview	Seaview	619
Wootton	Killingworth Castle	634
Wymondham	Berkeley Arms	635
York	Le Langhe	639

Restaurant Nathan Outlaw, Port Isaac

OUR TOP PICKS

Boutique boltholes by the sea

La Sablonnerie ⅩⅩ . . . . .Channel Islands/Sark 339
Nonsuch House 🏠 . . . . .Dartmouth/Kingswear 370
Rocksalt ⅩⅩ . . . . .Folkestone 396
Old Quay House 🏠 . . . . .Fowey 397
Seafood ⅩⅩⅩ . . . . .Padstow 523
Driftwood 🏠🏠 .Portscatho 538
Hell Bay 🏠🏠 . . . . .Scilly (Isles of) /Bryher. 563
Hotel Tresanton 🏠🏠 . . . . .St Mawes. 558
Pig on the Beach 🏠🏠 . . . . .Studland 587

Charming chocolate box
country pubs

Drunken Duck Inn 🍴 . . . . .Ambleside 252
Swan Inn 🍴 . . . . .Burford/Swinbrook. 318
Village Pub 🍴 .Cirencester/Barnsley. 359
Olive Branch & Beech House 🍴 . . . . .Clipsham. 360
Star Inn 🍴✿ . . . . .Helmsley/Harome 418
Punch Bowl Inn 🍴 . . . . .Kendal/Crosthwaite 438
The Wild Rabbit 🍴✿ . . . . .Kingham 442
Talbot Inn 🍴🦆 . . . . .Mells 490
Feathered Nest 🍴 . . . . .Stow-on-the-Wold/Nether Westcote 584
Beckford Arms 🍴 . . . . .Tisbury 595

Bunch of Grapes

Iconic country houses

Bath Priory 🏠 .Bath 264
Lords of the Manor 🏠 . . . . .Bourton-on-the-Water/Upper Slaughter 296
Buckland Manor 🏠 . . . . .Broadway 312
Maison Talbooth 🏠 . . . . .Dedham 372
Gravetye Manor 🏠 . . . . .East Grinstead 381
Hambleton Hall 🏠 . . . . .Oakham/Hambleton 513
Sharrow Bay Country House 🏠 . . . .Pooley Bridge 536
Gilpin H. & Lake House 🏠🏠 . . . . .Windermere/Bowness-on-Windermere 626

Regional stand-outs

Blagdon Manor ✗✗ . . . . .Ashwater 257
Wellington Arms 🍽 . . . . .Baughurst 270
Plough at Bolnhurst 🍽 . . . . .Bolnhurst 290
Great House ✗✗✗ . . . . .Lavenham 448
White Hart 🍽 .Oxford/Fyfield 522
ODE ✗ . . . . .Shaldon 567
Freemasons 🍽 . . . . .Wiswell 630
Little Barwick House ✗✗ . . . . .Yeovil/Barwick 636

Something a little different

Burgh Island 🏠 . . . . .Bigbury-on-Sea 277
Wiveton Farm Café ✗ . . . . .Blakeney 287
Cley Windmill 🏠 . . . . .Blakeney/Cley next the Sea 288
The Pig ✗ . . . . .Brockenhurst 314
Goods Shed ✗ . . . . .Canterbury 326
Oyster Box ✗ .Channel Islands/Jersey/St Brelade's Bay 336
No 131 ✗ . . . . .Cheltenham 345
Daffodil ✗✗ . . . . .Cheltenham 344
Fifteen Cornwall ✗✗ . . . . .Newquay/Watergate Bay 504
Porthminster Beach Café ✗ . . . . .St Ives 555
Café at Daylesford Organic ✗ . . . . . .Stow-on-the-Wold/Daylesford 583

The ultimate in luxury

Coworth Park 🏠🏠 . . . . .Ascot 255
Lucknam Park 🏠🏠 . . . . .Bath/Colerne 269
Slaughters Manor House 🏠🏠 . . . . . . .Bourton-on-the-Water/Lower Slaughter 296
Gidleigh Park 🏠🏠 . . . . .Chagford 328
Longueville Manor 🏠🏠 . . . . .Channel Islands/Jersey/St Saviour 339
Lime Wood 🏠🏠 . . . . .Lyndhurst 474
Whatley Manor 🏠🏠 . . . . .Malmesbury 476
Chewton Glen 🏠🏠 . . . . .New Milton 498
Belmond
   Le Manoir aux Quat' Saisons 🏠🏠 .Oxford/Great Milton 521
Cliveden House 🏠🏠 . . . . .Taplow 589

ABBEY DORE

Herefordshire – Regional map n° **10**-A3

▶ London 170 mi – Gloucester 39 mi – Hereford 15 mi

⅄ Toi et Moi   ≤ 🛋 🛋 🔥 **P**

CLASSIC FRENCH · RURAL It's not just the views that set this charming little hillside restaurant apart. The spacious, Scandinavian lodge style building is simply but
stylishly furnished, the atmosphere is delightfully relaxed and the monthly French
menu is refreshingly honest. Cooking is precise and flavours are pronounced.

Menu £ 35/45 (dinner)

*Holling Grange ⊠ HR2 0JJ – Northwest : 1.5 mi on Ewyas Harold Common rd
– ℰ 01981 240244 (booking essential) – www.toietmoi.co.uk – lunch only and
dinner Friday – Closed January-mid March, Sunday-Wednesday, dinner Thursday
and Saturday*

ABBOTSBURY

Dorset – Pop. 481 – Regional map n° **2**-B3

▶ London 146 mi – Bournemouth 44 mi – Weymouth 10 mi

🏠 Abbey House   🐾 ≤ 🛋 🕸 **P**

HISTORIC · COSY A characterful guesthouse-cum-tea-shop in a stunning location, with the ruins of an 11C abbey and a Benedictine watermill in its grounds.
Well-kept, classical bedrooms have feature beds and one has its bathroom in an
old monk's cell.

5 rooms ⊆ – 🛉£ 75/120 🛉🛉£ 75/125

Church St ⊠ DT3 4JJ – ℰ 01305 871330 – www.theabbeyhouse.co.uk

ABBOTS RIPTON – Cambridgeshire → See Huntingdon

ABINGDON

Oxfordshire – Pop. 38 262 – Regional map n° **6**-B2

▶ London 64 mi – Oxford 6 mi – Reading 25 mi

🏠 Rafters   🕸 **P**

FAMILY · MODERN An unassuming exterior conceals a stylish, modern hotel.
Smart bedrooms have a Scandic feel and excellent facilities; one even has a water
bed! The friendly owner serves homemade bread and local bacon and sausages at
breakfast.

4 rooms ⊆ – 🛉£ 60/69 🛉🛉£ 115/135

*Abingdon Rd, Marcham ⊠ OX13 6NU – West : 3 mi on A 415 – ℰ 01865 391298
– www.bnb-rafters.co.uk – Closed 2 weeks Christmas and New Year*

ABINGER COMMON

Surrey – Regional map n° **4**-D2

▶ London 30 mi – Guildford 12 mi – Dorking 6 mi

🍴 Abinger Hatch   🛋 🛋 **P**

TRADITIONAL BRITISH · RUSTIC 18C pub in a charming hamlet – with its low
beams, cosy corners and log fires it oozes country gentility. It's open throughout
the day, offering snacks, sharing boards and comfort dishes; come summer, the
outside kitchen is a hit.

Carte £ 23/30

*Abinger Ln ⊠ RH5 6HZ – ℰ 01306 730737 – www.theabingerhatch.com – Closed
25 December*

ALDEBURGH

Suffolk – Pop. 2 341 – Regional map n° **8**-D3

▶ London 97 mi – Ipswich 24 mi – Norwich 41 mi

🏠 Wentworth ⌃ ⌃ 🛋 🏡 ⛢ 🅿

TRADITIONAL · PERSONALISED The friendly, engaging team know all the regulars at this family-run seaside hotel. The conservatory and large front terrace are popular spots. Extremely comfortable bedrooms come with a copy of locally set 'Orlando the Marmalade Cat'. The formal dining room serves a traditional daily menu.

35 rooms (dinner included) ⊡ – ♦£ 82/120 ♦♦£ 135/300

Wentworth Rd ⌗ IP15 5BD – ℰ 01728 452312 – www.wentworth-aldeburgh.com

🏠 Brudenell ⌃ ⌃ 🏡 ⊡ 🛁

FAMILY · MODERN Contemporary hotel right on the beachfront, with a relaxed ambience and superb sea views; take it all in from the large terrace. New England style bedrooms come with modern bathrooms and up-to-date facilities. The informal, split-level bar-cum-restaurant offers an accessible menu of modern classics.

44 rooms ⊡ – ♦£ 90/130 ♦♦£ 160/320

The Parade ⌗ IP15 5BU – ℰ 01728 452071 – www.brudenellhotel.co.uk

🍴 Lighthouse 🏡 🆔

🕸 **MEDITERRANEAN CUISINE · BISTRO** Popular, long-standing, split-level eatery with bright yellow décor, amiable service and a laid-back feel. Menus change constantly, featuring fish from the boats 200m away and local, seasonal meats and vegetables. Cooking is rustic and flavoursome, and dishes arrive generously proportioned.

Menu £ 15 (lunch and early dinner) – Carte £ 20/35

77 High St ⌗ IP15 5AU – ℰ 01728 453377 (booking essential)
– www.lighthouserestaurant.co.uk – Closed 26 December and lunch 1 January

🍴 Aldeburgh Market 🔲

SEAFOOD · BISTRO Set in a shop brimming with local veg and fresh seafood; the best tables are in the bay window, with views across the street. Well-priced, flavoursome cooking and friendly service. Arrive early to try one of the tasty breakfasts.

Carte £ 18/37

170-172 High St ⌗ IP15 5EY – ℰ 01728 452520 – www.thealdeburghmarket.co.uk
– lunch only – Closed 25 December

ALDERLEY EDGE

Cheshire East – Pop. 5 280 – Regional map n° **11**-B3
▶ London 187 mi – Chester 34 mi – Manchester 14 mi

🏠 Alderley Edge 🛏 ⊡ 💱 🛁 🅿

BUSINESS · CLASSIC This well-run, early Victorian country house sits in an affluent village. Compact guest areas are smartly furnished. Bedrooms in the main house have the most character; those at the back are smaller but look out over the gardens.

50 rooms ⊡ – ♦£ 95/140 ♦♦£ 110/155 – 1 suite

Macclesfield Rd ⌗ SK9 7BJ – ℰ 01625 583033 – www.alderleyedgehotel.com
The Brasserie · Alderley – See restaurant listing

🍴🍴 Alderley 🛏 ⛢ 🆔 🅿

MODERN BRITISH · ELEGANT Set in a gothic style building in the grounds of a country house, this formal conservatory restaurant has a long-standing reputation. Modern British dishes feature some interesting twists; the wine list offers a good range of bordeaux.

Menu £ 28 (lunch) – Carte £ 46/50

Alderley Edge Hotel, Macclesfield Rd ⌗ SK9 7BJ – ℰ 01625 583033
– www.alderleyedgehotel.com – Closed Sunday dinner to non residents

✗ The Brasserie ⚫ AC

TRADITIONAL BRITISH · BRASSERIE An informal French-style brasserie with mirrored walls and leather banquettes, set within a country house hotel. Retro British dishes like prawn and crayfish cocktail, scampi in a basket and jam roly poly are given a modern twist.

Carte £ 26/39

Alderley Edge Hotel, Macclesfield Rd ⊠ SK9 7BJ – ℰ 01625 583033
– www.alderleyedgehotel.com – Closed Sunday

ALFRISTON

East Sussex – ⊠ Polegate – Pop. 829 – Regional map n° **5**-A3
▶ London 66 mi – Brighton 18 mi – Lewes 10 mi

✗✗ Wingrove House ⬅ 🛏 🏠 P

MODERN BRITISH · BRASSERIE This imposing colonial-style building conceals a spacious brasserie and a comfy lounge. It's personally run and has a relaxed, informal feel. Menus change seasonally and offer appealing, unfussy dishes with a modern British style. Bedrooms are stylish and understated; two have access to the heated balcony.

Menu £ 29/35

7 rooms ⊆ – †£ 100/200 ††£ 100/200

High St ⊠ BN26 5TD – ℰ 01323 870276 – www.wingrovehousealfriston.com
– dinner only and lunch Saturday and Sunday – Closed 25 December

ALKHAM

Kent – Pop. 351 – Regional map n° **5**-D2
▶ London 72 mi – Maidstone 37 mi – Dover 5 mi

🏠 Alkham Court ⬅ 🛏 🏠 🦆 P

FAMILY · RURAL Set on a hill, surrounded by mature grounds, is this delightful guesthouse with a hot tub and sauna. Homely, well-equipped bedrooms come with complimentary sherry and stylish bathrooms. The large conservatory has lovely country views.

4 rooms ⊆ – †£ 90/110 ††£ 140/180

Meggett Ln ⊠ CT15 7DG – Southwest : 1 mi by Alkham Valley Rd
– ℰ 01303 892056 – www.alkhamcourt.co.uk

✗✗ Marquis ⬅ 🛏 🏠 🦆 ⬆ P

MODERN CUISINE · DESIGN Fashionable former pub with a smart bar, a stylish dining room and a relaxed atmosphere. Accomplished cooking features classic combinations with original touches and modern presentation. The lunch menu is good value and they even have their own sparkling wine! Chic, sexy bedrooms boast luxurious bathrooms.

Menu £ 20/35 – Carte £ 31/46

10 rooms ⊆ – †£ 79/139 ††£ 99/169

Alkham Valley Rd ⊠ CT15 7DF – ℰ 01304 873410
– www.themarquisatalkham.co.uk

ALNWICK

Northumberland – Pop. 8 116 – Regional map n° **14**-B2
▶ London 320 mi – Edinburgh 86 mi – Newcastle upon Tyne 34 mi

🏠 West Acre House ⬅ 🦆 P

TOWNHOUSE · PERSONALISED Proudly run Edwardian villa with a beautifully maintained 1 acre garden. Well-proportioned rooms come with bold wallpapers, Arts and Crafts features and a keen eye for detail; choose a Georgian, Edwardian, Oriental or Parisian theme.

4 rooms ⊆ – †£ 95/120 ††£ 95/120

West Acres ⊠ NE66 2QA – East : 0.5 mi by A 1068 – ℰ 01665 510374
– www.westacrehouse.co.uk

Greycroft

TOWNHOUSE · GRAND LUXURY 19C house near the Garden and Castle, run by welcoming owners with good local knowledge. Individually styled bedrooms have good facilities and homely touches; the bright conservatory breakfast room overlooks a lovely walled garden.

6 rooms ⚏ – ♦£ 65/70 ♦♦£ 100/135

Croft Pl ⊠ NE66 1XU – via Prudhoe St – ℰ 01665 602127
– www.greycroftalnwick.co.uk – Closed Christmas and New Year

ALSTONEFIELD

Staffordshire – Pop. 274 – Regional map n° **10**-C1
▶ London 157 mi – Birmingham 66 mi – Stafford 34 mi

The George

TRADITIONAL CUISINE · PUB Simply furnished, 18C pub on the village green, with a roaring fire and a relaxed, cosy atmosphere; it has been in the same family for three generations. Daily changing menus offer well-priced, down-to-earth dishes.

Carte £ 23/44

⊠ DE6 2FX – ℰ 01335 310205 – www.thegeorgeatalstonefield.com – Closed 25 December

AMBERLEY

West Sussex – ⊠ Arundel – Pop. 586 – Regional map n° **4**-C2
▶ London 56 mi – Brighton 24 mi – Chichester 18 mi

Amberley Castle

LUXURY · HISTORIC Stunning 12C castle displaying original stonework, battlements and evidence of a moat. The charming grounds consist of lovely gardens, lakes and a croquet lawn, and are matched inside by a characterful array of rooms. Sumptuous bedrooms have a palpable sense of history; those in the main castle are the best.

19 rooms ⚏ – ♦£ 175/670 ♦♦£ 175/670 – 6 suites

⊠ BN18 9LT – Southwest : 0.5 mi on B 2139 – ℰ 01798 831992
– www.amberleycastle.co.uk

Queen's Room – See restaurant listing

Queen's Room

MODERN BRITISH · ELEGANT Within the walls of a stunning 12C castle is this elegant dining room with a barrel-vaulted ceiling, lancet windows and an open fire. Ambitious modern dishes arrive artfully presented. Henry VIII's wives all visited, hence its name.

Menu £ 35/68

Amberley Castle Hotel, ⊠ BN18 9LT – Southwest : 0.5 mi on B 2139
– ℰ 01798 831992 (booking essential) – www.amberleycastle.co.uk

AMBLESIDE

Cumbria – Pop. 2 529 – Regional map n° **12**-A2
▶ London 276 mi – Birmingham 162 mi – Carlisle 41 mi

The Samling

TRADITIONAL · CONTEMPORARY A former farmhouse in a stunning fellside position, looking southwards along Lake Windermere; take in the fantastic view from the outdoor hot tub. Bedrooms are highly individual and range from classical and characterful to bold and eye-catching; some are duplex suites. Service is relaxed but attentive.

11 rooms ⚏ – ♦£ 280/540 ♦♦£ 300/590 – 2 suites

Ambleside Rd ⊠ LA23 1LR – South : 1.5 mi on A 591 – ℰ 015394 31922
– www.thesamlinghotel.co.uk

❀ **The Samling** – See restaurant listing

⌂ Nanny Brow ♨ ⇐ 🛏 🗶 🅿

COUNTRY HOUSE · HISTORIC Charming Arts and Crafts house with views of the River Brathay and the Langdale Fells. Spacious, antique-furnished bedrooms sit above an elegant lounge. Original stained glass, wood panelling and impressive fireplaces feature.

14 rooms ☲ – †£ 115/265 ††£ 130/280

*Clappersgate ⊠ LA22 9NF – Southwest : 1.25 mi on A 593 – 𝒞 015394 33232
– www.nannybrow.co.uk*

⌂ Riverside ♨ ⇐ 🛏 🗶 🅿

TRADITIONAL · COSY A homely slate house in a peaceful riverside location; run by delightful owners. The steep, mature garden is filled with rhododendrons. Bedroom 2 has a four-poster, a whirlpool bath and water views. Breakfast is locally sourced.

6 rooms ☲ – †£ 110/120 ††£ 120

*Under Loughrigg ⊠ LA22 9LJ – West : 1mi by A 591 and A 593 – 𝒞 015394 32395
– www.riverside-at-ambleside.co.uk – Closed 7 December-24 January*

🗶🗶 The Samling ⇐ 🛏 🅿
❀

MODERN CUISINE · ROMANTIC Smart hotel restaurant which looks out over 66 acres of grounds and down along Lake Windermere. Cooking is modern, innovative and full of flavour and many ingredients come from their kitchen garden, which is part of an international seed exchange project. Well-executed dishes are impressively presented.

→ Scallop with oyster, seaweed, cucumber and wasabi. Fillet of beef with brassicas and truffle. Coconut, curry, mango and lime.

Menu £ 30/65

Ambleside Rd ⊠ LA23 1LR – South : 1.5 mi on A 591 – 𝒞 015394 31922 (booking essential) – www.thesamlinghotel.co.uk

🗶 Lake Road Kitchen

SCANDINAVIAN · NEIGHBOURHOOD The passionate chef-owner of this small restaurant used to work in Copenhagen and the concise daily menu features some excellent Nordic-inspired combinations. Well-crafted modern dishes use top Scandic and locally foraged produce.

Carte £ 44/60

Lake Rd ⊠ LA22 0AD – 𝒞 015394 22012 – www.lakeroadkitchen.co.uk – dinner only – Closed Monday and Tuesday

🗶 Old Stamp House

MODERN CUISINE · INTIMATE Named after William Wordsworth, the 'Distributor of Stamps' for Westmorland from 1813-1843. A stone floor and exposed beams set the scene for an intimate dining experience. Cooking is modern, complex and champions Cumbrian produce.

Menu £ 20 (lunch) – Carte £ 33/51

Church St ⊠ LA22 0BU – 𝒞 015394 32775 – www.oldstamphouse.com – Closed Christmas, 3-25 January, Sunday and Monday

🍴 Drunken Duck Inn ⇦ ⇐ 🛏 🅿

TRADITIONAL BRITISH · RURAL Attractive pub in the heart of the beautiful Lakeland countryside, with a characterful, fire-lit bar and two more formal dining rooms. Simple lunches are followed by elaborate dinners with prices to match; cooking is generous and service, attentive. Ales are brewed on-site. Boutique, country house bedrooms – some with patios – have large squashy beds and country views.

Carte £ 29/50

17 rooms ☲ – †£ 79/244 ††£ 105/325

*Barngates ⊠ LA22 0NG – Southwest : 3 mi by A 593 and B 5286 on Tarn Hows rd
– 𝒞 015394 36347 (booking essential at dinner) – www.drunkenduckinn.co.uk
– Closed 25 December*

AMERSHAM (Old Town)

Buckinghamshire – Pop. 23 086 – Regional map n° **6**-D2

▶ London 46 mi – Aylesbury 26 mi – Oxford 64 mi

XX Artichoke   AC 🅸⊘ ⇔

CREATIVE BRITISH · ELEGANT 16C red-brick house in a picturesque town. A narrow beamed room with cream-painted walls and polished tables leads through to a more modern extension complete with a semi-open kitchen. Ambitious modern dishes arrive nicely presented.

Menu £ 28 (weekday lunch)/68 – Carte lunch £ 42/48

9 Market Sq ⊠ HP7 0DF – ☎ 01494 726611 (booking essential at dinner)
– www.artichokerestaurant.co.uk – Closed 2 weeks late August, 1 week Easter,
1 week January, Christmas-New Year, Sunday and Monday

X Gilbey's   🅰️ AC ⇔

TRADITIONAL BRITISH · COSY Long-standing neighbourhood restaurant located in a 17C former school and consisting of three rustic rooms and a delightful terrace. It's rooted in tradition, from the furnishings to the food; homemade jams feature at afternoon tea.

Menu £ 23 (weekdays)/27 – Carte £ 33/58

1 Market Sq ⊠ HP7 0DF – ☎ 01494 727242 (booking essential)
– www.gilbeygroup.com – Closed 23-30 December

AMPLEFORTH – North Yorkshire ➜ See Helmsley

APPLEBY-IN-WESTMORLAND

Cumbria – Pop. 2 862 – Regional map n° **12**-B2

▶ London 285 mi – Carlisle 33 mi – Middlesbrough 58 mi

🏠 Tufton Arms   🕱 🅰️ P

TRADITIONAL · GRAND LUXURY 16C coaching inn, in an old market town; a popular place for fishing and shooting parties. Guest areas include two traditional lounges and a bar; chic bedrooms are a complete contrast with their bold, contemporary furnishings. The classical, cane-furnished restaurant offers an easy-going menu.

22 rooms ⊊ – ♦£ 60/80 ♦♦£ 140/250

Market Sq ⊠ CA16 6XA – ☎ 017683 51593 – www.tuftonarmshotel.co.uk – Closed 24-27 December

ARKENDALE

North Yorkshire – Regional map n° **22**-B2

▶ London 218 mi – York 17 mi – Knaresborough 4 mi

🍴 Blue Bell 🆕   ⇔ 🅰️ & P

TRADITIONAL BRITISH · COSY This might be a modern dining pub but it still has plenty of character, courtesy of hops hanging over the bar, sofas set in front of a wood burning stove and locals hanging out with their dogs. When it comes to the food, everything is homemade. Upstairs are four smart bedrooms with super king sized beds.

Carte £ 21/36

4 rooms ⊊ – ♦£ 85/150 ♦♦£ 85/150

Moor Ln ⊠ HG5 0QT – ☎ 01423 369242 – www.thebluebellatarkendale.co.uk
– Closed 9 January

ARLINGHAM

Gloucestershire – Pop. 459 – Regional map n° **2**-C1

▶ London 120 mi – Birmingham 69 mi – Bristol 34 mi

XX Old Passage Inn

SEAFOOD · FRIENDLY Sit out on the terrace or beside the window, surrounded by colourful art, and watch the famous Severn bore travel up the estuary. Extensive seafood menus offer everything from a fish pie to a fruits de mer platter or lobster direct from their saltwater tank. Simply furnished modern bedrooms share the view.

Menu £ 13 (weekday lunch) – Carte £ 34/61

2 rooms 🖙 – ♦£ 80/120 ♦♦£ 120/140

Passage Rd ⊠ GL2 7JR – West : 0.75 mi – 𝒞 01452 740547
– www.theoldpassage.com – Closed 25-26 December, Sunday dinner and Monday and dinner Tuesday-Wednesday January-February

ARMSCOTE

Warwickshire – Regional map n° **10**-C3
▶ London 98 mi – Birmingham 45 mi – Warwick 26 mi

🍺 Fuzzy Duck

TRADITIONAL CUISINE · PUB Siblings Adrian and Tania – also owners of the Baylis and Harding toiletries company – have taken this place from a boarded up boozer to a modern, fashionably attired dining pub. Seasonal British dishes – including plenty of pub classics – show respect for the local ingredients. Stylish boutique bedrooms.

Menu £ 24 (weekday lunch) – Carte £ 21/44

4 rooms 🖙 – ♦£ 110/160 ♦♦£ 110/160

Ilmington Rd ⊠ CV37 8DD – 𝒞 01608 682635 (booking advisable)
– www.fuzzyduckarmscote.com – Closed 26 December, Sunday dinner and Monday

ARNSIDE

Cumbria – Pop. 2 334 – Regional map n° **12**-A3
▶ London 257 mi – Kendal 12 mi – Lancaster 16 mi

🏠 Number 43

TRADITIONAL · GRAND LUXURY Stylishly converted Victorian townhouse boasting superb views over the estuary and fells. Contemporary bedrooms have smart bathrooms, quality furnishings, good facilities and plenty of extras. The comfortable open-plan lounge and dining room offers light meat and cheese sharing platters in the evening. Start the day with breakfast on the glass-enclosed terrace.

6 rooms 🖙 – ♦£ 90/145 ♦♦£ 125/185

43 The Promenade ⊠ LA5 0AA – 𝒞 01524 762761 – www.no43.org.uk

ARUNDEL

West Sussex – Pop. 3 285 – Regional map n° **4**-C2
▶ London 58 mi – Chichester 12 mi – Brighton 21 mi

XX Town House

MODERN CUISINE · ELEGANT If you're a fan of Renaissance architecture, head for this early 17C townhouse, where you'll find a gilt walnut panelled ceiling which was originally installed in the Medici Palace in Florence. Confidently executed, tried-and-tested dishes have a classic base. Bedrooms include a family room in the old attic.

Menu £ 18/30

5 rooms 🖙 – ♦£ 75/110 ♦♦£ 110/150

65 High St ⊠ BN18 9AJ – 𝒞 01903 883847 – www.thetownhouse.co.uk
– Closed 2 weeks Easter, 2 weeks October, 25-26 December, 1-2 January, Sunday and Monday

at Burpham Northeast: 3 mi by A27✉ Arundel

🗋 The George at Burpham   🛋 🅿

MODERN BRITISH · RUSTIC A local consortium headed by three local business-men saved this pub from closure and it's since been given a smart new look, to which beams, fires and a smugglers' wheel add character. The seasonal menu is full of tasty, popular classics.

Carte £ 25/43

Main St ✉ BN18 9RR – ℰ 01903 883131 – www.georgeatburpham.co.uk – Closed 25 December

ASCOT

Windsor and Maidenhead – Pop. 15 761 – Regional map n° **6**-D3
▶ London 37 mi – Reading 15 mi – Oxford 47 mi

🏨🏨 Coworth Park   🏝 🌜 ≤ 🛏 🖥 ⓦ 🛎 ⅃ᵇ ※ 🗗 ᖱ 🆎 🍴 🔧 🅿

COUNTRY HOUSE · GRAND LUXURY A luxurious 18C property set in 246 acres, with stylish, contemporary guest areas and beautiful bedrooms featuring bespoke furniture, marble bathrooms and excellent facilities; those in main house are the largest. Dine in the elegant restaurant or more causal brasserie, overlooking their championship polo fields. The superb spa has a 'living roof' of herbs and flowers.

70 rooms ⌷ – 🛏£ 281/787 🛏🛏£ 281/787 – 21 suites

London Rd ✉ SL5 7SE – East : 2.75 mi on A 329 – ℰ 01344 876600
– www.dorchestercollection.com/en/ascot/coworth-park
Coworth Park – See restaurant listing

XXXX Coworth Park   🎎 ≤ 🛋 ᖱ 🆎 ⇔ 🅿

MODERN CUISINE · ELEGANT A bright, elegant restaurant in a beautiful mansion house, with stylish tableware, an eye-catching centrepiece and a lovely terrace offering views over the manicured gardens. Cooking is accomplished and service is professional.

Menu £ 30 (weekday lunch)/85

Coworth Park Hotel, London Rd ✉ SL5 7SE – East : 2.75 mi on A 329
– ℰ 01344 876600 – www.dorchestercollection.com/en/ascot/coworth-park
– Closed Sunday dinner, Monday and Tuesday

XX Ascot Grill   🛋 🆎 🖳

MEATS AND GRILLS · FASHIONABLE Neighbourhood restaurant with a slick, minimalistic interior featuring leather, silk and velvet; full-length windows open onto a pleasant pavement terrace. Wide-ranging modern grill menu offers steak and seafood. Good value lunches.

Carte £ 19/50

6 Hermitage Par, High St ✉ SL5 7HE – ℰ 01344 622285 – www.ascotgrill.co.uk
– Closed 25-26 December, first week January and Monday

ASHBOURNE

Derbyshire – Pop. 8 377 – Regional map n° **9**-A2
▶ London 141 mi – Birmingham 45 mi – Manchester 46 mi – Sheffield 52 mi

🏨 Callow Hall   🏝 🌜 ≤ 🛏 🔧 🅿

TRADITIONAL · PERSONALISED Traditional Victorian country house in 30 acres of gardens, fields and woodland. Individually styled bedrooms boast original features, spacious bathrooms, and traditional fabrics and furnishings. Seasonal menus showcase local produce in classically based dishes with the occasional modern touch.

16 rooms ⌷ – 🛏£ 110/165 🛏🛏£ 125/165 – 1 suite

Mapleton Rd ✉ DE6 2AA – West : 0.75 mi by Union St (off Market Pl)
– ℰ 01335 300900 – www.callowhall.co.uk

ENGLAND

at Shirley Southeast: 5 mi by A515 and off A52

🗗 Saracen's Head

TRADITIONAL BRITISH · RUSTIC A rustic, open-plan dining pub opposite the village church, in a remote, picturesque village. Menus are chalked on blackboards above the open fire and offer an eclectic mix of generously portioned pub and restaurant-style classics.

Carte £ 21/41

Church Ln ⊠ DE6 3AS – ℰ 01335 360330 – www.saracens-head-shirley.co.uk

ASHBURTON

Devon – Pop. 3 346 – Regional map n° **1**-C2
▶ London 192 mi – Exeter 33 mi – Plymouth 41 mi

🏠 Agaric

TOWNHOUSE · THEMED Friendly owners welcome you to this rustic guesthouse on the main street with its comfortable, simply furnished bedrooms. The single is decorated in a Chinese style, while the best is Havana with its four-poster bed and roll top bath.

4 rooms ⊑ – ♦£ 58/90 ♦♦£ 120/140

36 North St ⊠ TQ13 7QD – ℰ 01364 654478
– www.agaricrestaurant.co.uk/bed-and-breakfast – Closed Christmas

ASHENDON

Buckinghamshire – Regional map n° **6**-C2
▶ London 82 mi – Oxford 35 mi – Northampton 59 mi

🗗 The Hundred of Ashendon

REGIONAL CUISINE · FRIENDLY In Saxon times, shires were divided into 'hundreds' for military and judicial purposes. This charming 17C inn keeps the concept alive by sourcing its produce from within its 'hundred'. Great value dishes arrive in hearty portions, packed full of flavour – and influences from Matt's time at St John are clear to see. Modest bedrooms are continually being upgraded.

Menu £ 14 (weekday lunch) – Carte £ 24/35

5 rooms ⊑ – ♦£ 55/85 ♦♦£ 70/100

Lower End ⊠ HP18 0HE – ℰ 01296 651296 – www.thehundred.co.uk – Closed 25 December, Sunday dinner and Monday

ASHFORD

Kent – Pop. 67 528 – Regional map n° **5**-C2
▶ London 56 mi – Canterbury 14 mi – Dover 24 mi

🏰 Eastwell Manor

LUXURY · HISTORIC Impressive manor house with Tudor origins, surrounded by beautifully manicured gardens and extensive parkland. Rebuilt in 1926 following a fire but some superb plaster ceilings and stone fireplaces remain. Characterful guest areas and luxurious bedrooms. Sizeable spa and golf course. Choice of wood-panelled restaurant complete with pianist or more casual brasserie and terrace.

42 rooms ⊑ – ♦£ 170/410 ♦♦£ 170/410 – 20 suites

Eastwell Park, Boughton Lees ⊠ TN25 4HR – North : 3 mi by A 28 on A 251
– ℰ 01233 213000 – www.eastwellmanor.co.uk

ASHFORD-IN-THE-WATER

Derbyshire – Regional map n° **9**-A1
▶ London 164 mi – Birmingham 87 mi – Leeds 72 mi

🏠 Riverside House   🏡 🛏 🎾 **P**

TRADITIONAL · COSY Charming former hunting lodge with gardens running down to the river. Comfy, individually styled bedrooms are named after flowers and birds: one is a four-poster and some have French doors opening onto garden terraces. Classical dining takes place over four different rooms. It has a homely feel throughout.

14 rooms ⌂ – ♦£ 145/195 ♦♦£ 145/195

Fennel St ✉ DE45 1QF – ☎ 01629 814275 – www.riversidehousehotel.co.uk

🏠 River Cottage   🛏 🎾 **P** 🛏

TRADITIONAL · COSY Traditional stone cottage by the River Wye, with delightful gardens and two terraces. Bedrooms mix modern and antique furnishings and mattresses are handmade. Locally sourced ingredients and homemade preserves feature at breakfast.

4 rooms ⌂ – ♦£ 79/125 ♦♦£ 100/125

Buxton Rd ✉ DE45 1QP – ☎ 01629 813327 – www.rivercottageashford.co.uk
– Closed December and January

ASHWATER

Devon – Regional map n° **1**-C2
▶ London 217 mi – Exeter 42 mi – Plymouth 36 mi

✗✗ Blagdon Manor   🍴 🐾 ⟨ 🛏 🏡 **P**

MODERN CUISINE · ROMANTIC Former farmhouse with delightful gardens; set in a peaceful rural location and proudly run by a husband and wife team. Comfortable restaurant with lovely countryside views and a large flagged terrace for summer dining. Unfussy, seasonal cooking; dishes are classically based with a modern touch. Immaculately kept, well-equipped bedrooms have stylish modern bathrooms.

Menu £ 35/40

6 rooms ⌂ – ♦£ 95/110 ♦♦£ 165/260

✉ EX21 5DF – Northwest : 2 mi by Holsworthy rd on Blagdon rd – ☎ 01409 211224 (booking essential) – www.blagdon.com – dinner only and Sunday lunch – Closed 2 weeks January, Monday and Tuesday

ASKHAM - Cumbria ➜ See Penrith

ASKRIGG

North Yorkshire – ✉ Leyburn – Pop. 1 002 – Regional map n° **13**-A1
▶ London 251 mi – Kendal 32 mi – York 63 mi

🏠 Yorebridge House   🛏 **P**

COUNTRY HOUSE · GRAND LUXURY Stylish former schoolmaster's house in a lovely Dales setting, with a snug bar and great country views. Bold modern bedrooms are themed around the owner's travels; those in the old schoolhouse have riverside patios and hot tubs.

12 rooms ⌂ – ♦£ 175/225 ♦♦£ 200/285

Bainbridge ✉ DL8 3EE – West : 1.25 mi – ☎ 01969 652060
– www.yorebridgehouse.com
Yorebridge House – See restaurant listing

✗✗ Yorebridge House   🛏 🏡 ⇔ **P**

MODERN BRITISH · INTIMATE Romantic restaurant set within an old schoolmaster's house and offering lovely countryside views. Concise menus evolve with the seasons and feature locally sourced produce; dishes are modern, flavoursome and attractively presented.

Menu £ 55

Yorebridge House Hotel, Bainbridge ✉ DL8 3EE – West : 1.25 mi
– ☎ 01969 652060 (bookings essential for non-residents)
– www.yorebridgehouse.com – dinner only

ASTON CANTLOW
Warwickshire – Pop. 1 843 – Regional map n° **10**-C3
▶ London 104 mi – Birmingham 30 mi – Leicester 46 mi

🍴 King's Head
MODERN CUISINE · RUSTIC Characterful black and white timbered inn in a picturesque village. Dine in the characterful beamed bar or the chic country restaurant. Choose from generously sized pub favourites or more modern dishes; local duck is a feature.
Carte £ 20/45
21 Bearley Rd ✉ B95 6HY – ☎ 01789 488242 – www.thekh.co.uk

ATTLEBOROUGH
Norfolk – Pop. 10 549 – Regional map n° **8**-C2
▶ London 101 mi – Norwich 19 mi – Ipswich 42 mi

✗ Mulberry Tree
MODERN CUISINE · BRASSERIE A casual, contemporary bar-cum-restaurant in an imposing Victorian property. The bar menu is popular at lunchtime, while the modern à la carte offers attractively presented, globally-influenced dishes. In summer, head through to the pleasant garden and terrace. Bedrooms are stylish and very comfortable.
Carte £ 23/37
7 rooms ⌚ – †£ 80 ††£ 106/110
*Station Rd ✉ NR17 2AS – ☎ 01953 452124 – www.the-mulberry-tree.co.uk
– Closed Christmas*

AUSTWICK
North Yorkshire – Pop. 463 – Regional map n° **13**-A2
▶ London 259 mi – Kendal 28 mi – Lancaster 20 mi – Leeds 46 mi

🏠 Traddock
COUNTRY HOUSE · PERSONALISED Unusually named after a horse trading paddock; a Georgian country house with Victorian additions – once a private residence. Inside it's traditional with bright, airy lounges and bedrooms boasting feature beds and country views. The formal dining room serves local produce in updated versions of old classics.
12 rooms ⌚ – †£ 95/155 ††£ 99/240
✉ LA2 8BY – ☎ 015242 51224 – www.thetraddock.co.uk

🏠 Austwick Hall
HISTORIC BUILDING · PERSONALISED Set in a delightful village on the edge of the Dales and surrounded by tiered gardens, is this characterful house built in 1590 for the Master of the Mint. The flagged hall has an impressive stained glass window framed by two columns and antiques abound. Nothing is too much trouble for the friendly owners.
4 rooms ⌚ – †£ 110/140 ††£ 125/155
Townhead Lane ✉ LA2 8BS – ☎ 015242 51794 – www.austwickhall.co.uk

AXMINSTER
Devon – Pop. 5 761 – Regional map n° **1**-D2
▶ London 156 mi – Exeter 27 mi – Lyme Regis 5 mi – Taunton 22 mi

✗ River Cottage Canteen
REGIONAL CUISINE · RUSTIC Busy restaurant, deli and coffee shop owned by Hugh Fearnley-Whittingstall. The slightly stark rear room was once a dance hall. Menus change twice-daily and offer gutsy, flavoursome country dishes which showcase local produce.
Carte £ 21/33
*Trinity Sq ✉ EX13 5AN – ☎ 01297 631715 – www.rivercottage.net/axminster
– Closed 25-26 December, dinner Sunday-Tuesday and Wednesday
November-April*

AYLESBURY

Buckinghamshire – Pop. 71 977 – Regional map n° **6**-C2

▶ London 46 mi – Birmingham 72 mi – Northampton 37 mi – Oxford 22 mi

🏰 Hartwell House

HISTORIC · CLASSIC An impressive palatial house set in 90 acres of parkland: the erstwhile residence of Louis XVIII, exiled King of France, and now owned by the National Trust. It boasts ornate furnishings, luxurious lounges, an intimate spa and magnificent antique-filled bedrooms. The formal restaurant offers traditional country house cooking and afternoon tea is a speciality.

46 rooms ⌂ – ♦£ 190/600 ♦♦£ 300/700 – 10 suites

Oxford Rd ⊠ HP17 8NR – Southwest : 2 mi on A 418 – ℰ *01296 747444*
– www.hartwell-house.com

AYLESFORD

Kent – Regional map n° **5**-B1

▶ London 37 mi – Maidstone 3 mi – Royal Tunbridge Wells 19 mi

✗✗ Hengist

MODERN BRITISH · FASHIONABLE Sit either on the rustic ground floor or on the boldly decorated first floor of this characterful 16C timbered house. Good-sized menus offer ambitious modern British dishes. In summer, find a spot on the terrace beside the stream.

Menu £ 15 (weekdays) – Carte £ 29/44

7-9 High St ⊠ ME20 7AX
– ℰ 01622 885800 – www.hengistrestaurant.co.uk
– Closed 26 December, Sunday dinner and Monday

AYLSHAM

Norfolk – Pop. 6 016 – Regional map n° **8**-D1

▶ London 128 mi – Norwich 13 mi – Ipswich 57 mi

🏠 Old Pump House

TOWNHOUSE · PERSONALISED This tastefully furnished Georgian house is named after the old village water pump which stands in the square outside. Spacious bedrooms have period furnishings and the open-plan lounge and breakfast room overlooks the lovely garden.

5 rooms ⌂ – ♦£ 85/100 ♦♦£ 100/125

2 Holman Rd ⊠ NR11 6BY – ℰ 01263 733789 – www.theoldpumphouse.com
– Closed Christmas

AYOT GREEN – Hertfordshire → See Welwyn

AYSGARTH

North Yorkshire – Regional map n° **22**-A1

▶ London 249 mi – York 56 mi – Ripon 28 mi

🏠 Stow House

COUNTRY HOUSE · PERSONALISED A Gothic-style residence built in 1876 for the Rev Stow, which sits in an enviable position looking down the valley. The owners have an extensive art collection and the smart retro bedrooms are named after pictures on their walls.

7 rooms ⌂ – ♦£ 100/132 ♦♦£ 110/175

⊠ DL8 3SR – East : 0.5 mi on A 684 – ℰ 01969 663635
– www.stowhouse.co.uk

🏠 Aysgarth Falls

MODERN BRITISH · INN Just up the road from the waterfalls, you'll find this homely roadside inn with three terraces. Menus evolve constantly and offer a mix of pub classics, homemade pizzas and more ambitious dishes; specials are often based around east coast fish. Contemporary bedrooms have views of the surrounding Dales.

Carte £ 20/37

✉ DL8 3SR - 𝒞 01969 663775 - www.aysgarthfallshotel.com - *Restricted opening in January*

BABBACOMBE - Torbay → See Torquay

BAGSHOT
Surrey – Pop. 5 430 – Regional map n° **4**-C1
▶ London 37 mi – Guildford 12 mi – Reading 17 mi

🏨 Pennyhill Park

LUXURY · CLASSIC Impressive 19C manor house in 123 acres, boasting one of Europe's best spas. Both the guest areas and bedrooms are spacious, with period furnishings and modern touches; feature bathrooms come with rain showers or glass baths. Dine in the elegant restaurant or the stylish brasserie which opens onto the garden.

123 rooms – ♦£ 255/455 ♦♦£ 255/455 – ☖£ 21 – 11 suites
London Rd ✉ GU19 5EU – Southwest : 1 mi on A 30 – 𝒞 01276 471774
– www.exclusivehotels.co.uk
The Latymer – See restaurant listing

🍴 The Latymer

MODERN CUISINE · CLASSIC DÉCOR Dark wood panelled walls and low beamed ceilings characterise this classical hotel dining room. Set menus offer 6 or 7 courses at lunch and 6 or 10 courses at dinner. Dishes are modern and eye-catching and service is swift.

Menu £ 70/100 – tasting menu only
Pennyhill Park Hotel, London Rd ✉ GU19 5EU – Southwest : 1 mi on A 30
– 𝒞 01276 471774 – www.exclusivehotels.co.uk – dinner only and lunch Thursday-Friday – Closed Monday and Tuesday

BALLASALLA → See Man (Isle of)

BAMBURGH
Northumberland – Pop. 279 – Regional map n° **14**-B1
▶ London 337 mi – Edinburgh 77 mi – Newcastle upon Tyne 51 mi

🏠 Lord Crewe Arms

INN · COSY Smart 17C former coaching inn, privately owned and superbly set in the shadow of a famous Norman castle. Comfy, cosy bedrooms have a modern feel, yet are in keeping with the age of the building. Characterful stone-walled bar and New England style restaurant serve brasserie dishes. Efficient service.

9 rooms ☖ – ♦£ 60/125 ♦♦£ 98/125
Front St ✉ NE69 7BL – 𝒞 01668 214243 – www.lord-crewe.co.uk – Closed 25 December

at Waren Mill West: 2.75 mi on B1342✉ Belford

🏨 Waren House

FAMILY · CLASSIC Personally run, antique-furnished country house set in beautiful, tranquil gardens. Bedrooms – some named after the owners' family members – mix classic and modern styles: some have four-posters and coastal views. Formal dining room boasts an ornate ceiling; traditional menus showcase local ingredients.

15 rooms ☖ – ♦£ 85/115 ♦♦£ 110/160 – 2 suites
✉ NE70 7EE – 𝒞 01668 214581 – www.warenhousehotel.co.uk

BAMPTON

Devon – Pop. 1 260 – Regional map n° **1**-D1

▶ London 189 mi – Exeter 18 mi – Minehead 21 mi – Taunton 15 mi

🏠 Swan

TRADITIONAL BRITISH · INN The Swan dates back to 1450, when it provided accommodation for craftsmen working on the village church. Its original inglenook fireplace and bread oven remain but the open-plan layout gives it an up-to-date feel. Unfussy pub classics arrive neatly presented. Smart, modern bedrooms are found on the 2nd floor.

Carte £ 22/36

3 rooms 🖙 – †£ 70/90 ††£ 85/90

Station Rd ✉ EX16 9NG – 𝒞 01398 332248 – www.theswan.co – Closed 25 December

BARNARD CASTLE

Durham – Pop. 7 040 – Regional map n° **14**-A3

▶ London 258 mi – Carlisle 63 mi – Leeds 68 mi – Middlesbrough 31 mi

at Greta Bridge Southeast: 4.5 mi off A66 ✉ Barnard Castle

🏠 Morritt

INN · PERSONALISED Attractive 19C inn on the site of an old Roman fort. The characterful interior cleverly blends the old and the new, with antiques and feature bedsteads offset by contemporary décor. The superb spa has a car garage theme. All-day snacks are served in the bar-bistro and there's a modern menu in the restaurant.

26 rooms 🖙 – †£ 75/105 ††£ 95/179 – 1 suite

✉ DL12 9SE – 𝒞 01833 627232 – www.themorritt.co.uk

Gilroy's – See restaurant listing

XX Gilroy's

MODERN CUISINE · CLASSIC DÉCOR Smart hotel dining room with a lovely parquet floor, wood-panelling and bold splashes of colour here and there. Dishes are modern, attractively presented and employ some complex techniques. Start with a drink by the fire in the cosy lounge.

Menu £ 39

Morritt Hotel, ✉ DL12 9SE – 𝒞 01833 627232 – www.themorritt.co.uk – dinner only

at Hutton Magna Southeast: 7.25 mi by A66

🏠 Oak Tree Inn

TRADITIONAL BRITISH · COSY Small but charming whitewashed pub with six tables flanked by green settles and a bench table for drinkers. It's run by a husband and wife team; he cooks, while she serves. Cooking is hearty and flavoursome with a rustic British style.

Carte £ 32/44

✉ DL11 7HH – 𝒞 01833 627371 (booking essential) – www.theoaktreehutton.co.uk – dinner only – Closed 24-27 and 31 December, 1-2 January and Monday

at Romaldkirk Northwest: 6 mi by A67 on B6277 ✉ Barnard Castle

🏠 Rose and Crown

TRADITIONAL BRITISH · INN Delightful Georgian inn overlooking three village greens, with a wonderfully characterful bar and a smart, wood-panelled dining room. Menus focus on British pub classics and showcase local, seasonal produce. Well-equipped bedrooms are spread between the main building, the courtyard and the "Monk's House".

Carte £ 23/40 **s**

14 rooms 🖙 – †£ 90/135 ††£ 115/160

✉ DL12 9EB – 𝒞 01833 650213 – www.rose-and-crown.co.uk – Closed Christmas

BARNSLEY – Gloucestershire → See Cirencester

BARRASFORD

Northumberland – Regional map n° **14**-A2

▶ London 309 mi – Newcastle upon Tyne 29 mi – Sunderland 42 mi
– Middlesbrough 66 mi

🏠 **Barrasford Arms**   ← 🛋 🏠 🅿

TRADITIONAL BRITISH · PUB Personally run 19C stone inn, close to Kielder Water and Hadrian's Wall. It has a traditional, homely atmosphere, with cosy fires and regular competitions for the locals. Pub classics are served at lunch, followed by more refined dishes at dinner. Bedrooms are comfortable and sensibly priced.
Menu £ 15 (weekday lunch) – Carte £ 25/33

7 rooms ☲ – 🛉£ 67 🛉🛉£ 87

✉ NE48 4AA – 𝒞 01434 681237 – www.barrasfordarms.co.uk
– Closed 24-26 December, Sunday dinner, Monday and bank holidays

BARTON-ON-SEA

Hampshire – Regional map n° **4**-A3

▶ London 108 mi – Bournemouth 11 mi – Southampton 24 mi – Winchester 35 mi

✕✕ **Pebble Beach**   ← ← 🏠 ⅆ 🆎 🅿

SEAFOOD · FASHIONABLE Head for the terrace of this split-level restaurant for impressive views to the Isle of Wight. Inside, the open kitchen takes pride of place and the fish tank gives a clue as to the menu. Assured classic cooking comes from an experienced chef. Bedrooms are smart and well-kept; the Penthouse has the views.
Carte £ 25/78

4 rooms ☲ – 🛉£ 70/80 🛉🛉£ 70/100

Marine Dr ✉ BH25 7DZ – 𝒞 01425 627777 – www.pebblebeach-uk.com

BARWICK – Somerset → See Yeovil

BASLOW

Derbyshire – Pop. 1 178 – Regional map n° **9**-A1

▶ London 158 mi – Matlock 10 mi – Manchester 35 mi – Sheffield 14 mi

🏨 **Cavendish**   🕆 ← 🛋 🕸 🏰 🅿

TRADITIONAL · PERSONALISED Elegant hotel on the Chatsworth Estate, boasting lovely parkland views. Bedrooms have a contemporary country house style and some of the furniture and paintings are from nearby Chatsworth House. The Garden Room offers an extensive menu along with afternoon teas; the formal restaurant serves classic fare.

24 rooms – 🛉£ 165/220 🛉🛉£ 215/340 – ☲ £ 19 – 1 suite

Church Ln ✉ DE45 1SP – on A 619 – 𝒞 01246 582311 – www.cavendish-hotel.net
The Gallery – See restaurant listing

🏠 **Heathy Lea**   ← 🛋 🕸 🅿

COUNTRY HOUSE · PERSONALISED 17C farmhouse owned by the Chatsworth Estate – which has access to the grounds through its garden gate. Cosy, comfortable bedrooms have views over the farmland. The estate farm shop provides much of the produce used at breakfast.

3 rooms ☲ – 🛉£ 60/80 🛉🛉£ 90/120

✉ DE45 1PQ – East : 0.75 mi on A 619 – 𝒞 01246 583842 – www.heathylea.co.uk
– Closed Christmas

XXX Fischer's at Baslow Hall

MODERN CUISINE · ELEGANT A fine Edwardian manor house with a country house feel, impressive formal grounds and a walled vegetable garden. The two dining rooms, with their ornate ceilings, offer a mix of classic and original modern dishes, prepared using skilful techniques; sit at the 'Kitchen Tasting Bench' to be part of the action. Bedrooms are charming – the garden rooms are the largest.
→ Tempura of quail with confit leg, toasted seeds and mirin aspic. Roast Derbyshire lamb with Wye Valley asparagus, chickpeas, lemon and crispy sweetbread. 'Black Forest'.

Menu £ 21 (weekday lunch)/72

11 rooms ⌂ – ♦£ 125/175 ♦♦£ 200/270 – 1 suite

Calver Rd ⊠ DE45 1RR – on A 623 – ℰ 01246 583259 (booking essential)
– www.fischers-baslowhall.co.uk – Closed 25-26 and 31 December

XXX The Gallery

MODERN BRITISH · CHIC Striking restaurant in an elegant hotel, which features a stylish mix of contemporary décor and antique furnishings. Dishes have a traditional base but techniques and presentation are modern. Service is detailed yet personable.

Menu £ 50

Cavendish Hotel, Church Ln ⊠ DE45 1SP – on A 619 – ℰ 01246 582311
– www.cavendish-hotel.net

X Rowley's

TRADITIONAL CUISINE · BRASSERIE Stone-built former blacksmith's; now a contemporary bar-restaurant with a small terrace and friendly service. Dine in the buzzy ground floor bar or more intimate upstairs rooms. Hearty, satisfying dishes have classic French roots.

Menu £ 17 (weekday lunch)/25 – Carte £ 27/36

Church St ⊠ DE45 1RY – ℰ 01246 583880 (booking advisable)
– www.rowleysrestaurant.co.uk – Closed 25 December, Sunday dinner and Monday

BASSENTHWAITE

Cumbria – Pop. 433 – Regional map n° **12**-A2
▶ London 300 mi – Carlisle 24 mi – Keswick 7 mi

🏠 Pheasant

INN · CLASSIC Characterful 16C coaching inn with comfy lounges and welcoming open fires. Bedrooms are spacious and retain a classic look appropriate to the building's age; some have lovely country outlooks. Have drinks amongst polished brass in the bar then make for the rustic oak-furnished bistro or more formal restaurant.

15 rooms ⌂ – ♦£ 95/115 ♦♦£ 120/200

⊠ CA13 9YE – Southwest : 3.25 mi by B 5291 on Wythop Mill Rd
– ℰ 017687 76234 – www.the-pheasant.co.uk – Closed 25 December

X Bistro at the Distillery

MODERN BRITISH · BISTRO Smart modern bistro in a former cattle shed; the other farm buildings now house a shop and a working gin, vodka and whisky distillery. Extensive lunches are followed by afternoon teas, with more ambitious dishes appearing at dinner.

Menu £ 20 (weekdays) – Carte £ 23/45

Bassenthwaite Lake ⊠ CA13 9SJ – West : 2.75 mi by A 591 on B 5291
– ℰ 017687 88850 (booking advisable) – www.bistroatthedistillery.com – Closed 25 December

BATH

Bath and North East Somerset – Pop. 94 782 – Regional map n° **2**-C2
▶ London 119 mi – Taunton 49 mi – Bristol 13 mi

Hotels

⌂ **Royal Crescent**　　　⟨ ⇤ ◻ ⬚ spa ⌂ ℔ ⊡ AC ⚑ ⇱

HISTORIC · ELEGANT Smartly refurbished Grade I listed building at the centre of the magnificent sweeping terrace. Ornate plasterwork, pastel shades and gilt-framed portraits evoke feelings of the Georgian era. The lovely spa is in an old gothic chapel.

45 rooms ☕ – ♦£ 265/495 ♦♦£ 265/495 – 12 suites
Town plan: C1-a - *16 Royal Cres* ✉ *BA1 2LS* – ℰ *01225 823333*
– *www.royalcrescent.co.uk*
Dower House – See restaurant listing

⌂ **Bath Priory**　　　　⇤ ⚒ ◻ ⬚ spa ⌂ ℔ ⊡ ⚑ ⚑ P

COUNTRY HOUSE · ELEGANT Two adjoining properties with large gardens, an outdoor pool and an intimate spa. Country house guest areas are filled with antiques and impressive oil paintings and the luxurious bedrooms blend the traditional with the modern. Dine in the elegant restaurant, the more informal Pantry or out on the terrace.

33 rooms – ♦£ 155/795 ♦♦£ 155/795 – ☕£ 20 – 6 suites
Town plan: A1-c - *Weston Rd* ✉ *BA1 2XT* – ℰ *01225 331922*
– *www.thebathpriory.co.uk*
❀ **Bath Priory** – See restaurant listing

⌂ **Gainsborough Bath Spa** ⓝ　　⚒ ◻ spa ⌂ ℔ ⊡ ⚑ ⚑ ⚑ P

THERMAL SPA · ELEGANT Set within two Grade II listed buildings, this hotel comes with an impressive state-of-the-art spa which taps into the original thermal springs. Three of the elegantly understated bedrooms also have thermal water supplied to their baths. Modern menus offer innovative dishes with some Asian flavours.

99 rooms – ♦£ 285/395 ♦♦£ 285/395 – ☕£ 25
Town plan: C2-a - *Beau St* ✉ *BA1 1QY* – ℰ *01225 358888*
– *www.thegainsboroughbathspa.co.uk*

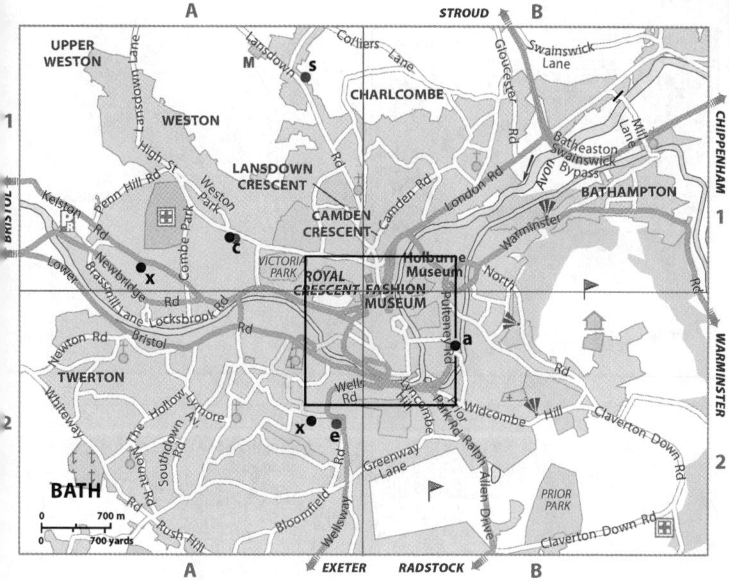

Queensberry

TOWNHOUSE · CLASSIC A series of Georgian townhouses in one of the oldest parts of the city, run by a friendly, well-versed team. Guest areas include a charming wood-panelled lounge and a chic bar with an extensive array of unusual spirits. Funky, individually designed bedrooms have smart designer touches and a host of extras.

29 rooms – 🚹£ 99/175 👫£ 125/420 – ☕£ 18

Town plan: C1-x - *Russel St ✉ BA1 2QF – ✆ 01225 447928*
– www.thequeensberry.co.uk

Olive Tree – See restaurant listing

Dukes

TOWNHOUSE · CLASSIC Two Grade I listed Palladian-style townhouses, built in 1789, with a friendly, informal feel. Bedrooms are named after famous Dukes and have period themes. If you've skipped dinner, they offer a late night cheeseboard and port.

17 rooms ☕ – 🚹£ 90/195 👫£ 90/195 – 4 suites

Town plan: D1-n - *Great Pulteney St ✉ BA2 4DN*
– ✆ 01225 787960 – www.dukesbath.co.uk
– Closed 23-29 December

Grays

TOWNHOUSE · PERSONALISED This boutique guesthouse is run by a very hands-on family team. The ground floor bedrooms are largest, while those at the top have a cosy feel. The décor is light and modern, featuring family antiques and good attention to detail.

12 rooms ☕ – 🚹£ 85/185 👫£ 110/205

Town plan: A2-x - *9 Upper Oldfield Pk ✉ BA2 3JX*
– ✆ 01225 403020 – www.graysbath.co.uk
– Closed 24-26 December

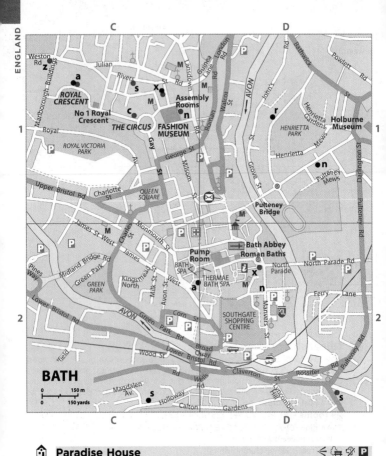

BATH

0   150 m
0   150 yards

🏠 **Paradise House** ⇐ 🛏 🛇 **P**

TOWNHOUSE · CLASSIC Elegant 18C house with award-winning gardens, set on Beechen Cliff, overlooking the city. The interior is charming and homely, with a cosy, classical lounge and bedrooms ranging from traditional four-posters to more modern styles.

12 rooms ♋ – ♦£89/220 ♦♦£89/240

Town plan: C2-s - *86-88 Holloway* ✉ *BA2 4PX* – *☎ 01225 317723* – *www.paradise-house.co.uk* – *Closed 24-25 December*

🏠 **Apsley House** 🛏 🛇 **P**

TOWNHOUSE · PERSONALISED Substantial 18C house built for the Duke of Wellington and still retaining many grand features. High-ceilinged guest areas have large fireplaces and chandeliers. Luxuriously appointed bedrooms display a subtle contemporary style.

12 rooms ♋ – ♦£135/205 ♦♦£150/220

Town plan: A1-x - *141 Newbridge Hill* ✉ *BA1 3PT* – *☎ 01225 336966* – *www.apsley-house.co.uk* – *Closed 24-26 December*

🟣 Follow our inspectors @MichelinGuideUK

🏠 Villa Magdala

TOWNHOUSE · CONTEMPORARY Victorian house named after Napier's 1868 victory, in an attractive residential area, overlooking a park. Smart, modern interior with two impressive staircases. Stylish, airy bedrooms have shuttered windows and feature wallpapers.

21 rooms ⊊ – ♦£ 119/249 ♦♦£ 139/349 – 1 suite

Town plan: D1-r - *Henrietta Rd* ⊠ *BA2 6LX* – ℰ *01225 466329*
- www.villamagdala.co.uk - Closed 1 week Christmas

🏠 Brindleys

TOWNHOUSE · DESIGN Victorian house tucked away in a residential street and concealing a surprisingly chic interior. Cosy lounge and neatly laid breakfast room. Tastefully decorated bedrooms in colour themes ranging from lavender to monochrome.

6 rooms ⊊ – ♦£ 85/165 ♦♦£ 110/195

Town plan: B2-a - *14 Pulteney Gdns* ⊠ *BA2 4HG* – ℰ *01225 310444*
- www.brindleysbath.co.uk - Closed 24-26 December

Restaurants

XXX Bath Priory

🕸 MODERN CUISINE · ELEGANT Start with an aperitif in the elegant open-fired drawing room, then head for the airy, orangery-style dining room with French doors opening onto the garden. An array of menus feature accomplished, boldly flavoured dishes which use some original combinations. Wines are well chosen but will push up the bill.

→ Seared scallops with girolles, pickled radish, apple and hazelnuts. Berkshire pork cheek, belly and shoulder with cheesy mash, spring onions and paprika jus. Bitter chocolate ginger snap with Earl Grey tea ice cream.

Menu £ 30/105

Town plan: A1-c - *Bath Priory Hotel, Weston Rd* ⊠ *BA1 2XT* – ℰ *01225 331922*
- www.thebathpriory.co.uk

XXX Dower House

MODERN CUISINE · ELEGANT Across the garden of a smart hotel is this elegant restaurant with gold and blue hues and a feature wall of hand-stitched silk. Dishes are modern and very visual; desserts are a highlight. 'Wine walls' display their finest bottles.

Carte £ 52/62

Town plan: C1-a - *Royal Crescent Hotel, 16 Royal Cres* ⊠ *BA1 2LS*
- ℰ 01225 823333 - www.royalcrescent.co.uk - dinner only

XX Olive Tree

MODERN CUISINE · INTIMATE A stylish, well-run restaurant in the basement of a boutique hotel, with a small bar and three dining rooms – all on different levels. Refined, classic dishes are created using fine ingredients and delivered in a modern style.

Menu £ 30/60 – Carte £ 38/51

Town plan: C1-x - *Queensberry Hotel, Russel St* ⊠ *BA1 2QF* – ℰ *01225 447928*
- www.olivetreebath.co.uk - dinner only and lunch Friday-Sunday

XX Allium

MODERN CUISINE · BRASSERIE A distinctly modern hotel restaurant, close to the river in the city centre. Confident, well-presented brasserie cooking is skilful and ambitious, with influences coming from Britain, Asia and the Med. Dine alfresco in the summer.

Menu £ 28 (lunch and early dinner) – Carte £ 22/50

Town plan: D2-x - *Abbey Hotel, 1 North Par* ⊠ *BA1 1LF* – ℰ *01225 461603*
(booking advisable) - www.abbeyhotelbath.co.uk

XX Menu Gordon Jones

MODERN CUISINE · SIMPLE Tiny restaurant comprising 8 tables and an open kitchen. Daily tasting menus showcase some unusual British ingredients such as beef tendons or rabbit kidneys. Complex modern dishes have interesting texture and flavour combinations.

Menu £ 45/65

Town plan: A2-e - 2 Wellsway ⊠ BA2 3AQ
- ℰ 01225 480871 (booking essential at dinner) - www.menugordonjones.co.uk
- Closed 2 weeks January, Christmas-New Year, Sunday and Monday

X Henry's 🆕

MODERN BRITISH · NEIGHBOURHOOD A laid-back bistro in a pretty pedestrianised street. It's simple yet appealing, with wooden furnishings and pictures of local scenes. Original modern dishes are packed with flavour and include some interesting vegetarian options.

Carte £ 28/35

Town plan: C1-n - ⊠ BA1 2QP - ℰ 01225 780055
- www.henrysrestaurantbath.com - Closed first week January, last 2 weeks July, 25-26 December, Sunday and Monday

X Circus 🆕

BRITISH TRADITIONAL · NEIGHBOURHOOD The small pavement terrace of this neighbourhood bistro is the perfect spot for people-watching in the historic heart of the city. Unfussy dishes use West Country produce and have a Mediterranean bias. Wines come from small growers.

Carte £ 20/34

Town plan: C1-c - 34 Brock St ⊠ BA1 2LN - ℰ 01225 466020 (bookings advisable at dinner) - www.thecircuscafeandrestaurant.co.uk - Closed 23 December-14 January and Sunday

🍴 Marlborough Tavern

TRADITIONAL BRITISH · NEIGHBOURHOOD 18C pub on the edge of Victoria Park, close to the Royal Crescent. Chic, fashionable interior with boldly patterned wallpapers and contemporary art. Carefully sourced ingredients feature in pub classics and interesting specials.

Menu £ 16 (lunch) - Carte £ 25/42

Town plan: C1-z - 35 Marlborough Buildings ⊠ BA1 2LY
- ℰ 01225 423731 - www.marlborough-tavern.com
- Closed 25 December

🍴 Chequers

TRADITIONAL CUISINE · NEIGHBOURHOOD Simply furnished pub set in a smart residential street, amid elegant Georgian terraces. Cooking is sophisticated and presentation, elaborate. The homemade bread is a highlight and creative desserts offer something a little different.

Carte £ 23/46

Town plan: C1-s - 50 Rivers St ⊠ BA1 2QA
- ℰ 01225 360017 - www.thechequersbath.com
- Closed 25 December

🍴 White Hart

TRADITIONAL CUISINE · SIMPLE Appealing pub on south east edge of the city centre, with a local following and a neighbourhood feel. Generous portions of hearty cooking; smaller tapas plates are also popular.

Menu £ 13 (weekday lunch) - Carte £ 30/40

Town plan: D2-s - Widcombe Hill ⊠ BA2 6AA
- ℰ 01225 338053 (booking essential at dinner) - www.whitehartbath.co.uk
- Closed 25-26 December, 1 January, Sunday dinner and bank holidays

Hare & Hounds

TRADITIONAL CUISINE • PUB A huge pub, more suited to a celebration with friends than a romantic dinner for two. Its hillside location affords superb views and its gardens and terrace come into their own in summer. Menus offer modern versions of classic dishes.

Carte £ 25/40

Town plan: A1-s - *Lansdown Rd ✉ BA1 5TJ - North : 1.5 mi on Lansdown Rd - ✆ 01225 482682 - www.hareandhoundsbath.com*

at Colerne Northeast: 6.5 mi by A4✉ Chippenham

Lucknam Park

GRAND LUXURY • CLASSIC A grand Palladian mansion with a mile-long tree-lined drive, rich, elegant décor, luxurious furnishings and sumptuous fabrics. Bedrooms are classically furnished and extremely comfortable. Top class facilities include an impressive spa and well-being centre, a renowned equestrian centre and a cookery school.

42 rooms - †£ 290/1145 ††£ 290/1145 - 5 suites

✉ SN14 8AZ - North : 0.5 mi on Marshfield rd - ✆ 01225 742777 - www.lucknampark.co.uk

✿ **Restaurant Hywel Jones by Lucknam Park • Brasserie** - See restaurant listing

XXXX Restaurant Hywel Jones by Lucknam Park

✿ MODERN BRITISH • ELEGANT An aperitif in the library of this impressive mansion is a fine prelude to a formal dinner in the opulent dining room. Service is professional and the kitchen, knowledgeable. Classical menus display modern European influences, with dishes expertly crafted from top quality produce - some from the estate.

→ Fillet of veal with sweetbreads glazed in pancetta and marinated salsify. Pembrokeshire sea bass with maple chicken wings and creamed sweetcorn. Tahitian vanilla crème brûlée with Gariguette strawberry salad and strawberry doughnuts.

Menu £ 85 (weekdays)/110

Lucknam Park Hotel, ✉ SN14 8AZ - North : 0.5 mi on Marshfield rd - ✆ 01225 742777 (booking essential) - www.lucknampark.co.uk - dinner only and Sunday lunch - Closed Monday

XX Brasserie

INTERNATIONAL • FASHIONABLE A stylish brasserie in a beautiful courtyard within Lucknam Park's state-of-the-art spa. There's a spacious bar-lounge and an airy dining room with full-length windows. Precise, modern cooking arrives in well-judged combinations and many healthy options are available. Dine on the charming terrace in summer.

Menu £ 23 (lunch) - Carte £ 30/79

Lucknam Park Hotel, ✉ SN14 8AZ - North : 0.5 mi on Marshfield rd - ✆ 01225 742777 - www.lucknampark.co.uk

at Monkton Combe Southeast: 4.5 mi by A36✉ Bath

Wheelwrights Arms

TRADITIONAL CUISINE • PUB Relax to the sound of birdsong at this charming stone inn; part of which was once a carpenter's workshop. Concise menus offer a selection of traditional dishes and sharing plates along with some more creative specials. As with the rest of the pub, the individually designed bedrooms are warm and welcoming.

Menu £ 12 (weekday lunch) - Carte £ 23/36 **s**

7 rooms - †£ 85/95 ††£ 95/160

Church Ln ✉ BA2 7HB - ✆ 01225 722287 - www.wheelwrightsarms.co.uk - Closed dinner 25-26 December and 1 January

at Combe Hay Southwest: 5 mi by A367 ⊠ Bath

ⓘ Wheatsheaf

MODERN BRITISH · COSY It began life as a farmhouse in 1576 but now boasts modern styling, typified by pink flock wallpaper and vivid art, and a relaxed atmosphere, helped on its way by open fires and the pub's resident spaniels. Flavourful, seasonal food is presented in a contemporary style. Bedrooms have a spacious, modern feel.

Menu £ 20/23 (weekdays) – Carte £ 26/48

3 rooms ⌸ – ♦£ 100/120 ♦♦£ 120/150

⊠ BA2 7EG – ℰ 01225 833504 – www.wheatsheafcombehay.com – Closed 10 days January, Sunday dinner and Monday except bank holidays

BAUGHURST

Hampshire – Regional map n° **4**-B1

▶ London 61 mi – Southampton 40 mi – Oxford 39 mi

ⓘ Wellington Arms

TRADITIONAL CUISINE · PUB This smart cream pub has its own herb and vegetable beds, keeps its own sheep, pigs, chickens and bees, and sources the rest of its meats from within 20 miles. Menus feature 6 dishes per course – supplemented by a selection of blackboard specials – and cooking is generous and satisfying. Smart, rustic bedrooms come with slate floors, sheepskin rugs and big, comfy beds.

Menu £ 16 (weekday lunch) – Carte £ 22/46

4 rooms ⌸ – ♦£ 100/200 ♦♦£ 100/200

Baughurst Rd ⊠ RG26 5LP – Southwest : 0.5 mi – ℰ 0118 982 0110 (booking essential) – www.thewellingtonarms.com – Closed Sunday dinner

BEACONSFIELD

Buckinghamshire – Pop. 13 797 – Regional map n° **6**-D3

▶ London 26 mi – Aylesbury 19 mi – Oxford 32 mi

🏨 Crazy Bear

LUXURY · DESIGN A discreet, unique hotel with sumptuous, over-the-top styling and idiosyncratic furnishings. Moody, masculine bedrooms blend original features with rich fabrics; some slightly less flamboyant bedrooms are located over the road. The lavishly styled 'English' restaurant offers extensive menus and uses produce from their farm shop, while sexy 'Thai' serves Asian cuisine.

32 rooms ⌸ – ♦£ 290/490 ♦♦£ 290/490

75 Wycombe End ⊠ HP9 1LX – ℰ 01494 673086 – www.crazybeargroup.co.uk

Thai – See restaurant listing

✗✗ Thai

THAI · FASHIONABLE Part of the Crazy Bear but in a separate building. It's extravagant, sexy and atmospheric, with chandeliers, flock wallpaper, snakeskin handrails and studded leather chairs. Thai dishes dominate, but influences are drawn from all over Asia.

Menu £ 30 (lunch) – Carte £ 27/62

Crazy Bear Hotel, 73 Wycombe End ⊠ HP9 1LX – ℰ 01494 673086 (booking essential) – www.crazybeargroup.co.uk – Closed Sunday lunch and Monday

ⓘ Garibaldi 🆕

TRADITIONAL BRITISH · INN A 17C inn owned by 46 shareholders, who banded together to keep their local alive. The surroundings are homely, the mood relaxed and the cooking classically based; Monday is Pie night and on Tuesday it's Cornish Mussels and Fries.

Carte £ 22/35

Hedsor Rd, Bourne End ⊠ SL8 5EE – Southwest : 3 mi by A 40 and B 4440 off A 4094 – ℰ 01628 522092 – www.garibaldipub.co.uk – Closed 26 December

ENGLAND

at Seer Green Northeast: 2.5 mi by A355

🍴 Jolly Cricketers   🏠 🅿

TRADITIONAL BRITISH · PUB Charming Victorian pub filled with a host of cricketing memorabilia; even the menu is divided into 'Openers', 'Main Play' and 'Sticky Wicket'. Cooking pleasingly balances the classics with more modern choices. Staff are welcoming.

Carte £ 25/41

24 Chalfont Rd ⊠ HP9 2YG – ℰ 01494 676308 (booking advisable)
– www.thejollycricketers.co.uk – closed Sunday dinner

BEAMINSTER

Dorset – Pop. 2 957 – Regional map n° **2**-B3
▶ London 154 mi – Dorchester 19 mi – Exeter 45 mi

🏠 BridgeHouse   🚕 🅿

HISTORIC BUILDING · CONTEMPORARY Hugely characterful 13C priests' house. Relax by an inglenook fireplace in one of the traditional flag-floored lounges. Bedrooms in the main house are spacious and have original features; those in the 'CoachHouse' are more modern.

13 rooms 🍴 – ♦£ 95/115 ♦♦£ 120/180

3 Prout Bridge ⊠ DT8 3AY – ℰ 01308 862200 – www.bridge-house.co.uk
Beaminster Brasserie – See restaurant listing

✕✕ Beaminster Brasserie   🚕 🏠 🅿

MODERN CUISINE · BRASSERIE Start with a fireside drink in the bar of this charming hotel, then head for the Georgian dining room, the conservatory or the covered terrace. Menus showcase local produce and dishes are fresh, vibrant and attractively presented.

Menu £ 14 (weekday lunch) – Carte £ 29/44

BridgeHouse Hotel, 3 Prout Bridge ⊠ DT8 3AY – ℰ 01308 862200
– www.bridge-house.co.uk

✕ Brassica 🆕

MEDITERRANEAN CUISINE · BISTRO Two pretty little 16C houses on the small town square: one is a homeware shop and the other a laid-back restaurant. Tasty, rustic cooking is full of flavour; influences are Mediterranean, with a particular focus on Spain and Italy.

Menu £ 19 (lunch) – Carte £ 23/39

3-4 The Square ⊠ DT8 3AS – ℰ 01308 538100 (booking essential)
– www.brassicarestaurant.co.uk – Closed Christmas, 2 weeks January, Sunday dinner and Monday

BEARSTED

Kent – Regional map n° **5**-B2
▶ London 39 mi – Maidstone 3 mi – Dover 40 mi

✕ Fish On The Green   🏠 ⅚ 🆔 🅿

SEAFOOD · NEIGHBOURHOOD Tucked away on a corner of the Green is this simply decorated restaurant with a pleasant terrace. Professional cooking focuses on fresh, tasty local seafood. The lunch menu is good value and service is polite and knowledgeable.

Menu £ 21 (lunch) – Carte £ 29/48

Church Ln, Bearsted Grn ⊠ ME14 4EJ – ℰ 01622 738300 (booking essential)
– www.fishonthegreen.com – Closed 25 December-mid January, Sunday dinner and Monday

BEAULIEU

Hampshire – ⊠ Brockenhurst – Pop. 726 – Regional map n° **4**-B2
▶ London 102 mi – Southampton 13 mi – Bournemouth 24 mi

🏠 Montagu Arms   🛒 🕸 ♨ 🅿️

INN · CLASSIC With its characterful parquet floors and wood panelling, this 18C inn has a timeless elegance. Traditional country house bedrooms marry antique furniture with modern facilities. The conservatory and terrace overlook the lovely gardens.

22 rooms ⬜ – ♦£139/244 ♦♦£159/369 – 4 suites

Palace Ln ⊠ *SO42 7ZL* – ✆ *01590 612324* – *www.montaguarmshotel.co.uk*
The Terrace · Monty's Inn – See restaurant listing

𝕏𝕏𝕏 The Terrace   🛒 🍴 ♻ 🅿️

MODERN BRITISH · TRADITIONAL DÉCOR This elegant dining room is found at the heart of an alluring 18C inn; sit on the terrace for views across the lovely gardens. Classically based dishes have a modern touch; fish is from the Solent and game from the New Forest.

Menu £30/75

Montagu Arms Hotel, Palace Ln ⊠ *SO42 7ZL* – ✆ *01590 612324*
– www.montaguarmshotel.co.uk – Closed Monday and lunch Tuesday

𝕏 Monty's Inn   🛒 ♿ 🅿️

TRADITIONAL BRITISH · INN Set within a large red-brick inn in a delightful village, this laid-back bar-restaurant is the perfect spot for a pint and a home-cooked classic. The eggs are from their own chickens, and meats are free range and from nearby farms.

Carte £21/38

Montagu Arms Hotel, Palace Ln ⊠ *SO42 7ZL* – ✆ *01590 612324*
– www.montaguarmshotel.co.uk

BEAUMONT – Saint Peter → See Channel Islands (Jersey)

BEELEY
Derbyshire – Pop. 165 – Regional map n° **9**-B1
▶ London 160 mi – Derby 26 mi – Sheffield 30 mi

🏠 Devonshire Arms   🎱 🍷 🍴 🕸 🅿️

TRADITIONAL BRITISH · INN Stone inn with a hugely characterful low-beamed bar and a bright modern brasserie extension with views of the village and stream. Have afternoon tea or choose from the lengthy classically based main menu; estate game is a speciality. Bedrooms in the inn and next door are cosy; those opposite are more modern.

Carte £23/35

14 rooms ⬜ – ♦£86/196 ♦♦£99/209

Devonshire Sq ⊠ *DE4 2NR* – ✆ *01629 733259 (booking advisable)*
– www.devonshirebeeley.co.uk

BELBROUGHTON
Worcestershire – Pop. 1 272 – Regional map n° **10**-C2
▶ London 122 mi – Worcester 19 mi – Birmingham 16 mi

🏠 The Queens   🍴 ♿ 🅿️

TRADITIONAL BRITISH · FRIENDLY This 16C pub might have been refurbished but its traditional look and feel remains – a conscious effort by the owners to respect the locals' preferences. Dishes are a mix of hearty pub favourites and more sophisticated classics.

Menu £13 (weekdays) – Carte £23/39

Queens Hill ⊠ *DY9 0DU* – ✆ *01562 730276* – *www.thequeensbelbroughton.co.uk*
– Closed 25 December and Sunday dinner

BELCHFORD
Lincolnshire – ⊠ Horncastle – Regional map n° **9**-C1
▶ London 169 mi – Lincoln 28 mi – Nottingham 62 mi

🍴 Blue Bell Inn   🏠 P

TRADITIONAL CUISINE · PUB Welcoming pub in a tiny hamlet in the Lincolnshire Wolds. A traditional bar with a copper-topped counter leads to a bright red dining room. Menus cover all bases, offering honest, home-cooked dishes which are big on flavour.

Carte £ 20/34

1 Main Rd ✉ LN9 6LQ – ☎ 01507 533602 – www.bluebellbelchford.co.uk – Closed 9-23 January

BELFORD

Northumberland – Pop. 1 258 – Regional map n° **14**-A1

▶ London 335 mi – Alnwick 15 mi – Newcastle upon Tyne 49 mi

🏠 Market Cross   ☆ 🛏 ⅍

TOWNHOUSE · PERSONALISED 200 year old stone townhouse close to the medieval cross in the market square; run by friendly, welcoming owners. Bright modern bedrooms come in neutral hues and feature Nespresso machines and complimentary sherry and Lindisfarne Mead. Local produce features at breakfast; dinner is by arrangement.

4 rooms � – ♦£ 60/100 ♦♦£ 80/110

1 Church St ✉ NE70 7LS – ☎ 01668 213013 – www.marketcrossbelford.co.uk – Closed 21-28 December

BELPER

Derbyshire – Pop. 23 417 – Regional map n° **9**-B2

▶ London 141 mi – Derby 10 mi – Nottingham 17 mi

🏠 Chevin Green Farm   ⅍ ≤ 🛏 ⅍ P

FAMILY · PERSONALISED Chevin Green has been in the family since 1929, when it was a working farm; the outbuildings are now homes, and the residents' families supply fresh produce to the farmhouse. The delightful owners have a passion for tea, so you'll find a great selection, alongside tea-themed artwork, ornaments and furnishings.

4 rooms ☲ – ♦£ 75 ♦♦£ 90

Chevin Rd ✉ DE56 2UN – West : 2 mi by A 517 and Farnah Green Rd – ☎ 01773 822328 – www.chevingreenfarm.com

BENENDEN

Kent – Pop. 787 – Regional map n° **5**-B2

▶ London 55 mi – Maidstone 16 mi – Hastings 23 mi

🏠 Ramsden Farm   ⅍ ≤ 🛏 ⅍ P ⊭

FAMILY · PERSONALISED Attractive clapboard house with a refreshingly relaxed air and modern styling. Bedrooms are spacious, with a slight New England look, and the luxurious bathrooms have underfloor heating. Have breakfast in the country kitchen or out on the terrace and take in lovely garden and countryside views.

3 rooms ☲ – ♦£ 95/120 ♦♦£ 95/120

Dingleden Ln ✉ TN17 4JT – Southeast : 1 mi by B 2086 – ☎ 01580 240203 – www.ramsdenfarmhouse.co.uk

BEPTON – West Sussex → See Midhurst

BERKHAMSTED

Hertfordshire – Pop. 20 641 – Regional map n° **7**-A2

▶ London 34 mi – Aylesbury 14 mi – St Albans 11 mi

XX The Gatsby

MODERN BRITISH · HISTORIC Charming cinema built in 1938 and sympathetically converted to incorporate a trendy art deco bar and glamorous restaurant. Dine among elegant columns and ornate plasterwork. Menus offer detailed, classically based dishes with modern twists.

Menu £ 15 (lunch and early dinner) – Carte £ 31/48

97 High St ⊠ HP4 2DG – ℰ 01442 870403 – www.thegatsby.net – Closed 25-26 December

BERRICK SALOME

Oxfordshire – Pop. 326 – Regional map n° **6**-B2

▶ London 50 mi – Oxford 13 mi – Aylesbury 22 mi

Chequers

TRADITIONAL BRITISH · FRIENDLY Delightful 17C pub with a spacious garden and a warm, welcoming interior with fresh flowers and candles on the tables and warming open fires. Hearty menus list British classics and at lunchtime they offer a good value 2 course menu.

Menu £ 10 (weekday lunch) – Carte £ 25/42

⊠ OX10 6JN – ℰ 01865 891118 – www.chequersberricksalome.co.uk – Closed 25 December, Sunday dinner and Tuesday

BERWICK-UPON-TWEED

Northumberland – Pop. 13 265 – Regional map n° **14**-A1

▶ London 349 mi – Edinburgh 57 mi – Newcastle upon Tyne 63 mi

Granary

TOWNHOUSE · PERSONALISED Discreet Georgian house on a side street near the river. Guest areas are on the first floor; breakfast features organic and Fairtrade produce. The 2nd floor bedrooms are bright and modern with eye-catching art and thoughtful extras.

3 rooms ⊇ – ♦£ 96 ♦♦£ 96/138

11 Bridge St ⊠ TD15 1ES – ℰ 01289 304403 – www.granaryguesthouse.co.uk

BEVERLEY

East Riding of Yorkshire – ⊠ Kingston-Upon-Hull – Pop. 30 587 – Regional map n° **13**-D2

▶ London 188 mi – Kingston-upon-Hull 8 mi – Leeds 52 mi

XX Westwood ⓝ

MODERN BRITISH · BRASSERIE The twins who own this smart modern brasserie clearly share the same vision. Appealing menus offer unfussy, recognisable dishes and the meats cooked 'a la plancha' are a hit. It sits in the wing of an impressive Georgian courthouse.

Menu £ 20 (weekdays) – Carte £ 27/49

New Walk ⊠ HU17 7AE – ℰ 01482 881999 (booking advisable)
– www.thewestwood.co.uk – Closed 27 December-13 January, Sunday dinner and Monday

XX Whites

CREATIVE · NEIGHBOURHOOD A small, keenly run neighbourhood restaurant by the old city walls; its plain décor contrasts nicely with its black wood tables and eye-catching glass art. Ambitious, creative, modern cooking is delivered in set menus of either 4 or 9 courses. Smart, contemporary bedrooms and rooftop terrace breakfasts.

Menu £ 25 (weekdays)/50

4 rooms ⊇ – ♦£ 75 ♦♦£ 95

12a North Bar Without ⊠ HU17 7AB – ℰ 01482 866121 (booking advisable)
– www.whitesrestaurant.co.uk – dinner only and Saturday lunch – Closed 1 week Christmas, 1 week August, Sunday and Monday

at Tickton Northeast: 3.5 mi by A1035 ✉ Kingston-Upon-Hull

🏠 Tickton Grange ✿ 🚗 🏋 🅿

COUNTRY HOUSE · CLASSIC A warm, welcoming, family-run hotel in an extended Georgian house – a popular wedding venue. Bedrooms are smart, stylish and up-to-date, while the spacious sitting room looks out over the immaculately kept gardens. Ambitious, modern cooking is served in the contemporary ground floor restaurant.

21 rooms ♋ – ♦£ 98/160 ♦♦£ 130/200

✉ HU17 9SH – on A 1035 – ☎ 01964 543666 – www.ticktongrange.co.uk

at South Dalton Northwest: 5 mi by A164 and B1248 ✉ Beverley

🍴 Pipe and Glass Inn (James Mackenzie) ⇦ 🚗 🏠 🎡 ⇦ 🅿
🐝

MODERN BRITISH · FRIENDLY Warm, bustling and inviting pub; very personally run by its experienced owners. Dishes are generously proportioned, carefully executed and flavourful, with judicious use of local, seasonal and traceable produce. Luxurious designer bedrooms boast the latest mod cons and have their own patios overlooking the estate woodland; breakfast is served in your room.

→ Cured salmon with pastrami spices, celeriac, pickled cucumber and sorrel. Rump of lamb with barley & beer risotto, mutton belly fritter, nettle and mint sauce. Raspberry and pistachio Bakewell tart with raspberry ripple ice cream.

Carte £ 24/57

5 rooms ♋ – ♦£ 155/190 ♦♦£ 190/225

West End ✉ HU17 7PN – ☎ 01430 810246 – www.pipeandglass.co.uk – Closed 2 weeks January, Sunday dinner and Monday except bank holidays

BEWDLEY

Worcestershire – Pop. 8 571 – Regional map n° **10**-B2
▶ London 130 mi – Worcester 16 mi – Birmingham 30 mi

🏠 Kateshill House 🚗 🍽 🅿

TOWNHOUSE · PERSONALISED This elegant Georgian manor house is surrounded by beautiful gardens; where you'll find a tree from the reign of King Henry VIII. Sumptuous, contemporary furnishings provide a subtle contrast to the house's original features.

8 rooms ♋ – ♦£ 75/85 ♦♦£ 90/110

Redhill ✉ DY12 2DR – South : 0.25 mi on B 4194 – ☎ 01299 401563 – www.kateshillhouse.co.uk

BIBURY

Gloucestershire – ✉ Cirencester – Pop. 570 – Regional map n° **2**-D1
▶ London 86 mi – Gloucester 26 mi – Oxford 30 mi

🏠 Swan ✿ 🚗 ➕ 🏋 🅿

INN · GRAND LUXURY Set in a delightful village, this ivy-clad coaching inn has a trout stream running through the garden and a cosy, characterful interior. Bedrooms mix cottagey character with contemporary touches; the best are in the annexes. The brasserie has an unusual log wall and opens onto a lovely flag-stoned courtyard.

22 rooms ♋ – ♦£ 150/210 ♦♦£ 170/210 – 4 suites

✉ GL7 5NW – ☎ 01285 740695 – www.cotswold-inns-hotels.co.uk/swan

🏠 Cotteswold House 🚗 🍽 🅿

FAMILY · PERSONALISED This pleasant guesthouse is set just outside picturesque Bibury and provides an ideal base for exploring the area. The Victorian façade conceals traditional, spotlessly kept bedrooms and the friendly owner offers a warm welcome.

3 rooms ♋ – ♦£ 65 ♦♦£ 90

Arlington ✉ GL7 5ND – on B 4425 – ☎ 01285 740609 – www.cotteswoldhouse.net

BIDBOROUGH

Kent – Regional map n° **5**-B2

▶ London 35 mi – Maidstone 29 mi – Royal Tunbridge Wells 7 mi

Kentish Hare

MODERN CUISINE · PUB Saved from development by local residents Lord and Lady Mills of Olympic Committee fame and run by the Tanner brothers, this smart pub features a hare theme, quirky wallpaper and an open kitchen. Tasty steaks from the Kamado grill.

Menu £ 22 (weekdays) – Carte £ 27/43

95 Bidborough Ridge ⊠ TN3 0XB – ℰ 01892 525709 – www.thekentishhare.com – Closed Sunday dinner and Monday except bank holidays

BIDDENDEN

Kent – Pop. 1 303 – Regional map n° **5**-C2

▶ London 52 mi – Maidstone 16 mi – Folkestone 29 mi

Barclay Farmhouse

TRADITIONAL · CLASSIC A converted farmhouse and barn in an acre of neatly kept gardens, complete with a duck pond. Comfortable bedrooms feature French oak furniture and characterful beams; extra touches include chocolate truffles on your pillow.

3 rooms – †£ 70/75 ††£ 90/95

Woolpack Corner ⊠ TN27 8BQ – South : 0.5 mi by A 262 on Benenden rd – ℰ 01580 292626 – www.barclayfarmhouse.co.uk

West House (Graham Garrett)

MODERN BRITISH · RUSTIC Characterful beamed restaurant with contemporary oil paintings and a wood-burning stove – one of a row of old weavers' cottages in a picturesque village. Original, modern dishes display global influences and the occasional playful touch, and top quality ingredients allow the natural flavours to shine through.

→ Cured mackerel with wood-roasted beetroot, pickled rhubarb, horseradish and smoked dashi. BBQ Middle White pork collar with celeriac consommé, apple and marigold. White chocolate and honeycomb parfait with dark chocolate sorbet.

Menu £ 25/45

28 High St ⊠ TN27 8AH – ℰ 01580 291341 – www.thewesthouserestaurant.co.uk – Closed Christmas, Saturday lunch, Sunday dinner and Monday

The Three Chimneys

CLASSIC CUISINE · PUB A delightful pub which dates back to 1420 and boasts dimly lit, low-beamed rooms, an old world feel and a charming terrace and garden. Dishes are mainly British based and there are some tempting local wines, ciders and ales on offer too. Bedrooms are at the end of the garden and open onto a private terrace.

Carte £ 25/40

5 rooms – †£ 80 ††£ 120/180

Hareplain Rd ⊠ TN27 8LW – West : 1.5 mi by A 262 – ℰ 01580 291472 (booking essential) – www.thethreechimneys.co.uk

BIDEFORD

Devon – Pop. 18 029 – Regional map n° **7**-C1

▶ London 231 mi – Exeter 43 mi – Plymouth 58 mi

Yeoldon House

COUNTRY HOUSE · PERSONALISED A delightfully run 19C house featuring original stained glass and wood-panelling. It's set in a peaceful riverbank location and the landscaped gardens offer lovely walks. Some of the cosy bedrooms have balconies with river views.

9 rooms – †£ 115/125 ††£ 125/140

Durrant Ln, Northam ⊠ EX39 2RL – North : 1.5 mi by B 3235 off A 386 – ℰ 01237 474400 – www.yeoldonhousehotel.co.uk – Closed Christmas

BIGBURY

Devon – Regional map n° **1**-C3

▶ London 195 mi – Exeter 41 mi – Plymouth 22 mi

✗ Oyster Shack   🛖 ᕀ 🅿

SEAFOOD · NEIGHBOURHOOD Former oyster farm with a small oyster bar and lounge, and a large terrace. The brightly decorated room is hung with fishing nets and centred around a large fish tank. Cooking is fresh and unfussy, focusing on shellfish and the daily catch.

Carte £ 24/49

Milburn Orchard Farm, Stakes Hill ✉ TQ7 4BE – East : 1 mi by Easton rd on Tidal rd – ☎ 01548 810876 (booking essential) – www.oystershack.co.uk
– Closed 3-31 January and Sunday dinner in winter

BIGBURY-ON-SEA

Devon – ✉ Kingsbridge – Pop. 220 – Regional map n° **1**-C3

▶ London 196 mi – Exeter 42 mi – Plymouth 23 mi

🏨 Burgh Island   ✿ ⅋ ⪤ 🕭 🏠 ✗ 🗗 ⅋ 🅿

HISTORIC · ART DÉCO Grade II listed house on its own island, accessed using the hotel's Land Rover (or tractor at high tide!). It has classic art deco styling throughout, from the guest areas to the individually designed bedrooms; some rooms have small balconies and most have excellent bay views. 1930s themed 'black tie' dinners take place in the ballroom; there's live music Weds and Sat.

25 rooms (dinner included) ☲ – ♦£ 310/665 ♦♦£ 400/665 – 12 suites

✉ TQ7 4BG – South : 0.5 mi by hotel transport – ☎ 01548 810514
– www.burghisland.com – Closed 2-15 January

🏠 Henley   ✿ ⅋ ⪤ 🕭 🅿

TRADITIONAL · PERSONALISED Not only is this extended cottage very personally run by its welcoming owners but it also affords superb views over Burgh Island and towards Bolt Tail. Charming bedrooms mix antique and modern furnishings and all share the wonderful view. Home-cooked meals are taken in the wicker-furnished conservatory.

5 rooms ☲ – ♦£ 90 ♦♦£ 120/150

Folly Hill ✉ TQ7 4AR – ☎ 01548 810240 – www.thehenleyhotel.co.uk – Closed November-mid March

BIGGLESWADE

Bedfordshire – Pop. 15 383 – Regional map n° **12**-B1

▶ London 46 mi – Bedford 12 mi – Luton 24 mi

✗✗ Croft Kitchen   🄰🄲

MODERN BRITISH · FRIENDLY Two enthusiastic brothers, of Indian and Scottish descent, run this simple little restaurant – one cooks and one serves. Creative modern dishes are attractively presented and subtle Indian spicing adds another dimension to the cooking.

Menu £ 31 (weekdays)/45

28 Palace St ✉ SG18 8DP
– ☎ 01767 601502 – www.thecroftbiggleswade.com
– Closed Monday-Tuesday, Sunday dinner and lunch Wednesday-Thursday

BILDESTON

Suffolk – Regional map n° **8**-C3

▶ London 85 mi – Bury St Edmunds 18 mi – Ipswich 15 mi

ENGLAND

🏠 Bildeston Crown   ☆ & P

INN · CONTEMPORARY A hugely characterful 15C wool merchant's with a lovely rear courtyard. The stylish, modern interior has warm colours and open fires. Luxurious bedrooms vary from florally feminine to bright and bold and all have designer furnishings. Choose from classic or adventurous dishes in the charming beamed dining room.

13 rooms ☞ – ♦£ 70/100 ♦♦£ 90/150

104 High St ✉ IP7 7EB – ☏ 01449 740510 – www.thebildestoncrown.com

BIRKENHEAD

Merseyside – Pop. 142 968 – Regional map n° **11**-A3
▶ London 208 mi – Liverpool 3 mi – Manchester 37 mi

✗✗✗ Fraiche (Marc Wilkinson)

❀ CREATIVE · DESIGN Enter into the cosy bar, where seasonal images are projected onto the wall, then head through to the boldly decorated restaurant which seats just 10 diners. Cooking is innovative and presentation is key – both the colours of the ingredients and the shape and style of the crockery play their part.
→ Celeriac lasagne, mushroom consommé and pear. Gressingham duck with charred asparagus and miso caramel. Rosemary ice cream with apple textures and tonka bean crisp.

Menu £ 85

11 Rose Mount, Oxton ✉ CH43 5SG – Southwest : 2.25 mi by A 552 and B 5151 – ☏ 0151 652 2914 (booking essential) – www.restaurantfraiche.com – dinner only and Sunday lunch – Closed 25 December, 1-7 July, Sunday dinner, Monday and Tuesday

BIRMINGHAM

West Midlands – Pop. 1 085 810 – Regional map n° **10**-C2
▶ London 122 mi – Bristol 91 mi – Newcastle upon Tyne 207 mi

Hotels

🏨 **Hyatt Regency**

BUSINESS · CONTEMPORARY An eye-catching, mirror-fronted, tower block hotel in a prime city centre location, with a covered link to the International Convention Centre. Spacious bedrooms have floor to ceiling windows and an excellent level of facilities. Aria restaurant, in the atrium, offers modern European menus.

319 rooms – †£ 95/220 ††£ 95/220 – ☲ £ 18 – 11 suites
Town plan: D2-a - *2 Bridge St* ⊠ *B1 2JZ* – ✆ *0121 643 1234*
– *www.birmingham.regency.hyatt.com*

🏨 **Malmaison**

BUSINESS · MODERN A stylish hotel with dark, moody décor, set on the site of the old Royal Mail sorting office next to designer clothing and homeware shops. Bedrooms are spacious and stylish; the Penny Black suite has a mini-cinema and a steam room. Dine from an accessible British menu in the bright, bustling brasserie.

192 rooms ☲ – †£ 80/250 ††£ 80/250 – 1 suite
Town plan: E2-e - *Mailbox, 1 Wharfside St* ⊠ *B1 1RD* – ✆ *0121 246 5000*
– *www.malmaison.com*

🏨 **Hotel La Tour**

BUSINESS · MODERN A striking modern building with spacious, stylish guest areas. With their media hubs and TV recording facilities, bedrooms are ideal for business travellers; Superiors come with baths which have TVs mounted above them. The informal chophouse serves an extensive menu of hearty, unfussy classics and steaks.

174 rooms – †£ 89/245 ††£ 89/245 – ☲ £ 18
Town plan: F2-a - *Albert St* ⊠ *B5 5JE* – ✆ *0121 718 8000* – *www.hotel-latour.co.uk*
– *Closed 23-30 December*

Hotel Du Vin

BUSINESS · DESIGN A characterful former eye hospital with a relaxed, shabby-chic style. Bright bedrooms are named after wine companies and estates; one suite boasts an 8 foot bed, two roll-top baths and a gym. Kick-back in the small cellar pub or comfy champagne bar; the classical bistro has a lively buzz and a French menu.

66 rooms – †£ 120/185 ††£ 130/195

Town plan: E1-e - *25 Church St ✉ B3 2NR* – *℘ 0844 736 4250*
– *www.hotelduvin.com*

Hotel Indigo

BUSINESS · DESIGN Stylish hotel located on the top three floors of the eye-catching 'Cube' building. Both the appealingly styled guest areas and vividly decorated bedrooms come with floor to ceiling windows. A smart steakhouse serves classic dishes and boasts a champagne bar, a terrace and a view from every table.

52 rooms – †£ 99/200 ††£ 140/210 – �)£ 16

Town plan: D3-x - *The Cube ✉ B1 1PR* – *℘ 0121 643 2010*
– *www.hotelindigobirmingham.com*

Restaurants

Simpsons (Andreas Antona & Luke Tipping)

MODERN CUISINE · FASHIONABLE Behind the walls of this suburban Georgian house is a sleek dining room and three contemporary bedrooms. Cooking has a clean, Scandic style and the visually appealing dishes are packed with flavour. Lunch sees a 2-choice set price menu; dinner a 4-course set price menu and a tasting option – some courses are served by the chefs. Desserts are satisfyingly traditional.
→ Sweetbreads with mushroom broth, charred onions, bone marrow and asparagus. Suckling pig with leeks, aubergine, apple and miso. Madagascan sugar espuma with Yorkshire rhubarb and gingerbread.

Menu £ 35/60

3 rooms �)– †£ 110 ††£ 110

Town plan: A2-e - *20 Highfield Rd, Edgbaston ✉ B15 3DU* – *℘ 0121 454 3434*
– *www.simpsonsrestaurant.co.uk* – *Closed Sunday dinner and bank holidays*

Purnell's (Glynn Purnell)

MODERN CUISINE · DESIGN Start in the comfy lounge, then head past the wine display to the vibrantly decorated dining room. Menus range from 3 to 9 courses and some of them offer swaps so you can try the chef's signature dishes. Sophisticated cooking ranges from classic to Scandic in style and flavours and textures marry perfectly.
→ Chicken liver parfait with red wine braised salsify and sour leaves. Loin of Balmoral venison, Bordelaise sauce, pommes dauphine and black truffle. Blood orange curd tartlet with honeycomb, frozen yoghurt and almond.

Menu £ 35 (weekday lunch)/88

Town plan: E1-b - *55 Cornwall St ✉ B3 2DH* – *℘ 0121 212 9799*
– *www.purnellsrestaurant.com* – *Closed 2 weeks August, 1 week Easter, 1 week Christmas, Saturday lunch, Sunday and Monday*

Adam's (Adam Stokes)

MODERN CUISINE · ELEGANT Adam's has moved just around the corner to larger premises. Enjoy a drink in the smart cocktail bar then move on to the bright, elegant restaurant with a subtle retro feel. Choose from a concise set menu or an 8 course tasting menu: top notch produce is used in carefully prepared dishes which have wonderfully bold complementary flavours and contrasting textures.
→ Veal sweetbread with air-dried ham, cauliflower, lemon and sorrel. Sea trout with artichoke, broad beans and garlic. Rhubarb with caramel and blood orange.

Menu £ 35/60

Town plan: E2-c - *New Oxford House, 16 Waterloo St ✉ B2 5UG*
– *℘ 0121 643 3745 (booking essential)* – *www.adamsrestaurant.co.uk*
– *Closed Christmas-New Year, Sunday and Monday*

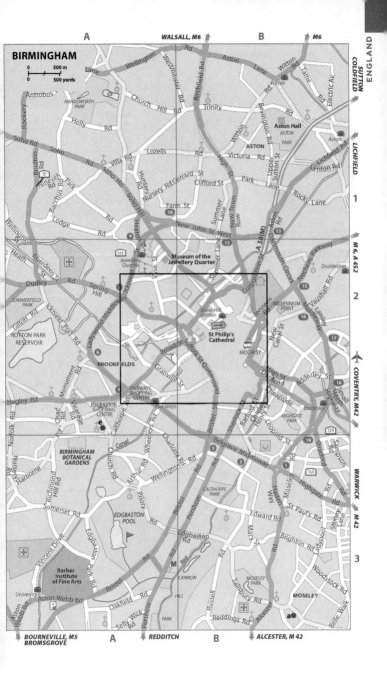

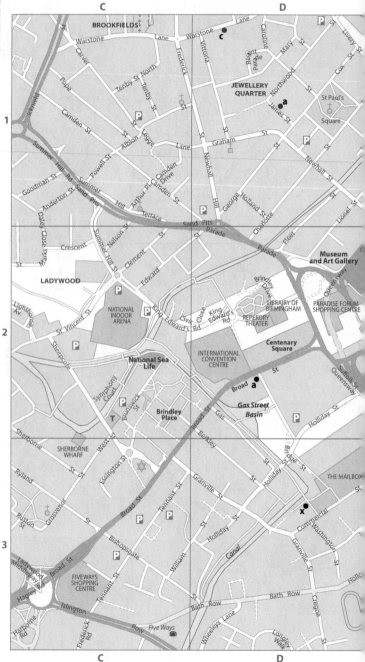

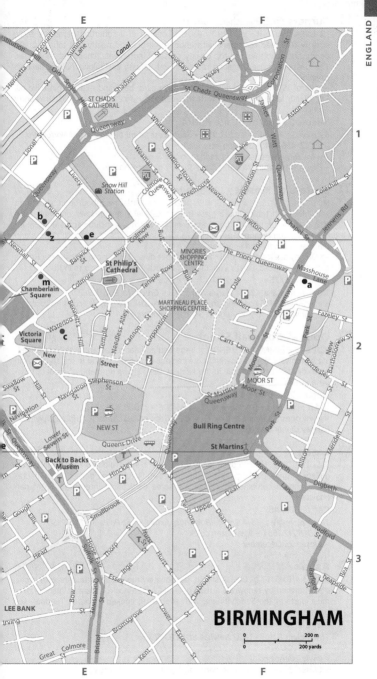

BIRMINGHAM

| 0 | | 200 m |
| 0 | | 200 yards |

XX Turners @ 69 (Richard Turner)   &. AC
MODERN BRITISH · NEIGHBOURHOOD Located in a suburban parade, a busy, smartly furnished restaurant with antique mirrors and neatly laid tables. Confidently crafted dishes use top quality seasonal ingredients, chosen at their peak. The classically based cooking is refined yet unfussy and allows natural flavours to shine.

→ Isle of Wight tomatoes with Innes Farm curd, basil and extra virgin olive oil. Salt-marsh lamb Wellington with rosemary jelly and lamb jus. Wild strawberry Arctic roll.

Menu £ 20 (lunch) – Carte £ 30/43

69 High St, Harborne ⊠ B17 9NS – Southwest : 4 mi by A 456 and Norfolk Rd
– 𝒞 0121 426 4440 (booking essential)
– www.turnersrestaurantbirmingham.co.uk
– Closed Christmas, New Year and Sunday dinner-Monday

XX Carters of Moseley (Brad Carter)   &. AC ⟨♡⟩
MODERN BRITISH · NEIGHBOURHOOD Lovely little neighbourhood restaurant with black ash tables and a glass-fronted cabinet running down one wall. Each dish is made up of three key components – which can include some unusual ingredients; combinations are well-balanced and flavours are intense. The young team are friendly and engaging.

→ Orkney scallop with coral roe and pepper dulse. Manx lamb with Jersey Royals and monk's beard. Goat's yoghurt with pistachio and Alphonso mango.

Menu £ 35/75

Town plan: B3-a - *2c St Mary's Row, Wake Green Rd ⊠ B13 9EZ*
– 𝒞 0121 449 8885 (booking advisable) – www.cartersofmoseley.co.uk – Closed 1-18 January, 30 July-16 August, Sunday and Monday

XX Opus at Cornwall Street   ☂ &. AC ⟨♡⟩ ⇔
MODERN CUISINE · DESIGN Very large and popular restaurant with floor to ceiling windows; enjoy an aperitif in the cocktail bar before dining in the stylish main room or at the chef's table in the kitchen. Daily changing menu of modern brasserie dishes.

Menu £ 20 – Carte £ 26/49

Town plan: E1-z - *54 Cornwall St ⊠ B3 2DE – 𝒞 0121 200 2323*
– www.opusrestaurant.co.uk – Closed 24 December-3 January, Saturday lunch, Sunday dinner and bank holidays

XX Lasan   AC ⟨♡⟩
INDIAN · DESIGN An industrial-style restaurant in an old Jewellery Quarter art gallery. Original cooking takes authentic Indian flavours and delivers them in creative modern combinations; there are some particularly interesting vegetarian choices.

Carte £ 28/45

Town plan: D1-a - *3-4 Dakota Buildings, James St, St Pauls Sq ⊠ B3 1SD*
– 𝒞 0121 212 3664 – www.lasan.co.uk
– Closed 25 December

XX Asha's   ☂ &. AC ⟨♡⟩ ⇔
INDIAN · EXOTIC DÉCOR A stylish, passionately run Indian restaurant with exotic décor; owned by renowned artiste/gourmet Asha Bhosle. Extensive menus cover most parts of the Subcontinent, with everything cooked to order. Tandoori kebabs are a speciality.

Menu £ 32 – Carte £ 19/68

Town plan: E2-m - *12-22 Newhall St ⊠ B3 3LX*
– 𝒞 0121 200 2767
– www.ashasuk.co.uk
– Closed 26 December, 1 January and lunch Saturday-Sunday

X **Two Cats Kitchen** ⓝ

REGIONAL CUISINE · SIMPLE Tucked away down an alley in the jewellery quarter is this small restaurant with exposed brickwork and stained glass windows. The 7 course set menu comprises artistically presented modern dishes of flavoursome New Baltic cuisine.

Menu £ 42 – tasting menu only

Town plan: D1-C - *27 Warstone Ln ✉ B18 6JQ - ☎ 0121 212 0070 (booking advisable) - www.twocatskitchen.com - dinner only and lunch Friday-Saturday - Closed 3 weeks Christmas-New Year, Sunday and Monday*

at National Exhibition Centre Southeast : 9 ½ m. on A 45✉ Birmingham

XX **Andy Waters** ⓝ   ዿ AC P

TRADITIONAL BRITISH · CHIC Unusually set in a shopping centre, beside the cinema, is this comfy, formal restaurant run by an experienced chef – ask for one of the booths. Traditional cooking is given a personal touch; the 2 course lunch menu is good value.

Menu £ 15 (lunch) – Carte £ 26/48

Floor One, Resorts World, Pendigo Way ✉ B40 1PU - ☎ 020 1273 1238 - www.watersrestaurant.co.uk - Closed 25 December

BISHOP'S STORTFORD

Hertfordshire – Pop. 37 838 – Regional map n° **7**-B2
▶ London 34 mi – Hertford 16 mi – Cambridge 27 mi

X **Water Lane**   ዿ AC

TRADITIONAL BRITISH · BISTRO Atmospheric restaurant set over two floors – with a cellar bar below – in the converted 18C Hawkes Brewery. Menus offer a range of rustic British and American dishes, from bubble and squeak to Bourbon-glazed ribs with chipotle slaw.

Carte £ 23/33

31 Water Ln ✉ CM23 2JZ - ☎ 01279 211888 - www.waterlane.co

X **Lemon Tree**   AC ⇔ P

REGIONAL CUISINE · FRIENDLY A friendly, passionately run little restaurant in a 200 year old house hidden in the town centre. Choose from several characterful dining areas. Seasonal menus offer unfussy classical dishes; the 'Taste of ...' menus are good value.

Carte £ 23/45

14-16 Water Ln ✉ CM23 2JZ - ☎ 01279 757788 - www.lemontree.co.uk - Closed 25-27 December, 1-2 January, bank holidays, dinner Sunday and Monday

BISPHAM GREEN

Lancashire – Regional map n° **11**-A2
▶ London 212 mi – Preston 15 mi – Liverpool 22 mi

🏠 **Eagle & Child**   🍴 🏠 P

TRADITIONAL BRITISH · COSY A 16C inn with all the requisite character of a 'proper' pub; sit in the charmingly small snug. Quality seasonal ingredients are used to create unfussy, boldly flavoured dishes. Before you leave, visit the delightful farm shop next door.

Menu £ 10 – Carte £ 21/43

Maltkiln Ln ✉ L40 3SG - ☎ 01257 462297 - www.ainscoughs.co.uk

BLACKBURN

Blackburn with Darwen – Pop. 117 963 – Regional map n° **11**-B2
▶ London 228 mi – Preston 11 mi – Manchester 24 mi

🍴 Clog & Billycock   🕭 ⅋ 🅿

TRADITIONAL BRITISH · PUB Spacious, modern, open-plan pub. Extensive menus offer plenty of choice and display a strong Lancastrian slant; cooking is rustic and generous. Most produce is sourced from within 25 miles.

Menu £ 14 (weekdays) – Carte £ 21/41

Billinge End Rd, Pleasington ✉ BB2 6QB – West : 2 mi by A 677 – ℰ 01254 201163 – www.theclogandbillycock.com

at Langho North: 4.5 mi on A666 ✉ Whalley

🏨 Northcote   🛏 ⅋ 🕭 ⅋ 🛁 🅿

COUNTRY HOUSE · ELEGANT This smart Victorian house sits on the edge of the Ribble Valley and is continually evolving and expanding. The individually designed bedrooms are spacious, stylish and sophisticated; all have queen or king-sized beds and some have garden terraces. Enjoy afternoon tea beside the fire in the lounge.

26 rooms ⌷ – ♦£ 220/565 ♦♦£ 260/605 – 1 suite

Northcote Rd ✉ BB6 8BE – North : 0.5 mi on A 59 at junction with A 666 – ℰ 01254 240555 – www.northcote.com

❀ **Northcote** – See restaurant listing

🍴🍴🍴 Northcote (Nigel Haworth)   ⅋ 🛏 ⅋ 🕭 🍷 ⅋ 🅿
❀

MODERN BRITISH · ELEGANT Elegant restaurant within a smart Victorian house. Refined, sophisticated cooking shows depth of flavour and a lightness of touch. Local and garden ingredients are the stars of the show. Watch the chefs in action from the glass-walled kitchen table or join them by taking part in one of the cookery classes.

➜ Bay leaf roast John Dory with apple vinegar. Rare breed milk-fed pork with Wyre Valley asparagus and garlic cream. Californian cherry 'Black Forest' and pine.

Menu £ 30 (lunch) – Carte £ 52/80

Northcote Hotel, Northcote Rd ✉ BB6 8BE – North : 0.5 mi on A 59 at junction with A 666 – ℰ 01254 240555 (booking essential) – www.northcote.com

at Mellor Northwest: 3.25 mi by A677 ✉ Blackburn

🏨 Stanley House   🏹 ⅋ 🛏 🕘 🐾 ⅋ ⅋ 🛁 🅿

LUXURY · DESIGN Attractive part-17C manor house boasting superb country views and a smart spa with four types of sauna. Bedrooms in the main house are elegant and feature original beams and mullioned windows; the 'Woodland Rooms' are more contemporary. Stylish 'Grill on the Hill' offers modern favourites and views over the garden towards the coast; 'Mr Fred's' serves simpler fare.

30 rooms ⌷ – ♦£ 155/250 ♦♦£ 190/275

✉ BB2 7NP – Southwest : 0.75 mi by A 677 and Further Ln – ℰ 01254 769200 – www.stanleyhouse.co.uk

BLACKPOOL

Blackpool – Pop. 147 663 – Regional map n° **11**-A2

▶ London 246 mi – Preston 17 mi – Liverpool 56 mi

🏠 Number One St Lukes   🛏 ⅋ 🅿

TOWNHOUSE · DESIGN A boutique guesthouse set close to the promenade and the Pleasure Beach and run by a very charming owner. Bedrooms are named after the town's piers: 'North' has an African feel and 'Central' has a white half-tester and a more feminine touch. There's also an outdoor hot tub and a mini pitch and putt green!

3 rooms ⌷ – ♦£ 75/130 ♦♦£ 100/135

1 St Lukes Rd ✉ FY4 2EL – ℰ 01253 343901 – www.numberoneblackpool.com

at Thornton Northeast: 5.5 mi by A584 -(BY)- on B5412 ⊠ Blackpool

✗✗ Twelve   🍷 🏠 ⚴

MODERN BRITISH · DESIGN Set beneath the sails of one of Europe's tallest working windmills is this passionately run cocktail bar and restaurant – which has an
urban, industrial feel courtesy of brick walls, exposed pipework and grey beams.
Good value menus offer modern dishes with the occasional innovative touch.
Menu £24/27 – Carte £24/38

Marsh Mill, Fleetwood Rd North ⊠ FY5 4JZ – ✆ 01253 821212
– www.twelve-restaurant.co.uk – dinner only and Sunday lunch – Closed first
2 weeks January and Monday

BLAGDON

North Somerset – Pop. 1 001 – Regional map n° **3**-B2
▶ London 132 mi – Taunton 35 mi – Bristol 14 mi

🏠 Seymour Arms ⓝ   ⇦ 🏠 ⟳ 🅿

MODERN BRITISH · INN Set in a small village in the Mendip Hills, overlooking a
Lake. Hole up beside the wood-burning stove with a pint of locally brewed ale.
The regularly changing menus are refreshingly concise and the unfussy, confidently prepared dishes have a modern British style. Up-to-date bedrooms are
simply furnished.
Carte £24/40
5 rooms 😋 – †£77/85 ††£95/105
Bath Rd ⊠ BS40 7TH – On A 368 – ✆ 01761 462279
– www.theseymourarmsblagdon.co.uk – Closed Monday lunch

BLAKENEY

Norfolk – ⊠ Holt – Pop. 801 – Regional map n° **8**-C1
▶ London 127 mi – King's Lynn 37 mi – Norwich 28 mi

🏨 Blakeney   👆 ≤ ⇦ 🔲 🐾 🛁 🛗 ⚴ 💪 🅿

FAMILY · CONTEMPORARY Traditional hotel in a great quayside location, affording views over the estuary and the salt marshes. It has various comfy lounges
and a bar with subtle modern touches. Some of the individually designed bedrooms have balconies or sea views. The formal dining room offers a good outlook
and a wide-ranging menu.
64 rooms 😋 – †£85/185 ††£170/370
The Quay ⊠ NR25 7NE – ✆ 01263 740797 – www.blakeneyhotel.co.uk

✗ Wiveton Farm Café   ≤ 🏠 🖥 🅿

REGIONAL CUISINE · FRIENDLY An extension of a farm shop, set down a dusty
track and run by a smiley young team. Light breakfasts and tasty, salad-based
lunches; weekends see 'Norfolk' tapas in the evenings. Take in glorious farm and
sea views from the terrace.
Carte £17/32
⊠ NR25 7TE – West : 0.5 mi on A149 – ✆ 01263 740515 – www.wivetonhall.co.uk
– lunch only and dinner Thursday-Saturday – Closed November-March

🏠 White Horse   ⇦ 🏠 🅿

TRADITIONAL CUISINE · INN A brick and flint pub near the harbour; if the sun's
shining, find a spot on the suntrap terrace. Inside it's bright and airy with pastel
colours and modern art. The menu champions local produce in tried-and-tested
combinations, with seafood a feature in summer. Smart bedrooms are named after nautical knots.
Carte £16/34
9 rooms 😋 – †£89/159 ††£99/159
4 High St ⊠ NR25 7AL – ✆ 01263 740574 (booking advisable)
– www.blakeneywhitehorse.co.uk – Closed 25 December

at Cley next the Sea East: 1.5 mi on A149 ✉ Holt

🏠 Cley Windmill

HISTORIC · COSY With its views over the marshes and river, this restored 18C windmill is a birdwatcher's paradise. Snug, characterful bedrooms are split between the mill, the stables and the boatshed. The flagstone dining room offers a set menu of homemade country dishes and the tea room opens in the summer months.

9 rooms ☑ – ♦£ 159/199 ♦♦£ 159/199
The Quay ✉ NR25 7RP – ℰ 01263 740209 – www.cleywindmill.co.uk

at Wiveton South: 1 mi by A149 on Wiveton Rd

🍴 Wiveton Bell

TRADITIONAL BRITISH · FASHIONABLE Modernised pub featuring beams, stripped floors and wood-burning stoves; with picnic tables out the front and a beautifully landscaped rear terrace. Seasonal menu offers pub classics, carefully crafted from quality local ingredients. Stylish, cosy bedrooms have smart bathrooms; continental breakfasts.

Carte £ 25/37
6 rooms ☑ – ♦£ 90/160 ♦♦£ 90/160
Blakeney Rd ✉ NR25 7TL – ℰ 01263 740101 (booking essential)
– www.wivetonbell.com

at Morston West: 1.5 mi on A149 ✉ Holt

🏠 Morston Hall

LUXURY · CLASSIC Attractive, personally run country house with manicured gardens, set in a small coastal hamlet. Comfy guest areas feature antiques and paintings. Bedrooms are split between the main house and an annexe – the latter are larger and have subtle contemporary touches. Service is keen and friendly.

13 rooms (dinner included) ☑ – ♦£ 240/300 ♦♦£ 380/400
The Street ✉ NR25 7AA – ℰ 01263 741041 – www.morstonhall.com
– Closed 1-29 January and 24-26 December
❀ **Morston Hall** – See restaurant listing

XX Morston Hall (Galton Blackiston)

❀ MODERN BRITISH · ELEGANT Set in an attractive country house surrounded by landscaped gardens: choose between a traditionally furnished room or a beautiful conservatory. The set 7 course daily menu (served at 8pm), offers well-balanced seasonal dishes. Cooking is classically based, sophisticated and exhibits a delicate, modern touch.

→ Brancaster lobster ravioli with King's Lynn tomatoes and Thornage Hall spinach. Holkham Estate venison Wellington with Norfolk asparagus, carrot purée and white pepper jus. Sherrington strawberries with yoghurt and buttermilk panna cotta.

Menu £ 68 – tasting menu only
Morston Hall Hotel, The Street ✉ NR25 7AA – ℰ 01263 741041 (booking essential)
– www.morstonhall.com – dinner only and Sunday lunch – Closed 1-29 January and 24-26 December

BLANCHLAND

Northumberland – Regional map n° **14**-A2
▶ London 286 mi – Newcastle upon Tyne 29 mi – Carlisle 50 mi

🏠 Lord Crewe Arms

TRADITIONAL · CONTEMPORARY This 12C abbot's priory has also spent time as a hunting lodge and a lead miners' hostelry. Its hugely characterful guest areas don't disappoint; smell the chicken roasting over the open fire in the barrel-ceilinged bar. Bedrooms have a modern country charm and come with bespoke furnishings and walkers' packs.

21 rooms ☑ – ♦£ 84/209 ♦♦£ 99/224 – 2 suites
The Square ✉ DH8 9SP – ℰ 01434 675469 – www.lordcrewearmsblanchland.co.uk
Bishop's Dining Room – See restaurant listing

Q60

INDULGE YOURSELF

INFINITI

EMPOWER THE DRIVE

Fuel economy figures for the Q60 range – subject to official homologation: mpg (l/100km).
Urban 18.7/29.4 (15.1/9.6), extra urban 36.4/50.4 (7.8/5.6), combined 27.0/40.4 (10.5/5.6),
CO_2 emissions 249-168 g/km.* Model shown: Infiniti Q60 3.0t available from 01.10.2016.
*Official homologated emission and fuel consumption figures for the Q60 range are not available
at the time of going to press. MPG figures are obtained from laboratory testing and are intended
for comparisons between vehicles and may not reflect real driving results. Optional equipment,
maintenance, driving behaviour, road and weather conditions may affect the results.

X **Bishop's Dining Room**

TRADITIONAL BRITISH · RUSTIC Bright, hunting-themed restaurant in a characterful hotel; the monks from the neighbouring abbey once dined here. Menus offer robust, flavoursome British dishes which feature kitchen garden, spit-roast and home-smoked produce.

Carte £ 18/33

Lord Crewe Arms Hotel, The Square ⊠ DH8 9SP – ℰ 01434 675469
– www.lordcrewearmsblanchland.co.uk

BLANDFORD FORUM

Dorset – Pop. 11 694 – Regional map n° **2**-C3

▶ London 124 mi – Dorchester 17 mi – Bournemouth 17 mi

at Tarrant Launceston Northeast: 5.5 mi by A354

🏠 **Launceston Farmhouse**

FAMILY · PERSONALISED Charming guesthouse on a working cattle farm, which is the friendly owner's childhood home. Stylish bedrooms can be reached via a wrought iron spiral staircase and feature period furniture, modern bathrooms and homely extras.

6 rooms ♁ – ♦£ 75/125 ♦♦£ 100/125

⊠ *DT11 8BY – ℰ 01258 830528 – www.launcestonfarm.co.uk*

at Farnham Northeast: 7.5 mi by A354⊠ Blandford Forum

🏠 **Farnham Farm House**

FAMILY · COSY Welcoming farmhouse on a 300 acre working farm, complete with a swimming pool and a holistic therapy centre. Homely, immaculately kept bedrooms have country views. Enjoy tea and cake on arrival; the eggs are from their own hens.

3 rooms ♁ – ♦£ 80 ♦♦£ 90/100

⊠ *DT11 8DG – North : 1 mi by Shaftesbury rd – ℰ 01725 516254*
– www.farnhamfarmhouse.co.uk – Closed 25-26 December

> Good quality cooking at a great price?
> Look out for the Bib Gourmand ⊛.

BLEDINGTON – Gloucestershire ➜ See Stow-on-the-Wold

BODIAM

East Sussex – Regional map n° **5**-B2

▶ London 58 mi – Lewes 29 mi – Hastings 13 mi

XX **Curlew**

MODERN BRITISH · DESIGN Contemporary restaurant behind a white clapboard pub façade, with funky cow print wallpaper and a Scandinavian feel. Menus are modern, the wine list promotes organic and biodynamic wines, and service is smooth and professional.

Menu £ 20 (weekdays) – Carte £ 31/46

Junction Rd ⊠ TN32 5UY – Northwest : 1.5 mi at junction with B 2244
– ℰ 01580 861394 – www.thecurlewrestaurant.co.uk – Closed 26 December,
1 January and Monday

BODMIN

Cornwall – Pop. 14 614 – Regional map n° **1**-B2

▶ London 270 mi – Newquay 18 mi – Plymouth 32 mi

ENGLAND

🏠 Bokiddick Farm   🖄 🛏 🕭 **P**

TRADITIONAL · TRADITIONAL A traditional farmhouse on a 180 acre working dairy farm – a warm welcome is guaranteed and they serve cream teas on arrival. Homely, spotlessly kept bedrooms come with super king sized beds and country views; the largest rooms are in the old barn. Hearty breakfasts are taken overlooking the garden.

3 rooms 🗷 – 🛉£ 55/65 🛉🛉£ 84/90

Lanivet ⊠ PL30 5HP – South : 5 mi by A 30 following signs for Lanhydrock and Bokiddick – 𝒞 01208 831481 – www.bokiddickfarm.co.uk – Closed Christmas

BOLLINGTON

Cheshire East – ⊠ Cheshire – Pop. 7 373 – Regional map n° **11**-B3
▶ London 178 mi – Stockport 11 mi – Manchester 22 mi

XX Oliver at Bollington Green

MODERN CUISINE · BISTRO A bright, personally-run neighbourhood restaurant, set just off the main road opposite a tiny village green. Interesting menus offer refined, balanced dishes packed with flavour; the bread, ice-cream and chocolates are all homemade.

Menu £ 20 (weekdays) – Carte £ 26/40

*22 High St ⊠ SK10 5PH – 𝒞 01625 575058 (booking advisable)
– www.oliveratbollingtongreen.com – dinner only and Sunday lunch – Closed Sunday dinner, Monday and Tuesday*

BOLNHURST

Bedford – Regional map n° **7**-A1
▶ London 64 mi – Bedford 8 mi – St Neots 7 mi

🍴 Plough at Bolnhurst   🕸 🛏 🍴 **P**

MODERN BRITISH · INN Charming whitewashed pub with a rustic bar, a modern restaurant, a lovely garden and a bustling atmosphere. Menus change with the seasons but always feature 28-day aged Aberdeenshire steaks, dishes containing Mediterranean ingredients like Sicilian black olives, and a great selection of wines and cheeses.

Menu £ 22 (weekdays) – Carte £ 31/52

*Kimbolton Rd ⊠ MK44 2EX – South : 0.5 mi on B 660 – 𝒞 01234 376274
– www.bolnhurst.com – Closed 2 weeks January, Sunday dinner and Monday*

BOLTON ABBEY

North Yorkshire – ⊠ Skipton – Pop. 117 – Regional map n° **13**-B2
▶ London 216 mi – Harrogate 18 mi – Skipton 6 mi

🏠 Devonshire Arms H. & Spa   🖄 ≼ 🛏 🖵 🕭 ⋒ ₤ 🛠 🕭 🎱 **P**

LUXURY · CLASSIC A charming coaching inn with a popular spa, set on the Duke and Duchess of Devonshire's 30,000 acre estate in the Yorkshire Dales. Comfy lounges display part of the owners' vast art collection and dogs are welcome. Bedrooms in the wing are bright, modern and compact; those in the inn are more traditional.

40 rooms 🗷 – 🛉£ 118/458 🛉🛉£ 135/475 – 2 suites

⊠ BD23 6AJ – 𝒞 01756 710441 – www.thedevonshirearms.co.uk

The Burlington · Brasserie – See restaurant listing

XXX The Burlington   🕸 ≼ 🛏 🛠 🕭 ✿ **P**

MODERN BRITISH · ELEGANT Elegant, antique-filled hotel dining room, hung with impressive oils; sit in the conservatory to overlook the Italian garden. Elaborate modern dishes utilise fine ingredients, with many coming from the kitchen garden and estate.

Menu £ 70

Devonshire Arms Hotel and Spa ⊠ BD23 6AJ – 𝒞 01756 710441 (booking essential) – www.thedevonshirearms.co.uk – dinner only

✗ Brasserie

TRADITIONAL BRITISH · RUSTIC Relaxed hotel brasserie with an attractive wine cellar; set opposite the kitchen garden. Sit on stripy banquettes in the bar or on red velour chairs in the dining room. The extensive à la carte offers satisfying brasserie classics.

Carte £ 31/60

Devonshire Arms Hotel and Spa ⊠ BD23 6AJ – ℰ 01756 718105
– www.devonshirebrasserie.co.uk

BORDON

Hampshire – Pop. 16 035 – Regional map n° **6**-C2
▶ London 54 mi – Southampton 42 mi – Portsmouth 29 mi

🏠 Groomes

COUNTRY HOUSE · CONTEMPORARY A part 17C former farmhouse set in 185 acres, which has been made 'green' by the installation of biomass boilers and solar panels. Spacious, modern bedrooms come with roll-top baths; it even has its own games room. Dining takes place at two communal tables – local produce features in dishes cooked on the Aga.

6 rooms ⊉ – †£ 90/150 ††£ 130/160

Frith End ⊠ GU35 0QR – North : 2.75 mi by A 325 on Frith End Sand Pit rd
– ℰ 01420 489858 – www.groomes.co.uk

BOROUGHBRIDGE

North Yorkshire – Pop. 3 610 – Regional map n° **13**-B2
▶ London 215 mi – Leeds 19 mi – York 16 mi

✗✗ thediningroom

MODERN BRITISH · INTIMATE Characterful bow-fronted cottage concealing an opulent bar-lounge and an intimate beamed dining room. Wide-ranging menus offer boldly flavoured, Mediterranean-influenced dishes and chargrilled meats. In summer, head for the terrace.

Menu £ 22 (weekdays) – Carte £ 26/45

20 St James's Sq ⊠ YO51 9AR – ℰ 01423 326426
– www.thediningroomonline.co.uk – dinner only and Sunday lunch
– Closed 26 December, 1 January, Sunday dinner and Monday

🛏 Grantham Arms

TRADITIONAL BRITISH · INN A proper roadside inn where the locals come to watch the latest sporting events. The all-encompassing menu ranges from pie and mash to pan-roasted duck. If gin's your thing, this is the place for you – there are over 30 varieties. Smart bedrooms come with contemporary oak furnishings and Egyptian cotton linen.

Menu £ 16 (lunch and early dinner) – Carte £ 21/30

7 rooms ⊉ – †£ 60/150 ††£ 70/150

Milby ⊠ YO51 9BW – North : 0.25 mi on B 6265 – ℰ 01423 323980
– www.granthamarms.co.uk

at Roecliffe West: 1 mi

🛏 Crown Inn

REGIONAL CUISINE · INN 14C inn in a delightful position by the village green. Menus offer pub classics alongside more ambitious dishes; if you can't decide on a dessert, try them all with the assiette of puddings. Well-appointed bedrooms come with feature beds, roll-top baths and plenty of extra touches.

Carte £ 25/43

4 rooms ⊉ – †£ 80/90 ††£ 100/120

⊠ YO51 9LY – ℰ 01423 322300 – www.crowninnroecliffe.co.uk

BOROUGHBRIDGE

at Lower Dunsforth Southeast : 4.25 mi by B 6265

🍴 The Dunsforth
MODERN BRITISH · PUB You can tailor your experience at this contemporary pub: if you like things lively, sit in its fire-lit front rooms; for a more intimate meal head for the smart restaurant. Menus offer admirable choice and value for money, and seasonality and freshness are key. Most dishes come with a modern twist.
Menu £ 20/45 – Carte £ 24/54
Mary Ln ⊠ YO26 9SA – ℰ 01423 320700 – www.thedunsforth.co.uk – Closed Sunday dinner and Monday-Tuesday

BOSCASTLE
Cornwall – Regional map n° **1**-B2
▶ London 260 mi – Exeter 59 mi – Plymouth 43 mi

🏠 Boscastle House
FAMILY · PERSONALISED Modern styling in a detached Victorian house with a calm, relaxing air. Bedrooms are light and spacious, with roll-top baths and walk-in showers. Hearty breakfasts feature home-baked muffins and banana bread. Tea and cake on arrival.
6 rooms ⊡ – ♦£ 60/90 ♦♦£ 100/140
Tintagel Rd ⊠ PL35 0AS – South : 0.75 mi on B 3263 – ℰ 01840 250654 – www.boscastlehouse.com – Closed 2 weeks Christmas

🏠 Old Rectory
COUNTRY HOUSE · ROMANTIC A lovely house with a Victorian walled garden; Thomas Hardy once stayed here. Bedrooms are characterful: one has a wood stove; another, a whirlpool bath. Breakfast includes bacon and sausages from the owner's pigs. Dinner is by arrangement.
4 rooms ⊡ – ♦£ 63/99 ♦♦£ 75/110
St Juliot ⊠ PL35 0BT – Northeast : 2.5 mi by B 3263 – ℰ 01840 250225 – www.stjuliot.com – Closed Christmas

BOSTON SPA
West Yorkshire – Pop. 4 662 – Regional map n° **13**-B2
▶ London 127 mi – Leeds 12 mi – York 16 mi

🏠 Four Gables
TRADITIONAL · ART DÉCO Grade II listed Arts and Crafts house with a smartly manicured garden and croquet lawn; hidden away down a private road. Cosy bedrooms have good comforts. Breakfast includes homemade breads and jams, as well as eggs from their hens.
4 rooms ⊡ – ♦£ 53/80 ♦♦£ 76/110
Oaks Ln ⊠ LS23 6DS – West : 0.25 mi by A 659 – ℰ 01937 845592 – www.fourgables.co.uk – Closed Christmas-New Year

BOUGHTON MONCHELSEA
Kent – Pop. 2 863 – Regional map n° **5**-B2
▶ London 40 mi – Maidstone 4 mi – Folkestone 36 mi

🍴🍴 Mulberry Tree
MODERN BRITISH · FRIENDLY This rurally located restaurant has lovely gardens, a large paved terrace and a surprisingly stylish interior. Modern British menus feature confidently prepared, imaginatively presented dishes and ingredients are well-sourced.
Menu £ 20 (weekdays) – Carte £ 29/43
Hermitage Ln. ⊠ ME17 4DA – South : 1.5 mi by Park Lane and East Hall Hill – ℰ 01622 749082 – www.themulberrytreekent.co.uk – Closed first 2 weeks January, Sunday dinner and Monday

ENGLAND

BOURN

Cambridgeshire – Pop. 669 – Regional map n° **8**-A3
▶ London 58 mi – Cambridge 10 mi – Peterborough 35 mi

🍴 **Willow Tree**
⁂ 🍴 🛜 **P**

MODERN BRITISH · PUB Quirky pub with a life-sized cow model outside and gilt mirrors, chandeliers and Louis XV style furniture inside. Cooking ranges from pub classics to more ambitious modern dishes; afternoon tea and a 'Deckchair' menu are served May-Sept.

Carte £ 16/42

29 High St ⊠ CB23 2SQ – ℰ 01954 719775 – www.thewillowtreebourn.com

BOURNEMOUTH

Bournemouth – Pop. 187 503 – Regional map n° **2**-D3
▶ London 114 mi – Dorchester 175 mi – Southampton 34 mi

🏨 **Miramar**
⌂ ≤ 🛜 🔁 ⅗ 🎿 **P**

TRADITIONAL · CLASSIC Late Edwardian villa intended as a summer residence for the Austrian ambassador – until WW1 intervened. Close to town yet boasting peaceful, award-winning gardens and superb sea views. Large, classical bedrooms; some with balconies. Traditional dinner menu and snacks in the bar or on the terrace.

43 rooms ⌑ – ♦£ 50/110 ♦♦£ 100/280

Town plan: C2-u - *19 Grove Rd, East Overcliff ⊠ BH1 3AL – ℰ 01202 556581*
– www.miramar-bournemouth.com

🏨 **Green House**
🔁 ⅗ 🎿 🎿 **P**

BUSINESS · DESIGN Bright, eco-friendly hotel set in a small Grade II listed property. Furnishings are reclaimed and wallpapers are printed using vegetable ink. They generate their own electricity and even use old cooking oil to power their car!

32 rooms ⌑ – ♦£ 99/149 ♦♦£ 99/179

Town plan: C2-n - *4 Grove Rd ⊠ BH1 3AX – ℰ 01202 498900*
– www.thegreenhousehotel.com

Arbor – See restaurant listing

🏨 **Chocolate**
🛜 🎿 **P**

TOWNHOUSE · PERSONALISED A unique, chocolate-themed hotel, owned by a chocolatier who runs regular workshops. Contemporary bedrooms come in browns and creams. The small lounge-bar features an automatic cocktail machine – they even serve 'choctails'.

15 rooms ⌑ – ♦£ 60/75 ♦♦£ 90/159

Town plan: A2-a - *5 Durley Rd ⊠ BH2 5JQ – ℰ 01202 556857*
– www.thechocolateboutiquehotel.co.uk

XX **Edge**
≤ 🛜 ⅗ 🆎 ⇄

MODERN BRITISH · DESIGN Stylish restaurant on the top levels of an apartment block, with floor to ceiling windows and excellent views over the town and Poole Bay. Seafood menus feature intricate modern dishes which are styled on classical combinations.

Menu £ 20 (weekday lunch) – Carte £ 28/52

Studland Dene (4th Floor), 2 Studland Rd, Alum Chine ⊠ BH4 8JA – Southwest : 2.25 mi by B 3066 off Alumhurst Rd – ℰ 01202 757007
– www.edgerestaurant.co.uk

XX **Neo** 🆕
🍷 ≤ 🛜 ⅗ 🆎 ⇄

MODERN BRITISH · BRASSERIE Have a cocktail on the ground floor of this unusual round building then head up to the restaurant for views of the gardens and pier. Appetising dishes change with the seasons; the Josper-grilled meats and Dorset lobster are hits.

Menu £ 23 (lunch and early dinner) – Carte £ 25/55

Town plan: B2-c - *Hermitage Hotel, Exeter Rd ⊠ BH2 5AH – ℰ 01202 203610*
– www.neorestaurant.co.uk

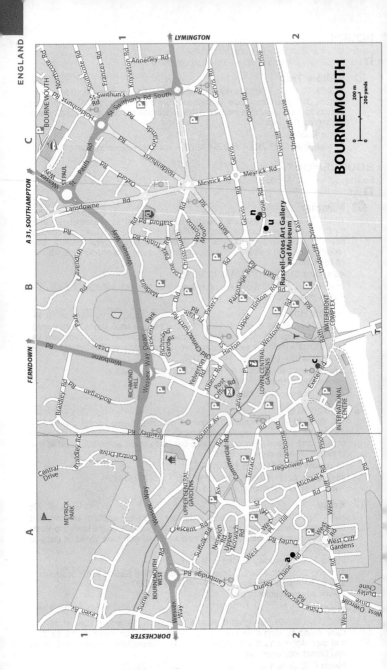

BOURNEMOUTH

Russell-Cotes Art Gallery and Museum

0   200 m
0   200 yards

LYMINGTON
A 31, SOUTHAMPTON
FERNDOWN
DORCHESTER

MEYRICK PARK
WEST CLIFF GARDENS
WATERFRONT COMPLEX
INTERNATIONAL CENTRE
UPPER CENTRAL GARDENS
LOWER CENTRAL GARDENS
WEST OVERCLIFF DRIVE
DURLEY CHINE

ST PAUL
BOURNEMOUTH WEST

Wessex Way
Leven Av.
Surrey Rd
Cambridge Rd
Central Drive
Braidley Rd
Bodorgan Rd
RICHMOND HILL
Richmond Gardens
Dean Park Crescent
Park Rd
Cavendish Rd
Madeira Rd
Lansdowne Rd
Oxford Rd
St Paul's Rd
Holdenhurst Rd
St Swithun's Rd South
Frances Rd
Knyveton Rd
Annerley Rd
Northcote Rd
St Swithun's Rd
Meyrick Rd
Gervis Rd
Grove Rd
Overcliff Drive
Underclff Drive
Bath Rd
Christchurch Rd
Mount
Stafford Rd
Lorne Park Rd
Trinity Rd
Old Christchurch Rd
St Peter's Rd
Parsonage Rd
Upper Hinton Rd
Hinton
Westover Rd
Exeter Rd
Gervis Pl.
Albert Rd
Yelverton Rd
Bourne Av.
Commercial Rd
Terrace
Priory Rd
Cranborne Rd
Tregonwell Rd
St Michael's Rd
West Cliff Rd
Durley Rd
Durley Chine Rd
West Cliff Crescent
West Overcliff Drive
Norwich Av.
Upper Norwich Rd
Suffolk Rd
Crescent Rd
Central Drive

ENGLAND

✗✗ Arbor   ♿ 🅿

MODERN CUISINE · CONTEMPORARY DÉCOR Located in an eco-friendly hotel, Arbor comes complete with a feature tree, FSC timbered floors, low energy induction cookers and honey bees on the roof. Modern menus display innovative touches and produce is local and sustainable.

Menu £20 (lunch) – Carte £23/42

Town plan: C2-n - Green House Hotel, 4 Grove Rd ⊠ BH1 3AX – *ℰ 01202 498900* – *www.arbor-restaurant.co.uk*

at Southbourne East : 3.75 mi. by A 35 on B 3059

⌂ Cliff House   🛌 ♿ 🕸 🅿

TOWNHOUSE · PERSONALISED A smartly refurbished 120 year old house which retains some of its original Victorian features. Comfortable bedrooms feature Smart TVs and coffee machines. The elegant, modern lounge-bar leads onto a landscaped garden and terrace.

14 rooms ☲ – †£45/75 ††£90/150

13 Belle Vue Rd ⊠ BH6 3DA
– ℰ 01202 424701 – www.cliffhouse-hotel.com
– Closed January

BOURTON-ON-THE-HILL – Gloucestershire ➜ See Moreton-in-Marsh

BOURTON-ON-THE-WATER

Gloucestershire – Pop. 3 296 – Regional map n° **2**-D1
▶ London 91 mi – Gloucester 24 mi – Oxford 36 mi

🏠 Coombe House   🛌 🕸 🅿 ⇥

TRADITIONAL · PERSONALISED Spacious 1920s detached house, not far from the delightful village centre. There's a traditional lounge and a first floor terrace for sunnier days; the breakfast room boasts full-length leaded windows and overlooks the attractive garden. Homely, immaculately kept bedrooms offer good comforts.

4 rooms ☲ – †£65/75 ††£80/95

⊠ GL54 2DT – *ℰ 01451 821966 – www.coombehouse.net*

✗✗ Dial House   ⇦ 🛌 🏠 🅿

MODERN FRENCH · COUNTRY HOUSE The oldest property in this charming village dates from the 17C and has lovely lawned gardens and a tranquil feel. The dining room has a black and white theme and serves skilfully prepared modern versions of French classics. Bedrooms are spread about the place and mix the traditional and the contemporary.

Menu £59 – bar lunch

14 rooms ☲ – †£129/229 ††£139/259

The Chestnuts, High St ⊠ GL54 2AN
– ℰ 01451 822244 – www.dialhousehotel.com
– Closed 1 week January, Monday and Tuesday

at Lower Slaughter Northwest: 1.75 mi by A429 ⊠ Cheltenham

🏨 Slaughters Country Inn   ⚡ 🛌 ♿ 🏋 🅿

INN · CONTEMPORARY Originally a crammer school for Eton College, this stone-built manor house is a good choice for families – and they welcome dogs too! It's relaxed and understated, with modern styling; the cosy bedrooms have feature walls and up-to-date facilities. The pub and restaurant serve British classics.

31 rooms ☲ – †£90/240 ††£90/240 – 7 suites

⊠ GL54 2HS – *ℰ 01451 822143*
– www.theslaughtersinn.co.uk

🏠 Slaughters Manor House 🐾 🛁 ✗ ☆ ⛟ P

LUXURY · CLASSIC A beautiful part-17C manor house built from warm Cotswold stone and surrounded by delightful grounds. Elegant bedrooms are split between the house and the stables: the former are individually styled, while the latter are more up-to-date – and two have private hot tubs. Guest areas are modern and stylish.

19 rooms 🖙 – 🛉£ 170/550 🛉🛉£ 170/550

✉ GL54 2HP – ☎ 01451 820456 – www.slaughtersmanor.co.uk

Slaughters Manor House – See restaurant listing

✗✗✗ Slaughters Manor House 🛁 🎐 ㅎ ⅏ ♻ P

MODERN CUISINE · CHIC An elegant dining room in a bright, airy extension of a fine manor house hotel, overlooking its lovely gardens. Immaculately laid tables have beautiful floral displays. Menus offer accomplished modern dishes with a classical base.

Menu £ 65 (dinner) – Carte lunch £ 22/39

Slaughters Manor House Hotel, ✉ GL54 2HP – ☎ 01451 820456
– www.slaughtersmanor.co.uk

at Upper Slaughter Northwest: 2.5 mi by A429✉ Bourton-On-The-Water

🏠 Lords of the Manor 🐾 🛁 ⛟ P

LUXURY · CLASSIC Charming 17C former rectory in a pretty Cotswold village, with beautiful gardens, superb views and a real sense of tranquility. Two luxurious sitting rooms and a bar with a 'nature' colour theme. Bedrooms have a fitting country house style and subtle contemporary touches. Staff are diligent and affable.

24 rooms 🖙 – 🛉£ 185/500 🛉🛉£ 195/510 – 2 suites

✉ GL54 2JD – ☎ 01451 820243 – www.lordsofthemanor.com

❀ **Lords of the Manor** – See restaurant listing

✗✗✗ Lords of the Manor 🛁 🎐 P
❀

MODERN CUISINE · CHIC Plush, formal dining room in a beautiful country house in a tranquil Cotswold village; enjoy an aperitif in the luxurious sitting rooms. Accomplished, understated dishes use well-judged, classical combinations and are executed using modern techniques. Service is professional and very personable.
→ Cornish crab with oyster cream and Oscietra caviar. Pot-roast squab pigeon with confit leg ravioli, foie gras, onion and gem lettuce. Coffee, mascarpone mousse and parfait with Amaretti biscuits and coffee bean ice cream.

Menu £ 73/85

Lords of the Manor Hotel, ✉ GL54 2JD – ☎ 01451 820243 (booking essential)
– www.lordsofthemanor.com – dinner only and lunch Saturday-Sunday

BOWLAND BRIDGE
Cumbria – Regional map n° **12**-A2_3
▶ London 269 mi – Carlisle 83 mi – Manchester 126 mi

🏠 Hare and Hounds   ♻ 🛁 🎐 P

TRADITIONAL BRITISH · PUB Charming, 17C Lakeland pub in a delightful village. Large front terrace leads through into a rustic, open-fired inner hung with old village photos and hop bines. Menus offer typical, hearty favourites and most produce is locally sourced. Bedrooms are well-equipped and elegant; some boast roll-top baths.

Carte £ 21/33

5 rooms 🖙 – 🛉£ 72/135 🛉🛉£ 95/145

✉ LA11 6NN – ☎ 015395 68333 – www.hareandhoundsbowlandbridge.co.uk
– Closed 25 December

BOWNESS-ON-WINDERMERE – Cumbria → See Windermere

BOYLESTONE
Derbyshire – Regional map n° **9**-A2
▶ London 142 mi – Derby 18 mi – Stoke on Trent 24 mi

✕✕ Lighthouse   🚫 🅿

MODERN BRITISH · DESIGN It may not be near the coast, but the Lighthouse does attract your attention. The self-taught chef prepares ambitious, complex dishes with good combinations of flavours and textures; the tasting menu, in particular, is a hit.

Carte £ 37/44

New Rd ⊠ DE6 5AA – behind Rose & Crown public house – ℰ 01335 330658
– www.the-lighthouse-restaurant.co.uk – dinner only – Closed Sunday-Tuesday

BRADFORD-ON-AVON
Wiltshire – Pop. 9 149 – Regional map n° **2**-C2
▶ London 118 mi – Bristol 24 mi – Salisbury 35 mi

🏠 Woolley Grange   ✿ 🐾 ≼ 🏡 🏠 ⌸ 🐷 🏊 ♨ ⛳ 🅿

COUNTRY HOUSE · CLASSIC Fine Jacobean manor house that's geared towards families, with a crèche, a kids' club, a games room and outdoor activities. For adults, there's a chic spa and some lovely country views. Smart bedrooms come in many styles. Accomplished, classical cooking is served in the restaurant and more relaxed orangery.

25 rooms ⌂ – ♦£ 95/265 ♦♦£ 120/290 – 6 suites

Woolley Green ⊠ BA15 1TX – Northeast : 0.75 mi by B 3107 on Woolley St
– ℰ 01225 864705 – www.woolleygrangehotel.co.uk

🏠 Timbrell's Yard 🆕   ✿

INN · CONTEMPORARY This Grade II listed riverside inn was once part of the old dye works. Bedrooms come in muted tones and feature reclaimed furnishings, quirky contemporary art and vintage touches; ask for a duplex room with river and church views. Enjoy appealing modern day classics in the rustic bar or restaurant.

17 rooms ⌂ – ♦£ 95/145 ♦♦£ 95/145

49 St Margaret's St ⊠ BA15 1DE – ℰ 01225 869492 – www.timbrellsyard.com

✕✕✕ Three Gables   🏠 🏠 ⇄

MODERN CUISINE · ELEGANT Personally and passionately run restaurant in a 350 year old house, with a lovely terrace and charming exposed stone and wattle and daub walls. Skilful, accomplished cooking; interesting, original dishes are based on classical combinations.

Menu £ 18/25 – Carte £ 34/51

St Margaret's St ⊠ BA15 1DA – ℰ 01225 781666 – www.thethreegables.com
– Closed 1-15 August, 1-11 January, 25-26 December, Sunday dinner, Monday and Tuesday

✕ Weaving Shed 🆕   🏠 🚫 🅰🅺

MODERN CUISINE · BRASSERIE Cast iron pillars and exposed lightbulbs give a nod to this old mill's weaving days. Well-spaced tables look out over a riverside terrace and you are encouraged to talk to the chefs in the open kitchen. Dishes are modern and appealing.

Carte £ 25/35

3 Bridge Yard, Kingston Mills ⊠ BA15 1EJ – ℰ 01225 866519
– www.weaving-shed.co.uk – Closed 25-26 December and Sunday dinner in winter

🍴 Bunch of Grapes 🆕   🍷 🍴

FRENCH · PUB A collaboration between 5 friends who love the food and wine of South West France. Rustic cooking focuses on the wood-fired Bertha oven and wines are imported directly from France. The place has an appealingly bijou, brocante feel.

Menu £ 16/22 – Carte £ 24/42

14 Silver St ⊠ BA15 1JY – ℰ 01225 938088 – www.thebunchofgrapes.com – Closed 25-26 December

ENGLAND

BRADWELL
Derbyshire – Pop. 1 416 – Regional map n° **9**-A1
▶ London 170 mi – Derby 43 mi – Liverpool 66 mi

⬧ Samuel Fox Country Inn ⬅ 🏠 **P**
MODERN BRITISH · PUB An attractive, light-stone pub with smart, cosy bedrooms and a dramatic, hilly backdrop: named after the inventor of the steel-ribbed umbrella, who was born in the village. Flavourful classic dishes have modern touches and make good use of seasonal local produce. Popular 7 course tasting menu.
Menu £ 20/49 – Carte £ 25/39
4 rooms ⌖ – ♦£ 75/95 ♦♦£ 100/130
Stretfield Rd ⊠ S33 9JT – ℰ 01433 621562 – www.samuelfox.co.uk – Closed 2-25 January, Sunday dinner, Monday, Tuesday and lunch Wednesday-Thursday

BRAITHWAITE – Cumbria → See Keswick

BRAMPFORD SPEKE – Devon → See Exeter

BRAMPTON
Cumbria – Pop. 4 229 – Regional map n° **12**-B1
▶ London 317 mi – Carlisle 9 mi – Newcastle upon Tyne 49 mi

🏠 Farlam Hall ✧ 🐾 ⬅ 🏠 **P**
TRADITIONAL · PERSONALISED A well-run, family-owned country house, whose origins can be traced back to the 1600s. Bedrooms are furnished with antiques but also have modern touches like Bose radios. The sumptuous dining room has a traditional daily menu and romantic views across a lake, while afternoon tea is served in the curio-filled lounges, overlooking the immaculate ornamental gardens.
12 rooms (dinner included) ⌖ – ♦£ 118/148 ♦♦£ 216/275
⊠ CA8 2NG – Southeast : 2.75 mi on A 689 – ℰ 016977 46234
– www.farlamhall.co.uk – Closed 8-27 January and 25-30 December

BRANCASTER STAITHE
Norfolk – Regional map n° **8**-C1
▶ London 131 mi – King's Lynn 25 mi – Norwich 40 mi

⬧ White Horse ⬅ ⬅ 🏠 **P**
CLASSIC CUISINE · PUB The rear views over the marshes and Scolt Head Island really make this pub. Choose from old favourites, tapas-style dishes and a few more ambitious offerings on the bar menu; or seasonally changing dishes supplemented by daily specials on the à la carte. Smart, New England style bedrooms – some with terraces.
Carte £ 26/38
15 rooms ⌖ – ♦£ 85/105 ♦♦£ 100/180
⊠ PE31 8BY – ℰ 01485 210262 (booking essential)
– www.whitehorsebrancaster.co.uk

BRAUGHING
Hertfordshire – Pop. 854 – Regional map n° **7**-B2
▶ London 33 mi – Hertford 12 mi – Stevenage 18 mi

⬧ Golden Fleece 🏠 🏠 **P**
TRADITIONAL BRITISH · INN Proudly run, part-16C pub with a spacious garden, a pretty terrace overlooking the village and striking period features including a vast inglenook fireplace. Comforting, country-style dishes include gluten and dairy free options.
Carte £ 22/38
20 Green End ⊠ SG11 2PG – ℰ 01920 823555 – www.goldenfleecebraughing.co.uk – Closed 25-26 December and Sunday dinner

BRAY

Windsor and Maidenhead – Pop. 8 121 – Regional map n° **6**-C3
▶ London 30 mi – Oxford 36 mi – Bristol 93 mi

XXXX **Waterside Inn** (Alain Roux)   ⊛ ⇦ ← AC IO ⇔ P

✿✿✿ CLASSIC FRENCH · ELEGANT An illustrious restaurant in a glorious spot on a
bank of the Thames, with a relaxed, elegant dining room and a delightful terrace
ideal for aperitifs. Service is charming and expertly structured. Carefully considered French menus reflect the seasons and use top quality luxury ingredients in
perfectly judged, sophisticated combinations. Bedrooms are chic and sumptuous.
→ Tronçonnettes de homard poêlées minute au Porto blanc. Filets de lapereau
grillés sur un fondant de céleri-rave, sauce à l'armagnac et aux marrons glacés.
Soufflé chaud aux mirabelles.

Menu £ 62 (weekday lunch)/160 – Carte £ 121/167
11 rooms ⌂ – †£ 245/550 ††£ 245/550 – 2 suites
Town plan: B1-s - Ferry Rd ⊠ SL6 2AT – ☎ 01628 620691 (booking essential)
– www.waterside-inn.co.uk – Closed 26 December-1 February and
Monday-Tuesday

XXX **Fat Duck** Ⓝ (Heston Blumenthal)   ⊛ AC P

✿✿✿ CREATIVE · MINIMALIST Heston Blumenthal takes you on a theatrical, multi-sen-
sory journey informed by a narrative which evokes memories of childhood. Cooking is inventive, playful and perfectly judged, and no matter how elaborate the
presentation, it is never at the expense of flavour. The experience is made all
the more enjoyable by the delightful staff.
→ Hot and cold tea. Duck à l'orange. Botrytis cinerea.

Menu £ 255 – tasting menu only
Town plan: B1-d - High St ⊠ SL6 2AQ – ☎ 01628 580333 (booking essential)
– www.thefatduck.co.uk – Closed 21 December-14 January, Sunday and Monday

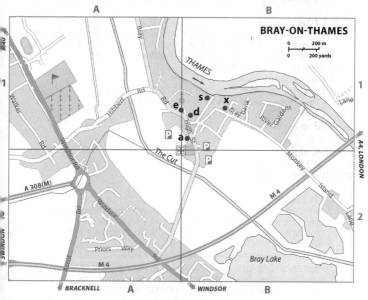

XX Caldesi in Campagna

ITALIAN · INTIMATE Sister of Café Caldesi in London, is this chic, sophisticated restaurant with a cosy conservatory and a lovely covered terrace – complete with a wood-fired oven. Flavoursome Italian dishes feature Tuscan and Sicilian specialities.

Menu £ 20 (lunch) – Carte £ 43/57

Town plan: B1-x - *Old Mill Ln* ⊠ *SL6 2BG* – ℰ *01628 788500* – *www.caldesi.com*
– *Closed Sunday dinner and Monday*

🛏 Hinds Head

❀ **TRADITIONAL BRITISH · TRADITIONAL DÉCOR** Listed 15C pub at the heart of a pretty village; its dark wood panelling and log fires giving it a characterful Georgian feel. Prime seasonal produce is used to create rich, satisfying dishes that are down-to-earth, fiercely British, carefully presented and big on flavour. Service is informed and engaging.

→ Venison carpaccio with horseradish, turnip, shallots and a caper dressing. Fillet of cod with wilted chard, onion, borage and mussel broth. Quaking pudding.

Menu £ 48 – Carte £ 34/51

Town plan: B1-e - *High St* ⊠ *SL6 2AB* – ℰ *01628 626151 (booking essential)*
– *www.hindsheadbray.com* – *Closed 25 December and Sunday dinner*

🛏 Royal Oak

❀ **TRADITIONAL BRITISH · DESIGN** A warm, welcoming beamed dining pub with a smart extension and an elegantly manicured herb garden. The appealing menu champions seasonal British produce. Cooking is skilled, confident and sensibly avoids over-elaboration; fish and game are handled deftly. Formal service provides a sense of occasion.

→ Smoked herring ravioli with leeks, chilli jam and curry sauce. Stone bass with chorizo, mussels and samphire. Caramel 'Snickers' with chocolate cremeux and peanut ice cream.

Menu £ 30 (lunch) – Carte £ 29/46

Paley Street ⊠ *SL6 3JN* – *Southwest : 3.5 mi by A 308 and A 330 on B 3024*
– ℰ *01628 620541* – *www.theroyaloakpaleystreet.com* – *Closed Sunday dinner*

🛏 Crown

TRADITIONAL BRITISH · PUB Charmingly restored 16C building; formerly two cottages and a bike shop! Drinkers mingle with diners, and dark columns, low beams and roaring fires create a cosy atmosphere. Carefully prepared British dishes are robust and flavoursome.

Carte £ 28/46

Town plan: B1-a - *High St* ⊠ *SL6 2AH* – ℰ *01628 621936*
– *www.thecrownatbray.com* – *Closed 25 December*

BRAYE → See Channel Islands (Alderney)

BRIDPORT

Dorset – Pop. 13 737 – Regional map n° **2**-B3
▶ London 150 mi – Exeter 38 mi – Taunton 33 mi

X Riverside

SEAFOOD · BISTRO Since 1964, this restaurant has offered unfussy seafood dishes crafted from local produce – much of it landed just 100m away. It sits beside the river on its own little island and is accessed via a bridge. Go for the daily specials.

Menu £ 26 (weekday lunch)/28 – Carte £ 26/56

West Bay ⊠ *DT6 4EZ* – *South : 1.75 mi by B 3157* – ℰ *01308 422011 (booking essential)* – *www.thefishrestaurant-westbay.co.uk* – *Closed December-mid February, Sunday dinner in winter and Monday except bank holidays*

at Burton Bradstock Southeast: 2 mi by B3157

XX **Seaside Boarding House** Ⓝ   ⇦ ⌂ ₺ **P**

TRADITIONAL BRITISH · CONTEMPORARY DÉCOR Stunningly located on the clifftop, this old hotel has been given a fresh new look. The bright, airy restaurant has a subtle maritime theme and a lovely terrace with sea views. Menus offer everything from a croque monsieur to lemon sole with samphire. Classically understated bedrooms come with claw-foot baths.

Menu £ 17 (weekday lunch) – Carte £ 25/42

7 rooms – ♦£ 160/215 ♦♦£ 180/235

Cliff Rd ✉ DT6 4RB – Southeast : 0.5 mi – ✆ 01308 897205
– www.theseasideboardinghouse.com

GOOD TIPS!

The jewel of the south coast is a city that knows how to have a good time, with plenty of cool, quirky hotels and restaurants. Enjoy vistas out over the Channel from your bedroom at **Drakes** or **A Room with a View**. **Terre à Terre** is a vegetarian's dream; pescatarians should book a table at **Little Fish Market**, while carnivores can head for **Coal Shed**.

BRIGHTON AND HOVE

Brighton and Hove – Pop. 229 700 – Regional map n° **5**-A3
▶ London 53 mi – Portsmouth 48 mi – Southampton 61 mi

Hotels

🏨 Hotel du Vin

BUSINESS · PERSONALISED Made up of various different buildings; the oldest being a former wine merchant's. Kick-back in the cavernous, gothic-style bar-lounge or out on the terrace. Bedrooms are richly decorated and have superb monsoon showers. The relaxed brasserie, with its hidden courtyard, serves French bistro classics.

49 rooms ⌴ – †£ 105/550 ††£ 105/550
Town plan: B2-a - *2-6 Ship St* ⊠ *BN1 1AD* – ℰ *01273 718588*
– *www.hotelduvin.com*

🏨 Drakes

TOWNHOUSE · DESIGN A pair of 18C townhouses on the promenade, with a smart cocktail bar. Chic, well-equipped bedrooms have wooden feature walls and sea or city views – one even has a bath in the bay window! Minimum 2 night stay at weekends.

20 rooms – †£ 120/160 ††£ 120/360 – ⌴ £ 15
Town plan: C2-u - *43-44 Marine Par* ⊠ *BN2 1PE* – ℰ *01273 696934*
– *www.drakesofbrighton.com*
The Restaurant at Drakes – See restaurant listing

🏨 A Room with a View

TOWNHOUSE · PERSONALISED Snuggle into a Hungarian goose down duvet and, if your room is at the front of this Regency townhouse, enjoy the views out over the Channel. All have Nespresso machines and a soft drink mini-bar; Room 10 has a roof terrace.

10 rooms ⌴ – †£ 59/95 ††£ 79/295
Town plan: C2-u - *41 Marine Par.* ⊠ *BN2 1PE*
– ℰ *01273 682885*
– *www.aroomwithaviewbrighton.com*

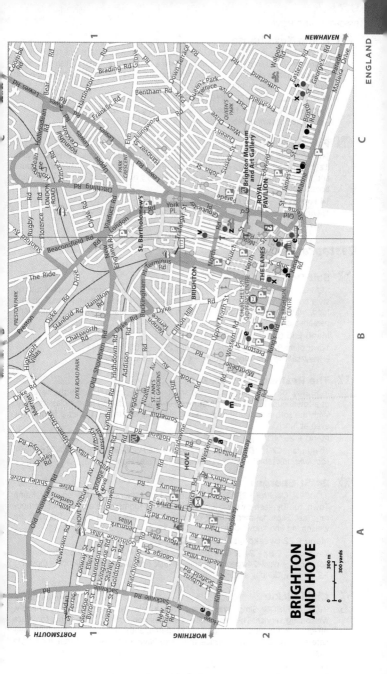

**BRIGHTON
AND HOVE**

NEWHAVEN

PORTSMOUTH

WORTHING

0   300 m
0   300 yards

303

🏠 Kemp Townhouse

TOWNHOUSE · MODERN A boutique townhouse with a basement breakfast room turned bar-lounge which opens onto a courtyard terrace. Stylish bedrooms have compact wet rooms; those at the front are larger and more comfortable and two have four-poster beds.

11 rooms ⌂ – ♦£ 75/115 ♦♦£ 135/205

Town plan: C2-n - *21 Atlingworth St* ⊠ *BN2 1PL* – *℘ 01273 681400*
– www.kemptownhousebrighton.com – Closed 24-26 December

🏠 Fab Guest

TOWNHOUSE · DESIGN Don't be fooled by the classic Georgian exterior; inside it's stylish and modern, with minimalist bedrooms displaying a mix of antiques and bespoke furnishings by local artists. There's no reception and no keys – just access codes.

14 rooms ⌂ – ♦£ 59/150 ♦♦£ 89/255

Town plan: C2-z - *9 Charlotte St* ⊠ *BN2 1AG* – *℘ 01273 625505*
– www.fabguest.co.uk – Closed Christmas

Restaurants

✗✗ Salt Room

SEAFOOD · FASHIONABLE This city hotspot has a lovely 'rustic-meets-industrial' style and has views from many of its tables and the terrace. Menus focus on seafood, with some fish cooked whole on the Josper grill. Service is attentive and personable.

Menu £ 15 (lunch) – Carte £ 24/42

Town plan: B2-s - *106 Kings Rd* ⊠ *BN1 2FY* – *℘ 01273 929488*
– www.saltroom-restaurant.co.uk – Closed 25-26 December

✗✗ The Restaurant at Drakes

MODERN BRITISH · INTIMATE Two small, intimate dining rooms in the basement of a townhouse hotel. Menus feature luxury ingredients and have a classical bent. With the soft, moody atmosphere and elegantly laid tables, there's a formal feel, even at lunch.

Menu £ 25/40

Town plan: C2-u - *Drakes Hotel, 43-44 Marine Par* ⊠ *BN2 1PE* – *℘ 01273 696934*
(booking advisable) – www.therestaurantatdrakes.co.uk

✗✗ 24 St Georges

MODERN CUISINE · BRASSERIE Shabby-chic restaurant on the edge of Kemp Town, run by keen owners; its three adjoining rooms have a stylish, contemporary feel. Seasonal menus offer complex, technically skilled dishes. The staff are welcoming and knowledgeable.

Menu £ 22 (weekdays) – Carte £ 28/43

Town plan: C2-x - *24 St George's Rd* ⊠ *BN2 1ED* – *℘ 01273 626060 (booking advisable) – www.24stgeorges.co.uk – dinner only and Saturday lunch – Closed 1-9 January, Sunday and Monday*

✗ Chilli Pickle

INDIAN · BISTRO Simple restaurant with a relaxed, buzzy vibe and friendly, welcoming service. The passionate chef uses good quality ingredients to create oft-changing menus of thoughtfully prepared, authentic Indian dishes with delicate spicing. Beside the terrace they also have a cart selling street food style snacks.

Menu £ 14/30 – Carte £ 21/34

Town plan: C2-z - *17 Jubilee St* ⊠ *BN1 1GE* – *℘ 01273 900383*
– www.thechillipickle.com – Closed 25-26 December

✗ Terre à Terre

VEGETARIAN · NEIGHBOURHOOD Relaxed, friendly restaurant decorated in warm burgundy colours. Appealing menu of generous, tasty, original vegetarian dishes which include items from Japan, China and South America. Mini épicerie sells wine, pasta and chutney.

Menu £ 35 – Carte £ 29/41

Town plan: C2-e - *71 East St* ⊠ *BN1 1HQ* – ☏ *01273 729051 (booking essential)* – *www.terreaterre.co.uk* – *Closed 25-26 December*

✗ Coal Shed

MEATS AND GRILLS · NEIGHBOURHOOD A keenly run, rustic steakhouse hidden away in the Brighton Lanes district. Cooking centres around the charcoal oven; they specialise in 35-day matured organic steaks but there's also a tasty selection of fresh fish dishes to try.

Menu £ 18 (weekdays) – Carte £ 25/50

Town plan: B2-x - *8 Boyces St* ⊠ *BN1 1AN* – ☏ *01273 322998* – *www.coalshed-restaurant.co.uk* – *Closed 25-26 December*

✗ 64°
🅐

MODERN BRITISH · SIMPLE If you like things fun and fuss-free, then this intimate modern restaurant is the place for you! Menus are divided into four – 'Meat', 'Fish', 'Veg' and 'Dessert' – and each section also has four choices. Cooking is simple but well-textured and flavoursome; most of the dining takes place at the counter.

Carte £ 23/32

Town plan: B2-c - *53 Meeting House Ln.* ⊠ *BN1 1HB* – ☏ *01273 770115 (booking essential)* – *www.64degrees.co.uk* – *Closed 25-26 December*

✗ Little Fish Market

SEAFOOD · SIMPLE Fish is the focus at this simple restaurant, set in a converted fishmonger's opposite the former Victorian fish market. The owner cooks alone in the kitchen and his set 4 course menu offers refined, interesting modern sea-food dishes.

Menu £ 50

Town plan: B2-m - *10 Upper Market St, Hove* ⊠ *BN3 1AS* – ☏ *01273 722213 (booking essential)* – *www.thelittlefishmarket.co.uk* – *dinner only and Saturday lunch* – *Closed 1 week April, 1 week August, 1 week September, 1 week December, Sunday and Monday*

✗ Gingerman

MODERN CUISINE · NEIGHBOURHOOD There's a smart Scandic feel to the deco-ration and an intimacy to the atmosphere at this long-standing neighbourhood restaurant. Lunch is fairly classical while the à la carte features more elaborate, innovative combinations.

Menu £ 20/37

Town plan: B2-a - *21a Norfolk Sq* ⊠ *BN1 2PD* – ☏ *01273 326688 (booking essential)* – *www.gingermanrestaurants.com* – *Closed 2 weeks winter, 25 December and Monday*

✗ The Set 🆕

MODERN BRITISH · RUSTIC Two communal tables make up the café, while the counter and tables behind form the restaurant. Exposed wood, brick and iron set the scene. Modern tasting plates reflect the seasons; the three restaurant me-nus comprise 4 set courses.

Menu £ 29/35 – Carte £ 16/20

Town plan: B2-e - *Artist Residence Hotel, 33 Regency Sq* ⊠ *BN1 2GG* – ☏ *01273 855572 (booking essential)* – *www.thesetrestaurant.com* – *Closed Sunday dinner and Monday*

✗ Market ⓝ 🄰 🍴 ♿

MODERN CUISINE · TAPAS BAR Bright green glazed tiles, a large counter and cheery hands-on service from the owners give this intimate space a vibrant feel. Cooking is equally colourful with punchy flavours; choose 4-5 small plates or one of the daily specials.

Carte £ 23/38

Town plan: A2-a - *42 Western Rd, Hove* ⊠ *BN3 1JD* – 🞉 *01273 823707 (booking advisable)* – *www.market-restaurantbar.co.uk*

✗ Silo ⓝ 🄰 ♿

MODERN CUISINE · RUSTIC The UK's first zero-waste restaurant: furnishings are made from reclaimed materials, plates are recycled from carrier bags, drinks are served in jam jars and food waste is composted and distributed back to suppliers. Choose a set menu – Plant, Dairy, Meat or Fish – or mix and match dishes as you please.

Menu £ 21/36 – Carte £ 26/36

Town plan: C2-v - *39 Upper Gardner St* ⊠ *BN1 4AN* – 🞉 *01273 674259 (booking essential at dinner)* – *www.silobrighton.com* – *lunch only and dinner Thursday-Saturday*

🅑 Ginger Dog 🍸 ♿

MODERN BRITISH · PUB A charming Victorian pub with a pleasingly shabby-chic feel. Ornately carved woodwork sits comfortably alongside more recent additions like bowler hat lampshades. Cooking has a modern British style and uses the latest techniques.

Menu £ 13 (weekdays) – Carte £ 26/40

Town plan: C2-s - *12 College Pl* ⊠ *BN2 1HN* – 🞉 *01273 620990*
– *www.gingermanrestaurants.com* – *Closed 25 December*

🅑 Ginger Pig 🍸 🛏

TRADITIONAL BRITISH · PUB Smart building by the seafront – formerly a hotel – boasting a mortar ship relief and a beautifully restored revolving door. Menus offer precise, flavoursome British dishes and vegetarians are well-catered for. Good value set lunch menu.

Menu £ 18 (weekdays) – Carte £ 23/44

Town plan: A2-e - *3 Hove St, Hove* ⊠ *BN3 2TR* – 🞉 *01273 736123*
– *www.gingermanrestaurants.com* – *Closed 25 December*

BRILL

Buckinghamshire – Pop. 1 141 – Regional map n° **11**-C2
▶ London 57 mi – Oxford 16 mi – Aylesbury 14 mi

🅑 Pointer ⓝ 🍴 🛏

TRADITIONAL BRITISH · INN Sit in one of two beamed dining rooms or beside the fire in one of the smaller rooms and take time to read the menu, which explains what they are currently growing in the gardens and using in the cooking. Rare breed meats come from their 240 acre farm; take something home from the adjoining butcher's shop.

Menu £ 18 (lunch) – Carte £ 26/59

27 Church St ⊠ *HP18 9RT* – . – 🞉 *01844 238339* – *www.thepointerbrill.co.uk*
– *Closed first week January and Monday*

BRISTOL

City of Bristol – Pop. 535 907 – Regional map n° **2**-C2
▶ London 121 mi – Birmingham 91 mi – Cardiff 43 mi

Hotels

🏨 Hotel du Vin
✿ ⬆ AC Ꮱ

BUSINESS · DESIGN Characterful 18C former sugar refinery with classical Hotel du Vin styling and a wine-theme running throughout. Dark-hued bedrooms and duplex suites boast Egyptian cotton linen – one room has twin roll-top baths. Cosy lounge-bar; French brasserie with a pleasant courtyard terrace for bistro classics.

40 rooms ☲ – †£ 119/205 ††£ 129/215
Town plan: C1-e - *The Sugar House* ✉ BS1 2NU – ☎ 0844 736 4252
– www.hotelduvin.com

🏨 Berwick Lodge
✿ 🛏 ⬆ ⌖ Ꮱ P

COUNTRY HOUSE · PERSONALISED A popular wedding and events venue, run by gregarious, hands-on owners. It's surrounded by 18 acres of grounds and offers views over Avonmouth and the Severn Bridge. Inside, original features combine with Eastern furnishings and mosaic tiles. The intimate restaurant has fine chandeliers and a modern menu.

14 rooms ☲ – †£ 99 ††£ 125/170
Berwick Dr ✉ BS10 7TD – Northwest : 5 mi by A 4018 – ☎ 0117 958 1590
– www.berwicklodge.co.uk

🏨 Number 38 Clifton
⬅ 🛏 ⌖

TOWNHOUSE · PERSONALISED Built in 1820, this substantial townhouse overlooks both the city and the Clifton Downs. Boutique bedrooms have coloured wood-panelled walls, Roberts radios and smart bathrooms with underfloor heating; the most luxurious are the loft suites, complete with copper baths. The rear terrace makes a great suntrap.

9 rooms ☲ – †£ 115/200 ††£ 115/235
Town plan: A1-a - *38 Upper Belgrave Rd ✉ BS8 2XN – ☎ 0117 946 6905*
– www.number38clifton.com

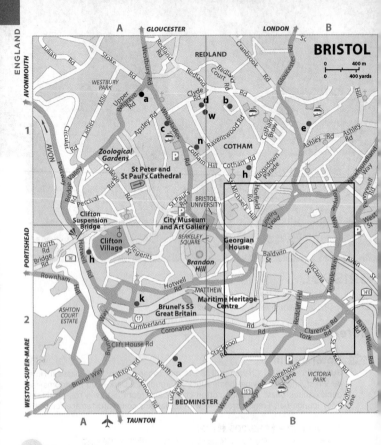

Restaurants

XXX Second Floor at Harvey Nichols

MODERN CUISINE · DESIGN A spacious and elegant light-filled restaurant with stylish gold décor. Good value lunch menu and concise à la carte offering original, modern dishes. Chic lounge bar for cocktails and light bites. Attentive service.

Menu £ 20 – Carte £ 31/41

Town plan: D1-a - *27 Philadelphia St, Quakers Friars, Cabot Circus* ⊠ *BS1 3BZ* – ℰ *0117 916 8898 – www.harveynichols.com – Closed 25 December, 1 January, Easter Sunday, Sunday and Monday dinner*

XX Casamia Ⓝ (Peter Sanchez-Iglesias)

CREATIVE · DESIGN Casamia sits in an impressive listed Victorian hospital over-looking Bathurst Basin; enter through the double glass doors, under an arch and past a table of produce, into a pared down, Scandic-style room. The passionate chefs personally deliver very skilfully prepared, highly creative, seasonal dishes.
→ Mackerel risotto. Lamb with Jersey Royals and nasturtium. Variations of rhubarb.

Menu £ 38/88 – tasting menu only

Town plan: C2-e - *The General, Lower Guinea St* ⊠ *BS1 6SY* – ℰ *0117 959 2884 (booking essential) – www.casamiarestaurant.co.uk – Closed 24 December-7 January, 3-6 May, 30 August-2 September, 25-29 October and Sunday-Tuesday*

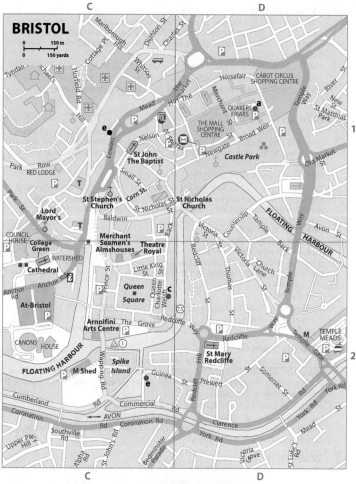

BRISTOL

XX **wilks** (James Wilkins)

MODERN BRITISH · FRIENDLY An appealing neighbourhood restaurant with a relaxed atmosphere and a simple, understated style. Well-balanced dishes display a lightness of touch and a real understanding of flavours – they are also refreshingly lacking in over-adornment. The meringue-based desserts have become something of a speciality.

→ Scottish langoustine tails with lemon purée and shellfish vinaigrette. Wild turbot with pancetta, asparagus, morels and Jersey Royal cream. Citrus meringue sphere with lemon curd, orange jelly and fresh yuzu sorbet.

Menu £ 25 (weekday lunch) – Carte £ 42/57

Town plan: A1-d - 1 Chandos Rd ⊠ BS6 6PG – ℰ 0117 973 7999 (booking essential) – www.wilksrestaurant.co.uk – Closed
23 December-14 January, 31 July-22 August, Monday, Tuesday and lunch Wednesday

✗✗ Spiny Lobster AC

SEAFOOD · BRASSERIE The Spiny Lobster brings a taste of the sea to the city. Enter through the fishmonger's to view the daily catch on a marble slab on your way to the leather-furnished dining room. Simply prepared dishes are cooked in the Josper oven.

Menu £ 18 (lunch and early dinner) – Carte £ 25/54

Town plan: A1-c - *128 Whiteladies Rd* ⊠ *BS8 2RS* – ℰ *0117 973 7384*
– www.thespinylobster.co.uk – Closed 25 December-4 January, Sunday and Monday

✗ Bulrush ⓝ I⊘ ⇔

BRITISH MODERN · BISTRO On looks alone, you might pass it by, but its simplicity is also part of its charm. A whitewashed wall divides the room in two and service is warm and engaging. Modern British dishes are boldly flavoured with the odd Asian touch.

Menu £ 15 (weekday lunch)/45 – Carte £ 27/35

Town plan: B1-h - *21 Cotham Rd South* ⊠ *BS6 5TZ* – ℰ *0117 329 0990 (booking essential) – www.bulrushrestaurant.co.uk – Closed 2 weeks January, 1 week April, 2 weeks August, Sunday, Monday and lunch Tuesday-Wednesday*

✗ No Man's Grace 🛋 AC 🍴

🤩 **MODERN BRITISH · NEIGHBOURHOOD** Simple neighbourhood restaurant run by an experienced young chef. Boldly flavoured small plates feature just 3 or 4 ingredients and have a classic heart and a modern touch. For something sweeter, pay a visit to the dessert bar, where every dish is matched with a dessert wine and a cocktail.

Carte £ 25/30

Town plan: AB1-w - *6 Chandos Rd* ⊠ *BS6 6PE* – ℰ *0117 974 4077*
– www.nomansgrace.com – dinner only and lunch Friday-Sunday – Closed 2 weeks August, 1st week January, Sunday dinner, Monday and Tuesday

✗ Adelina Yard ⓝ 🛋 ⅙ AC

MODERN CUISINE · INTIMATE The experienced chef-owners named their first restaurant after their old home. Well-presented, well-balanced modern dishes are brought to the tables by the chefs. Sit at the far end of the simple L-shaped room, overlooking the quay.

Menu £ 15 (weekdays) – Carte £ 32/47

Town plan: C2-c - *3 Queen Quay, Welsh Back* ⊠ *BS1 4SL* – ℰ *0117 911 2112 (booking advisable) – www.adelinayard.com – Closed 24 December-6 January, Sunday, Monday and bank holidays*

✗ Wallfish Bistro

CLASSIC CUISINE · BISTRO This friendly bistro is named after the West Country word for 'snail' and, satisfyingly, you'll find Herefordshire Wallfish on the menu. Careful, classical cooking focuses on good ingredients; fish from the day boats is popular.

Menu £ 14 (weekdays) – Carte £ 26/56

Town plan: A2-h - *112 Princess Victoria St, Clifton Village* ⊠ *BS8 4DB*
– ℰ 0117 973 5435 (booking advisable) – www.wallfishbistro.co.uk – Closed 23 December-12 January, Monday and Tuesday

✗ Bell's Diner & Bar Rooms 🍴

MEDITERRANEAN CUISINE · BISTRO A bustling city institution with a bohemian feel, which retains evidence of its old grocer's shop days. Flavoursome Mediterranean cooking shows a good understanding of ingredients; try the charcoal-grilled chicken oyster pinchos.

Carte £ 23/34

Town plan: B1-e - *1-3 York Rd, Montpelier* ⊠ *BS6 5QB* – ℰ *0117 924 0357 (bookings advisable at dinner) – www.bellsdiner.com – Closed 24-27 December, 1 January, Sunday and lunch Monday*

✗ Birch

TRADITIONAL BRITISH · SIMPLE Simple neighbourhood restaurant on a long, terraced street. Chef Sam's time at St John shows in his concise menu of rustic British dishes, which use lesser-known produce and are packed with flavour. Service is charming and attentive.

Carte £ 21/31

Town plan: A2-a - 47 Raleigh Rd ⊠ BS3 1QS – ✆ 0117 902 8326 (booking essential) – www.birchbristol.co – dinner only – Closed August, 2 weeks Christmas-New Year and Sunday-Tuesday

✗ Bellita

MEDITERRANEAN · TAPAS BAR Bellita will put a smile on your face with its bright décor and unpretentious atmosphere. The menu is all about sharing, with vibrant small plates inspired by the Med, the Middle East and North Africa. Try the 8 year old Galician beef.

Carte £ 14/29

Town plan: A1-n 34 Cotham Hill ⊠ BS6 6LA – ✆ 0117 923 8755 – www.bellita.co.uk – dinner only and lunch Thursday-Saturday – Closed 24-26 December and Sunday

🍴 Pump House

MODERN CUISINE · PUB A cavernous former pumping station for the adjacent docks; now a rustic pub with a smart mezzanine restaurant. Modern classics change with seasons; Thurs-Sat there's also a more refined tasting menu. Watch the boats from the terrace.

Carte £ 22/44

Town plan: A2-k - Merchants Rd ⊠ BS8 4PZ – ✆ 0117 927 2229 – www.the-pumphouse.com – Closed 25 December

🍴 Kensington Arms

TRADITIONAL BRITISH · PUB It might be painted 'stealth' grey but this smart Victorian-style pub stands out a mile for its warm neighbourhood atmosphere and great food. Daily menus have a strong British base and tick both the local and seasonal boxes.

Carte £ 20/39

Town plan: B1-b - ⊠ BS6 6NP – ✆ 0117 944 6444 – www.thekensingtonarms.co.uk – Closed 25-26 December

at Long Ashton Southwest: 2.5 mi by A370 off B3128

🍴 Bird in Hand

TRADITIONAL BRITISH · COSY Tiny country pub with three small but smartly decorated rooms. Quirky touches include an antelope's head and a wall covered in pages from Mrs Beeton's Book of Household Management. Menus offer tasty, carefully cooked British dishes which let local and foraged ingredients speak for themselves.

Carte £ 25/31

17 Weston Rd ⊠ BS41 9LA – ✆ 01275 395222 (booking essential at dinner) – www.bird-in-hand.co.uk

BROADSTAIRS

Kent – Pop. 23 632 – Regional map n° **5**-D1

▷ London 77 mi – Canterbury 18 mi – Ramsgate 2 mi

🏠 Belvidere Place

TOWNHOUSE · PERSONALISED Centrally located Georgian house with a charming owner, green credentials and an eclectic, individual style. Bohemian, shabby-chic lounge boasts a retro football table. Spacious bedrooms mix modern facilities with older antique furnishings.

5 rooms ⌂ – ♥£ 140 ♥♥£ 160/200

Belvedere Rd ⊠ CT10 1PF – ✆ 01843 579850 – www.belvidereplace.co.uk – Closed 25-26 December

✗ Albariño   AC 🍷

SPANISH · TAPAS BAR Run by a husband and wife team and named after her favourite wine. Freshly prepared, full-flavoured tapas dishes; 3 per person will suffice – let the chef choose. Counter seating for 7. Good views of the Channel.

Carte £ 15/28

29 Albion St ⊠ CT10 1LX – 𝒞 01843 600991 – www.albarinorestaurant.co.uk – dinner only and Saturday lunch – Closed 25-26 December, 1 January and Sunday

✗ Wyatt & Jones   ← AC 🖳

MODERN BRITISH · BISTRO Follow the narrow road under the arch, towards the harbour; here you'll find 3 old fishermen's cottages with pleasant sea views. Appealing menus keep things regional, with local lobsters a speciality; start with some tempting nibbles.

Menu £ 19 (weekday lunch) – Carte £ 25/42

23-27 Harbour St ⊠ CT10 1EU – 𝒞 01843 865126 – www.wyattandjones.co.uk – Closed 25-26 December, Monday and Tuesday

BROADWAY

Worcestershire – Pop. 2 496 – Regional map n° **10**-C3

▶ London 93 mi – Birmingham 36 mi – Oxford 38 mi

🏛 Buckland Manor   🐾 ✿ ⅋ ← 🛏 ✗ ⅋ P

HISTORIC · CLASSIC With its 13C origins, beautiful gardens and peaceful hamlet setting, this is one of England's most charming country houses. The elegant interior comprises tastefully appointed country house bedrooms and traditionally furnished lounges featuring wood panelling and big open fires. The formal restaurant has garden views and offers classical cooking with modern touches.

15 rooms �يₐ – †£ 175/555 ††£ 195/575

Buckland ⊠ WR12 7LY – Southwest : 2.25 mi by B 4632 – 𝒞 01386 852626 – www.bucklandmanor.com

🏠 Dormy House   ✿ ⅋ 🛏 🖥 🕛 ⅋ ♨ & AC P

LUXURY · CONTEMPORARY Behind the original farmhouse façade you'll find a modern interior and a luxurious spa. The odd beam and fireplace remain but bold contemporary fabrics and designer furnishings now feature too; wood and stone play a big part and the atmosphere is laid-back. The Potting Shed has an informal bistro feel and the stylish Garden Room offers a more sophisticated alternative.

38 rooms ⊑ – †£ 245/285 ††£ 255/295 – 10 suites

Willersey Hill ⊠ WR12 7LF – East : 4 mi by A 44 – 𝒞 01386 852711 – www.dormyhouse.co.uk

🏠 Foxhill Manor   ✿ ⅋ ← 🛏 🚻 & AC P

COUNTRY HOUSE · DESIGN Once home to Henry Maudslay, who died in the Dam Busters raid; a Grade II listed Arts and Crafts house, where guests are made to feel as if they're staying in a private home. Striking bedrooms have first class facilities – 'Oak' has his and hers baths with a view. Modern 4 course menus are discussed with the chef; after dinner, relax on bean bags in front of the 74" TV.

8 rooms ⊑ – †£ 295/650 ††£ 295/650 – 2 suites

Farncombe Estate ⊠ WR12 7LJ – East : 3.75 mi by A 44 – 𝒞 01386 852711 – www.foxhillmanor.com

🏠 The Fish   ✿ 🛏 & P

TRADITIONAL · PERSONALISED Up until the 16C the Benedictine monks kept their fish stocks in the local hillside caves – hence its name. Guest areas are set in a wood-clad building and include a British brasserie specialising in meats and grills. Scandinavian-style bedrooms are set in various outbuildings and have lovely country views.

67 rooms ⊑ – †£ 85/125 ††£ 100/155 – 3 suites

Farncombe Estate ⊠ WR12 7LJ – East : 4 mi by A 44 – 𝒞 01386 858000 – www.thefishhotel.co.uk/

East House 🅿

HISTORIC · PERSONALISED Beautifully furnished, 18C former farmhouse in lovely mature gardens, with wood-burning stoves and a welcoming feel. Sumptuous beamed bedrooms mix antique furniture with modern technology; superb bathrooms have underfloor heating. The Jacobean Suite is the biggest room, with a four-poster and garden views.

4 rooms 🖙 – ♦£ 185/225 ♦♦£ 185/225

162 High St ⊠ WR12 7AJ – ☎ 01386 853789 – www.easthouseuk.com

Mill Hay House 🅿

HISTORIC · ELEGANT This lovely 17C house, tucked away on the edge of the village, comes with beautiful gardens overlooking a lake. With just three individually furnished bedrooms, the atmosphere is intimate, and guests are treated as family friends.

3 rooms 🖙 – ♦£ 165/225 ♦♦£ 185/245

Snowshill Rd ⊠ WR12 7JS – South : 0.5 mi – ☎ 01386 852498 – www.millhay.co.uk – Closed Christmas-New Year

Windrush House 🅿

FAMILY · COSY Welcoming guesthouse in a pretty village. Individually decorated bedrooms have bold feature walls: some use Laura Ashley designs and have wrought iron beds; four-poster 'Snowshill' is the best. Homemade jams feature at breakfast.

5 rooms 🖙 – ♦£ 75/90 ♦♦£ 85/105

Station Rd ⊠ WR12 7DE – ☎ 01386 853577 – www.windrushhouse.com

Olive Branch 🅿

TOWNHOUSE · COSY Welcoming guesthouse run by an experienced husband and wife team. Pleasantly cluttered bedrooms with thoughtful extras; one has a small veranda. Rustic, characterful dining room with homemade cakes, breads and muesli at breakfast.

8 rooms 🖙 – ♦£ 72/78 ♦♦£ 102/112

78 High St ⊠ WR12 7AJ – ☎ 01386 853440 – www.theolivebranch-broadway.com

XX Russell's 🅿

MODERN BRITISH · FASHIONABLE An attractive Cotswold stone house in the centre of the village, with a smart brasserie-style interior and both a front and rear terrace. Choose from a constantly evolving selection of modern British dishes. Service is relaxed and friendly and bedrooms are stylish – there's even a spacious suite!

Menu £ 22 (weekdays) – Carte £ 28/51

7 rooms 🖙 – ♦£ 120/300 ♦♦£ 120/300

20 High St ⊠ WR12 7DT – ☎ 01386 853555 – www.russellsofbroadway.co.uk – Closed Sunday dinner and bank holidays

BROCKENHURST

Hampshire – Pop. 3 552 – Regional map n° **4**-A2
▶ London 99 mi – Winchester 27 mi – Southampton 14 mi

The Pig 🅿

COUNTRY HOUSE · GRAND LUXURY This smart manor house hotel follows a philosophy of removing barriers and bringing nature indoors. Characterful bedrooms are divided between the house and a stable block, and boast distressed wood floors, chunky furnishings and large squashy beds. The comfy lounges and dining room have a shabby-chic style.

31 rooms – ♦£ 155/435 ♦♦£ 155/435 – 🖙 £ 15

Beaulieu Rd ⊠ SO42 7QL – East : 1 mi on B 3055 – ☎ 01590 622354 – www.thepighotel.com

The Pig – See restaurant listing

Cloud

TRADITIONAL · COSY Well-kept hotel made up of four cottages, set on the edge of a pretty New Forest village. It has a homely feel, from the cosy lounges to the immaculately kept bedrooms; a collection of photos in the bar attest to the owner's past as a tiller girl. The restaurant and conservatory offer traditional menus.

18 rooms (dinner included) ♨ – ♦£ 116/125 ♦♦£ 192/250

Meerut Rd ✉ SO42 7TD – ☎ 01590 622165 – www.cloudhotel.co.uk
– Closed 27 December-13 January

Daisybank Cottage

LUXURY · PERSONALISED A charming Arts and Crafts house built in 1902. Modern bedrooms come with seating areas; one room opens onto an internal courtyard and another, onto a terrace. Aga-cooked breakfasts come in English, Irish and American versions.

7 rooms ♨ – ♦£ 85/135 ♦♦£ 100/150

Sway Rd ✉ SO42 7SG – South : 0.5 mi on B 3055 – ☎ 01590 622086
– www.bedandbreakfast-newforest.co.uk

✗ The Pig

TRADITIONAL BRITISH · BRASSERIE A delightful conservatory with plants dotted about, an eclectic collection of old tables and chairs, and a bustling atmosphere. The forager and kitchen gardener supply what's best and any ingredients they can't get themselves are sourced from within 25 miles. Cooking is unfussy, wholesome and British-based.

Carte £ 27/44

The Pig Hotel, Beaulieu Rd ✉ SO42 7QL – East : 1 mi on B 3055 – ☎ 01590 622354
– www.thepighotel.com

BROMESWELL – Suffolk → See Woodbridge

BROUGHTON

North Yorkshire – Regional map n° **13**-A2
▶ London 228 mi – York 46 mi – Skipton 4 mi

Bull

REGIONAL CUISINE · PUB The big, solid-looking Bull is part of the Ribble Valley Inns group. Expect real ales and local meats and cheeses, as well as traditional British dishes, rediscovered classics and the sort of puddings that make you feel patriotic.

Menu £ 14 (weekdays) – Carte £ 22/46

✉ BD23 3AE – ☎ 01756 792065 – www.thebullatbroughton.com

BROUGHTON GIFFORD

Wiltshire – Pop. 851 – Regional map n° **2**-C2
▶ London 109 mi – Bristol 31 mi – Cardiff 64 mi

The Fox

TRADITIONAL BRITISH · COSY Raising the profile of this pub, both locally and farther afield, has been a labour of love for its young owner. Cooking is simple, unfussy and fresh, and uses what's in the garden: salad leaves, fruits, chickens and pigs.

Menu £ 18 (weekday lunch) – Carte £ 22/46

The Street ✉ SN12 8PN – ☎ 01225 782949 – www.thefox-broughtongifford.co.uk
– Closed 2-8 January and Monday

BRUNTINGTHORPE

Leicestershire – Regional map n° **9**-B3
▶ London 96 mi – Leicester 10 mi – Birmingham 67 mi

The Joiners ⓟ

TRADITIONAL BRITISH · RUSTIC Beams and a tiled floor bring 17C character to this dining pub but designer wallpaper and fresh flower displays give it a chic overall feel. There's plenty of choice on the menus, with the likes of pork rillettes or pot-roast pheasant.

Menu £ 16 (weekday lunch) – Carte £ 25/35

Church Walk ⊠ LE17 5QH – ℰ 0116 247 8258 (booking essential)
– www.thejoinersarms.co.uk – Closed Sunday dinner and Monday

BRUTON

Somerset – Pop. 2 984 – Regional map n° **2**-C2
▶ London 118 mi – Bristol 27 mi – Salisbury 35 mi

✗ Roth Bar & Grill 🍷 🛏 🛖 �& 🗔 ⓟ

TRADITIONAL BRITISH · DESIGN The converted outbuildings of a working farm now house this charming restaurant with its striking modern art exhibitions. Beef, pork and lamb from the farm are aged in their salting room. Be sure to try the caramelised lemonade.

Carte £ 22/46

Durslade Farm, Dropping Ln ⊠ BA10 0NL – Southeast : 0.5 mi on B 3081
– ℰ 01749 814700 (booking advisable) – www.rothbarandgrill.co.uk – lunch only and dinner Friday-Saturday – Closed first week January, 25-26 December and Monday except bank holidays

✗ At The Chapel 🔄 🛖 🗔

MEDITERRANEAN CUISINE · DESIGN Stylish, informal restaurant in a former 18C chapel, with a bakery to one side and a wine shop to the other. Daily menus offer rustic, Mediterranean-influenced dishes; specialities include wood-fired breads, pizzas and cakes. The chic club lounge and cocktail bar opens at weekends. Bedrooms are luxurious.

Carte £ 21/57

8 rooms – †£ 125 ††£ 250

High St ⊠ BA10 0AE – ℰ 01749 814070 (booking advisable)
– www.atthechapel.co.uk

Your discoveries and comments help us improve the guide. Please let us know about your experiences – good or bad!

BRYHER → See Scilly (Isles of)

BUCKDEN

Cambridgeshire – Pop. 2 385 – Regional map n° **8**-A2
▶ London 65 mi – Cambridge 20 mi – Northampton 31 mi

🏠 George 🏡 🖥 🍽 🛝 ⓟ

HISTORIC · PERSONALISED Delightfully restored part black and white, part red-brick coaching inn. Original flag floors mix with modern furnishings, creating a stylish, understated feel. The simple yet tastefully decorated bedrooms are named after famous 'Georges'. Classic brasserie dishes feature in the restaurant.

12 rooms ⊊ – †£ 95/150 ††£ 120/150

High St ⊠ PE19 5XA – ℰ 01480 812300 – www.thegeorgebuckden.com

BUDE

Cornwall – Pop. 5 091 – Regional map n° **1**-B2
▶ London 252 mi – Exeter 51 mi – Plymouth 50 mi

🏨 Beach   ♤ ⪦ 🖃 🕸 🅿

BOUTIQUE HOTEL · CONTEMPORARY Spacious New England style hotel with views over the Atlantic Ocean and a pleasingly laid-back feel. Contemporary bedrooms have limed oak furnishings and all the latest mod cons; 'Deluxe' boast rolltop baths and either a terrace or a balcony. The smart brasserie offers a menu of classic dishes and grills.

16 rooms ⌕ – ♦£ 128/238 ♦♦£ 140/250

Summerleaze Cres. ⊠ EX23 8HL – ℰ 01288 389800 – www.thebeachatbude.co.uk
– Closed 24-26 December

BUDLEIGH SALTERTON
Devon – Pop. 5 185 – Regional map n° **1**-D2
▶ London 182 mi - Exeter 16 mi - Plymouth 55 mi

🏨 Heath Close   ♤ 🛏 🕸 🅿 ⇄

FAMILY · PERSONALISED Smart detached house with a lovely rear garden. The open-plan lounge and dining room are stylish and modern. Good-sized bedrooms display personal touches and bathrooms have underfloor heating. The welcoming owners offer tea and cake on arrival and traditional home-cooked dinners on Friday and Saturday.

5 rooms ⌕ – ♦£ 75 ♦♦£ 105

3 Lansdowne Rd ⊠ EX9 6AH – West : 1 mi by B 3178 – ℰ 01395 444337
– www.heathclose.com

🏨 Rosehill   🛏 🕸 🅿

COUNTRY HOUSE · PERSONALISED After a tasty breakfast of French toast, eggs royale or smoked salmon, relax on the veranda, by the monkey puzzle tree. Bright, airy bedrooms come with king-sized beds and homemade treats. The owner also runs cookery courses.

4 rooms ⌕ – ♦£ 120/150 ♦♦£ 120/150

30 West Hill ⊠ EX9 6BU – entrance via West Hil Ln – ℰ 01395 444031
– www.rosehillroomsandcookery.co.uk – Closed Christmas

🏨 Long Range   🛏 ♿ 🕸 🅿

FAMILY · PERSONALISED Spotlessly kept guesthouse with a large garden, set on a quiet street. Choice of two lounges; one in a conservatory and complete with a small bar. Unfussy, brightly coloured bedrooms have good facilities; those to the rear can see the sea.

9 rooms ⌕ – ♦£ 74/80 ♦♦£ 108/140

5 Vales Rd ⊠ EX9 6HS – by Raleigh Rd – ℰ 01395 443321
– www.thelongrangehotel.co.uk – Restricted opening in winter

BUNBURY
Cheshire East – Pop. 1 308 – Regional map n° **11**-A3
▶ London 183 mi - Chester 24 mi - Manchester 44 mi

🍴 Yew Tree Inn   🏡 🅿

TRADITIONAL BRITISH · PUB Handsome part red-brick, part black and white timbered pub with a pleasingly relaxed feel, a lovely terrace and numerous snug, quirky rooms. They host a quarterly farmers' market and cooking is – unsurprisingly – seasonal and local.

Carte £ 21/37

Long Ln, Spurstow ⊠ CW6 9RD – ℰ 01829 260274
– www.theyewtreebunbury.com

BUNGAY
Suffolk – Pop. 5 127 – Regional map n° **8**-D2
▶ London 108 mi - Ipswich 38 mi - Cambridge 105 mi

🏠 Castle Inn ⇦ 🛋 🅿

REGIONAL CUISINE · PUB Sky-blue pub, formerly known as The White Lion, with an open-plan dining area and an intimate rear bar. Fresh, simple and seasonal country based cooking; the Innkeeper's platter of local produce is a perennial favourite. Tasty homemade cakes and cookies on display. Homely, comfortable bedrooms.

Menu £ 20 (lunch) – Carte dinner £ 20/32

4 rooms ⌑ – ♦£ 70/75 ♦♦£ 95

35 Earsham St ✉ NR35 1AF – ☎ 01986 892283 – www.thecastleinn.net – Closed 25 December, Sunday dinner and Monday in winter

BUNTINGFORD

Hertfordshire – Pop. 4 948 – Regional map n° **12**-B2

▶ London 51 mi – Stevenage 10 mi – Saffron Walden 15 mi

🍴 Buntingford Kitchen ⓝ

MODERN BRITISH · INTIMATE At 450 years old, this sweet little restaurant has plenty of character, from its thick walls and wonky beams to its hidden first floor sitting room. Choose from 4 choices per course; flavours are classical but techniques are modern.

Menu £ 30 (dinner) – Carte £ 30/35

69 High St ✉ SG9 9AE – ☎ 01763 661389 – www.thebuntingfordkitchen.com – dinner only and Sunday lunch – Closed 21-31 December and Monday-Wednesday

BURCHETT'S GREEN

Windsor and Maidenhead – Pop. 306 – Regional map n° **11**-C3

▶ London 32 mi – Oxford 35 mi – Reading 11 mi

🏠 Crown (Simon Bonwick) 🍴 🅿

🔆 **REGIONAL CUISINE · RUSTIC** The Crown is very personally and passionately run by the Bonwick family and comes with a small bar and two intimate, open-fired dining rooms. The refined, deftly prepared dishes – six per course – are decided upon daily; the options are diverse and appealing, with flavours clearly defined.

→ Rillettes of Lop pig with pickles. Slow-cooked salt marsh lamb with roasting juices. White chocolate and praline cadeau.

Carte £ 20/30

✉ SL6 6QZ – ☎ 01628 824079 – www.thecrownburchettsgreen.com – Closed first 2 weeks August, Sunday dinner, Wednesday lunch, Monday and Tuesday

BURFORD

Oxfordshire – Pop. 1 171 – Regional map n° **6**-A2

▶ London 76 mi – Oxford 20 mi – Birmingham 55 mi

🏠 Burford House 🍴

TRADITIONAL · GRAND LUXURY The welcome is warm at this delightful part-timbered 17C house, where spacious, comfy bedrooms – including 3 four-posters – mix traditional styling with contemporary touches. Cosy sitting rooms and a lovely terrace for afternoon tea.

6 rooms ⌑ – ♦£ 115/190 ♦♦£ 145/240

99 High St ✉ OX18 4QA – ☎ 01993 823151 – www.burfordhouse.co.uk

🏠 Lamb Inn ⇦ 🍴 🛋 🕩 🅿

TRADITIONAL BRITISH · COSY Delightful collection of 15C weavers' cottages with a gloriously cosy feel. The elegant, candlelit dining room offers a tasting menu and an à la carte of classic dishes; a simpler menu is served in the bar and sitting rooms. Chatty service. Charming, individually furnished bedrooms; 'Rosie' has a private garden.

Menu £ 25 (lunch) – Carte £ 28/51

17 rooms ⌑ – ♦£ 140/275 ♦♦£ 140/275

Sheep St ✉ OX18 4LR – ☎ 01993 823155 – www.cotswold-inns-hotels.co.uk/the-lamb-inn

at Swinbrook East: 2.75 mi by A40 ⊠ Burford

🅿 Swan Inn   ⇔ 🛏 🎍 🅿

MODERN BRITISH · PUB Wisteria-clad, honey-coloured pub on the riverbank, boasting a lovely garden filled with fruit trees. The charming interior displays an open oak frame and exposed stone walls hung with old lithographs and hand-made walking sticks. The daily menu showcases the latest local produce and features modern takes on older recipes. Well-appointed bedrooms have a luxurious feel.

Carte £ 25/44

11 rooms ⌂ – 🛉£ 110/180 🛉🛉£ 125/195

⊠ OX18 4DY – ☏ 01993 823339 – www.theswanswinbrook.co.uk – Closed 25-26 December

at Shilton Southeast : 2.5 mi by A40 off B4020

🅿 Rose & Crown   🎍 🅿

TRADITIONAL CUISINE · RUSTIC Charming Cotswold stone pub with flickering fires, exposed beams and a welcoming owner. Meats are from local farms and game, from nearby shoots. Gutsy country cooking is full of flavour and reasonably priced; Sunday lunch is popular.

Carte £ 21/40

⊠ OX18 4AB – ☏ 01993 842280 – www.shiltonroseandcrown.com – Closed 25 December

BURNHAM MARKET
Norfolk – Pop. 877 – Regional map n° **8**-C1
▶ London 128 mi – Norwich 36 mi – Cambridge 71 mi

🏠 Hoste   ⌂ 🛏 🎍 ⅙ ♨ 🅿

INN · PERSONALISED Personally and passionately run is this greatly extended former inn at the heart of a picturesque village. Stylish, luxurious bedrooms in the main building and two annexes; smart beauty and wellness spa in the wing. The extensive restaurant comprises an appealing bar, four dining rooms and a courtyard garden.

62 rooms ⌂ – 🛉£ 120/235 🛉🛉£ 140/275

The Green ⊠ PE31 8HD – ☏ 01328 738777 – www.thehoste.com

BURPHAM – West Sussex → See Arundel

BURTON-UPON-TRENT
Staffordshire – Pop. 72 299 – Regional map n° **10**-C1
▶ London 128 mi – Stafford 27 mi – Leicester 27 mi

✗ 99 Station Street

TRADITIONAL BRITISH · NEIGHBOURHOOD Amongst the vast brewing towers is this bright, boldly decorated neighbourhood restaurant, run by two experienced locals. They make everything on the premises daily and showcase regional ingredients; try the mature rare breed meats.

Menu £ 14 (weekday lunch) – Carte £ 24/36

99 Station St ⊠ DE14 1BT – ☏ 01283 516859 – www.99stationstreet.com – Closed Monday, Tuesday, Sunday dinner and Wednesday lunch

BURY
Greater Manchester – Pop. 77 211 – Regional map n° **11**-B2
▶ London 211 mi – Manchester 9 mi – Liverpool 35 mi

Ⅹ Waggon ⇔ 🅿

🛞 **TRADITIONAL BRITISH · NEIGHBOURHOOD** Both the building and the décor may be unassuming and understated but the focus at the Waggon is where it matters – on the food. Classical dishes change with the seasons and the experienced chef clearly knows how to get the best out of his ingredients. The mid-week 'Market' menu offers excellent value.

Menu £ 18 (weekdays) – Carte £ 21/38

131 Bury and Rochdale Old Rd, Birtle ⊠ BL9 6UE – East : 2 mi on B 6222 – 𝒞 01706 622955 – www.thewaggonatbirtle.co.uk – dinner only and lunch Thursday, Friday and Sunday – Closed 2 weeks summer, first week January, Monday and Tuesday

BURY ST EDMUNDS
Suffolk – Pop. 41 113 – Regional map n° **8**-C2
▶ London 79 mi – Ipswich 26 mi – Cambridge 27 mi

🏠 Angel 🔁 ♿ 🔌 🅿

HISTORIC · PERSONALISED The creeper-clad Georgian façade hides a surprisingly stylish hotel. Relax in the atmospheric bar or smart lounges. Individually designed bedrooms offer either classic four-poster luxury or come with funky décor and iPod docks.

74 rooms ⌿ – ♦£ 120/333 ♦♦£ 120/333

3 Angel Hill ⊠ IP33 1LT – 𝒞 01284 714000 – www.theangel.co.uk

Eaterie – See restaurant listing

ⅩⅩ Maison Bleue 🐝

SEAFOOD · NEIGHBOURHOOD Passionately run neighbourhood restaurant in a converted 17C house, with a smart blue canopy, wooden panelling and impressive fish sculptures. Menus focus on seafood; cooking is modern in style but with classic influences and Gallic and Asian touches; you must try the excellent French cheeses.

Menu £ 20 (weekday lunch)/37 – Carte £ 35/55

30-31 Churchgate St ⊠ IP33 1RG – 𝒞 01284 760623 – www.maisonbleue.co.uk – Closed 3 weeks January, 2 weeks summer, Sunday and Monday

ⅩⅩ 1921 🅝

MODERN CUISINE · INTIMATE A fine period house located at 19-21 Angel Hill; its smart, modern facelift complements the original beams and red-brick inglenook fireplace. Cooking displays a modern flair, with some interesting combinations. Good value set lunch menu.

Menu £ 21 (lunch) – Carte £ 28/43

19-21 Angel Hill ⊠ IP33 1UZ – 𝒞 01284 704870 – www.nineteen-twentyone.co.uk – Closed 1 week Christmas and Sunday

Ⅹ Pea Porridge

🛞 **MODERN BRITISH · BISTRO** A charming former bakery in two 19C cottages, with its original bread oven still in situ. Tasty country cooking is led by the seasons and has a Mediterranean bias; many dishes are cooked in the wood-fired oven. It has a stylish, rustic look and a homely feel – its name is a reference to the old town green.

Menu £ 19/27 (weekdays) – Carte £ 25/36

28-29 Cannon St ⊠ IP33 1JR – 𝒞 01284 700200 (booking advisable) – www.peaporridge.co.uk – Closed first week January, 2 weeks summer, last week December, Sunday-Monday and lunch Tuesday and Wednesday

Ⅹ Eaterie 🅿

TRADITIONAL BRITISH · BRASSERIE An airy two-roomed bistro set within an attractive 15C coaching inn where Dickens once stayed. There's an impressive modern chandelier and a display of the owner's contemporary art. Tasty British brasserie dishes use local produce.

Menu £ 22 (lunch) – Carte dinner £ 22/49

Angel Hotel, 3 Angel Hill ⊠ IP33 1LT – 𝒞 01284 714000 – www.theangel.co.uk

at Ixworth Northeast: 7 mi by A143 ⊠ Bury St Edmunds

✗✗ Theobalds

TRADITIONAL BRITISH · NEIGHBOURHOOD Part-16C cottage in a charming village, with a cosy, fire-lit lounge and a beamed dining room. Professionally run by a husband and wife and a jolly chef. Monthly changing menus offer heartwarming, well-presented, traditional dishes.

Menu £ 30/34

68 High St ⊠ IP31 2HJ – 𝒞 01359 231707 – www.theobaldsrestaurant.co.uk
– dinner only and lunch Friday and Sunday – Closed 1 week spring, 1 week autumn, Monday and dinner Sunday

at Horringer Southwest: 3 mi on A143 ⊠ Bury St Edmunds

🏰 Ickworth   🏠 🐾 ⬅ 🛏 🖼 ✗ 🔲 🛉 🕊 Ⓟ

HISTORIC · CLASSIC This family-orientated hotel occupies the east wing of a grand 200 year old mansion set in 1,800 acres: former home of the 7th Marquess of Bristol and now owned by the National Trust. It features huge art-filled lounges, antique-furnished bedrooms and luxurious suites. Dine in the formal restaurant or in the impressive orangery, which serves relaxed meals and high teas.

39 rooms ☕ – 🛉£ 175/275 🛉🛉£ 225/500 – 12 suites
⊠ IP29 5QE – 𝒞 01284 735350 – www.ickworthhotel.co.uk

BUTLERS CROSS
Buckinghamshire – Regional map n° **11**-C2
▶ London 64 mi – Aylesbury 8 mi – Milton Keynes 44 mi

🍴 Russell Arms ⓝ   🍽 Ⓟ

TRADITIONAL BRITISH · INN You'll find walkers relaxing at the tables to the side and a large terrace to the rear. Daily coffee mornings are followed by a great value lunchtime 'plat du jour' and on Fridays they host children's tea parties. The chef knows how to get the best out of his ingredients and dishes are packed with flavour.

Carte £ 25/34

2 Chalkshire Rd ⊠ HP17 0TS – 𝒞 01296 624411 – www.therussellarms.co.uk
– Closed 25-26 December and Monday

BUTTERMERE
Cumbria – Pop. 139 – Regional map n° **12**-A2
▶ London 306 mi – Carlisle 35 mi – Kendal 43 mi

🏡 Wood House   🏠 🐾 ⬅ 🛏 ✗ Ⓟ

TRADITIONAL · CLASSIC Charming part-16C house with Victorian additions and lovely gardens, in a wonderfully serene lakeside setting. Welcoming owners, stunning views and no TVs to disturb the peace! Classical lounge and cosy dining room with a communal antique table, silver cutlery and cut crystal glassware.

3 rooms ☕ – 🛉£ 55/70 🛉🛉£ 110/130
⊠ CA13 9XA – Northwest : 0.5 mi on B 5289 – 𝒞 017687 70208
– www.wdhse.co.uk – Closed November-February

CALLINGTON
Cornwall – Pop. 4 698 – Regional map n° **1**-C2
▶ London 237 mi – Exeter 53 mi – Plymouth 15 mi

🏡 Cadson Manor   🐾 ⬅ 🛏 ✗ Ⓟ

COUNTRY HOUSE · PERSONALISED Welcoming guesthouse on a 600 year old working farm, with views over an iron age settlement. Cosy, individually furnished bedrooms feature antiques, fresh flowers and a decanter of sherry. Rayburncooked breakfasts include weekly specials.

4 rooms ☕ – 🛉£ 85/125 🛉🛉£ 125/135
⊠ PL17 7HW – Southwest : 2.75 mi by A 390 – 𝒞 01579 383969
– www.cadsonmanor.co.uk – Closed Christmas

✗✗ Langmans

MODERN BRITISH · INTIMATE Langmans is run by a husband and wife and dining here is an all-night affair. Pre-dinner drinks with your fellow guests are followed by a tasting menu in the formal dining room; cooking is refined and they have a great cheese selection.

Menu £ 45

3 Church St ✉ PL17 7RE – ☎ 01579 384933 (booking essential)
– www.langmansrestaurant.co.uk – dinner only – Closed Sunday-Wednesday

CALNE

Wiltshire – Pop. 17 274 – Regional map n° **2**-C2
▶ London 91 mi – Bristol 33 mi – Southampton 63 mi

at Compton Bassett Northeast: 4.5 mi by A4

🍴 White Horse Inn   ⇦ 🛏 🏠 🅿

MODERN BRITISH · FRIENDLY The White Horse dates back over a century: the cosy bar is where you'll find the regulars, while most diners head for the rustic room next door. For traditionalists there are pub classics; for those with more adventurous tastes there's the à la carte. Beyond the garden are 8 snug, simply furnished bedrooms.

Menu £ 15 (weekday lunch) – Carte £ 21/49

8 rooms ☲ – ♦£ 75/85 ♦♦£ 85/110

✉ SN11 8RG – ☎ 01249 813118 – www.whitehorse-comptonbassett.co.uk – Closed 25 December, Sunday dinner and Monday

CAMBER – East Sussex ➔ See Rye

CAMBRIDGE

Cambridgeshire – Pop. 123 867 – Regional map n° **8**-B3
▶ London 55 mi – Birmingham 101 mi – Ipswich 54 mi

Hotels

🏨 Hotel du Vin 　　　　　　　　　　　　　　 ⌖ 🖭 ⅏ 🆎 🔧

TOWNHOUSE · GRAND LUXURY Stylish hotel set over a row of 16C and 17C ex-university owned buildings. Original quarry tiled floors and wood-panelled walls feature, along with plenty of passages, nooks and crannies. Chic, modern bedrooms – one even has its own cinema. Clubby bar and an appealing brasserie with a Gallic-led menu.

41 rooms – †£ 185/220 ††£ 205/255 – ⌸ £ 17
Town plan: B3-e - *15-19 Trumpington St* ✉ CB2 1QA – ℰ 01223 227330
– *www.hotelduvin.com*

Restaurants

XXX Midsummer House (Daniel Clifford)　　　　 ఔ 🍴 ⅊⒴ ⇄

ఔ ఔ MODERN CUISINE · ELEGANT A stylish restaurant in an idyllic location on Midsummer Common; enjoy an aperitif in the first floor lounge overlooking the River Cam. Set 7 or 10 course menus (with 5 courses also available at lunch). Creative, highly accomplished cooking showcases top quality produce and flavours are well-balanced, with the main ingredient of each dish allowed to shine.

→ Sea scallop with Granny Smith, celeriac and truffle. Roast Anjou pigeon with crispy leg, wild garlic and morels. Passion fruit with yoghurt sorbet and dark chocolate.

Menu £ 48/105

Town plan: B1-a - *Midsummer Common* ✉ CB4 1HA
– ℰ 01223 369299 – *www.midsummerhouse.co.uk*
– *Closed 2 weeks December, Sunday, Monday and lunch Tuesday*

 The symbol ఔ denotes a particularly interesting wine list.

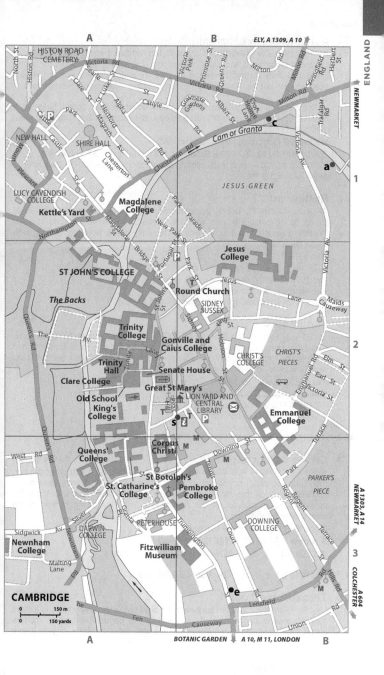

CAMBRIDGE

ENGLAND

ELY, A 1309, A 10
NEWMARKET
NEWMARKET

HISTON ROAD CEMETERY

North St.
Histon Rd.
Castle St.
Union
Pleasant
Searle St.
Park St.
Clare St.
Alpha Rd.
Hertford St.
Magrath Av.
Victoria Rd.
Carlyle Rd.
Grasmere Gardens
Albert St.
Green St.
Victoria Rd.
Primrose St.
Victoria Park
Milton Rd.
Milton Rd.
Cross Home Lane
Herbert St.
Spring field Rd.
Trafalgar Rd.
Victoria Av.

NEW HALL
SHIRE HALL
Chesterton Lane
LUCY CAVENDISH COLLEGE
Northampton St.
Kettle's Yard
Magdalene College
Magdalene Bridge
Chesterton Rd.
Cam or Granta
c

a

JESUS GREEN

New Park St.
Park Parade
Portugal Pl.
ST JOHN'S COLLEGE
The Backs
Queens' Rd.
The Av.
Trinity College
Trinity Hall
Clare College
St. John's St.
Trinity Lane
Round Church
Jesus Lane
Jesus College
Maids Causeway
SIDNEY SUSSEX
Sidney St.
Gonville and Caius College
Senate House
Great St Mary's
Old School
King's College
Sidney St.
Hobson St.
CHRIST'S COLLEGE
CHRIST'S PIECES
Emmanuel Rd.
Elm St.
Earl St.
Victoria St.
LION YARD AND CENTRAL LIBRARY
T
T
S
i
P
Emmanuel College
Parker's Terrace

West Rd.
Queens' Rd.
Queens' College
St. Catharine's College
Silver St.
Darwin College
Grange
Newnham College
Sidgwick Av.
Newnham Rd.
Malting Lane
Fen
Corpus Christi
St Botolph's
Pembroke College
PETERHOUSE
Downing St.
Tennis Court
Trumpington St.
M
M
M
DOWNING COLLEGE
Regent St.
PARKER'S PIECE
Park Terrace

Fitzwilliam Museum
e
Lensfield Rd.
Union Rd.
Causeway
Hills Rd.
M

A 1303, A 14
NEWMARKET
A 604
COLCHESTER

BOTANIC GARDEN
A 10, M 11, LONDON

0   150 m
0   150 yards

A   B

323

XX Alimentum (Mark Poynton)   ⊛ ☂ & 🄰🄲 ⇔
❀

BRITISH MODERN · MINIMALIST Sleek, stylish restaurant with a spacious cocktail bar and a striking red and black dining room. Top quality ingredients are showcased in skilfully crafted dishes and flavours are clearly defined. Cooking is classically based but has innovative modern touches. The early evening menu is good value.

→ Roast scallop curry with apple, cumin dahl, coriander and yoghurt. Sirloin with beef fat potato, veal sweetbreads, parsley and mushroom. BBQ orange parfait, mojito and liquorice.

Menu £ 29 (lunch and early dinner)/65

152-154 Hills Rd ⊠ CB2 8PB - Southeast : 1.5 mi by Regent St on Hills Rd
- ℰ 01223 413000 - www.restaurantalimentum.co.uk - Closed 24-30 December and bank holiday Mondays

XX Restaurant 22   🄰🄲 ⇔

FRENCH · NEIGHBOURHOOD A converted Victorian townhouse with a formal dining room; personally run, with ten tables set with flowers and candles. Monthly changing, four course menu of classically based, flavourful cooking with Italian influences.

Menu £ 40

Town plan: B1-c - *22 Chesterton Rd ⊠ CB4 3AX*
- ℰ 01223 351880 (booking essential)
- www.restaurant22.co.uk - dinner only
- Closed 24 December-2 January, Sunday and Monday

🍴 Pint Shop 🄽   🏠 &

BRITISH TRADITIONAL · PUB 'MEAT. BEER. BREAD.' is written on the window – and that pretty much sums this place up. Cooking is gutsy and satisfying and the charcoal grill takes centre stage. To accompany are 10 keg beers, 6 cask beers and over 70 different gins.

Menu £ 13 (lunch and early dinner) - Carte £ 20/35

Town plan: B2-s - *10 Peas Hill ⊠ CB2 3NP*
- ℰ 01223 352293 - www.pintshop.co.uk
- Closed 25-26 December and 1 January

at Horningsea Northeast: 4 mi by A1303 and B1047⊠ Cambridge

🍴 Crown & Punchbowl   ⇔ 🛏 ⇔ 🅿

MODERN BRITISH · PUB Watch your head on the beams as you enter the bar, then take your pick from several different seating areas. Start with rustic bread and zingy olive oil then move on to modern seasonal dishes or one of the wide-ranging specials chalked on the fish board. Cosy, welcoming bedrooms are named after local writers.

Menu £ 19 (weekdays) - Carte £ 24/38

5 rooms - ♦£ 120/130 ♦♦£ 120/130 - ⊊ £ 10
⊠ CB25 9JG - ℰ 01223 860643 - www.cambscuisine.com

at Madingley West: 4.5 mi by A1303⊠ Cambridge

🍴 Three Horseshoes   ⊛ 🛏 🏠 📖 🅿

MODERN CUISINE · PUB An appealing thatched pub with a lively bar and a more formal conservatory restaurant overlooking the garden. Ambitious, modern dishes have international influences and the wine list is well-chosen, with plenty available by the glass.

Carte £ 25/45

High St ⊠ CB23 8AB
- ℰ 01954 210221 (booking advisable) - www.threehorseshoesmadingley.com
- Closed Sunday dinner November-February

at Little Wilbraham East: 7.25 mi by A1303 ✉ Cambridge

⌂ Hole in the Wall   🗣 🅿

MODERN BRITISH · PUB A charming 16C pub with a cosy, fire-lit, beamed bar. The regularly changing, seasonal menu offers European flavours presented in a modern fashion; dishes are prepared with zeal by the young chef-owner, a past MasterChef finalist. Excellent value lunch menu; tasting menus available in the evening.

Menu £ 20/35

2 High St ✉ CB21 5JY – ℰ 01223 812282 (booking advisable)
– www.holeinthewallcambridge.com – Closed 2 weeks January, Sunday dinner, Monday and Tuesday lunch

CAMELFORD

Cornwall – Pop. 2 335 – Regional map n° **1**-B2
▶ London 376 mi – Truro 57 mi – Plymouth 69 mi

⌂ Pendragon Country House   ⌂ ⌂ 🅿

COUNTRY HOUSE · COSY This former vicarage is run by an extremely enthusiastic couple and offers views across the fields to the church it once served. There's always a jigsaw on the go in the period furnished drawing room and Cornish artwork features throughout. Home-baked breads, homemade cake and local produce feature.

7 rooms ⌂ – ♦£ 65/115 ♦♦£ 105/150

Davidstow ✉ PL32 9XR – Northeast : 3.5 mi by A 39 on A 395 – ℰ 01840 261131
– www.pendragoncountryhouse.com – Closed 23-27 December

CANTERBURY

Kent – Pop. 54 880 – Regional map n° **5**-D2
▶ London 59 mi – Brighton 76 mi – Dover 15 mi

⌂ Abode Canterbury   ⌂ ⌂ ⌂ ⌂ ⌂ ⌂ 🅿

HISTORIC BUILDING · PERSONALISED Centrally located former coaching inn; heavily beamed, yet with a stylish, boutique feel. Comfy champagne bar and atmospheric first floor lounge. Contemporary bedrooms come in 4 categories: 'Enviable' and 'Fabulous' are the most luxurious.

72 rooms – ♦£ 95/195 ♦♦£ 125/225 – ⌂ £ 15 – 1 suite

30-33 High St ✉ CT1 2RX – ℰ 01227 766266 – www.abodecanterbury.co.uk
County – See restaurant listing

XX County   ⌂ ⌂ ⌂ ⌂

MODERN BRITISH · DESIGN Spacious, modern restaurant divided in two by a smart, glass-walled wine cellar. Accomplished, contemporary cooking is stylishly presented, with classic combinations of ingredients interpreted in a modern fashion. Private chef's table.

Menu £ 20 (lunch and early dinner) – Carte £ 38/48

Abode Canterbury Hotel, High St ✉ CT1 2RX – ℰ 01227 826684
– www.abodecanterbury.co.uk – Closed Sunday dinner

XX Ambrette   ⌂ ⌂

INDIAN · TRENDY This modern restaurant is hidden away, just off the main street. A striking tiled floor leads through to a spacious, moodily lit room. Local ingredients – some foraged from the woods – feature in deftly spiced Anglo-Indian dishes.

Menu £ 25 (lunch) – Carte £ 30/55

14-15 Beer Cart Ln ✉ CT1 2NY – ℰ 01227 200777 – www.theambrette.co.uk

✗ Deesons

TRADITIONAL BRITISH · TRADITIONAL DÉCOR Charming building in the shadow of the cathedral, with a dark, rustic interior decked out with old wood furnishings. Hearty British cooking uses ingredients from the owner's smallholding; at lunch they also serve small plates.

Carte £ 29/41

25-26 Sun St ✉ *CT1 2HX* – *℘ 01227 767854* – *www.deesonsrestaurant.co.uk*
– Closed 26 December

✗ Goods Shed

TRADITIONAL BRITISH · RUSTIC Daily farmers' market and food hall in an early Victorian locomotive shed, selling an excellent variety of organic, free range and homemade produce. Hearty, rustic, daily changing dishes are served at scrubbed wooden tables.

Carte £ 27/43

Station Rd West, St Dunstans ✉ *CT2 8AN* – *℘ 01227 459153*
– www.thegoodsshed.net – Closed 25-26 December, 1-2 January, Sunday dinner and Monday

CARBIS BAY – Cornwall → See St Ives

CARLYON BAY – Cornwall → See St Austell

CARTHORPE
North Yorkshire – Regional map n° **13**-B1
▶ London 228 mi – Leeds 49 mi – York 34 mi

🏠 Fox and Hounds

TRADITIONAL BRITISH · PUB This traditional country pub has an open-fired bar packed with memorabilia and a bright dining room with an old forge on display. Good-sized menu offers unfussy home-cooked dishes. Local organic and homemade products are for sale.

Menu £ 16 (weekdays) – Carte £ 23/44

✉ *DL8 2LG* – *℘ 01845 567433* – *www.foxandhoundscarthorpe.co.uk* – *Closed first 2 weeks January, 25 December and Monday*

CARTMEL – Cumbria → See Grange-over-Sands

CASTLE COMBE
Wiltshire – Pop. 347 – Regional map n° **2**-C2
▶ London 110 mi – Bristol 23 mi – Chippenham 6 mi

🏰 Manor House H. and Golf Club

LUXURY · ELEGANT Fine period manor house in 365 acres of formal gardens and parkland. The interior exudes immense charm and style, with characterful oak panelling and a host of open-fired lounges. Uniquely styled, luxurious bedrooms are split between the main house and mews cottages. Book ahead for one of the event days.

50 rooms ☟ – ♦£ 215/445 ♦♦£ 215/445 – 8 suites
✉ *SN14 7HR* – *℘ 01249 782206* – *www.manorhouse.co.uk*
❀ **Bybrook** – See restaurant listing

🏠 Castle Inn

HISTORIC · COSY Delightful 12C former inn set in a charming village, with two small, cosy lounges and a pubby dining room where rustic features blend with contemporary touches. Dishes range from old favourites to more sophisticated choices. Bedrooms mix old beams with modern furnishings; some have four-posters.

11 rooms ☟ – ♦£ 94/170 ♦♦£ 135/199
✉ *SN14 7HN* – *℘ 01249 783030* – *www.castle-inn.info* – *Closed 25 December*

✗✗✗ Bybrook ⌷ 🅿

🏵 **MODERN BRITISH · ELEGANT** Spacious dining room within a charming 14C manor house, in 365 acres of formal gardens and parkland. Large, well-spaced tables are immaculately laid. Menus offer refined, carefully prepared dishes with a classical base and modern overtones, and feature local and kitchen garden produce. Smooth service.

→ Mackerel with marinated beetroot, oyster fritter and potato & horseradish mousse. Wiltshire lamb with peas, garlic leaves, girolles, parmesan gnocchi and lamb jus. Amalfi lemon tart with baby basil and raspberry sorbet.

Menu £ 30/66

Manor House Hotel and Golf Club, ✉ SN14 7HR – ℰ 01249 782206
– www.manorhouse.co.uk – dinner only and Sunday lunch

CASTLE EDEN
Durham – Regional map n° **14**-B3
▶ London 265 mi – Newcastle upon Tyne 28 mi – York 62 mi

🍴 Castle Eden Inn 🏠 🅿

TRADITIONAL BRITISH · PUB A former coaching inn on what was once the main road to London: local gossip says that Dick Turpin was once tied up outside! The experienced owners offer a wide choice of dishes and the 'monthly specials' menu offers great value.

Menu £ 15 (weekdays) – Carte £ 23/42

Stockton Rd ✉ TS27 4SD – ℰ 01429 835137 – *www.castleedeninn.com – Closed Sunday dinner*

CATEL/CASTEL → See Channel Islands (Guernsey)

CAXTON
Cambridgeshire – Pop. 572 – Regional map n° **8**-A3
▶ London 58 mi – Cambridge 15 mi – Bedford 22 mi

🍴 No 77 🅿

THAI · PUB The cream and blue exterior of No 77 leads to a rustic interior with blue velvet cushioned chairs from an old cinema. An extensive list of Thai dishes includes popular Kantok sharing platters and there's a cinema club on Sundays.

Carte £ 16/37

77 Ermine St ✉ CB23 3PQ – ℰ 01954 269577 – *www.77cambridge.com – Closed Tuesday lunch and Monday*

CERNE ABBAS
Dorset – Pop. 784 – Regional map n° **2**-C3
▶ London 132 mi – Bristol - 60 mi – Cardiff 115 mi

🍴 New Inn ⇐ ⌷ 🏠 🅿

TRADITIONAL BRITISH · FRIENDLY This delightful village is home to the famous Chalk Giant, as well as this 16C part-flint inn. It's a charming place with a relaxed ambience and menus which mix the modern and the traditional. Spacious, stylish bedrooms are split between the pub and the courtyard and some are duplex suites.

Menu £ 16 (weekday lunch) – Carte £ 24/42

12 rooms ⌷ – †£ 85/140 ††£ 95/170

14 Long St ✉ DT2 7JF – ℰ 01300 341274 – *www.thenewinncerneabbas.co.uk – Closed 25-26 December*

CHADDESLEY CORBETT
Worcestershire – Pop. 1 440 – Regional map n° **10**-B2
▶ London 123 mi – Worcester 16 mi – Leicester 62 mi

🏨 Brockencote Hall

HISTORIC · CONTEMPORARY Professionally run 19C mansion with the feel of a French château; its long driveway leads past a lake and grazing cattle. Inside, period features blend well with contemporary country house furnishings and bold colour schemes. Bedrooms are spacious and well-equipped and some have pleasant park views.

21 rooms ⊊ – 🛏£ 105/325 🛏🛏£ 125/375

✉ DY10 4PY – On A 448 – ☎ 01562 777876 – www.brockencotehall.com

The Chaddesley – See restaurant listing

XXX The Chaddesley

MODERN CUISINE · ELEGANT Elegant restaurant in an impressive 19C mansion. Smartly laid tables overlook the gardens; in summer, head for the terrace. Accomplished cooking relies on classic combinations but uses modern techniques and dishes are nicely presented.

Menu £ 33 (weekdays)/65 **s**

Brockencote Hall Hotel, ✉ DY10 4PY – On A 448 – ☎ 01562 777876
– www.brockencotehall.com

CHAGFORD

Devon – Pop. 1 020 – Regional map n° **1**-C2

🚉 London 218 mi – Exeter 17 mi – Plymouth 27 mi

🏨 Gidleigh Park

LUXURY · ELEGANT An impressive black and white, timbered Arts and Crafts house with lovely tiered gardens and Teign Valley views. Luxurious sitting and drawing rooms have a classic country house feel but a contemporary edge. Wonderfully comfortable bedrooms echo this, with their appealing mix of styles. Service is superb.

24 rooms ⊊ – 🛏£ 225/1315 🛏🛏£ 250/1340 – 1 suite

✉ TQ13 8HH – Northwest : 2 mi by Gidleigh Rd – ☎ 01647 432367
– www.gidleigh.co.uk – Closed 3-15 January

❀❀ **Gidleigh Park** – See restaurant listing

XXXX Gidleigh Park

❀❀ **CREATIVE · ELEGANT** Within a grand Edwardian house you'll find three intimate dining rooms with well-spaced tables and colourful armchairs. Innovative modern cooking combines French, local and kitchen garden produce in well-thought-out combinations. Preparation is skilful and the chef's personality really shines through.

➔ Cornish lobster with cuttlefish film, carrot sorbet, lobster curd and citrus. Lamb with smoked ricotta, morels, nasturtium oil and garlic. Frozen yeast cream with milk skin, caramel ganache, Horlicks and walnuts.

Menu £ 40/130

Gidleigh Park Hotel, ✉ TQ13 8HH – Northwest : 2 mi by Gidleigh Rd
– ☎ 01647 432367 (booking essential) – www.gidleigh.co.uk – Closed 3-15 January

at Sandypark Northeast: 2.25 mi on A382✉ Chagford

🏨 Mill End

TRADITIONAL · PERSONALISED Whitewashed former mill off a quiet country road: once home to Frank Whittle, inventor of the jet engine. Comfy, cosy lounges with beams and open fires. Contemporary bedrooms have bold feature walls and colourful throws. Bright dining room offers classical dishes prepared using local produce.

15 rooms ⊊ – 🛏£ 75/195 🛏🛏£ 125/210 – 1 suite

✉ TQ13 8JN – On A 382 – ☎ 01647 432282 – www.millendhotel.com – Closed 5-21 January

Parford Well

🦢 🛏 🍴 **P** 🛏

TRADITIONAL · COSY Well-kept guesthouse with superb mature gardens. Homely lounge with a wood-burning stove, books and games. Two small breakfast rooms; one communal and one with a table for two. Individually decorated bedrooms offer pleasant country views.

3 rooms ☕ – 🕴£ 85/110 🕴🕴£ 95/110

✉ TQ13 8JW – On Drewsteignton rd – ✆ 01647 433353 – www.parfordwell.co.uk – restricted opening in winter

CHANNEL ISLANDS

Regional map n° **3**-B2

ALDERNEY

Alderney – Pop. 2 400 – Regional map n° **3**-B1

Braye

🏠 **Braye Beach**

☆ 🦢 ⇦ 🏠 🔲 ⑨ 🏛 **P**

COUNTRY HOUSE · MODERN Stylish hotel on Braye beach, just a stone's throw from the harbour. The vaulted basement houses two lounges and a 19-seater cinema; above is a modern bar with a delightful terrace. Bedrooms are beech-furnished, and some have balconies and bay views. The formal restaurant showcases local island seafood.

27 rooms ♡ – ♦£ 95/155 ♦♦£ 130/210

Braye St. ✉ GY9 3XT – ℰ 01481 824300 – www.brayebeach.com

GUERNSEY

Guernsey – Pop. 58 867 – Regional map n° **3**-A2

Castel

🏠 **Cobo Bay**

☆ ⇦ 🏠 ⑨ 🔲 **P**

FAMILY · MODERN Modern hotel set on the peaceful side of the island and well run by the 3rd generation of the family. Bright, stylish bedrooms come with fresh fruit, irons, safes and bathrobes – some have large balconies overlooking the sandy bay. Smart dining room; sit on the spacious terrace for lovely sunset views.

34 rooms ♡ – ♦£ 59/89 ♦♦£ 99/159

Cobo Coast Rd ✉ GY5 7HB
– ℰ 01481 257102 – www.cobobayhotel.com
– Closed 1 January-21 March

Fermain Bay

🏠 **Fermain Valley**

☆ ⇦ 🛏 🔲 ⑨ 🔲 占 ⑨ 🏛 **P**

LUXURY · MODERN Stylish hotel with beautiful gardens, hidden in a picturesque valley and affording pleasant bay views through the trees. Well-equipped bedrooms are widely dispersed; the 'Gold' rooms have balconies. Dine with a view in Ocean or from a steakhouse menu – accompanied by cocktails – in contemporary Rock Garden.

45 rooms ♡ – ♦£ 95/225 ♦♦£ 110/240

Fermain Ln ✉ GY1 1ZZ
– ℰ 01481 235666 – www.fermainvalley.com

Kings Mills

⫚ Fleur du Jardin ⇦ 🏚 🏠 🍴 🅿

TRADITIONAL CUISINE · INN Attractive inn with a stylish terrace, lovely land-scaped gardens and several charming, adjoining rustic rooms. The menu ranges from homemade burgers to sea bass and tasty island seafood specials. Stylish bedrooms have a New England theme, and there's even a heated outdoor pool.

Menu £ 13 (lunch and early dinner) – Carte £ 20/37

13 rooms ⌂ – ♦£ 62/92 ♦♦£ 84/189 – 2 suites

Grand Moulins ✉ GY5 7JT – ☏ 01481 257996 – www.fleurdujardin.com – Closed dinner 25 December and 1 January

St Martin

✗✗ Auberge ⇐ 🏚 🏠 🅿

MODERN CUISINE · FRIENDLY Long-standing restaurant in a great location. Sim-ple interior with a bar and well-spaced tables; concertina doors open onto a lovely terrace, which offers views across to the other islands. Classical menu fea-tures plenty of island seafood.

Menu £ 13 (lunch and early dinner) – Carte £ 26/42

Jerbourg Rd ✉ GY4 6BH – ☏ 01481 238485 (booking essential)
– www.theauberge.gg – Closed 25-26 December and 1 January

St Peter Port

🏨 Old Government House H. & Spa 🎐 🏚 🍴 📶 🐾 ♨ ☒ 🔥 🄰🄲 🔥

LUXURY · CLASSIC Fine, classically furnished 18C building, with many of its 🅿 original features restored, including a glorious ballroom. Individually styled bed-rooms have padded walls, modern bathrooms and a personal touch. Relax in the well-equipped spa or outdoor pool. Authentic Indian cooking in The Curry Room. The smart yet informal brasserie has a delightful terrace.

62 rooms ⌂ – ♦£ 183/545 ♦♦£ 183/545 – 1 suite

Town plan: A1-a · *St Ann's Pl ✉ GY1 2NU – ☏ 01481 724921*
– www.theoghhotel.com

🏨 Duke of Richmond 🎐 ⇐ ☒ ☒ 🄰🄲 🔥

BUSINESS · CONTEMPORARY Contemporary hotel with a bright reception area and a stylish lounge ideal for afternoon tea. Smart, modern bedrooms; some with balconies. Relax in the secluded pool or on the patio overlooking the 19C Candie Gardens. A chic bar with leopard print furnishings leads to the restaurant and terrace.

73 rooms ⌂ – ♦£ 152/184 ♦♦£ 152/184 – 1 suite

Town plan: A1-s · *Cambridge Pk. ✉ GY1 1UY – ☏ 01481 726221*
– www.dukeofrichmond.com

🏨 La Frégate 🎐 ⇐ 🏚 ☒ 🔥 🔥 🅿

TOWNHOUSE · CONTEMPORARY Greatly extended 18C property offering stun-ning panoramic views across the harbour and out towards the island of Herm. Bedrooms have a clean contemporary style; go for one with a balcony or terrace. Extensive menus feature modern international dishes. Breakfast on the terrace is hard to beat.

22 rooms ⌂ – ♦£ 100 ♦♦£ 200/260 – 1 suite

Town plan: A1-b · *Beauregard Ln, Les Cotils ✉ GY1 1UT – ☏ 01481 724624*
– www.lafregatehotel.com

🏨 Duke of Normandie 🎐 🔥 🅿

BUSINESS · FUNCTIONAL A former German HQ during the WW2 invasions; su-perbly located in the centre of town. Modern designer bedrooms display bright colours and have a comfy, cosy feel; some are set in the courtyard. The smart lounge and bar are decorated with historical island memorabilia and serve tradi-tional international dishes.

37 rooms ⌂ – ♦£ 49/89 ♦♦£ 89/149

Town plan: A1-c · *Lefebvre St ✉ GY1 2JP – ☏ 01481 721431*
– www.dukeofnormandie.com

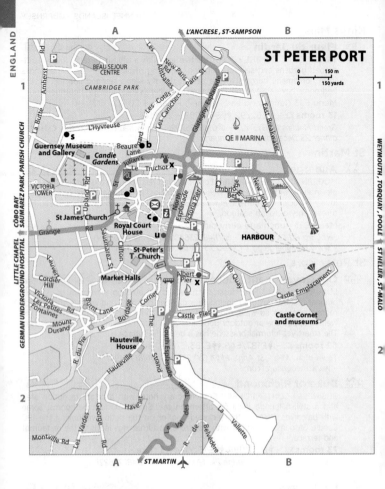

L'ANCRESE, ST-SAMPSON

ST PETER PORT

0   150 m
0   150 yards

BEAU SEJOUR
CENTRE

CAMBRIDGE PARK

L'Hyvreuse

Guernsey Museum
and Gallery

Candie
Gardens

Beaure ● **b**

Lane

x

r

QE II MARINA

VICTORIA
TOWER

● **a**

St James'Church

● **c**

u

Royal Court
House

St-Peter's
T' Church

HARBOUR

Market Halls

Albert
Pier **x**

Fish Quay

Castle Emplacement

**Castle Cornet
and museums**

Hauteville
House

Castle Pier

Montville Rd

ST MARTIN

XX Nautique

FRENCH · INTIMATE A former sailmaker's warehouse on the quayside with a stylish, nautically themed interior and a pleasant marina view; ask for a window seat. The large menu offers generously sized classic dishes, with daily fish specials a feature.

Menu £16 (weekday lunch) – Carte £29/57

Town plan: A1-u - *Quay Steps* ⊠ *GY1 2LE* – *ℰ 01481 721714*
– www.lenautiquerestaurant.co.uk – Closed Saturday lunch and Sunday

XX Pier 17

TRADITIONAL BRITISH · FASHIONABLE Set at the end of a substantial stone pier in the centre of Guernsey harbour. The conservatory extension affords superb water views and the two terraces catch the last of the sun's rays. Tasty, traditionally based, seasonal dishes.

Menu £16 (weekday lunch)/36 – Carte £28/42

Town plan: A2-x - *Albert Pier* ⊠ *GY1 1AD* – *ℰ 01481 720823*
*– www.pier17restaurant.com – Closed 25-26 December and Sunday,
September-April*

332

XX Red   🍽 AC

MEATS AND GRILLS · FASHIONABLE Popular harbourfront restaurant run by an experienced owner; the first floor cocktail lounge is a real hit. Its name refers to 'red' wines and 'red' meat, with the large menu focusing on top quality char-grilled Scottish steaks.

Menu £16 (weekday lunch)/34 – Carte £20/40

Town plan: A1-r - *61 Le Poulet* ✉ GY1 1WL – 𝒞 01481 700299 *(booking essential)* – www.red.gg – *Closed 25 December, Saturday lunch and Sunday*

XX Absolute End   🍴

MODERN CUISINE · ROMANTIC This cosy, formal restaurant is located at the quieter end of town. Menus offer a good selection of hearty, classically based seafood dishes. The linen-clad dining room leads up to a small first floor bar-lounge and roof terrace.

Menu £16 (lunch) – Carte £24/47

St Georges Esplanade ✉ GY1 2BG – *North : 0.75 mi by Glategny Esplanade* – 𝒞 01481 723822 *(booking advisable)* – www.absoluteend.com – *Closed Sunday*

XX Pavilion in the Park   🍴 AC P

MODERN CUISINE · BRASSERIE Light, spacious restaurant set within the St Pierre Park hotel, overlooking the gardens. The larger-than-life chef prepares extensive all-day menus using the best of the island's produce. Champagne afternoon teas are a feature.

Menu £17 (lunch)/28 – Carte £23/32

St Pierre Park, Rohais ✉ GY1 1FD – *West : 1.5 mi by Grange Rd* – 𝒞 01481 736676 – www.thepavilion.co.gg – *lunch only and dinner Friday-Saturday – Closed Tuesday*

🍴 Swan Inn   🍴

TRADITIONAL BRITISH · PUB Smart Victorian pub with a bottle-green façade, a traditional bar complete with a coal fire and a formal first floor dining room. The same menu is served throughout, offering plenty of choice, with hearty main courses and nursery puddings.

Carte £21/30

Town plan: A1-x - *St Julian's Ave* ✉ GY1 1WA – 𝒞 01481 728969 – *Closed 25 December, Sunday and Monday*

St Saviour

▶ St Peter Port 4 mi

🏠 Farmhouse   🍴 ⇔ 🍴 🛀 AC 🏊 🧖 P

LUXURY · MODERN Former farm restyled in a boutique vein. Stylish, sumptuous bedrooms come with hi-tech amenities and the bathrooms have heated floors. The pleasant garden features a pool, a terrace and a kitchen garden. Contemporary cooking has an international edge and uses the island's finest produce in eclectic ways.

14 rooms ♔ – ♦£79/179 ♦♦£179/279

Route des Bas Courtils ✉ GY7 9YF – 𝒞 01481 264181 – www.thefarmhouse.gg

HERM

Herm – Pop. 60 – Regional map n° **3**-A2

🏠 White House   🌳 🐾 ⇐ 🍴 🍴 🍴

TRADITIONAL · PERSONALISED The only hotel on this tranquil, car-free island. Comfy, airy bedrooms are split between the house and various annexes; there are no clocks, TVs or radios. The open-fired lounge offers bay and island views; vast tropical gardens come with tennis courts and a pool. Traditional dining room offers plenty of seafood; popular pub-cum-brasserie serves more modern dishes.

40 rooms (dinner included) ♔ – ♦£72/137 ♦♦£144/260

✉ GY1 3HR – 𝒞 01481 750075 – www.herm.com – *Closed October-March*

JERSEY

ENGLAND

C.I. – Pop. 85 150 – Regional map n° **3**-B2

Beaumont

✗✗ Mark Jordan at the Beach ≤ 🏠 **P**

MEDITERRANEAN CUISINE · NEIGHBOURHOOD Modern brasserie with a small lounge and bar; a paved terrace with bay views; and a dining room with heavy wood tables, modern seashore paintings and animal ornaments. Menus showcase island produce and fish from local waters. Cooking is refined but hearty, mixing tasty brasserie and restaurant style dishes.

Menu £ 25/28 – Carte £ 28/44

La Plage, La Route de la Haule ✉ *JE3 7YD* – *☎ 01534 780180*
– www.markjordanatthebeach.com – Closed 6-21 November and Mondays except in summer

Gorey

 St Helier 4 mi

🏠 Moorings ☆ ≤

TRADITIONAL · PERSONALISED Keenly run hotel below the ramparts of Mont Or-gueil castle, overlooking the harbour. Leather-furnished first floor lounge. Modern bedrooms in cream, brown and purple colour schemes; some have small balconies. Formal restaurant or casual bistro and terrace for comfort dishes and seafood specials.

15 rooms ☑ – ♦£ 70/100 ♦♦£ 139/171

Gorey Pier ✉ *JE3 6EW* – *☎ 01534 853633 – www.themooringshotel.com*

Walker's – See restaurant listing

✗✗ Sumas ≤ 🏠 **AC**

MODERN CUISINE · TRENDY A well-known restaurant in a whitewashed house, with a smart heated terrace affording lovely harbour views. Modern European dishes feature island produce. The monthly changing lunch and midweek dinner menus represent good value.

Menu £ 23 (weekdays) – Carte £ 28/48

Gorey Hill ✉ *JE3 6ET* – *☎ 01534 853291 (booking essential)*
– www.sumasrestaurant.com – Closed 21 December-19 January and Sunday dinner

✗✗ Walker's **AC**

TRADITIONAL CUISINE · FRIENDLY Formal hotel restaurant with a modern lounge, harbour views and local artwork on display. Good value menus offer well-prepared, unashamedly traditional dishes in tried-and-tested combinations and feature the odd personal twist.

Menu £ 25 – Carte £ 33/65

Moorings Hotel, Gorey Pier ✉ *JE3 6EW* – *☎ 01534 853633*
– www.themooringshotel.com – dinner only and Sunday lunch

✗ Crab Shack Gorey ≤ 🏠

SEAFOOD · FASHIONABLE Laid-back, friendly restaurant with a decked terrace and superb views over the harbour. The pared-down, rustic interior is decorated with nautical memorabilia. Unfussy menus have a Mediterranean edge and focus on locally caught seafood.

Carte £ 18/28

La Route de la Cote ✉ *JE3 6DR* – *☎ 01534 850830 (booking advisable)*
– www.jerseycrabshack.com – Closed 25-26 December, 1 January and Monday

🍴 Bass and Lobster 🏠 **AC** **P**

TRADITIONAL CUISINE · PUB A bright, modern 'foodhouse' close to the beach, with a small decked terrace. Seasonal island produce is simply cooked to create immensely flavourful dishes; fresh, tasty seafood and shellfish dominate the menu. Smooth, effective service.

Menu £ 16/19 – Carte £ 29/56

Gorey Coast Rd ✉ *JE3 6EU* – *☎ 01534 859590 – www.bassandlobster.com*
– Closed 26 December, 1 January, Monday and Sunday lunch May-November

ENGLAND

Green Island

✗ Green Island 🏠

MEDITERRANEAN CUISINE · FRIENDLY Friendly, personally run restaurant with a terrace and beachside kiosk; the southernmost restaurant in the British Isles. Mediterranean-influenced dishes and seafood specials showcase island produce. Flavours are bold and perfectly judged.

Menu £ 17/27 – Carte £ 33/47

St Clement ⊠ JE2 6LS – ℰ 01534 857787 (booking essential)
– www.greenisland.je – Closed 23 December-1 March, Sunday dinner and Monday

Grouville

▶ St Helier 3 mi

✗ Café Poste 🏠 🔖 🅿

MEDITERRANEAN CUISINE · BISTRO Popular all-day restaurant – formerly a post office – with a vast array of curios, a wood burning stove and a French country kitchen feel. Choose from an eclectic Mediterranean menu and daily specials; breakfast is served at weekends.

Menu £ 20 (lunch and early dinner) – Carte £ 31/45

La Rue de la ville es Renauds ⊠ JE3 9FY – ℰ 01534 859696
– www.cafeposte.co.uk – Closed 11-27 November, Monday and Tuesday

La Haule

🏠 La Haule Manor ← 🛏 🏊 🛏 🅿

TOWNHOUSE · ELEGANT Attractive Georgian house overlooking the fort and bay, with a lovely terrace, a good-sized pool and neat lawned gardens. Stylish guest areas and spacious bedrooms mix modern and antique furnishings; those in the wing are the largest.

16 rooms ☒ – ♦£ 80/220 ♦♦£ 107/220

St Aubin's Bay ⊠ JE3 8BS – ℰ 01534 741426 – www.lahaulemanor.com

La Pulente

▶ St Helier 7 mi

🏠 Atlantic

GRAND LUXURY · CONTEMPORARY Stylish hotel with well-manicured grounds, set in a superb location overlooking St Ouen's Bay. Public areas are understated, with tiled floors, exposed brick, water features and a relaxed, intimate feel. Bedrooms are cool and fresh: some have a patio; others, a balcony. Attentive, personable staff.

50 rooms ☒ – ♦£ 130/280 ♦♦£ 150/340 – 1 suite

Le Mont de la Pulente ⊠ JE3 8HE – on B 35 – ℰ 01534 744101
– www.theatlantichotel.com – Closed 3 January-2 February

❀ **Ocean** – See restaurant listing

✗✗✗ Ocean

❀ **MODERN CUISINE · LUXURY** Elegant, well-run dining room with a fresh, understated feel, set in a stunning position overlooking St Ouen's Bay. Delicious, well-crafted dishes make use of fine ingredients from the island and display a real understanding of flavour. Smooth, professional service and a relaxed, friendly atmosphere.

→ Pan-seared red mullet with foie gras, ratatouille and olive crumb. Assiette of Jersey beef with lobster ravioli and beef Marmite. Flavours of mojito with kalamansi foam and mint ice cream.

Menu £ 28/65

Atlantic Hotel, Le Mont de la Pulente ⊠ JE3 8HE – on B 35 – ℰ 01534 744101 (booking essential) – www.theatlantichotel.com/dining
– Closed 3 January-2 February

Rozel Bay

▶ St Helier 6 mi

🏨 Chateau La Chaire   🏠 🐾 🛏 🛋 🅿

HISTORIC · CLASSIC Attractive 19C house surrounded by peaceful gardens and mature woodland. Traditionally styled guest areas and more modern, well-equipped bedrooms: 2nd floor rooms are cosy; 1st floor rooms are larger and some have balconies. Formal restaurant with a conservatory and terrace offers classics with a twist.

14 rooms ⌷ – †£ 90/125 ††£ 125/325 – 2 suites

Rozel Valley ⊠ JE3 6AJ – ℰ 01534 863354 – www.chateau-la-chaire.co.uk

🍺 Rozel   🛏 🛋 🖥 🅿

TRADITIONAL CUISINE · PUB Cosy pub run by the same owners as the neighbouring hotel. The upstairs dining room has distant sea views but, come summer, the garden is the place to be. Cooking is traditional and homely and ales are from the island's Liberation Brewery.

Carte £ 22/31

Rozel Valley ⊠ JE3 6AJ – ℰ 01534 863438 – www.rozelpubanddining.co.uk

St Aubin

▶ St Helier 4 mi

🏨 Panorama   ≤ 🛏 🕸

TRADITIONAL · PERSONALISED Immaculate hotel with Georgian origins, colourful gardens and stunning views over the fort and bay. It's largely traditional throughout. Afternoon tea is served in the conservatory on arrival and over 1,400 teapots are on display.

14 rooms ⌷ – †£ 50/100 ††£ 100/172

La Rue du Crocquet ⊠ JE3 8BZ – ℰ 01534 742429 – www.panoramajersey.com – Closed November-early April

St Brelade's Bay

▶ St Helier 6 mi

🏨 L'Horizon Beach H & Spa   🏠 ≤ 🕸 ⊕ 🕸 🛁 🍴 ⊡ ⅇ ⚒ 🕸 ⚓ 🅿

LUXURY · GRAND LUXURY Long-standing hotel located right on the beachfront and boasting stunning views over the bay. Luxurious interior with extensive guest areas and subtle modern styling. Choose a deluxe bedroom, as they come with balconies and sea views. Stylish, formal restaurant; modern British menus focus on local seafood.

106 rooms ⌷ – †£ 75/200 ††£ 95/305 – 6 suites

⊠ JE3 8EF – ℰ 01534 743101 – www.handpickedhotels.co.uk/lhorizon

🏨 St Brelade's Bay   🏠 ≤ 🛏 ⌶ 🕸 🕸 🛁 🍴 ⊡ ⚒ 🕸 ⚓ 🅿

FAMILY · GRAND LUXURY Smart seafront hotel with charming tropical gardens and panoramic views across the bay. A modernised lounge and contemporary bedrooms fit well alongside original parquet floors and ornate plaster ceilings. Excellent health club. Formal restaurant offers impressive sea views and a classical menu.

74 rooms ⌷ – †£ 93/145 ††£ 140/290 – 5 suites

La Route de la Baie ⊠ JE3 8EF – ℰ 01534 746141 – www.stbreladesbayhotel.com

🍴 Oyster Box   ≤ 🛋 ⅇ 🅰🅲

SEAFOOD · BRASSERIE Glass-fronted eatery with pleasant heated terrace, set on the promenade and affording superb views over St Brelade's Bay. Stylish, airy interior hung with sail cloths and fishermen's floats. Laid-back, friendly service. Accessible seasonal menu features plenty of fish and shellfish; oysters are a speciality.

Menu £ 18 (weekdays) – Carte £ 25/56

La Route de la Baie ⊠ JE3 8EF – ℰ 01534 850888 (booking essential) – www.oysterbox.co.uk – Closed 25-26 December, 1 January, dinner Sunday-Monday October-April and Monday lunch

X **Jersey Crab Shack St Brelade's Bay** ⇐ 🗺 👍 AIC

SEAFOOD · BISTRO A scaled down version of next door Oyster Box, superbly sited on the beachfront; sit in a cosy booth or on a bench outside. Accessible modern dishes of prime island produce, with seafood a speciality. Relaxed, family-friendly atmosphere.

Menu £ 15 (weekdays) – Carte £ 18/33

*La Route de la Baie ⊠ JE3 8EF – ℰ 01534 850855 (booking advisable)
– www.jerseycrabshack.com – Closed 25-26 December, 1 January and Monday dinner except bank holidays*

St Helier

🏨 **Grand Jersey** ⇑ ⇐ 🗺 🕥 🛁 ⊡ 👍 AIC ⅍ 🛁

LUXURY · MODERN Welcoming hotel with a large terrace overlooking the bay. The stylish interior incorporates a chic champagne bar, a well-equipped spa and a corporate cinema. Contemporary bedrooms come in bold colours; some have balconies and sea views. Watch TV footage from the kitchen in intimate Tassili; Victoria's serves brasserie dishes.

123 rooms ⊊ – ♦£ 94/190 ♦♦£ 119/225

Town plan: A1-u – *The Esplanade ⊠ JE2 3QA – ℰ 01534 722301
– www.grandjersey.com*

🏨 **Club Hotel & Spa** 🗺 🕥 🕥 ⊡ AIC ⅍ 🛁 P

LUXURY · MODERN Modern hotel with stylish guest areas, an honesty bar and a split-level breakfast room. Contemporary bedrooms have floor to ceiling windows and good facilities. Relax in the smart spa or on the terrace beside the small outdoor pool.

46 rooms ⊊ – ♦£ 89/299 ♦♦£ 89/299 – 4 suites

Town plan: B2-e – *Green St ⊠ JE2 4UH – ℰ 01534 876500
– www.theclubjersey.com – Closed 24-30 December*

⚜ **Bohemia** – See restaurant listing

XXX **Bohemia** 🍸 👍 AIC 🖵 🀄 P
⚜

MODERN CUISINE · FASHIONABLE Marble-fronted hotel restaurant with a chic cocktail bar and an intimate dining room. The emphasis is on tasting menus, with both pescatarian and vegetarian options available. Cooking is modern, vibrant and has a lightness of touch; original texture and flavour combinations feature.

→ Oyster, cucumber, dill and caviar. Anjou pigeon with onion, liquorice, girolles and pastrami on toast. Chocolate and hazelnut sphere with pear, prune & Armagnac.

Menu £ 29 (weekday lunch)/59

Town plan: B2-e - *Club Hotel & Spa, Green St ⊠ JE2 4UH – ℰ 01534 880588 (booking advisable) – www.bohemiajersey.com – Closed 24-30 December*

XX **Ormer by Shaun Rankin** 🗺 👍 AIC 🖵 ⇔
⚜

MODERN CUISINE · DESIGN This elegant restaurant features bold blue banquettes and yellow leather chairs, and is named after a rare shellfish found in local waters. Cooking is refined and assured and uses only the very best seasonal island produce. Inside, it's intimate yet buzzy, and there's a pavement terrace for warmer days.

→ Jersey lobster ravioli with scallops and crab & tomato bisque. Venison with parsnip purée, quinoa, Medjool date and smoked chocolate tortellini. Camembert with orange marmalade, pecan nuts, milk foam and salted caramel.

Menu £ 25 (lunch) – Carte £ 47/62

Town plan: B1-2-c - *7-11 Don St ⊠ JE2 4SP – ℰ 01534 725100 (booking advisable) – www.ormerjersey.com – Closed 25 December, 1 January, Sunday and bank holidays*

☰ Banjo 🍴 ⇔ ⊡ & 🗚 ⇔

INTERNATIONAL · BRASSERIE Substantial former gentlemen's club with an ornate façade; the banjo belonging to the owner's great grandfather is displayed in a glass-fronted wine cellar. The appealing, wide-ranging menu features everything from brasserie classics to sushi. Stylish bedrooms have Nespresso machines and Bose sound systems.

Menu £ 18 (weekdays) – Carte £ 25/44

4 rooms – ♦£ 100/190 ♦♦£ 100/190 – ⌂ £ 10

Town plan: B1-a - 8 Beresford St ⊠ JE2 4WN
– ℰ 01534 850890 – www.banjojersey.com
– Closed 25-26 December and Sunday

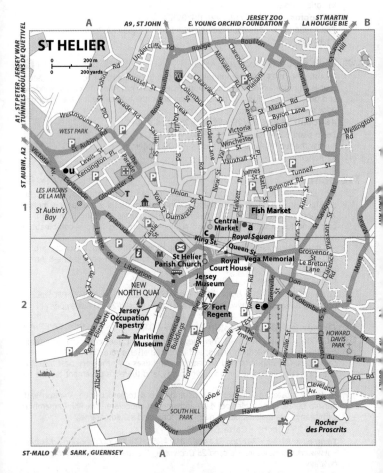

St Saviour

▶ St Helier 1 mi

🏠🏠🏠 Longueville Manor   🍴 ⅀ ⒑₅ ※ 🖵 ⚑ 🅿

LUXURY · CLASSIC Iconic 13C manor house, which is very personally and professionally run. Comfortable, country house guest areas have a modern edge.
Bedrooms come in either classic or contemporary styles and all are well-
equipped. Relax in the lovely pool, on the charming terrace or in the 6 acres of
delightful gardens.

28 rooms ⚌ – 🛏£ 135/575 🛏🛏£ 195/575 – 2 suites

*Longueville Rd ⊠ JE2 7WF – on A 3 – ☏ 01534 725501
– www.longuevillemanor.com – Closed 3-18 January*

Longueville Manor – See restaurant listing

XXX Longueville Manor   🕸 🍴 🔒 🅿

MODERN CUISINE · ELEGANT Set within a charming manor house; dine in the
characterful 15C oak-panelled room, the brighter Garden Room or on the terrace.
Daily menus champion island produce; seafood is a feature and many of the ingredients are foraged for or come from the impressive kitchen garden. Classical
dishes have a modern edge.

Menu £ 25 (weekday lunch) **s** – Carte £ 60/76

*Longueville Manor Hotel, Longueville Rd ⊠ JE2 7WF – on A 3 – ☏ 01534 725501
(booking advisable) – www.longuevillemanor.com – Closed 3-18 January*

SARK

Sark – Pop. 550 – Regional map n° **3**-A2

🏠🏠🏠 Stocks   🏞 🕸 🍴 🔒 ⅀ ⅃₅

COUNTRY HOUSE · ELEGANT Set facing a wooded valley; a very personally run
former farmhouse that's undergone a smart transformation. Immaculately kept,
well-equipped, classical bedrooms. Small gym, arty island shop and fantastic
wine cellar. Formal gardens have a split-level pool and jacuzzi. Eat in the panelled
dining room, in the bistro or on the terrace; local island produce features.

23 rooms ⚌ – 🛏£ 243/308 🛏🛏£ 260/325 – 5 suites

⊠ GY10 1SD – ☏ 01481 832001 – www.stockshotel.com – Closed January-February

XX La Sablonnerie   🍴 🕸 🍴 🔒

SEAFOOD · COSY Charming, whitewashed 16C former farmhouse with beautiful
gardens. Cosy, beamed interior with a comfortable lounge for aperitifs. Regularly
changing, five course menu offers a classic style of cooking using produce from
their own farm. Prompt service. Neat, tidy bedrooms; Room 14, in the former
stables, is the best.

Carte £ 25/47

22 rooms ⚌ – 🛏£ 50/98 🛏🛏£ 100/195 – 2 suites

*Little Sark ⊠ GY9 OSD – ☏ 01481 832061 (booking essential)
– www.lasablonnerie.com – Closed mid October-mid April*

CHARLTON

West Sussex – Regional map n° **4**-C2

▶ London 72 mi – Chichester 7 mi – Southampton 39 mi

🗓 Fox Goes Free   🍴 🍴 🔒 🅿

TRADITIONAL CUISINE · RUSTIC Charming 17C flint pub with a superb garden
and terrace and a lovely outlook. Original features include exposed stone walls,
low beamed ceilings and brick floors. Dishes range from simple pub classics to
more substantial local offerings; some are to share. Clean, unfussy bedrooms; a
few with low beamed ceilings.

Carte £ 21/44

5 rooms ⚌ – 🛏£ 70/180 🛏🛏£ 95/180

⊠ PO18 OHU – ☏ 01243 811461 – www.thefoxgoesfree.com

CHARMOUTH

Dorset – Pop. 1 352 – Regional map n° **2**-B3

▶ London 157 mi – Dorchester 22 mi – Exeter 31 mi

🏠 Abbots House   🛖 ⌷ P

TOWNHOUSE · GRAND LUXURY This cosy guesthouse dates back to 1480 and was originally an annexe of Forde Abbey. It has a beamed, wood-panelled lounge and a conservatory breakfast room overlooking a model railway in the garden. Bedrooms are bright and modern.

4 rooms ⌷ – ♦£ 110/130 ♦♦£ 120/140

The Street ⌷ *DT6 6QF – ℰ 01297 560339 – www.abbotshouse.co.uk – Closed January and last 2 weeks December*

CHARWELTON – Northamptonshire ➔ See Daventry

CHATTON

Northumberland – Pop. 438 – Regional map n° **14**-A1

▶ London 336 mi – Sunderland 63 mi – Newcastle upon Tyne 52 mi

🏠 Chatton Park House   🐾 🛖 ⌷ ⌷ P

TRADITIONAL · PERSONALISED Charming 1730s house in 6 acres of formal gardens. It has a smart parquet-floored hallway, a huge open-fired sitting room and spacious bedrooms which blend modern décor and original features. Excellent breakfasts use local produce.

5 rooms ⌷ – ♦£ 100/175 ♦♦£ 100/189

⌷ *NE66 5RA – East : 1 mi on B 6348 – ℰ 01688 215507 – www.chattonpark.com – Closed November-March*

CHELMONDISTON – Suffolk ➔ See Ipswich

GOOD TIPS!

This pretty spa town on the edge of the Cotswolds is renowned for its splendid Regency architecture, two examples being the elegant, Grade II listed **Malmaison** hotel and the chic, centrally located **Hotel du Vin**. The grounds of the magnificent, part-15C **Ellenborough Park** hotel stretch down to Cheltenham's famous racecourse, home of the Gold Cup.

CHELTENHAM

Gloucestershire – Pop. 116 447 – Regional map n° **2**-C1
▶ London 99 mi – Gloucester 9 mi – Birmingham 48 mi

Hotels

🏨 **Ellenborough Park**   ☆ ⅗ 🛏 🏊 🕭 🛖 🗗 ⬆ 👌 🗛 🐾 🅿

LUXURY · ELEGANT Part-15C timbered manor house, with stone annexes, an understated Indian-themed spa and large grounds stretching down to the racecourse. Beautifully furnished guest areas have an elegant, classical style. Nina Campbell designed bedrooms have superb bathrooms, the latest mod cons and plenty of extras. Dine in the sophisticated restaurant or informal brasserie.

61 rooms ☲ – ♦£ 169/285 ♦♦£ 169/744
Southam Rd ✉ *GL52 3NJ – Northeast : 2.75 mi on B 4632 –* 📞 *01242 545454*
– www.ellenboroughpark.com
The Beaufort – See restaurant listing

🏨 **Hotel du Vin**   ☆ 🗗 ⬆ 👌 🗛 🅿

TOWNHOUSE · THEMED Attractive Regency house in an affluent residential area. Inside it's chic and laid-back, with a leather-furnished bar and a comfy lounge. Some of the individually designed, well-equipped, wine-themed bedrooms have baths in the room. The French bistro features an eye-catching wine glass chandelier.

49 rooms ☲ – ♦£ 115/185 ♦♦£ 155/595 – 1 suite
Town plan: A1-c *- Parabola Rd* ✉ *GL50 3AQ –* 📞 *01242 588450*
– www.hotelduvin.com

🏨 **Malmaison**   ☆ 🗁 🕭 🗗 👌 🗛 🅿

TOWNHOUSE · MODERN Chic Regency townhouse, where stylish modern guest areas are hung with an impressive collection of contemporary art. Light wood furnished bedrooms come with Nespresso machines, complimentary mini bars and in-room info on an iPod touch. Dine on British dishes at marble-topped tables or on one of two terraces.

61 rooms – ♦£ 145/525 ♦♦£ 145/525 – ☲ £ 15
Town plan: A2-r *- Bayshill Rd* ✉ *GL50 3AS –* 📞 *01242 527788*
– www.malmaison.com

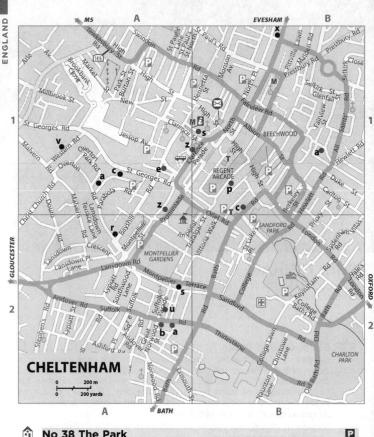

🏠 No 38 The Park   P

TOWNHOUSE · DESIGN Behind the attractive Georgian façade is a very original, tastefully designed hotel with a relaxed atmosphere and supremely comfortable furnishings. Bedrooms come with coffee machines and vast walk-in showers or feature baths.

13 rooms 🖙 - 🛉£ 110/315 🛉🛉£ 120/325

Town plan: B1-x *38 Evesham Rd* ✉ *GL52 2AH* - ☎ *01242 248656*
- *www.no38thepark.com*

🏠 Beaumont House   🖨 ❀ P

TOWNHOUSE · CONTEMPORARY Your hosts here are warm and welcoming, just like the hotel. The lounge and breakfast room are comfortably and classically furnished, while the bedrooms are more contemporary; there are two themed rooms – Africa and Asia.

16 rooms 🖙 - 🛉£ 75/275 🛉🛉£ 98/275

56 Shurdington Rd ✉ *GL53 0JE* - *South : 1.5 mi on A 46* - ☎ *01242 223311*
- *www.bhhotel.co.uk*

 If you are looking for particularly charming accommodation, book a hotel shown in red: 🏨, 🏠... 🏚🏚.

🏠 Wyastone Townhouse   🍴 🅿

TOWNHOUSE · CONTEMPORARY Nothing is too much trouble for the charming young owner of this attractive townhouse. Inside, contemporary décor blends with period features. Bedrooms – split between the house and the courtyard – are surprisingly spacious.

16 rooms 🍽 – 🛏£ 75/95 🛏🛏£ 115/165

Town plan: A1-a - *Parabola Rd* ✉ GL50 3BG – ☎ 01242 245549
– www.wyastonehotel.co.uk – *Closed 23 December-1 January*

🏠 Butlers   🚭 🍴 🅿

TOWNHOUSE · PERSONALISED The bedrooms of this tastefully furnished Victorian townhouse are named after famous butlers – a theme which continues in the classical lounge and breakfast room. There's also an interesting collection of hats about the place!

9 rooms 🍽 – 🛏£ 75/95 🛏🛏£ 95/120

Town plan: A1-v - *Western Rd* ✉ GL50 3RN – ☎ 01242 570771
– www.butlers-hotel.co.uk

🏠 Georgian House   🍴 🅿

TRADITIONAL · CLASSIC The experienced owner of this terraced Georgian townhouse looks after his guests very personally – which is why so many come back time and again. The décor and furnishings respect the house's age; one of the rooms is a four-poster.

3 rooms 🍽 – 🛏£ 80/95 🛏🛏£ 95/120

Town plan: A2-s - *77 Montpellier Terr* ✉ GL50 1XA – ☎ 01242 515577
– www.georgianhouse.net – *Closed 19 December-15 January*

🏠 Detmore House   🐾 🚭 🍴 🅿

COUNTRY HOUSE · CONTEMPORARY Peace and tranquility reign at this 1840s country house, which is accessed via a private drive and offers pleasant rural views. Bedrooms are modern and comfortable – 'Oak' is the best. Breakfast is served at a fine oak table.

4 rooms 🍽 – 🛏£ 75/95 🛏🛏£ 95/110

London Rd, Charlton Kings ✉ GL52 6UT – *Southeast : 2.5 mi by A 40*
– ☎ 01242 582868 – www.detmorehouse.com – *Closed Christmas and New Year*

Restaurants

🍴🍴🍴 Le Champignon Sauvage (David Everitt-Matthias)   🅰🅲

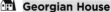 MODERN CUISINE · INTIMATE The chef has cooked here passionately and proudly for 30 years, creating dishes with classic French roots and a personal touch. Visually impressive and boldly flavoured, they often feature foraged ingredients such as dandelion or burdock. Come at lunchtime or midweek to take advantage of the good value set menus.

→ Parfait and rillettes of rabbit with carrot and Muscat jelly. Fillet of Cinderford lamb, lamb breast, anchovy cream, dandelion and burdock. Thai-spiced mango cream with Thai green curry sorbet.

Menu £ 32/63

Town plan: A2-a - *24-28 Suffolk Rd* ✉ GL50 2AQ – ☎ 01242 573449
– www.lechampignonsauvage.co.uk – *Closed 3 weeks June, 10 days Christmas, Sunday and Monday*

🍴🍴🍴 The Beaufort   🚭 ♿ 🅰🅲 🍷 🅿

MODERN CUISINE · INTIMATE With its Tudor stone fireplaces, original oak wood panelling and stained glass windows, this characterful hotel restaurant lends itself to sophisticated dining. Cooking is modern and accomplished and relies on local ingredients.

Menu £ 45 **s**

Ellenborough Park Hotel, Southam Rd ✉ GL52 3NJ – *Northeast : 2.75 mi on B 4632* – ☎ 01242 545454 – www.ellenboroughpark.com – *dinner only and Sunday lunch* – *Closed Sunday dinner and Monday*

XXX Lumière ⓐⓒ

MODERN CUISINE · INTIMATE Friendly, personally run restaurant; its unassuming exterior concealing a long, stylish room decorated with mirrors. Seasonal dishes are modern and intricate with the occasional playful twist – desserts are often the highlight.

Menu £30/60

Town plan: AB1-z - *Clarence Par* ⊠ *GL50 3PA* – ℰ *01242 222200 (booking essential) – www.lumiere.cc – dinner only and lunch Friday-Saturday – Closed 2 weeks January, 2 weeks summer, Sunday and Monday*

XX Daffodil 🍷 ⓖ ⓐⓒ 🈸

MODERN BRITISH · BRASSERIE A delightful 1920s art deco cinema: the tables are in the old stalls, the kitchens are in the screen area and the stylish lounge is up on the balcony. A slick team serve classic brasserie dishes include steaks from the Josper grill. Buy something to take home from their deli – they even sell live lobsters!

Menu £14 (lunch and early dinner) – Carte £26/50

Town plan: A2-u - *18-20 Suffolk Par* ⊠ *GL50 2AE* – ℰ *01242 700055 – www.thedaffodil.com – Closed 25-26 December, Sunday and lunch Monday-Thursday*

XX Curry Corner 🈷 ⓐⓒ � ⇔

BANGLADESHI · NEIGHBOURHOOD Long-standing, family-run restaurant in a smart Regency townhouse. Authentic, flavoursome dishes take their influences from across Bangladesh, India and Persia. Imported spices are ground and roasted every morning.

Menu £20 (weekday dinner) – Carte £23/34

Town plan: B1-a - *133 Fairview Rd* ⊠ *GL52 2EX* – ℰ *01242 528449 – www.thecurrycorner.com – Closed 25 December, Friday lunch and Monday except bank holidays*

XX White Spoon ⓝ

MODERN BRITISH · ELEGANT Hidden away in the town centre, down a tiny passageway, is this impressive Regency building with lovely views of Cheltenham Minster. The passionate, knowledgeable chef-owner is an advocate of modern techniques and natural flavours.

Menu £12 (weekday lunch) – Carte £31/45

Town plan: B1-s - *8 Well Walk* ⊠ *GL50 3JX* – ℰ *01242 228555 – www.thewhitespoon.co.uk – Closed Sunday dinner, Monday and Tuesday*

XX Prithvi ⓐⓒ ⅄

INDIAN · DESIGN This smart Indian restaurant is a refreshing break from the norm, with its ambitious owner, designer décor, detailed service and refined cooking. Reinvented Indian and Bangladeshi dishes are presented in a sophisticated manner.

Menu £19/43 – Carte £26/36

Town plan: B1-c *37 Bath Rd* ⊠ *GL53 7HG* – ℰ *01242 226229 (booking essential at dinner) – www.prithvirestaurant.com – Closed 18 December-4 January and 1-7 August*

XX Bhoomi ⓐⓒ ⅄ ⇔

INDIAN · ROMANTIC Its name means 'earth' in the Keralan dialect and the cooking focuses on southeast India. The preparation and presentation may have been subtly modernised but the essence of each dish remains. The room has a plush, luxurious feel.

Carte £26/35

Town plan: A2-b - *52 Suffolk Rd* ⊠ *GL50 2AQ* – ℰ *01242 222010 – www.bhoomi.co.uk – Closed 25 December-9 January, Easter Sunday, Monday and lunch Tuesday-Thursday*

XX Koloshi

INDIAN · INTIMATE Former pub, set by the reservoir; now a spacious Indian restaurant, its name meaning 'water carrying vessel' in Hindi. Visual, vibrant cooking is full of flavour; good vegetarian selection. Smartly attired staff provide professional service.

Menu £ 10 (weekday lunch) – Carte £ 19/34

London Rd ⊠ GL54 4HG – Southeast : 2.5 mi on A 40 – 𝒞 01242 516400
– www.koloshi.co.uk – Closed 25-26 December and Monday

X No 131

MEATS AND GRILLS · BISTRO The columned exterior of this fine 1820s building overlooks an attractive park. Inside, original features remain but it now has a cool, contemporary style, with impressive modern artwork featuring throughout. The menu lists well-prepared, unfussy classics, with steaks cooked on the Josper grill a feature at dinner. Bedrooms are individually and tastefully furnished.

Menu £ 18 (weekday lunch) – Carte £ 29/55

11 rooms � – †£ 150/365 ††£ 150/365

Town plan: A1-z - *131 Promenade ⊠ GL50 1NW – 𝒞 01242 822939 (booking essential) – www.no131.com*

X Purslane

MODERN BRITISH · INTIMATE A stylishly minimalistic neighbourhood restaurant with relaxed, efficient service. Fresh seafood from Cornwall and Scotland is combined with good quality, locally sourced ingredients to produce interesting, original dishes.

Menu £ 26 (lunch and early dinner)/38

Town plan: B1-p - *16 Rodney Rd ⊠ GL50 1JJ – 𝒞 01242 321639*
– www.purslane-restaurant.co.uk – Closed 2 weeks January, 2 weeks August, Sunday and Monday

X The Tavern

MEATS AND GRILLS · FASHIONABLE Rustic, all-day eatery with a strong American theme, split over two floors and featuring large tables and bench seating suited to sharing. Stools set around the open kitchen make up the chef's table. Accessible menu offers the likes of sliders, chilli cheese dogs and steaks to share. Chatty service.

Menu £ 10 (weekday lunch) – Carte £ 24/36

Town plan: A1-e - *5 Royal Well Pl ⊠ GL50 3DN – 𝒞 01242 221212*
– www.thetaverncheltenham.com – Closed 25-26 December

⏚ Royal Oak

BRITISH TRADITIONAL · RUSTIC This was once owned by batting legend Tom Graveney, hence the 'Pavilion' function room. Lunch offers tasty, satisfying dishes like kedgeree, while dinner steps things up a level. Sit in the cosy bar, dark wood dining room or heated garden.

Carte £ 23/45

The Burgage, Prestbury ⊠ GL52 3DL – Northeast : 2 mi by A 435, off B 4075
– 𝒞 01242 522344 – www.royal-oak-prestbury.co.uk – Closed 25 December

at Shurdington Southwest: 3.75 mi on A46 ⊠ Cheltenham

🏠 Greenway

COUNTRY HOUSE · CLASSIC 16C ivy-clad manor house, set in 8 acres of peaceful grounds and offering pleasant views over the hills. Comfy drawing rooms and well-equipped bedrooms have a pleasant country house style. Enjoy a laid-back brasserie-style lunch on the terrace of the lovely spa. The oak-panelled restaurant offers classic dishes with modern overtones and overlooks the lily pond.

21 rooms ⊯ – †£ 139/409 ††£ 149/419 – 1 suite

⊠ GL51 4UG – 𝒞 01242 862352 – www.thegreenwayhotelandspa.com

ENGLAND

at Piff's Elm Northwest: 4 mi on A4019

🍴 **Gloucester Old Spot**   🏠 ♿ 🅿

BRITISH TRADITIONAL · RUSTIC Cosy, relaxing inn with a snug, quarry-tiled bar, a baronial dining room and open fires aplenty. Menus offer tasty, seasonal dishes, with rare breed pork a speciality. Nursery puddings. Cheery, welcoming staff.

Menu £ 14 (weekday lunch) – Carte £ 25/40

Tewkesbury Rd ⊠ GL51 9SY – ℰ 01242 680321 – www.thegloucesteroldspot.co.uk – Closed 25-26 December

GOOD TIPS!

There is evidence of Chester's Roman origins all around the city; not least, its two miles of ancient walls. It is also known for its black & white half-timbered buildings, like the Grade II listed **Chester Grosvenor** hotel – home to Simon Radley's Michelin Starred restaurant. Carnivores will appreciate the quality of the meat on offer **Upstairs at the Grill**.

CHESTER

Cheshire West and Chester – Pop. 86 011 – Regional map n° **11**-A3
▶ London 207 mi – Manchester 40 mi – Liverpool 21 mi

Hotels

🏨 **Chester Grosvenor**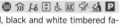

GRAND LUXURY · CLASSIC 19C hotel with a grand, black and white timbered façade, a stunning Rococo chocolate shop and a buzzy lounge serving all-day snacks. Stylish bedrooms blend traditional furnishings and modern fabrics; luxurious, marble-floored bathrooms.

80 rooms �があ – ♦£165/330 ♦♦£190/330 – 6 suites
Town plan: B2-a - *Eastgate* ⊠ *CH1 1LT* – ℰ *01244 324024*
- www.chestergrosvenor.com - Closed 25 December
❀ **Simon Radley at Chester Grosvenor • La Brasserie** – See restaurant listing

🏨 **Oddfellows**

TOWNHOUSE · DESIGN It was originally an Oddfellows Hall built in 1676 to help the poor but its name also suits its unique, quirky styling. Well-equipped, contemporary bedrooms include some duplex suites: some have circular beds and others, double roll-top baths. The garden-themed restaurant serves unfussy Mediterranean dishes.

18 rooms ☑ – ♦£100/250 ♦♦£100/250
Town plan: A2-c - *20 Lower Bridge St* ⊠ *CH1 1RS* – ℰ *01244 345454*
- www.oddfellowschester.com - Closed 25 December

🏠 **Edgar House**

TOWNHOUSE · ELEGANT A charming 17C house by the city walls, in the historic heart of Chester. The delightful garden overlooks the River Dee and the bright, modern bedrooms have raised-up beds so you can see the water. An honesty bar is housed in an old telephone box and the rustic dining room offers a traditional menu.

7 rooms – ♦£169/229 ♦♦£169/229 – ☑ £15
Town plan: B2-h - *22 City Walls* ⊠ *CH1 1SB* – ℰ *01244 347007*
- www.edgarhouse.co.uk - Closed 2 weeks Janaury

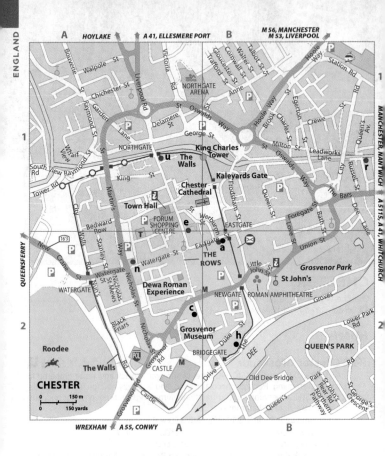

A HOYLAKE | A 41, ELLESMERE PORT | M 56, MANCHESTER M 53, LIVERPOOL | B

MANCHESTER, NANTWICH | A5115, A 41, WHITCHURCH

QUEENSFERRY

NORTHGATE ARENA
King Charles' Tower
The Walls
Kaleyards Gate
Chester Cathedral
Town Hall
FORUM SHOPPING CENTRE
EASTGATE
THE ROWS
Grosvenor Park
St John's
Dewa Roman Experience
NEWGATE ROMAN AMPHITHEATRE
WATERGATE
Black Friars
Grosvenor Museum
BRIDGEGATE
Roodee
The Walls
CHESTER CASTLE
QUEEN'S PARK
Old Dee Bridge
CHESTER
0   150 m
0   150 yards

WREXHAM | A 55, CONWY   A | B

Restaurants

XXXX Simon Radley at Chester Grosvenor

MODERN CUISINE · LUXURY Elegant restaurant with a fresh, classic feel, a stylish cocktail lounge and an impressive wine cellar. Confident cooking shows respect for ingredients, bringing together clean, clear flavours in sophisticated dishes that display interesting, innovative touches. Formal and detailed service.

→ Heritage potato with Loomswood duck ragout, fondant liver and titbits. Charred sirloin of beef with cheek bresaola, smoked onion pickles and cracked pepper. Crisp chocolate shell with apple dacquoise and calvados toffee.

Menu £ 75/99

Town plan: B2-a - Chester Grosvenor Hotel, Eastgate ⊠ CH1 1LT
- ℰ 01244 324024
- www.chestergrosvenor.com
- dinner only
- Closed 25 December, Sunday and Monday

✗✗ Upstairs at the Grill ⬥ 🍽 AC ⬥

MEATS AND GRILLS · BISTRO Smart restaurant offering prime quality steaks – including porterhouse and bone-in fillet or rib-eye; the 5 week dry-aged cuts are from premium Welsh beef. Eat in the moody cocktail bar or downstairs amongst the cow paraphernalia.

Carte £ 22/51

Town plan: A2-n - *70 Watergate St* ✉ *CH1 2LA* – ✆ *01244 344883*
– www.upstairsatthegrill.co.uk – dinner only and lunch Thursday-Sunday – Closed 25 December and 1 January

✗✗ La Brasserie 🍸 ♿ AC 🖥 P

INTERNATIONAL · BRASSERIE Parisian-style brasserie with a hand-painted glass skylight, mirrors, brass rails and colourful light fittings; sit on a leather banquette or in a booth. Refined British, French and Mediterranean dishes are cooked on the Josper grill.

Carte £ 31/52

Town plan: B2-a - *Chester Grosvenor Hotel, Eastgate* ✉ *CH1 1LT*
– ✆ 01244 324024 – www.chestergrosvenor.com – Closed 25 December

✗ Joseph Benjamin 🖥

😊 **MODERN CUISINE · BISTRO** This personally and passionately run bistro is named after its owners, Joe and Ben. The light, simple décor mirrors the style of cooking and the monthly menu offers tasty, well-judged dishes. They serve breakfast, lunch, coffee and homemade pastries and, from Thursday to Saturday, intimate candlelit dinners.

Carte £ 20/35

Town plan: A1-u - *134-140 Northgate St* ✉ *CH1 2HT* – ✆ *01244 344295 (booking essential) – www.josephbenjamin.co.uk – lunch only and dinner Thursday-Saturday – Closed 25 December-1 January and Monday*

✗ Chef's Table AC 🖥

MODERN BRITISH · SIMPLE Intimate café-cum-bistro in the city centre. They open from early 'til late, offering breakfast, snacks, sandwiches and full meals – there are no real boundaries! The vibe is pleasingly laid-back and they will do anything to help.

Menu £ 18 (lunch) – Carte £ 28/46

Town plan: A1-2-e - *4 Music Hall Passage* ✉ *CH1 2EU* – ✆ *01244 403040 (booking essential) – www.chefstablechester.co.uk – Closed Monday*

✗ Sticky Walnut

MODERN BRITISH · SIMPLE Run by a confident young team, a quirky, slightly bohemian restaurant in a residential parade of shops. Concise menus feature quality ingredients in a mix of British, French and Italian dishes; the breads and pastas are all homemade.

Carte £ 23/38

11 Charles St ✉ *CH2 3AZ – Northeast : 1 mi by Hoole Way (A 56) off Faulkner St – ✆ 01244 400400 (booking essential at dinner) – www.stickywalnut.com – Closed 25-26 December*

✗ Artichoke 🍸 🏠 ♿ AC 🖥

MODERN CUISINE · BISTRO Sit outside beside the canal towpath or inside the Victorian mill building, where you'll find original beams, bare brick walls and a contemporary cocktail bar. Cooking ranges from homemade cakes to seasonal 3 course meals.

Carte £ 20/34

Town plan: B1-r - *The Steam Mill, Steam Mill St* ✉ *CH3 5AN* – ✆ *01244 329229 – www.artichokechester.co.uk – Closed 25-26 December*

X Porta 🏠 🍽

SPANISH · TAPAS BAR Close to the city wall, behind a narrow terrace, is this cosy, characterful little tapas bar. It has no phone number or reservation system, but it does offer generous, tasty dishes which are served by a friendly young team.

Carte £ 10/21

Town plan: A1-u - *140 Northgate St* ✉ *CH1 2HT* – ✆ *01244 344295 (bookings not accepted)* – *www.portatapas.co.uk* – *dinner only* – *Closed 25 December-1 January*

CHESTERFIELD

Derbyshire – Pop. 88 483 – Regional map n° **9**-B1

▶ London 149 mi – Derby 47 mi – Manchester 44 mi

🏨 Casa 🔊 🖪 ⑤ Æ 🌮 🕍 🅿

BUSINESS · MODERN Modern hotel with 11 state-of-the-art meeting rooms and a smart bar with a heated terrace. Sizeable bedrooms are furnished in autumnal colours and come with useful extras; some of the suites have balconies and outdoor hot tubs.

100 rooms 🖵 – ♦£ 105/150 ♦♦£ 120/165

Lockoford Ln ✉ *S41 7JB* – *North : 1 mi off A 61* – ✆ *01246 245999*
– *www.casahotels.com*

Cocina – See restaurant listing

XX Cocina 🍷 ⑤ Æ 🅿

MEDITERRANEAN CUISINE · BRASSERIE Stylish hotel restaurant with a well-stocked cocktail bar. Mediterranean menus have a strong Spanish influence; try the tapas or the mature steaks from the Josper oven. Organic rare breed beef comes from the owners' 350 acre farm.

Menu £ 22 (early dinner) – Carte £ 28/47

Casa Hotel, Lockoford Ln ✉ *S41 7JB* – *North : 1 mi off A 61* – ✆ *01246 245999*
– *www.casahotels.com* – *dinner only and Sunday lunch*

CHEW MAGNA

Bath and North East Somerset – Pop. 1 149 – Regional map n° **2**-C2

▶ London 128 mi – Bristol 9 mi – Cardiff 52 mi

X Salt & Malt ⇐ 🏠 ⑤ Æ 🔲 🅿

SEAFOOD · FRIENDLY Smart lakeside eatery with lovely views over the water. They're open all day for breakfast, coffee and cakes, light lunches and cream teas. The evening menu steps things up a gear; fish and chips are the focus and the thing to go for.

Carte £ 14/29

Walley Ln, Chew Stoke ✉ *BS40 8TF* – *South : 1.25 mi by Bishop Sutton rd and Denny Rd* – ✆ *01275 333345* – *www.saltmalt.com* – *Closed Sunday dinner*

🍴 Pony & Trap (Josh Eggleton) 🍴 🏠 🅿

🕸 **MODERN BRITISH · COSY** A cosy whitewashed pub with a characterful bar featuring church pews and an old range – and superb countryside views from the rustic dining room and terrace. Twice-daily menu of extremely fresh, seasonal produce, including locally sourced, hung and smoked meats and fish. Classical cooking with bold flavours.

➜ Chargrilled pigeon breast with bresaola, carrot, walnut and apple. 47-day aged South Devon rib-eye with grilled bone marrow and chips. Sticky ale pudding with salted caramel sauce and stout ice cream.

Carte £ 25/44

Knowle Hill, New Town ✉ *BS40 8TQ* – *South : 1.25 mi on Bishop Sutton rd*
– ✆ *01275 332627 (booking essential)* – *www.theponyandtrap.co.uk* – *Closed 25 December, dinner 26, 31 December and 1 January, Monday except December and bank holidays*

CHICHESTER

ENGLAND

West Sussex – Pop. 28 657 – Regional map n° **4**-C2
▶ London 69 mi – Brighton 31 mi – Portsmouth 18 mi

🏠 Chichester Harbour   ⌂ ⊡ ⅍ ᴬ 🅿

BUSINESS · MODERN Grade II listed former home to one of Nelson's men. Some impressive Georgian features remain, including a cantilevered wrought iron stair-case. Stylish, up-to-date bedrooms and a spacious, contemporary bar. Airy brasse-rie offers a modern European menu, with meat and game from the nearby estate.
37 rooms ☲ – †£ 99/190 ††£ 125/300
57 North St ✉ PO19 1NH – ℰ 01243 778000 – www.theshiphotel.net

✗ Amelie and Friends   🛖

MODERN CUISINE · SIMPLE City centre brasserie-style restaurant with contem-porary white décor; sit in the smaller room overlooking the walled garden ter-race. The cheerful, efficient team serve everything from brasserie classics through to Asian-inspired dishes.
Carte £ 24/35
31 North St ✉ PO19 1LY – ℰ 01243 771444 (booking essential at dinner)
– www.amelieandfriends.com – Closed 25-26 December, 1 January and Sunday dinner

at Mid Lavant North: 2 mi on A286

🏠 Rooks Hill   ⅍ 🅿

COUNTRY HOUSE · PERSONALISED Grade II listed house with a pleasant view across to the Goodwood estate. Relax on the charming courtyard terrace or next to the wood burner in the cosy sitting room. Individually decorated bed-rooms have contemporary touches.
4 rooms ☲ – †£ 95/125 ††£ 115/175
Lavant Rd ✉ PO18 0BQ – ℰ 01243 528400 – www.rookshill.co.uk

🍽 Earl of March   🛖 ✿ 🅿

TRADITIONAL CUISINE · PUB This 18C inn offers the perfect blend of contempo-rary styling and relaxed country character. Good quality seasonal produce is showcased in British-based dishes. Find a spot on the terrace to take in the amazing South Downs views.
Menu £ 22 (lunch and early dinner) – Carte £ 30/40
✉ PO18 0BQ – ℰ 01243 533993 – www.theearlofmarch.com

An important business lunch or dinner with friends?
The symbol ✿ indicates restaurants with private rooms.

at Tangmere East: 2 mi by A27 ✉ Chichester

✗✗ Cassons   🅿

MODERN CUISINE · RUSTIC Passionately run restaurant with exposed brick, wooden beams and a rustic feel. Boldly flavoured dishes are generously propor-tioned. Cooking is classically based but employs modern techniques. The regular gourmet evenings are a hit.
Menu £ 39 (dinner) – Carte lunch £ 39/45
Arundel Rd ✉ PO18 0DU – Northwest : 0.25 mi off A 27 (westbound)
– ℰ 01243 773294 – www.cassonsrestaurant.co.uk
– Closed 25-30 December, Tuesday lunch, Sunday dinner and Monday

at West Ashling Northwest: 4.5 mi by B2178 and B2146

⊨ Richmond Arms ⇔ 🏠 P

INTERNATIONAL · RUSTIC Appealing, laid-back country pub opposite a duck pond in a lovely little village. The menu offers an appealing mix, from freshly sliced hams and local steaks to game from the family estate in Anglesey; many meats are cooked on the rotisserie or the Japanese robata grill. Two luxurious bedrooms are above.

Carte £ 22/44

2 rooms ♙ – ♦£ 115/145 ♦♦£ 115/145

Mill Rd ✉ PO18 8EA – ℰ 01243 572046 – www.therichmondarms.co.uk – Closed Christmas-New Year, last week July, first week November, Sunday dinner, Monday and Tuesday

at Funtington Northwest: 4.75 mi by B2178 on B2146✉ Chichester

XX Hallidays P

CLASSIC CUISINE · INTIMATE Characterful thatched cottage comprising a series of interconnecting rooms with low beams. The chef knows a thing or two about sourcing good ingredients and his menu changes regularly. Cooking is skilful and classically based.

Menu £ 24 (weekday lunch)/37 – Carte lunch £ 31/41

Watery Ln ✉ PO18 9LF – ℰ 01243 575331 – www.hallidays.info.co.uk – Closed 2 weeks August, 1 week March, 1 week Christmas-New Year, Saturday lunch, Sunday dinner, Monday and Tuesday

CHIDDINGFOLD

Surrey – Pop. 2 211 – Regional map n° **4**-C2
▶ London 47 mi – Guildford 10 mi – Brighton 62 mi

⊨ Swan Inn ⇔ 🏠 & AC P

MODERN CUISINE · INN It might be over 200 years old but the Swan has a modern feel and its 11 comfy bedrooms are equally stylish. The extensive menu changes a little each day and offers a mix of pub and restaurant style dishes. Unsurprisingly, on sunny days, the stepped rear terrace is a popular spot.

Carte £ 22/45

11 rooms ♙ – ♦£ 74/195 ♦♦£ 74/195

Petworth Rd ✉ GU8 4TY – ℰ 01428 684688 – www.theswaninnchiddingfold.com

CHIEVELEY

West Berkshire – Regional map n° **6**-B3
▶ London 60 mi – Newbury 5 mi – Swindon 25 mi

⊨ Crab & Boar ⇔ 🏠 & P

TRADITIONAL BRITISH · INN A pretty 17C pub with a thatch and red tile roof, leaded windows and a lovely terrace. British dishes are rooted in tradition yet have a modern edge; go for one of the game or seafood specials. Sunday lunch is an event and the Garden Kitchen offers outside snacks. Many of the stylish bedrooms have hot tubs.

Carte £ 26/45

14 rooms ♙ – ♦£ 110/210 ♦♦£ 110/210

Wantage Rd ✉ RG20 8UE – West : 2.5 mi by School Rd on B 4494 – ℰ 01635 247550 – www.crabandboar.com

CHILCOMPTON

Somerset – Pop. 2 062 – Regional map n° **4**-C2
▶ London 125 mi – Taunton 45 mi – Bristol 16 mi

ENGLAND

Redan Inn

MODERN BRITISH · PUB This smartly refurbished pub displays an impressive selection of old curios. The concise weekly menu offers an enticing mix of accomplished dishes. They cure their own meats, make their own sausages and use apples from the garden for their chutney. Service is relaxed and engaging and bedrooms are stylish.

Menu £ 15/20 – Carte £ 23/44

8 rooms ⌂ – †£ 80/160 ††£ 90/170

Fry's Well ⊠ BA3 4HA – ℰ 01761 258560 – www.theredaninn.co.uk

CHILLATON – Devon → See Tavistock

CHILLINGTON

Devon – Regional map n° **1**-C3

▶ London 217 mi – Plymouth 26 mi – Torquay 22 mi

whitehouse

COUNTRY HOUSE · CONTEMPORARY Attractive Georgian house run in a relaxed manner. Stylish bedrooms are boldly decorated and feature a mix of modern and retro furnishings; all have heavy handmade beds and smart bathrooms. The breakfast room overlooks the gardens.

6 rooms ⌂ – †£ 190/260 ††£ 190/260

⊠ TQ7 2JX – ℰ 01548 580505 – www.whitehousedevon.com

CHINNOR

Oxfordshire – Pop. 5 473 – Regional map n° **6**-C2

▶ London 45 mi – Oxford 19 mi – Birmingham 88 mi

at Sprigg's Alley Southeast: 2.5 mi by Bledlow Ridge rd⊠ Chinnor

Sir Charles Napier

MODERN BRITISH · COSY An attractive flint pub in a small hillside hamlet, with a hint of eccentricity in its décor. In summer, relax on the pleasant terrace or in the delightful gardens; in winter, sit beside the log fire. Boldly flavoured dishes are prepared with skill and capture flavours to their full.

→ Diver-caught scallops with brawn croquette, apple and beurre noisette. Goosnargh duck with confit leg terrine, salsify and sweet wine jus. Rhubarb crumble soufflé with rhubarb & ginger ice cream.

Menu £ 20 (weekdays) – Carte £ 39/56

Sprigs Holly ⊠ OX39 4BX – ℰ 01494 483011 (booking advisable)
– www.sircharlesnapier.co.uk – Closed 24-26 December, Sunday dinner
and Monday except bank holidays

CHIPPING CAMPDEN

Gloucestershire – Pop. 2 037 – Regional map n° **2**-D1

▶ London 93 mi – Gloucester 35 mi – Birmingham 44 mi

Cotswold House H. and Spa

TOWNHOUSE · CONTEMPORARY A set of stylish Regency townhouses with lovely gardens, boldly decorated lounges hung with eclectic modern art, and a fine spiral staircase winding upwards towards luxurious modern bedrooms. Eat in the laid-back grill restaurant.

25 rooms ⌂ – †£ 100/250 ††£ 150/500 – 3 suites

The Square ⊠ GL55 6AN – ℰ 01386 840330 – www.cotswoldhouse.com

Dining Room – See restaurant listing

🏠 Kings ⚙ 🅿

TOWNHOUSE · CLASSIC Beautiful Cotswold stone townhouse with a stylish boutique interior. Bedrooms in the main house mix antiques with modern facilities – some boast sleigh beds; rooms in the cottage at the end of the garden are more up-to-date.

18 rooms ☑ – ♦£ 95/229 ♦♦£ 105/305

The Square ✉ *GL55 6AW –* ☏ *01386 840256 – www.kingscampden.co.uk*
Kings – See restaurant listing

🏠 Seymour House ⚙ 🅿

TOWNHOUSE · PERSONALISED Welcoming Cotswold stone house with early 18C origins, a lovely garden and a pretty breakfast terrace. It's tastefully furnished throughout, with a classical, understated style; fine furnishings, artwork and antiques feature.

5 rooms ☑ – ♦£ 90 ♦♦£ 100/150

High St ✉ *GL55 6AG –* ☏ *01386 840064 – www.seymourhousebandb.co.uk*
– Closed Christmas-New Year

✗✗ Kings ⚙ 🏠 🖥 ↻ 🅿

MODERN CUISINE · RUSTIC An appealing, rustic restaurant in a stylish boutique townhouse. Exposed stone walls, wooden beams and a large inglenook fireplace feature. Modern British menus use top quality ingredients and dishes are refined and flavoursome.

Menu £ 15/33

Kings Hotel, The Square ✉ *GL55 6AW –* ☏ *01386 840256*
– www.kingscampden.co.uk

✗ Chef"s Dozen 🏠

MODERN BRITISH · FRIENDLY This intimate restaurant and shady terrace sit close to the square and are run by a local chef with a passion for wild and organic ingredients. Dishes are modern, creative and attractive; this is inspired field-to-fork cooking.

Menu £ 28 (weekdays)/45

Island House, High St ✉ *GL55 6AL –* ☏ *01386 840598 (booking advisable)*
– www.thechefsdozen.co.uk – dinner only and lunch Friday-Saturday – Closed 23 January-11 February, 25-26 December, Sunday and Monday

✗ Dining Room ⚙ 🏠 AC ↻ 🅿

TRADITIONAL CUISINE · BISTRO This relaxed, informal restaurant is found within a Regency townhouse hotel. Open all day, it serves breakfast and afternoon tea as well as an appealing, bistro-style menu of modern dishes including steaks, burgers and charcuterie.

Menu £ 17 (weekday lunch) – Carte £ 27/49

Cotswold House Hotel and Spa, The Square ✉ *GL55 6AN –* ☏ *01386 840330*
– www.cotswoldhouse.com

at Ebrington East: 2 mi by B4035

🏠 Ebrington Arms ⇦ ⚙ 🏠 🅿

MODERN CUISINE · COSY Set in a charming chocolate box village, a proper village local with a beamed, flag-floored bar at its hub. Choose from pub classics on the blackboard or more elaborate dishes on the à la carte. Be sure to try one of the ales brewed to their own recipe. Bedrooms have country views and thoughtful extras.

Carte £ 26/41

5 rooms ☑ – ♦£ 100/140 ♦♦£ 110/150

✉ *GL55 6NH –* ☏ *01386 593223 – www.thebringtonarms.co.uk – Closed 25 December*

at Weston-sub-Edge Northwest : 3 mi. by B 4081 and B 4035 on B 4632

🏠 Seagrave Arms   ⇦ 🛏 🅿

MODERN BRITISH · PUB A handsome building of Cotswold stone, with a cosy, fire-warmed bar and two traditional dining rooms. Attractively presented, refined modern dishes use well-judged combinations of ingredients from the local larder. Bedrooms are classic in style; opt for the suite, with its spacious bathroom and roll-top bath.

Menu £ 15 (lunch and early dinner) – Carte £ 30/42

8 rooms ☑ – ♥£ 70/155 ♥♥£ 80/165

Friday St ⊠ GL55 6QH – ℰ 01386 840192 – www.seagravearms.co.uk

CHIPPING NORTON

Oxfordshire – Pop. 5 719 – Regional map n° **6**-A1

▶ London 77 mi – Oxford 22 mi – Stow-on-the-Wold 9 mi

❌ Wild Thyme   ⇦

TRADITIONAL BRITISH · COSY A cosy, keenly run restaurant with rustic tables; No. 10, in the window, is the best. Wholesome regional British cooking has Mediterranean influences, with tasty homemade breads and game in season. Simply appointed bedrooms; the friendly owners go out of their way to ensure their guests' comfort.

Menu £ 25 (weekdays)/40

3 rooms ☑ – ♥£ 65/75 ♥♥£ 75/95

10 New St ⊠ OX7 5LJ – ℰ 01608 645060 (booking advisable) – www.wildthymerestaurant.co.uk – Closed first week January, Sunday and Monday

CHIPPING ONGAR

Essex – Pop. 6 093 – Regional map n° **7**-B2

▶ London 28 mi – Chelmsford 12 mi – Harlow 10 mi

❌❌ Smith's   🅰🅲 🅿

SEAFOOD · BRASSERIE Long-standing, locally acclaimed seafood restaurant with a buzzy atmosphere. The à la carte and extensive daily set menu offer dishes ranging from Cornish squid to Scottish smoked salmon. Lobster, cooked several ways, is a speciality.

Menu £ 27/30 – Carte £ 32/67

Fyfield Rd ⊠ CM5 0AL – ℰ 01277 365578 (booking essential) – www.smithsrestaurants.com – Closed 25-26 December 1 January and Monday lunch

CHIPSTEAD

Kent – Regional map n° **5**-B1

▶ London 27 mi – Maidstone 37 mi – Guildford 66 mi

🏠 George & Dragon   🍴 🛏 ↺ 🅿

MODERN BRITISH · PUB Superbly set, 450 year old inn with a beamed bar and a wonky-floored upstairs dining room. Delightful garden with terrace and children's play area. The menu is a roll call of seasonal English classics; herbs and salad are home-grown.

Carte £ 20/39

39 High St ⊠ TN13 2RW – ℰ 01732 779019 – www.georgeanddragonchipstead.com

CHOBHAM

Surrey – Pop. 2 771 – Regional map n° **4**-C1

▶ London 32 mi – Guildford 16 mi – Birmingham 127 mi

✗✗✗ Stovell's   🏠 AC ♿ **P**

MODERN BRITISH · INTIMATE The owner of this characterful 16C farmhouse has put Chobham firmly on the culinary map. Creative, often intricate dishes use top quality ingredients. Highlights include the bespoke tasting menu and dishes from the wood-fired grill.

Menu £ 18 (weekday lunch)/45

125 Windsor Rd ⊠ GU24 8QS – North : 0.75 mi on B 383 – ☎ 01276 858000
(booking essential) – www.stovells.com – Closed first 2 weeks January,
21-23 August, 26-27 December, Saturday lunch, Sunday dinner and Monday

CHOLMONDELEY

Cheshire East – Regional map n° **11**-A3

▶ London 178 mi – Chester 26 mi – Manchester 80 mi

🍴 Cholmondeley Arms   ⇦ 🏠 🏠 🔋 **P**

TRADITIONAL BRITISH · RUSTIC The eponymous estate's old schoolhouse, with high, vaulted ceilings, large windows and roaring fires. Modern pub favourites might include calves' liver or homemade lamb faggots. Gin lovers will be in clover with more than 200 from which to choose. The 6 comfy bedrooms are in the Old Headmaster's House.

Carte £ 22/34

6 rooms ♀ – ♦£ 65/85 ♦♦£ 85/100

Wrenbury Rd ⊠ SY14 8HN – ☎ 01829 720300 – www.cholmondeleyarms.co.uk

CHRISTCHURCH

Dorset – Pop. 54 210 – Regional map n° **2**-D3

▶ London 111 mi – Dorchester 58 mi – Bournemouth 6 mi

🏨 Christchurch Harbour   🏖 ⇦ 🏠 🖼 ⑨ 🐎 ⮕ ♿ AC ⚡ 🔋 **P**

BUSINESS · CONTEMPORARY Don't be fooled by the unassuming exterior; inside is a cool, chic hotel with a smart basement spa – its waterside location reflected in the modern, nautical-inspired décor. Some bedrooms have waterfront terraces or balconies. Both of the restaurants open onto delightful terraces with far-reaching views.

64 rooms ♀ – ♦£ 130/179 ♦♦£ 130/179

95 Mudeford ⊠ BH23 3NT – East : 2 mi by B 3059 – ☎ 01202 483434
– www.christchurch-harbour-hotel.co.uk

Jetty – See restaurant listing

🏨 Captain's Club   🏖 ⇦ 🏠 ⑨ 🐎 ⮕ ♿ AC ⚡ **P**

BUSINESS · CONTEMPORARY Striking modern building with art deco and nautical influences, set in a lovely riverside spot – floor to ceiling windows offer fantastic views. Bedrooms are sleek and contemporary; some are three-roomed suites. The restaurant offers all-day menus. Relax in the stylish spa or out on the water in their boat.

29 rooms ♀ – ♦£ 179/269 ♦♦£ 199/289 – 12 suites

Wick Ferry, Wick Ln ⊠ BH23 1HU – ☎ 01202 475111 – www.captainsclubhotel.com

🏠 Kings Arms   ⮕ ♿ ⚡ 🔋 **P**

TOWNHOUSE · GRAND LUXURY This lovingly restored Georgian inn stands opposite the bowling green and castle ruins, and has been given a smart modern makeover. Guest areas have a chic yet characterful feel and the boutique-style bedrooms are well-appointed.

20 rooms (dinner included) ♀ – ♦£ 68/119 ♦♦£ 75/169

18 Castle St ⊠ BH23 1DT – ☎ 01202 588933 – www.thekings-christchurch.co.uk

Kings Arms – See restaurant listing

🏠 Druid House 🛏 🗟 P

FAMILY · PERSONALISED Hidden behind an unassuming exterior, a bright, well-kept house that's passionately run and great value for money. Bedrooms are bright and modern; some of those in the newer wing open out onto a small terrace. Excellent breakfasts include a buffet and hot specials such as muffins with poached eggs and bacon.

10 rooms ⌂ – †£ 98/135 ††£ 98/155

26 Sopers Ln ⊠ BH23 1JE – ℰ 01202 485615 – www.druid-house.co.uk

XX Splinters ✧

CLASSIC CUISINE · BISTRO A very traditional family-run restaurant, named after the splinters the carpenters got when building the booths! Choose from several cosy, characterful rooms. Cooking is wholesome and classical with rich, tasty sauces a feature.

Menu £ 20 (weekday dinner) – Carte £ 22/46

12 Church St ⊠ BH23 1BW – ℰ 01202 483454 – www.splinters.uk.com
– Closed 1-13 January, Sunday and Monday

XX Jetty ≤ 🛆 ᬉ 🆎 P

MODERN BRITISH · DESIGN Set within the grounds of the Christchurch Harbour hotel, this contemporary, eco-friendly restaurant offers fantastic water views. Appealing menus reflect what's available locally, with fish from nearby waters and game from the forest.

Menu £ 25 (weekdays) – Carte £ 32/70

Christchurch Harbour Hotel, 95 Mudeford ⊠ BH23 3NT – East : 2 mi by B 3059
– ℰ 01202 400950 – www.thejetty.co.uk

X Kings Arms ᬉ 🆎 ✧

TRADITIONAL BRITISH · BRASSERIE Smart hotel brasserie offering gutsy cooking. The £ 15 weekly menu is made up of produce sourced from within 15 miles; Friday is 'Fizz 'n' Chips' night and they also offer afternoon tea. Start with a cocktail in the stylish bar.

Menu £ 15 (lunch and early dinner) – Carte £ 24/40

Kings Arms Hotel, 18 Castle St ⊠ BH23 1DT – ℰ 01202 588933
– www.thekings-christchurch.co.uk

CHURCHILL

Oxfordshire – Pop. 502 – Regional map n° **6**-A1

▶ London 79 mi – Oxford 23 mi – Cheltenham 29 mi

🍺 Chequers 🛆 ᬉ ✧ P

TRADITIONAL CUISINE · PUB Welcoming sandstone pub in the heart of the village; it's a vital part of the community and the owners have got the formula just right. The bar is stocked with local ales; gutsy, traditional dishes include steaks cooked on the Josper grill.

Menu £ 15 (weekday lunch) – Carte £ 21/40

Church Rd ⊠ OX7 6NJ – ℰ 01608 659393 – www.thechequerschurchill.com
– Closed 25 December

CHURCH ENSTONE

Oxfordshire – Regional map n° **6**-B1

▶ London 72 mi – Oxford 38 mi – Banbury 13 mi

🍺 Crown Inn 🛆

TRADITIONAL BRITISH · PUB 17C inn set among pretty stone houses in a picturesque village. Sit in the slate-floored conservatory, the beamed dining room or the rustic bar. Meat, fruit and veg come from local farms; seafood is a speciality, as is the steak pie.

Menu £ 19 (weekdays) – Carte £ 20/34

Mill Ln ⊠ OX7 4NN – ℰ 01608 677262 – www.crowninnenstone.co.uk – Closed
25-26 December, 1 January and Sunday dinner

CIRENCESTER

Gloucestershire – Pop. 16 325 – Regional map n° **2**-D1

▶ London 97 mi – Gloucester 19 mi – Oxford 37 mi

Kings Head

HISTORIC · DESIGN A former coaching inn built from local stone, set overlooking the Market Place. Original features attest to its age but it's now a stylish, modern hotel offering spacious bedrooms with all the latest mod cons. The popular restaurant offers hearty classics and Cotswold beef cooked on the Robata grill.

45 rooms – ♥£ 110/255 ♥♥£ 110/255 – ☑ £ 18

24 Market Pl ✉ GL7 2NR – ✆ 01285 700900 – www.kingshead-hotel.co.uk

No 12

TOWNHOUSE · PERSONALISED This 16C townhouse provides plenty of contrasts: its Georgian façade hides a modern interior and the large bedrooms blend stylish furnishings with original features. In summer, breakfast on organic products in the delightful garden.

4 rooms ☑ – ♥£ 100/110 ♥♥£ 130/150

12 Park St ✉ GL7 2BW – ✆ 01285 640232 – www.no12cirencester.co.uk

Old Brewhouse

TOWNHOUSE · PERSONALISED 17C former brewhouse in busy central spot, with a characterful cluttered interior and two stone-walled breakfast rooms. Choose between cottage-style bedrooms – most with wrought iron beds – or more modern rooms set around a small courtyard.

9 rooms ☑ – ♥£ 75/90 ♥♥£ 85/100

7 London Rd ✉ GL7 2PU – ✆ 01285 656099 – www.theoldbrewhouse.com
– Closed 24 December-2 January

Made by Bob

MEDITERRANEAN CUISINE · FASHIONABLE The name says it all: Bob makes most of the products himself – be it for the informal eatery or the crammed deli – and the rest of the ingredients are organic and locally sourced. Service is bright and breezy, and the flexible daily menus are appealing. If you can't find a seat, they also do takeaway.

Carte £ 25/40

The Corn Hall, 26 Market Pl ✉ GL7 2NY – ✆ 01285 641818 (bookings not accepted)
– www.foodmadebybob.com – lunch only and dinner Thursday-Friday – Closed
25-26 December, 1 January and Sunday

Jesse's Bistro

TRADITIONAL CUISINE · COSY This rustic bistro is hidden away in a little courtyard behind the Jesse Smith butcher's shop. Local meat and veg feature alongside Cornish fish and good use is made of the wood-fired oven. Beams and flagstones give it a cosy feel.

Menu £ 20 (weekday lunch) – Carte £ 29/50

14 Blackjack St ✉ GL7 2AA – ✆ 01285 641497 – www.jessesbistro.co.uk – Closed
Monday dinner and Sunday

at Barnsley Northeast: 4 mi by A429 on B4425 ✉ Cirencester

Barnsley House

HISTORIC · GRAND LUXURY 17C Cotswold manor house with a wonderfully relaxed vibe, set in the midst of beautiful gardens styled by Rosemary Verey. A very stylish interior blends original features with modern touches, from the open-fired lounges to the chic bedrooms; there's also a spa and even a cinema in the grounds.

18 rooms ☑ – ♥£ 280/550 ♥♥£ 300/650 – 8 suites

✉ GL7 5EE – ✆ 01285 740000 – www.barnsleyhouse.com

The Potager – See restaurant listing

✗✗ The Potager

MEDITERRANEAN CUISINE · FASHIONABLE Understated hotel restaurant with a pleasant garden outlook and a laid-back feel. Influencing more than just the name, the kitchen gardens inform what's on the menu each day. Unfussy cooking has Mediterranean overtones; don't miss the freshly baked breads with herb-infused oils and salsa verde.

Carte £ 25/53

Barnsley House Hotel, ✉ GL7 5EE – ℰ 01285 740000 – www.barnsleyhouse.com

🍴 Village Pub

TRADITIONAL BRITISH · DESIGN With an interior straight out of any country homes magazine, this place has the cosy, open-fired, village pub vibe down to a tee. It has four intimate rooms and a carefully manicured terrace. Appealing modern British dishes and irresistible nibbles feature locally sourced meats, charcuterie from Highgrove and comforting desserts. Bedrooms are tastefully styled.

Carte £ 23/40

6 rooms ☲ – †£ 89/159 ††£ 99/169
✉ GL7 5EF – ℰ 01285 740421 (booking essential) – www.thevillagepub.co.uk

at Sapperton West: 5 mi by A419 ✉ Cirencester

🍴 The Bell

TRADITIONAL CUISINE · RUSTIC Charming and characterful Cotswold pub with flagged floors, exposed stone, an abundance of beams and warming log fires. Menus offer the expected burger or fish and chips, as well as dishes which show off more of the chef's skills.

Carte £ 23/39

✉ GL7 6LE – ℰ 01285 760298 – www.bellsapperton.co.uk – Closed 25 December and Sunday dinner

CLANFIELD

Oxfordshire – Pop. 1 709 – Regional map n° **6**-A2
▶ London 75 mi – Oxford 24 mi – Bristol 60 mi

🏨 Cotswold Plough

TRADITIONAL · CLASSIC Charming 16C wool merchant's house in the heart of a pretty village, with an antique-furnished lounge and a characterful bar boasting two open fires and over 180 types of gin. Bedrooms in the main house are cosy with mullioned windows; those in the extension are more spacious. 3 of the rooms have four-posters.

11 rooms ☲ – †£ 89/120 ††£ 115/175
Bourton Rd ✉ OX18 2RB – on A 4095 – ℰ 01367 810222
– www.cotswoldploughhotel.com – Closed 24-27 December
Cotswold Plough – See restaurant listing

✗✗ Cotswold Plough

TRADITIONAL BRITISH · FRIENDLY Set within a 16C hotel, a lovely three-roomed restaurant with beamed ceilings, relaxed service and a comfortingly traditional feel. Classical menus provide plenty of appeal and all of the wines are available by the glass or carafe.

Carte £ 23/45

Cotswold Plough Hotel, Bourton Rd ✉ OX18 2RB – on A 4095 – ℰ 01367 810222
– www.cotswoldploughhotel.com – Closed 24-27 December

CLAVERING

Essex – Pop. 882 – Regional map n° **7**-B2
▶ London 44 mi – Colchester 44 mi – Cambridge 25 mi

🍴 **Cricketers**   ⇐ 🛋 🚗 **P**

INTERNATIONAL · INN Deceptively spacious pub set close to the cricket pitch in a sleepy village. Bread is baked daily, specials are chalked on a board above the fire and the cooking mixes British and Italian influences. The owners' son, Jamie Oliver, supplies fruit, veg and herbs from his organic garden. Bedrooms are welcoming.
Carte £ 22/42

20 rooms 🖵 – 🛏£ 70/75 🛏🛏£ 95/135

✉ CB11 4QT – ✆ 01799 550442 (booking essential) – www.thecricketers.co.uk
– Closed 25-26 December

CLEARWELL
Gloucestershire – Regional map n° **2**-C1
🚇 London 138 mi – Gloucester 22 mi – Bristol 31 mi

🏠 **Tudor Farmhouse**   ⇧ 🛋 🛁 **P**

COUNTRY HOUSE · CONTEMPORARY A group of converted farm buildings in the heart of the Forest of Dean. Two cosy dining rooms serving carefully prepared, interesting dishes are found in the old farmhouse and, above them, characterful bedrooms with old beams and wonky floors. More modern bedrooms are housed in two of the outbuildings.

20 rooms 🖵 – 🛏£ 100/230 🛏🛏£ 100/230 – 5 suites

High St ✉ GL16 8JS – ✆ 01594 833046 – www.tudorfarmhousehotel.co.uk

CLEESTANTON – Shropshire → See Ludlow

CLEY-NEXT-THE-SEA – Norfolk → See Blakeney

CLIFTON – Cumbria → See Penrith

CLIPSHAM
Rutland – Pop. 120 – Regional map n° **9**-C2
🚇 London 101 mi – Leicester 35 mi – Nottingham 38 mi

🍴 **Olive Branch & Beech House**   ⇐ 🚗 🛁 🎬 **P**

TRADITIONAL BRITISH · PUB Characterful village pub made up of a series of small rooms which feature open fires and exposed beams. The selection of rustic British dishes changes daily, reflecting the seasons and keeping things fiercely local. These are accompanied by real ales, homemade lemonade and vodka made from hedgerow berries. Bedrooms, across the road, are cosy and thoughtfully finished.
Menu £ 19/33 – Carte £ 27/46

6 rooms 🖵 – 🛏£ 98/165 🛏🛏£ 115/195

Main St ✉ LE15 7SH – ✆ 01780 410355 (booking essential)
– www.theolivebranchpub.com

CLOVELLY
Devon – Pop. 439 – Regional map n° **1**-B1
🚇 London 241 mi – Exeter 52 mi – Penzance 92 mi

🏠 **Red Lion**   ⇧ ⇐ 🚗 **P**

TRADITIONAL · COSY Traditional inn set in a wonderful location under the cliffs, right on the harbourfront. Good-sized, comfortable bedrooms all have sea views; the newest and largest rooms are in the converted sail loft. Enjoy classic dishes and a superb vista in the dining room; lighter snacks are served in the bar.

17 rooms 🖵 – 🛏£ 131/165 🛏🛏£ 131/165

The Quay ✉ EX39 5TF – ✆ 01237 431237 – www.stayatclovelly.co.uk/red-lion

CLYST HYDON
Devon – Regional map n° **1**-D2
🚇 London 188 mi – Exeter 12 mi – Bristol 74 mi

Five Bells Inn

TRADITIONAL BRITISH · PUB Pretty, thatched, Grade II listed pub, deep in the Devon countryside. Experienced chef uses the finest local ingredients in well-balanced dishes with real clarity of flavour. Blackboard of pub favourites and a more creative à la carte. Set lunch menu is excellent value for money. Smooth, friendly service.

Menu £15 (weekday lunch) – Carte £30/42

✉ EX15 2NT – West : 0.5 mi on Clyst St Lawrence rd – ☏ 01884 277288 (bookings advisable at dinner) – www.fivebells.uk.com

COGGESHALL

Essex – Pop. 3 919 – Regional map n° **7**-C2

▶ London 49 mi – Colchester 9 mi – Cambridge 49 mi

XX Ranfield's Brasserie

INTERNATIONAL · BRASSERIE Characterful 16C building on the market square; its walls packed with pictures and prints. Globally-influenced dishes are made up of lots of different ingredients. Service is warm and welcoming and it has a loyal local following.

Menu £13 (lunch and early dinner)/55 – Carte £29/43

4-6 Stoneham St ✉ CO6 1TT – ☏ 01376 561453 – www.ranfieldsbrasserie.co.uk
– Closed first week January

at Pattiswick Northwest: 3 mi by A120 (Braintree Rd) ✉ Coggeshall

Compasses at Pattiswick

TRADITIONAL BRITISH · PUB Remote pub with far-reaching views; make the most of these with a seat in the garden. Smart, spacious interior with open fires, chatty staff and a warm, relaxing feel. Wide-ranging menu of traditional English dishes and nursery puddings.

Carte £23/39

Compasses Rd ✉ CM77 8BG – ☏ 01376 561322 – www.thecompassespattiswick.co.uk

COLCHESTER

Essex – Pop. 119 441 – Regional map n° **7**-D2

▶ London 52 mi – Cambridge 48 mi – Ipswich 18 mi

Greyfriars

HISTORIC · ELEGANT It took five years to convert this former monastery into the fine hotel that it is today. Stunning public areas include beautiful rooms hung with Murano chandeliers, and the bedrooms are a curious mix of the simple and the ostentatious. Dine on complex dishes in the old chapel, under stained glass windows.

26 rooms – ♦£120 ♦♦£140/350 – 17 suites

High St ✉ CO1 1UG – ☏ 01206 575913 – www.greyfriarscolchester.co.uk

XX Memoirs

MODERN BRITISH · ELEGANT The town's old Victorian library is a grand, impressive place, with high beamed ceilings, wood-panelled walls and a big stone tablet depicting the Great Exhibition of 1853. The equally large menu of classics has Portuguese touches.

Menu £17/19 (weekdays) – Carte £25/85

65 West Stockwell St ✉ CO1 1HE – ☏ 01206 562400
– www.memoirscolchester.co.uk – Closed Sunday

X Church Street Tavern

TRADITIONAL BRITISH · BRASSERIE Modern brasserie run in a relaxed, efficient manner. The trendy, shabby-chic bar serves cocktails and light bites. The upstairs restaurant offers British classics with Mediterranean influences; the early evening menu is great value.

Menu £20 (lunch and early dinner) – Carte £19/40

3 Church St ✉ CO1 1NF – ☏ 01206 564325 – www.churchstreettavern.co.uk
– Closed 25-26 December, first week January, Sunday dinner, Monday and Tuesday

COLERNE – Wiltshire ➜ See Bath

COLSTON BASSETT
Nottinghamshire – Pop. 239 – Regional map n° **9**-B2
▶ London 129 mi – Nottingham 15 mi – Sheffield 51 mi

🍴 The Martins Arms 🚗 🏡 **P**
TRADITIONAL CUISINE · **CHIC** Creeper-clad pub in a charming village, with a cosy, fire-lit bar and period furnished dining rooms. The menu has a meaty, masculine base, with a mix of classical and more modern dishes, and plenty of local game in season.
Carte £ 32/53
School Ln ✉ *NG12 3FD – ℰ 01949 81361 – www.themartinsarms.co.uk – Closed dinner 25 December*

COLYFORD
Devon – Pop. 563 – Regional map n° **1**-D2
▶ London 168 mi – Exeter 21 mi – Taunton 30 mi

🏠 Swallows Eaves ☆ 🚗 🛁 **P**
TRADITIONAL · **PERSONALISED** Smart creamwashed house clad with wisteria, located in the heart of a pretty village. Bright bedrooms come with books, wi-fi and views over the gardens or the Axe Valley. Relax in the comfy lounge or out on the terrace. The light, airy restaurant serves traditional dishes of locally sourced produce.
7 rooms 🖵 – ♦£ 85/95 ♦♦£ 115/145
Swan Hill Rd ✉ *EX24 6QJ – ℰ 01297 553184 – www.swallowseaves.co.uk*

COMBE HAY – Bath and North East Somerset ➜ See Bath

COMPTON BASSETT – Wiltshire ➜ See Calne

CONDOVER – Shropshire ➜ See Shrewsbury

COOKHAM
Windsor and Maidenhead – ✉ Maidenhead – Pop. 5 304 – Regional map n° **6**-C3
▶ London 32 mi – Oxford 31 mi – Reading 16 mi

🍴 White Oak 🚗 🏡 **P**

TRADITIONAL BRITISH · **FRIENDLY** One could argue about whether this is a contemporary pub or a pubby restaurant, as it's set up quite formally, but what is in no doubt is the warmth of the welcome and the affection in which the place is held by its many regulars. Cooking is carefully executed and full of flavour. Great value 'Menu Auberge'.
Menu £ 15/19 – Carte £ 21/37
Pound Ln ✉ *SL6 9QE – ℰ 01628 523043 – www.thewhiteoak.co.uk – Closed Sunday dinner*

CORBRIDGE
Northumberland – Pop. 2 946 – Regional map n° **14**-A2
▶ London 300 mi – Durham 34 mi – Newcastle upon Tyne 18 mi

🍴 Duke of Wellington ⇔ ⇜ 🏡 ♿ **P**
TRADITIONAL BRITISH · **DESIGN** Smart, modern country style pub looking out over the Tyne Valley – head straight for the terrace on sunnier days. Pub classics sit alongside more adventurous dishes such as saddle of roe deer; breakfast includes local eggs Benedict. Stylish, luxurious bedrooms feature characterful exposed beams.
Menu £ 15 (weekdays) – Carte £ 26/43 **s**
7 rooms 🖵 – ♦£ 85/100 ♦♦£ 110/140
Newton ✉ *NE43 7UL – East : 3.5 mi by A 69 – ℰ 01661 844446
– www.thedukeofwellingtoninn.co.uk*

CORFE CASTLE

Dorset – Pop. 1 355 – Regional map n° **2**-C3
▶ London 129 mi – Bournemouth 18 mi – Weymouth 23 mi

⌂ Mortons House

FAMILY · PERSONALISED An Elizabethan manor house built in the shape of an "E" to honour the Queen. The castle ruins are close above it and a steam railway runs just below. Bedrooms are classical and well-kept; one has a Victorian bath and four are in an annexe. Have lunch in the bar or lounges and dinner in the panelled restaurant.

23 rooms ☲ – ♦£ 90/125 ♦♦£ 160 – 2 suites
45 East St ✉ BH20 5EE – ☎ 01929 480988 – www.mortonshouse.co.uk

CORNHILL-ON-TWEED

Northumberland – Pop. 347 – Regional map n° **14**-A1
▶ London 345 mi – Edinburgh 49 mi – Newcastle upon Tyne 59 mi

⌂ Tillmouth Park

COUNTRY HOUSE · HISTORIC Late Victorian country house set in 15 acres of prime shooting and fishing country. The welcoming interior comes with grand staircases, wood panelling and characterful stained glass. Traditional guest areas have lovely views; the most popular bedrooms boast four-poster beds. Cooking is fittingly classical.

14 rooms ☲ – ♦£ 79/225 ♦♦£ 175/245
*✉ TD12 4UU – Northeast : 2.5 mi on A 698 – ☎ 01890 882255
– www.tillmouthpark.co.uk – Closed 1 February-2 April*

CORSE LAWN – Worcestershire → See Tewkesbury (Glos.)

CORSHAM

Wiltshire – Pop. 13 432 – Regional map n° **2**-C2
▶ London 103 mi – Bristol 31 mi – Cardiff 64 mi

⌂ Methuen Arms

MODERN BRITISH · INN A substantial pub set over three storeys, with a columned porch and a pleasant courtyard terrace. Sit in the 'Little Room' by the bar, the flag floored 'Nott Room' or the characterful restaurant – and dine on modern British dishes.

Menu £ 20 (weekdays) – Carte £ 27/47
14 rooms ☲ – ♦£ 90/125 ♦♦£ 110/175
2 High St ✉ SN13 0HB – ☎ 01249 717060 – www.themethuenarms.com – Closed 25 December

CORTON DENHAM

Somerset – ✉ Sherborne – Pop. 210 – Regional map n° **2**-C3
▶ London 123 mi – Bristol 36 mi – Cardiff 110 mi

⌂ Queens Arms

MODERN BRITISH · PUB This hub-of-the-village pub hosts plenty of events and comes with plush bedrooms. The menu lists food 'metres' and much of the produce is from their smallholding; choose from small plates, pub classics and more elaborate dishes. The bar is topped with tempting treats and they do a great trade in afternoon tea.

Carte £ 26/43
8 rooms ☲ – ♦£ 90/135 ♦♦£ 115/135
✉ DT9 4LR – ☎ 01963 220317 (booking advisable) – www.thequeensarms.com

COTEBROOK

Cheshire West and Chester – Regional map n° **11**-A3
▶ London 186 mi – Chester 13 mi – Manchester 33 mi

🍴 Fox and Barrel   🚗 🏠 🅿️

TRADITIONAL BRITISH · PUB Well-run pub with wood-panelled walls, heaving bookshelves and a smart terrace. The constantly evolving menu offers originality and interest, with sensibly priced dishes arriving neatly presented and generously sized.

Carte £ 21/35

Foxbank ⊠ CW6 9DZ – ℰ 01829 760529 – www.foxandbarrel.co.uk – Closed dinner 25-26 December and 1 January

COVERACK
Cornwall – Regional map n° **1**-A3
▶ London 300 mi – Penzance 25 mi – Truro 27 mi

🏠 Bay   📡 ⬩ 🚗 ♿ 🅿️

COUNTRY HOUSE · COSY Imposing, family-run country house located in a pretty fishing village and boasting views over the bay. Homely lounge and bar. Spotless, modern bedrooms with a slight New England edge. Dining room and conservatory offer a classical daily menu and local seafood specials.

14 rooms (dinner included) ⌷ – 🛏️£ 85/220 🛏️🛏️£ 100/270

North Corner ⊠ TR12 6TF – ℰ 01326 280464 – www.thebayhotel.co.uk – Closed 1-22 December and 3 January-mid March

COWAN BRIDGE
Lancashire – Regional map n° **11**-B1
▶ London 263 mi – Lancaster 18 mi – Carlisle 61 mi

🏠 Hipping Hall   🚗 🅿️

COUNTRY HOUSE · GRAND LUXURY Charming part 15/16C blacksmith's named after the stepping (or 'hipping') stones over the beck by the old washhouse. Sleek white bedrooms in the main house; the best rooms are in two outbuildings and are spacious and contemporary.

15 rooms ⌷ – 🛏️£ 169/419 🛏️🛏️£ 169/419 – 3 suites

On A 65 ⊠ LA6 2JJ – ℰ 015242 71187 – www.hippinghall.com

Hipping Hall – See restaurant listing

🍴🍴 Hipping Hall   🚗 🅿️

MODERN CUISINE · ROMANTIC A formal, airy hotel restaurant with a superb beamed ceiling, a minstrel's gallery and a medieval feel. Choose between a fixed price menu and a 7 course tasting menu: creative, original dishes come with matching wine pairings.

Menu £ 30/55

Hipping Hall Hotel, on A 65 ⊠ LA6 2JJ – ℰ 015242 71187 (booking essential) – www.hippinghall.com – dinner only and lunch Saturday-Sunday

COWLEY
Gloucestershire – Regional map n° **2**-C1
▶ London 105 mi – Gloucester 14 mi – Cheltenham 6 mi

🏠 Cowley Manor   📡 🐕 🚗 ⚒️ 🖥️ 🌐 🎱 🧖 💆 ⬅️ 🏊 ⛱️ 🅿️

LUXURY · CONTEMPORARY Impressive Regency house in 55 acres, with beautiful formal gardens, a superb spa, and lake views from some of the bedrooms. Original features and retro furnishings mix with bold colours and modern fittings to create a laid-back, understated vibe. The carved wood panelling in the restaurant is a feature.

30 rooms ⌷ – 🛏️£ 200/575 🛏️🛏️£ 230/575 – 8 suites

⊠ GL53 9NL – ℰ 01242 870900 – www.cowleymanor.com

CRANBROOK
Kent – Pop. 4 225 – Regional map n° **5**-B2
▶ London 53 mi – Maidstone 15 mi – Hastings 19 mi

Cloth Hall Oast

HISTORIC · PERSONALISED Superbly restored oast house that was rebuilt in 2001. Antiques, family photos and fine artwork fill the drawing room. Bedrooms are well-equipped but retain some original character; one boasts a splendid four-poster bed. Communal breakfasts at an antique table set below restored rafters in the main hall.

3 rooms ⌂ – ♦£ 65/80 ♦♦£ 95/125

Coursehorn Ln ⊠ TN17 3NR - East : 1 mi by Tenterden rd – ℰ 01580 712220 – www.clothhalloast.co.uk – Closed Christmas

CRAWLEY

Oxfordshire – Regional map n° **6**-A1
▶ London 111 mi – Oxford 23 mi – Cheltenham 46 mi

Lamb Inn

MODERN BRITISH · FRIENDLY This pretty stone pub, in a lovely village, is a hit with one and all. Roaring log fires and a friendly team welcome you into the charming bar, where old milk churns act as tables. Top quality regional produce includes rare breeds.

Carte £ 28/42

Steep Hill ⊠ OX29 9TW – ℰ 01993 708792 – www.lambcrawley.co.uk – Closed Monday and Tuesday

CRAYKE

North Yorkshire – Regional map n° **13**-C2
▶ London 217 mi – York 16 mi – Sheffield 70 mi

Durham Ox

TRADITIONAL BRITISH · PUB Characterful 300 year old pub located in a sleepy hamlet next to Crayke Castle. Menus change regularly and offer hearty dishes of fresh seafood, local meats and Crayke game – with 40-day dry-aged steaks a speciality. Bedrooms are set in old farm cottages; the split-level suite has a jacuzzi bath.

Menu £ 18 (weekday lunch) – Carte £ 21/46

6 rooms ⌂ – ♦£ 70/90 ♦♦£ 90/120

Westway ⊠ YO61 4TE – ℰ 01347 821506 (booking advisable) – www.thedurhamox.com

CREWE

Cheshire East – Pop. 71 722 – Regional map n° **11**-B3
▶ London 174 mi – Chester 40 mi – Manchester 36 mi

Crewe Hall

BUSINESS · HISTORIC A tree-lined drive leads up to this impressive 19C mansion designed by Edward Barry. Dramatic Jacobean features provide plenty of character in the main house and lovely chapel, while bedrooms and events rooms in the extensions are stylish and contemporary. The modern brasserie offers a menu to match.

117 rooms ⌂ – ♦£ 87/307 ♦♦£ 99/319 – 4 suites

Weston Road ⊠ CW1 6UZ – Southeast : 1.75 mi on A 5020 – ℰ 01270 253333 – www.qhotels.co.uk

CRICKLADE

Wiltshire – Regional map n° **2**-D1
▶ London 89 mi – Bristol 54 mi – Cardiff 87 mi

🏠 Red Lion

TRADITIONAL BRITISH · RUSTIC Traditional 17C pub just off the Thames path with a characterful, low-beamed bar. Classic cooking makes good use of local produce; burgers are a speciality. They smoke some of their own meats and fish and even brew their own ales on-site. Comfortable, well-equipped bedrooms are found in the old stables.

Carte £ 22/36

5 rooms 🖃 - 🛉£ 85 🛉🛉£ 85

74 High St ⊠ SN6 6DD - ℰ 01793 750776 - www.theredlioncricklade.co.uk

CROCKERTON - Wiltshire → See Warminster

CROMER

Norfolk - Pop. 7 949 - Regional map n° **8**-D1

▶ London 132 mi - Kings Lynn 43 mi - Norwich 23 mi

✗ No1 Cromer

FISH AND CHIPS · SIMPLE This is fish and chips with a difference: looking out over the beach and pier and offering everything from fresh fish and battered local sausages to cockle popcorn and mushy pea fritters. Potatoes are from their farm and the varieties change throughout the year. Head up to the bistro for some tasty fish tapas.

Carte £ 17/29

1 New St ⊠ NR27 9HP - ℰ 01263 515983 - www.no1cromer.com - Closed 1 week November, 2 weeks January and 24-25 December

CROPSTON

Leicestershire - Regional map n° **9**-B2

▶ London 106 mi - Leicester 6 mi - Sheffield 67 mi

🏡 Horseshoe Cottage Farm

FAMILY · CLASSIC Well-run, extended farmhouse and outbuildings, beside Bradgate Country Park. Traditional bedrooms with beams, exposed stonework and coordinating fabrics. Small breakfast room and a larger, high-ceilinged drawing room, with a solid oak table where communal dinners are served; local and garden produce features.

3 rooms 🖃 - 🛉£ 65/70 🛉🛉£ 100/110

Roecliffe Rd, Hallgates ⊠ LE7 7HQ - Northwest : 1 mi on Woodhouse Eaves rd - ℰ 0116 235 0038 - www.horseshoecottagefarm.com

CROSTHWAITE - Cumbria → See Kendal

CRUDWELL - Wiltshire → See Malmesbury

CRUNDALE

Kent - Regional map n° **9**-C2

▶ London 62 mi - Canterbury 10 mi - Folkestone 19 mi

🏠 Compasses Inn

CLASSIC CUISINE · PUB An enthusiastically run 1420s pub. The characterful bar has hop-hung beams and inglenook fireplaces and the large dining room opens onto the garden. The set menu offers comfort dishes while the à la carte shows a little more finesse.

Menu £ 18 (weekday lunch) - Carte £ 26/37

Sole Street ⊠ CT4 7ES - Northwest : 1.25 mi - ℰ 01227 700300 - www.thecompassescrundale.co.uk - Closed Sunday dinner and Monday

CUCKFIELD

West Sussex - Pop. 3 500 - Regional map n° **4**-D2

▶ London 37 mi - Lewes 35 mi - Brighton 25 mi

Ockenden Manor

HISTORIC · CLASSIC Part-Elizabethan manor house in 9 acres of parkland. Kick-back in the cosy panelled bar or beside the grand fireplace in the elegant drawing room. Stay in a characterful period bedroom or one of the modern rooms above the chic spa.

28 rooms ⌷ – †£ 139/239 ††£ 179/279 – 3 suites

Ockenden Ln ⊠ RH17 5LD – ℰ 01444 416111 – www.ockenden-manor.co.uk

Ockenden Manor – See restaurant listing

Ockenden Manor

CLASSIC CUISINE · CLASSIC DÉCOR A contemporary orangery-style dining room within a manor house hotel; it opens onto the gardens and affords pleasant views over the South Downs. The passionate chef uses seasonal local produce to create appealing, original menus.

Menu £ 21 (weekday lunch)/60

Ockenden Manor Hotel, Ockenden Ln ⊠ RH17 5LD – ℰ 01444 416111 (booking essential) – www.ockenden-manor.co.uk

CUNDALL

North Yorkshire – Regional map n° **13**-B2

▶ London 222 mi – York 29 mi – Leeds 36 mi

Cundall Lodge Farm

COUNTRY HOUSE · RURAL Grade II listed Georgian farmhouse on a working arable farm; its 150 acres include a stretch of the River Swale. Country bedrooms come with homemade shortbread and Roberts radios. The friendly owners have great local knowledge.

3 rooms ⌷ – †£ 55/65 ††£ 85/100

⊠ YO61 2RN – Northwest : 0.5 mi on Asenby rd – ℰ 01423 360203
– www.cundall-lodgefarm.co.uk – Closed February and Christmas

DALTON-IN-FURNESS

Cumbria – Pop. 7 827 – Regional map n° **12**-A3

▶ London 283 mi – Barrow-in-Furness 3 mi – Kendal 30 mi

Clarence House

FAMILY · CLASSIC The majority of guests here are repeat customers – which says a lot about the way the family run it. Relax in the peaceful, mature gardens or in one of the plush sitting rooms. Some bedrooms come with jacuzzis or four-posters.

28 rooms ⌷ – †£ 105 ††£ 140

Skelgate ⊠ LA15 8BQ – ℰ 01229 462508 – www.clarencehouse-hotel.com
– Closed 26 December

Clarence House – See restaurant listing

Clarence House

MODERN BRITISH · FAMILY This is a proper country house hotel restaurant with luxurious furnishings and willing service. Dishes are traditionally based but are modern in their execution. They use the finest Cumbrian meats, so steak is always a good bet.

Carte £ 30/46

Clarence House Hotel, Skelgate ⊠ LA15 8BQ – ℰ 01229 462508
– www.clarencehouse-hotel.co.uk – Closed 26 December

DARLEY ABBEY – Derby → See Derby

DARLINGTON

Darlington – Pop. 92 363 – Regional map n° **13**-B1

▶ London 251 mi – Leeds 61 mi – Newcastle upon Tyne 35 mi

⌂ Houndgate Townhouse 🏠 ⌂ ⌂ ⌂ ⌂

TOWNHOUSE · CONTEMPORARY This smart Georgian townhouse – formerly a registry office – is set on a quiet square in the heart of town. Inside, stylish colour schemes and contemporary furnishings create a boutique feel; bedroom Two has a bath in the room. The bistro has comfy booths, a terrace and a menu of modern classics.

8 rooms ⊇ – ♦£ 72/135 ♦♦£ 72/145

11 Houndgate ⊠ DL1 5RF – ℰ 01325 486011 – www.houndgatetownhouse.co.uk

⌂ Clow Beck House 🏠 ⌂ ⌂ ⌂ ⌂ ⌂ P

FAMILY · COSY Collection of converted farm buildings not far from the River Tees. Welcoming owners and a homely interior. Immaculately kept, tastefully furnished bedrooms come with iPod docks, bathrobes and chocolates; the larger ones have dressing rooms. Home-cooked dinners, with a puzzle supplied while you wait.

13 rooms ⊇ – ♦£ 90 ♦♦£ 145

Monk End Farm, Croft-on-Tees ⊠ DL2 2SP – South : 5.25 mi by A 167 off Barton rd – ℰ 01325 721075 – www.clowbeckhouse.co.uk – Closed 24 December-3 January

at Hurworth-on-Tees South: 5.5 mi by A167

🏠 Rockliffe Hall 🏠 ⌂ ⌂ ⌂ ⌂ ⌂ ⌂ ⌂ ⌂ ⌂ ⌂ ⌂ ⌂ P

LUXURY · MODERN Impressive red-brick manor house in 376 acres of grounds, complete with a championship golf course and extensive, state-of-the-art leisure facilities. The original Victorian house has grand guest areas and characterful bedrooms; rooms in the extensions are more modern. Dining options include ambitious restaurant menus, modern brasserie dishes, classics and grills.

61 rooms ⊇ – ♦£ 210/295 ♦♦£ 265/440

⊠ DL2 2DU – ℰ 01325 729999 – www.rockliffehall.com

The Orangery – See restaurant listing

🍴🍴 The Orangery 🏠 ⌂ ⌂ P

MODERN CUISINE · INTIMATE An elegant glass extension to a smart country house hotel. Choose from several set menus including vegetarian, pescatarian and surprise options. Dishes are carefully crafted and eye-catching, with contrasting textures and flavours.

Menu £ 55

Rockcliffe Hall Hotel, ⊠ DL2 2DU – ℰ 01325 729999 – www.rockliffehall.com – dinner only – Closed Sunday and Monday

🍴 Bay Horse 🏠 ⌂ ⌂ P

MODERN CUISINE · PUB A smart and cosy dining pub in a delightful village, with beams, open fires, antique furnishings and a warm, welcoming feel. Wide-ranging menus offer ambitious dishes with distinctive flavours, and friendly locals provide charming service.

Menu £ 15 (weekday lunch) – Carte £ 32/52

45 The Green ⊠ DL2 2AA – ℰ 01325 720663 – www.thebayhorsehurworth.com – Closed 25-26 December

at Summerhouse Northwest: 6.5 mi by A68 on B6279

🍴🍴 Raby Hunt (James Close) 🏠 ⌂ P

❀❀ **MODERN BRITISH · INTIMATE** A former drovers' inn in a rural hamlet and originally part of the Raby Estate, this was a favourite finishing point for the old hunt. It's now an elegantly decorated family-run restaurant, where a passionate self-taught chef uses first class ingredients to create original dishes which leave you impatient for the next. Contemporary bedrooms are set in the old stables.

➔ Raw scallop with avocado and grapefruit. Lamb in two servings. Black olive, chocolate and sheep's yoghurt.

Menu £ 70/80 – tasting menu only

2 rooms ⊇ – ♦£ 125/150 ♦♦£ 125/150

⊠ DL2 3UD – ℰ 01325 374237 (booking essential) – www.rabyhuntrestaurant.co.uk – dinner only and Saturday lunch – Closed 1 week spring, 1 week autumn, 25-26 December, 1 January and Sunday-Tuesday

at Headlam Northwest: 8 mi by A67 ⊠ Gainford

🏨 Headlam Hall   🏡 🐾 ⬳ 📶 🖼 🗔 🌐 🛁 💆 🍽 ♿ 🎱 🅿

FAMILY · HISTORIC Family-run manor house with delightful walled gardens, set in a secluded countryside spot. Spacious sitting rooms are furnished with antiques. Well-equipped bedrooms are a mix of the traditional (in the original house) and the more contemporary. The bright conservatory restaurant offers classic dishes.

38 rooms ⊇ – ♦£ 100/200 ♦♦£ 130/230 – 4 suites
⊠ DL2 3HA – ☎ 01325 730238 – www.headlamhall.co.uk
– Closed 24-27 December

DARSHAM

Suffolk – Regional map n° **15**-D2
▶ London 106 mi – Ipswich 27 mi – Norwich 33 mi

🍴 Darsham Nurseries Café 🆕   📶 🏡 ♿ 🛍 🍽 ⇄ 🅿

INTERNATIONAL · SIMPLE In 2014, the owners of this nursery opened a smart gift shop and a small café. Expect colourful, richly flavoured small plates of garden produce, with Mediterranean and Middle Eastern leanings. On Sundays they only serve brunch.

Carte £ 16/31

Main Rd ⊠ IP17 3PW – (on A 12) – ☎ 01728 667022 (booking essential)
– www.darshamnurseries.co.uk – lunch only and dinner Friday-Saturday in summer – Closed 25 December-9 January

DARTMOUTH

Devon – Pop. 6 008 – Regional map n° **1**-C3
▶ London 236 mi – Exeter 36 mi – Plymouth 35 mi

🏨 Dart Marina   🏡 ⬳ 🗔 🛁 ⊡ ♿ 🅿

TRADITIONAL · DESIGN Once an old boat works and chandlery, now a relaxed, modern hotel with a small spa and leisure centre. Smart, contemporary bedrooms have lovely outlooks over either the river or marina – many also boast balconies. The stylish, formal restaurant offers up-to-date versions of British classics.

53 rooms ⊇ – ♦£ 115/155 ♦♦£170/425 – 4 suites
Sandquay Rd ⊠ TQ6 9PH – ☎ 01803 832580 – www.dartmarina.com

🍴🍴 Seahorse   🏡 🅰🅲

SEAFOOD · CHIC Smart restaurant in a lovely spot on the embankment; sit outside looking over the estuary or inside, beside the glass-walled kitchen. Seafood orientated menus have a Mediterranean bias; whole fish cooked on the Josper grill are a hit.

Menu £ 20 (lunch and early dinner) – Carte £ 31/60

5 South Embankment ⊠ TQ6 9BH – ☎ 01803 835147 (booking essential)
– www.seahorserestaurant.co.uk – Closed Monday and Sunday dinner

🍴 Rockfish   🅰🅲 ⇄

SEAFOOD · NEIGHBOURHOOD Buzzy 'beach shack' style eatery run by a chatty team. Good old comfort dishes arrive in paper-lined baskets and rely on sustainable produce. Closely set tables have paper cloths proclaiming 'fish so fresh, tomorrow's are still in the sea'.

Carte £ 16/39

8 South Embankment ⊠ TQ6 9BH
– ☎ 01803 832800 (bookings not accepted) – www.rockfishdevon.co.uk
– Closed 25 December

at Kingswear East: via lower ferry ⊠ Dartmouth

⌂ **Nonsuch House**   ⤲ ⟨ 🛌 🎯

TOWNHOUSE · CLASSIC Charming Edwardian house run by friendly hands-on owners; boasting lovely views over the castle, town and sea. Bright Mediterranean-style décor blends nicely with original features. Bedrooms are spacious and well-appointed and one has a small balcony. Tea and homemade cake on arrival; local, seasonal cooking and excellent views from the conservatory dining room.

4 rooms ⌂ – 🛉£ 75/150 🛉🛉£ 115/195

Church Hill ⊠ *TQ6 0BX – from lower ferry take first right onto Church Hill before Steam Packet Inn –* ℰ *01803 752829 – www.nonsuch-house.co.uk – Closed January*

at Strete Southwest: 4.5 mi on A379 ⊠ Dartmouth

🏠 **Strete Barton House**   ⟍ ⟨ 🛌 🎯 **P**

HISTORIC · PERSONALISED Attractive part-16C manor house in a quiet village, with partial views over the rooftops to the sea. The contemporary interior has a personal style; bedrooms come with bold feature walls and modern facilities. Homemade cake is served on arrival and top quality local ingredients feature at breakfast.

6 rooms ⌂ – 🛉£ 105/165 🛉🛉£ 105/165

Totnes Rd ⊠ *TQ6 0RU –* ℰ *01803 770364 – www.stretebarton.co.uk – Closed 2 weeks January*

✗ **Laughing Monk**

TRADITIONAL CUISINE · BISTRO Built in 1839 as the village schoolhouse; the original wooden floor and a huge stone fireplace remain. Tasty, traditional dishes feature meats from nearby farms and seafood from local waters; cooking is unfussy and uses classical pairings.

Menu £ 26 – Carte £ 30/50

Totnes Rd ⊠ *TQ6 0RN –* ℰ *01803 770639 – www.thelaughingmonkdevon.co.uk – dinner only – Closed December, January, Sunday and Monday*

DATCHWORTH

Hertfordshire – Pop. 1 210 – Regional map n° **7**-B2
▶ London 31 mi – Hertford 7 mi – Stevenage 6 mi

🍴 **Tilbury**   🛌 🏡 **P**

TRADITIONAL CUISINE · TRADITIONAL DÉCOR Charming 18C inn run by two brothers, set just off the village green. There's something for everyone here: pub classics will please traditionalists, while dishes like maple-roasted guinea fowl really showcase the kitchen's skills.

Carte £ 24/39

1 Watton Rd ⊠ *SG3 6TB –* ℰ *01483 815550 – www.thetilbury.co.uk – Closed Monday and Sunday dinner*

DAVENTRY

Northamptonshire – Pop. 23 879 – Regional map n° **9**-B3
▶ London 79 mi – Northampton 13 mi – Leicester 31 mi

🏰 **Fawsley Hall**   ⤲ ⟋ ⟨ 🛌 📺 🕙 🐎 🛋 ✗ ⟟ 🎯 🏊 **P**

LUXURY · CLASSIC Set in 2,000 peaceful acres, a luxurious Tudor manor house with Georgian and Victorian extensions. Have afternoon tea in the Great Hall or unwind in the exclusive leisure club and spa. Smart, well-appointed bedrooms vary from wing to wing. Have lunch in the courtyard and dinner in the atmospheric restaurant.

60 rooms ⌂ – 🛉£ 125/225 🛉🛉£ 145/245 – 2 suites

Fawsley ⊠ *NN11 3BA – South : 6.5 mi by A 45 off A 361 –* ℰ *01327 892000 – www.handpicked.co.uk/fawsley*

at Staverton Southwest: 2.75 mi by A45 off A425 ⊠ Daventry

🏠 Colledges House &↓ ⅍ P

TRADITIONAL · PERSONALISED Lovely 17C thatched cottage and barn, run by an equally charming owner. The cosy lounge is filled with antiques and curios; the conservatory is a pleasant spot come summer. Traditional bedrooms have floral fabrics and good extras.

3 rooms ⌇ – ♦£ 70 ♦♦£ 99

Oakham Ln ⊠ NN11 6JQ – off Glebe Ln – ℰ 01327 702737
– www.colledgeshouse.co.uk

at Charwelton South : 6.25 mi by A 45 on A 361

🍴 Fox & Hounds ❿ ⌂ P

TRADITIONAL BRITISH · PUB The Fox & Hounds was built in 1871, refurbished by its owners – the Charwelton villagers – in 2013 and welcomed an experienced new chef and managers in 2016. Alongside pub favourites are dishes with European and Indian influences.

Menu £ 16 (weekdays) – Carte £ 24/42

Banbury Rd ⊠ NN11 3YY – ℰ 01327 260611 – www.foxandhoundscharwelton.co.uk
– Closed 25 December, 2 weeks January and Sunday dinner

DAYLESFORD – Gloucestershire → See Stow-on-the-Wold

DEAL

Kent – Pop. 30 555 – Regional map n° **5**-D2
▶ London 78 mi – Canterbury 19 mi – Dover 8 mi

🏠 Number One ⅍

TOWNHOUSE · MODERN Stylish guesthouse near the promenade, run by an enthusiastic owner. Bedrooms have bold wallpapers, fine linen and luxury bathrooms with tower showers. A delightful breakfast room hosts award-winning breakfasts of Kentish produce.

4 rooms ⌇ – ♦£ 73/100 ♦♦£ 83/110

1 Ranelagh Rd ⊠ CT14 7BG – ℰ 01304 364459 – www.numberonebandb.co.uk

✗ Victuals & Co

MODERN BRITISH · BISTRO You'll find this enthusiastically run restaurant down a narrow passageway – its name a reference to the victuallers who once supplied the local ships. Classic dishes are given modern twists; the set menu represents good value.

Menu £ 19 (lunch) – Carte £ 33/48

St Georges Passage ⊠ CT14 6TA – ℰ 01304 374389 – www.victualsandco.com
– Closed January, Monday-Wednesday except bank holiday Mondays and lunch Thursday-Friday

at Worth Northwest: 5 mi by A258

🏠 Solley Farm House &↓ ⅍ P

FAMILY · PERSONALISED Attractive 300 year old house overlooking the duck pond and run by a charming owner. In the beamed lounge, a vast inglenook fireplace takes centre stage; colour-themed bedrooms come with great extras. Have breakfast on the terrace.

3 rooms ⌇ – ♦£ 105/115 ♦♦£ 155/165

The Street ⊠ CT14 0DG – ℰ 01304 613701 – www.solleyfarmhouse.co.uk

DEDHAM

Essex – ⊠ Colchester – Pop. 719 – Regional map n° **7**-D2
▶ London 63 mi – Colchester 8 mi – Ipswich 12 mi

🏠 Maison Talbooth   ⬡ ⬡ ⬡ ⬡ ⬡ ⬡ P

LUXURY · PERSONALISED Charming, part-Georgian house in rolling countryside, with a modern, country house feel and views over the river valley. Individually decorated bedrooms boast quality furnishings and come in a mix of classical and contemporary styles. Seek out the tennis court and lovely, year-round heated swimming pool.

12 rooms ⬡ – ✚£ 225/425 ✚✚£ 225/425

Stratford Rd ✉ *CO7 6HN – West : 0.5 mi – ✆ 01206 322367 – www.milsomhotels.com*

Le Talbooth – See restaurant listing

🏠 Milsoms   ⬡ ⬡ ⬡ ⬡ P

TRADITIONAL · MODERN A late 19C country house with modern additions, over-looking Dedham Vale; its interior is stylish and contemporary, with comfortable and well-equipped New England style bedrooms. All-day dining from an appealing menu in the airy bar-restaurant with its covered terrace.

15 rooms ⬡ – ✚£ 135/210 ✚✚£ 135/210

Stratford Rd ✉ *CO7 6HW – West : 0.75 mi – ✆ 01206 322795 – www.milsomhotels.com*

🍴🍴🍴 Le Talbooth   ⬡ ⬡ ⬡ ⬡ ⬡ P

MODERN BRITISH · LUXURY Delightful hotel restaurant with numerous private rooms and a lovely terrace, in an attractive riverside setting. To celebrate its 60th birthday, it was cleverly and subtly updated, with a zinc bar and stunning Italian chandeliers. Menus are light and modern, and are accompanied by a well-chosen wine list.

Menu £ 31 (weekday lunch) – Carte £ 40/62

Gun Hill ✉ *CO7 6HN – West : 0.75 mi – ✆ 01206 323150 – www.milsomhotels.com – Closed Sunday dinner October-May*

🍴 Sun Inn   ⬡ ⬡ ⬡ ⬡ P

ITALIAN · INN Characterful yellow inn with an appealing shabby-chic style, located in a picturesque spot in the heart of Constable Country. The monthly menu offers generous Italian-inspired dishes and the well-chosen wine list offers plenty by the glass. Bedrooms are cosy – two have a modern New England style.

Carte £ 19/40

7 rooms ⬡ – ✚£ 90/130 ✚✚£ 145

High St ✉ *CO7 6DF – ✆ 01206 323351 – www.thesuninndedham.com – Closed 25-26 December*

DELPH

Greater Manchester – Pop. 2 224 – Regional map n° **11**-B2

▶ London 215 mi – Manchester 13 mi – Leeds 31 mi

🍴 Old Bell Inn   ⬡ P

TRADITIONAL BRITISH · TRADITIONAL DÉCOR 18C coaching inn set high up on the moors, with a cosy bar, a smart modern brasserie and well-kept bedrooms. Choose from sharing platters, hearty pub favourites, 35 day matured steaks and more modern set menus. Their gin selection features over 500 different types and is the biggest in the world.

Menu £ 25 (lunch and early dinner) – Carte £ 22/44

18 rooms ⬡ – ✚£ 60/70 ✚✚£ 95/125

Huddersfield Rd ✉ *OL3 5EG – ✆ 01457 870130 – www.theoldbellinn.co.uk*

DENHAM

Buckinghamshire – Pop. 1 432 – Regional map n° **6**-D3

▶ London 20 mi – Buckingham 42 mi – Oxford 41 mi

🍺 **Swan Inn**   ⇔ 🏡 **P**

TRADITIONAL BRITISH · PUB Located in a picture postcard village; a wisteria-clad, red-brick Georgian pub with a pleasant terrace and mature gardens. Menus change with the seasons and offer plenty of interest – the side dishes are appealing and pudding is a must.

Carte £ 23/43

Village Rd ⊠ *UB9 5BH* – ✆ *01895 832085 (booking essential)*
– *www.swaninndenham.co.uk*

DERBY

Derby – Pop. 255 394 – Regional map n° **9**-B2
▶ London 132 mi – Birmingham 40 mi – Manchester 49 mi

X **Ibérico World Tapas**   🕭 🗚 🍽

😊 MEDITERRANEAN CUISINE · FRIENDLY It's all in the name: the main concept is Spanish, with plenty of tapas dishes and Spanish classics, but there's also a more global feel, courtesy of Mediterranean-style décor and some dishes with Asian origins. The imported hams are a must-try, and the lunch and early evening menus are excellent value.

Menu £ 12 (weekdays) – Carte £ 13/40

9-11 Bold Ln ⊠ *DE1 3NT*
– ✆ *01332 345456* – *www.ibericotapas.com*
– *Closed 1-5 January and Sunday*

at Darley Abbey North: 2.5 mi off A6⊠ Derby

XX **Darleys**   🗚 🕭🕉 **P**

MODERN CUISINE · FRIENDLY Popular weir-side restaurant, located in the old canteen of a 19C silk mill. Start with drinks in the modern bar-lounge or on the attractive terrace. Good value lunches are followed by more ambitious European dishes in the evening.

Menu £ 25 (lunch) – Carte £ 34/45

Darley Abbey Mill ⊠ *DE22 1DZ*
– ✆ *01332 364987 (booking advisable)* – *www.darleys.com*
– *Closed 25 December-10 January, Sunday dinner and bank holidays*

DEVIZES

Wiltshire – Pop. 18 064 – Regional map n° **2**-C2
▶ London 98 mi – Bristol 38 mi – Salisbury 25 mi

🏠 **Blounts Court Farm**   🐾 ⇔ 🎋 **P**

COUNTRY HOUSE · PERSONALISED Delightfully run farmhouse on a 150 acre working farm; the village cricket team play in one of their fields! The snug interior consists of a cosy lounge and a spacious breakfast room filled with clocks and curios. Warm, well-kept bedrooms show good attention to detail. Pastel artwork and country photos abound.

3 rooms ⊆ – ♦£ 56/60 ♦♦£ 88/98

Coxhill Ln, Potterne ⊠ *SN10 5PH* – *South : 2.25 mi by A 360* – ✆ *01380 727180*
– *www.blountscourtfarm.co.uk*

Prices quoted after the symbol ♦ refer to the lowest rate for a single room in low season, followed by the highest rate in high season. The same principle applies to the symbol ♦♦ for a double room.

at Rowde Northwest: 2 mi by A361 on A342✉ Devizes

🍴 George & Dragon ⇦ 🛏 🏠 🅿

SEAFOOD · PUB Rustic and cosy 16C coaching inn with open fires, solid stone floors and wooden beams. The oft-changing menu has a strong emphasis on seafood, with fish delivered daily from Cornwall. Old-world charm meets modern facilities in the individually designed bedrooms.

Menu £20 – Carte £26/43

3 rooms 🖵 – 🛉£75/125 🛉🛉£75/125

High St ✉ SN10 2PN – 𝒞 01380 723053 – www.thegeorgeanddragonrowde.co.uk – Closed Sunday dinner

DIDSBURY – Greater Manchester → See Manchester

DITCHLING

East Sussex – Pop. 1 476 – Regional map n° **4**-D2
▶ London 48 mi – Brighton and Hove 10 mi – Hastings 40 mi

🏠 Tovey Lodge ⅛ ⪡ 🛏 🖫 🎝 🥂 🅿

COUNTRY HOUSE · PERSONALISED Well-appointed guesthouse with mature gardens and views over the South Downs. Smart bedrooms have modern facilities; Maple, with its balcony, is the best. Beyond the communal breakfast room you'll find a swimming pool and sauna.

5 rooms 🖵 – 🛉£99/165 🛉🛉£109/190

Underhill Ln ✉ BN6 8XE – South : 1 mi by B 2112 off Ditchling Beacon rd – 𝒞 01273 256156 – www.toveylodge.co.uk – Closed January

DODDINGTON

Kent – Regional map n° **5**-C2
▶ London 50 mi – Maidstone 15 mi – Canterbury 16 mi

🏠 Old Vicarage ⅛ 🛏 🥂 🅿

FAMILY · CLASSIC Grade II listed former vicarage with 16C origins, where wood and stone blend with modern furnishings. There's an impressive galleried hall and a striking antique breakfast table. Bedrooms feature coffee machines and Bose sound systems.

5 rooms 🖵 – 🛉£65/75 🛉🛉£85/105

Church Hill ✉ ME9 0BD – 𝒞 01795 886136 – www.oldvicaragedoddington.co.uk – Closed 24 December-2 January

DOGMERSFIELD

Hampshire – Regional map n° **4**-C1
▶ London 44 mi – Winchester 29 mi – Southampton 41 mi

🏨 Four Seasons 🏋 ⅛ ⪡ 🛏 🖫 🕸 🎝 ♨ 🍽 🖻 🛗 🛝 🕢 🎛 🅿

LUXURY · CLASSIC An attractive part-Georgian house in 350 acres of parkland, where you can try your hand at all manner of outdoor pursuits. Luxurious bedrooms are well-equipped and come with marble bathrooms. A superb spa is found in the converted coach house. Seasons, the contemporary restaurant, offers sophisticated modern dishes, while the casual bistro offers steaks and grills.

133 rooms – 🛉£265/550 🛉🛉£265/550 – 🖵£25 – 21 suites

Dogmersfield Park, Chalky Ln ✉ RG27 8TD – 𝒞 01252 853000 – www.fourseasons.com/hampshire

DOLTON

Devon – Pop. 687 – Regional map n° **2**-C2
▶ London 214 mi – Exeter 36 mi – Bristol 97 mi

ENGLAND

🍴 Rams Head Inn ⓝ ⇦ 🛏 P

TRADITIONAL CUISINE · INN The Rams Head has a cosy, characterful feel. Enjoy a drink by the inglenook fireplace in the large beamed bar or head for the traditional dining room. Dishes are a mix of old favourites and more restaurant-style dishes; the daily changing suet pudding is a hit. Simply furnished bedrooms have a modern feel.

Carte £ 23/35

9 rooms – 🛆£ 50/59 🛆🛆£ 89/99

South St ✉ EX19 8QS – ℰ01805 804255 – www.theramsheadinn.co.uk – Closed February and lunch Monday

DONCASTER

South Yorkshire – Pop. 109 805 – Regional map n° **13**-C3
▶ London 173 mi – Sheffield 19 mi – Nottingham 46 mi

🏨 Mount Pleasant ⌂ ⇩ 🛆 🛇 🛆 P

BUSINESS · CONTEMPORARY Well-run hotel with smart, spacious, individually styled bedrooms – many with feature beds, jacuzzi baths and even saunas; try a room with a five-poster or glass bed. Good range of beauty treatments in the spa. Characterful bar and a formal restaurant with an impressive wall tapestry; extensive, classic menu.

67 rooms ⌂ – 🛆£ 79/119 🛆🛆£ 99/139 – 7 suites

Great North Rd ✉ DN11 0HW – Southeast : 6 mi on A 638 – ℰ01302 868696 – www.mountpleasant.co.uk – Closed 24-25 December

DONHEAD-ST-ANDREW

Wiltshire – Regional map n° **2**-C3
▶ London 115 mi – Bournemouth 34 mi – Bath 37 mi

🍴 The Forester ⇩ 🛏 P

TRADITIONAL BRITISH · RUSTIC Gloriously rustic, 13C thatched pub, hidden down narrow lanes in a delightful village. Exposed stone walls and vast open fires feature throughout. Seasonal menus showcase well-prepared, flavoursome dishes with a classical country base and a refined edge; they also offer a daily seafood selection.

Menu £ 19 (weekdays) – Carte £ 27/47

Lower St ✉ SP7 9EE – ℰ01747 828038 – www.theforesterdonheadstandrew.co.uk – Closed Sunday dinner and Monday except bank holidays

DORCHESTER

Dorset – Pop. 19 060 – Regional map n° **2**-C3
▶ London 135 mi – Bournemouth 27 mi – Southampton 54 mi

🏨 Little Court ⇩ 🛆 🛇 🛇 P

TRADITIONAL · CLASSIC Lutyens-style house boasting Edwardian wood and brickwork, leaded windows and mature gardens with a pool and tennis court. Bedrooms display original features and modern furnishings; one has a four-poster bed.

8 rooms ⌂ – 🛆£ 119 🛆🛆£ 129

5 Westleaze, Charminster ✉ DT2 9PZ – North : 1 mi by B3147, turning right at Loders garage – ℰ01305 261576 – www.littlecourt.net – Closed 22 December-2 January

🏨 Westwood House 🛇

TOWNHOUSE · COSY Georgian townhouse built in 1815 by Lord Illchester. Spotlessly kept bedrooms have bold colours, king-sized beds and fridges containing fresh milk. The sunny drawing room opens onto a conservatory where hearty breakfasts are served.

6 rooms ⌂ – 🛆£ 65/75 🛆🛆£ 75/95

29 High St West ✉ DT1 1UP – ℰ01305 268018 – www.westwoodhouse.co.uk – Closed 31 December-5 January

XX Yalbury Cottage ⇔ 🖚 🅿

TRADITIONAL BRITISH · RUSTIC This very proudly and personally run restaurant is set within an old thatched cottage and has a snug beamed interior. Cooking is traditional, gutsy and flavoursome. Produce is sourced from within 9 miles and the menu evolves as new ingredients become available. Well-kept cottagey bedrooms are located in a wing.

Menu £ 33/38

8 rooms ⌑ – †£ 70/85 ††£ 99/120

Lower Bockhampton ⊠ DT2 8PZ – East : 3.75 mi by A 35 – ℰ 01305 262382 (booking essential) – www.yalburycottage.com – dinner only and Sunday lunch residents only Sunday-Monday dinner – Closed Christmas-mid January

XX Sienna 🔲

MODERN CUISINE · COSY This unassuming high street restaurant is run by a keen young chef. Terse menu descriptions belie the complexity of the dishes, which are modern and ambitious both in flavour and presentation. It has just five tables, so book ahead.

Carte £ 26/42

36 High West St ⊠ DT1 1UP – ℰ 01305 250022 (booking essential) – www.siennadorchester.co.uk – Closed 25-26 December, 1 January, Sunday and Monday

at Winterbourne Steepleton West: 4.75 mi by B3150 and A35 on B3159⊠ Dorchester

🏠 Old Rectory 🖚 🛇 🅿 🛏

TRADITIONAL · PERSONALISED A proudly run, attractive stone rectory in a pretty village. It's immaculately kept, from the comfy lounge and conservatory breakfast room to the homely bedrooms and smart bathrooms. Cross the brook to enter the mature gardens.

4 rooms ⌑ – †£ 70 ††£ 80/110

⊠ DT2 9LG – ℰ 01305 889468 – www.theoldrectorybandb.co.uk – Closed 1 week Christmas

DORKING

Surrey – Pop. 17 098 – Regional map n° **4**-D2

▶ London 26 mi – Guildford 12 mi – Brighton 39 mi

X Two to Four 🔲 ⇔

MODERN CUISINE · COSY This Grade II listed property sports contemporary décor, although beams bear witness to its history and provide a rustic feel. It's friendly, informal and cosy at night. Adventurous dishes take their influences from far and wide.

Menu £ 16 (weekday lunch)/19 – Carte £ 29/48

2-4 West St ⊠ RH4 1BL – ℰ 01306 889923 – www.2to4.co.uk – Closed 25 December-early January and Sunday

DORRIDGE

West Midlands – ⊠ Birmingham – Regional map n° **10**-C2

▶ London 109 mi – Birmingham 11 mi – Warwick 11 mi

XX Forest ⇔ 🍴 ♿ 🔲 🗔 ⇔ 🅿

MODERN BRITISH · DESIGN Surprisingly stylish restaurant located in a 19C hotel opposite the railway station: choose the bar-lounge for unfussy classics or head to the dining room for ambitious dishes with interesting modern twists. Cooking is accomplished and well-judged. Comfortable, contemporary bedrooms complete the picture.

Carte £ 20/33

12 rooms ⌑ – †£ 105/120 ††£ 115/130

25 Station Approach ⊠ B93 8JA – ℰ 01564 772120 – www.forest-hotel.com – Closed 25 December and Sunday dinner

DOUGLAS - Douglas ➜ See Man (Isle of)

DOVER
Kent – Pop. 41 709 – Regional map n° **5**-D2
▶ London 76 mi – Maidstone 43 mi – Brighton 105 mi

🏨 Wallett's Court
HISTORIC · PERSONALISED Family-run country house with 16C origins, in a peaceful setting. Guest areas are heavily beamed and bedrooms are traditional and characterful. The annexe rooms are more modern, with the converted grain store and Victorian bath house the most unusual. Classic menus are offered in the atmospheric restaurant.

14 rooms ⌂ – ♥£ 95/165 ♥♥£ 150/250

West Cliffe, St Margaret's at Cliffe ⊠ CT15 6EW – Northeast : 3.5 mi by A 258 on St Margaret's at Cliffe rd – ☎ 01304 852424 – www.wallettscourt.com

DREWSTEIGNTON
Devon – Pop. 668 – Regional map n° **1**-C2
▶ London 190 mi – Exeter 15 mi – Plymouth 56 mi

XX Old Inn
MODERN BRITISH · INTIMATE Olive green former pub in the centre of a lovely Devonshire village. It has two small, cosy dining rooms and a parquet-floored lounge with modern art for sale on the walls and a wood-burning stove in the large inglenook fireplace. A concise menu offers hearty, classical dishes. Bedrooms are simply furnished.

Menu £ 52

3 rooms ⌂ – ♥£ 80/90 ♥♥£ 100/110

⊠ EX6 6QR – ☎ 01647 281276 (booking essential) – www.old-inn.co.uk – dinner only and lunch Friday-Saturday – Closed Sunday-Tuesday

DRIGHLINGTON
West Yorkshire – Regional map n° **13**-B2
▶ London 196 mi – Leeds 7 mi – Manchester 35 mi

XX Prashad
INDIAN VEGETARIAN · NEIGHBOURHOOD Stylish former pub with wooden panels from India fronting the bar; head upstairs to admire the huge picture of a Mumbai street scene. Authentic vegetarian dishes range from enticing street food to more original creations, with influences from Southern India and Gujarat; be sure to try the dosas.

Menu £ 16/34 – Carte £ 21/37

137 Whitehall Rd ⊠ BD11 1AT – ☎ 0113 285 2037 – www.prashad.co.uk – dinner only and lunch Saturday-Sunday

DROXFORD
Hampshire – Pop. 675 – Regional map n° **4**-B2
▶ London 79 mi – Southampton 21 mi – Portsmouth 16 mi

🍴 Bakers Arms
TRADITIONAL BRITISH · PUB A traditional pub with a loyal local following. It's small and cosy with wooden beams, exposed bricks and an open fire – and it also doubles as the village post office. Cooking is simple and classical; the midweek menu is good value.

Menu £ 15 (weekdays) – Carte £ 25/35

High St ⊠ SO32 3PA – ☎ 01489 877533 – www.thebakersarmsdroxford.com – Closed Sunday dinner

DULVERTON
Somerset – Pop. 1 052 – Regional map n° **2**-A2
▶ London 198 mi – Taunton 27 mi – Exeter 27 mi

ENGLAND

377

🏠 Woods   🐝 🛗

MODERN BRITISH · PUB Former bakery, with a cosy, hugely characterful interior. Tasty, carefully prepared dishes offer more than just the usual pub fare. Provenance is taken seriously, with quality local ingredients including meat from the owner's farm.

Carte £ 23/33

4 Banks Sq ⊠ TA22 9BU – ℰ 01398 324007 (bookings advisable at dinner)
– www.woodsdulverton.co.uk – Closed 25 December, dinner 26 December and 1 January

DUMMER

Hampshire – Pop. 466 – Regional map n° **6**-B2
▶ London 57 mi – Winchester 15 mi – Reading 25 mi

🏠 Sun Inn 🔘   🚗 🛗 🅿

MODERN BRITISH · PUB Its location on the A30 isn't ideal and it's not a particularly pretty place, but all of that pales into insignificance when you try the food. Alongside the usual pub classics you'll find some more ambitious modern choices. Good ingredients are carefully prepared and dishes are well-balanced and interesting.

Carte £ 22/40

Winchester Rd ⊠ RG25 2DJ – (on A 30) – ℰ 01256 397234
– www.suninndummer.com – Closed 25 December and dinner 26 December, 1 January and Sunday

DUNSFORD

Devon – Regional map n° **1**-C2
▶ London 206 mi – Exeter 8 mi – Plymouth 40 mi

🏡 Weeke Barton   ✿ 🌿 🚗 🅿 🍴

HISTORIC · CONTEMPORARY The owners of this 15C Devonshire longhouse are friendly and laid-back, and the place itself has a funky yet cosy feel. The interior combines old world character with stylish furnishings, and bedrooms are modern and minimalistic. Rustic, home-cooked dishes feature in the communal dining room.

5 rooms ☑ – 🛏£ 100/120 🛏🛏£ 110/130

⊠ EX6 7HH – Southeast : 1.5 mi by B 3212 and Christow rd, turning right up unmarked road after river bridge – ℰ 01647 253505 – www.weekebarton.com – Closed Christmas and New Year

DUNSTER

Somerset – Pop. 408 – Regional map n° **2**-A2
▶ London 185 mi – Taunton 23 mi – Exeter 44 mi

🏡 Luttrell Arms 🔘   ✿ 🚗 🏋

HISTORIC · PERSONALISED A stone built 15C inn – once a hostelry for monks – with open fires, period features and a small medieval courtyard. Bedrooms are named after local landmarks: one has an ornate plaster fireplace; another a four-poster and an impressive timbered ceiling. Traditional dishes are served in the formal restaurant.

28 rooms ☑ – 🛏£ 70/100 🛏🛏£ 140/195

32-36 High St ⊠ TA24 6SG – ℰ 01653 821555 – www.luttrellarms.co.uk

🏡 Spears Cross   🌸 🅿

HISTORIC · CLASSIC Built in 1460 and reputedly the oldest house in the street. Charming bedrooms feature traditional William Morris and Sanderson furnishings; one has elm panelling. Over 50 wines and malt whiskies for sale, with Champagne offered at breakfast.

4 rooms ☑ – 🛏£ 70 🛏🛏£ 97/107

West St ⊠ TA24 6SN – ℰ 01643 821439 – www.spearscross.co.uk – Closed 31 December-1 February

DURHAM

Durham – Pop. 47 785 – Regional map n° **14**-B3

▶ London 267 mi – Newcastle upon Tyne 20 mi – Leeds 77 mi

🏠 The Town House   ✕ 🛋 ⚹ 🅰🄺 ✍

TOWNHOUSE · DESIGN Attractive Georgian townhouse with lavishly decorated rooms: the lounge has purple velvet furnishings and there's a mahogany bar. Sumptuous bedrooms feature bathrooms with underfloor heating; those in the garden annexe have hot tubs. Intimate restaurant serving classic British dishes, with steaks a speciality.

11 rooms ☑ – ♦£ 90/250 ♦♦£ 90/250

Town plan: B2-x - *34 Old Elvet* ⊠ *DH1 3HN* – *℘ 0191 384 1037*
– *www.thetownhousedurham.com* – *Closed 1 January*

🏠 Castle View   ✍

TOWNHOUSE · COSY Attractive Georgian townhouse beside a Norman castle on a steep cobbled hill; reputedly a former vicarage. Large bedrooms have modern monochrome colour schemes, good facilities and smart bathrooms. Have breakfast on the terrace in summer.

5 rooms ☑ – ♦£ 80/100 ♦♦£ 100/120

Town plan: A2-e - *4 Crossgate* ⊠ *DH1 4PS* – *℘ 0191 386 8852*
– *www.castle-view.co.uk* – *Closed 18 December-13 January*

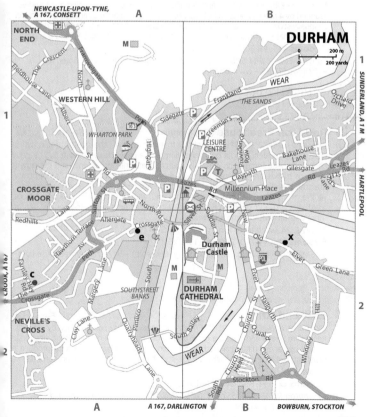

XX **DH1**   🕭 🕙 🅿

MODERN CUISINE · INTIMATE An intimate restaurant on the lower floor of a large Victorian house overlooking the city. An array of choices mean everything from a weekly market menu to a vegetarian tasting menu; dishes are modern and full of flavour.

Menu £ 35/60 – Carte approx. £ 42

Town plan: A2-c *The Avenue* ⊠ *DH1 4DX –* ℰ *0191 384 6655*
– www.restaurantdh1.co.uk – dinner only – Closed 2 weeks October, first week January, 25-26 December, Sunday and Monday

XX **Finbarr's** 🔟   🛉 ⇔ 🅿

MODERN BRITISH · BISTRO Finbarr's has relocated to a converted farm building on the edge of the city – it's a place familiar to the owners, who both worked here previously. Menus offer plenty of choice and the hearty brasserie cooking suits the area well.

Menu £ 20 (weekday lunch)/22 (weekday dinner) – Carte £ 26/47

Aykley Heads House, Aykley Heads ⊠ *DH1 5TS – Northwest : 1.5 ml by A 691 and B 6532. –* ℰ *0191 307 7033 – www.finbarrsrestaurant.co.uk – Closed first week January and 25-26 December*

EARL STONHAM

Suffolk – Regional map n° **8**-C3
▶ London 91 mi – Ipswich 12 mi – Colchester 33 mi

🏠 **Bays Farm**   🕭 🛏 🕊 🅿

FAMILY · PERSONALISED A delightful 17C farmhouse run by charming hosts and surrounded by 4 acres of beautifully landscaped gardens. Smart, modern bedrooms are individually styled – 'The Hayloft' is the most luxurious and the stand-alone wooden Shepherd's Hut has its own decked terrace. Breakfast features homemade bread and jam.

5 rooms � – ♦£ 70/120 ♦♦£ 80/130

Forward Grn ⊠ *IP14 5HU – Northwest : 1 mi by A1120 on Broad Green rd –* ℰ *01449 711286 – www.baysfarmsuffolk.co.uk*

EAST CHISENBURY

Wiltshire – Regional map n° **2**-D2
▶ London 92 mi – Bristol 51 mi – Southampton 53 mi

🍴 **Red Lion Freehouse** (Guy Manning)   ⇔ 🛏 🛉 ⇔ 🅿

😋 CLASSIC CUISINE · SIMPLE Delightful thatched pub off the beaten track, with a pretty little garden, simple country styling and a cosy, characterful feel. The daily changing menu focuses on carefully sourced, seasonal ingredients and the down-to-earth dishes are precisely composed and packed with flavour. Set opposite, are smart, well-equipped bedrooms with private terraces – all have river views.
→ Warm crab tart with dressed fennel and watercress salad. Steamed turbot, roast gurnard and cod "bouillabaisse" with violet artichokes and rouille. Lemon meringue tart with thyme ice cream.

Menu £ 24 (weekday lunch) – Carte £ 34/50

5 rooms ⊆ – ♦£ 130/250 ♦♦£ 130/250

⊠ *SN9 6AQ –* ℰ *01980 671124 (booking advisable) – www.redlionfreehouse.com*

EAST END

Hampshire – Regional map n° **4**-A3
▶ London 100 mi – Southampton 21 mi – Bristol 85 mi

🍴 **East End Arms**   ⇔ 🛉 🅿

TRADITIONAL BRITISH · RUSTIC This traditional country pub is owned by John Illsley of Dire Straits and boasts a great display of photos from his personal collection in its shabby bar and pine-furnished dining room. Concise menus feature local produce in satisfying British dishes. Modern cottage-style bedrooms provide a smart contrast.

Carte £ 24/42

5 rooms ⊆ – ♦£ 85/100 ♦♦£ 110/130

Lymington Rd ⊠ *SO41 5SY –* ℰ *01590 626223 – www.eastendarms.co.uk – Closed Sunday dinner*

EAST GRINSTEAD

West Sussex – Pop. 29 084 – Regional map n° **4**-D2

▶ London 48 mi – Chichester 50 mi – Maidstone 37 mi

🏛 Gravetye Manor ♨ ⟨ 🛌 🗱 🅿

LUXURY · CLASSIC A quintessential English country house set in a forest and surrounded by 35 acres of glorious gardens. Ornate Elizabethan ceilings and fireplaces dominate beautifully furnished lounges, which provide the perfect spot for afternoon tea. Bedrooms are luxurious and service is personalised and detailed.

17 rooms ☒ – ∲£ 170/220 ∲∲£ 260/525 – 1 suite

Vowels Ln ⌧ RH19 4LJ – Southwest : 4.5 mi by B 2110 taking second turn left towards West Hoathly – ℰ 01342 810567 – www.gravetyemanor.co.uk

❀ **Gravetye Manor** – See restaurant listing

☓☓☓ Gravetye Manor ⟨ 🛌 ⇔ 🅿

❀ **MODERN BRITISH · TRADITIONAL DÉCOR** A charming country house dining room with wood-panelled walls, fresh flowers and a cosy, traditional feel. Classically based menus use excellent quality produce from the kitchen garden to create refined, flavourful dishes, with desserts a highlight. Well-chosen wine list and polished, professional service.

→ Dorset crab with sorrel, brown crab emulsion and Exmoor caviar. Rump of English veal with sweetbreads, Jerusalem artichoke, leek and gremolata. Gooseberry crumble soufflé with gooseberry & mint compote and clotted cream ice cream.

Menu £ 28/68

Gravetye Manor Hotel, Vowels Ln ⌧ RH19 4LJ – ℰ 01342 810567 (booking essential) – www.gravetyemanor.co.uk

EAST HADDON

Northamptonshire – Regional map n° **9**-B3

▶ London 76 mi – Northampton 13 mi – Birmingham 47 mi

🍴 Red Lion ⟨ 🛌 🍽 ♿ 🅿

TRADITIONAL CUISINE · PUB Thatched honey-stone inn at the heart of an attractive village, boasting pretty gardens and a pleasing mix of exposed wood, brick and slate. Drinkers are welcome but it's the food that's the focus here, with a seasonal menu offering an eclectic mix of tasty dishes including perennial favourite, slow-cooked beef in red wine. Enthusiastic service and chic, cosy bedrooms.

Carte £ 21/40

7 rooms ☒ – ∲£ 80/95 ∲∲£ 95/110

Main St ⌧ NN6 8BU – ℰ 01604 770223 – www.redlioneasthaddon.co.uk – Closed 25 December

EAST HENDRED

Oxfordshire – Regional map n° **6**-B3

▶ London 70 mi – Oxford 18 mi – Reading 37 mi

🍴 Eyston Arms 🍽 ♿ 🅿

INTERNATIONAL · PUB Set in a largely estate-owned village; an inviting modern pub where several low-beamed rooms are set around an inglenook fireplace. Local workers pop in for the 'business dish of the day' and Maria's blackboard lists the specials.

Carte £ 26/53

High St ⌧ OX12 8JY – ℰ 01235 833320 – www.eystonarms.co.uk – Closed 25 December

EAST HOATHLY

East Sussex – Pop. 893 – Regional map n° **5**-B3

▶ London 60 mi – Brighton 16 mi – Hastings 25 mi

🏠 Old Whyly ☆ 🐾 🛏 ⌿ ※ 🅿 🍽

TRADITIONAL · PERSONALISED Charming red-brick house built in 1760, set in beautiful grounds and very personally run by its delightful owner. Guest areas mix the classic and the contemporary. Bedrooms are individually designed around a subtle theme: choose from Tulip, French or Chinese. The minimalist dining room offers a daily changing 3 course dinner, and homemade yoghurts and jams at breakfast.

4 rooms ☲ – 🛉£ 90/145 🛉🛉£ 98/145

London Rd ⊠ BN8 6EL – Northwest : 0.5 mi, turning right by post box on right and then taking centre drive – 𝒞 01825 840216 – www.oldwhyly.co.uk

EAST WITTERING

West Sussex – Pop. 5 647 – Regional map n° **4**-C3
▶ London 86 mi – Chichester 7 mi – Brighton 62 mi

✗ Samphire

TRADITIONAL BRITISH · SIMPLE A brightly decorated bistro with a shabby-chic beach café style, set 100 metres from the sea. Freshly caught seafood comes from the local day boats and meats are from the surrounding countryside. Cooking is unfussy and good value.

Menu £ 16 (lunch) – Carte £ 24/38

57 Shore Rd ⊠ PO20 8DY – 𝒞 01243 672754 – www.samphireeastwittering.co.uk – Closed 2 weeks January, Christmas and Sunday

EAST WITTON

North Yorkshire – ⊠ Leyburn – Regional map n° **13**-B1
▶ London 238 mi – York 45 mi – Harrogate 29 mi

🏨 Blue Lion ⇦ 🛏 🏡 & 🛈 🅿

TRADITIONAL CUISINE · PUB Charming, characterful countryside pub. Daily-changing menu features a tasty mix of classic and modern dishes, all with seasonality and traceability at their core. Bedrooms – in the pub and outbuildings – are warm and cosy.

Menu £ 16 (weekday lunch) – Carte £ 26/45 **s**

15 rooms ☲ – 🛉£ 79/130 🛉🛉£ 94/145

⊠ *DL8 4SN – 𝒞 01969 624273 (booking essential) – www.thebluelion.co.uk*

EASTBOURNE

East Sussex – Pop. 109 185 – Regional map n° **5**-B3
▶ London 68 mi – Brighton 25 mi – Dover 61 mi

🏨 Grand ☆ ⇐ 🛏 ⌿ 🖼 🕸 🏠 🎧 🔁 & 🚼 🏋 🅿

LUXURY · CLASSIC Built in 1875 and offering all its name promises, the Grand retains many original features including ornate plasterwork, columned corridors and a Great Hall. The delightful gardens feature a superb outdoor pool and sun terrace. Bedrooms are spacious and classical – it's worth paying extra for a sea view. Dine in formal Mirabelle or the more accessible Garden Restaurant.

152 rooms ☲ – 🛉£ 160/220 🛉🛉£ 180/250 – 13 suites

King Edward's Par. ⊠ BN21 4EQ – 𝒞 01323 412345 – www.grandeastbourne.com

🏠 Ocklynge Manor 🛏 ⌿ 🅿 🍽

HISTORIC · PERSONALISED Sit in the small summerhouse and admire the beautiful mature gardens of this charming, traditional guesthouse. Mabel Lucie Attwell – the illustrator of 'Peter Pan and Wendy' – once lived here. Homemade cake is served on arrival.

3 rooms ☲ – 🛉£ 60/110 🛉🛉£ 100/130

Mill Rd ⊠ BN21 2PG – Northwest : 2 mi by A 259 and A 2270 – 𝒞 01323 734121 – www.ocklyngemanor.co.uk

EASTGATE
Durham – Regional map n° **14**-A3
▶ London 288 mi – Durham 27 mi – Newcastle upon Tyne 35 mi

🏠 Horsley Hall
HISTORIC · PERSONALISED Characterful 14C hunting lodge built for the Bishop of Durham, featuring impressive stained glass and a baronial hallway. Two of the cosy bedrooms have Edwardian bathrooms and many offer valley views. Have afternoon tea in the revolving garden pod and dinner under an ornate ceiling; game is a speciality.

9 rooms ⌂ – †£ 85/95 ††£ 140/160

✉ DL13 2LJ – Southeast : 1 mi by A 689 – ☎ 01388 517239 – www.horsleyhall.co.uk
– Closed 22 December-4 January

EBRINGTON – Gloucestershire → See Chipping Campden

ECKINGTON – Worcestershire → See Pershore

ECKINGTON
Derbyshire – Pop. 16 684 – Regional map n° **9**-B1
▶ London 155 mi – Derby 35 mi – Sheffield 10 mi

🍴 Devonshire Arms
TRADITIONAL BRITISH · DESIGN Sit on the small terrace or in one of three cosy, simply laid rooms. Cooking is fittingly understated: tried-and-tested British dishes are packed with flavour and equal effort is put into the classics as the more adventurous dishes.

Menu £ 28 (weekdays) – Carte £ 26/42

Lightwood Ln, Middle Handley ✉ S21 5RN – Southwest : 2 mi by B 6052 on Middle Handley rd – ☎ 01246 434800 – www.devonshirearmsmiddlehandley.com
– Closed Monday except bank holiday lunch and dinner Sunday

🍴 Inn at Troway
TRADITIONAL BRITISH · PUB Early Victorian pub in a picturesque location, offering delightful countryside views. The extensive menu offers satisfyingly hearty dishes and desserts often have a playful element. There's also a fine selection of local ales.

Carte £ 21/34

Snowdon Ln, Troway ✉ S21 5RU – West : 3.5 mi by B 6052 on B 6056
– ☎ 01246 417666 – www.relaxeatanddrink.co.uk

EDINGTON
Wiltshire – Regional map n° **2**-C2
▶ London 105 mi – Bristol 43 mi – Cardiff 76 mi

🍴 Three Daggers
MODERN BRITISH · COSY Attractive pub with original wood beams and flagstones, and a large conservatory overlooking the garden. The accessible menu always features a homemade soup and a 'pie of the day', and the Huntsman's and Fisherman's sharing platters are extremely popular. Charming bedrooms feature bespoke oak furnishings.

Carte £ 23/41

3 rooms ⌂ – †£ 85/110 ††£ 85/165

47 Westbury Rd ✉ BA13 4PG – ☎ 01380 830940 – www.threedaggers.co.uk

EGHAM
Surrey – Pop. 25 996 – Regional map n° **4**-C1
▶ London 22 mi – Guildford 23 mi – Oxford 49 mi

🏠 Great Fosters ⌂ ⌘ ⚒ ✕ ⚕ ✦ ⚒ 🅿

BUSINESS · ELEGANT Striking Elizabethan manor built as a hunting lodge for Henry VIII, boasting 50 acres of gardens, a beautiful parterre and an amphitheatre. The charming interior displays characterful original detailing. Bedrooms come with feature beds and a flamboyant touch; those in the annexes are more modern. Dine on steaks from the Josper grill or more formally in the Tudor Room.

43 rooms – ♦£180/205 ♦♦£195/315 – ⌑£20 – 3 suites

Stroude Rd ⊠ TW20 9UR – South : 1.25 mi by B 388 – ℰ 01784 433822
– www.greatfosters.co.uk

⚙ **Tudor Room** – See restaurant listing

🍴🍴🍴 Tudor Room ⚙ ⌘ ⚕ 🅿

⚙ **MODERN CUISINE · INTIMATE** An intimate hotel dining room with mullioned windows, burgundy décor and large tapestries on the walls. The menu might be concise but dishes are interesting, accomplished and full of flavour. Cooking is sophisticated but not over-complicated and the kitchen garden provides many of the ingredients.

➜ Scallop, broccoli, truffle and hazelnut. Turbot with gnocchi, peas and clams. Gariguette strawberries with tarragon, meringue and cream.

Menu £32/58 – tasting menu only

Great Fosters Hotel, Stroude Rd ⊠ TW20 9UR – South : 1.25 mi by B 388
– ℰ 01784 433822 (booking essential) – www.greatfosters.co.uk – dinner only and lunch Thursday-Friday – Closed Sunday-Tuesday

EGTON

North Yorkshire – Regional map n° **13**-C1
▶ London 250 mi – York 45 mi – Leeds 72 mi

🍴 Wheatsheaf Inn ⌂ 🅿

TRADITIONAL BRITISH · INN Family-run, late 17C inn on the edge of the picturesque North Yorkshire Moors. Menu offers a real taste of Yorkshire with fresh, hearty dishes like lambs' kidneys, local steak, Whitby scampi and game sourced from within 2 miles.

Carte £24/36

⊠ YO21 1TZ – ℰ 01947 895271 – www.wheatsheafegton.com – Closed 25 December and Monday

ELDERSFIELD

Worcestershire – Regional map n° **10**-B3
▶ London 124 mi – Worcester 23 mi – Gloucester 10 mi

🍴 Butchers Arms (James Winter) ⌘ 🅿

⚙ **MODERN BRITISH · RUSTIC** A sweet rural inn with two cosy dining rooms and a small bar, where the beams are fringed with hop bines and villagers meet for a pint at the end of the day. The chef, who cooks alone, has a great appreciation for natural ingredients and knows how to use them to create simple yet wonderfully well-flavoured dishes.

➜ Grilled octopus with steamed pork dumpling, ginger and coriander. Fillet of turbot with slow-roasted pork shoulder, buttered spinach and fondant potato. Brown sugar doughnuts with chocolate and caramel ice cream.

Carte £39/53

Lime Street ⊠ GL19 4NX – Southeast : 1 mi – ℰ 01452 840381 (booking essential) – www.thebutchersarms.net – dinner only and lunch Friday-Sunday – Closed 1 week early January, 1 week late August, Sunday dinner, Monday and bank holidays

ELLASTONE

Staffordshire – Regional map n° **10**-C1
▶ London 148 mi – Stafford 22 mi – Birmingham 49 mi

☺ Duncombe Arms   🛏 🍴 ♿ 🅿

TRADITIONAL BRITISH · COSY A stylish dining pub owned by the Hon. Johnny Greenall – of the famous brewing family – and his wife, a descendant of the Duncombe family after which the pub is named. There are several cosy rooms to choose from, each with their own identity. Menus mix pub classics with more ambitious restaurant-style dishes.
Carte £ 24/47

Main Road ⊠ DE6 2GZ – ☎ 01335 324275 – www.duncombearms.co.uk

ELLEL
Lancashire – Regional map n° **11**-A1
▶ London 240 mi – Lancaster 6 mi – Manchester 51 mi

☺ Bay Horse Inn   🛏 🍴 🅿

REGIONAL CUISINE · PUB Cosy, homely pub in a pleasant rural location, with a characterful interior and an attractive terrace. Seasonal, locally sourced produce is crafted into classic, tried-and-tested dishes. The Lancashire cheeseboard is a speciality.
Menu £ 20 (weekdays)/24 **s** – Carte £ 20/43 **s**

Bay Horse Ln, Bay Horse ⊠ LA2 0HR – South 1.5 mi by A 6 on Quernmore rd – ☎ 01524 791204 – www.bayhorseinn.com – Closed Monday except bank holiday lunch and Tuesday

ELMTON
Derbyshire – Regional map n° **9**-B1
▶ London 155 mi – Derby 34 mi – Sheffield 21 mi

☺ Elm Tree   🛏 🍴 ♻ 🅿

TRADITIONAL CUISINE · PUB 18C stone pub with a brightly lit bar, characterful beamed rooms, a wood-burning stove and a large garden. The good value menu offers pub classics presented in a modern manner, with most ingredients sourced from within 10 miles.
Menu £ 15 (weekday lunch) – Carte £ 18/40

⊠ S80 4LS – ☎ 01909 721261 – www.elmtreeelmton.co.uk – Closed Tuesday

ELSTREE
Hertfordshire – Pop. 1 986 – Regional map n° **7**-A2
▶ London 24 mi – Hertford 32 mi – Watford 11 mi

🏨 Laura Ashley-The Manor H. Elstree   🍴 🛏 ♿ 🍽 🛎 🅿

HISTORIC · GRAND LUXURY An eye-catching, timbered Edwardian house which showcases the latest fabrics, furnishings and fittings from the famous company. Well-equipped bedrooms: the largest and most characterful are in the main house. The intimate, formal restaurant offers modern cooking and views over the extensive gardens.
49 rooms � – †£ 129/179 ††£ 129/179

Barnet Ln ⊠ WD6 3RE – ☎ 020 8327 4700 – www.lauraashleyhotels.com/elstree

ELTERWATER
Cumbria – Regional map n° **21**-A2
▶ London 279 mi – Carlisle 46 mi – Kendal 18 mi

✕✕ The Eltermere ⓝ   ↩ ← 🛏 🅿

MODERN BRITISH · CLASSIC DÉCOR Take in lovely lake and mountain views from this handsome 17C farmhouse, where you'll find three elegantly furnished dining-cum-sitting rooms, a darkly decorated fire-lit bar and 12 capacious bedrooms. Cooking is fresh, unfussy and appealing, and many of the leaves and berries come from the attractive garden.
Menu £ 20/29 – Carte £ 30/40

12 rooms ⊡ – †£ 130/280 ††£ 145/295

⊠ LA22 9HY – At edge of village on Coniston rd – ☎ 015394 37207 – www.eltermere.co.uk – Closed 23-27 December and 2-16 January

ELTON
Cambridgeshire – Regional map n° **8**-A2
▶ London 84 mi – Cambridge 39 mi – Bedford 40 mi

Crown Inn   ⇦ 🛏 **P**

TRADITIONAL BRITISH · PUB 17C honey-stone pub in a delightful country parish, with a thatched roof, a cosy inglenook fireplace in the bar and a laid-back feel. Extensive menus offer homely British dishes which arrive in generous portions. Bedrooms are smart and individually styled – some have feature beds or roll-top baths.
Carte £ 24/35

8 rooms ⌂ – ♦£ 68/75 ♦♦£ 110/145
8 Duck St ⊠ *PE8 6RQ* – *ℰ 01832 280232* – *www.thecrowninn.org*

ELTON-ON-THE-HILL
Nottinghamshire – Regional map n° **9**-B2
▶ London 121 mi – Nottingham 15 mi – Lincoln 35 mi

The Grange   ⇦ 🛏 🍴 **P** 🚲

FAMILY · COSY What better way to start your holiday than in this charming Georgian farmhouse with a slice of homemade cake? The owners are lovely, the gardens are delightful and the country views are superb. Bedrooms are homely and come with good facilities and thoughtful touches; one is accessed via a spiral staircase.

3 rooms ⌂ – ♦£ 50/59 ♦♦£ 80/89
Sutton Ln. ⊠ *NG13 9LA* – *ℰ 07887 952181*
– www.thegrangebedandbreakfastnotts.co.uk

ELY
Cambridgeshire – Pop. 19 090 – Regional map n° **8**-B2
▶ London 74 mi – Cambridge 16 mi – Norwich 60 mi

Poets House   🍴 🛏 🖬 � 🅰🅲 🍴 🧖 **P**

TOWNHOUSE · MODERN A series of 19C townhouses set opposite the cathedral. Spacious, boutique bedrooms come with beautiful bathrooms, good extras and a moody feel. The modern bar overlooks the pretty walled garden and also offers afternoon tea. Dine on ambitious dishes, which include plenty of vegetarian options.

21 rooms ⌂ – ♦£ 139/229 ♦♦£ 139/229
St Mary's St ⊠ *CB7 4EY* – *ℰ 01353 887777* – *www.poetshouse.uk.com*

at Sutton Gault West: 8 mi by A142 off B1381⊠ Ely

Anchor Inn   ⇦ 🛏 🍴 **P**

REGIONAL CUISINE · PUB Riverside pub dating back to 1650 and the creation of the Hundred Foot Wash. Tempting menu complemented by daily fish specials. For a pleasant river outlook head for the wood-panelled rooms to the front of the bar. Neat, pine-furnished bedrooms include two suites; one with river views.
Menu £ 15 (weekday lunch)/35 – Carte £ 25/44

4 rooms ⌂ – ♦£ 60/135 ♦♦£ 65/145
⊠ *CB6 2BD* – *ℰ 01353 778537* – *www.anchor-inn-restaurant.co.uk*

at Little Thetford South: 2.75 mi by A10⊠ Ely

Springfields   🛏 🧖 **P** 🚲

TRADITIONAL · PERSONALISED Delightfully run, curio-filled bungalow in pleasant gardens. Immaculately kept bedrooms have different coloured Toile de Jouy wallpapers and plenty of extra touches. Enjoy breakfast among the Cranberry Glass collection or in the courtyard.

3 rooms ⌂ – ♦£ 60 ♦♦£ 85
Ely Rd ⊠ *CB6 3HJ - North : 0.5 mi on A 10* – *ℰ 01353 663637*
– www.smoothhound.co.uk/hotels/springfields – *Closed Christmas-New Year*

EMSWORTH

Hampshire - Pop. 18 777 - Regional map n° **4**-B2

▶ London 75 mi - Southampton 22 mi - Portsmouth 10 mi

XX 36 on the Quay   ⇔ ≤ ଐ ⇕

MODERN BRITISH · ELEGANT Long-standing, intimate restaurant and conservatory bar-lounge in a quayside cottage with pleasant harbour views. Concise menus offer elaborate modern dishes in some unusual combinations and foraged ingredients feature highly. Stylish bedrooms have good comforts; be ready to order breakfast at check-in.

Menu £ 24/65

4 rooms ⌑ - ♦£ 75/90 ♦♦£ 100/120

47 South St, The Quay ⊠ PO10 7EG - ℰ 01243 375592 (booking advisable)
- www.36onthequay.co.uk - Closed 2 weeks January, 1 week May, 1 week October, 24-27 December, Sunday and Monday

X Fat Olives   ⋒

MODERN BRITISH · RUSTIC This sweet 17C fisherman's cottage sits in a characterful coastal town, in a road leading down to the harbour. It's run by a charming couple and has a rustic modern feel, courtesy of locally crafted tables and upholstered chairs. Classic British dishes have a modern edge and rely on small local suppliers.

Menu £ 21 (lunch) - Carte £ 30/46

30 South St ⊠ PO10 7EH - ℰ 01243 377914 (booking essential)
- www.fatolives.co.uk - Closed 2 weeks late June, Christmas, New Year, Sunday and Monday

EPPING

Essex - Pop. 10 289 - Regional map n° **7**-B2

▶ London 23 mi - Colchester 41 mi - Chelmsford 18 mi

XX Haywards   & 🆑 ⇔ 🅿

MODERN CUISINE · INTIMATE This proudly run restaurant is the realisation of a couple's dream. A hammerbeam ceiling and cherry wood tables set the scene. Appealing dishes follow the seasons and flavours are well-balanced. Service is extremely welcoming.

Menu £ 31 (weekday lunch)/45

111 Bell Common ⊠ CM16 4DZ - Southwest : 1 mi by B 1393 and Theydon Rd
- ℰ 01992 577350 - www.haywardsrestaurant.co.uk - Closed 1-24 January and Sunday dinner-Wednesday lunch

EPSOM

Surrey - Pop. 31 474 - Regional map n° **4**-D1

▶ London 14 mi - Guildford 21 mi - Reading 41 mi

XXX Le Raj   🆑

BANGLADESHI · CHIC A local institution run by a larger-than-life owner. It has a comfy bar-lounge and a smart restaurant where wooden panels are picked out with gold leaf. White-gloved waiters serve carefully prepared, authentic Bangladeshi dishes.

Carte £ 25/35

211 Fir Tree Rd, Epsom Downs ⊠ KT17 3LB - Southeast : 2 mi by B 289 and B 284 on B 291 - ℰ 01737 371371 - www.lerajrestaurant.co.uk

ERMINGTON

Devon - Regional map n° **1**-C2

▶ London 216 mi - Exeter 36 mi - Plymouth 11 mi

✗✗ Plantation House

MODERN CUISINE · INTIMATE Georgian former rectory in a pleasant country spot, with a small drinks terrace, an open-fired lounge and two dining rooms: one formal, with black furnishings; one more relaxed, with polished wood tables. Interesting modern menus feature local produce. Stylish bedrooms come with fresh milk and homemade cake.

Menu £ 40 **s**

8 rooms ⌂ – ♯£ 80/120 ♯♯£ 115/230

Totnes Rd ⌂ PL21 9NS – Southwest : 0.5 mi on A 3121 – ℰ 01548 831100 (bookings essential for non-residents) – www.plantationhousehotel.co.uk – dinner only

---

ESHOTT – Northd. ➜ See Morpeth

ETTINGTON
Warwickshire – Pop. 1 039 – Regional map n° **10**-C3
▶ London 95 mi – Warwick 12 mi – Leicester 48 mi

🏠 Chequers Inn

TRADITIONAL CUISINE · PUB Chandeliers, brushed velvet furniture and Regency chairs set at chequered tables mean this is not your typical pub. Menus display a broad international style; dishes range from British classics to others with a Mediterranean bent.

Carte £ 22/38

91 Banbury Rd ⌂ CV37 7SR – ℰ 01789 740387
– www.the-chequers-ettington.co.uk – Closed Sunday dinner and Monday

---

EVERSHOT
Dorset – ⌂ Dorchester – Pop. 225 – Regional map n° **2**-C3
▶ London 149 mi – Dorchester 12 mi – Taunton 30 mi

🏨 Summer Lodge

LUXURY · ELEGANT Attractive former dower house in mature gardens, featuring a smart wellness centre, a pool and a tennis court. Plush, individually designed bedrooms come with marble bathrooms and the country house guest areas display heavy fabrics and antiques – the drawing room was designed by Thomas Hardy. The formal dining room offers classical cuisine and a superb wine list.

24 rooms ⌂ – ♯£ 235/745 ♯♯£ 235/745 – 4 suites

9 Fore St ⌂ DT2 0JR – ℰ 01935 482000 – www.summerlodgehotel.com

🏠 Acorn Inn

INN · CLASSIC The historic Acorn Inn was mentioned in 'Tess of the d'Urbervilles' and to this day is the hub of the village. Cosy, individually appointed bedrooms have fabric-covered walls – some have four-posters and the attic is perfect for families. Dine in the classic restaurant or the locals bar with its skittle alley.

10 rooms ⌂ – ♯£ 89/210 ♯♯£ 99/220 – 1 suite

28 Fore St ⌂ DT2 0JW – ℰ 01935 83228 – www.acorn-inn.co.uk

🏠 Wooden Cabbage

COUNTRY HOUSE · COSY The unusual name comes from the local term for a stunted oak tree. An attractive former gamekeeper's cottage, it sits in a quiet spot and has lovely countryside views from its pretty bedrooms and tropical plant filled orangery.

3 rooms ⌂ – ♯£ 100/120 ♯♯£ 110/125

⌂ DT2 0QA – ℰ 01935 83362 – www.woodencabbage.co.uk

EWEN
Gloucestershire – Pop. 257 – Regional map n° **4**-C1
▶ London 91 mi – Gloucester 22 mi – Stroud 17 mi

🍴 Wild Duck ❶   🛎 P

TRADITIONAL CUISINE · RUSTIC The Wild Duck is a charming place, both inside and out. Snack on charcuterie sliced on the ornate slicer behind the bar, choose a healthy option such as soy-glazed mackerel or really push the boat out with the duck for two to share.

Menu £ 15 (weekday lunch) – Carte £ 22/38

Drakes Island ⊠ GL7 6BY – ℰ 01285 770310 – www.thewildduckewen.com

EXETER

Devon – Pop. 113 507 – Regional map n° **1**-D2

▶ London 201 mi – Plymouth 46 mi – Bristol 83 mi

🏨 Abode Exeter   🔄 ⬆ ⅃ 🐾 ⅏

HISTORIC · MODERN An attractive Georgian property in the shadow of the cathedral. The stylish interior features an all-day café, a pub and a chic cocktail bar. Some of the smart, boldly coloured bedrooms have roll-top baths with cathedral views.

53 rooms ⊡ – ♦£ 79/199 ♦♦£ 89/249 – 1 suite

Town plan: AB1-z - *Cathedral Yard ⊠ EX1 1HD – ℰ 01392 319955*
– www.abodehotels.co.uk

The Restaurant – See restaurant listing

🏨 Southernhay House   🍸 🍴 🛎 ⅏

TOWNHOUSE · CONTEMPORARY Attractive Georgian townhouse with original ceiling roses and ornate coving. Smart, compact guest areas include a stylish lounge and a bar with bright blue furniture. Warmly decorated bedrooms have sumptuous beds, luxurious fabrics and chic bathrooms. The small dining room offers British-based menus.

10 rooms ⊡ – ♦£ 150/260 ♦♦£ 150/260

Town plan: B2-x - *36 Southernhay East ⊠ EX1 1NX – ℰ 01392 435324*
– www.southernhayhouse.com

✕✕ The Restaurant   ⅃ AC

INTERNATIONAL · FRIENDLY Contemporary hotel restaurant with well-spaced tables and huge mirrors on the walls; ask to sit by the window for a view of the cathedral. Modern menus feature European influences – the tasting menu offers the most elaborate dishes.

Menu £ 17/20 – Carte £ 39/55

Town plan: AB1-z - *Abode Exeter Hotel, Cathedral Yard ⊠ EX1 1HD*
– ℰ 01392 223638 – www.abodeexeter.co.uk

🍴 Rusty Bike   ⅃

TRADITIONAL BRITISH · PUB A bohemian pub which appeals to lovers of traditional British food. Daily changing menus feature hearty, masculine dishes. They butcher rare breed pigs on-site, cure their own bresaola and smoke their own ham. Sit in the cosy snug.

Carte £ 28/41

Town plan: B1-x - *67 Howell Rd ⊠ EX4 4LZ – ℰ 01392 214440*
– www.rustybike-exeter.co.uk – dinner only and Sunday lunch – Closed
24-25 December, 1 January and Sunday dinner

at Brampford Speke North: 5 mi by A377

🍴 Lazy Toad Inn   🍴 🛎 ⅃ P

REGIONAL CUISINE · COSY In winter, sit under a lovely oak-beamed ceiling beside an inviting log fire; in summer, head for the beautiful walled garden or charming cobbled courtyard. Hearty British dishes showcase produce from the garden and polytunnel.

Carte £ 16/38

⊠ EX5 5DP – ℰ 01392 841591 – www.thelazytoad.com – Closed 1 week January,
Sunday dinner and Monday

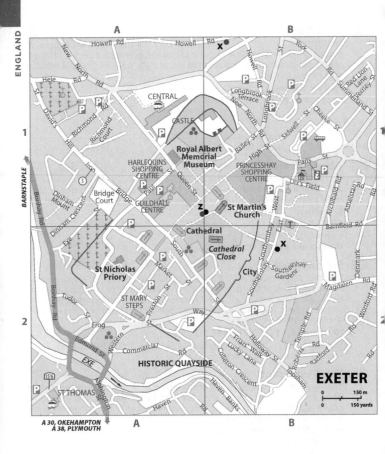

BARNSTAPLE

EXETER

0   150 m
0   150 yards

A 30, OKEHAMPTON
A 38, PLYMOUTH

EXMOUTH

Devon – Pop. 34 432 – Regional map n° **1**-D2
▶ London 175 mi – Exeter 12 mi – Cardiff 114 mi

✗ **Les Saveurs**

TRADITIONAL CUISINE · BISTRO Traditional restaurant owned and run by a French chef and his family. Menus are unashamedly classical and feature dishes from their homeland; seafood features highly - most of it caught by the chef himself. Don't miss the lemon tart.

Carte £ 33/44

9 Tower St ✉ EX8 1NT – ℰ 01395 269459 – www.lessaveurs.co.uk – dinner only – Closed early January-mid February, Sunday and Monday

EYDON

Northamptonshire – Pop. 422 – Regional map n° **16**-B3
▶ London 77 mi – Northampton 18 mi – Birmingham 55 mi

Royal Oak

MODERN CUISINE • PUB Characterful 17C pub owned by a local farming family. There are four different dining areas, plus a courtyard terrace. Choose ambitious modern dishes from the à la carte or stick with the classics on the good value set lunch menu.

Menu £10 (lunch) – Carte £27/47

6 Lime Av ✉ NN11 3PG – ✆ 01327 263167 – www.theroyaloakateydon.co.uk – Closed dinner Monday-Tuesday

FALMOUTH

Cornwall – Pop. 22 686 – Regional map n° **1**-A3

London 308 mi – Truro 11 mi – Penzance 26 mi

Dolvean House

TOWNHOUSE • CLASSIC Victorian house built in 1870; its homely lounge has lots of local guide books and magazines. Neat breakfast room. Good-sized bedrooms with thoughtful touches; Room 9, with a big bay window, is the best.

10 rooms – †£40/55 ††£80/110

Town plan: B2-n - *50 Melvill Rd ✉ TR11 4DQ – ✆ 01326 313658 – www.dolvean.co.uk – Closed first 2 weeks November and 22-28 December*

Chelsea House

TOWNHOUSE • PERSONALISED An imposing Edwardian house in a quiet residential street close to the beaches. It's a trendy spot where retro furnishings fuse with vibrant fabrics to create a modish, boutique feel. Bedrooms on the top floors have good sea views.

9 rooms – †£80/125 ††£88/138

Town plan: B2-e - *2 Emslie Rd ✉ TR11 4BG – ✆ 01326 212230 – www.chelseahousehotel.com*

Rick Stein's Fish

SEAFOOD • BRASSERIE With their own special beef dripping batter and fish chilli burgers to takeaway, this is more than your usual fish 'n' chips. Head inside and, alongside your favourites, you'll find the likes of dressed crab, fruits de mer and cod curry.

Menu £12 (lunch and early dinner) – Carte £23/39

Town plan: B2-a - *Discovery Quay ✉ TR11 3XA – ✆ 01841 532700 (booking advisable) – www.rickstein.com – Closed 25-26 December*

Oliver's

TRADITIONAL • NEIGHBOURHOOD Although it's just a few paces from the water, Oliver's is known more for its game than anything else. Good value lunches are followed by more ambitious dinners. It's a simple place, run with plenty of passion, and a hit with the locals.

Menu £22/40 – Carte £26/39

Town plan: B1-s - *33 High St ✉ TR11 2AD – ✆ 01326 218138 – www.oliversfalmouth.com – Closed Christmas-New Year, Sunday and Monday*

at Maenporth Beach South: 3.75 mi by Pennance Rd

Cove

MODERN CUISINE • ROMANTIC A bright, stylish restaurant in a smart glass-fronted building overlooking the beach, the cove and St Anthony's Head. The modern dining room leads through to a lovely split-level terrace with a retractable roof. Menus are contemporary, with a strong seafood base and some Asian influences.

Menu £20 – Carte £25/40

Maenporth Beach ✉ TR11 5HN – ✆ 01326 251136 – www.thecovemaenporth.co.uk – Closed 25 December

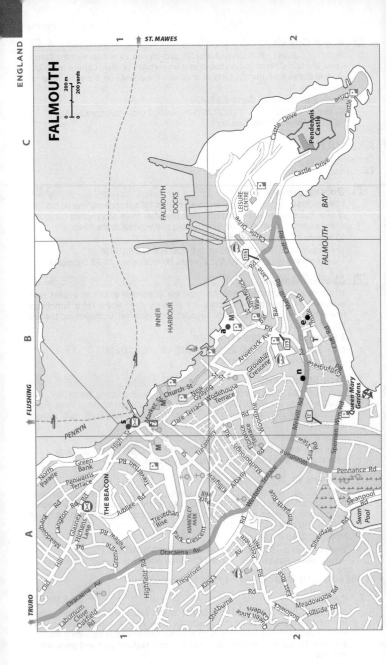

FALMOUTH

0   200 m
0   200 yards

ST. MAWES

1

2

FLUSHING

PENRYN

TRURO

INNER HARBOUR

FALMOUTH DOCKS

FALMOUTH BAY

Pendennis Castle

Castle Drive

Castle Drive

Castle Drive

LEISURE CENTRE

Cliff Rd

Bar Rd

Melville Rd

Gyllyngvase Rd

Queen Mary Gardens

Gyllyngvase Rd

Cliff Rd

Spernen Wyn Rd

Woodlane

Sea View Rd

Melville Rd

Pennance Rd

Swanpool Rd

Swan Pool

Silverdale Rd

Boslowick Rd

Meadowside Rd

Hillside Rd

Green Anne Gardens

Shelburne Rd

East St

King's Rd

Penmere Rise

Pennance Rd

Dracaena Av.

Tregenver

Highfield Rd

Dracaena Av.

Oakfield Rd

Laburnum Close

Old Hill

Meadowbank Rd

Langton Rd

Glasney Rd

Hichen's Lane

Pellow Rd

Grenville Rd

Trevethan Rise

Jubilee Rd

Park Hill

Killigrew Rd

KIMBERLEY PARK

Park Crescent

Marlborough Rd

Albany Rd

Western Terrace

Trelawney Rd

Woodlane Terrace

Clare Terrace

Wodehouse Terrace

New Stilling St

Church St

Market St

High St

North Parade

Green Bank

Penwerris Terrace

Trevethan Rd

THE BEACON

Arwenack Av.

Grovehill Crescent

Gyllyng St

Grommack Way

Bar Rd

Meadowbank Rd

A

B

C

1

2

FARINGDON

Oxfordshire – Pop. 7 121 – Regional map n° **6**-A2

▶ London 81 mi – Oxford 19 mi – Bristol 55 mi

🏠 Sudbury House

BUSINESS · FUNCTIONAL Corporate hotel in 9 acres of grounds, not far from the Folly Tower. The eight meeting rooms include a 100-seater tiered lecture theatre. Bedrooms are modern and functional with smart bathrooms. Have snacks in the bar, wood-fired specialities in relaxed Magnolia or more elaborate dishes in Restaurant 56.

50 rooms – ♟£124/450 ♟♟£144/470 – ☑£13

56 London St. ⊠ SN7 7AA – ☎ 01367 241272 – www.sudburyhouse.co.uk – Closed 2-16 January

Restaurant 56 – See restaurant listing

XXX Restaurant 56

MODERN CUISINE · ELEGANT Georgian manor house in the grounds of a corporate hotel – its wood-panelling and red fabrics give it a smart, formal feel. Attractive dishes are crafted from good quality produce; cooking is classically based with a modern edge.

Menu £45/95

Sudbury House Hotel, 56 London St ⊠ SN7 7AA – ☎ 01367 245389 (booking advisable) – www.restaurant56.co.uk – dinner only – Closed 2-16 January, Sunday and Monday

FARNBOROUGH

Hampshire – Pop. 65 034 – Regional map n° **4**-C1

▶ London 41 mi – Winchester 33 mi – Southampton 44 mi

🏠 Aviator

BUSINESS · MODERN Eye-catching modern hotel overlooking Farnborough Airport with a striking circular atrium, a stylish cocktail bar and an American burger joint. Sleek, good-sized bedrooms feature light wood and modern facilities. The contemporary restaurant serves modern British dishes and steaks from the Josper grill.

169 rooms ☑ – ♟£145/245 ♟♟£155/470

55 Farnborough Rd ⊠ GU14 6EL – Southwest : 1 mi on A 325 – ☎ 01252 555890 – www.aviatorbytag.com

FARNHAM – Dorset ➜ See Blandford Forum

FAVERSHAM

Kent – Pop. 19 829 – Regional map n° **5**-C1

▶ London 52 mi – Maidstone 21 mi – Dover 26 mi

XXX Read's

TRADITIONAL CUISINE · ELEGANT An elegant Georgian manor house in landscaped grounds, with traditional country house styling, antique furnishings and lovely oil paintings. Classically based dishes have subtle modern touches and make use of seasonal produce from the walled kitchen garden and the nearby quay. Comfortable bedrooms are full of period charm and thoughtful extras provide a sense of luxury.

Menu £28/60

6 rooms ☑ – ♟£140/195 ♟♟£180/210

Macknade Manor, Canterbury Rd ⊠ ME13 8XE – East : 1 mi on A 2 – ☎ 01795 535344 – www.reads.com – Closed 2 weeks early September, 1 week early January, 25-26 December, Sunday and Monday

at Oare Northwest: 2.5 mi by A2 off B2045

🍴 Three Mariners   🦽 🛋 **P**

TRADITIONAL BRITISH · PUB Welcoming 500 year old pub set in a sleepy hamlet and boasting views across the marshes to the estuary. Constantly evolving menus offer an extensive range of British and Mediterranean-influenced dishes.
Menu £ 14/22 – Carte £ 20/36

2 Church Rd ⊠ ME13 0QA – ℰ 01795 533633 – www.thethreemarinersoare.co.uk
– Closed dinner 24-25 December

FELIXKIRK
North Yorkshire – Regional map n° **13**-B1
▶ London 228 mi – York 42 mi – Harrogate 29 mi

🍴 Carpenter's Arms   🥢 🦽 🛋 占 🗔 **P**

TRADITIONAL BRITISH · PUB A proper village pub with 18C origins, set in a village mentioned in the Domesday Book. Choose from blackboard specials or a wide-ranging menu of seasonal dishes, and be sure to save room for pudding. Stylishly appointed, well-equipped bedrooms overlook the Vale of Mowbray – as does the lovely terrace.
Carte £ 26/53

10 rooms � – ♦£ 95/160 ♦♦£ 120/185
⊠ YO7 2DP – ℰ 01845 537369 – www.thecarpentersarmsfelixkirk.com

FENCE
Lancashire – Pop. 1 459 – Regional map n° **11**-B2
▶ London 240 mi – Skipton 17 mi – Burnley 5 mi

🍴 White Swan   🛋 占 **P**

😊 MODERN BRITISH · SIMPLE Traditional pub owned by Timothy Taylor's brewery: you're always guaranteed a perfect, crystal-clear pint here – and the food is just as good. Concise set menus offer a well-crafted daily selection of flavoursome modern dishes. The cheeseboard with homemade crackers and truffle honey is well worth a try.
Carte £ 26/36

300 Wheatley Lane Rd ⊠ BB12 9QA – ℰ 01282 611773
– www.whiteswanatfence.co.uk – Closed Sunday dinner and Monday

FERMAIN BAY → See Channel Islands (Guernsey)

FERRENSBY – North Yorkshire → See Knaresborough

FILEY
North Yorkshire – Pop. 6 530 – Regional map n° **13**-D2
▶ London 240 mi – York 40 mi – Leeds 66 mi

🏠 All Seasons   🚫

TOWNHOUSE · PERSONALISED This unassuming Victorian terraced house – just a stone's throw from the sea – conceals a smart, stylish interior, where no detail is forgotten. The cosy lounge is filled with magazines and local info, and bedrooms are bright, comfy and immaculately kept. You are welcomed with homemade cake and brownies.

6 rooms ⊠ – ♦£ 65/100 ♦♦£ 85/110
11 Rutland St ⊠ YO14 9JA – ℰ 01723 515321 – www.allseasonsfiley.co.uk – Closed 24-26 December

FILKINS
Oxfordshire – Pop. 434 – Regional map n° **6**-A2
▶ London 78 mi – Oxford 23 mi – Bristol 59 mi

🍴 **Five Alls** 🔁 🛏 🏠 🅿

TRADITIONAL BRITISH · PUB Like its curious logo, this pub has it all: an open-fired bar where they serve snacks and takeaway burgers; a locals bar stocked with fine ales; three antique-furnished dining rooms; and a terrace and a garden with an Aunt Sally area. The menu is satisfyingly traditional and bedrooms are modern and cosy.

Menu £18 (weekdays) – Carte £27/43

9 rooms ☑ – ♦£75/90 ♦♦£90/150

✉ GL7 3JQ – ☎01367 860875 – www.thefiveallsfilkins.co.uk – Closed 25 December and Sunday dinner

FIVEHEAD

Somerset – Pop. 609 – Regional map n° **2**-B3
▶ London 140 mi – Taunton 10 mi – Bristol 63 mi

XX **Langford Fivehead** 🔁 🌭 🔁 🛏 ✕ 🅿

MODERN CUISINE · INTIMATE Beautiful, personally run country house with 13C origins, set in 7 acres of well-tended gardens. With its antique panelling, old stone fireplaces and mullioned windows, it conveys a real sense of history. The talented chef cooks modern, balanced, highly seasonal dishes with lovely flavours. Bedrooms are tastefully furnished and many have four-poster beds.

Menu £28/38

6 rooms ☑ – ♦£125/275 ♦♦£140/290

Lower Swell ✉ TA3 6PH – East : 0.5 mi by Westport rd on Swell rd – ☎01460 282020 (booking essential) – www.langfordfivehead.co.uk – dinner only and lunch Wednesday-Friday – Closed 2 January-3 February, 25-26 December, Sunday and Monday

FLAUNDEN

Hertfordshire – Pop. 5 468 – Regional map n° **7**-A2
▶ London 35 mi – Hertford 26 mi – Oxford 43 mi

🍴 **Bricklayers Arms** 🛏 🏠 🅿

TRADITIONAL CUISINE · INN Smart pub tucked away in a small hamlet. There are no snacks, just hearty, French-inspired dishes and old-school puddings. The wine list is a labour of love, featuring boutique Australian wines, and Sunday lunch is a real family affair.

Menu £17 (weekdays) – Carte £25/44

Hogpits Bottom ✉ HP3 0PH – ☎01442 833322 – www.bricklayersarms.com – Closed 25 December

FLETCHING

East Sussex – Pop. 301 – Regional map n° **5**-A2
▶ London 45 mi – Lewes 10 mi – Brighton 20 mi

🍴 **Griffin Inn** 🕸 🔁 🛏 🏠 🅿

TRADITIONAL BRITISH · CLASSIC DÉCOR Hugely characterful coaching inn, under the same ownership for over 30 years. There's a sizeable garden and a terrace with a wood-burning oven for summer BBQs. Menus feature British classics and some Mediterranean influences. Individually decorated bedrooms are accessed via narrow, sloping corridors.

Carte £26/44

13 rooms ☑ – ♦£70/80 ♦♦£85/155

✉ TN22 3SS – ☎01825 722890 – www.thegriffininn.co.uk – Closed 25 December

FOLKESTONE

Kent – Pop. 51 337 – Regional map n° **5**-D2
▶ London 76 mi – Maidstone 33 mi – Dover 8 mi

⊞ 10 to12 Folkestone

TOWNHOUSE · MODERN Classic Victorian end-of-terrace house, close to the seafront. It's run by friendly owners and is the perfect place to stop before getting the ferry. Bedrooms are particularly spacious and are appointed in a simple, modern manner.

10 rooms �てい – †£ 90/110 ††£ 100/120

10-12 Langhorne Gdns ✉ CT20 2EA – ℰ 01303 210127
– www.10to12folkestone.co.uk – Closed 1 week Christmas

XX Rocksalt

SEAFOOD · DESIGN Set within a stylish harbourfront eco-building affording lovely sea views. Smart cantilevered dining room with full-length windows opening onto a terrace; semi open air bar upstairs. Menus mix seafood and local meats; veg is from their farm. Nearby, bedrooms boast antique beds, Egyptian cotton linen and wet rooms.

Menu £ 22 (weekday lunch) – Carte £ 27/60

4 rooms ☲ – †£ 85/115 ††£ 85/115

4-5 Fish Market ✉ CT19 6AA – ℰ 01303 212070 – www.rocksaltfolkestone.co.uk
– Closed Sunday dinner

FONTHILL BISHOP

Wiltshire – Regional map n° **2**-C2
▶ London 101 mi – Salisbury 15 mi – Bath 29 mi

X Riverbarn

MODERN CUISINE · SIMPLE Two riverside cottages in a characterful village. Dining takes place in a series of beamed, low-ceilinged rooms adorned with copper pans and prints. Two brothers create carefully prepared, flavoursome dishes, which their parents bring to the table. Simple, comfortable bedrooms are found in the old barn.

Menu £ 20 (lunch) – Carte £ 25/43

4 rooms ☲ – †£ 65/70 ††£ 80/155

✉ SP3 5SF – ℰ 01747 820232 (bookings advisable at dinner)
– www.theriverbarn.org.uk – lunch only and dinner Thursday-Saturday – Closed
26 December-mid January and Monday

FONTMELL MAGNA

Dorset – Pop. 333 – Regional map n° **2**-C3
▶ London 115 mi – Salisbury 24 mi – Bournemouth 28 mi

⊞ Fontmell

MODERN CUISINE · PUB Stylish, modern pub with a simple front bar; the smart dining room straddles the brook, so keep an eye out for otters. Daily menus offer an eclectic mix of carefully executed dishes, from Mediterranean to Thai. Bedrooms are named after butterflies; Mallyshag is particularly spacious, with a roll-top bath.

Carte £ 25/46

6 rooms ☲ – †£ 95/175 ††£ 105/185

✉ SP7 0PA – ℰ 01747 811441 – www.thefontmell.com – Closed 26 December

FORDINGBRIDGE

Hampshire – Pop. 4 474 – Regional map n° **4**-A2
▶ London 101 mi – Winchester 30 mi – Salisbury 11 mi

⊞ Three Lions

FAMILY · COSY A former farmhouse and pub in a small hamlet. Homely bedrooms are split between this and various outbuildings; those in the garden are the largest and come with French windows and outdoor seating. Blackboard menus offer classically inspired Anglo-French dishes crafted from local, seasonal produce.

7 rooms ☲ – †£ 79 ††£ 125

Stuckton Rd, Stuckton ✉ SP6 2HF – Southeast : 1 mi by B 3078 – ℰ 01425 652489
– www.thethreelionsrestaurant.co.uk – Closed last 2 weeks February

FOREST GREEN

Surrey – Pop. 1 843 – Regional map n° **4**-D2

▶ London 34 mi – Guildford 13 mi – Horsham 10 mi

🍴 Parrot Inn

TRADITIONAL CUISINE · RUSTIC Characterful 17C pub on the village green. They serve meats from their farm, run their own butchery courses, and sell homemade breads, cakes and preserves in their neighbouring farm shop. Be sure to try the tasty raised pastry pies.

Carte £ 22/36

✉ RH5 5RZ – ☎ 01306 621339 – www.theparrot.co.uk – Closed 25 December and Sunday dinner

FOTHERINGHAY

Northamptonshire – Regional map n° **9**-C2

▶ London 87 mi – Northampton 34 mi – Peterborough 12 mi

🍴 Falcon Inn

TRADITIONAL CUISINE · PUB An attractive stone inn with a nice terrace and garden. Good ingredients feature in a wide range of flavoursome dishes and local game is a feature. You'll find the regulars playing darts in the tap bar and diners in the conservatory.

Menu £ 16 (weekdays) – Carte £ 23/39

✉ PE8 5HZ – ☎ 01832 226254 – www.thefalcon-inn.co.uk – Closed Sunday dinner September-May

FOWEY

Cornwall – Pop. 2 131 – Regional map n° **1**-B2

▶ London 277 mi – Truro 22 mi – Plymouth 34 mi

🏨 Fowey Hall

COUNTRY HOUSE · PERSONALISED A striking 19C manor house with an ornate lounge and a mix of traditional and modern bedrooms. It's set high above the village and has lovely views. Families are well-catered for and an informal feel pervades. There's an oak-panelled restaurant reserved for adults and a conservatory for those with children.

36 rooms ☲ – ♦£ 190/750 ♦♦£ 190/750 – 11 suites

Hanson Dr ✉ PL23 1ET – West : 0.5 mi off A 3082 – ☎ 01726 833866
– www.foweyhallhotel.co.uk

🏠 Old Quay House

TOWNHOUSE · CONTEMPORARY 19C former seamen's mission in a pretty harbour village; now a characterful boutique hotel with a laid-back feel and a lovely riverside terrace. Bedrooms have an understated contemporary style; most have balconies and water views.

11 rooms ☲ – ♦£ 105/140 ♦♦£ 145/355

28 Fore St ✉ PL23 1AQ – ☎ 01726 833302 – www.theoldquayhouse.com
– Closed 1-20 December

Q – See restaurant listing

🍴🍴 Q

MODERN CUISINE · FRIENDLY Bright hotel restaurant with wood framed mirrors, comfy furnishings and a glorious terrace with harbour views. Light lunches and more sophisticated dinners of modern, flavoursome dishes; fish is from Looe and shellfish from Fowey.

Menu £ 33 (dinner) – Carte lunch £ 28/49

Old Quay House Hotel, 28 Fore St ✉ PL23 1AQ – ☎ 01726 833302
– www.theoldquayhouse.com – Closed 1-20 December and lunch October-April

ℵ The Globe ⇦

TRADITIONAL BRITISH · COSY A 400 year old posting house run by lifelong friends and refurbished by local craftsmen. The food keeps things pleasingly regional too, with bread from the adjacent bakery, fish from the nearby harbour, meats from a local farm and beer from St Austell. Bedrooms are comfy and cosy.

Menu £ 19 (weekday lunch) – Carte £ 28/45

4 rooms ⌱ – ♦£ 90/120 ♦♦£ 90/120

24 Fore St ⊠ PL23 1AQ – ℰ 01726 337076 – www.theglobefowey.co.uk

at Golant North: 3 mi by B3269⊠ Fowey

🏠 Cormorant ☆ ⅋ ⋖ 🖴 🖭 🖻 🕸 ⑩ 🅿

COUNTRY HOUSE · PERSONALISED Well-run hotel in a superb waterside position. At only one room deep, all of its bedrooms overlook the estuary; the superior rooms boast balconies. Appealing seasonal menus feature local meats and seafood dishes. Light lunches offered in the formal restaurant or on the terrace.

14 rooms ⌱ – ♦£ 65/160 ♦♦£ 85/190

⊠ PL23 1LL – ℰ 01726 833426 – www.cormoranthotel.co.uk

FOXHAM

Wiltshire – Regional map n° **2**-C2

◰ London 94 mi – Bristol 28 mi – Cardiff 61 mi

🍴 Foxham Inn ⇦ 🖭 ⌕ 🅿

CLASSIC CUISINE · SIMPLE Family-run pub in a sleepy Wiltshire village. A semi-covered terrace overlooks the fields and inside there's a cosy bar and a light, airy restaurant in a conservatory extension. Dishes are uniformly priced, and everything from the condiments to the ice creams is homemade. Bedrooms are warm and homely.

Carte £ 27/42

2 rooms ⌱ – ♦£ 75 ♦♦£ 90

⊠ SN15 4NQ – ℰ 01249 740665 (booking advisable) – www.thefoxhaminn.co.uk – Closed 2 weeks early January, Sunday dinner and Monday

FREATHY

Cornwall – Regional map n° **1**-C2

◰ London 235 mi – Truro 51 mi – Plymouth 9 mi

ℵ The View ⋖ 🖭 🅿

MODERN BRITISH · SIMPLE Charming and informal converted café perched on a cliff, with coastal views. Relaxed daytime vibe; more atmospheric in the evening. Assured, confident, generous cooking and friendly service. Plenty of seafood and tasty homemade bread.

Menu £ 15 (lunch) – Carte £ 32/40

⊠ PL10 1JY – East : 1 mi – ℰ 01752 822345 – www.theview-restaurant.co.uk – Closed February, Monday and Tuesday

FRILSHAM – West Berkshire → See Yattendon

FRITHSDEN

Hertfordshire – Regional map n° **7**-A2

◰ London 33 mi – St Albans 11 mi – Aylesbury 16 mi

🍴 Alford Arms 🖭 🅿

TRADITIONAL BRITISH · INN Attractive Victorian pub beside the village green. The traditional British menu follows the seasons closely, with salads and fish featuring in the summer and game and comfort dishes in the winter; go for one of the tempting specials.

Carte £ 22/40

⊠ HP1 3DD – ℰ 01442 864480 – www.alfordarmsfrithsden.co.uk – Closed 25-26 December

FROGGATT
Derbyshire – Regional map n° **9**-A1

▶ London 167 mi – Derby 6 mi – Sheffield 11 mi

🍽 Chequers Inn

TRADITIONAL BRITISH · PUB Traditional 16C inn built right into the stone boulders of Froggatt Edge and boasting a direct path up to the peak. Cooking is unfussy, tasty and largely classical, with more imaginative specials on the blackboard. Comfortable bedrooms; Number One, to the rear, is the quietest.

Carte £ 26/39

7 rooms ⌷ – †£ 109/119 ††£ 109/119

Hope Valley ⌧ S32 3ZJ – On A 625 – ℰ 01433 630231
– www.chequers-froggatt.com – Closed 25 December

FROME
Somerset – Pop. 26 203 – Regional map n° **2**-C2

▶ London 118 mi – Taunton 51 mi – Bristol 24 mi

🏨 Babington House

LUXURY · TRENDY Behind this country house's classic Georgian façade is a cool, fashionable hotel with bold colour schemes, modern understated bedrooms and a bohemian feel. Unwind in the luxurious lounges or in the beautiful spa with its superb fitness area and pool. The Orangery offers an accessible menu of Italian-influenced dishes which showcase ingredients from the walled garden.

33 rooms – †£ 240/365 ††£ 240/365 – ⌷ £ 17 – 11 suites

Babington ⌧ BA11 3RW – Northwest : 6.5 mi by A 362 on Vobster rd
– ℰ 01373 812266 – www.babingtonhouse.co.uk

FULLER STREET
Essex – Pop. 50 – Regional map n° **7**-C2

▶ London 52 mi – Chelmsford 8 mi – Colchester 23 mi

🍽 Square & Compasses

MODERN BRITISH · PUB A hugely characterful pub hidden down rural lanes: run with a passion by its welcoming owners. One menu lists classic dishes; the other features more adventurous choices, including fish caught off the Essex coast and local game in season.

Carte £ 19/33

⌧ CM3 2BB – ℰ 01245 361477 (booking essential)
– www.thesquareandcompasses.co.uk

FULMER
Buckinghamshire – Pop. 230 – Regional map n° **6**-D3

▶ London 21 mi – Aylesbury 26 mi – Reading 25 mi

🍽 Black Horse

TRADITIONAL BRITISH · PUB Whitewashed village pub with thick walls, cosy alcoves, a wood-burning stove and a gem of a garden for sunny days. The stylish, formal dining area is hung with delightful portraits. Dishes include sharing boards, small plates and grills. Uniquely styled bedrooms have spacious, modern bathrooms.

Carte £ 26/43

2 rooms – †£ 120/150 ††£ 120/150

Windmill Rd ⌧ SL3 6HD – ℰ 01753 663183 – www.theblackhorsefulmer.co.uk
– Closed 25 December and Sunday dinner

FUNTINGTON – West Sussex ➡ See Chichester

FYFIELD
Essex – Pop. 737 – Regional map n° **7**-B2

▶ London 33 mi – Chelmsford 14 mi – Cambridge 44 mi

🍴 Queens Head   🚪 🏠 ⟷ 🅿️

MODERN CUISINE · PUB Characterful village pub with a pretty rear garden leading down to the river. The inviting interior features original 16C beams and fireplaces. Menus change regularly and offer a good choice of classics and blackboard specials.

Menu £ 22 (weekdays) – Carte £ 28/47

Queen St ⊠ CM5 0RY – 𝒞 01277 899231 – www.thequeensheadfyfield.co.uk
– Closed 26 December and Mondays

FYFIELD – Oxfordshire ➜ See Oxford

GEDNEY DYKE

Lincolnshire – Pop. 320 – Regional map n° **9**-D2
▶ London 112 mi – Peterborough 28 mi – Cambridge 32 mi

✕✕ Chequers   🏠 ♿ 🅿️

MODERN BRITISH · FRIENDLY Formerly a pub, now a stylish modern bar and restaurant with a smart conservatory extension opening onto a pavement terrace. They are enthusiastic about using the wealth of produce on their doorstep; the set menus represent good value.

Menu £ 20

Main St ⊠ PE12 0AJ – 𝒞 01406 366700 – www.the-chequers.co.uk – Closed first 2 weeks January, Sunday dinner, Monday and Tuesday

GERRARDS CROSS

Buckinghamshire – Pop. 20 633 – Regional map n° **6**-D3
▶ London 22 mi – Aylesbury 22 mi – Reading 27 mi

🍴 Three Oaks   🚪 🏠 🅿️

😊   MODERN BRITISH · PUB An appealing, well-run pub in a rural location, with several stylishly decorated rooms: dine in the brighter room overlooking the terrace and pretty garden. Cooking is tasty, satisfying and seasonal, and they offer particularly good value set lunch and dinner menus. The bright young staff are eager to please.

Menu £ 12/19 (weekdays) – Carte £ 23/36

Austenwood Ln ⊠ SL9 8NL – Northwest : 0.75 mi by A 413 on Gold Hill rd
– 𝒞 01753 899016 – www.thethreeoaksgx.co.uk – Closed Sunday dinner

GESTINGTHORPE

Essex – Regional map n° **7**-C2
▶ London 65 mi – Colchester 20 mi – Ipswich 29 mi

🍴 Pheasant   ⟸ 🚪 🅿️

TRADITIONAL BRITISH · PUB A true country inn centring around sustainability, where they grow vegetables and keep chickens and bees. Simple cooking offers traditional, heartwarming dishes and the inviting, low-beamed bar and takeaway fish & chips keep the locals happy. Stylish, modern bedrooms; those to the rear have country views.

Carte £ 25/41

5 rooms ⊑ – 🛉£ 125/155 🛉🛉£ 155/185

⊠ CO9 3AU – South : 0.75 mi by Church St on Halstead rd – 𝒞 01787 465010
– www.thepheasant.net – Closed January and Monday in winter

GILLINGHAM

Dorset – Pop. 11 278 – Regional map n° **2**-C3
▶ London 116 mi – Bournemouth 34 mi – Bristol 46 mi

🏠 Stock Hill Country House ☆ 🐾 🛏 🏠 ✗ 🛁 🅿

TRADITIONAL · CLASSIC Personally-run Georgian country house with later extensions, set in attractive mature grounds. Classical lounges boast heavy fabrics and antiques. Spacious bedrooms – in the main house and stables – display a mix of cottagey and country house styles; all have good facilities. The formal two-roomed restaurant has its own kitchen garden and serves Austrian cuisine.

9 rooms (dinner included) ☺ – 🛇£ 130/175 🛇🛇£ 295/325

Stock Hill ✉ SP8 5NR – West : 1.5 mi on B 3081 – ℰ 01747 823626
– www.stockhillhouse.co.uk

GISBURN
Lancashire – Regional map n° **11**-B2
▶ London 242 mi – Bradford 28 mi – Skipton 12 mi

🏠 Park House ⇦ 🛁 🅿

TOWNHOUSE · CLASSIC Imposing Victorian house with a classical open-fired drawing room and a small library leading to a hidden stepped garden. Bedrooms mix antique and more modern furnishings. Good breakfast selection; tea and homemade cake served on arrival.

6 rooms ☺ – 🛇£ 55/90 🛇🛇£ 65/120

13 Church View ✉ BB7 4HG – ℰ 01200 445269 – www.parkhousegisburn.co.uk
– Closed December-February

✗ La Locanda

ITALIAN · NEIGHBOURHOOD A charming low-beamed, flag-floored restaurant run by a keen couple: a little corner of Italy in Lancashire. Extensive menu of hearty homemade dishes; try the tasty pastas. Top quality local and imported produce; well-chosen wine list.

Carte £ 19/34

Main St ✉ BB7 4HH – ℰ 01200 445303 – www.lalocanda.co.uk – Closed
25 December, 1 January and lunch Monday-Wednesday

GLINTON – Peterborough → See Peterborough

GODSHILL – Isle of Wight → See Wight (Isle of)

GOLANT Cornwall → See Fowey

GOREY → See Channel Islands (Jersey)

GORING
Oxfordshire – Pop. 4 193 – Regional map n° **6**-B3
▶ London 56 mi – Oxford 16 mi – Reading 12 mi

🍽 Miller of Mansfield ⇦ 🏠

MODERN BRITISH · FRIENDLY Large 18C inn on the banks of the Thames; sit in one of two cosy bar rooms, in the dining room or out on the terrace. Dishes range from homemade sausage rolls to poached lobster salad. The homemade bread and skilfully prepared desserts are a highlight. Bedrooms blend modern furnishings with original features.

Menu £ 16 (weekday lunch) – Carte £ 29/41

13 rooms ☺ – 🛇£ 70/140 🛇🛇£ 100/195

High St ✉ RG8 9AW – ℰ 01491 872829 – www.millerofmansfield.com

GRANGE-OVER-SANDS
Cumbria – Pop. 4 788 – Regional map n° **12**-A3
▶ London 268 mi – Kendal 13 mi – Lancaster 24 mi

⌂ Clare House   ♔ ⊰ ⇎ ⅏ P

FAMILY · PERSONALISED Family-run Victorian house set in lovely gardens, over-looking Morecambe Bay. Two classical sitting rooms. Stylish, boldly coloured bed-rooms in the main house and smaller, simpler rooms with balconies in the wing. The smart, modern dining room offers traditional daily menus.

18 rooms (dinner included) 🖾 – ✚£ 75/132 ✚✚£ 150/165

Park Rd ⊠ LA11 7HQ – ℰ 015395 33026 – www.clarehousehotel.co.uk – Closed 17 December-mid March

at Cartmel Northwest: 3 mi⊠ Grange-Over-Sands

✖✖✖ L'Enclume (Simon Rogan)   ⇦ ⇎ 🆒

ℰℰ **CREATIVE · RUSTIC** A fervently run, stone-built former smithy in an attractive village. Inventive modern cooking has a superb balance of textures and flavours and a pleasing lightness. Home-grown and foraged ingredients feature. Smart, comfortable bedrooms are spread about the village and breakfast is taken at Ro-gan & Company.

→ Aged rose veal in coal oil with shallots and wood sorrel. Native lobster with broad beans, leek and elderflower. Gooseberry, buttermilk and oxalis.

Menu £ 49/130 – tasting menu only

16 rooms 🖾 – ✚£ 90/129 ✚✚£ 129/229

Cavendish St ⊠ LA11 6PZ – ℰ 015395 36362 (booking essential) – www.lenclume.co.uk – Closed 2-15 January and Monday lunch

✖ Rogan & Company   ♿

MODERN BRITISH · NEIGHBOURHOOD The informal cousin to L'Enclume, set in a converted cottage by a lovely stream. The rustic, open-plan interior has dark wood beams and you can watch the chefs at the kitchen pass. Modern dishes rely on local, seasonal produce.

Menu £ 24 (lunch) – Carte £ 32/49

The Square ⊠ LA11 6QD – ℰ 015395 35917 – www.roganandcompany.co.uk – Closed 2 January

GRANTHAM

Lincolnshire – Pop. 41 998 – Regional map n° **9**-C2

▶ London 113 mi – Lincoln 29 mi – Nottingham 24 mi

✖✖ Harry's Place   P

TRADITIONAL BRITISH · COSY Long-standing, intimate restaurant in a former farmhouse: it consists of just 3 tables and is personally run by a dedicated and delightful husband and wife team. Warm, welcoming feel, with fresh flowers, can-dles and antiques. Classically based menus offer 2 choices per course. Good cheese selection.

Carte £ 57/70

17 High St, Great Gonerby ⊠ NG31 8JS – Northwest : 2 mi on B 1174 – ℰ 01476 561780 (booking essential) – Closed Christmas and New Year, 2 weeks August, Sunday and Monday

at Hough-on-the-Hill North: 6.75 mi by A607⊠ Grantham

✖✖ Brownlow Arms   ⇦ 🍴 🆒 P

BRITISH MODERN · INN Characterful former shooting lodge for the nearby Bel-ton Estate, with wood-panelled walls and large open fireplaces. Lengthy menu and specials list offer classically based dishes with modern presentation. Lovely terrace and friendly service. Delightful bedrooms are furnished with contempo-rary fabrics and period pieces.

Carte £ 30/50

5 rooms 🖾 – ✚£ 70/85 ✚✚£ 110/125

High Rd ⊠ NG32 2AZ – ℰ 01400 250234 – www.thebrownlowarms.com – Closed 25-26 December, 1 January, Sunday dinner, Monday, Tuesday lunch and bank holidays

GRASMERE

Cumbria – Regional map n° **12**-A2

▶ London 282 mi – Carlisle 43 mi – Kendal 18 mi

🏠 Rothay Garden　　　　　　　🌤 🛏 🎎 🛗 **P**

COUNTRY HOUSE · CONTEMPORARY Slate-built Lakeland house with modern extensions, which include a spa and a copper-roofed conservatory restaurant with a lovely outlook and a classically based menu. Bedrooms are stylish and contemporary – many have king-sized beds and some have balconies or patios; the Loft Suites are the best.

30 rooms ⌤ – ♦£ 115/125 ♦♦£ 151/281

Broadgate ✉ *LA22 9RJ – ℰ 015394 35334 – www.rothaygarden.com*

🏠 Forest Side 🅝　　　　　　🌿 ⬅ 🛏 **P**

COUNTRY HOUSE · ELEGANT Enjoy afternoon tea in the elegant fire-lit lounge while admiring the view over the deer-filled grounds towards the mountains. Both the guest areas and bedrooms have a modern country house style and there's a laid back feel throughout.

20 rooms ⌤ – ♦£ 159/374 ♦♦£ 209/409

Keswick Rd ✉ *LA22 9RN – On A 591 – ℰ 015394 35250 – www.theforestside.com*
❀ **Forest Side** – See restaurant listing

🏠 Grasmere　　　　　　　　🌤 🛏 **P**

TRADITIONAL · PERSONALISED This welcoming Victorian country house sits close to the village centre and comes with original features and traditional décor. The bright bedrooms are named after writers and are immaculately kept. The dining room overlooks the garden and the River Rothay which meanders through it.

11 rooms ⌤ – ♦£ 64/69 ♦♦£ 118/148

Broadgate ✉ *LA22 9TA – ℰ 015394 35277 – www.grasmerehotel.co.uk*
– Restricted opening in winter

🏠 Moss Grove Organic　　　　　　🌿 **P**

COUNTRY HOUSE · MODERN Laid-back house with a stylish interior featuring many reclaimed furnishings. Funky bedrooms boast large beds, Bose sound systems and whirlpool baths. Organic breakfasts include tasty veggie options; help yourself from the kitchen.

11 rooms ⌤ – ♦£ 84/164 ♦♦£ 99/265

✉ *LA22 9SW – ℰ 015394 35251 – www.mossgrove.com – Closed 24-25 December*

🏠 Oak Bank　　　　　　　　🛏 🌿 **P**

TRADITIONAL · PERSONALISED Passionately run Victorian house with a pretty rear garden. Relax beside the converted range in the sitting room or next to the open fire in the lounge-bar. Modern bedrooms have comfortable beds, bold fabrics and bright colours.

13 rooms ⌤ – ♦£ 102/127 ♦♦£ 116/175

Broadgate ✉ *LA22 9TA – ℰ 015394 35217 – www.lakedistricthotel.co.uk – Closed 2-19 January and 18-26 December*

Dining Room – See restaurant listing

🍴🍴 Forest Side 🅝　　　　　⬅ 🛏 🍷 ⇔ **P**

❀ MODERN BRITISH · CHIC Sit in deep leather armchairs and take in the view over the 48 acre hotel grounds. With produce originating from the walled garden and foraged from the surrounding area, their strapline 'inspired by the Cumbrian landscape' is spot on. Scandic-style dishes are creative and modern with a deceptive simplicity.

→ Salt cod with radishes, nasturtium and cured ham broth. Herdwick hogget with Heritage potatoes and hedgerow clippings. Preserved blueberries, sorrel and goat's yoghurt.

Menu £ 35/75

Keswick Rd ✉ *LA22 9RN – On A 591 – ℰ 015394 35250 (booking advisable) – www.theforestside.com – Closed lunch Monday and Tuesday*

ENGLAND

✗✗ Dining Room 🛌 🅿

MODERN CUISINE · CHIC Split-roomed hotel restaurant in a Victorian house, with a pleasant conservatory overlooking the garden. The concise daily menu features interesting modern dishes crafted from seasonal Lakeland produce; everything is made in-house.

Menu £ 22/60

Oak Bank Hotel, Broadgate ✉ LA22 9TA – 𝒞 015394 55217 (booking essential) – www.lakedistricthotel.co.uk – Closed 2-19 January and 17-26 December

GRASSINGTON

North Yorkshire – ✉ Skipton – Pop. 1 126 – Regional map n° **13**-A2
▶ London 240 mi – Bradford 30 mi – Burnley 28 mi – Leeds 37 mi

✗✗ Grassington House ⇦ 🛖 🅿

MODERN BRITISH · BRASSERIE Georgian house with a large bar-lounge, two dining rooms and delightful service. Classical menus display Mediterranean touches and include their home-bred pork. Smart, modern bedrooms; No.6 has a roll-top bath in the room. Home-cured bacon or sausages are offered at breakfast and they host regular wine dinners.

Menu £ 18 (lunch and early dinner)/45 – Carte £ 25/41

9 rooms 🖵 – ♦£ 105 ♦♦£ 120/140

5 The Square ✉ BD23 5AQ – 𝒞 01756 752406 – www.grassingtonhousehotel.co.uk – Closed 25 December

---

 Can't choose between two similar establishments in the same town? We list them in order of preference, within each category.

GREAT BIRCHAM

Norfolk – Regional map n° **8**-C1
▶ London 115 mi – Hunstanton 10 mi – King's Lynn 15 mi

🏠 King's Head 🍴 🛖 ⚒ 🅿

INN · PERSONALISED This family run inn dates from the Edwardian era and is well-located for the north Norfolk coast and the Sandringham Estate. Individually decorated bedrooms are contemporary in style. Enjoy a pub classic and a G&T from the 'gin wall' in the cosy bar or choose from more modern dishes in the restaurant.

12 rooms 🖵 – ♦£ 90/170 ♦♦£ 95/175

✉ PE31 6RJ – 𝒞 01485 578265 – www.the-kings-head-bircham.co.uk

GREAT DUNMOW

Essex – Pop. 7 749 – Regional map n° **7**-C2
▶ London 42 mi – Cambridge 27 mi – Chelmsford 13 mi – Colchester 24 mi

✗ Square 1 🆎 ⇔

MODERN CUISINE · FRIENDLY Pretty little whitewashed building; once a 14C monastic reading room. Much original character remains in the form of exposed beams and low ceilings; which contrast with vibrant modern art. Unfussy monthly menu has Mediterranean leanings.

Menu £ 15 (lunch) – Carte £ 24/36

15 High St. ✉ CM6 1AB – 𝒞 01371 859922 – www.square1restaurant.co.uk – Closed 25-26 December and Sunday dinner

GREAT LIMBER

Lincolnshire – Pop. 271 – Regional map n° **9**-C1
▶ London 172 mi – Lincoln 31 mi – Grimsby 13 mi

🛏 **New Inn**

MODERN CUISINE · INN Smart modern pub with a stylish terrace. The bar is a hit with the locals, while the lounge is the perfect spot for a fireside G&T before dinner in the contemporary restaurant. Carefully prepared, sophisticated dishes have a modern touch. Smart bedrooms exceed expectations; some are in a barn conversion.

Carte £ 25/38

10 rooms ♤ – ♦£ 90/135 ♦♦£ 96/135

2 High St ⊠ DN37 8JL – ℰ 01469 569998 – www.thenewinngreatlimber.co.uk
– Closed Monday lunch

GREAT MALVERN

Worcestershire – Pop. 36 770 – Regional map n° **10**-B3
▶ London 127 mi – Birmingham 34 mi – Cardiff 66 mi – Gloucester 24 mi

🏠 **Cotford**

TOWNHOUSE · CONTEMPORARY The owners of this 1851 Gothic-style house (built for the Bishop of Worcester), put a lot of effort into getting things right. It mixes the traditional and the contemporary and has stylish bedrooms and a chic black and pink bar.

15 rooms ♤ – ♦£ 70/89 ♦♦£ 130/145

51 Graham Rd ⊠ WR14 2HU – ℰ 01684 572427 – www.cotfordhotel.co.uk

L' Amuse Bouche – See restaurant listing

XX **L' Amuse Bouche**

TRADITIONAL CUISINE · CONTEMPORARY DÉCOR Start with an aperitif in the stylish bar or traditional lounge of this Gothic hotel, then head for the contemporary dining room overlooking the gardens. Boldly flavoured, classically based dishes have a subtle modern touch.

Carte £ 31/42

Cotford Hotel, 51 Graham Rd ⊠ WR14 2HU – ℰ 01684 572427
– www.cotfordhotel.co.uk – dinner only and Sunday lunch

at Welland Southeast: 5 mi on B4208

🛏 **The Inn at Welland**

TRADITIONAL BRITISH · CONTEMPORARY DÉCOR The owners have turned this pub from wreck to "by 'eck!" Inside it's light, open and stylish, with charming features and designer touches; outside there's a landscaped garden and a smart decked terrace. Pub classics sit alongside more adventurous dishes – all tasty, generous of portion and sensibly priced.

Carte £ 25/43

Hook Bank ⊠ WR13 6LN – East : 1 mi on A 4104 – ℰ 01684 592317
– www.theinnatwelland.co.uk – Closed 25-26 December, Sunday dinner and Monday

GREAT MILTON – Oxfordshire → See Oxford

GREAT MISSENDEN

Buckinghamshire – Pop. 7 980 – Regional map n° **6**-C2
▶ London 34 mi – Aylesbury 10 mi – Maidenhead 19 mi – Oxford 35 mi

🛏 **Nags Head**

TRADITIONAL BRITISH · PUB Traditional 15C inn whose features include original oak beams, thick brick walls and an inglenook fireplace. Gallic charm mixes with British classics on the interesting menus and service is keen and cheerful. Bedrooms are stylish and modern (Number One is the best), and breakfasts are tasty.

Menu £ 17 (weekdays) – Carte £ 26/49

6 rooms ♤ – ♦£ 75/115 ♦♦£ 75/115

London Rd ⊠ HP16 0DG – Southeast : 1.5 mi by A 413 and Holmer Green rd.
– ℰ 01494 862200 – www.nagsheadbucks.com – Closed 25 December

GREAT TEW

Oxfordshire – Pop. 145 – Regional map n° **10**-B1

▶ London 75 mi – Oxford 21 mi – Birmingham 50 mi

🏠 Soho Farmhouse 🅽

RESORT · DESIGN Set in 100 acres of rolling countryside, this exclusive resort offers everything you could want. Luxurious self-contained cabins are dotted about the estate and come with wellies and bikes. There's a range of different restaurants and breakfast is transported on a milk float and cooked outside your door. Unwind in the stunning spa or the outside pool set within a lake.

44 rooms – 🛏£ 210/220 🛏🛏£ 365/385 – ☑£ 12 – 18 suites

✉ OX7 4JS – South 0.75 mi by New Rd and Ledwell Ln. – ☎ 01608 691000
– www.sohofarmhouse.com

GREAT YELDHAM

Essex – Pop. 1 844 – Regional map n° **7**-C2

▶ London 64 mi – Cambridge 28 mi – Colchester 20 mi

✕✕ White Hart

MODERN BRITISH · ROMANTIC Charming 16C house with a characterful interior. The large, open-fired bar with its wonky floors and exposed beams serves unfussy favourites, while the elegant restaurant offers a refined, modern menu of skilfully prepared dishes which are full of flavour. Bedrooms are stylish, modern and comfortable.

Carte £ 30/49

13 rooms ☑ – 🛏£ 70/90 🛏🛏£ 90/180

Poole St ✉ CO9 4HJ – ☎ 01787 237250 (booking advisable)
– www.whitehartyeldham.co.uk – Closed 1-18 January, dinner 25-26 December, Monday and lunch Tuesday

GREEN ISLAND → See Channel Islands (Jersey)

GREETHAM

Rutland – Regional map n° **9**-C2

▶ London 101 mi – Birmingham 86 mi – Nottingham 38 mi

🍺 Wheatsheaf Inn

TRADITIONAL BRITISH · FAMILY The aroma of fresh bread is the first thing you notice at this simple, family-friendly country pub. Cooking is unfussy and traditionally based; cheaper cuts keep prices sensible and desserts are a must. It's run by a charming couple.

Menu £ 17 (weekday lunch) – Carte £ 23/32

1 Stretton Rd ✉ LE15 7NP – ☎ 01572 812325 – www.wheatsheaf-greetham.co.uk
– Closed first 2 weeks January, Sunday dinner and Monday except bank holidays

GRETA BRIDGE – Durham → See Barnard Castle

GRETTON – Gloucestershire → See Winchcombe

GRIMSTON – Norfolk → See King's Lynn

GRINSHILL – Shropshire → See Shrewsbury

GROUVILLE → See Channel Islands (Jersey)

GUILDFORD

Surrey – Pop. 77 057 – Regional map n° **4**-C1

▶ London 33 mi – Brighton 43 mi – Reading 27 mi – Southampton 49 mi

at Shere East: 6.75 mi by A246 off A25 ⊠ Guildford

✗✗ Kinghams 🛖 🅿

MODERN BRITISH · RUSTIC Characterful 17C creeper-clad cottage with a cosy low-beamed interior and a pleasant terrace. Cooking has a classic foundation, with plenty of fish specials and game in season. The good value 2 course menu includes a side dish too.

Menu £ 18 (weekdays) – Carte £ 31/42

Gomshall Ln ⊠ *GU5 9HE* – ℰ *01483 202168* – *www.kinghams-restaurant.co.uk*
– Closed 25 December-5 January, Sunday dinner and Monday

GULWORTHY – Devon ➜ See Tavistock

GUNTHORPE

Nottinghamshire – Pop. 646 – Regional map n° **9**-B2
▶ London 132 mi – Nottingham 12 mi – Newark-on-Trent 13 mi

✗ Tom Brown's Brasserie 🛖 & 🄰🄲 🅿

MODERN CUISINE · BRASSERIE Stylish modern restaurant in an old Victorian schoolhouse beside the river. Tables are spread over several different areas – including a mezzanine – and the team are friendly and efficient. Dishes are fresh, tasty and well-presented.

Menu £ 18 (lunch and early dinner) – Carte £ 25/48

The Old School House, Trentside ⊠ *NG14 7FB* – ℰ *0115 966 3642*
– www.tombrowns.co.uk – Closed dinner 25-26 December and 1 January

GURNARD ➜ See Wight (Isle of)

HADLEIGH

Suffolk – Pop. 8 150 – Regional map n° **8**-C3
▶ London 72 mi – Cambridge 49 mi – Colchester 17 mi – Ipswich 10 mi

🏠 Edge Hall 🚐 ⅋ 🅿 🛏

TOWNHOUSE · CLASSIC A lovely Queen Anne style house with a Georgian brick façade, dating from 1453 and supposedly the oldest house in town. Bedrooms are spacious and furnished with antiques. The breakfast room overlooks the delightful garden.

6 rooms ⌧ – ✝£ 55/70 ✝✝£ 90/150

2 High St ⊠ *IP7 5AP* – ℰ *01473 822458* – *www.edgehall.co.uk* – *Closed 23-29 December*

🏠 Hadleigh Ram 🛖 & ♿

MODERN CUISINE · RUSTIC Stylish, contemporary dining pub with neatly laid tables. Elaborate modern cooking features lots of ingredients in some original combinations. If you've come just for a drink you'll feel most at home on the attractive terrace.

Menu £ 22 (weekdays) – Carte £ 28/43

5 Market Pl ⊠ *IP7 5DL* – ℰ *01473 822880* – *www.thehadleighram.co.uk* – *Closed 26-27 December and Sunday dinner*

HALFORD

Warwickshire – Pop. 301 – Regional map n° **10**-C3
▶ London 94 mi – Oxford 43 mi – Stratford-upon-Avon 8 mi

🏠 Old Manor House ⅌ 🚐 ⅋ 🅿

COUNTRY HOUSE · HISTORIC Characterful part-timbered house in a pleasant spot next to the River Stour. Well-appointed drawing room with garden views and an antique-furnished breakfast room with a large inglenook. Appealing period style bedrooms have rich fabrics.

3 rooms ⌧ – ✝£ 75/85 ✝✝£ 100/110

Queens St ⊠ *CV36 5BT* – ℰ *01789 740264* – *www.oldmanor-halford.co.uk*

HALIFAX
West Yorkshire – Pop. 88 134 – Regional map n° **13**-B2
► London 206 mi – Leeds 17 mi – Manchester 31 mi – Bradford 10 mi

Holdsworth House
HISTORIC · COSY Attractive 17C property with beautiful gardens and a parterre within its old stone walls. Characterful rooms feature original wood panelling and mullioned windows; bedrooms are contemporary. The three-roomed restaurant offers a mix of homely classics and more refined dishes – all use local produce.
38 rooms ☐ – †£100/125 ††£125/150 – 4 suites
Holdsworth Rd ✉ HX2 9TG – North : 3 mi by A 629 and Shay Ln
– ✆ 01422 240024 – www.holdsworthhouse.co.uk

Ricci's Tapas & Cicchetti
MEDITERRANEAN CUISINE · FASHIONABLE Modern tapas restaurant with a buzzy vibe, run by a bright, breezy team. Sit on the spacious terrace, at a wooden table or on white leather stools at the metal-topped bar. The Spanish and Italian small plates are perfect for sharing.
Carte £ 20/32
F Mill, Ground Floor, Dean Clough, (Gate 9) ✉ HX3 5AX – ✆ 01422 410204
– www.riccistapasandcicchetti.co.uk – Closed 25 December-1 January

Shibden Mill Inn
MODERN BRITISH · COSY A former corn mill set in a tranquil, deep-sided valley, with beamed ceilings, welcoming fires and lots of cosy corners. Menus offer plenty of choice, with pub favourites alongside more ambitious dishes. Well-drilled staff. Comfy, individually furnished bedrooms; choose Room 14 if it's luxury you're after.
Menu £ 14 (lunch and early dinner) **s** – Carte £ 22/40 **s**
11 rooms ☐ – †£ 90/165 ††£ 95/195
Shibden Mill Fold ✉ HX3 7UL – ✆ 01422 365840 – www.shibdenmillinn.com
– Closed 25-26 December and 1 January

HALSETOWN – Cornwall → See St Ives

HALTWHISTLE
Northumberland – Pop. 3 791 – Regional map n° **14**-A2
► London 335 mi – Carlisle 22 mi – Newcastle upon Tyne 37 mi

Ashcroft
FAMILY · CLASSIC A family-run early Victorian vicarage, with beautiful award-winning gardens. The spacious interior retains many of its original features and smoothly blends the classic with the contemporary. Some of the bedrooms have roof terraces.
9 rooms ☐ – †£ 72/90 ††£ 84/110
Lantys Lonnen ✉ NE49 0DA – ✆ 01434 320213 – www.ashcroftguesthouse.co.uk
– Closed 25 December

HAMBLE-LE-RICE
Hampshire – Pop. 4 695 – Regional map n° **4**-B2
► London 87 mi – Birmingham 149 mi – Leeds 243 mi – Sheffield 213 mi

Bugle
TRADITIONAL BRITISH · PUB Set in a charming spot in a quaint little village, this Grade II listed building has views over the river and is popular with the sailing community. Choose from small plates, pub classics or more interesting dishes on the main menu.
Menu £ 18 (weekday lunch) – Carte £ 22/36 **s**
High St ✉ SO31 4HA – ✆ 023 8045 3000 (booking advisable)
– www.idealcollection.co.uk/buglehamble

HAMBLETON - Rutland → See Oakham

HAMPTON IN ARDEN
West Midlands - Pop. 1 678 - Regional map n° **10**-C2
▶ London 113 mi - Birmingham 15 mi - Coventry 11 mi

🏠 Hampton Manor

HISTORIC · GRAND LUXURY An early Victorian gothic-style manor house set in 45 acres of mature grounds - it was built for Sir Robert Peel's son. Contemporary décor blends with characterful original plasterwork and wood panelling in various lounges and drawing rooms. Spacious bedrooms have a smart modern style and superb bathrooms.

15 rooms - 🛏£160/370 🛏£160/370 - ☷£15 - 3 suites
Shadowbrook Ln ⊠ B92 ODQ - ✆ 01675 446080 - www.hamptonmanor.com
❀ **Peel's** - See restaurant listing

🍴🍴🍴 Peel's
❀
CREATIVE BRITISH · ELEGANT This elegant dining room is situated within an impressive manor house and features beautiful plasterwork, oak panelling and hand-painted Chinoiserie wallpaper. Modern dishes come from a confident kitchen and feature refined, original combinations with some playful elements. Service is pitched perfectly.
→ Foie gras, bacon jam and pickled onions. Turbot on the bone with mussels, mushrooms and wild garlic. Passion fruit, liquorice and white chocolate.
Menu £55/80

Hampton Manor Hotel, Shadowbrook Ln ⊠ B92 ODQ - ✆ 01675 446080 (booking essential) - www.hamptonmanor.com - dinner only - Closed Sunday and Monday

HAMPTON POYLE
Oxfordshire - Pop. 106 - Regional map n° **6**-B2
▶ London 68 mi - Birmingham 72 mi - Barnet 71 mi - Ealing 57 mi

🍴 Bell at Hampton Poyle
MEDITERRANEAN CUISINE · PUB Almost Mediterranean in its style, with a very visual kitchen that includes a wood-burning oven. The seasonal menu offers everything from meze, homemade pizza and charcuterie boards to pub staples, steaks and seafood. Bright, fresh bedrooms are located above the bar and in a neighbouring cottage.
Menu £10 (weekdays) - Carte £27/44
9 rooms ☷ - 🛏£95/130 🛏£120/155
11 Oxford Rd ⊠ OX5 2QD - ✆ 01865 376242 - www.thebellathamptonpoyle.co.uk

HAROME - North Yorkshire → See Helmsley

HARROGATE
North Yorkshire - Pop. 73 576 - Regional map n° **13**-B2
▶ London 211 mi - Bradford 18 mi - Leeds 15 mi - Newcastle upon Tyne 76 mi

🏠 Rudding Park
LUXURY · DESIGN Sizeable hotel set in 250 acres; the old Victorian church and Grade I listed manor house are used for events. Sleek bedrooms are in a wing - the best boast media hubs, touch lighting and jacuzzis. Relax in the smart spa, the cinema or on one of the terraces. Modern menus showcase produce from within 20 miles.
90 rooms ☷ - 🛏£154/437 🛏£180/459 - 7 suites
Rudding Park, Follifoot ⊠ HG3 1JH - Southeast : 3.75 mi by A 661
- ✆ 01423 871350 - www.ruddingpark.com

ENGLAND

🏨 Hotel du Vin

☆ 🖭 & 🛁

TOWNHOUSE · DESIGN Smart hotel with a small basement spa, set in a terrace of Georgian houses overlooking the green. Inside it has a stylish, boutique-style feel; the attic rooms boast huge bathrooms with 'his and hers' roll-top baths. Have a drink at the smart zinc bar before dinner in the chic French bistro or the courtyard.

49 rooms – 🛏£ 110/360 🛏🛏£ 110/360 – ☲ £ 17
Town plan: A2-a - *Prospect Pl* ✉ *HG1 1LB* – ☏ *01423 856800*
– *www.hotelduvin.com*

🏨 West Park

☆ 🛋 🖭 & AC

INN · CONTEMPORARY It might still look like a pub but once inside you'll find a stylish, contemporary hotel. Bedrooms have the latest mod cons, including coffee machines; the suites overlook the park and have small balconies. The lively open-plan bar and modern restaurant serve an extensive list of brasserie favourites.

25 rooms – 🛏£ 125/300 🛏🛏£ 125/300 – ☲ £ 10 – 2 suites
Town plan: A2-w - *19 West Park Rd* ✉ *HG1 1BJ* – ☏ *01423 524471*
– *www.thewestparkhotel.com*

🏨 Ascot House

☆ 🛁 P

TOWNHOUSE · COSY A family-run Victorian property – once home to W H Baxter, inventor of the 'knapping' machine (used in road-making). Original features include ornate plasterwork, coving and an impressive stained glass window; floral fabrics and king-sized beds feature. The traditional restaurant has a classic menu to match.

19 rooms ☲ – 🛏£ 59/99 🛏🛏£ 89/160
Town plan: A1-z - *53 King's Rd* ✉ *HG1 5HJ* – ☏ *01423 531005*
– *www.ascothouse.com*

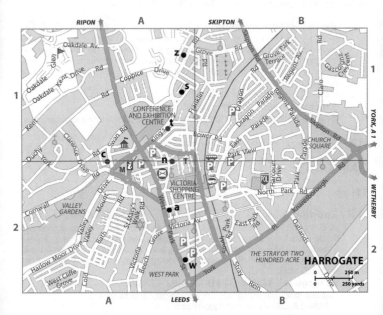

🏠 Brookfield House   🕸 P

TOWNHOUSE · CONTEMPORARY A well-run, three-storey Victorian townhouse
on a quiet street. Modern bedrooms come in light hues: the first floor rooms are
bright and airy, while the top floor rooms are cosy and intimate – all have fridges
and ironing boards.

6 rooms ⌂ – ♦£ 65/95 ♦♦£ 75/105

Town plan: A1-s - 5 Alexandra Rd ⌧ HG1 5JS – ℰ 01423 506646
– www.brookfieldhousehotel.co.uk – Closed 2 weeks Christmas-New Year

XX Orchid   🏆 🏠 AC ⇔ P

ASIAN · FASHIONABLE Below the chic cocktail bar is a spacious room with
etched glass screens, Asian artefacts and a TV screening live kitchen action. The
extensive pan-Asian menu indicates the dishes' origins and spiciness; Sunday
lunch is a buffet.

Menu £ 15 (weekday lunch) – Carte £ 20/38

Town plan: A1-2-c - 28 Swan Rd ⌧ HG1 2SE – ℰ 01423 560425
– www.orchidrestaurant.co.uk – Closed 25-26 December and Saturday lunch

X Norse   🏠 AC

SCANDINAVIAN · SIMPLE During the day it's a café called Baltzersen's; in the
evening it reopens as Norse. Choose 2 or 3 savoury dishes plus a dessert from
the concise menu. Flavoursome Nordic cooking includes the likes of Norwegian
skrei and woof fish.

Carte £ 19/40

Town plan: A1-2-n - 22 Oxford St ⌧ HG1 1PU – ℰ 01423 202363
– www.norserestaurant.co.uk – dinner only – Closed 4 days Christmas-New Year,
23-27 January, Sunday and Monday

X Stuzzi 🆕   🏠 🖵 🍴

ITALIAN · TRENDY A great little place comprising a deli, a café and an osteria,
and serving homemade cakes, topped focaccia and fresh, authentic Italian small
plates. It's run with passion by a young but experienced team and it's great
value too.

Carte £ 18/24

Town plan: A1-t - 46b King's Rd ⌧ HG1 5JW – ℰ 01423 705852 – Closed Sunday
dinner and Monday

at Kettlesing West: 6.5 mi by A 59⌧ Harrogate

🏠 Cold Cotes   🌢 🛒 🕸 P

TRADITIONAL · COSY A remote former farmhouse bordered by colourful gardens. Bedrooms are in the outbuildings: those in the barn are suites with lounges
and private terraces. Local produce features at breakfast – try the bacon and onion relish sandwich.

7 rooms ⌂ – ♦£ 75/99 ♦♦£ 85/109

Cold Cotes Rd, Felliscliffe ⌧ HG3 2LW – West : 1 mi by A 59 – ℰ 01423 770937
– www.coldcotes.com – Closed February

HARTINGTON

Derbyshire – ⌧ Buxton – Pop. 1 604 – Regional map n° **9**-A1
▶ London 168 mi – Derby 36 mi – Manchester 40 mi – Sheffield 34 mi

🏠 Biggin Hall   🏠 🌢 ⪕ 🛒 P

TRADITIONAL · COSY Characterful house with traditional, rustic appeal. Many
guests follow the Tissington and High Peak Trails: bike storage and picnics are
offered. Classical, low-beamed bedrooms in the main house; brighter rooms in
the barns. Pleasant garden views and homely cooking in the dining room .

21 rooms ⌂ – ♦£ 70/100 ♦♦£ 90/140

Biggin ⌧ SK17 0DH – Southeast : 2 mi by B 5054 – ℰ 01298 84451
– www.bigginhall.co.uk

HARWICH

Essex – Pop. 19 738 – Regional map n° **7**-D2

▶ London 78 mi – Chelmsford 41 mi – Colchester 20 mi – Ipswich 23 mi

🏚 Pier at Harwich ⇐ P

TOWNHOUSE · PERSONALISED A Victorian hotel by the quayside, built to accommodate rail travellers waiting to board their cruise liners; it's ideal if you're catching the ferry. Some of the stylish New England style bedrooms have views of the port. Dine on seafood dishes in the brasserie or Nordic inspired snacks overlooking the pier.

14 rooms ☲ – ♥£ 130/170 ♥♥£ 130/200

The Quay ✉ *CO12 3HH* – ☏ *01255 241212* – *www.milsomhotels.com*

The Pier – See restaurant listing

XX The Pier ⇐ 🛗 🆎 ⇔ P

SEAFOOD · CONTEMPORARY DÉCOR This comfortable hotel brasserie boasts a terrific balcony with attractive port and North Sea views. The seafood-oriented menu offers a mix of grills and modern classics, with much of the fish landed locally.

Carte £ 27/64 **s**

Pier at Harwich Hotel, The Quay ✉ *CO12 3HH* – ☏ *01255 241212*
– www.milsomhotels.com

HASELBURY PLUCKNETT

Somerset – Pop. 744 – Regional map n° **2**-B3

▶ London 140 mi – Taunton 24 mi – Yeovil 8 mi

🍴 White Horse 🛗

MEDITERRANEAN CUISINE · PUB Traditional village pub with dried hops hung on exposed beams, a mix of wood and flagged floors, and a fire at either end. Most produce comes from within 50 miles; alongside British classics, you'll find Gallic and Mediterranean dishes.

Menu £ 17 – Carte £ 21/36

North St ✉ *TA18 7RJ* – ☏ *01460 78873* – *www.thewhitehorsehaselbury.co.uk*
– Closed Sunday dinner and Monday

HASTINGS and ST LEONARDS

East Sussex – Pop. 91 053 – Regional map n° **5**-B3

▶ London 65 mi – Brighton 37 mi – Folkestone 37 mi – Maidstone 34 mi

🏠 Zanzibar ✕ ⅏ P

TOWNHOUSE · DESIGN An enthusiastically run Victorian seafront property with a stylish boutique interior. The chic restaurant faces the sea and leads through to a delightful tiered terrace. Bedrooms are named and themed after places the owner has visited on his travels; 'Japan' has an authentic small, square spa bath in the room.

8 rooms ☲ – ♥£ 99/199 ♥♥£ 99/349

Town plan: A2-c - *9 Eversfield Pl* ✉ *TN37 6BY* – ☏ *01424 460109*
– www.zanzibarhotel.co.uk

Old Rectory ⇐ ⅏ P

TOWNHOUSE · ELEGANT A delightful Georgian house with beautiful tiered gardens, set next to the church at the bottom of the hill, just a short walk from the sea. No expense has been spared inside, with hand-painted feature walls, bespoke designer furnishings and luxurious styling. They smoke the fish and cure the bacon on-site.

8 rooms ☲ – ♥£ 90/115 ♥♥£ 110/165

Town plan: C1-r - *Harold Rd, Old Town* ✉ *TN35 5ND* – ☏ *01424 422410*
– www.theoldrectoryhastings.co.uk – Closed 2 weeks January and 1 week Christmas

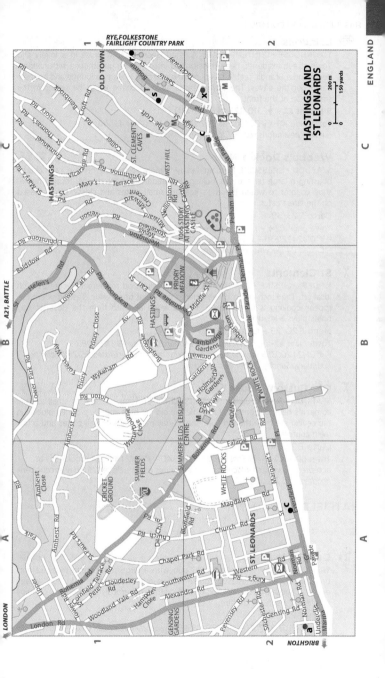

HASTINGS AND
ST LEONARDS

0 ——— 200 m
0 ——— 150 yards

RYE, FOLKESTONE
FAIRLIGHT COUNTRY PARK

OLD TOWN

HASTINGS

ST. CLEMENT'S
CAVES

1066 STORY
AT HASTINGS
CASTLE

PRIORY
MEADOW

SUMMERFIELDS LEISURE
CENTRE

SUMMER
FIELDS

CRICKET
GROUND

WHITE ROCKS

ST. LEONARDS

Magdalen

A21, BATTLE

LONDON

BRIGHTON

413

🏠 Laindons

TOWNHOUSE · CONTEMPORARY A listed Georgian townhouse in a lovely Old Town street; inside it's been transformed into a stylish guesthouse with nautical décor and a Scandic feel. A steep, narrow staircase leads to a lounge and honesty bar under the eaves. The owner roasts his own coffee which he serves in the small shop at the front.

5 rooms ☑ – 🛏£ 110/125 🛏🛏£ 125/140
Town plan: C1-s - 23 High St ⊠ TN34 3EY – 𝒞 01424 437710
– www.thelaindons.com – Closed Christmas

🍴 Webbe's Rock-a-Nore

SEAFOOD · BRASSERIE Bustling family-friendly restaurant on the promenade, boasting a large terrace overlooking the Stade. Sit at the marble-topped horse-shoe counter to watch the chefs prepare small plates and classic dishes based on the latest catch.

Carte £ 23/39
Town plan: C2-x - 1 Rock-a-Nore ⊠ TN34 3DW
– 𝒞 01424 721650 – www.webbesrestaurants.co.uk
– Closed 24 December-13 January

🍴 St Clements

MODERN CUISINE · BISTRO Pleasant neighbourhood restaurant decorated with local art. The lunch and midweek menus represent good value. Tasty modern European cooking is unfussy with a rustic edge and fish from the Hastings day boats plays a key role.

Menu £ 20/29 – Carte £ 26/50
Town plan: A2-a - 3 Mercatoria, St Leonards on Sea ⊠ TN38 0EB
– 𝒞 01424 200355 – www.stclementsrestaurant.co.uk – Closed 25-26 December, 1 January, Sunday dinner and Monday

🍴 Old Custom House 🆕

SEAFOOD · SIMPLE Built in 1725, this former Customs House is as small as they come. It's been designed to resemble the old net huts and the wooden blocks on the ceiling are from the old pier. The all-day menu offers small plates and a few main courses.

Carte £ 22/34
Town plan: C2-c - 19 East Par ⊠ TN34 3AL – 𝒞 01424 447724 (bookings not accepted) – www.theoldcustomhousehastings.co.uk – Closed Monday except bank holidays and Tuesday

HATFIELD BROAD OAK

Essex – Pop. 916 – Regional map n° **7**-B2
▶ London 35 mi – Bishop's Stortford 8 mi – Colchester 34 mi

🍴 Duke's Head

TRADITIONAL BRITISH · COSY 17C pub with a large terrace and pleasant garden, run by an enthusiastic couple who support local clubs and host village events. Choose from a selection of well-crafted, generously sized dishes, or enjoy nibbles on a sofa by the fire.

Carte £ 22/30
High St ⊠ CM22 7HH – 𝒞 01279 718598 – www.thedukeshead.co.uk – Closed 25-26 December

HATFIELD PEVEREL

Essex – Pop. 3 251 – Regional map n° **7**-C2
▶ London 39 mi – Chelmsford 8 mi – Maldon 12 mi

XX Blue Strawberry Bistrot 🛜 🅿️

TRADITIONAL BRITISH · INTIMATE A creeper-clad, red-brick restaurant with a labyrinth of characterful, old-fashioned rooms full of ornaments. Extensive menus offer traditional, keenly priced cooking which is wholesome and satisfying. Polite service.

Menu £ 15/20 (weekdays) – Carte £ 22/40

The Street ⊠ CM3 2DW – 𝒞 01245 381333 – www.bluestrawberrybistrot.co.uk – Closed 26 December and Sunday dinner

HATHERSAGE

Derbyshire – Pop. 2 018 – Regional map n° **9**-A1

▶ London 177 mi – Derby 39 mi – Manchester 34 mi – Sheffield 11 mi

🏠 George 🍽️ 🧖 🅿️

TRADITIONAL · COSY Eye-catching 14C coaching inn where modern furnishings blend nicely with traditional stone walls and exposed beams. Relax in the open-fired lounge or small cocktail bar. Smart, pastel-hued bedrooms are bright and contemporary.

24 rooms ☐ – ♥£ 75/140 ♥♥£ 95/180

Main Rd ⊠ S32 1BB – 𝒞 01433 650436 – www.george-hotel.net

George's – See restaurant listing

XX George's 🅿️

TRADITIONAL BRITISH · CHIC Formally laid restaurant decorated in subtle pastel shades and set within a 14C coaching inn. Extensive menus have a largely British base and dishes are classically grounded with modern touches. Cooking is refined and flavoursome.

Menu £ 20/38

George Hotel, Main Rd ⊠ S32 1BB – 𝒞 01433 650436 – www.george-hotel.net

HAUGHTON MOSS

Cheshire East – Regional map n° **11**-A3

▶ London 180 mi – Manchester 41 mi – Chester 17 mi

🍽️ Nag's Head 🛏️ 🛜 ♿ 🅿️

TRADITIONAL BRITISH · PUB Characterful timbered pub in a peaceful hamlet; sit at a table made from a shotgun or in the delightful garden overlooking the bowling green. Local produce features in regional specialities, pub classics and dishes from the charcoal grill.

Menu £ 14 (weekdays) – Carte £ 22/46

Long Ln ⊠ CW6 9RN – 𝒞 01829 260265 – www.nagsheadhaughton.co.uk

HAWES

North Yorkshire – Pop. 887 – Regional map n° **13**-A1

▶ London 253 mi – Kendal 27 mi – Leeds 72 mi – Newcastle upon Tyne 76 mi

🏠 Stone House ♞ 🐾 ⋖ 🛏️ 🅿️

COUNTRY HOUSE · COSY Characterful stone house built in 1908. Guest areas include a pleasant drawing room with an oak-panelled fireplace and a small billiard-room-cum-library. Bedrooms vary in size and décor; some have conservatories and are ideal for those with dogs. The traditional beamed dining room offers a classical menu.

24 rooms ☐ – ♥£ 78/199 ♥♥£ 145/205

Sedbusk ⊠ DL8 3PT – North : 1 mi by Muker rd – 𝒞 01969 667571 – www.stonehousehotel.co.uk – Closed January and mid-week December

HAWKSHEAD

Cumbria – ⊠ Ambleside – Pop. 570 – Regional map n° **12**-A2

▶ London 283 mi – Carlisle 52 mi – Kendal 19 mi

West Vale

TRADITIONAL · PERSONALISED Welcoming slate house boasting lovely countryside views; run by keen owners. Two comfy lounges and a smart country house style room for hearty breakfasts. Good-sized bedrooms have a warm, boutique style; 7 and 8, on the top floor, are the best. Tea and cake on arrival, and plenty of extra touches.

7 rooms ⌨ – †£ 90/105 ††£ 90/170

Far Sawrey ✉ LA22 0LQ – Southeast : 2 mi on B 5285 – ☎ 015394 42817
– www.westvalecountryhouse.co.uk – Closed 25-26 December and restricted opening 3 January-4 February

HAWNBY

North Yorkshire – ✉ Helmsley – Regional map n° **13**-C1
▶ London 245 mi – Middlesbrough 27 mi – Newcastle upon Tyne 69 mi – York 30 mi

Laskill Country House

TRADITIONAL · PERSONALISED A delightful stone house draped with wisteria. It's remotely set and very personally run, with a welcoming house party atmosphere. There's a cosy open-fired lounge and a communal dining room where they serve meat from the family farm. Simple bedrooms have country views and there's even a hot tub in the garden.

3 rooms ⌨ – †£ 65 ††£ 100/125

Easterside, Laskill ✉ YO62 5NB – Northeast : 2.25 mi by Osmotherley rd
– ☎ 01439 798265 – www.laskillcountryhouse.co.uk – Closed 24-25 December

HAWORTH

West Yorkshire – ✉ Keighley – Pop. 6 379 – Regional map n° **13**-A2
▶ London 213 mi – Burnley 22 mi – Leeds 22 mi – Manchester 34 mi

Ashmount Country House

COUNTRY HOUSE · PERSONALISED Substantial Victorian house built by the Brontë sisters' physician. Luxurious bedrooms have state-of-the-art bathrooms – some with hot tubs. Original features include impressive stained glass paintings and an intricate plaster ceiling in the dining room; menus mix classics with more modern dishes.

12 rooms ⌨ – †£ 75/150 ††£ 95/275

Mytholmes Ln ✉ BD22 8EZ – ☎ 01535 645726 – www.ashmounthaworth.co.uk

HAYDON BRIDGE – Northumberland ➜ See Hexham

HAYWARDS HEATH

West Sussex – Pop. 33 845 – Regional map n° **4**-D2
▶ London 39 mi – Croydon 30 mi – Barnet 53 mi – Ealing 50 mi

XX Jeremy's at Borde Hill

MODERN CUISINE · FRIENDLY Converted stable block with exposed rafters, contemporary sculptures, vivid artwork and delightful views towards the Victorian walled garden. Interesting, modern European dishes and a good value 'menu of the day'. Regular gourmet nights.

Menu £ 20 (weekdays) – Carte £ 32/43

Borde Hill Gdns ✉ RH16 1XP – North : 1.75 mi by B 2028 and Balcombe Rd on Borde Hill Ln. – ☎ 01444 441102 – www.jeremysrestaurant.co.uk – Closed 1-15 January, Monday except bank holidays and Sunday dinner

HEADLAM – Durham ➜ See Darlington

HEATHROW AIRPORT – Greater London ➜ See London

HEDLEY ON THE HILL

Northumberland – Regional map n° **14**-A2
▶ London 293 mi – Newcastle upon Tyne 16 mi – Sunderland 26 mi – South Shields 26 mi

🍴 Feathers Inn   🏠 🅿

TRADITIONAL BRITISH · PUB Traditional stone inn set on a steep hill in the heart of a rural village. Daily changing menu of hearty British classics, cooked using carefully sourced regional produce, with meat and game to the fore. Relaxed, friendly atmosphere.

Carte £ 18/33

✉ NE43 7SW - 𝒞 01661 843607 - www.thefeathers.net - Closed first 2 weeks January, Sunday dinner, Monday except bank holidays and lunch Tuesday-Wednesday

HELMSLEY

North Yorkshire - Pop. 1 515 - Regional map n° **13**-C1

▶ London 239 mi - Leeds 51 mi - Middlesbrough 28 mi - York 24 mi

🏨 Feversham Arms H. & Verbena Spa   🛏 ⌛ ⊕ 🏠 ▣ ♨ 🚗

TRADITIONAL · CONTEMPORARY 19C former coaching inn with a lovely stone façade. Relax on the terrace beside the outdoor pool; the spa is superb and boasts a salt vapour room and an ice cave. Be sure to book one of the stylish newer bedrooms; many have stoves or fires.

33 rooms ⌷ - †£ 110/450 ††£ 120/510 - 21 suites

1-8 High St ✉ YO62 5AG - 𝒞 01439 770766 - www.fevershamarmshotel.com

The Weathervane - See restaurant listing

🏨 Black Swan   🛏 ♨ 🅿

HISTORIC · PERSONALISED Set overlooking the historic marketplace, The Black Swan is one of the country's best known coaching inns. The charming interior features beamed lounges, a modern bar and a tea shop. Bedrooms are a mix of characterful and contemporary. On Friday and Saturday nights, dinner is included in the rate.

45 rooms ⌷ - †£ 140/235 ††£ 155/250 - 1 suite

Market Pl ✉ YO62 5BJ - 𝒞 01439 770466 - www.blackswan-helmsley.co.uk

Gallery - See restaurant listing

🏠 No.54   🛏 ⌗ 🅿

TOWNHOUSE · COSY Charming Victorian terraced house near the main square. The three cosy, simply decorated bedrooms are set around a courtyard garden. Communal breakfasts feature good quality local produce, with honey from their bees in Lincolnshire.

3 rooms ⌷ - †£ 70/85 ††£ 100/130

54 Bondgate ✉ YO62 5EZ - 𝒞 01439 771533 - www.no54.co.uk - Closed Christmas-New Year

✕✕ The Weathervane

MODERN CUISINE · BRASSERIE Modern hotel restaurant with a pleasingly laid-back style. In summer, have lunch in the garden or on the poolside terrace. Dishes feature the latest local produce and cooking is refined and accurate; the tasting menu is worth a try.

Menu £ 48 - Carte £ 40/59 - bar lunch Monday-Saturday

Feversham Arms Hotel, 1-8 High St ✉ YO62 5AG - 𝒞 01439 770766
- www.fevershamarmshotel.com

✕✕ Gallery   ⊞ 🛏 🍽 🅿

CREATIVE · ELEGANT Bright, modern restaurant within a historic 15C coaching inn; its walls are filled with artwork for sale and at dinner, the plate becomes the canvas. Attractive, modern dishes have a classical base; the tasting menu is a highlight.

Carte £ 44/53

Black Swan Hotel, Market Pl ✉ YO62 5BJ - 𝒞 01439 770466
- www.blackswan-helmsley.co.uk - dinner only and Sunday lunch

ENGLAND

at Wombleton East: 4 mi by A170

🛏 Plough Inn

TRADITIONAL CUISINE · PUB 16C inn, popular with locals, serving tasty traditional dishes, including game in season. Prices are laudably low and service, friendly and relaxed. Sit in the hugely characterful restaurant, which is kept cosy by wood burners.

Carte £ 22/37

Main St ✉ YO62 7RW
– ☎ 01751 431356 – www.theploughinnatwombleton.co.uk
– Closed 25 December and Monday lunch

at Harome Southeast: 2.75 mi by A170✉ York

🏨 Pheasant

TRADITIONAL · PERSONALISED An attractive hotel in a picturesque hamlet, with a delightful duck pond and a mill stream close by. Beautiful, very comfortable lounges and spacious, well-furnished bedrooms; Rudland – running the width of the building and with views of the pond – is one of the best. Pleasant service. Excellent breakfasts.

16 rooms ☲ – 🛏£ 90/165 🛏🛏£ 170/260
Mill St ✉ YO62 5JG – ☎ 01439 771241
– www.thepheasanthotel.com
Pheasant – See restaurant listing

🏠 Cross House Lodge

COUNTRY HOUSE · DESIGN These sympathetically converted farm buildings have a rustic ski-chalet style and ultra-stylish, individually decorated bedrooms; one boasts a snooker table; another, a bed suspended on ropes. Relax in the open-plan, split-level lounge; excellent breakfasts are taken in the dramatic beamed 'Wheelhouse'.

9 rooms ☲ – 🛏£ 150/260 🛏🛏£ 150/260
High St ✉ YO62 5JE – ☎ 01439 770397 – www.thestaratharome.co.uk
❀ **Star Inn** – See restaurant listing

XX Pheasant

MODERN BRITISH · COSY Elegant hotel dining room with both classical and contemporary touches – along with a less formal conservatory and a lovely terrace overlooking the village duck pond. Appealing menus of seasonal dishes with a classical base and a modern touch. Skilful, knowledgeable cooking; smooth, assured service.

Menu £ 24/40 – Carte £ 39/65

Pheasant Hotel, Mill St ✉ YO62 5JG – ☎ 01439 771241
– www.thepheasanthotel.com

🛏 Star Inn (Andrew Pern)

❀ **MODERN BRITISH · INN** 14C thatched pub with a delightful terrace, a low-ceilinged bar and a brasserie-like restaurant with a chef's table. Dishes have assured flavours and a skilled, classical style; they use the very best of local produce, including veg from the kitchen garden and meats from their own pigs and chickens.

→ Grilled black pudding with pan-fried foie gras and Pickering watercress. Pot-roast squab pigeon with pickled beetroot and charred leek. A celebration of Tomlinson's Yorkshire rhubarb.

Menu £ 25 (weekdays) – Carte £ 33/56

High St ✉ YO62 5JE – ☎ 01439 770397 (booking essential)
– www.thestaratharome.co.uk
– Closed Monday lunch except bank holidays

at Ampleforth Southwest: 4.5 mi by A170 off B1257 ⊠ Helmsley

🏠 Shallowdale House ⚐ ⅏ ⪡ 🛋 ℀ 🅿

TRADITIONAL · CLASSIC A remotely set, personally run house with a well-tended garden and stunning views of the Howardian Hills. Charming, antique-furnished interior, with an open-fired sitting room and good-sized bedrooms decorated in bright, Mediterranean tones. Four course set menu of home-cooked fare.

3 rooms ⌂ – ♦£ 110/125 ♦♦£ 130/155

⊠ YO62 4DY – West : 0.5 mi – ℰ 01439 788325 – www.shallowdalehouse.co.uk
– Closed Christmas-New Year

at Scawton West : 5 m. by B 1257 ⊠ Helmsley

✗✗ The Hare Inn ♿ 🅿

MODERN CUISINE · COSY Exposed brick and beams give this 13C inn a pubby feel but despite its appearance this is now a restaurant. The self-taught chef offers 3 set menus of creative, accomplished dishes which are attractively presented and full of flavour.

Menu £ 30 (weekdays)/60

⊠ YO7 2HG – ℰ 01845 597769 (booking essential) – www.thehare-inn.com
– Closed 3 weeks January, 1 week June, 1 week November, Sunday dinner, Monday and Tuesday

HELPERBY

North Yorkshire – Regional map n° **13**-B2
▶ London 220 mi – Leeds 36 mi – Sheffield 70 mi – Manchester 81 mi

🍴 Oak Tree Inn ⪢ 🛖 ♿ ♻ 🅿

TRADITIONAL BRITISH · INN A pub of two halves, with a large bar, a tap room and two snugs in the main building, and a smart dining room in the old hay barn. Cooking is based around the Bertha charcoal oven, with steaks, chops, poultry and fish to the fore. Chic modern bedrooms come with 'Yorkie' bars and spa baths.

Carte £ 20/45

6 rooms ⌂ – ♦£ 75/125 ♦♦£ 100/150

Raskelf Rd ⊠ YO61 2PH – ℰ 01423 789189 – www.theoaktreehelperby.com

HELSTON

Cornwall – Pop. 11 311 – Regional map n° **1**-A3
▶ London 280 mi – Birmingham 275 mi – Croydon 288 mi – Barnet 293 mi

at Trelowarren Southeast: 4 mi by A394 and A3083 on B3293 ⊠ Helston

✗ New Yard 🛖 🅿

MODERN BRITISH · RUSTIC Converted 17C stable building adjoining a craft gallery. Spacious, rustic room with timbered walls and doors opening onto the terrace. Seasonal menu uses quality Cornish produce; breads and ice creams are homemade. Friendly service.

Carte £ 19/31

Trelowarren Estate ⊠ TR12 6AF – ℰ 01326 221595 (bookings advisable at dinner)
– www.trelowarren.com – Closed 3 weeks January, Monday and Tuesday October-Easter

HEMINGFORD GREY – Cambridgeshire ➜ See Huntingdon

HENFIELD

West Sussex – Pop. 4 527 – Regional map n° **4**-D2
▶ London 47 mi – Brighton 10 mi – Worthing 11 mi

🏨 Ginger Fox ⛲ 🛋 ♿ 🅿️

CLASSIC CUISINE · PUB Spot the fox running across the thatched roof and you know you're in the right place. Monthly changing menu offers good value, flavourful dishes, with a popular vegetarian tasting plate. Desserts are a highlight, so save space.

Menu £ 15 (weekday lunch) – Carte £ 25/45

Muddleswood Rd, Albourne ✉ BN6 9EA – Southwest : 3 mi on A 281
– ☎ 01273 857888 – www.gingermanrestaurants.com
– Closed 25 December

HENLEY – West Sussex ➜ See Midhurst

HENLEY-IN-ARDEN

Warwickshire – Pop. 2 846 – Regional map n° **10**-C3
▶ London 104 mi – Birmingham 15 mi – Stratford-upon-Avon 8 mi – Warwick 8 mi

🍴🍴 Cheal's of Henley Ⓝ ♿

MODERN CUISINE · ELEGANT A 400 year old house on the high street, which has been smartly refurbished yet retains plenty of character – it's leased by a local couple and run by their son. Complex modern cooking relies on classic flavour combinations.

Menu £ 30/50

65 High St ✉ B95 5BX – ☎ 01564 793856 – www.chealsofhenley.co.uk – Closed 2 weeks August, 1 week Easter, Christmas-New Year, Sunday dinner, Monday and Tuesday

🏨 Bluebell 🛋 🅿️

MODERN BRITISH · ROMANTIC This unusual high street pub displays an intriguing mix of rustic character and formal elegance. The chef uses top local ingredients in refined, seasonal dishes and there's a wide range of wines, beers and cocktails available too.

Carte £ 23/39

93 High St ✉ B95 5AT – ☎ 01564 793049 – www.bluebellhenley.co.uk – Closed Monday

HENLEY-ON-THAMES

Oxfordshire – Pop. 11 494 – Regional map n° **6**-C3
▶ London 40 mi – Oxford 23 mi – Croydon 44 mi – Barnet 46 mi

🏨 Hotel du Vin 🍴 ♿ 🆎 ⚒ 🅿️

BUSINESS · MODERN Characterful 1857 building that was formerly the Brakspear Brewery. Stylish bedrooms include airy doubles and duplex suites: one features two roll-top tubs and a great view of the church; others boast heated balconies and outdoor baths. Choose from a list of brasserie classics and over 400 wines in the bistro.

43 rooms – 🛏£ 130/300 🛏£ 130/300 – 🍽£ 17 – 2 suites
New St. ✉ RG9 2BP – ☎ 01491 848400 – www.hotelduvin.com

🍴🍴 Shaun Dickens at The Boathouse 🛋 ♿ 🆎

MODERN BRITISH · FRIENDLY This modern restaurant is sure to please with its floor to ceiling glass doors and decked terrace overlooking the Thames. The young chef-owner offers an array of menus; attractively presented dishes centre around local ingredients.

Menu £ 26/69 – Carte £ 40/49

Station Rd ✉ RG9 1AZ – ☎ 01491 577937 – www.shaundickens.co.uk – Closed 25-26 December, Monday and Tuesday

X **Luscombes at The Golden Ball**

TRADITIONAL CUISINE · FRIENDLY A pretty former pub – now a cosy restaurant that's popular with the locals. Appealing menus offer tasty, well-executed modern classics; the afternoon tea with homemade preserves is a hit. Service is friendly and attentive.

Menu £15 (weekday lunch) – Carte £28/45

Lower Assendon ⊠ RG9 6AH – Northwest : 0.75 mi by A 4130 on B 480
– ℰ 01491 574157 – www.luscombes.co.uk

⑂ **Three Tuns**

TRADITIONAL BRITISH · PUB Pretty, red-brick, town centre pub with a lively, open-fired front bar and a formal dining room for a more intimate meal. Seasonal, traditional dishes are well-presented, satisfying and full of flavour. Homemade bread. Friendly service.

Menu £12 (weekday lunch) – Carte £25/42

5 Market Pl ⊠ RG9 2AA – ℰ 01491 410138 – www.threetunshenley.co.uk – Closed 25 December and Sunday dinner

at Shiplake South: 2 mi on A4155

XX **Orwells**

MODERN BRITISH · RUSTIC This 18C building may look like a rural inn but inside it has a modern, formal feel. Creative cooking uses top quality produce and flavours are pronounced. It's named after George Orwell, who spent his childhood in the area.

Menu £15 (weekdays) – Carte £40/54

Shiplake Row ⊠ RG9 4DP – West 0.5 mi on Binfield Heath rd. – ℰ 0118 940 3673
– www.orwellsatshiplake.co.uk – Closed first 2 weeks January, first 2 weeks September, 1 week June, Sunday dinner, Tuesday and Monday except bank holidays

⑂ **Plowden Arms**

TRADITIONAL BRITISH · FAMILY An appealing pub with a delightful garden; inside, open fires, flickering candles and hop bines set the scene. The large blackboard offers tasty snacks and the interesting main menu features a number of Eliza Acton inspired dishes.

Carte £24/42

Reading Rd ⊠ RG9 4BX – ℰ 0118 940 2794 – www.plowdenarmsshiplake.co.uk
– Closed Monday except bank holidays

HEREFORD

Herefordshire – Pop. 60 415 – Regional map n° **10**-B3
▶ London 133 mi – Birmingham 51 mi – Cardiff 56 mi

🏠 **Castle House**

TOWNHOUSE · CONTEMPORARY This elegant Georgian house sits close to the cathedral. An impressive staircase leads to warmly furnished bedrooms of various sizes; some overlook the old castle moat. More contemporary rooms can be found in nearby 'Number 25'.

24 rooms �??? – ♦£110/140 ♦♦£150/250

Castle St ⊠ HR1 2NW – ℰ 01432 356321 – www.castlehse.co.uk

Castle House – See restaurant listing

🏠 **Somerville House**

TOWNHOUSE · CLASSIC A Victorian villa with cathedral views and an enclosed garden; home-grown apples, plums and pears are used to make the breakfast preserves. Bedrooms on the first floor are the most spacious; all have mini-bars and good facilities.

12 rooms �??? – ♦£60/92 ♦♦£80/125

12 Bodenham Rd ⊠ HR1 2TS – Northeast : 0.75 mi by A 465 and Southbank Rd.
– ℰ 01432 273991 – www.somervillehouse.net

XX Castle House
MODERN CUISINE · ELEGANT This elegant restaurant looks out over the hotel gardens and across the old moat of Hereford Castle. Classic dishes are reinvented in a modern manner and ingredients from Herefordshire feature highly. Menus offer plenty of choice.

Carte £ 20/47

Castle House Hotel, Castle St ⊠ HR1 2NW – ℰ 01432 356321
– www.castlehse.co.uk

HERNE BAY
Kent – Pop. 38 385 – Regional map n° **5**-D1
London 65 mi – Maidenhead 33 mi – Dover 25 mi

X Le Petit Poisson
SEAFOOD · NEIGHBOURHOOD Head straight for the terrace of this whitewashed building opposite the town pier. The split-level interior boasts flagged floors, exposed brick and eye-catching art. Constantly evolving blackboard menus offer unfussy seafood dishes.

Menu £ 13 (weekday lunch) – Carte £ 22/34

Pier Approach, Central Par. ⊠ CT6 5JN – ℰ 01227 361199
– www.lepetitpoisson.co.uk – Closed 25-26 December, 1 January, Sunday dinner and Monday except bank holidays when closed Tuesday

HERSTMONCEUX
East Sussex – Pop. 1 130 – Regional map n° **5**-B3
London 63 mi – Eastbourne 12 mi – Hastings 14 mi – Lewes 16 mi

XX Sundial
CLASSIC FRENCH · TRADITIONAL DÉCOR With its original leaded windows and beamed ceiling, this characterful 16C cottage is a real hit with the locals. Service is structured and the room is formally laid. Rich, classic French dishes use luxurious seasonal ingredients.

Menu £ 28/43

Gardner St ⊠ BN27 4LA – ℰ 01323 832217 – www.sundialrestaurant.co.uk – Closed Sunday dinner and Monday

at Wartling Southeast: 3.75 mi by A271 on Wartling rd⊠ Herstmonceux

Wartling Place
COUNTRY HOUSE · CLASSIC A charming part-Georgian house with a homely feel, set in three acres of mature grounds and run by a delightful owner. Two of the bedrooms have four-poster beds; DAB radios and iPod docks provide a contrast to the antique furniture.

4 rooms ⊡ – †£ 95/115 ††£ 135/165

⊠ BN27 1RY – ℰ 01323 832590 – www.wartlingplace.co.uk

HESWALL
Mersey. – Pop. 29 977 – Regional map n° **20**-A3
London 212 mi – Birkenhead 12 mi – Chester 14 mi – Liverpool 11 mi

X Burnt Truffle ⓝ
BRITISH MODERN · BISTRO A friendly team run this sweet modern bistro. Menus offer a good range of original dishes with global influences. Start with the sourdough bread with truffle and walnut butter and be sure to save room for the delicious desserts.

Menu £ 18 (lunch) – Carte dinner £ 23/39

106 Telegraph Rd ⊠ CH60 0AQ – ℰ 0151 342 1111 – www.burnttruffle.net – Closed 25-27 December

HETHE
Oxfordshire – Regional map n° **6**-B1
London 114 mi – Oxford 36 mi – Northampton 45 mi

🛏️ **Muddy Duck** 🍴 🛋️ 🚫 AC P

MODERN CUISINE · FRIENDLY An unpretentious local with a happy feel and ul-tra-smiley staff, this modernised mellow stone pub stays true to its traditional roots. Pub staples and more adventurous choices on the menu, with dishes from the wood-fired oven in summer.

Carte £ 23/60

Main St ✉ OX27 8ES – ☎ 01869 278099 – www.themuddyduckpub.co.uk – Closed Sunday dinner

HETTON

North Yorkshire – Regional map n° **13**-N2

▶ London 229 mi – Leeds 31 mi – York 48 mi

🛏️ **Angel Inn** 🏵️ 🔄 AC P

MODERN CUISINE · PUB For a casual dinner, sit in the appealing Brasserie area of this 18C inn and pick something from the daily specials board; for a special evening out, book the Restaurant and choose from more refined, imaginative dishes. Classical bedrooms are found in the Barn Lodgings and more modern rooms in Sycamore Bank.

Carte £ 27/45

9 rooms 🗠 – 🛉£ 135/185 🛉🛉£ 150/200

*✉ BD23 6LT – ☎ 01756 730263 (booking essential) – www.angelhetton.co.uk
– Closed 2 weeks January and 25 December*

HEXHAM

Northumberland – Pop. 11 388 – Regional map n° **14**-A2

▶ London 304 mi – Carlisle 37 mi – Newcastle upon Tyne 21 mi

XX **Bouchon** 🔄

CLASSIC FRENCH · INTIMATE Well-run French restaurant with a simply styled ground floor room and a more romantic first floor with opulent purple furnish-ings. Excellent value set price lunch menu and more ambitious à la carte. Classic French dishes use local produce.

Menu £ 15 (weekday lunch) – Carte £ 22/38

*4-6 Gilesgate ✉ NE46 3NJ – ☎ 01434 609943 – www.bouchonbistrot.co.uk
– Closed 24-26 December, Sunday and bank holidays*

🛏️ **Rat Inn** 🛋️ P

TRADITIONAL BRITISH · PUB Traditional 18C drovers' inn with wooden beams, an open range and a multi-level garden boasting arbours and Tyne Valley views. The daily changing blackboard menu showcases interesting dishes; the rib of beef for two is a must.

Carte £ 22/42

*Anick ✉ NE46 4LN – Northeast : 1.75 mi by A 6079 – ☎ 01434 602814
– www.theratinn.com – Closed 25 December, Monday except bank holidays and Sunday dinner*

at Haydon Bridge West: 7.5 mi on A69 ✉ Hexham

🏰 **Langley Castle**

HISTORIC BUILDING · CLASSIC Impressive 14C castle in 12 acres; its charming guest areas feature stone walls, tapestries and heraldic shields. Characterful bed-rooms, some with four-posters; Castle View rooms are more uniform in style. Modern, international menus in the romantic dining room or in the glass cube overlooking the gardens.

27 rooms 🗠 – 🛉£ 130/220 🛉🛉£ 159/279

*Langley-on-Tyne ✉ NE47 5LU – South : 2 mi by Alston rd on A 686
– ☎ 01434 688888 – www.langleycastle.com*

HIGHCLERE

Hampshire – ✉ Newbury – Pop. 2 409 – Regional map n° **4**-B1

▶ London 69 mi – Newbury 5 mi – Reading 25 mi

🍴 Yew Tree   ⇦ 🖧 🛏 ⇔ 🅿️

TRADITIONAL BRITISH · INN An attractive 17C inn with a pretty terrace, a wel-coming open-fired bar and three low-beamed dining rooms. Dishes are listed on the menu by size. Classically based recipes are given modern twists and include some interesting vegetarian options. Cosy bedrooms come with good mod cons and smart wet rooms.

Carte £ 24/49

8 rooms ⌸ – 🛉£ 95/130 🛉🛉£ 95/130
*Hollington Cross, Andover Rd ⊠ RG20 9SE – South : 1 mi on A 343
– 𝒞 01635 253360 – www.theyewtree.co.uk*

HIGHCLIFFE
Dorset – Regional map n° **2**-D3
▶ London 112 mi – Bournemouth 10 mi – Salisbury 21 mi – Southampton 26 mi

🏠 Lord Bute   🌣 🆎 ♨ 🅿️

BUSINESS · PERSONALISED Some of the suites in this elegant hotel stand where the original 18C entrance lodges to Highcliffe Castle (home of Lord Bute), were once located. Bedrooms are well-appointed and decorated in a contemporary style. The smart restaurant and courtyard offer classical menus and host jazz and cabaret evenings.

13 rooms ⌸ – 🛉£ 125/245 🛉🛉£ 125/245 – 2 suites
179-185 Lymington Rd ⊠ BH23 4JS – 𝒞 01425 278884 – www.lordbute.co.uk

HIGHER BURWARDSLEY
Cheshire West and Chester – Regional map n° **20**-A3
▶ London 183 mi – Chester 10 mi – Liverpool 28 mi

🍴 Pheasant Inn   ⇦ 🐾 ⇐ 🖧 🛏 🅿️

TRADITIONAL BRITISH · PUB Well-run, modern pub set atop a sandstone es-carpment, with views across the Cheshire Plains. The menu focuses on simple pub classics, with no-nonsense cooking and clear, gutsy flavours. Spacious, beamed bedrooms in the main building; more modern rooms with views in the barn. Staff are keen to please.

Carte £ 20/38

12 rooms ⌸ – 🛉£ 95/110 🛉🛉£ 105/145
⊠ CH3 9PF – 𝒞 01829 770434 – www.thepheasantinn.co.uk

HINCKLEY
Leicestershire – Pop. 45 249 – Regional map n° **9**-B2
▶ London 103 mi – Birmingham 31 mi – Leicester 14 mi

✕✕ 34 Windsor St   🛏 🆎 🅿️

MODERN CUISINE · FASHIONABLE This stylish modern restaurant is well-run by an experienced, hands-on owner. It has a relaxed feel and a smart chill-out ter-race to the rear. Cooking is also contemporary; the 8 course tasting menu shows the kitchen's ambition.

Menu £ 16 (lunch) – Carte £ 29/52

*34 Windsor St ⊠ LE10 2EF – Southeast : 2.25 mi by B 4669 off B 578
– 𝒞 01455 234342 – www.34windsorst.com – Closed 1-3 January, 27-28 December, Monday and Tuesday*

HINTLESHAM – Suffolk ➜ See Ipswich

HINTON ST GEORGE
Somerset – Regional map n° **2**-B3
▶ London 138 mi – Taunton 21 mi – Weymouth 41 mi – Yeovil 13 mi

Lord Poulett Arms

MODERN BRITISH · RURAL Characterful pub with open fires and beams fringed with hop bines; outside it's just as charming, with a lavender-framed terrace, a boules pitch and a secret garden. Creative cooking has a British base but also displays a wide range of influences. Stylish bedrooms come with feature beds and Roberts radios.

Menu £16 (lunch and early dinner) – Carte £26/38

4 rooms �). – †£60/65 ††£85/95

High St ✉ TA17 8SE – ✆01460 73149 – www.lordpoulettarms.com – Closed 25-26 December and 1 January

HITCHIN

Hertfordshire – Pop. 34 266 – Regional map n° **7**-A2

▶ London 40 mi – Bedford 14 mi – Cambridge 26 mi – Luton 9 mi

✗ hermitage rd

MODERN BRITISH · BRASSERIE A vast, open-plan brasserie with a cocktail bar and a vibrant, buzzy atmosphere; sit in the booths at the back. The menu offers something for everyone, with mussels or oysters from their own beds, sharing boards and some great steaks.

Menu £15 (weekday lunch) – Carte £26/43

20-21 Hermitage Rd ✉ SG5 1BT – ✆01462 433603 (booking essential) – www.hermitagerd.co.uk – Closed 25-26 December

HOLCOMBE

Somerset – Regional map n° **2**-C2

▶ London 119 mi – Birmingham 106 mi – Leeds 228 mi – Sheffield 198 mi

Holcombe Inn

MODERN BRITISH · RUSTIC Charming 17C inn set in the heart of the Somerset countryside, with a lovely south-facing garden and a peaceful air. Menus offer quite a range of dishes, from good old pub classics to more sophisticated offerings. Bedrooms are luxuriously appointed; some boast views over Downside Abbey.

Carte £29/44

10 rooms ☲ – †£75/125 ††£100/145

Stratton Rd ✉ BA3 5EB – West : 0.25 mi on Stratton-on-the-Fosse rd – ✆01761 232478 – www.holcombeinn.co.uk

HOLKHAM

Norfolk – Regional map n° **8**-C1

▶ London 124 mi – King's Lynn 32 mi – Norwich 39 mi

Victoria

INN · COSY An extended flint inn with a relaxed, modern style, large lawned gardens and pleasant country views, set close to the beach at the gates of Holkham Hall. Stylish bedrooms – some in 'Ancient House' across the road. Dine on traditional British dishes overlooking the marshes of the adjacent nature reserve.

20 rooms ☲ – †£95/155 ††£125/240

Park Rd ✉ NR23 1RG – ✆01328 711008 – www.holkham.co.uk/victoria

HOLLINGBOURNE

Kent – Regional map n° **5**-C2

▶ London 43 mi – Maidstone 7 mi – Faversham 23 mi

The Windmill

TRADITIONAL BRITISH · PUB With its giant inglenook fireplace and low-slung beams, the Windmill is as characterful as they come. You'll find tempting bar snacks, sharing roasts on Sundays and, alongside the hearty British classics, some more refined dishes too.

Menu £ 15 (weekday lunch) – Carte £ 27/40

32 Eyhorne St ⊠ ME17 1TR – ℰ 01622 889000
– www.thewindmillbyrichardphillips.co.uk

HOLMFIRTH

West Yorkshire – Pop. 21 706 – Regional map n° **13**-B3
London 187 mi – Leeds 35 mi – Sheffield 32 mi – Manchester 25 mi

Sunnybank

TOWNHOUSE · ELEGANT Attractive Victorian house with lovely gardens and great views; hidden up a narrow road in the village where 'Last of the Summer Wine' was filmed. Cosy bedrooms have a personal touch. Look out for the original stained glass window.

6 rooms ⌂ – ♦£ 68/105 ♦♦£ 78/115

78 Upperthong Ln ⊠ HD9 3BQ – Northwest : 0.5 mi by A 6024 – ℰ 01484 684065
– www.sunnybankguesthouse.co.uk

HOLT

Norfolk – Pop. 3 550 – Regional map n° **8**-C1
London 124 mi – Norwich 22 mi – King's Lynn 34 mi

Byfords

TOWNHOUSE · MODERN Grade II listed, 15C flint house. Stunning bedrooms come with feature beds, underfloor heating and plenty of extras. Numerous characterful rooms incorporate a deli, a café and a restaurant. Light meals are served during the day and more substantial dishes in the evening; it's a real hit with the locals.

17 rooms ⌂ – ♦£ 125/175 ♦♦£ 155/205

Shirehall Plain ⊠ NR25 6BG – ℰ 01263 711400 – www.byfords.org.uk

HOLT

Wiltshire – Pop. 1 532 – Regional map n° **4**-C2
London 109 mi – Yeovil 46 mi – Taunton 65 mi

Tollgate Inn

TRADITIONAL CUISINE · PUB If there was an award for the most welcoming pub, then this village inn would surely be the winner. The attentive staff pitch things just right, from the cheery hello to the charming personal touches in the cosy bedrooms. Cooking keeps things simple – as befits a pub – with hearty, flavoursome dishes.

Carte £ 18/41

5 rooms ⌂ – ♦£ 50/80 ♦♦£ 60/120

Ham Grn ⊠ BA14 6PX – ℰ 01225 782326 – www.tollgateinn.co.uk – Closed
25 December and Sunday dinner

HOLYPORT

Windsor and Maidenhead – Regional map n° **6**-C3
London 30 mi – Birmingham 107 mi – Bristol 93 mi – Croydon 37 mi

Belgian Arms

TRADITIONAL BRITISH · PUB Pretty 17C inn tucked away just off the village green, next to a pond fringed by willow trees. Gutsy pub dishes include tempting bar snacks and heartwarming desserts. It's a real locals' local, so there's always plenty going on.

Carte £ 28/39

Holyport St ⊠ SL6 2JR – ℰ 01628 634468 – www.thebelgianarms.com
– Closed Monday

HONITON

Devon – Pop. 11 483 – Regional map n° **1**-D2

▶ London 186 mi – Exeter 17 mi – Southampton 93 mi – Taunton 18 mi

🏚️ The Pig ⓝ   🏇 🐾 ≼ 🍴 🏠 🐾 🅿️

COUNTRY HOUSE · CONTEMPORARY A hugely impressive Elizabethan mansion. Inside it's been completely redesigned, with the historic entrance hall now being a bar. Bedrooms in the house boast wonderful country views; those in the old stables retain original features such as their partitions. Dine in the elegant restaurant or the old garden folly, which showcase local and garden produce.

27 rooms – 🛏️£ 145/325 🛏️🛏️£ 145/325 – 🍽️£ 15

Gittisham ✉️ *EX14 3AD – Southwest : 5 mi by A 30 and B 3177 –* ☎️ *01404 540400 – www.thepighotel.com*

🍴 Holt

REGIONAL CUISINE · PUB A rustic, family-run pub, where their passion for food is almost palpable. The regularly changing menu features regional and homemade produce, with meats and fish smoked and cured on-site; ales are from their nearby family brewery.

Carte £ 27/35

178 High St ✉️ *EX14 1LA –* ☎️ *01404 47707 – www.theholt-honiton.com – Closed 25-26 December, 1 January, Sunday and Monday*

🍴 Railway   ≼ 🏠 & 🅿️

MEDITERRANEAN CUISINE · INN Smart, modern pub with a horseshoe bar, an open kitchen and a decked terrace. Authentic, affordable Mediterranean cooking features homemade pastas, brick-fired pizzas and well-cooked steaks. An eclectic wine list and an olive oil top-up service add to the fun, and comfortable bedrooms complete the picture.

Menu £ 16 (weekday lunch) – Carte £ 24/34

3 rooms 🍽️ – 🛏️£ 85/95 🛏️🛏️£ 95/110

Queen St ✉️ *EX14 1HE –* ☎️ *01404 47976 – www.therailwayhoniton.co.uk – Closed 25-26 December, Sunday and Monday*

HOOK

Hampshire – Pop. 7 934 – Regional map n° **4**-B1

▶ London 47 mi – Oxford 39 mi – Reading 13 mi – Southampton 31 mi

🏚️ Tylney Hall   🏇 🐾 🍴 🛁 🎞️ 🐾 🏌️ 🎾 & 🏊 🅿️

LUXURY · CLASSIC Impressively restored 19C mansion full of period grandeur. Bedrooms are split between the main house and courtyard: the former are traditionally furnished with period features; the latter benefit from views over the delightful gardens, designed by Jekyll. The formal panelled restaurant offers classic dishes.

112 rooms 🍽️ – 🛏️£ 230/520 🛏️🛏️£ 250/540 – 20 suites

Rotherwick ✉️ *RG27 9AZ – Northwest : 2.5 mi by A 30 and Newnham Rd on Ridge Ln –* ☎️ *01256 764881 – www.tylneyhall.com*

HOPE

Derbyshire – ✉️ Sheffield – Regional map n° **9**-A1

▶ London 180 mi – Derby 50 mi – Manchester 31 mi – Sheffield 15 mi

🏚️ Losehill House   🏇 🐾 ≼ 🍴 🏠 🎞️ 🐾 🔁 🎾 🏊 🅿️

TRADITIONAL · PERSONALISED Peacefully located former walkers' hostel affording wonderful views up to Win Hill; in summer it's a popular wedding venue. It has an airy open-plan lounge-bar and bright modern bedrooms. Unwind in the spa or in the hot tub on the terrace. The formally laid restaurant offers classic dishes with a modern edge.

23 rooms 🍽️ – 🛏️£ 160/180 🛏️🛏️£ 195/265

Lose Hill Ln, Edale Rd ✉️ *S33 6AF – North : 1 mi by Edale Rd –* ☎️ *01433 621219 – www.losehillhouse.co.uk*

🏠 **Underleigh House**   🌿 ⟨ 🛏 ⌀ **P**

TRADITIONAL · PERSONALISED Former Derbyshire longhouse and shippon with far-reaching views; the gregarious owner offers a friendly welcome. Traditional bedrooms, some opening onto the garden. Communal breakfasts include home-made preserves, bread and muesli.

5 rooms ⌑ – � £ 75/105 �£ 95/125

Losehill Ln, Hope Valley ✉ S33 6AF – North : 1 mi by Edale Rd – 𝒞 01433 621372 – www.underleighhouse.co.uk – Closed Christmas-New Year and January

HOPTON HEATH

Shropshire – Regional map n° **10**-A2

▶ London 162 mi – Birmingham 66 mi – Leeds 152 mi – Sheffield 131 mi

🏠 **Hopton House**   🌿 ⟨ 🛏 ⅙ **P**

COUNTRY HOUSE · PERSONALISED An unassuming former granary backed by a wild flower meadow and the Shropshire Hills. Stylish bedrooms come with sofas and double-ended baths. One room has a balcony; one has a terrace – and they all come with a freshly baked cake.

2 rooms ⌑ – � £ 120/130 �£ 120/130

✉ SY7 0QD – On Clun rd – 𝒞 01547 530885 – www.shropshirebreakfast.co.uk

HORLEY

Surrey – Pop. 22 693 – Regional map n° **4**-D2

▶ London 27 mi – Brighton 26 mi – Royal Tunbridge Wells 22 mi

🏛 **Langshott Manor**   🌿 🛏 ⌀ **P**

HISTORIC · PERSONALISED Characterful 16C manor house set amidst roses, vines and ponds. The traditional exterior contrasts with contemporary furnishings and many of the bedrooms have fireplaces, four-posters or balconies. Afternoon tea is a feature.

22 rooms – � £ 99/319 �£ 99/319 – ⌑ £ 17 – 1 suite

Langshott ✉ RH6 9LN – North : 0.5 mi by A 23 turning right at Chequers Hotel onto Ladbroke Rd – 𝒞 01293 786680 – www.alexanderhotels.com

Mulberry – See restaurant listing

XX **Mulberry**   🛏 🍴 **AC** 🔲 **P**

MODERN BRITISH · CHIC Smart hotel dining room set within a Part-Elizabethan manor house. Well-presented dishes have a classical heart but are given personal twists by the experienced team. They use many herbs, fruits and vegetables from the gardens.

Menu £ 35/50

Langshott Manor Hotel, Langshott ✉ RH6 9LN – North : 0.5 mi by A 23 turning right at Chequers Hotel onto Ladbroke Rd – 𝒞 01293 786680 – www.langshottmanor.com

HORNCASTLE

Lincolnshire – Pop. 6 815 – Regional map n° **9**-C1

▶ London 143 mi – Lincoln 22 mi – Nottingham 62 mi

XX **Magpies**   ⟨ ⅙ **AC**

TRADITIONAL BRITISH · FAMILY Three adjoining 18C cottages; now a cosy, family-run restaurant which hosts regular gourmet and wine dinners. Hearty, classically based dishes are attractively presented; don't miss the tasty homemade canapés and breads. Modern bedrooms have bold floral feature walls and impressive bathrooms.

Menu £ 16 (weekday lunch)/49

3 rooms ⌑ – � £ 70/80 �£ 110/130

71-75 East St ✉ LN9 6AA – 𝒞 01507 527004 – www.magpiesrestaurant.co.uk – Closed 26-30 December, 1-5 January, Saturday lunch, Monday and Tuesday

HORNDON ON THE HILL

Thurrock – Pop. 1 596 – Regional map n° **7**-C3

▶ London 25 mi – Chelmsford 22 mi – Maidstone 34 mi – Southend-on-Sea 16 mi

🏠 Bell Inn   ← 🛏 🅿

TRADITIONAL BRITISH · INN A characterful 15C coaching inn, run by the same family for over 70 years; look out for the hot cross buns hanging from the bar. Cooking uses quality produce to create classically based dishes with a modern touch. Pub bedrooms are traditional in style, while those in Hill House are thoroughly modern.

Carte £ 22/41

27 rooms ⌷ – ∮£ 65/140 ∮∮£ 70/145

High Rd ⌧ SS17 8LD – ℰ 01375 642463 – www.bell-inn.co.uk – Closed 25-26 December and bank holidays

HORNING

Norfolk – Pop. 1 098 – Regional map n° **8**-D1

▶ London 121 mi – Great Yarmouth 16 mi – Norwich 11 mi

🍴 Bure River Cottage

SEAFOOD · FRIENDLY Friendly restaurant tucked away in a lovely riverside village that's famed for its boating. Informal, L-shaped room with modern tables and chairs. Blackboard menu features fresh, carefully cooked fish and shellfish; much from Lowestoft.

Carte £ 24/50

27 Lower St ⌧ NR12 8AA – ℰ 01692 631421 (booking advisable) – www.burerivercottagerestaurant.co.uk – dinner only – Closed 25 December-13 February, Sunday and Monday

HORNINGSEA – Cambridgeshire → See Cambridge

HORN'S CROSS

Devon – Regional map n° **1**-C1

▶ London 222 mi – Barnstaple 15 mi – Exeter 46 mi

🏠 Roundhouse   🛏 ℀ 🅿 ⇥

TRADITIONAL · COSY Spacious, welcoming guesthouse on the site of a 13C corn mill, with neat gardens and donkeys in the paddock. Guest areas are comfortable and homely and bedrooms are immaculately kept – ask for the round room on the first floor.

3 rooms ⌷ – ∮£ 50 ∮∮£ 65/70

⌧ EX39 5DN – West : 1 mi on A 39 – ℰ 01237 451687 – www.the-round-house.co.uk

HORRINGER – Suffolk → See Bury St Edmunds

HORSHAM

West Sussex – Pop. 48 041 – Regional map n° **4**-D2

▶ London 39 mi – Brighton 23 mi – Guildford 20 mi – Lewes 25 mi

🍴 Restaurant Tristan (Tristan Mason)   🖳
❀ MODERN BRITISH · RUSTIC A characterful beamed dining room on the first floor of a 16C town centre property. Carefully crafted, creative dishes are delivered with a modern touch; ingredients are excellent and flavours, distinct and well-matched. Service is enthusiastic and friendly and the atmosphere, refreshingly relaxed.

→ Duck egg 64° with asparagus. Fillet of lamb with kid pastilla, goat's cheese and turnip. Rhubarb soufflé with liquorice, rose and gin.

Menu £ 25/45

Stans Way, East St ⌧ RH12 1HU – ℰ 01403 255688 – www.restauranttristan.co.uk – Closed 25 December,1 January, Sunday and Monday

at Rowhook Northwest: 4 mi by A264 and A281 off A29 ⊠ Horsham

🍴 Chequers Inn   ⟨⟩ 🛏 🚗 🅿

TRADITIONAL BRITISH · COSY Part-15C inn with a charming open-fired, stone-floored bar and an unusual dining room extension. The chef-owner grows, forages for or shoots the majority of his produce. Classical menus.

Carte £ 26/41

⊠ RH12 3PY – 𝒞 01403 790480 – www.thechequersrowhook.com – Closed 25 December and Sunday dinner

HORSTED KEYNES

West Sussex – Pop. 1 180 – Regional map n° **4**-D2

▶ London 40 mi – Brighton 23 mi – Guildford 48 mi – Canterbury 75 mi

🍴 Crown Inn   ⇔ ⟨⟩ 🛏 🚗 🅿

CLASSIC CUISINE · PUB With its beams and feature inglenook, the front bar of this pub is full of character, while the smart dining room houses a grand piano, played on Friday nights. Classical dishes form the core of the menu, with more ambitious, seasonal specials. Simple bedrooms have views of the green; one is a four-poster.

Carte £ 25/44

4 rooms � – ♦£ 75/90 ♦♦£ 90/110

The Green ⊠ RH17 7AW – 𝒞 01825 791609 – www.thecrown-horstedkeynes.co.uk – Closed Sunday dinner and Monday January-June

HOUGH-ON-THE-HILL – Lincolnshire → See Grantham

HUCCOMBE

Devon – Regional map n° **1**-C3

▶ London 217 mi – Bristol 121 mi – Cardiff 152 mi – Plymouth 30 mi

🏠 Huccombe House   🌳 ⟨ 🛏 🛇 🅿 ⟼

FAMILY · PERSONALISED Converted Victorian school – the owner herself once went to school here! Pleasant lounge with high beamed ceilings and huge windows affording countryside views. Large bedrooms with sleigh beds made up with Egyptian cotton linen. Aga-cooked breakfasts at the communal table or on the patio.

3 rooms � – ♦£ 80 ♦♦£ 95

⊠ TQ7 2EP – 𝒞 01548 580669 – www.southdevonbandb.co.uk

HUDDERSFIELD

West Yorkshire – Pop. 162 949 – Regional map n° **13**-B3

▶ London 191 mi – Bradford 11 mi – Leeds 15 mi – Manchester 25 mi

✕✕ Eric's

MODERN CUISINE · NEIGHBOURHOOD Contemporary neighbourhood restaurant offering seasonal menus of appealing modern dishes packed with bold, distinct flavours. Great value lunch and early evening menu. On selected Saturdays they host brunch or afternoon tea events.

Menu £ 17 (weekday lunch)/25 – Carte £ 33/44

73-75 Lidgets St, Lindley ⊠ HD3 3JP – Northwest : 3.25 mi by A 629 and Birchencliffe Hill Rd. – 𝒞 01484 646416 (booking advisable) – www.ericsrestaurant.co.uk – Closed Monday except December and Sunday dinner

HULLBRIDGE

Essex – Pop. 6 097 – Regional map n° **7**-C2_3

▶ London 40 mi – Southend on Sea 10 mi – Chelmsford 13 mi

☓ Anchor

MODERN CUISINE · BRASSERIE A large, busy, open-plan restaurant with modern décor, a sleek bar and a superb terrace; sit here or in the Orangery for views of the River Crouch. The à la carte offers a wide range of tasty seasonal British dishes and there's an excellent value set price weekday menu too. Summer barbecues. Friendly service.

Menu £ 16 (weekdays) – Carte £ 26/40

Ferry Rd ⊠ SS5 6ND – ℰ 01702 230777 – www.theanchorhullbridge.co.uk
– Closed 25 December

HUMSHAUGH

Northumberland – Regional map n° **14**-A2

▶ London 290 mi – Birmingham 220 mi – Glasgow 132 mi

⌂ Carraw

FAMILY · PERSONALISED Converted farmhouse and barn on the foundations of Hadrian's Wall, with a bright pine-furnished breakfast room and an open-fired lounge which opens onto a terrace. Some bedrooms have exposed stone and beams; others are more modern.

8 rooms ⌂ – ♦£ 68/85 ♦♦£ 88/110

Carraw Farm, Military Rd ⊠ NE46 4DB – West : 5 mi on B 6318 – ℰ 01434 689857
– www.carraw.co.uk

HUNSDON

Hertfordshire – Regional map n° **7**-B2

▶ London 26 mi – Bishop's Stortford 8 mi – Harlow 7 mi

🍽 Fox and Hounds

TRADITIONAL BRITISH · PUB Sizeable pub with a large garden and a rustic interior. Menus are British at heart, with Mediterranean influences, and offer tasty, unfussy dishes that display a clear understanding of flavours. Pastas are homemade, they smoke their own fish and the Josper grill is a hit. Desserts are not to be missed.

Menu £ 15 (weekdays) – Carte £ 24/43

2 High St ⊠ SG12 8NH – ℰ 01279 843999 – www.foxandhounds-hunsdon.co.uk
– Closed 25-26 December, Sunday dinner and Monday

HUNSTANTON

Norfolk – Pop. 8 704 – Regional map n° **8**-B1

▶ London 120 mi – Cambridge 60 mi – Norwich 45 mi

⌂ Lodge

FAMILY · PERSONALISED After a day at the beach head for this laid-back hotel and one of its modern, well-equipped bedrooms; go for a suite for views over the rooftops to the sea. Dine in the smart, cosy bar or head through to the more formal, intimate dining room; the menu offers a mix of pub classics and Italian-based dishes.

16 rooms ⌂ – ♦£ 75/95 ♦♦£ 120/140

Old Hunstanton Rd ⊠ PE36 6HX – Northeast : 1.5 mi on A 149 – ℰ 01485 532896
– www.thelodgehunstanton.co.uk

⌂ No. 33

LUXURY · DESIGN A Victorian house with an unusual façade, set in a peaceful street. Designer touches feature throughout, from the cosy open-fired lounge to the boutique bedrooms with their creative feature walls; some even have baths in the room.

5 rooms ⌂ – ♦£ 90/185 ♦♦£ 90/185

33 Northgate ⊠ PE36 6AP – ℰ 01485 524352 – www.33hunstanton.co.uk

XX **The Neptune** (Kevin Mangeolles) ⇔ 🅿️
🅢

MODERN CUISINE · FRIENDLY Very personally run, attractive, red-brick former pub. New England style interior with a rattan-furnished bar and large nautical photographs in the dining room. The constantly evolving menu relies on the latest local produce to arrive at the door. Presentation is modern; service is relaxed and efficient. Comfy bedrooms have Nespresso machines and thoughtful extras.
→ Brancaster lobster and star anise mousse with pea purée. Duck with almond praline, red cabbage, butternut squash and dauphine potatoes. Colombian white chocolate mousse with strawberries and Campari jelly.
Menu £ 59

5 rooms ⌧ – †£ 110/135 ††£ 160/195

85 Old Hunstanton Rd, Old Hunstanton ⊠ PE36 6HZ – Northeast : 1.5 mi on A 149 – ℰ 01485 532122 – www.theneptune.co.uk – dinner only and Sunday lunch – Closed 3 weeks January, 1 week May, 1 week November, 26 December and Monday

Our selection of hotels, guesthouses and restaurants change every year, so change your MICHELIN Guide every year!

HUNSTRETE

Bath and North East Somerset – Regional map n° **2**-C2
▶ London 124 mi – Bath 10 mi – Bournemouth 75 mi – Exeter 77 mi

🏠 **The Pig** ⅏ ⇔ 🛏 & ⅏ 🅿️

COUNTRY HOUSE · PERSONALISED Nestled in the Mendip Hills, with deer roaming around the parkland, this Grade II listed house is all about getting back to nature. It has a relaxed, friendly atmosphere and extremely comfortable bedrooms which feature handmade beds and fine linens; some are in converted sheds in the walled vegetable garden.

29 rooms – †£ 155/300 ††£ 155/300 – ⌧ £ 15 – 1 suite

Hunstrete House ⊠ BS39 4NS – ℰ 01761 490490 – www.thepighotel.com
The Pig – See restaurant listing

XX **The Pig** 🍷 🛏 🛖 & ⇔ 🅿️

TRADITIONAL CUISINE · BRASSERIE This rustic hotel conservatory takes things back to nature with pots of fresh herbs placed on wooden tables and chimney pots filled with flowering shrubs. The extremely knowledgeable team serve dishes which showcase ingredients from their extensive gardens, along with produce sourced from within 25 miles.
Carte £ 26/45

The Pig Hotel, Hunstrete House ⊠ BS39 4NS – ℰ 01761 490490 (booking essential) – www.thepighotel.com

HUNTINGDON

Cambridgeshire – Pop. 23 937 – Regional map n° **8**-A2
▶ London 69 mi – Bedford 21 mi – Cambridge 16 mi

🏠 **Old Bridge** 🛖 🅰️🅲 ⅏ 🅿️

TOWNHOUSE · GRAND LUXURY Attractive 18C former bank next to the River Ouse; its bright, contemporary décor cleverly blended with the property's original features. Individually styled, up-to-date bedrooms; some with four-poster beds. Cosy oak-panelled bar, conservatory restaurant with a lovely terrace and a superbly stocked wine shop.

24 rooms ⌧ – †£ 95/175 ††£ 125/250

1 High St ⊠ PE29 3TQ – ℰ 01480 424300 – www.huntsbridge.com

Abbots Ripton North: 6.5 mi by B1514 and A141 on B1090

🏠 **Abbot's Elm** 🐝 ⇆ 🛏 ♿ 🅿

MODERN CUISINE · FRIENDLY A modern reconstruction of an attractive 17C pub, with a spacious open-plan layout, homely touches and a vaulted, oak-beamed roof. Extensive menus offer hearty, flavoursome cooking; the wine list is a labour of love and the cosy, comfy bedrooms come with fluffy bathrobes and complimentary mineral water.

Carte £ 20/43

3 rooms ⌂ – ♦£ 65/70 ♦♦£ 80/90

Moat Ln ✉ *PE28 2PA* – ✆ *01487 773773* – *www.theabbotselm.co.uk* – *Closed Sunday dinner*

at Hemingford Grey Southeast: 5 mi by A1198 off A14 ✉ Huntingdon

🏠 **The Cock** 🛏 🏡 🅿

TRADITIONAL CUISINE · PUB A homely 17C country pub with a split-level bar and a spacious dining room; run by an experienced team. Tried-and-tested British cooking includes good value lunches, daily fish specials and a repertoire of over 100 types of sausage.

Menu £ 14 (weekday lunch) – Carte £ 23/37

47 High St ✉ *PE28 9BJ* – ✆ *01480 463609 (booking essential)* – *www.cambscuisine.com*

HURSTPIERPOINT

Pop. 12 730 – Regional map n° **4**-D2
▶ London 45 mi – Croydon 35 mi – Barnet 87 mi – Ealing 69 mi

🍴 **Fig Tree**

TRADITIONAL BRITISH · COSY This attractive Victorian house sits in a pretty high street and has been personally run by David and Monika since 2006; as such, it has a loyal local following. Traditional home-cooked dishes are flavoursome and good value.

Menu £ 20/24 – Carte £ 25/45

120 High St ✉ *BN6 9PX* – ✆ *01273 832183* – *www.figtreerestaurant.co.uk* – *Closed 2 weeks January, Tuesday lunch, Sunday dinner and Monday*

HURWORTH-ON-TEES – Darlington ➔ See Darlington

HUTTON MAGNA – Durham ➔ See Barnard Castle

ICKHAM

Kent – Regional map n° **9**-D2
▶ London 67 mi – Canterbury 6 mi – Dover 16 mi

🏠 **Duke William** ⓝ ⇆ 🛏 🏡 ♿

MODERN BRITISH · PUB The smart exterior has more of a city than a country look but inside it has a good old neighbourhood vibe. Keenly priced menus list time-honoured classics everyone knows and loves. Cosy up on fur throw covered benches by the fire, then stay the night in one of the smart yet casual bedrooms.

Carte £ 22/46

4 rooms ⌂ – ♦£ 100 ♦♦£ 100

The Street ✉ *CT3 1QP* – ✆ *01227 721308* – *www.thedukewilliamickham.com*

ILFRACOMBE

Devon – Pop. 11 184 – Regional map n° **1**-C1
▶ London 218 mi – Barnstaple 13 mi – Exeter 53 mi

🏠 Westwood ⟨ P

FAMILY · DESIGN Perched on the hillside overlooking the rooftops, this appealingly styled Victorian house offers warm décor and an eclectic mix of modern and retro furniture. Spacious bedrooms boast bold feature wallpaper; those to the front are the best.

5 rooms ⌷ – ♦£ 85/125 ♦♦£ 85/125

Torrs Pk ⊠ EX34 8AZ – ☏ 01271 867443 – www.west-wood.co.uk

✗✗ Quay ⟨ AC

MODERN BRITISH · DESIGN Long-standing restaurant on the harbourside; one of the first floor rooms overlooks the sea. It's owned by local lad Damien Hirst, who designed everything from the uniform to the crockery. Menus focus on local fish and Devon beef.

Carte £ 27/45

11 The Quay ⊠ EX34 9EQ – ☏ 01271 868090 – www.11thequay.co.uk – Closed 4-17 January

✗ Thomas Carr @ The Olive Room ⟨ 🏵

🌸 **SEAFOOD · RUSTIC** A simple, homely restaurant set in a 19C townhouse and run by an experienced local chef. Ultra-fresh seafood is the focus, with dishes only confirmed once the day boat deliveries come in. Cooking is creative, with distinct flavours, and each dish comprises just 4 or 5 complementary ingredients. Bedrooms have a pleasant period feel and some have great views over the town.

→ Beetroot-cured Loch Duart salmon with Gentleman's Relish. Roast scallop with watercress, hazelnut and lemon oil. Chocolate tart with caramel, pistachios, honeycomb and praline ice cream.

Menu £ 45/65 – Carte £ 32/42

5 rooms ⌷ – ♦£ 50/85 ♦♦£ 94/105

56 Fore St ⊠ EX34 9DJ – ☏ 01271 867831 (booking essential)
– www.thomascarrchef.co.uk – dinner only and lunch Friday-Saturday
– Closed January and Monday

✗ La Gendarmerie

MODERN CUISINE · RUSTIC Once a police station, now a simple little restaurant with exposed stone walls and an intimate feel; personally run by a husband and wife team. Concise, daily changing menu showcases market produce in precise, skilfully executed combinations.

Menu £ 28/35

63 Fore St ⊠ EX34 9ED – ☏ 01271 865984 (booking advisable)
– www.lagendarmerie.co.uk – dinner only – Closed November,
Tuesday-Wednesday October-March and Monday

ILKLEY

West Yorkshire – Pop. 14 809 – Regional map n° **13**-B2
▶ London 210 mi – Bradford 13 mi – Harrogate 17 mi – Leeds 16 mi

✗✗✗ Box Tree AC 🏵 ⟺

🌸 **MODERN BRITISH · ELEGANT** An iconic Yorkshire restaurant established back in 1962. It's set in two charming sandstone cottages and has a plush, antique-furnished lounge and two luxurious dining rooms. Cooking is refined and skilful, with a classical French base, and dishes are light and delicate. Only the best ingredients are used.

→ Smoked ox tongue & oxtail terrine with horseradish cream and pickled onion. Stone bass with parsley, wild garlic and confit chicken wings. Granny Smith soufflé with calvados sauce.

Menu £ 35/65

37 Church St ⊠ LS29 9DR – on A 65 – ☏ 01943 608484 – www.theboxtree.co.uk
– dinner only and lunch Friday-Sunday – Closed 26-30 December, 1-7 January,
Sunday dinner and Monday-Tuesday

INGHAM

Norfolk – Pop. 376 – Regional map n° **8**-D1

▶ London 139 mi – Norwich 25 mi – Ipswich 65 mi – Lowestoft 30 mi

⏸ Ingham Swan ⇦ 🛋 P

MODERN BRITISH · PUB An attractive thatched pub with flint walls and exposed wooden beams. There's an array of menus – including a good value 'menu du jour' – all of which feature produce from their farm; eye-catching dishes are made up of many different elements. Bedrooms come with muted colour schemes and designer furnishings.

Menu £ 17 (weekday lunch)/28 **s** – Carte £ 27/45 **s**

4 rooms 🖙 – †£ 85/165 ††£ 95/195

Sea Palling Rd ✉ *NR12 9AB*
– ✆ 01692 581099 (booking essential at dinner) – www.theinghamswan.co.uk
– Closed 25-26 December

IPSWICH

Suffolk – Pop. 144 957 – Regional map n° **8**-C3

▶ London 77 mi – Redbridge 64 mi – Romford 59 mi – Norwich 45 mi

🏨 Salthouse Harbour ⇦ 🔼 ♿ P

BUSINESS · PERSONALISED Stylish former salt warehouse – its trendy lobby-lounge boasts floor to ceiling windows and great marina views. Modern boutique bedrooms have well-appointed bathrooms; some feature chaise longues, copper slipper baths or balconies.

70 rooms 🖙 – †£ 135/185 ††£ 159/250

1 Neptune Quay ✉ *IP4 1AX – ✆ 01473 226789 – www.salthouseharbour.co.uk*
Eaterie – See restaurant listing

🏨 Kesgrave Hall 🌳 🏡 🛋 ♿ 👗 P

HISTORIC · MODERN An impressive house built in 1812, with a delightful terrace overlooking large lawned gardens to a 38 acre wood. Stylish lounges have a relaxed, urban-chic feel. Luxurious bedrooms boast quality furnishings, modern facilities and stylish bathrooms. The busy brasserie offers a European menu.

23 rooms 🖙 – †£ 115/315 ††£ 135/315

Hall Rd, Kesgrave ✉ *IP5 2PU – East : 4.75 mi by A 1214 on Bealings rd*
– ✆ 01473 333471 – www.kesgravehall.com

✕✕ Trongs

CHINESE · FRIENDLY Brightly painted restaurant filled with flowers and candles. The owners are from Hanoi: the parents and one son cook – his brother runs front of house. The extensive menu specialises in vibrant dishes from northern China; try the spring rolls.

Carte £ 21/46

23 St Nicholas St ✉ *IP1 1TW – ✆ 01473 256833 – Closed 3 weeks August and Sunday*

✕ Eaterie ⇦ 🛋 ♿ P

MODERN CUISINE · BRASSERIE Modern hotel brasserie in an old salt warehouse, with a zinc-topped bar, gold pillars, modern art and padded booths. Tasty brasserie dishes and numerous specials focus largely on seafood. Eat on the terrace, overlooking the marina.

Menu £ 18 (lunch) – Carte dinner £ 25/40

Salthouse Harbour Hotel, 1 Neptune Quay ✉ *IP4 1AX – ✆ 01473 226789 (bookings advisable at dinner) – www.salthouseharbour.co.uk*

at Chelmondiston Southeast : 6 mi by A 137 on B 1456

✗ Red Lion   🛋 & ♻ 🅿

TRADITIONAL CUISINE · BISTRO Smartly refurbished former pub with a few comfy chairs in the bar and two dining rooms furnished with dark wood tables and Lloyd Loom chairs. Menus offer a broad range of dishes and daily specials. The bubbly owner leads the service.

Carte £ 23/31

Main St ⊠ IP9 1DX – ℰ 01473 780400 – www.chelmondistonredlion.co.uk – Closed Sunday and Monday

at Hintlesham West: 5 mi by A1214 on A1071⊠ Ipswich

🏠 Hintlesham Hall   ⚑ ⌁ ⪦ 🛏 🖿 📶 & ♨ 🅿

COUNTRY HOUSE · CLASSIC Impressive Georgian manor house with 16C roots; the original ornate plasterwork and gold leaf inlaid cornicing remain. Bedrooms in the main house are grand; the courtyard rooms are more modern and some have terraces. Dine in the impressive 'Salon' or wood-panelled 'Parlour'; fresh herbs come from the garden.

32 rooms – 🛉£ 85/395 🛉🛉£ 85/395 – ⌂ £ 19 – 1 suite

⊠ IP8 3NS – West : 0.25 mi on A 1071 – ℰ 01473 652334

– www.hintleshamhall.com

IRBY

Merseyside – Regional map n° **11**-A3

▶ London 212 mi – Liverpool 12 mi – Manchester 46 mi – Stoke-on-Trent 56 mi

✗✗ Da Piero   🕝

ITALIAN · FAMILY The passionate owners of Da Piero extend a very warm welcome to one and all. The wide-ranging menu takes its influences from Sicily, where the chef grew up, and from Northern Italy, the birthplace of his mother. Portions are hearty.

Carte £ 23/45

5-7 Mill Hill Rd ⊠ CH61 4UB – ℰ 0151 648 7373 (booking essential)
– www.dapiero.co.uk – dinner only – Closed 1 week January, Sunday and Monday

IRONBRIDGE

Telford and Wrekin – Pop. 1 560 – Regional map n° **10**-B2

▶ London 135 mi – Birmingham 36 mi – Shrewsbury 18 mi

🏠 Library House   🛏 ⅏

TOWNHOUSE · PERSONALISED Attractive former library, just a stone's throw from the famous bridge. It has a farmhouse-style breakfast room and a homely lounge where books sit on the old library shelves. Tastefully furnished bedrooms are named after poets.

3 rooms ⌂ – 🛉£ 75/90 🛉🛉£ 95/120

11 Severn Bank ⊠ TF8 7AN – ℰ 01952 432299 – www.libraryhouse.com

✗✗ Restaurant Severn

TRADITIONAL BRITISH · COSY Traditional little restaurant with a loyal following; enter down a narrow side passage into a cosy low-beamed room. Classic dishes rely on seasonal local produce. It's run by a couple: she cooks starters and desserts; he cooks the mains.

Menu £ 26

33 High St. ⊠ TF8 7AG – ℰ 01952 432233 (booking essential)
– www.restaurantsevern.co.uk – dinner only – Closed 1 week January, 1 week August, Sunday, Monday and Tuesday

IRTHINGTON

Cumbria – Regional map n° **12**-B1

▶ London 314 mi – Newcastle upon Tyne 54 mi – Sunderland 67 mi – Carlisle 8 mi

Golden Fleece
⇔ 🛏 🍴 P

TRADITIONAL BRITISH · COSY Find a spot beside the wood-burning stove and choose from a list of tasty pub classics, juicy mature steaks and proper pub puddings, and be sure to try something from the selection of local ales too. Comfy, cosy bedrooms are named after the words Cumbrian shepherds once used to count their sheep.

Carte £ 23/45

8 rooms ☑ – 🛉£ 85/95 🛉🛉£ 95

*Ruleholme ✉ CA6 4NF – Southeast : 1.5 mi off A 689 – ☎ 01228 573686
– www.thegoldenfleececumbria.co.uk – Closed 1-7 January*

ISLEHAM

Cambridgeshire – Pop. 2 228 – Regional map n° **8**-B2
▶ London 73 mi – Cambridge 20 mi – Norwich 49 mi

✗ Merry Monk
🍴 ⇔ P

TRADITIONAL BRITISH · NEIGHBOURHOOD Originally 17C cottages, with time spent as a pub, this is now a quirky, rustic restaurant with beamed ceilings and farmhouse kitchen style décor. Hearty, flavoursome dishes use local produce and are given a personal twist by the chef.

Menu £ 19 (lunch) – Carte £ 28/46

*30 West St ✉ CB7 5SB – ☎ 01638 780900 – www.merry-monk.co.uk – Closed
25-26 December*

ISLE OF MAN – I.O.M. ➜ See Man (Isle of)

ITTERINGHAM

Norfolk – ✉ Aylsham – Regional map n° **8**-C1
▶ London 126 mi – Cromer 11 mi – Norwich 17 mi

Walpole Arms
🛏 🍴 P

MODERN BRITISH · PUB A pretty 18C inn in a sleepy little village, with a surprisingly modern yet sympathetically designed interior. Refined modern dishes champion local ingredients and feature produce from their own farm; rare breed beef is a speciality.

Carte £ 18/39

*The Common ✉ NR11 7AR – ☎ 01263 587258 – www.thewalpolearms.co.uk
– Closed 25 December and Sunday dinner in winter*

IXWORTH – Suffolk ➜ See Bury St Edmunds

KELMSCOTT

Oxfordshire – Regional map n° **10**-A2
▶ London 78 mi – Oxford 25 mi – Cirencester 17 mi

Plough 🆕
⇔ 🛏 🍴

TRADITIONAL CUISINE · RURAL The 16C Plough has all the character you would expect of a pub its age, with rough stone walls, open fires and a cottage-style garden. Traditional menus list dishes you'll know and love, from buck rarebit to devilled lambs' kidneys.

Carte £ 27/43

8 rooms – 🛉£ 100/120 🛉🛉£ 110/130

*✉ GL7 3HG – ☎ 01367 253543 – www.theploughinnkelmscott.com – Closed
Monday dinner*

KELVEDON

Essex – Pop. 4 717 – Regional map n° **7**-C2
▶ London 56 mi – Colchester 11 mi – Chelmsford 14 mi

✗ George & Dragon

🛜 🅿

MODERN BRITISH · MINIMALIST Bright and welcoming former pub with a sleek, contemporary style encompassing topiary planters, marble tiled floors, antique mirrors and art deco pictures. Simple, well-priced menu with locally caught fish specials. Pretty terrace.

Carte £ 24/34

*Coggleshall Rd ⊠ CO5 9PL – Northwest : 2 mi on B 1024 – ℰ 01376 561797
– www.georgeanddragonkelvedon.co.uk – Closed 25 December-2 January, Sunday and Monday*

KENDAL

Cumbria – Pop. 28 586 – Regional map n° **12**-B2
▶ London 270 mi – Bradford 64 mi – Burnley 63 mi – Carlisle 49 mi

🏠 Beech House

�… ✗ 🅿

TOWNHOUSE · PERSONALISED Pretty, three-storey Georgian house set just out of town. Modern, open-plan lounge with comfy sofas and communal breakfast tables. Bright, airy, pine-furnished bedrooms with up-to-date bathrooms. Welcoming owners.

5 rooms ⌂ – ♦£ 60/75 ♦♦£ 80/100
*40 Greenside ⊠ LA9 4LD – By All Hallows Ln – ℰ 01539 720385
– www.beechhouse-kendal.co.uk – Closed 1 week Christmas*

✗ Sawadee Thai

THAI · NEIGHBOURHOOD The staff, dressed in authentic Thai silks, provide a very warm welcome at this smart neighbourhood restaurant. The appealing menu offers flavoursome dishes ranging from Tom Yam soup to Som Tam Thai salad and Geng Ba Jungle curry.

Menu £ 20 – Carte £ 13/32

*54 Stramongate ⊠ LA9 4BD – ℰ 01539 722944 – www.kendalthairestaurant.com
– dinner only – Closed 24-31 December and Monday*

at Crosthwaite West: 5.25 mi by All Hallows Ln ⊠ Kendal

🏠 Punch Bowl Inn

⇔ ⇐ 🛜 🅿

TRADITIONAL BRITISH · INN Charming 17C inn set in the picturesque Lyth Valley, boasting antiques, cosy fires and exposed wood beams; dine either in the rustic bar or the more formal restaurant. Cooking has a classical base but also features some modern touches; dishes display a degree of complexity that you wouldn't usually find in a pub. Luxury bedrooms boast quality linens and roll-top baths.

Carte £ 26/39

9 rooms ⌂ – ♦£ 85/229 ♦♦£ 105/305
⊠ LA8 8HR – ℰ 015395 68237 – www.the-punchbowl.co.uk

KENILWORTH

Warwickshire – Pop. 22 413 – Regional map n° **10**-C2
▶ London 102 mi – Birmingham 19 mi – Coventry 5 mi – Leicester 32 mi

🏠 Cross at Kenilworth (Adam Bennett)

🚋 🛜 🤝 🆎 🅘 ⇔ 🅿

🏵 **CLASSIC CUISINE · ELEGANT** Smartly furnished pub with eager, welcoming staff. Skilfully executed, classical cooking uses prime seasonal ingredients, and dishes not only look impressive but taste good too. Sit in the back room to watch the kitchen in action. The bright and airy room next door used to be a classroom.
→ Scallop ravioli with sea vegetables and smoked fish cream. Fillet of venison with haggis, potato terrine, lingonberries and Laphroaig sauce. Chocolate and candied orange tart with blood orange sorbet.

Menu £ 30 (lunch) – Carte £ 42/55

*16 New St ⊠ CV8 2EZ – ℰ 01926 853840 – www.thecrosskenilworth.co.uk
– Closed Sunday dinner and bank holidays*

KENTISBURY

Devon – Regional map n° **1**-C1

▶ London 220 mi – Exeter 58 mi – Barnstaple 10 mi

⌂ Kentisbury Grange   ⟰ ⌸ **P**

COUNTRY HOUSE · DESIGN This Victorian country house may have a Grade II listing but it's been smartly decked out with designer fabrics and furnishings in the colours of its original stained glass windows. Go for one of the chic, detached Garden Suites.

16 rooms (dinner included) ⌷ – ∲£ 125/260 ∲∲£ 125/260

✉ EX31 4NL – Southeast : 1 mi by B 3229 on A39 – ℰ 01271 882295
– www.kentisburygrange.co.uk

Coach House by Michael Caines – See restaurant listing

✗✗ Coach House by Michael Caines   ⌸ ⟐ **P**

MODERN CUISINE · DESIGN This smart hotel restaurant has a lovely walnut and marble bar counter, a funky lounge under the eaves and an elegant dining room featuring plush blue velvet booths. Flavoursome modern dishes use local meats and south coast fish.

Menu £ 25/45

Kentisbury Grange Hotel, ✉ EX31 4NL – Southeast : 1 mi by B 3229 on A39
– ℰ 01271 882295 – www.kentisburygrange.co.uk

KENTON

Devon – Regional map n° **1**-D2

▶ London 200 mi – Bristol 85 mi – Exeter 8 mi

✗✗ Rodean

TRADITIONAL BRITISH · NEIGHBOURHOOD Family-run restaurant – once a butcher's shop – overlooking a tiny village green. There's a small bar-lounge and two beamed dining rooms with dark wood panelling. Constantly evolving menus have a classical base and a modern edge.

Menu £ 18 – Carte £ 27/48

The Triangle ✉ EX6 8LS – ℰ 01626 890195 (booking advisable)
– www.rodeanrestaurant.co.uk – dinner only and Sunday lunch – Closed Sunday dinner and Monday

KERNE BRIDGE – Herefordshire → See Ross-on-Wye

KERRIDGE

Cheshire East – Regional map n° **11**-B3

▶ London 179 mi – Manchester 24 mi – Macclesfield 4 mi

⌂ Lord Clyde   ⌸ **P**

MODERN CUISINE · PUB A small, keenly run village pub with a simple, rustic interior. The cooking is a complete contrast, offering extremely creative, eye-catching modern dishes which use a wide range of complex techniques. The tasting menus are popular.

Carte £ 28/46

36 Clarke Ln ✉ SK10 5AH – ℰ 01625 562123 – www.thelordclyde.co.uk – Closed Sunday dinner and Monday lunch

KESWICK

Cumbria – Pop. 4 984 – Regional map n° **12**-A2

▶ London 294 mi – Carlisle 31 mi – Kendal 30 mi

⌂ Inn on the Square ⓝ   ☐ 🚹 🏃

TOWNHOUSE · CONTEMPORARY This classic 19C coaching inn stands proudly on the square. Inside it's surprisingly modern, with bright, bold furnishings, a cocktail bar and a cosy pub. Bedrooms have top facilities and locally made beds; some have sheep murals!

34 rooms ☐ – 🛏£ 141 🛏🛏£ 141/282

Market Sq ⊠ CA12 5JF – ℰ 017687 73333 – www.innonthesquare.co.uk

Brossen – See restaurant listing

⌂ Lairbeck   🌿 🛏 🕸 🅿

TRADITIONAL · PERSONALISED An attractive Victorian house in the suburbs – its mature garden boasting a huge Sequoia Redwood. Inside it has an original barley-twist staircase and a galleried landing. Bedrooms come in a mix of styles; some have lovely views.

14 rooms ☐ – 🛏£ 59/103 🛏🛏£ 118/160

Vicarage Hill ⊠ CA12 5QB – Northwest : 1 mi by Main St and Crossthwaite Rd – ℰ 017687 73373 – www.lairbeckhotel-keswick.co.uk – Closed Christmas-New Year

⌂ Howe Keld   🕸 🕸

TOWNHOUSE · CONTEMPORARY Howe Keld means 'mountain spring' and this Victorian house has strong eco and ethical credentials. Boutique bedrooms are furnished with locally crafted pieces made using reclaimed wood; the best rooms have bay windows and fell views.

12 rooms ☐ – 🛏£ 55/85 🛏🛏£ 112/130

5-7 The Heads ⊠ CA12 5ES – ℰ 017687 72417 – www.howekeld.co.uk

✗✗ Morrel's

MODERN BRITISH · BRASSERIE Popular local eatery with scrubbed wood flooring, etched glass dividers and a buzzy atmosphere. Seasonally changing dishes have subtle Mediterranean influences; some come in two sizes. Good value menus.

Menu £ 22 – Carte £ 23/35

34 Lake Rd ⊠ CA12 5DQ – ℰ 017687 72666 – www.morrels.co.uk – dinner only – Closed 24-26 December, 4-17 January and Monday

✗✗ Brossen ⓝ   🕸 🆎

STEAKHOUSE · FRIENDLY Meaning 'stuffed' in Cumbrian, Brossen is a sleek, Scandic-style steakhouse in a smartly refurbished coaching inn. Local steaks are the focus, although there are plenty of other choices too, from rotisserie chicken to venison.

Carte £ 24/75

Inn on the Square, Market Sq ⊠ CA12 5JF – ℰ 017687 73333 – www.innonthesquare.co.uk

at Braithwaite West: 2 mi by A66 on B5292 ⊠ Keswick

✗✗ Cottage in the Wood   ⇦ 🕸 < 🛏 🏡 🅿

MODERN BRITISH · ROMANTIC A keenly run restaurant in a superb forest setting, with a lovely terrace and great views over the fells and valley below; sit and watch the birds and squirrels as you eat. Concise, ambitious set menus are supplemented by a tasting menu at dinner and many ingredients are foraged from the surrounding forest. Bedrooms are contemporary; some have whirlpool baths.

Menu £ 30/65 **s**

10 rooms ☐ – 🛏£ 88/96 🛏🛏£ 110/205

Magic Hill, Whinlatter Forest ⊠ CA12 5TW – Northwest : 1.75 mi on B 5292 – ℰ 017687 78409 (bookings essential for non-residents) – www.thecottageinthewood.co.uk – Closed 2-23 January, Sunday, Monday and lunch Tuesday-Wednesday

KETTERING

Northamptonshire – Pop. 56 226 – Regional map n° **9**-C3
▶ London 88 mi – Birmingham 54 mi – Northampton 24 mi

at Rushton Northwest : 3.5 mi by A 14 and Rushton Rd

🏨 **Rushton Hall**   🦢 🛋 🔟 ⑩ 🎢 🌡 ⌘ 🎰 ☐ ♿ ⅏ 🛎 🅿

HISTORIC · ELEGANT An imposing 15C house with stunning architecture, in 28 acres of countryside. The Grand Hall features huge stained glass windows and an impressive fireplace. Luxurious, classically furnished bedrooms in the house and converted stable block.

46 rooms ⌿ – ♦£ 150/380 ♦♦£ 170/400 – 3 suites

✉ NN14 1RR – ☎ 01536 713001 – www.rushtonhall.com

Tresham – See restaurant listing

🍴🍴🍴 **Tresham**   ⌘ 🅿

MODERN CUISINE · ELEGANT Named after the man who built the magnificent mansion in which this grand restaurant resides; enjoy an aperitif in the impressive Grand Hall. Ornate plaster ceiling and wood panelled walls. Elaborate modern cooking and formal service.

Menu £ 55

Rushton Hall Hotel, ✉ NN14 1RR – ☎ 01536 713001 – www.rushtonhall.com
– dinner only

KETTLESING – North Yorkshire → See Harrogate

KEYSTON

Cambridgeshire – ✉ Huntingdon – Pop. 257 – Regional map n° **8**-A2

🛣 London 75 mi – Cambridge 29 mi – Northampton 24 mi

🍴 **Pheasant**   ៦៦ 🛖 🅿
ⓐ

TRADITIONAL BRITISH · PUB Hidden away in a sleepy hamlet, this is a big pub with enormous character; think exposed beams, hunting scenes, John Bull wallpaper and a stuffed albino pheasant. Wide-ranging seasonal menu includes a 'classic' section; excellent value set menu. Warm, attentive staff and delightful rear terrace.

Menu £ 15 (lunch and early dinner) – Carte £ 24/40

Village Loop Rd ✉ PE28 0RE – ☎ 01832 710241 (booking essential)
– www.thepheasant-keyston.co.uk – Closed 2-15 January, Sunday dinner and Monday

KIBWORTH BEAUCHAMP

Leicestershire – ✉ Leicester – Pop. 3 550 – Regional map n° **9**-B2

🛣 London 85 mi – Birmingham 49 mi – Leicester 6 mi

🍴 **Lighthouse**   🗄

SEAFOOD · NEIGHBOURHOOD With its coastal pictures and nautical knick-knacks, the Lighthouse is fittingly named. The emphasis is on seafood and the flexible menu offers many dishes in both small and large portions; the 'Nibbles' are a popular choice.

Menu £ 18 (weekdays) – Carte £ 14/35

9 Station St ✉ LE8 0LN – ☎ 0116 279 6260 (booking essential)
– www.lighthousekibworth.co.uk – dinner only – Closed Sunday, Monday and bank holidays

KIBWORTH HARCOURT

Leicestershire – Regional map n° **9**-B2

🛣 London 101 mi – Leicester 9 mi – Birmingham 50 mi

🍴 **Boboli**   🛖 🅰🅲 🅿

ITALIAN · NEIGHBOURHOOD Buzzy, laid-back Italian restaurant with a sunny terrace; formerly a pub, it has a central bar and dining on 3 levels. Extensive selection of seasonally inspired dishes; flavours are bold and portions, large. Satisfyingly affordable wines.

Menu £ 15 (weekday lunch) – Carte £ 16/35

88 Main St ✉ LE8 0NQ – ☎ 0116 279 3303 – www.bobolirestaurant.co.uk – Closed 25-26 December and 1 January

KILNDOWN

Kent – Regional map n° **8**-B2

▶ London 48 mi – Canterbury 38 mi – Hastings 20 mi

ⅼ☐ Globe & Rainbow ⓝ

MODERN BRITISH · SIMPLE The décor is modest but the cooking is refined. Dishes show a real understanding of classic techniques and prime ingredients are simply married with one or two others in order to let them shine; look out for the côte du boeuf to share.

Menu £ 20 (lunch) – Carte dinner £ 27/40

Ranters Ln ⊠ TN17 2SG – ℰ 01892 890803 (booking advisable)
– www.globeandrainbow.co.uk
– Closed Sunday dinner and Monday

KILPECK

Herefordshire – Regional map n° **10**-A3

▶ London 132 mi – Birmingham 71 mi – Liverpool 123 mi – Cardiff 47 mi

ⅼ☐ Kilpeck Inn

TRADITIONAL CUISINE · PUB A popular pub which narrowly escaped being turned into private housing thanks to the villagers' valiantly fought 'Save Our Pub' campaign. Its spacious interior and bedrooms are smart, modern and characterful, with impressive green credentials. Menus offer locally sourced meats and old fashioned puddings.

Carte £ 20/35

4 rooms �*立* – †£ 70/100 ††£ 80/110

⊠ HR2 9DN – ℰ 01981 570464 – www.kilpeckinn.com
– Closed 25 December

KINGHAM

Oxfordshire – Pop. 547 – Regional map n° **6**-A1

▶ London 81 mi – Gloucester 32 mi – Oxford 25 mi – Cardiff 91 mi

🏠 Mill House

TRADITIONAL · CLASSIC Smartly converted flour mill owned by a couple from the village; set in 10 acres of well-maintained gardens which lead down to a brook – opt for a bedroom with a terrace overlooking the lawns. Have a drink in the bright wood-furnished bar or on the terrace, before heading to dinner in the formal restaurant.

21 rooms ⊊ – †£ 107/152 ††£ 120/165

⊠ OX7 6UH – ℰ 01608 658188 – www.millhousehotel.co.uk

ⅼ☐ The Wild Rabbit

MODERN BRITISH · ELEGANT Just down the road from the Daylesford Farm Shop is the Bamford family's lovely stone pub with a subtle leporine theme. Well-judged modern cooking is packed with flavour and has plenty of appeal – aside from the 40-day matured charcoal-grilled steak, this is restaurant food, with ingredients arranged in delicious layers of flavours. Bedrooms are delightfully understated.

→ Roast breast of quail with Morteau sausage, smoked shallot and verjus reduction. Newlyn sole with organic leeks, scallop ceviche and truffle purée. Passion fruit soufflé with iced coconut.

Carte £ 38/55

13 rooms ⊊ – †£ 160/335 ††£ 175/350

Church St ⊠ OX7 6YA – ℰ 01608 658389 (booking advisable)
– www.thewildrabbit.co.uk
– Closed first 2 weeks January

🍽 Kingham Plough   ⇔ 🛋 ♿ 🅿

MODERN BRITISH · PUB Rustic, laid-back pub and restaurant located on the green in an unspoilt Cotswold village. It's run by a friendly team and an experienced chef-owner. The snack menu offers tasty classics, while the seasonal à la carte evolves as new ingredients arrive. Comfy bedrooms await: numbers 2 and 4 are the best.

Carte £ 32/44

6 rooms 🖵 – 🛉£ 110/150 🛉🛉£ 145/195

The Green ✉ *OX7 6YD – 𝒞 01608 658327 – www.thekinghamplough.co.uk – Closed 25 December*

KING'S LYNN

Norfolk – Pop. 46 093 – Regional map n° **8**-B1

▶ London 103 mi – Cambridge 45 mi – Leicester 75 mi – Norwich 44 mi

🏠 Bank House   ← 🍽

TOWNHOUSE · COSY A charming Grade II Georgian townhouse on the quayside; it was once a wine merchant's house and later the place where Barclays Bank was founded. Cosy bedrooms mix modern fabrics with antique furnishings; bathrooms are luxurious.

12 rooms 🖵 – 🛉£ 85/120 🛉🛉£ 115/220

King's Staithe Sq ✉ *PE30 1RD – 𝒞 01553 660492 – www.thebankhouse.co.uk*

Bank House – See restaurant listing

🍴 Market Bistro   🛋 ♿

MODERN BRITISH · BISTRO 17C beams and a fireplace remain but this relaxed bistro is more up-to-date than its exterior suggests. Fresh, unfussy cooking uses passionately sourced local produce and modern techniques. The chef's wife looks after the service.

Menu £ 17 (weekday lunch) – Carte £ 24/37

11 Saturday Market Pl ✉ *PE30 5DQ – 𝒞 01553 771483 – www.marketbistro.co.uk – Closed 26 December, 1 and 7-14 January, Sunday, Monday and lunch Tuesday*

🍴 Bank House 🅝   ← 🛋 ♿ 🖥 ⇔

MODERN CUISINE · BRASSERIE This Georgian townhouse was also once a bank. Dine in the contemporary former kitchen, the billiard room or the old banking hall, from a menu of British classics and Mediterranean-inspired fare. Colourful dishes burst with flavour.

Carte £ 20/37

Bank House Hotel, King's Staithe Sq ✉ *PE30 1RD – 𝒞 01553 660492 – www.thebankhouse.co.uk*

at Grimston East: 6.25 mi by A148

🏠 Congham Hall   🌱 ← 🛒 🖼 🛎 🐾 🌿 🧖 🅿

COUNTRY HOUSE · ELEGANT Part-Georgian country house in 30 acres of peaceful grounds. Guest areas include a snug bar and a spacious drawing room with a subtle modern style. Opt for a lovely Garden Room by the spa, overlooking the flower or herb gardens.

26 rooms – 🛉£ 135/325 🛉🛉£ 135/325 – 🖵 £ 15 – 2 suites

Lynn Rd. ✉ *PE32 1AH – 𝒞 01485 600250 – www.conghamhallhotel.co.uk*

Congham Hall – See restaurant listing

🍴🍴🍴 Congham Hall   ← 🛒 🛋 🅰🅲 🖥 ⇔ 🅿

MODERN CUISINE · INTIMATE Start with a drink in the elegant hotel bar, then head for the spacious dining room with its super terrace and garden views. Appealing menus have something to please everyone, from good old classics to more modern fare.

Carte £ 29/47

Congham Hall Hotel, Lynn Rd. ✉ *PE32 1AH – 𝒞 01485 600250 – www.conghamhallhotel.co.uk*

KINGS MILLS → See Channel Islands (Guernsey)

KING'S SUTTON

Northamptonshire – Pop. 2 069 – Regional map n° **16**-B3

▶ London 74 mi – Northampton 28 mi – Birmingham 56 mi

🍴 White Horse ⓝ   P

MODERN BRITISH · PUB Pretty sandstone pub run by a keen young couple. The self-taught chef makes everything from scratch and always tries to exceed his guests' expectations. Produce is fresh and local and follows a 'when it's gone, it's gone' approach.

Menu £ 14 (lunch) – Carte £ 22/40

2 The Square ✉ OX17 3RF – ☎ 01295 812440 – www.whitehorseks.co.uk – Closed 27-30 December, Sunday dinner and Monday

KINGSBRIDGE

Devon – Pop. 6 116 – Regional map n° **1**-C3

▶ London 236 mi – Exeter 36 mi – Plymouth 24 mi – Torquay 21 mi

🏰 Buckland-Tout-Saints   ⌂ ⅏ ≤ ⇎ 🏡 ♨ P

HISTORIC · CLASSIC Appealing Queen Anne mansion set in large, peaceful grounds. Traditional, antique-furnished interior with wood-panelling in many rooms. Bedrooms vary in shape and size; some have a classic country house feel and others are more contemporary. Choice of two dining rooms offering accomplished dishes.

16 rooms ⌂ – ♦£ 89/315 ♦♦£ 99/315 – 2 suites

Goveton ✉ TQ7 2DS – Northeast : 3 mi by A 381 – ☎ 01548 853055 – www.tout-saints.co.uk

KINGSTON-UPON-HULL

Kingston upon Hull – Pop. 284 321 – Regional map n° **13**-D2

▶ London 183 mi – Leeds 61 mi – Nottingham 94 mi – Sheffield 68 mi

🍴🍴 1884 Dock Street Kitchen   🕭 AC

MODERN BRITISH · FASHIONABLE A red-brick former ropery by the marina: built in 1884, it is now a stylish brasserie with a smart leather-furnished bar, an open kitchen and a buzzing feel. Appealing menus of modernised British classics, with a popular grill section.

Menu £ 21/25 – Carte £ 34/55

Humber Dock St, Hull Marina ✉ HU1 1TB – ☎ 01482 222260 – www.1884dockstreetkitchen.co.uk – Closed 2-5 January, Sunday dinner and Monday lunch

KINGSWEAR – Devon → See Dartmouth

KIRKBY LONSDALE

Cumbria – Pop. 1 843 – Regional map n° **12**-B3

▶ London 259 mi – Carlisle 62 mi – Kendal 13 mi – Lancaster 17 mi

🏰 Royal   ⌂

TRADITIONAL · CONTEMPORARY Well-run Georgian hotel overlooking a characterful town square. The décor is a mix of modern and shabby-chic, and the owner has a keen eye for detail. Bedrooms are spacious; some have free-standing baths in the room. Snug, open-fired lounge and an all-day brasserie serving classics and wood-fired pizzas.

14 rooms ⌂ – ♦£ 63/150 ♦♦£ 95/190

Main St ✉ LA6 2AE – ☎ 015242 71966 – www.royalhotelkirkbylonsdale.co.uk

⌂ **Plato's**   ⚲

TOWNHOUSE · PERSONALISED Georgian-style townhouse once home to Plato Harrison wine merchants. Tastefully decorated bedrooms blend modern furnishings with period charm and come with thoughtful extras. The all-day coffee-shop-cum-café offers an extensive range of modern, international dishes ranging from tapas to tasting boards.

10 rooms ⌕ – ♦£ 72/162 ♦♦£ 88/196

2 Mill Brow ⊠ *LA6 2AT* – *℘015242 74180* – *www.platoskirkbylonsdale.co.uk*

🍴 **Sun Inn**   ⇦ ⑩

TRADITIONAL BRITISH · PUB 17C inn with a characterful beamed bar and a smartly furnished restaurant which comes into its own in the evening. Menus are concise; bar snacks are served throughout the day and dinner is a serious affair. Smart modern bedrooms boast quality linens and thoughtful extras – the breakfasts are delicious.

Menu £ 29 (dinner) – Carte lunch £ 26/38

11 rooms ⌕ – ♦£ 82/144 ♦♦£ 114/189

6 Market St ⊠ *LA6 2AU* – *℘015242 71965* – *www.sun-inn.info* – *Closed 25 December*

at Lupton Northwest: 4.75 mi on A65

🍴 **Plough**   ⇦ 🏠 ♿ 🅿

TRADITIONAL BRITISH · PUB A homely former coaching inn with exposed beams and open fires, set on the main road from the Lake District to North Yorkshire. Sit in the shabby-chic bar or smarter pink-hued restaurant and choose from an appealing list of traditionally-based dishes. Smart, individually styled bedrooms boast roll-top baths.

Carte £ 20/44

6 rooms ⌕ – ♦£ 85/195 ♦♦£ 99/195

Cow Brow ⊠ *LA6 1PJ* – *℘015395 67700* – *www.theploughatlupton.co.uk*

KIRKBY STEPHEN
Cumbria – Pop. 1 522 – Regional map n° **12**-B2
▶ London 296 mi – Carlisle 46 mi – Darlington 37 mi – Kendal 28 mi

⌂ **Augill Castle**   ⚲ 🐕 ⇐ 🛋 🍽 🏊 🅿

FAMILY · CLASSIC A carefully restored, castellated country house filled with period furniture and antiques. It has three interconnecting sitting rooms with vast open fires and a dining room with an ornate plaster ceiling; traditional dishes are taken at a communal table. Many bedrooms have four-poster beds or roll-top baths.

15 rooms ⌕ – ♦£ 160 ♦♦£ 160/240

⊠ *CA17 4DE* – *Northeast : 4.25 mi by A 685* – *℘017683 41937* – *www.stayinacastle.com*

KIRKBY THORE
Cumbria – Pop. 758 – Regional map n° **12**-B2
▶ London 275 mi – Preston 68 mi – Sunderland 68 mi – Newcastle upon Tyne 68 mi

🍴 **Bridge**   ♿ 🅰🅲 🖥 🅿

TRADITIONAL CUISINE · BISTRO A remodelled roadside pub with a bright extension and a bistro feel, which is keenly run by a husband and wife team. Cooking has a likeable simplicity, with the odd Asian touch, and there's a tempting display of cakes on the counter.

Menu £ 14 (weekday lunch) – Carte £ 19/39

⊠ *CA10 1UZ* – *on A66* – *℘017683 62766* – *www.thebridgebistro.co.uk* – *Closed Sunday dinner*

KIRKBYMOORSIDE
North Yorkshire – Pop. 2 751 – Regional map n° **13**-C1
▶ London 244 mi – Leeds 61 mi – Scarborough 26 mi – York 33 mi

🏠 Cornmill

HISTORIC · TRADITIONAL Charming 18C cornmill with a pleasant courtyard and gardens; look for the mill race running beneath the glass panel in the characterful breakfast room. The cosy lounge and elegant bedrooms are set in the old farmhouse and stables.

5 rooms 🖵 - 🛉£ 58/75 🛉🛉£ 85/110

Kirby Mills ✉ YO62 6NP - East : 0.5 mi by A 170 - 📞 01751 432000
- www.kirbymills.co.uk

KIRKWHELPINGTON

Northumberland – ✉ Morpeth – Pop. 353 – Regional map n° **14**-A2
▶ London 305 mi – Carlisle 46 mi – Newcastle upon Tyne 20 mi

🏠 Shieldhall

HISTORIC · COSY Early 17C farmhouse and outbuildings, where Capability Brown's uncle once lived. Mix of rustic and country house guest areas; library-lounge has garden views. Individually styled bedrooms, with furniture handmade by the owner. Beamed, flag-floored dining room for classical British dishes and Aga-cooked breakfasts.

4 rooms 🖵 - 🛉£ 68/98 🛉🛉£ 68/98

Wallington ✉ NE61 4AQ - Southeast : 2.5 mi by A 696 on B 6342
- 📞 01830 540387 - www.shieldhallguesthouse.co.uk - Closed
November-February

KIRTLINGTON

Oxfordshire – Regional map n° **6**-B2
▶ London 70 mi – Bicester 11 mi – Oxford 16 mi

🏠 Dashwood

TRADITIONAL · MODERN Grade II listed former pub and barn, built in classic Cotswold stone; popular with visitors to Bicester Village. Clean, fresh, uncluttered bedrooms are decorated in a contemporary style; Room 1 is the best, with air con and a spacious bathroom. Modern European menu served in informal, ground floor restaurant.

12 rooms - 🛉£ 90/110 🛉🛉£ 110/135 - 🖵 £ 12

South Green, Heyford Rd ✉ OX5 3HJ - 📞 01869 352707
- www.thedashwood.co.uk - Closed 1-3 January

KNARESBOROUGH

North Yorkshire – Pop. 15 484 – Regional map n° **13**-B2
▶ London 217 mi – Bradford 21 mi – Harrogate 3 mi – Leeds 18 mi

at Ferrensby Northeast: 3 mi on A6055

✕✕ General Tarleton

TRADITIONAL BRITISH · INN Characterful 18C coaching inn with low beams and exposed stone walls; most sit in the main room but there's also a glass-roofed courtyard and a large terrace for warmer days. Hearty dishes champion Yorkshire produce. Bedrooms feature solid oak furnishings and come with home-baked biscuits.

Menu £ 15 (lunch and early dinner) - Carte £ 25/44

13 rooms 🖵 - 🛉£ 75/95 🛉🛉£ 129/150

Boroughbridge Rd ✉ HG5 0PZ - 📞 01423 340284 - www.generaltarleton.co.uk

KNOWSTONE

Devon – ✉ South Molton – Regional map n° **1**-C1
▶ London 183 mi – Bristol 78 mi – Cardiff 109 mi – Plymouth 78 mi

🍴 **Masons Arms** (Mark Dodson) 🛏 🍴 🅿

CLASSIC FRENCH · PUB Pretty 13C inn, in a secluded Exmoor village, with a cosy bar and a bright dining room featuring a celestial ceiling mural. The experienced owners offer attractively presented, sophisticated French and British classics. Ingredients are top class and flavours are pronounced and assured. Service is charming.

→ Seared peppered tuna with oriental salad. Breast of guinea fowl with confit leg cannelloni and morel cream sauce. Chocolate and passion fruit délice with raspberry sorbet.

Menu £ 25 (lunch) – Carte £ 40/50

✉ EX36 4RY – ☎ 01398 341231 (booking essential)
– www.masonsarmsdevon.co.uk – Closed first week January, 1 week mid-February, 10 days August-September, Sunday dinner and Monday

LA HAULE → See Channel Islands (Jersey)

LANCASTER
Lancashire – Pop. 48 085 – Regional map n° **11**-A1
▶ London 252 mi – Blackpool 26 mi – Bradford 62 mi – Burnley 44 mi

🏠 **Ashton** 🛏 🎇 🅿

TRADITIONAL · MODERN Georgian house surrounded by lawned gardens; stylishly decorated and personally run by a friendly owner. Good-sized boldly coloured bedrooms feature a blend of modern and antique furniture. Meat, fish or cheese dinner platters by arrangement.

5 rooms ☲ – ♦£ 115/135 ♦♦£ 135/185

Wyresdale Rd ✉ LA1 3JJ – Southeast : 1.25 mi by A 6 on Clitheroe rd
– ☎ 01524 68460 – www.theashtonlancaster.com

LANGAR
Nottinghamshire – Regional map n° **9**-B2
▶ London 132 mi – Boston 45 mi – Leicester 25 mi – Lincoln 37 mi

🏠 **Langar Hall** 🎇 🐾 ⬅ 🛏 🍴 🅿

TRADITIONAL · HISTORIC Characterful Georgian manor surrounded by over 20 acres of pastoral land and ponds; its antique-furnished bedrooms named after those who've featured in the house's history. Dine by candlelight in the elegant, pillared dining room; classically based cooking features veg from the kitchen garden and local game.

12 rooms ☲ – ♦£ 100/160 ♦♦£ 125/225 – 1 suite

✉ NG13 9HG – ☎ 01949 860559 – www.langarhall.co.uk

LANGHO – Lancashire → See Blackburn

LANGTHWAITE – North Yorkshire → See Reeth

LA PULENTE → See Channel Islands (Jersey)

LAPWORTH
Warwickshire – Pop. 2 100 – Regional map n° **10**-C2
▶ London 108 mi – Birmingham 23 mi – Leicester 47 mi – Coventry 19 mi

🍴 **Boot Inn** 🛏 🍴 🅿

TRADITIONAL BRITISH · PUB A big, buzzy pub boasting a large terrace, a traditional quarry-floored bar and a modern restaurant. Dishes range from sandwiches, picnic boards and sharing plates to more sophisticated specials. You can eat in a tepee in the summer!

Menu £ 15 (lunch and early dinner) – Carte £ 24/40

Old Warwick Rd ✉ B94 6JU – ☎ 01564 782464 (booking essential)
– www.bootinnlapworth.co.uk

LAVENHAM

Suffolk – ⊠ Sudbury – Pop. 1 413 – Regional map n° **8**-C3
▶ London 66 mi – Cambridge 39 mi – Colchester 22 mi – Ipswich 19 mi

⌂ The Swan at Lavenham H & Spa ⚘ 🍴 🌐 🐾 🛁 🅿

HISTORIC · PERSONALISED A characterful 15C coaching inn with several delightful lounges, a hugely atmospheric bar and a smart spa with a terrace. Beamed bedrooms have a subtle contemporary style. Dine on classics in the smart brasserie or on more modern dishes beneath a minstrels' gallery – with piano accompaniment at weekends.

45 rooms ☖ – ♦£110/155 ♦♦£185/360 – 1 suite
High St ⊠ CO10 9QA – ℰ 01787 247477 – www.theswanatlavenham.co.uk
Brasserie – See restaurant listing

XXX Great House ⇔ 🍴

CLASSIC FRENCH · ELEGANT Passionately run restaurant on the main square of an attractive town; its impressive Georgian façade concealing a timbered house with 14C origins. Choose between two dining rooms and a smart enclosed terrace. Concise menus offer ambitious dishes with worldwide influences and a French heart. Stylish, contemporary décor blends well with the old beams in the bedrooms.

Menu £25/37 – Carte £42/54
5 rooms – ♦£99/125 ♦♦£140/215 – ☖ £12 – 2 suites
Market Pl ⊠ CO10 9QZ – ℰ 01787 247431 – www.greathouse.co.uk – Closed 3 weeks January, 2 weeks summer, Sunday dinner, Monday and lunch Tuesday

XX Brasserie 🍴 🍴 🅿

MODERN CUISINE · RUSTIC Smart restaurant offering a classic bistro menu. Modern furnishings blend with the more traditional elements of the historic inn in which it resides. In winter, sit by the fire; in summer, sit on the terrace overlooking the gardens.

Carte £24/42
*Swan Hotel, High St ⊠ CO10 9QA – ℰ 01787 247477
– www.theswanatlavenham.co.uk*

at Preston St Mary Northeast 2.75 mi by A 1141

🍴 Six Bells 🍴 🅿

TRADITIONAL CUISINE · PUB An attractive brick and timber pub in a small hamlet. Heavy timbers are hung with tankards, open fires punctuate brick walls and a hunting theme runs throughout. Restaurant-style dishes are carefully and confidently prepared.

Menu £12 (weekday lunch) – Carte £22/31
*The Street ⊠ CO10 9NG – ℰ 01787 247440 – www.thesixbellspreston.com
– Closed Monday and Tuesday*

LEDBURY

Herefordshire – Pop. 8 862 – Regional map n° **10**-B3
▶ London 119 mi – Birmingham 53 mi – Bristol 58 mi

XX Verzon ⇔ ⇐ 🍴 🍴 ♿ 🅿

MODERN BRITISH · CHIC A smartly restored Georgian manor house with a laid-back vibe. The chic restaurant offers a menu of precisely prepared, classic British dishes. It's owned by the local Chase Distillery, so the gins and vodkas are well worth a try. Most of the seductively styled bedrooms have a country view.

Menu £25 (weekday lunch) – Carte £28/54
8 rooms ☖ – ♦£80/90 ♦♦£90/150
*Hereford Rd ⊠ HR8 2PZ – Northwest: 3.25 mi on A438 – ℰ 01531 670381
– www.verzonhouse.com*

LEEBOTWOOD

Shropshire – Regional map n° **18**-B2

▶ London 171 mi – Shrewsbury 10 mi – Birmingham 55 mi

🍺 The Pound Inn ⓝ   🛋 🛋 ⚐ Ⓟ

TRADITIONAL CUISINE · NEIGHBOURHOOD It might have been modernised inside but there's still plenty of character to be found, courtesy of flagged floors, a large inglenook fireplace and a wooden bar. Choose from a small list of classics or some more ambitious options.

Carte £ 23/30

✉ SY6 6ND – ☎ 01694 751477 – www.thepound.org.uk – Closed first 2 weeks November, Sunday dinner and Monday

LEEDS

Kent – Regional map n° **5**-C2

▶ London 41 mi – Ealing 53 mi – Stratford 41 mi – Bromley 33 mi

🏠 Leeds Castle   ✿ ☜ ≼ 🛋 ▣ ⚐ ✂ 🛋 Ⓟ

HISTORIC BUILDING · PERSONALISED This unique accommodation is found in the grounds of 900 year old Leeds Castle. Stay in smart, modern bedrooms in the 1920s stable block or in a more historic room in the Maiden's Tower (an old Tudor bakehouse beside the castle). The timbered café morphs into a candlelit restaurant in the evening.

22 rooms ☲ – ♟£ 75/100 ♟♟£ 100/200

Broomfield Gate ✉ ME17 1PL – Southeast 3 mi by A 20 – ☎ 01622 767823 – www.leeds-castle.co.uk – Closed 24-26 December

LEEDS

West Yorkshire – Pop. 751 485 – Regional map n° **13**-B2

▶ London 204 mi – Liverpool 75 mi – Manchester 43 mi – Newcastle upon Tyne 95 mi

Hotels

Malmaison

BUSINESS · DESIGN Chic, boutique hotel in the former offices of the city's tram and bus department; hence the name of the stylish suite, 'Depot'. Generously sized bedrooms have warm colour schemes and good comforts. Smart, intimate guest areas include a relaxing bar and a modern take on a brasserie.

100 rooms – ♦£ 115/195 ♦♦£ 115/195 – ♀£ 15 – 1 suite
Town plan: A2-n - 1 Swinegate ✉ LS1 4AG – ℰ 0113 398 1000
– www.malmaison.com

Quebecs

BUSINESS · ELEGANT Interesting 19C building – formerly a Liberal Club; its original features include wood-panelling, a curvaceous oak staircase and stained glass windows depicting districts of Leeds. Bedrooms blend the classic with the contemporary.

44 rooms – ♦£ 75/285 ♦♦£ 75/285 – ♀£ 16
Town plan: A2-a - 9 Quebec St ✉ LS1 2HA – ℰ 0113 244 8989
– www.quebecshotel.co.uk
– Closed 23-27 December

42 The Calls

BUSINESS · CONTEMPORARY Converted 18C grain mill on the banks of the River Aire. Many of the well-equipped bedrooms come complete with original beams, steel girders or industrial machinery; go for a room with a river view. Breakfasts are comprehensive.

41 rooms – ♦£ 85/180 ♦♦£ 99/210 – ♀£ 16
Town plan: B2-z - 42 The Calls ✉ LS2 7EW – ℰ 0113 244 0099
– www.42thecalls.co.uk – Closed 3 days Christmas
Brasserie Forty 4 – See restaurant listing

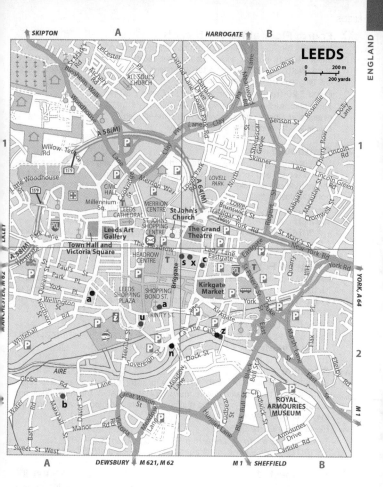

LEEDS

0   200 m
0   200 yards

Restaurants

XX The Man Behind the Curtain (Michael O'Hare)   AC
😸
MODERN CUISINE · FASHIONABLE A unique, very individually styled restaurant with a minimalist interior and bold graffiti artwork, set on the top floor of a privately owned fashion store. Accomplished, highly skilled cooking uses very original, creative combinations – and the artful presentation is equally striking.
→ Hand-dived scallops, chorizo oil and grains. Pork jowl, oysters, cinders. Praline, passion fruit, meringue.

Menu £ 45/75 – tasting menu only

Town plan: B2-c - *3rd Floor, Flannels, 68-78 Vicar Ln* ✉ *LS1 7JH*
- ☎ *0113 243 2376 (booking essential)* – *www.themanbehindthecurtain.co.uk*
- *dinner only and lunch Friday-Saturday – Closed 17 December-9 January and Sunday-Tuesday*

451

XX Fourth Floor at Harvey Nichols 🍸 ☆ AC 🕸

MODERN BRITISH · BRASSERIE Bright, stylish dining room with rooftop views, metal fretwork screens and a Scandic feel; located on the top floor of a chic store. Watch the chefs prepare tasty, modern, globally influenced dishes. Pleasant service is from a smart team.

Menu £ 20 (lunch and early dinner) – Carte £ 30/48

Town plan: AB2-s - 107-111 Briggate ⊠ LS1 6AZ – ℰ 0113 204 8000 (booking essential at lunch) – www.harveynichols.com – Closed 25 December, 1 January, Easter Sunday and dinner Sunday-Monday

XX Crafthouse ≤ ☆ 🕭 AC 🕸 ⇔

MODERN CUISINE · DESIGN Located in the Trinity shopping centre, with a wrap-around terrace and rooftop views. It has a bright, modern feel; the open kitchen and marble counter take centre stage. Menus offer European classics and meats from the Josper grill.

Menu £ 24 (lunch and early dinner) – Carte £ 26/40

Town plan: A2-a - Trinity Leeds (5th Floor), 70 Boar Ln ⊠ LS1 6HW – ℰ 0113 897 0444 – www.crafthouse-restaurant.co.uk – Closed 25 December and 1 January

XX Brasserie Forty 4 ☆ AC 🕸 ⇔

INTERNATIONAL · BRASSERIE Contemporary hotel brasserie and a bright, stylish bar, set in an old 18C warehouse. Tables are spread amongst steel girders; sit by the window for a river view. Straightforward, up-to-date cooking displays European influences.

Menu £ 20 (weekdays) – Carte £ 24/35

Town plan: B2-z - 42 The Calls Hotel, 42 The Calls ⊠ LS2 7EW – ℰ 0113 244 0099 – www.42thecalls.co.uk – Closed 3 days Christmas

XX Angelica 🍸 ≤ ☆ AC

MODERN CUISINE · BRASSERIE Set above its sister 'Crafthouse' and also boasting a superb terrace and skyline views. The large bar is the focal point and cocktails are a speciality. Cooking is simple, modern and global – and, pleasingly, they're open all day.

Menu £ 15 – Carte £ 25/47

Town plan: A2-a - Trinity Leeds (6th Floor), 70 Boar Ln ⊠ LS1 6HW – ℰ 0113 897 0444 – www.angelica-restaurant.co.uk – Closed 25 December

X Bundobust 🆕 ☆ ⅙ AC 🗏

INDIAN VEGETARIAN · EXOTIC DÉCOR The simplicity is part of the fun: order at the bar, grab a paper plate and some plastic cutlery, find a space on the communal benches and get stuck in! Authentic vegetarian street food includes delicious masala dosas and okra fries.

Carte £ 12/16

Town plan: A2-u - 6 Mill Hill ⊠ LS1 5DQ – ℰ 0113 243 1248 – www.bundobust.com – Closed 25-26 December and 1 January

X Ox Club 🆕 AC

BARBECUE · SIMPLE A former mill houses this multi-floor venue comprising a beer hall, cocktail bar, event space and restaurant. The latter boasts a wood-fired grill imported from the USA; rustic, smoky-flavoured dishes showcase Yorkshire ingredients.

Carte £ 21/27

Town plan: B2-x - Bramleys Yard, The Headrow ⊠ LS1 6PU
– ℰ 07470 359961 – www.oxclub.co.uk
– dinner only and lunch Saturday-Sunday
– Closed 25-26 December, Sunday dinner and Monday

⚹ Foundry   🍴 🗚

TRADITIONAL CUISINE · WINE BAR Simply styled bistro-cum-wine bar on the site of the legendary steel foundry, with a vaulted ceiling, ornate bar and laid-back feel. Wine box ends and 'squashed' bottles feature. Classic dishes include plenty of specials.

Menu £ 15 (weekday lunch) – Carte £ 21/39

Town plan: **A2-b** - *1 Saw Mill Yard, The Round Foundry* ✉ *LS11 5WH*
– ☎ *0113 245 0390* – *www.thefoundrywinebar.co.uk*
– *Closed first week January, last week August, 25-26 December, Saturday lunch, Sunday and Monday*

⚹ Tharavadu   🎯

INDIAN · EXOTIC DÉCOR A simple-looking restaurant with seascape murals. The extensive menu offers superbly spiced, colourful Keralan specialities and re-fined street food – the dosas are a hit. Service is bright and friendly and dishes arrive swiftly.

Carte £ 17/31

Town plan: **A2-u** - *7-8 Mill Hill* ✉ *LS1 5DQ*
– ☎ *0113 244 0500 (booking essential)* – *www.tharavadurestaurants.com*
– *Closed 24-27 December and Sunday*

🍴 Cross Keys   🍴

TRADITIONAL BRITISH · FRIENDLY Traditional brick-built pub: a watering hole for foundry workers in the 19C. Cosy and welcoming with beams, flagged floors and wood-burning stoves. It gets busy, so book ahead. Hearty, straightforward, British cooking; popular Sunday lunch.

Carte £ 21/36

Town plan: **A2-b** - *107 Water Ln, The Round Foundry* ✉ *LS11 5WD*
– ☎ *0113 243 3711 (booking essential)*
– *www.the-crosskeys.com*
– *Closed 25-26 December and 1 January*

LEICESTER

Leicester – Pop. 443 760 – Regional map n° **9**-B2
▶ London 107 mi – Birmingham 43 mi – Nottingham 26 mi

🏨 Hotel Maiyango   ❀ 🖃 ⅙ 🗚 ❦ 🕹

BUSINESS · MODERN Privately owned city centre hotel in a 150 year old shoe factory. The interior is stylish and the trendy bar boasts a terrace overlooking the rooftops. Spacious, individually designed bedrooms have bespoke wood fur-nishings and a colonial feel. The oriental restaurant serves global dishes with In-dian spicing.

14 rooms – 🛏£ 79/139 🛏🛏£ 79/139 – ⌸ £ 8 – 1 suite
Town plan: **A1-a** - *13-21 St Nicholas Pl* ✉ *LE1 4LD*
– ☎ *0116 251 8898* – *www.maiyango.com*
– *Closed 25-26 December*

⚹⚹ Chutney Ivy   ⅙ 🗚 🎯 🍷

INDIAN · FASHIONABLE Keenly run former warehouse with a smart industrial feel; its floor to ceiling windows open onto the pavement. Mix of modern and classic dishes, with influences from Hyderabad, Goa and Bengal. Watch the chefs in the open kitchen.

Menu £ 17 – Carte £ 16/33

Town plan: **B1-x** - *41 Halford St* ✉ *LE1 1TR* – ☎ *0116 251 1889*
– *www.chutneyivy.com* – *dinner only* – *Closed 25-26 December,1 January and Sunday*

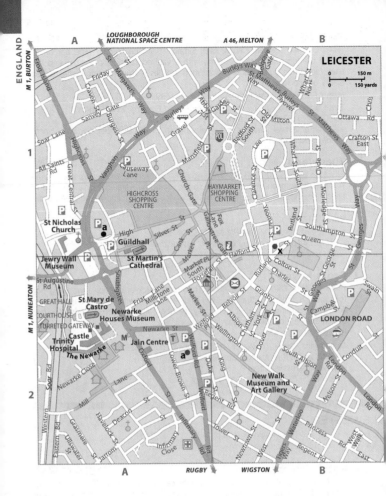

LEICESTER

X **Shivalli**   AC ⍩

INDIAN VEGETARIAN · SIMPLE Simple, part-panelled restaurant with Indian artefacts on the walls. Appealing South Indian, vegetarian menu with most dishes
also suitable for vegans. Tasty, authentic cooking with honest flavours. Good
value thalis and buffet lunches.

Carte £ 11/21

Town plan: A2-a - 21 Welford Rd ⊠ LE2 7AD – 𝒞 0116 255 0137
- www.shivallirestaurant.com – Closed 25 December, Sunday dinner and Monday

LEIGH-ON-SEA

Southend-on-Sea – Regional map n° **7**-C3
▶ London 37 mi – Basildon 9 mi – Chelmsford 18 mi

XX Sandbank

INTERNATIONAL · NEIGHBOURHOOD Former bank in a parade of shops; now a spacious restaurant with a high ceiling, a classic black and white theme and a tropical fish tank in a dramatic feature wall. Wide-ranging menu of well-presented dishes with clear flavours.

Menu £ 16 (weekdays)/35 – Carte £ 24/44

1470 London Rd ⊠ SS9 2UR – ℰ 01702 719000 – www.sandbankrestaurant.co.uk
– Closed Sunday dinner and Monday

LEINTWARDINE

Herefordshire – ⊠ Craven Arms – Regional map n° **10**-A2
▶ London 156 mi – Birmingham 55 mi – Hereford 24 mi – Worcester 40 mi

🏠 The Lion

TRADITIONAL BRITISH · CLASSIC DÉCOR 18C inn on the banks of the River Teme, next to an attractive medieval bridge. It's relaxed and stylish with a proper bar and a slightly smarter dining room with river views. Dishes are nicely presented and local produce plays a big part. Smart bedrooms have up-to-date facilities; some have river views.

Carte £ 20/36

8 rooms ⌁ – ♦£ 75/85 ♦♦£ 100/120

⊠ SY7 0JZ – ℰ 01547 540203 – www.thelionleintwardine.co.uk – Closed 25 December

LEVISHAM – North Yorkshire → See Pickering

LEWANNICK

Cornwall – Regional map n° **1**-B2
▶ London 243 mi – Bristol 127 mi – Plymouth 24 mi

🏠 Coombeshead Farm ⓝ

Set on a working farm, in 66 acres of meadows and woodland, this former farmhouse offers accommodation and communal dining for just 12 guests. Menus offer a mix of small and large sharing dishes; the owners' aim is to bring diners closer to where raw ingredients are produced. They also run cookery workshops.

5 rooms ⌁ – ♦£ 110 ♦♦£ 175/185

⊠ PL15 7QQ Southeast : 0.7 mi by Callington/North Hill rd and Trelaske rd on Congdons Shop rd. – ℰ 01566 782009 – www.coombesheadfarm.co.uk – Closed Monday and Tuesday

LEWDOWN

Devon – Regional map n° **1**-C2
▶ London 238 mi – Exeter 37 mi – Plymouth 29 mi

🏠 Lewtrenchard Manor

HISTORIC · ELEGANT Hugely impressive Grade II listed Jacobean manor house in mature grounds. The characterful antique-furnished interior features huge fireplaces, ornate oak panelling, intricately designed ceilings and mullioned windows. Bedrooms are spacious and well-equipped; those in the coach house are the most modern.

14 rooms ⌁ – ♦£ 165/205 ♦♦£ 200/250 – 1 suite

⊠ EX20 4PN – South : 0.75 mi by Lewtrenchard rd – ℰ 01566 783222
– www.lewtrenchard.co.uk

Lewtrenchard Manor – See restaurant listing

XX Lewtrenchard Manor

MODERN BRITISH · INTIMATE Intimate wood-panelled dining room in a Jacobean manor house. Cooking is contrastingly modern yet refreshingly unadorned; flavoursome garden produce features. For a more unique experience book 'Purple Carrot' (the chef's table).

Menu £ 26/50

Lewtrenchard Manor Hotel, ⊠ EX20 4PN – South : 0.75 mi by Lewtrenchard rd
– ℰ 01566 783222 (booking essential) – www.lewtrenchard.co.uk

LEWES

East Sussex – Pop. 17 297 – Regional map n° **5**-A3

▶ London 53 mi – Brighton 8 mi – Hastings 29 mi – Maidstone 43 mi

at East Chiltington Northwest: 5.5 mi by A275 and B2116 off Novington

Lane✉ Lewes

🍽 Jolly Sportsman
         😮 🍴 🛎 🅰🅲 🅿

TRADITIONAL BRITISH · RUSTIC Down a myriad of country lanes is this olive green pub, which attracts the locals in their droves. Choose from interesting bar bites, a rustic British-based à la carte, a good value set menu and blackboard specials which come and go.

Menu £ 15 (weekday lunch) – Carte £ 28/41

Chapel Ln ✉ BN7 3BA – ℰ 01273 890400 (booking essential)
– www.thejollysportsman.com – Closed 25 December, Sunday dinner and Monday

LEYBURN

North Yorkshire – Pop. 2 183 – Regional map n° **13**-B1

▶ London 251 mi – Darlington 25 mi – Kendal 43 mi – Leeds 53 mi

🏠 Clyde House
         🚫

TOWNHOUSE · PERSONALISED 18C former coaching inn on the main market square, run by an experienced owner and immaculately kept throughout. Small, cosy sitting room and cottagey breakfast room. Smart, comfortable bedrooms with good quality soft furnishings, hair dryers and bathrobes. Extensive buffet and 'full Yorkshire' breakfasts.

5 rooms 🛏 – ♦£ 55/60 ♦♦£ 85/95

5 Railway St ✉ DL8 5AY – ℰ 01969 623941 – www.clydehouse.com – Closed 8-21 January

🍴 Saddle Room
         🍴 ♿ 🛋 🔄

TRADITIONAL BRITISH · BISTRO Located within an area of parkland close to the 'Forbidden Corner', is this converted stable decked out with equine paraphernalia – ask for a table in a stall! Unfussy, classical menus are offered from breakfast through to dinner.

Carte £ 22/51

Tupgill Park, Coverdale ✉ DL8 4TJ – Southwest : 2.5 mi by Coverham rd
– ℰ 01969 640596 – www.thesaddleroom.co.uk – Closed Sunday dinner

🍽 Sandpiper Inn
         🍴 🛎 🅿

TRADITIONAL BRITISH · PUB A friendly Yorkshire welcome is extended at this characterful, stone-built, part-16C pub just off the main square. Subtle, refined cooking offers a modern take on the classics and the skilled kitchen prides itself on the provenance of its ingredients. Two country-chic style bedrooms offer excellent comforts.

Carte £ 25/44 **s**

2 rooms 🛏 – ♦£ 80/90 ♦♦£ 90/100

Market Pl ✉ DL8 5AT – ℰ 01969 622206 – www.sandpiperinn.co.uk – Closed 2 weeks January, Tuesday in winter and Monday

LICHFIELD

Staffordshire – Pop. 32 877 – Regional map n° **10**-C2

▶ London 128 mi – Birmingham 16 mi – Derby 23 mi

🏰 Swinfen Hall
         🍴 ✂ 🚫 ⛳ 🅿

COUNTRY HOUSE · HISTORIC Grade II listed Georgian mansion with an impressive façade, set in 100 acres. Original features abound, including a stucco ceiling in the magnificent foyer. Individually styled bedrooms; extras include fruit and freshly baked shortbread.

17 rooms 🛏 – ♦£ 175/335 ♦♦£ 200/375 – 1 suite

✉ WS14 9RE – Southeast : 2.75 mi by A 5206 on A 38 – ℰ 01543 481494
– www.swinfenhallhotel.co.uk – Restricted opening between Christmas and New Year

Four Seasons – See restaurant listing

🏠 Netherstowe House   🍴 🛏 ⬚ 🏊 ℗

COUNTRY HOUSE · CLASSIC Extensively restored 19C country house, professionally run by a family team. Period lounges and luxurious bedrooms come with antique furnishings and original fireplaces; modern apartments complete with kitchenettes are located in the grounds. The elegant formal restaurant offers ambitious modern cooking.

24 rooms ☲ – 🛉£ 115/165 🛉🛉£ 115/165 – 10 suites

Netherstowe Ln ✉ WS13 6AY – Northeast : 1.75 mi following signs for A 51 and A 38, off Eastern Ave – ☏ 01543 254270 – www.netherstowehouse.com

🏠 St Johns House   🛏 🏊 ℗

TOWNHOUSE · CONTEMPORARY Impressive Regency townhouse fronted by large columns. Enter through a beautiful tiled hallway into a contemporary drawing room with ornate cornicing and chandeliers. Individually styled bedrooms have a modern, understated feel.

9 rooms ☲ – 🛉£ 75/95 🛉🛉£ 99/120

28 St John St ✉ WS13 6PB – ☏ 01543 252080 – www.stjohnshouse.co.uk – Closed 25-30 December

XX Four Seasons   🛏 🍷 ℗

MODERN BRITISH · CLASSIC DÉCOR An impressive classical dining room with original wood panelling and a superbly ornate ceiling, set within the grand surroundings of Swinfen Hall. Elaborate modern cooking uses meat from the estate and veg and herbs from the walled garden.

Menu £ 38/52

Swinfen Hall Hotel, ✉ WS14 9RE – Southeast : 2.75 mi by A 5206 on A 38 – ☏ 01543 481494 – www.swinfenhallhotel.co.uk – Closed Sunday dinner and Monday

X Wine House   ♿

TRADITIONAL CUISINE · NEIGHBOURHOOD This smart red-brick house has an open-fired bar at one end and a dining room at the other. Lunch sees good value comfort dishes, while dinner puts steaks and seafood to the fore. It's named after its impressive glass wine cellar.

Menu £ 14 (weekday lunch) – Carte £ 25/50

27 Bird St ✉ WS13 6PW – ☏ 01543 419999 – www.thewinehouselichfield.co.uk – Closed Sunday dinner

at Wall South: 2.75 mi by A5127

🍴 The Trooper   🛏 🌿 ♿ ℗

TRADITIONAL CUISINE · FRIENDLY Feast like a Roman general after battle on mature steaks including local rump, Kobe beef and rare breed steaks which go up to 20oz. Tasty pizzas cooked to order in a wood-fired oven. Grab a seat on the terrace when the weather allows.

Menu £ 12 (weekday lunch) – Carte £ 17/41

Watling St ✉ WS14 0AN – ☏ 01543 480413 – www.thetrooperwall.co.uk

LICKFOLD – West Sussex → See Petworth

LIFTON

Devon – Pop. 1 180 – Regional map n° **1**-C2

▶ London 238 mi – Bude 24 mi – Exeter 37 mi – Launceston 4 mi

🏠 Arundell Arms   🍴 🛏 🌿 ℗

TRADITIONAL · COSY Family-run roadside coaching inn with cosy, traditional bedrooms and access to 20 miles of private fishing on the River Tamar and its tributaries. The characterful lounge and bar serve a brasserie menu, while the restaurant – which overlooks the terrace and gardens – offers classical fare.

25 rooms ☲ – 🛉£ 115/120 🛉🛉£ 160/180

Fore St ✉ PL16 0AA – ☏ 01566 784666 – www.arundellarms.com

LINCOLN

Lincolnshire – Pop. 100 160 – Regional map n° **9**-C1

▶ London 140 mi – Leeds 73 mi – Nottingham 38 mi

⌂ The Rest

TOWNHOUSE · CONTEMPORARY With direct access to the bedrooms from the street, guests can come and go freely at this laid-back hotel. Breakfast is served in the coffee shop-cum-bar. Chic bedrooms feature bespoke furnishings and bathrooms with heated floors.

10 rooms ⌂ – ♦£ 84/129 ♦♦£ 84/149

Town plan: B1-t - *55A Steep Hill* ✉ *LN2 1LR* – ℰ *01522 247888*
– *www.theresthotellincoln.co.uk*

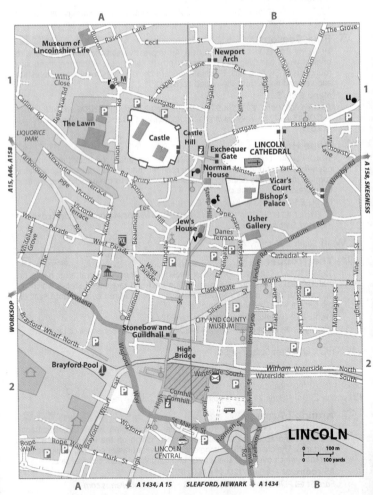

🏠 St Clements Lodge   ⅌ 🅿 ⇌

TOWNHOUSE · PERSONALISED Cosy, Edwardian-style house close to the cathedral and castle (where you can view the Magna Carta). Cheerful owners offer good old-fashioned hospitality. Spacious, well-equipped bedrooms have pine furnishings and a homely feel.

3 rooms ⌂ – 🛏£ 70 🛏🛏£ 85/90

Town plan: B1-u - *21 Langworthgate* ✉ *LN2 4AD* – ℰ *01522 521532*
– *www.stclementslodge.co.uk*

✕✕ Jews House   ⇄

MODERN CUISINE · COSY At the bottom of a steep cobbled hill is this cosy stone house dating from 1150; reputedly Europe's oldest surviving dwelling. Bold, ambitious dishes display an eclectic mix of influences – the tasting menu is a hit. Service is charming.

Menu £ 20 (lunch) – Carte £ 31/44

Town plan: B1-v - *15 The Strait* ✉ *LN2 1JD* – ℰ *01522 524851*
– *www.jewshouserestaurant.co.uk* – *Closed 2 weeks January, 2 weeks July, 1 week November, Sunday, Monday and lunch Tuesday*

✕ Bronze Pig   🖢 ⇄

MODERN BRITISH · DESIGN This former pop-up, run by an Irishman and a Sicilian, has taken root. It's split over 4 rooms and is decorated with country scenes and colourful chairs. The modern menu offers 5 choices per course and reflects what's in season.

Carte £ 34/54

Town plan: A1-r - *4 Burton Rd* ✉ *LN1 3LB* – ℰ *01522 524817*
– *www.thebronzepig.co.uk* – *dinner only and lunch Saturday-Sunday* – *Closed Monday and Tuesday*

🍽 Wig & Mitre   🄰🄲 🖢 ⇄

TRADITIONAL BRITISH · PUB Well-established pub with a cosy bar, period dining rooms and an airy beamed restaurant. Menus offer classical dishes with the odd Mediterranean or Asian influence, alongside daily specials, hearty breakfasts and over 20 wines by the glass.

Menu £ 18 (weekdays) – Carte £ 19/52

Town plan: B1-r - *30-32 Steep Hill* ✉ *LN2 1LU* – ℰ *01522 535190*
– *www.wigandmitre.com* – *Closed 25 December*

LISKEARD

Cornwall – Pop. 9 237 – Regional map n° **1**-B2

▶ London 261 mi – Exeter 59 mi – Plymouth 19 mi – Truro 37 mi

🏠 Pencubitt Country House   🐾 🐕 ⌂ ⅌ 🅿

TRADITIONAL · PERSONALISED Sympathetically restored Victorian property with delightful views over the gardens and countryside – take it all in from the veranda or from the balcony in bedroom 3. Look out too for the original windows and staircase in the lovely hall. They offer home-cooked dinners, cream teas and picnics by arrangement.

9 rooms ⌂ – 🛏£ 55/90 🛏🛏£ 75/120

Station Rd ✉ *PL14 4EB* – *South : 0.5 mi by B 3254 on Lamellion rd*
– ℰ *01579 342694* – *www.pencubitt.com* – *Closed January and February*

LISS

Hampshire – Pop. 6 248 – Regional map n° **4**-C2

▶ London 53 mi – Bristol 104 mi – Cardiff 137 mi – Plymouth 184 mi

✕✕ Madhuban   🄰🄲

INDIAN · FRIENDLY Smartly furnished restaurant owned by three enthusiastic brothers. The focus is on fresh north Indian dishes; most of which can be prepared to the desired heat – the menu provides a useful glossary of terms. They also sell their sauces.

Carte £ 14/24

94 Station Rd ✉ *GU33 7AQ* – ℰ *01730 893363* – *www.madhubanrestaurant.co.uk*
– *Closed 25-26 December and Friday lunch*

ENGLAND

LITTLE BEDWYN – Wiltshire → See Marlborough

LITTLE COXWELL
Oxfordshire – Pop. 132 – Regional map n° **6**-A2
▶ London 79 mi – Sheffield 158 mi – Derby 120 mi – York 202 mi

Eagle Tavern
TRADITIONAL BRITISH · TRADITIONAL DÉCOR This welcoming pub was built in 1901 for the farmers of this sleepy hamlet and, although it might look a little different now, a convivial atmosphere still reigns. The self-taught chef cooks the kind of food he likes to eat, including dishes from his homeland, Slovakia. Spacious bedrooms are spotlessly kept.
Menu £ 16 (weekday lunch) – Carte £ 23/36
6 rooms ⌂ – ♦£ 60/90 ♦♦£ 70/100
✉ SN7 7LW – ☎ 01367 241879 – www.eagletavern.co.uk – Closed Sunday dinner and Monday

LITTLE DUNMOW
Essex – Pop. 2 190 – Regional map n° **13**-C2
▶ London 46 mi – Colchester 25 mi – Cambridge 36 mi

Flitch of Bacon ⑩
BRITISH MODERN · PUB This is a place where the serving team are confident and the chef is experienced. An extensive range of modern dishes are allied with the odd pub classic: good ingredients are used in accomplished ways, flavour combinations are great and presentation is top notch. Contemporary bedrooms are boldly decorated.
Carte £ 28/53
3 rooms ⌂ – ♦£ 160 ♦♦£ 160
✉ CM6 3HT – ☎ 01371 821660 (booking essential) – www.flitchofbacon.co.uk – Closed first week January

LITTLE ECCLESTON
Lancashire – Regional map n° **11**-A2
▶ London 238 mi – Liverpool - 55 mi – Leeds 83 mi – Manchester 51 mi

Cartford Inn
TRADITIONAL CUISINE · PUB The Cartford Inn stands next to small toll bridge on the River Wyre and comes complete with a deli and farm shop. Cooking is gutsy and satisfying and many of the tried-and-tested classics come with a twist. The owner played a big part in the interior design, particularly the bold, boutique bedrooms.
Carte £ 24/39
15 rooms ⌂ – ♦£ 75/130 ♦♦£ 125/230
Cartford Ln ✉ PR3 0YP – ☎ 01995 670166 – www.thecartfordinn.co.uk – Closed 25 December and Monday lunch except bank holidays

LITTLE MARLOW – Buckinghamshire → See Marlow

LITTLE THETFORD – Cambridgeshire → See Ely

LITTLE WILBRAHAM – Cambridgeshire → See Cambridge

LITTLETON – Hants. → See Winchester

LITTLEHAMPTON
West Sussex – Pop. 55 706 – Regional map n° **4**-C3
▶ London 64 mi – Brighton 18 mi – Portsmouth 31 mi

460

🏠 Bailiffscourt H. & Spa 🏠 🐾 🛏️ 🏡 🏊 🗓️ ⊕ 🏠 ᒪ₅ 🍴 🏋️ 🅿️

COUNTRY HOUSE · HISTORIC Charming, reconstructed medieval manor in immaculately kept gardens. Bedrooms are split between the main house and the outbuildings; the newer rooms are in the grounds and are more suited to families. Beautiful spa facility. Classic country house cooking served in the formal dining room.

39 rooms ⌑ – ∤£ 199 ∤∤£ 229/499

Climping St, Climping ✉ *BN17 5RW* – *West : 2.75 mi by A 259* – ☏ *01903 723511*
– www.hshotels.co.uk

LIVERPOOL

Merseyside – Pop. 552 267 – Regional map n° **11**-A3

▶ London 219 mi – Birmingham 103 mi – Leeds 75 mi – Manchester 35 mi

🏠 Aloft Liverpool 🏠 ᒪ₅ ⊟ 🛗 ᵃᶜ 🏋️

HISTORIC · DESIGN Relaxed hotel in the Grade II listed Royal Insurance building in the centre of the city. It features stunning original panelling, stained glass and ornate plasterwork, alongside colourful contemporary décor and the latest mod cons. An open lounge with a pool table leads to the New York style restaurant.

116 rooms – ∤£ 60/250 ∤∤£ 85/250 – ⌑ £ 10

Town plan: B2-s – *1 North John St* ✉ *L2 5QW* – ☏ *0151 294 4050*
– www.aloftliverpool.com

🏠 Hope Street 🏠 ᒪ₅ ⊟ 🛗 🏋️

TOWNHOUSE · DESIGN Minimalist boutique hotel in two adjoining buildings. Bedrooms in the former carriage works have a slightly rustic edge, while those in the old police station are more modern; the top floor suites offer stunning skyline views. The spacious restaurant is divided by large shards of glass and offers modern fare.

89 rooms ⌑ – ∤£ 101/200 ∤∤£ 113/212

Town plan: C2-a - *40 Hope St* ✉ *L1 9DA* – ☏ *0151 709 3000*
– www.hopestreethotel.co.uk

🏠 Hard Days Night 🏠 ⊟ 🛗 ᵃᶜ 🍴 🏋️

LUXURY · DESIGN Unique Beatles-themed hotel – their story recounted in artwork from doorstep to rooftop – with contemporary bedrooms featuring original works, and suites styled around Lennon and McCartney. Blakes, named after the designer of the Sgt. Pepper album cover, features a modern brasserie menu.

110 rooms – ∤£ 90/270 ∤∤£ 90/290 – ⌑ £ 16 – 2 suites

Town plan: B2-b - *Central Buildings, North John St* ✉ *L2 6RR* – ☏ *0151 236 1964*
– www.harddaysnighthotel.com

🏠 2 Blackburne Terrace 🍴 🅿️

LUXURY · ELEGANT A delightful Georgian house with plenty of personality. Individually styled bedrooms come with top quality beds, free-standing baths and extras such as fresh fruit and cut flowers. Modern art features in the large sitting room.

4 rooms ⌑ – ∤£ 160/180 ∤∤£ 160/230

Town plan: D3-c - *2 Blackburne Terr* ✉ *L8 7PJ* – ☏ *0151 708 5474*
– www.2blackburneterrace.com – *Closed mid December- early January*

𝕏𝕏𝕏 The Art School 🛗 ᵃᶜ 🅾️ 🕸️ ⇔

MODERN BRITISH · ELEGANT Bright red chairs contrast with crisp white tablecloths at this elegant restaurant, where a huge glass roof floods the room with light. The experienced local chef carefully prepares a bewildering array of colourful modern dishes.

Menu £ 29/69

Town plan: D2-s - *1 Sugnall St* ✉ *L7 7DX* – ☏ *0151 230 8600*
– www.theartschoolrestaurant.co.uk – *Closed 25-26 December,*
1 January, 1-4 August, Sunday and Monday

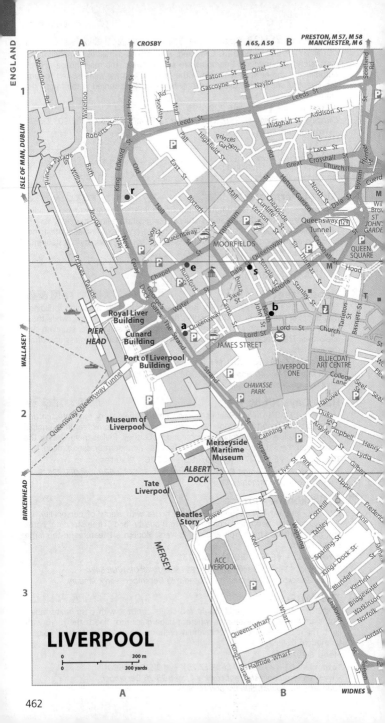

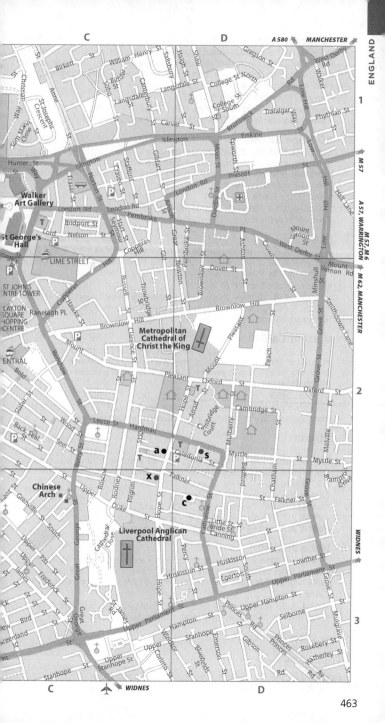

A 580 ↗ MANCHESTER

C

D

1

2

3

West Derby Rd

Walker

Gregson St

College St North

College St South

William Henry St

Saltsbury

Shaw

Halgh St

Langsdale St

Birkett

Soho

Biddar

Canterbury

Langsdale St

Carver

Brunswick

Low Hill

Trafalgar Way

Phythian St

St Josephs Crescent

Anne

Christian

St

Tom Mann Close

Way

Islington

Moss St

Erskine

Epworth St

Prescot

↗ M 57

Hunter St

St Way

Fraser

Islington

Norton St

Crayen

Stafford

Gildart

Great

London Rd

Daulby

▸ A 57, WARRINGTON

M 57, M 6

Walker Art Gallery

London Rd

London Rd

Bridport St

Pembroke

Seymour St

St Anne

St Josephs

Copperas Hill

West Derby

Mount Vernon

▸ M 57, M 62, MANCHESTER

St George's Hall

T

Lord Nelson St

LIME STREET

Copperas Hill

Hart

Russell St

Great Newton St

Dover St

Mount Vernon Rd

P

ST JOHN'S CENTRE TOWER

Copperas

Hawke St

Trowbridge St

Brownlow

Ashton

Cownl

Minshull

Grove St

Smithdown Lane

CLAYTON SQUARE SHOPPING CENTRE

Ranelagh Pl.

Brownlow Hill

Brownlow Hill

Pleasant

Peach

Oxford

St

CENTRAL

Mount

Renshaw

Metropolitan Cathedral of Christ the King

Mount

Oxford

Melville

Bold

Pleasant

Oxford St

Pl.

Leece St

Hardman

a •

T

Cambridge Court

Cambridge St

Cambridge St

Mulberry

Back Seel St

Wood St

Seel St

Berry

T

Arrad

Hope St

Caledonia

P

s •

Myrtle

Bedford

Chatham

St

Myrtle St

Brampton Drive

Roscoe

x •

Falkner

Falkner St

Chinese Arch

Grenville St South

Upper

Rodney

Pilgrim

Duke

c •

Catharine

Little St

Bride St

Canning

Hope St

St James

Upper Pitt

Upper Frederick

Great George

Cathedral Close

Liverpool Anglican Cathedral

Percy

Huskisson

Huskisson St

Egerton

Lowther St

Upper Parliament St

Grove St

Bird

Greenland

St James Rd

Great George

Hope St

Upper Parliament St

Upper Parliament St

Princes

Windsor

Hampton

Stanhope

Emerson

Bluefields

Upper Hampton St

Princes Rd

Selborne

Gibson

Princes

Rosebery

Mulgrave

▸ WIDNES

Stanhope

Upper Stanhope St

Upper Comus St

Hatherley

Rd

↙ WIDNES

C

D

463

XXX Panoramic 34 ≼ 🛦 AC

MODERN BRITISH · FASHIONABLE On the 34th floor of the city's highest sky-scraper you'll find this elegant restaurant with under-lit tables and fabulous 360° views. Ambitious dishes arrive swiftly and are attractively presented; the lunch menu offers good value.

Menu £ 27 (lunch) – Carte £ 37/47

Town plan: A1-r - West Tower (34th floor), Brook St ⊠ L3 9PJ – ✆ 0151 236 5534
– www.panoramic34.com – Closed 25-26 December, 1 January and Monday

XX 60 Hope Street AC ⇔

REGIONAL CUISINE · BRASSERIE An attractive Grade II listed Georgian house concealing a well-established modern brasserie with battleship grey walls and a smart basement wine bar. Menus feature interesting regional dishes; the set se-lection provides good value.

Menu £ 30 – Carte £ 35/57

Town plan: C3-x - 60 Hope St ⊠ L1 9BZ – ✆ 0151 707 6060
– www.60hopestreet.com – Closed 26 December

X Spire AC

MODERN BRITISH · BISTRO Simple neighbourhood restaurant set in the Penny Lane area of the city. Good value, understated menus offer regional and modern European dishes. Flavoursome cooking and friendly service.

Menu £ 17/19 – Carte £ 26/40

1 Church Rd ⊠ L15 9EA – Southeast : 3.5 mi by Upper Parliament St (A 562)
– ✆ 0151 734 5040 – www.spirerestaurant.co.uk – Closed 25-26 December,
1-7 January, Sunday and lunch Saturday and Monday

X Vincent Café 🆕 🍷 🛖 🛦 AC 🖵 ⇔

ASIAN INFLUENCES · BRASSERIE Start with a cocktail at the striking copper-fronted bar, then head through to the buzzy, glamorous brasserie. Menus offer something for everyone at any time of the day, including brasserie classics, North African dishes and sushi.

Carte £ 25/53

Town plan: A2-e - Walker House, Exchange Flags ⊠ L2 3YL – ✆ 0151 236 1331
(bookings advisable at dinner) – www.vincentcafeandcocktailbar.com

X Etsu 🆕 🛖 🛦

JAPANESE · FRIENDLY Behind a rather ordinary looking exterior lies a vibrant little restaurant. The three chefs have over 60 years' experience between them and carefully create authentic Japanese dishes which are great value – the sushi is a highlight.

Carte £ 18/32

Town plan: A2-a - Beetham Plaza, 25 The Strand ⊠ L2 0XJ – (Off Brunswick St)
– ✆ 0151 236 7530 (booking essential) – www.etsu-restaurant.co.uk – Closed
Monday and lunch Wednesday, Saturday and Sunday

X Neon Jamón

SPANISH · TAPAS BAR In the bustling Penny Lane, you'll find this equally buzzy, informal tapas bar. Service is friendly and obliging, and dishes are carefully pre-pared and full of flavour. Sit at the counter or a table backed by bare brick walls.

Carte £ 18/33

12 Smithdown Pl ⊠ L15 9EH – Southeast : 3.5 mi by Upper Parliament St (A 562)
– ✆ 0151 734 3840 (bookings not accepted) – www.neonjamon.com

LONG ASHTON - North Somerset → See Bristol

LONG COMPTON
Warwickshire – ⊠ Shipston-On-Stour – Pop. 705 – Regional map n° **10**-C3
▶ London 81 mi – Birmingham 53 mi – Liverpool 147 mi – Bristol 72 mi

🍴 Red Lion　　　　　⇦ 🛏 🎍 P

TRADITIONAL BRITISH · FRIENDLY 18C former coaching inn with flag floors, log fires and a warm, modern feel. Seasonal menu of tasty, home-cooked pub classics, with more adventurous daily specials. Keen service. Good-sized garden and children's play area. Stylish bedrooms have a contemporary, country-chic feel and a good level of facilities.

Menu £14 (lunch and early dinner) – Carte £27/36

5 rooms ⌂ – ✦£60/65 ✦✦£95/150

Main St ⊠ CV36 5JS – ℰ 01608 684221 – www.redlion-longcompton.co.uk

LONG CRENDON

Buckinghamshire – ⊠ Aylesbury – Pop. 2 335 – Regional map n° **6**-C2

▶ London 50 mi – Aylesbury 11 mi – Oxford 15 mi – Birmingham 82 mi

🍴 Mole & Chicken　　　⇦ 🛏 🎍 ⅙ P

INTERNATIONAL · RURAL A charming pub built in 1831 as part of a local farm workers' estate, with low wonky ceilings, open fires and a large garden offering commanding country views. The menu features classic British dishes and heartwarming puddings. Staff are friendly and there are five cosy bedrooms in the adjoining house.

Carte £24/37

5 rooms ⌂ – ✦£95 ✦✦£125

Easington ⊠ HP18 8EY – North 0.5 mi by Dorton rd – ℰ 01844 208387 – www.themoleandchicken.co.uk – Closed 25 December

LONG MELFORD

Suffolk – Pop. 2 898 – Regional map n° **8**-C3

▶ London 62 mi – Cambridge 34 mi – Colchester 18 mi – Ipswich 24 mi

✕✕ Scutchers　　　　　AC

TRADITIONAL CUISINE · RUSTIC This converted medieval hall house is now a smart, personally run restaurant. Cooking is skilful, classical and full of flavour; everything from the bread to the sorbet is homemade. The wine list features some top class producers.

Carte £32/52

Westgate St ⊠ CO10 9DP – on A 1092 – ℰ 01787 310200 – www.scutchers.com – Closed 2 weeks Christmas and Sunday-Wednesday

🍴 Swan ⓝ　　　　　⇦ 🛏 🎍 🗄

MODERN CUISINE · PUB Smart double-fronted pub in a characterful old wool town. The appealing menu provides plenty of choice, ranging from refined French classics to dishes with an Asian bent. From the flavoursome cooking to the eye-catching décor and stylish bedrooms, this is a place where you can really see that they care.

Carte £26/53

8 rooms ⌂ – ✦£95/165 ✦✦£125/175

Hall St ⊠ CO10 9JQ – ℰ 01787 464545 – www.longmelfordswan.co.uk

LONG SUTTON

Somerset – ⊠ Langport – Regional map n° **2**-B3

▶ London 131 mi – Bristol 39 mi – Cardiff 83 mi – Bournemouth 64 mi

🍴 Devonshire Arms　　　⇦ 🛏 🎍 ⇔ P

REGIONAL CUISINE · INN A striking Grade II listed former hunting lodge overlooking the village green. Wing-back chairs sit by an open fire and blue panelled walls are broken up by bold wallpaper. Appealing menus follow the seasons: stick with British classics or choose something Mediterranean. Bedrooms are modern and well-furnished.

Carte £25/36

9 rooms ⌂ – ✦£90/155 ✦✦£105/155

⊠ TA10 9LP – ℰ 01458 241271 – www.thedevonshirearms.com – Closed 25-26 December

LONG WHATTON

Leicestershire - Pop. 1 124 - Regional map n° **9**-B2

London 120 mi - Birmingham 43 mi - Liverpool 101 mi - Leeds 84 mi

Royal Oak

TRADITIONAL BRITISH • PUB A smartly modernised pub in a sleepy village not far from East Midlands Airport. Menus offer plenty of choice, from sharing platters and pub favourites to ambitious main courses; some with Indian or Italian influences. Well-equipped, up-to-date bedrooms are in an adjacent block; one has a whirlpool bath.

Menu £ 13 (weekday dinner) - Carte £ 21/38

7 rooms - †£ 69/89 ††£ 79/99

The Green ✉ LE12 5BD - ✆ 01509 843694 - www.theroyaloaklongwhatton.co.uk

LONGHORSLEY - Northumberland ➜ See Morpeth

LONG ROCK

Cornwall - Pop. 570 - Regional map n° **1**-B2

London 284 mi - Truro 26 mi - Exeter 109 mi

Mexico Inn (N)

TRADITIONAL BRITISH • FRIENDLY This roadside inn is run by an experienced local couple. It has a touch of the shabby-chic about it, with a wood-burner in the bar and a sunnier room to the rear; there's a lovely suntrap terrace too. Cooking is gutsy and flavourful.

Carte £ 20/28

4 Riverside ✉ TR20 8JD - ✆ 01736 710625 - www.themexicoinn.com - Closed 1 week early February, Sunday dinner and Monday

LONGSTOCK

Hampshire - ✉ Stockbridge - Regional map n° **4**-B2

London 74 mi - Bristol 77 mi - Cardiff 110 mi - Plymouth 148 mi

Peat Spade Inn

TRADITIONAL BRITISH • COSY An attractive 19C inn in the heart of the Test Valley, with fishing rights on the nearby river. Menus mix pub classics with more interesting dishes. In the evening, find a spot on the lovely terrace and cosy up beside the fire-pit. Charming bedrooms are split between the inn and an old barn.

Carte £ 26/43

8 rooms - †£ 110/145 ††£ 110/145

Village Street ✉ SO20 6DR - ✆ 01264 810612 - www.peatspadeinn.co.uk

LOOE

Cornwall - Pop. 5 112 - Regional map n° **1**-B2

London 264 mi - Plymouth 23 mi - Truro 39 mi

Beach House

FAMILY • PERSONALISED A personally run, detached house in a fantastic spot on the edge of town, looking out to sea. Bedrooms are immaculately kept; Fistral, with its balcony, is the best. The breakfast room is on the first floor and offers super views.

5 rooms - †£ 70/135 ††£ 85/135

Marine Dr, Hannafore ✉ PL13 2DH - Southwest : 0.75 mi by Quay Rd - ✆ 01503 262598 - www.thebeachhouselooe.co.uk - Closed Christmas

LORTON

Cumbria - Regional map n° **12**-A2

London 302 mi - Carlisle 33 mi - Lancaster 71 mi

New House Farm ⬅ 🏠 🍽 P

TRADITIONAL · COSY Part-17C former farmhouse with several beamed, open-fired lounges, a hot tub boasting fell views and a tea room in the old cow byres. Richly furnished bedrooms have king or super king sized beds and some feature double jacuzzis.

5 rooms ⌂ – 🛉£ 50/90 🛉🛉£ 100/180

✉ CA13 9UU – South : 1.25 mi on B 5289 – 𝒞 07841 159818
– www.newhouse-farm.co.uk

LOSTWITHIEL
Cornwall – Pop. 2 659 – Regional map n° **1**-B2
▶ London 244 mi – Bristol 148 mi – Cardiff 179 mi – Plymouth 32 mi

✕✕ Asquiths

MODERN CUISINE · INTIMATE Smartly converted shop with exposed stone walls hung with modern Cornish art, funky lampshades and contemporary styling. Confidently executed dishes feature some original flavour combinations. The atmosphere is relaxed and intimate.

Carte £ 26/33

19 North St ✉ PL22 0EF – 𝒞 01208 871714 – www.asquithsrestaurant.co.uk
– dinner only – Closed first 2 weeks January, Sunday and Monday

LOUGHBOROUGH
Leicestershire – Pop. 59 932 – Regional map n° **9**-B2
▶ London 117 mi – Birmingham 41 mi – Leicester 11 mi

✕✕ John's House (John Duffin) P
❀

MODERN CUISINE · RUSTIC A 16C farmhouse where the eponymous and talented John was born and now cooks; his family also own the surrounding farm with its shop, café, petting farm and motor museum. Produce from the surrounding fields is used to create original, interesting dishes which show a real understanding of textures and flavours.

→ Heritage carrots with ox tongue, crème fraîche and mint. Stonehurst hogget with wood blewits and charred onions. Violet cream with meringue and yoghurt.

Menu £ 28 (weekday lunch)/70

Stonehurst Farm, 139 Loughborough Rd, Mountsorrel ✉ LE12 7AR – Southeast : 4.5 mi by A 6 – 𝒞 01509 415569 (booking essential at dinner)
– www.johnshouse.co.uk – Closed Sunday and Monday

✕ Blacksmiths Arms ♿ P

TRADITIONAL CUISINE · FRIENDLY A former pub and, before that, a blacksmith's forge, built in 1753; now a stylish eatery with a sunny terrace, friendly service and a laid-back feel. Menus include all the favourites and cooking is straightforward, fresh and tasty.

Carte £ 20/40

North St, Barrow-upon-Soar ✉ LE12 8PP – Southeast : 3 mi by A 6
– 𝒞 01509 413100 – www.blacksmiths1753.co.uk – Closed Sunday dinner and Monday

LOUTH
Lincolnshire – Pop. 16 419 – Regional map n° **9**-D1
▶ London 156 mi – Boston 34 mi – Grimsby 17 mi – Lincoln 26 mi

Brackenborough ✕ 🍴 🍽 ♨ P

BUSINESS · PERSONALISED Contemporary hotel with a relaxed feel and a warm, personal style. Spacious, individually designed bedrooms have bold feature walls, Egyptian cotton linen and the latest mod cons; executive rooms come with jacuzzi baths. The bistro and conservatory lounge-bar serve grills and classics with a modern twist.

24 rooms ⌂ – 🛉£ 103/118 🛉🛉£ 111/124

Cordeaux Corner, Brackenborough ✉ LN11 0SZ – North : 2 mi by A 16
– 𝒞 01507 609169 – www.oakridgehotels.co.uk

XX **14 Upgate** 🅝

MODERN · INTIMATE This elegant townhouse conversion seats 12 diners at 6 polished tables. The modern 7 course set menu changes weekly and presents some unusual twists and turns along the way. Start with a drink in the first floor sitting room.

Menu £ 45 – tasting menu only

14 Upgate ✉ *LN11 9ET* – ✆ *01507 610610* – *www.14upgate.co.uk* – *dinner only*
– *Closed 25 December-1 February and Sunday-Tuesday*

LOVINGTON

Somerset – Regional map n° **2**-C2
▶ London 126 mi – Bristol 30 mi – Taunton 33 mi

X **Pilgrims**   ⇦ 🏠 **P**

MODERN BRITISH · RUSTIC Cosy, hugely characterful restaurant with low-beamed ceilings, flagged floors and a roaring fire; run by a passionate husband and wife team. Well-prepared, classical dishes are made with quality local produce. Comfortable, contemporary bedrooms, luxurious bathrooms and substantial breakfasts.

Carte £ 28/46

5 rooms ☕ – 🛉£ 80/130 🛉🛉£ 95/130

✉ *BA7 7PT* – ✆ *01963 240597* – *www.thepilgrimsatlovington.co.uk* – *dinner only and lunch Friday-Saturday* – *Closed Sunday and Monday*

LOW FELL

Tyne and Wear – Regional map n° **14**-B2
▶ London 272 mi – Newcastle upon Tyne 5 mi – Durham 15 mi

🏠 **Eslington Villa**   ⭐ 🍴 ⅍ 🖘 **P**

TRADITIONAL · PERSONALISED Comprising two red-brick Victorian houses in the city suburbs. It's well-run by its hand-on owners and has a relaxed atmosphere and a surprisingly large rear garden. Individually styled bedrooms have a contemporary edge. Dine from a traditional menu with modern twists in the dining room or conservatory.

18 rooms ☕ – 🛉£ 80/90 🛉🛉£ 100/120

8 Station Rd ✉ *NE9 6DR* – *West : 0.75 mi by Belle Vue Bank, turning left at T junction, right at roundabout then taking first turn right*
– ✆ *0191 487 6017* – *www.eslingtonvilla.co.uk*
– *Closed 25-26 December and 1 January*

LOW ROW – North Yorkshire ➜ See Reeth

LOWER BEEDING

West Sussex – Regional map n° **4**-D2
▶ London 40 mi – Brighton 20 mi – Guildford 25 mi – Southampton 67 mi

🏨 **South Lodge**   ⅋ ⟨ 🍴 🖼 🛆 ⅍ 🖭 ⅃ 🖘 **P**

LUXURY · HISTORIC Intricate carved fireplaces and ornate ceilings are on display in this Victorian mansion, which affords superb South Downs views from its 93 acres. Bedrooms are beautifully appointed; some are traditional and others more modern.

84 rooms ☕ – 🛉£ 195/300 🛉🛉£ 195/375 – 4 suites

Brighton Rd ✉ *RH13 6PS* – *South : 1.5 mi by B 2110 on A 281* – ✆ *01403 891711*
– *www.southlodgehotel.co.uk* – *Closed 1-14 January*

The Pass • Camellia – See restaurant listing

XX The Pass 🛏 AC 🅿

CREATIVE · FASHIONABLE A unique hotel restaurant where high level tables provide a ringside seat for the chef's at work; they both present and explain their own dishes. Cooking takes its inspiration from art and is creative, colourful and playful.
Menu £ 30/90 – tasting menu only
South Lodge Hotel, Brighton Rd ⊠ RH13 6PS – South : 1.5 mi by B 2110 on A 281 – ℰ 01403 891711 (number of covers limited, pre-book) – www.southlodgehotel.co.uk – Closed first 2 weeks January, Monday and Tuesday

XX Camellia ◁ 🛏 🛆 🅿

MODERN CUISINE · ELEGANT Named after the tree which covers the front of the house, Camellia occupies three wood-panelled rooms with grand fireplaces and chandeliers. Refined modern dishes are light but boldly flavoured and use produce from the walled garden.
Carte £ 38/66
South Lodge Hotel, Brighton Rd ⊠ RH13 6PS – South : 1.5 mi by B 2110 on A 281 – ℰ 01403 891711 – www.southlodgehotel.co.uk – Closed 1-14 January

🍴 Crabtree 🛏 🛆 ৬ 🅿

TRADITIONAL CUISINE · PUB A family-run affair with a cosy, lived-in feel, warming fires and cheery, helpful staff. Traditional English dishes come with a touch of refinement and plenty of flavour, and the wine list is well-priced and full of helpful information.
Menu £ 15 (weekdays) – Carte £ 25/40
Brighton Rd ⊠ RH13 6PT – South : 1.5 mi by B 2110 on A 281 – ℰ 01403 892666 – www.crabtreesussex.com – Closed Sunday dinner

LOWER DUNSFORTH – North Yorkshire → See Boroughbridge

LOWER ODDINGTON – Gloucestershire → See Stow-on-the-Wold

LOWER PEOVER
Cheshire East – Regional map n° **20**-B3
▶ London 181 mi – Chester 25 mi – Liverpool 35 mi

🍴 Bells of Peover 🛏 🛆 🅿

MEDITERRANEAN CUISINE · PUB 16C coaching inn set down a narrow cobbled lane; its regulars once included Generals Eisenhower and Patton. It has a cosy bar, three tastefully decorated dining rooms and a smart terrace. Italian, Greek and Turkish dishes feature.
Carte £ 24/40
The Cobbles ⊠ WA16 9PZ – ℰ 01565 722269 – www.thebellsofpeover.com

LOWER SLAUGHTER – Gloucestershire → See Bourton-on-the-Water

LUDLOW
Shropshire – Pop. 10 515 – Regional map n° **10**-B2
▶ London 162 mi – Birmingham 39 mi – Hereford 24 mi

🏡 Fishmore Hall 🌖 ◁ 🛏 🕉 🔄 ৬ 🅿

COUNTRY HOUSE · DESIGN Whitewashed Georgian mansion in half an acre of mature gardens, just out of town. Original features mix with modern fittings to create a boutique country house feel. Smart bedrooms have bold wallpapers, stylish bathrooms and good views.
15 rooms ヱ – †£ 110/210 ††£ 150/250
Fishmore Rd ⊠ SY8 3DP – North : 1.5 mi by B 4361 and Kidderminster rd on Fishmore Rd – ℰ 01584 875148 – www.fishmorehall.co.uk
Forelles – See restaurant listing

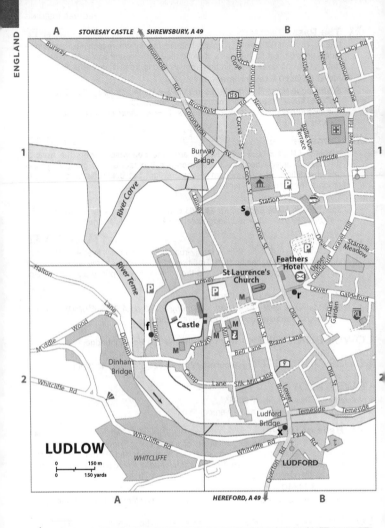

A STOKESAY CASTLE SHREWSBURY, A 49 B

HEREFORD, A 49

LUDLOW

0   150 m
0   150 yards

WHITCLIFFE

LUDFORD

🏠 **Overton Grange**   🏃 🛁 ⛷ 🛏 📺 🐾 ♨ 🅿

TRADITIONAL · CLASSIC Well-maintained Edwardian country house where sub-tle modern touches sit alongside original features. Well-equipped bedrooms and smart bathrooms. Good-sized pool, sauna and 2 treatment rooms. Dining rooms offer immaculately laid tables and countryside views; cooking has a refined French base.

14 rooms 🍽 – 🛏£ 99/199 🛏🛏£ 119/249

*Old Hereford Rd ⊠ SY8 4AD – South : 1.75 mi on B 4361 – 𝒞 01584 873500
– www.overtongrangehotel.com – Closed 28 December-9 January*

If you want the special atmosphere of a pub,
look for the 🍺 symbol.

XX Forelles

MODERN CUISINE · ELEGANT Appealing conservatory restaurant named after the pear tree outside, with lovely views over the hotel gardens. Attractively presented dishes use local produce and modern techniques, and feature good flavour and texture combinations.

Menu £ 49

Fishmore Hall Hotel, ⊠ SY8 3DP – North : 1.5 mi by B 4361 and Kidderminster rd on Fishmore Rd – ℰ 01584 875148 – www.fishmorehall.co.uk – Closed Sunday and Monday

XX Old Downton Lodge

MODERN CUISINE · RURAL Supremely characterful farm buildings, dating from medieval to Georgian times and set on the 5,500 acre Downton Estate. Cooking is modern and original; choose from a 5 or 7 course menu in the 13C barn. Bedrooms combine period features with modern amenities; 7 and 8, with their antique four-posters, are best.

Menu £ 45/55

10 rooms ⊊ – †£ 125/250 ††£ 125/250

Downton on the Rock ⊠ SY8 2HU – West : 7.5 mi by A 49, off A 4113 – ℰ 01568 771826 (booking essential) – www.olddowntonlodge.com – dinner only – Closed 22-27 December, February, Sunday and Monday

XX Mortimers ⓝ

MODERN BRITISH · ELEGANT A local forest gives this 16C townhouse restaurant its name. It has plenty of character, courtesy of exposed stone, sloping floors and lovely wood panelling. Concise set menus offer classically rooted dishes with a personal touch.

Menu £ 20/40

Town plan: B1-s - *17 Corve St ⊠ SY8 1DA – ℰ 01584 872325 – www.mortimersludlow.co.uk – Closed 29 January-10 February, 1-12 October, Sunday and Monday*

X French Pantry

FRENCH · COSY Pretty little café-cum-bistro on a paved side street, selling produce and wines imported from Parisian markets. Authentic Gallic dishes are crafted from local and French ingredients. Cooking is rustic, hearty and full of flavour.

Menu £ 22 (dinner) – Carte lunch £ 23/33

Town plan: B2-r - *15 Tower St. ⊠ SY8 1RL – ℰ 01584 879133 (booking essential) – www.thefrenchpantry.co.uk – Closed 1-5 January and Sunday*

X Green Café

MODERN BRITISH · SIMPLE A modest little eatery with a delightful waterside terrace, set in a charming 14C watermill on the banks of the River Teme. The concise lunch menu offers unfussy daily dishes which showcase British ingredients in simple, flavoursome combinations. Outside of lunch hours they serve coffee and cake.

Carte £ 16/25

Town plan: A2-f - *Mill on the Green ⊠ SY8 1EG – ℰ 01584 879872 (booking advisable) – www.thegreencafe.co.uk – lunch only and dinner Friday-Saturday June-September – Closed 4-22 January, 23-26 December and Monday*

⊓ Charlton Arms

TRADITIONAL BRITISH · RUSTIC Claude Bosi is arguably the man who put Ludlow on the map and this pub in a commanding position on the banks of the River Teme is owned by his brother Cedric and Cedric's wife, Amy. Menus have something for everyone and dishes are good value and full of flavour. Up-to-date bedrooms; most have river outlooks.

Carte £ 17/35

9 rooms ⊊ – †£ 90/110 ††£ 100/160

Town plan: B2-x - *Ludford Bridge ⊠ SY8 1PJ – ℰ 01584 872813 – www.thecharltonarms.co.uk – Closed 25-26 December*

at Cleestanton Northeast: 5.5 mi by A4117 and B4364

Timberstone ✿ ⅗ ⋖ 🖨 ⅌ 🅿

COUNTRY HOUSE · PERSONALISED This pair of cosy 17C cottages offer a wonderfully peaceful atmosphere and lovely rural views. Beamed bedrooms come with stylish modern bathrooms; one room even has its own balcony. Dine around the large farmhouse table – there's always a good selection, which includes many organic or home-grown options.

4 rooms ☑ – ♦£ 65/98 ♦♦£ 98/100

✉ SY8 3EL – ☎ 01584 823519 – www.timberstoneludlow.co.uk

LUND

East Riding of Yorkshire – Regional map n° **13**-C2

▶ London 213 mi – Leeds 61 mi – Sheffield 64 mi – Bradford 67 mi

Wellington Inn 🛜 ⅗ 🅿

TRADITIONAL BRITISH · FRIENDLY Well-run pub with beamed, open-fired bars and more formal, linen-laid dining rooms. Experienced kitchen uses quality ingredients in dishes that are generous, both in flavour and portion. Efficient service. Good selection of Yorkshire beers.

Carte £ 30/39

19 The Green ✉ YO25 9TE – ☎ 01377 217294 – www.thewellingtoninn.co.uk
– Closed 25 December, 1 January, Sunday dinner and Monday

LUPTON – Cumbria ➜ See Kirkby Lonsdale

LURGASHALL

West Sussex – Regional map n° **4**-C2

▶ London 49 mi – Bristol 124 mi – Cardiff 157 mi – Plymouth 197 mi

Barn at Roundhurst ✿ ⅗ 🖨 ⅋ ⅌ 🅿

HISTORIC · ELEGANT Beautifully restored mid-17C threshing barn, on a 250 acre working farm in the South Downs. Characterful bedrooms – in the old outbuildings – are designed by the owner and come with homemade biscuits and luxurious bathrooms. The spacious lounge features fresh flowers, sculptures and modern art. Meals use eggs and meats from the farm, along with other local ingredients.

6 rooms ☑ – ♦£ 90/200 ♦♦£ 90/220

Lower Roundhurst Farm, Jobson's Ln ✉ GU27 3BY – Northwest : 3 mi by Haslemere rd – ☎ 01428 642535 – www.thebarnatroundhurst.com

Noah's Ark Inn 🖨 🛜 🅿

TRADITIONAL CUISINE · COSY A quintessentially English pub in a picturesque village green location; its garden overlooks the cricket pitch. The gloriously rustic interior features a bar, a baronial-style room with cosy sofas and 'The Restaurant' with its large inglenook fireplace. Generous dishes keep things in the traditional vein.

Carte £ 25/36

The Green ✉ GU28 9ET – ☎ 01428 707346 – www.noahsarkinn.co.uk

LUTON

Luton – Pop. 211 228 – Regional map n° **7**-A2

▶ London 35 mi – Cambridge 36 mi – Ipswich 93 mi – Oxford 45 mi

Luton Hoo ✿ ⅗ ⋖ 🖨 🖥 🖳 📶 🛉 🎿 ⅋ 🗄 ⅙ ⛷ 🅿

GRAND LUXURY · HISTORIC Stunning 18C house in over 1,000 acres of gardens; some designed by Capability Brown. The main mansion boasts an impressive hallway, numerous beautifully furnished drawing rooms and classical, luxurious bedrooms. The marble-filled Wernher restaurant offers sophisticated modern cuisine. The old stable block houses the smart spa and the casual, contemporary brasserie.

135 rooms ☑ – ♦£ 180/340 ♦♦£ 200/340 – 9 suites

The Mansion House ✉ LU1 3TQ – Southeast : 2.5 mi by A 505 on A 1081
– ☎ 01582 734437 – www.lutonhoo.com

LYDDINGTON – Rutland ➜ See Uppingham

LYDFORD

Devon – ⊠ Okehampton – Pop. 1 734 – Regional map n° **1**-C2
▶ London 234 mi – Exeter 33 mi – Plymouth 25 mi

⫚ **Dartmoor Inn**   ⇦ 🛏 ⇧ **P**

MODERN BRITISH · PUB Rustic pub with a shabby-chic style. Low ceilings add a
cosy feel, while artwork provides a modern touch. Classic dishes are satisfying and
full of flavour and there is an emphasis on local produce; Devon Ruby Red beef
and dishes from the charcoal grill are the specialities. Spacious, elegant bedrooms.
Menu £ 13 (weekdays)/27 – Carte £ 21/46

3 rooms ⌷ – ♦£ 65/100 ♦♦£ 100/140

Moorside ⊠ EX20 4AY – East : 1 mi on A 386 – ☏ 01822 820221
– www.dartmoorinn.com – Closed Sunday dinner and Monday

LYME REGIS

Dorset – Pop. 4 712 – Regional map n° **2**-B3
▶ London 160 mi – Dorchester 25 mi – Exeter 31 mi – Taunton 27 mi

🏠 **Alexandra**   🌲 ⫷ 🛏 🛏 🖫 **P**

BOUTIQUE HOTEL · CONTEMPORARY 18C dower house with superb views over
the Cobb and out to sea. There's a small terrace and a lookout tower (for hire)
in the lovely gardens. The lounges and bedrooms are contemporary; No.12 has a
large bay window to take in the views. Modern menus are served in the formal
restaurant and conservatory.

26 rooms ⌷ – ♦£ 95 ♦♦£ 180/250

Pound St ⊠ DT7 3HZ – ☏ 01297 442010 – www.hotelalexandra.co.uk – Closed
3-29 January

🏠 **HIX Townhouse**

TOWNHOUSE · QUIRKY Georgian townhouse with stylishly understated bedrooms designed around various themes, including hunting and sailing; two rooms
have lounges and two have terraces. There's a communal kitchen and breakfast is
delivered in a hamper.

8 rooms ⌷ – ♦£ 100/155 ♦♦£ 110/165

1 Pound St ⊠ D17 3HZ – ☏ 01297 442499 – www.hixtownhouse.co.uk – Closed
January

𝒳 **HIX Oyster & Fish House**   ⇦ 🛏 ৬ 🕼

SEAFOOD · SIMPLE Modern, Scandic-style restaurant with a chef's table, a terrace and breathtaking views over Lyme Bay and the Cobb. Menus focus on the
latest catch brought in by the day boats and dishes have a likeable simplicity.
Service is charming.

Carte £ 24/41

Lister Gdns, Cobb Rd ⊠ DT7 3JP – ☏ 01297 446910 (booking essential)
– www.hixoysterandfishhouse.co.uk – Closed 3-29 January, 25-26 December,
Monday and dinner Sunday November-March

LYMINGTON

Hampshire – Pop. 15 218 – Regional map n° **4**-A3
▶ London 103 mi – Bournemouth 18 mi – Southampton 19 mi – Winchester 32 mi

🏠 **Stanwell House**   🌲 🛏

TOWNHOUSE · GRAND LUXURY An attractive 18C house. Tastefully designed
bedrooms are comfy and well-equipped: those in the original house are the
most characterful; those in the extension are more contemporary. Dine on modern British dishes in the formal bistro; the restaurant offers small plates of New
Forest produce. The trendy wine bar is themed around Sir Ben Ainslie, who
once lived here.

29 rooms ⌷ – ♦£ 109/145 ♦♦£ 109/145 – 7 suites

14-15 High St ⊠ SO41 9AA – ☏ 01590 677123 – www.stanwellhouse.com

✗✗ Elderflower   ⇐ ⑩

MODERN CUISINE · FAMILY Their motto is 'quintessentially British, with a sprinkling of French', and that's just what you'll find at this proudly run restaurant. Cooking is playful and imaginative, with elderflower always featuring somewhere on the menu. Bedrooms are simply appointed and the quay is just a stone's throw away.

Carte £ 34/45

3 rooms � – ♦£ 69/95 ♦♦£ 85/95

4-5 Quay St ⊠ SO41 3AS – 𝒞 01590 676908 – www.elderflowerrestaurant.co.uk – Closed Sunday dinner and Monday

LYMM

Warrington – Pop. 11 608 – Regional map n° **11**-B3
▶ London 190 mi – Liverpool 26 mi – Leeds 62 mi – Sheffield 68 mi

🍴 Church Green   🛏 🛋 🅿

MODERN BRITISH · PUB A double-fronted pub beside Lymm Dam, with an attractive decked terrace and a kitchen garden. Choose from an extensive list of small plates, an appealing set selection or a grill menu where you choose a cut, then add sauce and extras.

Menu £ 30 (weekdays) – Carte £ 28/58

Higher Ln ⊠ WA13 0AP – on A 56 – 𝒞 01925 752068 (booking essential) – www.thechurchgreen.co.uk – Closed 25 December

LYNDHURST

Hampshire – Pop. 2 347 – Regional map n° **4**-A2
▶ London 95 mi – Bournemouth 20 mi – Southampton 10 mi – Winchester 23 mi

🏨 Lime Wood   🛀 ⇐ 🛏 🖥 🌐 🍵 ⅃ᴢ 📶 ᴊ 🅿

LUXURY · ELEGANT Impressive Georgian mansion with a stunning spa topped by a herb garden roof. Stylish guest lounges have quality fabrics and furnishings; one is set around a courtyard and features a retractable glass roof. Beautifully furnished bedrooms boast luxurious marble-tiled bathrooms, and many have New Forest views.

33 rooms – ♦£ 330/485 ♦♦£ 330/485 – ☕ £ 25 – 14 suites

Beaulieu Rd ⊠ SO43 7FZ – Southeast : 1 mi by A 35 on B 3056 – 𝒞 023 8028 7177 – www.limewoodhotel.co.uk

Hartnett Holder & Co – See restaurant listing

✗✗ Hartnett Holder & Co   🛏 🛋 ᴊ 🅿

ITALIAN · ELEGANT Elegant restaurant in an impressive Georgian mansion, offering a relaxed, clubby feel and views over the delightful grounds. The main menu lists Italian favourites like pizzetta, pastas and risottos as well as authentic fish and meat dishes. The sharing menu offers the likes of whole duck 'family-style'.

Menu £ 25 (weekday lunch) – Carte £ 24/68

Lime Wood Hotel, Beaulieu Rd ⊠ SO43 7FZ – Southeast : 1 mi by A 35 on B 3056 – 𝒞 023 8028 7177 – www.limewood.co.uk

LYNMOUTH – Devon ➜ See Lynton

LYNTON

Devon – Pop. 1 157 – Regional map n° **1**-C1
▶ London 206 mi – Exeter 59 mi – Taunton 44 mi

🏠 Hewitt's - Villa Spaldi   🏵 🛀 ⇐ 🛏 🍽 🅿

HISTORIC · CLASSIC Splendid cliffside Arts and Crafts house in mature gardens. Antique-furnished bedrooms have up-to-date facilities, sea views and smart modern bathrooms. Informal weekday meals in wood-panelled bar; fine dining on Friday and Saturday evenings. High tea, with its homemade scones and excellent tea selection, is a must and the terrace is a delightful spot for breakfast.

8 rooms – ♦£ 95/115 ♦♦£ 140/180 – ☕ £ 14

North Walk ⊠ EX35 6HJ – 𝒞 01598 752293 – www.hewittshotel.com – Closed October-March

🏠 Castle Hill

FAMILY · PERSONALISED Stone-built house on the main street of this popular tourist village. Spacious, simply decorated bedrooms; 3 of the 7 have their own sitting area. Lounge with plenty of local info and a large fish tank. Friendly owners.

7 rooms 🖵 – ♦£ 50/75 ♦♦£ 75/95

Castle Hill ⊠ EX35 6JA – ℰ 01598 752291 – www.castlehill.biz

at Lynmouth East: 1 mi

🏠 Shelley's

TRADITIONAL · COSY A bright, keenly run hotel overlooking the sea; the eponymous poet honeymooned here in 1812. Traditionally styled guest areas include a homely lounge and a formally laid breakfast room with coastal views. Good-sized bedrooms.

11 rooms 🖵 – ♦£ 85/125 ♦♦£ 85/125

8 Watersmeet Rd ⊠ EX35 6EP – ℰ 01598 753219 – www.shelleyshotel.co.uk – Closed November-February

at Martinhoe West: 4.25 mi via Coast rd (toll) ⊠ Barnstaple

🏠 Old Rectory

TRADITIONAL · ELEGANT Built in the 19C for a rector of Martinhoe's 11C church, this quiet country retreat is in a charming spot, with a well-tended 3 acre garden and a cascading brook. Fresh, bright bedrooms are modern, yet retain period touches: Heddon and Paddock are two of the best. Comfortable dining room; simple home-cooking.

11 rooms (dinner included) 🖵 – ♦£ 175/255 ♦♦£ 190/270

⊠ EX31 4QT – ℰ 01598 763368 – www.oldrectoryhotel.co.uk – Closed November-March

MADINGLEY – Cambridgeshire → See Cambridge

MAENPORTH BEACH – Cornwall → See Falmouth

MAIDENCOMBE – Torbay → See Torquay

MAIDENHEAD

Windsor and Maidenhead – Pop. 63 580 – Regional map n° **6**-C3
▶ London 33 mi – Oxford 32 mi – Reading 13 mi

🏠 Fredrick's

BUSINESS · CLASSIC It's hard to imagine that this smart red-brick hotel – with its stylish spa – was once an inn. It's classically styled, with a marble reception, a clubby bar and a formal restaurant serving modern French dishes. Bedrooms have panelled walls and bespoke wooden furnishings, and most overlook the gardens.

37 rooms 🖵 – ♦£ 119/179 ♦♦£ 129/189 – 1 suite

Shoppenhangers Rd ⊠ SL6 2PZ – ℰ 01628 581000 – www.fredricks-hotel.co.uk

✗✗ Boulters Riverside Brasserie

MODERN BRITISH · BRASSERIE Stylish modern eatery beside a lock, on a small island in the Thames. Full-length windows open onto the terrace; superb river views. Menu offers dishes ranging from fish and chips to roast partridge, with mature steaks and lighter salads.

Menu £ 16 (lunch) – Carte £ 28/44

Boulters Lock Island ⊠ SL6 8PE – Northeast : 2.25 mi by A 4094 – ℰ 01628 621291 – www.boultersrestaurant.co.uk – Closed 27-30 December and Sunday dinner

MAIDEN NEWTON

Dorset – Regional map n° **2**-C3
▶ London 144 mi – Bristol 93 mi – Cardiff 113 mi – Southampton 66 mi

XX Le Petit Canard

TRADITIONAL BRITISH · COSY This double-fronted former shop has a welcoming feel, with its cosy beamed interior and flickering candlelight. Run by a husband and wife team, it offers a seasonal menu of classic dishes; tasty duck and homemade bread feature.

Menu £ 34

Dorchester Rd ⊠ DT2 0BE – ℰ 01300 320536 – www.le-petit-canard.co.uk – dinner only and Sunday lunch – Closed 2 weeks January, Sunday dinner, alternate Sunday lunch and Monday

MAIDENSGROVE

Oxfordshire – ⊠ Henley-On-Thames – Pop. 1 572 – Regional map n° **6**-C3
▶ London 43 mi – Oxford 23 mi – Reading 15 mi

🍴 Five Horseshoes   🛏 🛎 P

TRADITIONAL BRITISH · NEIGHBOURHOOD Charming 17C inn – a walkers' paradise – boasting a large garden and terrace with delightful country views and a wood-fired oven used for bespoke pizzas. Cooking is wholesome, with plenty of meaty dishes and a good value set lunch.

Menu £ 13 (weekday lunch) – Carte £ 23/43

⊠ RG9 6EX – ℰ 01491 641282 – www.thefivehorseshoes.co.uk – Closed Monday except bank holidays

MALDON

Essex – Pop. 21 462 – Regional map n° **7**-C3
▶ London 42 mi – Chelmsford 9 mi – Colchester 17 mi

XX Rubino Kitchen   🖥 P

MODERN BRITISH · COSY Tiny restaurant hidden away on Chigborough Farm; it's much older than it looks and has a rustic cosiness. Choose 2-5 courses from a selection of 9 fresh, flavoursome, weekly dishes. Cooking mixes English and Italian influences.

Menu £ 40 (dinner) – Carte lunch £ 17/24

Chigborough Farm, Chigborough Rd, Heybridge ⊠ CM9 4RE – East : 2.5 mi by B 1022 off B 1026 – ℰ 01621 855579 (booking essential) – www.rubinokitchen.co.uk – Closed Sunday dinner, Monday and Tuesday

MALMESBURY

Wiltshire – Pop. 6 318 – Regional map n° **2**-C2
▶ London 108 mi – Bristol 28 mi – Gloucester 24 mi – Swindon 19 mi

🏨 Whatley Manor   🐾 ← 🛏 📺 💷 🗿 🖴 ⊡ 🕭 🚿 P

LUXURY · CONTEMPORARY Charming Cotswold stone country house in 12 acres of beautiful formal gardens. Guest areas include a delightful wood-panelled sitting room, a stunning spa, a top class business centre and a private cinema. Luxurious, individually decorated bedrooms have a chic, contemporary feel and sumptuous bathrooms.

23 rooms ☕ – ♦£ 325/895 ♦♦£ 325/895 – 8 suites

Easton Grey ⊠ SN16 0RB – West : 2.25 mi on B 4040 – ℰ 01666 822888 – www.whatleymanor.com – Closed 2-6 January

    ❀❀ **The Dining Room · Le Mazot** – See restaurant listing

XXX The Dining Room

🕄🕄 **MODERN CUISINE · ELEGANT** Sophisticated country house restaurant overlooking the kitchen garden. Choose between three 6 course set menus, where original modern dishes demonstrate the technical skill of the chefs, who have an excellent understanding of combinations. Clearly defined flavours are complemented by some interesting wines.

→ Caramelised foie gras with compressed pear, ginger and sauternes sauce. Poached & roast veal with slow-braised cheek and hazelnut. Prune & orange soufflé with prune & mandarin ice cream and iced mandarin bonbon.

Menu £ 116 **s** – tasting menu only

Whatley Manor Hotel, Easton Grey ⊠ SN16 0RB – West : 2.25 mi on B 4040
– ℰ 01666 822888 (booking essential) – www.whatleymanor.com – dinner only
– Closed 2-6 January, Monday and Tuesday

XX Le Mazot

MODERN CUISINE · RUSTIC The less formal dining option at a delightful country hotel. With a comfy laid-back feel, wood panelling and carvings, it brings to mind a traditional Swiss chalet. Dishes have a modern edge and feature the occasional Swiss speciality.

Menu £ 25 (weekday lunch) – Carte £ 31/54 **s**

Whatley Manor Hotel, Easton Grey ⊠ SN16 0RB – West : 2.25 mi on B 4040
– ℰ 01666 822888 – www.whatleymanor.com – Closed 2-6 January

at Crudwell North: 4 mi on A429⊠ Malmesbury

🏠 The Rectory

COUNTRY HOUSE · CONTEMPORARY Classical 18C former rectory with high ceilings, period features and a laid-back feel. Stylish fabrics and contemporary furnishings in the lounge and bar. Bedrooms boast bold feature walls, iPod docks, Roberts radios and some antiques. Oak-panelled dining room offers carefully cooked modern dishes.

12 rooms ⊑ – 💲£ 95/205 💲💲£ 105/205
⊠ SN16 9EP – ℰ 01666 577194 – www.therectoryhotel.com

🍴 Potting Shed Pub

REGIONAL CUISINE · COSY Spacious, light-filled pub with contemporary décor, exposed beams and a relaxing feel. Monthly changing menus offer wholesome, satisfying dishes, with vegetables and herbs from their garden.

Carte £ 25/32

The Street ⊠ SN16 9EW – ℰ 01666 577833 – www.thepottingshedpub.com

MALTBY

Stockton-on-Tees – Regional map n° **14**-B3
▶ London 251 mi – Liverpool 141 mi – Leeds 69 mi – Sheffield 101 mi

🍴 Chadwicks Inn

TRADITIONAL BRITISH · NEIGHBOURHOOD This pub dates back over 200 years and was a favourite haunt of the Spitfire pilots before their missions. The à la carte menu features ambitious, intricate dishes and is supplemented by a good value set selection. The live acoustic evenings are popular, as are the wine and tapas evenings.

Menu £ 14 (weekday lunch)/28 – Carte £ 31/50

High Ln ⊠ TS8 0BG – ℰ 01642 590300 (booking advisable)
– www.chadwicksinnmaltby.co.uk – Closed 26 December, 1 January and Monday except bank holidays

MALTON

North Yorkshire – Pop. 4 888 – Regional map n° **13**-C2
▶ London 234 mi – Pickering 9 mi – Scarborough 23 mi

🏨 Talbot   ⬥ 🛏 ♿ 🅿

HISTORIC · CLASSIC Early 17C hunting lodge owned by the Fitzwilliam Estate, featuring an impressive wooden staircase and country house style rooms filled with family artefacts. Traditional bedrooms have smart marble bathrooms. Dine in the grand restaurant or in the rustic modern brasserie in the glass-enclosed courtyard.

26 rooms ⌷ – ♦£ 105/165 ♦♦£ 105/165

Yorkersgate ✉ *YO17 7AJ –* 𝒞 *01653 639096 – www.talbotmalton.co.uk*

Wentworth – See restaurant listing

XX Wentworth   🛏 ♿ 🍴 🅿

MODERN BRITISH · CLASSIC DÉCOR Grand country house restaurant with an elegant chandelier, heavy drapes and fine paintings. Good quality local and estate ingredients feature in carefully prepared, classically-based dishes. Service is amiable, from a charming team.

Carte £ 27/44

Talbot Hotel, Yorkersgate ✉ *YO17 7AJ –* 𝒞 *01653 639096 (booking advisable) – www.talbotmalton.co.uk – dinner only and Sunday lunch*

🍴 New Malton

TRADITIONAL BRITISH · PUB 18C stone pub with open fires, reclaimed furniture and photos of old town scenes. A good-sized menu offers hearty pub classics with the odd more adventurous dish thrown in; cooking is unfussy and flavoursome with an appealing Northern bias.

Carte £ 18/32

2-4 Market Pl ✉ *YO17 7LX –* 𝒞 *01653 693998 – www.thenewmalton.co.uk – Closed 25-26 December and 1 January*

MAN (Isle of)
I.O.M. – Pop. 80 058 – Regional map n° **11**-B1

Ballasalla

X Abbey   🛏 🏕 🍴 🅿

MODERN BRITISH · FRIENDLY An appealing former pub that was once a judge's house and a jam factory. Inside it's a cosy mix of the old and new; outside, a delightful terrace overlooks the abbey gardens. Careful modern British cooking showcases homemade produce.

Menu £ 28 (lunch) – Carte £ 26/65

Rushen Abbey, Mill Rd ✉ *IM9 3DB –* 𝒞 *01624 822393 – www.theabbey.im – Closed 10 January-13 February*

Douglas

🏨 Claremont   ✿ ⬥ ▣ 🍴 🛁

BUSINESS · FUNCTIONAL Smart, modern hotel made up of several Victorian seaside properties. Bedrooms have good quality dark wood furnishings, Hungarian duck feather pillows, superb wet rooms, and state-of-the-art TV and audio equipment. The large brasserie-style restaurant serves modern dishes, which are presented by a cheery team.

56 rooms ⌷ – ♦£ 95/180 ♦♦£ 120/260

18-22 Loch Promenade ✉ *IM1 2LX –* 𝒞 *01624 617068 – www.claremont.im*

🏨 Regency   ✿ ⬥ ▣ 🍴 🛁

TRADITIONAL · PERSONALISED Restored Victorian townhouse featuring wood panelling, stained glass and a substantial collection of seascape watercolours. Bedrooms are well-equipped for business travellers and mobile phones and iPads are available on loan.

38 rooms ⌷ – ♦£ 85/140 ♦♦£ 115/195 – 4 suites

Queens Promenade ✉ *IM2 4NN –* 𝒞 *01624 680680 – www.regency.im*

⌂ Inglewood

TOWNHOUSE · FUNCTIONAL Modern hotel at the quieter end of the promenade; the front-facing rooms enjoy views over the bay. Spacious bedrooms have chunky, contemporary furnishings, leather armchairs and modern shower rooms. Well-stocked residents' bar.

16 rooms ⌸ – ♦£ 43/85 ♦♦£ 85/125

26 Palace Terr, Queens Promenade ⊠ *IM2 4NF –* ☏ *01624 674734*
– www.inglewoodhotel-isleofman.com – Closed mid-end October and Christmas-New Year

XX Portofino

INTERNATIONAL · DESIGN This proudly run restaurant is on the ground floor of a chic apartment block on the harbour's edge. Menus offer classical international dishes with lots of Italian choices and verbally presented specials. Tables are smartly laid.

Menu £ 12 (weekdays)/29 – Carte £ 28/50

Quay West ⊠ *IM1 5AG –* ☏ *01624 617755 – www.portofino.im – Closed 25 December, Saturday lunch and Sunday*

XX Macfarlane's

MODERN BRITISH · COSY Small restaurant in the heart of town, run by a personable couple. Sit in high-sided booths or on tall banquettes. Unfussy menus rely on fresh local produce; the blackboard specials have fresh fish and shellfish to the fore.

Menu £ 15 (weekday lunch) – Carte £ 28/54

24 Duke St ⊠ *IM1 2AY –* ☏ *01624 624777 (booking essential)*
– www.macfarlanes.im – dinner only and lunch Thursday-Friday – Closed 2 weeks late July-early August, Saturday lunch, Sunday and Monday

X Tanroagan

SEAFOOD · BISTRO Friendly restaurant off the quayside, with seafaring décor and a cosy feel. Fish from the island's day boats are simply cooked, making the most of their natural flavours. Portions are hearty; bread, desserts and ice creams are homemade.

Menu £ 17 (weekday lunch) – Carte £ 27/54

9 Ridgeway St ⊠ *IM1 1EW –* ☏ *01624 612355 – www.tanroagan.co.uk – Closed 25-26 December and Sunday*

Ramsey

🏠 River House

TRADITIONAL · PERSONALISED Attractive Georgian country house in an idyllic riverside setting; its bright, spacious interior filled with antique furnishings and objets d'art. Traditional bedrooms come with floral fabrics, knick-knacks and large baths.

4 rooms ⌸ – ♦£ 70/90 ♦♦£ 95/140

⊠ *IM8 3DA – North : 0.25 mi by A 9 turning left immediately after bridge*
– ☏ *01624 816412 – www.theriverhouse-iom.com*

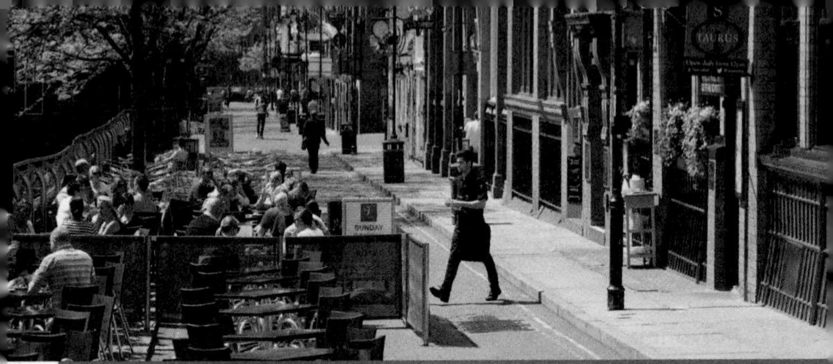

GOOD TIPS!

The Manchester dining scene has exploded in recent years and now offers a vibrancy and diversity unrivalled outside of London. Sample tasty, authentic tapas at **El Gato Negro** in the city centre; try modern Indian cuisine at **Asha's**; or enjoy the best of British at **Damson** restaurant, part of the Salford Quays – symbol of this cool city's continued regeneration.

MANCHESTER

Greater Manchester – Pop. 510 746 – Regional map n° **11**-B2
London 202 mi – Birmingham 86 mi – Glasgow 221 mi – Leeds 43 mi

Hotels

Lowry

LUXURY • DESIGN Modern and hugely spacious, with excellent facilities, an impressive spa and a minimalist feel: art displays and exhibitions feature throughout. Stylish bedrooms with oversized windows; some have river views. The airy first floor restaurant serves a wide-ranging menu.

165 rooms – £ 119/739 £ 119/739 – £ 22 – 7 suites

Town plan: A1-n - *50 Dearmans Pl, Chapel Wharf, Salford M3 5LH - 0161 827 4000 – www.thelowryhotel.com*

Radisson Blu Edwardian

BUSINESS • GRAND LUXURY This 14 floor hotel cleverly incorporates the façade of the former Free Trade Hall and has a great pool and spa. Bedrooms are contemporary – some have part-covered verandas; the Valentino Suite is the best and offers superb views. Sultry 'Opus One' is popular for afternoon tea, cocktails and seasonal modern dinners. Informal 'Steak and Lobster' serves an all-day menu.

263 rooms – £ 140/360 £ 140/360 – £ 21 – 4 suites

Town plan: A2-a - *Free Trade Hall, Peter St M2 5GP – 0161 835 9929 - www.radissonblu-edwardian.com*

Hotel Gotham

LUXURY • ELEGANT This Grade II listed former bank has something of a Manhattan-style exterior, hence its name. Stylish modern bedrooms have black and white prints of Manchester and New York on the walls and some have projected 'wonderwalls' instead of windows. The delightful all-day dining room serves English classics.

60 rooms – £ 129/500 £ 149/500

Town plan: B2-e - *100 King St M2 4WU – 0161 413 0000 - www.hotelgotham.co.uk*

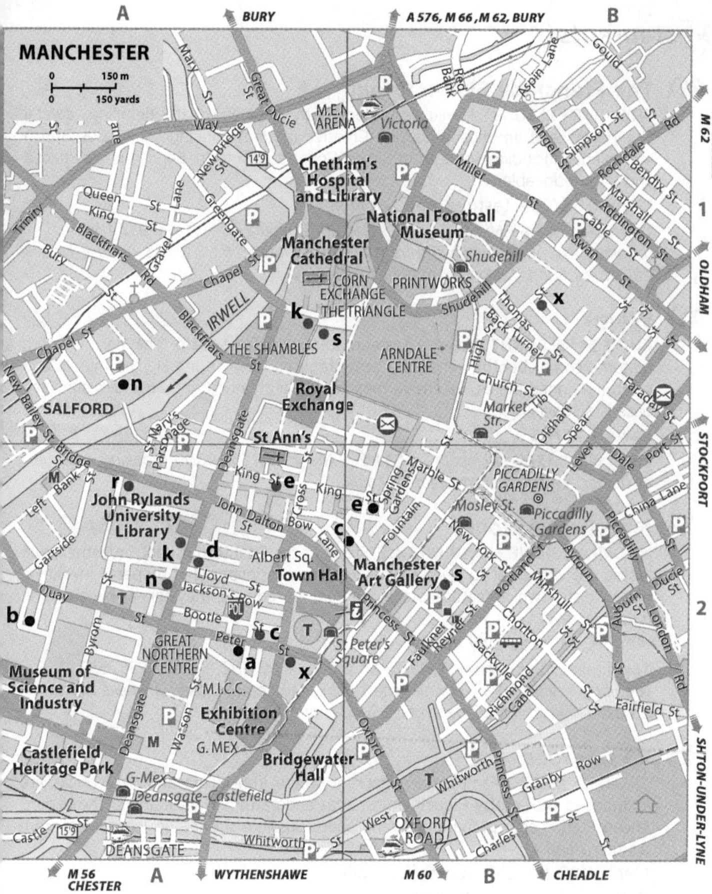

King Street Townhouse

TOWNHOUSE • CONTEMPORARY A boutique townhouse in an impressive Italianate building designed in 1872 by local architect Edward Salomons. Stylish bedrooms have super king sized beds and top quality furnishings. Relax in the infinity plunge pool looking out across the rooftops then sit on bold red banquettes and enjoy bistro classics.

40 rooms – †£ 150/210 ††£ 150/420 – ☕ £ 18

Town plan: B2-c - *10 Booth St ✉ M2 4AW - ✆ 0161 667 0707 - www.kingstreettownhouse.co.uk*

Great John Street

HISTORIC • CONTEMPORARY This stylish, boutique hotel was once a wonderful Victorian schoolhouse; you can hold a meeting in the old Headmaster's study! All of the bedrooms are duplex suites with roll-top baths. Relax on the roof terrace with its cocktail bar and hot-tub. There's no restaurant but they do offer room service.

30 rooms – †£ 210/340 ††£ 210/340 – ☕ £ 18

Town plan: A2-b - *Great John St ✉ M3 4FD - ✆ 0161 831 3211 - www.greatjohnstreet.co.uk*

ENGLAND

Restaurants

XXX The French by Simon Rogan   AC

CREATIVE · ELEGANT Iconic restaurant with original ornate detailing, crystal chandeliers and an unusual carpet. Creative modern cooking showcases British ingredients, including some from Simon Rogan's own farm. Service is well-paced and knowledgeable.

Menu £ 65/85 – tasting menu only

Town plan: A2-x – Midland Hotel. Peter St. ✉ M60 2DS – ℰ 0161 932 4198 (booking essential) – www.the-french.co.uk – Closed first 2 weeks August, 1 week Christmas, Sunday, Monday and lunch Tuesday

XXX Wings   AC

CHINESE · ELEGANT Well-run restaurant off a busy square. The narrow room features comfy booths, terracotta army replicas, Hong Kong skyline murals and celebrity-signed plates. Extensive menus offer authentic Cantonese dim sum; sea bass is a speciality.

Carte £ 25/63

Town plan: A2-d - 1 Lincoln Sq ✉ M2 5LN – ℰ 0161 834 9000 (booking essential at dinner) – www.wingsrestaurant.co.uk

XX Manchester House   🍽 🏠 ⅙ AC 🕐 ⇔

MODERN CUISINE · FASHIONABLE Step out the lift into this cool, industrial style restaurant with floor to ceiling windows. The passionate chef prepares inventive, playful dishes which feature lots of different ingredients; they serve only a tasting menu Sat eve.

Menu £ 28 (weekday lunch) – Carte approx. £ 70

Town plan: A2-r - Tower 12, 18-22 Bridge St ✉ M3 3BZ – ℰ 0161 835 2557 (booking advisable) – www.manchesterhouse.uk.com – Closed 2 weeks January, 2 weeks August, 25-26 December, Sunday and Monday

XX 63 Degrees   🏠 ⅙ AC

FRENCH · BISTRO Family-run restaurant where iron pillars and bare bricks are juxtaposed with pretty French lampshades and patterned wallpapers. The experienced French chef prepares accomplished, classic dishes using ingredients from his homeland.

Menu £ 20 (lunch) – Carte £ 27/60

Town plan: B1-x - 104 High Street ✉ M4 1HQ – ℰ 0161 832 5438 – www.63degrees.co.uk – Closed Monday

XX Mr Cooper's   🍽 ⅙ AC 🍽

MODERN CUISINE · BRASSERIE This unique restaurant is inspired by Thomas Cooper's house and gardens, which stood here until 1819. Start with drinks in the 'library', then dine in the indoor 'garden'. Dishes are modern and flavoursome with global influences.

Menu £ 20/24 – Carte £ 29/46

Town plan: A2-x - Midland Hotel, Peter St ✉ M60 2DS – ℰ 0161 932 4198 – www.mrcoopershouseandgarden.co.uk

XX Asha's 🆕   🍽 ⅙ AC 🕐

INDIAN · ELEGANT Start in the intimately lit basement cocktail bar then move up to the exotic, glamorous restaurant. The modern Indian menu offers both 'Classic' and 'Creative' curries; kebabs are a specialty, as is the traditional masala recipe.

Menu £ 21 (weekday lunch) – Carte £ 26/34

Town plan: A2-c - 47 Peter St ✉ M2 3NG – ℰ 0161 832 5309 – www.ashasrestaurant.co.uk

✗✗ Australasia 🍷 AC 🍽

MODERN CUISINE · TRENDY Fun, fashionable basement restaurant on the site of the old Manchester Evening News; come for cocktails, small plates, sushi, DJs and a clubby vibe. Vibrant dishes have European, Pacific Rim and Asian influences. Helpful staff.

Menu £16 (weekday lunch) – Carte £25/78

Town plan: A2-k - 1 The Avenue, Spinningfields ✉ M3 3AP – ℰ 0161 831 0288 – www.australasia.uk.com – Closed 25-26 December and 1 January

✗✗ San Carlo Bottega 🍷 ≤ & AC 🖵 🍽

ITALIAN · TAPAS BAR Take time out from shopping at Selfridges to relax in the elegant cocktail bar or long, brasserie-like dining room, which offers views across to the Cathedral. Tasty cicchetti dishes use fine Italian produce and arrive as they're ready.

Carte £20/30

Town plan: A1-s - Selfridges (2nd floor), 1 Exchange Square Central ✉ M3 1BD – ℰ 0161 838 0571 – www.sancarlobottega.co.uk – Closed 25 December

✗ El Gato Negro 🆕 🕸 🍷 & AC 🍽
🕸

SPANISH · TAPAS BAR 'The Black Cat' sits in a three storey building in a pedestrianised street. The ground floor bar offers snacks and charcuterie, the first floor houses an industrial-style dining room and the third floor boasts a cocktail bar with a retractable roof. Appealing tapas dishes include meats from the Josper grill.

Carte £17/31

Town plan: A2-e - 52 King St ✉ M2 4LY – ℰ 0161 694 8585 (booking essential) – www.elgatonegrotapas.com – Closed Christmas

✗ Second Floor Brasserie at Harvey Nichols 🕸 🍷 & AC 🖵 🍽

MODERN BRITISH · DESIGN Take a break from shopping and head for this relaxed restaurant with huge windows overlooking the street below. Choose from small plates, seasonal mains and steaks from the charcoal grill; they also serve brunch and afternoon tea.

Carte £20/39

Town plan: A1-k - 21 New Cathedral St ✉ M1 1AD – ℰ 0161 828 8898 – www.harveynichols.com – Closed 25 December, 1 January, Easter Sunday and dinner Sunday-Monday

✗ Hawksmoor Manchester 🍷 & AC

MEATS AND GRILLS · BISTRO A large former probate office with plenty of charm and character. Have a bespoke beer and snacks at the bar or head through to the high-ceilinged dining room. The bovine-based menu offers steaks for one or to share, from 500g-1kg.

Menu £25/28 – Carte £23/60

Town plan: A2-n - 184-186 Deansgate ✉ M3 3WB – ℰ 0161 836 6980 – www.thehawksmoor.com

✗ Yuzu AC

JAPANESE · SIMPLE Climb the steps to the upper floor of this converted Victorian warehouse, where you'll find an open kitchen, a counter and four communal tables. The Japanese cooking is fresh, authentic and healthy; the dumplings are delicious.

Carte £10/21

Town plan: B2-s 39 Faulkner St ✉ M1 4EE – ℰ 0161 236 4159 (booking advisable) – www.yuzumanchester.co.uk – Closed Christmas-New Year, Sunday and Monday

at West Didsbury South : 4.75 mi by A 5103✉ Manchester

✗ Rose Garden

TRADITIONAL CUISINE · NEIGHBOURHOOD This stylish little restaurant is a family project, with siblings and parents all involved, from the design and installation to the day-to-day running. Tasty modern dishes use top ingredients and there's a good value set menu Sun-Weds.

Carte £27/42

218 Burton Rd ✉ M20 2LW – ℰ 0161 478 0747 – www.therosegardendidsbury.com – dinner only – Closed 25-26 December and 1 January

ENGLAND

at Didsbury South: 5.5 mi by A5103 on A5145⊠ Manchester

🏠 Didsbury House   ♿ P

LUXURY · PERSONALISED A whitewashed Victorian villa with original features and a boutique feel – look out for the impressive stained glass window. Stylish, well-appointed bedrooms include duplex suites. There's no designated restaurant area but you can dine from an accessible menu in the bar and lounges or in your room. They also own similarly styled Eleven Didsbury Park, just down the road.

27 rooms – 🛏£100/150 🛏£100/150 – ⌷ £16 – 2 suites

Didsbury Pk ⊠ M20 5LJ – South : 1.5 mi on A 5145 – ℰ 0161 448 2200
– www.didsburyhouse.com

at Salford Quays Southwest: 2.25 mi by A56 off A5063⊠ Manchester

XX Damson   🍷 < ♿ AC 🎔

MODERN CUISINE · FASHIONABLE Enter into the sleek MediaCityUK – home of the BBC – and head for this smart first floor restaurant on the quayside. The elaborate à la carte menu offers refined, modern dishes and the full-length windows afford great water views.

Menu £25 (weekdays) – Carte £32/50

Orange Building, Media City ⊠ M50 2HF – ℰ 0161 660 3615
– www.damsonrestaurant.co.uk – Closed Monday and Sunday dinner

---

MANSFIELD

Nottinghamshire – Pop. 77 551 – Regional map n° **9**-B1
▶ London 143 mi – Chesterfield 12 mi – Worksop 14 mi

XX No.4 Wood Street   AC ⇔ P

TRADITIONAL BRITISH · RUSTIC Modern restaurant on the first floor of a converted warehouse. Exposed stone walls and chunky wood furniture give it a rustic feel. Classical cooking has clearly defined flavours. Start with a speciality gin in the spacious lounge.

Menu £16/39

4 Wood St ⊠ NG18 1QA – ℰ 01623 424824 (booking advisable)
– www.4woodstreet.co.uk – Closed Sunday dinner, Monday and Tuesday

MARAZION

Cornwall – ⊠ Penzance – Pop. 1 294 – Regional map n° **1**-A3
▶ London 318 mi – Penzance 3 mi – Truro 26 mi

🏠 Mount Haven   ⋔ < 🛏 🛋 P

COUNTRY HOUSE · PERSONALISED Small hotel overlooking St Michael's Bay, with a spacious bar and a lounge featuring Indian fabrics and artefacts. Contemporary bedrooms come with good modern amenities and most have a balcony and a view. Bright, attractive dining room offers elaborate modern dishes with ambitious flavour combinations.

18 rooms ⌷ – 🛏£90/140 🛏£130/240

Turnpike Rd ⊠ TR17 0DQ – East : 0.25 mi – ℰ 01736 710249
– www.mounthaven.co.uk – Closed 20 December-10 February

X Ben's Cornish Kitchen   ♿

MODERN CUISINE · SIMPLE Rustic family-run eatery; sit upstairs for views over the rooftops to St Michael's Mount. Unfussy lunches are followed by sophisticated dinners, which feature some interesting flavour combinations. They offer 25 wines by the glass.

Menu £20/29

West End ⊠ TR17 0EL – ℰ 01736 719200 – www.benscornishkitchen.com – Closed 25-26 December, 1 January, Sunday and Monday

at Perranuthnoe Southeast: 1.75 mi by A394 ✉ Penzance

🏠 Ednovean Farm   ⌖ ⌖ ⌖ ⌖ P

FAMILY · PERSONALISED 17C granite barn in a tranquil spot overlooking the bay and surrounded by 22 acres of sub-tropical gardens and paddocks. Individually styled bedrooms feature local toiletries; the Blue Room has a French bed, a roll-top bath and a terrace. Complimentary sherry is left in the hall. Have a range-cooked breakfast at the oak table or a continental selection in bed.

3 rooms ☲ – ♦£ 110/140 ♦♦£ 110/140

✉ TR20 9LZ – ☎ 01736 711883 – www.ednoveanfarm.co.uk – Closed Christmas

🍸 Victoria Inn   ⇔ 🏠 P

CLASSIC CUISINE · PUB A well-established, bright pink pub, in a small village close to the sea; the owner is a local returned home. Menus stick mainly to the classics and fish, landed at nearby Newlyn, is in abundance. Be sure to save room for one of the tasty puddings! Cosy, unfussy bedrooms have a seaside feel.

Carte £ 25/41

2 rooms ☲ – ♦£ 75/85 ♦♦£ 75/85

✉ TR20 9NP – ☎ 01736 710309 – www.victoriainn-penzance.co.uk – Closed 25 December and 1 January

MARGATE

Kent – Pop. 61 223 – Regional map n° **5**-D1

▶ London 74 mi – Canterbury 17 mi – Dover 21 mi – Maidstone 43 mi

🏨 Sands   ⌖ ⌖ ⌖ ⌖ 🆎 ⌖ ⌖ P

BOUTIQUE HOTEL · PERSONALISED Set between the high street and the sea – a smartly refurbished hotel, with extremely stylish bedrooms. Have a cocktail in the white leather furnished lounge-bar overlooking the beach before watching the sun go down from the roof terrace. The brasserie serves modern British dishes and also shares the view.

20 rooms ☲ – ♦£ 120/200 ♦♦£ 120/200

16 Marine Dr ✉ CT9 1DH – (entrance on High St) – ☎ 01843 228228 – www.sandshotelmargate.co.uk

🏠 Crescent Victoria   ⌖ ⌖ ⌖

TOWNHOUSE · PERSONALISED Classic Georgian terraced house with pleasant views over the Winter Gardens and Margate Sands. Most of the bedrooms share the outlook and all are boldly decorated and come with quality linens and very comfortable beds. The modern cellar restaurant has a suntrap terrace and serves an all-encompassing menu.

14 rooms ☲ – ♦£ 60/120 ♦♦£ 85/180

25-26 Ford Cres ✉ CT9 1HX – ☎ 01843 230375 – www.crescentvictoria.co.uk

🏠 Reading Rooms   ⌖

TOWNHOUSE · PERSONALISED Passionately run guesthouse with original plaster walls and worn woodwork. Three bedrooms – one per floor – boast distressed furniture, super-comfy beds, huge bathrooms and Square views. Extensive breakfasts are served in your room.

3 rooms ☲ – ♦£ 95/180 ♦♦£ 95/180

31 Hawley Sq ✉ CT9 1PH – ☎ 01843 225166 – www.thereadingroomsmargate.co.uk

🍴 Ambrette Margate   🆎 ⌖ P

INDIAN · COSY Quirky restaurant with modest surroundings. The concise menu showcases Kentish produce in an original modern style; freshly prepared dishes offer well-balanced flavours and subtle Indian spicing – you won't find any curries here!

Menu £ 21 (lunch) – Carte £ 31/52

44 King St ✉ CT9 1QE – ☎ 01843 231504 – www.theambrette.co.uk – Closed Monday in winter

MARKET RASEN

Lincolnshire – Pop. 4 773 – Regional map n° **9**-C1

London 158 mi – Nottingham 54 mi – Kingston upon Hull 37 mi – Sheffield 53 mi

Advocate Arms

TRADITIONAL BRITISH • INN Former hotel close to the market square, with an original revolving door and a smart, modern interior divided by etched glass walls. Lunch sticks to good old pub classics and at dinner, mature local steaks are a speciality; they also serve breakfast and afternoon tea. Bedrooms are spacious and well-equipped.

Menu £ 19 (weekday lunch) – Carte £ 20/43

10 rooms – †£ 50/90 ††£ 50/130 – ☕£ 8

2 Queen St ✉ LN8 3EH – ✆ 01673 842364 – www.advocatearms.co.uk – Closed Sunday dinner except in December

MARLBOROUGH

Wiltshire – Pop. 8 092 – Regional map n° **2**-D2

London 84 mi – Bristol 47 mi – Southampton 40 mi – Swindon 12 mi

at Little Bedwyn East: 9.5 mi by A4 ✉ Marlborough

XX Harrow at Little Bedwyn (Roger Jones)

✿ MODERN CUISINE • INTIMATE A red-brick former pub off the beaten track, with an intimate, understated style; look out for the wine bottle capsule pictures. Assured cooking has a classical base but there are plenty of modern elements too. The comprehensive wine list champions the New World and they offer wine pairings with every menu.

→ Sashimi of diver-caught Orkney scallops with English asparagus and Périgord truffle. Grey leg partridge with game bonbon, apple sauce and cabbage. Tasting of Yorkshire rhubarb.

Menu £ 30/50

✉ SN8 3JP – ✆ 01672 870871 – www.theharrowatlittlebedwyn.com – Closed 25 December-4 January and Sunday-Tuesday

at West Overton West: 4 mi on A4

Bell

MODERN BRITISH • PUB A simple, friendly pub, rescued from oblivion by a local couple, who hired an experienced pair to run it. The menu mixes pub classics with Mediterranean-influenced dishes; presentation is modern but not at the expense of flavour.

Carte £ 23/40

Bath Rd ✉ SN8 1QD – ✆ 01672 861099 – www.thebellwestoverton.co.uk – Closed Sunday dinner and Monday except bank holidays

MARLDON

Devon – Pop. 1 906 – Regional map n° **1**-C2

London 193 mi – Plymouth 30 mi – Torbay 3 mi – Exeter 23 mi

Church House Inn

TRADITIONAL BRITISH • PUB A charming, well-run inn with wooden beams, open fires and eye-catching Strawberry Gothic windows. Several blackboards offer a range of classically based dishes with Mediterranean influences, including tapas and sharing plates.

Carte £ 24/38

Village Rd ✉ TQ3 1SL – ✆ 01803 558279 – www.churchhousemarldon.com – Closed 25 December and dinner 26 December

MARLOW

Buckinghamshire – Pop. 14 823 – Regional map n° **6**-C3

London 35 mi – Aylesbury 22 mi – Oxford 29 mi – Reading 14 mi

🏨 Compleat Angler ✿ ⪕ 🛏 ▣ AC 🛁 P

TRADITIONAL · CLASSIC Well-kept hotel in an idyllic spot on the Thames, with views of the weir and the chain bridge. Comfy, corporate-style bedrooms blend classic furnishings with contemporary fabrics: some have balconies – go for a Feature Room. The restaurants offer modern British and South Indian cooking overlooking the river.

64 rooms ☕ – 🛉£125/275 🛉🛉£125/300 – 3 suites

Marlow Bridge, Bisham Rd ✉ SL7 1RG – ☎ 0344 879 9128
– www.macdonald-hotels.co.uk/compleatangler

Sindhu – See restaurant listing

XX Sindhu ⪕ AC 🕙 P

INDIAN · INTIMATE Traditional stained glass and dark wood blend with bold modern fabrics in this glitzy waterside restaurant within a smart hotel. Authentic South Indian cooking is confidently spiced and features specialities from the tandoor oven.

Menu £20 (lunch) – Carte £22/35

Compleat Angler Hotel, Marlow Bridge, Bisham Rd ✉ SL7 1RG – ☎ 01628 405405
– www.sindhurestaurant.co.uk

XX Vanilla Pod 🏛 AC 🕙 ⇌

FRENCH · INTIMATE An intimate, well-established restaurant in T. S. Eliot's former home, featuring a plush interior and smartly laid tables. The chef works alone, cooking ambitious dishes with classical French foundations and original touches.

Menu £20/45 **s**

31 West St ✉ SL7 2LS – ☎ 01628 898101 (booking essential)
– www.thevanillapod.co.uk – Closed 24 December-8 January, Sunday, Monday and bank holidays

🛏 Hand and Flowers (Tom Kerridge) ⪕ P

🏵🏵 **MODERN BRITISH · FRIENDLY** A pretty little pub with low beams, flagged floors and a characterful lounge bar for pre and post-dinner drinks. Classic dishes display assured flavours, with quality ingredients marrying perfectly to turn the simple into the sublime. A lucky few get to dine without booking at the metal-topped bar counter. Bedrooms are beautifully furnished; some have outdoor jacuzzis.
➜ Duck liver parfait with orange chutney and toasted brioche. Wiltshire pork with pickled cabbage, garlic sausage and malted cheek beignet. Chocolate and ale cake with salted caramel and muscovado ice cream.

Menu £20 (weekday lunch) – Carte £48/66

8 rooms ☕ – 🛉£140/190 🛉🛉£140/190

126 West St. ✉ SL7 2BP – ☎ 01628 482277 (booking essential)
– www.thehandandflowers.co.uk – Closed 24-26 December

🛏 The Coach

🏵 **MODERN BRITISH · FRIENDLY** Tom Kerridge's second pub offers a casual modern approach to dining. There are no starters or main courses, just flavoursome 'Meat' and 'No Meat' dishes that arrive as they're ready and are designed for sharing. Rotisserie dishes are a speciality and they also serve tasty breakfasts and coffee and cake.

Carte £17/35

3 West St ✉ SL7 2LS (bookings not accepted) – www.thecoachmarlow.co.uk
– Closed 25 December

🛏 Royal Oak 🛏 🏛 P

MODERN BRITISH · PUB Part-17C, country-chic pub with a herb garden, a petanque pitch and a pleasant terrace. Set close to the M40 and M4, it's an ideal London getaway. Cooking is British-led; wash down an ox cheek pasty with a pint of local Rebellion ale.

Carte £22/42

Frieth Rd, Bovingdon Green ✉ SL7 2JF – West : 1.25 mi by A 4155
– ☎ 01628 488611 – www.royaloakmarlow.co.uk – Closed 25-26 December

at Little Marlow East: 3 mi on A4155

🏚 Queens Head   🍴 🅿

TRADITIONAL BRITISH · FRIENDLY A charming 16C pub with a keen owner and friendly staff; popular with walkers. The light lunch menu offers sandwiches and pub classics; the regularly changing à la carte features produce from local farms, forages and shoots.

Carte £ 25/39

Pound Ln ⊠ SL7 3SR – ℰ 01628 482927 – www.marlowslittlesecret.co.uk – Closed 25-26 December

MARTINHOE – Devon ➜ See Lynton

MARTON CUM GRAFTON
North Yorkshire – Regional map n° **13**-B2
▶ London 206 mi – Birmingham 136 mi – Liverpool 103 mi – Leeds 28 mi

🏚 Punch Bowl Inn   🍴 🏠 ♻ 🅿

TRADITIONAL BRITISH · RUSTIC A delightful crescent-shaped, part-14C inn, comprising several little rooms and a lovely terrace. The all-encompassing menu includes a seafood platter and a Yorkshire board, along with excellent fish and chips and rib-eye steak.

Carte £ 23/50

⊠ YO51 9QY – ℰ 01423 322519 – www.thepunchbowlmartoncumgrafton.com

MARTON
Cheshire East – Regional map n° **20**-B3
▶ London 180 mi – Chester 34 mi – Manchester 26 mi

✗ La Popote ⓝ   🍴 🏠 ♿ 🅿

CLASSIC FRENCH · BISTRO With its French-themed prints and bistro feel, this is the perfect destination for Francophiles; ask for a table overlooking the garden or head for the terrace. The menu is a roll-call of tasty Gallic classics; lunch is good value.

Menu £ 20 (weekday lunch) – Carte £ 24/48

⊠ SK11 9HF – ℰ 01260 224785 (booking essential) – www.la-popote.co.uk – Closed Sunday dinner, Monday and Tuesday

MARTON
Shropshire – Regional map n° **10**-A2
▶ London 181 mi – Leeds 133 mi – Sheffield 132 mi – Manchester 95 mi

🏚 Sun Inn   🏠 🅿

TRADITIONAL CUISINE · PUB A traditional, family-run country pub on the English-Welsh border, with a cosy bar and a brightly painted restaurant. The concise, regularly changing menu offers comforting home-cooked dishes which include some tasty fish specials.

Carte £ 24/38

⊠ SY21 8JP – ℰ 01938 561211 – www.suninn.org.uk – Closed Sunday dinner, Monday and lunch Tuesday

MASHAM
North Yorkshire – ⊠ Ripon – Pop. 1 205 – Regional map n° **13**-B1
▶ London 231 mi – Leeds 38 mi – Middlesbrough 37 mi – York 32 mi

🏰 Swinton Park   🌿 ≤ 🍴 🎬 🔄 ♿ 🏋 🅿

HISTORIC · CLASSIC 17C castle with Georgian and Victorian additions, set on a 22,000 acre estate. The grand interior features open fires, ornate plasterwork, oil portraits and antiques. Try your hand at shooting, fishing, riding, falconry or cooking.

31 rooms (dinner included) ⊡ – †£ 195 ††£ 195/405 – 4 suites
Swinton ⊠ HG4 4JH – Southwest : 1 mi – ℰ 01765 680900 – www.swintonpark.com
Samuels – See restaurant listing

𝕏𝕏𝕏𝕏 Samuels   ≤ 🚗 ⅋ 🕙 ⇆ 🅿

MODERN BRITISH · ELEGANT Set within a castle, a beautiful rococo-style dining room with an ornate gilt ceiling and park views. Well-spaced tables are adorned with lilies. Complex modern cooking uses produce from the huge kitchen gardens and local suppliers.

Menu £ 58

Swinton Park Hotel, Swinton ⊠ HG4 4JH – Southwest : 1 mi – ☎ 01765 680900
(booking essential) – www.swintonpark.com – dinner only and lunch Saturday-Sunday

𝕏𝕏 Vennell's

TRADITIONAL BRITISH · INTIMATE This personally run restaurant has purple walls, boldly patterned chairs and a striking feature wall – at weekends, sit downstairs surrounded by local art. Seasonal menus offer 4 choices per course and cooking has a modern edge.

Menu £ 35 **s**

7 Silver St ⊠ HG4 4DX – ☎ 01765 689000 (booking essential)
– www.vennellsrestaurant.co.uk – dinner only and Sunday lunch – Closed first
2 weeks January, 1 week Easter, 1 week August, Sunday dinner and Monday

MATFIELD
Regional map n° **5**-B2
▶ London 43 mi – Maidstone 15 mi – Royal Tunbridge Wells 6 mi

🍽 Wheelwrights Arms   🏡 🅿

TRADITIONAL BRITISH · RUSTIC 17C former Kentish farmhouse: outside it's all clapboard and colourful flower baskets; inside it's rustic with low beamed ceilings crammed with hanging hops. Expect an abundance of local, seasonal produce in classic dishes.

Carte £ 22/43

The Green ⊠ TN12 7JX – ☎ 01892 722129
– www.thewheelwrightsarmsfreehouse.co.uk – Closed Sunday dinner and Monday

MATLOCK
Derbyshire – Pop. 14 956 – Regional map n° **9**-B1
▶ London 150 mi – Sheffield 23 mi – Derby 19 mi

𝕏𝕏 Stones   🏡

MODERN BRITISH · NEIGHBOURHOOD Negotiate the steep steps down to this small riverside restaurant and head for the front room with its floor to ceiling windows. Unfussy, modern British dishes are attractively presented and display the odd Mediterranean touch.

Menu £ 22/49

1C Dale Rd ⊠ DE4 3LT – ☎ 01629 56061 (booking advisable)
– www.stones-restaurant.co.uk – Closed 25 December-5 January, Sunday, Monday
and lunch Tuesday

MAWGAN PORTH – Cornwall → See Newquay

MELLOR – Lancashire → See Blackburn

MELLOR
Greater Manchester – Regional map n° **11**-B3
▶ London 185 mi – Bristol 163 mi – Cardiff 184 mi – Plymouth 277 mi

🍽 Oddfellows   🏡 🅿

TRADITIONAL BRITISH · PUB Oddies – as it is known locally – has a light, uncluttered feel, with wood burning stoves adding an element of cosiness. The appealing, daily changing menu offers tasty, locally sourced 'British food with a modern twist'.

Carte £ 17/35

Moor End Rd ⊠ SK6 5PT – ☎ 0161 449 7826 – www.oddfellowsmellor.com
– Closed Monday except bank holidays

MELLS

Somerset – Pop. 2 222 – Regional map n° **2**-C2

▶ London 117 mi – Bath 16 mi – Frome 3 mi

🍴🛏 Talbot Inn
😊

MODERN BRITISH · RUSTIC Characterful 15C coaching inn with a cobbled court-yard, a cosy sitting room with an open fire, a snug bar offering real ales and an elegant Grill Room to keep carnivores happy at weekends. Delightful bedrooms are well-priced and understated in style. Food is seasonal, modern and full of flavour; and staff may be casually attired, but their manner is anything but.

Carte £ 24/34

8 rooms ☑ – 🛉£ 100/160 🛉🛉£ 100/160

Selwood St ⊠ BA11 3PN – 𝒞 01373 812254 – www.talbotinn.com

MELTON MOWBRAY

Leicestershire – Pop. 27 158 – Regional map n° **9**-B2

▶ London 113 mi – Leicester 15 mi – Northampton 45 mi – Nottingham 18 mi

🏰 Stapleford Park

HISTORIC · PERSONALISED Beautiful stately home in 500 acres of landscaped grounds, with grand drawing rooms, a lovely leather-furnished bar, exceedingly comfortable bedrooms and marble bathrooms. The extensive leisure facilities are a replica of those at Buckingham Palace! Ornate rococo dining room; mix of classic and modern dishes.

55 rooms ☑ – 🛉£ 110/140 🛉🛉£ 180/280 – 3 suites

*⊠ LE14 2EF – East : 5 mi by B 676 on Stapleford rd – 𝒞 01572 787000
– www.staplefordpark.com*

MEVAGISSEY

Cornwall – Pop. 2 117 – Regional map n° **1**-B3

▶ London 287 mi – Newquay 21 mi – Plymouth 44 mi – Truro 20 mi

🏠 Trevalsa Court

HISTORIC · PERSONALISED Charming Arts and Crafts style house which combines dark wood panelling and stone fireplaces with bright modern art and bold soft furnishings. Most of the well-appointed bedrooms have coastal views. The oak-panelled dining room looks onto the lovely terrace and garden, and dishes showcase local produce.

14 rooms ☑ – 🛉£ 65/115 🛉🛉£ 120/265

*School Hill ⊠ PL26 6TH – East : 0.5 mi – 𝒞 01726 842468
– www.trevalsa-hotel.co.uk – Closed January and December*

🏠 Pebble House

TOWNHOUSE · PERSONALISED This impressive three-storey property looks out over the bay to Chapel Point and all but one of its stylish, luxurious bedrooms share the view. Guests are welcomed with champagne and in summer they serve afternoon tea on the terrace. Breakfasts are extensive and the keen owners are very hands-on.

6 rooms ☑ – 🛉£ 120/215 🛉🛉£ 120/215

*Polkirt Hill ⊠ PL26 6UX – South : 0.5 mi on Porthmellon rd – 𝒞 01726 844466
– www.pebblehousecornwall.co.uk – Closed late November-Christmas*

MID LAVANT – West Sussex ➜ See Chichester

MIDDLESBROUGH

Middlesbrough – Pop. 174 700 – Regional map n° **14**-B3

▶ London 246 mi – Leeds 66 mi – Newcastle upon Tyne 41 mi

✗ Brasserie Hudson Quay ⇐ 🏠 � 🎧 ⅈ℗ 🅿

TRADITIONAL BRITISH · BRASSERIE Be sure to find a window seat or a spot on the terrace so you can look out over Hudson Quay's old docks. Dinner offers a mix of sharing plates and brasserie classics. On the last Sunday of every month they host 'Jazz on the Quay'.

Carte £ 29/60

Windward Way ✉ TS2 1QG – East : 0.5 mi by A 66 – ☎ 01642 261166
– www.brasseriehudsonquay.com

MIDDLETON TYAS

North Yorkshire – Pop. 581 – Regional map n° **13**-B1
▶ London 235 mi – York 47 mi – Darlington 10 mi

✗✗ The Coach House at Middleton Lodge ⇐ 🛏 🏠 ⅈ℗ ⇔ 🅿

MODERN BRITISH · DESIGN A stylishly converted coach house to the Georgian mansion where the owner grew up. The dining area is in the former stables and the bar is where the coaches once parked. Concise, constantly evolving menus feature produce from within 40 miles. Contemporary bedrooms come with roll-top baths and Roberts radios.

Menu £ 25 (weekday lunch) – Carte £ 34/48
14 rooms ⌂ – ♦£ 135/190 ♦♦£ 155/220

Kneeton Ln ✉ DL10 6NJ – Northwest : 1 mi on Barton rd – ☎ 01325 377977
– www.middletonlodge.co.uk/coachhouse – Closed 26 December, 2-10 January,
Monday and Tuesday

MIDHURST

West Sussex – Pop. 4 914 – Regional map n° **4**-C2
▶ London 57 mi – Brighton 38 mi – Chichester 12 mi – Southampton 41 mi

🏨 Spread Eagle ✗ 🏠 🔲 ⑩ 🐎 ⅃♨ 🔥 🅿

HISTORIC · TRADITIONAL Part-15C coaching inn retaining plenty of its original character and decked out with antiques, tapestries and gleaming brass – although there's also a modern, well-equipped spa. Bedrooms are traditional. Dine next to an inglenook fireplace under wooden beams and look out for the Christmas puddings too!

39 rooms ⌂ – ♦£ 89/250 ♦♦£ 109/279 – 3 suites
South St ✉ GU29 9NH – ☎ 01730 816911 – www.hshotels.co.uk

🏨 Church House 🛏 ⅋

TOWNHOUSE · PERSONALISED An enthusiastically run townhouse; the main part dates from 1383 and features low beams and oak pillars. Bedrooms are quirky and luxurious; the best are 'Silver', with its slipper bath and 'Gaudi', with its vaulted ceiling and sleigh bed.

5 rooms ⌂ – ♦£ 80/100 ♦♦£ 140/160
Church Hill ✉ GU29 9NX – ☎ 01730 812990 – www.churchhousemidhurst.com
– Closed Christmas

at Henley North: 4.5 mi by A286

🍽 Duke of Cumberland Arms 🛏 🏠 🅿

TRADITIONAL BRITISH · COSY A hidden gem, nestled in pretty tiered gardens with trickling streams, trout ponds and splendid South Downs views. Sit in the cosy bar or more modern dining area which opens onto a terrace. Appealing menus offer carefully prepared seasonal dishes: lunch sees pub classics and dinner shifts things up a gear.

Carte £ 28/51

✉ GU27 3HQ – ☎ 01428 652280 – www.dukeofcumberland.com – Closed
25-26 December and dinner Sunday-Monday

at Bepton Southwest: 2.5 mi by A286 on Bepton rd ⊠ Midhurst

🏠 **Park House** ✿ 🐾 🏊 ▣ 🛖 ⌿ 🖳 🕙 🎾 ♨ 🎾 ♿ ⚒ 🅿

COUNTRY HOUSE · CONTEMPORARY Family-run country house with a light modern style and smart spa and leisure facilities. Spacious, homely bedrooms are split between this and South Downs Cottage; they come in neutral hues and most have views of the well-tended gardens and golf course. The stylish conservatory restaurant serves modern menus.

21 rooms ☑ – ♦£ 135/430 ♦♦£ 135/430 – 1 suite
⊠ GU29 0JB – ℰ 01730 819000 – www.parkhousehotel.com – Closed 24-26 December

MILFIELD

Northumberland – Regional map n° **14**-A1
▶ London 336 mi – Glasgow 118 mi – Edinburgh 72 mi – Aberdeen 204 mi

🍴 **Red Lion Inn** ⇦ 🏠 ⌿ 🅿

TRADITIONAL BRITISH · NEIGHBOURHOOD Set close to the Scottish border, this former coaching inn really is the heart of the village. It has a traditional look and feel, matched by a classical menu which makes good use of the larders of Scotland and England – and you definitely won't leave hungry! Bedrooms are homely; most are in wooden lodges.

Carte £ 19/30
5 rooms ☑ – ♦£ 45 ♦♦£ 80
Main Rd ⊠ NE71 6JD – ℰ 01668 216224 (booking advisable)
– www.redlionmilfield.co.uk – Closed 1 January and 25 December

MILFORD-ON-SEA

Hampshire – ⊠ Lymington – Pop. 4 348 – Regional map n° **4**-A3
▶ London 109 mi – Bournemouth 15 mi – Southampton 24 mi – Winchester 37 mi

🍴 **Verveine** ♿

SEAFOOD · FRIENDLY Bright, New England style restaurant fronted by a fish-monger's. Breads are baked twice-daily, veg is from the raised beds and smoking takes place on-site. The focus is on wonderfully fresh fish and cooking is accurate and original.

Menu £ 17 (lunch) – Carte £ 32/55
98 High St ⊠ SO41 0QE – ℰ 01590 642176 – www.verveine.co.uk – Closed Sunday and Monday

MILSTEAD

Kent – Pop. 264 – Regional map n° **5**-C1
▶ London 46 mi – Maidstone 29 mi – Canterbury 19 mi

🍴 **Red Lion** 🏠 ⌿ 🅿

CLASSIC FRENCH · PUB Simple, cosy country pub, personally run by an experienced couple. Ever-changing blackboard menu offers French-influenced country cooking. Dishes are honest, wholesome and richly flavoured.

Carte £ 24/42
Rawling St ⊠ ME9 0RT – ℰ 01795 830279 (booking advisable)
– www.theredlionmilstead.co.uk – Closed Sunday and Monday

MILTON ABBOT – Devon ➜ See Tavistock

MILTON KEYNES

Milton Keynes – Pop. 171 750 – Regional map n° **6**-C1
▶ London 56 mi – Bedford 16 mi – Birmingham 72 mi – Northampton 18 mi

ENGLAND

XX Brasserie Blanc

CLASSIC FRENCH · BRASSERIE Bustling French brasserie and a small shop, set within a striking modern building and accessed via a revolving 1930s mahogany door. Friendly team and a lively, buzzy atmosphere. Menus focus on tasty, wholesome, classic brasserie dishes.

Menu £14 (weekday lunch) – Carte £20/39

Chelsea House, 301 Avebury Blvd ⊠ MK9 2GA – ✆ 01908 546590 (booking essential) – www.brasserieblanc.com

X Jamie's Italian

ITALIAN · FAMILY Busy, buzzy restaurant with a laid-back, family-friendly feel. The passionate team serve flavoursome, rustic Italian dishes; all of the pasta is made on-site. For a quieter time, head for the upstairs floor, which opens at the weekend.

Menu £20/40 – Carte £20/49

3-5 Silbury Arcade ⊠ MK9 3AG – ✆ 01908 769011 (booking advisable) – www.jamiesitalian.com – Closed 25-26 December and Easter Sunday

MINEHEAD

Somerset – Pop. 11 981 – Regional map n° **2**-A2

▶ London 187 mi – Bristol 64 mi – Exeter 43 mi – Taunton 25 mi

⌂ Channel House

TRADITIONAL · CLASSIC Passionately run, detached Edwardian house in an elevated position, with the sea just visible through its mature gardens. Comfy lounge and a cosy bar. Immaculately kept bedrooms have a modern edge; Rooms 7 and 8 are the most comfortable. Traditional, daily changing dinner menu and comprehensive breakfasts.

8 rooms (dinner included) 🖙 – †£123 ††£206

Church Path ⊠ TA24 5QG – off Northfield Dr – ✆ 01643 703229 – www.channelhouse.co.uk – Closed November-February

MINSTER

Kent – Regional map n° **5**-D1

▶ London 73 mi – Canterbury 14 mi – Dover 21 mi – Brighton 103 mi

X Corner House

TRADITIONAL BRITISH · NEIGHBOURHOOD Pass the stone bar inset with a cart wheel, and the small lounge and terrace, to the characterful dining room with its low beamed ceiling and quarry tiled floor. Classic recipes use good quality produce; the dishes for two are a hit. Bedrooms have smart feature walls and modern facilities.

Menu £17 (lunch) – Carte £29/34

2 rooms – †£75/90 ††£75/90 – 🖙 £8

42 Station Rd ⊠ CT12 4BZ – ✆ 01843 823000 – www.cornerhouserestaurants.co.uk – Closed dinner Sunday, Monday and lunch Tuesday

MINSTER LOVELL

Oxfordshire – Pop. 1 236 – Regional map n° **6**-A2

▶ London 74 mi – Birmingham 87 mi – Bristol 67 mi – Sheffield 151 mi

⌂⌂ Minster Mill

BUSINESS · FUNCTIONAL Charming 17C Cotswold stone mill on the riverbank, with admirable eco-credentials. The open-fired lounge has a minstrels' gallery. Smart, well-appointed bedrooms come with robes and sloe gin and the best boast riverside terraces. Meals are taken at the Old Swan, their sister establishment.

52 rooms 🖙 – †£155/375 ††£175/395

⊠ OX29 0RN – ✆ 01993 774441 – www.oldswanandminstermill.com

🏠 Old Swan   ⬅ 🍴 🏠 **P**

TRADITIONAL CUISINE · SIMPLE Smart inn with parquet floors, roaring open fires and garden games. Large herb plots contribute to unfussy pub classics; tasty daily specials feature fish from the Brixham day boats. Bedrooms boast period furnishings and mod cons, and some have feature bathrooms.

Carte £ 25/43

14 rooms ☟ – 🚹£ 165/375 🚻£ 185/395

✉ OX29 0RN – ☎ 01993 774441 – www.oldswanandminstermill.com

MISTLEY
Essex – Pop. 1 696 – Regional map n° **7**-D2
▶ London 69 mi – Colchester 11 mi – Ipswich 14 mi

✕ Mistley Thorn   ⬅ 🖥 **P**

INTERNATIONAL · FRIENDLY A bright, modern restaurant with an informal feel, in a historic coastal town. The appealing menu offers something for everyone, with seafood a speciality and plenty of local mussels and oysters. Smart bedrooms offer up-to-date facilities; some have river views. There's also a homeware/wine shop and cookery school.

Menu £ 18 (weekday lunch) – Carte £ 23/39

11 rooms ☟ – 🚹£ 75/110 🚻£ 105/125

High St ✉ CO11 1HE – ☎ 01206 392821 – www.mistleythorn.co.uk – Closed 25 December

MITTON – Lancashire ➡ See Whalley

MOBBERLEY
Cheshire East – Pop. 2 034 – Regional map n° **20**-B3
▶ London 188 mi – Chester 29 mi – Manchester 17 mi

🏠 Church Inn   🍴 🏠 **P**

TRADITIONAL CUISINE · COSY 18C brick pub beside the bowling green, offering lovely views of the 12C church from its terrace. Regularly changing menus reflect the seasons, with light dishes in summer and hearty stews in winter. Hand-pumped local beers feature.

Carte £ 21/44

Church Ln ✉ WA16 7RD – ☎ 01565 873178 – www.churchinnmobberley.co.uk

MONKTON COMBE – Bath and North East Somerset ➡ See Bath

MONKTON FARLEIGH
Wiltshire – Pop. 460 – Regional map n° **2**-C2
▶ London 112 mi – Exeter 103 mi – Cheltenham 58 mi

🏠 Muddy Duck   ⬅ 🍴 🏠 **P**

TRADITIONAL CUISINE · PUB This is reputedly Wiltshire's most haunted pub. From the outside it looks like a manor house and inside it's full of character, with a giant inglenook fireplace and a stylish, rustic dining room. Concise menus offer classic British dishes. Opt for a duplex bedroom, which has a snug with a wood burning stove.

Menu £ 15 (weekday lunch) – Carte £ 24/44

5 rooms ☟ – 🚹£ 100/250 🚻£ 120/250

42 Monkton Farleigh ✉ BA15 2QN – ☎ 01225 858705
– www.themuddyduckbath.co.uk

MORETONHAMPSTEAD
Devon – ✉ Newton Abbot – Pop. 1 339 – Regional map n° **1**-C2
▶ London 213 mi – Exeter 13 mi – Plymouth 30 mi

🍴 The Horse   🏮 ♿

MEDITERRANEAN CUISINE · PUB Pub with rustic, flag-floored rooms and a sunny, Mediterranean-style courtyard. Tasty, unfussy dishes offer more than a hint of Italy. Thin crust pizzas are baked in a custom-built oven.

Carte £ 18/37

7 George St ⊠ TQ13 8PG – ℰ 01647 440242 – www.thehorsedartmoor.co.uk
– Closed 25 December and Monday lunch

MORETON-IN-MARSH

Gloucestershire – Pop. 3 493 – Regional map n° **2**-D1
▶ London 86 mi – Birmingham 40 mi – Gloucester 31 mi – Oxford 29 mi

🏨 Manor House   ♠ 🛏 🖭 ♿ 🎿 🅿

INN · ELEGANT Part-16C manor house with a smart interior which mixes old beams and inglenook fireplaces with modern fabrics and contemporary art. Chic, stylish bedrooms boast bold décor and feature walls; those in the main house are the most characterful. Dine in the sophisticated restaurant or classical brasserie.

35 rooms � – ♦£ 80/190 ♦♦£ 130/390 – 1 suite

High St ⊠ GL56 0LJ – ℰ 01608 650501 – www.cotswold-inns-hotels.co.uk
Mulberry – See restaurant listing

🏚 Old School   🛏 ℅ 🅿

COUNTRY HOUSE · PERSONALISED Change pace at this laid-back, stone-built hotel – formerly a school – where you can relax in the gardens over a game of boules or croquet. The impressive upstairs lounge features an exposed A-frame ceiling and original ecclesiastical windows; bright, modern bedrooms offer a high level of facilities.

4 rooms �}) – ♦£ 100/130 ♦♦£ 130/150

Little Compton ⊠ GL56 0SL – East : 3.75 mi on A 44 – ℰ 01608 674588
– www.theoldschoolbedandbreakfast.com

✕✕✕ Mulberry   🛏 ♿ 🅰 🅿

MODERN BRITISH · DESIGN Formal restaurant with an enclosed walled garden, set within a part-16C manor house. Cooking is modern and adventurous and features some challenging combinations – choose between a 4 course set menu and an 8 course tasting menu.

Menu £ 45/60

Manor House Hotel, High St ⊠ GL56 0LJ – ℰ 01608 650501
– www.cotswold-inns-hotels.co.uk – dinner only and Sunday lunch

at Bourton-on-the-Hill West: 2 mi on A44⊠ Moreton-In-Marsh

🍴 Horse & Groom   ⇔ 🛏 🏮 🅿

🎖 **TRADITIONAL CUISINE · PUB** Listed Cotswold stone property in a pretty village set high on the hillside; it's run by two brothers, who grew up working in their parents' pub. Study the daily changing blackboard menu then order at the bar. Unfussy dishes are good value, fresh and flavoursome. Individually decorated bedrooms are stylish and contemporary – and breakfast is well worth getting up for.

Carte £ 22/37

5 rooms ⊋ – ♦£ 80 ♦♦£ 96/170

⊠ GL56 9AQ – ℰ 01386 700413 (booking essential) – www.horseandgroom.info
– Closed 25, 31 December and Sunday dinner except bank holidays

MORPETH

Northumberland – Pop. 14 403 – Regional map n° **14**-B2
▶ London 301 mi – Edinburgh 93 mi – Newcastle upon Tyne 15 mi

at Eshott North: 8.5 mi by A1 ✉ Morpeth

🏠 Eshott Hall

COUNTRY HOUSE · CLASSIC Attractive Georgian manor house in a quiet, rural location – yet only 5min from the A1. Classically stylish guest areas. Smart, modern bedrooms boast warm fabrics, antique furniture and good facilities. Formal dining room offers contemporary menus; local produce includes fruit and veg from the kitchen garden.

17 rooms 🖵 – 🛉£ 70/135 🛉🛉£ 99/185

✉ NE65 9EN – 𝒞 01670 787454 – www.eshotthall.co.uk

at Longhorsley Northwest: 6.5 mi by A192 on A697 ✉ Morpeth

🏠 Thistleyhaugh Farm

FAMILY · COSY Attractive Georgian farmhouse, set off the beaten track on a 750 acre organic farm, with the River Coquet flowing through its grounds. Cosy, open-fired lounge and antique-filled dining room. Spacious, comfortable bedrooms – most have luxurious bathrooms with feature baths. Communal dinners; home-cooking features beef and lamb from the farm. Charming owners.

5 rooms 🖵 – 🛉£ 70/90 🛉🛉£ 100

✉ NE65 8RG – Northwest : 3.75 mi by A 697 and Todburn rd taking first right turn – 𝒞 01665 570629 – www.thistleyhaugh.co.uk – Closed Christmas-1 February

MORSTON – Norfolk → See Blakeney

MOULTON

Suffolk – Regional map n° **8**-B2

▶ London 64 mi – Ipswich 42 mi – Cambridge 14 mi

🍴 Packhorse Inn

MODERN CUISINE · PUB A smart modern pub in a pretty village, named after the 15C flint bridge which spans the river. Cooking keeps things classical, with the focus firmly on the ingredients' natural flavours; for dessert, the assiettes are a good way to go. Bedrooms are ultra-stylish with quality furnishings and roll-top baths.

Menu £ 19 (weekday lunch) – Carte £ 28/41

8 rooms 🖵 – 🛉£ 85/225 🛉🛉£ 100/250

Bridge St ✉ CB8 8SP – 𝒞 01638 751818 – www.thepackhorseinn.com

MOUSEHOLE

Cornwall – ✉ Penzance – Regional map n° **1**-A3

▶ London 321 mi – Penzance 3 mi – Truro 29 mi

🍴 2 Fore Street

SEAFOOD · FRIENDLY Friendly café-cum-bistro with a delightful courtyard terrace and garden. All-day menus offer everything from coffee and cake to a full meal, with brunch a feature at weekends. Tasty, unfussy dishes are guided by the day's catch.

Carte £ 25/35

2 Fore St ✉ TR19 6PF – 𝒞 01736 731164 (booking essential at dinner)
– www.2forestreet.co.uk – Closed January and Monday in winter

🍴 Old Coastguard

MEDITERRANEAN CUISINE · BISTRO Old coastguard's cottage in a small fishing village, with a laid-back, open-plan interior, a sub-tropical garden and views towards St Clement's Isle. Well-presented brasserie dishes display a Mediterranean edge; great wine selection. Individually styled bedrooms – some with balconies, most with sea views.

Menu £ 24 – Carte £ 26/36 **s**

14 rooms 🖵 – 🛉£ 100/165 🛉🛉£ 135/225

The Parade ✉ TR19 6PR – 𝒞 01736 731222 – www.oldcoastguardhotel.co.uk
– Closed 25 December and early January

MULLION

Cornwall – ✉ Helston – Pop. 1 955 – Regional map n° **1**-A3

▶ London 287 mi – Birmingham 282 mi – Croydon 295 mi – Barnet 300 mi

🏠 **Polurrian Bay** ⚗ ⟨ 🛏 🏠 ⤴ 🖥 🐾 ✕ 🕭 ⚘ 🅿

HISTORIC BUILDING · CONTEMPORARY Imposing Victorian hotel with 12 acres of grounds, set in a commanding clifftop position. The spacious modern interior is geared towards families, with a crèche, a games room and a cinema. Most of the bright bedrooms boast views across Mount's Bay. Unfussy menus showcase seasonal, local produce.

41 rooms ⌂ – †£ 120/560 ††£ 120/560

✉ TR12 7EN – ℰ 01326 240421 – www.polurrianhotel.com

MURCOTT

Oxfordshire – ✉ Kidlington – Pop. 1 293 – Regional map n° **6**-B2

▶ London 70 mi – Oxford 14 mi – Witney 20 mi

🍴 **Nut Tree** (Mike North) ⤴ 🏠 🅿
❀

TRADITIONAL BRITISH · RUSTIC Characterful thatched pub with a cosy bar and a smart restaurant. The appealing menus change constantly, relying on the latest seasonal ingredients to arrive at the door, and produce is organic, free range or wild wherever possible; they even rear rare breed pigs. Combinations are classical and satisfying.

➜ Terrine of foie gras and duck confit with apple salad, hazelnut and balsamic purée. Olive oil poached fillet of halibut, green herb risotto and fennel salad. Rhubarb and star anise soufflé with rhubarb & custard ice cream.

Carte £ 34/59

Main St ✉ OX5 2RE – ℰ 01865 331253 – www.nuttreeinn.co.uk – Closed 27 December-11 January, Sunday dinner and Monday

NAILSWORTH

Gloucestershire – Pop. 7 728 – Regional map n° **2**-C1

▶ London 110 mi – Bristol 30 mi – Swindon 28 mi

✕✕ **Wild Garlic** ⟻ 🗛

MODERN BRITISH · INTIMATE This attractive little restaurant offers something for everyone. One room is a rustic tapas bar with a south-facing terrace and a menu of Spanish favourites; the second is a modern restaurant serving a concise à la carte and a biweekly tasting menu. Three stylish, well-equipped bedrooms complete the picture.

Carte £ 29/47

3 rooms ⌂ – †£ 80/120 ††£ 90/130

3 Cossack Sq ✉ GL6 0DB – ℰ 01453 832615 – www.wild-garlic.co.uk – Closed 2-9 January and Sunday dinner-Tuesday

NATIONAL EXHIBITION CENTRE – W. Mids. ➜ See Birmingham

NETHER BURROW

Lancashire – ✉ Kirkby Lonsdale – Regional map n° **11**-B1

▶ London 257 mi – Liverpool 73 mi – Leeds 101 mi – Manchester 68 mi

🍴 **Highwayman** 🏠 🕭 🅿

REGIONAL CUISINE · PUB Sizeable 18C coaching inn with an open-fired bar and a lovely terrace. A rustic, no-nonsense approach to food makes for well-crafted, flavourful dishes. Produce is local and seasonal, with Lancashire hotpot a perennial favourite.

Menu £ 14 (weekdays) – Carte £ 22/46

✉ LA6 2RJ – ℰ 015242 73338 – www.highwaymaninn.co.uk

NETHER WESTCOTE – Gloucestershire → See Stow-on-the-Wold

NETLEY MARSH – Hampshire → See Southampton

NEW MILTON
Hampshire – Pop. 19 969 – Regional map n° **4**-A3
▶ London 106 mi – Bournemouth 12 mi – Southampton 21 mi – Winchester 34 mi

⛪ Chewton Glen
GRAND LUXURY · CLASSIC Professionally run country house with an impressive spa, set in 130 acres of New Forest parkland – try a host of outdoor pursuits, including croquet, archery and clay pigeon shooting. Luxurious bedrooms range from classic to contemporary; opt for one with a balcony or terrace, or try a unique Treehouse suite.
70 rooms – ♦£ 325/747 ♦♦£ 325/747 – ☑£ 26 – 15 suites
Christchurch Rd ⊠ BH25 6QS – West : 2 mi by A 337 and Ringwood Rd on Chewton Farm Rd – ✆ 01425 275341 – www.chewtonglen.com
Dining Room – See restaurant listing

XXX Dining Room
MODERN BRITISH · ELEGANT Stylish hotel restaurant comprising five impressive rooms, including one with wines displayed in illuminated cases. The seasonally inspired à la carte offers classically based dishes of garden produce which are prepared in a refined manner; from Friday-Sunday they also serve specials from the trolley.
Menu £ 27 (weekday lunch) **s** – Carte £ 42/75 **s**
Chewton Glen Hotel, Christchurch Rd ⊠ BH25 6QS – West : 2 mi by A 337 and Ringwood Rd on Chewton Farm Rd – ✆ 01425 275341 – www.chewtonglen.com

NEW ROMNEY
Kent – Regional map n° **5**-C2
▶ London 71 mi – Brighton 60 mi – Folkestone 17 mi – Maidstone 36 mi

Romney Bay House
HISTORIC · ART DÉCO Built by Sir Clough Williams-Ellis in the 1920s, for actress Hedda Hopper, and accessed via a private coast road. Open-fired drawing room with honesty bar; first floor lounge has a telescope and lovely views out to sea. Homely bedrooms. Conservatory dining room offers a daily, seafood-based menu.
10 rooms ☑ – ♦£ 75/95 ♦♦£ 95/164
Coast Rd, Littlestone ⊠ TN28 8QY – East : 2.25 mi by B 2071 – ✆ 01797 364747 – www.romneybayhousehotel.co.uk – Closed 1 week Christmas and first week January

NEWARK-ON-TRENT
Nottinghamshire – Pop. 37 084 – Regional map n° **9**-C1
▶ London 127 mi – Lincoln 16 mi – Nottingham 20 mi – Sheffield 42 mi

Grange
TOWNHOUSE · PERSONALISED Personally run hotel with a small terrace and award-winning gardens. The main house has mock Tudor gables, a Victorian-style bar and lounge, and a smart restaurant decorated with antique plates and cutlery. Individually styled bedrooms are split between this and a second house, and offer good comforts.
19 rooms ☑ – ♦£ 85/110 ♦♦£ 100/165
73 London Rd ⊠ NG24 1RZ – South : 0.5 mi on Grantham rd (B 6326) – ✆ 01636 703399 – www.grangenewark.co.uk – Closed 22 December-6 January

at Norwell North: 7.25 mi by A1

🏠 Willoughby House

HISTORIC · PERSONALISED A three-storey red-brick farmhouse and converted stables, with a chic, stylish interior, a small open-fired lounge and a deep red breakfast room. Bedrooms feature good quality furnishings and antiques, along with contemporary artwork and homemade flapjacks. The owner has a keen eye for detail.

5 rooms � - ♦£ 65/95 ♦♦£ 95/115

Main St ✉ NG23 6JN - ☎ 01636 636266 - www.willoughbyhousebandb.co.uk

NEWBOTTLE

Tyne and Wear – Regional map n° **14**-B2

▶ London 268 mi – Newcastle upon Tyne 14 mi – Sunderland 6 mi

🏠 Hideaway at Herrington Hill   ⊰ ⇦ ⅍ 🅿

FAMILY · REGIONAL The charming owners really look after their guests at this spacious former shooting lodge, built in 1838 for the Earl of Durham. Bedrooms blend period features and modern amenities. The Garden Room is largest, with views of the grounds.

3 rooms ☲ - ♦£ 85/150 ♦♦£ 85/150

High Ln ✉ DH4 4NH - West : 1 mi - ☎ 07730 957795
- www.hideawayatherringtonhill.com

NEWBURY

West Berkshire – Pop. 38 762 – Regional map n° **6**-B3

▶ London 67 mi – Reading 17 mi – Bristol 66 mi – Oxford 28 mi

🏨 The Vineyard   ⇦ 🖼 🔳 ⅍ ㎙ 🔼 🆎 🔩 🅿

BUSINESS · CLASSIC Extended former hunting lodge with over 1,000 pieces of art and a striking fire and water feature. Some bedrooms have a country house style, while others are more contemporary; all boast smart marble bathrooms. The owner also has a vineyard in California, hence the stunning wine vault and the wine-themed bar.

49 rooms - ♦£ 225/660 ♦♦£ 275/660 - ☲£ 21 – 32 suites

Stockcross ✉ RG20 8JU - Northwest : 2 mi by A 4 on B 4000 - ☎ 01635 528770
- www.the-vineyard.co.uk

The Vineyard – See restaurant listing

🏨 Donnington Valley H. & Spa   ⚒ ⇦ 🖼 🔳 ㊙ ⅍ ㎙ 🔼 ⅚ 🆎 🔩 🅿

BUSINESS · FUNCTIONAL Modern business-orientated hotel on the outskirts of town; its large grounds include a golf course. Guest areas are spacious and stylishly furnished and there's a well-equipped gym and spa. Smart bedrooms offer a high level of facilities. The restaurant has an unusual pyramid roof and offers modern fare.

111 rooms ☲ - ♦£ 99/188 ♦♦£ 99/299

Old Oxford Rd, Donnington ✉ RG14 3AG - North : 1.75 mi by A 4 off B 4494
- ☎ 01635 551199 - www.donningtonvalley.co.uk

✕✕✕ The Vineyard   ⅋ ⇦ ⅚ 🆎 🍴 🅿

MODERN CUISINE · ELEGANT Smart hotel restaurant split over two levels. Accomplished, classical dishes are attractively presented; choose between a set and a tasting menu. They offer over 100 wines by the glass – some are from their own Californian vineyard.

Menu £ 29/65

Vineyard Hotel, Stockcross ✉ RG20 8JU - Northwest : 2 mi on B 4000
- ☎ 01635 528770 - www.the-vineyard.co.uk

✗ Woodspeen (John Campbell)   � 🅿

❀ MODERN CUISINE · FASHIONABLE Despite being set in an old pub, this smart neighbourhood eatery has more of a bistro feel, courtesy of its Scandic styling and bright, modern thatched extension. Mouth-watering seasonal dishes feature local and garden produce; flavour is paramount and dishes have a comforting, modern classic style.

→ Roast scallops with confit chicken and shallots. Pan-fried sea bass with parmesan gnocchi, braised fennel and potted shrimp dressing. Rhubarb and ginger with buttermilk & vanilla parfait.

Menu £ 25 (lunch and early dinner) – Carte £ 36/62

Lambourn Rd, Bagnor ⊠ RG20 8BN – Northwest : 2 mi by A 4 and Station Rd - signed Watermill Theatre – ℰ 01635 265070 – www.thewoodspeen.com – Closed Sunday dinner and Monday

🛏 The Newbury   🚭 🆎

TRADITIONAL BRITISH · SIMPLE A relaxed, trendy pub behind a traditional façade. There's an experienced team in charge and a lively buzz when it's busy. Dishes range from pub classics to more adventurous offerings; head upstairs for pizza fresh from the oven.

Carte £ 24/40

137 Bartholomew St ⊠ RG14 5HB – ℰ 01635 49000 – www.thenewburypub.co.uk

NEWBY BRIDGE

Cumbria – Regional map n° **12**-A3

▶ London 270 mi – Kendal 16 mi – Lancaster 27 mi

🏨 Lakeside   ✿ ⪡ 🚪 📺 ⦾ 🎐 ₤₅ 🔄 💆 ♨ 🅿

TRADITIONAL · CLASSIC Superbly situated hotel on the water's edge. Extremely comfy guest areas have a traditional style. Bedrooms are smart and modern – some have four-poster beds and great views. Relax in the spa and leisure club, then dine in the stylish modern brasserie or more traditional dining room; and be sure to find time for afternoon tea in the conservatory, overlooking the lake.

74 rooms ⌷ – ♦£ 155/165 ♦♦£ 195/205 – 7 suites

Lakeside ⊠ LA12 8AT – Northeast : 1 mi on Hawkshead rd – ℰ 015395 30001 - www.lakesidehotel.co.uk – Closed 3-20 January

🏠 Knoll   ✿ 🚪 ♨ 🅿

TRADITIONAL · GRAND LUXURY Keenly run, slate-built Edwardian house opposite the lake, with a smart interior that blends classic and modern styles. Comfy, leather-furnished lounge. Good-sized bedrooms with bold décor and modern bathrooms; 'The Retreat' has a private entrance and hot tub. Simple dining room displays heart-themed art.

9 rooms ⌷ – ♦£ 75/118 ♦♦£ 90/160

Lakeside ⊠ LA12 8AU – Northeast : 1.25 mi on Hawkshead rd – ℰ 015395 31347 - www.theknoll-lakeside.co.uk – Closed 22-27, 31 December and 1 January

NEWCASTLE UPON TYNE

Tyne and Wear – Pop. 268 064 – Regional map n° **14**-B2

▶ London 276 mi – Edinburgh 105 mi – Leeds 95 mi

🏨 Jesmond Dene House   🕭 🚪 🔄 ₤ ♨ 💆 🅿

LUXURY · MODERN Stone-built Arts and Crafts house in a peaceful city dene; originally owned by the Armstrong family. Characterful guest areas with wood panelling, local art and striking original fireplaces. Individually furnished bedrooms have bold feature walls, modern facilities and smart bathrooms with underfloor heating.

40 rooms ⌷ – ♦£ 125/165 ♦♦£ 140/220

Jesmond Dene Rd ⊠ NE2 2EY – Northeast : 1.5 mi by B 1318 off A 189 - ℰ 0191 212 3000 – www.jesmonddenehouse.co.uk

Jesmond Dene House – See restaurant listing

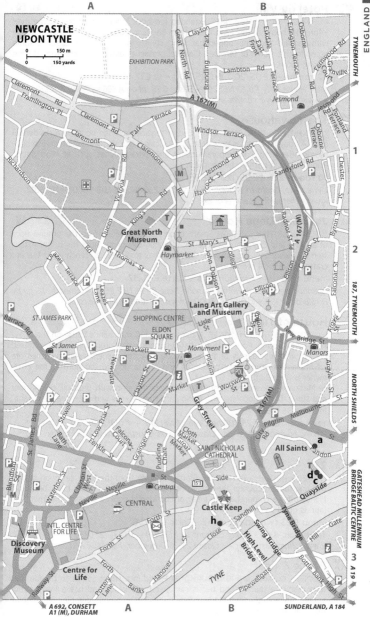

NEWCASTLE UPON TYNE

0 ——— 150 m
0 ——— 150 yards

EXHIBITION PARK

Great North Rd

Claremont Rd
Framlington Pl
Claremont Rd
Claremont Pl
Claremont
Richardson

Clayton
Brandling Park
Lambton Rd
A 167(M)
Windsor Terrace

Esk dale
East Front
Ellington Terrace
Osborne Rd
Fern wood Rd
Grville
Granville Ct
Jesmond
Portland Rd
Osborne Terrace
Portland Terrace

Jesmond Rd West
Sandyford Rd
Hancock St
King's Rd

Chester St

Great North Museum
Haymarket
M
T

St Mary's Pl
John Dobson St
College
Radnor St
A 167(M)
Ellison St
Ellison Pl
Camden St
Byron St
Falconar St

Queen St
St Thomas' St
Leazes Terrace
Leazes Lane

Laing Art Gallery and Museum
Lisle St

ST JAMES PARK
St James
Barrack Rd

SHOPPING CENTRE
ELDON SQUARE
Blackett St
Newgate St
Clayton St
Market St

Monument
Pilgrim St
Worswick St

New Bridge St
Manors
Argyle St

St James' Rd
Stowell St
Bath Lane
Low Friar St
Frankle St
Falconar's Court
Pudding Chare
Granger St

SAINT NICHOLAS CATHEDRAL
Cloth Market
Groat Market

City Rd
Pilgrim St
Melbourne St
Landon

All Saints
a

Blenheim St
Waterloo St
Clayton St West
Neville St
Neville St

CENTRAL
Central
153
Side

Grey Street
A 167(M)

d
c
Quayside

INTL. CENTRE FOR LIFE

Discovery Museum

Centre for Life

Castle Keep
h
Sandhill
Close

Swing Bridge
High Level Bridge
Tyne Bridge
Bottle Bank
High St
Hill Gate

Railway St
Forth St
Pottery Lane
Banks
Forth St
Hanover St

TYNE
Pipewellgate

A 692, CONSETT
A1 (M), DURHAM

SUNDERLAND, A 184

🏨 Hotel du Vin   ✕ 🖥 & AC P

BUSINESS · CONTEMPORARY Extended red-brick building overlooking the river – formerly home to the Tyne Tees Steam Shipping Company. Characterful lounge with gas fire and zinc-topped bar. Chic, stylish, wine-themed bedrooms; some boast feature baths or terraces. Classical brasserie features a glass-fronted wine tasting room.

42 rooms – 🛏£ 95/200 🛏🛏£ 95/200 – ☷ £ 17

Allan House, City Rd ✉ NE1 2BE – East : 0.75 mi on A 186 – ✆ 0191 229 2200 – www.hotelduvin.com/newcastle

🏨 The Townhouse

TOWNHOUSE · CONTEMPORARY End of terrace Victorian house in a residential area. All-day café serves breakfast, snacks, cakes and the like. Smart, stylish bedrooms offer bold, contemporary décor and extra touches such as iPod docks; Room 10 has a bath in the bedroom.

10 rooms ☷ – 🛏£ 95/120 🛏🛏£ 95/120

1 West Ave, Gosforth ✉ NE3 4ES – North : 2.5 mi by B 1318 – ✆ 0191 285 6812 – www.thetownhousehotel.co.uk

✕✕✕ Jesmond Dene House   🚗 🏠 & ⓘ♡ P

MODERN BRITISH · DESIGN Smart, understated restaurant on the ground floor of an Arts and Crafts house hotel in a tranquil city dene. Sit in the bright extension for views over the gardens. Classic dishes may have a French heart but are crafted from local produce.

Menu £ 20 (weekday lunch) **s** – Carte £ 31/57

Jesmond Dene House Hotel, Jesmond Dene Rd ✉ NE2 2EY – Northeast : 1.5 mi by B 1318 off A 189 – ✆ 0191 212 3000 – www.jesmonddenehouse.co.uk

✕✕ House of Tides (Kenny Atkinson)   & ⓘ♡
🕸

MODERN CUISINE · INTIMATE A characterful 16C merchant's house on the quayside. The ground floor features flagged floors, cast iron pillars and exposed bricks, while upstairs is bright and modern. Accomplished, creative dishes are well-balanced, attractively presented and give a nod to the north – the chef-owner is a local after all!

→ Mackerel, gooseberries, lemon and mustard. Lamb with broccoli, onion, mint and sorrel. Dark chocolate with Gariguette strawberries and roast tea ice cream.

Menu £ 35/68

Town plan: B3-h - *28-30 The Close ✉ NE1 3RF – ✆ 0191 230 3720 – www.houseoftides.co.uk – Closed 2 weeks Christmas-New Year, Sunday and Monday*

✕✕ 21   🍸 & AC ⓘ♡ ⇄

MODERN BRITISH · BRASSERIE Start with a gin from the large selection behind the zinc-topped counter then head through to the smart red and black brasserie. Menus offer a comprehensive array of confidently cooked classics; the 'menu du jour' is good value.

Menu £ 23 (weekday lunch) – Carte £ 29/56

Town plan: B3-a - *Trinity Gardens ✉ NE1 2HH – ✆ 0191 222 0755 – www.21newcastle.co.uk – Closed 25-26 December, 1 January and Easter Monday*

✕✕ Peace & Loaf   & AC

MODERN CUISINE · NEIGHBOURHOOD Found in a smart suburban parade, this fashionable restaurant and bar is set over three levels and has a lively atmosphere. Attractively presented modern dishes are ambitious, complex and employ many different cooking techniques.

Menu £ 20 (lunch and early dinner) – Carte £ 34/55

217 Jesmond Rd, Jesmond ✉ NE2 1LA – Northeast : 1.5 mi by A 1058 – ✆ 0191 281 5222 – www.peaceandloaf.co.uk – Closed 25-26 December, 1 January and Sunday dinner

X **Caffé Vivo**   &. AC 畳 📶

ITALIAN · BRASSERIE In a converted quayside warehouse – also home to a theatre. Zinc ducting and steel pillars give it an industrial feel, while hams, salamis
and oils add a touch of the Mediterranean. Simple, satisfying cooking of classic
Italian dishes.

Menu £ 20 – Carte £ 24/42

Town plan: B3-d - *29 Broad Chare* ✉ *NE1 3DQ* – ℰ *0191 232 1331*
– www.caffevivo.co.uk – Closed Sunday and bank holidays

🏠 **Broad Chare**   AC

😊 TRADITIONAL BRITISH · PUB Owned by Terry Laybourne and next to its sister
operation, Caffé Vivo. Sit in the snug ground floor bar or upstairs dining room.
Choose from a snack menu of 'Geordie Tapas', an appealing 'on toast' selection,
hearty daily specials and tasty nursery puddings. Over 40 ales, including some
which are custom-made.

Carte £ 21/37

Town plan: B3-c - *25 Broad Chare* ✉ *NE1 3DQ* – ℰ *0191 211 2144 (booking*
advisable) – www.thebroadchare.co.uk – Closed 25-26 December and Sunday
dinner

at Ponteland Northwest: 8.25 mi by A167 on A696✉ Newcastle Upon Tyne

XX **Haveli**   🍷 &. AC ↩

INDIAN · FASHIONABLE Haveli means 'grand house' and this neighbourhood
restaurant is certainly very smart. Influences come from all over India; try one of
the chef's signature curries. Staff combine personality with professionalism.

Menu £ 18 (early dinner) – Carte £ 15/34

3-5 Broadway, Darras Hall ✉ *NE20 9PW Ponteland – Southwest : 1.5 mi by B*
6323 off Darras Hall Estate rd – ℰ *01661 872727 – www.haveliponteland.com*
– dinner only

NEWHAVEN

Derbyshire – Regional map n° **9**-A1

▶ London 159 mi – Leeds 84 mi – Manchester 38 mi – Derby 22 mi

🏠 **The Smithy**   🐾 🛏 🍽 **P** 🚭

FAMILY · PERSONALISED Friendly owners keep the blacksmith theme alive at
this cosy guesthouse. Tools and the old forge are found in the rustic breakfast
room; while the bedrooms come with wrought-iron beds and are named Anvil,
Swage, Bellows and Forge.

4 rooms ☑ – 🛉£ 50 🛉🛉£ 95

✉ *SK17 0DT – South : 1 mi on A 515* – ℰ *01298 84548*
– www.thesmithybedandbreakfast.co.uk

NEWLYN

Cornwall – Pop. 3 536 – Regional map n° **1**-A3

▶ London 288 mi – Camborne 16 mi – Saint Austell 44 mi – Falmouth 29 mi

🏠 **Tolcarne Inn**   🌿 **P**

😊 SEAFOOD · TRADITIONAL DÉCOR An unassuming, family-run pub behind the sea
wall. Inside it's narrow and cosy, with 18C beams, a wood-burning stove and a long
bar. The experienced chef offers appealing, flavoursome dishes which centre
around fresh, locally landed fish and shellfish – go for the turbot if it's on the menu.

Carte £ 23/38

Tolcarne Pl ✉ *TR18 5PR* – ℰ *01736 363074 – www.tolcarneinn.co.uk*

NEWPORT – Isle of Wight → See Wight (Isle of)

NEWPORT PAGNELL

Milton Keynes – Pop. 15 118 – Regional map n° **11**-C1

▶ London 87 mi – Northampton 31 mi – Oxford 69 mi

✗ East House 🆕

POLISH · SIMPLE The clue is in the name: this homely, two-roomed restaurant with wine box motif wallpaper offers authentic Polish and Eastern European cuisine. Flavoursome dishes are crafted from scratch and it's worth checking out the vodkas too!

Carte £ 20/42

8 St John St. ⊠ *MK16 8HN –* ☎ *01908 616080 – www.theeasthouse.co.uk – Closed 24 December-1 January*

NEWQUAY

Cornwall – Pop. 20 189 – Regional map n° **1**-A2

▶ London 291 mi – Exeter 83 mi – Penzance 34 mi – Plymouth 48 mi

✗ Chapter 1 🆕

MODERN BRITISH · NEIGHBOURHOOD Set in a parade of shops in the heart of town, with recycled mix and match furnishings, filament lighting and copper ducting. The keen young chef creates adventurous British dishes, with new ideas trialled on Wednesday nights.

Carte £ 27/36

Morfa Hall, Cliff Rd ⊠ *TR7 1SG –* ☎ *01637 499263 – www.chapter1restaurant.co.uk*

at Watergate Bay Northeast: 3 mi by A3059 on B3276⊠ Newquay

🏠 Watergate Bay   ✿ ← 🖼 🌐 🖭 � 🏃 ⚄ 🅿

FAMILY · CONTEMPORARY A long-standing seaside hotel where fresh, contemporary bedrooms range from standards to family suites; some have freestanding baths with sea outlooks. The beautiful infinity pool and hot tub share the view and there's direct beach access, beach changing rooms and even a surfboard store. Dine in the bar, the laid-back sandy-floored café or the smart modern brasserie.

69 rooms ⊡ – ♦£ 120/315 ♦♦£ 160/420

On The Beach ⊠ *TR8 4AA –* ☎ *01637 860543 – www.watergatebay.co.uk*

Zacry's – See restaurant listing

✗✗ Fifteen Cornwall   ☙ ← ⅞ 🖵 ⇔

ITALIAN · TRENDY Lively beachfront restaurant with fabulous bay views; a social enterprise where the profits go to their registered charity, who train disengaged adults to become chefs. Unfussy Italian menus have a Cornish twist and feature homemade pastas and steaks from the Josper grill. They open for breakfast too.

Menu £ 32/65 – Carte £ 42/53

On The Beach ⊠ *TR8 4AA –* ☎ *01637 861000 (booking essential)*
– www.fifteencornwall.co.uk

✗✗ Zacry's 🆕   ☙ ⌂ 🆎 🖵

MODERN BRITISH · CHIC Set within a seaside hotel, a lively brasserie with a modish feel. There's lots of choice on the menu, which draws on the chef's love of American and fusion cuisine; cooking is full of flavour and the charcoal oven plays a key role.

Menu £ 30/37 – Carte £ 24/44

Watergate Bay Hotel, On The Beach ⊠ *TQ8 4AA –* ☎ *01637 861231*
– www.zacrys.com – dinner only

at Mawgan Porth Northeast: 6 mi by A3059 on B3276

🏠 Scarlet   ☙ ← 🖳 🖼 🌐 ⊡ ⅄ 🅿

LUXURY · MODERN Eco-centric, adults only hotel set high on a cliff and boasting stunning coastal views. Modern bar and lounges, and a great spa offering extensive treatments. Bedrooms range from 'Just Right' to 'Indulgent' and have unusual open-plan bathrooms and a cool, Scandic style – every room has a terrace and sea view.

37 rooms ⊡ – ♦£ 190/530 ♦♦£ 210/550

Tredragon Rd ⊠ *TR8 4DQ –* ☎ *01637 861800 – www.scarlethotel.co.uk – Closed 3-29 January*

Scarlet – See restaurant listing

🏠 Bedruthan   🌳 ⟨ 🛴 ⟰ ▣ 🆒 ⛱ ✕ ▣ ♿ ⼝ ⛷ 🅿

FAMILY · CONTEMPORARY Unassuming hotel set in an elevated position over-looking the shore and boasting direct access to the beach. The interior is surpris-ingly contemporary and bedrooms are bright. Facilities and activities are family-orientated but the cocktail bar and lounge are set aside for adults. Interesting modern menus in Herring and accessible, family-focused dining in Wild Café.

89 rooms ⌂ - ♦£ 79/149 ♦♦£ 139/279 - 10 suites

✉ TR8 4BU – Northeast : 0.5 mi on B 3276 – 𝒞 01637 860860
– www.bedruthan.com – Closed Christmas-February

✕✕ Scarlet   ⟨ 🛖 ♿ 🅿

MODERN BRITISH · DESIGN Contemporary hotel restaurant with huge windows offering stunning coastal views; start with a drink on the lovely terrace or in the chic bar. Concise daily menus promote small local suppliers; cooking is light, modern and seasonal.

Menu £ 24/45

Scarlet Hotel, Tredragon Rd ✉ TR8 4DQ – 𝒞 01637 861800 (bookings essential for non-residents) – www.scarlethotel.co.uk – Closed 3-29 January

NEWTON LONGVILLE

Buckinghamshire – Pop. 1 846 – Regional map n° **6**-C1
▶ London 52 mi – Birmingham 77 mi – Bristol 110 mi – Cardiff 144 mi

🍴 Crooked Billet   🛖 🛖 🎮 🅿

REGIONAL CUISINE · NEIGHBOURHOOD Delightful 17C thatched pub with an in-viting fire-lit bar. Choose between pub classics on the bar menu or more modern dishes on the à la carte; the tasty meat and fish sharing platters are a hit. Service is attentive and personable.

Carte £ 24/45

2 Westbrook End ✉ MK17 0DF – 𝒞 01908 373936
– www.thecrookedbilletmiltonkeynes.co.uk

NEWTON-ON-OUSE

North Yorkshire – Pop. 599 – Regional map n° **22**-B2
▶ London 211 mi – York 11 mi – Manchester 77 mi

🍴 Dawnay Arms   🛖 🛖 🎮 🅿

MODERN BRITISH · PUB A handsome pub with stone floors, low beams, open fires and all manner of bric-a-brac – its delightful dining room has views over the garden and down to the river. Gutsy, well executed British dishes include plenty of local game.

Menu £ 14 (weekday lunch) – Carte £ 18/49

✉ YO30 2BR – 𝒞 01347 848345 – www.thedawnayatnewton.co.uk – Closed Sunday dinner and Monday except bank holidays

NOMANSLAND

Hampshire – Regional map n° **2**-D3
▶ London 96 mi – Bournemouth 26 mi – Salisbury 13 mi – Southampton 14 mi

✕✕ Les Mirabelles   🐝 🛖 🏧

CLASSIC FRENCH · FRIENDLY This bright, modern restaurant overlooks the common and is enthusiastically run by a welcoming Frenchman. The well-bal-anced menu features unfussy, classic Gallic dishes and the superb wine selection lists over 3,000 bins!

Menu £ 20 (weekdays) – Carte £ 30/49

Forest Edge Rd ✉ SP5 2BN – 𝒞 01794 390205 – www.lesmirabelles.co.uk
– Closed 22 December-13 January, 1 week May, 1 week September, Sunday and Monday

NORTH BOVEY

Devon – ⊠ Newton Abbot – Pop. 254 – Regional map n° **1**-C2

▶ London 197 mi – Plymouth 41 mi – Torbay 23 mi – Exeter 15 mi

🏨 Bovey Castle

HISTORIC · CLASSIC An impressive manor house on an extensive country estate, beautifully set within Dartmoor National Park. It has a relaxed, homely feel; bedrooms have contemporary touches but still retain their classic edge. The restaurant has a modern menu of local seasonal produce and the brasserie offers British classics.

64 rooms ⊇ – ♦£ 139/199 ♦♦£ 179/279 – 4 suites

⊠ TQ13 8RE – Northwest : 2 mi by Postbridge rd, bearing left at fork just out of village – ℰ 01647 445000 – www.boveycastle.com

🏨 Gate House

HISTORIC · COSY Charming 15C medieval hall house in the heart of an attractive village, boasting a characterful thatched roof, a large oak door and a lovely country garden with a small pool. Homely lounge, cosy low-beamed breakfast room and simple, spotlessly kept bedrooms, some with moor views. Charming owners.

3 rooms ⊇ – ♦£ 55 ♦♦£ 90/92

⊠ TQ13 8RB – just off village green, past "Ring of Bells" public house
– ℰ 01647 440479 – www.gatehouseondartmoor.com – Closed 24-26 December

NORTH LOPHAM

Norfolk – Regional map n° **8**-C2

▶ London 98 mi – Norwich 34 mi – Ipswich 31 mi – Bury Saint Edmunds 20 mi

🏨 Church Farm House

FAMILY · PERSONALISED Characterful thatched farmhouse in the shadow of the village church, with lovely gardens and a terrace for summer breakfasts. The comfy conservatory and spacious beamed lounge are filled with antiques and musical curios; bedrooms are traditional. The charming owners prepare homely meals of local produce.

3 rooms ⊇ – ♦£ 55/75 ♦♦£ 110

Church Rd ⊠ IP22 2LP – ℰ 01379 687270 – www.churchfarmhouse.org – Closed January-mid February

NORTH SHIELDS

Tyne and Wear – Pop. 39 042 – Regional map n° **14**-B2

▶ London 288 mi – Newcastle upon Tyne 9 mi – Sunderland 14 mi – Middlesbrough 39 mi

🍴 Irvins Brasserie

CLASSIC CUISINE · BRASSERIE Busy, informal restaurant in an old industrial building on the historic fish quay; brick walls and exposed pipes feature. The experienced chef has worked in a variety of places – menus are appealing and eclectic, with personal twists.

Menu £ 12 (weekday lunch) – Carte £ 17/35

The Richard Irvin Building, Union Quay ⊠ NE30 1HJ – ℰ 0191 296 3238
– www.irvinsbrasserie.co.uk – Closed Monday and Tuesday

🍴 River Cafe on the Tyne

TRADITIONAL BRITISH · BISTRO Laid-back restaurant run by a friendly local team, set above a pub in the North Shields fish quay. The daily changing à la carte offers unfussy, bistro-style dishes of fresh local produce, including fish from the market on the quayside. The 3 course set lunch and early dinner menu is a steal.

Menu £ 8 (lunch and early dinner) – Carte £ 19/33

51 Bell St, Fish Quay ⊠ NE30 1HF – ℰ 0191 296 6168 (booking advisable)
– www.rivercafeonthetyne.co.uk – Closed 25-26 December, 1-2 January, Monday, Sunday dinner and Tuesday lunch

Staith House 🛖 ♿

TRADITIONAL BRITISH · PUB There's a pleasing no-frills feel to this cosy quay-side pub with its portholes and nautical charts. Bypass classics like burger and chips in favour of fish or shellfish straight from the sea; cooking is robust, tasty and well-priced.

Carte £ 21/43

57 Low Lights ⊠ NE30 1JA – 𝒞 0191 270 8441 (booking essential at dinner) – www.thestaithhouse.co.uk – Closed 25-26 December and 1-2 January

NORTH WALSHAM
Norfolk – Pop. 12 463 – Regional map n° **8**-D1
▶ London 133 mi – Norwich 15 mi – Ipswich 61 mi – Lowestoft 34 mi

🏠 Beechwood ☆ 🚗 **P**

TOWNHOUSE · CLASSIC A red-brick, creeper-clad, part-Georgian property with classical furnishings and bright, eye-catching colour schemes. Period bedrooms vary in size and comfort – many have feature beds and the best have terraces onto the lovely gardens. A '10 Mile Menu' offers local ingredients in modern Mediterranean dishes.

18 rooms 🖙 – 🛉£ 70/90 🛉🛉£ 100/175

20 Cromer Rd ⊠ NR28 0HD – 𝒞 01692 403231 – www.beechwood-hotel.co.uk

NORTHAW
Hertfordshire – Regional map n° **7**-B2
▶ London 22 mi – St Albans 13 mi – Welwyn Garden City 10 mi

Sun at Northaw 🚗 🛖 **P**

TRADITIONAL BRITISH · PUB A restored, whitewashed, part-16C inn which sits by the village green; passionately run and contemporary in style, it's deceptively spacious, with a traditional edge. Hearty, unfussy, flavoursome cooking uses seasonal East of England produce, and beers and ciders are equally local. Friendly service.

Carte £ 24/33

1 Judges Hill ⊠ EN6 4NL – 𝒞 01707 655507 – www.thesunatnorthaw.co.uk – Closed Sunday dinner and Monday except bank holidays when closed Tuesday

NORTHLEACH
Gloucestershire – Pop. 1 854 – Regional map n° **2**-D1
▶ London 87 mi – Birmingham 73 mi – Bristol 54 mi – Coventry 47 mi

Wheatsheaf Inn 🔄 🛖 ♻ **P**

TRADITIONAL BRITISH · INN Smart 17C coaching inn with a pretty tiered terrace and two traditional dining rooms, one either side of the stone-floored, open-fired bar. The same menu is available throughout, offering classical dishes and something to suit every taste. Stylish, contemporary bedrooms have quirky touches and feature interesting French flea market finds; some have baths in the rooms.

Menu £ 13 (weekday lunch) – Carte £ 24/46

14 rooms 🖙 – 🛉£ 120/220 🛉🛉£ 120/220

West End ⊠ GL50 3EZ – 𝒞 01451 860244 – www.cotswoldswheatsheaf.com

NORTHMOOR
Oxfordshire – Regional map n° **6**-B2
▶ London 111 mi – Oxford 23 mi – Gloucester 73 mi

Red Lion 🚗 **P**

TRADITIONAL BRITISH · FRIENDLY Extremely welcoming pub owned by the villagers and run by an experienced young couple and a friendly team. Low beams, open fires and fresh flowers abound and the menu is a great mix of pub classics and more modern daily specials.

Carte £ 23/37

Standlake Rd ⊠ OX29 5SX – 𝒞 01865 300301 – www.theredlionnorthmoor.com – Closed Sunday dinner

NORTON DISNEY

Lincolnshire – Regional map n° **9**-C1

▶ London 134 mi – Nottingham 30 mi – Lincoln 13 mi

🏠 Brills Farm   ⇧ ⇦ 🖨 🛇 **P**

FAMILY · PERSONALISED Charming Georgian farmhouse in a commanding hilltop position on a 2,000 acre working farm. Elegant country bedrooms have period wallpapers, goose down duvets and lovely rural views. Tasty Aga-cooked dinners are served by arrangement (min. 6 people) at an antique table; the bacon is from their farm.

3 rooms ⌂ – 🛉£ 69 🛉🛉£ 98

Brills Hill ⊠ LN6 9JN – West : 2 mi on Newark Rd – ℰ 01636 892311
– www.brillsfarm-bedandbreakfast.co.uk – Closed Christmas-New Year

NORWELL – Nottinghamshire → See Newark-on-Trent

NORWICH

Norfolk – Pop. 186 682 – Regional map n° **8**-D2

▶ London 109 mi – Kingston-upon-Hull 148 mi – Leicester 117 mi

🏠 38 St Giles   🛇 **P**

TOWNHOUSE · PERSONALISED City centre townhouse where boutique styling blends with original features. Elegant, uncluttered bedrooms boast high ceilings and wood panelling, along with silk curtains, handmade mattresses and quality linen. Excellent breakfasts.

8 rooms ⌂ – 🛉£ 95/120 🛉🛉£ 110/245

Town plan: A1-x *– 38 St Giles St ⊠ NR2 1LL – ℰ 01603 662944*
– www.38stgiles.co.uk – Closed 24-27 December

🏠 Catton Old Hall   🖨 🛇 **P**

HISTORIC · PERSONALISED Attractive, personally run, 17C merchant's house with a characterful interior. Individually designed bedrooms include 5 feature rooms; Anna Sewell, with exposed rafters and a vast four-poster, is the best.

7 rooms ⌂ – 🛉£ 99/150 🛉🛉£ 99/150

Lodge Ln, Old Catton ⊠ NR6 7HG – North : 3.5 mi by Catton Grove Rd off St Faiths Rd – ℰ 01603 419379 – www.catton-hall.co.uk

XX Roger Hickman's   ⒶⒸ

MODERN CUISINE · INTIMATE Personally run restaurant in a historic part of the city, with soft hues, modern art and romantic corners. Service is attentive yet unobtrusive. Cooking is modern, intricate and displays respect for ingredients' natural flavours.

Menu £ 25/45

Town plan: A1-c *79 Upper St Giles St ⊠ NR2 1AB – ℰ 01603 633522*
– www.rogerhickmansrestaurant.com – Closed 2 weeks Christmas, Sunday and Monday

XX Bishop's   ⒶⒸ

TRADITIONAL BRITISH · ROMANTIC Intimate restaurant of only eight tables, in a 15C building with a country-chic décor of floral prints, oval mirrors, crystal chandeliers and silk curtains. Simply presented, traditional dishes. Efficient service.

Menu £ 15/35

Town plan: A1-a *8-10 St Andrew's Hill ⊠ NR2 1AD – ℰ 01603 767321 (booking essential) – www.bishopsrestaurant.co.uk – Closed Sunday and Monday*

X Benedicts   ✿

MODERN CUISINE · BISTRO A huge window lets in lots of light and white wood-panelled walls keep things suitably down-to-earth. Tried-and-tested combinations are given subtle modern touches and cooking shows respect for good quality Norfolk ingredients.

Menu £ 20/36

Town plan: A1-b *9 St Benedicts Street ⊠ NR2 4PE – ℰ 01603 926080*
– www.restaurantbenedicts.com – Closed 24 December-7January, Sunday and Monday

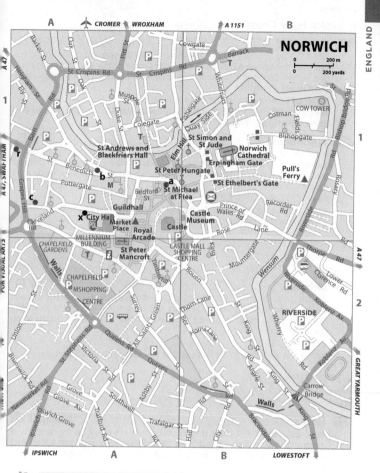

🏠 Georgian Townhouse ⬅️ 🍴 🛋️ 🚗 AC 🔌 🔄 P

TRADITIONAL CUISINE · NEIGHBOURHOOD Laid-back pub with a flexible menu: choose small plates to start or to share; dishes 'for the table' for 2 or 4; or something for yourself 'from the store'. Fruit and veg is home-grown and they home-smoke cheese and spit-roast and flame-grill meats. Bold, retro-style bedrooms have fridges and coffee machines.

Carte £ 20/41

22 rooms ☕ – †£ 85/160 ††£ 95/170

30-34 Unthank Rd ⊠ NR2 2RB – West : 0.5 mi by A 147 – ℘ 01603 615655
– www.thegeorgiantownhousenorwich.com

🏠 Reindeer 🛋️ AC 🔄 P

TRADITIONAL CUISINE · PUB Rustic neighbourhood pub with a keen local following. Plenty of space is kept aside for drinkers, who have 10 real ales to choose from. Straightforward, proudly British cooking employs lesser-used cuts and offers plenty of sharing dishes.

Carte £ 20/32

Town plan: A1-r *10 Dereham Rd ⊠ NR2 4AY – Northwest : 0.5 mi by A 147*
– ℘ 01603 612995 – www.thereindeerpub.co.uk – Closed 25-26 December and Monday

ENGLAND

at Stoke Holy Cross South: 5.75 mi by A140 ⊠ Norwich

✕✕ Stoke Mill

TRADITIONAL CUISINE · HISTORIC Characterful 700 year old mill spanning the River Tas; the adjoining building is where the Colman family started making mustard in 1814. Confidently prepared, classically based dishes use good ingredients and flavours are distinct.

Menu £ 17 (weekday lunch) – Carte £ 32/49

Mill Rd ⊠ NR14 8PA – ℘ 01508 493337 – www.stokemill.co.uk – Closed Sunday dinner, Monday and Tuesday

ⁱ◫ Wildebeest

MODERN BRITISH · PUB A smart dining pub run by one of the locals. Comfy leather chairs are set at chunky tree trunk tables. Cooking is modern and refined and the colourful dishes blend many different ingredients to create pleasing contrasts of flavour.

Menu £ 17/28 – Carte £ 32/47

82-86 Norwich Rd ⊠ NR14 8QJ – ℘ 01508 492497 (booking essential) – www.thewildebeest.co.uk – Closed 25-26 December

NOSS MAYO

Devon – Regional map n° **1**-C3

▶ London 217 mi – Plymouth 11 mi – Torbay 32 mi – Exeter 45 mi

ⁱ◫ Ship Inn

TRADITIONAL BRITISH · PUB Large, busy, well-run pub with characterful, nautical décor and wonderful waterside views from its peaceful spot on the Yealm Estuary. Appealing menu of unfussy pub classics. Bright, friendly service. Keep an eye on the tide!

Carte £ 22/33

⊠ PL8 1EW – ℘ 01752 872387 – www.nossmayo.com – Closed 25 December

NOTTINGHAM

Nottingham – Pop. 289 301 – Regional map n° **9**-B2

▶ London 135 mi – Birmingham 50 mi – Leeds 74 mi – Leicester 27 mi

⌂⌂ Hart's

BUSINESS · DESIGN Sophisticated, boutique-style hotel built on the ramparts of a medieval castle. Compact bedrooms have modern bathrooms and a high level of facilities; some open onto garden terraces. The small bar-lounge doubles as a breakfast room.

32 rooms – ♦£ 134/179 ♦♦£ 134/179 – ⌧ £ 14 – 2 suites

Town plan: A2-e - *Standard Hill, Park Row ⊠ NG1 6FN – ℘ 0115 988 1900 – www.hartsnottingham.co.uk*

Hart's – See restaurant listing

✕✕✕ Restaurant Sat Bains

❀❀ **CREATIVE · INTIMATE** Smart restaurant with an intimate atmosphere and slick service; incongruously located near a flyover. 7 and 10 course tasting menus feature refined, highly original dishes with distinct, carefully balanced flavours. Book a table in the 6-seater 'Nucleus' dining room to best see the kitchen's creativity. Bedrooms are modern and individually styled; some have feature beds.

→ Scallop curry '1999/2016'. Wood-fired aged Goosnargh duck with parsnip, pear, olive and raisin. Chocolate 'Grand Cru', toast and sea salt.

Menu £ 85/125 – tasting menu only

8 rooms ⌧ – ♦£ 140/285 ♦♦£ 140/285 – 4 suites

Trentside, Lenton Ln ⊠ NG7 2SA – Southwest : 3.5 mi by A 610, A 6005 and A 52 – ℘ 0115 986 6566 (booking essential) – www.restaurantsatbains.com – Closed 2 weeks August, 2 weeks late December-early January, 1 week April and Sunday-Tuesday

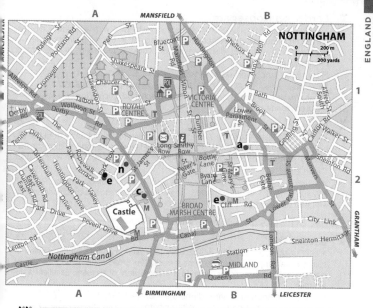

MANSFIELD

NOTTINGHAM

0   200 m
0   200 yards

BIRMINGHAM   LEICESTER

GRANTHAM

XX Hart's

🛖 🔥 🖫 🥂 ⇄

MODERN BRITISH · FASHIONABLE Contemporary restaurant in the A&E department of the old city hospital; ask to sit in one of the central booths. British brasserie dishes feature on the daily menu and cooking is flavourful and well-priced. Lighter snacks are also served.

Menu £ 24/28 (weekdays) – Carte £ 30/43

Town plan: A2-e Hart's Hotel, Standard Ct., Park Row ⊠ NG1 6GN – ℰ 0115 988 1900
– www.hartsnottingham.co.uk – Closed 1 January and dinner 25-26 December

XX World Service

🍽 🛖 ⇄

INTERNATIONAL · CHIC Hidden in the extension of a Georgian property and accessed via an Indonesian-inspired courtyard garden. It has a clubby, colonial feel, with panelled walls and cases of archaeological artefacts. Appealing dishes have global influences.

Menu £ 22 (lunch) – Carte £ 27/52

Town plan: A2-c - Newdigate House, Castlegate ⊠ NG1 6AF – ℰ 0115 847 5587
– www.worldservicerestaurant.com – Closed 1-5 January and Sunday dinner

XX MemSaab

🖫 🎯 ⇄

INDIAN · EXOTIC DÉCOR Professionally run restaurant with eye-catching artwork and a wooden 'Gateway of India'. Original, authentic cooking has a distinct North Indian influence. Spicing is well-judged and dishes from the charcoal grill are a highlight.

Carte £ 19/38

Town plan: A2-n - 12-14 Maid Marian Way ⊠ NG1 6HS – ℰ 0115 957 0009
– www.mem-saab.co.uk – dinner only – Closed 25 December

X Ibérico World Tapas

🖫 🍴

☺

MEDITERRANEAN CUISINE · FASHIONABLE Lively, well-run restaurant hidden away in the basement of the former city jail and law courts, with a vaulted ceiling, colourful Moorish tiles and ornate fretwork. Tapas menu with 'Spanish' and 'World' sections; skilful cooking is full of flavour. Friendly staff offer good recommendations.

Menu £ 13 (weekdays) s – Carte £ 13/25 s

Town plan: B2-e The Shire Hall, High Pavement ⊠ NG1 1HN – ℰ 0115 941 0410
(booking essential at dinner) – www.ibericotapas.com – Closed 1-5 January and Sunday

511

✗ Larder on Goosegate

TRADITIONAL BRITISH · RUSTIC Appealing restaurant with a shabby-chic feel, on the first floor of a listed Victorian building; sit in the window for a view of the street below. Unfussy dishes are skilfully cooked, good value and very tasty; the steaks are a hit.

Menu £ 15 (lunch and early dinner) – Carte £ 23/36

*Town plan: B1-a - 1st Floor, 16-22 Goosegate ✉ NG1 1FE – ℰ 0115 950 0111
– www.thelarderongoosegate.co.uk – dinner only and lunch Friday-Sunday
– Closed Monday*

✗ Lime

INDIAN · NEIGHBOURHOOD Bright, modern Indian restaurant away from the city centre; personally run by the cheery owner. Flavoursome food with distinctive spicing. Non-alcoholic bar, and no corkage fee if you bring your own wine or beer.

Carte £ 15/30

*4-6 Upminster Dr, Nuthall ✉ NG16 1PT – Northwest : 4.5 mi by Alfreton Rd, A 610 and A 6002 – ℰ 0115 975 0005 – www.lime-restaurant.co.uk – dinner only
– Closed 25 December*

at West Bridgford *Southeast: 1.75 mi by A60✉ Nottingham*

✗ escabeche

MEDITERRANEAN CUISINE · FRIENDLY Informal, modern, Mediterranean-inspired restaurant with a sunny front terrace. The broad main menu lists vibrant, well-presented tapas dishes, offering a great variety of flavours. Excellent value set menu.

Menu £ 10 (lunch and early dinner) **s** – Carte £ 13/24

27 Bridgford Rd ✉ NG2 6AU – ℰ 0115 981 7010 – www.escabeche.co.uk – Closed 25-26 December and 1 January

at Plumtree *Southeast: 5.75 mi by A60 off A606✉ Nottingham*

✗✗ Perkins

MODERN BRITISH · FRIENDLY Formerly a Victorian railway station, now a bright family-run brasserie; find a spot in the conservatory overlooking the railway line. Menus evolve daily and the modern British cooking features home-smoked fish, game and cheeses.

Menu £ 14/20 (weekdays) – Carte £ 27/40

Old Railway Station, Station Rd ✉ NG12 5NA – ℰ 0115 937 3695 (booking advisable) – www.perkinsrestaurant.co.uk – Closed Sunday dinner

at Ruddington *South : 5.5 mi on A 60✉ Nottinghamshire*

⌂ Ruddington Arms

TRADITIONAL CUISINE · NEIGHBOURHOOD This dramatically refurbished, faux-industrial style pub is found in a sleepy village. Flavoursome dishes cater for one and all, with everything from pub classics to more adventurous offerings. Tasty marmalades and chutneys are for sale.

Menu £ 17 (weekdays) – Carte £ 19/34

56 Wilford Rd ✉ NG11 6EQ – ℰ 0115 984 1628 – www.theruddingtonarms.com

at Stapleford *Southwest: 5.5 mi by A52✉ Nottingham*

✗✗ Crème

TRADITIONAL BRITISH · NEIGHBOURHOOD Well-run neighbourhood restaurant with a spacious, comfortable lounge area and a stylish, modern, formally laid dining room. Seasonally changing, modern British menu; well-presented dishes are served by friendly staff.

Menu £ 18 (weekday lunch)/21 – Carte £ 23/33

*12 Toton Ln ✉ NG9 7HA – ℰ 0115 939 7422 (booking advisable)
– www.cremerestaurant.co.uk – Closed 25-26 and 31 December, Saturday lunch, Sunday dinner and Monday*

at Sherwood Business Park Northwest: 10 mi by A611 off
A608 ⊠ Nottingham

🏨 Dakota
BUSINESS · MODERN An eye-catching black glass cube in the heart of a business park by the M1. Spacious modern bedrooms have good facilities and walk-in showers; executive rooms have super king sized beds and extras such as bathrobes and chocolates. The roomy, laid-back restaurant offers an international grill-style menu.

92 rooms - ♦£ 89/179 ♦♦£ 89/179 - ⊊ £ 14

Lake View Dr ⊠ NG15 0EA – ℰ 01623 727670 – www.dakotanottingham.co.uk

NUN MONKTON
North Yorkshire – Regional map n° **22**-B2
▶ London 207 mi – York 11 mi – Leeds 29 mi

🍴 Alice Hawthorn Inn 🄽
MODERN CUISINE · PUB This smart, stylish pub sits on a picturesque village green complete with a duck pond, grazing cattle and the country's tallest maypole. Choose from pub classics and sharing boards at lunch or more refined modern dishes at dinner.

Menu £ 20 (lunch and early dinner) – Carte £ 28/39

*The Green ⊠ YO26 8EW – ℰ 01423 330303 – www.thealicehawthorn.com
– Closed Sunday dinner, Monday and Tuesday lunch*

OAKHAM
Rutland – Pop. 10 922 – Regional map n° **9**-C2
▶ London 103 mi – Leicester 26 mi – Northampton 35 mi

at Hambleton East: 3 mi by A606 ⊠ Oakham

🏨 Hambleton Hall
LUXURY · CLASSIC Beautiful Victorian manor house in a peaceful location, with mature grounds sloping down to Rutland Water. Classical country house drawing rooms boast heavy drapes, open fires and antiques. Good-sized bedrooms are designed by the owner herself and come with a host of thoughtful extras. Service is engaging.

16 rooms ⊊ - ♦£ 195/510 ♦♦£ 270/560 – 1 suite

⊠ LE15 8TH – ℰ 01572 756991 – www.hambletonhall.com
❀ **Hambleton Hall** – See restaurant listing

XXX Hambleton Hall
❀
CLASSIC CUISINE · COUNTRY HOUSE A traditional dining room in a lovely Victorian manor house, boasting superb views over Rutland Water. Accomplished cooking marries together a host of top quality seasonal ingredients. Gallic dishes are classically based but display the occasional modern touch; the delicious bread is from their artisan bakery.
→ Spring morels with wild garlic and Hambleton's poached hen's egg. Loin and breast of lamb with pepper stew and dumplings. Gariguette strawberries with champagne sorbet and hibiscus.

Menu £ 38 (weekday lunch)/68

Hambleton Hall Hotel, ⊠ LE15 8TH – ℰ 01572 756991 – www.hambletonhall.com

🍴 Finch's Arms
TRADITIONAL BRITISH · PUB Quaint stone inn with a characterful bar, two very stylish dining rooms and a delightful terrace overlooking Rutland Water. Assured, seasonal dishes rely on local produce; desserts are satisfyingly old school and afternoon tea is also an option. Modern bedrooms complete the picture.

Menu £ 14 (weekday lunch) – Carte £ 22/43

10 rooms ⊊ - ♦£ 75/100 ♦♦£ 80/130

Oakham Rd ⊠ LE15 8TL – ℰ 01572 756575 – www.finchsarms.co.uk

OARE – Kent → See Faversham

OLD ALRESFORD
Hampshire – Pop. 577 – Regional map n° **6**-B2
▶ London 62 mi – Winchester 8 mi – Southampton 20 mi

X **Pulpo Negro** ⓝ 🛱 🗛 ▤
😊 SPANISH · TAPAS BAR A characterful, well run restaurant in an old townhouse in the heart of the town; its name translates as the Black Octopus. Stylish interior with exposed brick, rough floorboards, an open kitchen and a relaxed atmosphere. Tasty authentic Spanish tapas is accompanied by a good choice of Spanish wines.
Carte £ 12/26
28 Broad St ⊠ SO24 9AQ – ℰ 01962 732262 (booking essential)
– www.pulponegro.co.uk – Closed 25-26 December, 1 January, Sunday and Monday

OLD BURGHCLERE
Hampshire – ⊠ Newbury – Regional map n° **4**-B1
▶ London 77 mi – Bristol 76 mi – Newbury 10 mi – Reading 27 mi

XX **Dew Pond** < 🛱 ⇔ 🅿
CLASSIC FRENCH · COSY A part-16C farmhouse with well-tended gardens leading down to a dew pond. The longstanding restaurant is family owned and run and serves classic French cooking; enjoy an aperitif on the terrace, overlooking the real Watership Down.
Menu £ 36
⊠ RG20 9LH – ℰ 01635 278408 – www.dewpond.co.uk – dinner only – Closed 2 weeks Christmas-New Year, Sunday and Monday

OLDHAM
Greater Manchester – Pop. 96 555 – Regional map n° **11**-B2
▶ London 212 mi – Leeds 36 mi – Manchester 7 mi – Sheffield 38 mi

XX **Dining Room** ⓝ 🍹 🅿
MODERN BRITISH · DESIGN Tucked away to the back of a pub, this small but stylish restaurant is a destination in its own right. Refined modern dishes are skilfully prepared and have Mediterranean influences; the 7 course tasting menu is a good option.
Carte £ 34/47
White Hart Inn, 51 Stockport Rd, Lydgate ⊠ OL4 4JJ – East : 3 mi by A 669 on A 6050 – ℰ 01457 872566 (booking advisable) – www.thewhitehart.co.uk – dinner only and Sunday lunch – Closed 1 January, 26 December, Sunday dinner and Monday

🍽 **White Hart Inn** ⇦ ⇔ 🅿
MODERN BRITISH · CLASSIC DÉCOR The original part of this stone-built inn dates from 1788 but there's always something new going on here. With its formal restaurant, private dining room, large function room and smart bedrooms, it can be a busy place. The menu offers a good range of refined pub classics, many with a Mediterranean slant.
Menu £ 14 (weekdays) – Carte £ 25/42
17 rooms ☑ – ♦£ 85/120 ♦♦£ 125/165
51 Stockport Rd, Lydgate ⊠ OL4 4JJ – East : 3 mi by A 669 on A 6050 – ℰ 01457 872566 – www.thewhitehart.co.uk – Closed 1 January and 26 December
Dining Room – See restaurant listing

OLDSTEAD
North Yorkshire – Regional map n° **13**-C2
▶ London 235 mi – Leeds 54 mi – Sheffield 86 mi

ENGLAND

XX **Black Swan** (Tommy Banks)   🕸 ⇔ 🍸 🚪 🎥 🅿

🏵 MODERN BRITISH · FAMILY The Black Swan is owned by a family who've farmed in the area for generations. Enjoy an aperitif in the characterful bar, then head upstairs to the restaurant. Modern menus are driven by meats from their farm and produce grown in the garden; cooking is highly skilled and dishes are carefully presented. Antique-furnished bedrooms have smart bathrooms and private patios.
→ Crapaudine beetroot slow-cooked in beef fat. Hogget with Jerusalem artichoke and hispi cabbage. Heather honey with vinegar and elderflower.

Menu £ 60/85

9 rooms 🖵 - †£ 160/280 ††£ 160/280

✉ YO61 4BL - ℰ 01347 868387 (bookings essential for non-residents)
- www.blackswanoldstead.co.uk - dinner only and Saturday lunch - Closed Sunday

OMBERSLEY
Worcestershire - Pop. 623 - Regional map n° **10**-B3
▶ London 128 mi - Birmingham 25 mi - Coventry 41 mi

XX **Venture In**

TRADITIONAL BRITISH · COSY A hugely characterful black and white timbered house with 15C origins and a large inglenook fireplace in the bar. Cooking is classically based but has modern overtones and there's always a good choice of specials available.

Menu £ 32 (lunch)/42

Main St ✉ WR9 0EW - ℰ 01905 620552 - www.theventurein.co.uk - Closed 2 weeks August, 1 week March, 1 week June, 1 week Christmas, Monday and dinner Sunday

ORFORD
Suffolk - ✉ Woodbridge - Pop. 1 153 - Regional map n° **8**-D3
▶ London 103 mi - Ipswich 22 mi - Norwich 52 mi

🏠 **Crown and Castle**   🚪 🅿

HISTORIC · PERSONALISED It is thought that the original 12C inn which stood on this site was built into the walls of neighbouring Orford Castle. The latest incarnation, a Tudor-style house, is run in a relaxed yet professional manner. Most of the well-furnished bedrooms are in chalets - many have terraces and distant sea views.

21 rooms 🖵 - †£ 127/200 ††£ 145/215 - 1 suite

✉ IP12 2LJ - ℰ 01394 450205 - www.crownandcastle.co.uk

Crown and Castle - See restaurant listing

XX **Crown and Castle**   🕸 🚪 ⇆ 🅿

MODERN CUISINE · CONTEMPORARY DÉCOR A relaxed hotel restaurant decorated with eclectic art. Cooking mixes British and Italian traditions; try the lunchtime cicchetti or the cooked-to-order steak and kidney pie. Fish is landed at the nearby quay and service is efficient.

Carte £ 29/44

Crown and Castle Hotel, ✉ IP12 2LJ - ℰ 01394 450205 (booking essential at dinner) - www.crownandcastle.co.uk - Closed lunch 31 December

OSMOTHERLEY
North Yorkshire - ✉ Northallerton - Pop. 668 - Regional map n° **13**-B1
▶ London 245 mi - Darlington 25 mi - Leeds 49 mi - Middlesbrough 20 mi

🏠 **Golden Lion**   ⇔

TRADITIONAL BRITISH · PUB 18C stone inn set in a historic village in the North York Moors; make for the atmospheric bar which offers over 80 different whiskies. Cooking is traditional and satisfying, with filling dishes on the main menu and more ambitious weekly specials. Modern bedrooms have heavy oak furnishings and good facilities.

Carte £ 23/33

7 rooms 🖵 - †£ 75 ††£ 95/100

6 West End ✉ DL6 3AA - ℰ 01609 883526 - www.goldenlionosmotherley.co.uk
- Closed 25 December, lunch Monday and Tuesday except bank holidays

OSWESTRY

Shropshire – Pop. 16 660 – Regional map n° **10**-A1

▶ London 182 mi – Birmingham 66 mi – Chester 28 mi

✗✗ Sebastians ⇦ 🅿

TRADITIONAL CUISINE · COSY Housed in three characterful 17C cottages, Sebastians is a long-standing restaurant with an open fire, lots of beams and bags of charm. Cooking uses good ingredients and is classically based, and you'll be well looked after by the team. Many of the cosy, characterful bedrooms are set around a courtyard.

Menu £ 45

6 rooms – ♦£ 75 ♦♦£ 85 – ⚏£ 12

45 Willow St ⊠ *SY11 1AQ* – ℰ *01691 655444* – *www.sebastians-hotel.co.uk* – *dinner only* – *Closed 25-26 December, 1 January, Sunday and Monday*

✗✗ Townhouse 🍷 ⇦ 🏠 ⛓ 🕐 ⇦

MODERN BRITISH · FRIENDLY Contemporary restaurant in a Georgian townhouse. There's a flamboyant cocktail bar, a sunny terrace and an airy dining room featuring glitzy chandeliers. Classical cooking has a modern edge and dishes are attractively presented.

Menu £ 13/20 – Carte £ 32/44

35 Willow St ⊠ *SY11 1AQ* – ℰ *01691 659499* – *www.townhouseoswestry.com* – *Closed Sunday dinner and Monday*

at Rhydycroesau West: 3.5 mi on B4580 ⊠ Oswestry

🏠 Pen-Y-Dyffryn ⇧ 🐾 ⇐ 🏠 🅿

TRADITIONAL · COSY An early Victorian rectory in a peaceful countryside setting, with a pretty garden and a lovely outlook. Classical lounges feature antique furnishings and roaring fires. Bedrooms have subtle modern touches and the Coach House rooms come with private terraces. Daily menus use local and organic produce.

12 rooms ⚏ – ♦£ 99/105 ♦♦£ 136/198

⊠ *SY10 7JD* – ℰ *01691 653700* – *www.peny.co.uk* – *Closed 14 December-15 January*

OUSTON

Durham – Regional map n° **14**-B2

▶ London 197 mi – Cardiff 141 mi – Swansea 177 mi – Gloucester 241 mi

🏠 Low Urpeth Farm 🐾 ⇦ 🍽 🅿

FAMILY · PERSONALISED A stone-built Victorian farmhouse on a working arable farm: a very welcoming place, full of warmth and run with pride. Cakes and biscuits are served on arrival in the traditional, antique-furnished lounge; breakfast features homemade bread and preserves, and the spacious, comfy bedrooms have country views.

3 rooms ⚏ – ♦£ 55/60 ♦♦£ 80/87

⊠ *DH2 1BD* – *North : 1 mi on Kibblesworth rd* – ℰ *0191 410 2901* – *www.lowurpeth.co.uk* – *Closed Christmas and New Year*

OVERTON

Hampshire – Pop. 3 318 – Regional map n° **6**-B1

▶ London 63 mi – Winchester 15 mi – Southampton 30 mi

🍴 White Hart 🅝 ⇦ 🏠 ⛓ 🅿

TRADITIONAL CUISINE · RUSTIC The lounge has retained its original stone fireplace and the dining room its characterful wood panelling and parquet floor but there's also a more modern extension, an attractive terrace and 12 cosy boutique-style bedrooms. Menus offer something for one and all, from the traditional to the more adventurous.

Carte £ 20/38

12 rooms ⚏ – ♦£ 85/140 ♦♦£ 90/150

London Rd ⊠ *RG25 3NW* – ℰ *01256 771431* – *www.whitehartoverton.co.uk*

OXFORD

Oxfordshire – Pop. 159 994 – Regional map n° **6**-B2
▶ London 59 mi – Birmingham 63 mi – Brighton 105 mi – Bristol 73 mi

Hotels

🏨 Randolph

HISTORIC · CLASSIC This grand old lady exudes immense charm and character, and comes complete with an intricate wrought iron staircase and plush modern bedrooms. Have a cocktail in the magnificent bar or afternoon tea in the drawing room beneath Sir Osbert Lancaster oils. The impressive formal dining room offers classic menus.

151 rooms ⊑ – ♦£ 200/350 ♦♦£ 250/400 – 9 suites
Town plan: C1-n - *Beaumont St.* ✉ OX1 2LN – ✆ 0344 879 9132
– www.macdonaldhotels.co.uk/randolph – Restricted opening at Christmas

🏨 Malmaison

BUSINESS · HISTORIC Unique hotel in the 13C castle prison, where a pleasant rooftop terrace contrasts with a moody interior. The most characterful bedrooms are in the old A Wing cells; feature rooms are in the Governor's House and House of Correction. The basement brasserie serves an accessible menu, with steaks a speciality.

95 rooms – ♦£ 120/240 ♦♦£ 120/240 – ⊑ £ 14 – 3 suites
Town plan: C2-a - *Oxford Castle, 3 New Rd* ✉ OX1 1AY – ✆ 01865 268400
– www.malmaison.com

🏨 Old Bank

LUXURY · MODERN Warm, welcoming hotel in the heart of the city: once the area's first bank. It has a smart neo-classical façade and plenty of style. Elegant bedrooms have modern furnishings and eclectic artwork – those higher up boast great views.

42 rooms – ♦£ 158/330 ♦♦£ 158/330 – ⊑ £ 15 – 1 suite
Town plan: D2-s - *92-94 High St* ✉ OX1 4BJ – ✆ 01865 799599
– www.oldbank-hotel.co.uk
Quod – See restaurant listing

517

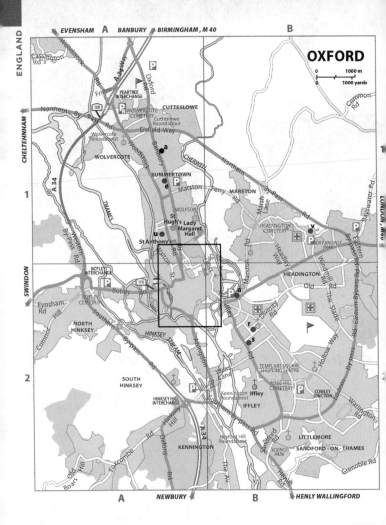

OXFORD

🏠 Old Parsonage

🏠 🍴 🛗 🅰🅲 🚭 🅿

TOWNHOUSE · PERSONALISED This ivy-clad sandstone parsonage sits in the historic town centre and dates from the 1660s. Enter into the original house via a pretty terrace; inside it's chic and modern – bold greys and purples feature in the bedrooms, along with the latest mod cons. Appealing menus offer classic British comfort food.

35 rooms – 🛏£ 195/340 🛏🛏£ 195/340 – ☕ £ 20

Town plan: C1-p - *1 Banbury Rd* ⊠ *OX2 6NN* - ☎ *01865 310210*
- *www.oldparsonage-hotel.co.uk*

 Is breakfast included? If it is, the cup symbol ☕ appears after the number of rooms.

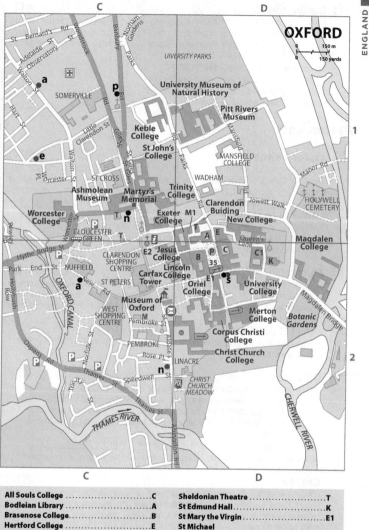

OXFORD

All Souls College C	Sheldonian Theatre ....T
Bodleian Library ....A	St Edmund Hall...K
Brasenose College.......................................B	St Mary the Virgin.......................................E1
Hertford College ....E	St Michael
Museum of the History	at the Northgate E2
of Science M1	
Queen's College (The) C1	Radcliffe Square...35
Radcliffe Camera..P	

🏠 Burlington House   ⚐ ⚒ **P**

TOWNHOUSE · CONTEMPORARY Handsome former merchant's house dating from 1889. Smart lounge with guest info overlooks a Japanese courtyard garden. Individually styled, modern bedrooms feature vivid wallpaper. Homemade bread and fresh fruit and juices at breakfast.

16 rooms ⚐ – †£ 70/99 ††£ 91/160

Town plan: A1-a - *374 Banbury Rd* ✉ *OX2 7PP*
- ☎ *01865 513513* – *www.burlington-house.co.uk*
- *Closed 21 December-2 January*

Restaurants

XX Oxford Kitchen   ⚑ **AC**

MODERN BRITISH · MINIMALIST Bright, modern neighbourhood restaurant hidden in a parade of shops in trendy Summertown. Menus list appealing, original dishes with a modern British base and cooking is refined and flavoursome. Come at the weekend for brunch.

Menu £ 23 (weekdays)/50 – Carte £ 30/54

Town plan: A1-e - *215 Banbury Rd, Summertown* ✉ *OX2 7HQ*
- ☎ *01865 511149* – *www.theoxfordkitchen.co.uk*
- *Closed 2-16 January, Sunday dinner and Monday*

XX Quod   ⚐ ⚒ **AC** 🖥 ⚒ **P**

INTERNATIONAL · BRASSERIE Buzzy brasserie in an old banking hall (now a stylish hotel). It's open from early 'til late and has a lovely terrace to the rear. Modern menus offer a mix of Italian and European dishes, along with twice-daily blackboard specials.

Menu £ 13 (lunch and early dinner) – Carte £ 23/46

Town plan: D2-s - *Old Bank Hotel, 92-94 High St* ✉ *OX1 4BJ* – ☎ *01865 799599*
- *www.quod.co.uk*

X Oli's Thai

🏵 **THAI · FRIENDLY** This lovely little restaurant is set off the beaten track, in an up-and-coming residential area. Start with a drink on the patio then make for the cool, relaxed restaurant; if you haven't booked, try for a seat at the counter. The concise menu offers fresh, meticulously prepared, vibrantly flavoured dishes.

Carte £ 15/26

Town plan: B2-r - *38 Magdalen Rd* ✉ *OX4 1RB* – ☎ *01865 790223 (booking essential)* – *www.olisthai.com* – *Closed Tuesday dinner, Sunday and Monday*

X Branca   ⚑ **AC**

ITALIAN · BISTRO Bustling restaurant with a spacious, modern interior and French doors opening onto a courtyard terrace. The menu is a roll call of Italian classics; portions are generous and lunch deals, good value. Friendly young staff; adjoining deli.

Menu £ 14 (weekday lunch) – Carte £ 18/39

Town plan: C1-a - *111 Walton St.* ✉ *OX2 6AJ* – ☎ *01865 556111* – *www.branca.co.uk*

X Shanghai 30's

CHINESE · ELEGANT Delightful, colonial-style restaurant in a characterful 15C building; the rooms are listed and feature wood panelling and ornate plaster ceilings. Menus offer a wide range of authentic Chinese dishes; don't miss the fiery Sichuan section.

Menu £ 12/23 – Carte £ 16/53

Town plan: C2-n - *82 St Aldates* ✉ *OX1 1RA* – ☎ *01865 242230*
- *www.shanghai30s.com* – *Closed 19th December-8th January and Monday lunch*

Al Shami

LEBANESE • NEIGHBOURHOOD Smart, established neighbourhood restaurant serving well-priced, tasty Middle Eastern food. Beautiful, ornate ceiling in rear dining room. Lengthy menu offers wide range of authentic Lebanese dishes.

Menu £ 15/22 - Carte £ 13/19

Town plan: C1-e - *25 Walton Cres ✉ OX1 2JG - ✆ 01865 310066 - www.al-shami.co.uk*

Magdalen Arms

TRADITIONAL BRITISH • PUB Buzzy battleship-grey pub boasting quirky old standard lamps, an eclectic collection of 1920s posters, board games and a bar billiards table. The experienced chef uses local ingredients to create flavoursome, good value dishes. Be sure to try the delicious fresh juices and homemade lemonade.

Carte £ 23/33

Town plan: B2-s - *243 Iffley Rd ✉ OX4 1SJ - ✆ 01865 243159 - www.magdalenarms.co.uk - Closed 24-26 December, 1 January, Monday lunch and bank holidays*

The Anchor

TRADITIONAL BRITISH • PUB Not your typical pub, with subtle art deco styling and black and white dining room floor tiles. The main menu offers largely British classics with some Mediterranean influences as well as morning coffee and cakes and weekend brunches.

Carte £ 22/69

Town plan: A1-u - *2 Hayfield Rd ✉ OX2 6TT - ✆ 01865 510282 - www.theanchoroxford.com*

Black Boy

INTERNATIONAL • NEIGHBOURHOOD This sizeable pub serves unfussy, sensibly priced pub classics with a French edge; be sure to start with the tasty homemade bread. Alternatively, opt for cocktails and mix and match tapas at the bar. The Sunday roasts are popular.

Carte £ 25/41

Town plan: B1-v - *91 Old High St, Headington ✉ OX3 9HT - ✆ 01865 741137 - www.theblackboy.uk.com - Closed 26 December and 1 January*

at Toot Baldon Southeast: 5.5 mi by B480 ✉ Oxford

Mole Inn

REGIONAL CUISINE • PUB Popular pub with a pleasant terrace, beautiful gardens and a warm, welcoming atmosphere. The appealing menu caters for all tastes and appetites; sourcing is taken seriously and dishes disappear from the menu as ingredients are used up.

Menu £ 23 - Carte approx. £ 32

✉ OX44 9NG - ✆ 01865 340001 (booking advisable) - www.themoleinn.com - Closed 25 December

at Great Milton Southeast: 12 mi by A40 off A329 ✉ Oxford

Belmond Le Manoir aux Quat' Saisons

GRAND LUXURY • PERSONALISED Majestic, part-15C country house offering the ultimate in guest services. Bedrooms are extremely comfortable - those in the Garden Wing are the most luxurious and have subtle themes. Relax by an open fire in the sumptuous sitting rooms or out on the delightful terrace overlooking the pristine gardens.

32 rooms - †£ 570/880 ††£ 570/880 - 14 suites

Church Rd ✉ OX44 7PD - ✆ 01844 278881 - www.belmond.com

✿✿ **Belmond Le Manoir aux Quat' Saisons** - See restaurant listing

XXXX Belmond Le Manoir aux Quat' Saisons (Raymond Blanc) 🕸

🕸🕸 FRENCH · LUXURY Elegant beamed restaurant in a truly 🏛 AC ↔ P luxurious hotel; head for the large conservatory overlooking the lovely gardens. French-inspired cooking uses seasonal garden produce and dishes are prepared with skill, clarity and a lightness of touch. Choose from the monthly à la carte or one of two superb tasting menus.

→ Confit of salmon with cucumber, mouli and horseradish. Sea bass with langoustine, smoked mash and star anise. Exotic fruit raviole with kaffir lime and coconut jus.

Menu £ 82/159 – Carte £ 98/120

Church Rd ✉ OX44 7PD – ℰ 01844 278881 (booking essential)
– www.belmond.com

at Fyfield Southwest: 9.5 mi by A420 ✉ Abingdon

🍴 White Hart 🏛 🎍 P

TRADITIONAL BRITISH · PUB An intriguing 15C chantry house with a cosy open-fired bar, a minstrels' gallery and an impressive three-storey high vaulted dining room; not forgetting a pleasant terrace. The diverse range of dishes is guided by produce from the vegetable plot. Save room for one of the excellent desserts.

Menu £ 17 (weekday lunch) – Carte £ 28/41

Main Rd ✉ OX13 5LW – ℰ 01865 390585 – www.whitehart-fyfield.com – Closed Monday except bank holidays

PADSTOW

Cornwall – Pop. 2 449 – Regional map n° **1**-B2
▶ London 288 mi – Exeter 78 mi – Plymouth 45 mi – Truro 23 mi

🏠 Padstow Townhouse 🆕 P

TOWNHOUSE · ELEGANT Everything's been thought of at this beautiful 18C townhouse. Six luxurious, individually styled suites come with top quality linens and bespoke toiletries made by local company St Kitts. There's an honesty bar in the kitchen pantry and the delicious breakfasts are taken at their nearby Italian restaurant.

6 rooms – 🛏£ 175/335 🛏🛏£ 280/380

Town plan: A1-s - *16/18 High St ✉ PL28 8BB – ℰ 01841 550950*
– www.paul-ainsworth.co.uk – Closed 23-26 December
🕸 **Paul Ainsworth at No.6** – See restaurant listing

🏠 Treverbyn House ← 🏛 ⌘ P ⇥

TOWNHOUSE · PERSONALISED Charming Edwardian house built for a wine merchant and run by a delightful owner. Comfy bedrooms feature interesting furniture from local sale rooms; one has a huge roll-top bath and all have harbour views – the Turret Room is the best. Have breakfast in your bedroom, the dining room or the garden.

3 rooms ⌷ – 🛏£ 100 🛏🛏£ 130

Town plan: B1-e - *Station Rd ✉ PL28 8DA – ℰ 01841 532855*
– www.treverbynhouse.com – Closed November-March

🏠 Althea Library ⌘ P

FAMILY · TRADITIONAL Grade II listed former Sunday school and library, just 5min from the harbour. Homely lounge and breakfast room; pine-furnished bedrooms. In summer, the Aga-cooked breakfasts are served on the terrace, next to the pond and water feature.

3 rooms ⌷ – 🛏£ 78/100 🛏🛏£ 98/122

Town plan: A1-g - *27 High St ✉ PL28 8BB – (access via 64 Church St.)*
– ℰ 01841 532717 – www.althealibrary.co.uk – Closed 8-28 February, 29 April-3rd May and 18 December

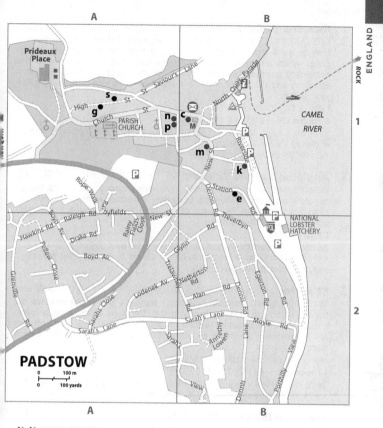

✗✗✗ Seafood

⇦ 🕭 AC P

SEAFOOD · ROMANTIC Stylish, laid-back, local institution – dominated by a large pewter-topped bar. Daily menus showcase fresh fish and shellfish. Classic dishes sit alongside those influenced by Rick Stein's travels; perhaps Singapore chilli crab or Madras fish curry. New England style bedrooms boast good quality furnishings; some have terraces or balconies and estuary views.

Menu £40 (lunch) – Carte £40/86

16 rooms ⌣ – ♦£154/270 ♦♦£154/314

Town plan: B1-k - *Riverside* ⊠ PL28 8BY – ℰ 01841 532700 *(booking essential)* – www.rickstein.com – *Closed 25-26 December*

✗ Paul Ainsworth at No.6

❀ MODERN CUISINE · COSY A delightful Georgian townhouse on a harbour back-water, with a relaxed, buzzy vibe; run by a friendly, enthusiastic team. Seasonal modern cooking displays originality and the occasional playful element, and textures and flavours are bold yet refined. Try the 'Fairground Tale' for dessert.
➙ Raw scallops with kimchi-style cabbage and Gentleman's Relish. Cornish chap with crackling, roast cauliflower and smoked eel. Valrhona chocolate with pistachio, olive oil sponge and Caramac.

Menu £26 (lunch) – Carte £51/68

Town plan: A1-n *6 Middle St* ⊠ PL28 8AP – ℰ 01841 532093
– www.number6inpadstow.co.uk – *Closed 7 January-6 February, 24-26 December, Sunday and Monday*

� Rick Stein's Café
😊

INTERNATIONAL · BISTRO A deceptively large café hidden behind a tiny shop front on a side street. Concise, seasonally changing menus offer tasty, unfussy dishes which display influences from Thailand, Morocco and the Med. The homemade bread is worth a try, as are the great value set menus. Bedrooms are comfy and simply furnished; have breakfast in the café or the small court-yard garden.

Menu £ 24 – Carte £ 23/36

3 rooms 🖵 – †£ 113/154 ††£ 113/160

Town plan: A1-p - *10 Middle St* ✉ *PL28 8AP* – ✆ *01841 532700 (booking essential at dinner)* – *www.rickstein.com*
– *Closed 24-26 December and 1 May*

� Appleton's at the Vineyard 🅝

MEDITERRANEAN CUISINE · FRIENDLY An enterprising couple bought this old mill and planted over 11,000 vines. Enjoy their homemade wines, ciders and apple juices while sitting on the terrace, gazing down the valley and dining on fresh, unfussy Italian-influenced dishes.

Carte £ 27/43

Trevibban Mill, Dark Ln ✉ *PL27 7SE – South : 3.5mi by A 389 off B 3274*
– ✆ 01841 541413 – www.trevibbanmill.com – Closed January, Monday, Tuesday and dinner Sunday and Wednesday

� St Petroc's

SEAFOOD · BISTRO Attractive house on a steep hill, with an oak-furnished bis-tro and terraces to both the front and rear. The menu offers simply prepared classics with an emphasis on seafood and grills. Smart, well-appointed bedrooms are split between the house and an annexe – where you'll also find a small lounge and library.

Menu £ 15 (lunch) – Carte £ 29/44

14 rooms 🖵 – †£ 160/250 ††£ 160/250

Town plan: B1-m - *4 New St* ✉ *PL28 8EA* – ✆ *01841 532700 (booking essential)*
– www.rickstein.com – Closed 24-26 December

� Prawn on the Lawn 🅝

SEAFOOD · TAPAS BAR If you like seafood then you'll love this modern fish-mongers-cum-seafood bar with its beautiful display of super-fresh fish out front and its tasty tapas-style sharing plates of shellfish and fish. It's cosy, with some counter seating.

Carte £ 28/54

Town plan: B1-c - *11 Duke St* ✉ *PL28 8AB* – ✆ *01841 532223 (booking advisable)*
– www.prawnonthelawn.com – Closed 2 January-7 February, Sunday October-Easter and Monday

PAINSWICK

Gloucestershire – Pop. 1 762 – Regional map n° **4**-C1
▶ London 104 mi – Gloucester 8 mi – Bristol 35 mi

🏠 The Painswick 🅝

HISTORIC · PERSONALISED A wonderful Regency house in the heart of a de-lightful village. A lovely inner hall leads to a relaxed, stylish sitting room but the jewel in the crown is the magnificent wisteria-clad stone terrace with valley views – the perfect spot for afternoon tea. Immaculate bedrooms have an understated designer feel.

16 rooms – †£ 119/269 ††£ 344/369 – 🖵 £ 17 – 1 suite
Kemps Ln ✉ *GL6 6YB* – ✆ *01452 813688 – www.thepainswick.co.uk*
The Painswick – See restaurant listing

XX **The Painswick** Ⓝ 🍴🛋️🅿️

MODERN BRITISH · BRASSERIE Pass the hams hanging on the walls and the coffee tables by the wood-burning oven (where the bread is cooked), into the bright parquet-floored dining room with blue leather chairs. Unfussy modern cooking follows the seasons; the charcuterie board is worth a try. Dine on the terrace to enjoy Slad Valley views.

Carte £ 32/50

The Painswick Hotel, Kemps Ln ⊠ GL6 6YB – ℰ 01452 813688
– www.thepainswick.co.uk

PATELEY BRIDGE
North Yorkshire – ⊠ Harrogate – Pop. 1 432 – Regional map n° **13**-B2
▶ London 225 mi – Leeds 28 mi – York 32 mi

XXX **Yorke Arms** (Frances Atkins) 🕸️🔄🍴🛋️🅿️

❀ MODERN CUISINE · FRIENDLY Charming, part-17C former shooting lodge overlooking the village green and run in a friendly, professional manner. Traditional, antique-furnished restaurant with a beamed ceiling and open fires. Measured and accomplished classical cooking demonstrates a good understanding of flavours; presentation is contemporary. Bedrooms have a subtle modern style and good comforts.

→ Quail cooked in hay with jasmine, lychee and raisin. Dry-aged loin, shoulder and leg of pork with pineapple. Tarragon with strawberry and caramelised white chocolate.

Menu £ 45 (weekday lunch)/85 – Carte £ 49/65

16 rooms ☑️ – 🛏️£ 250/275 🛏️🛏️£ 345/430 – 4 suites

Ramsgill-in-Nidderdale ⊠ HG3 5RL – Northwest : 5 mi by Low Wath Rd
– ℰ 01423 755243 – www.yorke-arms.co.uk – Closed Sunday and Monday except
bank holidays

PATRICK BROMPTON
North Yorkshire – ⊠ Bedale – Regional map n° **13**-B1
▶ London 242 mi – Newcastle upon Tyne 58 mi – York 43 mi

🏠 **Elmfield House** 🔄🍴🅿️

TRADITIONAL · FUNCTIONAL Spacious former gamekeeper's house in a peaceful farmland setting, complete with a fishing lake and a 14 acre forest. Guests are welcomed into the conservatory-cum-breakfast-room with homemade cake. Bedrooms are warm and welcoming.

4 rooms ☑️ – 🛏️£ 65/77 🛏️🛏️£ 80/92

Arrathorne ⊠ DL8 1NE – Northwest : 2.25 mi by A 684 on Richmond rd
– ℰ 01677 450558 – www.elmfieldhouse.co.uk

PATTISWICK – Essex → See Coggeshall

PENN
Buckinghamshire – Pop. 3 779 – Regional map n° **6**-D2
▶ London 31 mi – High Wycombe 4 mi – Oxford 36 mi

🍴 **Old Queens Head** 🍴🛋️🅿️

TRADITIONAL BRITISH · PUB Smart country pub purchased in 1666 by one of the King's physicians; find a spot on the paved terrace or take in the view from the dining room. Choose from a selection of 'small' and 'big' plates, many with influences from the Med.

Carte £ 23/39

Hammersley Ln ⊠ HP10 8EY – ℰ 01494 813371 – www.oldqueensheadpenn.co.uk

PENRITH
Cumbria – Pop. 15 181 – Regional map n° **12**-B2
▶ London 290 mi – Carlisle 24 mi – Kendal 31 mi – Lancaster 48 mi

Brooklands

TRADITIONAL · PERSONALISED This Victorian terraced house is located close to the town centre and is run by warm, welcoming owners. It has a traditional, antique-furnished hall and a smart breakfast room with marble-topped tables. Homely bedrooms come with fridges and robes; one has a locally crafted four-poster bed.

6 rooms 🖙 – ♦£ 40/70 ♦♦£ 80/90

2 Portland Pl ⊠ CA11 7QN – ℰ 01768 863395 – www.brooklandsguesthouse.com – Closed Christmas and New Year

✗ Four&Twenty 🅝

MODERN BRITISH · FRIENDLY Come at lunch for a good value menu; come at dinner for a more substantial à la carte. Well-executed, unfussy cooking is a mix of traditional and modern British. The bright, capacious room is simply furnished – it used to be a bank.

Menu £ 16 (weekday lunch) – Carte £ 24/46

42 King St ⊠ CA11 7AY – ℰ 01768 210231 – www.fourandtwentypenrith.co.uk – Closed Sunday and Monday

at Temple Sowerby East: 6.75 mi by A66⊠ Penrith

Temple Sowerby House

COUNTRY HOUSE · CLASSIC An attractive, enthusiastically run, red-brick Georgian mansion with spacious, classically styled guest areas. Traditional country house bedrooms boast antique furnishings and contemporary facilities. Ambitious, modern menus of local, seasonal produce are served overlooking the enclosed lawned gardens.

12 rooms 🖙 – ♦£ 105/145 ♦♦£ 145/175

⊠ CA10 1RZ – ℰ 017683 61578 – www.templesowerby.com – Closed Christmas

at Clifton Southeast: 3 mi on A6

🏠 George and Dragon

TRADITIONAL CUISINE · INN Whitewashed coaching inn with a characterful 18C bar and modern, brasserie-style restaurant. Appealing dishes feature vegetables from the garden, game from the moors and organic meats from the Lowther Estate farms. Modern bedrooms showcase furniture and paintings from the family's collection.

Menu £ 15 (weekdays) – Carte £ 25/36

11 rooms 🖙 – ♦£ 85/119 ♦♦£ 95/155

⊠ CA10 2ER – ℰ 01768 865381 – www.georgeanddragonclifton.co.uk – Closed 26 December

at Askham South: 6 mi by A6

Askham Hall

COUNTRY HOUSE · HISTORIC At the edge of the Lowther Estate you'll find this fine, family-run castle dating from the 1300s. It's been stylishly yet sympathetically refurbished and its spacious rooms are full of original features and old family furnishings.

15 rooms 🖙 – ♦£ 138/308 ♦♦£ 150/320

⊠ CA10 2PF – ℰ 01931 712350 – www.askhamhall.co.uk – Closed 3 January-mid February and Christmas

Askham Hall – See restaurant listing

✗✗ Askham Hall 🅝

REGIONAL CUISINE · INTIMATE Relax by the fire before heading through to the modish country house restaurant with its bright tiled floor and elegant panelled private room. Concise menus showcase meats from their farm and veg from their superb kitchen garden.

Menu £ 50/65

⊠ CA10 2PF – ℰ 01931 712350 (booking essential) – www.askhamhall.co.uk – dinner only – Closed 3 January-mid February, Christmas, Sunday and Monday

PENSHURST

Kent – Pop. 708 – Regional map n° **5**-B2

▶ London 40 mi – Royal Tunbridge Wells 7 mi – Maidstone 22 mi

🛏 **Leicester Arms**   🔄 ⬆ 🅿

TRADITIONAL BRITISH · INN Sympathetically refurbished 16C former coaching inn offering an evolving menu of rustic and satisfying pub classics. Sit in the garden room: a large bright space with a lovely rural view. Bedrooms are furnished in a contemporary style; ask for Room 8, which is the biggest, with the best outlook.

Carte £ 23/59

13 rooms � – ♦£ 69/99 ♦♦£ 79/139

High St ✉ *TN11 8BT* – *ℰ 01892 871617* – *www.theleicesterarmshotel.com*

PENZANCE

Cornwall – Pop. 16 336 – Regional map n° **1**-A3

▶ London 319 mi – Exeter 113 mi – Plymouth 77 mi – Taunton 155 mi

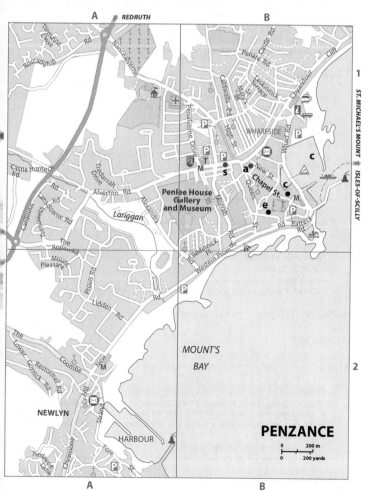

PENZANCE

🏠 Chapel House ⓝ   ← 🛏

TOWNHOUSE · GRAND LUXURY A smartly refurbished 18C house with a pretty walled garden. Sumptuous lounges are filled with modern art and there's a fabulous basement dining room where they serve breakfast and pre-booked weekend meals. Bedrooms have a cool, understated elegance and sea views: all feature fresh flowers and hand-crafted oak furnishings and one has a bathroom with a retractable roof!

6 rooms – 🛏£ 90/160 🛏🛏£ 120/190
Town plan: B1-c - Chapel St ✉ TR18 4AQ - 𝒫 01736 362024
– www.chapelhouse.pz.co.uk

🏠 Chy-An-Mor   ← 🛏 🌿 🅿

TOWNHOUSE · PERSONALISED This fine Georgian townhouse overlooks the promenade; fittingly, its name means 'House of the Sea'. Bedrooms have lovely soft furnishings – two have 6ft cast iron beds. In the evening, twinkling garden lights welcome you home and at breakfast they offer homemade muffins, Scotch pancakes and granola sundaes.

9 rooms 🛏 – 🛏£ 47/70 🛏🛏£ 82/96
Town plan: B1-e - 15 Regent Terr ✉ TR18 4DW - 𝒫 01736 363441
– www.chyanmor.co.uk – Closed November-March

✗✗ Shore ⓝ

SEAFOOD · INTIMATE The name refers to the cooking rather than the location of this small bistro. The experienced chef works alone: his produce is ethically sourced and many of his precisely prepared dishes have Mediterranean or Asian influences.

Menu £ 24 (lunch) – Carte £ 32/35
Town plan: B1-s - 13-14 Alverton St ✉ TR18 2QP
– 𝒫 01736 362444 (booking advisable) – www.theshorerestaurant.uk – Closed 2 weeks January, Sunday and Monday

✗✗ Harris's

TRADITIONAL CUISINE · CLASSIC DÉCOR Long-standing, split-level restaurant with a spiral staircase and an unusual Welsh black metal plate ceiling; run by a keen husband and wife. Classical cooking uses seasonal Cornish produce; try the steamed lobster when it's in season.

Carte £ 31/47
Town plan: B1-a - 46 New St ✉ TR18 2LZ
– 𝒫 01736 364408
– www.harrissrestaurant.co.uk
– Closed 3 weeks winter, 25-26 December, Sunday and Monday

PERRANUTHNOE – Cornwall → See Marazion

PERSHORE

Worcestershire – Pop. 7 125 – Regional map n° **10**-C3
▶ London 106 mi – Birmingham 33 mi – Worcester 8 mi

🏠 Barn   🐾 ← 🛏 ✗ 🌿 🅿 🚭

TRADITIONAL · COSY A hugely characterful series of hillside outbuildings, run by a charming owner. There's a homely beamed lounge and three warmly decorated bedrooms; one even boasts a sauna. The apple juice comes from the fruit trees in the garden.

3 rooms 🛏 – 🛏£ 65/75 🛏🛏£ 90/95
Pensham Hill House, Pensham ✉ WR10 3HA – Southeast : 1 mi by B 4084
– 𝒫 01386 555270
– www.pensham-barn.co.uk

at Tillington West: 1 mi on A272

🍽 Horse Guards Inn　　　　　　　⇔ 🚗 🏠

REGIONAL · RUSTIC In the heart of a quiet village sits this charming mid-17C inn, with views over the valley from its lavender-filled garden. Cooking mixes the rustic and the more elaborate and local seafood stands out. Service is chatty and willing. Bedrooms are charmingly understated; families can book the cottage next door.

Carte £ 21/38

3 rooms ☺ – 🛇£ 100/135 🛇🛇£ 100/150

Upperton Rd ✉ GU28 9AF – ℰ 01798 342332 – www.thehorseguardsinn.co.uk – Closed 25-26 December

at Lickfold Northwest : 6 mi by A 272 ✉ Petworth

✗✗ Lickfold Inn　　　　　　　　🚗 ♿ 🅿

MODERN BRITISH · COSY A pretty Grade II listed brick and timber pub with a characterful lounge-bar serving small plates and a formal first floor restaurant. Terse descriptions hide the true complexities of the innovative dishes, which echo the seasons and are given a touch of theatre. Staff are friendly and eager to please.

Menu £ 25 (lunch) – Carte £ 33/55

Highstead Ln ✉ GU28 9EY – ℰ 01789 532535 (booking essential) – www.thelickfoldinn.co.uk – Closed 2 weeks January, Sunday dinner, Monday except bank holidays and Tuesday

PICKERING

North Yorkshire – Pop. 6 588 – Regional map n° **13**-C1

▶ London 237 mi – Middlesbrough 43 mi – Scarborough 19 mi – York 25 mi

🏠 White Swan Inn　　　　　　　　⚗ 🅿

HISTORIC · COSY Characterful 17C coaching inn – its cosy bar and lounge decorated in modern hues. Bedrooms are appealing and come with smart bathrooms; those in the outbuildings have heated stone floors and one even has a bath in the lounge. The brasserie-style restaurant specialises in meats and grills.

21 rooms ☺ – 🛇£ 119/149 🛇🛇£ 149/179 – 2 suites

Market Pl ✉ YO18 7AA – ℰ 01751 472288 – www.white-swan.co.uk

🏠 17 Burgate　　　　　　　　　🚗 🅿

TOWNHOUSE · PERSONALISED The stained glass window on the stairway of this classic Georgian townhouse is a talking point and the garden behind is a pleasant place to relax. Bedrooms are spacious and individually styled. Local ingredients feature at breakfast.

3 rooms ☺ – 🛇£ 90/95 🛇🛇£ 90/110

17 Burgate ✉ YO18 7AU – ℰ 01751 473463 – www.17burgate.co.uk – Restricted opening in spring and winter

at Levisham Northeast: 6.5 mi by A169 ✉ Pickering

🏠 Moorlands Country House　　　　⚗ 🐾 ⪡ 🚗 ♞ 🅿

TRADITIONAL · PERSONALISED 19C restored vicarage in the heart of the national park, boasting superb views down the valley. Spacious, well-maintained interior with a classically decorated lounge and flowery wallpapers. Comfortable bedrooms boast rich colour schemes; one has a four-poster bed. Traditional three course dinners. Menu changes daily.

4 rooms ☺ – 🛇£ 100/120 🛇🛇£ 160/180

✉ YO18 7NL – ℰ 01751 460229 – www.moorlandslevisham.co.uk – Closed November-April, minimum 2 night stay

at Sinnington Northwest: 4 mi by A170 ⊠ York

Fox and Hounds

TRADITIONAL BRITISH · PUB It's always a good sign if a pub has regulars and this pretty, traditional 18C inn has plenty. What keeps them coming back is the generously proportioned, hearty Yorkshire cooking: pub classics, slow braises and plenty of game in season. Stay the night in one of the homely, individually decorated bedrooms.
Carte £ 24/48
10 rooms ⊈ – ♦£ 59/84 ♦♦£ 70/140
Main St ⊠ YO62 6SQ – ℰ 01751 431577 – www.thefoxandhoundsinn.co.uk – Closed 25-27 December

PICKHILL
North Yorkshire – ⊠ Thirsk – Pop. 401 – Regional map n° **13**-B1
▶ London 229 mi – Leeds 41 mi Middlesbrough 30 mi – York 34 mi

Nags Head Country Inn

TRADITIONAL CUISINE · PUB Quirky pub with a rustic open-fired bar filled with over 700 framed ties and a dining room with booths and hunting prints. Blackboard menus list plenty of classics, accompanied by seasonal vegetables and a jug of gravy; the owner is an avid shooter, so game season is a good time to visit. Bedrooms are cosy.
Carte £ 16/35
7 rooms ⊈ – ♦£ 60/80 ♦♦£ 80/120
⊠ YO7 4JG – ℰ 01845 567391 – www.nagsheadpickhill.co.uk – Closed 25 December

PIFF'S ELM - Gloucestershire → See Cheltenham

PILSLEY
Derbyshire – Regional map n° **9**-A1
▶ London 161 mi – Manchester 37 mi – Sheffield 22 mi – Nottingham 20 mi

Devonshire Arms

TRADITIONAL BRITISH · INN Traditional pub dishes get a makeover on the menu sourced from the Chatsworth Estate; servings are generous and dishes, satisfyingly filling. The stylish, contemporary bedrooms were designed by the Duchess of Devonshire. Stock up in the nearby Chatsworth Farm shop before going home.
Carte £ 21/36
13 rooms ⊈ – ♦£ 76/203 ♦♦£ 89/219
⊠ DE45 1UL – ℰ 01246 583258 (booking advisable) – www.devonshirepilsley.co.uk

PLUMTREE - Nottinghamshire → See Nottingham

PLYMOUTH
Plymouth – Pop. 234 982 – Regional map n° **1**-C2
▶ London 242 mi – Bristol 124 mi – Southampton 161 mi

XX Greedy Goose

MODERN BRITISH · ELEGANT Smart restaurant housed in a delightful building dating from 1482 and named after the children's book 'Chocolate Mousse for Greedy Goose'. Cooking is modern and flavoursome and the local beef is superb. Sit in the 'quad' in summer.
Menu £ 12 (lunch and early dinner) – Carte £ 25/56
Town plan: B1-n - *Prysten House, Finewell St ⊠ PL1 2AE – ℰ 01752 252001 – www.thegreedygoose.co.uk – Closed Christmas, Sunday and Monday*

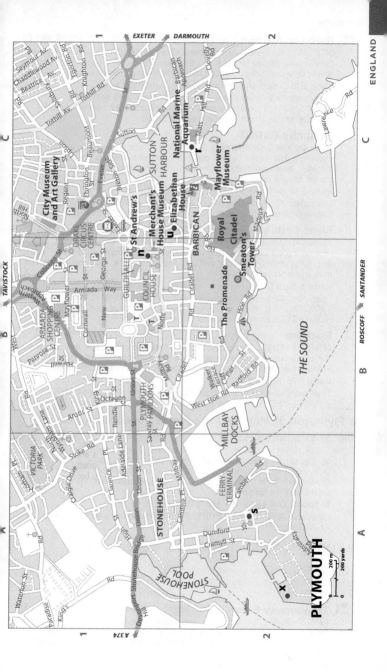

ENGLAND

EXETER   DARMOUTH

City Museum
and Art Gallery

National Marine
Aquarium

St Andrew's

Merchant's
House Museum

SUTTON
HARBOUR

TAVISTOCK

Elizabethan
House

Mayflower
Museum

BARBICAN

DRAKE
CIRCUS
CENTRE

GUILDHALL

COUNCIL
HOUSE

Royal
Citadel

ARMADA
SHOPPING
CENTRE

Armada   Way

Smeaton's
Tower

The Promenade

THE SOUND

Amada Way

ROSCOFF   SANTANDER

VICTORIA
PARK

PLYMOUTH
PAVILIONS

STONEHOUSE

MILLBAY
DOCKS

FERRY
TERMINAL

STONEHOUSE
POOL

Devonport Stonehouse Bridge

PLYMOUTH

XX Barbican Kitchen

INTERNATIONAL · DESIGN An informal eatery in the Plymouth Gin Distillery (where gin was once distilled for the Navy). Brasserie menus offer a good choice of simply cooked dishes, with classic comfort food to the fore; vegetarians are well catered for.

Menu £16 (lunch and early dinner) – Carte £23/38 **s**

Town plan: C1-u - *Black Friars Distillery, 60 Southside St* ⊠ *PL1 2LQ*
– *℘ 01752 604448 (booking advisable) – www.barbicankitchen.com – Closed 25-26 December, dinner 31 December and Sunday*

X Samphire Bush ◍

SEAFOOD · NEIGHBOURHOOD Seafood is the name of the game at this friendly restaurant. The Yealm oysters and Fowey mussels are a good bet, as are the monkfish dishes and fruits de mer platters. Cooking is unfussy and flavoursome; the set menu is great value.

Menu £16 (weekdays) – Carte £22/36

Town plan: A2-s - *36 Admiralty St* ⊠ *PL1 3RU* – *℘ 01752 253247*
– *www.thesamphirebush.co.uk – Closed Sunday, Monday and lunch Tuesday*

X River Cottage Canteen & Deli

REGIONAL CUISINE · BISTRO Large, buzzy restaurant and deli in an impressive spot on the old dockside; thick stone walls and reclaimed wood give it a rustic feel. Gutsy dishes showcase wild and organic produce; most ingredients come from within 50 miles.

Carte £20/43

Town plan: A2-x - *No 1 Brew House, Royal William Yard* ⊠ *PL1 3QQ*
– *℘ 01752 252702 (booking essential) – www.rivercottage.net/canteens/plymouth*
– *Closed 25 December and Sunday dinner*

X Rockfish

SEAFOOD · RUSTIC This buzzy quayside shack is ideal for those in 'holiday mode'. The rustic interior features reclaimed wood, hull-shaped banquettes and seaside snaps. Simply prepared seafood sits on greaseproof paper, atop stainless steel plates.

Carte £26/39

Town plan: C2-r - *Sutton Harbour, Cox Side, 3 Rope Walk* ⊠ *PL4 0LB*
– *℘ 01752 255974 – www.therockfish.co.uk – Closed 25 December*

at Plympton St Maurice East: 6 mi by A374 on B3416 ⊠ Plymouth

🏠 St Elizabeth's House

TRADITIONAL · MODERN This former convent is now a family-run boutique hotel. Eye-catching fabrics add splashes of colour to the spacious bedrooms and many come with feature bathrooms; you can watch TV from the spa bath in the St Elizabeth Suite. Have a drink at the pewter-topped bar then dine formally overlooking the gardens.

15 rooms 🖵 – ♦£99/139 ♦♦£109/179 – 1 suite

Longbrook St ⊠ *PL7 1NJ* – *℘ 01752 344840 – www.stelizabeths.co.uk – Closed 24-26 December*

PLYMPTON ST MAURICE Devon – Plymouth → See Plymouth

POLPERRO

Cornwall – ⊠ Looe – Regional map n° **1**-B2
▶ London 238 mi – Birmingham 223 mi – Bristol 142 mi – Cardiff 173 mi

🏠 Trenderway Farm

FAMILY · RURAL 16C farmhouse and outbuildings set in 206 acres of working farmland. Well-appointed bedrooms come in a mix of styles and some have seating areas and kitchenettes. A cream tea is served on arrival and breakfast is cooked on the Aga.

7 rooms 🖵 – ♦£99/189 ♦♦£99/189

⊠ *PL13 2LY – Northeast : 2 mi by A 387 – ℘ 01503 272214*
– *www.trenderwayfarm.co.uk*

PONTELAND – Northumberland → See Newcastle upon Tyne

POOLE
Poole – Pop. 154 718 – Regional map n° **2**-C3
▶ London 116 mi – Bournemouth 4 mi – Dorchester 23 mi – Southampton 36 mi

🏨 Hotel du Vin   ☆ & AC ⅀ P

TOWNHOUSE · MODERN A strikingly extended Queen Anne property in the old town. Smart guest areas have eye-catching wine-themed murals; stylish, modern bedrooms are named after wine or champagne houses – one boasts an 8ft bed and twin roll-top baths. Local produce features in classic French dishes and there's a 300 bin wine list.

38 rooms ⅂ – ♦£ 99/129 ♦♦£ 109/179

Town plan: A2-a 7-11 Thames St. ✉ BH15 1JN – ℰ 0844 748 9265
– www.hotelduvin.com

🏨 Harbour Heights   ☆ ← ⬆ AC ⅀ ⅄ P

HISTORIC · CONTEMPORARY 1920s whitewashed hotel, perched on the hillside, overlooking Poole Bay and Brownsea Island; the modern lounge-bar boasts a superb three-tiered terrace which makes the most of the view. Contemporary bedrooms come with good mod cons and smart bathrooms. The open-plan restaurant serves a modern menu.

38 rooms ⅂ – ♦£ 80 ♦♦£ 90/290

Haven Rd, Sandbanks ✉ BH13 7LW – Southeast : 3 mi by A 35 and B 3369
– ℰ 01202 707272 – www.harbourheights.com

XX Rick Stein ⓝ   ← & AC ℉⅄

SEAFOOD · FASHIONABLE Rick may be expanding his empire but he's keeping his fishy theme. The large menu offers everything from cod and chips to seafood platters and all his classics are there, including turbot hollandaise and plaice alla carlina. Start with a drink in the sleek bar then enjoy superb sea views from the restaurant.

Menu £ 25 (weekday lunch) – Carte £ 31/73

10-14 Banks Rd, Sandbanks ✉ BH13 7QB – Southeast : 4.75 mi by B 3068 and
Sandbanks Rd – ℰ 01202 283000 (booking essential) – www.rickstein.com

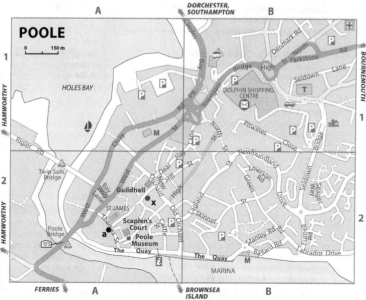

XX Isabel's

INTERNATIONAL · NEIGHBOURHOOD Lovingly run restaurant in a former chemist's shop, where the old shelving is still in situ. Grab a booth in the characterful red dining room or make for the basement room which opens onto the garden. Hearty French dishes feature.

Menu £ 35 (weekdays) – Carte £ 30/40

32 Station Rd, Lower Parkstone ⊠ BH14 8UD – East : 2 mi by B 3069 off A 35 – ℰ 01202 747885 (booking essential) – www.isabelsrestaurant.co.uk – dinner only – Closed 25-26 December, 1-2 January, Sunday and Monday

XX Guildhall Tavern

SEAFOOD · BISTRO Proudly run restaurant opposite the Guildhall, with a bright, cheery interior and a nautical theme. Tasty, classical French dishes are generously proportioned and largely seafood-based. They also host monthly gourmet evenings.

Menu £ 20/26 – Carte £ 29/62

Town plan: A2-x - *15 Market St ⊠ BH15 1NB – ℰ 01202 671717 (booking advisable) – www.guildhalltavern.co.uk – Closed 25 December-6 January, 2 weeks April, 2 weeks July, Sunday and Monday*

POOLEY BRIDGE

Cumbria – Regional map n° **12**-B2

▶ London 294 mi – Carlisle 25 mi – Keswick 16 mi

🏨 Sharrow Bay Country House

COUNTRY HOUSE · CLASSIC Long-standing, celebrated Victorian villa in mature gardens and woodland; beautifully located on the shore of Lake Ullswater. It has a traditional country house style throughout, with extremely charming drawing rooms and a great sense of tranquillity. Comfortable bedrooms have a classic, cottagey feel.

17 rooms ⊊ – †£ 150/520 ††£ 150/520

Ullswater ⊠ CA10 2LZ – South : 2 mi on Howtown Rd – ℰ 017684 86301 – www.sharrowbay.co.uk

Sharrow Bay Country House – See restaurant listing

XxX Sharrow Bay Country House

CLASSIC CUISINE · ELEGANT Two delightful dining rooms in a beautifully located, traditional country house; 'Lakeside' has superb views over Lake Ullswater. Service is formal and dishes are as classic as they come; don't miss the 'icky sticky toffee pudding'.

Menu £ 65

Sharrow Bay Country House Hotel, Ullswater ⊠ CA10 2LZ – South : 2 mi on Howtown Rd – ℰ 017684 86301 (booking essential) – www.sharrowbay.co.uk

PORLOCK

Somerset – ⊠ Minehead – Pop. 1 395 – Regional map n° **2**-A2

▶ London 190 mi – Bristol 67 mi – Exeter 46 mi – Taunton 28 mi

🏨 Oaks

TRADITIONAL · CLASSIC Imposing Edwardian house with great views over the weir and bay; the builder quarried the stone used to build it himself. The antique-filled entrance hall boasts a beautiful parquet floor and the large bedrooms come with fresh fruit and smart bathrooms. The dining room offers a classical daily menu and views from every table; care is served on arrival in the snug lounge.

7 rooms ⊊ – †£ 100/120 ††£ 170/190

⊠ TA24 8ES – ℰ 01643 862265 – www.oakshotel.co.uk – Closed November-March

🏠 Cross Lane House ☆ 🛏 🛖 🅿

HISTORIC · PERSONALISED A very stylishly restored farmhouse and outbuildings dating from 1484; a short walk from the South West Coastal Path. Inside the old and the new have been cleverly blended, with great attention paid to detail. Cake is served on arrival and afternoon tea is a feature; there is even a small gift shop! The intimate formal restaurant offers a concise menu of modern dishes.

4 rooms 🖵 – 🛉£ 140/200 🛉🛉£ 170/210

Allerford ✉ TA24 8HW – *East : 1.25 mi on A 39* – ✆ 01643 863276
– www.crosslanehouse.com – Closed 3 January-12 February and 1 week mid-November

PORT ISAAC
Cornwall – Regional map n° **1**-B2
▶ London 264 mi – Plymouth 50 mi – Newquay 24 mi

✗✗ Restaurant Nathan Outlaw (Nathan Outlaw) ⪕ ⏺

❀❀ **SEAFOOD · INTIMATE** A smart yet casual restaurant in a great headland location – the views from the first floor dining room are stunning. No-choice set menus focus on ultra-fresh fish and shellfish landed at the nearby harbour. Classical combinations are very carefully crafted, keeping the focus firmly on the main ingredient.
➜ Raw scallops, preserved herring, chilli, onion and bacon. Gurnard and Porthilly sauce. Spiced quince and hazelnut tart.

Menu £ 59/119

6 New Rd ✉ PL29 3SB – ✆ 01208 880896 *(booking essential)*
– www.nathan-outlaw.com – dinner only and lunch Friday-Saturday – Closed January and Sunday-Tuesday

✗ Outlaw's Fish Kitchen 🍴

❀ **SEAFOOD · INTIMATE** This intimate 15C building has low ceilings and wonky walls and is found in the heart of this famous harbourside fishing village. The day boats guide the menu, which offers a delicious mix of old favourites and appealing small plates – 3 or 4 dishes should suffice. Cornish gins, beers and wines also feature.
➜ Ginger-cured mackerel with beetroot chutney and basil yoghurt. Port Isaac crab on toast with celeriac and apple dressing. Rhubarb & almond sponge with poached rhubarb and crème fraîche.

Menu £ 43 (dinner) – Carte £ 13/32

✉ PL29 3RH – ✆ 01208 881183 *(booking essential at dinner)*
– www.outlaws.co.uk/fishkitchen – Closed January, Monday October-May and Sunday

PORTHLEVEN
Cornwall – Pop. 3 059 – Regional map n° **1**-A3
▶ London 284 mi – Helston 3 mi – Penzance 12 mi

✗✗ Kota ⇦

☺ **ASIAN INFLUENCES · RUSTIC** Welcoming harbourside granary with thick stone walls, a tiled floor and an array of wood furnishings; its name means 'shellfish' in Maori. Menus mix unfussy and more elaborate dishes and display subtle Asian influences courtesy of the owner's Chinese and Malaysian background. Many of the ingredients are foraged. Bedrooms are simply furnished – one overlooks the harbour.

Menu £ 21 – Carte £ 24/40
2 rooms 🖵 – 🛉£ 60/90 🛉🛉£ 75/100

Harbour Head ✉ TR13 9JA – ✆ 01326 562407 – *www.kotarestaurant.co.uk – dinner only – Closed 1 January-10 February, 25-26 December, Sunday and Monday*

ⅩⅩ Rick Stein Fish and Shellfish   ⅙ ⊞

SEAFOOD · FASHIONABLE This old harbourside clay store has been transformed
into a smart restaurant with floor to ceiling windows and a first floor terrace. Top
quality seafood small plates are inspired by Rick Stein's travels and sharing is encouraged.

Menu £ 22 (lunch and early dinner) – Carte £ 25/38

Mount Pleasant Rd ⊠ TR13 9JS – 𝒞 01326 565636 – www.rickstein.com – Closed
25 December, Sunday dinner and Monday in winter

Ⅹ Square   ⌂

MODERN CUISINE · SIMPLE Small harbourside bistro: in summer, bag a table on
the terrace; in winter, cosy up and watch the waves crash on the harbour wall.
Coffee and cakes are followed by snacks and sharing platters, with more struc-
ture at dinner. Well-prepared modern classics have punchy flavours; go for the
freshly landed seafood.

Menu £ 20/22 – Carte £ 26/35

7 Fore St ⊠ TR13 9HQ – 𝒞 01326 573911 – www.thesquareatporthleven.co.uk
– Closed Sunday in winter

PORTLOE

Cornwall – Regional map n° **1**-B3
▶ London 296 mi – Plymouth 51 mi – Truro 15 mi

⌂ Lugger   ⌖ ≤ ⅍ 🅿

INN · PERSONALISED This 17C smugglers' inn sits in a picturesque fishing village and affords dramatic views over the rugged bay. It's snug and cosy
throughout, with open fires, low ceilings and friendly, personal service. Have a
drink on the terrace and dinner in the elegant dining room, which serves seafood fresh from the bay.

23 rooms ⚌ – †£ 95/185 ††£ 135/225

⊠ *TR2 5RD – 𝒞 01872 501322 – www.luggerhotel.co.uk*

PORTSCATHO

Cornwall – ⊠ Truro – Regional map n° **1**-B3
▶ London 298 mi – Plymouth 55 mi – Truro 16 mi

⌂ Driftwood   ⅋ ≤ ⌸ ⅍ 🅿

COUNTRY HOUSE · PERSONALISED Charming clifftop hotel looking out over
mature grounds, which stretch down to the shore and a private beach. Stylish,
contemporary guest areas are decorated with pieces of driftwood. Smart bedrooms – in the main house and annexed cottages – have a good level of modern
facilities; some have decked terraces.

15 rooms ⚌ – †£ 153/243 ††£ 180/285

Rosevine ⊠ TR2 5EW – North : 2 mi by A 3078 – 𝒞 01872 580644
– www.driftwoodhotel.co.uk – Closed 8 December-5 February

❀ **Driftwood** – See restaurant listing

⌂ Rosevine   ⌖ ≤ ⌸ ⌂ ▣ ⋈ ⅍ ⅋ 🅿

COUNTRY HOUSE · ELEGANT Dramatically refurbished country house overlooking the sea, with modern guest areas and stylish bedrooms featuring kitchenettes. They cater strongly for families: children have their own lounge, they offer
family high tea and the large grounds have a pool and play area. The all-day
brasserie uses local produce.

15 suites – ††£ 150/395 – ⚌ £ 10

Rosevine ⊠ TR2 5EW – North : 2 mi by A 3078 – 𝒞 01872 580206
– www.rosevine.co.uk – Closed mid November-early December and January

✗✗ ☸ Driftwood ⟨ 🚗 🅿

MODERN CUISINE · DESIGN Bright, New England style restaurant in an attractive house, in a peaceful clifftop setting; it's delightfully run by a friendly, efficient team and boasts superb views out to sea. Unfussy, modern, seasonally pertinent dishes display technical adroitness and feature excellent flavour and texture combinations.

→ Glazed pork cheek with clotted cream boudin blanc, puffed crackling, rhubarb and cider. Seared turbot with slow-cooked cuttlefish, gem lettuce, peas and hollandaise. 'Thunder and Lightning' tart, saffron jelly and ginger beer.

Menu £ 60

Driftwood Hotel, Rosevine ⊠ TR2 5EW – North : 2 mi by A 3078
– ☏ 01872 580644 (booking essential) – www.driftwoodhotel.co.uk – dinner only
– Closed 8 December-5 February

PORTSMOUTH and SOUTHSEA

Portsmouth – Pop. 238 137 – Regional map n° **4**-B3
▶ London 78 mi – Brighton 48 mi – Salisbury 44 mi – Southampton 21 mi

🏠 Clarence 🄰🄲 ⅏ 🅿

TOWNHOUSE · PERSONALISED Immaculately kept, bay windowed house, just a short walk from the sea. Bedrooms come in various sizes and feature contemporary décor, superb modern bathrooms and pleasing extra touches; some have a TV inset in the bathroom wall.

8 rooms ⌷ – ♦£ 99/159 ♦♦£ 99/245

Clarence Rd, Southsea ⊠ PO5 2LQ – ☏ 023 9200 9777
– www.theclarencehotel.co.uk

✗✗ Restaurant 27

MODERN BRITISH · NEIGHBOURHOOD This long-standing, elegant restaurant is professionally and passionately run by its owner-chef. Contemporary cooking has a slightly Scandic style; attractively presented dishes taste as good as they look and are full of flavour.

Menu £ 50

27a South Par, Southsea ⊠ PO5 2JF – ☏ 023 9287 6272 (booking advisable)
– www.restaurant27.com – dinner only and Sunday lunch
– Closed 25-26 December, Sunday dinner, Monday and Tuesday

POSTBRIDGE

Devon – Regional map n° **1**-C2
▶ London 207 mi – Exeter 21 mi – Plymouth 21 mi

🏠 Lydgate House 🕭 🐾 ⟨ 🚗 🅿

TRADITIONAL · COSY Personally run whitewashed house, set in a secluded spot high on the moors and accessed via a narrow track. Homely, cosy lounge and conservatory restaurant offering home-cooked local produce. Bedrooms are named after birds; many offer lovely views over the 36 acre grounds and the East Dart River.

7 rooms ⌷ – ♦£ 50/61 ♦♦£ 95/132

⊠ PL20 6TJ – ☏ 01822 880209 – www.lydgatehouse.co.uk – Closed January

PULHAM MARKET

Norfolk – ⊠ Diss – Pop. 722 – Regional map n° **8**-C2
▶ London 106 mi – Cambridge 58 mi – Ipswich 29 mi – Norwich 16 mi

🏠 Old Bakery 🚗 ⅏ 🅿

TOWNHOUSE · CLASSIC Pretty 16C former bakery just off the green. The characterful interior features exposed beams and inglenooks. There's a homely lounge and breakfast room and good-sized bedrooms with modern facilities. Don't miss the 'Baker's Breakfast'.

5 rooms ⌷ – ♦£ 65/90 ♦♦£ 85/105

Church Walk ⊠ IP21 4SL – ☏ 01379 676492 – www.theoldbakery.net – Closed Christmas-New Year

RAINHAM
Medway – Regional map n° **5**-C1

▶ London 14 mi – Basildon 16 mi – Dartford 9 mi

XX Barn

TRADITIONAL CUISINE · RUSTIC A black and white timbered barn which was transported from Essex and reconstructed on this site; its heavy beams and open fires give it a rustic feel. The enthusiastic owner and his team offer a menu of elaborate modern dishes.

Menu £ 25 (weekday lunch) **s** – Carte £ 30/47 **s**

507 Lower Rainham Rd ✉ ME8 7TN – North : 1.75 mi by Station Rd – 𝒞 01634 361363 – www.thebarnrestaurant.co.uk – Closed 25-26 December, 1 January, Saturday lunch, Sunday dinner, Monday and bank holidays

RAMSBOTTOM
Greater Manchester – Pop. 17 872 – Regional map n° **11**-B2

▶ London 223 mi – Blackpool 39 mi – Burnley 12 mi – Leeds 46 mi

X Levanter

SPANISH · TAPAS BAR Joe has a passion for all things Spanish – he's even a trained flamenco guitarist – so, unsurprisingly, his sweet little tapas bar has an authentic feel. The menu is dictated by market produce; be sure to try some of the freshly sliced Iberico ham. He also owns the nearby Basque-style Baratxuri pintxo bar.

Carte £ 20/25

10 Square St ✉ BL0 9BE – 𝒞 01706 551530 (bookings not accepted) – www.levanterfinefoods.co.uk – Closed Monday, Tuesday and lunch Wednesday

RAMSBURY
Wiltshire – Pop. 1 540 – Regional map n° **2**-D2

▶ London 73 mi – Bristol 53 mi – Cardiff 86 mi – Plymouth 172 mi

Bell

MODERN CUISINE · INN Charming 16C pub with stylish, well-appointed bedrooms. Dine on pub favourites among hop-covered beams in the open-fired bar or sit on smart tartan banquettes in the crisply laid dining room and choose from more ambitious, accomplished dishes. You'll find the locals at the back in 'Café Bella'.

Carte £ 25/52

9 rooms ⌂ – ♦£ 110/120 ♦♦£ 130/170

The Square ✉ SN8 2PE – 𝒞 01672 520230 – www.ramsbury.com – Closed 25 December

RAMSEY – Ramsey ➡ See Man (Isle of)

RAMSHOLT
Suffolk – Regional map n° **8**-D3

▶ London 96 mi – Norwich 54 mi – Ipswich 17 mi – Colchester 38 mi

Ramsholt Arms

TRADITIONAL BRITISH · SIMPLE Honest, well-priced pub food and Suffolk ales in a great location. This striking inn is set against the spectacular backdrop of the River Deben; particularly magnificent at sunset and on summer days. Plenty of room on the terrace.

Carte £ 20/31

Dock Rd ✉ IP12 3AB – 𝒞 01394 411209 – www.theramsholtarms.com – Closed weekdays January-mid February and Monday-Wednesday dinner October-April

READING
Reading – Pop. 218 705 – Regional map n° **6**-C3

▶ London 43 mi – Oxford 29 mi – Bristol 78 mi

The Forbury 🏠 ⊡ ⅊ ⚹ ⚐ 🅿

TOWNHOUSE · GRAND LUXURY An impressive former civic hall overlooking Forbury Square Gardens; now a smart townhouse hotel where contemporary designs meet with original features. Luxurious bedrooms come with Nespresso machines, fridges and Bang & Olufsen electronics. The chic basement bar and restaurant offer modern menus.

23 rooms ⌱ – †£ 157/240 ††£ 157/300

26 Forbury ⊠ RG1 3EJ – ℰ 0118 952 7770 – www.theforburyhotel.co.uk

Holiday Inn 🏠 ⬚ ⅊ ⅃ ⊡ ⅊ ⒶⒸ ⚹ ⇔

BUSINESS · MODERN Conveniently located for the M4, with spacious open-plan guest areas, smart function facilities and a well-equipped leisure club. Stylish, uniform bedrooms come with good facilities and compact, up-to-date bathrooms. Have snacks in the comfy lounge or classic dishes in the formal split-level restaurant.

174 rooms ⌱ – †£ 65/189 ††£ 65/189

Wharfedale Rd, Winnersh Triangle ⊠ RG41 5TS – Southeast : 4.5 mi by A 4 and A 3290 off Winnerish rd – ℰ 0118 944 0444 – www.hireadinghotel.com

Forbury's 🐟 🕅 ⅊ ⒶⒸ ⇔

MODERN CUISINE · FASHIONABLE In a city centre square near the law courts, with a pleasant terrace, a leather-furnished bar-lounge and a smart, spacious dining room decorated with wine paraphernalia. Menus offer French-inspired dishes. Popular monthly wine events.

Menu £ 17 (weekday lunch)/28 – Carte £ 32/54

1 Forbury Sq ⊠ RG1 3BB – ℰ 0118 957 4044 – www.forburys.co.uk – Closed 1-6 January

London Street Brasserie 🕅 ⅊ 🕅

TRADITIONAL CUISINE · BRASSERIE Bright, 200 year old building which was once a post office; the two decked terraces and some of the first floor tables overlook the River Kennet. The extensive menu offers something for everyone and dishes are stout and satisfying.

Menu £ 17 (lunch and early dinner) – Carte £ 31/53

2-4 London St ⊠ RG1 4PN – ℰ 0118 950 5036 (booking essential) – www.londonstbrasserie.co.uk – Closed 25 December

at Sonning-on-Thames Northeast: 4.25 mi by A4 on B4446

French Horn ⇔ ⋖ ⅊ ⅊ ⒶⒸ ⇔ 🅿

TRADITIONAL BRITISH · ELEGANT Beautifully located, 200 year old coaching inn, set on a bank of the Thames fringed by weeping willows; on sunny days head for the splendid terrace. The formal dining room has delightful views over the river and gardens and offers a classical menu of dishes from yesteryear – a gueridon trolley adds to the theatre. The cosy bedrooms are also traditionally appointed.

Menu £ 23 (weekdays)/60 – Carte £ 44/80 **s**

21 rooms ⌱ – †£ 135/185 ††£ 170/225 – 4 suites

⊠ RG4 6TN – ℰ 0118 969 2204 – www.thefrenchhorn.co.uk – Closed 1-2 January and dinner 25-26 December

at Shinfield South: 4.25 mi on A327 ⊠ Reading

L'Ortolan ⅊ ⅃ⓥ ⇔ 🅿

FRENCH · INTIMATE Beautiful, red-brick former vicarage with stylish, modern décor, several private dining rooms and a conservatory-lounge overlooking a lovely garden. Cooking is confident and passionate, with well-crafted, classically based dishes showing flair, originality and some playful, artistic touches.

→ Scallops with pea, mint and bergamot. Loin of lamb with sweetbreads, wild garlic, artichoke and lamb jus. Salted chocolate rock with coffee marshmallow and blueberries.

Menu £ 32/65

Church Ln ⊠ RG2 9BY – ℰ 0118 988 8500 – www.lortolan.com – Closed 25 December-3 January, Sunday and Monday

541

REDDITCH

Worcestershire – Pop. 81 919 – Regional map n° **10**-C2
▶ London 111 mi – Birmingham 15 mi

⌂ Old Rectory   ⚡ 🐾 🚕 🛁 P

TRADITIONAL · PERSONALISED A part-Elizabethan, part-Georgian former rectory set in well-tended gardens. Guest areas have a cosy, country house feel. Bedrooms are split between the house and stables; the latter, with their exposed beams, are the most characterful. Dine in the bright conservatory restaurant overlooking the garden.

10 rooms ☲ – ♦£ 79/150 ♦♦£ 94/288

Ipsley Lane, Ipsley ✉ *B98 0AP – Southeast : 2.5 mi by A 4023 off B 4497
– ✆ 01527 523000 – www.theoldrectory-hotel.co.uk*

REDHILL

Surrey – Pop. 34 498 – Regional map n° **4**-D2
▶ London 22 mi – Brighton 31 mi – Guildford 20 mi – Maidstone 34 mi

🍴 The Pendleton in St Johns   🏠 P

CLASSIC CUISINE · DESIGN A buzzing atmosphere and friendly service are guaranteed at this smart pub. Menus have plenty of South American influences, courtesy of the Brazilian chef, and on summer evenings they serve pizzas on the terrace from the van outside.

Carte £ 25/39

26 Pendleton Rd, St Johns ✉ *RH1 6QF – South : 1 mi by A 23 and Pendleton Rd
– ✆ 01737 760212 (bookings advisable at dinner) – www.thependleton.co.uk
– Closed 25 December-2 January, Sunday dinner, Monday*

REEPHAM

Norfolk – Pop. 2 405 – Regional map n° **15**-C1
▶ London 129 mi – Norwich 13 mi – Ipswich 59 mi

🍴 Dial House   ↩ 🏠 🍽 ⇔

TRADITIONAL CUISINE · SIMPLE An attractive Georgian house in a pretty village; all of its furniture, fabrics and antiques are for sale. Dine in the endearing Garden Room or in the Aga Room, where you can watch them making pancakes. Cooking is simple, fresh and tasty. Charming bedrooms are named after places from the Grand Tour.

Carte £ 19/29

8 rooms – ♦£ 155/190 ♦♦£ 155/190

7 Market Pl ✉ *NR10 4JJ – ✆ 01603 879900 – www.thedialhouse.org.uk*

REETH

North Yorkshire – Pop. 724 – Regional map n° **13**-B1
▶ London 253 mi – Leeds 53 mi – Middlesbrough 36 mi – Newcastle upon Tyne 61 mi

🏠 Burgoyne   ⚡ ≼ 🚕 P

TRADITIONAL · CLASSIC A late Georgian house with a cosy, comforting feel, set in a lovely spot overlooking the village green and the Yorkshire Dales. The two lounges are filled with antiques and vases of flowers. Bedrooms are individually styled and traditionally appointed. The elegant dining room offers an all-encompassing menu.

10 rooms ☲ – ♦£ 93/203 ♦♦£ 110/220

On The Green ✉ *DL11 6SN – ✆ 01748 884292 – www.theburgoyne.co.uk
– Restricted opening in January*

at Low Row West: 4 mi on B6270

🏠 Punch Bowl Inn   ⇔ ≤ 🏠 P

TRADITIONAL CUISINE · PUB Deep in the heart of Swaledale is this traditional 17C stone inn, which is a popular stop-off point for walkers looking to refuel on hearty, classic dishes; come at dinner for some more refined, interesting choices. Supremely comfortable bedrooms have a fresh, modern style and all have dramatic views.

Carte £ 20/39

11 rooms ⏰ – 🛏£ 81/102 🛏🛏£ 95/125

✉ DL11 6PF – ☏ 01748 886233 – www.pblnn.co.uk – Closed 25 December

at Langthwaite Northwest: 3.25 mi on Langthwaite rd✉ Reeth

🏠 Charles Bathurst Inn   ⇔ 🐕 ≤ 🏠 ⟳ P

TRADITIONAL CUISINE · PUB Characterful 18C hostelry, set in a peaceful hillside village and offering commanding rural views. Lunchtime sees hearty British pub classics, while more elaborate dishes follow in the evening, with plenty of fish and game in season. Local beers include Black Sheep Ale. Bedrooms are spacious and comfortable.

Carte £ 22/42

19 rooms ⏰ – 🛏£ 81/102 🛏🛏£ 95/130

✉ DL11 6EN – ☏ 0333 700 0779 – www.cbinn.co.uk – Closed 25 December

REIGATE

Surrey – Pop. 22 123 – Regional map n° **4**-D2

▶ London 26 mi – Brighton 33 mi – Guildford 20 mi – Maidstone 38 mi

✕✕ Tony Tobin @ The Dining Room   🆎 🔊

CLASSIC CUISINE · ELEGANT Chic, contemporary restaurant with a comfortable atmosphere and professional staff. Cooking demonstrates the chef's classical background whilst also incorporating some international influences. Most plump for the 5 course tasting menu.

Menu £ 28 (weekday dinner)/40

59a High St (1st Floor) ✉ RH2 9AE – ☏ 01737 226650
– www.tonytobinrestaurants.co.uk – Closed 23 December-4 January, Saturday lunch, Sunday dinner and bank holidays

✕ Barbe   🆎

CLASSIC FRENCH · NEIGHBOURHOOD A long-standing French bistro with a cheery owner and a huge local following. Two main dining areas are strewn with Gallic memorabilia. Simply laid, tightly packed tables. Classical, bi-monthly menu.

Menu £ 22/35

71 Bell St ✉ RH2 7AN – ☏ 01737 241966 – www.labarbe.co.uk – Closed 26-28 December, 1 January, Saturday lunch, Sunday dinner and bank holiday Mondays

RETFORD

Nottinghamshire – Pop. 22 023 – Regional map n° **9**-B1

▶ London 148 mi – Lincoln 23 mi – Nottingham 31 mi – Sheffield 27 mi

🏠 Barns Country Guesthouse   🐕 🚪 🚫 P

TRADITIONAL · PERSONALISED 18C barn with a pleasant garden and a traditionally styled interior. The oak-beamed breakfast room is furnished with old dressers and Regency-style tables and chairs. Country bedrooms have good rural outlooks; one has a four-poster.

6 rooms ⏰ – 🛏£ 40/68 🛏🛏£ 65/76

Morton Farm, Babworth ✉ DN22 8HA – Southwest : 2.25 mi by A 620 on B 6420
– ☏ 01777 706336 – www.thebarns.co.uk – Closed Christmas-New Year

RHYDYCROESAU – Shropshire → See Oswestry

RIBCHESTER
Lancashire – Pop. 888 – Regional map n° **11**-B2
▶ London 229 mi – Blackburn 7 mi – Manchester 41 mi

XxX Angels   🍽 & P

MODERN CUISINE · INTIMATE Smartly converted roadside pub with a cocktail bar and comfy lounge seating. Two formally dressed dining rooms offer a comfortable, intimate dining experience. Classic dishes with a modern edge are tasty, well-balanced and good value.

Menu £ 23 (weekdays)/38 – Carte £ 35/47

Fleet Street Ln ⊠ PR3 3ZA – Northwest : 1.5 mi by B 6245 (Longridge Rd)
– ☎ 01254 820212 – www.angelsribchester.co.uk
– dinner only and Sunday lunch
– Closed Monday

RICHMOND
North Yorkshire – Pop. 8 413 – Regional map n° **13**-B1
▶ London 243 mi – Leeds 53 mi – Middlesbrough 26 mi – Newcastle upon Tyne 44 mi

🏠 Easby Hall   🕊 < 🛏 P 🛏

COUNTRY HOUSE · PERSONALISED The views of the church, the abbey ruins and the hills are as stunning as this part-18C hall itself. There are two gardens, an orchard, a kitchen garden and a paddock – and even stables for your horse! Inside it's elegant and luxurious. Tea and scones or cocktails are served on arrival, depending on the time.

3 rooms ⌛ – 🛏£ 150 🛏🛏£ 180

Easby ⊠ DL10 7EU – Southeast : 2.5 mi by A 6108 off B 6271 – ☎ 01748 826066
– www.easbyhall.com

XX Frenchgate   🛏 🏡 P

MODERN CUISINE · INTIMATE Part-dating from the 17C, with two open-fired lounges filled with vivid art, a simply furnished dining room and a lovely terrace and walled garden. Modern, ambitious dishes. Immaculately kept, well-equipped bedrooms; breakfast features local bacon and sausages, and preserves made from berries picked nearby.

Menu £ 25/39

9 rooms ⌛ – 🛏£ 88/198 🛏🛏£ 118/250

59-61 Frenchgate ⊠ DL10 7AE – ☎ 01748 822087 – www.thefrenchgate.co.uk

at Whashton Northwest : 4.5 mi by A 6108 off Ravensworth rd

🏠 Hack & Spade ⓝ   🍴 🛏 🏡 P

INN · PERSONALISED The unusual name is a reference to the copper and lead mines that used to operate in the area. Extremely spacious bedrooms are tastefully done out with traditional furnishings and modern comforts. The beamed, open-fired restaurant has a homely feel; a short menu of home-cooked favourites is served Thurs-Sat.

5 rooms ⌛ – 🛏£ 120/140 🛏🛏£ 120/140

⊠ DL11 7JL – ☎ 01748 823721 – www.hackandspade.com – Closed 24-26 and 31 December and January.

RIMPTON
Somerset – Pop. 235 – Regional map n° **2**-C3
▶ London 126 mi – Bath 50 mi – Bournemouth 44 mi – Exeter 57 mi

🍽 White Post
⇔ 🛋 🕭 ♿ 🅿

CLASSIC CUISINE · PUB On the Dorset/Somerset border, with stunning views of the West Country. Plenty of pub classics alongside more imaginative creations and quirky touches like piggy nibbles and the Sunday roast board: surely every carnivore's dream dish? Bedrooms are simply furnished: ask for Dorset, which has the best views.

Carte £ 26/46

3 rooms ⌂ – ♦£ 80 ♦♦£ 95

✉ BA22 8AR – ☎ 01935 851525 – www.thewhitepost.com – Closed Sunday dinner and Monday

RIPLEY
North Yorkshire – ✉ Harrogate – Pop. 193 – Regional map n° **13**-B2
▶ London 213 mi – Bradford 21 mi – Leeds 18 mi – Newcastle upon Tyne 79 mi

🏠 Boar's Head
♟ 🛋 ✗ 🅿

INN · COSY 18C creeper-clad coaching inn, set in an estate-owned village and reputedly furnished from the nearby castle's attics. Family portraits and knick-knacks fill the lounges. Comfy bedrooms are found in the inn, the courtyard and an adjacent house. The all-encompassing menu is served in various different rooms.

25 rooms ⌂ – ♦£ 85/125 ♦♦£ 100/150

✉ HG3 3AY – ☎ 01423 771888 – www.boarsheadripley.co.uk

RIPLEY
Surrey – Pop. 2 041 – Regional map n° **4**-C1
▶ London 24 mi – Croydon 22 mi – Barnet 46 mi – Ealing 28 mi

🏠 Broadway Barn
🛋 ✗

TOWNHOUSE · DESIGN This charming double-fronted house spent time as an antiques shop before being converted into a guesthouse. The large open-fired lounge leads to a conservatory breakfast room which overlooks a well-tended garden. Bedrooms display good attention to detail and come with thoughtful extras.

4 rooms ⌂ – ♦£ 110/120 ♦♦£ 110/120

High St ✉ GU23 6AQ – ☎ 01483 223200 – www.broadwaybarn.com

✗✗✗ Drake's
🛋 🍽

MODERN CUISINE · INTIMATE A red-brick Georgian building with a double-sided clock above the door and a drinks terrace overlooking a beautiful garden. The panelled bar leads to an elegant modern dining room. Cooking is creative, accomplished and very visual.

Menu £ 30/60

The Clock House, High St ✉ GU23 6AQ – ☎ 01483 224777
– www.drakesrestaurant.co.uk – Closed 2 weeks August, 1 week January, 1 week Christmas, Tuesday lunch, Sunday and Monday

🍽 Anchor
🛋 ♿ 🅿

CLASSIC CUISINE · CONTEMPORARY DÉCOR A smart yet rustic pub with a 400 year history, polished slate floors and on-trend grey walls; it's nowhere near the water but it is close to a famous cycle route, which explains the bicycle-themed interior. Classic dishes like slow-cooked leg of guinea fowl are carefully executed and bursting with flavour.

Menu £ 19 (weekday lunch) – Carte £ 24/39

High St ✉ GU23 6AE – ☎ 01483 211866 – www.ripleyanchor.co.uk – Closed Monday

RIPON
North Yorkshire – Pop. 16 363 – Regional map n° **13**-B2
▶ London 222 mi – Leeds 26 mi – Middlesbrough 35 mi – York 23 mi

Bay Tree Farm

TRADITIONAL · COSY 18C sandstone barn on a working beef farm, with a smartly furnished farmhouse interior and country views. The open-fired lounge is hung with farm implements and opens onto the garden. The welcoming owners always make time to talk.

6 rooms ⌂ – ♦£ 50/80 ♦♦£ 90/110

Aldfield ⊠ HG4 3BE – Southwest : 3.75 mi by B6265 – ℰ 01765 620394
– www.baytreefarm.co.uk

ROCHDALE

Greater Manchester – Pop. 107 926 – Regional map n° **11**-B2
▶ London 224 mi – Blackpool 40 mi – Burnley 11 mi – Leeds 45 mi

XX Peacock Room at The Crimble

MODERN CUISINE · CHIC A winding drive leads up to this Victorian house; by-pass the pub and head for the cocktail bar. The restaurant boasts a mirrored-ceiling and two striking chandeliers. Constantly evolving modern menus rely on classic combinations.

Menu £ 17 (weekdays)/20 – Carte £ 27/42

Crimble Ln, Bamford ⊠ OL11 4AD – West : 2 mi on B 6222 – ℰ 01706 368591
– www.thepeacockroom.com – Closed Monday, Tuesday and lunch Saturday

XX Nutters

MODERN BRITISH · FRIENDLY Enthusiastically run restaurant in a beautiful old manor house – a popular spot for afternoon tea. Appealing menus list modern British dishes with international influences. Can't decide? Go for the 6 course 'Surprise' menu.

Menu £ 17 (weekday lunch)/44 – Carte £ 26/45

Edenfield Rd, Norden ⊠ OL12 7TT – West : 3.5 mi on A 680 – ℰ 01706 650167
– www.nuttersrestaurant.com – Closed 27-28 December, 2-3 January and Monday

ROCK

Cornwall – ⊠ Wadebridge – Pop. 4 593 – Regional map n° **1**-B2
▶ London 266 mi – Newquay 24 mi – Tintagel 14 mi – Truro 32 mi

St Enodoc

FAMILY · PERSONALISED Beautifully located hotel boasting stunning bay views. There's a strong New England feel throughout, courtesy of striped sofas and pastel coloured woodwork. Most of the contemporary, well-appointed bedrooms have a sea outlook.

20 rooms ⌂ – ♦£ 153/195 ♦♦£ 185/295

⊠ PL27 6LA – ℰ 01208 863394 – www.enodoc-hotel.co.uk
St Enodoc – See restaurant listing

XX Dining Room

MODERN BRITISH · NEIGHBOURHOOD Immaculately kept, understated restaurant with modern seascapes on the walls; run by a friendly, family-led team. Flavoursome, classically based cooking features local seasonal produce. Everything is homemade, including the butter.

Carte £ 38/47

Pavilion Buildings, Rock Rd ⊠ PL27 6JS – ℰ 01208 862622 (booking essential)
– www.thediningroomrock.co.uk – dinner only – Closed 4 weeks
January-February, 2 weeks November, Monday except bank holidays and Tuesday

X St Enodoc

MODERN CUISINE · FRIENDLY Enjoy great views over the estuary from the floor to ceiling windows of the brasserie or out on the terrace. Cooking is unfussy and full of flavour, with the occasional Spanish touch. Try the fresh shellfish from nearby Porthilly.

Menu £ 25/35

St Enodoc Hotel, ⊠ PL27 6LA – ℰ 01208 863394 – www.enodoc-hotel.co.uk

Mariners

TRADITIONAL CUISINE • PUB Two of Cornwall's top ambassadors - Sharp's Brewery and Nathan Outlaw - have come together to run this pub. Satisfying dishes feature local seafood and top quality meats. Sit on the terrace for stunning views of the Camel Estuary.

Carte £ 25/43

Slipway ✉ PL27 6LD - ✆ 01208 863679 - www.marinersrock.com - Closed 25 December

ROECLIFFE - North Yorkshire

→ See Boroughbridge

ROMALDKIRK - Durham

→ See Barnard Castle

ROMSEY

Hampshire - Pop. 16 998 - Regional map n° **4**-A2

London 82 mi - Bournemouth 28 mi - Salisbury 16 mi - Southampton 8 mi

White Horse

INN • CONTEMPORARY Smartly refurbished coaching inn; one of only 12 in the country to have continuously served as a hotel since the 14C - maybe even earlier! Guest areas feature beams, exposed brick and inglenook fireplaces. Well-equipped modern bedrooms include two duplex suites. The extensive brasserie menu suits all tastes.

31 rooms - †£ 95/105 ††£ 115/295 - ☕ £ 15 - 2 suites

Market Pl ✉ SO51 8ZJ - ✆ 01794 512431 - www.thewhitehorseromsey.co.uk

Three Tuns

TRADITIONAL BRITISH • PUB Cosy 300 year old pub off the market square. Original features include oak beams and a central bar which divides the place in two - head left if you want to dine. Classic pub dishes are generously proportioned and full of flavour.

Carte £ 23/31

58 Middlebridge St ✉ SO51 8HL - ✆ 01794 512639 - www.the3tunsromsey.co.uk - Closed 25-26 December

ROSS-ON-WYE

Herefordshire - Pop. 10 582 - Regional map n° **10**-B3

London 118 mi - Gloucester 15 mi - Birmingham 61 mi

Wilton Court

HISTORIC • COSY An attractive part-Elizabethan house just out of town, on the banks of the River Wye. Comfortable bedrooms have a subtle modern style - those to the front have river views. Tasty breakfasts feature homemade preserves. For dinner there's a choice of two different rooms; classic menus utilise local produce.

11 rooms ☕ - †£ 100/155 ††£ 135/185

Wilton Ln, Wilton ✉ HR9 6AQ - West : 0.75 mi by B 4260 - ✆ 01989 562569 - www.wiltoncourthotel.com - Closed 2-22 January

Bridge House

TOWNHOUSE • ELEGANT You get a lot more than you bargained for at this 18C townhouse: original features combine with chic, stylish furnishings; there's a superb view of the town and the River Wye; and the ruins of Castle Wilton border the grounds.

6 rooms ☕ - †£ 79/105 ††£ 105/125

Wilton ✉ HR9 6AA - West : 0.75 mi by B 4260 - ✆ 01989 562655 - www.bridgehouserossonwye.co.uk - Closed 19 December-8 January, minimum 2 nights stay at weekends

at Upton Bishop Northeast: 3 mi by A40 on B4221

🍴 Moody Cow 🛖 🅿

TRADITIONAL BRITISH · FRIENDLY A traditional country pub serving classic dishes to match the surroundings. What the food may lack in originality, it makes up for with quality ingredients, careful cooking and distinct flavours. Friendly owners run the place with a passion.

Carte £ 22/40

✉ HR9 7TT – ☎ 01989 780470 – www.moodycowpub.co.uk – *Closed 1-14 January, Sunday dinner and Monday*

at Walford South: 3 mi on B4234

🍴 Mill Race 🛏 🛖 ♿ 🅿

TRADITIONAL BRITISH · PUB It might not look like a village pub but there's definitely an atmosphere of relaxed contentment. Simple cooking uses produce from their estate and farm and lets ingredients speak for themselves; try the steaks from the charcoal oven.

Carte £ 23/35

✉ HR9 5QS – ☎ 01989 562891 – www.millrace.info

at Kerne Bridge South: 3.75 mi on B4234 ✉ Ross-On-Wye

🏠 Lumleys 🛏 🅿 ⇗

TRADITIONAL · COSY Double-fronted brick house with colourful gardens; formerly the village pub, now a cosy, characterful guesthouse run with love and care. It has cluttered, homely bedrooms, a comfy first floor lounge and a drying room for walkers.

3 rooms ⌿ – 🛏 £ 70/80 🛏🛏 £ 70/80

✉ HR9 5QT – ☎ 01600 890040 – www.thelumleys.co.uk

ROWDE – Wiltshire → See Devizes

ROWHOOK – West Sussex → See Horsham

ROWSLEY

Derbyshire – ✉ Matlock – Pop. 451 – Regional map n° **9**-A1

▶ London 157 mi – Derby 23 mi – Manchester 40 mi – Nottingham 30 mi

🏠 Peacock 🛏 🅿

TRADITIONAL · PERSONALISED Characterful 17C Dower House of the Duchess of Rutland, with gardens leading down to the river. There's a snug open-fired sitting room and a characterful bar with stone walls, wood-panelling and a large peacock mural. Bedrooms mix antique furnishings with modern facilities and service is top notch.

15 rooms ⌿ – 🛏 £ 120/135 🛏🛏 £ 190/250

Bakewell Rd ✉ DE4 2EB – ☎ 01629 733518 – www.thepeacockatrowsley.com – *Closed first 2 weeks January*

Peacock – See restaurant listing

🏠 East Lodge 🌳 🦢 🛏 🛖 ♿ 🍽 🧖 🅿

TRADITIONAL · PERSONALISED 17C hunting lodge surrounded by 10 acres of landscaped gardens dotted with ponds. Guest areas are elegant and well-appointed. Many of the bedrooms have great views; the two 'Luxury' rooms come with four-poster beds and TVs in the bathrooms. The formal dining room boasts a delightful chef's table.

12 rooms ⌿ – 🛏 £ 115/265 🛏🛏 £ 115/265

Main St ✉ DE4 2EF – ☎ 01629 734474 – www.eastlodge.com

✖✖ Peacock

MODERN CUISINE · CHIC Elegant hotel restaurant where old mullioned stone windows, oak Mousey Thompson furnishings and antique oil paintings are juxtaposed with modern lighting and contemporary art. Classic dishes at lunch are followed by more complex, elaborate combinations comprising lots of ingredients in the evening.

Carte £ 37/62

Peacock Hotel, Bakewell Rd ⊠ DE4 2EB – ℰ 01629 733518
– www.thepeacockatrowsley.com – Closed first 2 weeks January, 24-26 December and Sunday dinner

ROYAL LEAMINGTON SPA

Warwickshire – Pop. 55 733 – Regional map n° **10**-D3
▶ London 99 mi – Birmingham 23 mi – Coventry 9 mi – Leicester 33 mi

🏠 Mallory Court

LUXURY · CLASSIC Part-Edwardian house in Lutyens' style, with lovely gardens. Classic lounges display fine antiques and quality furnishings. Fresh flowers and fruit feature in the bedrooms; those in the main house are in keeping with the building's age.

43 rooms ☲ – ✦£ 139/550 ✦✦£ 165/595

Harbury Ln, Bishop's Tachbrook ⊠ CV33 9QB – South : 2.25 mi by B 4087 (Tachbrook Rd) – ℰ 01926 330214 – www.mallory.co.uk
Dining Room at Mallory • Brasserie at Mallory – See restaurant listing

🏠 Adams

TOWNHOUSE · CLASSIC Attractive, double-fronted Regency house run by passionate owners. Classically styled bedrooms come with extra touches; those to the rear are smaller but quieter. The smart, bay-windowed lounge has a small bar and ornate cornicing.

12 rooms ☲ – ✦£ 83/93 ✦✦£ 89/99

22 Avenue Rd ⊠ CV31 3PQ – ℰ 01926 450742 – www.adams-hotel.co.uk – Closed 23 December-2 January

✖✖✖ Dining Room at Mallory

MODERN BRITISH · INTIMATE Elegant wood-panelled dining room hidden within a lovely country house and looking out over its delightful grounds. Herbs, vegetables and soft fruits come from the kitchen garden. Cooking is modern; the simplest dishes are the best.

Menu £ 33 (lunch)/50

Mallory Court Hotel, Harbury Ln, Bishop's Tachbrook ⊠ CV33 9QB – South : 2.25 mi by B 4087 (Tachbrook Rd) – ℰ 01926 330214 (booking essential)
– www.mallory.co.uk – Closed Saturday lunch

✖✖ Restaurant 23

MODERN CUISINE · CHIC Smart restaurant with a chic cocktail bar and a stylish, elegant dining room, which is intimately candlelit at dinner. Modern cooking has classical European tendencies and is attractively presented. Top quality ingredients are the focus.

Menu £ 25 (lunch and early dinner) – Carte £ 42/57

34 Hamilton Terr ⊠ CV32 4LY – ℰ 01926 422422 (booking advisable)
– www.restaurant23.co.uk – Closed 25-26 December, 1 January, Sunday and Monday

✖✖ Brasserie at Mallory

MODERN CUISINE · BRASSERIE Smart brasserie in a charming country house. The bar-lounge has striking black art deco features and the airy conservatory dining room looks out over the pretty walled garden. Wide-ranging modern British menus follow the seasons.

Menu £ 23 (weekday lunch) – Carte £ 22/45

Mallory Court Hotel, Harbury Ln, Bishop's Tachbrook ⊠ CV33 9QB – South : 2.25 mi by B 4087 (Tachbrook Rd) – ℰ 01926 453939 (booking essential)
– www.mallory.co.uk – Closed Sunday dinner

✗ Oscar's

CLASSIC FRENCH · BISTRO Friendly French bistro with two rustic rooms down-stairs and a third above; the walls busy with pictures. There's a buzzy atmosphere, especially on the good value 'Auberge' nights, and the classic Gallic dishes are truly satisfying.

Menu £ 13 (weekday lunch)/20 – Carte £ 28/41

39 Chandos St ⊠ CV32 4RL – ℰ 01926 452807 (booking essential)
– www.oscarsfrenchbistro.co.uk – Closed Sunday and Monday

ROYAL TUNBRIDGE WELLS

Kent – Pop. 57 772 – Regional map n° **5**-B2

▶ London 36 mi – Brighton 33 mi – Folkestone 46 mi – Hastings 27 mi

🏠 Hotel du Vin

☆ 🛏 🖻 🖄 🅿

TOWNHOUSE · PERSONALISED Attractive Georgian property in the town centre, boasting southerly views over Calverley Park. It's wine-themed throughout, with a well-stocked clubby bar, two comfy lounges and contemporary bedrooms; some have emperor-sized beds and baths in the rooms. The rustic bistro and terrace serve French cuisine.

34 rooms – ♦£ 109/200 ♦♦£ 120/220 – � £ 17

Crescent Rd ⊠ TN1 2LY – ℰ 0844 748 9266 – www.hotelduvin.com

🏠 Tunbridge Wells

🖄

TOWNHOUSE · ELEGANT This longstanding hotel sits at the centre of the Pantiles, a Georgian colonnade which leads to the famous well. Bedrooms are modern and stylish – most have French antique walnut beds with Hypnos mattresses.

20 rooms � – ♦£ 75/85 ♦♦£ 110/195

58 The Pantiles ⊠ TN2 5TD – ℰ 01892 530501 – www.thetunbridgewellshotel.com

Eating House – See restaurant listing

🏠 Danehurst

🕸 🅿

TRADITIONAL · PERSONALISED Attractive Edwardian house with a pleasant terrace and koi carp pond; set in a peaceful residential area. Furnishings are top quality and show good attention to detail. The charming owners make the tasty bread and jam for breakfast.

4 rooms � – ♦£ 105/155 ♦♦£ 115/175

41 Lower Green Rd, Rusthall ⊠ TN4 8TW – West : 1.75 mi by A 264
– ℰ 01892 527739 – www.danehurst.net – Closed 20 December-2 January

✗✗✗ Thackeray's

🖼 ⬦

MODERN BRITISH · INTIMATE A softly illuminated clapboard house; the oldest in town and once home to the eponymous author. Classic dishes have modern elements and feature lots of different ingredients. The moody first floor private rooms showcase local art.

Menu £ 20/55

85 London Rd ⊠ TN1 1EA – ℰ 01892 511921 – www.thackerays-restaurant.co.uk
– Closed Sunday dinner and Monday

✗ Eating House 🅝

🖼 🔲

MODERN BRITISH · BRASSERIE A French bistro themed restaurant overlooking the historic Pantiles parade, with a large terrace that comes into its own in the summer. Lunch sees classics like steak frites; dinner offers refined modern dishes packed with flavour.

Menu £ 20 (weekdays)/28 – Carte £ 22/41

Tunbridge Wells Hotel, 58 The Pantiles ⊠ TN2 5TD – ℰ 01892 530501
– www.thetunbridgewellshotel.com

The Beacon 🆕
≤ 🍴 🛏 ♻ 🅿

MODERN CUISINE · PUB The Beacon is stunningly built into a stone escarpment and has fantastic views over the town. It's set over three levels and its original decorative features include carved wood and stained glass. Classic pub dishes are driven by the latest seasonal ingredients and have bold flavours and comforting feel.

Menu £17 (weekdays) – Carte £25/41

Tea Garden Ln ⊠ TN3 9JH – ℰ 01892 524252 – www.the-beacon.co.uk – Closed Sunday dinner and Monday

Black Pig
🛏

MODERN BRITISH · FRIENDLY The black façade may feel quite austere but inside it's quite the opposite, courtesy of a friendly team, a laid-back vibe and rustic shabby-chic styling. Dishes are gutsy and full-flavoured and there's even a 'PIG Heaven' section.

Menu £15 (weekdays)/30 – Carte £22/40

18 Grove Hill Rd ⊠ TN1 1RZ – ℰ 01892 523030 – www.theblackpig.net – Closed 26 December and 1 January

at Southborough North : 2 m. on A 26

🍴 Twenty Six Test Kitchen 🆕
♻

MODERN CUISINE · BISTRO A homely, rustic restaurant overlooking the village green – it has 26 seats, 26 light bulbs hanging from the ceiling and 26 stars fixed to the window! Satisfying, seasonal modern dishes; you'll wish you could try everything on the menu.

Menu £22 (weekday dinner)/50 – Carte £26/36

15a Church Rd ⊠ TN4 0RX – ℰ 01892 544607 – www.thetwenty-six.co.uk – Closed Sunday, Monday and lunch Tuesday-Friday

at Speldhurst Northwest: 3.5 mi by A26

George & Dragon
🛏 ♿ 🅿

TRADITIONAL BRITISH · PUB Hugely characterful Wealden Hall house dating back to 1212 and boasting an impressive beamed ceiling and an unusual Queen's post. Generous cooking uses local, organic produce, offering pub classics alongside more elaborate dishes.

Carte £26/46

Speldhurst Hill ⊠ TN3 0NN – ℰ 01892 863125 – www.speldhurst.com

ROZEL BAY – Saint Martin → See Channel Islands (Jersey)

RUDDINGTON – Nottinghamshire → See Nottingham

RUGBY
Warwickshire – Pop. 70 628 – Regional map n° **10**-D2
▶ London 88 mi – Birmingham 33 mi – Northampton 20 mi

🍴🍴 Ferguson's
🛏 ♿

MODERN CUISINE · CLASSIC DÉCOR Have light bites on the terrace or head into the airy contemporary interior, where glass and light wood feature. Understated menu descriptions give little away – cooking is carefully prepared and ambitious with modern overtones.

Menu £35

7A Eastfield Pl ⊠ CV21 3AT – ℰ 01788 550222 – www.fergusonsrugby.co.uk – Closed 25-26 December, 1 January, Sunday and Monday

RUSHLAKE GREEN
East Sussex – ⊠ Heathfield – Regional map n° **5**-B2
▶ London 54 mi – Brighton 26 mi – Eastbourne 13 mi

⌂ Stone House
HISTORIC · PERSONALISED Beautiful gardens lead up to this charming part-15C house, set in 1,000 acres of tranquil grounds. It's been in the family for 500 years and is very personally run. The traditional country house interior features original staircases, wood-panelling and antiques; some of the individually decorated bedrooms have four-poster beds. Classic menus use kitchen garden produce.

7 rooms ⌂ – ♦£ 145/165 ♦♦£ 160/310 – 1 suite

✉ TN21 9QJ – (Northeast corner of the green) – ✆ 01435 830553
– www.stonehousesussex.co.uk – Closed 23 December-3 January and
17 February-10 March

RUSHTON – Northamptonshire ➜ See Kettering

RYE
East Sussex – Pop. 3 708 – Regional map n° **5**-C2
▶ London 61 mi – Brighton 49 mi – Folkestone 27 mi – Maidstone 33 mi

⌂ George in Rye
INN · DESIGN A deceptively large, centrally located coaching inn offering an attractive blend of the old and the new. Stylish bedrooms have bold modern colour schemes and good facilities. There's a characterful beamed bar, a cosy wood-panelled lounge and a smart restaurant. Steaks are the highlight of the grill menu.

34 rooms ⌂ – ♦£ 135/325 ♦♦£ 135/325

98 High St. ✉ TN31 7JT – ✆ 01797 222114 – www.thegeorgeinrye.com

⌂ Mermaid Inn
INN · HISTORIC One of England's oldest coaching inns, which offers immense charm and character, from its heavy beams and carved wooden fireplaces to its tapestries, false stairways and priests' holes. Formal dining features mainly local fish and game. The owner has been looking after guests here for over three decades.

31 rooms ⌂ – ♦£ 90/150 ♦♦£ 150/220

Mermaid St. ✉ TN31 7EY – ✆ 01797 223065 – www.mermaidinn.com

⌂ Jeake's House
TOWNHOUSE · PERSONALISED Three 17C houses joined together over time, set down a cobbled lane. A former wool store and Quaker meeting place, it is set apart by its substantial charm. Characterful beamed rooms are warmly decorated and filled with antiques.

11 rooms ⌂ – ♦£ 90/120 ♦♦£ 120/150

Mermaid St. ✉ TN31 7ET – ✆ 01797 222828 – www.jeakeshouse.com

⌂ Willow Tree House
TOWNHOUSE · COSY 300 year old boathouse on the main road into town. Comfy bedrooms are decorated in warm colours and are tastefully furnished; those at the top have exposed beams. Substantial breakfasts are served in a conservatory-style room.

6 rooms ⌂ – ♦£ 90/121 ♦♦£ 90/145

113 Winchelsea Rd. ✉ TN31 7EL – South : 0.5 mi on A 259 – ✆ 01797 227820
– www.willow-tree-house.com – Closed 20-30 October and 24-30 December

✗ Webbe's at The Fish Café
SEAFOOD · BISTRO Relaxed café in a former antiques warehouse and teddy bear factory, with terracotta-coloured brick walls, a small counter and a cookery school above. Extensive menus offer simply prepared seafood from the Rye and Hastings day boats.

Carte £ 25/40

17 Tower St. ✉ TN31 7AT – ✆ 01797 222226 – www.webbesrestaurants.co.uk
– Closed 24th December-17th January

✗ **Tuscan Kitchen Rye**

ITALIAN · RUSTIC Centrally located, with dark wood tables, studded leather chairs, Italian memorabilia and even a stuffed wild boar. Rustic, classical cooking with everything homemade. The olive oil comes from the family farm in Tuscany.

Carte £ 20/34

8 Lion St ⊠ TN31 7LB – ℰ 01797 223269 (booking advisable)
– www.tuscankitchenrye.co.uk – dinner only and lunch Friday and Sunday
– Closed Monday and Tuesday

at Camber Southeast: 4.25 mi by A259⊠ Rye

🏠 **Gallivant** AC 🔱 P

BOUTIQUE HOTEL · SEASIDE Laid-back hotel opposite Camber Sands, run by a friendly team. Relax by the fire in the New England style lounge. Bedrooms come in blues and whites, with distressed wood furniture and modern facilities; some have decked terraces.

20 rooms ⌂ – 🛏£ 95/260 🛏🛏£ 95/260

New Lydd Rd. ⊠ TN31 7RB – ℰ 01797 225057 – www.thegallivant.co.uk
Gallivant – See restaurant listing

✗ **Gallivant** 🌤 AC P

MODERN BRITISH · BISTRO Informal hotel bistro with distressed wood furniture, white and blue hues and a pleasant covered terrace. Appealing all-day menus keep local seafood to the fore; refreshingly, the good value two-choice set menu is always available.

Menu £ 16 (weekday lunch) – Carte £ 27/40

Gallivant Hotel, New Lydd Rd. ⊠ TN31 7RB – ℰ 01797 225057
– www.thegallivant.co.uk

RYHALL

Rutland – Pop. 1 459 – Regional map n° **9**-C2
▶ London 94 mi – Leicester 35 mi – Nottingham 45 mi

✗✗ **Wicked Witch** 🍴 ⅄ P

CLASSIC CUISINE · NEIGHBOURHOOD A smart former pub with dark wood panelling, purple walls and a relaxed formality; one owner cooks and the other serves. Seasonal menus have a classic base but combinations are original and there's a real emphasis on presentation.

Menu £ 15/25

Bridge St ⊠ PE9 4HH – ℰ 01780 763649 – www.thewickedwitchexperience.co.uk
– Closed Sunday dinner and Monday

ST ALBANS

Hertfordshire – Pop. 82 146 – Regional map n° **7**-A2
▶ London 27 mi – Cambridge 41 mi – Luton 10 mi

🏠 **St Michael's Manor** 🍴 ⅄ AC ⅗ 🔱 P

TOWNHOUSE · PERSONALISED Part-16C William and Mary manor house with well-kept gardens and lake views. Characterful guest areas display contemporary touches. Bedrooms are well-appointed; those in the Garden Wing are the most modern and some have terraces.

30 rooms ⌂ – 🛏£ 110/320 🛏🛏£ 135/340 – 1 suite

St Michael's Village, Fishpool St ⊠ AL3 4RY – ℰ 01727 864444
– www.stmichaelsmanor.com
Lake – See restaurant listing

XX THOMPSON St Albans 🏠 ᕃ ᴀᴄ ᑏⓋ

MODERN CUISINE · INTIMATE Come on a Sunday for 'lobster and steak' night or any day of the week for refined, tasty dishes with a modern edge. Three contemporary dining rooms feature bold artwork from the local gallery. Try the lesser-known wines by the glass.

Menu £ 19 (weekday lunch)/25 – Carte £ 38/55

2 Hatfield Rd ⊠ AL1 3RP – 𝒞 01727 730777 – www.thompsonstalbans.co.uk
– Closed 2-12 January, Sunday dinner, Monday and lunch Tuesday

XX Lake ⪡ 🏠 🏠 ᕃ ᴀᴄ ᴘ

MODERN CUISINE · ELEGANT Spacious, airy orangery in a family-owned manor house, which looks out over well-tended gardens and a lake. Daily changing dishes feature contemporary twists; the Lake Menu is good value. Formal service comes from a chatty team.

Menu £ 19 (weekdays) – Carte £ 33/59

St Michael's Manor Hotel, St Michael's Village, Fishpool St ⊠ AL3 4RY
– 𝒞 01727 864444 – www.lakerestaurant.co.uk

ST AUBIN → See Channel Islands (Jersey)

ST AUSTELL
Cornwall – Pop. 23 864 – Regional map n° **1**-B2
▶ London 281 mi – Newquay 16 mi – Plymouth 38 mi – Truro 14 mi

⌂ Anchorage House 🏠 🏠 🖼 🏠 ᴸᵃ ⅍ ᴘ

FAMILY · PERSONALISED Modern guesthouse owned by an ex-Canadian Naval Commander. Afternoon tea is served in the comfy lounge. Charming, antique-filled bedrooms boast modern fabrics, state-of-the-art bathrooms and plenty of extras. Facilities include an indoor pool, a gym, a sauna and a chill-out lounge. The conservatory dining room offers simple, home-cooked dishes. The owners are lovely.

5 rooms ⌕ – ♦£ 75/85 ♦♦£ 110/140

Nettles Corner, Boscundle ⊠ PL25 3RH – East : 2.75 mi by A 390
– 𝒞 01726 814071 – www.anchoragehouse.co.uk – Closed 15 November-15 March

at Carlyon Bay East: 2.5 mi by A3601⊠ St Austell

XX Brett@Austell's

MODERN CUISINE · NEIGHBOURHOOD Keenly run neighbourhood restaurant with a brightly lit, mirror-filled interior. Modern seasonal menus showcase local produce in elaborate, confidently executed dishes with original touches. They open at 10am for coffee and cake.

Menu £ 28 – Carte £ 31/41

10 Beach Rd ⊠ PL25 3PH – 𝒞 01726 813888 – www.austells.co.uk – dinner only and Sunday lunch – Closed first 2 weeks January and Monday

ST BRELADE'S BAY → See Channel Islands (Jersey)

ST EWE
Cornwall – Regional map n° **1**-B3
▶ London 258 mi – Bristol 161 mi – Cardiff 192 mi – Plymouth 46 mi

⌂ Lower Barns 🏠 🐿 🏠 ᕃ ⅍ ᴘ

FAMILY · ELEGANT The gregarious owner extends a warm welcome at this stylishly converted 18C granite barn (formerly part of the Heligan Estate). Quirky, vibrantly decorated bedrooms are spread about the place and a hot tub on the decking overlooks the garden. Home-cooked dinners are served in the 'shack'.

6 rooms ⌕ – ♦£ 85/100 ♦♦£ 115/225

Bosue ⊠ PL26 6ET – North : 1.25 mi by Crosswyn rd, St Austell rd and signed off St Mawes rd – 𝒞 01726 844881 – www.lowerbarns.co.uk

ST HELENS → See Wight (Isle of)

ST HELIER → See Channel Islands (Jersey)

ST IVES
Cornwall – Pop. 9 966 – Regional map n° **1**-A3
▶ London 319 mi – Penzance 10 mi – Truro 25 mi

No 27
HISTORIC · PERSONALISED Unusually for St Ives, this stylishly restored Georgian house has its own car park... even more unusually, it also owns the beach beneath it! Bedrooms are modern and appealing. Take in a view of the bay from the airy breakfast room.
9 rooms ☑ – ♦£ 65/135 ♦♦£ 85/155
Town plan: A2-n - *27 The Terrace* ⊠ TR26 2BP – ℰ 01736 797450
– www.27theterrace.co.uk

Blue Hayes
HISTORIC · PERSONALISED Built in 1922 for Professor Whitnall, a surgeon friend of Edward III. Comfy bedrooms: one with French doors onto a roof terrace; another with a four-poster and a balcony. Single course dinner available. Breakfast on the terrace in summer.
6 rooms ☑ – ♦£ 130/216 ♦♦£ 190/270
Town plan: B2-u - *Trelyon Ave* ⊠ TR26 2AD – ℰ 01736 797129
– www.bluehayes.co.uk – Closed November-February

Trevose Harbour House
TOWNHOUSE · GRAND LUXURY The experienced owners have decorated this stylish townhouse themselves, so you'll find lots of personal touches alongside an unusual mix of designer and upcycled furnishings. Breakfast features local produce and is a real highlight. They have 3 parking spaces reserved at the nearby station.
6 rooms ☑ – ♦£ 145/265 ♦♦£ 155/275
Town plan: AB2-t - *22 The Warren* ⊠ TR26 2EA – ℰ 01736 793267
– www.trevosehouse.co.uk – Closed mid December-March

XX Alba
MODERN BRITISH · ROMANTIC A former lifeboat station in a great harbourside location. Dishes are European in base with a modern slant – go for one of the fish specials. The ground floor cocktail bar offers small plates and a good range of wines by the glass.
Menu £ 19 – Carte £ 21/49
Town plan: A1-d *Old Lifeboat House, The Wharf* ⊠ TR26 1LF – ℰ 01736 797222
– www.thealbarestaurant.com – dinner only – Closed 25-26 December

X Porthminster Beach Café
SEAFOOD · FASHIONABLE Charming 1930s beach house in a superb location overlooking Porthminster Sands. It's hung with Cornish artwork, has a nautical style and leads out onto a large heated terrace. The seasonal seafood menu offers unfussy, vibrantly flavoured dishes with Asian influences. Service is relaxed and friendly.
Carte £ 26/55
Town plan: B2-p - *Porthminster Beach* ⊠ TR26 2EB – ℰ 01736 795352 (booking advisable) – www.porthminstercafe.co.uk – Closed 1-13 January

X Black Rock
REGIONAL CUISINE · NEIGHBOURHOOD A relaxed, modern bistro with a semi-open kitchen and contemporary art. The regularly changing menu places its emphasis on local seafood and the owner is a third generation fisherman so has lots of local contacts. Cooking is gutsy and big on flavour; come before 7pm for a good value 3 course selection.
Menu £ 17 – Carte £ 25/38
Town plan: A1-v - *Market Pl* ⊠ TR26 1RZ – ℰ 01736 791911 (booking advisable) – www.theblackrockstives.co.uk – dinner only – Closed November-February, Sunday and restricted opening in winter

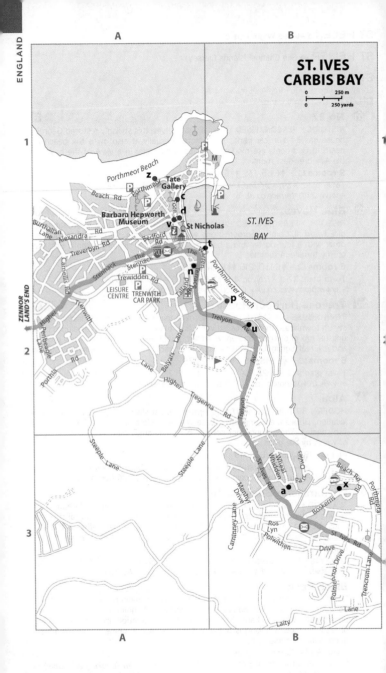

ST. IVES
CARBIS BAY

0   250 m
0   250 yards

Porthmeor Beach

z

Tate Gallery

Beach Rd

c

Barbara Hepworth Museum

Burthallan Lane

Alexandra Rd

d

v

St Nicholas

ST. IVES
BAY

Treverbyn Rd

Bedford Rd

Canells Rd

Stennack

Trewidden Rd

t

Higher Trenwith

n

Porthminster Beach

Penbeagle Lane

LEISURE CENTRE

TRENWITH CAR PARK

Talland

p

Trelyon

u

Portha Rd

Bellair Lane

Higher Tregenna Rd

ZENNOR LAND'S END

Steeple Lane

Steeple Lane

Wheal Whidden

St Ives Rd

Beach Rd

a

x

Porthrepta Rd

Menhyr Drive

Carninney Lane

Boskerris

Ros Lyn

Polwithen Drive

St Ives Rd

Palmeshtal Drive

Trencrom Lane

Laity

Lane

ENGLAND

X **Porthmeor Café Bar** ≤ 🏠 🛋 🎦

MODERN CUISINE · NEIGHBOURHOOD A popular beachfront café where you can sit inside, on the terrace or in heated pods. They offer breakfast, cakes, Mediterranean small plates and a few more substantial dishes too. Every table has a great view, especially at sunset.

Carte £ 21/32

Town plan: A1-z - Porthmeor Beach ⊠ TR26 1JZ - 𝒞 01736 793366 (booking essential at dinner) - www.porthmeor-beach.co.uk - Closed November-March

X **Porthminster Kitchen** 🆕 🍷 ≤ 🏠 🛋 🎦

MODERN CUISINE · NEIGHBOURHOOD Follow the narrow staircase up to this contemporary bistro and you'll be rewarded with glorious harbour views from both the restaurant and terrace. The all-day menu offers light, fresh, global cuisine with a focus on local seafood.

Carte £ 20/30

Town plan: A1-c - The Wharf ⊠ TR26 1LG - 𝒞 01736 799874
- www.porthminster.kitchen

at Carbis Bay South: 1.75 mi on A3074 ⊠ St Ives

🏨 **Boskerris** ≤ 🖼 🛇 🅿

FAMILY · CONTEMPORARY A passionately run hotel with a light and airy feel. The French-style lounge-bar leads out onto a huge terrace with panoramic views of Carbis Bay. Uncluttered bedrooms come in cool modern designs and some have baths for two.

15 rooms ☑ - ♦£ 113/210 ♦♦£ 150/280

Town plan: B3-x - Boskerris Rd ⊠ TR26 2NQ - 𝒞 01736 795295
- www.boskerrishotel.co.uk - Closed mid-November-March

🏨 **Beachcroft** ≤ 🖼 🛇 🅿

LUXURY · PERSONALISED Set in an elevated position, with stunning views across the bay. Contemporary interior with subtle 1920s touches. Comfy, understated bedrooms have bespoke furnishings and luxurious bathrooms. Have your breakfast on the delightful terrace.

5 rooms ☑ - ♦£ 120/160 ♦♦£ 140/200

Town plan: B3-a - Valley Rd ⊠ TR26 2QS - 𝒞 01736 794442
- www.beachcroftstives.co.uk - Closed November-March except New Year

at Halsetown Southwest: 1.5 mi on B3311

🍴 **Halsetown Inn** 🏠 🅿

MODERN CUISINE · FRIENDLY A slightly quirky pub, a short drive from St Ives; there are various little areas to sit in, as well as a lovely suntrap terrace. Menus change every 6-8 weeks and offer an interesting selection of dishes enlivened with some global flavours - with a particular nod towards Asia. Service is warm and friendly.

Menu £ 16 (weekday lunch) - Carte £ 23/38

⊠ TR26 3NA - 𝒞 01736 795583 - www.halsetowninn.co.uk - Closed January and Sunday dinner

ST KEVERNE

Cornwall - Pop. 939 - Regional map n° **1**-A3
▶ London 302 mi - Penzance 26 mi - Truro 28 mi

🏨 **Old Temperance House** 🛇 🍽

TOWNHOUSE · CONTEMPORARY This pretty pink-washed cottage framed by olive trees was once a 15C temperance house. The interior is contemporary and immaculately kept. Bright bedrooms are named after alcoholic drinks and display thoughtful touches. Fresh fruit and produce from the local butcher features at breakfast.

4 rooms ☑ - ♦£ 65/70 ♦♦£ 89/95

The Square ⊠ TR12 6NA - 𝒞 01326 280986 - www.oldtemperancehouse.co.uk

🍴 Greenhouse

REGIONAL CUISINE · RUSTIC Simple eatery in a sleepy little village, where they sell their own bread and meringues. Daily blackboard menus are centred around local, organic and gluten free produce. Cooking is unfussy and flavoursome and seafood is a feature.

Carte £ 21/34

6 High St. ✉ *TR12 6NN –* ☎ *01326 280800 (booking advisable) – www.tgor.co.uk – dinner only and occasional Sunday lunch – Closed last 3 weeks January*

ST KEW

Cornwall – Regional map n° **1**-B2
▶ London 265 mi – Newquay 20 mi – Liskeard 24 mi

🍴 St Kew Inn   🍴 🏠 **P**

TRADITIONAL BRITISH · PUB A characterful country pub with a lovely garden and patio heaters, set in a quintessentially English location. Menus offer a wide range of appealing, good value dishes. Be sure to order a beer from the wooden casks behind the bar.

Carte £ 24/36

✉ *PL30 3HB –* ☎ *01208 841259 – www.stkewinn.co.uk – Closed 25-26 December*

ST MARTIN → See Channel Islands (Guernsey)

ST MARY'S → See Scilly (Isles of)

ST MAWES

Cornwall – ✉ Truro – Regional map n° **1**-B3
▶ London 299 mi – Plymouth 56 mi – Truro 18 mi

🏨 Hotel Tresanton   🐾 ⟨ 🏃 🧖 **P**

TOWNHOUSE · GRAND LUXURY Set in a collection of old fishermen's cottages and a former yacht club. Elegant, nautically themed guest areas include an intimate bar and a movie room. Understated bedrooms – some in cottages – have a high level of facilities and superb sea views. The lovely split-level terrace shares the outlook.

30 rooms 🖵 – ♦£ 234/243 ♦♦£ 260/360 – 4 suites

27 Lower Castle Rd ✉ *TR2 5DR –* ☎ *01326 270055 – www.tresanton.com – Closed 2 weeks January*

Restaurant Tresanton – See restaurant listing

🏨 Idle Rocks   ⟨ ⟨ 🏃 **P**

BOUTIQUE HOTEL · PERSONALISED Boutique hotel on the water's edge, with fabulous views over the harbour and the estuary. The décor is personalised and local art is displayed throughout. Cosy, contemporary bedrooms have pleasing subtle touches and are well-equipped. The relaxed restaurant has bay views, a modern menu and a superb terrace.

20 rooms 🖵 – ♦£ 200/380 ♦♦£ 200/380

Harbourside ✉ *TR2 5AN –* ☎ *01326 270270 – www.idlerocks.com – Closed 5-29 January*

🏠 St Mawes 🆕   ⟨ ⟨

BOUTIQUE HOTEL · CONTEMPORARY A smart refurbishment has revived this classic harbourside hotel, leaving it with a cool and trendy vibe. Bedrooms are understated and immaculately kept and the restful lounge boasts squashy sofas and opens onto a small balcony. The lively front restaurant serves fresh seafood and wood-fired pizzas.

7 rooms – ♦£ 130/285 ♦♦£ 130/285

Harbourside ✉ *TR2 5DN –* ☎ *01326 270170 – www.stmaweshotel.com*

XX Restaurant Tresanton ⟨ 🏠 P

MODERN BRITISH · FASHIONABLE Take in superb bay views from this bright hotel restaurant, which has attractive mosaic flooring and a nautical theme. Daily menus offer unfussy dishes crafted from quality local produce and seafood is a feature. The large terrace is a popular spot, especially when they're hosting their summer BBQs.

Menu £ 27 (lunch) – Carte £ 40/62

Hotel Tresanton, 27 Lower Castle Rd ⊠ TR2 5DR – ℰ 01326 270055 (booking essential) – www.tresanton.com – Closed 2 weeks January

X Watch House ⟨ ⅋

MEDITERRANEAN CUISINE · SIMPLE Old Customs and Excise watch house on the quayside, with a nautically styled interior, friendly service and harbour views. Light lunches and substantial dinners; unfussy cooking follows a Mediterranean theme – try the tasty fish specials.

Menu £ 22/30 – Carte £ 23/38

1 The Square ⊠ TR2 5DJ – ℰ 01326 270038 – www.watchhousestmawes.co.uk – Closed 25-26 December and Sunday dinner-Tuesday except Easter-September

ST MELLION

Cornwall – Regional map n° **1**-C2

▶ London 225 mi – Bristol 129 mi – Cardiff 160 mi – Plymouth 13 mi

🏠 Pentillie Castle 🏰 🦢 ⟨ 🛏 🧺 ⅋ 🎾 P

COUNTRY HOUSE · HISTORIC 17C house – later transformed into a castle – set in 2,000 acres overlooking the river. Spacious, elegant bedrooms have antique furnishings, luxurious bathrooms and some great views. Classical guest areas include a dining room with a crystal chandelier; traditional dinners require a minimum of 6 guests.

9 rooms ⊅ – ♦£ 110/235 ♦♦£ 125/250

⊠ PL12 6QD – Southeast : 1 mi by A 388 on Cargreen rd – ℰ 01579 350044 – www.pentillie.co.uk

ST OSYTH

Essex – Pop. 2 118 – Regional map n° **7**-D2

▶ London 83 mi – Colchester 12 mi – Clacton-on-Sea 5 mi

🏠 Park Hall 🦢 🛏 ⅋ 🎾 P

HISTORIC · PERSONALISED Charming 14C former monastery with a homely feel, surrounded by 400 acres of arable farmland. Characterful bedrooms come with good extras, and antiques and ornaments abound. Seek out the hidden seating areas in the large gardens.

4 rooms ⊅ – ♦£ 75/110 ♦♦£ 130/190

Bypass Rd ⊠ CO16 8HG – East : 1.5 mi on B 1027 – ℰ 01255 820922 – www.parkhall.info

ST PETER PORT → See Channel Islands (Guernsey)

ST SAVIOUR → See Channel Islands (Jersey)

ST SAVIOUR → See Channel Islands (Guernsey)

ST TUDY

Cornwall – Pop. 604 – Regional map n° **1**-B2

▶ London 239 mi – Truro 32 mi – Exeter 64 mi

🍴 St Tudy Inn ⓝ 🏠 ⅋ P

TRADITIONAL BRITISH · FRIENDLY A lovingly restored pub in a pretty village. Inside there's a labyrinth of cosy rooms with fresh flowers, open fires and rustic, modish overtones. Food is unfussy, seasonal and satisfying and arrives beautifully presented; the 3 course midweek menu is good value. The chef is passionate and service is friendly.

Carte £ 25/36

⊠ PL30 3NN – ℰ 01208 850656 – www.sttudyinn.com – Closed 25-26 December

SALCOMBE

Devon – Pop. 1 893 – Regional map n° **1**-C3
▶ London 243 mi – Exeter 43 mi – Plymouth 27 mi – Torquay 28 mi

🏨 Salcombe Harbour
☆ ⟨ 🔲 💿 🛜 ♨ 🔄 ♿ 🧖 🅿

LUXURY · CONTEMPORARY Take in views of the estuary from this contemporary seaside hotel, with its sleek, nautical edge. Stylish bedrooms come with Nespresso machines and tablets; many also have balconies. For relaxation there's a chic spa and even a cinema! The restaurant offers modern menus, with local seafood a feature.

50 rooms ⌂ – ♦£ 99/295 ♦♦£ 145/495 – 1 suite
Cliff Rd ⌂ TQ8 8JH – ℰ 01548 844444 – www.salcombe-harbour-hotel.co.uk

🏨 South Sands
⟨ ♿ 🅿

FAMILY · GRAND LUXURY Stylish hotel by the water's edge, with a subtle New England theme running throughout and South Sands views. Small, modern bar and lounges. Smart bedrooms have heavy wood furnishings and good facilities; opt for one with a balcony.

27 rooms ⌂ – ♦£ 170/475 ♦♦£ 170/475 – 5 suites
Bolt Head ⌂ TQ8 8LL – Southwest : 1.25 mi – ℰ 01548 845900
– www.southsands.com
Beachside – See restaurant listing

🍴🍴 Beachside
⟨ 🍴 ♿ 🆎 🅿

SEAFOOD · FASHIONABLE Large, airy hotel restaurant with full-length windows opening onto a delightful decked terrace overlooking the bay. Modern, daily changing menus offer a good mix of unfussy, flavoursome dishes, with plenty of fresh seafood options.

Menu £ 28
South Sands Hotel, Bolt Head ⌂ TQ8 8LL – Southwest : 1.25 mi – ℰ 01548 845900
(booking advisable) – www.southsands.com

at Soar Mill Cove Southwest: 4.25 mi by A381⌂ Salcombe

🏨 Soar Mill Cove
☆ 🏊 ⟨ 🍸 🍴 🔲 ♨ 🔄 🍴 🏕 🅿

FAMILY · PERSONALISED Family-run hotel built from local slate and stone; delightfully set above a secluded cove. Relax in the modern lounge or smart bar. Spacious bedrooms come in bright, contemporary styles; half have private patios and sea views. Blue-hued restaurant offers a modern menu and a lovely outlook from every table.

22 rooms ⌂ – ♦£ 99/200 ♦♦£ 149/269
⌂ TQ7 3DS – ℰ 01548 561566 – www.soarmillcove.co.uk – Closed
1 January-14 February

SALFORD QUAYS – Gtr Manchester → See Manchester

SALISBURY

Wiltshire – Pop. 44 748 – Regional map n° **2**-D3
▶ London 91 mi – Bournemouth 28 mi – Bristol 53 mi – Southampton 23 mi

🍴🍴 Anokaa
🆎 🍷

INDIAN · DESIGN A smart Indian restaurant that's a little different, with colour-changing lights and interesting water features. Originality is also expressed in the extensive menu: expect dishes like spiced crushed scallops or duck jaalsha.

Menu £ 17 (early dinner) – Carte £ 23/59
60 Fisherton St ⌂ SP2 7RB – ℰ 01722 414142 – www.anokaa.com

ENGLAND

at Teffont Evias West: 10.25 mi by A36 and A30 on B3089 ⊠ Salisbury

🏠 **Howard's House** 🏡 🐾 🖨 🛜 🅿

COUNTRY HOUSE · COSY This charming Grade II listed dower house stands in a beautiful English village; the eponymous 'Howard' was a tenant here for 20yrs. Bright, airy bedrooms have an understated feel and offer village or garden views. The dining room has a sophisticated menu and its French windows open onto a sheltered terrace. Good old-fashioned hospitality is provided by a family team.

9 rooms ⊐ – †£120 ††£190/225

⊠ SP3 5RJ – ℰ 01722 716392 – www.howardshousehotel.co.uk – Closed 23-26 December

SALTWOOD

Kent – Regional map n° **5**-C2

▶ London 65 mi – Maidstone 30 mi – Margate 37 mi

✗ **Saltwood on the Green** 🍸 🖳

MODERN BRITISH · FRIENDLY A former village store run by a charismatic American chef. It has a relaxed, modish style and a bar laden with cakes. Appealing, highly original dishes are flavourful and healthy. It's open for breakfast through to cocktails.

Menu £16 (weekday lunch) – Carte £27/43

The Green ⊠ CT21 4PS – ℰ 01303 237800 (booking advisable) – www.saltwoodrestaurant.co.uk – Closed 1 week September, 24-30 December and Sunday dinner-Tuesday

SANCTON

East Riding of Yorkshire – Pop. 286 – Regional map n° **13**-C2

▶ London 194 mi – York 23 mi – Hull 20 mi

🏮 **Star** 🛜 🕭 🕼 🅿

MODERN CUISINE · FRIENDLY A personally run pub in a small village, with a cosy bar and two smart dining rooms. Homemade nibbles and hearty, boldly flavoured dishes, with regional suppliers proudly listed on a blackboard. Staff are young, local and full of smiles.

Menu £17 (weekday lunch) – Carte £26/42

King St ⊠ YO43 4QP – ℰ 01430 827269 – www.thestaratsancton.co.uk – Closed Monday

SANDIACRE

Derbyshire – Pop. 9 600 – Regional map n° **9**-B2

▶ London 123 mi – Birmingham 46 mi – Leeds 75 mi – Sheffield 45 mi

✗✗ **La Rock** 🕭 🆎

MODERN BRITISH · RUSTIC Charming, personally run restaurant with an airy feel – it was once a butcher's. Exposed brick walls and antler chandeliers feature. Cooking combines classical flavours with modern techniques; home-grown fruits are well utilised.

Menu £29 (weekday lunch) – Carte £36/53

4 Bridge St ⊠ NG10 5QT – ℰ 0115 939 9833 – www.larockrestaurant.co.uk – Closed 24 December-mid January, Monday, Tuesday and lunch Wednesday

SANDSEND – North Yorkshire ➜ See Whitby

SANDYPARK – Devon ➜ See Chagford

SAPPERTON – Gloucestershire ➜ See Cirencester

SAWDON – North Yorkshire ➜ See Scarborough

SAWLEY

Lancashire – Pop. 237 – Regional map n° **11**-B2

▶ London 242 mi – Blackpool 39 mi – Leeds 44 mi – Liverpool 54 mi

🍽️ Spread Eagle ⬅️ P

TRADITIONAL CUISINE · TRADITIONAL DÉCOR Very much at the heart of the community is this stylish, characterful pub with lovely river views. Cooking is gutsy and flavourful with pub favourites available in two sizes, classic main courses, and platters and tapas-style nibbles perfect for sharing. Comfortable bedrooms have smart, modern bathrooms.

Carte £ 20/32

7 rooms ☲ – ♦£ 65/95 ♦♦£ 85/140

✉ BB7 4NH – ☎ 01200 441202 – www.spreadeaglesawley.co.uk

SAXILBY
Lincolnshire – Pop. 3 992 – Regional map n° **9**-C1
▶ London 145 mi – Lincoln 7 mi – Newark-on-Trent 22 mi

🏠 Canal View ✿ P

FAMILY · HOMELY Guests are welcomed to this pleasant guesthouse with a cup of tea and a slice of homemade cake. Neat bedrooms come with fridges, goose feather duvets and Egyptian cotton linen. As the name suggests, it has a view over the canal.

3 rooms ☲ – ♦£ 52/79 ♦♦£ 69/79

Lincoln Rd ✉ LN1 2NF – on A 57 – ☎ 01522 704475 – www.canal-view.co.uk

SCARBOROUGH
North Yorkshire – Pop. 61 749 – Regional map n° **13**-D1
▶ London 253 mi – Kingston-upon-Hull 47 mi – Leeds 67 mi – Middlesbrough 52 mi

🏨 Crown Spa

TRADITIONAL · SEASIDE 19C landmark hotel, in a prime position on the headland of a Victorian seaside town. Contemporary guest areas, superb leisure facilities and state-of-the-art meeting rooms. Smart bedrooms feature bespoke furnishings and the latest mod cons. Informal, bistro-style dining is split over four different rooms.

115 rooms – ♦£ 53/150 ♦♦£ 63/250 – ☲ £ 10 – 2 suites

8-10 Esplanade ✉ YO11 2AG – ☎ 01723 357400 – www.crownspahotel.com

🏨 Ox Pasture Hall

TRADITIONAL · COSY This charming creeper-clad farmhouse in set in 17 acres of landscaped grounds and is a popular venue for weddings. Guest areas are stylish and contemporary. Bedrooms are well-equipped – those in the courtyard wing are the most modern and afford the best views. Dine from a modern menu in the formal restaurant or choose from hearty, unfussy dishes in the bistro.

32 rooms ☲ – ♦£ 95/145 ♦♦£ 110/390

Lady Edith's Dr, Raincliffe Woods ✉ YO12 5TD – West : 3.25 mi by A 171 following signs for Raincliffe Woods – ☎ 01723 365295 – www.oxpasturehallhotel.com

🏠 Alexander

TOWNHOUSE · COSY 1930s red-brick house at the popular North Beach end of town. The well-kept lounge and cocktail bar are traditional styled; bedrooms are more contemporary and have a clean, uncluttered style – extras include robes, biscuits and seaside rock. The linen-laid dining room offers a 3 choice set menu; local seafood is a highlight. Homemade shortbread is served on arrival.

8 rooms ☲ – ♦£ 56/60 ♦♦£ 77/93

33 Burniston Rd ✉ YO12 6PG – ☎ 01723 363178
– www.alexanderhotelscarborough.co.uk – Closed mid October-mid March

🍴 Lanterna

ITALIAN · NEIGHBOURHOOD Long-standing, passionately run neighbourhood restaurant with homely décor and a loyal local following. Extensive menu of classic Italian dishes and a sizeable truffle selection – but go for one of the expertly cooked fish specials.

Carte £ 33/44

33 Queen St ✉ YO11 1HQ – ☎ 01723 363616 – www.lanterna-ristorante.co.uk – dinner only – Closed last 2 weeks October, 25-26 December, 1 January, Sunday and Monday

✗ Jeremy's

MODERN BRITISH · NEIGHBOURHOOD This smart, buzzy bistro started life as a 1930s butcher's shop, and the original tiles on the walls and floors still remain. Flavoursome, classically based dishes have Asian touches and come courtesy of an assured, confident chef.

Carte £ 28/47

33 Victoria Park Ave ⊠ YO12 7TR – ℰ 01723 363871 (booking essential) – www.jeremys.co – dinner only and Sunday lunch – Closed first week January, 1 week May, 1 week October, Sunday dinner, Monday and Tuesday

✗ Green Room

MODERN BRITISH · BISTRO With its green front, this traditional family-run bistro certainly stands out. The son cooks while mum serves out front. Hearty cooking has a classical base and dishes are packed with flavour; the early evening set menu is a steal.

Menu £ 10 (weekday dinner) – Carte £ 30/44

138 Victoria Rd ⊠ YO11 1SL – ℰ 01723 501801 – www.thegreenroomrestaurant.com – dinner only – Closed Sunday and Monday

at Sawdon Southwest: 10 mi by A170 ⊠ Scarborough

ᵢⒹ Anvil Inn

TRADITIONAL BRITISH · PUB Charming former smithy, with its bellows, tools, forge and anvil still in situ. Classical cooking uses regional produce and features the odd international influence; Sunday lunch is a hit. The intimate restaurant has just 7 tables.

Carte £ 25/39

Main St ⊠ YO13 9DY – ℰ 01723 859896 – www.theanvilinnsawdon.co.uk – dinner only and lunch Saturday-Sunday – Closed 25-26 December, 1 January, Monday and Tuesday

SCAWTON – North Yorkshire → See Helmsley

SCILLY (Isles of)

Cornwall – Regional map n° **1**-A3

▶ London 295 mi – Camborne 23 mi – Saint Austell 52 mi – Falmouth 36 mi

Bryher

Cornwall – Pop. 78

🏠 Hell Bay

BOUTIQUE HOTEL · PERSONALISED Several charming, New England style buildings arranged around a central courtyard, with a contemporary, nautical-style interior displaying an impressive collection of modern art. Immaculately kept bedrooms come with plenty of thoughtful extras. The fabulous coastal location allows for far-reaching views.

25 rooms (dinner included) ⊡ – †£ 116/397 ††£ 210/660 – 14 suites

⊠ TR23 0PR – ℰ 01720 422947 – www.hellbay.co.uk – Closed November-February

Hell Bay – See restaurant listing

🏠 Bank Cottage

FAMILY · PERSONALISED Friendly guesthouse with a sub-tropical garden, a koi carp pond and a rowing boat. The lounge boasts an honesty bar and artefacts from shipwrecks. Bedrooms are simple and compact – one has a roof terrace. There's free use of the kitchen.

4 rooms ⊡ – †£ 62/64 ††£ 124/128

⊠ TR23 0PR – ℰ 01720 422612 – www.bank-cottage.com – Closed November-April

✗✗ Hell Bay ⟨ 🛏 🏠

MODERN CUISINE · FRIENDLY Hotel restaurant with a relaxed 'boat house' feel. Light, Mediterranean-influenced lunches in the bar, courtyard or terrace. Dinner steps things up a gear, with unfussy, modern dishes displaying fresh ingredients and clear flavours.

Menu £ 45 (dinner) – Carte lunch £ 27/42

Hell Bay Hotel, ✉ TR23 0PR – ☎ 01720 422947 (booking essential)
– www.hellbay.co.uk – Closed November-February

St Martin's

Cornwall – Pop. 113 – Regional map n° **1**-A3

🏠 Karma St Martin's ☂ 🛁 ⟨ 🚗 🏠 &

FAMILY · PERSONALISED The owner of Karma Resorts spent time on the Isles of Scilly when he was young and its sandy white beaches and clear blue waters fit the group's ethos perfectly. The hotel resembles a row of cottages and has a bright, calming feel; Indonesian-style furniture is a feature. The modern menu is all-encompassing.

30 rooms ♄ – 🛏£ 190 🛏🛏£ 240/305 – 4 suites

Lower Town ✉ TR25 0QW – ☎ 01720 422368 – www.karmaroyalgroup.com
– Closed November-March

St Mary's

Cornwall – Pop. 1 607

🏠 Star Castle ☂ 🛁 ⟨ 🚗 ☒ ✗ 🏌

HISTORIC BUILDING · TRADITIONAL Elizabethan castle in the shape of an 8-pointed star. Well-appointed, classical bedrooms and brighter garden suites – some with harbour or island views. 17C staircase leads from the stone ramparts to the charming Dungeon bar. Fabulous fireplace and kitchen garden produce in the dining room. Seafood menus in the conservatory.

38 rooms ♄ – 🛏£ 75/147 🛏🛏£ 150/278 – 4 suites

The Garrison ✉ TR21 0JA – ☎ 01720 422317 – www.star-castle.co.uk
– Closed 2 January-12 February

🏠 Atlantic ☂ ⟨ 🏠 &

INN · FUNCTIONAL Former Customs Office in a charming bay setting, affording lovely views across the harbour. Bedrooms – accessed through twisty passages – are well-equipped, and many share the view. There's a comfortable lounge and a small bar, along with a wicker-furnished restaurant which offers an accessible menu.

21 rooms ♄ – 🛏£ 120/200 🛏🛏£ 120/200

Hugh St, Hugh Town ✉ TR21 0PL – ☎ 01720 422417
– www.atlantichotelscilly.co.uk
– Closed November-February

🏠 Evergreen Cottage

FAMILY · COSY 300 year old captain's cottage with colourful window boxes, set in the heart of town. The interior is cosy, with a small, low-ceilinged lounge and breakfast room. The modest oak-furnished bedrooms are compact but spotlessly kept.

5 rooms ♄ – 🛏£ 40/43 🛏🛏£ 80/86

Parade, Hugh Town ✉ TR21 0LP – ☎ 01720 422711
– www.evergreencottageguesthouse.co.uk – Closed 1 week February and Christmas-New Year

Tresco

Cornwall – Pop. 167

🏨 Sea Garden Cottages   🕭 ≤ 🖶 🖾 🕉 𝄡 ℀ ℥

HOLIDAY HOTEL · CONTEMPORARY A smart aparthotel divided into New England style 'cottages'. Each has an open-plan kitchen and lounge with a terrace; the first floor bedroom opens onto a balcony offering stunning views over Old Grimsby Quay and Blockhouse Point.

9 rooms ☍ – ♦£ 262/338 ♦♦£ 350/450

Old Grimsby ⊠ TR24 0QQ – 𝒞 01720 422849 – www.tresco.co.uk – Closed November-mid March

Ruin Beach Café – See restaurant listing

🏨 New Inn   𝄡 ≤ 🖙 🗶

INN · COSY Stone-built inn boasting a large terrace, an appealing outdoor pool and pleasant coastal views. Bedrooms are bright, fresh and very comfy. Regular live music events attract guests from near and far. The hugely characterful bar and restaurant offer accessible menus.

16 rooms ☍ – ♦£ 80/150 ♦♦£ 160/300

New Grimsby ⊠ TR24 0QQ – 𝒞 01720 422849 – www.tresco.co.uk – Closed November to February

𝄐 Ruin Beach Café   ≤ 🖙 🖳

MEDITERRANEAN CUISINE · RUSTIC Relaxed beachside restaurant in an old smugglers cottage – part of an aparthotel. The rustic room is decorated with striking Cornish art and opens onto a terrace with superb St Martin views. Colourful Mediterranean dishes have big, bold flavours; seafood and pizzas from the wood-burning oven are a hit.

Carte £ 19/37

Sea Garden Cottages Hotel, Old Grimsby ⊠ TR24 0QQ – 𝒞 01720 424849 (booking essential) – www.tresco.co.uk – Closed November-mid March

SEAHAM

Durham – Pop. 22 373 – Regional map n° **14**-B2

▶ London 284 mi – Newcastle upon Tyne 17 mi – Leeds 84 mi

🏨 Seaham Hall   𝄡 🖶 🖾 ⊕ 🕉 𝄡 🔲 ꆤ 🅰 ℀ 🔱 🅿

LUXURY · CONTEMPORARY An imposing, part-18C mansion which combines grand original features with striking modern styling. Bedrooms are spacious and contemporary, and come with luxurious touches such as Nespresso machines. There's a chic lounge; a grill restaurant complete with velour booths and a zinc-topped bar; and a stylish Asian restaurant set within the impressively equipped spa.

20 rooms ☍ – ♦£ 195/295 ♦♦£ 195/295 – 4 suites

Lord Byron's Walk ⊠ SR7 7AG – North : 1.5 mi by B 1287 – 𝒞 0191 516 1400 – www.seaham-hall.com

SEAHOUSES

Northumberland – Regional map n° **14**-B1

▶ London 328 mi – Edinburgh 80 mi – Newcastle upon Tyne 46 mi

🏨 Olde Ship   𝄡 ≤ ℀ 🔱 🅿

TRADITIONAL · COSY A long-standing, family-run stone inn, in a popular seaside town; full to bursting with nautical memorabilia. The cosy former farmhouse offers comfy, individually designed bedrooms; those in the annexe are bigger with better views but less character. The formal dining room serves a simple, traditional menu.

18 rooms ☍ – ♦£ 47/94 ♦♦£ 94/130

9 Main St ⊠ NE68 7RD – 𝒞 01665 720200 – www.seahouses.co.uk – Closed December-February

🏠 St Cuthbert's House   ♿ 🚭 🅿

HISTORIC · GRAND LUXURY Former Georgian Presbyterian chapel, with comfortable modern bedrooms, a homely lounge and a wood-furnished breakfast room; large arched windows and many original features remain. The friendly, welcoming owners often host music nights.

6 rooms 🛏 – 🛏£ 90/125 🛏🛏£ 90/125

192 Main St ⊠ NE68 7UB – Southwest : 0.5 mi by Beadnell rd on North Sunderland rd – 𝒞 01665 720456 – www.stcuthbertshouse.com – Restricted opening in winter

SEASALTER – Kent ➜ See Whitstable

SEAVIEW – Isle of Wight ➜ See Wight (Isle of)

SEDGEFORD
Norfolk – Pop. 613 – Regional map n° **8**-B1
▶ London 121 mi – Norwich 42 mi – Hunstanton 5 mi

🏠 Magazine Wood   🐾 ⬱ 🛋 🚭 🅿

LUXURY · CONTEMPORARY Stylish guesthouse on a family farm beside the Peddars Way. Luxuriously appointed bedrooms come with dining areas, continental breakfasts and terraces overlooking the fields; you can order a newspaper or a cooked breakfast online.

3 rooms 🛏 – 🛏£ 105/145 🛏🛏£ 105/145

Peddars Way ⊠ PE36 5LW – East : 0.75 mi on B 1454 – 𝒞 01485 570422 – www.magazinewood.co.uk – Closed Christmas (minimum two night stay at weekends)

SEER GREEN – Buckinghamshire ➜ See Beaconsfield

SENNEN COVE
Cornwall – Pop. 410 – Regional map n° **1**-A3
▶ London 316 mi – Truro 37 mi – Exeter 119 mi

🍴 Ben Tunnicliffe Sennen Cove   ⬱ 🌳 ♿ 🖥 🅿

CLASSIC CUISINE · SIMPLE Just along from Land's End, you'll find this modern brick and glass eatery, superbly located overlooking a lovely sandy cove. Tasty, unfussy dishes showcase fresh local ingredients, including seafood from the nearby day boats.

Carte £ 22/40

Sennen Cove ⊠ TR19 7BT – 𝒞 01736 871191 (bookings advisable at dinner) – www.benatsennen.com – Closed January

SETTLE
North Yorkshire – Pop. 3 621 – Regional map n° **22**-A2
▶ London 238 mi – Leeds 41 mi – Kendal 30 mi

🏠 Falcon Manor ⓝ   ⚘ 🛋 🌳 🏋 🅿

COUNTRY HOUSE · DESIGN Just out of town is this fine stone manor house with partial Fell views. It's owned by an interior designer, who has added some flamboyant touches to its Gothic Victorian architecture; it's worth paying the extra to stay in the huge Rafters Suite. Dine on modern classics in the snug bar or bright brasserie.

16 rooms 🛏 – 🛏£ 75/225 🛏🛏£ 95/225

Skipton Rd ⊠ BD24 9BD – South : 0.25 mi on B 6479 – 𝒞 01729 823814 – www.falconmanor.co.uk

SHAFTESBURY
Dorset – Pop. 7 314 – Regional map n° **2**-C3
▶ London 115 mi – Bournemouth 31 mi – Bristol 47 mi – Dorchester 29 mi

⌂ Fleur de Lys

TRADITIONAL · CLASSIC Keenly run, creeper-clad stone house in a lovely market town. Comfortable, well-kept bedrooms are named after grape varieties and each comes with its own laptop. The cosy lounge features a mahogany bar. Dine from traditional menus either in the L-shaped restaurant or on the wood-furnished terrace.

8 rooms ⌷ – †£ 80/110 ††£ 100/175

Bleke St ⊠ SP7 8AW – ℰ 01747 853717 – www.lafleurdelys.co.uk – Closed 2 weeks January

⌂ Retreat

TRADITIONAL · CLASSIC Pretty Georgian house on a narrow street in a delightful market town; built for a local doctor on the old site of a school for poor boys. Wood-furnished breakfast room and immaculately kept bedrooms with good facilities. Charming owner.

9 rooms ⌷ – †£ 47/70 ††£ 93/95

47 Bell St ⊠ SP7 8AE – ℰ 01747 850372 – www.the-retreat.co.uk – Closed 28 December-31 January

SHALDON

Devon – Pop. 1 762 – Regional map n° 1-D2

▶ London 188 mi – Exeter 16 mi – Torquay 7 mi – Paignton 13 mi

✗ ODE

MODERN BRITISH · NEIGHBOURHOOD Proudly run neighbourhood restaurant in a glass-fronted Georgian house on a narrow village street. It has a strong sustainable and organic ethos, sourcing recycled glassware, biodynamic wines and produce from small local suppliers and foragers. Simple dishes are precisely prepared and attractively presented.

Menu £ 35/55

21 Fore St ⊠ TQ14 0DE – ℰ 01626 873977 (booking essential) – www.odetruefood.com – dinner only – Closed October, 25-26 December, Sunday-Tuesday and bank holidays

SHANKLIN - Isle of Wight → See Wight (Isle of)

SHEFFIELD

South Yorkshire – Pop. 518 090 – Regional map n° 13-B3

▶ London 174 mi – Leeds 36 mi – Liverpool 80 mi – Manchester 41 mi

⌂ Leopold

BUSINESS · PERSONALISED Evidence of this hotel's past can be seen in the boys grammar school photos hung throughout and in the Victorian wood-panelling in its meeting rooms. Contemporary bedrooms have fridges and iPod docks; some overlook the rear courtyard.

90 rooms – †£ 99/179 ††£ 99/179 – ⌷ £ 13 – 14 suites

2 Leopold St ⊠ S1 2GZ – ℰ 0114 252 4000 – www.leopoldhotels.com – Closed 23-27 December

⌂ Halifax Hall

HISTORIC · MODERN Set just out of town is this converted Victorian mansion which, in a previous life, provided student accommodation. Good-sized, modern bedrooms feature bold décor; the suites are the largest and also have a lounge area. The restaurant offers classic dishes and has a terrace overlooking the gardens.

38 rooms ⌷ – †£ 85 ††£ 95

Endcliffe Vale Rd ⊠ S10 3ER – Southwest : 2 mi by B 6547 and Clarkehouse Rd – ℰ 0114 222 8810 – www.halifaxhall.co.uk

🏠 Brocco on the Park ⑩ ☆ 🏠 ఈ 🐾 🅿

TOWNHOUSE · MODERN Broccos's claim to fame is that Picasso once stayed here! It's a compact place, set by a roundabout, overlooking a park, and it has plenty of style and individuality. Bedrooms have light colour schemes and a chic modern feel. The all-day restaurant with its heated terrace offers a real mix of dishes.

8 rooms – †£ 85/120 ††£ 85/230 – ☑ £ 9

92 Brocco Bank ⊠ S11 8RS – Southwest : 2 mi by B 6547 and Clarkehouse Rd – 𝒞 0114 266 1233 – www.brocco.co.uk – Closed 1 week January

XxX Old Vicarage 🍴 🅿

MODERN CUISINE · FAMILY Long-standing restaurant with a loyal following, set in a former Victorian vicarage; dine in the traditional front room or the fairy light festooned conservatory. Set price menus offer classic dishes presented in a modern style.

Menu £ 40 (lunch)/60

Ridgeway Moor ⊠ S12 3XW – Southeast : 6.75 mi by A 6135 (signed Hyde Park) and B 6054 on Marsh Lane rd. – 𝒞 0114 247 5814 – www.theoldvicarage.co.uk – Closed 26 December-4 January, last week July, Saturday lunch, Sunday, Monday and Tuesday after bank holidays

XX Rafters

MODERN BRITISH · CLASSIC DÉCOR If you're looking to celebrate a special occasion, this long-standing restaurant is the perfect place. The room might have a classic feel but the food is modern. Dishes are attractively presented and show respect for natural flavours.

Menu £ 44/60

220 Oakbrook Rd, Nether Green ⊠ S11 7ED – West : 2.5 mi by A 57 and Fulwood rd, turning left onto Hangingwater Rd – 𝒞 0114 230 4819 – www.raftersrestaurant.co.uk – dinner only and Sunday lunch – Closed 1-10 January and 22-30 August

X Nonnas 🏠 ఈ 🄰🄲

ITALIAN · NEIGHBOURHOOD Long-standing Italian restaurant with a lively atmosphere. The extensive menu offers old favourites, from antipasti and sharing dishes to tasty homemade pastas and stews. You can also stop by for coffee and homemade cake in the bar.

Carte £ 22/40

535-541 Ecclesall Rd ⊠ S11 8PR – Southwest : 2.25 mi on A 625 – 𝒞 0114 268 6166 – www.nonnas.co.uk – Closed 25 December and 1 January

X Milestone ఈ

MODERN CUISINE · NEIGHBOURHOOD Spacious 18C former pub set over two floors, in a regenerated area of the city. An array of regularly changing, seasonal menus offer modern, boldly flavoured dishes; presentation mixes the traditional and the contemporary.

Menu £ 13 – Carte £ 23/38

84 Green Ln ⊠ S3 8SE – North : 1.25 mi by A 61 off Mowbray St – 𝒞 0114 272 8327 – www.the-milestone.co.uk – Closed 25-26 December and 1 January

SHELLEY

West Yorkshire – Regional map n° **13**-B3

▶ London 185 mi – Leeds 22 mi – Manchester 37 mi – Sheffield 22 mi

XX Three Acres ⇦ 🍴 🏠 🄰🄲 🅿

TRADITIONAL BRITISH · RUSTIC Traditional stone inn on top of the moors, with a maze of charmingly cluttered low-beamed dining rooms. Choose from a large, traditional menu which features plenty of steak and rotisserie dishes. Bedrooms are warmly decorated; those in the adjacent cottages are the most modern and also the most peaceful.

Carte £ 29/58

17 rooms ☑ – †£ 50/100 ††£ 80/150

Roydhouse ⊠ HD8 8LR – Northeast : 1.5 mi on Flockton rd – 𝒞 01484 602606 (booking essential) – www.3acres.com – Closed dinner 25-26 December, lunch 31 December and dinner 1 January

SHERBORNE

Dorset – Pop. 9 523 – Regional map n° **2**-C3
▶ London 128 mi – Bournemouth 39 mi – Dorchester 19 mi – Salisbury 36 mi

✗ The Green 🛱 ⇔

MODERN BRITISH · BISTRO Pretty Grade II listed stone property at the top of the hill, with a traditional bistro style, an inglenook fireplace and ecclesiastical panelling. Concise à la carte and a good value set lunch; classical, confident, satisfying cooking.

Menu £ 20 (weekdays) – Carte £ 31/46

3 The Green ⊠ DT9 3HY – ℰ 01935 813821 – www.greenrestaurant.co.uk
– Closed 25-26 December, Sunday and Monday

SHERE – Surrey → See Guildford

SHERINGHAM

Norfolk – Pop. 7 367 – Regional map n° **8**-C1
▶ London 136 mi – Cromer 5 mi – Norwich 27 mi

🏠 Ashbourne House 🛏 🛇 🍽

TOWNHOUSE · PERSONALISED Well-appointed guesthouse in an elevated position; its large, landscaped garden has access to the clifftop. Two of the homely, comfortable bedrooms have coastal views. Local bacon and sausages feature at breakfast, which is taken beside an impressive fireplace in the wood-panelled breakfast room.

4 rooms ☑ – ♦£ 60/65 ♦♦£ 80/85

1 Nelson Rd ⊠ NR26 8BT – ℰ 01263 821555
– www.ashbournehousesheringham.co.uk – Closed 21 December-3 January

SHERWOOD BUSINESS PARK – Nottinghamshire → See Nottingham

SHILTON – Oxfordshire → See Burford

SHINFIELD – Wokingham → See Reading

SHIPLAKE – Oxfordshire → See Henley-on-Thames

SHIRLEY – Derbyshire → See Ashbourne

SHOTTLE

Derbyshire – Regional map n° **9**-B2
▶ London 140 mi – Sheffield 33 mi – Derby 13 mi

🏠 Dannah Farm Country House 🐾 🛏 🛇 🅿

TRADITIONAL · PERSONALISED 18C stone farmhouse on a 154 acre working farm owned by the Chatsworth Estate; its outbuildings converted into spacious, well-equipped bedrooms. Many rooms have spa baths and the Granary and Studio Suites have hot tubs and terraces.

8 rooms ☑ – ♦£ 95/105 ♦♦£ 185/295

Bowmans Ln. ⊠ DE56 2DR – North : 0.25 mi by Alport rd – ℰ 01773 550273
– www.dannah.co.uk – Closed 24-26 December

SHREWSBURY

Shropshire – Pop. 71 715 – Regional map n° **10**-B2
▶ London 164 mi – Birmingham 48 mi – Chester 43 mi – Derby 67 mi

🏠 Lion and Pheasant

HISTORIC · CONTEMPORARY A collection of adjoining 16C and 18C townhouses on a famous medieval street. Inside it's modern, quirky and understated. Chic bedrooms – designed by the owner's daughter – have a boutique French feel; the rear rooms are quieter.

22 rooms ⌂ – ♦£99/210 ♦♦£120/225

49-50 Wyle Cop ⊠ SY1 1XJ – ℰ01743 770345 – www.lionandpheasant.co.uk – Closed 25-26 December

Lion and Pheasant – See restaurant listing

🍴 Lion and Pheasant

MODERN BRITISH · FASHIONABLE Head through the hotel's café-bar and up the stairs to this cosy beamed restaurant. Carefully prepared dishes rely on quality ingredients and have a subtle modern touch. Another more formally set room is also opened at weekends.

Menu £25 (early dinner) – Carte £27/41

Lion and Pheasant Hotel, 49-50 Wyle Cop ⊠ SY1 1XJ – ℰ01743 770345 – www.lionandpheasant.co.uk – Closed 25-26 December

at Grinshill North: 7.5 mi by A49 ⊠ Shrewsbury

🍴 Inn at Grinshill

TRADITIONAL BRITISH · INN Family-owned and very personally run, this inn stands in the middle of a pretty Shropshire village and its food revolves around the seasons. A cosy bar plays host to walkers and locals while the contemporary restaurant has a view to the kitchen. Six pretty bedrooms are individually decorated and comfortable.

Carte £20/36 **s**

6 rooms ⌂ – ♦£70/90 ♦♦£90/120

The High St ⊠ SY4 3BL – ℰ01939 220410 – www.theinnatgrinshill.co.uk – Closed first week January, Sunday dinner, Monday and Tuesday

at Upton Magna East : 6 mi by A 5064 off B 4380

🍴 The Haughmond

TRADITIONAL CUISINE · PUB A stylish dining pub complete with a 'Village Shop', smart modern bedrooms and a recurring stag theme. Lunchtime sees a good value selection of pub classics, the evening menus are more ambitious and at weekends they open Basil's – an 18-seater restaurant offering a sophisticated 5 course set menu.

Carte £24/46

5 rooms ⌂ – ♦£72/90 ♦♦£90/120

⊠ SY4 4TZ – ℰ01743 709918 – www.thehaughmond.co.uk – Closed 25 December and 1 January

at Condover South: 5 mi by A49

🏠 Grove Farm House

COUNTRY HOUSE · PERSONALISED The friendly owners of this 18C farmhouse have opened up their family home. Bedrooms are pleasantly furnished and come with well-equipped bathrooms and country views. Extensive breakfasts showcase local and homemade choices.

4 rooms ⌂ – ♦£70/75 ♦♦£90/95

⊠ SY5 7BH – South : 0.75 mi on Dorrington rd – ℰ01743 718544 – www.grovefarmhouse.com

SHREWTON

Wiltshire – Pop. 1 723 – Regional map n° **2**-D2
▶ London 91 mi – Bristol 53 mi – Southampton 52 mi – Reading 69 mi

🏠 Rollestone Manor

COUNTRY HOUSE · PERSONALISED Grade II listed house on a part-working farm just outside the village; reputed to once have been the home of Jane Seymour's family. Good-sized, antique-furnished bedrooms offer modern facilities; one even has a bath mounted on top of a plinth in the room. The contemporary restaurant serves modern classics.

7 rooms ⌧ – †£ 80/90 ††£ 90/105

⌧ SP3 4HF – Southeast : 0.5 mi on A 360 – ✆ 01980 620216
– www.rollestonemanor.com – Closed 24-26 December

SHURDINGTON – Gloucestershire ➜ See Cheltenham

SIBFORD GOWER
Oxfordshire – Regional map n° **6**-B1
▶ London 82 mi – Oxford 28 mi – Cheltenham 40 mi

🍺 Wykham Arms

TRADITIONAL BRITISH · PUB 17C thatched pub with sand-coloured stone walls, set down narrow country lanes in a small village. Menus feature local produce and offer everything from light bites to the full 3 courses. There's a good choice of wines by the glass.

Carte £ 25/34

Temple Mill Rd ⌧ OX15 5RX – ✆ 01295 788808 – www.wykhamarms.co.uk
– Closed Monday except bank holidays

SIDFORD – Devon ➜ See Sidmouth

SIDLESHAM
West Sussex – Regional map n° **4**-C3
▶ London 84 mi – Bristol 137 mi – Cardiff 170 mi – Plymouth 187 mi

🏠 Landseer House

FAMILY · ELEGANT Tastefully furnished guesthouse, with numerous antiques and pleasant views of the surrounding wetlands. Contemporary bedrooms; go for Room 1 – the most luxurious. Those in the garden have their own terraces and kitchens.

6 rooms ⌧ – †£ 95/300 ††£ 100/300

Cow Ln ⌧ PO20 7LN – South : 1.5 mi by B 2145 and Keynor Ln – ✆ 01243 641525
– www.landseerhouse.co.uk

🍺 Crab & Lobster

SEAFOOD · PUB This sympathetically modernised inn is superbly located within the striking landscape of Pagham Harbour Nature Reserve. Well-presented, seafood-focused dishes are at the restaurant end of the scale, although lunch also sees sandwiches and salads. Comfortable bedrooms have a modern, minimalist style.

Menu £ 27 (weekday lunch) – Carte £ 31/52

5 rooms ⌧ – †£ 90/100 ††£ 165/300

Mill Ln ⌧ PO20 7NB – ✆ 01243 641233 (booking advisable) – www.crab-lobster.co.uk

SIDMOUTH
Devon – Pop. 12 569 – Regional map n° **1**-D2
▶ London 176 mi – Exeter 14 mi – Taunton 27 mi – Weymouth 45 mi

🏨 Riviera

TRADITIONAL · PERSONALISED This characterful Regency hotel stands proudly on the promenade and has been family run for over 40 years. The marble entrance hall leads through to modern guest areas. Classical bedrooms come in blues and golds and many have bay windows and sea views. Menus are traditional and cream teas are a speciality.

26 rooms (dinner included) ⌧ – †£ 109/194 ††£ 218/436

The Esplanade ⌧ EX10 8AY – ✆ 01395 515201 – www.hotelriviera.co.uk – Closed
2 January-17 February

at Sidford North: 2 mi ⊠ Sidmouth

✕✕ Salty Monk ⇦ 🖶 🛱 🖪 🅿

REGIONAL CUISINE · INTIMATE Smart, proudly run restaurant in an old 16C salt house, featuring striking purple woodwork and a pleasant blend of the old and new. The Abbots Den offers a casual brasserie menu, while the Garden Room serves more elaborate modern dishes. Bedrooms have good extras and there's a gym and hot tub in the garden.

Menu £ 25 (weekdays)/45 – Carte £ 24/50

6 rooms ⌑ – 🛉£ 85/150 🛉🛉£ 130/195

Church St ⊠ EX10 9QP – on A 3052 – 𝒞 01395 513174 (booking essential)
– www.saltymonk.co.uk – dinner only and lunch Thursday-Sunday
– Closed January, 2 weeks November and Monday

SINNINGTON – North Yorkshire ➜ See Pickering

SISSINGHURST

Kent – Regional map n° **5**-B2

▶ London 50 mi – Maidstone 13 mi – Ashford 18 mi

🍽 The Milk House ⇦ 🖶 🛱 🕭 🅿

TRADITIONAL BRITISH · PUB Turn right into the bar with its soft sofas, huge fire and appetising grazing menu; turn left into the dining room for a seasonal list of modern British dishes. Pub classics are available in both areas and in the summer they serve wood-fired pizzas in the garden. Bedrooms are smart and contemporary.

Carte £ 19/44

4 rooms ⌑ – 🛉£ 80/140 🛉🛉£ 80/140

The Street ⊠ TN17 2JG – 𝒞 01580 720200 – www.themilkhouse.co.uk

---

SLALEY – Northumberland ➜ See Hexham

SNAPE

Suffolk – Pop. 1 509 – Regional map n° **8**-D3

▶ London 113 mi – Ipswich 19 mi – Norwich 50 mi

🍽 Crown Inn ⇦ 🖶 🛱 🅿

REGIONAL CUISINE · PUB The affable owners of this characterful 15C former smugglers' inn grow fruit and vegetables and raise various animals, which provide much of the meat for their constantly evolving menus; the rosettes in the bar come from showing their Gloucester Old Spot pigs. Rustic bedrooms have beams and sloping floors.

Carte £ 20/36

2 rooms ⌑ – 🛉£ 70/90 🛉🛉£ 70/90

Bridge Rd ⊠ IP17 1SL – 𝒞 01728 688324 – www.snape-crown.co.uk

---

SNETTISHAM

Norfolk – Pop. 2 570 – Regional map n° **8**-B1

▶ London 113 mi – King's Lynn 13 mi – Norwich 44 mi

🍽 Rose and Crown ⇦ 🖶 🛱 🕭 🅿

TRADITIONAL CUISINE · PUB 14C pub featuring a warren of rooms with uneven floors and low beamed ceilings. Gutsy cooking uses locally sourced produce, with globally influenced dishes alongside trusty pub classics. Impressive children's adventure fort. Modern bedrooms are decorated in sunny colours, and offer a good level of facilities.

Carte £ 21/38

16 rooms ⌑ – 🛉£ 100/120 🛉🛉£ 120/140

Old Church Rd ⊠ PE31 7LX – 𝒞 01485 541382
– www.roseandcrownsnettisham.co.uk – Closed 25 December

SOAR MILL COVE - Devon → See Salcombe

SOMERTON
Somerset – Pop. 4 133 – Regional map n° **2**-B2
▶ London 138 mi – Bristol 32 mi – Taunton 17 mi

🏠 White Hart

MEDITERRANEAN CUISINE · RUSTIC A 16C inn on the village's main market square; its beautiful parquet-floored entrance leads to six characterful rooms, including 'the barn' where you can watch the chefs at work. Seasonal food centres around the wood burning oven. Bedrooms are cosy and modern; Room 3, with a bath centre stage, is the best.
Carte £ 22/33
8 rooms – 🛏£ 85/135 🛏🛏£ 85/135 – ⌂£ 11
Market Pl ⊠ TA11 7LX – ℰ 01458 272273 – www.whitehartsomerton.com

SONNING-ON-THAMES - Wokingham → See Reading

SOUTH BRENT
Devon – Pop. 2 559 – Regional map n° **7**-C2
▶ London 201 mi – Exeter 29 mi – Plymouth 17 mi

🏠 Glazebrook House

COUNTRY HOUSE · PERSONALISED A stunning 150 year old property set in 4 acres of peaceful grounds. It's been delightfully refurbished and features a lovely teak parquet floor and an eclectic mix of décor. Beautifully appointed, boutique bedrooms are named after characters from 'Alice in Wonderland'. Menus offer seasonal British dishes.
8 rooms ⌂ – 🛏£ 140/160 🛏🛏£ 140/290
⊠ TQ10 9JE – Southwest : 0.5 mi by Exeter Rd – ℰ 01364 73322
– www.glazebrookhouse.com – Closed 3 weeks January

SOUTH DALTON - East Riding of Yorkshire → See Beverley

SOUTH FERRIBY
North Lincolnshire – Pop. 651 – Regional map n° **13**-C3
▶ London 180 mi – Kingston upon Hull 13 mi – Lincoln 39 mi

🏠 Hope & Anchor

TRADITIONAL BRITISH · PUB Rustic, nautically-themed pub with Humber views. Well-priced, tasty British dishes showcase fish from Grimsby, fruit and veg from their smallholding and meats from the Lake District – which are aged in a glass-fronted drying cabinet.
Carte £ 18/42
⊠ DN18 6JQ – ℰ 01652 635334 (booking advisable)
– www.thehopeandanchorpub.co.uk – Closed 1-7 January and Monday except bank holidays

SOUTH MOLTON
Devon – Pop. 5 108 – Regional map n° **7**-C1
▶ London 197 mi – Barnstaple 11 mi – Bristol 81 mi

🏠 Ashley House

HISTORIC · PERSONALISED You'll be warmly welcomed into this snug guesthouse, set next to the village green. It dates from 1879 and is named after the majestic ash tree out the front. Bedrooms are homely; dramatic photos of the local area hang on the walls.
3 rooms ⌂ – 🛏£ 65/95 🛏🛏£ 75/105
3 Paradise Lawn ⊠ EX36 3DJ – ℰ 01769 573444
– www.ashleyhousebedandbreakfast.com

ENGLAND

SOUTH POOL
Devon – Regional map n° **1**-C3
▶ London 218 mi – Plymouth 26 mi – Torbay 25 mi – Exeter 46 mi

🍴 **Millbrook Inn**   ⌂

TRADITIONAL CUISINE · PUB A passionately run, appealingly worn pub squeezed in between the houses on a narrow village street. Sit in the cosy low-beamed interior or on one of two terraces. Cooking is traditional and hearty with Mediterranean influences.
Carte £ 26/50
✉ TQ7 2RW – ☎ 01548 531581 – www.millbrookinnsouthpool.co.uk

SOUTH RAUCEBY
Lincolnshire – Pop. 335 – Regional map n° **9**-C2
▶ London 131 mi – Nottingham 40 mi – Leicester 54 mi

🍴 **Bustard Inn**   ⌂ & 🅿

MODERN CUISINE · PUB Grade II listed inn set in a peaceful hamlet, with a light and airy flag-floored bar and a spacious, beamed restaurant. Good value lunch menu and a more ambitious à la carte offering modern English dishes. Satisfying desserts.
Menu £ 15 (weekday lunch) – Carte £ 22/45
44 Main St ✉ NG34 8QG – ☎ 01529 488250 – www.thebustardinn.co.uk – Closed 1 January, Sunday dinner and Monday except bank holidays

SOUTHAMPTON
Southampton – Pop. 253'651 – Regional map n° **4**-B2
▶ London 87 mi – Bristol 79 mi – Plymouth 161 mi

🏠 **Pig in the Wall**   AC � 🅿

TOWNHOUSE · PERSONALISED Delightfully run, early 19C property that's been lovingly restored. The rustic lounge-cum-deli serves superb breakfasts and light meals; for something more substantial they will chauffeur you to their sister restaurant. Smart, boutique bedrooms come with antiques, super-comfy beds and Egyptian cotton linen.
12 rooms – ♦£ 155/190 ♦♦£ 155/190 – ☲ £ 10
8 Western Esplanade ✉ SO14 2AZ – ☎ 023 8063 6900 – www.thepighotel.co.uk

🍴 **White Star Tavern, Dining and Rooms**   ⚑ ⇦ ⌂ & AC ⌂

TRADITIONAL BRITISH · INN Eye-catching black pub with vast windows and a smart pavement terrace, set in the lively maritime district. Choose between all-day small plates from the blackboard or meaty dishes on the modern British à la carte. Smart modern bedrooms, named after yachts and liners, boast good facilities and extra touches.
Menu £ 16 (lunch) – Carte £ 23/43
16 rooms – ♦£ 80/135 ♦♦£ 80/135 – ☲ £ 11
✉ SO14 3DJ – ☎ 023 8082 1990 – www.whitestartavern.co.uk

at Netley Marsh West: 6.5 mi by A33 off A336

🏠 **Hotel TerraVina**   ⚒ ⇦ ⌂ & AC ⅝ ♨ 🅿

BUSINESS · MODERN Victorian red-brick house with wood-clad extensions, in a peaceful New Forest location. Brown and orange hues create a relaxed Mediterranean feel. Bedrooms have superb bedding, good facilities and thoughtful extras; some have roof terraces.
11 rooms ☲ – ♦£ 155/165 ♦♦£ 165/265
174 Woodlands Rd ✉ SO40 7GL – ☎ 023 8029 3784 – www.hotelterravina.co.uk
Restaurant TerraVina – See restaurant listing

574

☼☼ Restaurant TerraVina   🕸 🛏 🛖 ﾠ 🅰🅲 🅿

MODERN CUISINE · BRASSERIE Modern hotel restaurant with a glass-fronted wine cave and a covered terrace. Lunch sticks to the classics, while dinner introduces more imaginative dishes and a 6 course tasting menu. The sommelier offers some original wine pairings.

Menu £27 (weekday lunch) – Carte £36/53

Hotel TerraVina, 174 Woodlands Rd ✉ SO40 7GL – ℰ 023 8029 3784
– www.hotelterravina.co.uk

SOUTHBOROUGH – Kent → See Royal Tunbridge Wells

SOUTHBOURNE – Bournemouth → See Bournemouth

SOUTHPORT
Merseyside – Pop. 91 703 – Regional map n° **11**-A2
▶ London 221 mi – Liverpool 25 mi – Manchester 38 mi – Preston 19 mi

🏠 Vincent   ꜰ 🖭 🛖 🅰🅲 🍴 ♨ 🚗

BUSINESS · DESIGN Striking glass, steel and stone hotel beside the gardens and bandstand. Stylish, boutique interior with chic bar, fitness room and spa. Sleek, modern bedrooms come in dark colours, boasting Nespresso machines and deep Japanese soaking tubs.

59 rooms – 🛉£96/208 🛉🛉£96/208 – ⬒ £10 – 2 suites
98 Lord St. ✉ PR8 1JR – ℰ 01704 883800 – www.thevincenthotel.com
V-Café - See restaurant listing

☼ V-Café   🛖 🅰🅲 🖳

ASIAN INFLUENCES · BRASSERIE Relaxed café in a striking modern hotel, its glass façade overlooking the street. Open all-day and offering everything from sushi at the counter to 3 courses of globally influenced dishes.

Carte £26/56

Vincent Hotel, 98 Lord St. ✉ PR8 1JR – ℰ 01704 883800
– www.thevincenthotel.com

☼ Bistrot Vérité   🛖 🅰🅲

CLASSIC FRENCH · FRIENDLY Simple neighbourhood bistro with panelled walls and candles; sit on the red banquette which runs down one side. Gutsy, traditional French cooking, with desserts a speciality. Friendly, efficient service.

Menu £18 (lunch) – Carte £24/43

7 Liverpool Rd, Birkdale ✉ PR8 4AR – South : 1.5 mi by A 565 – ℰ 01704 564199
(booking essential) – www.bistrotverite.co.uk – Closed 1 week summer, 1 week
winter, 25-26 December, 1 January, Sunday, Monday and lunch Tuesday

SOUTHROP
Gloucestershire – Regional map n° **2**-D1
▶ London 87 mi – Birmingham 77 mi – Bristol 60 mi – Sheffield 146 mi

🏠 Swan   ✿

TRADITIONAL BRITISH · NEIGHBOURHOOD Delightful Virginia creeper clad inn set in a quintessential Cotswold village in the Leach Valley. With its characterful low-beamed rooms and charming service, it's popular with locals and visitors alike. Dishes are mainly British-based and feature garden produce; try the delicious homemade bread.

Menu £16 (weekdays) – Carte £24/47

✉ GL7 3NU – ℰ 01367 850205 – www.theswanatsouthrop.co.uk – Closed
25 December

SOUTHWOLD
Suffolk – Pop. 1 098 – Regional map n° **8**-D2
▶ London 108 mi – Great Yarmouth 24 mi – Ipswich 35 mi – Norwich 34 mi

🏘️ Swan ☂ 🛏️ 🖥️ ⚐ ♨️ **P**

HISTORIC BUILDING · PERSONALISED Attractive 17C coaching inn set in the town centre, close to the brewery. The cosy lounge and bar display subtle modern touches. Bedrooms are a mix: some are traditional, some are boldly coloured and some are charming. The grand dining room is hung with portraits and chandeliers and has a modern European menu. They are closing for the first half of 2017 for a reburbishment.

42 rooms ☂ – ♦£ 120/150 ♦♦£ 185/235 – 2 suites

Market Pl. ✉ IP18 6EG – ☎ 01502 722186 – www.adnams.co.uk

🏠 Crown ♟️ ☂ ♨️ **P**

INN · CONTEMPORARY A few doors down from its sister, the Swan, is this 17C coaching inn with an appealingly relaxed feel. Bedrooms have a modern New England style; those to the rear are the quietest. Have a pint of Adnams in the tiny nautically-themed bar, a stone's throw from their brewery. Daily menus keep things traditional.

14 rooms ☂ – ♦£ 99/175 ♦♦£ 215/285

90 High St ✉ IP18 6DP – ☎ 01502 722275 – www.adnams.co.uk/hotels

SOWERBY BRIDGE

West Yorkshire – ✉ Halifax – Pop. 4 601 – Regional map n° **13**-A2

▶ London 211 mi – Bradford 10 mi – Burnley 35 mi – Manchester 32 mi

✗✗ Gimbals

MODERN CUISINE · BISTRO Personally and passionately run restaurant on the high street of a former mill town; look out for the eye-catching illuminated window display. Modern monthly menus have subtle Mediterranean influences and the desserts are a real highlight.

Menu £ 19 (weekday dinner)/25 – Carte £ 23/42

76 Wharf St ✉ HX6 2AF – ☎ 01422 839329 – www.gimbals.co.uk – dinner only – Closed 25-27 December, 1-2 January, Sunday and Monday

SPARKWELL

Devon – Regional map n° **1**-C2

▶ London 210 mi – Bristol 114 mi – Cardiff 145 mi – Plymouth 10 mi

🍽️ Treby Arms (Anton Piotrowski) 🛋️ 🚻 **P**
🏵️

MODERN CUISINE · RUSTIC A quotation chalked on the timbers warns that 'you can't please all of the people all of the time' but they seem to be doing a pretty good job! Carefully prepared, clearly flavoured modern dishes are visually appealing and often feature a playful twist; the 'Taster' menus best demonstrate the chef's talent.

➜ Chilli and soya glazed gurnard with parsley root, Marmite purée and sesame. Roe deer, venison shoulder, chilli con carne, toasted wild rice foam and aubergine. Double Decker with Guinness ice cream and passion fruit.

Menu £ 18 (weekday lunch)/80 – Carte £ 30/55

✉ PL7 5DD – ☎ 01752 837363 (booking essential) – www.thetrebyarms.co.uk

SPARSHOLT – Hampshire ➜ See Winchester

SPARSHOLT

Oxfordshire – Regional map n° **6**-A3

▶ London 77 mi – Oxford 21 mi – Swindon 17 mi

🍽️ Star Inn ⇦ 🚻 **P**

MODERN CUISINE · FRIENDLY Lovingly restored, flint-walled inn at the very heart of village life. Have a drink on the squashy sofas by the wood-burning stove then dine overlooking the garden. Carefully prepared, appealing dishes range from comforting to adventurous and game features highly. Comfy bedrooms are located in the barn behind.

Carte £ 29/48

8 rooms ☂ – ♦£ 85/115 ♦♦£ 95/135

Watery Ln ✉ OX12 9PL – ☎ 01235 751873 – www.thestarsparsholt.co.uk – Closed 4-11 January

SPELDHURST - Kent ➔ See Royal Tunbridge Wells

SPRIGG'S ALLEY - Oxfordshire ➔ See Chinnor

ENGLAND

STADDLEBRIDGE
North Yorkshire – Regional map n° **13**-B1
▶ London 236 mi – Leeds 48 mi – York 34 mi

XX Cleveland Tontine ⇦ ⇧ 🅿

TRADITIONAL BRITISH · BISTRO This established basement bistro is something of a local institution. Start with a drink in the champagne and cocktail bar then make for the characterful bistro or airy conservatory. Quirky modern bedrooms boast bold wallpapers and free-standing baths. Yorkshire meets France on the classically based menus.

Menu £ 20 (lunch and early dinner) – Carte £ 31/56

7 rooms ⌑ – ♦£ 143/203 ♦♦£ 150/210

✉ DL6 3JB – On southbound carriageway of A 19 – ℰ 01609 882671
– www.theclevelandtontine.co.uk

STADHAMPTON
Oxfordshire – Pop. 702 – Regional map n° **6**-B2
▶ London 53 mi – Aylesbury 18 mi – Oxford 10 mi

🏠 Crazy Bear ☆ 🛏 🐕 🛤 🅿

LUXURY · MODERN Wacky converted pub with a London bus reception, a characterful bar, a smart glasshouse and even a Zen garden. Sumptuous, quirky bedrooms are spread about the place; some have padded walls and infinity baths. Eat in 'Thai' or flamboyant 'English', with its mirrored walls and classic British and French dishes.

18 rooms ⌑ – ♦£ 199/399 ♦♦£ 199/399

Bear Ln ✉ OX44 7UR – Off Wallingford rd – ℰ 01865 890714
– www.crazybeargroup.co.uk

Thai – See restaurant listing

XX Thai 🛏 🏠 ⇧ 🅿

THAI · INTIMATE Cosy hotel restaurant in an intimate basement room, with ornate silk hangings and 8 tables topped with polished brass. Flavoursome, authentic dishes are skilfully prepared by a Thai chef; the 10 and 12 plate sharing menus are popular.

Menu £ 30 – Carte £ 19/45

Crazy Bear Hotel, Bear Ln ✉ OX44 7UR – Off Wallingford rd – ℰ 01865 890714
(booking essential) – www.crazybeargroup.co.uk

STAFFORD
Staffordshire – Pop. 68 472 – Regional map n° **10**-C1
▶ London 142 mi – Birmingham 26 mi – Stoke-on-Trent 17 mi

🏠 Moat House ☆ 🛏 🔁 ⅙ AC 🐕 🛤 🅿

BUSINESS · CLASSIC The original 15C farmhouse is now a pub and the sympathetically added extensions house characterful wood-panelled lounges, attractively furnished modern bedrooms and an orangery restaurant. There's a duck pond to the front and a canal to the rear. It's been owned and run by the same family for many years.

41 rooms ⌑ – ♦£ 102/170 ♦♦£ 135/190 – 1 suite

Lower Penkridge Rd, Acton Trussell ✉ ST17 0RJ – South : 3.75 mi by A 449
– ℰ 01785 712217 – www.moathouse.co.uk – Closed 25 December
Orangery – See restaurant listing

🏠 The Swan
☆ 🔲 ⚓ 🐾 **P**

INN · CONTEMPORARY This 17C coaching inn is found among some impressive old buildings, including a neighbouring Jacobean townhouse. Inside it's stylish and contemporary with up-to-date bedrooms. The brasserie offers a large menu of modern classics and there's also a coffee shop and two bars which share a pleasant terrace.

31 rooms ⌑ – 🛆£ 60/100 🛆🛆£ 80/120

46 Greengate St ⌧ ST16 2JA – ℰ 01785 258142 – www.theswanstafford.co.uk – Closed 24-25 December

✗✗ Orangery
🚪 ⚓ 🔠 ⑩ **P**

MODERN BRITISH · ELEGANT Head to this attractive hotel restaurant for views over the leafy garden to the barges gliding by on the canal. Cooking is modern British and dishes are accomplished and well-judged; the tasting menu is a hit with the regulars.

Menu £ 21 (lunch and early dinner) – Carte £ 32/49

Moat House Hotel, Lower Penkridge Rd, Acton Trussell ⌧ ST17 0RJ – South: 3.75 mi by A 449 – ℰ 01785 712217 – www.moathouse.co.uk – Closed 25 December

STALISFIELD
Kent – Regional map n° **5**-C2

▶ London 51 mi – Canterbury 17 mi – Maidstone 15 mi

🍽 Plough
🚪 🏠 **P**

TRADITIONAL BRITISH · RUSTIC Rurally set, 15C pub with thick walls, exposed beams, farming implements and hop bines. The usual suspects on the bar snack menu; more ambitious dishes on the à la carte. Nursery puddings and an impressive range of Kentish real ales.

Menu £ 14 (weekday lunch) – Carte £ 23/33

⌧ ME13 0HY – ℰ 01795 890256 – www.theploughinnstalisfield.co.uk – Closed Monday except bank holidays

STAMFORD
Lincolnshire – Pop. 22 574 – Regional map n° **9**-C2

▶ London 92 mi – Leicester 31 mi – Lincoln 50 mi – Nottingham 45 mi

🏠 George of Stamford
☆ 🚪 🔠 **P**

INN · COSY This characterful coaching inn dates back over 500 years and, despite its bedrooms having a surprisingly contemporary feel, it still offers good old-fashioned hospitality. There are plenty of places to relax, with various bars, lounges and a walled garden. Dine in the laid-back Garden Room or the more formal restaurant – both spill out into the lovely courtyard in summer.

45 rooms ⌑ – 🛆£ 120/140 🛆🛆£ 195/320 – 1 suite

71 St Martins ⌧ PE9 2LB – ℰ 01780 750750 – www.georgehotelofstamford.com

The Oak Panelled Restaurant – See restaurant listing

🏠 William Cecil
☆ 🚪 🏠 ⚓ 🔠 **P**

COUNTRY HOUSE · HISTORIC This 17C stone rectory is named after the 1st Baron Burghley and is where they filmed Pride and Prejudice. Inside it's shabbychic, with Colonial-style bedrooms featuring wood carvings and pastoral scene wallpaper. The restaurant has intimate, Regency-style booths; be sure to have afternoon tea on the terrace.

27 rooms ⌑ – 🛆£ 85/190 🛆🛆£ 85/190 – 1 suite

High St, St Martins ⌧ PE9 2LJ – ℰ 01780 750070 – www.thewilliamcecil.co.uk

🏠 Crown
☆ 🏠 🔠 **P**

HISTORIC · GRAND LUXURY Former coaching inn set in a historic market town. Bedrooms in the main house have a funky, boutique style; those in the townhouse and cottage are larger with a more classical feel. Dine in the modern cocktail bar, in one of the cosy lounges, in the quieter rear dining room or out on the large terrace.

28 rooms ⌑ – 🛆£ 85/165 🛆🛆£ 95/185

All Saints Pl. ⌧ PE9 2AG – ℰ 01780 763136 – www.thecrownhotelstamford.co.uk

XXX **The Oak Panelled Restaurant**

TRADITIONAL BRITISH · INN Smart dress is required in this lovely oak-panelled dining room, which is found at the heart of an equally charming 16C coaching inn. Classical menus are largely British based with a few international influences. Alongside their speciality beef carving trolley, there are also 'cheese' and 'sweet' trolleys.
Menu £ 28 (weekday lunch) – Carte £ 43/77
George of Stamford Hotel, 71 St Martins ⊠ PE9 2LB – ℰ 01780 750750
– www.georgehotelofstamford.com

X **Zada** ℕ

TURKISH · NEIGHBOURHOOD Its name means 'fortunate' and the locals are lucky to have it in town. Turkish rugs hang on exposed stone walls and fresh bread is made behind the counter. The menu features all the favourites, from hummus and kebabs to baklava.
Carte £ 19/31
13 St Mary's Hill ⊠ PE9 2DP – ℰ 01780 766848 – www.zadarestaurant.co.uk
– dinner only and lunch Saturday-Sunday – Closed 25 December

🏠 **Bull & Swan**

TRADITIONAL BRITISH · INN A stone-built medieval hall house which was converted into an inn during the 1600s and later taken over by a former coachman to the Earl of Exeter in 1739. Dishes range from sharing slates to regional classics and local steaks. Like the characterful beamed bar, bedrooms have a traditional feel.
Carte £ 25/42
9 rooms ⊊ – ♦£ 90/160 ♦♦£ 100/180
St Martins ⊠ PE9 2LJ – ℰ 01780 766412 – www.thebullandswan.co.uk

STANFORD DINGLEY
West Berkshire – Pop. 179 – Regional map n° **6**-B3
▶ London 52 mi – Sheffield 168 mi – Nottingham 130 mi – Bristol 69 mi

🏠 **Bull Inn**

BRITISH TRADITIONAL · RUSTIC Locals and their dogs gather in the rustic bar of this beamed 15C inn, while the garden plays host to alfresco diners, chickens and the annual village dog show. The experienced chef-owner offers a wide range of tasty dishes; 'beer tapas' allows you to sample local ales and bedrooms are cosy and great value.
Carte £ 24/49
5 rooms – ♦£ 70/80 ♦♦£ 70/80 – ⊊ £ 12
Cock Ln ⊠ RG7 6LS – ℰ 0118 974 4582 – www.thebullinnstanforddingley.co.uk

STANHOE
Norfolk – Pop. 289 – Regional map n° **8**-C1
▶ London 124 mi – Norwich 36 mi – Kings Lynn 18 mi

🏠 **Duck Inn**

TRADITIONAL CUISINE · INN Fairy lights decorate the picket fence and ducks waddle over from the pond round the corner. Enjoy Elgood's ales and bar bites in the buzzy slate-floored bar or go for fresh fish dishes or thick, juicy local steaks in one of three relaxed, rustic dining rooms. Bedrooms are cosy and well-kept.
Carte £ 23/46
2 rooms ⊊ – ♦£ 80/90 ♦♦£ 100/150
Burnham Rd ⊠ PE31 8QD – ℰ 01485 518330 – www.duckinn.co.uk – Closed 25 December

STANNINGTON
Northumberland – Regional map n° **14**-B2
▶ London 288 mi – Morpeth 7 mi – Newcastle upon Tyne 9 mi

🛏️ St Mary's Inn   🍽️ 🏡 ♿ 🅿️

TRADITIONAL CUISINE · PUB Spacious pub in the striking red-brick offices of the old St Mary's Hospital. The experienced owners offer hearty dishes that people will know and love; meat and fish are cooked on the lumpwood charcoal grill and afternoon tea is a hit. Bright, airy bedrooms feature ultra-modern bathrooms and local art.

Carte £ 19/31

11 rooms ☲ – ♛£ 80/140 ♛♛£ 90/150

St Mary's Ln, St Mary's Park ✉ *NE61 6BL – West : 2.5 mi by Saltwick rd*
– ✆ 01670 293293 – www.stmarysinn.co.uk

STANSTED MOUNTFITCHET

Essex – Pop. 6 669 – Regional map n° **7**-B2
▶ London 39 mi – Chelmsford 23 mi – Cambridge 29 mi

🏠 Linden House   🏡 ⊘ 🖥️

TOWNHOUSE · ROMANTIC This part-timbered former antique shop is now a smart hotel. Bedrooms have a pleasing mix of classic and modern elements and most come with a bath in the room. The bar is characterised by dark wood and has a shabby-chic, masculine feel. The rustic restaurant offers a concise selection of country classics.

9 rooms – ♛£ 90/135 ♛♛£ 90/135 – ☲ £ 10

1-3 Silver St ✉ *CM24 8HA – ✆ 01279 813003 – www.lindenhousestansted.co.uk*

🏘️ Chimneys   🅿️

TOWNHOUSE · COSY Charming 17C house with low-beamed ceilings and cosy guest areas. Pine-furnished bedrooms have a modern cottagey style and come with homely touches. Tasty breakfasts include Manx kippers and smoked haddock with poached eggs.

3 rooms ☲ – ♛£ 59/68 ♛♛£ 85/90

44 Lower St ✉ *CM24 8LR – on B 1351 – ✆ 01279 813388*
– www.chimneysguesthouse.co.uk

STANTON

Suffolk – Pop. 2 073 – Regional map n° **8**-C2
▶ London 88 mi – Cambridge 38 mi – Ipswich 40 mi – King's Lynn 38 mi

🍴 Leaping Hare   🍷 🏡 ♿ 🅿️

MODERN BRITISH · BISTRO This beautiful 17C timber-framed barn sits at the centre of a 7 acre vineyard. Carefully judged cooking relies on well-sourced, seasonal ingredients; many from their own farm. Sit on the lovely terrace and try the interesting all-day light bites or choose something from the more substantial daily menu.

Menu £ 22 (weekdays)/28 – Carte £ 29/39

Wyken Vineyards ✉ *IP31 2DW – South : 1.25 mi by Wyken Rd – ✆ 01359 250287*
(booking essential) – www.wykenvineyards.co.uk – lunch only and dinner
Friday-Saturday – Closed 25 December-5 January

STAPLEFORD – Nottinghamshire ➔ See Nottingham

STAVERTON – Northamptonshire ➔ See Daventry

STILTON

Cambridgeshire – ✉ Peterborough – Pop. 2 455 – Regional map n° **8**-A2
▶ London 76 mi – Cambridge 30 mi – Northampton 43 mi – Peterborough 6 mi

⌂ Bell Inn   ☆ ⌂ & ⅍ ⚿ P

INN · COSY Historic coaching inn with a characterful beamed lounge and bar; run by a hospitable, hands-on owner. Comfy bedrooms have a traditional feel – some feature original beams or four-posters and those in the old smithy overlook the garden. The first floor restaurant offers a seasonal, classically based menu.

22 rooms ⌷ – ♦£ 85 ♦♦£ 110/145

Great North Rd ⌧ PE7 3RA – 𝒞 01733 241066 – www.thebellstilton.co.uk – Closed 25 December

STOCKBRIDGE

Hampshire – Pop. 570 – Regional map n° **4**-B2

▶ London 75 mi – Salisbury 14 mi – Southampton 19 mi – Winchester 9 mi

🍴 Greyhound on the Test   ⇐ ⌂ ⌂ P

MODERN BRITISH · PUB Mustard-coloured pub with over a mile of River Test fishing rights to the rear. Low beams and wood burning stoves abound and elegant décor gives it a French bistro feel. The appealing range of dishes includes modern small plates, a selection 'on toast' and a classical daily menu; the chef will also cook your catch. Homely bedrooms have large showers and quality bedding.

Menu £ 15 (weekday lunch) – Carte £ 22/59

10 rooms ⌷ – ♦£ 90/150 ♦♦£ 145/240

31 High St ⌧ SO20 6EY – 𝒞 01264 810833 (booking advisable) – www.thegreyhoundonthetest.co.uk – Closed 25-26 December

STOCKPORT

Greater Manchester – Pop. 105 878 – Regional map n° **11**-B3

▶ London 201 mi – Liverpool 42 mi – Leeds 50 mi – Sheffield 52 mi

✕✕ Damson   ⌂ Ⓐ 🍴

MODERN BRITISH · NEIGHBOURHOOD The décor of this understated neighbourhood restaurant takes in oversized damson-coloured lampshades and boldly patterned velour chairs. Choose from a great selection of menus, which offer classic combinations with modern touches.

Menu £ 25/40 – Carte £ 32/50

113 Heaton Moor Rd ⌧ SK4 4HY – Northwest : 3 mi by A 6 on B 5169 – 𝒞 0161 432 4666 – www.damsonrestaurant.co.uk – Closed 26 December, 1 January, lunch Monday and Saturday

✕ brassicagrill

😊 MODERN BRITISH · NEIGHBOURHOOD The walls of this neighbourhood restaurant are filled with old lithographs of brassica plants and tea lights twinkle on the tables in the evening. Cooking is honest, flavoursome and good value; be sure to try the 'stout' ice cream. The team have worked together for many years and it shows.

Menu £ 14 – Carte £ 17/42

27 Shaw Rd ⌧ SK4 4AG – Northwest : 2.5 mi by A 6 off B 5169 – 𝒞 0161 442 6730 – www.brassicagrill.com – Closed 25-26 December, 1 January, Monday and Sunday dinner

STOKE BY NAYLAND

Suffolk – Regional map n° **8**-C3

▶ London 70 mi – Bury St Edmunds 24 mi – Cambridge 54 mi – Colchester 11 mi

🍴 Crown   ⅍ ⇐ ⌂ ⌂ P

REGIONAL CUISINE · PUB Smart, relaxed pub in a great spot overlooking the Box and Stour river valleys. Globally influenced menus feature produce from local farms and estates, with seafood from the east coast. Well-priced wine list with over 25 wines by the glass. Large, luxurious, superbly equipped bedrooms with king or super king sized beds; some have French windows and terraces.

Carte £ 20/43

11 rooms ⌷ – ♦£ 95/130 ♦♦£ 140/260

⌧ CO6 4SE – 𝒞 01206 262001 – www.crowninn.net – Closed 25-26 December

STOKE HOLY CROSS - Norfolk → See Norwich

STOKE POGES
Buckinghamshire - Pop. 3 962 - Regional map n° **6**-D3
▶ London 23 mi - Bristol 99 mi - Croydon 44 mi

🏨 Stoke Park
LUXURY · CLASSIC Grade I listed Palladian property - once home to the Penn family, who created England's first country club. Extensive sporting activities, impressive spa and characterful guest areas. Mix of chic and luxurious 'Feature' bedrooms.

49 rooms - ♦£ 199/330 ♦♦£ 220/380 - ☱£ 25 - 1 suite
Park Rd ✉ SL2 4PG - Southwest : 0.75 mi on B 416 - ✆ 01753 717171
- www.stokepark.com - Closed 3-6 January and 25-26 December
Humphry's - See restaurant listing

🏨 Stoke Place
HISTORIC · MODERN 17C Queen Anne mansion, set by a large lake and surrounded by delightful gardens and parkland. Quirky guest areas display bold wallpapers and original furnishings. Uniquely styled bedrooms are spread about the house and grounds.

39 rooms - ♦£ 95/250 ♦♦£ 95/250 - ☱£ 16
Stoke Green ✉ SL2 4HT - South : 0.5 mi by B 416 - ✆ 01753 534790
- www.stokeplace.co.uk
Seasons - See restaurant listing

XXXX Humphry's
MODERN BRITISH · ELEGANT Impressive hotel dining room named after 18C landscape gardener Humphry Repton, who designed the surrounding gardens; the lake and parkland views are superb. Classically based dishes are presented in a modern style. Service is professional.

Menu £ 25/68
Stoke Park Hotel, Park Rd ✉ SL2 4PG - ✆ 01753 717171 (booking essential)
- www.humphrysrestaurant.co.uk - Closed 3-6 January, 25-26 December, Monday, Tuesday and lunch Wednesday-Thursday

XX Seasons
MODERN CUISINE · ELEGANT Smart hotel dining room overlooking a lake and gardens designed by Capability Brown. Modern menus rely on good quality local ingredients and many dishes uses herbs, vegetables or fruit from the kitchen garden. Service is attentive.

Menu £ 24 (lunch)/45
Stoke Park Hotel, Stoke Green ✉ SL2 4HT - South : 0.5 mi by B 416
- ✆ 01753 534790 - www.stokeplace.co.uk - Closed Sunday dinner and Monday

STON EASTON
Somerset - Pop. 579 - Regional map n° **2**-C2
▶ London 131 mi - Bath 12 mi - Bristol 11 mi - Wells 7 mi

🏨 Ston Easton Park
GRAND LUXURY · ELEGANT Striking Palladian mansion in 36 acres of delightful grounds. Fine rooms of epic proportions are filled with antiques, curios and impressive flower arrangements. Many of the bedrooms have coronet or four-poster beds; three are set in a cottage. Classic menus showcase produce from the Victorian kitchen garden.

23 rooms ☱ - ♦£ 115/379 ♦♦£ 149/399 - 2 suites
✉ BA3 4DF - ✆ 01761 241631 - www.stoneaston.co.uk

STOW-ON-THE-WOLD
Gloucestershire - Pop. 2 042 - Regional map n° **2**-D1
▶ London 86 mi - Gloucester 27 mi - Birmingham 44 mi - Oxford 30 mi

🏠 Number Four at Stow

BUSINESS · CONTEMPORARY Contemporary, open-plan hotel; so named as it's the fourth this experienced family own. The comfy lounge boasts bold brushed velvet seating, while the bright, compact bedrooms feature smart leather headboards, cream furniture and modern facilities. The comfortable brasserie offers a classical menu.

18 rooms ☲ – ♦£ 100/150 ♦♦£ 120/185 – 3 suites

Fosseway ✉ GL54 1JX – South : 1.25 mi by A 429 on A 424 – ℰ 01451 830297
– www.hotelnumberfour.co.uk – Closed 23-31 December

🏠 Number Nine

FAMILY · COSY Expect a warm welcome at this ivy-clad, 18C stone house, close to the historic town square. The cosy lounge and breakfast room boast exposed stone walls, open fireplaces and dark wood beams. A winding staircase leads up to the pleasant wood-furnished bedrooms, which come with plenty of extras.

3 rooms ☲ – ♦£ 50/65 ♦♦£ 75/85

9 Park St ✉ GL54 1AQ – ℰ 01451 870333 – www.number-nine.info

XX Old Butchers

CLASSIC CUISINE · FRIENDLY An old butcher's shop with quirky décor, colourful chairs and ice bucket and colander lampshades. The menu offers plenty of choice from old favourites to dishes with a Mediterranean slant. The 'bin end' wine list is worth a look.

Carte £ 23/45

7 Park St ✉ GL54 1AQ – ℰ 01451 831700 – www.theoldbutchers.com

at Lower Oddington East: 3 mi by A436 ✉ Stow-On-The-Wold

🍴 Fox Inn

TRADITIONAL BRITISH · PUB Creeper-clad, quintessentially English pub at the heart of a peaceful Cotswold village, with beamed ceilings, solid stone walls, flagged floors and plenty of cosy nooks and crannies. The menu focuses on carefully prepared, tasty British classics and the comfortable bedrooms are individually furnished.

Carte £ 20/43

3 rooms ☲ – ♦£ 85/100 ♦♦£ 85/100

✉ GL56 0UR – ℰ 01451 870555 (booking essential) – www.foxinn.net – Closed Sunday dinner and Monday

at Daylesford East: 3.5 mi by A436 ✉ Stow-On-The-Wold

X Café at Daylesford Organic

MODERN BRITISH · FASHIONABLE Stylish café attached to a farm shop; its rustic interior boasting an open charcoal grill and a wood-fired oven. Throughout the day, tuck into light dishes and small plates; at night, candle-lit suppers step things up a gear. Everything is organic, with much of the produce coming from the farm.

Carte £ 25/49

✉ GL56 0YG – ℰ 01608 731700 (bookings not accepted) – www.daylesford.com
– lunch only and dinner Friday-Saturday – Closed 25-26 December and 1 January

at Bledington Southeast: 4 mi by A436 on B4450

🍴 Kings Head Inn

TRADITIONAL BRITISH · INN Charming 16C former cider house on a picturesque village green, bisected by a stream filled with bobbing ducks. Appealing bar snacks include pheasant in a basket; pub classics and some interesting modern dishes on the à la carte. Large bar with a vast inglenook fireplace. Cosy bedrooms.

Carte £ 25/40

12 rooms ☲ – ♦£ 75/100 ♦♦£ 100/130

The Green ✉ OX7 6XQ – ℰ 01608 658365 – www.kingsheadinn.net – Closed 25-26 December

at Nether Westcote Southeast: 4.75 mi by A429 and A424

îⓌ **Feathered Nest** ⌾ ⇦ ≼ ⇦ ㎕ ⅋ 🅿

MODERN CUISINE · INN Smart pub with a laid-back bar, a rustic snug, a casual conservatory and a formal dining room. Sit on quirky horse saddle stools and sample unfussy dishes from the daily blackboard or head through to elegant antique tables for more complex offerings; the wine list features over 200 bins. Comfy bedrooms boast antiques, quality linens and roll-top baths. The views are superb.
Menu £ 25 (weekday lunch) – Carte £ 44/65

4 rooms ⌕ – †£ 195/245 ††£ 210/260

✉ OX7 6SD – ℰ 01993 833030 – www.thefeatherednestinn.co.uk – Closed 1 week February, 1 week July, 1 week October, 25 December Monday and Tuesday

STRATFORD ST MARY

Suffolk – Pop. 701 – Regional map n° **15**-C3
▶ London 67 mi – Ipswich 11 mi – Colchester 9 mi

îⓌ **Swan** Ⓝ ⇦ ㎕ 🅿

CLASSIC CUISINE · PUB A homely 16C coaching inn overlooking the river, with characterful low beams, whitewashed walls and open fires. The short menu changes daily and uses local ingredients in time-honoured ways. Each dish is matched to a wine and an ale.
Carte £ 23/40

Lower St ✉ CO7 6JR – ℰ 01206 321244 – www.stratfordswan.com – Closed Monday and Tuesday

STRATFORD-UPON-AVON

Warwickshire – Pop. 27 830 – Regional map n° **10**-C3
▶ London 96 mi – Birmingham 23 mi – Coventry 18 mi – Leicester 44 mi

🏠 **Arden** ⅁ 🆔 ⅋ 🔆 🅿

BUSINESS · MODERN Set in a great location opposite the theatre, with a split-level terrace overlooking the river. There's a smart bar-lounge and a second plush lounge for afternoon tea. Twisty corridors lead to stylish bedrooms in vibrant colour schemes.

45 rooms ⌕ – †£ 128/153 ††£ 155/205

Town plan: B2-x - Waterside ✉ CV37 6BA – ℰ 01789 298682
– www.theardenhotelstratford.com

Waterside Brasserie – See restaurant listing

🏠 **White Sails** ⇦ 🆔 ⅋ 🅿

LUXURY · GRAND LUXURY Detached Edwardian house; look out for the 'Sail' signs. Leather-furnished lounge with local info, a Nespresso machine and a decanter of sherry. Smart bedrooms with superb bathrooms and good extras. Comprehensive buffet breakfasts.

4 rooms ⌕ – †£ 90/115 ††£ 105/130

85 Evesham Rd ✉ CV37 9BE – Southwest : 1 mi on B 439 – ℰ 01789 550469
– www.white-sails.co.uk – Closed Christmas-New Year

🏠 **Cherry Trees** ⇦ ⅋ 🅿

TOWNHOUSE · PERSONALISED Hidden away close to the river, beside the Butterfly Farm. Spacious bedrooms come with good extras; two have small conservatories and overlook the attractively landscaped garden. Homemade bread and granola feature at breakfast.

3 rooms ⌕ – †£ 115/135 ††£ 115/135

Town plan: B2-e - Swan's Nest Ln ✉ CV37 7LS – ℰ 01789 292989
– www.cherrytrees-stratford.co.uk – Closed December-March

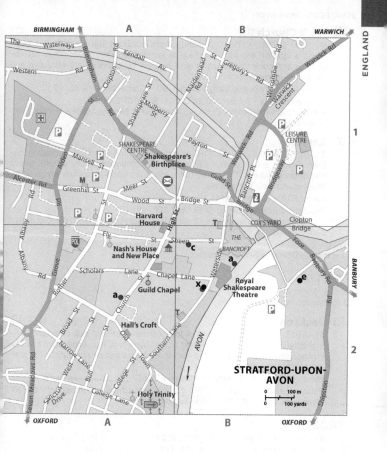

BIRMINGHAM   A   B   WARWICH

STRATFORD-UPON-AVON

0   100 m
0   100 yards

OXFORD   A   B   OXFORD

✗✗ Waterside Brasserie   🏡 ౹ AC 🅿

INTERNATIONAL · BRASSERIE Contemporary hotel brasserie with purple chairs and doors that open onto a landscaped terrace overlooking the river. Light bites at lunch are followed by well-presented British brasserie classics at dinner; the set menu is good value.

Menu £ 20 – Carte £ 36/50

Town plan: B2-x - *Arden Hotel, Waterside* ⊠ *CV37 6BA*
- ☎ *01789 298682*
- *www.theardenhotelstratford.com*

✗✗ Rooftop   ⟨ 🏡 ౹ 🕮

TRADITIONAL CUISINE · DESIGN Curvaceous open-plan restaurant with a lovely terrace, set on top of the Royal Shakespeare Theatre and boasting great views over the canal basin, river and gardens. Menus offer brasserie classics with some European influences.

Menu £ 25 (dinner) – Carte lunch £ 21/31

Town plan: B2-a - *Royal Shakespeare Theatre, Waterside* ⊠ *CV37 6BB*
- ☎ *01789 403449*
- *www.rsc.org.uk/eat*
- *Closed 25 December and Sunday dinner*

585

XX **No 9 Church St.**

MODERN BRITISH · BISTRO A friendly, cosy restaurant in a 400 year old town-house a little off the main streets. The experienced chef-owner offers flavour-some British cooking with an original modern twist. Dishes are attractive and use lots of ingredients.

Menu £ 14 (lunch and early dinner)/60 – Carte dinner £ 25/43

Town plan: A2-a - *9 Church St ⊠ CV37 6HB* – ℰ *01789 415522*
- www.no9churchst.com – Closed 25 December-3 January, Sunday, Monday and bank holidays

X **Lambs**

TRADITIONAL CUISINE · RUSTIC Attractive 16C house with an interesting his-tory; dine on one of several intimate levels, surrounded by characterful beams and original features. The classic bistro menu lists simply, carefully prepared fa-vourites and daily fish specials.

Menu £ 19 – Carte £ 24/41

Town plan: B2-c - *12 Sheep St ⊠ CV37 6EF* – ℰ *01789 292554*
- www.lambsrestaurant.co.uk – Closed 25-26 December and lunch Monday except bank holidays

STRETE – Devon → See Dartmouth

STRETTON

Rutland – Regional map n° **9**-C2
▶ London 100 mi – Leicester 33 mi – Nottingham 37 mi

🍴 **Jackson Stops Inn**

TRADITIONAL BRITISH · RUSTIC A lovely stone and thatch pub comprising sev-eral different seating areas, including a small open-fired bar, a cosy barn and sev-eral beamed rooms. Choose from the list of classics and pub favourites; the shar-ing boards are a hit.

Menu £ 15 (weekday lunch) – Carte £ 25/37

Rookery La ⊠ LE15 7RA – ℰ *01780 410237* – *www.thejacksonstops.com* – *Closed Monday except bank holidays and Sunday dinner*

STROUD

Gloucestershire – Pop. 32 670 – Regional map n° **2**-C1
▶ London 113 mi – Bristol 30 mi – Gloucester 9 mi

🏠 **The Bear of Rodborough**

INN · TRADITIONAL There's plenty of character to this 17C coaching inn, which stands on Rodborough Common and affords pleasant country views. The cosy beamed lounge and bar provide an atmospheric setting for a casual meal, while the more formal library offers modern cuisine. Bedrooms are stylish and con-temporary.

45 rooms ⊡ – †£ 80/150 ††£ 90/200

Rodborough Common ⊠ GL5 5DE – *Southeast : 2 mi by A 419 on Butterow Hill rd*
– ℰ 01453 878522 – www.cotswold-inns-hotels.co.uk

🍴 **Bell Inn ①**

MODERN BRITISH · INN This Grade II listed stone inn dates back to the 16C and its delightful terrace and conservatory afford great countryside views. Interesting modern dishes showcase produce from the chef-owner's allotment and there's a great vegetarian selection. Make a night of it by staying in one of the homely bedrooms.

Carte £ 20/32

2 rooms ⊡ – †£ 90 ††£ 130

Bell Ln, Selsley ⊠ GL5 5LY – *Southwest : 2 mi by A 419 and on B 4048*
– ℰ 01453 753801 – www.thebellinnselsley.com – Closed Sunday dinner

🍴 Bisley House

TRADITIONAL CUISINE · FRIENDLY Stroud's oldest pub has been given a new lease of life and now sports a bright, modern look, with tiled floors, white walls – and not a beam or a horse brass in sight! The menu changes almost daily and cooking is simple, fresh and tasty.

Carte £ 23/33

Middle St ⊠ GL5 1DZ – ℰ 01453 751328 – www.bisleyhousecafe.co.uk – Closed Monday

STUDLAND

Dorset – Pop. 299 – Regional map n° **2**-C3

▶ London 135 mi – Bournemouth 25 mi – Southampton 53 mi – Weymouth 29 mi

🏠 Pig on the Beach

COUNTRY HOUSE · GRAND LUXURY Delightful country house with commanding coastal views and lovely gardens leading down to the sea. It has a relaxed, shabby-chic style and the furnishings are a pleasing mix of the old and the new. For something a little different, stay in an old gardener's bothy or dovecote. Staff are extremely welcoming.

23 rooms – ♦£ 145/310 ♦♦£ 145/310 – ☷ £ 15

Manor Rd ⊠ BH19 3AU – ℰ 01929 450288 – www.thepighotel.com

Pig on the Beach – See restaurant listing

✗ Pig on the Beach

REGIONAL CUISINE · FRIENDLY Set within a large, plant-filled conservatory in a delightful country house; a rustic, shabby-chic restaurant where the wonderful kitchen garden informs the menu and additional produce comes from within 25 miles. Cooking is light and fresh and is accompanied by superb views over the lawns to Studland Bay.

Carte £ 25/47

Manor Rd ⊠ BH19 3AU – ℰ 01929 450288 – www.thepighotel.com

✗ Shell Bay

SEAFOOD · BISTRO Simply furnished seafood restaurant with a decked terrace; superbly set on the waterfront and boasting views over the water to Brownsea Island – all tables have a view. The daily menu mixes the classical with the more adventurous.

Carte £ 26/50

Ferry Rd ⊠ BH19 3BA – North : 3 mi or via car ferry from Sandbanks – ℰ 01929 450363 (booking essential) – www.shellbay.net – Closed December-February

SUMMERHOUSE – Darlington → See Darlington

SUNBURY ON THAMES

Surrey – Pop. 27 415 – Regional map n° **4**-C1

▶ London 16 mi – Croydon 38 mi – Barnet 44 mi – Ealing 10 mi

✗✗ Indian Zest

INDIAN · NEIGHBOURHOOD Pleasant restaurant with two small terraces, in a building dating back over 450 years. Pretty interior with black and white photos of Colonial India and a fine array of polo mallets. Large, interesting dishes originate from all over India.

Menu £ 11 (lunch)/36 – Carte £ 19/32

21 Thames St ⊠ TW16 5QF – ℰ 01932 765000 – www.indianzest.co.uk – Closed dinner 25 December and lunch 26 December

SUNNINGDALE

Windsor and Maidenhead – Regional map n° **6**-D3

▶ London 33 mi – Croydon 39 mi – Barnet 46 mi – Ealing 22 mi

SUNNINGDALE

ENGLAND

XXX Bluebells

MODERN CUISINE · INTIMATE The smart façade of this professionally run restaurant is matched by a sophisticated interior, where white leather furnishings stand out against dark green walls. Beautifully presented dishes are crafted using modern techniques.

Menu £ 26/37 – Carte dinner £ 37/49

*Shrubbs Hill, London Rd ⊠ SL5 0LE – Northeast : 0.75 mi on A 30
– ℰ 01344 622722 – www.bluebells-restaurant.com – Closed 1-12 January,
25-26 December, Sunday dinner and Monday*

SUNNISIDE

Tyne and Wear – Regional map n° **14**-B2

▶ London 283 mi – Newcastle upon Tyne 6 mi – Sunderland 16 mi – Middlesbrough 41 mi

Hedley Hall

TRADITIONAL · COSY Stone-built former farmhouse in a quiet location close to the Beamish Open Air Museum. Formal, linen-laid breakfast room and a comfy lounge with a large conservatory extension. Good-sized bedrooms offer pleasant countryside views.

4 rooms ⌂ – ♦£ 70/80 ♦♦£ 100

*Hedley Ln ⊠ NE16 5EH – South : 2 mi by A 6076 – ℰ 01207 231835
– www.hedleyhall.com – Closed Christmas-New Year*

SUTTON

Central Bedfordshire – Pop. 299 – Regional map n° **7**-B1

▶ London 47 mi – Cambridge 35 mi – Huntingdon 22 mi

John O'Gaunt Inn

TRADITIONAL CUISINE · COSY Well-run by experienced owners, this is a cosy, honest village inn with a fire-warmed bar, a smart dining room and delightful gardens overlooking wheat fields. The tried-and-tested menu includes some tasty 'Crumps Butchers' steaks.

Carte £ 24/40

*30 High St ⊠ SG19 2NE – ℰ 01767 260377 – www.johnogauntsutton.co.uk
– Closed Monday except bank holidays and Sunday dinner*

SUTTON COLDFIELD

West Midlands – Pop. 109 015 – Regional map n° **10**-C2

▶ London 124 mi – Birmingham 8 mi – Coventry 29 mi

New Hall

HISTORIC · ELEGANT Despite its name, this is one of the oldest inhabited moated houses in England, dating back to the 13C. Mature, topiary-filled grounds give way to a characterful interior of wood panelling and stained glass. Bedrooms are luxurious. A mix of classic and modern dishes are offered in the restaurant.

60 rooms ⌂ – ♦£ 106/184 ♦♦£ 116/194 – 5 suites

*Walmley Rd ⊠ B76 1QX – Southeast : 2.5 mi by A 5127 off Wylde Green Rd
– ℰ 0845 072 7577 – www.handpickedhotels.co.uk/newhall*

SUTTON COURTENAY

Oxfordshire – Pop. 2 421 – Regional map n° **6**-B2

▶ London 72 mi – Bristol 77 mi – Coventry 70 mi

Fish

TRADITIONAL CUISINE · FRIENDLY A taste of France in Oxfordshire: expect French pictures, French music and charming Gallic service. Robust country cooking offers both French and British classics; ask for wine recommendations. Sit in the lovely garden or conservatory.

Menu £ 16 (weekdays)/19 – Carte £ 27/48

*4 Appleford Rd ⊠ OX14 4NQ – ℰ 01235 848242 – www.thefishatsuttoncourtenay.co.uk
– Closed January, Monday except bank holidays and Sunday dinner*

588

SUTTON GAULT - Cambridgeshire → See Ely

SWAFFHAM

Norfolk – Pop. 6 734 – Regional map n° **8**-C2

▶ London 97 mi – Cambridge 46 mi – King's Lynn 16 mi – Norwich 27 mi

Strattons　　　　　　　　　　　　　　　🏠 ⬅ 🅿

TOWNHOUSE · PERSONALISED Laid-back, eco-friendly hotel in an eye-catching 17C villa with Victorian additions. Quirky, individually styled bedrooms are spread about the place: some are duplex; some have terraces or courtyards. The rustic basement restaurant serves modern British dishes; on quieter days, breakfast is taken in their deli.

14 rooms ☲ – ♦£ 92/230 ♦♦£ 99/250

4 Ash Cl ✉ PE37 7NH – ☎ 01760 723845 – www.strattonshotel.com – Closed 21-27 December

SWAY

Hampshire – Pop. 2 294 – Regional map n° **4**-A3

▶ London 96 mi – Bournemouth 15 mi – Lymington 5 mi

Manor at Sway　　　　　　　　　　　　　　　🏠 ⬅ 🅿

FAMILY · PERSONALISED The Manor is set in the centre of a busy New Forest village and comes with a delightful rear garden where a mature Cedar of Lebanon takes centre stage. Inside it's bold and bright, with cosy modern bedrooms and Hypnos beds. The showy dining room has flock wallpaper, black tables and a French-inspired menu.

15 rooms ☲ – ♦£ 90 ♦♦£ 170

Station Rd ✉ SO41 1QE – ☎ 01590 682754 – www.themanoratsway.com

SWINBROOK - Oxfordshire → See Burford

TALATON

Devon – Regional map n° **1**-D2

▶ London 165 mi – Bristol 76 mi – Exeter 14 mi

Larkbeare Grange　　　　　　　　　　　　🌿 ⬅ 🅿

FAMILY · PERSONALISED A friendly, experienced couple run this well-kept house. Start the day with homemade yoghurt and preserves, and end it beside the wood-burner in the cosy lounge. Bedrooms feature stripped pine furnishings and floral fabrics.

4 rooms ☲ – ♦£ 85/125 ♦♦£ 110/175

Larkbeare ✉ EX5 2RY – South : 1.5 mi by Fairmile rd – ☎ 01404 822069 – www.larkbeare.net

TANGMERE - West Sussex → See Chichester

TAPLOW

Buckinghamshire – Pop. 518 – Regional map n° **6**-C3

▶ London 33 mi – Maidenhead 2 mi – Oxford 36 mi – Reading 12 mi

Cliveden House　　　　　　🌿 ⬅ 🏊 📺 ⏺ 🧖 ♨ 🅿

HISTORIC · CLASSIC Stunning Grade I listed, 19C stately home in a superb location, boasting views over the formal parterre and National Trust gardens towards the Thames. The opulent interior boasts sumptuous antique-filled lounges and luxuriously appointed bedrooms. Unwind in the smart spa then take a picnic or afternoon tea hamper and kick-back in style on one of their vintage launches.

44 rooms ☲ – ♦£ 495/750 ♦♦£ 495/750 – 6 suites

✉ SL6 0JF – North : 2 mi by Berry Hill – ☎ 01628 668561
– www.clivedenhouse.co.uk

André Garrett at Cliveden House · Astor Grill – See restaurant listing

✗✗✗ André Garrett at Cliveden House   錣 ≼ 🛏 🕦 ⇄ 🅿

MODERN CUISINE · LUXURY A grand hotel dining room with views over the par-terre garden. Classic recipes are brought up-to-date in refined, well-presented dishes where local and seasonal produce feature highly. These are accompanied by a superb wine list.

Menu £ 33 (weekday lunch)/98

Cliveden House, ✉ SL6 0JF – North : 2 mi by Berry Hill – 𝒞 01628 607100 – www.clivedenhouse.co.uk/restaurant

✗ Astor Grill ⓝ   🛏 🚟 🅿

TRADITIONAL BRITISH · BISTRO Set in the former stable wing: a small hotel restaurant complete with its old horse rail, an equestrian theme and a delightful terrace. The menu is a roll-call of English classics, with grills a specialty; be sure to try the trifle.

Carte £ 33/60

Cliveden House, ✉ SL6 0JF – North : 2 mi by Berry Hill – 𝒞 01628 607107 – www.clivedenhouse.co.uk

TARR STEPS
Somerset – Regional map n° **2**-A2
▶ London 191 mi – Taunton 31 mi – Tiverton 20 mi

🍴 Tarr Farm Inn   ⇆ 🛏 🚟 🅿

TRADITIONAL BRITISH · RUSTIC Cosy beamed pub in an idyllic riverside spot, over-looking a 1000 BC, stone-slab clapper bridge. If it's sunny, head for the garden for afternoon tea; if not, make for the narrow bar or cosy restaurant for everything from potted shrimps to Devon Ruby steak. Bedrooms are comfy and well-equipped.

Carte £ 23/41

9 rooms ☷ – ♦£ 75/90 ♦♦£ 100/150
✉ TA22 9PY – 𝒞 01643 851507 – www.tarrfarm.co.uk – Closed 1-13 February

TAUNTON
Somerset – Pop. 60 479 – Regional map n° **2**-B3
▶ London 168 mi – Bournemouth 69 mi – Bristol 50 mi – Exeter 37 mi

🏰 Castle   🍸 🛏 🔁 🏋 🅿

HISTORIC BUILDING · CLASSIC Part-12C, wisteria-clad Norman castle with impressive gardens, a keep and two wells. It's been run by the Chapman family for three generations and retains a fittingly traditional style. Well-kept, individually decorated bedrooms. Castle Bow serves modern dishes; relaxed Brazz offers brasserie classics.

44 rooms ☷ – ♦£ 89/125 ♦♦£ 120/225
Castle Grn ✉ TA1 1NF – 𝒞 01823 272671 – www.the-castle-hotel.com
Castle Bow Bar & Grill – See restaurant listing

✗✗ Castle Bow Bar & Grill   🛏 🅰🅲 🅿

MODERN CUISINE · FRIENDLY Elegant, art deco style restaurant in the old snooker room of a Norman castle. Regularly changing menus showcase top quality regional produce. Well-balanced dishes are classically based yet refined, and feature some playful modern touches.

Carte £ 34/52

Castle Hotel, Castle Grn ✉ TA1 1NF – 𝒞 01823 328328 (booking advisable) – www.castlebow.com – dinner only – Closed Sunday, Monday and Tuesday

✗✗ Willow Tree   🚟 ⇄

MODERN CUISINE · INTIMATE Intimate restaurant in a 17C townhouse, featuring exposed beams and a large inglenook fireplace. Daily menus evolve with the seasons and blend a robust classical base with artful, innovative ideas. Service is friendly and efficient.

Menu £ 28/33

3 Tower Ln ✉ TA1 4AR – 𝒞 01823 352835 (booking essential) – www.thewillowtreerestaurant.com – dinner only – Closed January, August, Sunday, Monday and Thursday

✗✗ Mint and Mustard   ⅙ 🄰🄲

INDIAN · FASHIONABLE Smart glass doors lead to a teak-furnished lounge and a contemporary, split-level restaurant in shades of green and mustard. Highly original, modern dishes with Keralan influences; the lunchtime thalis offer great value for money.

Menu £ 31/56 – Carte £ 17/32

10 Station Rd ⊠ TA1 1NH – ℰ 01823 330770 – www.mintandmustard.com – Closed 25-26 December and 1 January

✗ Augustus   🛖

MODERN BRITISH · BISTRO A simple little bistro run by an experienced chef and featuring a conservatory terrace with a retractable roof. Good-sized menu of hearty, unfussy dishes which mix French, British and some Asian influences. Bright and breezy service.

Carte £ 21/39

3 The Courtyard, St James St. ⊠ TA1 1JR – ℰ 01823 324354 (booking essential) – www.augustustaunton.co.uk – Closed 23 December-2 January, Sunday and Monday

TAVISTOCK
Devon – Pop. 12 280 – Regional map n° **1**-C2
▶ London 239 mi – Exeter 38 mi – Plymouth 16 mi

🏠 Rockmount   🅿

TOWNHOUSE · CONTEMPORARY 1920s house with a contrastingly contemporary interior, set beside the Tavistock viaduct and overlooking the town's rooftops. Individually furnished bedrooms are compact but come with plenty of extras. Breakfast is brought to your room.

5 rooms ⌂ – ∮£ 75/95 ∮∮£ 85/130

Drake Rd ⊠ PL19 0AX – ℰ 01822 611039 – www.rockmount-tavistock.com

🍴 Cornish Arms   🛖 ⅙
(❀)
TRADITIONAL CUISINE · COSY It might have been refurbished but the Cornish Arms is still a pleasingly traditional pub and its quarry-tiled bar is invariably filled with regulars playing darts and watching football. The ambitious, talented chef prepares a range of tasty classic and modern dishes, and attractive, sophisticated desserts.

Carte £ 20/40

15 West St ⊠ PL19 8AN – ℰ 01822 612145 – www.thecornisharmstavistock.co.uk – Closed dinner 24 December

at Gulworthy West: 3 mi on A390 ⊠ Tavistock

✗✗ Horn of Plenty   ⇔ 🌭 ⋜ 🍴 🛖 🄰🄲 ⇔ 🅿

MODERN CUISINE · ELEGANT Extremely friendly restaurant in an attractive creeper-clad country house, which offers lovely moor and valley views; ask for a window table. The modern menu has wide-ranging influences – the tasting menu best showcases the chef's talent. Bedrooms are bright and modern and many have balconies or terraces.

Menu £ 20 (lunch)/65

16 rooms ⌂ – ∮£ 100/235 ∮∮£ 110/245

Gulworthy ⊠ PL19 8JD – Northwest : 1 mi by B 3362 – ℰ 01822 832528 – www.thehornofplenty.co.uk

at Milton Abbot Northwest: 6 mi on B3362 ⊠ Tavistock

🏠 Hotel Endsleigh   🌭 ⋜ 🍴 🅿

HISTORIC · CLASSIC Restored Regency lodge in an idyllic rural setting; spacious guest areas offer wonderful countryside views and have a warm, classical style with a contemporary edge. Comfortable, antique-furnished bedrooms boast an understated elegance; choose one overlooking the magnificent gardens.

17 rooms ⌂ – ∮£ 170/500 ∮∮£ 190/500 – 3 suites

⊠ PL19 0PQ – Southwest : 1 mi – ℰ 01822 870000 – www.hotelendsleigh.com
Restaurant Endsleigh – See restaurant listing

XX Restaurant Endsleigh ≤ 🏠 🏠 & P

MODERN CUISINE · INTIMATE Elegant, wood-panelled restaurant in a peacefully located hotel; ask for a window table for superb countryside views. Classic cooking with a modern edge; dishes are neatly presented and flavoursome, with local produce to the fore. Attentive service, with a pleasant degree of informality.

Menu £ 26 (lunch)/44 – Carte £ 26/50

Hotel Endsleigh, ⊠ PL19 0PQ – Southwest : 1 mi – ℰ 01822 870000 (bookings essential for non-residents) – www.hotelendsleigh.com

at Chillaton Northwest: 6.25 mi by Chillaton rd⊠ Tavistock

🏠 Tor Cottage 🦋 ≤ 🏠 🍴 ⁄ P

TRADITIONAL · CLASSIC Remotely set cottage in 28 hillside acres, with peaceful gardens and a lovely outdoor pool. Bedrooms, most in converted outhouses, boast small kitchenettes and wood burning stoves. Breakfast is taken on the terrace or in the conservatory. Charming owner.

5 rooms ⊡ – ♦£ 98 ♦♦£ 150/155

⊠ PL16 0JE – Southwest : 0.75 mi by Tavistock rd, turning right at bridle path – ℰ 01822 860248 – www.torcottage.co.uk – Closed mid-December-1 February (minimum 2 night stay)

TEFFONT EVIAS – Wiltshire → See Salisbury

TEMPLE SOWERBY – Cumbria → See Penrith

TENTERDEN

Kent – Pop. 7 118 – Regional map n° **5**-C2

▶ London 57 mi – Folkestone 26 mi – Hastings 21 mi – Maidstone 19 mi

XX Swan Wine Kitchen 🏠 🅰🅲 ⇔ P

😊 **MODERN BRITISH · FRIENDLY** This rustic modern restaurant sits above the shop in the Chapel Down vineyard and boasts a cosy lounge and a lovely rooftop terrace with views over the vines; naturally, wines from the vineyard feature. Refined cooking is full of flavour and relies on just a few ingredients. The midweek menu is good value.

Menu £ 22 (weekdays)/25 – Carte £ 28/37

Chapel Down Winery, Small Hythe Rd ⊠ TN30 7NG – ℰ 01580 761616 – www.illbemother.co.uk – Closed dinner Sunday-Wednesday

TETBURY

Gloucestershire – Pop. 5 250 – Regional map n° **2**-C1

▶ London 113 mi – Bristol 27 mi – Gloucester 19 mi

🏠 Calcot Manor 🏡 🦋 🏠 🍴 📺 🕪 🎐 🎰 ✕ 🚶 ⁄ 🛁 P

FAMILY · CONTEMPORARY Impressive collection of converted farm buildings in a peaceful country setting, comprising ancient barns, old stables and a characterful farmhouse. Comfy lounges and stylish bedrooms have good mod cons; the outbuildings house a crèche, conference rooms and a superb spa complex. The laid-back conservatory offers classical dishes and there's a popular pub in the grounds.

35 rooms ⊡ – ♦£ 174/339 ♦♦£ 199/364 – 1 suite

Calcot ⊠ GL8 8YJ – West : 3.5 mi on A 4135 – ℰ 01666 890391 – www.calcot.co

Gumstool Inn – See restaurant listing

🏠 The Close 🏡 🏠 🛁 P

TOWNHOUSE · CONTEMPORARY The rear garden and courtyard of this 16C townhouse provide the perfect spot on a warm summer's day. Bold colours and contemporary furnishings blend well with the building's period features; look out for the superb cupola ceiling in the bar. Choose from a list of classics in the brasserie or a selection of refined, modern dishes in the more sophisticated restaurant.

18 rooms ⊡ – ♦£ 110/150 ♦♦£ 180/200

Long St ⊠ GL8 8AQ – ℰ 01666 502272 – www.cotswold-inns-hotels.co.uk

⌂ Gumstool Inn   🖨 🛏 P

TRADITIONAL CUISINE · CONTEMPORARY DÉCOR Set in the grounds of Calcot Manor; an attractive outbuilding with a contemporary 'Country Living' style. A flexible menu offers snacks, two sizes of starter and hearty British main courses; the open fire with a chargrill is a feature.

Carte £ 21/41

Calcot Manor Hotel, Calcot ⊠ GL8 8YJ – West : 3.5 mi on A 4135
– ℰ 01666 890391 – www.calcot.co

TEWKESBURY

Gloucestershire – Pop. 19 778 – Regional map n° **2**-C1
▶ London 108 mi – Birmingham 39 mi – Gloucester 11 mi

at Corse Lawn Southwest: 6 mi by A38 and A438 on B4211⊠ Gloucester

🏠 Corse Lawn House   ⛲ 🖨 🖼 ※ 🏋 P

COUNTRY HOUSE · CLASSIC Elegant Grade II listed Queen Anne house, just off the village green and fronted by a pond. The traditionally appointed interior features open fires and antiques; some of the spacious bedrooms have four-poster or half-tester beds. Dine from classical menus in the formal restaurant or characterful bistro-bar.

18 rooms � – ♥£ 75/100 ♥♥£ 100/180 – 3 suites
⊠ GL19 4LZ – ℰ 01452 780771 – www.corselawn.com – Closed 24-26 December

THETFORD

Norfolk – Pop. 24 833 – Regional map n° **15**-C2
▶ London 87 mi – Norwich 30 mi – Ipswich 34 mi

✗ The Mulberry 🅽   🛏

MEDITERRANEAN CUISINE · NEIGHBOURHOOD A bell tinkles as you enter this delightful stone property and the charming owner welcomes you in. The dining room leads through to a conservatory and a walled garden complete with a mulberry tree. Cooking is gutsy and boldly flavoured.

Carte £ 26/37

11 Raymond St ⊠ IP24 2EA – ℰ 01842 824122 (booking advisable)
– www.mulberrythetford.co.uk – dinner only – Closed 31 July- 4 August,
26-30 December, Sunday and Monday

THORNBURY

South Gloucestershire – ⊠ Bristol – Pop. 11 687 – Regional map n° **2**-C1
▶ London 128 mi – Bristol 12 mi – Gloucester 23 mi – Swindon 43 mi

🏠 Thornbury Castle   🌳 🖨 ⅙ 🏋 P

HISTORIC · CLASSIC Impressive 16C castle with a long and illustrious history; Henry VIII stayed here on his honeymoon with Anne Boleyn! Characterful, baronial style bedrooms feature mullioned windows, wall tapestries, beams and huge fireplaces.

28 rooms � – ♥£ 189/600 ♥♥£ 189/600 – 3 suites
Castle St ⊠ BS35 1HH – ℰ 01454 281182 – www.thornburycastle.co.uk
Thornbury Castle – See restaurant listing

✗✗ Thornbury Castle   🖨 ⅙ 🕪 P

MODERN CUISINE · ELEGANT Sited in a tower within the main 16C part of Thornbury Castle; a small, partly wood-panelled, circular room decorated in deep red, with coats of arms and an impressive fireplace. Elegantly laid tables; elaborate, modern dishes.

Menu £ 22 (weekdays)/50 – Carte £ 34/49

Thornbury Castle Hotel, Castle St ⊠ BS35 1HH – ℰ 01454 281182
– www.thornburycastle.co.uk

THORNTON - Lancashire → See Blackpool

THORNTON HOUGH
Merseyside – Regional map n° **11**-A3
▶ London 215 mi – Birkenhead 12 mi – Chester 17 mi – Liverpool 12 mi

🏨 Thornton Hall   🛬 📺 ☝ 🕸 ↯ & ♨ 🛁 **P**
BUSINESS · CLASSIC Extended manor house on the Wirral Peninsula. Wood panelling and stained glass feature in the main house, along with some luxurious bedrooms – the remainder are more contemporary, with balconies or terraces. Impressively equipped spa.

62 rooms – ♦£ 75/250 ♦♦£ 85/250 – ☕ £ 15 – 1 suite
Neston Rd ⊠ CH63 1JF – On B 5136 – ℰ 0151 336 3938
– www.thorntonhallhotel.com

Lawns – See restaurant listing

XX Lawns   🛬 & 🎦 ⇆ **P**
MODERN CUISINE · ELEGANT Grand hotel restaurant with oak-panelled walls, overlooking the lawns; formerly the house's billiard room. Chandeliers hang from the embossed leather ceiling. Elaborate modern cooking shows respect for local ingredients. Friendly service.

Menu £ 25 (weekday lunch) – Carte £ 45/55
Thornton Hall Hotel, Neston Rd ⊠ CH63 1JF – On B 5136 – ℰ 0151 336 3938
(booking essential) – www.lawnsrestaurant.com – Closed Sunday and Monday

THORPE MARKET
Norfolk – ⊠ North Walsham – Regional map n° **8**-D1
▶ London 134 mi – Norwich 20 mi – Ipswich 63 mi – Lowestoft 39 mi

🍺 Gunton Arms   ⇆ ≼ 🛬 🏠 ⇆ **P**
🐕 MODERN BRITISH · INN Charming pub overlooking the 1,000 acre Gunton Estate deer park. Enjoy a tasty homemade snack over a game of pool or darts in the bar or make for a gnarled wood table by the fireplace in the flag-floored Elk Room. Dishes are fiercely seasonal; some – such as the Aberdeen Angus steaks – are cooked over the fire. Well-equipped bedrooms have a stylish, country house feel.
Carte £ 23/40

12 rooms ☕ – ♦£ 85/89 ♦♦£ 95/240
Gunton Park ⊠ NR11 8TZ – South : 1 mi on A 149 – ℰ 01263 832010 (booking advisable) – www.theguntonarms.co.uk – Closed 25 December

THUNDER BRIDGE
West Yorkshire – Regional map n° **13**-B3
▶ London 185 mi – Leeds 22 mi – Huddersfield 7 mi

🍺 Woodman Inn   ⇆ 🏠 ⇆ **P**
TRADITIONAL BRITISH · INN Dark stone pub in a lovely wooded South Pennine valley, run by a local father and son. Menus strike a great balance between pub and restaurant style dishes; start with the Yorkshire tapas sharing plate and end with a comforting pudding. Smart, modern country bedrooms include a 3 level suite.

Menu £ 28 (weekday dinner) – Carte £ 27/48
19 rooms ☕ – ♦£ 50/90 ♦♦£ 65/100
⊠ HD8 0PX – ℰ 01484 605778 – www.woodman-inn.com

THURSFORD GREEN
Norfolk – Regional map n° **8**-C1
▶ London 120 mi – Fakenham 7 mi – Norwich 29 mi

🏠 Holly Lodge   🌳 🐕 🛏 ✂ P

TRADITIONAL · COSY Remotely set 18C house surrounded by delightful gardens.
Bedrooms are located in the old stable block and boast exposed beams, feature
beds and numerous extra touches. Communal breakfasts in the smart conservatory use local and homemade produce; home-cooked dinners are from a daily
changing set menu.

3 rooms 🍽 – 🛉£ 80/110 🛉🛉£ 100/130

The Street ✉ *NR21 0AS* – ☎ *01328 878465* – *www.hollylodgeguesthouse.co.uk*
– Restricted opening January-March

THURSLEY
Surrey – Regional map n° **4**-C2

▶ London 40 mi – Birmingham 144 mi – Bristol 115 mi – Ealing 43 mi

🍴 Three Horseshoes   🛏 🏠 P

TRADITIONAL CUISINE · CLASSIC DÉCOR There's no doubting this pub is at the
heart of the community – the locals clubbed together to save it from developers.
Hearty meals are high on flavour yet low on price. Real fires and fresh flowers
give it a homely feel.

Carte £ 23/44

Dye House Rd ✉ *GU8 6QD* – ☎ *01252 703268*
– www.threehorseshoesthursley.com – Closed Sunday dinner

TICEHURST
East Sussex – ✉ Wadhurst – Pop. 1 705 – Regional map n° **5**-B2

▶ London 49 mi – Brighton 44 mi – Folkestone 38 mi – Hastings 15 mi

🍴 Bell   🍴 🛏 🏠 🛗 ⟳ P

TRADITIONAL BRITISH · INN With top hats as lampshades, tubas in the loos and
a dining room called 'The Stable with a Table', quirky is this 16C coaching inn's
middle name. Seasonal menus offer proper pub food, and the rustic bedrooms
– many with their own silver birch tree – share the pub's idiosyncratic charm.

Carte £ 25/44

11 rooms 🍽 – 🛉£ 150/295 🛉🛉£ 150/295

High St ✉ *TN5 7AS* – ☎ *01580 200234 (booking advisable)*
– www.thebellinticehurst.com

TICKTON – East Riding of Yorkshire ➔ See Beverley

TILLINGTON – West Sussex ➔ See Petworth

TISBURY
Wiltshire – Pop. 2 178 – Regional map n° **2**-C3

▶ London 103 mi – Bristol 45 mi – Cardiff 87 mi – Torbay 98 mi

🍴 Beckford Arms   🍴 🛏 🏠 ⟳ P

TRADITIONAL CUISINE · FRIENDLY Charming 18C inn with a beamed dining
room, a rustic bar and a lovely country house sitting room – where films are
screened on Sundays. There's a delightful terrace and garden with hammocks, a
petanque pitch and even a dog bath. Tasty, unfussy classics and country-style
dishes. Tasteful bedrooms provide thoughtful comforts. Smart duplex suites, a
3min drive away.

Carte £ 24/35

10 rooms 🍽 – 🛉£ 95/130 🛉🛉£ 95/130

Fonthill Gifford ✉ *SP3 6PX – Northwest : 2 mi by Greenwich Rd*
– ☎ 01747 870385 (booking essential) – www.beckfordarms.com – Closed
25 December

TITCHWELL
Norfolk – Pop. 99 – Regional map n° **8**-C1

▶ London 128 mi – King's Lynn 25 mi – Boston 56 mi – Wisbech 36 mi

🏠 Titchwell Manor ⚐ 🛏 ♿ 🛇 🅿

COUNTRY HOUSE · GRAND LUXURY This attractive brick farmhouse has a stylish interior, where bare floorboards and seaside photos feature. Bedrooms in the grounds are modern, colourful and originally styled; those in the main house are slightly more conservative.

27 rooms ☑ – †£ 99/155 ††£ 99/225

✉ PE31 8BB – 𝒞 01485 210221 – www.titchwellmanor.com

The Conservatory – See restaurant listing

🏠 Briarfields ⚐ 🛏 🛋 ♿ 🅿

FAMILY · MODERN In winter, sink into a sofa by the cosy fire; in summer, relax in the secluded courtyard beside the pond or on the deck overlooking the salt marshes and the sea. Bedrooms are modern and immaculately kept; some open onto the garden.

23 rooms ☑ – †£ 80/85 ††£ 115/140

Main Street ✉ PE31 8BB – 𝒞 01485 210742 – www.briarfieldshotelnorfolk.co.uk

✗✗ The Conservatory ⚐ 🛋 ♿ 🅰 🅿

MODERN CUISINE · FASHIONABLE An appealing hotel restaurant offering plenty of choice. The trendy 'Eating Rooms' area offers sea views and comfort food. The smart 'Conservatory' area offers two more ambitious, accomplished menus of interesting modern dishes.

Menu £ 10 (weekday lunch) – Carte £ 20/49 **s**

Titchwell Manor Hotel, ✉ PE31 8BB – 𝒞 01485 210221 – www.titchwellmanor.com

TITLEY

Herefordshire – ✉ Kington – Regional map n° **10**-A3

▶ London 176 mi – Plymouth 196 mi – Torbay 175 mi – Exeter 159 mi

🍴 Stagg Inn ⬅ ⚐ 🛋 🍷 🅿

MODERN BRITISH · PUB Deep in rural Herefordshire, at the meeting point of two drover's roads, sits this characterful, part-medieval, part-Victorian pub. Seasonal menus offer tried-and-tested combinations; be sure to save room for one of the generous desserts. The cosy pub bedrooms can be noisy; opt for one in the former vicarage.

Carte £ 32/42

6 rooms ☑ – †£ 60/120 ††£ 100/140

✉ HR5 3RL – 𝒞 01544 230221 (booking essential) – www.thestagg.co.uk
– Closed 1-4 January, 1-8 March, 1-17 November, 25-27 December, Monday and Tuesday

TOLLARD ROYAL

Wiltshire – Regional map n° **2**-C3

▶ London 118 mi – Bristol 63 mi – Southampton 40 mi – Portsmouth 59 mi

🍴 King John Inn ⬅ ⚐ 🛋 🅿

REGIONAL CUISINE · PUB Modern black and white hunting photos line the walls and provide a clue both to the cooking and the clientele. The short daily menu is printed on brown paper and lists the origin of ingredients; start with the tasty homemade bread.

Menu £ 22 (weekday lunch) – Carte £ 26/51

8 rooms ☑ – †£ 90/190 ††£ 90/190

✉ SP5 5PS – 𝒞 01725 516207 – www.kingjohninn.co.uk – Closed 25 December

TOOT BALDON – Oxfordshire → See Oxford

TOPSHAM

Devon – ✉ Exeter – Pop. 3 730 – Regional map n° **1**-D2

▶ London 175 mi – Torbay 26 mi – Exeter 4 mi – Torquay 24 mi

✗✗ Salutation Inn ⇔ 🏠 ♿ 🔲 🛁

MODERN CUISINE · DESIGN 1720s coaching inn with a surprisingly contemporary interior. The glass-covered courtyard serves breakfast, light lunch and afternoon tea, while the stylish dining room offers nicely balanced weekly 4, 6 and 8 course menus of well-judged modern cooking. Bedrooms are similarly up-to-date and understated.

Menu £ 24 (lunch)/40

6 rooms ♀ – ♦£ 120/210 ♦♦£ 140/230

68 Fore St ⊠ EX3 0HL – ✆ 01392 873060 (booking essential at dinner)
– www.salutationtopsham.co.uk

TORQUAY

Torbay – Pop. 49 094 – Regional map n° **1**-C-D2
▶ London 223 mi – Exeter 23 mi – Plymouth 32 mi

🏠 Marstan 🚪 ⤬ 🍽 🅿

TOWNHOUSE · PERSONALISED Keenly run Victorian villa in a quiet part of town, with an opulent lounge, a pool, a hot tub and a lovely suntrap terrace. Comfy bedrooms have warm red décor and sumptuous fabrics. Substantial breakfasts include homemade granola.

9 rooms ♀ – ♦£ 65/110 ♦♦£ 89/170

Town plan: C2-a - *Meadfoot Sea Rd ⊠ TQ1 2LQ – ✆ 01803 292837*
– www.marstanhotel.co.uk – Closed November-18 March except
23 December-2 January

🏠 Somerville 🚪 🍽 🅿

TRADITIONAL · PERSONALISED Set on the hillside, a short stroll from town, a traditional-looking hotel with a warm, welcoming interior. Bedrooms have good mod cons – Room 12 has direct garden access and is the only room to have breakfast served on the terrace.

9 rooms ♀ – ♦£ 65/90 ♦♦£ 75/150

Town plan: C1-u - *515 Babbacombe Rd. ⊠ TQ1 1HJ – ✆ 01803 294755*
– www.somervillehotel.co.uk – Closed 15 November-8 December

🏠 Kingston House 🆎 🍽 🅿

FAMILY · CONTEMPORARY This enthusiastically run Victorian guesthouse comes with plenty of thoughtful touches, like fresh flowers displayed in the hallway, homemade scones served by the fire on arrival and locally made chocolates left in the bedrooms.

5 rooms ♀ – ♦£ 75/105 ♦♦£ 85/120

Town plan: A1-n - *75 Avenue Rd ⊠ TQ2 5LL – ✆ 01803 212760*
– www.kingstonhousetorquay.co.uk – Closed 20 December-6 January

✗✗ The Elephant (Simon Hulstone)
❀

MODERN BRITISH · FASHIONABLE For over 10 years the dedicated chef-owner has proudly run this bright, modern restaurant, which sits in a Georgian terrace overlooking the harbour. Menus offer well-judged, beautifully presented dishes with no unnecessary elaboration. Ingredients are top notch – most come from their 96 acre farm near Brixham.

→ Celeriac & pig's cheek with horseradish and pancetta. Fillet of beef with asparagus, morels and madeira jus. Caramelised lemon and passion fruit tart.

Menu £ 17 (lunch) – Carte £ 35/42

Town plan: B2-e - *3-4 Beacon Terr ⊠ TQ1 2BH – ✆ 01803 200044*
– www.elephantrestaurant.co.uk – Closed 1-19 January, Sunday and Monday

✗✗ Orange Tree

CLASSIC FRENCH · NEIGHBOURHOOD A homely, split-level restaurant set down a narrow town centre backstreet. The seasonally evolving menu is made up of classically based, French-influenced dishes, which are carefully prepared and rely on fresh, local produce.

Menu £ 48 – Carte £ 27/45

Town plan: B2-u - *14-16 Parkhill Rd ⊠ TQ1 2AL – ✆ 01803 213936 (booking essential) – www.orangetreerestaurant.co.uk – dinner only – Closed 2 weeks January, 2 weeks October-November, Sunday and Monday*

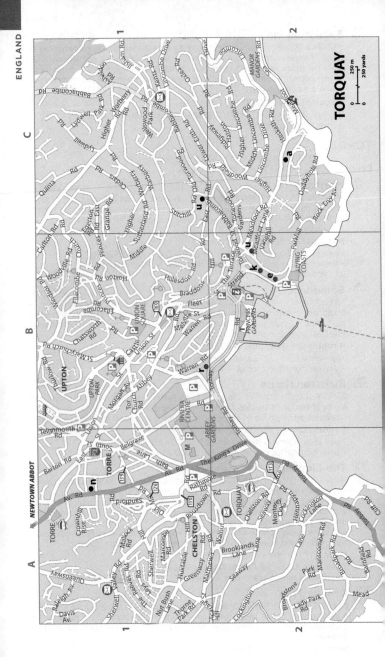

TORQUAY

0 — 250 m
0 — 250 yards

Ⅹ On the Rocks   ⪕ 🏠

MODERN BRITISH · BISTRO Two local lads opened this lovely restaurant overlooking Torbay. It's modern and laid-back, with a split-level room and furniture made from reclaimed scaffold boards. Appealing menus champion produce from the bay and the fields above.

Menu £13 (weekday dinner)/28 – Carte £20/49

Town plan: B1-r *1 Abbey Cres.* ✉ TQ2 5HB – 𝒞 01803 203666 *(bookings advisable at dinner) – www.ontherocks-torquay.co.uk – Closed 26 December and 1 January*

Ⅹ Number 7   AC

SEAFOOD · BISTRO Personally run bistro in a terrace of Regency houses. The walls are covered with fish-related photos and artefacts, as well as extensive blackboard menus of seafood fresh from the Brixham day boats; the simplest dishes are the best.

Carte £23/45

Town plan: B2-e *- 7 Beacon Terr.* ✉ TQ1 2BH – 𝒞 01803 295055 *(booking advisable) – www.no7-fish.com – dinner only and lunch Wednesday-Saturday – Closed 2 weeks February, 1 week November, Christmas-New Year, Monday November-May and Sunday October-June*

Ⅹ Harbour Kitchen 🆕   🍸 ⪕ 🏠

SEAFOOD · BISTRO A laid-back eatery on the harbourside; sit on the pavement terrace or at high communal tables for cocktails and snacks or head for the first floor for a more intimate atmosphere. Regularly changing menus keep their focus on seafood.

Carte £17/36

Town plan: B2-k *- 16 Victoria Par* ✉ TQ1 2BB – 𝒞 01803 211075 *- www.harbourkitchen.co.uk – Closed lunch October-April except December*

at Maidencombe North: 3.5 mi by A379 ✉ Torquay

🏠 Orestone Manor   🖈 🦢 ⪕ 🛏 🏠 🌿 🍴 🅿

TRADITIONAL · PERSONALISED Characterful house set amongst thick shrubbery and mature trees. It has a colonial feel courtesy of dark wood furnishings and Oriental and African artefacts. Most of the individually designed bedrooms have sea or country views. Menus are classical – dine in the restaurant, the conservatory or on the terrace.

14 rooms 🖙 – ♦£110/150 ♦♦£150/190

Rockhouse Ln ✉ TQ1 4SX – 𝒞 01803 328098 – www.orestonemanor.com – Closed 3-30 January

at Babbacombe Northeast: 2 mi on A379

🏠 Cary Arms   🖈 ⪕ 🏠 🅿

INN · UNIQUE Built into the cliffside, this inn is wonderfully located and has great views out to sea. Sumptuous, well-equipped bedrooms have a New England style and include garden suites and duplex beach huts. There's a nautically-themed residents' lounge, a characterful bar and a terrace reaching down to the shore.

12 rooms 🖙 – ♦£195/295 ♦♦£295/450

Babbacombe Beach ✉ TQ1 3LX – East : 0.25 mi by Beach Rd. – 𝒞 01803 327110 *- www.caryarms.co.uk*

TOTNES

Devon – Pop. 8 076 – Regional map n° **1**-C2

▶ London 224 mi – Exeter 24 mi – Plymouth 23 mi – Torquay 9 mi

🏠 Royal Seven Stars   🖈 🍴 🅿

HISTORIC · PERSONALISED Centrally located, 17C coaching inn; the characterful glass-roofed, flag-floored reception was once the carriage entrance. Smart colonial-style lounge. Well-equipped, individually designed bedrooms mix the old and the new; some have jacuzzi baths. Snacks in the bars or on the terrace; brasserie dishes in TQ9.

21 rooms 🖙 – ♦£91/120 ♦♦£125/156

The Plains ✉ TQ9 5DD – 𝒞 01803 862125 – www.royalsevenstars.co.uk

TOWCESTER

Northamptonshire – Pop. 9 057 – Regional map n° **9**-B3

▶ London 70 mi – Birmingham 50 mi – Northampton 9 mi – Oxford 36 mi

✗✗ Vine House ⇦ ⇔ 🅿

MODERN CUISINE · INTIMATE A pair of pretty stone cottages in this tranquil village: dating from the 17C and home to a passionately run restaurant decorated with foodie photos. Daily changing, fixed price menu of accomplished modern dishes, deftly made using good quality ingredients. Cosy beamed bedrooms are named after grape vines.

Menu £ 33

6 rooms ☲ – ♦£ 69/85 ♦♦£ 95/110

100 High St, Paulerspury ⊠ NN12 7NA – Southeast : 4 mi by A 5 – ℰ 01327 811267 (booking advisable) – www.vinehousehotel.com – Closed 1 week January, Sunday and lunch Monday

TREBURLEY

Cornwall – Pop. 252 – Regional map n° **1**-B2

▶ London 359 mi – Truro 83 mi – Plymouth 35 mi

🏚 Springer Spaniel 🍴 🅿

MODERN CUISINE · PUB Unassuming-looking roadside pub in a small hamlet, where three cosy rooms are filled with scrubbed wooden tables. It might feel like your village local but, when it comes to the food, expect bold flavours and colourful combinations.

Menu £ 20 (weekdays) – Carte £ 20/43

⊠ PL15 9NS – ℰ 01579 370424 – www.thespringerspaniel.org.uk – Closed Monday

TREGONY

Cornwall – Pop. 768 – Regional map n° **1**-B3

▶ London 416 mi – Truro 14 mi – Plymouth 78 mi

🏠 Hay Barton ⇔ ✗ ✗ 🅿 ⇎

COUNTRY HOUSE · COSY The owner has lived in this warm, cosy farmhouse since the 1960s and still keeps some cattle. Country-style bedrooms come with Roberts radios and plenty to read; two antique bath tubs. Cornish produce features at breakfast.

3 rooms ☲ – ♦£ 65/75 ♦♦£ 85/95

⊠ TR2 5TF – South : 1 mi on A 3078 – ℰ 01872 530288 – www.haybarton.com

TRELOWARREN – Cornwall ➜ See Helston

TRENT

Dorset – Regional map n° **2**-C3

▶ London 128 mi – Southampton 67 mi – Bristol 39 mi – Bournemouth 46 mi

🏚 Rose & Crown ⇦ ⇔ 🍴 & 🔄 🅿

MODERN CUISINE · RUSTIC Sit in the characterful 'Buffs Bar' or the bright conservatory of this part-thatched 14C pub. Tasty country cooking is the order of the day – bypass the pub classics and go for the likes of pig's head with apple purée or calves' liver with sage fritters. Bedrooms come with patios overlooking the countryside.

Carte £ 24/39

3 rooms ☲ – ♦£ 65/105 ♦♦£ 75/125

⊠ DT9 4SL – ℰ 01935 850776 – www.theroseandcrowntrent.co.uk – Closed 25-26 December

TRESCO → See Scilly (Isles of)

TRISCOMBE
Somerset – Regional map n° **2**-B2

▶ London 163 mi – Bristol 50 mi – Swansea 116 mi – Exeter 42 mi

🍴 Blue Ball Inn   ⇦ 🍴 🏠 ♿ 🅿

MODERN CUISINE · RUSTIC Characterful 15C barn in the Quantock Hills, with exposed rafters, open fires and a lovely tiered garden. Lunchtime sandwiches and pub classics provide fuel for passing walkers, while dinner offers original, modern dishes. A pretty thatched cottage houses comfy bedrooms named 'Pheasant', 'Hind' and 'Stag'.

Carte £ 23/35

3 rooms ☑ – ♦£ 65/75 ♦♦£ 75/95

✉ TA4 3HE – ☎ 01984 618242 – www.blueballinn.info – Closed 25 December, dinner 1 January and Sunday dinner

TRURO
Cornwall – Pop. 20 332 – Regional map n° **1**-B3

▶ London 295 mi – Exeter 87 mi – Penzance 26 mi – Plymouth 52 mi

🏨 Mannings   ⇪ ♿ ⅏ 🅿

BUSINESS · MODERN Imposing hotel located in the city centre, close to the cathedral. Boutique bedrooms are bright, modern and stylish; spacious apartment-style rooms – in the neighbouring mews – boast over-sized beds and galley kitchens. There's a chic cocktail bar and a stylish restaurant offering an eclectic all-day menu.

42 rooms ☑ – ♦£ 80/135 ♦♦£ 105/135

Lemon St ✉ TR1 2QB – ☎ 01872 270345 – www.manningshotels.co.uk – Closed Christmas

✗✗ Tabb's

MODERN BRITISH · NEIGHBOURHOOD A series of lilac-painted rooms with matching chairs, in a small former pub. The appealing menu lists refined, classically based dishes where good quality produce shines through. Tasty tapas-style lunches offer three dishes for £ 12.

Menu £ 25 – Carte £ 31/39

85 Kenwyn St ✉ TR1 3BZ – ☎ 01872 262110 (booking essential at lunch) – www.tabbs.co.uk – Closed 1 week January, 1 week October, Saturday lunch, Sunday dinner and Monday

✗ Saffron   ♿ 🗐

TRADITIONAL CUISINE · RUSTIC Smart rustic restaurant in the city's heart, run by a charming owner. There's a snug bar to the front, a lovely open room behind and pots of fresh flowers throughout. A blackboard lists what's in season, which is reflected on the menu.

Menu £ 13 (weekday lunch)/20 – Carte £ 25/35

5 Quay St ✉ TR1 2HB – ☎ 01872 263771 – www.saffronrestauranttruro.co.uk – Closed 25-26 December, Monday dinner January-April, Sunday and bank holidays

TUDDENHAM
Suffolk – Pop. 400 – Regional map n° **8**-B2

▶ London 76 mi – Birmingham 120 mi – Sheffield 152 mi – Croydon 96 mi

✗✗ Tuddenham Mill   ⇦ 🍴 ⇪ 🅿

CREATIVE BRITISH · INTIMATE Delightful 18C watermill overlooking the millpond; the old workings are still in situ in the stylish bar and there's a beamed restaurant with black furnishings above. Cooking features quality seasonal produce in unusual, innovative combinations. Some of the trendy bedrooms are in attractive outbuildings.

Menu £ 20 (weekdays)/50 – Carte dinner £ 35/48

15 rooms ☑ – ♦£ 185/395 ♦♦£ 185/395

High St ✉ IP28 6SQ – ☎ 01638 713552 – www.tuddenhammill.co.uk

TURNERS HILL

West Sussex – Pop. 885 – Regional map n° **4**-D2

▶ London 33 mi – Brighton 24 mi – Crawley 7 mi

🏠🏠🏠 Alexander House

COUNTRY HOUSE · ELEGANT A stunning 18C country house in extensive grounds – once owned by Percy Shelley's family. The superb spa has 21 treatment rooms and a Grecian pool. Spacious bedrooms are well-equipped; the contemporary Cedar Lodge Suites have mood lighting and either a balcony or terrace. Dine in the brasserie or formal AG's.

58 rooms – ♦£ 145/695 ♦♦£ 145/695 – ☲£ 15 – 3 suites

East St ⊠ RH10 4QD – East : 1 mi on B 2110 – ℰ 01342 714914
– www.alexanderhouse.co.uk

AG's – See restaurant listing

XXX AG's

MODERN CUISINE · CHIC Have drinks in the champagne bar before dinner by the marble fireplace in the formal restaurant of this fabulous 18C country house. Cooking follows the seasons and presentation and flavour combinations are modern and original.

Menu £ 50

Alexander House Hotel, East St ⊠ RH10 4QD – East : 1 mi on B 2110
– ℰ 01342 714914 (booking essential) – www.alexanderhouse.co.uk – dinner only and Sunday lunch

TWO BRIDGES

Devon – ⊠ Yelverton – Regional map n° **1**-C2

▶ London 226 mi – Exeter 25 mi – Plymouth 17 mi

🏠🏠 Prince Hall

TRADITIONAL · COSY Remote former hunting lodge with a welcoming, shabby-chic interior and wide-ranging views. Dogs are welcome throughout, except in the bright restaurant, where you'll find vibrantly flavoured dishes with Mediterranean influences. Homely bedrooms display subtle modern touches; some overlook the moor.

8 rooms ☲ – ♦£ 150/170 ♦♦£ 170/190

⊠ PL20 6SA – East : 1 mi on B 3357 – ℰ 01822 890403 – www.princehall.co.uk

TYNEMOUTH

Tyne and Wear – Pop. 67 519 – Regional map n° **14**-B2

▶ London 290 mi – Newcastle upon Tyne 8 mi – Sunderland 7 mi

🏠🏠 Grand

TRADITIONAL · CLASSIC A Victorian hotel with superb sea views: the Duchess of Northumberland's one-time holiday home. Original features include an impressive staircase. Bedrooms are either traditionally styled and spacious or smaller and more modern; 222 has a four-poster and jacuzzi. Classical dining room with a menu to match.

46 rooms ☲ – ♦£ 69/170 ♦♦£ 79/205

14 Grand Par. ⊠ NE30 4ER – ℰ 0191 293 6666 – www.grandhotel-uk.com

🏠 Martineau

TOWNHOUSE · GRAND LUXURY Attractive 18C red brick house named after Harriet Martineau. Cosy, individually furnished bedrooms come with thoughtful extras; two offer pleasant Tyne views. Superb communal breakfasts or a pre-ordered hamper in your room.

4 rooms ☲ – ♦£ 80 ♦♦£ 100

57 Front St ⊠ NE30 4BX – ℰ 0191 257 9038 – www.martineau-house.co.uk
– Closed 23-29 December

UCKFIELD

East Sussex – Pop. 15 213 – Regional map n° **5**-A2

▶ London 45 mi – Brighton 17 mi – Eastbourne 20 mi – Maidstone 34 mi

🏠 Horsted Place   🐦 🦆 ⟨ 🛏 🖼 🛋 ✖ 🖥 🧖 🦺 🅿

HISTORIC · CLASSIC Impressive country house in Victorian Gothic style. The tiled entrance hall leads to an impressive main gallery, where ornate sitting rooms are furnished with fine antiques. Individually styled bedrooms are well-equipped; most have great views over the parkland. The formal dining room offers a classical menu.

20 rooms ⌑ – 🛉£ 145/375 🛉🛉£ 145/375 – 5 suites

Little Horsted ✉ *TN22 5TS – South : 2.5 mi by B 2102 and A 22 on A 26 – ☎ 01825 750581 – www.horstedplace.co.uk – Closed first week January*

UFFORD

Suffolk – Regional map n° **8**-D3

▶ London 92 mi – Ipswich 12 mi – Colchester 31 mi

🏠 Ufford Crown   🛏 🛋 🅿

TRADITIONAL BRITISH · FRIENDLY A welcoming former coaching inn run by an enthusiastic husband and wife team. The daily menu of hearty, honest cooking includes a great grill section and some Mediterranean-inspired dishes. Portions are generous and service is keen.

Carte £ 22/41

High St ✉ *IP13 6EL – ☎ 01394 461030 – www.theuffordcrown.com – Closed Tuesday*

UPPER SLAUGHTER – Gloucestershire → See Bourton-on-the-Water

UPPER SOUTH WRAXALL

Wiltshire – Regional map n° **2**-C2

▶ London 108 mi – Swindon 30 mi – Bath 8 mi

🏠 Longs Arms   🛏 🛋 ⅙ 🅿
🐸

TRADITIONAL BRITISH · PUB Handsome, bay-windowed, Bath stone pub opposite a medieval church in a sleepy village. Traditional British dishes are full-flavoured, hearty and satisfying; everything is homemade and they smoke their own meats and fish. Dine in the characterful area in front of the bar. Warm, friendly service.

Carte £ 17/42

✉ *BA15 2SB – ☎ 01225 864450 (booking essential) – www.thelongsarms.com – Closed 3 weeks January,1 week September, Sunday dinner and Monday*

UPPINGHAM

Rutland – Pop. 4 745 – Regional map n° **9**-C2

▶ London 101 mi – Leicester 19 mi – Northampton 28 mi – Nottingham 35 mi

✕✕ Lake Isle   🐦 🖙 🛋 🄰🄺 ⇆ 🅿

CLASSIC CUISINE · FRIENDLY Characterful 18C town centre property accessed via a narrow passageway and very personally run by experienced owners. It has a cosy lounge and a heavy wood-furnished dining room. Light lunches are followed by much more elaborate modern dinners. Bedrooms come with good extras and some have whirlpool baths.

Carte £ 27/45

12 rooms ⌑ – 🛉£ 65/75 🛉🛉£ 90/130

16 High St East ✉ *LE15 9PZ – ☎ 01572 822951 – www.lakeisle.co.uk – Closed Sunday dinner and Monday lunch*

ENGLAND

at Lyddington South: 2 mi by A6003 ⊠ Uppingham

🍴 Marquess of Exeter   ⟨⇔ 🛏 🏠 ⅙ ⇄ Ⓟ

TRADITIONAL BRITISH · PUB Attractive 16C thatched pub with a cosy bar, characterful exposed beams, inglenook fireplaces and a rustic dining room. The daily changing menu offers tasty, classical combinations of local, home-grown and home-reared produce. Comfortable bedrooms are located across the car park.

Menu £ 14 (weekday lunch) – Carte £ 25/39

17 rooms ⌙ – †£ 80/100 ††£ 100/135

52 Main St ⊠ LE15 9LT – ℰ 01572 822477 – www.marquessexeter.co.uk – Closed 25 December

🍴 Old White Hart   ⟨⇔ 🛏 🏠 ⅙ Ⓟ

TRADITIONAL CUISINE · PUB This pub offers all you'd expect from a traditional 17C coaching inn – and a lot more besides. It's got the chocolate box village setting, the open fires and the seasonal menu of hearty, classic dishes; but also gives you a relaxing ambience, charming service, a 10-piste petanque pitch and stylish bedrooms.

Carte £ 12/37

10 rooms ⌙ – †£ 75/85 ††£ 100/110

51 Main St ⊠ LE15 9LR – ℰ 01572 821703 – www.oldwhitehart.co.uk – Closed 25 December and Sunday dinner in winter

UPTON BISHOP – Herefordshire → See Ross-on-Wye

UPTON GREY
Hampshire – Pop. 449 – Regional map n° **6**-B1
▶ London 50 mi – Winchester 25 mi – Southampton 37 mi

🍴 Hoddington Arms ⓝ   🛏 🏠 ⅙ Ⓟ

TRADITIONAL BRITISH · RUSTIC Sit in the lovely garden, the smart cabana or the characterful, laid-back pub – the restored barn area is particularly atmospheric. Lunch offers pub classics while dinner sees the likes of venison scotch egg or braised lamb shoulder.

Carte £ 24/42

Bidden Rd ⊠ RG25 2RL – ℰ 01256 862371 – www.hoddingtonarms.co.uk – Closed 26 December, 1 January and Sunday dinner

UPTON MAGNA – Shropshire → See Shrewsbury

VENTNOR – Isle of Wight → See Wight (Isle of)

VERYAN
Cornwall – ⊠ Truro – Pop. 877 – Regional map n° **1**-B3
▶ London 291 mi – St Austell 13 mi – Truro 13 mi

🏚 Nare   🏹 🐕 ⟨ 🛏 ⅄ 🗖 🏠 ᒪᚴ 🍽 🖵 Ⓟ

COUNTRY HOUSE · CLASSIC Personally run, classic country house with a stunning bay outlook; take it in from the pool or hot tub. Most bedrooms have views and some have patios or balconies. Have afternoon tea in the drawing room followed by canapés in the bar, then choose from either a traditional daily menu in the dining room or more modern fare in Quarterdeck.

37 rooms ⌙ – †£ 150/290 ††£ 290/835 – 7 suites

Carne Beach ⊠ TR2 5PF – Southwest : 1.25 mi – ℰ 01872 501111 – www.narehotel.co.uk

VIRGINSTOW
Devon – Regional map n° **1**-C2
▶ London 227 mi – Bideford 25 mi – Exeter 41 mi – Launceston 11 mi

🏠 Percy's   🕸 🐾 < 🍴 🏠 **P**

TRADITIONAL · COSY Stone house in 130 acres of fields and woodland. The owners grow veg, breed racehorses, rear pigs and sheep, and sell wool, skins and produce. Spacious, comfy bedrooms in the former barn – some have jacuzzi baths. Set menu of traditional dishes in the formal dining room; ingredients are from the estate.

7 rooms ♑ – ♦£ 150/230 ♦♦£ 150/230

Coombeshead Estate ⊠ EX21 5EA – Southwest : 1.75 mi on Tower Hill rd
– 🕾 01409 211236 – www.percys.co.uk

WADDESDON

Buckinghamshire – ⊠ Aylesbury – Pop. 1 797 – Regional map n° **6**-C2
▶ London 51 mi – Aylesbury 5 mi – Northampton 32 mi – Oxford 31 mi

🍴🍴 Five Arrows   < 🍴 🏠 ⇔ **P**

TRADITIONAL BRITISH · INN A half-timbered house on the Rothschild Estate, with Elizabethan chimney stacks, attractive gabling and mullioned windows (its name is derived from the Rothschild family emblem). Contemporary country house bedrooms are split between the main house and the courtyard. Local game is a highlight in the restaurant.

Menu £ 16 (weekday lunch) – Carte £ 29/45

16 rooms ♑ – ♦£ 69/105 ♦♦£ 89/235

High St ⊠ HP18 0JE – 🕾 01296 651727 – www.waddesdon.org.uk/fivearrows

WADDINGTON

Lancashire – Pop. 3 992 – Regional map n° **20**-B2
▶ London 237 mi – Lancaster 24 mi – Manchester 36 mi

🍴 Higher Buck 🆕   < 🏠 & **P**

TRADITIONAL CUISINE · FRIENDLY A smartly refurbished pub with pastel-painted wood panelling and modern furnishings, in a lovely Ribble Valley village. Bag a spot at one of the U-shaped banquettes or on the sunny terrace overlooking the Square and dine on reassuringly robust, seasonal dishes. Service is friendly and stylish bedrooms await.

Carte £ 22/42

7 rooms ♑ – ♦£ 65/115 ♦♦£ 90/115

The Square ⊠ BB7 3HZ – 🕾 01200 423226 – www.higherbuck.com – Closed 25 December

WADEBRIDGE

Cornwall – Pop. 6 599 – Regional map n° **1**-B2
▶ London 245 mi – Truro 26 mi – Newquay 19 mi

🏠 Trewornan Manor 🆕   🕸 < 🍴 🍴 🌿 **P**

COUNTRY HOUSE · ELEGANT Stunning Grade II listed 13C manor house set in 25 acres beside the River Amble, with over 8 acres of delightfully manicured gardens. Sumptuous, ultra-chic bedrooms all have views of the grounds. Welcoming young owners offer cream tea by the fire in the restful sitting room and fresh home-cooked breakfasts.

5 rooms ♑ – ♦£ 110/170 ♦♦£ 120/190

Trewornan Bridge, St Minver ⊠ PL27 6EX – North : 1.75 mi on B3314 (Rock rd)
– 🕾 01208 812359 – www.trewornanmanor.co.uk

🍴 Ship Inn   🏠

TRADITIONAL CUISINE · COSY This 16C inn is one of the oldest public houses in town and has a real community feel. The menu offers something for everyone, mixing pub classics with more modern dishes. Choose a seat in one of the three cosy, low-beamed rooms.

Carte £ 21/33

Gonvena Hill ⊠ PL27 6DF – 🕾 01208 813845 – www.shipinnwadebridge.com
– Closed Sunday dinner in winter.

WALBERSWICK
Suffolk – Pop. 380 – Regional map n° **8**-D2
▶ London 115 mi – Norwich 31 mi – Ipswich 31 mi – Lowestoft 16 mi

⌂ Anchor   ⊞ ⇦ 🛏 🛏 � 🅿

TRADITIONAL CUISINE · PUB Welcoming, relaxing pub in an Arts and Crafts building; its sizeable garden features a wood-fired oven and seaward views. Global flavours feature alongside British classics – try some of their home-baked bread. If you're staying the night, choose a wood-clad chalet in the garden. Breakfasts are impressive.
Menu £ 12 (weekday lunch) – Carte £ 23/35
10 rooms ⌂ – †£ 95/125 ††£ 100/160
Main St ✉ *IP18 6UA* – ℰ *01502 722112* – *www.anchoratwalberswick.com* – *Closed 25 December*

WALFORD – Herefordshire ➜ See Ross-on-Wye

WALL – Staffordshire ➜ See Lichfield

WAREHAM
Dorset – Pop. 5 496 – Regional map n° **2**-C3
▶ London 123 mi – Bournemouth 13 mi – Weymouth 19 mi

🏠 Priory   ⇗ ⅗ ≼ 🛏 🛏 ⅗ 🅿

HISTORIC BUILDING · CLASSIC Delightfully located part-16C priory, which is proudly and personally run. Have afternoon tea on the terrace, overlooking the beautifully manicured gardens and on towards the river – here, peace and tranquility reign. The country house inspired bedrooms are charming; those in the 'Boathouse' are the most luxurious. Dress smartly for dinner in the formal candlelit cellar.
18 rooms ⌂ – †£ 176/304 ††£ 220/380 – 2 suites
Church Grn ✉ *BH20 4ND* – ℰ *01929 551666* – *www.theprioryhotel.co.uk*

🏠 Gold Court House   🛏 ⅗ 🅿

HISTORIC BUILDING · CLASSIC Charmingly run Georgian house in a small square off the high street; which stands on the foundations of a 13C goldsmith's house. It has a fire-lit lounge, a lovely breakfast room with garden views and traditional, restful bedrooms.
3 rooms ⌂ – †£ 70 ††£ 85
St John's Hill ✉ *BH20 4LZ* – ℰ *01929 553320* – *www.goldcourthouse.co.uk* – *Closed 25 December-2 January*

WAREN MILL – Northumberland ➜ See Bamburgh

WARKWORTH
Northumberland – Regional map n° **14**-B2
▶ London 316 mi – Alnwick 7 mi – Morpeth 24 mi

🏠 Roxbro House   🅿

TOWNHOUSE · GRAND LUXURY 'Elegant' and 'opulent' are suitable adjectives to describe these two houses in the shadow of Warkworth Castle, where boutique bedrooms mix modern facilities with antique furniture. Choose between two comfy lounges – one with an honesty bar; tasty breakfasts are served in a conservatory-style room.
6 rooms ⌂ – †£ 65/99 ††£ 65/140
5 Castle Terr ✉ *NE65 0UP* – ℰ *01665 711416* – *www.roxbrohouse.co.uk* – *Closed 24-28 December*

WARMINGHAM
Cheshire East – Regional map n° **11**-B3
▶ London 174 mi – Birmingham 61 mi – Manchester 33 mi – Bristol 143 mi

🍺 Bear's Paw

TRADITIONAL BRITISH · INN Handsome 19C inn with a spacious, wood-panelled bar and a huge array of local ales. The menu will please all appetites, with everything from nibbles, salads and deli boards to European dishes, pub favourites and steaks you can cook yourself on a hot stone. Stylish, good value bedrooms.

Carte £ 20/41

17 rooms ⌂ – ♦£ 105/135 ♦♦£ 115/145

School Ln ⌂ CW11 3QN – ℘ 01270 526317 – www.thebearspaw.co.uk

WARMINSTER

Wiltshire – Pop. 17 490 – Regional map n° **2**-C2

▶ London 111 mi – Bristol 29 mi – Exeter 74 mi – Southampton 47 mi

🍺 Weymouth Arms

TRADITIONAL BRITISH · NEIGHBOURHOOD Grade II listed building with plenty of history. It's immensely characterful, with wood panelling, antiques and lithographs, as well as two fireplaces originally intended for nearby Longleat House. Cooking is fresh and fittingly traditional. Cosy bedrooms have charming original fittings.

Carte £ 21/45

6 rooms ⌂ – ♦£ 70/90 ♦♦£ 80/95

12 Emwell St ⌂ BA12 8JA – ℘ 01985 216995 – www.weymoutharms.co.uk – Closed Monday-Wednesday lunch

at Crockerton South: 2 mi by A350

🍺 Bath Arms

TRADITIONAL BRITISH · RUSTIC This down-to-earth pub was once part of the Longleat Estate. The daily menu features snacks, grills and classic pub dishes, along with a selection of specials; try the legendary sticky beef with braised red cabbage. The two ultra-spacious, contemporary bedrooms are amusingly named 'Left' and 'Right'.

Carte £ 24/33

2 rooms ⌂ – ♦£ 80/110 ♦♦£ 80/110

Clay St ⌂ BA12 8AJ – On Shearwater rd – ℘ 01985 212262
– www.batharmscrockerton.co.uk – Closed Sunday dinner in winter

WARTLING – East Sussex ➜ See Herstmonceux

WARWICK

Warwickshire – Pop. 31 345 – Regional map n° **10**-C3

▶ London 96 mi – Birmingham 20 mi – Coventry 11 mi – Leicester 34 mi

🍴 Tailors

MODERN CUISINE · INTIMATE As well as a tailor's, this intimate restaurant was once a fishmonger's, a butcher's and a casino! It's run by two ambitious chefs, who offer good value modern lunches, and elaborate dinners which feature unusual flavour combinations.

Menu £ 18 (lunch)/40

22 Market Pl ⌂ CV34 4SL – ℘ 01926 410590 – www.tailorsrestaurant.co.uk
– Closed Christmas, Sunday and Monday

WATCHET

Somerset – Pop. 3 581 – Regional map n° **2**-B2

▶ London 174 mi – Bristol 60 mi – Exeter 49 mi – Cardiff 86 mi

🏠 Swain House

TOWNHOUSE · PERSONALISED In the characterful high street of this coastal town, you'll find this super smart guesthouse with spacious bedrooms and a sleek yet cosy feel. Parts of famous paintings make up feature walls and all have roll-top baths and rain showers.

4 rooms ⌂ – ♦£ 115 ♦♦£ 135

48 Swain St ⌂ TA23 0AG – ℘ 01984 631038 – www.swain-house.com

WATERGATE BAY – Cornwall → See Newquay

WATERMILLOCK – Cumbria → See Pooley Bridge

WATFORD
Hertfordshire – Pop. 131 982 – Regional map n° **7**-A2
▶ London 20 mi – Hertford 36 mi – Luton 32 mi

🏨🏨🏨 Grove

BUSINESS · MODERN An impressive Grade II listed country house in 300 acres, with elegant lounges and smart, contemporary bedrooms – some with balconies. There's a superb spa and an outdoor pool, as well as tennis, croquet, golf and volleyball facilities. Fine dining in Colette's; casual meals in Stables; buffets in Glasshouse.

214 rooms 🖙 – 🛉£ 260/545 🛉🛉£ 285/570 – 6 suites

Chandler's Cross ✉ *WD3 4TG – Northwest : 2 mi on A 411 – ℰ 01923 807807
– www.thegrove.co.uk*

Colette's · Stables – See restaurant listing

🍴🍴🍴 Colette's

MODERN CUISINE · DESIGN A sleek, contemporary hotel restaurant with high ceilings and large windows overlooking the grounds. Complex modern dishes feature imaginative combinations; choose between set 5 and 8 course menus.

Menu £ 75/85

Grove Hotel, Chandler's Cross ✉ *WD3 4TG – Northwest : 2 mi on A 411
– ℰ 01923 296015 – www.thegrove.co.uk – dinner only – Closed Sunday-Monday
except Sunday dinner on bank holidays*

🍴🍴 Stables

INTERNATIONAL · RUSTIC Informal, New England style restaurant in the clubhouse of an impressive Grade II listed country house. It boasts its own sports bar, has pleasant views over the golf course and offers a gutsy British menu with plenty of grills.

Carte £ 27/44

Grove Hotel, Chandler's Cross ✉ *WD3 4TG – Northwest : 2 mi on A 411
– ℰ 01923 296010 – www.thegrove.co.uk*

WATLINGTON
Oxfordshire – Pop. 2 139 – Regional map n° **6**-C2
▶ London 45 mi – Birmingham 89 mi – Bristol 88 mi – Sheffield 153 mi

🍴 Fat Fox Inn

TRADITIONAL BRITISH · COSY In the heart of a busy market village; a 19C pub run with honesty and integrity by experienced owners. The menu reflects what they themselves like to eat, covering all bases from potted mackerel to pheasant pie. Fight the cats for a seat by the wood burning range, then settle in to one of the cosy bedrooms.

Carte £ 25/35

9 rooms 🖙 – 🛉£ 65/109 🛉🛉£ 75/119

13 Shireburn St ✉ *OX49 5BU – ℰ 01491 613040 – www.thefatfoxinn.co.uk – Closed
dinner 25 December and 1 January*

WATTON
Norfolk – Pop. 7 435 – Regional map n° **8**-C2
▶ London 95 mi – Norwich 22 mi – Swaffham 10 mi

🍴🍴 Café at Brovey Lair

SEAFOOD · INTIMATE Dining here has more of a dinner party atmosphere than a restaurant feel. The spacious conservatory has an open kitchen with stool seating and a teppan-yaki grill. The no-choice set menu revolves around seafood and Asian flavours. Well-appointed bedrooms are situated beside the pool in lovely gardens.

Menu £ 53

3 rooms 🖙 – 🛉£ 105 🛉🛉£ 120

Carbrooke Rd., Ovington ✉ *IP25 6SD – Northeast : 1.75 mi by A 1075
– ℰ 01953 882706 – www.broveylair.com – Closed 25 December and 1 January*

WEDMORE
Somerset – Pop. 1 409 – Regional map n° **2**-B2
▶ London 155 mi – Bristol 23 mi – Cardiff 67 mi – Plymouth 100 mi

Swan
TRADITIONAL BRITISH · INN Spacious 18C coaching inn with a buzzy bar, a comfy restaurant and an open-plan kitchen with an appealing display of freshly baked breads linking the two. Good quality British ingredients match the seasons and daily changing dishes are unfussy and flavoursome. Stylish bedrooms complete the picture.
Carte £ 23/39
7 rooms ☑ – ♦£ 85/125 ♦♦£ 85/125
Cheddar Rd ✉ *BS28 4EQ – ☏ 01934 710337 (booking essential)*
– www.theswanwedmore.com – Closed 25 December

WELBURN
North Yorkshire – Regional map n° **13**-C2
▶ London 225 mi – Leeds 40 mi – York 14 mi

Crown and Cushion
CLASSIC CUISINE · FRIENDLY Well run 18C pub two miles from Castle Howard. The menu champions local meats and the kitchen's pride and joy is its charcoal-fired rotis-serie. Dishes are hearty, sandwiches are doorstops, and puddings are of the nursery variety.
Carte £ 25/43
✉ *YO60 7DZ – ☏ 01653 618777 – www.thecrownandcushionwelburn.com*

WELLAND – Worcestershire ➜ See Great Malvern

WELLINGHAM
Norfolk – Regional map n° **8**-C1
▶ London 120 mi – King's Lynn 29 mi – Norwich 28 mi

Manor House Farm
WORKING FARM · CLASSIC Attractive, wisteria-clad farmhouse with large gardens, set by a church in a beautifully peaceful spot. Spacious, airy bedrooms are located in the former stables. Home-grown and home-reared produce is served at breakfast.
3 rooms ☑ – ♦£ 70/75 ♦♦£ 120/130
✉ *PE32 2TH – ☏ 01328 838227 – www.manor-house-farm.co.uk*

WELLS
Somerset – Pop. 10 536 – Regional map n° **2**-C2
▶ London 132 mi – Bristol 20 mi – Southampton 68 mi – Taunton 28 mi

Swan
INN · ELEGANT 15C former coaching inn with a good outlook onto the famous cathedral; its charming interior has subtle contemporary touches, particularly in the lounge and bar. Comfortable, stylish, well-equipped bedrooms and an opulent 'Cathedral Suite'. The formal, wood-panelled restaurant serves classic dishes.
48 rooms ☑ – ♦£ 82/114 ♦♦£ 116/500 – 1 suite
11 Sadler St ✉ *BA5 2RX – ☏ 01749 836300 – www.swanhotelwells.co.uk*

Beryl
COUNTRY HOUSE · CLASSIC A fine 19C country house in 13 acres of mature gardens, complete with a pond and a swimming pool. The delightful drawing rooms are packed with antiques and curios from the owner's travels. Go for one of the four-poster bedrooms.
13 rooms ☑ – ♦£ 75/95 ♦♦£ 100/160
✉ *BA5 3JP – East : 1.25 mi by B 3139 off Hawkers Lane – ☏ 01749 678738*
– www.beryl-wells.co.uk – Closed 23-30 December

🏠 Stoberry House

TRADITIONAL · PERSONALISED 18C coach house with a delightful walled garden, overlooking Glastonbury Tor. Large lounge with a baby grand piano and antique furniture. Breakfast is an event, with 7 homemade breads, a porridge menu and lots of cooked dishes. Immaculately kept bedrooms come with fresh flowers, chocolates and a pillow menu.

5 rooms ⌂ - 🛏£ 75/110 🛏🛏£ 95/155

Stoberry Park ✉ BA5 3LD - Northeast : 0.5 mi by A 39 on College Rd
- ☏ 01749 672906 - www.stoberryhouse.co.uk
- Closed Christmas and New Year.

WELLS-NEXT-THE-SEA

Norfolk - Pop. 2 165 - Regional map n° **8**-C1
▶ London 122 mi - Cromer 22 mi - Norwich 38 mi

🏠 Crown

INN · MODERN Characterful 16C former coaching inn located in the centre of town, overlooking the green. Individually styled bedrooms blend classical furniture with more modern décor and facilities. Dine from an accessible menu in the charming bar, orangery or dining room.

17 rooms ⌂ - 🛏£ 80/240 🛏🛏£ 100/260

The Buttlands ✉ NR23 1EX - ☏ 01328 710209
- www.flyingkiwiinns.co.uk

at Wighton Southeast: 2.5 mi by A149

🏠 Meadowview

FAMILY · MODERN Set in the centre of a peaceful village, this smart, modern guesthouse is the perfect place to unwind, as its neat garden boasts a hot tub and a comfy seating area overlooking a meadow. Breakfast is cooked on the Aga in the country kitchen.

5 rooms ⌂ - 🛏£ 100/120 🛏🛏£ 100/120

53 High St ✉ NR23 1PF - ☏ 01328 821527 - www.meadow-view.net

WELWYN

Hertfordshire - Pop. 3 497 - Regional map n° **7**-B2
▶ London 31 mi - Bedford 31 mi - Cambridge 31 mi

🏠 Tewin Bury Farm

BUSINESS · GRAND LUXURY A collection of converted farm buildings on a 400 acre working farm, next to a nature reserve. Rustic interior with comfy oak-furnished bedrooms in various wings. The function room is in an impressive tithe barn beside the old mill race.

36 rooms ⌂ - 🛏£ 124/164 🛏🛏£ 139/179

✉ AL6 0JB - Southeast : 3.5 mi by A 1000 on B 1000 - ☏ 01438 717793
- www.tewinbury.co.uk
Williams' - See restaurant listing

✕ Williams'

MODERN BRITISH · RUSTIC A characterful, rustic hotel restaurant in an old timber chicken shed on a working farm; black and white photos of farm life adorn the walls. Fresh, well-executed, modern dishes are pleasing to the eye as well as the taste buds.

Menu £ 17 (weekday lunch)/35 - Carte £ 25/40

Tewin Bury Farm Hotel, ✉ AL6 0JB - Southeast : 3.5 mi by A 1000 on B 1000
- ☏ 01438 717793 - www.tewinbury.co.uk

at Ayot Green Southwest: 2.5 mi by B 197

🏠 Waggoners   🍴 🛋 🅿

FRENCH · PUB A delightful 17C pub on the edge of the Brocket Hall Estate, with a welcoming owner, a charming young team and a pleasant, buzzy atmosphere. Choose from unfussy pub dishes or a more ambitious French-based à la carte.

Menu £ 15 (weekday lunch)/26 – Carte £ 25/53

Brickwall Cl ⊠ AL6 9AA – ℰ 01707 324241 (booking advisable)
– www.thewaggoners.co.uk – Closed Sunday dinner

WENTBRIDGE

West Yorkshire – ⊠ Pontefract – Regional map n° **13**-B3
▶ London 183 mi – Leeds 19 mi – Nottingham 55 mi – Sheffield 28 mi

🏨 Wentbridge House   🍴 🍴 🛋 🅱 ♨ 🅿

COUNTRY HOUSE · GRAND LUXURY Personally run, bay-windowed house, dating back to the 19C and surrounded by 20 acres of immaculate gardens. Bedrooms are a mix of characterful, wood-panelled period styles and spacious modern designs with up-to-date facilities. Classical menu in the formal restaurant; more modern dishes in the smart brasserie.

41 rooms ☲ – ♦£ 85/105 ♦♦£ 115/135

Old Great North Rd. ⊠ WF8 3JJ – ℰ 01977 620444
– www.wentbridgehouse.co.uk

WEST ASHLING – West Sussex → See Chicester

WEST BRIDGFORD – Nottinghamshire → See Nottingham

WEST BYFLEET

Surrey – Regional map n° **7**-C1
▶ London 32 mi – Epsom 15 mi – Woking 4 mi

XX London House 🆕   🕭 🏧

MODERN BRITISH · FASHIONABLE A pleasant neighbourhood restaurant in a busy parade of shops; where white walls are hung with modern art. Colourful modern dishes take their influences from Britain and the Med. Top quality ingredients include local rare breed pork.

Menu £ 23/39

30 Station Approach ⊠ KT14 6NF – ℰ 01932 482026
– www.restaurantlondonhouse.co.uk – Closed 2 weeks August, 1 week January, Sunday dinner, Monday and Tuesday lunch

WEST DIDSBURY – Greater Manchester → See Manchester

WEST END

Surrey – ⊠ Guildford – Pop. 4 135 – Regional map n° **4**-C1
▶ London 37 mi – Bracknell 7 mi – Camberley 5 mi – Guildford 8 mi

🏠 The Inn West End   🐴 ⇐ 🍴 🛋 🕭 🅿

TRADITIONAL CUISINE · PUB A big-hearted, recently refurbished pub offering genuine hospitality and a lively atmosphere. Wide-ranging menus offer generously proportioned, seasonal dishes with robust flavours and original touches. The wine shop specialises in European wines. Smart boutique bedrooms complete the picture.

Menu £ 16 (weekday lunch)/28 – Carte £ 25/49

12 rooms ☲ – ♦£ 125/150 ♦♦£ 125/150

42 Guildford Rd ⊠ GU24 9PW – on A 322 – ℰ 01276 858652 – www.the-inn.co.uk

WEST HATCH

Wiltshire – Regional map n° **2**-C3
▶ London 104 mi – Swindon 88 mi – Salisbury 28 mi

Pythouse Kitchen Garden, Café and Pantry 🖢 🛋 ⅏ 🖥 P

TRADITIONAL BRITISH · SIMPLE Simple, rustic café in a former potting shed, serving breakfast, coffee, lunch and afternoon tea; order in the well-stocked shop. Tasty, unfussy cooking uses seasonal produce from the charming 18C walled garden. Save room for some cake!

Carte £ 18/28

⊠ SP3 6PA – ℰ 01747 870444 (booking advisable)
– www.pythousekitchengarden.co.uk – lunch only and dinner Friday-Saturday
– Closed 25-26 December and 1 January

WEST HOATHLY

West Sussex – Pop. 709 – Regional map n° **4**-D2
▶ London 36 mi – Bristol 141 mi – Croydon 26 mi – Barnet 78 mi

Cat Inn 🖢 🛋 P

TRADITIONAL BRITISH · COSY Popular with the locals and very much a village pub, with beamed ceilings, pewter tankards, open fires and plenty of cosy corners. Carefully executed, good value cooking focuses on tasty pub classics like locally smoked ham, egg and chips or steak, mushroom and ale pie. Service is friendly and efficient – and four tastefully decorated bedrooms complete the picture.

Carte £ 23/42

4 rooms ⌧ – †£ 95/120 ††£ 125/165

Queen's Sq ⊠ RH19 4PP – ℰ 01342 810369 – www.catinn.co.uk
– Closed 25 December and Sunday dinner

WEST MALLING

Kent – Pop. 2 266 – Regional map n° **5**-B1
▶ London 35 mi – Maidstone 7 mi – Royal Tunbridge Wells 14 mi

Swan 🛞 🛋 ⅏ 🌀

MODERN CUISINE · FASHIONABLE An informal 15C coaching inn where original beams blend with stylish furnishings and there are smart bars both upstairs and downstairs. Modern European menus offer flavoursome combinations (side dishes are required); brunch is a hit.

Menu £ 18 (weekdays)/50 – Carte £ 27/43

35 Swan St. ⊠ ME19 6JU – ℰ 01732 521910 (booking essential)
– www.theswanwestmalling.co.uk – Closed 1 January

WEST MEON

Hampshire – Regional map n° **4**-B2
▶ London 74 mi – Southampton 27 mi – Portsmouth 21 mi – Basingstoke 32 mi

Thomas Lord 🖢 🛋 P

TRADITIONAL CUISINE · PUB A smartly refurbished early 19C pub, named after the founder of Lord's Cricket Ground and decorated with cricketing memorabilia. The atmosphere is warm and welcoming, there's a lovely garden with a wood-burning stove, and the menu perfectly balances the classics with some more adventurous offerings.

Carte £ 28/49

High St ⊠ GU32 1LN – ℰ 01730 829244 – www.thethomaslord.co.uk – Closed 25 December

WEST OVERTON – Wiltshire → See Marlborough

WEST TANFIELD

North Yorkshire – ⊠ Ripon – Pop. 293 – Regional map n° **13**-B2
▶ London 237 mi – Darlington 29 mi – Leeds 32 mi – Middlesbrough 39 mi

⌂ Old Coach House 🛏 🧖 P

TOWNHOUSE · MODERN Smart 18C coach house nestled between the Dales and the Moors. Bedrooms differ in size but all have a bright modern style and are furnished by local craftsmen. The breakfast room overlooks the fountain in the courtyard garden.

8 rooms ⌂ – †£ 65/105 ††£ 85/115

2 Stable Cottage, North Stainley ⌂ HG4 3HT – Southeast : 1 mi on A 6108
– 𝓒 07912 632296 – www.oldcoachhouse.info

WEST WITTERING

West Sussex – Pop. 875 – Regional map n° **4**-C3
▶ London 87 mi – Southampton 38 mi – Brighton and Hove 41 mi

✗ Beach House ⇦ 🏛 🖥 P

TRADITIONAL CUISINE · FRIENDLY It might be 10 minutes' from the beach but the Beach House definitely has a seaside feel, with its large veranda, shuttered windows and scrubbed wooden tables. Tasty breakfasts, coffee and cakes morph into fresh, bistro-style dishes later in the day. Bedrooms are bright and modern with a New England style.

Carte £ 22/41

7 rooms ⌂ – †£ 85/100 ††£ 120/140

Rookwood Rd ⌂ PO20 8LT – 𝓒 01243 514800 (booking advisable)
– www.beachhse.co.uk – Closed 3 weeks January and Monday-Tuesday
November-April

WEST WITTON

North Yorkshire – ⌂ Leyburn – Regional map n° **13**-B1
▶ London 241 mi – Kendal 39 mi – Leeds 60 mi – Newcastle upon Tyne 65 mi

⌂ Wensleydale Heifer ✿ 🏛 🎦 P

TRADITIONAL · PERSONALISED Pretty, whitewashed former pub on the main street of the village. Quirky, themed bedrooms boast quality linen and the latest mod cons. Characterful lounge has a roaring fire. Dine in the fish bar or at clothed tables in the beamed restaurant; cooking has a strong seafood base.

13 rooms ⌂ – †£ 80/140 ††£ 140/240

⌂ DL8 4LS – 𝓒 01969 622322 – www.wensleydaleheifer.co.uk

WESTON-SUB-EDGE – Gloucestershire ➙ See Chipping Campden

WESTONBIRT

Gloucestershire – Regional map n° **2**-C1
▶ London 104 mi – Bristol 24 mi – Cardiff 57 mi – Plymouth 144 mi

🏠 Hare & Hounds ✿ 🛏 🗙 ⚹ 🛁 P

COUNTRY HOUSE · CONTEMPORARY Attractive former farmhouse with lovely gardens, set between Highgrove House and the National Arboretum. The country house style interior features several lounges and a small library; bedrooms blend modern fabrics with period furniture – half are located in the old outbuildings. Formal Beaufort offers classical dishes with a modern edge, while Jack Hare's serves a pub-style menu and real ales.

42 rooms ⌂ – †£ 80/110 ††£ 130/370 – 3 suites

⌂ GL8 8QL – on A 433 – 𝓒 01666 881000 – www.cotswold-inns-hotels.co.uk

WESTFIELD

East Sussex – Pop. 1 509 – Regional map n° **5**-B3
▶ London 66 mi – Brighton 38 mi – Folkestone 45 mi – Maidstone 30 mi

XX **Wild Mushroom**   🖴 **P**

CLASSIC FRENCH · ELEGANT Keenly run restaurant in an old 17C farmhouse, with a contemporary brown and green theme and an intimate conservatory lounge-bar. Classic French menus continually evolve and feature well-presented, tried-and-tested combinations.

Menu £ 23 (weekday lunch) – Carte dinner £ 39/43

Woodgate House, Westfield Ln. ⊠ TN35 4SB – Southwest : 0.5 mi on A 28 – ℰ 01424 751137 (booking essential) – www.webbesrestaurants.co.uk – Closed 2-18 January, 2-10 November 25-27 December, Sunday dinner, Monday and Tuesday

WESTLETON

Suffolk – ⊠ Saxmundham – Pop. 349 – Regional map n° **8**-D2

▶ London 97 mi – Cambridge 72 mi – Ipswich 28 mi – Norwich 31 mi

🍴 **Westleton Crown**   ⇦ 🖴 🍴 & 🛈♥ **P**

MODERN BRITISH · PUB Good-looking, 17C former coaching inn with an appealing terrace and garden, set in a pretty little village. Welcoming beamed bar with open fires; more modern conservatory. Seasonal menu, with special diets well-catered for. Uncluttered bedrooms are named after birds found on the adjacent RSPB nature reserve.

Carte £ 26/39

34 rooms �addedbreakfast – ♦£ 90/100 ♦♦£ 95/215

The Street ⊠ IP17 3AD – ℰ 01728 648777 – www.westletoncrown.co.uk

WESTON-SUPER-MARE

North Somerset – Pop. 83 641 – Regional map n° **2**-B2

▶ London 147 mi – Bristol 24 mi – Taunton 32 mi

XX **Duets**   🅰🅲

TRADITIONAL BRITISH · NEIGHBOURHOOD A husband and wife team duet here, with him in the kitchen and her out front; there's also always a duet dish to share. Carefully prepared classical dishes follow the seasons. It's more modern inside than the exterior suggests.

Menu £ 19 (weekday lunch)/33 – Carte approx. £ 36

103 Upper Bristol Rd. ⊠ BS22 8ND – Northeast : 1.75 mi by Bristol Rd Lower – ℰ 01934 413428 (booking essential at lunch) – www.duets.co.uk – Closed 1 week spring, 1 week summer, 1 week winter, Sunday dinner, Monday and Tuesday

X **Mint and Mustard**   🅰🅲

INDIAN · NEIGHBOURHOOD Modern, friendly restaurant with eye-catching Indian art. The extensive menu includes tandoori dishes from the north, biryanis from Hyderabad and fish dishes from Kerala, where the owner grew up. Herbs and spices are well-balanced.

Carte £ 14/29

45 Oxford St ⊠ BS23 1TN – ℰ 01934 626363 – www.mintandmustard.com – Closed 25 December

X **Cove**   ⇦ 🍴 & 🖳

TRADITIONAL BRITISH · BRASSERIE Every table at Cove has views over the bay to Knightstone Island but, when the weather's good, the terrace is the place to be. Come for coffee and cake, try the good value set menus or visit on a Friday for grill and fish night.

Menu £ 15 (lunch)/20 – Carte £ 20/32

Birnbeck Rd ⊠ BS23 2BX – Northwest : 1.5 mi by A 370 and Knightstone Rd – ℰ 01934 418217 – www.the-cove.co.uk – Closed 25 December

WHALLEY

Lancashire – ⊠ Blackburn – Pop. 3 230 – Regional map n° **11**-B2

▶ London 233 mi – Blackpool 32 mi – Burnley 12 mi – Manchester 28 mi

X **Food by Breda Murphy**   🛋 🐧 **P**

TRADITIONAL CUISINE · NEIGHBOURHOOD Set opposite the station, with a
smart shop selling gadgets and books and a deli counter for cakes, coffee and
takeaway meals. The bright, modern restaurant offers tasty home-cooked
lunches; it's occasionally open for dinner events.

Carte £ 23/34

Abbots Ct, 41 Station Rd ✉ BB7 9RH – ✆ 01254 823446
– www.foodbybredamurphy.com – lunch only – Closed 24 December-7 January,
Sunday and Monday

at Mitton Northwest: 2.5 mi on B6246✉ Whalley

🍴 **Three Fishes**   🛋 🐧 **P**

REGIONAL CUISINE · PUB 'Regional' and 'local' are the buzzwords at this behemoth
of a country pub. Expect shrimps from Morecambe Bay, Ribble Valley beef and Fleetwood fish, with specialities like hotpot and cheese soufflé firmly rooted in the region.

Menu £ 14 (weekdays) – Carte £ 22/47

Mitton Rd ✉ BB7 9PQ – ✆ 01254 826888 – www.thethreefishes.com

WHIMPLE
Devon – Regional map n° **1**-D2
▶ London 166 mi – Bristol 81 mi – Cardiff 112 mi – Plymouth 52 mi

🏠 **Woodhayes Country House**   🦢 🛏 ⌘ **P**

HISTORIC · GRAND LUXURY 18C yellow-washed house with mature grounds, in
a peaceful village. Small comfy lounge, where tea and cake are served on arrival.
Good-sized bedrooms with simple, neutral décor and modern facilities. Order
breakfast the night before.

6 rooms ⌂ – 🛏£ 85/165 🛏🛏£ 85/165

Woodhayes Ln ✉ EX5 2TQ – ✆ 01404 823120 – www.woodhayescountryhouse.co.uk

WHITBY
North Yorkshire – Pop. 13 213 – Regional map n° **13**-C1
▶ London 257 mi – Middlesbrough 31 mi – Scarborough 21 mi – York 45 mi

🏨🏨 **Raithwaite Hall**   🎋 🛏 📺 ⊛ 🐾 🏋 🖃 🐧 🏊 **P**

LUXURY · CONTEMPORARY Modern resort hotel with a smart spa, set in 80 acres of
delightful parkland. Stylish bedrooms are spread about the place: some are in a modern mock-castle, some are in cottages and others are in a house overlooking the lake.
Brace serves a modern menu, while informal Hunters offers brasserie-style dishes.

81 rooms ⌂ – 🛏£ 124/414 🛏🛏£ 135/425

Sandsend Rd ✉ YO21 3ST – West : 2 mi on A 197 – ✆ 01947 661661
– www.raithwaiteestate.com

🏨 **Dillons of Whitby**   🛏 ⌘ **P**

TOWNHOUSE · DESIGN Charming Victorian townhouse built for a sea captain, set opposite the beautiful Pannett Park. Immaculately kept bedrooms are individually themed
and feature Egyptian cotton linens. Extensive breakfasts are something of an event.

5 rooms ⌂ – 🛏£ 75/105 🛏🛏£ 85/130

14 Chubb Hill Rd ✉ YO21 1JU – ✆ 01947 600290 – www.dillonsofwhitby.co.uk

at Sandsend Northwest: 3 mi on A174✉ Whitby

XX **Estbek House**   🐾 🔙

SEAFOOD · FRIENDLY Personally run Regency house close to the beach, with a
lovely front terrace and an elegant dining room. The basement bar overlooks the
kitchen and doubles as a breakfast room. Menus offer unfussy dishes of sustainable wild fish from local waters. Smart bedrooms come with stylish bathrooms.

Carte £ 36/57

5 rooms ⌂ – 🛏£ 90/165 🛏🛏£ 125/200

East Row ✉ YO21 3SU – ✆ 01947 893424 – www.estbekhouse.co.uk – dinner only
– Closed January-9 February

WHITE WALTHAM
Windsor and Maidenhead – Pop. 349 – Regional map n° **6**-C3
▶ London 54 mi – Maidenhead 10 mi – Reading 16 mi

⊓⃞ Beehive ⛱ ⏦ 🅿

CLASSIC CUISINE · PUB A traditional English pub overlooking the cricket pitch, where you'll find local drinkers in the bar and a comfy, light-filled dining room. Eye-catching daily dishes are full of flavour and exhibit a staunch sense of Britishness.

Carte £ 27/45

Waltham Rd ⊠ SL6 3SH – 𝒞 01628 822877 – www.thebeehivewhitewaltham.com – Closed Sunday dinner

WHITEHAVEN
Cumbria – Pop. 23 986 – Regional map n° **12**-A2
▶ London 332 mi – Carlisle 39 mi – Keswick 28 mi – Penrith 47 mi

✗✗ Zest 🅿

MODERN BRITISH · FRIENDLY An unassuming exterior conceals a stylish red-hued room with spotted chairs, stripy booths and a lively atmosphere. The extensive modern menu has an Asian edge and they are known for their excellent selection of Cumbrian steaks.

Carte £ 18/37

Low Rd ⊠ CA28 9HS – South : 0.5 mi on B 5345 (St Bees) – 𝒞 01946 692848 – www.zestwhitehaven.com – dinner only – Closed 25 December, 1 January and Sunday-Tuesday

WHITEWELL
Lancashire – ⊠ Clitheroe – Pop. 5 617 – Regional map n° **11**-B2
▶ London 281 mi – Lancaster 31 mi – Leeds 55 mi – Manchester 41 mi

🏠 Inn at Whitewell ⩤ ⟵ 🅿

INN · PERSONALISED 14C creeper-clad inn, high on the banks of the river, with stunning valley views. Spacious bedrooms are split between the inn and a nearby coach house – some are traditional, with four-posters and antique baths; others more contemporary.

23 rooms �ⷩ – ♦£ 95/210 ♦♦£ 132/260

Forest of Bowland ⊠ BB7 3AT – 𝒞 01200 448222 – www.innatwhitewell.com
Inn at Whitewell – See restaurant listing

✗✗ Inn at Whitewell ⩤ ⟵ ⛱ ⏦ ♿ 🅿

TRADITIONAL BRITISH · CLASSIC DÉCOR 14C inn in the heart of the Trough of Bowland. Antique furniture and a valley view make the bar the most atmospheric place to sit. For a more formal meal, head to the smart dining room. Classic menus of wholesome, regionally inspired dishes.

Carte £ 30/41

Inn at Whitewell, Forest of Bowland ⊠ BB7 3AT – 𝒞 01200 448222 – www.innatwhitewell.com

WHITSTABLE
Kent – Pop. 32 100 – Regional map n° **5**-C1
▶ London 68 mi – Dover 24 mi – Maidstone 37 mi – Margate 12 mi

🏠 Crescent Turner ⛲ ⩤ ⟵ ⊗ 🅿

COUNTRY HOUSE · ELEGANT Smart rural retreat named after the artist, who painted the local landscapes. Their strapline is 'British, Boutique and Unique' and with its bold furnishings, it's exactly that. Take in sea views from the terrace, have a drink in the inviting lounge or make for the conservatory for a modern British dish.

17 rooms �\u14vⷩ – ♦£ 60/130 ♦♦£ 99/150

Wraik Hill ⊠ CT5 3BY – Southwest : 2.75mi by B 2205 off A 290 – 𝒞 01227 263506 – www.crescentturner.co.uk

XX East Coast Dining Room 🛋 🛆 🗚

MODERN CUISINE · NEIGHBOURHOOD Find a spot on the terrace or head inside, where you'll find reupholstered chairs from the 1960s and '70s. Concise, modern menus offer fresh, flavoursome dishes with a subtle Asian slant; the fish dishes are always a popular choice.

Menu £13 (weekday lunch)/22 – Carte £27/38

101 Tankerton Rd ⊠ CT5 2AJ – East : 1 mi on B 2205 – ✆ 01227 281180
– www.eastcoastdiningroom.co.uk – Closed 25 December, 1 January, Sunday dinner, Monday and Tuesday

X JoJo's 🛋 🖻 🗚

MEDITERRANEAN CUISINE · BISTRO Unusually converted from a supermarket, this buzzy coffee shop and restaurant offers good views over the Thames Estuary. The self-taught chef offers a large menu of meze, sharing boards and Mediterranean dishes – the hummus is hit.

Carte £20/35

2 Herne Bay Rd ⊠ CT5 2LQ – East : 1.75 mi by B 2205 – ✆ 01227 274591
– www.jojosrestaurant.co.uk – Closed Sunday dinner-Wednesday

X Whitstable Oyster Company ← 🛋

SEAFOOD · RUSTIC An old seafront oyster warehouse with a rustic interior and a great informal atmosphere. Blackboards list simply prepared seafood dishes; from Sept-Dec try oysters from their own beds – the lower staircase leads to the seedling pool.

Carte £30/59

Royal Native Oyster Stores, Horsebridge ⊠ CT5 1BU – ✆ 01227 276856 (booking essential) – www.whitstableoystercompany.com – Closed 25-26 December and lunch Monday-Thursday November-January

at Seasalter Southwest: 2 mi by B2205⊠ Whitstable

🛏 The Sportsman (Steve Harris) 🛋 🅿
❀❀

MODERN BRITISH · PUB An unassuming-looking pub serving excellent food: dishes feature four or five complementary ingredients and are carefully prepared; flavours are well-judged and presentation is original. The full tasting menu must be booked in advance but the 5 course option can be ordered on arrival.
→ Slip sole grilled in seaweed butter. Roast saddle of lamb with mint sauce. Dark chocolate and salted caramel tart with vanilla ice cream.

Carte £37/45

Faversham Rd ⊠ CT5 4BP – Southwest : 2 mi following coast rd
– ✆ 01227 273370 (booking advisable) – www.thesportsmanseasalter.co.uk
– Closed 25-26 December, 1 January, Sunday dinner and Monday

WHITTLESFORD

Cambridgeshire – Regional map n° **8**-B3
▶ London 50 mi – Cambridge 11 mi – Peterborough 46 mi

🛏 Tickell Arms ❀ 🛋 🛋 🛆 🗚 🅿

TRADITIONAL BRITISH · PUB Large pub with an orangery-style extension overlooking a pond. Fish is delivered 6 days a week; on Tuesdays diners can select their own cuts for 'Steak and Chop' night; and on Sundays they leave freshly roasted potatoes on the bar.

Menu £14 (weekdays)/19 – Carte £23/39

1 North Rd ⊠ CB22 4NZ – ✆ 01223 833025 – www.cambscuisine.com

Our selection of hotels, guesthouses and restaurants change every year, so change your MICHELIN Guide every year!

WIGHT (Isle of)

Isle of Wight – Pop. 138 500 – Regional map n° **4**-A/B 3

Godshill

🕸 Taverners   🍴 🏠 **P**

TRADITIONAL BRITISH · PUB Passionately run roadside pub with its own deli selling homemade produce. The main menu lists pub classics like burgers and pies but the more ambitious daily blackboard specials are the ones to go for. Ingredients are local and home-grown.

Carte £ 17/28

High St ✉ PO38 3HZ – 𝒞 01983 840707 – www.thetavernersgodshill.co.uk
– Closed first 3 weeks January

Gurnard

🍴 Little Gloster   ⇦ ≤ 🍴 🏠 **P**

TRADITIONAL CUISINE · RUSTIC Set in a great spot among the beach huts, with lovely views over The Solent. Have a cocktail on the terrace then head inside to the tables by the kitchen or the relaxed, shabby chic dining room. Unfussy, flavoursome cooking uses island produce. Stylish bedrooms have a fresh nautical theme and superb views.

Carte £ 26/48

3 rooms �), – ∮£ 100/220 ∮∮£ 100/220

31 Marsh Rd ✉ PO31 8JQ – 𝒞 01983 298776 – www.thelittlegloster.com – Closed 1 January-early February, Tuesday-Wednesday in low season, Sunday dinner and Monday

Newport

🍴 Thompson's 🅽   ♿

MODERN BRITISH · TRENDY A stylish yet relaxed restaurant in the centre of town; try to book one of the three tables in front of the open kitchen. Original cooking makes good use of island ingredients and exhibits some interesting flavour combinations.

Menu £ 22 (lunch) – Carte £ 29/55

11 Town Ln ✉ PO30 1JU – 𝒞 01983 526118 – www.robertthompson.co.uk – Closed 25-29 December, 2 weeks February, 1 week September, 2 weeks November, Sunday and Monday

St Helens

🍴 Dans Kitchen   🅥

TRADITIONAL CUISINE · FRIENDLY Old corner shop in a lovely location overlooking the village green. Simple wood furnishings, scatter cushions and nautical pictures feature. Traditional, hearty dishes showcase island produce; blackboard specials include the daily catch.

Menu £ 15 (weekday lunch) – Carte £ 25/48

Lower Green Rd ✉ PO33 1TS – 𝒞 01983 872303 – www.danskitcheniow.co.uk – Closed 3 weeks January, 1 week June, 1 week October, Sunday, Monday and Tuesday lunch

Seaview

🏠 Seaview   ⬍ ♿

TRADITIONAL · QUIRKY A long-standing seaside hotel with a laid-back feel – its interesting interior filled with nautical charts, maritime photos and model ships. Bright, comfy bedrooms come in various styles; some are in annexes and several are suites.

29 rooms ☟ – ∮£ 80/170 ∮∮£ 95/190 – 6 suites

High St ✉ PO34 5EX – 𝒞 01983 612711 – www.seaviewhotel.co.uk – Closed 24-27 December

🍴 **Seaview** – See restaurant listing

XX Seaview

MODERN BRITISH · CLASSIC DÉCOR The seafaring décor gives a clue as to the focus at this boldly decorated hotel restaurant. Classically based seafood dishes are well-prepared and come in a choice of two sizes. The 'Naval Mess' and 'Pump Room' provide simpler alternatives and the crab ramekin has become something of an institution.

Menu £ 28 – Carte £ 22/37

Seaview Hotel, High St ⊠ PO34 5EX – ✆ 01983 612711 (booking essential) – www.seaviewhotel.co.uk – Closed 24-27 December and Sunday dinner October-May

Shanklin

⌂ Rylstone Manor

COUNTRY HOUSE · CLASSIC This attractive part-Victorian house sits in the town's historic gardens and was originally a gift from the Queen to one of her physicians. The classical interior has a warm, cosy feel and is furnished with antiques. Carefully prepared dishes are served in the formally laid dining room.

9 rooms ⌂ – ♦£ 68/120 ♦♦£ 135/165

Rylstone Gdns ⊠ PO37 6RG – ✆ 01983 862806 – www.rylstone-manor.co.uk – Closed 6 November-6 February

Ventnor

⌂⌂⌂ Royal

TRADITIONAL · CLASSIC A sympathetically restored Victorian house with mature lawned gardens and a heated outdoor pool. The interior has a bygone elegance with hints of modernity. Traditional bedrooms have good facilities and some offer lovely sea views.

52 rooms ⌂ – ♦£ 95/125 ♦♦£ 150/290

Belgrave Rd ⊠ PO38 1JJ – ✆ 01983 852186 – www.royalhoteliow.co.uk
Royal Hotel – See restaurant listing

⌂ Hillside

COUNTRY HOUSE · UNIQUE Set high above the town, this wonderful thatched Georgian house has a beautiful terrace and superb sea views. The Danish owner has fused period furnishings with clean-lined Scandinavian styling, and displays over 350 pieces of CoBrA and Scandinavian art. Everything is immaculate and the linens are top quality. Frequently changing menus use local and garden produce.

14 rooms ⌂ – ♦£ 78/143 ♦♦£ 156/206

151 Mitchell Ave ⊠ PO38 1DR – ✆ 01983 852271 – www.hillsideventnor.co.uk

XX Royal Hotel ⓝ

CLASSIC CUISINE · ELEGANT Set within an elegant hotel is this fittingly grand dining room hung with portraits and chandeliers. Good value light lunches are followed by more sophisticated dinners where old favourites are offered alongside more modern dishes.

Menu 40 – Carte £ 22/39

Royal Hotel, Belgrave Rd ⊠ PO38 1JJ – ✆ 01983 852186 – www.royalhoteliow.co.uk – dinner only and Sunday lunch – Closed 2 weeks January

X Ale and Oyster ⓝ

TRADITIONAL BRITISH · BISTRO This relaxed little bistro sits in a super spot on the esplanade, looking out to sea, and is run by a friendly, experienced team. Enjoy a light lunch on the terrace or come in the evening for the likes of local lobster linguine.

Carte £ 30/44

The Esplanade ⊠ PO38 1JX – ✆ 01983 857025 – www.thealeandoyster.co.uk – Closed 3 weeks January, 1 week November, Monday and Tuesday in winter

ENGLAND

Yarmouth

🏠 The George   ⇐ 🐾 &

INN · CLASSIC Set in the shadow of the castle, this cosy 17C inn blends subtle modern touches with characterful period features. Bedrooms vary in shape and style: some are wood-panelled; some have luxurious bathrooms; some open onto the garden or have spacious balconies – and many have excellent Solent views.

17 rooms ⌓ – †£ 180/360 ††£ 195/375

Quay St ✉ PO41 0PE – ☎ 01983 760331 – www.thegeorge.co.uk

Isla's • Isla's Conservatory – See restaurant listing

XXX Isla's ⓝ   & AC

MODERN CUISINE · DESIGN At the heart of an old inn you'll find this stylishly understated restaurant with large linen-laid tables and detailed service. The three no-choice set menus change with the seasons – cooking is precise, modern and sophisticated.

Menu £ 45/75

The George Hotel, Quay St ✉ PO41 0PE – ☎ 01983 760331 (booking essential) – www.thegeorge.co.uk – dinner only – Closed Tuesday in Winter, Sunday and Monday

X Isla's Conservatory   ⇐ 🐾 🏡 & AC

TRADITIONAL BRITISH · BRASSERIE Hidden at the back of the George hotel is this modern conservatory with a lovely garden leading down to the water's edge. Flexible brasserie-style menus offer tasty nibbles and a choice of dish size; ingredients are local and organic.

Carte £ 29/45

The George Hotel, Quay St ✉ PO41 0PE – ☎ 01983 760331 – www.thegeorge.co.uk

WIGHTON – Norfolk ➜ See Wells-Next-The-Sea

WILLIAN

Hertfordshire – Pop. 326 – Regional map n° **7**-B2

▶ London 38 mi – Croydon 48 mi – Barnet 24 mi – Ealing 37 mi

🍴 Fox   🐾 🏡 🅿

MODERN BRITISH · FRIENDLY A popular, bright and airy pub with a sheltered terrace, set right in the heart of the village. Dishes are modern and there's a good choice of seafood and game in season; if you can't decide, try the 'Fox Slate' for two.

Carte £ 23/35

✉ SG6 2AE – ☎ 01462 480233 – www.foxatwillian.co.uk

WILMINGTON

Regional map n° **6**-C3

▶ London 17 mi – Royal Tunbridge Wells 28 mi – Maidstone 24 mi

🏠 Rowhill Grange   ☆ 🐾 🔟 ⑩ 🏊 ♨ ⊡ & ⅋ 🛁 🅿

COUNTRY HOUSE · MODERN An early 19C house set in 15 acres of pretty gardens, with smart modern bedrooms in dark, bold hues. The fantastic spa has 9 treatment rooms, a large gym and a superb swimming pool, along with a separate infinity pool with a waterfall. RG's serves fresh seasonal dishes – try the grills.

38 rooms – †£ 129/209 ††£ 139/209 – ⌓ £ 16

✉ DA2 7QH – Southwest : 2 mi on Hextable rd (B 258) – ☎ 01322 615136 – www.rowhillgrange.com

WIMBORNE MINSTER

Dorset – Pop. 15 174 – Regional map n° **2**-C3

▶ London 112 mi – Dorchester 23 mi – Bournemouth 10 mi

ℵ Tickled Pig

MODERN BRITISH · BISTRO Charmingly run restaurant in the heart of a pretty market town, with a modern country interior, a deli, a lovely terrace and a laid-back feel. Daily brown paper menus feature home-grown veg and home-reared pork; their mantra is 'taking food back to its roots'. Cooking is vibrant, flavourful and unfussy.

Menu £ 20 (weekdays) – Carte £ 24/38

26 West Borough ⊠ BH21 1NF – ℰ 01202 886778 – www.thetickledpig.co.uk
– Closed 25-26 December and 1 January

ℵ Number 9 ⓝ

TRADITIONAL BRITISH · RUSTIC Low ceilings, exposed brick walls and bare floorboards give this pleasant little restaurant a cosy feel and fairy lights at the windows add to the mood. Carefully cooked, classical dishes – like roasted pheasant – are full of flavour. Three small but stylish bedrooms are sponsored by Farrow & Ball.

Carte £ 23/44

3 rooms ⌕ – ♦£ 70/90 ♦♦£ 110/120

9 West Borough ⊠ BH21 1LT – ℰ 01202 887557 – www.number9wimborne.co.uk

WINCHCOMBE

Gloucestershire – Pop. 4 538 – Regional map n° **2**-D1

▶ London 100 mi – Gloucester 26 mi – Oxford 43 mi – Birmingham 43 mi

ℵℵ 5 North St (Marcus Ashenford)

£ₒₚ **MODERN BRITISH · COSY** Established neighbourhood restaurant that's very personally run by a husband and wife team. Low-beamed ceilings and burgundy walls provide an intimate feel. Menus change with the seasons and feature regional ingredients in classic combinations. Assured, well-crafted dishes are guaranteed to be full of flavour.

→ Scallop with ham hock, piccalilli and pineapple. Sea bass with duck egg pasta, baby fennel and cauliflower & truffle purée. Chocolate and thyme panna cotta with mango sorbet.

Menu £ 30/54

5 North St ⊠ GL54 5LH
– ℰ 01242 604566 – www.5northstreetrestaurant.co.uk
– Closed 2 weeks January, 1 week August, Monday, Tuesday lunch and Sunday dinner

ℵℵ Wesley House

TRADITIONAL CUISINE · RUSTIC Characterful 15C house with lots of beams, a cosy open-fired bar and a smart rear dining room and conservatory. Cooking is classical and flavourful, and service is relaxed and cheery; simpler meals are served in their next door wine bar. The cosy bedrooms have a comfortingly traditional feel.

Menu £ 20/28 – Carte £ 29/46

5 rooms ⌕ – ♦£ 70/95 ♦♦£ 85/110

High St ⊠ GL54 5LJ – ℰ 01242 602366 – www.wesleyhouse.co.uk – Closed 26 December, Sunday dinner and Monday

at Gretton Northwest: 2 mi by B4632 and B4078

ℍ Royal Oak

TRADITIONAL BRITISH · RUSTIC In summer, head for the large garden, with its chickens, kids' play area, tennis court and passing steam trains; in winter, sit in one of two snug dining rooms or in the conservatory. Local produce features in honest, traditional dishes.

Carte £ 24/42

⊠ GL54 5EP – ℰ 01242 604999 – www.royaloakgretton.co.uk

WINCHESTER

Hampshire – Pop. 45 184 – Regional map n° **4**-B2

▶ London 72 mi – Bristol 76 mi – Oxford 52 mi

🏨 Hotel du Vin   ⇗ ⇛ AC ♨ P

TOWNHOUSE · CONTEMPORARY Attractive Georgian house dating from 1715, and the first ever Hotel du Vin. Wine-themed bedrooms, split between the house and garden, are stylish and well-equipped; some have baths in the room. The characterful split-level bistro offers unfussy French cooking and – as hoped – an excellent wine selection.

24 rooms ⌸ – ♦£ 169/239 ♦♦£ 179/249

Town plan: A2-c - *14 Southgate St* ⊠ *SO23 9EF*

– ✆ *01962 841414*

– *www.hotelduvin.com*

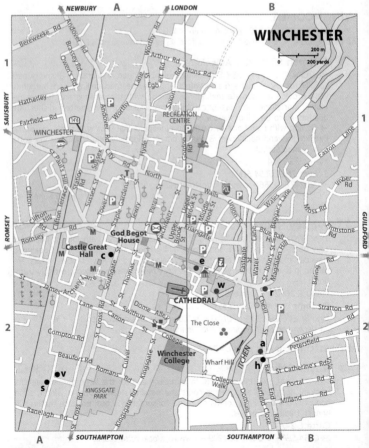

ENGLAND

🏠 Giffard House 🦒 🅿

TOWNHOUSE · CLASSIC Imposing Victorian house in a quiet road. Spacious, classically styled guest areas include a comfy drawing room, modern bar and formal breakfast room. Individually styled bedrooms boast quality furnishings and good facilities.

13 rooms ☑ – 🛉£ 81/132 🛉🛉£ 107/144

Town plan: A2-s - 50 Christchurch Rd ✉ SO23 9SU – ☎ 01962 852628
– www.giffardhotelwinchester.co.uk
– Closed 24 December-2 January

🏠 29 Christchurch Road 🦒 🍽

TOWNHOUSE · PERSONALISED Spacious, Regency-style guesthouse with a pretty walled garden, set in an attractive residential area close to town. It's immaculately kept throughout, from the homely bedrooms to the fire-lit lounge and elegant breakfast room.

3 rooms ☑ – 🛉£ 75/90 🛉🛉£ 95/105

Town plan: A2-v - 29 Christchurch Rd. ✉ SO23 9SU – ☎ 01962 868661
– www.bedbreakfastwinchester.co.uk

🏠 Black Hole

TOWNHOUSE · PERSONALISED This three-storey guesthouse is fashioned on an 18C prison – the Black Hole of Calcutta – and comes with heavy prison doors, framed prints of history's villains and themed wallpapers. The top floor terrace has city rooftop views.

10 rooms ☑ – 🛉£ 85/110 🛉🛉£ 85/110

Town plan: B2-h - Wharf Hill ✉ SO23 9NP – ☎ 01962 807010
– www.blackholebb.co.uk

XX Rick Stein ♿ 🄰🄲

SEAFOOD · ELEGANT Winchester's high street is the location of the first outpost of the Stein empire outside Cornwall: a smart restaurant with a large open kitchen. Simply cooked fish and seafood dishes have some Asian influences; good value set lunch.

Menu £ 20 (lunch) – Carte £ 31/72

Town plan: B2-e - 7-8 High St ✉ SO23 9JX – ☎ 01962 353535
– www.rickstein.com – Closed 25 December

XX Chesil Rectory 🗂 ✿

MODERN CUISINE · HISTORIC This double-gabled wattle and daub house dates from the 15C and its characterful interior takes in heavily beamed ceilings and a large inglenook fireplace. Appealing menus offer classic British dishes with the odd Mediterranean touch.

Menu £ 17 (lunch and early dinner)/22 – Carte £ 27/38

Town plan: B2-r - Chesil St. ✉ SO23 0HU – ☎ 01962 851555
– www.chesilrectory.co.uk – Closed 25-26 December and 1 January

X Black Rat 🏡 ✿

❀ MODERN CUISINE · RUSTIC This unassuming building conceals a quirky, bohemian-style interior with a small bar, a lounge and a two-roomed restaurant. Refined, classically based cooking displays Mediterranean influences and modern twists. The four wicker-roofed booths on the rear terrace are an unusual feature.
→ Lamb sweetbreads with peas, burnt onion oil, yoghurt and charred onion rings. Breast of guinea fowl with artichoke, broad beans and carrot & tonka bean purée. Madeleines with butterscotch sauce.

Carte £ 30/52

Town plan: B2-a - 88 Chesil St. ✉ SO23 0HX – ☎ 01962 844465
– www.theblackrat.co.uk – dinner only and lunch Saturday-Sunday – Closed 2 weeks December-January, 1 week spring and 1 week autumn

623

Ⅹ River Cottage Canteen   🔥 🆎

TRADITIONAL BRITISH · RUSTIC A delightful restaurant set within a 200 year old silk mill in the Abbey Gardens. The lower floor has an open kitchen and the upper floor has exposed timbers and rope lights. Seasonal regional produce is at the core of the menu and dishes are hearty and rustic; the small plates and sharing boards are popular.

Menu £ 16 (weekday lunch)/25 – Carte £ 22/43

Town plan: **B2-w** - *Abbey Mill, Abbey Mill Gardens* ⊠ *SO23 9GH*
– 𝒫 01962 457747 (booking essential) – www.rivercottage.net – Closed
25-26 December, Sunday dinner and Monday

at Littleton Northwest: 2.5 mi by B3049 ⊠ Winchester

🛏 Running Horse   🛌 🚽 🏠 🔥 🅿

TRADITIONAL CUISINE · FRIENDLY A smart, grey-painted pub with a straw-roofed cabana at the front (heated, very cosy and it can be booked!) The menu is concise and constantly evolving and dishes are fuss-free and big on flavour. Service is pleasingly unpretentious and the simple bedrooms are arranged around the garden, motel-style.

Carte £ 23/35

15 rooms � – ♦£ 80/130 ♦♦£ 80/130

88 Main Rd ⊠ *SO22 6QS – 𝒫 01962 880218 – www.runninghorseinn.co.uk*
– Closed dinner 25 December

at Sparsholt Northwest: 3.5 mi by B3049 ⊠ Winchester

🏯 Lainston House   🍃 ⪪ 🚽 ℔ Ⅹ 🧖 🅿

COUNTRY HOUSE · CONTEMPORARY Impressive 17C William and Mary manor house with attractive gardens and a striking avenue of lime trees. Clubby wood-panelled bar and modern drawing room; bedrooms are spacious and contemporary. Relax over a game of tennis, croquet or boules – or brush up on your culinary skills at the cookery school.

50 rooms – ♦£ 165/265 ♦♦£ 165/265 – ⊠£ 21 – 3 suites

Woodman Ln ⊠ *SO21 2LT – 𝒫 01962 776088 – www.lainstonhouse.com*
Avenue – See restaurant listing

ⅩⅩⅩ Avenue   ⪪ 🚽 🏠 🔥 🕙 ⟳ 🅿

CREATIVE · CHIC Formal dining room within an impressive 17C country house; named after the mile-long avenue of lime trees it overlooks. Cooking is modern, original and creative and uses lots of produce from the kitchen garden; try the tasting menu.

Menu £ 33 (weekday lunch)/58 – Carte approx. £ 58

Lainston House Hotel, Woodman Ln ⊠ *SO21 2LT – 𝒫 01962 776088*
– www.lainstonhouse.com – Closed Saturday lunch in winter

WINDERMERE

Cumbria – Pop. 5 243 – Regional map n° **12**-A2
▶ London 279 mi – Carlisle 56 mi – Kendal 12 mi

🏯 Holbeck Ghyll   🍃 ⪪ 🚽 🏛 Ⅹ 🧖 🅿

TRADITIONAL · CLASSIC A charming stone-built Victorian hunting lodge, set in 15 acres and boasting stunning views over the lake and mountains. Traditional guest areas feature antiques and warming open fires. Well-equipped bedrooms range from classical to contemporary in style; Miss Potter, complete with a hot tub, is the best.

31 rooms ⊠ – ♦£ 129/425 ♦♦£ 169/625 – 4 suites

Holbeck Ln ⊠ *LA23 1LU – Northwest : 3.25 mi by A 591 – 𝒫 015394 32375*
– www.holbeckghyll.com – Closed first 2 weeks January
Holbeck Ghyll – See restaurant listing

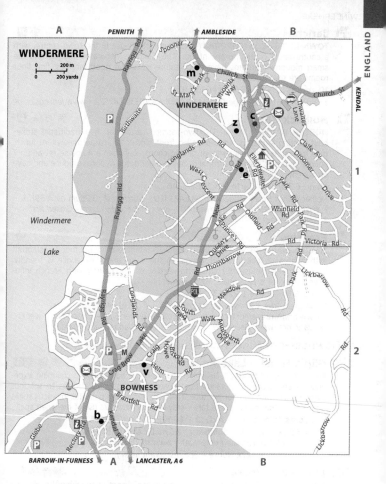

⌂ Windermere Suites   ⌘ 🅿

LUXURY · DESIGN Spacious Edwardian house with a seductive interior. Funky, sexy bedrooms boast bold modern décor, iPod docks and walk-in wardrobes. Huge bathrooms feature TVs and colour-changing lights. Breakfast is served in your room.

8 rooms ⊑ – ♦£ 180/200 ♦♦£ 180/270

Town plan: B1-e - *New Rd* ⊠ *LA23 2LA* – ℰ *015394 47672*
– *www.windermeresuites.co.uk* – *Closed 24-25 December*

⌂ Cedar Manor   ♤ ⌂ ⌘ 🅿

TRADITIONAL · PERSONALISED Victorian house with a cedar tree in the garden; it was built by a former minister and has ecclesiastical influences. Contemporary country house bedrooms display locally made furniture – some have spa baths or views and the Coach House suite has a private terrace. Appealing menus use local produce.

10 rooms ⊑ – ♦£ 115/425 ♦♦£ 135/425 – 2 suites

Town plan: B1-m - *Ambleside Rd* ⊠ *LA23 1AX* – ℰ *015394 43192*
– *www.cedarmanor.co.uk* – *Closed 2-19 January and 11-26 December*

Jerichos

TOWNHOUSE · CONTEMPORARY Victorian slate house in the town centre, with a contrastingly contemporary interior. The lounge is decorated in silver and the smart modern bedrooms have bold feature walls and good facilities; first floor rooms are the largest.

10 rooms ⌱ – †£ 65/75 ††£ 105/170

Town plan: B1-z - *College Rd* ✉ *LA23 1BX* – ✆ *015394 42522* – *www.jerichos.co.uk*

XX Holbeck Ghyll

MODERN BRITISH · ROMANTIC Two-roomed restaurant in a traditional stone-built hunting lodge; its wood-panelled front room offers superb views. At lunch, dine from a flexible à la carte; at dinner, choose between a 4 course set and a 7 course 'gourmet' menu. Seasonal dishes use good quality local produce and have an adventurous feel.

Menu £ 30/88 – Carte lunch £ 36/46

Holbeck Ghyll Hotel, Holbeck Ln ✉ *LA23 1LU* – *Northwest : 3.25 mi by A 591* – ✆ *015394 32375 (booking advisable)* – *www.holbeckghyll.com* – *Closed first 2 weeks January*

X Francine's

TRADITIONAL BRITISH · NEIGHBOURHOOD Intimate neighbourhood restaurant with a homely feel; local art hangs on the walls and the service is friendly. Wide-ranging menus offer straightforward classical cooking with French influences; the chef is passionate about game.

Menu £ 17 – Carte £ 22/63

Town plan: B1-c - *27 Main Rd* ✉ *LA23 1DX* – ✆ *015394 44088* – *www.francinesrestaurantwindermere.co.uk* – *dinner only* – *Closed last 2 weeks January, first week December, 25-26 December, 1 January and Monday*

at Bowness-on-Windermere South: 1 mi ✉ Windermere

Gilpin Hotel & Lake House

LUXURY · PERSONALISED Delightful country house hotel run by a charming, experienced family. Bedrooms range from contemporary country doubles to spacious garden suites with outdoor hot tubs. There are even more peaceful, luxurious suites a mile down the road beside a tarn – stay here for exclusive use of the smart spa.

31 rooms (dinner included) ⌱ – †£ 195/535 ††£ 295/575

Crook Rd ✉ *LA23 3NE* – *Southeast : 2.5 mi by A 5074 on B 5284* – ✆ *015394 88818 (booking essential)* – *www.thegilpin.co.uk*

❀ **Gilpin Hotel & Lake House** – See restaurant listing

Linthwaite House

TRADITIONAL · GRAND LUXURY Set in a peaceful spot overlooking the lake and fells and surrounded by 14 acres of beautiful grounds. Guest areas are cosy and stylish and the service is polished and personable. Smart modern bedrooms feature mood lighting; some come with terraces and hot tubs and number 31 has a retractable glass roof.

30 rooms ⌱ – †£ 124/582 ††£ 124/582

Crook Rd ✉ *LA23 3JA* – *South : 0.75 mi by A 5074 on B 5284* – ✆ *015394 88600* – *www.linthwaite.com*

Linthwaite House – See restaurant listing

Laura Ashley-Belsfield

COUNTRY HOUSE · GRAND LUXURY A Victorian mansion built in Italianate style, perched overlooking Lake Windermere. An eye-catching glass and steel reception opens into four elegant lounges, where contemporary décor marries with original features. Every piece of furniture, every fabric and every ornament is made by Laura Ashley. Dine from classic menus in the all-day brasserie or formal restaurant.

62 rooms ⌱ – †£ 189/239 ††£ 199/399 – 6 suites

Town plan: A2-b - *Kendal Rd* ✉ *LA23 3EL* – ✆ *015394 42448* – *www.lauraashleyhotels.com/thebelsfield*

🏠 Lindeth Howe ☆ 🦢 ← 🛏 🖼 🕰 📶 ⬅ ⚙ 🅿

TRADITIONAL · CLASSIC An attractive country house once bought by Beatrix Potter for her mother. It has a clubby bar, a homely lounge and pleasant views from the drawing room. Bedrooms are traditional: the top floor rooms have the best views, while the suites are more contemporary. The classical restaurant offers a modern menu.

35 rooms ☷ – ♦£ 95/130 ♦♦£ 160/360 – 2 suites

Lindeth Dr. Longtail Hill ✉ LA23 3JF – South : 1.25 mi by A 5074 on B 5284 – ✆ 015394 45759 – www.lindeth-howe.co.uk – Closed 3-16 January

🏠 Storrs Hall 🆕 ☆ 🦢 ← 🛏 🎣 🅿

HISTORIC · CLASSIC The gardens of this striking part-Georgian country house sweep down to the lake shore and their private jetty. The décor combines the old and the new, while a striking cupola adds a touch of grandeur – as does the polished dark wood and stained glass bar. Dine in the elegant dining room or bright conservatory.

29 rooms ☷ – ♦£ 129/149 ♦♦£ 286 – 1 suite

✉ LA23 3LG – South : 2 mi on A 592 – ✆ 015394 47111 – www.storrshall.com

🏠 Ryebeck ☆ 🦢 🛏 ⬅ ⚙ 🅿

FAMILY · ELEGANT Have afternoon tea on the terrace, looking over the gardens and down to the famous lake. Some of the bright, airy bedrooms share the view and some have patios or Juliet balconies. Kick-back in one of the cosy lounges then head to the dining room for tasty Cumbrian produce in a mix of classic and Asian dishes.

26 rooms ☷ – ♦£ 70/170 ♦♦£ 90/250

Lyth Valley Rd ✉ LA23 3JP – South : 0.75 mi on A 5074 – ✆ 015394 88195 – www.ryebeck.com – Closed 1 week in January

🏠 Angel Inn ☆ 🛏 🏠 🆎 🅿

INN · MODERN A cosy creamwashed inn just off the main street, with a large open-fired lounge and comfortable, contemporary bedrooms – two are in an annexed 18C cottage with lake views. Dine on classic pub dishes or sharing plates in the welcoming bar or minimalistic dining room, or head for the terraced garden in summer.

13 rooms ☷ – ♦£ 75/110 ♦♦£ 90/180

Town plan: A2-v - *Helm Rd ✉ LA23 3BU – ✆ 015394 44080 – www.theangelinnbowness.com – Closed 24-25 December*

𝕏𝕏𝕏 Gilpin Hotel & Lake House 🛏 🏠 ⬅ 🅿
✿

MODERN CUISINE · ELEGANT A series of intimate, individually styled dining rooms in a charming country house hotel; start with an aperitif in the comfy lounge or funky bar. Precisely prepared, original dishes are very attractively presented and provide a fitting sense of occasion; some have interesting spicing. Service is excellent.

→ Chilli-glazed poached lobster. Cartmel Valley venison with venison dumpling, aubergine purée, root vegetables and charred baby gem. Medjool date and milk chocolate bar with apple cannelloni and milk sorbet.

Menu £ 65/90

Gilpin Hotel & Lake House Hotel, Crook Rd ✉ LA23 3NE – Southeast : 2.5 mi by A 5074 on B 5284 – ✆ 015394 88818 (booking essential) – www.thegilpin.co.uk

𝕏𝕏𝕏 Linthwaite House ← 🛏 🅿

MODERN CUISINE · ROMANTIC Contemporary country house restaurant – sit in the intimate Mirror Room with its romantic booths or in the airy, bay-windowed former billiard room. Constantly evolving menus showcase Lakeland produce; cooking is modern and complex.

Menu £ 25/75

Linthwaite House Hotel, Crook Rd ✉ LA23 3JA – South : 0.75 mi by A 5074 on B 5284 – ✆ 015394 88600 – www.linthwaite.com

ENGLAND

🍴 **Brown Horse Inn**   ⇦ 🛜 **P**

TRADITIONAL BRITISH · PUB Shabby-chic coaching inn with a lovely split-level terrace. Seasonal menus feature unfussy, generous dishes and more adventurous specials. Much of the produce is from their fields out the back and they brew their own
beers too. Bedrooms are a mix of classic and boutique styles; some have terraces.
Carte £ 22/49

9 rooms ⊇ – †£ 55/110 ††£ 80/150

✉ *LA23 3NR – On A 5074 – ℰ 015394 43443 – www.thebrownhorseinn.co.uk*

WINDSOR

Windsor and Maidenhead – Pop. 31 225 – Regional map n° **6**-D3
▶ London 28 mi – Reading 19 mi – Southampton 59 mi

🏨 **Macdonald Windsor**   ⌖ ⊡ ⌖ ⟨AC⟩ 🛁 🚗

BUSINESS · DESIGN Set in a former department store opposite the Guildhall. Pass
through attractive open-plan guest areas up to contemporary bedrooms with a high
level of facilities and bold masculine hues; two have balconies overlooking the castle.
The modern brasserie specialises in mature Scottish beef from the Josper grill.

120 rooms – †£ 180/450 ††£ 180/450 – ⊇ £ 20

Town plan: B1-2-r - *23 High St.* ✉ *SL4 1LH – ℰ 01753 483100*
– www.macdonald-hotels.co.uk/windsor

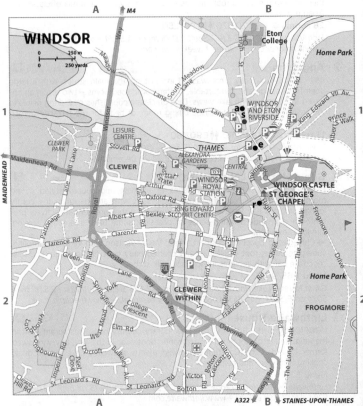

Sir Christopher Wren's House

HISTORIC · CONTEMPORARY Impressive house on the riverbank, built by Wren in 1676 as his family home. Characterful guest areas have high ceilings, panelled walls and bold modern furnishings. Some of the stylish bedrooms are beamed and some have balconies and river views. The modern restaurant has a lovely Thames outlook.

98 rooms ☑ – ∲£ 110/190 ∲∲£ 130/360 – 3 suites

Town plan: B1-e - *Thames St* ✉ SL4 1PX – ☏ 01753 442400 – www.sarova.com

Christopher

INN · CONTEMPORARY 18C brick-built coaching inn close to Eton College; cross the footbridge over the Thames to reach the castle. Contemporary bedrooms are spread about the main building and a mews; guest areas have an informal feel. The brightly coloured bistro offers international menus with subtle North African influences.

34 rooms – ∲£ 120/150 ∲∲£ 140/250 – ☑ £ 16

Town plan: B1-a - *110 High St, Eton* ✉ SL4 6AN – ☏ 01753 852359
– www.thechristopher.co.uk

X Gilbey's

TRADITIONAL CUISINE · BISTRO Opened by the Gilbey family in 1975, as the first wine bar outside London. It's relaxed and friendly, with an airy conservatory and terrace. Carefully cooked French and British dishes are accompanied by an interesting wine selection.

Menu £ 18 (weekday lunch)/30 – Carte £ 32/58

Town plan: B1-s - *82-83 High St* ✉ SL4 6AF – ☏ 01753 854921
– www.gilbeygroup.com – Closed 23-29 December and Monday lunch

Greene Oak

MODERN CUISINE · DESIGN Set close to the racecourse is this 'country pub and eating house', with its smart sun-trap terrace. Refined modern dishes show a good level of technical skill, textures and flavours are well-balanced, and portions are satisfying.

Carte £ 26/49

Oakley Green ✉ SL4 5UW – *West : 3 mi by A 308 on B 3024* – ☏ 01753 864294
– www.thegreeneoak.co.uk – Closed Sunday dinner

WINSFORD

Somerset – ✉ Minehead – Pop. 270 – Regional map n° **2**-A2
◪ London 194 mi – Taunton 32 mi – Exeter 31 mi

Royal Oak Inn

TRADITIONAL BRITISH · RUSTIC Delightful 12C farmhouse and dairy, beside a ford in a charming little village. Sit in the dining room or the rustic bar with its wood-furnished dining area and enjoy well-executed British classics and tasty desserts. Spacious country bedrooms come with huge bathrooms; most have four-poster beds.

Carte £ 23/35

8 rooms ☑ – ∲£ 75/95 ∲∲£ 100/140

Halse Ln ✉ TA24 7JE – ☏ 01643 851455 – www.royaloakexmoor.co.uk

WINSTER – Cumbria → See Windermere

WINSTER

Derbyshire – Pop. 1 787 – Regional map n° **9**-A1
◪ London 153 mi – Derby 25 mi – Matlock 5 mi

Old Shoulder of Mutton

LUXURY · TRADITIONAL This old village pub closed in 1916 but its name and character have been kept and it's been transformed into a stylish, cosy guesthouse. Beams and handmade furniture abound and local produce features at breakfast. (Min 2 nights stay).

3 rooms ☑ – ∲£ 110/125 ∲∲£ 125/140

West Bank ✉ DE4 2DQ – ☏ 01629 650005 – www.oldshoulderofmutton.co.uk
– Closed December-February

WINSTON

Durham – Regional map n° **14**-A3

▶ London 244 mi – Darlington 10 mi – York 56 mi

🍴 Bridgewater Arms   🏡 🅿

SEAFOOD · COSY This traditional pub spent the first hundred years of its life as a school; look out for the copperplate alphabet. The chef is known for his seafood and dishes are unashamedly classic, accurately executed and extremely satisfying.

Carte £ 22/59

✉ DL2 3RN – ℰ 01325 730302 – www.thebridgewaterarms.com – Closed 25-26 December, 1 January, Sunday and Monday

---

WINTERBOURNE STEEPLETON – Dorset → See Dorchester

WINTERINGHAM

North Lincolnshire – ✉ Scunthorpe – Pop. 1 000 – Regional map n° **13**-C3

▶ London 176 mi – Scunthorpe 8 mi – Sheffield 67 mi

🍽️🍽️🍽️ Winteringham Fields   ⇦ ⇧ 🅿

MODERN CUISINE · INTIMATE Characterful 16C house in a remote location, featuring an elegant dining room and several private rooms. The chef adopts a modern approach to cooking and many ingredients come from their own smallholding. The 'Menu Surprise' consists of 7 or 9 courses and there's also a 4 course set priced menu at lunch. Some of the antique-furnished bedrooms are set in the courtyard.

Menu £ 45/85

15 rooms � – 🛏£ 150 🛏🛏£ 180/220

1 Silver St ✉ DN15 9ND – ℰ 01724 733096 (booking essential) – www.winteringhamfields.co.uk – Closed 3 weeks August, Christmas, 1 week January, Sunday and Monday

---

WISWELL

Lancashire – Regional map n° **11**-B2

▶ London 232 mi – Preston 49 mi – Manchester 28 mi

🍴 Freemasons   🎱 🏡 ♿ ⇧

MODERN BRITISH · PUB A delightful pub, hidden away on a narrow lane, with flagged floors, low beams and open fires downstairs, and elegant, antique-furnished, country house style dining rooms upstairs. The interesting menu features modern versions of traditional pub dishes and cooking is refined and skilful. Charming service.

Menu £ 25 (lunch and early dinner) – Carte £ 38/62

8 Vicarage Fold ✉ BB7 9DF – ℰ 01254 822218 – www.freemasonsatwiswell.com – Closed 2-14 January and Monday-Tuesday except bank holidays

---

WITHAM ON THE HILL

Lincolnshire – Pop. 260 – Regional map n° **9**-C2

▶ London 99 mi – Lincoln 42 mi – Leicester 40 mi

🍴 Six Bells   ⇦ 🏡 ♿ 🍸 🅿

TRADITIONAL CUISINE · FRIENDLY This pub's spacious courtyard is an obvious draw and the bright, stylish interior keeps things cheery whatever the weather. Choose hand-crafted pizzas cooked in the wood-burning oven in the bar or something more sophisticated from the main menu. Bedrooms are very stylishly appointed; Hayloft is the best.

Menu £ 13 (weekday lunch)/17 – Carte £ 22/37

3 rooms ⊂⊃ – 🛏£ 65/130 🛏🛏£ 80/150

✉ PE10 0JH – ℰ 01778 590360 – www.sixbellswitham.co.uk – Closed 1-9 January, Sunday dinner and Monday in winter

WIVETON – Norfolk → See Blakeney

WOBURN
✉ Milton Keynes – Pop. 1 534 – Regional map n° **7**-A2
▶ London 49 mi – Bedford 13 mi – Northampton 24 mi

🏠 The Woburn
HISTORIC · CLASSIC The Woburn Estate comprises a 3,000 acre deer park, an abbey and this 18C coaching inn. Charming guest areas include a cosy bar and brasserie-style Olivier's. This is where afternoon tea was popularised in the 1840s. The best of the bedrooms are the themed suites and those in the 300yr old beamed Cottages.

55 rooms ☲ – ♦£ 153/305 ♦♦£ 185/305 – 9 suites
George St ✉ MK17 9PX – ℰ 01525 290441 – www.thewoburnhotel.co.uk

✗✗ Paris House
CREATIVE · INTIMATE A beautiful mock-Tudor house, built in Paris and reassembled in this idyllic location; enjoy an aperitif on the terrace while watching the deer. Cooking is a mix of Asian dishes and British classics given ambitious modern makeovers.

Menu £ 43/109

Woburn Park ✉ MK17 9QP – Southeast : 2.25 mi on A 4012 – ℰ 01525 290692 (booking essential) – www.parishouse.co.uk – Closed dinner 24 December-4 January and Sunday dinner-Tuesday

WOLD NEWTON
East Riding of Yorkshire – Regional map n° **13**-D2
▶ London 229 mi – Bridlington 25 mi – Scarborough 13 mi

🏠 Wold Cottage
COUNTRY HOUSE · ELEGANT A fine Georgian manor house and outbuildings in 300 acres of peaceful farmland, which guests are encouraged to explore. Personal items abound in the elegant, tastefully furnished interior. Sizeable bedrooms boast luxurious soft furnishings and antiques; some have four-posters – the courtyard rooms are simpler.

6 rooms ☲ – ♦£ 65/90 ♦♦£ 100/150
✉ YO25 3HL – South : 0.5 mi on Thwing rd – ℰ 01262 470696 – www.woldcottage.com

WOLVERHAMPTON
Staffordshire – Pop. 210 319 – Regional map n° **10**-C2
▶ London 140 mi – Birmingham 17 mi – Stafford 17 mi

✗✗ Bilash
INDIAN · FAMILY This smart contemporary restaurant is well-established and has several generations of the same family involved. Appealing, original menus offer South Indian and Bangladeshi dishes, crafted only from local and home-made produce.

Menu £ 10 (lunch)/45 – Carte £ 22/38

No 2 Cheapside ✉ WV1 1TU – ℰ 01902 427762 – www.thebilash.co.uk – Closed 1 January, 25-27 December and Sunday

WOMBLETON – North Yorkshire → See Helmsley

WOODBRIDGE
Suffolk – Pop. 11 341 – Regional map n° **8**-D3
▶ London 81 mi – Ipswich 8 mi – Great Yarmouth 45 mi

🏠 Seckford Hall

HISTORIC · DESIGN This part-Tudor country house in attractive gardens was reputedly once visited by Elizabeth I – she would hardly recognise it now, with its bold champagne bar, stylish sitting rooms and creatively designed modern bedrooms. The linen-laid restaurant offers a seasonal menu of modern classics.

32 rooms ⌔ – ♦£ 75/140 ♦♦£ 110/340 – 7 suites

✉ IP13 6NU – Southwest : 1.25 mi by A 12 – 𝒞 01394 385678 – www.seckford.co.uk

X Riverside

MODERN CUISINE · BISTRO A restaurant, cinema and theatre in one – where many menus include entrance to a film. It's light and airy, with full-length windows, a terrace and a marble counter topped with fresh bread. At lunch they serve mix and match tapas boards.

Carte £ 25/40

Quayside ✉ IP12 1BH – 𝒞 01394 382174 (booking advisable)
– www.theriverside.co.uk – Closed 25-26 December, 1 January and Sunday dinner

🍴 Crown

TRADITIONAL CUISINE · PUB A modern dining pub in the town centre, with a smart granite-floored bar and four different dining areas. Seasonal menus of well-presented, modern classics, with plenty of shellfish; the set menu is particularly good value. Polite, friendly service. Minimalist, very cosy bedrooms boast good facilities.

Menu £ 15 (weekdays) – Carte £ 26/46

10 rooms ⌔ – ♦£ 100/200 ♦♦£ 100/200

Thoroughfare ✉ IP12 1AD – 𝒞 01394 384242 – www.thecrownatwoodbridge.co.uk

at Bromeswell Northeast: 2.5 mi by B1438 off A1152

🍴 Unruly Pig ⓝ

MODERN CUISINE · PUB This cosy open-fired pub is far from unruly, with its wooden panelling and interesting art. The Mediterranean-inspired cooking offers plenty of choice, the set menus are good value and there's usually a daily main course for £ 10.

Menu £ 15 (weekday lunch)/25 – Carte £ 27/38

Orford Rd ✉ IP12 2PU – 𝒞 01394 460310 (booking advisable)
– www.theunrulypig.co.uk – Closed Sunday dinner and Monday

WOODSTOCK

Oxfordshire – Pop. 2 389 – Regional map n° **6**-B2
▶ London 65 mi – Gloucester 47 mi – Oxford 8 mi

🏠 Feathers

TOWNHOUSE · ELEGANT Stylish 17C house boasting individually styled bedrooms with boutique twists: some have feature walls; others, bold fabrics and modern art. The bar-lounge and walled terrace offer a casual menu and a fabulous gin selection. The formal dining room serves classically based dishes with a creative, original edge.

21 rooms ⌔ – ♦£ 125/425 ♦♦£ 145/445 – 5 suites

Market St ✉ OX20 1SX – 𝒞 01993 812291 – www.feathers.co.uk

🏠 Kings Arms

TRADITIONAL · MODERN Keenly run, contemporary hotel in the heart of a busy market town. Its immaculately kept interior displays a good eye for detail; cosy up and enjoy a drink in the open-fired bar. Sleek, stylish bedrooms are named after English kings.

15 rooms ⌔ – ♦£ 85 ♦♦£ 150/160

19 Market St ✉ OX20 1SU – 𝒞 01993 813636 – www.kingshotelwoodstock.co.uk

Kings Arms – See restaurant listing

✗ Kings Arms

MODERN BRITISH · BISTRO Spacious hotel restaurant with a large glass atrium, a striking black and white tiled floor and a welcoming open fire. Robust, flavoursome British dishes come with modern twists. They offer a good value set lunch and early evening menu.

Menu £ 12 (weekday lunch) – Carte £ 23/35

19 Market St ⊠ OX20 1SU – ℰ 01993 813636 – www.kingshotelwoodstock.co.uk

🍴 Crown   ⇦ 🏠

MEDITERRANEAN CUISINE · FRIENDLY It might have 18C origins but the Crown is not your typical coaching inn, with its bright, almost greenhouse-style dining room complete with an attractive Belgian tiled floor. Fresh, light cooking takes its influences from the Med and makes good use of the wood-fired oven. Bedrooms are beautifully appointed.

Carte £ 20/32

5 rooms – ♦£ 175/250 ♦♦£ 175/250

31 High St ⊠ OX20 1TE – ℰ 01993 813339 – www.thecrownwoodstock.com

WOOLACOMBE

Devon – Pop. 840 – Regional map n° **7**-C1

▶ London 237 mi – Exeter 55 mi – Barnstaple 15 mi

✗ NC@EX34

MODERN BRITISH · INTIMATE Rustic restaurant which reflects the owner's personality; the 6 counter seats are always in demand. Choose 7 or 9 courses from the daily set menu and go for the wine pairings. Skilful modern cooking uses seasonal Devon produce.

Menu £ 75/95

South St ⊠ EX34 7BB – ℰ 01271 871187 (booking essential)
– www.noelcorston.com – dinner only – Closed November-Easter and Sunday-Tuesday

WOOLER

Northumberland – Pop. 1 983 – Regional map n° **14**-A1

▶ London 337 mi – Morpeth 31 mi – Newcastle Upon Tyne 47 mi

🏠 Firwood   🐾 ⇦ ⚘ 🅿

TRADITIONAL · COSY Bay-windowed dower house in a peaceful setting, with a beautiful tiled hall, a comfy lounge and lovely countryside views. Spacious bedrooms are furnished in a simple period style. The friendly owners are a font of local knowledge.

3 rooms ⌣ – ♦£ 60 ♦♦£ 90

Middleton Hall ⊠ NE71 6RD – South : 1.75 mi by Earle rd on Middleton Hall rd
– ℰ 01668 283699 – www.firwoodhouse.co.uk – Closed 1 December-13 February

WOOLHOPE

Herefordshire – Regional map n° **10**-B3

▶ London 137 mi – Hereford 8 mi – Birmingham 72 mi

🍴 Butchers Arms   ⇦ 🏠 🅿

TRADITIONAL CUISINE · RUSTIC Unfussy, classical cooking, with game in season, plenty of offal, tasty home-baked bread and hearty, reasonably priced dishes. The décor is traditional too, with a welcoming log fire, wattle walls and low-slung beams.

Menu £ 9 (weekday lunch) – Carte £ 25/37

⊠ HR1 4RF – ℰ 01432 860281 – www.butchersarmswoolhope.com – Closed Sunday dinner in winter and Monday except bank holidays

WOOTTON

Oxfordshire – Regional map n° **6**-B2

▶ London 61 mi – Bedford 5 mi – Northampton 30 mi

Killingworth Castle

TRADITIONAL BRITISH • RUSTIC A welcoming roadside inn dating from the 16C, set just outside the village centre. The chatty staff know what they're doing and food is great value, especially the dish of the day. Interesting menus champion local produce; here they bake their own breads, butcher their own meats and brew their own beers. Retire to one of the spacious bedrooms feeling suitably fortified.

Carte £ 20/49

8 rooms – †£ 99/170 ††£ 99/180

Glympton Rd ✉ OX20 1EJ – ✆ 01993 811401 – www.thekillingworthcastle.com – Closed 25 December

WORCESTER

Worcestershire – Pop. 100 153 – Regional map n° **10**-B3

London 124 mi – Birmingham 26 mi – Cheltenham 25 mi

Old Rectifying House

TRADITIONAL BRITISH • PUB You'll find shabby-chic décor, easy-going staff and a cocktail list in this striking mock-Tudor building overlooking Worcester Bridge and the River Severn. Most dishes have a British slant, but there's the odd international influence too.

Carte £ 24/43

North Par. ✉ WR1 3NN – ✆ 01905 619622 – www.theoldrec.co.uk – Closed Monday except bank holidays and 25 December

WORKSOP

Nottinghamshire – Pop. 41 820 – Regional map n° **9**-B1

London 160 mi – Sheffield 20 mi – Nottingham 37 mi

Browns

TRADITIONAL • COSY Cross the ford to this keenly run, cosy cottage, which dates back to 1730. Lovely garden with mature fruit trees. Bedrooms are in the old cow shed; all have four-posters and open onto a large decked terrace. Appealing breakfast menu.

3 rooms – †£ 59/69 ††£ 89/99

Old Orchard Cottage, Holbeck Ln, Holbeck. ✉ S80 3NF – Southwest : 4.5 mi by A 60 – ✆ 01909 720659 – www.brownsholbeck.co.uk – Closed 24 December-2 January

WORTH

Kent → See Deal

WRINGTON

North Somerset – Pop. 1 918 – Regional map n° **2**-B2

London 130 mi – Bristol 12 mi – Weston-super-Mare 12 mi

The Ethicurean

MODERN BRITISH • SIMPLE Two rustic, informal glasshouses in a beautifully restored Victorian walled garden; fresh produce leads the daily menu and they strive to be 'ethical' and 'epicurean'. They serve everything from coffee and cake to 5 set courses.

Menu £ 28 (lunch)/41 – Carte lunch £ 21/40

Barley Wood Walled Garden, Long Ln ✉ BS40 5SA – East : 1.25 mi by School Rd on Redhill rd – ✆ 01934 863713 (booking essential) – www.theethicurean.com – Closed 2 weeks January, Sunday dinner and Monday

WROTHAM

Kent – Pop. 1 767 – Regional map n° **5**-B1

London 27 mi – Sevenoaks 9 mi – Maidstone 12 mi

The Bull ⇦ ⇔ P

TRADITIONAL BRITISH · RUSTIC This 14C inn might look a little plain but give it a chance and it will grow on you. The restaurant offers a traditional à la carte but most come for the Bull Pit menu, which is served in the bar and courtyard and features a host of meats cooked on the American-style BBQ. Bedrooms are smart and up-to-date.
Carte £ 31/44

11 rooms – ∱£ 69/139 ∱∱£ 79/159 – ⊊ £ 8

Bull Ln. ⊠ *TN15 7RF* – ℰ *01732 789800* – *www.thebullhotel.com* – *Closed 1 January*

WYMESWOLD

Leicestershire – Regional map n° **9**-B2
▶ London 118 mi – Leicester 17 mi – Nottingham 14 mi

✗ hammer & pincers 🏠 P

TRADITIONAL CUISINE · RUSTIC Formerly the village forge (the old water pump can still be seen at the back), then a pub, and now a rustic restaurant. Menus mix classic British and Italian influences; the 8 course grazing menu is the most modern and creative.
Menu £ 23 (weekdays) – Carte dinner £ 29/46

5 East Rd ⊠ *LE12 6ST* – ℰ *01509 880735* – *www.hammerandpincers.co.uk* – *Closed 25 December, Sunday dinner and Monday*

WYMONDHAM

Leicestershire – Pop. 600 – Regional map n° **9**-C2
▶ London 107 mi – Norwich 11 mi – Bury Saint Edmunds 34 mi

Berkeley Arms 🏠 & ⇔ P

TRADITIONAL BRITISH · PUB Attractive 16C village pub run by an experienced local couple; turn left for the low-beamed bar or right for the dining room. Appealing, gutsy dishes rely on seasonal local produce and are constantly evolving; alongside British favourites you'll find the likes of mallard with poached pears. Service is relaxed.
Menu £ 16 (weekday lunch)/19 – Carte £ 25/43

59 Main St ⊠ *LE14 2AG* – ℰ *01572 787587 (booking essential)* – *www.theberkeleyarms.co.uk* – *Closed first 2 weeks January, 2 weeks summer, Sunday dinner and Monday*

WYNYARD

Stockton-on-Tees – Regional map n° **14**-B3
▶ London 250 mi – Middlesbrough 10 mi – Durham 16 mi

Wynyard Hall 🍴 🐾 ⇐ 🛏 🕸 🛋 🖥 & ⅋ 🛁 P

COUNTRY HOUSE · ELEGANT Impressive Georgian mansion built for the Marquis of Londonderry; its smart spa overlooks a lake. Traditional bedrooms in the main house and more modern lodges spread about the vast grounds. Classical guest areas feature stained glass, open fires and antiques. The formal dining room offers modern classics.
22 rooms ⊊ – ∱£ 99/275 ∱∱£ 99/275 – 3 suites

⊠ *TS22 5NF* – ℰ *01740 644811* – *www.wynyardhall.co.uk*

YARM

Stockton-on-Tees – Pop. 19 184 – Regional map n° **14**-B3
▶ London 239 mi – Middlesbrough 9 mi – Durham 30 mi

Judges Country House 🐾 🛏 🛁 ⅋ 🛁 P

COUNTRY HOUSE · CLASSIC Victorian judge's house with wood panelling, antiques and ornaments; set in well-kept gardens. Traditional country house bedrooms offer a high level of facilities, bright modern bathrooms and extra touches such as fresh fruit, flowers and even goldfish! There's a welcoming atmosphere and service is pleasant.
21 rooms ⊊ – ∱£ 125/215 ∱∱£ 235/245

Kirklevington Hall, Kirklevington ⊠ *TS15 9LW* – *South : 1.5 mi on A 67* – ℰ *01642 789000* – *www.judgeshotel.co.uk*

Judges Country House – See restaurant listing

XXX Judges Country House

MODERN CUISINE · TRADITIONAL DÉCOR Formal, two-roomed restaurant on the ground floor of a traditional country house hotel; the conservatory extension has a lovely outlook over the lawns. Modern, well-prepared dishes are simple and straightforward, yet full of flavour.

Menu £20/25 – Carte £31/57

Judges Country House, Kirklevington Hall, Kirklevington ⊠ TS15 9LW – South : 1.5 mi on A 67 – 𝒞 01642 789000 – www.judgeshotel.co.uk

X Muse

INTERNATIONAL · BRASSERIE Smart, modern continental café: bright and busy, with a pavement terrace in the summer. Extensive menu offers international brasserie dishes from lunchtime salads to pasta and grills; very good value set price menu of simpler dishes.

Menu £14 (lunch and early dinner) – Carte £23/46

104b High St ⊠ TS15 9AU – 𝒞 01642 788558 (booking advisable) – www.museyarm.com – Closed 25 December, 1 January and Sunday dinner

YARMOUTH – Isle of Wight → See Wight (Isle of)

YATTENDON

West Berkshire – ⊠ Newbury – Pop. 288 – Regional map n° **6**-B3
▶ London 54 mi – Bristol 68 mi – Newbury 9 mi

❢🄳 Royal Oak

TRADITIONAL BRITISH · INN A red-brick pub bursting with country charm, set in a picture postcard village; you'll find a heavily beamed bar with a roaring fire at its hub. Menus offer honest British dishes and traditional puddings. Country house style bedrooms are named after guns and even have their own gun cabinets.

Menu £15 (weekday lunch) – Carte £26/47

10 rooms ⌂ – ♦£95/135 ♦♦£95/135

The Square ⊠ RG18 0UF – 𝒞 01635 201325 (booking advisable) – www.royaloakyattendon.co.uk

at Frilsham South: 1 mi by Frilsham rd on Bucklebury rd⊠ Yattendon

❢🄳 Pot Kiln

TRADITIONAL BRITISH · COSY Head for the cosy bar and order a pint of Brick Kiln beer then follow the delicious aromas through to the dining area, where flavoursome British dishes arrive in gutsy portions. On summer Sundays they fire up the outdoor pizza oven.

Carte £28/42

⊠ RG18 0XX – 𝒞 01635 201366 – www.potkiln.org – Closed 25 December

YEOVIL

Somerset – Pop. 45 784 – Regional map n° **2**-B3
▶ London 130 mi – Taunton 28 mi – Bristol 42 mi

at Barwick South: 2 mi by A30 off A37⊠ Yeovil

XX Little Barwick House

MODERN BRITISH · INTIMATE Attractive Georgian dower house on the outskirts of town, run by a hospitable husband and wife team. Relax on deep sofas before heading into the elegant dining room with its huge window and heavy drapes. Cooking is classical, satisfying and full of flavour – a carefully chosen wine list accompanies. Charming, comfortably furnished bedrooms, each with its own character.

Menu £30/49

7 rooms ⌂ – ♦£75/140 ♦♦£100/170

⊠ BA22 9TD – 𝒞 01935 423902 (booking essential) – www.littlebarwickhouse.co.uk – Closed 26 December-27 January, dinner Sunday, Monday and lunch Tuesday

GOOD TIPS!

In the tourist capital of the North, every cobbled twist and turn reveals another historic building. A stone's throw from the magnificent York Minster cathedral is the **Judge's Lodging**; once a doctor's house and now a characterful hotel. Follow the ancient city walls to the Museum Gardens and the **Star Inn The City**, where chargrilled meats are a highlight.

YORK

York – Pop. 198 900 – Regional map n° **13**-C2

▶ London 213 mi – Leeds 28 mi – Newcastle upon Tyne 86 mi

Hotels

🏠 Grand H. & Spa York   ♤ 🖾 🕥 🏠 ᒪ🗗 🖃 ᬓ 🔼 ᬚ 🅿

BUSINESS · CONTEMPORARY Original features blend with contemporary décor in the grand former offices of the North Eastern Railway Company. Spacious, modern bedrooms are well-equipped and there's an impressive spa and leisure facility in the cellar. The formal, two-roomed restaurant serves ambitious modern dishes.

208 rooms ⌑ – ♦£ 148/318 ♦♦£ 148/318 – 13 suites
Town plan: A2-v - Station Rise ✉ YO1 6HT – ℰ 01904 380038
– www.thegrandyork.co.uk

🏠 Middlethorpe Hall   ♤ ≼ 📠 🖾 🏠 ᒪ🗗 🖃 ᬓ 🔼 🅿

HISTORIC · CLASSIC A William and Mary House dating from 1699, set in 20 acres of impressive parkland. The elegant sitting room has French-style furnishings, oil paintings and flower displays. Antique-filled bedrooms are split between the house and the courtyard. Classic cooking uses luxury ingredients and kitchen garden produce.

29 rooms ⌑ – ♦£ 143/205 ♦♦£ 205/287 – 9 suites
Bishopthorpe Rd ✉ YO23 2GB – South : 1.75 mi – ℰ 01904 641241
– www.middlethorpe.com

🏠 Grange   ♤ ᬚ 🅿

TOWNHOUSE · ELEGANT Well-run, Grade II listed Regency hotel with a grand portico entrance. Inside, flower arrangements and horse racing memorabilia abound. Choose between traditional bedrooms – some with four-posters – or more up-to-date rooms with TVs in the bathrooms. The informal basement brasserie serves a classical menu.

41 rooms ⌑ – ♦£ 110/150 ♦♦£ 140/175 – 1 suite
Town plan: A1-u - ✉ YO30 6AA – ℰ 01904 644744
– www.grangehotel.co.uk

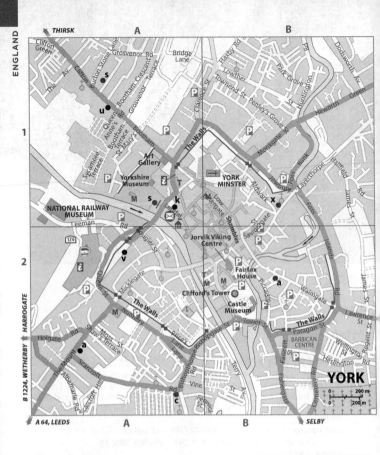

🏨 Hotel du Vin ✿ 🛏 🖥 ♿ AC 🧖 🅿

TOWNHOUSE · CONTEMPORARY An 18C former orphanage with a Georgian-style annexe, set on the edge of city. The stylish interior features two snug lounges, a chic champagne bar and a glass-roofed courtyard for afternoon tea. Well-equipped bedrooms are wine-themed and they offer an imaginative wine list in the popular French bistro.

44 rooms – ♥£100/320 ♥♥£100/320 – ☲£15

Town plan: A2-a *89 The Mount* ⊠ *YO24 1AX* – ℰ *01904 557350*
– *www.hotelduvin.com*

🏨 Judge's Lodging ✿ 🛋 🍴

HISTORIC · CONTEMPORARY Built for a doctor in 1706 and later used by judges sitting at the nearby court. Rooms in the main building have high ceilings and antique furnishings; the terrace rooms are more modern with smart shower rooms. It also has a wonderfully characterful barrel-ceilinged bar and a stylish brasserie and terrace.

23 rooms ☲ – ♥£119/144 ♥♥£119/190

Town plan: A1-k *9 Lendal* ⊠ *YO1 8AQ* – *West : 1 mi by A 59*
– ℰ *01904 638733*
– *www.judgeslodgingyork.co.uk*

🏠 Bishops   🐾 🅿

TRADITIONAL · PERSONALISED This centrally located Victorian guesthouse is run by a welcoming couple (he was once a professional footballer for Sunderland). Well-kept bedrooms vary in shape and size; some have four-posters. Local produce is served at breakfast.

10 rooms 🛏 – ♦£ 45/60 ♦♦£ 75/140

✉ YO24 4DF – Southwest : 1 mi on A 59 – ✆ 01904 628000
– www.bishopsyork.co.uk – Closed 1 week Christmas

Restaurants

XX **Star Inn The City**   🏕 ᯤ AK 🖥 ⇔

MODERN BRITISH · DESIGN A buzzy all-day brasserie set in an old brick engine house, in a delightful riverside spot beside the Museum Gardens. Well-judged dishes are modern yet gutsy and showcase top Yorkshire produce – the char-grilled meats are a highlight.

Menu £ 22 (weekday lunch) – Carte £ 30/56

Town plan: A1-s – ✉ YO1 7DR – ✆ 01904 619208 – www.starinnthecity.co.uk

XX **Melton's**   AK 🖤 ⇔

MODERN BRITISH · NEIGHBOURHOOD A cosy-looking shop conversion in the suburbs. The walls are covered in murals of ingredients and happy diners, which is fitting as local produce features highly and the restaurant is well-regarded. Cooking is fresh and flavoursome.

Menu £ 26 (lunch and early dinner)/45 – Carte £ 31/42

Town plan: A2-c – 7 Scarcroft Rd ✉ YO23 1ND – ✆ 01904 634341 (booking essential) – www.meltonsrestaurant.co.uk – Closed 3 weeks Christmas, Sunday and Monday

XX **The Park**   AK 🅿

MODERN CUISINE · NEIGHBOURHOOD Adam Jackson has moved his restaurant to a quiet residential suburb of York; it's set within a hotel and is run by a chatty, knowledgeable team. The seasonal 6 course menu features complex, eye-catching dishes comprising many flavours.

Menu £ 55

Town plan: A1-s - Marmadukes Hotel, 4-5 St Peters Grove, Bootham ✉ YO30 6AQ – ✆ 01904 540903 – www.theparkrestaurant.co.uk – dinner only – Closed 24-26 December, 2 weeks January, 2 weeks summer, Sunday and Monday

X **Le Cochon Aveugle**

MODERN CUISINE · BISTRO An appealingly rustic bistro with striking chequerboard flooring and a unique style: it's a tiny place, with just 7 tables, but that's all part of its charm. The 'surprise' menu offers original modern dishes which feature some interesting combinations. Service is charming and well-paced.

Menu £ 40/60 – tasting menu only

Town plan: B2-a – ✉ YO1 9TX – ✆ 01904 640222 (booking essential) – www.lecochonaveugle.uk – dinner only – Closed 3 weeks January and Sunday-Monday

X **Le Langhe**   🍸 🏕 ⇔

🆕 **ITALIAN · RUSTIC** To the front, an upmarket deli sells imported Italian produce, while behind there's a small dining room and terrace serving an extensive selection of unfussy Italian dishes. The 4 course lunch with wine is great value and there are some interesting wines on offer. The rustic upstairs room is open Fri and Sat.

Menu £ 25 (lunch)/42 – Carte £ 24/36

Town plan: B1-x – ✉ YO1 7PW – ✆ 01904 622584 (booking advisable) – www.lelanghe.co.uk – lunch only and dinner Friday-Saturday – Closed first 2 weeks January, Easter Sunday, 25-27 December, Monday and Tuesday

ZENNOR

Cornwall – Regional map n° **1**-A3

▶ London 289 mi – Truro 30 mi – Plymouth 82 mi

🍴 **Gurnard's Head** ⚉ ⇔ ⇪ **P**

REGIONAL CUISINE · INN Surrounded by nothing but fields and livestock; a dog-friendly pub with shabby-chic décor, blazing fires and a relaxed, cosy feel. Menus rely on regional and foraged produce and the wine list offers some interesting choices by the glass. Compact bedrooms feature good quality linen and colourful throws.

Menu £ 19 (weekday lunch)/23 – Carte £ 26/32

7 rooms ⌂ – ♦£ 95/140 ♦♦£ 165/230

Treen ✉ *TR26 3DE – West : 1.5 mi on B 3306 – ℰ 01736 796928 (booking advisable) – www.gurnardshead.co.uk – Closed 24-25 December and 4 days early December*

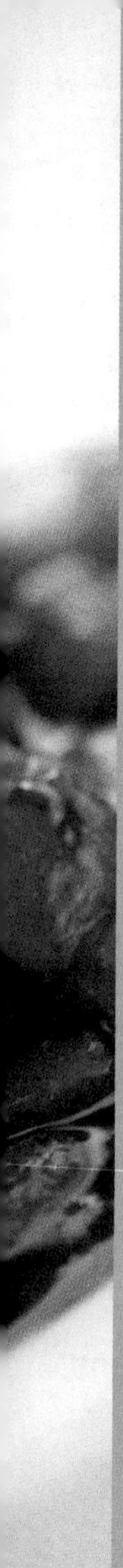

SCOTLAND

Scotland may be small, but its variety is immense.
The vivacity of Glasgow can seem a thousand miles
from the vast peatland wilderness of Caithness; the arty
vibe of Georgian Edinburgh a world away from the
remote and tranquil Ardnamurchan peninsula. Wide
golden sands trim the Atlantic at South Harris, and the
coastline of the Highlands boasts empty islands and
turquoise waters. Meantime, Fife's coast draws golf
fans to St Andrews and the more secretive delights
of East Neuk, an area of fishing villages and stone
harbours. Wherever you travel, a sense of a dramatic
history prevails in the shape of castles, cathedrals and
rugged lochside monuments to the heroes of old.

Food and drink embraces the traditional too, typified
by Speyside's famous Malt Whisky Trail. And what
better than Highland game, fresh fish from the Tweed
or haggis, neeps and tatties to complement a grand
Scottish hike? The country's glorious natural larder
yields such jewels as Spring lamb from the Borders,
Perthshire venison, fresh fish and shellfish from the
Western Highlands and Aberdeen Angus beef.

• Michelin Road map n° 501,
  502 and 713
• Michelin Green Guide:
  Great Britain

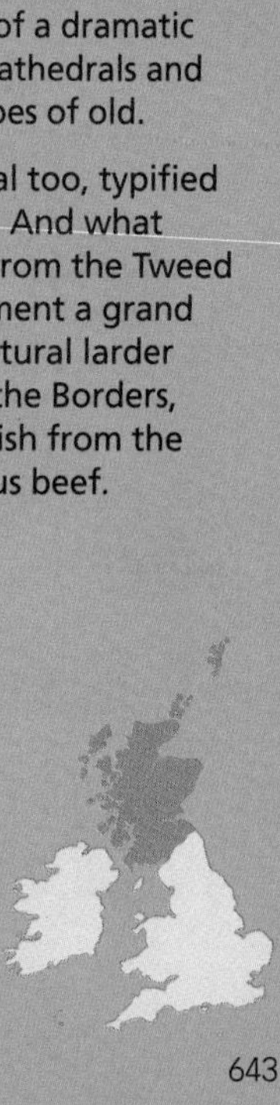

IOB/Loop Images/age fotostock

CENTRAL SCOTLAND
(plans **16**)

EAST
DUNBARTONSHIRE

WEST
DUNBARTONSHIRE

Balloch

FALKIRK

Dunblane

Stirling

Dunoon

Rothesay

NORTH
LANARKSHIRE

Glasgow

Giffnock

High Blantyre

Fairlie

NORTH
AYRSHIRE

Lochranza

Dalry

EAST
AYRSHIRE

Brodick

Gatehead

SOUTH

Lamlash

Troon

Sorn

Isle of Arran

Ayr

LANARK

Cumnock

Sanquhar

2

Turnberry

SOUTH
AYRSHIRE

Thornhill

Ballantrae

DUMFRIES

Portpatrick

Castle Douglas

Kirkcudbright

Luce Bay

3

Kilbrannan Sound

Firth of Clyde

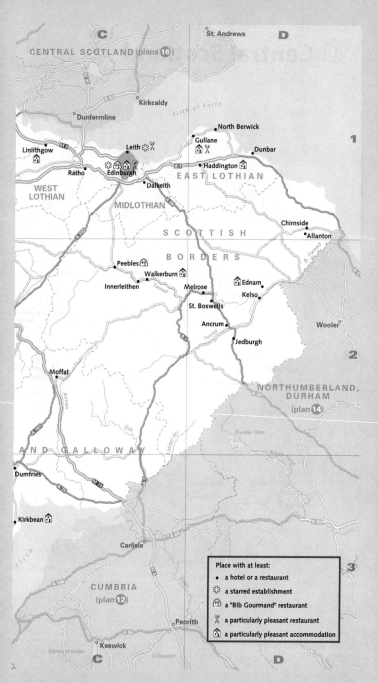

Place with at least:
- • a hotel or a restaurant
- ❀ a starred establishment
- 😊 a "Bib Gourmand" restaurant
- ✗ a particularly pleasant restaurant
- 🏠 a particularly pleasant accommodation

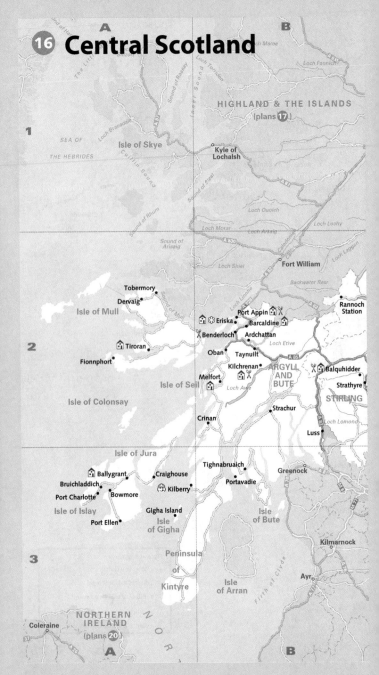

HIGHLAND & THE ISLANDS
(plans 17)

SEA OF
THE HEBRIDES

Isle of Skye

Kyle of
Lochalsh

Loch Brandale

Fort William

Backwater Resr

Tobermory

Dervaig

Isle of Mull

Rannoch
Station

Port Appin
Eriska
Barcaldine
Benderloch
Ardchattan

Tiroran

Oban

Taynuilt

Loch Etive

Balquhidder

Fionnphort

Kilchrenan

ARGYLL
AND
BUTE

Strathyre

Melfort

STIRLING

Isle of Seil

Loch Awe

Isle of Colonsay

Strachur

Loch Lomond

Crinan

Luss

Isle of Jura

Tighnabruaich

Greenock

Ballygrant

Craighouse

Bruichladdich

Kilberry

Portavadie

Port Charlotte

Bowmore

Gigha Island

Isle
of Bute

Isle of Islay

Port Ellen

Isle
of Gigha

Kilmarnock

Peninsula

of

Isle
of Arran

Ayr

Kintyre

NORTHERN
IRELAND
(plans 20)

Coleraine

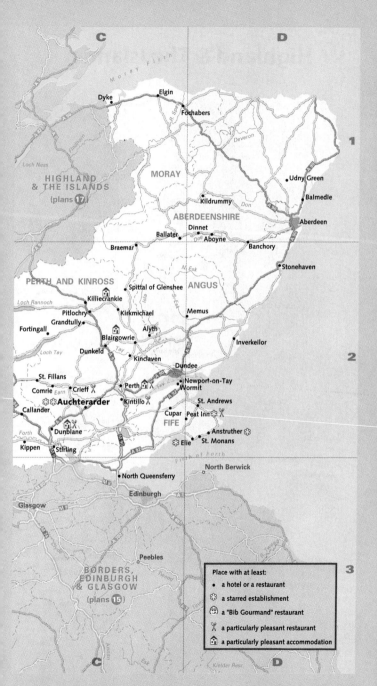

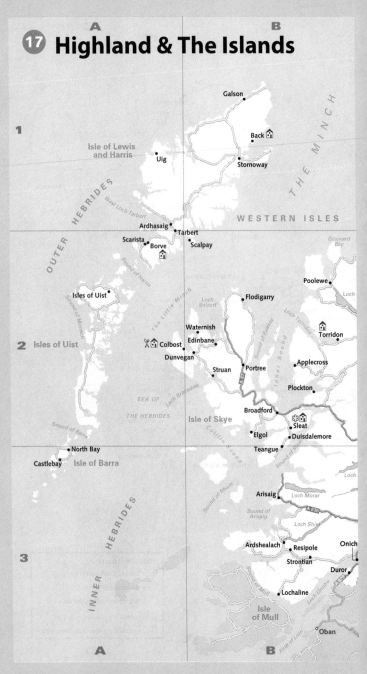

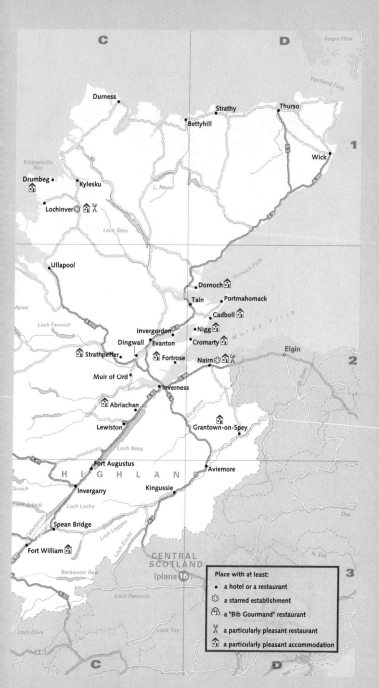

Durness

Strathy

Thurso

Bettyhill

Wick

Eddrachillis
Bay

Drumbeg

Kylesku

L. Naver

Lochinver

Loch Shin

Dornoch Firth

Ullapool

Dornoch

Tain

Portmahomack

Cadboll

Loch Fannich

Invergordon

Nigg

Dingwall

Evanton

Cromarty

Moray Firth

Elgin

Strathpeffer

Fortrose

Nairn

Muir of Ord

Inverness

Abriachan

Lewiston

Grantown-on-Spey

Loch Ness

H I G H L A N D

Fort Augustus

Aviemore

Invergarry

Kingussie

Loch Lochy

Spean Bridge

Loch Laggan

Loch Eicht

Fort William

CENTRAL
SCOTLAND
(plans 16)

Backwater Res.

N. Esk

Loch Rannoch

Loch Etive

Loch Tay

Place with at least:	
●	a hotel or a restaurant
✿	a starred establishment
🍴	a "Bib Gourmand" restaurant
✗	a particularly pleasant restaurant
🏠	a particularly pleasant accommodation

Shetland & Orkney 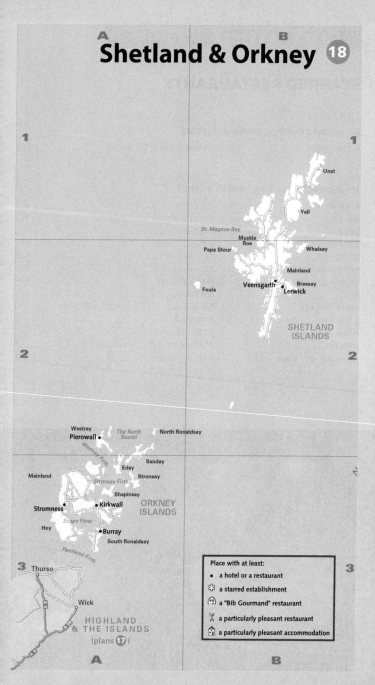 18

Unst

Yell

St. Magnus Bay

Muckle
Roe

Papa Stour

Whalsay

Mainland

Foula

Veensgarth •

Bressay
Lerwick

SHETLAND
ISLANDS

Westray
Pierowall •

*The North
Sound*

North Ronaldsay

Westray Firth

Sanday

Eday

Stronsay

Mainland

Stronsay Firth

Shapinsay

Stromness

• **Kirkwall**

ORKNEY
ISLANDS

Scapa Flow

Hoy

• **Burray**

South Ronaldsay

Pentland Firth

Thurso

Wick

HIGHLAND
& THE ISLANDS
(plans 17)

Place with at least:

• a hotel or a restaurant

✿ a starred establishment

☺ a "Bib Gourmand" restaurant

✗ a particularly pleasant restaurant

🏠 a particularly pleasant accommodation

FOOD NOT TO BE MISSED

STARRED RESTAURANTS

❀ ❀

Excellent cooking, worth a detour!

Auchterarder . . . . .Andrew Fairlie at Gleneagles 662

❀

High quality cooking, worth a stop!

Anstruther . . . . .The Cellar 659
Balloch . . . . .Martin Wishart at Loch Lomond 663
Dalry . . . . .Braidwoods 672
Edinburgh 21212 683
Edinburgh . . . . .Number One 683
Edinburgh / Leith. . . . . .Kitchin 688
Edinburgh / Leith. . . . . .Martin Wishart 688
Elie . . . . .Sangster's 689
Eriska (Isle of) .Isle of Eriska 690
Lochinver. . . . . .Albannach 713
Nairn. . . . . .Boath House 717
Peat Inn . . . . .The Peat Inn 721
Skye (Isle of) / Sleat . . . . .Kinloch Lodge 735

Michelin

OUR TOP PICKS

BIB GOURMANDS ⊛
Good quality, good value cooking

Edinburgh	Dogs	686
Edinburgh	Galvin Brasserie De Luxe	685
Edinburgh	Passorn	686
Edinburgh	The Scran and Scallie **N**	688
Glasgow	The Gannet	698
Glasgow	Ox and Finch	699
Glasgow	Stravaigin	699
Kintyre (Peninsula) / Kilberry	Kilberry Inn	707
Peebles	Osso	722

A sense of golfing history

Gleneagles 🏠🏠🏠	Auchterarder	661
Cameron House 🏠🏠🏠	Balloch	663
Old Course H. Golf Resort & Spa 🏠🏠🏠	St Andrews	729
Trump Turnberry 🏠🏠🏠🏠	Turnberry	743

Charming guesthouses

Ardtorna 🏠	Barcaldine	665
Factor's House 🏠	Cromarty	670
Blar na Leisg at Drumbeg House 🏠	Drumbeg	673
Dulaig 🏠	Grantown-on-Spey	700
Letham House 🏠	Haddington	701
Hillstone Lodge 🏠	Skye (Isle of)/Colbost	733
Craigvar 🏠	Strathpeffer	739
Wemyss House 🏠	Tain/Nigg	740

Known for their welcome

No.26 The Crescent 🏠............Ayr.. 662

Cosses Country House 🏠.........Ballantrae.................................. 663

Grange 🏠.......................Fort William............................... 691

15 Glasgow 🏠...................Glasgow.................................... 695

Edenwater House 🏠.............Kelso/Ednam................................ 706

Roineabhal 🏠...................Kilchrenan................................. 706

Something a little different

Monachyle Mhor 🍴🍴..............Balquhidder................................ 664

Gardeners Cottage 🍴...........Edinburgh.................................. 687

The Honours 🍴🍴.................Edinburgh.................................. 684

Timberyard 🍴..................Edinburgh.................................. 685

Seafood 🍴🍴....................St Andrews................................. 731

Craig Millar at 16 West End 🍴🍴......St Monans.................................. 732

Michelin

Michelin

Hideaways

Loch Ness Lodge 命命 . . . . Abriachan 658
Kilmichael Country House 命命 . . . . . . Arran (Isle of)/Brodick 661
Cavens 命 . . . . Kirkbean 708
Tiroran House 命 . . . . Mull (Isle of)/Tiroran 716
Airds 命命 . . . . Port Appin 727
Knockinaam Lodge 命命 . . . . Portpatrick 728
Kinloch Lodge 命命 . . . . Skye (Isle of)/Sleat 735
Glenmorangie House 命 . . . . Tain/Cadboll 740

Ultimate luxury

Glenapp Castle 命命命 . . . . Ballantrae 662
Kinloch House 命命命 . . . . Blairgowrie 667
Cromlix 命命命 . . . . Dunblane 674
Isle of Eriska 命命命 . . . . Eriska (Isle of) 690
Inverlochy Castle 命命命 . . . . Fort William 691
Greywalls 命命 . . . . Gullane 701
Torridon 命命命 . . . . Torridon 742

ABERDEEN

Aberdeen City – Pop. 195 021 – Regional map n° **16**-D1

▶ Edinburgh 126 mi – Dundee 65 mi – Dunfermline 112 mi

The Chester

TOWNHOUSE · CONTEMPORARY This smart boutique townhouse fits perfectly in this wealthy residential area. Sleek, contemporary bedrooms come with the latest mod cons (including Apple TV), and show a keen eye for detail. The cocktail bar and restaurant are set over three levels; seafood and grills from the Josper oven are a highlight.

50 rooms 🖙 – ♦£ 99/185 ♦♦£ 119/220 – 2 suites

Town plan: A2-v - *59-63 Queens Rd* ⊠ *AB15 4YP* – 𝒞 *01224 327777*

– *www.chester-hotel.com*

Malmaison

BUSINESS · DESIGN In a smart city suburb and built around a period property – now the height of urban chic. Black, slate-floored reception adorned with bagpipes and kilts; stylish bar with a whisky cellar. Funky, modern bedrooms have atmospheric lighting. High-ceilinged brasserie serves modern dishes, with steaks a speciality.

79 rooms – ♦£ 79/179 ♦♦£ 79/179 – 🖙 £ 16

Town plan: A2-e - *49-53 Queens Rd* ⊠ *AB15 4YP* – 𝒞 *01224 327370*

– *www.malmaison.com*

bauhaus

BUSINESS · MINIMALIST Set just off the main street; its functional, minimalist style is in keeping with the Bauhaus school of design. Stylish, colour-coded bedrooms have sharp, clean lines and an uncluttered feel – 'Gropius' and 'Kandinsky' are the best.

39 rooms 🖙 – ♦£ 65/90 ♦♦£ 75/210 – 1 suite

Town plan: C2-r - *52-60 Langstane Pl.* ⊠ *AB11 6EN* – 𝒞 *01224 212122*

– *www.thebauhaus.co.uk*

Fusion

MODERN CUISINE · FASHIONABLE Modernised granite townhouse featuring an airy bar with lime green furniture and a more intimate mezzanine restaurant. Choose between a concise set menu and a 5 course tasting selection. Service is attentive and knowledgeable.

Menu £ 25 – Carte £ 22/26

Town plan: C1-c - *10 North Silver St* ⊠ *AB10 1RL* – 𝒞 *01224 652959*

– *www.fusionbarbistro.com* – *dinner only and Saturday lunch* – *Closed 1-5 January, Sunday and Monday*

Silver Darling

SEAFOOD · FRIENDLY Attractively set at the port entrance, on the top floor of the castellated former customs house. Floor to ceiling windows make the most of the superb view. Neatly presented, classical dishes; excellent quality seafood is a highlight.

Menu £ 27 (weekday lunch) – Carte £ 34/67

Pocra Quay, North Pier ⊠ *AB11 5DQ* – *Southeast : 1.5 mi by Milner St, St Clement St and York St* – 𝒞 *01224 576229* – *www.thesilverdarling.co.uk* – *Closed 2 weeks Christmas-New Year, Saturday lunch in winter and Sunday*

Rendezvous at Nargile

TURKISH · NEIGHBOURHOOD Bright neighbourhood restaurant run by a cheerful team. All-day menus are great for sharing. Well-spiced dishes have Middle Eastern flavours – particularly Turkish; the meze and banquet meals are a highlight and the baklava are homemade.

Menu £ 16 (early dinner) – Carte £ 25/36

Town plan: A2-b - *106-108 Forest Ave* ⊠ *AB15 4UP* – 𝒞 *01224 323700*

– *www.rendezvousatnargile.co.uk* – *Closed 25-26 December and 1-2 January*

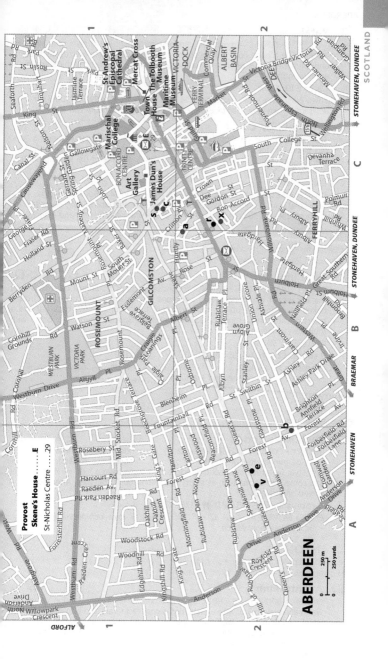

ABERDEEN

Provost Skene's House ...... E
St-Nicholas Centre 29

X Yatai

JAPANESE · SIMPLE Atmospheric Japanese restaurant in the style of a laid-back izakaya. The ground floor has a wooden counter and a robata grill; upstairs is airy and intimate. Menus offer tasty, authentic dishes – the sushi, sashimi and maki are highlights.

Carte £ 19/48

Town plan: C2-x - *53 Langstane Pl* ⊠ *AB11 6EN* – ℰ *01224 592355 (booking advisable)* – *www.yatai.co.uk* – *Closed 25 December-5 January and Monday*

X Yorokobi by CJ

JAPANESE · INTIMATE Popular Japanese restaurant with a name meaning 'joyous bliss'; C is for chef and J is for Jang, who takes on that role. Flavourful, authentic, good value Japanese and Korean dishes; try one of the sizzling platters or a Korean pot dish.

Carte £ 18/35

Town plan: BC2-a - *51 Huntly St* ⊠ *AB10 1TH* – ℰ *01224 566002 (booking advisable)* – *www.yorokobibycj.co.uk* – *dinner only and lunch Friday-Saturday* – *Closed 2 weeks summer, 2 weeks Christmas-New Year, Sunday and Monday*

ABOYNE
Aberdeenshire – Pop. 2 602 – Regional map n° **16**-D1
▶ Edinburgh 131 mi – Aberdeen 30 mi – Dundee 68 mi

🏠 Boat Inn

TRADITIONAL CUISINE · FRIENDLY Concise menu of traditional bar meals with the occasional international dish; portions are generous and there are freshly baked cakes for sale on the counter. Bright front room, a cosy back bar and a smart private dining room called the Pine Loft. Spacious bedrooms come with their own kitchenettes.

Carte £ 18/36

8 rooms ⊵ – ♦£ 65/95 ♦♦£ 75/110

Charleston Rd ⊠ *AB34 5EL* – ℰ *01339 886137* – *www.theboatinnaboyne.co.uk* – *Closed 25-26 December and 1 January*

ABRIACHAN
Highland – Pop. 120 – Regional map n° **17**-C2
▶ Edinburgh 167 mi – Dunfermline 153 mi – Dundee 148 mi

🏠 Loch Ness Lodge

LUXURY · CONTEMPORARY Passionately run modern country house, set in 18 acres of immaculately kept grounds overlooking Loch Ness. A classic-contemporary style features throughout. Spacious bedrooms have a high level of facilities and come with extras such as sherry and Penhaligon's toiletries. Afternoon tea is served on arrival.

6 rooms ⊵ – ♦£ 105/260 ♦♦£ 175/330

Brachla ⊠ *IV3 8LA* – *on A 82* – ℰ *01456 459469* – *www.loch-ness-lodge.com* – *Closed November-March*

ALLANTON
The Scottish Borders – Regional map n° **15**-D1
▶ Edinburgh 52 mi – Dumfries 92 mi – Glasgow 98 mi

🏠 Allanton Inn

MODERN BRITISH · FRIENDLY Striking stone inn in a conservation village. It's warm and welcoming, with a rustic bar, a cosy restaurant and bright, simply furnished bedrooms. Thoughtfully prepared modern dishes are crafted from local farm meats and Eyemouth fish. The regional cheeses are a hit, as is the pretty garden with country views.

Carte £ 17/38

6 rooms ⊵ – ♦£ 65/95 ♦♦£ 75/95

⊠ *TD11 3JZ* – ℰ *01890 818260* – *www.allantoninn.co.uk*

ALYTH

Perth and Kinross – Pop. 2 403 – Regional map n° **16**-C2
▶ Edinburgh 63 mi – Aberdeen 69 mi – Dundee 16 mi – Perth 21 mi

⌂ Tigh Na Leigh ☆ ⇦ ▣

LUXURY · MODERN An imposing Victorian house run in a relaxed yet professional manner. The interior is surprisingly modern – guest areas are inviting and contemporary bedrooms boast feature beds and great bathrooms with spa baths. The kitchen garden informs the unfussy modern menu; enjoy the lovely garden view while dining.

5 rooms ⌫ – ♦£ 54 ♦♦£ 92/130

22-24 Airlie St ✉ PH11 8AJ – ☎ 01828 632372 – www.tighnaleigh.co.uk – Closed 4 December-31 January

ANCRUM

The Scottish Borders – Regional map n° **15**-D2
▶ Edinburgh 44 mi – Glasgow 87 mi – Carlisle 55 mi – Perth 92 mi

▯ Ancrum Cross Keys ⇦ 😤 ♿

MODERN BRITISH · PUB What sets this place apart is the food – this is carefully crafted, tasty cooking with a refined edge; sit in the larger of the dining rooms to watch the chef at work. The man in charge also owns the nearby Scottish Borders Brewery.

Carte £ 21/32

The Green ✉ TD8 6XH – ☎ 01835 830242 – www.ancrumcrosskeys.com – Closed Monday, Tuesday and lunch Wednesday

ANSTRUTHER

Fife – Pop. 3 446 – Regional map n° **16**-D2
▶ Edinburgh 46 mi – Dundee 23 mi – Glasgow 77 mi

✗✗ The Cellar (Billy Boyter)
❀

MODERN CUISINE · RUSTIC Previously a smokehouse and a cooperage – now an iconic restaurant with exposed beams, stone walls and a cosy, characterful feel; pleasingly run by a local lad. Delicious, deftly prepared dishes are light, well-balanced and have subtle modern influences. Service is friendly and the atmosphere is relaxed.

→ East Neuk crab with cured cod, smoked shrimp jelly and cucumber juice. Lamb with goat's curd, hay-baked kohlrabi and wild garlic. Crowdie cheesecake mousse, white chocolate Aero, tarragon and yogurt sorbet.

Menu £ 28/48

✉ KY10 3AA – ☎ 01333 310378 (booking essential)
– www.thecellaranstruther.co.uk – Closed first 3 weeks January, 10 days May, 10 days September, 24-26 December, lunch Wednesday-Thursday October-March and Monday-Tuesday

APPLECROSS

Highland – Regional map n° **17**-B2
▶ Edinburgh 233 mi – Inverness 80 mi – Fort William 104 mi

✗ Applecross Walled Garden ⇦ 😤 ♿ ▣

TRADITIONAL CUISINE · FRIENDLY Set in a former potting shed in a 17C walled garden – where much of the produce is grown. A small counter displays homemade cakes. Light lunches are followed at dinner by more original dishes with clearly defined natural flavours.

Carte £ 18/36

✉ IV54 8ND – North : 0.5 mi – ☎ 01520 744440 – www.applecrossgarden.co.uk – Closed November-February

🏠 Applecross Inn   ⟻ ⟨ 🛏 🏠 ♿ 🅿

SEAFOOD · INN Unpretentious inn with friendly service and a bustling atmosphere; take the scenic route over the hair-raising, single-track Bealach na Ba, with its stunning views and hairpin bends to reach it. Dine on the freshest of seafood, often caught within sight of the door. Simple bedrooms have marvellous sea views.

Carte £ 16/40

7 rooms ☱ – 👤£ 80/100 👥£ 120/140

Shore St ✉ *IV54 8LR* – ☎ *01520 744262 (booking essential)*
– www.applecross.uk.com/inn – Closed 25 December and 1 January

ARDCHATTAN

Argyll and Bute – Regional map n° **16**-B2
▶ Edinburgh 123 mi – Glasgow 98 mi – Oban 12 mi

🏠 Blarcreen House   🏠 🐾 ⟨ 🛏 🍽 🅿

RURAL · HOMELY Friendly Victorian former farmhouse set in a tranquil location down a single track and boasting superb views over Loch Etive. Homely lounge and comfy bedrooms: two with four-posters and double-aspects; all with robes, fridges and fresh milk. Lovely dining room offers a daily menu of home-cooked dishes.

3 rooms ☱ – 👤£ 90/110 👥£ 110/130

✉ *PA37 1RG – East : 1 mi past Ardchattan Priory and gardens on Bonawe rd*
– ☎ 01631 750272 – www.blarcreenhouse.com – Closed Christmas and New Year

ARDHASAIG – Western Isles ➡ See Lewis and Harris (Isle of)

ARDSHEALACH

Highland – Regional map n° **29**-B3
▶ Edinburgh 152 mi – Fort William 46 mi – Oban 62 mi

🏠 Ardshealach Lodge ⓝ   🏠 🐾 ⟨ 🛏 🅿

TRADITIONAL · PERSONALISED Smart Victorian former hunting lodge in 22 acres of grounds; in a fabulous location on the Ardamurchan Peninsula overlooking Loch Sheil. Traditional bedrooms; ask for one at the front. Wide range of classic dishes served in the restaurant, with fruit, veg and herbs from the garden. Non-resident diners welcome.

3 rooms ☱ – 👤£ 50 👥£ 100

✉ *PH36 4JL – On A 861 – ☎ 01967 431399 – www.ardshealach-lodge.co.uk*

ARISAIG

Highland – Regional map n° **17**-B3
▶ Edinburgh 178 mi – Fort William 36 mi – Oban 80 mi

🏠 Arisaig House   🏠 🐾 ⟨ 🛏 🍽 🅿

COUNTRY HOUSE · PERSONALISED Attractive Victorian country house surrounded by mature grounds which lead down to the sea. Bedrooms retain their traditional feel and the building's original features are enhanced by a fine collection of artwork. Classic menus use ingredients from the kitchen garden, nearby estates and local waters.

14 rooms ☱ – 👤£ 85/120 👥£ 165/235

Beasdale ✉ *PH39 4NR – East : 2.5 mi by A 830 – ☎ 01687 450730*
– www.arisaighouse.co.uk – Closed November-April

ARRAN (Isle of)

North Ayrshire – Pop. 4 629 – Regional map n° **15**-A2
▶ Edinburgh 83 mi – Glasgow 37 mi – Oban 67 mi

Brodick

⌂ Kilmichael Country House   ⌖ ≤ 🖼 P

COUNTRY HOUSE · CLASSIC A sympathetically restored 17C house – reputedly the oldest house on the Isle of Arran – delightfully located in a peaceful glen and surrounded by mountains. Comfortable bedrooms are furnished with antiques; those in the converted stable block offer a little more comfort and privacy.

5 rooms ☲ – †£ 75/98 ††£ 120/205

Glen Cloy ⊠ *KA27 8BY – West : 1 mi by Shore Rd, taking left turn opposite Golf Club –* ℰ *01770 302219 – www.kilmichael.com – Closed November-Easter*

Lamlash

⌂ Glenisle   ⌖ ≤ 🖼 ᚱ ℅ P

TRADITIONAL · COSY Attractive whitewashed former inn, boasting views over the bay to Holy Island. It has an open-plan bar-lounge and a small snug. Bright, airy bedrooms come in natural hues; one covers the whole top floor and has a roll-top bath. The rustic dining room and terrace offer fresh, simple, homely cooking.

13 rooms ☲ – †£ 94/98 ††£ 129/228

Shore Rd. ⊠ *KA27 8LY –* ℰ *01770 600559 – www.glenislehotel.com*

Lochranza

⌂ Apple Lodge   ⌖ ≤ 🖼 ℅ P 🍴

TRADITIONAL · CLASSIC Former manse with attractive gardens, in a quiet hamlet surrounded by mountains. Traditionally decorated, comfortable and personally run, with many regular guests. Bedrooms have pleasant views; Apple Cottage is a self-contained garden suite. 3 course menu of classic, home-cooked dishes served by candlelight.

4 rooms ☲ – †£ 50 ††£ 78/90

⊠ *KA27 8HJ –* ℰ *01770 830229 – www.applelodgearran.co.uk – Closed 15 December-15 January*

AUCHTERARDER

Perth and Kinross – Pop. 4 206 – Regional map n° **16**-C2
▶ Edinburgh 55 mi – Glasgow 46 mi – Aberdeen 102 mi

⌂⌂⌂ Gleneagles   ⌖ ≤ 🖼 🖼 🖼 ⑳ 🦊 ᛚᚴ ℀ 🖼 ᚴ 🚲 🏊 P

GRAND LUXURY · ART DÉCO World-famous resort hotel with a renowned championship golf course, majestic art deco styling, an elegant interior and luxurious bedrooms. Excellent leisure facilities include a state-of-the-art spa, a popular equestrian centre and a gun-dog school. Strathearn offers a classical menu and superb estate views. All-day Deseo serves Mediterranean-influenced dishes and tapas.

232 rooms ☲ – †£ 365/585 ††£ 365/585 – 16 suites

⊠ *PH3 1NF – Southwest : 2 mi by A 824 on A 823 –* ℰ *01764 662231 – www.gleneagles.com*

❀❀ **Andrew Fairlie at Gleneagles** – See restaurant listing

⌂ Cairn   ⌖ 🖼 ℅ 🏊 P

COUNTRY HOUSE · DESIGN Glitzy lodge with pleasant gardens and a monochrome theme. There's a piano in the hall and an elegant bar with white tub chairs. Stylish modern bedrooms feature black ash furnishings and coffee machines. The chic restaurant has studded leather walls, twisty chandeliers and sumptuous leather seating.

14 rooms ☲ – †£ 99/280 ††£ 99/280

Orchill Rd ⊠ *PH3 1LX – West : 0.5 mi by Townhead Rd and Western Rd –* ℰ *01764 662634 – www.cairnlodge.co.uk*

XXXX Andrew Fairlie at Gleneagles   🕹 AC 🕪 P

🕸🕸 CREATIVE FRENCH · LUXURY An elegant restaurant hung with portraits of its famous chef. The à la carte focuses on refined French classics, with home-smoked lobster a signature dish, while the 8 course dégustation menu showcases their top picks 'en miniature'. Much of the produce is from their walled garden. Accomplished, carefully balanced cooking is coupled with professional, good-humoured service.

→ Home-smoked lobster, lime and herb butter. Roast loin of roe deer with venison tartare, bonbon and port jus. Passion fruit soufflé with piña colada sorbet and rum sauce.

Menu £ 95/125

*Gleneagles Hotel, ⊠ PH3 1NF – Southwest : 2 mi by A 824 on A 823
– 𝒞 01764 694267 – www.andrewfairlie.co.uk – dinner only – Closed 3-28 January, 25-26 December and Sunday*

AVIEMORE
Highland – Pop. 3 147 – Regional map n° **17**-D3
▶ Edinburgh 129 mi – Inverness 29 mi – Perth 85 mi

🏠 Old Minister's Guest House   🖨 ⅋ P

TRADITIONAL · PERSONALISED A 19C stone-built manse with unusual carved wood animals out the front and pretty gardens leading down to the river. The smart lounge has deep sofas and an honesty bar and the stylish bedrooms are spacious and well-appointed.

5 rooms ⌂ – †£ 120/125 ††£ 145/150

*Rothiemurchus ⊠ PH22 1QH – Southeast : 1 mi on B 970 – 𝒞 01479 812181
– www.theoldministershouse.co.uk*

AYR
South Ayrshire – Pop. 46 849 – Regional map n° **15**-A2
▶ Edinburgh 82 mi – Glasgow 36 mi – Dumfries 60 mi

🏠 No.26 The Crescent   ⅋

TOWNHOUSE · PERSONALISED Well-run Victorian terraced house, displaying a pleasing mix of traditional features and modern décor. Bedrooms are individually furnished; the best has a four-poster. Smoked haddock with poached eggs is a speciality at breakfast.

5 rooms ⌂ – †£ 70/95 ††£ 85/110

26 Bellevue Cres ⊠ KA7 2DR – 𝒞 01292 287329 – www.26crescent.co.uk – Closed 23-30 December

BACK – Western Isles → See Lewis and Harris (Isle of)

BALLANTRAE
South Ayrshire – ⊠ Girvan – Pop. 672 – Regional map n° **15**-A2
▶ Edinburgh 115 mi – Ayr 33 mi – Stranraer 18 mi

🏰 Glenapp Castle   🕳 🕸 ← 🖨 ⅋ ⬆ P

HISTORIC BUILDING · CLASSIC A long wooded drive leads to this stunning baronial castle with beautifully manicured gardens and Ailsa Craig views; it's personally run and the service is charming. The grand antique-filled interior has oak-panelled hallways, luxurious, impressively proportioned lounges and handsomely appointed bedrooms. The elegant dining room showcases local and garden ingredients.

23 rooms (dinner included) ⌂ – †£ 220/430 ††£ 350/570 – 4 suites
*⊠ KA26 0NZ – South : 1 mi by A 77 taking first right turn after bridge
– 𝒞 01465 831212 – www.glenappcastle.com*

🏠 Cosses Country House ✿ 🐾 ♿ 🅿

TRADITIONAL · COSY A 17C shooting lodge with lovely gardens, in an idyllic rural location. Immaculately kept bedrooms and suites – two in the old stables and byre – boast iPod docks, fresh flowers and underfloor heated bathrooms. Homemade cake is served on arrival in the kitchen, dining room or garden, and the 4 course, single-choice set dinners showcase local and garden produce.

3 rooms ☲ – †£ 85/105 ††£ 110/140

✉ KA26 0LR – East : 2.25 mi by A 77 (South) taking first turn left after bridge
– ✆ 01465 831363 – www.cossescountryhouse.com – Restricted opening in winter

BALLATER

Aberdeenshire – Pop. 1 533 – Regional map n° **16**-C1
▶ Edinburgh 111 mi – Aberdeen 41 mi – Inverness 70 mi – Perth 67 mi

🏠 Auld Kirk 🅿

HISTORIC · PERSONALISED Striking granite building – a church from 1870-1938; the bar-lounge still has the original stained glass windows. Bright, modern bedrooms with bold furnishings. Comprehensive breakfasts; the 'spirit of ecstasy' sculpture is a talking point!

7 rooms ☲ – †£ 80/110 ††£ 115/140

Braemar Rd ✉ AB35 5RQ – ✆ 01339 755762 – www.theauldkirk.com – Closed Christmas

🏠 Moorside House ♿ 🌾 🅿

TRADITIONAL · CLASSIC Traditional 19C former manse with a large garden, simple, homely bedrooms and a comfortable lounge filled with books about the local area. Original Victorian features include ornate cornicing and an attractive pine staircase. Hearty breakfasts feature homemade bread, muffins, muesli and preserves.

9 rooms ☲ – †£ 50 ††£ 70

26 Braemar Rd ✉ AB35 5RL – ✆ 01339 755492 – www.moorsidehouse.co.uk
– Closed October-Easter

BALLOCH

West Dunbartonshire – Regional map n° **15**-B1
▶ Edinburgh 72 mi – Glasgow 20 mi – Stirling 30 mi

🏰 Cameron House ✿ 🐾 ≼ ♿ 🖼 🖵 🌐 🔈 ⅙ ✕ 🔲 ₺ ⅍ 📻 🎿 🅿

SPA AND WELLNESS · CONTEMPORARY An extensive Victorian house and lodges set in 250 acres on the shore of Loch Lomond. Excellent leisure facilities include a spa, a golf course, a launch and a seaplane. Bedrooms are modern and moody, aside from the Whisky Suites which are more traditional. There are several dining options, including the informal Claret Jug bar and masculine grill restaurant Camerons.

134 rooms ☲ – †£ 155/425 ††£ 165/435 – 11 suites – ††£ 540/1079

Loch Lomond ✉ G83 8QZ – Northwest : 1.5 mi by A 811 on A 82 – ✆ 01389 755565
– www.cameronhouse.co.uk

❀ Martin Wishart at Loch Lomond • Boat House – See restaurant listing

XXX Martin Wishart at Loch Lomond ≼ ♿ ₺ 📻 🍴 🅿

❀ MODERN CUISINE · CHIC Smart restaurant in a lochside resort hotel, offering superb water and mountain views. Seasonal modern menus showcase Scottish ingredients in well-judged, creative combinations. Cooking is accomplished and dishes are attractively presented. The tasting menus include a 6 course vegetarian option.

→ Foie gras mousse with apricots, nuts, seeds and oloroso sherry. Fillet of turbot with smoked cockles, mushrooms and wild garlic. Crème fraîche parfait with mango and passion fruit.

Menu £ 32/95

Cameron House Hotel, Loch Lomond ✉ G83 8QZ – Northwest : 1.5 mi by A 811 on
A 82 – ✆ 01389 722504 (booking essential) – www.mwlochlomond.co.uk – Closed
1-14 January, Monday, Tuesday and lunch Wednesday

✗✗ Boat House

MEDITERRANEAN CUISINE · BISTRO Relaxed, buzzy restaurant in the grounds of Cameron House. The décor has a New England feel and its doors open out onto a jetty; bag a spot on the terrace if you can. Unfussy Mediterranean dishes include fresh Loch Fyne seafood.

Carte £ 22/47

Cameron House Hotel, Loch Lomond ⊠ G83 8QZ – Northwest : 1.5 mi by A 811 on A 82 – ✆ 01389 722585 – www.cameronhouse.co.uk

BALLYGRANT – Argyll and Bute → See Islay (Isle of)

BALMEDIE

Aberdeenshire – Pop. 2 534 – Regional map n° **16**-D1
▶ Edinburgh 137 mi – Aberdeen 7 mi – Peterhead 24 mi

🏠🏠🏠 Trump International Golf Links Scotland

LUXURY · MODERN Intimate hotel with a Championship links golf course, set on a 2,200 acre estate. The hotel is split between an 18C stone house and a lodge and features plush fabrics and opulent furnishings. Large bedrooms have arabesque furnishings and offer all you could want. The intimate restaurant serves a modern menu.

19 rooms � – ♦£ 225/365 ♦♦£ 250/390

MacLeod House and Lodge, Menie Estate ⊠ AB23 8YE – ✆ 01358 743300 – www.trumpgolfscotland.com – Closed 1-14 January

🏠 Cock and Bull

TRADITIONAL BRITISH · RUSTIC Quirky pub with a profusion of knick-knacks; dine in the cosy, open-fired lounge, the formal dining room or the airy conservatory. Menus offer a mix of pub classics and well-presented restaurant style dishes. Some of the contemporary bedrooms are in a nearby annexe; there's a complimentary shuttle service.

Menu £ 18 – Carte £ 21/34

6 rooms – ♦£ 75/95 ♦♦£ 75/110 – ⊟ £ 10

Ellon Rd, Blairton ⊠ AB23 8XY – North : 1 mi on A 90 – ✆ 01358 743249 – www.thecockandbull.co.uk – Closed 26-27 December and 1-2 January

BALQUHIDDER

Stirling – Regional map n° **16**-B2
▶ Edinburgh 70 mi – Stirling 29 mi – Perth 42 mi

🏠 Monachyle Mhor

TRADITIONAL · PERSONALISED A former farmhouse, located in a beautiful, very remote glen. Contemporary furnishings blend with original features in the reception, lounge and cosy bar. Smart, modern bedrooms boast slate-tiled bathrooms with underfloor heating; those in the main house afford great views over the Braes of Balquhidder.

16 rooms ⊟ – ♦£ 185/256 ♦♦£ 195/265

⊠ FK19 8PQ – West : 3.75 mi – ✆ 01877 384622 – www.mhor.net – Closed 5-25 January

Monachyle Mhor – See restaurant listing

✗✗ Monachyle Mhor

MODERN CUISINE · INTIMATE In the rurally set hotel of the same name is this candlelit conservatory restaurant with a warm, relaxing ambience and views of the glen. The set price menu features produce reared on the family farm and grown in the kitchen garden; cooking is modern and accomplished, with lots of natural flavours.

Menu £ 30/59

Monachyle Mhor Hotel, ⊠ FK19 8PQ – West : 3.75 mi – ✆ 01877 384622 (booking essential) – www.mhor.net – Closed 5-25 January

✗ Mhor 84

TRADITIONAL CUISINE · TRADITIONAL DÉCOR Food is served all day at this laid-back restaurant, where you're greeted by a welcoming team and a case bursting with cakes from their bakery. Produce from their farm features in hearty, unfussy dishes and things step up a gear on the daily changing dinner menu. Simple bedrooms boast extremely comfy beds.

Carte £ 27/52

11 rooms – †£ 80 ††£ 80 – ☱ £ 12

Kingshouse ⊠ FK19 8NY – East: 2 mi at junction with A 84 – ℰ 01877 384646
– www.mhor.net

BANCHORY

Aberdeenshire – Pop. 7 278 – Regional map n° **16**-D2
▶ Edinburgh 118 mi – Aberdeen 17 mi – Dundee 55 mi – Inverness 94 mi

⌂ Tor-Na-Coille

HISTORIC · PERSONALISED Well-run mansion dating from 1873 and surrounded by mature grounds. The décor blends the modern with the classic, and original cornicing, fireplaces and staircases feature. Bedrooms boast stylish wallpapers and bright, bold furnishings. The intimate restaurant showcases Scottish produce in up-to-date dishes.

25 rooms ☱ – †£ 100/115 ††£ 125/200

Inchmarlo Rd ⊠ AB31 4AB – West : 0.5 mi on A 93 – ℰ 01330 822242
– www.tornacoille.com

✗ Cowshed

MODERN CUISINE · MINIMALIST Impressive modern building with a cavernous dining room and countryside views. Simple, good value lunches, followed by more ambitious evening menus; meat and game is from the surrounding estates. Cookery classes available.

Carte £ 17/35

Raemoir Rd ⊠ AB31 5QB – North : 1.5 mi on A 980 – ℰ 01330 820813 (booking advisable) – www.cowshedrestaurant.co.uk – Closed 1-10 January

BARCALDINE

Argyll and Bute – Regional map n° **16**-B2
▶ Edinburgh 124 mi – Glasgow 98 mi – Oban 12 mi

⌂ Ardtorna

LUXURY · CONTEMPORARY An ultra-modern guesthouse in a stunning spot, with lovely views of the lochs and mountains – and amazing sunsets. Immaculate bedrooms have plenty of space in which to relax, perhaps with a complimentary glass of whisky. Home-baked scones are served on arrival. The charming owners also offer archery lessons.

4 rooms ☱ – †£ 99/160 ††£ 99/170

Mill Farm ⊠ PA37 1SE – Southwest : 1.5 mi on A 828 – ℰ 01631 720125
– www.ardtorna.co.uk – Closed mid November-mid March

⌂ Barcaldine Castle 🆕

HISTORIC BUILDING · PERSONALISED This lochside castle was built in 1609 and is packed with history. Charming bedrooms have period furnishings – one even has a dressing area in a turret. Breakfast is served in the Great Hall, complete with stags' heads and cannons!

6 rooms ☱ – †£ 155/220 ††£ 180/245

⊠ PA37 1SA – West : 3.5 mi by A 828 – ℰ 01631 720598
– www.barcaldinecastle.co.uk – Closed January-February

BARRA (Isle of)

Western Isles – ⊠ Castlebay – Regional map n° **17**-A3
▶ Edinburgh 126 mi – Glasgow 101 mi

SCOTLAND

Castlebay

🏨 Castlebay

TRADITIONAL · REGIONAL Homely hotel boasting excellent castle and island views – the hub of the island community. Bedrooms are a mix of styles: the newer rooms feature subtle tartan fabrics and 'MacNeil' has harbour views. There's a cosy lounge, a busy locals bar and a linen-clad dining room serving seafood specials.

15 rooms 🖵 – ♦£60/70 ♦♦£95/195

✉ HS9 5XD – ☎ 01871 810223 – www.castlebayhotel.com – Closed
22 December-8 January

🏨 Grianamul

TRADITIONAL · COSY Pale yellow dormer bungalow at the heart of a small hamlet – a homely place run by caring owners. There's a comfortable lounge and sunny breakfast room where huge, satisfying breakfasts are served. Bedrooms are bright and spacious,

3 rooms 🖵 – ♦£50 ♦♦£70

✉ HS9 5XD – ☎ 01871 810416 – www.isleofbarraaccommodation.com – Closed
October-March

North Bay

🏨 Heathbank

TRADITIONAL · PERSONALISED Former Presbyterian Church, now a smart, modern, well-run hotel that's popular with locals and visitors alike. A bright, airy bar forms the hotel's hub and, along with the dining room, serves straightforward, local seafood orientated menus. Good-sized bedrooms are light, airy and up-to-date.

5 rooms 🖵 – ♦£70/95 ♦♦£110/130

✉ HS9 5YQ – ☎ 01871 890266 – www.barrahotel.co.uk

BENDERLOCH

Argyll and Bute – Regional map n° **27**-B2

▶ Edinburgh 120 mi – Glasgow 94 mi – Oban 8 mi

🍴 Hawthorn ⓝ

BRITISH MODERN · NEIGHBOURHOOD Modern art blends with exposed stone walls at this rustic former croft – look out for the 'Wishing Wall' and leave a coin for luck. Generous, gutsy cooking is full of flavour; local produce includes Argyll meats and Mallaig fish.

Carte £21/40

5 Keils Crofts ✉ PA37 1QS – Northwest : 0.5 mi by A 828 on Tralee rd
– ☎ 01631 720777 (booking advisable) – www.hawthorn-restaurant.co.uk – dinner
only and lunch Friday-Sunday – Closed November-Easter

BETTYHILL

Highland – Regional map n° **17**-C1

▶ Edinburgh 246 mi – Glasgow 260 mi – Thurso 30 mi

🍴 Côte du Nord

CREATIVE · INTIMATE Intimate restaurant of just 3 tables; converted from an old school house by a local doctor-cum-self-taught-chef. Modern, innovative cooking; the 10-12 course menu features local and foraged ingredients and salt from evaporated seawater.

Menu £39

The School House, Kirtomy ✉ KW14 7TB – East : 4 mi by A 836 – ☎ 01641 521773
(booking essential) – www.cotedunord.co.uk – dinner only – Closed
October-March, Sunday-Tuesday and Thursday

BLAIRGOWRIE

Perth and Kinross – Pop. 8 954 – Regional map n° **16**-C2

▶ Edinburgh 60 mi – Dundee 19 mi – Perth 16 mi

Kinloch House 🐾 ⋖ 🛏 🏠 🅿

FAMILY · PERSONALISED Imposing ivy-clad country house in a tranquil, elevated setting, with beautiful walled gardens to the rear and 25 acres of grounds. Smart oak-panelled hall and a vast array of welcoming guest areas complete with log fires and antiques. Classical bedrooms are well-appointed and immaculately maintained.

15 rooms ☕ – ♦£ 125/225 ♦♦£ 200/340 – 1 suite

✉ PH10 6SG – West : 3 mi on A 923 – ℰ 01250 884237 – www.kinlochhouse.com
– Closed 14-29 December

Kinloch House – See restaurant listing

🏠 Gilmore House 🏠 🅿

TRADITIONAL · COSY Proudly run, stone-built house with a pretty, flower-filled entrance. Antlers, deer heads and old lithographs fill the walls. The first floor lounge has a good outlook; complimentary sherry and whisky are left out for a traditional nightcap. Immaculately kept modern bedrooms and plentiful breakfasts.

3 rooms ☕ – ♦£ 45/57 ♦♦£ 75/84

Perth Rd ✉ PH10 6EJ – Southwest : 0.5 mi on A 93 – ℰ 01250 872791
– www.gilmorehouse.co.uk

XXX Kinloch House ⋖ 🛏 🅿

TRADITIONAL CUISINE · INTIMATE Formal hotel dining room with twinkling chandeliers and smartly dressed tables. Start with drinks in the clubby bar or cosy, open-fired sitting room. The latest local, seasonal produce informs the daily menu – maybe West Coast crab or Perthshire venison. Dishes are well-crafted, traditional and flavoursome.

Menu £ 21/58

Kinloch House Hotel, ✉ PH10 6SG – West : 3 mi on A 923 – ℰ 01250 884237
– www.kinlochhouse.com – Closed 14-29 December

🍴 Dalmore Inn 🛏 🍽 🅿

TRADITIONAL CUISINE · PUB Traditional-looking pub with a surprisingly stylish interior, where brightly coloured walls are juxtaposed with old stonework. Good value cooking is unfussy and full of flavour; everything is freshly prepared using Scottish produce.

Menu £ 10 (weekday lunch) – Carte £ 20/44

Perth Rd ✉ PH10 6QB – Southwest : 1.5 mi on A 93 – ℰ 01250 871088
– www.dalmoreinn.com – Closed 25 December and 1-2 January

BORVE – Western Isles ➔ See Lewis and Harris (Isle of)

BOWMORE – Argyll and Bute ➔ See Islay (Isle of)

BRAEMAR
Aberdeenshire – Pop. 500 – Regional map n° **16**-C2
▶ Edinburgh 85 mi – Aberdeen 58 mi – Dundee 51 mi – Perth 51 mi

🏠 Callater Lodge 🛏 🏠 🅿

FAMILY · COSY A Victorian granite house on the village outskirts, with colourful, uplifting décor. Cosy up in an armchair by the fire then head past the old British Rail posters in the hallway to the immaculately kept bedrooms. Local wood features in the bright bathrooms and regional ingredients are used at breakfast.

6 rooms ☕ – ♦£ 55 ♦♦£ 95

9 Glenshee Rd ✉ AB35 5YQ – ℰ 01339 741275 – www.callaterlodge.co.uk – Closed
1 week Christmas

BROADFORD – Highland ➔ See Skye (Isle of)

BRODICK – North Ayrshire ➔ See Arran (Isle of)

BROUGHTY FERRY – Dundee City ➔ See Dundee

BRUICHLADDICH – Argyll and Bute → See Islay (Isle of)

BUNCHREW – Highland → See Inverness

BURRAY – Orkney Islands → See Orkney Islands (Mainland)

CADBOLL – Highland → See Tain

CALLANDER

Stirling – Pop. 3 077 – Regional map n° **16**-C2
▶ Edinburgh 52 mi – Glasgow 43 mi – Oban 71 mi – Perth 41 mi

Roman Camp

COUNTRY HOUSE · CLASSIC Pretty pink house – a former 17C hunting lodge – set by the river among well-tended gardens. Traditional bedrooms with a subtle contemporary edge and smart, marble-tiled bathrooms. Characterful panelled library and chapel. Charming service.

15 rooms �

 – †£ 110/160 ††£ 160/230 – 3 suites
Main St ✉ FK17 8BG – ℰ 01877 330003 – www.romancamphotel.co.uk
Roman Camp – See restaurant listing

Westerton

TOWNHOUSE · PERSONALISED Homely stone house run by delightful owners, with a colourful garden sweeping down to the river – take it all in from the pleasant terrace. Spotlessly kept bedrooms have wrought iron beds and good mod cons; some have mountain views.

3 rooms � – †£ 80/125 ††£ 85/130
Leny Rd ✉ FK17 8AJ – ℰ 01877 330147 – www.westertonhouse.co.uk – Closed November-April

XXX Roman Camp

MODERN CUISINE · ELEGANT Enjoy drinks and canapés in the characterful lounge or library of this charming riverside hotel, before dinner in the formal restaurant. Ambitious, modern, well-presented cooking; choose the tasting menu for the best value.

Menu £ 29/55 – Carte £ 48/73
Roman Camp Hotel, Main St ✉ FK17 8BG – ℰ 01877 330003 (bookings essential for non-residents) – www.romancamphotel.co.uk

X Mhor Fish

SEAFOOD · FRIENDLY Take the left door to eat in at this all-day fish and chip shop or choose the right door if you're here for a takeaway. The chips are cooked in beef dripping and the pies and bread are from their bakery just over the road.
Carte £ 11/36
75-77 Main St ✉ FK17 8DX – ℰ 01877 330213 – www.mhor.net – Closed 25-26 December, 1 January and Monday in winter except bank holidays

CASTLE DOUGLAS

Dumfries and Galloway – Pop. 4 174 – Regional map n° **15**-B3
▶ Edinburgh 98 mi – Ayr 49 mi – Dumfries 18 mi – Stranraer 57 mi

Douglas House

TOWNHOUSE · PERSONALISED An attractive 19C townhouse run by experienced owners. Comfy, individually decorated bedrooms have a modern edge. The lounge-cum-breakfast-room is light and airy; breakfast offers plenty of choice and features only local produce.

4 rooms �

 – †£ 40 ††£ 77/85
63 Queen St ✉ DG7 1HS – ℰ 01556 503262 – www.douglas-house.com

CASTLEBAY – Western Isles → See Barra (Isle of)

CHIRNSIDE
The Scottish Borders – ✉ Duns – Pop. 1 459 – Regional map n° **15**-D1
▶ Edinburgh 52 mi – Berwick-upon-Tweed 8 mi – Glasgow 95 mi
– Newcastle upon Tyne 70 mi

🏠 Chirnside Hall

HISTORIC BUILDING · CLASSIC Sizeable 1834 country house with a lovely re-volving door and beautiful views over the Cheviots. Grand lounges have original cornicing and huge fireplaces. Bedrooms are cosy and classical; some have four-poster beds. Local, seasonal dishes are served in the traditional dining room.
10 rooms ⌂ – ♦£ 100/195 ♦♦£ 170/195

✉ TD11 3LD – East : 1.75 mi on A 6105 – ☏ 01890 818219
– www.chirnsidehallhotel.com – Closed March

COLBOST – Highland → See Skye (Isle of)

COMRIE
Perth and Kinross – Pop. 1 927 – Regional map n° **16**-C2
▶ Edinburgh 66 mi – Glasgow 56 mi – Oban 70 mi – Perth 24 mi

🏠 Royal
TRADITIONAL · PERSONALISED Charming coaching inn dating back to the 18C and set at the heart of a riverside town. Cosy bar and lovely open-fired library with squashy sofas. Well-appointed bedrooms; some with four-posters and an-tiques. Relaxed, personable service.
11 rooms ⌂ – ♦£ 90/110 ♦♦£ 150/190

Melville Sq ✉ PH6 2DN – ☏ 01764 679200 – www.royalhotel.co.uk – Closed 25-26 December
Royal – See restaurant listing

✕✕ Royal
TRADITIONAL CUISINE · COSY An intimate dining room and bright conserva-tory, set within a stylishly decorated coaching inn. Concise menu of classically based dishes with modern touches. Produce is seasonal and locally sourced; the mussels and steaks are superb.
Carte £ 20/37

Royal Hotel, Melville Sq ✉ PH6 2DN – ☏ 01764 679200 – www.royalhotel.co.uk
– Closed 25-26 December

CRAIGHOUSE – Argyll and Bute → See Jura (Isle of)

CRIEFF
Perth and Kinross – Pop. 7 368 – Regional map n° **16**-C2
▶ Edinburgh 60 mi – Glasgow 50 mi – Oban 76 mi – Perth 18 mi

✕✕ Yann's at Glenearn House

CLASSIC FRENCH · BISTRO Busy restaurant in a Victorian house, with a delight-ful lounge and a large bistro-style dining room hung with French prints. Gallic cooking makes good use of Scottish produce and Savoyard sharing dishes are a speciality. Comfy, cosy bedrooms have good facilities and a relaxed, bohemian style. Pleasant team.
Carte £ 22/33
4 rooms ⌂ – ♦£ 75 ♦♦£ 95/100

Perth Rd ✉ PH7 3EQ – on A 85 – ☏ 01764 650111
– www.yannsatglenearnhouse.com – dinner only and lunch Friday-Sunday
– Closed 2 weeks October and 25-26 December

at Muthill South: 3 mi by A822

✗ Barley Bree ⟵ 🅿

CLASSIC CUISINE · RUSTIC Intimate coaching inn at the centre of a busy village, with a spacious fire-lit sitting room and a dining room hung with angling memorabilia. Classical cooking utilises local ingredients and arrives in a modern manner. Service is friendly and bedrooms are comfortable and well-thought-out.

Menu £ 16 (weekday lunch) – Carte £ 29/44 **s**

6 rooms ⌂ – ♦£ 70/85 ♦♦£ 88/112

6 Willoughby St ⊠ PH5 2AB – ✆ 01764 681451 (booking advisable)
– www.barleybree.com – Closed Christmas, Monday and Tuesday

CRINAN

Argyll and Bute – ⊠ Lochgilphead – Regional map n° **16**-B2
▶ Edinburgh 137 mi – Glasgow 91 mi – Oban 36 mi

🏠 Crinan ⚡ ⟵ 🛏 ⬆ 🅿

TRADITIONAL · PERSONALISED Built in the 19C to accommodate the Laird of Jura's business associates. Some of the simply furnished bedrooms have balconies and lovely Sound views. The small coffee shop sells homemade cakes, the 3rd floor bar has a superb terrace, and the large wood-panelled bar-restaurant offers an appealing seafood menu.

20 rooms ⌂ – ♦£ 100/170 ♦♦£ 110/280

⊠ PA31 8SR – ✆ 01546 830261 – www.crinanhotel.com – Closed January and Christmas

Westward – See restaurant listing

✗✗ Westward ⟵ 🛏 🅿

SEAFOOD · FORMAL Set within a welcoming, family-run hotel and boasting lovely views out over the Sound of Jura. Concise, seafood-based menus rely on local and island produce; langoustines are landed daily from Loch Crinan, right beside the hotel.

Menu £ 40

Crinan Hotel, ⊠ PA31 8SR – ✆ 01546 830261 – www.crinanhotel.com – dinner only
– Closed January and Christmas

CROMARTY

Highland – Pop. 726 – Regional map n° **17**-C2
▶ Edinburgh 177 mi – Inverness 23 mi – Fort William 88 mi

🏠 Factor's House ⚡ 🐕 🛏 ✂ 🅿

LUXURY · PERSONALISED This late Georgian house is very passionately run by a charming owner. It sits in a peaceful spot on the edge of an attractive town and offers pleasant sea views from its mature gardens. Bedrooms have a subtle contemporary style and good extras. Breakfast and dinner are taken around a farmhouse table; the latter is four courses and features accomplished home cooking.

3 rooms ⌂ – ♦£ 100/110 ♦♦£ 115/140

Denny Rd ⊠ IV11 8YT – ✆ 01381 600394 – www.thefactorshouse.com – Closed Christmas-New Year

✗ Sutor Creek Cafe

TRADITIONAL CUISINE · FRIENDLY A great little eatery hidden away by the harbour in a well-preserved coastal town. Wonderfully seasonal cooking features seafood from the local boats and pizzas from the wood-fired oven. It's run by a friendly, experienced couple.

Carte £ 22/47

21 Bank St ⊠ IV11 8YE – ✆ 01381 600855 (booking essential)
– www.sutorcreek.co.uk – Closed January, Monday-Wednesday September-April

CUMNOCK

East Ayrshire – Pop. 9 039 – Regional map n° **15**-B2
▶ Edinburgh 85 mi – Glasgow 38 mi – Dumfries 44 mi – Carlisle 88 mi

⌂ Dumfries House Lodge   🛏 ⅋ ⚅ **P**

COUNTRY HOUSE · PERSONALISED Set at the entrance to the 2,000 acre Dumfries Estate is this stylish country house hotel, formerly a factor's house and steading. There are two cosy lounges and a billiard room and some of the furniture is from the original manor house. Bedrooms are designed by the Duchess of Cornwall's sister.

22 rooms 🖙 – ♦£ 85/100 ♦♦£ 110/120

Dumfries House ⊠ KA18 2NJ – West : 1.5 mi on A 70 – ☎ 01290 429920
– www.dumfrieshouselodge.co.uk – Closed 23-27 December and
31-December-3 January

CUPAR

Fife – Pop. 9 339 – Regional map n° **16**-C2
▶ Edinburgh 45 mi – Dundee 15 mi – Perth 23 mi

⌂⌂ Ferrymuir Stables   🛏 ⅋ **P** 🛏

LUXURY · CONTEMPORARY The old stables of Ferrymuir House date from 1800 – but you'd never know. The hub of the house is a light, spacious orangery overlooking the stable yard. Modern bedrooms come with designer furnishings, smart wet rooms and Netbooks.

3 rooms 🖙 – ♦£ 55/75 ♦♦£ 100/120

Beechgrove Rise ⊠ KY15 5DT – West : 1 mi by Bonnygate (A91) and West Park
Rd off Westfield Rd – ☎ 01334 657579 – www.ferrymuirstables.co.uk

XX Ostlers Close

TRADITIONAL CUISINE · INTIMATE Cosy, cottagey little restaurant hidden away down a narrow alley. It's been personally run since 1981 and service is warm and chatty. Classic cooking features local ingredients, including mushrooms foraged for by the owner-chef.

Carte £ 39/50

25 Bonnygate ⊠ KY15 4BU – ☎ 01334 655574 – www.ostlersclose.co.uk – dinner
only and Saturday lunch – Closed 2 weeks April, 25-26 December, 1-2 January,
Sunday and Monday

DALKEITH

Midlothian – Pop. 12 342 – Regional map n° **15**-C1
▶ Edinburgh 6 mi – London 374 mi – Glasgow 51 mi – Manchester 208 mi

🍴 Sun Inn   ⇔ & 🗔 **P**

TRADITIONAL CUISINE · PUB A 17C blacksmith's with two large open-fired rooms; their wood and stone walls hung with modern black and white photos. Extensive menus feature good quality local produce – lunch keeps things simple but appealing and dinner is more ambitious. Smart bedrooms boast handmade furniture and Egyptian cotton linen.

Menu £ 11 (lunch and early dinner) – Carte £ 20/49

5 rooms 🖙 – ♦£ 75/100 ♦♦£ 95/150

Lothian Bridge ⊠ EH22 4TR – Southwest : 2 mi by A 6094 and B 6392 on A 7
– ☎ 0131 663 2456 – www.thesuninnedinburgh.co.uk – Closed 26 December and
1 January

DALRY

North Ayrshire – Regional map n° **15**-A1
▶ Edinburgh 70 mi – Ayr 21 mi – Glasgow 25 mi

⌂⌂ Lochwood Farm Steading   🐾 ⇐ 🛏 ⅋ **P**

COUNTRY HOUSE · PERSONALISED A remotely set farmhouse on a 100 acre dairy farm; it boasts impressive panoramic views. Luxuriously appointed bedrooms are split between an old barn and a wooden house – two have private hot tubs. Breakfast is served by candlelight!

5 rooms 🖙 – ♦£ 125/145 ♦♦£ 125/145

Saltcoats ⊠ KA21 6NG – Southwest : 5 mi by A 737 and Saltcoats rd
– ☎ 01294 552529 – www.lochwoodfarm.co.uk – Closed Christmas-New Year

XX Braidwoods (Keith Braidwood) [P]

CLASSIC CUISINE · COSY An old crofter's cottage hidden away in the country-side; it's cosy and charming, with just a handful of tables in each of its two rooms. Concise menus offer confident, classical cooking using good quality seasonal ingredients and dishes have clearly defined flavours. It's personally run by experienced owners.

→ Grilled Wester Ross scallops with baby leeks and Arran mustard butter sauce. Loin of roe deer with wild mushrooms, celeriac and artichoke purée. Iced heather honey parfait with poached rhubarb and puff candy.

Menu £ 26/50

Drumastle Mill Cottage ⊠ KA24 4LN – Southwest : 1.5 mi by A 737 on Saltcoats rd – ℰ 01294 833544 (booking essential) – www.braidwoods.co.uk – Closed 25 December-29 January, 2 weeks September, Sunday dinner, Monday, Tuesday lunch and Sunday from May-mid September

DERVAIG – Argyll and Bute → See Mull (Isle of)

DINGWALL

Highland – Pop. 5 491 – Regional map n° **17**-C2
▶ Edinburgh 172 mi – Inverness 14 mi – Glasgow 182 mi – Aberdeen 115 mi

XX Café India Brasserie [AC]

INDIAN · NEIGHBOURHOOD Well-run Indian restaurant close to the town centre. Small lounge and several dining areas separated by etched glass screens. Good range of authentic, regional dishes, with tasty Thalis, set menus for 2+ and good value two course lunches.

Menu £ 9 (weekday lunch) – Carte £ 16/32

Lockhart House, Tulloch St ⊠ IV15 9JZ – ℰ 01349 862552 – www.cafeindiadingwall.co.uk – Closed 25 December

DINNET

Aberdeenshire – Regional map n° **16**-D1
▶ Edinburgh 114 mi – London 517 mi – Glasgow 134 mi – Bradford 325 mi

Glendavan House

FAMILY · CLASSIC Set in 9 lochside acres, this former shooting lodge is somewhere to get away from it all. Two of the three bedrooms are very large suites; all are tastefully furnished with antiques and memorabilia. Delicious communal breakfasts.

3 rooms ☲ – ♦£ 95/125 ♦♦£ 120/160

⊠ AB34 5LU – Northwest : 3 mi by A 97 on B 9119 – ℰ 01339 881610 – www.glendavanhouse.com

DORNOCH

Highland – Pop. 1 208 – Regional map n° **17**-D2
▶ Edinburgh 219 mi – Inverness 63 mi – Wick 65 mi

Links House

LUXURY · CONTEMPORARY This restored 19C manse sits opposite the first tee of the Royal Dornoch Golf Club. Enjoy a dram from the honesty bar in the pine-panelled library or have tea and cake in the antique-furnished sitting room. Some of the beautifully furnished bedrooms feature bespoke tweed fabrics. The elegant orangery boasts an impressive stone fireplace and an elaborate 4 course menu.

8 rooms ☲ – ♦£ 285/320 ♦♦£ 285/360

Golf Rd ⊠ IV25 3LW – ℰ 01862 810279 – www.linkshousedornoch.com – Closed 4 January-18 March and 25-27 December

🏠 2 Quail ⚹ ⚹

TOWNHOUSE · PERSONALISED A bijou terraced house built in 1898 for a sea captain. Intimate bedrooms are furnished with antiques – in a Victorian style – and one has a wrought iron bedstead. The small open-fired library-lounge boasts a large array of vintage books. Daily changing set dinners are offered by arrangement.

3 rooms ☑ – †£ 80/105 ††£ 90/115

Castle St ⊠ IV25 3SN – ℰ 01862 811811 – www.2quail.com – Closed 2 weeks February-March and Christmas

DRUMBEG

Highland – Regional map n° **17**-C1

▶ Edinburgh 262 mi – Inverness 105 mi – Ullapool 48 mi

🏠 Blar na Leisg at Drumbeg House ⚹ 🛥 ⬕ 🖼 ⚹ 🅿 🚬

FAMILY · MODERN This remotely set Edwardian house affords lovely loch views. The large open-fired sitting room is filled with a vast array of books; and impressive modern art and Bauhaus-style furnishings feature throughout. Bedrooms are spacious and luxuriously appointed. Highland beef and game birds are a speciality at dinner, which is served in a smart, contemporary dining room.

5 rooms ☑ – †£ 80/160 ††£ 160

✉ IV27 4NW – *Take first right on entering village from Kylesku direction* – *ℰ 01571 833325 – www.blarnaleisg.com*

DUISDALEMORE – Highland ➜ See Skye (Isle of)

DUMFRIES

Dumfries and Galloway – Pop. 32 914 – Regional map n° **15**-C3

▶ Edinburgh 80 mi – Ayr 59 mi – Carlisle 34 mi – Glasgow 79 mi

🏠 Hazeldean House ⬕ ⚹ 🅿

TOWNHOUSE · PERSONALISED Victorian villa built in 1898, with a lovely garden, a curio-filled lounge and a conservatory breakfast room. Victorian-themed bedrooms – three with four posters; the basement room has a nautical cabin style.

6 rooms ☑ – †£ 38/45 ††£ 62/66

4 Moffat Rd ⊠ DG1 1NJ – ℰ 01387 266178 – www.hazeldeanhouse.com

🏠 Hamilton House ⚹ 🅿

TOWNHOUSE · PERSONALISED Converted Victorian townhouse next to a bowls club, with a large conservatory lounge and neat breakfast tables overlooking the tennis courts. Large bedrooms come with power showers and combine the classical with the contemporary.

7 rooms ☑ – †£ 40/50 ††£ 60/65

12 Moffat Rd ⊠ DG1 1NJ – ℰ 01387 266606 – www.hamiltonhousedumfries.co.uk – *Closed 24 December-3 January*

DUNBAR

East Lothian – Pop. 8 486 – Regional map n° **15**-D1

▶ Edinburgh 30 mi – Glasgow 76 mi – London 369 mi

🍴 Creel

TRADITIONAL CUISINE · BISTRO An unassuming, cosy former pub with a wood-panelled ceiling and walls. The experienced chef creates good value, full-flavoured dishes, with fresh fish and shellfish from the adjacent harbour. Friendly service.

Menu £ 17/28

The Harbour, 25 Lamer St ⊠ EH42 1HG – ℰ 01368 863279 (booking essential) – *www.creelrestaurant.co.uk – Closed Sunday dinner-Wednesday lunch*

DUNBLANE

Stirling – Pop. 8 811 – Regional map n° **16**-C2

▶ Edinburgh 42 mi – Glasgow 33 mi – Perth 29 mi

🏠 Cromlix   🐾 🚗 🍽 🛗 P

COUNTRY HOUSE · MODERN This grand country house, owned by Andy Murray, has elegantly appointed sitting rooms, a whisky room, a chapel and a superb games room, as well as a smart tennis court in its 30 acre grounds. Luxurious, antique-furnished bedrooms feature modern touches while also respecting the original style of the house.

16 rooms ☷ – †£ 180/275 †††£ 275/695 – 5 suites

Kinbuck ✉ FK15 9JT – North : 3.5 mi on B 8033 – ✆ 01786 822125
– www.cromlix.com

Chez Roux – See restaurant listing

XX Chez Roux   🚗 🏡 🛗 P

FRENCH · BRASSERIE Light and spacious conservatory restaurant in a magnificent country house hotel. Smart, yet relaxed, it's a hit with locals and tourists alike thanks to the enthusiastic service and good value, flavoursome cooking. Classic French dishes might include soufflé Suissesse, chateaubriand or tarte au citron.

Menu £ 32 – Carte £ 36/54

Cromlix Hotel, Kinbuck ✉ FK15 9JT – North : 3.5 mi on B 8033 – ✆ 01786 822125
– www.cromlix.com

DUNDEE

Dundee City – Pop. 147 285 – Regional map n° **16**-C2
▶ Edinburgh 63 mi – London 458 mi – Glasgow 76 mi – Newcastle upon Tyne 163 mi

🏠 Apex City Quay   ☆ ← 🖥 🕭 🐾 🛗 🛗 🛗 🍽 🏋 P

BUSINESS · MODERN Modern waterfront hotel with good business facilities and an atmospheric spa; located in an up-and-coming area. Well-proportioned, contemporary bedrooms boast king-sized beds and oversized windows that look out towards the city or marina. Vast bar-lounge and spacious brasserie with an accessible menu.

151 rooms ☷ – †£ 85/130 †††£ 105/150 – 6 suites

Town plan: B2-a *- 1 West Victoria Dock Rd ✉ DD1 3JP – ✆ 01382 202404*
– www.apexhotels.co.uk

🏠 Malmaison   ☆ 🛗 🛗 AC 🏋

CHAIN · CONTEMPORARY The best feature of this lovingly restored hotel is the wrought iron cantilevered staircase topped by a domed ceiling. Contemporary bedrooms come in striking bold colours and have a masculine feel. The all-day bar serves cocktails and nibbles and there's a DJ at weekends; the brasserie offers a grill menu.

91 rooms – †£ 75/315 †††£ 75/315 – ☷ £ 16

Town plan: B2-s *- 44 Whitehall Cres ✉ DD1 4AY – ✆ 01382 339715*
– www.malmaison.com

🏠 Balmuirfield House   🚗 P

COUNTRY HOUSE · COSY A double-fronted stone dower house built in 1904; Dighty Water runs past the bottom of the garden. Inside it's spacious and homely, with a cosy open-fired lounge. Two of the bedrooms have four-posters and one has an antique bath.

4 rooms ☷ – †£ 60/75 †††£ 80/95

Harestane Rd ✉ DD3 0NU – North : 3.5 mi by A 929, A 90, Claverhouse rd and Old Glamis rd. – ✆ 01382 819655 – www.balmuirfieldhouse.com

XX Castlehill   🛗

MODERN CUISINE · INTIMATE Smart designer restaurant close to the waterfront; its décor celebrates the history of the city. Modern dishes feature some innovative flavour combinations and have playful touches – the concise evening menu is the most imaginative.

Menu £ 15/36

Town plan: B2-c *- 22 Exchange St ✉ DD1 3DL – ✆ 01382 220008*
– www.castlehillrestaurant.co.uk – Closed Sunday and Monday

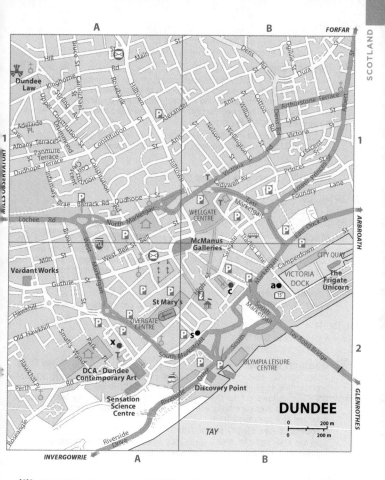

✗✗ Playwright

🍸 AC 🕸

MODERN BRITISH · FASHIONABLE Smart, modern bar and restaurant in an imposing 19C grey-stone building beside the Rep Theatre. Seasonal menus offer modern interpretations of classical dishes and everything from the bread to ice cream is made in-house. Great value lunch.

Menu £ 18/20 – Carte £ 44/50

Town plan: A2-x – 11 Tay Sq, South Tay St. ⊠ DD1 1PB – ℰ 01382 223113
– www.theplaywright.co.uk – Closed 25-26 December, 1-3 January and Sunday

at Broughty Ferry East : 4.5 mi by A 930

✗✗ Tayberry 🆕

🖵

MODERN BRITISH · FRIENDLY An unassuming roadside property overlooking the mouth of the Tay. The keen young chef offers fresh, tasty cooking with original modern touches and local and foraged ingredients play a key role. Service is engaging and attentive.

Menu £ 22/36

594 Brook St ⊠ DD5 2EA – ℰ 01382 698280 – www.tayberryrestaurant.com
– Closed Sunday dinner and Monday

DUNKELD
Perth and Kinross – Pop. 1 005 – Regional map n° **16**-C2
▶ Edinburgh 58 mi – Aberdeen 88 mi – Inverness 98 mi – Perth 14 mi

🏠 Letter Farm   🐾 🍴 🕸 **P**

FAMILY · TRADITIONAL A traditional farmhouse on a family-run stock farm, nestled between Butterstone Loch and the Loch of Lowes Nature Reserve. There's a welcoming open-fired lounge and a homely communal breakfast room. Comfortable, immaculately kept bedrooms come with king-sized beds and good extras.

3 rooms ⌂ – 🛏£ 55 🛏🛏£ 90

Loch of the Lowes ✉ PH8 0HH – Northeast : 3 mi by A 923 on Loch of Lowes rd – 𝒞 01350 724254 – www.letterfarmdunkeld.co.uk – Closed late November-early May

DUNVEGAN – Highland ➜ See Skye (Isle of)

DURNESS
Highland – Regional map n° **17**-C1
▶ Edinburgh 266 mi – Thurso 78 mi – Ullapool 71 mi

🏠 Mackay's   🕸 **P**

FAMILY · MODERN This smart grey stone house sits at the most north-westerly point of the mainland. It has a light, airy lounge and a cosy open-fired snug. The owner is a textile designer and this shows in the bedrooms, which have a stylish, rustic feel.

7 rooms ⌂ – 🛏£ 110 🛏🛏£ 129/139

✉ IV27 4PN – 𝒞 01971 511202 – www.visitdurness.com – Closed October-April

DUROR
Highland – Regional map n° **17**-B3
▶ Edinburgh 131 mi – Ballachulish 7 mi – Oban 26 mi

🏠 Bealach House   🌳 🐾 ⩶ 🍴 🕸 **P**

TRADITIONAL · PERSONALISED A former crofter's house in a superb location, accessed via an unpaved driveway with breathtaking forest and mountain scenery – keep an eye out for the deer! Snug conservatory and cosy bedrooms; the homely guest areas are hung with tapestries. The classical daily changing menu is served at a communal table.

3 rooms ⌂ – 🛏£ 60/80 🛏🛏£ 90/110

Salachan Glen ✉ PA38 4BW – South : 4.5 mi by A 828 – 𝒞 01631 740298 – www.bealachhouse.co.uk – Closed November-February

DYKE
Moray – Regional map n° **16**-C1
▶ Edinburgh 163 mi – London 564 mi – Aberdeen 81 mi – Glasgow 177 mi

🏠 Old Kirk   🐾 🍴 🕸 **P**

HISTORIC · DESIGN A peacefully set, converted 1856 church, surrounded by grain fields. It has an airy interior, a cosy library and a comfortable open-fired lounge with a pretty stained glass window. Charming, individually decorated bedrooms boast original stonework and arched windows; one has a carved four-poster bed.

3 rooms ⌂ – 🛏£ 85/95 🛏🛏£ 85/95

✉ IV36 2TL – Northeast : 0.5 mi – 𝒞 01309 641414 – www.oldkirk.co.uk

EDDLESTON – The Scottish Borders ➜ See Peebles

EDINBANE – Highland ➜ See Skye (Isle of)

GOOD TIPS!

A cool, cosmopolitan city with stunning scenery and a colourful history, Scotland's capital is home to Michelin-Starred restaurants as well as busy wine bars and bistros, with global flavours including Korean, Italian and Thai. The famous Royal Mile is the location of the luxurious **G & V** hotel, while the **Sheraton Grand** has views of the iconic castle.

EDINBURGH

City of Edinburgh – Pop. 459 366 – Regional map n° **15**-C1
London 397 mi – Glasgow 46 mi – Newcastle upon Tyne 120 mi – Aberdeen 126 mi

Hotels

Balmoral

GRAND LUXURY • CLASSIC Renowned Edwardian hotel which provides for the modern traveller whilst retaining its old-fashioned charm. Bedrooms are classical with a subtle contemporary edge; JK Rowling completed the final Harry Potter book in the top suite! Live harp music accompanies afternoon tea in the Palm Court and 'Scotch' offers over 460 malts. Dine on modern dishes or brasserie classics.

188 rooms – †£ 190/595 ††£ 190/595 – £ 27 – 20 suites

Town plan: G2-n – *EH2 2EQ* – *0131 556 2414* – *www.roccofortehotels.com*

Number One – See restaurant listing

Sheraton Grand H. & Spa

GRAND LUXURY • MODERN Spacious modern hotel with castle views from some rooms. Sleek, stylish bedrooms boast strong comforts, the latest mod cons and smart bathrooms with mood lighting. An impressive four-storey glass cube houses the stunning spa.

269 rooms – †£ 170/650 ††£ 170/650 – £ 22 – 12 suites

Town plan: F2-v – *1 Festival Sq* *EH3 9SR* – *0131 229 9131* – *www.sheratonedinburgh.co.uk*

One Square – See restaurant listing

Waldorf Astoria Edinburgh The Caledonian

HISTORIC • DESIGN Smart hotel in the old railway terminus: have afternoon tea on the former forecourt or cocktails where the trains once pulled in. Sumptuous modern bedrooms have excellent facilities; ask for a castle view. Unwind in the UK's first Guerlain spa, then dine in the grand French salon or luxurious brasserie.

241 rooms – †£ 169/759 ††£ 169/759 – 6 suites

Town plan: F2-x – *Princes St* *EH1 2AB* – *0131 222 8888* – *www.waldorfastoriaedinburgh.com*

Galvin Brasserie De Luxe • The Pompadour by Galvin – See restaurant listing

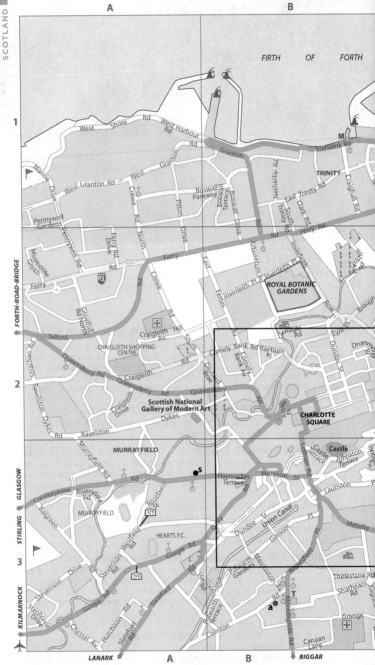

FIRTH OF FORTH

TRINITY

West Shore Rd
West Harbour Rd
West Granton Rd
Granton
Starbank Rd
M

Netherby Rd
East Trinity Rd
Craighall Rd

West Granton Rd
West Granton Rd
Boswall Parkway
Boswall Terrace
Boswall Drive
South Trinity Rd
Clark Rd
East Trinity Rd

Marine Drive
Pennywell Gardens
Muirhouse Green
Pennywell Rd
Ferry Rd Drive
Pilton Drive
North
Crewe Rd
Ferry Rd
Arboretum Rd
Fettes
Inverleith Pl
Inverleith Pl
Inverleith
Inverleith

Groathill Rd North
Ferry Rd
Crewe Rd
Ferry
POL

ROYAL BOTANIC GARDENS

Telford
Craigleith Hill Av.
South
Craigleith Rd
Comely Bank Rd
Raeburn Pl
Dundas St
Drummond Pl

CRAIGLEITH SHOPPING CENTRE
Queensferry Rd
Craigleith Rd
Comely Bank Av.
Denotes
Eyre
Brough

Strachan Rd
Queensferry Rd
Craigleith Drive
Queensferry Rd
Orchard Brae
Ann fe Rd
Dundas St

Ravelston Dykes Rd
Queensferry Rd
Dykes

Scottish National Gallery of Modern Art

CHARLOTTE SQUARE

FORTH-ROAD-BRIDGE

Ravelston Rd
Ravelston

MURRAYFIELD

Castle Terrace
Castle
Johnston Terrace

Murrayfield Rd
Roseburn St
Rd
Haymarket Terrace
Morrison St
Lothian Rd
Lauriston

GLASGOW

Corstorphine Rd
Riversdale Rd
Balgreen
MURRAYFIELD
129
Rd
Spey
Dundee St
Union Canal
Gilmore Pl
Melville

STIRLING

HEARTS F.C.
Westfield
Gorgie Rd
156

Stenhouse Drive
Balgreen
Stevenson Drive
Stevenson Rd
Harrison Rd
Ponwaith Gardens
Merchiston Av.
Bruntsfield

KILMARNOCK

Chesser Av.
Gorgie Rd
Hutchison Rd
Slateford Rd
Colinton Rd
Morningside Rd
Thirlestane Rd
Strathearn Rd
Grange

T
a

Canaan Lane

LANARK
A
B
BIGGAR

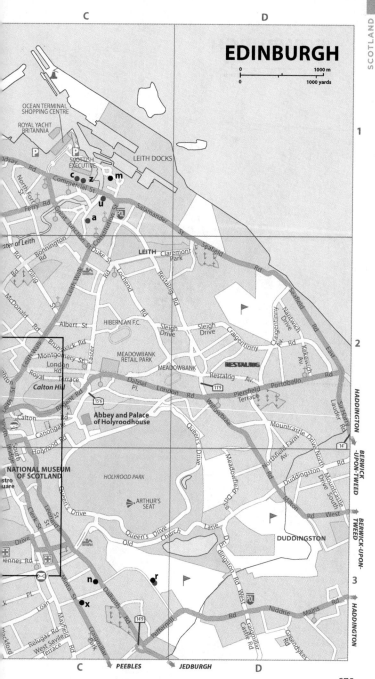

EDINBURGH

0   1000 m
0   1000 yards

C   **D**

OCEAN TERMINAL
SHOPPING CENTRE
ROYAL YACHT
BRITANNIA

P
P
SCOTTISH
EXECUTIVE   LEITH DOCKS

1

dsay   Rd
North Fort   St
Ferry   Rd
c ● z ●   ● m
Commercial   St
u
● a
Great   Junction   St
Salamander   St
POL

ater of Leith
Bonnington   Rd
Rd
Pilrig
McDonald   Rd
Leith   Walk
Duke   St
LEITH   Claremont
Park
Spatfield   St
Seafield   Rd
Nantwich   Drive
Kekewich   Av.
East   Rd

Albert   St
HIBERNIAN F.C.
Lochend   Rd
Restalrig   Rd
Sleigh
Drive
Sleigh
Drive
Craigentinny
RESTALRIG

2

Brunswick   Rd
Montgomery   St
Easter   Rd
MEADOWBANK
RETAIL PARK
MEADOWBANK
Restalrig   Av.
London   Rd
London   Rd
119
Piersfield
Terrace
Portobello
Lauder   Rd
Sheriff   Rd
HADDINGTON

Calton   Hill
London
Royal
Terrace
Dalziel
Pl.
Mountcastle   Drive
14

Calton
Regent   Rd
156
Abbey and Palace
of Holyroodhouse
Willowbrae
Northfield   Farm
Northfield   Av.
Mountcastle   Drive   North
BERWICK
-UPON-TWEED

South
Bridge
Canongate
Holyrood   Rd
Queen's   Drive
Meadowfield   Rd
Duddingston   Rd
Mountcastle   Drive   South

NATIONAL MUSEUM
OF SCOTLAND
stro
uare
HOLYROOD PARK
▶ ARTHUR'S
SEAT
Meadowfield   Dr
Duddingston   Rd   West
DUDDINGSTON
BERWICK-UPON-
TWEED

Clerk   St
Drive
ennes   Rd
Queen's   Drive
Old   Church   Lane
Duddingston   Rd
Niddrie   Mains   Rd

k   Pl.
Loan
● x
n ●
● r
Peffermill   Rd
POL
Craigmillar   Castle   Rd
Greendykes
3
HADDINGTON

Mayfield   Rd
Relugas   Rd
West Saville
Terrace
Dalkeith   Rd
Craigmillar
Park
149
Peffermill

C   PEEBLES   JEDBURGH   **D**

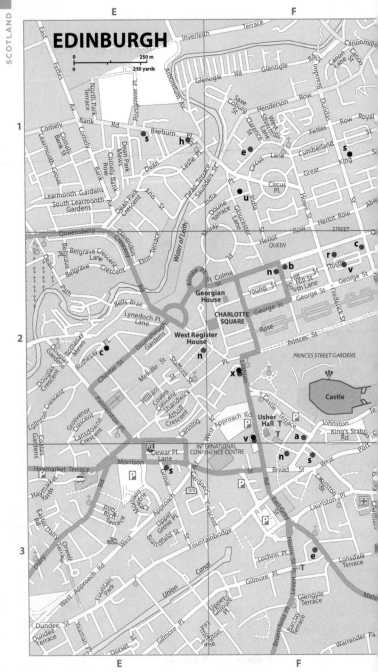

EDINBURGH

0   250 m
0   250 yards

Castle

Georgian House

West Register House

CHARLOTTE SQUARE

PRINCES STREET GARDENS

Usher Hall

INTERNATIONAL CONFERENCE CENTRE

E

F

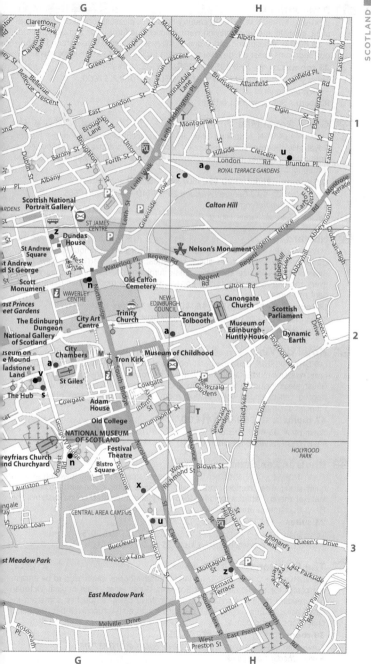

Prestonfield

LUXURY · PERSONALISED 17C country house in a pleasant rural spot, with an opulent, dimly lit interior displaying warm colours, fine furnishings and old tapestries – it's hugely atmospheric and is one of the most romantic hotels around. Luxurious bedrooms boast a high level of modern facilities and service is excellent.

23 rooms – ♦£ 295/395 ♦♦£ 295/395 – 5 suites

Town plan: C3-r - *Priestfield Rd* ⊠ *EH16 5UT* – ℰ *0131 225 7800*
– *www.prestonfield.com*

Rhubarb – See restaurant listing

G & V Royal Mile

LUXURY · DESIGN A striking hotel in a great central location on the historic Royal Mile. Bedrooms on the upper floors have impressive city skyline views. Bold colour schemes, modern furnishings and clever design features can be seen throughout.

136 rooms – ♦£ 150/390 ♦♦£ 150/390 – ⌚£ 21 – / suites

Town plan: G2-v - *1 George IV Bridge* ⊠ *EH1 1AD* – ℰ *0131 220 6666*
– *www.gandvhotel.com*

Cucina – See restaurant listing

Howard

TOWNHOUSE · CLASSIC A series of three Georgian townhouses with many characterful original features still in situ; situated in the heart of the New Town. Bedrooms vary in size and have classic furnishings and a contemporary edge; every room is assigned a butler. Formal dining from modern menus in the elegant restaurant.

18 rooms ⌚ – ♦£ 120/450 ♦♦£ 140/450 – 3 suites

Town plan: F1-s - *34 Great King St* ⊠ *EH3 6QH* – ℰ *0131 557 3500*
– *www.thehoward.com*

Hotel du Vin

LUXURY · DESIGN Boutique hotel located close to the Royal Mile, featuring unique modern murals and wine-themed bedrooms furnished with dark wood. Guest areas include a whisky snug and a mezzanine bar complete with glass-fronted cellars and a wine tasting room. The traditional bistro offers classic French cooking.

47 rooms ⌚ – ♦£ 90/300 ♦♦£ 90/300

Town plan: G3-n - *11 Bristo Pl* ⊠ *EH1 1EZ* – ℰ *0131 247 4900*
– *www.hotelduvin.com/edinburgh*

Chester Residence

TOWNHOUSE · CONTEMPORARY A series of smart Georgian townhouses in a quiet street. The luxurious, individually furnished suites come with kitchens and state-of-the-art facilities include video entry and integrated sound systems; the Mews apartments are the best.

23 suites – ♦♦£ 135/325 – ⌚£ 12

Town plan: E2-c - *9 Rothesay Pl* ⊠ *EH3 7SL* – ℰ *0131 226 2075*
– *www.chester-residence.com* – *Closed 23-26 December*

The Dunstane

TOWNHOUSE · CONTEMPORARY An impressive house which used to be a training centre for the Royal Bank of Scotland. Guest areas retain original Victorian features and the smart modern bedrooms have designer touches; some are located across a busy road. Small restaurant with a stylish cocktail bar; the menu champions local produce.

38 rooms ⌚ – ♦£ 79/229 ♦♦£ 99/259

Town plan: A3-s - *4 West Coates* ⊠ *EH12 5JQ* – ℰ *0131 337 6169*
– *www.thedunstane.co.uk*

Six Brunton Place 🛏 ⚭

TOWNHOUSE · CONTEMPORARY This late Georgian townhouse – run by a charming owner – was once home to Frederick Ritchie, who designed the One O'Clock Gun and Time Ball. Inside you'll find flagged floors, columns, marble fireplaces and a cantilevered stone staircase; these contrast with contemporary furnishings and vibrant modern art.

4 rooms ⌂ – ♦£ 89/159 ♦♦£ 109/199

Town plan: H1-u - *6 Brunton Place* ✉ *EH7 5EG* - ☎ *0131 622 0042*
– *www.sixbruntonplace.com*

94 DR ⚭ 🅿

TOWNHOUSE · PERSONALISED Charming owners welcome you to this very stylish and individual hotel in a Victorian terraced house. Bedrooms are well-equipped, there's a retro lounge with an honesty bar and breakfast is served in the conservatory with its decked terrace.

6 rooms ⌂ – ♦£ 90/145 ♦♦£ 100/225

Town plan: C3-n - *94 Dalkeith Rd* ✉ *EH16 5AF* - ☎ *0131 662 9265*
– *www.94dr.com* – *Closed 4-18 January and 25-26 December*

23 Mayfield 🛏 ⚭ 🅿

TRADITIONAL · CLASSIC Lovingly restored Victorian house with a very welcoming, helpful owner and an outdoor hot tub. Spacious lounge has an honesty bar and a collection of old and rare books. Sumptuous bedrooms come with coordinated soft furnishings, some mahogany features and luxurious bathrooms. Extravagant breakfast choices.

7 rooms ⌂ – ♦£ 85/165 ♦♦£ 99/189

Town plan: C3-x - *23 Mayfield Gdns* ✉ *EH9 2BX* - ☎ *0131 667 5806*
– *www.23mayfield.co.uk*

Restaurants

𝕏𝕏𝕏 Number One 🐾 ⅗ 🆎 ⑩

� MODERN CUISINE · INTIMATE A stylish, long-standing restaurant with a chic cocktail bar, set in the basement of a grand hotel. Richly upholstered banquettes and red lacquered walls give it a plush, luxurious feel. Cooking is modern and intricate and prime Scottish ingredients are key. Service is professional and has personality.

→ Balmoral smoked salmon with lemon butter, quail's egg and caviar. Roast veal sweetbread with Wye Valley asparagus, morels and madeira sauce. Valrhona chocolate tart '2001', praline and white chocolate.

Menu £ 75

Town plan: G2-n - *Balmoral Hotel, 1 Princes St* ✉ *EH2 2EQ* - ☎ *0131 557 6727*
– *www.roccofortehotels.com* – *dinner only* – *Closed 2 weeks mid-January*

𝕏𝕏𝕏 21212 (Paul Kitching) ⇦ ⅗ 🆎 ⑩ ⇧

� CREATIVE · ELEGANT Stunningly refurbished Georgian townhouse designed by William Playfair. The glass-fronted kitchen is the focal point of the stylish, high-ceilinged dining room. Cooking is skilful, innovative and features quirky combinations; '21212' reflects the number of dishes per course at lunch – at dinner it's '31313'. Some of the luxurious bedrooms overlook the Firth of Forth.

→ Barley & cardamom, cheese & onion, pimento & mushrooms. Sea bass ratatouille, scallop, caviar and pine nuts. Creamy vanilla rice pudding, kiwi, pears & dill with peanut butter custard.

Menu £ 32/75 **s**

4 rooms ⌂ – ♦£ 95/295 ♦♦£ 95/295

Town plan: H1-c - *3 Royal Terr* ✉ *EH7 5AB* - ☎ *0345 222 1212 (booking essential)*
– *www.21212restaurant.co.uk* – *Closed 10 days January, 10 days summer, Sunday and Monday*

XXX Rhubarb 🐕 👄 ⅙ AC P

MODERN CUISINE · ELEGANT Two sumptuous, richly decorated dining rooms set within a romantic 17C country house; so named as this was the first place in Scotland where rhubarb was grown. The concise menu lists modern dishes with some innovative touches and is accompanied by an interesting wine list, with a great selection by the glass.

Menu £ 20/36 – Carte £ 36/70

Town plan: C3-r - *Prestonfield Hotel, Priestfield Rd* ✉ *EH16 5UT* – ☏ *0131 225 1333* – *www.prestonfield.com*

XXX The Pompadour by Galvin ⅙ AC 🕠 P

FRENCH · CHIC A grand, first floor hotel restaurant which opened in the 1920s and is modelled on a French salon. Classic Gallic dishes showcase Scottish produce, using techniques introduced by Escoffier, and are executed with a lightness of touch.

Carte £ 47/67

Town plan: F2-x - *Waldorf Astoria Edinburgh The Caledonian, Princes St* ✉ *EH1 2AB* – ☏ *0131 222 8975* – *www.galvinrestaurants.com* – *dinner only and Friday lunch* – *Closed 1-16 January, Sunday and Monday*

XX Castle Terrace ⅙ AC 🕠

MODERN CUISINE · INTIMATE Set in the shadow of the castle is this bright, contemporary restaurant with hand-painted wallpapers and a mural depicting the Edinburgh skyline. Cooking is ambitious with a playful element. The wine list offers plenty of choice.

Menu £ 30/65

Town plan: F2-a - *33-35 Castle Terr* ✉ *EH1 2EL* – ☏ *0131 229 1222* – *www.castleterracerestaurant.com* – *Closed Christmas, New Year, 1 week April, 1 week July, 1 week October, Sunday and Monday*

XX Mark Greenaway 🐕 ⇦

MODERN CUISINE · INTIMATE Smart restaurant located in an old Georgian bank – they store their wine in the old vault. The well-travelled chef employs interesting texture and flavour combinations. Dishes are modern, ambitious and attractively presented.

Menu £ 25 (lunch and early dinner)/66 – Carte £ 38/57

Town plan: F2-b - *69 North Castle St* ✉ *EH2 3LJ* – ☏ *0131 226 1155 (booking advisable)* – *www.markgreenaway.com* – *Closed 25-26 December, 1-2 January, Sunday and Monday*

XX The Honours AC 🐕

CLASSIC CUISINE · BRASSERIE Bustling brasserie with a smart, stylish interior and a pleasingly informal atmosphere. Classical brasserie menus have French leanings but always offer some Scottish dishes too; meats cooked on the Josper grill are popular.

Menu £ 23 (lunch and early dinner) – Carte £ 37/70

Town plan: F2-n - *58A North Castle St* ✉ *EH2 3LU* – ☏ *0131 220 2513* – *www.thehonours.co.uk* – *Closed 25-26 December, 1-3 January, Sunday and Monday*

XX Cucina 🌲 ⅙ AC 🐕

ITALIAN · DESIGN A buzzy mezzanine restaurant in a chic hotel, featuring red and blue glass-topped tables and striking kaleidoscope-effect blocks on the walls. Italian dishes follow the seasons – some are classically based and others are more modern.

Menu £ 19 (lunch) – Carte £ 23/50

Town plan: G2-v - *G & V Royal Mile Hotel, 1 George IV Bridge* ✉ *EH1 1AD* – ☏ *0131 220 6666* – *www.gandvhotel.com*

XX One Square

TRADITIONAL CUISINE · CLASSIC DÉCOR So named because it covers one side of the square, this smart hotel restaurant offers casual dining from an all-encompassing menu, accompanied by views towards Edinburgh Castle. Its stylish bar stocks over 50 varieties of gin.

Menu £ 17 (lunch and early dinner) – Carte £ 28/97

Town plan: F2-v - *Sheraton Grand Hotel & Spa, 1 Festival Sq* ⊠ *EH3 9SR*
– ✆ *0131 221 6422 – www.onesquareedinburgh.co.uk*

XX Ondine

SEAFOOD · BRASSERIE Smart, lively restaurant dominated by an impressive horseshoe bar and a crustacean counter. Classic menus showcase prime Scottish seafood in tasty, straightforward dishes which let the ingredients shine. Service is well-structured.

Menu £ 22 (lunch and early dinner) – Carte £ 32/74

Town plan: G2-s - *2 George IV Bridge (1st floor)* ⊠ *EH1 1AD*
– ✆ *0131 226 1888 – www.ondinerestaurant.co.uk*
– Closed 1 week early January and 24-26 December

XX Galvin Brasserie De Luxe

FRENCH · BRASSERIE It's accurately described by its name: a simply styled restaurant which looks like a brasserie of old, but with the addition of a smart shellfish counter and formal service. There's an appealing à la carte and a good value two-choice daily set selection; dishes are refined, flavoursome and of a good size.

Menu £ 19 – Carte £ 27/50

Town plan: F2-x - *Waldorf Astoria Edinburgh The Caledonian, Princes St*
⊠ *EH1 2AB –* ✆ *0131 222 8988 – www.galvinrestaurants.com*

XX Forth Floor at Harvey Nichols

MODERN CUISINE · FASHIONABLE A buzzy fourth floor eatery and terrace offering wonderful rooftop views. Dine on accomplished modern dishes in the restaurant or on old favourites in the all-day bistro. Arrive early and start with a drink in the smart cocktail bar.

Menu £ 30 (lunch and early dinner) – Carte £ 34/44

Town plan: G2-z - *30-34 St Andrew Sq* ⊠ *EH2 2AD –* ✆ *0131 524 8350*
– www.harveynichols.com – Closed 25 December, 1 January and dinner Sunday-Monday

XX Angels with Bagpipes

MODERN CUISINE · BISTRO Small, stylish restaurant named after the wooden sculpture in St Giles Cathedral, opposite. Dishes are more elaborate than the menu implies; modern interpretations of Scottish classics could include 'haggis, neeps and tattiesgine'.

Menu £ 20 (lunch) – Carte £ 29/54

Town plan: G2-a - *343 High St, Royal Mile* ⊠ *EH1 1PW –* ✆ *0131 220 1111*
– www.angelswithbagpipes.co.uk – Closed 4-19 January and 24-26 December

X Timberyard

MODERN CUISINE · RUSTIC Trendy warehouse restaurant; its spacious, rustic interior incorporating wooden floors and wood-burning stoves. Scandic-influenced menu offers 'bites', 'small' and 'large' sizes, with some home-smoked dishes and an emphasis on distinct, punchy flavours. Cocktails are made with vegetable purées and foraged herbs.

Menu £ 27 (lunch and early dinner)/55

Town plan: F3-s - *10 Lady Lawson St* ⊠ *EH3 9DS –* ✆ *0131 221 1222 (booking essential at dinner) – www.timberyard.co – Closed Christmas, 1 week April, 1 week October, Sunday and Monday*

𝕏 Aizle   ⓥ

MODERN CUISINE · SIMPLE Modest little suburban restaurant whose name means 'ember' or 'spark'. Well-balanced, skilfully prepared dishes are, in effect, a surprise, as the set menu is presented as a long list of ingredients – the month's 'harvest'.

Menu £ 45

Town plan: H3-z - *107-109 St Leonard's St* ⊠ *EH8 9QY* – ⌀ *0131 662 9349*
– *www.aizle.co.uk* – *dinner only* – *Closed 1-18 January, 3-18 July, 25-31 December, Monday and Tuesday except in August*

𝕏 Passorn

THAI · FRIENDLY The staff are super-friendly at this extremely popular neighbourhood restaurant, whose name means 'Angel'. Authentic menus feature Thai classics and old family recipes; the seafood dishes are a highlight and presentation is first class. Spices and other ingredients are flown in from Thailand.

Menu £ 16 (weekday lunch) – Carte £ 24/37

Town plan: F3-e *23-23a Brougham Pl* ⊠ *EH3 9JU* – ⌀ *0131 229 1537 (booking essential)*
– *www.passornthai.com* – *Closed 25-26 December, 1-2 January, Sunday and Monday lunch*

𝕏 Dogs

TRADITIONAL CUISINE · BISTRO Cosy, slightly bohemian-style eatery on the first floor of a classic Georgian mid-terrace, with two high-ceilinged, shabby chic dining rooms and an appealing bar. Robust, good value comfort food is crafted from local, seasonal produce; dishes such as cock-a-leekie soup and devilled ox livers feature.

Carte £ 12/25

Town plan: F2-c - *110 Hanover St (1st Floor)* ⊠ *EH2 1DR* – ⌀ *0131 220 1208*
– *www.thedogsonline.co.uk* – *Closed 25 December and 1 January*

𝕏 The Atelier

MEDITERRANEAN CUISINE · BISTRO Attractive little restaurant with bright orange chairs and a stone feature wall. The chef is Polish but his dishes have French and Italian influences; fresh ingredients are prepared with care and cooking has a subtle modern slant.

Menu £ 18 (lunch) – Carte £ 27/47

Town plan: E3-s *159 Morrison St* ⊠ *EH3 8AG* – ⌀ *0131 629 5040*
– *www.theatelierrestaurant.co.uk* – *Closed 2-3 weeks January, 25-26 December and Monday*

𝕏 Field Grill House 🆕

MEATS AND GRILLS · NEIGHBOURHOOD Large pictures of sheep, pigs, cows and chickens give a clue as to the cooking: the extensive à la carte focuses on grilled meats, with 35-day aged beef sourced from an independent Borders butcher's. The set menus are good value.

Menu £ 16/17 – Carte £ 25/42

Town plan: E1-h - *1-3 Raeburn Pl, Stockbridge* ⊠ *EH4 1HU* – ⌀ *0131 332 9977*
– *www.fieldgrillhouse.co.uk* – *Closed 2 weeks January and Monday*

𝕏 Edinburgh Larder Bistro   🅰🅲

REGIONAL CUISINE · BISTRO Sustainability and provenance are key here: the tables are crafted from scaffold boards, old lobster creels act as lampshades and each month they feature a different local, organic animal on the menu, which is used from nose to tail.

Menu £ 15 (lunch and early dinner) – Carte £ 25/36

Town plan: E2-n - *1a Alva St* ⊠ *EH2 4PH* – ⌀ *0131 225 4599*
– *www.edinburghlarder.co.uk* – *Closed 1 January, Sunday and Monday*

𝕏 Purslane

MODERN CUISINE · NEIGHBOURHOOD Set in a residential area, in the basement of a terraced Georgian house; an intimate restaurant of just 7 tables, with wallpaper featuring a pine tree motif. The chef carefully prepares modern dishes using well-practiced techniques.

Menu £ 26 (lunch and early dinner)/38

Town plan: F1-e *33a St Stephen St* ⊠ *EH3 5AH* – ⌀ *0131 226 3500 (booking essential)*
– *www.purslanerestaurant.co.uk* – *Closed 25-26 December, 1 January and Monday*

✗ Gardener's Cottage

TRADITIONAL CUISINE · RUSTIC This quirky little eatery was once home to a royal gardener. Two cosy, simply furnished rooms have long communal tables. Lunch is light and dinner offers an 8 course set menu; much of the produce comes from the kitchen garden.

Menu £ 50 (dinner) – Carte lunch £ 16/24

Town plan: H1-a - 1 Royal Terrace Gdns ✉ EH7 5DX – ☎ 0131 558 1221 (bookings advisable at dinner) - www.thegardenerscottage.co - Closed Tuesday

✗ Field

MODERN CUISINE · SIMPLE A rustic restaurant run by two young owners, comprising just 8 tables – which are overlooked by a huge canvas of a prized cow. The appealing menu changes slightly each day, offering original modern cooking with a playful element.

Menu £ 17 (lunch and early dinner) – Carte £ 22/40

Town plan: G3-x - 41 West Nicholson St ✉ EH8 9DB – ☎ 0131 667 7010 - www.fieldrestaurant.co.uk - Closed Monday

✗ Bon Vivant   🏵 🍷

TRADITIONAL CUISINE · WINE BAR A relaxed wine bar in the city backstreets, with a dimly lit interior, tightly packed tables and a cheery, welcoming team. The appealing, twice daily menu has an eclectic mix of influences; start with some of the bite-sized nibbles.

Carte £ 17/35

Town plan: F2-v - 55 Thistle St ✉ EH2 1DY – ☎ 0131 225 3275 - www.bonvivantedinburgh.co.uk - Closed 25-26 December and 1 January

✗ Kanpai

JAPANESE · SIMPLE Uncluttered, modern Japanese restaurant with a smart sushi bar and cheerful service. Colourful, elaborate dishes have clean, well-defined flavours; the menu is designed to help novices feel confident and experts feel at home.

Carte £ 13/38

Town plan: F3-n - 8-10 Grindlay St ✉ EH3 9AS – ☎ 0131 228 1602 - www.kanpaisushi.co.uk - Closed Monday

✗ Kim's Mini Meals   🕙 🖤 ✉

KOREAN · SIMPLE A delightfully quirky little eatery filled with bric-a-brac and offering good value, authentic Korean home cooking. Classic dishes like bulgogi, dolsot and jjigae come with your choice of meat or vegetables as the main ingredient.

Carte approx. £ 18

Town plan: G3-u - 5 Buccleuch St ✉ EH8 9JN – ☎ 0131 629 7951 (booking essential at dinner)

✗ Bia Bistrot   🗔

CLASSIC CUISINE · NEIGHBOURHOOD A simple, good value neighbourhood bistro with a buzzy vibe. Unfussy, flavoursome dishes range in their influences due to the friendly owners' Irish-Scottish and French-Spanish heritages; they are husband and wife and cook together.

Menu £ 10 (lunch and early dinner) – Carte £ 19/34

Town plan: B3-a 19 Colinton Rd ✉ EH10 5DP – ☎ 0131 452 8453 - www.biabistrot.co.uk - Closed first week January, 1 week July, Sunday and Monday

✗ Café St Honoré

CLASSIC FRENCH · BISTRO Long-standing French bistro, tucked away down a side street. The interior is cosy, with wooden marquetry, mirrors on the walls and tightly packed tables. Traditional Gallic menus use Scottish produce and they even smoke their own salmon.

Menu £ 15/23 – Carte £ 28/45

Town plan: F2-r - 34 North West Thistle Street Ln. ✉ EH2 1EA – ☎ 0131 226 2211 (booking essential) - www.cafesthonore.com - Closed 24-26 December and 1-2 January

✗ Wedgwood 🔤 🔟

MODERN CUISINE · FRIENDLY Atmospheric bistro hidden away at the bottom of the Royal Mile. Well-presented dishes showcase produce foraged from the surrounding countryside and feature some original, modern combinations. It's personally run by a friendly team.

Menu £ 15 (lunch) – Carte £ 33/53

Town plan: H2-a - *267 Canongate* ✉ *EH8 8BQ* – ☎ *0131 558 8737*
– www.wedgwoodtherestaurant.co.uk – Closed 2-22 January and 25-26 December

🍴 The Scran & Scallie ♿ 🔤

TRADITIONAL BRITISH · NEIGHBOURHOOD The more casual venture from Tom Kitchin, located in a smart, village-like suburb. It has a wood-furnished bar and a dining room which blends rustic and contemporary décor. Extensive menus follow a 'Nature to Plate' philosophy and focus on the classical and the local.

Menu £ 15 (weekday lunch) – Carte £ 23/46

Town plan: E1-s - *1 Comely Bank Rd, Stockbridge* ✉ *EH4 1DT* – ☎ *0131 332 6281*
(booking advisable) – www.scranandscallie.com – Closed 25 December

at Leith

🏨 Malmaison ♤ 🛏 🖥 ♿ 🍽 🏋 🅿

BUSINESS · CONTEMPORARY Impressive former seamen's mission located on the quayside; the first of the Malmaison hotels. The décor is a mix of bold stripes and contrasting black and white themes. Comfy, well-equipped bedrooms; one with a four-poster and a tartan roll-top bath. Intimate bar and a popular French brasserie and terrace.

100 rooms – ♦£ 89/300 ♦♦£ 89/300 – ☐ £ 14

Town plan: C1-m - *1 Tower Pl* ✉ *EH6 7BZ* – ☎ *0131 285 1478*
– www.malmaison.com

✗✗✗ Martin Wishart ♿ 🔤 🔟

ⓈⒼ MODERN CUISINE · ELEGANT This elegant, modern restaurant is becoming something of an Edinburgh institution. Choose between three 6 course menus – Classic, Seafood and Vegetarian – and a concise à la carte. Top ingredients are used in well-judged, flavourful combinations; dishes are classically based but have elaborate, original touches.

→ Langoustine with kohlrabi, vanilla and passion fruit. Roast breast and pastilla of duck with red cabbage, beetroot, macadamia and redcurrant. Mangaro chocolate dome with banana, yuzu and almond ice cream.

Menu £ 29 (weekday lunch)/75 – Carte approx. £ 75

Town plan: C1-u - *54 The Shore* ✉ *EH6 6RA* – ☎ *0131 553 3557 (booking essential)*
– www.martin-wishart.co.uk – Closed 31 December-18 January, 18-19 October,
25-26 December, Sunday and Monday

✗✗ Kitchin (Tom Kitchin) ♿ 🔤 🔟 ⇔

ⓈⒼ MODERN CUISINE · DESIGN Set in a smart, converted whisky warehouse. 'From nature to plate' is the eponymous chef-owner's motto and the use of natural features like bark wall coverings, alongside the more traditional Harris tweed, reflect his passion for using the freshest and best quality Scottish ingredients. Refined, generously proportioned classic French dishes are packed with vivid flavours.

→ Isle of Cumbrae oysters prepared six ways. Highland hogget with roasted & raw artichoke and black olive. Tomlinson's Farm rhubarb crumble soufflé with vanilla ice cream.

Menu £ 30 (lunch) – Carte £ 70/87

Town plan: C1-z - *78 Commercial Quay* ✉ *EH6 6LX* – ☎ *0131 555 1755 (booking essential) – www.thekitchin.com – Closed 23 December-13 January, 4-8 April, 25-29 July, 10-14 October, Sunday and Monday*

XX Norn

AC

MODERN CUISINE · FASHIONABLE A young couple run this modern restaurant, where the chefs serve the dishes themselves. Creative cooking showcases produce from small Scottish suppliers along with items they have foraged. Lunch is 3 courses and dinner either 4 or 7.

Menu £ 20/40 – tasting menu only

Town plan: C1-a - 50-54 Henderson St ⊠ EH6 6DE – ℰ 0131 629 2525 (booking advisable) – www.nornrestaurant.com – Closed Sunday-Monday and lunch Tuesday-Wednesday

XX Bistro Provence

ሌ

CLASSIC FRENCH · BISTRO This converted warehouse brings a taste of France to the cobbled quayside of Leith. It's very personally run by a gregarious owner and a welcoming team, and offers an appealing range of unfussy dishes with Provençal leanings.

Menu £ 10/28

Town plan: C1-c - 88 Commercial St ⊠ EH6 6LX – ℰ 0131 344 4295 – www.bistroprovence.co.uk – Closed 3-15 July and Monday

EDNAM – The Scottish Borders → See Kelso

ELGIN

Moray – Pop. 23 128 – Regional map n° **16**-C1

▶ Edinburgh 198 mi – Aberdeen 68 mi – Fraserburgh 61 mi – Inverness 39 mi

🏠 Mansion House

⇪ 🚅 🖫 🕅 ⌟ ⁄ ⚙ 🐾 P

HISTORIC BUILDING · CLASSIC Victorian country house in pleasant gardens. The beautiful Georgian-style drawing room has a grand piano and there's a snooker table in the 'wee bar'. Bedrooms are luxurious – some have sleigh beds, four-posters or river views. The classically furnished, formal dining room offers an eclectic mix of dishes.

26 rooms ☷ – ♛£ 107/134 ♛♛£ 164/212

The Haugh ⊠ IV30 1AW – via Haugh Rd – ℰ 01343 548811 – www.mansionhousehotel.co.uk – Closed 25 December

ELIE

Fife – Pop. 942 – Regional map n° **16**-D2

▶ Edinburgh 44 mi – Dundee 24 mi – St Andrews 13 mi

XX Sangster's (Bruce Sangster)
£3

CLASSIC CUISINE · COSY A sweet little restaurant in a sleepy coastal hamlet; slickly run by a husband and wife. The well-respected chef uses Scotland's natural larder and willingly embraces new ideas. Appealing, flavoursome dishes are well-proportioned, carefully executed and have modern overtones: the simplest dishes are the best.

→ Seared scallops with chilli, ginger and lemongrass & galangal dressing. Roast breast of Gressingham duck with duck leg bonbon, garlic chips and hazelnut. Chocolate cremeux with poached pear and vanilla ice cream.

Menu £ 42

51 High St ⊠ KY9 1BZ – ℰ 01333 331001 (booking essential) – www.sangsters.co.uk – dinner only and Sunday lunch – Closed January-mid February, 1 week November, 25-26 December, Sunday dinner, Monday and Tuesday November-March

ERISKA (Isle of)

Argyll and Bute – ⊠ Oban – Regional map n° **16**-B2

▶ Edinburgh 127 mi – Glasgow 104 mi – Oban 12 mi

🏠 Isle of Eriska

GRAND LUXURY · PERSONALISED 19C baronial mansion in an idyllic spot on a private island, boasting fantastic views over Lismore and the mountains; pleasingly, it's family run. Open-fired guest areas display modern touches and the spa and leisure facilities are superb. Bedrooms are bright, stylish and well-equipped; some feature hot tubs. Pub classics in informal all-day brasserie, The Deck.

23 rooms ♨ – †£ 205/230 ††£ 350/480 – 7 suites

Benderloch ✉ PA37 1SD – ℰ 01631 720371 – www.eriska-hotel.co.uk – Closed 3-20 January

✸ **Isle of Eriska** – See restaurant listing

✕✕✕ Isle of Eriska

✸ **MODERN CUISINE · ELEGANT** Set in a country house on a private island, this dining room and conservatory offer enviable views. Cooking is modern and understated, with well-defined flavours; its emphasis on the finest Scottish ingredients, many of which come directly from the kitchen garden. For the full experience go for the tasting menu.

➜ Smoked ham hock with slow-cooked hen's egg, fermented cabbage and garden brassica. Glenfinnan Estate venison with crapaudine beetroot, brown butter mousseline and kale. Yoghurt parfait with ginger, pear and sorrel.

Menu £ 55

Isle of Eriska Hotel, Benderloch ✉ PA37 1SD – ℰ 01631 720371 (bookings essential for non-residents) – www.eriska-hotel.co.uk – dinner only – Closed 3-20 January

EVANTON

Highland – Regional map n° **17**-C2

▶ Edinburgh 171 mi – Inverness 17 mi – Dingwall 7 mi

🏠 Kiltearn House

COUNTRY HOUSE · CONTEMPORARY This large sandstone former manse sits in a quiet spot, yet only a few minutes from the A9. It has a classical sitting room and a conservatory breakfast room; bedrooms are more modern – two have views over Cromarty Firth.

5 rooms ♨ – †£ 60/120 ††£ 96/200

✉ IV16 9UY – South : 1 mi by B 817 on Kiltearn Burial Ground rd – ℰ 01349 830617 – www.kiltearn.co.uk – Closed 25 December

FAIRLIE

North Ayrshire – Pop. 1 424 – Regional map n° **15**-A1

▶ Edinburgh 79 mi – London 434 mi – Glasgow 34 mi

✕ Catch at Fins

SEAFOOD · RUSTIC Seafood is the order of the day – with crab, lobster and mackerel from Largs – but there's also beech-smoked produce from the next door smokery. Sit in the cosy bothy or spacious conservatory and bring a bottle from the farm shop.

Carte £ 17/42

Fencebay Fisheries, Fencefoot Farm ✉ KA29 0EG – South : 1.5 mi on A 78 – ℰ 01475 568989 (booking essential) – www.fencebay.com – Closed 26 December, 1-2 January, Sunday dinner-Wednesday

FIONNPHORT – Argyll and Bute ➜ See Mull (Isle of)

FLODIGARRY – Highland ➜ See Skye (Isle of)

FOCHABERS

Moray – Pop. 1 728 – Regional map n° **16**-C1

▶ Edinburgh 175 mi – London 580 mi – Aberdeen 56 mi – Inverness 48 mi

🏠 Trochelhill Country House   ⌕ 🛏 ✕ 🎾 P

COUNTRY HOUSE · CLASSIC Whitewashed Victorian house; well-run by friendly owners who serve tea and cake on arrival. Spacious bedrooms feature modern bathrooms with walk-in showers; two have roll-top baths. Breakfast includes haggis, black pudding and homemade bread.

3 rooms ⌂ – ♦£70/110 ♦♦£110

✉ IV32 7LN – West : 2.75 mi by A 96 off B 9015 – ✆ 01343 821267
– www.trochelhill.co.uk

FORT AUGUSTUS

Highland – Pop. 621 – Regional map n° **17**-C3
▶ Edinburgh 158 mi – Inverness 34 mi – Fort William 32 mi

🏠 The Lovat   🛏 ⬆ & P

TRADITIONAL · PERSONALISED A professionally run Victorian house which has been given a bold, stylish makeover. Bedrooms are a mix of the classic – with feature beds and antique furnishings – and the contemporary, with vibrant colours and feature wallpapers.

28 rooms ⌂ – ♦£80/200 ♦♦£100/300

✉ PH32 4DU – ✆ 01456 459250 – www.thelovat.com

Station Road · Brasserie – See restaurant listing

✕✕ Station Road   🛏 & P

MODERN CUISINE · INTIMATE Light, spacious hotel dining room with views up the Great Glen and a formal feel. It's only open for dinner and offers a 5 course, no-choice set menu. Elaborate modern cooking features adventurous texture and flavour combinations.

Menu £45 – tasting menu only

The Lovat Hotel, ✉ PH32 4DU – ✆ 01456 459250 (booking essential)
– www.thelovat.com – dinner only – Closed November-Easter and Sunday-Tuesday

✕ Brasserie   🛏 🌳 &

MODERN CUISINE · FRIENDLY Modern brasserie at the side of a hotel, with a large lawned garden and picnic benches; it offers informal yet surprisingly sophisticated dining. Classically based dishes are given a modern makeover and feature good ingredients.

Carte £27/49

The Lovat Hotel, ✉ PH32 4DU – ✆ 01456 459250 – www.thelovat.com

FORT WILLIAM

Highland – Pop. 5 883 – Regional map n° **17**-C3
▶ Edinburgh 133 mi – Glasgow 104 mi – Inverness 68 mi – Oban 50 mi

🏰 Inverlochy Castle   ⌕ ≤ 🛏 ✕ P

GRAND LUXURY · CLASSIC Striking castellated house in beautiful grounds, boasting stunning views over the loch to Glenfinnan. The classical country house interior comprises sumptuous open-fired lounges and a grand hall with an impressive ceiling mural. Elegant bedrooms offer the height of luxury; mod cons include mirrored TVs.

18 rooms ⌂ – ♦£280/695 ♦♦£335/695 – 2 suites

Torlundy ✉ PH33 6SN – Northeast : 3 mi on A 82 – ✆ 01397 702177
– www.inverlochycastlehotel.com

Inverlochy Castle – See restaurant listing

🏠 Grange   ⌕ ≤ 🛏 🎾 P 🚗

TOWNHOUSE · PERSONALISED Delightful Victorian house with an attractive garden and immaculate interior, set in a quiet residential area. The beautiful lounge displays fine fabrics and the lovely breakfast room boasts Queen Anne style chairs. Bedrooms are extremely well appointed, with smart bathrooms.

3 rooms ⌂ – ♦£140/160 ♦♦£145/180

Grange Rd. ✉ PH33 6JF – South : 0.75 mi by A 82 and Ashburn Ln
– ✆ 01397 705516 – www.grangefortwilliam.com – Closed November-mid March

XXXX Inverlochy Castle ⇐ ⇐ P

MODERN CUISINE · LUXURY Set within a striking castle in the shadow of Ben Nevis and offering stunning loch views. Two candlelit dining rooms are filled with period sideboards and polished silver. The daily set menu showcases top quality Scottish produce.

Menu £ 67 – tasting menu only

Inverlochy Castle Hotel, Torlundy ⊠ PH33 6SN – Northeast : 3 mi on A 82 – ℰ 01397 702177 (booking essential) – www.inverlochycastlehotel.com – dinner only

X Lime Tree An Ealdhain ⇔ ⇐ ⇐ ৬ P

MODERN CUISINE · RUSTIC Attractive 19C manse – now an informally run restaurant and art gallery, where the owner's pieces are displayed and two public exhibitions are held each year. Rustic dining room with exposed beams and an open kitchen; cooking is fresh and modern. Simply furnished bedrooms – ask for one with a view of Loch Linnhe.

Carte £ 29/37

9 rooms ⊡ – ♦£ 70/135 ♦♦£ 70/135

Achintore Rd ⊠ PH33 6RQ – ℰ 01397 701806 – www.limetreefortwilliam.co.uk – dinner only – Closed November, last 3 weeks January and 24-27 December

X Crannog ⇐ ৬

SEAFOOD · COSY Popular restaurant with a bright red roof and a colourful boat-like interior; set on the pier above Loch Linnhe – try to get a table by the window. Fresh local fish and shellfish are simply prepared. The 2 course lunch is good value.

Menu £ 15 (lunch) – Carte £ 28/41

Town Pier ⊠ PH33 6DB – ℰ 01397 705589 (booking essential) – www.crannog.net – Closed 25-26 December and 1 January

FORTINGALL

Perth and Kinross – Regional map n° **16**-C2
▶ Edinburgh 84 mi – Perth 40 mi – Pitlochry 23 mi

🏠 Fortingall ⇧ ⇐ ⇐ P

TRADITIONAL · PERSONALISED Stylish Arts and Crafts house on a tranquil private estate, boasting lovely country views. The interior is delightful, with its snug open-fired bar and cosy sitting rooms filled with Scottish country knick-knacks. Bedrooms are modern but in keeping with the building's age. Dining is formal and classical.

10 rooms ⊡ – ♦£ 90/180 ♦♦£ 90/180

⊠ PH15 2NQ – ℰ 01887 830367 – www.fortingall.com

FORTROSE

Highland – Pop. 1 367 – Regional map n° **17**-C2
▶ Edinburgh 166 mi – London 571 mi – Inverness 12 mi – Elgin 48 mi

🏠 Water's Edge ⇐ ⇐ ⇗ P

LUXURY · PERSONALISED Smart, personally run guesthouse with attractive gardens and stunning views over the Moray Firth. Immaculately kept guest areas include a small lounge and an adjoining antique-furnished breakfast room. Classically stylish first floor bedrooms open out onto a roof terrace – keep an eye out for the dolphins!

3 rooms ⊡ – ♦£ 150/160 ♦♦£ 150/160

Canonbury Ter ⊠ IV10 8TT – On A 832 – ℰ 01381 621202 – www.watersedge.uk.com – Closed mid October-April

GALSON – Western Isles → See Lewis and Harris (Isle of)

GATEHEAD
East Ayrshire – ⊠ East Ayrshire – Regional map n° **15**-B2
▶ Edinburgh 72 mi – Glasgow 25 mi – Kilmarnock 5 mi

Cochrane Inn   P
TRADITIONAL CUISINE · PUB This ivy-covered pub is surprisingly bright and modern inside, with its copper lampshades, coal-effect gas fires and striking contemporary art. It offers a good range of tasty, generously priced dishes; the Express Menu is a steal.
Menu £ 15 (lunch and early dinner) – Carte £ 20/38
45 Main Rd ⊠ KA2 0AP – ℰ 01563 570122 – www.costley-hotels.co.uk

GATTONSIDE – The Scottish Borders → See Melrose

GIFFNOCK
East Renfrewshire – Pop. 12 156 – Regional map n° **15**-B1
▶ Glasgow 7 mi – Edinburgh 46 mi – London 404 mi

Catch   ♿ A/C
FISH AND CHIPS · SIMPLE Modern fish and chip shop with exposed brick walls and nautical styling; sit in a booth to take in all the action from the large open kitchen. Fresh, sustainably sourced fish comes in crisp batter and is accompanied by twice-cooked chips.
Carte £ 15/45
186 Fenwick Rd ⊠ G46 6XF – ℰ 0141 638 9169 (bookings advisable at dinner) – www.catchfishandchips.co.uk

GIGHA (Isle of)
Argyll and Bute – Regional map n° **16**-A3
▶ Edinburgh 168 mi – Oban 74 mi – Dunoon 100 mi

The Boathouse   P
SEAFOOD · RUSTIC This 300 year old boathouse is set on a small community-owned island, overlooking the water. Whitewashed stone walls and beamed ceilings enhance the rustic feel. Menus cater for all, centring around fresh seafood and local meats.
Carte £ 17/51
Ardminish Bay ⊠ PA41 7AA – ℰ 01583 505123 – www.boathousegigha.co.uk – Closed November-Easter

GOOD TIPS!

This former industrial powerhouse has been reborn as a cultural and commercial hub, with a lively dining scene to boot. History is all around: enjoy a stay in the stunning **Blythswood Square** hotel – once the RAC HQ. Modernity comes in the form of creative, cutting-edge restaurants like **Cail Bruich** and Bib Gourmand awarded neighbourhood restaurant, **The Gannet**.

GLASGOW

Glasgow City – Pop. 590 507 – Regional map n° **15**-B1
▶ Edinburgh 46 mi – Ayr 38 mi – Dumbarton 20 mi

Hotels

🏨 Hotel du Vin at One Devonshire Gardens   ♿ ♨

TOWNHOUSE · ELEGANT Collection of adjoining townhouses boasting original 19C stained glass, wood panelling and a labyrinth of corridors. Furnished in dark, opulent shades but with a modern, country house air. Luxurious bedrooms; one with a small gym and sauna.

49 rooms – ♦£ 109/249 ♦♦£ 109/249 – ☕ £ 18 – 3 suites
1 Devonshire Gdns ⊠ G12 OUX – Northwest : 2.5 mi by A 82 (Great Western Rd) – ℰ 0141 378 0385 – www.hotelduvin.com
Bistro – See restaurant listing

🏨 Blythswood Square   🆘 ♨ ♨ 🛏 ⬆ ♿ 🅰🅲 ♨

HISTORIC · DESIGN Stunning property on a delightful Georgian square; once the Scottish RAC HQ. Modern décor contrasts with original fittings. Dark, moody bedrooms have marble bathrooms; the Penthouse Suite features a bed adapted from a snooker table.

100 rooms ☕ – ♦£ 120/280 ♦♦£ 120/280 – 1 suite
Town plan: C2-n - 11 Blythswood Sq ⊠ G2 4AD – ℰ 0141 248 8888 – www.blythswoodsquare.com
Blythswood Square – See restaurant listing

🏨 Malmaison   ⬆ ♿ ♨

BUSINESS · CONTEMPORARY Impressive-looking former church with moody, masculine décor. Stylish, boldly coloured bedrooms offer good facilities; some are duplex suites. The Big Yin Suite – named after Billy Connolly – has a roll-top bath in the room.

72 rooms ☕ – ♦£ 117/330 ♦♦£ 129/340 – 8 suites
Town plan: C2-c - 278 West George St ⊠ G2 4LL – ℰ 0141 572 1000 – www.malmaison.com
The Honours – See restaurant listing

⌂ Grasshoppers

BUSINESS · DESIGN Unusually located, on the 6th floor of the Victorian railway station building; the lounge overlooks what is the largest glass roof in Europe. Stylish, well-designed bedrooms with bespoke Scandinavian-style furnishings and Scottish art. Smart, compact shower rooms. Three course suppers for residents only.

29 rooms ⌕ – ♦£ 75/105 ♦♦£ 85/125

Town plan: C2-r - *Caledonian Chambers (6th Floor), 87 Union St* ⌧ *G1 3TA* – ℰ *0141 222 2666* – *www.grasshoppersglasgow.com* – *Closed 3 days Christmas*

15 Glasgow

TOWNHOUSE · PERSONALISED Delightful Victorian townhouse set on a quiet square. Characterful original features include mosaic floors and ornate cornicing. Extremely spacious bedrooms boast top quality furnishings and underfloor heating in their bathrooms.

5 rooms ⌕ – ♦£ 120/150 ♦♦£ 130/170

Town plan: B2-s - *15 Woodside Pl.* ⌧ *G3 7QL* – ℰ *0141 332 1263* – *www.15glasgow.com*

Restaurants

XXX Brian Maule at Chardon d'Or

MODERN CUISINE · ELEGANT Georgian townhouse in the city's heart, with original pillars, ornate carved ceilings and white walls hung with vibrant modern art. Classical cooking with a modern edge; luxurious ingredients and large portions. Friendly, efficient service.

Menu £ 21 (lunch and early dinner) – Carte £ 45/58

Town plan: C2-b - *176 West Regent St.* ⌧ *G2 4RL* – ℰ *0141 248 3801* – *www.brianmaule.com* – *Closed 25 December, 1 January, Sunday and bank holidays*

XXX Bistro

MODERN CUISINE · ELEGANT Elegant oak-panelled restaurant in a luxurious hotel. The three rooms are dark, moody and richly appointed, and there's a lovely lounge and whisky snug. Choose from well-prepared classics or more ambitious offerings on the degustation menu.

Menu £ 22 (lunch and early dinner) – Carte £ 38/64

Hotel du Vin at One Devonshire Gardens, 1 Devonshire Gdns ⌧ *G12 OUX* – *Northwest : 2.5 mi by A 82 (Great Western Rd)* – ℰ *0141 378 0385* – *www.hotelduvin.com*

XX The Honours

MODERN CUISINE · CLASSIC DÉCOR Intimate brasserie named after the Scottish Crown Jewels and set in the crypt of an old Greek Orthodox church. Sit on leather banquettes under a vaulted ceiling and beside gilded columns. Classic brasserie dishes have a modern edge.

Menu £ 19 (lunch and early dinner) – Carte £ 27/51

Town plan: C2-c - *Malmaison Hotel, 278 West George St* ⌧ *G2 4LL* – ℰ *0141 572 1001* – *www.thehonours.co.uk*

XX Cail Bruich

MODERN CUISINE · INTIMATE High ceilinged restaurant with red leather banquettes and low hanging copper lamps. Menus range from a market selection to tasting options; cooking is modern and creative, with BBQ dishes a specialty. Its name means 'to eat well'.

Menu £ 21 (lunch and early dinner)/25 – Carte £ 32/48

Town plan: A1-a - *725 Great Western Rd.* ⌧ *G12 8QX* – ℰ *0141 334 6265 (booking advisable)* – *www.cailbruich.co.uk* – *Closed 25-26 December, 1-2 January and lunch Monday-Tuesday*

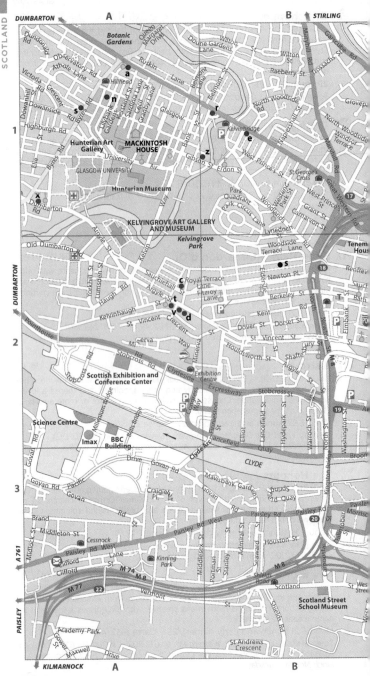

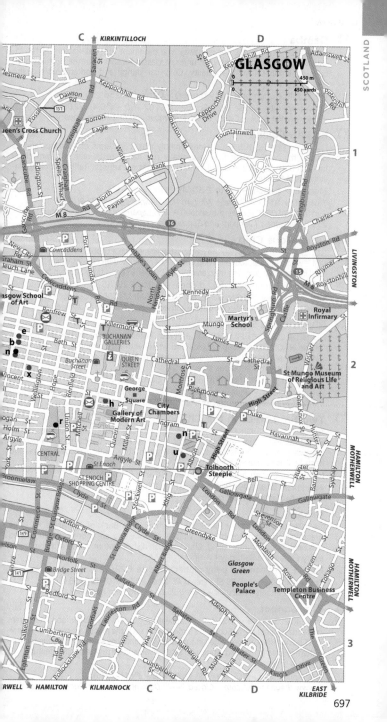

C *KIRKINTILLOCH* D

GLASGOW

0 _____ 450 m
0 _____ 450 yards

XX Gamba

SEAFOOD · BRASSERIE Tucked away in a basement but well-known by the locals. Appealing seafood menu of unfussy, classical dishes with the odd Asian influence; lemon sole is a speciality. Cosy bar-lounge and contemporary dining room hung with fish prints.

Menu £ 19 (lunch and early dinner) – Carte £ 25/56

Town plan: C2-x - 225a West George St. ⊠ G2 2ND – 𝒞 0141 572 0899
- www.gamba.co.uk – Closed 25-26 December and first week January

XX La Parmigiana

ITALIAN · NEIGHBOURHOOD Unashamedly classic in terms of its décor and its dishes, this well-regarded, professionally run Italian restaurant is approaching its 40th birthday. Red walls, white linen and efficient service. Refined cooking delivers bold flavours.

Menu £ 17 (lunch) – Carte £ 30/49

Town plan: B1-r - 447 Great Western Rd, Kelvinbridge ⊠ G12 8HH
- 𝒞 0141 334 0686 (booking essential) – www.laparmigiana.co.uk – Closed 25-26 December, 1 January and Sunday dinner

XX Ubiquitous Chip

MODERN CUISINE · BISTRO An iconic establishment on a cobbled street. The restaurant – with its ponds, fountains and greenery – offers modern classics which showcase local ingredients, while the mezzanine-level brasserie serves tasty Scottish favourites.

Menu £ 16 (lunch) – Carte £ 29/65

Town plan: A1-n 12 Ashton Ln ⊠ G12 8SJ – 𝒞 0141 334 5007 (bookings advisable at dinner) – www.ubiquitouschip.co.uk – Closed 25 December and 1 January

XX Blythswood Square

MODERN CUISINE · FASHIONABLE Stylish hotel restaurant in the ballroom of the old RAC building; chic in black and white, with a zinc-topped bar and Harris Tweed banquettes. Classic menu with meats from the Josper grill. Desserts showcase the kitchen's ambitious side.

Menu £ 19 (lunch and early dinner) – Carte £ 18/52

Town plan: C2-n - Blythswood Square Hotel, 11 Blythswood Sq ⊠ G2 4AD
- 𝒞 0141 248 8888 – www.blythswoodsquare.com

XX Two Fat Ladies in the City

TRADITIONAL CUISINE · CLASSIC DÉCOR Intimate restaurant which resembles an old-fashioned brasserie, courtesy of its wooden floor, banquettes and mirrors. Classically based dishes are straightforward in style, with a modern edge, and fresh Scottish seafood is a feature.

Menu £ 18 (lunch and early dinner) – Carte £ 30/56

Town plan: C2-e - 118a Blythswood St ⊠ G2 4EG – 𝒞 0141 847 0088
- www.twofatladiesrestaurant.com

XX Urban

TRADITIONAL BRITISH · BRASSERIE Formerly the Bank of England's HQ. The grand dining room has booths, vibrant artwork and an impressive illuminated glass and wrought iron ceiling. Classic British dishes feature, along with live music every Friday and Saturday evening.

Menu £ 17 (lunch and early dinner) – Carte £ 22/47

Town plan: C2-h - 23-25 St Vincent Pl. ⊠ G1 2DT – 𝒞 0141 248 5636
- www.urbanbrasserie.co.uk – Closed 25 December and 1 January

X The Gannet

MODERN BRITISH · RUSTIC This appealingly rustic neighbourhood restaurant makes passionate use of Scotland's larder and as such, the menus are constantly evolving. Classic dishes are presented in a modern style and they are brought to the table by a charming team. Exposed stone, untreated wood and corrugated iron all feature.

Carte £ 28/39

Town plan: A2-t - 1155 Argyle St ⊠ G3 8TB – 𝒞 0141 204 2081
- www.thegannetgla.com – Closed 24-27 December, Sunday dinner and Monday

✗ Ox and Finch
🔄 MODERN BRITISH · DESIGN A bright, breezy team run this likeable rustic restaurant, with its tile-backed open kitchen and wines displayed in a huge metal cage. The Scottish and European small plates will tempt one and all: cooking centres around old favourites but with added modern twists, and the flavours really shine through.

Carte £ 16/28

Town plan: A2-c - 920 Sauchiehall St ⊠ G3 7TF – ℰ 0141 339 8627
– www.oxandfinch.com – Closed 25-26 December and 1-2 January

✗ Turnip & Enjoy ⓝ
MODERN BRITISH · NEIGHBOURHOOD You can't help but like this sweet neighbourhood restaurant with its sage green walls and wonderful ceiling mouldings. Service is friendly and the food rustic, with classical flavours presented in a modern way; desserts are a highlight.

Menu £ 17/20 (weekdays) – Carte £ 27/83

Town plan: B1-e - 393-395 Great Western Rd ⊠ G4 9HY – ℰ 0141 334 6622
– www.turnipandenjoy.co.uk – Closed Monday and Tuesday lunch

✗ Porter & Rye
MEATS AND GRILLS · TRENDY Small, well-run loft style operation where wooden floors and exposed bricks blend with steel balustrades and glass screens. Menus offer creative modern small plates and a good range of aged Scottish steaks, from onglet to porterhouse.

Carte £ 23/91

Town plan: A2-v - 1131 Argyle St ⊠ G3 8ND – ℰ 0141 572 1212 (booking advisable)
– www.porterandrye.com – Closed 25 December and 1 January

✗ Stravaigin
🔄 INTERNATIONAL · SIMPLE Well-run eatery with a relaxed shabby-chic style, a bustling café bar and plenty of nooks and crannies. Interesting menus uphold the motto 'think global, eat local', with dishes ranging from carefully prepared Scottish favourites to tasty Asian-inspired fare. Monthly 'theme' nights range from haggis to tapas.

Carte £ 27/40

Town plan: B1-z - 28 Gibson St, ⊠ G12 8NX – ℰ 0141 334 2665 (booking essential at dinner) – www.stravaigin.co.uk – Closed 25 December and 1 January

✗ Two Fat Ladies West End
SEAFOOD · NEIGHBOURHOOD Quirky neighbourhood restaurant – the first in the Fat Ladies group – with red velour banquettes, bold blue and gold décor, and a semi open plan kitchen in the window. Cooking is simple and to the point, focusing on classical fish dishes.

Menu £ 16 (lunch and early dinner) – Carte £ 27/40

Town plan: A1-x - 88 Dumbarton Rd ⊠ G11 6NX – ℰ 0141 339 1944
– www.twofatladiesrestaurant.com – Closed 25-26 December and 1-2 January

✗ Dhabba
INDIAN · FASHIONABLE Stylish restaurant in the heart of the Merchant City. Menus focus on northern India, with interesting breads and lots of tandoor dishes. Its name refers to a roadside diner and its walls are decorated with photos of street scenes.

Menu £ 10 (weekday lunch) – Carte £ 19/38

Town plan: D2-u - 44 Candleriggs ⊠ G1 1LE – ℰ 0141 553 1249
– www.thedhabba.com – Closed 25 December and 1 January

✗ Hanoi Bike Shop
VIETNAMESE · SIMPLE Relaxed Vietnamese café; head to the lighter upstairs room with its fine array of lanterns. Simple menu of classic Vietnamese dishes including street food like rice paper summer rolls. Charming, knowledgeable staff offer recommendations.

Carte £ 18/26

Town plan: A1-s - 8 Ruthven Ln ⊠ G12 9BG – Off Byres Rd – ℰ 0141 334 7165
– www.thehanoibikeshop.co.uk – Closed 25th December and 1st January

✗ **Dakhin**   ♿ ⓥ

SOUTH INDIAN · SIMPLE It's all about the cooking at this modest, brightly decorated restaurant: authentic, southern Indian dishes might include seafood from Kerala, lamb curry from Tamil Nadu, and their speciality, dosas – available with a variety of fillings.

Menu £ 15 (weekday lunch) – Carte £ 17/34

Town plan: D2-n - 89 Candleriggs ⊠ G1 1NP - ℰ 0141 553 2585
– www.dakhin.com – Closed 25 December and 1 January

✗ **Cafezique**   ♿ 🅰 ▭

MODERN CUISINE · BISTRO Buzzy eatery with stone walls, wood floors and striking monotone screen prints. All-day breakfasts and Mediterranean light bites are followed by vibrant dishes in two sizes at dinner. Many ingredients come from their deli next door.

Carte £ 21/28

66 Hyndland St ⊠ G11 5PT – Northwest : 2.5 mi by A 82, B 808 and Highburgh Rd
– ℰ 0141 339 7180 – www.delizique.com – Closed 25-26 December and 1 January

🍴 **The Finnieston**   🍸 🌳 ♿

SEAFOOD · FRIENDLY Small, cosy pub specialising in Scottish seafood and gin cocktails; with an intriguing ceiling, a welcoming fire and lots of booths. Dishes are light, tasty and neatly presented, relying on just a few ingredients so that flavours are clear.

Carte £ 23/37

Town plan: A2-d - 1125 Argyle St ⊠ G3 8ND - ℰ 0141 222 2884
– www.thefinniestonbar.com – Closed 25-26 December and 1 January

🍴 **Salisbury**   🅰

MODERN BRITISH · NEIGHBOURHOOD A bijou pub on the south side of the city. Its interior is modern and cosy, the staff are friendly, and the monthly menu has an eclectic mix of Scottish and international flavours. Local seafood is given an original modern twist.

Menu £ 10 (lunch) – Carte £ 23/34

72 Nithsdale Rd ⊠ G41 2AN – Southwest : 2.5 mi by A 8 and A 77
– ℰ 0141 423 0084 – www.thesalisbury.co.uk – Closed 25 December and 1 January

GRANDTULLY

Perth and Kinross – Pop. 750 – Regional map n° **16**-C2
▶ Edinburgh 70 mi – London 475 mi – Glasgow 84 mi – Dundee 51 mi

🍴 **Inn on the Tay**   ⇔ 🛏 🌳 ♿ 🅿

TRADITIONAL CUISINE · FRIENDLY A smart modern inn on the banks of the Tay. There's a snug bar and a large dining room with superb views over the water. Burgers and gourmet sandwiches fill the lunch menu, while in the evening, satisfying tried-and-tested classics feature. The owners are cheery and welcoming and the bedrooms, comfy and cosy.

Carte £ 20/38

6 rooms ⌷ – ♦£ 70/110 ♦♦£ 110
⊠ PH9 0PL – ℰ 01887 840760 – www.theinnonthetay.co.uk

GRANTOWN-ON-SPEY

Highland – Pop. 2 428 – Regional map n° **17**-D2
▶ Edinburgh 143 mi – Inverness 34 mi – Perth 99 mi

🏠 **Dulaig**   🛏 � 🅿

TRADITIONAL · CLASSIC Small, detached, personally run guesthouse, built in 1910 and tastefully furnished with original Arts and Crafts pieces. Modern fabrics and an uncluttered feel in the comfortable bedrooms. Tea and homemade cake on arrival. Communal breakfasts include home-baked bread and muffins.

3 rooms ⌷ – ♦£ 120/140 ♦♦£ 160/180
Seafield Ave ⊠ PH26 3JF – ℰ 01479 872065 – www.thedulaig.com
– Closed 17 December-8 January

GULLANE

East Lothian – Pop. 2 568 – Regional map n° **15**-C1

▶ Edinburgh 20 mi – London 384 mi

🏠 Greywalls   🏖 ≼ 🛏 ✗ 🍸 🏊 🅿

COUNTRY HOUSE · CLASSIC A long-standing, classic Edwardian country house by Lutyens, in a superb location adjoining the famous Muirfield golf course and overlooking the Firth of Forth. Classically styled, antique-furnished bedrooms and a cosy library. Assured, professional service. Delightful formal gardens designed by Jekyll.

23 rooms ☟ – †£ 95/125 ††£ 245/370

Duncur Rd, Muirfield ⊠ EH31 2EG – Northeast : 0.75 mi by A 198
– ☎ 01620 842144 – www.greywalls.co.uk

Chez Roux – See restaurant listing

✗✗ La Potinière   ♿ 🅿

TRADITIONAL CUISINE · COSY Sweet little restaurant with white walls and striking red curtains. Concise, regularly changing menus of carefully prepared, classical dishes; lunch is good value and their homemade bread is renowned. The two owners share the cooking.

Menu £ 20/43

Main St ⊠ EH31 2AA – ☎ 01620 843214 (booking essential)
– www.lapotiniere.co.uk – Closed January, 24-26 December, Sunday dinner,
Monday, Tuesday and bank holidays

✗✗ Chez Roux   ≼ 🛏 ⇄ 🅿

FRENCH · INTIMATE A formal restaurant set in a classic country house hotel; enjoy an aperitif in the lounge or in the delightful Jekyll-designed gardens before dining with a superb view over the Muirfield golf course. Classical French menus have a Roux signature style and feature tried-and-tested classics with a modern edge.

Menu £ 30/32 – Carte £ 33/48

Greywalls Hotel, Duncur Rd, Muirfield ⊠ EH31 2EG – Northeast : 0.75 mi by A 198
– ☎ 01620 842144 (bookings essential for non-residents) – www.greywalls.co.uk

HADDINGTON

East Lothian – Pop. 9 064 – Regional map n° **15**-D1

▶ Edinburgh 17 mi – Hawick 53 mi – Newcastle upon Tyne 101 mi

🏠 Letham House   🎣 🏖 🛏 🍸 🅿

COUNTRY HOUSE · CLASSIC A classically proportioned former laird's house dating from 1645 and lovingly restored by the current owners. Luxurious bedrooms feature antique furniture, beautiful fabrics and modern, well-equipped bathrooms. Dine with your fellow guests: 3 courses of seasonal local produce are tailored to requirements.

5 rooms ☟ – †£ 95/125 ††£ 130/195

⊠ EH41 3SS – West : 1.25 mi on B 6471 – ☎ 01620 820055
– www.lethamhouse.com

HARRIS – Highland ➜ See Lewis and Harris (Isle of)

HIGH BLANTYRE

South Lanarkshire – Regional map n° **25**-B1

▶ Edinburgh 47 mi – Glasgow 16 mi – Dumfries 69 mi

🏰 Crossbasket Castle ⓝ   🎣 🛏 🏊 🅿

HISTORIC BUILDING · PERSONALISED With its 15C origins and sumptuous furnishings, this beautiful castle is a popular spot for weddings. There are elegant drawing rooms, a baronial-style library and an ornately decorated dining room. Bedrooms vary in size and are named after former custodians; the Tower Suite is set over numerous floors.

9 rooms ☟ – †£ 230/253 ††£ 260/395 – 2 suites

Stoneymeadow Rd ⊠ G72 9UE – Southwest : 1 mi by B 7012 – ☎ 01698 829461
– www.crossbasketcastle.com

INNERLEITHEN

The Scottish Borders – Pop. 3 031 – Regional map n° **15**-C2

▶ Edinburgh 31 mi – Dumfries 57 mi – Glasgow 60 mi

⌂ Caddon View   ☆ 🛏 🕸 🅿

TOWNHOUSE · PERSONALISED Substantial Victorian house with a large garden and a cosy open-fired lounge; run by a hospitable couple. Individually decorated bedrooms have modern touches – 'Yarrow' is the most spacious and 'Moorfoot' has the best view. The bright, airy dining room offers a daily set menu of produce from the Tweed Valley.

8 rooms 🖵 – †£ 52/85 ††£ 70/110

14 Pirn Rd. ✉ EH44 6HH – ☎ 01896 830208 – www.caddonview.co.uk – Closed 25-26 December

INVERGARRY

Highland – ✉ Inverness – Regional map n° **17**-C3

▶ Edinburgh 159 mi – Fort William 25 mi – Inverness 43 mi – Kyle of Lochalsh 50 mi

⌂⌂⌂ Glengarry Castle   ☆ 🦢 ← 🛏 🕸 🅿

COUNTRY HOUSE · HISTORIC Family-run Victorian house built in a baronial style and named after the ruined castle in its 60 acre grounds. Two large, open-fired sitting rooms are filled with stuffed wild animals. Classical bedrooms are individually designed; some come with four-poster beds. Dine formally, from a 4 course Scottish menu.

26 rooms 🖵 – †£ 85/130 ††£ 145/230

✉ PH35 4HW – South : 0.75 mi on A 82 – ☎ 01809 501254 – www.glengarry.net – Closed 5 November-23 March

INVERKEILOR

Angus – ✉ Arbroath – Pop. 902 – Regional map n° **16**-D2

▶ Edinburgh 85 mi – Aberdeen 32 mi – Dundee 22 mi

XX Gordon's   ← 🛏 🅿

MODERN CUISINE · INTIMATE Long-standing, passionately run restaurant with stone walls, open fires and exposed beams. The wife oversees the service and the husband and son are in the kitchen. The concise menu lists carefully prepared classic dishes which use local seasonal produce. Bedrooms are smart, modern and well-kept.

Menu £ 34/57

5 rooms 🖵 – †£ 110/160 ††£ 110/160

32 Main St ✉ DD11 5RN – ☎ 01241 830364 (booking essential) – www.gordonsrestaurant.co.uk – dinner only and Sunday lunch – Closed January and Monday

INVERNESS

Highland – Pop. 48 201 – Regional map n° **17**-C2

▶ Edinburgh 156 mi – Aberdeen 107 mi – Dundee 134 mi

⌂⌂ Rocpool Reserve   🅿

BUSINESS · DESIGN Stylish boutique hotel with a chic lounge and a sexy split-level bar. Minimalist bedrooms come with emperor-sized beds and are graded 'Hip', 'Chic', 'Decadent' and 'Extra Decadent'; some have terraces, hot tubs or saunas.

11 rooms 🖵 – †£ 195/395 ††£ 230/395

Town plan: B2-r - *14 Culduthel Rd ✉ IV2 4AG – ☎ 01463 240089 – www.rocpool.com*

Chez Roux – See restaurant listing

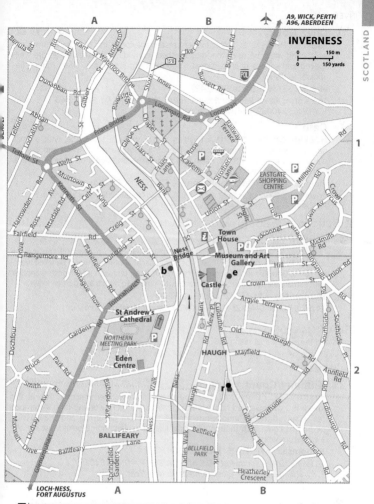

INVERNESS

A9, WICK, PERTH
A96, ABERDEEN

LOCH-NESS,
FORT AUGUSTUS

🏠 Trafford Bank   🌿 ⅌ P

HISTORIC · PERSONALISED 19C house with a modern, bohemian style. Original features include a tiled entrance and cast iron banister. Bedrooms come with iPod docks and decanters of sherry. Breakfast arrives on local china and includes haggis and tattie scones.

5 rooms ☲ – �£ 90/110 ♙♙£ 94/140

96 Fairfield Rd ⊠ IV3 5LL – West : 0.75 mi by A 82 and Harrowden Rd – ℰ 01463 241414
– www.traffordbankguesthouse.co.uk – Closed mid-November to mid-January

✗✗ Rocpool   🄰🄲

MODERN BRITISH · FRIENDLY Well-run restaurant on the banks of the River Ness; close to town and popular with the locals. Wide-ranging menus offer vibrant, colourful dishes that are full of flavour and have a distinct Mediterranean edge. The room has a modish feel.

Menu £ 16 (weekday lunch) – Carte £ 24/43

Town plan: A2-b - 1 Ness Walk ⊠ IV3 5NE – ℰ 01463 717274
– www.rocpoolrestaurant.com – Closed 25-26 December, 1-3 January and Sunday

XX Chez Roux

FRENCH · MINIMALIST Smart modern restaurant consisting of three rooms; their walls hung with photos of the Roux brothers' early days. Polished tables are well-spaced and service is professional. The French-inspired menu offers robust, fla-voursome dishes.

Menu £ 33/35 – Carte £ 34/49

Town plan: B2-r - *Rocpool Reserve Hotel, 14 Culduthel Rd* ⊠ *IV2 4AG – ℰ 01463 240089 – www.rocpool.com*

X Café 1

MODERN BRITISH · BISTRO A bustling bistro opposite the castle, with a small bar and two modern dining rooms. There's a good value set lunch and a more elaborate à la carte with an Asian and Mediterranean edge. Pork, beef and lamb come from their own croft.

Menu £ 12 (lunch and early dinner)/32 – Carte £ 23/41

Town plan: B2-e - *Castle St* ⊠ *IV2 3FA* – *ℰ 01463 226200* - *www.cafe1.net – Closed 25-26 December, 1-2 January and Sunday*

at Bunchrew West: 3 mi on A862 ⊠ Inverness

🏠 Bunchrew House

HISTORIC · CLASSIC Impressive 17C Scottish mansion, in a beautiful spot on the shore of Beauly Firth. Clubby, cosy, open-fired bar and intimate, wood-panelled drawing room. Good-sized, traditionally styled bedrooms; one with a four-poster, another with estuary views. Classical restaurant, with a menu to match and garden views.

16 rooms ⌑ – ♦£ 130/250 ♦♦£ 140/260

⊠ *IV3 8TA* – *ℰ 01463 234917* – *www.bunchrewhousehotel.com*

ISLAY (Isle of)

Argyll and Bute – Regional map n° **16**-A3

▶ Edinburgh 164 mi – London 518 mi – Greenock 117 mi – Irvine 132 mi

Ballygrant

🏠 Kilmeny Country House

TRADITIONAL · PERSONALISED You won't find a warmer welcome than at this lovely 18C whitewashed house which sits on a 300 acre working farm. Afternoon tea is served in the antique-furnished sitting room on arrival and the classical bedrooms come with thoughtful extras like binoculars, home-baked biscuits and a miniature whisky.

5 rooms ⌑ – ♦£ 85/95 ♦♦£ 125/168

⊠ *PA45 7QW – Southwest : 0.5 mi on A 846 – ℰ 01496 840668 – www.kilmeny.co.uk – Closed Christmas-New Year*

Bowmore

🏠 Harbour Inn

INN · STYLISH The owners of this pretty inn also run the neighbouring distillery. Stylish bedrooms blend the classic and the contemporary, with wood panelling, tartan throws and Islay slate bathrooms. The bar and lounge are full of character.

7 rooms ⌑ – ♦£ 85/130 ♦♦£ 105/170

The Square ⊠ *PA43 7JR* – *ℰ 01496 810330 – www.harbour-inn.com – Closed 21 December-12 January*

Harbour Inn – See restaurant listing

XX Harbour Inn

BRITISH MODERN · BRASSERIE A bright, airy restaurant within a whitewashed inn; ask for a window table for impressive loch views. Lunch offers traditional dishes, while dinner has a more modern edge. Whisky fans should try the tasting menu and whisky flight.

Menu £ 35 (dinner) – Carte £ 24/75

Harbour Inn, The Square ⊠ *PA43 7JR* – *ℰ 01496 810330 (booking essential) – www.harbour-inn.com – Closed 21 December-12 January*

Bruichladdich

Regional map n° **27**-A3

🏠 **Kentraw Farmhouse** 🆕

FAMILY · CONTEMPORARY An 18C former croft with panoramic loch views; the owner was a local gamekeeper for many years and now runs tours around the island. Spacious bedrooms feature solid oak furnishings – ask for one at the front to wake up to the view.

3 rooms ⌧ – ♦£ 85/140 ♦♦£ 85/140

✉ *PA49 7UN – North : 1 mi on A 847 – ℰ 01496 850643 – www.kentraw.com*

Port Charlotte

🏠 **Port Charlotte**

TRADITIONAL · PERSONALISED Waterside hotel packed full of modern art. Large lounge with a wood burning stove and a cosy bar hung with old island photos. Bedrooms display traditional furniture and modern colour schemes; most have a sea view. Good mix of meat and fish dishes in the restaurant.

10 rooms ⌧ – ♦£ 135 ♦♦£ 210

Main St ✉ *PA48 7TU – ℰ 01496 850360 – www.portcharlottehotel.co.uk – Closed 24-26 December*

Port Ellen

🏠 **Glenegedale House**

TRADITIONAL · PERSONALISED This passionately run former factor's house is handy for the airport. It has a boldly decorated lounge, a sunny morning room and stylish bedrooms with funky feature walls. Breakfast is an event – try the porridge with Laphroaig whisky!

4 rooms ⌧ – ♦£ 100/130 ♦♦£ 120/160

✉ *PA42 7AS – Northwest : 4.75 mi on A 846 – ℰ 01496 300400*
– www.glenegedalehouse.co.uk – Closed Christmas-New Year

JEDBURGH

The Scottish Borders – Pop. 4 030 – Regional map n° **15**-D2

▶ Edinburgh 48 mi – Carlisle 54 mi – Newcastle upon Tyne 57 mi

🏠 **Willow Court**

TOWNHOUSE · PERSONALISED Contemporary guesthouse looking out over the town's rooftops. Comfortable ground floor bedrooms offer a light, stylish space and come with iPod docks, DVD players and smart modern bathrooms. Communal breakfasts feature eggs from their own hens. Take time for yourself in the conservatory or out on the patio.

3 rooms ⌧ – ♦£ 75/80 ♦♦£ 80/90

The Friars ✉ *TD8 6BN – ℰ 01835 863702 – www.willowcourtjedburgh.co.uk*

JURA (Isle of)

Argyll and Bute – Regional map n° **27**-A3

▶ Edinburgh 196 mi – Glasgow 150 mi – Oban 100 mi

Craighouse

Regional map n° **27**-A3

🏠 **Jura** 🆕

FAMILY · CLASSIC An 18C drover's cottage on an unspoilt island, which sits in a beautiful spot beside the distillery, looking out over the bay. Bedrooms are simply furnished and those to the front have the view. Menus are traditional (go for the local lobster or langoustines) – and keep an eye out for the murals in the bar.

17 rooms ⌧ – ♦£ 65/105 ♦♦£ 105/130

✉ *PA60 7XU – ℰ 01496 820243 – www.jurahotel.co.uk – Closed 1 week Christmas*

KELSO
The Scottish Borders – Pop. 5 639 – Regional map n° **15**-D2
▶ Edinburgh 44 mi – Hawick 21 mi – Newcastle upon Tyne 68 mi

Roxburghe
HISTORIC · ELEGANT Characterful Jacobean-style mansion owned by the Duke of Roxburghe, set in extensive parkland and boasting a fly fishing school and a golf course. Plush guest areas display antiques and heirlooms. The 'Feature' bedrooms are luxurious; rooms in the courtyard are more modern. Chez Roux offers formal fine dining.

22 rooms ⌷ – †£ 150/365 ††£ 225/365 – 2 suites

Heiton ✉ TD5 8JZ – Southwest : 3.5 mi by A 698 – ✆ 01573 450331
– www.roxburghe-hotel.com

at Ednam North: 2.25 mi on B6461✉ Kelso

Edenwater House
LUXURY · CLASSIC This delightful house is run by an equally charming couple. Relax in the lovely garden beside the stream or in one of the antique-filled lounges, before heading up to one of the tastefully furnished, individually styled bedrooms. The dining room overlooks a meadow and offers a traditional menu Thursday-Saturday, with wine-themed suppers in the cellar on Wednesdays.

4 rooms ⌷ – †£ 70/80 ††£ 98/125

✉ TD5 7QL – Off Stichill rd – ✆ 01573 224070 – www.edenwaterhouse.co.uk
– Closed 1 December-12 March

KILBERRY – Argyll and Bute ➜ See Kintyre (Peninsula)

KILCHRENAN
Argyll and Bute – ✉ Taynuilt – Regional map n° **16**-B2
▶ Edinburgh 117 mi – Glasgow 87 mi – Oban 18 mi

Ardanaiseig
COUNTRY HOUSE · PERSONALISED Follow a 4 mile track through azalea-filled grounds and you'll end up at this romantic country house with stunning loch and mountain views. The impressive lounge features Corinthian pillars and the bedrooms are packed with antiques.

19 rooms – †£ 135/478 ††£ 185/478 – ⌷ £ 33 – 1 suite

✉ PA35 1HE – Northeast : 4 mi – ✆ 01866 833333 – www.ardanaiseig.com
Ardanaiseig – See restaurant listing

Roineabhal
COUNTRY HOUSE · COSY This charming stone and log house was built by the owners themselves. Relax in the open-fired lounge or lovely riverside garden. Bedrooms are immaculate – two are up a spiral staircase and all have access to a roll-top bath with views. Local produce is served in the homely breakfast room. (Min. 2 night stay.)

3 rooms ⌷ – †£ 83 ††£ 110

✉ PA35 1HD – ✆ 01866 833207 – www.roineabhal.com – Closed November-Easter

XX Ardanaiseig 🅽
BRITISH MODERN · ELEGANT Take time to admire the lovely loch view from the wood-panelled drawing room of this romantic country house before dining in the traditional restaurant. Confidently prepared dishes are classically based with a modern Scottish twist.

Menu £ 20/50 – Carte £ 25/44

Ardanaiseig Hotel, ✉ PA35 1HE – Northeast : 4 mi – ✆ 01866 833333 (booking essential) – www.ardanaiseig.com – dinner only

KILDRUMMY
Aberdeenshire – Regional map n° **16**-D1
▶ Edinburgh 137 mi – Aberdeen 35 mi

🍴 Kildrummy Inn ⇦ 🅿

TRADITIONAL BRITISH · COSY 19C coaching inn with a dining room, a conservatory and a lovely open-fired bar where you can cosy up in an armchair and sample the local whiskies. Set menus list modern main courses and more classical desserts. Cosy, contemporary bedrooms offer all you could want. They also have 4 miles of fishing rights.

Menu £ 35

4 rooms ⌂ – ♦£ 89/99 ♦♦£ 89/99

✉ AB33 8QS – North : 0.5 mi on A 97 – ✆ 01975 571227
– www.kildrummyinn.co.uk – dinner only and Sunday lunch – Closed January and Tuesday

KILLIECRANKIE – Perth and Kinross → See Pitlochry

KINCLAVEN
Perth and Kinross – ✉ Stanley – Pop. 394 – Regional map n° **16**-C2
▷ Edinburgh 55 mi – London 456 mi – Belfast 127 mi – Dundee 21 mi

🏛 Ballathie House ✿ 🐾 ⇐ 🚗 🛏 🛝 🅿

COUNTRY HOUSE · CLASSIC Mid-19C shooting lodge located on a peaceful estate of several hundred acres, on the banks of the River Tay. Bedrooms in the main house are the most characterful; the Riverside Rooms are more contemporary. The dining room has delightful river views and offers a concise menu of seasonal, regional produce.

41 rooms ⌂ – ♦£ 75/200 ♦♦£ 95/400 – 3 suites

Stanley ✉ PH1 4QN – ✆ 01250 883268 – www.ballathiehousehotel.com

KINGUSSIE
Highland – Pop. 1 476 – Regional map n° **17**-C3
▷ Edinburgh 117 mi – Inverness 41 mi – Perth 73 mi

🍴🍴 Cross at Kingussie ⇦ 🐾 🚗 🛝 🅿

MODERN BRITISH · RUSTIC 19C tweed mill in four acres of wooded grounds. Enjoy drinks on the terrace or in the first floor lounge then head to the smart dining room with It's low beams, antiques and ornaments. Cooking is modern British/Scottish and is attractively presented. Pleasant, pine-furnished bedrooms have thoughtful extras.

Menu £ 25/55

8 rooms ⌂ – ♦£ 100/200 ♦♦£ 120/280

Tweed Mill Brae, Ardbroilach Rd ✉ PH21 1LB – ✆ 01540 661166 (booking essential at lunch) – www.thecross.co.uk – Closed January and Christmas

KINTILLO – Perth and Kinross → See Perth

KINTYRE (Peninsula)
Argyll and Bute – Regional map n° **16**-B3
▷ Edinburgh 165 mi – London 515 mi – Dundee 164 mi – Paisley 111 mi

Kilberry

🍴 Kilberry Inn ⇦ 🐾 🅿
😊
REGIONAL CUISINE · INN Remotely set former croft house whose striking red roof stands out against whitewashed walls. Inside you'll find wooden beams, stone walls, open fires and a mix of bare and linen-laid tables. Classic dishes are crafted from carefully sourced local produce and meat and fish are smoked in-house. Modern bedrooms are named after nearby islands; one has an outdoor hot tub.

Carte £ 23/37

5 rooms (dinner included) ⌂ – ♦£ 130 ♦♦£ 215

✉ PA29 6YD – ✆ 01880 770223 (booking essential at dinner)
– www.kilberryinn.com – dinner only and lunch Thursday-Sunday – Closed January-mid March, Christmas and Monday

KIPPEN

Stirling – Pop. 1 026 – Regional map n° **16**-C2

▶ Edinburgh 50 mi – Glasgow 41 mi – Stirling 10 mi

🍴📖 The Inn at Kippen ⇦ 🏡 **P**

TRADITIONAL CUISINE · FRIENDLY Bigger than it looks from the outside; bright and subtly modernised on the inside, with simply furnished, contemporary bedrooms upstairs. The owners are keen to respect Scottish traditions and take full advantage of the bounteous local larder. Dishes are attractively presented in an elaborate, modern style.

Carte £ 20/49

4 rooms ⌲ – 🛉£ 65/85 🛉🛉£ 75/135

Fore Rd ✉ *FK8 3DT* – ☎ *01786 870500* – *www.theinnatkippen.co.uk* – *Closed 3-4 January*

KIRKBEAN

Dumfries and Galloway – Regional map n° **15**-C3

▶ Edinburgh 92 mi – Dumfries 13 mi – Kirkcudbright 29 mi

🏠 Cavens ✿ 🕭 ⇦ 🖙 ᴅ **P**

LUXURY · PERSONALISED Attractive 18C country house in 20 acres of mature grounds. Relax in the cosy, book-filled Green Room or the elegant drawing room with its grand piano. Luxurious 'Estate' bedrooms boast views over the Solway Firth, while the comfy 'Country' rooms have a simpler style. The linen-clad dining room offers an unfussy daily menu of local produce; complimentary afternoon tea.

7 rooms ⌲ – 🛉£ 80/150 🛉🛉£ 90/220

✉ *DG2 8AA* – ☎ *01387 880234* – *www.cavens.com* – *Closed January-February*

KIRKCUDBRIGHT

Dumfries and Galloway – Pop. 3 352 – Regional map n° **15**-B3

▶ Edinburgh 105 mi – London 369 mi – Glasgow 90 mi – Liverpool 185 mi

🏨 Selkirk Arms 🖙 **P**

TRADITIONAL · PERSONALISED Well-run 18C coaching inn, where Robert Burns reputedly wrote the Selkirk Grace. Bedrooms are spacious and comfortable – some are in the courtyard. Light lunches are served in the busy bar, which displays paintings of local scenes.

16 rooms – 🛉£ 79/84 🛉🛉£ 98/110 – 2 suites

High St ✉ *DG6 4JG* – ☎ *01557 330402* – *www.selkirkarmshotel.co.uk* – *Closed 24-26 December*

Artistas – See restaurant listing

🏨 Gladstone House ✿ 🖙 🍽

TOWNHOUSE · COSY Attractive 18C former merchant's house with friendly owners. Comfy, antique-furnished lounge. Simple, pastel-hued bedrooms with seating areas by the windows and views over the rooftops. 3 course dinner of local produce, tailored around guests' preferences.

3 rooms ⌲ – 🛉£ 67 🛉🛉£ 80

48 High St ✉ *DG6 4JX* – ☎ *01557 331734* – *www.kirkcudbrightgladstone.com* – *Closed 2 weeks January-February and Christmas*

🏨 Glenholme Country House ✿ ⇦ 🖙 🍽 **P**

COUNTRY HOUSE · CLASSIC Take in mountain views from this stone house's spacious garden. Inside, it has a cosy, eye-catching style and there's a large book and music library in place of TVs. Bedrooms are themed around Victorian political figures. The dining room features Chinese furnishings and meals are tailored to guests' tastes.

4 rooms ⌲ – 🛉£ 90/100 🛉🛉£ 110/125

Tongland Rd ✉ *DG6 4UU* – *Northeast : 1 mi on A 711* – ☎ *01557 339422* – *www.glenholmecountryhouse.com* – *Closed Christmas-New Year*

SCOTLAND

✗ Artistas &⬚♿🅿

MODERN BRITISH · FRIENDLY Relaxed, brasserie-style restaurant in a traditional coaching inn. Extensive menus mix classic and modern dishes. They are very passionate about using local produce; the Kirkcudbright scallops and Galloway Beef are worth a try.

Carte £ 21/38

Selkirk Arms Hotel, High St ⊠ DG6 4JG – 𝒞 01557 330402
– www.selkirkarmshotel.co.uk – dinner only and Sunday lunch – Closed
24-26 December except lunch 25 December

KIRKMICHAEL

Perth and Kinross – Regional map n° **16**-C2
▶ Edinburgh 73 mi – Aberdeen 85 mi – Inverness 102 mi – Perth 29 mi

🛏 Strathardle Inn ⬅⬚🏠🅿

TRADITIONAL CUISINE · PUB 18C drovers' inn opposite the river. Regulars and their dogs gather in the cosy bar and those after a hearty meal head for the dining room. Lunch focuses on pub favourites, while dinner offers grills and roasts; some Scottish dishes always feature too. Modern bedrooms make a great base for exploring the area.

Carte £ 20/34

8 rooms 😋 – 🛏£ 50/60 🛏🛏£ 85/95

⊠ PH10 7NS – On A 924 – 𝒞 01250 881224 – www.strathardleinn.co.uk

KYLESKU

Highland – Regional map n° **17**-C1
▶ Edinburgh 256 mi – Inverness 100 mi – Ullapool 34 mi

🛏 Kylesku ⬅⬚🏠

REGIONAL CUISINE · INN Breathtaking views of Loch Glendhu and the mountains make this 17C coaching inn an essential stop-off point. Fresh seafood is the way to go, with langoustines and mussels landed 200 yards away. Relax on the waterside terrace then make for one of the cosy bedrooms; two have balconies with panoramic views.

Carte £ 24/59

11 rooms 😋 – 🛏£ 73/105 🛏🛏£ 110/170

⊠ IV27 4HW – 𝒞 01971 502231 – www.kyleskuhotel.co.uk – Closed late November-mid February

LEITH – City of Edinburgh ➜ See Edinburgh

LERWICK ➜ See Shetland Islands (Mainland)

LEWIS AND HARRIS (ISLE OF)

Western Isles – Regional map n° **17**-A1

LEWIS

Western Isles – Regional map n° **17**-A1
▶ Edinburgh 210 mi – London 611 mi – Dundee 192 mi

Back

🏠 Broad Bay House   ≼ 🛋 ఉ 🕸 🅿

LUXURY · CONTEMPORARY Delightful guesthouse with a decked terrace and a garden leading down to the beach. Luxurious interior features an open-plan, Scandinavian-style lounge and a dining area with panoramic views. Modern, oak-furnished bedrooms come with super king sized beds, sliding doors onto private terraces and great extras.

4 rooms ☲ – 🛉£ 139 🛉🛉£ 179

✉ HS2 0LQ – Northeast : 1 mi on B 895 – ✆ 01851 820990
– www.broadbayhouse.co.uk – Closed October-March

Galson

🏠 Galson Farm   🏡 🐾 ≼ 🛋 🅿

TRADITIONAL · CLASSIC Welcoming guesthouse in a wonderfully remote location, boasting views out across the Atlantic. Traditional, homely guest areas and cosy bedrooms. The owner also operates the village post office from just inside the porch. Freshly prepared, home-cooked meals.

4 rooms ☲ – 🛉£ 91 🛉🛉£ 105

South Galson ✉ HS2 0SH – ✆ 01851 850492 – www.galsonfarm.co.uk

Stornoway

🏠 Braighe House   ≼ 🛋 🕸 🅿

TRADITIONAL · PERSONALISED Smart dormer bungalow with a neat garden and a relaxed, modern interior. Immaculately kept bedrooms come with mineral water and chocolates; 'Deluxe' rooms have sleigh beds and sea outlooks. Complimentary port. Diverse, appealing breakfasts.

4 rooms ☲ – 🛉£ 135 🛉🛉£ 149

20 Braighe Rd ✉ HS2 0BQ – Southeast : 3 mi on A 866 – ✆ 01851 705287
– www.braighehouse.co.uk – Closed October-March

Our selection of hotels, guesthouses and restaurants change every year, so change your MICHELIN Guide every year!

Uig

✕✕ Auberge Carnish ⟵ ♨ ≼ 🅿

TRADITIONAL CUISINE · FRIENDLY Modern, timber-clad building with decking all around, set in an idyllic position above the sweeping sands of Uig Bay. Lewis produce features in satisfying, classically based dishes with a twist; daily specials are usually seafood-based. Spacious, minimalist bedrooms have stylish bathrooms and stunning views.

Menu £ 32/38

4 rooms 🖙 – 🛉£ 115/125 🛉🛉£ 130/145

5 Carnish ✉ HS2 9EX – Southwest : 3.25 mi – 𝒫 01851 672459 (booking essential) – www.aubergecarnish.co.uk – dinner only – Closed December-mid February

HARRIS

Western Isles – Regional map n° **17**-A1
▶ Edinburgh 261 mi – London 638 mi – Dundee 242 mi

Ardhasaig

✕✕ Ardhasaig House ⟵ ♨ ≼ 🅿

REGIONAL CUISINE · FRIENDLY Purpose-built house that's been in the family for over 100 years. Modern, airy bar-lounge; flag-floored dining room with antique tables and dramatic bay and mountain views. Set menu offers local meats and seafood. Cosy bedrooms; the one in the stone lodge is the best.

Menu £ 58

6 rooms 🖙 – 🛉£ 70/110 🛉🛉£ 140

✉ HS3 3AJ – 𝒫 01859 502500 (booking essential) – www.ardhasaig.co.uk – dinner only – Closed November, January and February

Borve

🏠 Pairc an t-Srath ⌂ ♨ ≼ 🔛 🅿

FAMILY · PERSONALISED Welcoming guesthouse on a working croft, with views out over the Sound of Taransay. Comfy, open-fired lounge has a chaise longue; the intimate dining room offers delicious home-cooked meals and wonderful vistas. Extremely friendly owners serve tea and homemade cake on arrival. Immaculate bedrooms feature smart oak furniture and brightly coloured Harris Tweed fabrics.

4 rooms 🖙 – 🛉£ 54/82 🛉🛉£ 108

✉ HS3 3HT – 𝒫 01859 550386 – www.paircant-srath.co.uk – Closed 2 weeks October-November and Christmas-New Year

Scalpay

🏠 Hirta House ≼ 🕸 🅿 ⇄

TRADITIONAL · PERSONALISED Simple, characterful guesthouse in a small fishing village. Loch and mountain views from the lounge and conservatory. One traditional four-poster bedroom; two more modern rooms – one with a round bed. Nautically themed breakfast room.

3 rooms 🖙 – 🛉£ 75 🛉🛉£ 85/95

✉ HS4 3XZ – 𝒫 01859 540394 – www.hirtahouse.co.uk

Scarista

🏠 Scarista House ⌂ ♨ ≼ 🔛 🅿

TRADITIONAL · CLASSIC 19C former manse boasting amazing bay and mountain views. Caring owners; cosy, homely interior with open-fired library and drawing room. Traditional bedrooms, those at the rear are best. Classically inspired menu features garden produce.

6 rooms 🖙 – 🛉£ 125/160 🛉🛉£ 200/245

✉ HS3 3HX – 𝒫 01859 550238 – www.scaristahouse.com – Closed 21 December-31 January and restricted opening in winter

SCOTLAND

Tarbert

Ceol na Mara

⬩ ⬩ ⬩ ⬩ ⬩ **P**

TRADITIONAL · CLASSIC Former crofter's cottage – one of only three on the island with three storeys. Spacious, homely interior. Various well-kept lounges and good-sized, comfy bedrooms. Stunning lochside location.

4 rooms ⌕ – ♦£ 80 ♦♦£ 100/120

7 Direcleit ⊠ HS3 3DP – South : 1 mi by A 859 – ☎ 01859 502464
– www.ceolnamara.com

LEWISTON

Highland – Regional map n° **17**-C2
▶ Edinburgh 172 mi – London 553 mi – Dundee 153 mi

🍴 Loch Ness Inn

⬩ ⬩ ⬩ **P**

TRADITIONAL CUISINE · INN There are two parts to this pub: the small Brewery Bar, home to locals and walkers fresh from the Great Glen Way; and the open-plan Lewiston restaurant with its wood burning stove and bright timbered beams. Hearty, robust, flavoursome dishes champion Scottish produce. Bedrooms are spacious and comfortable.

Carte £ 20/36

12 rooms ⌕ – ♦£ 55/89 ♦♦£ 75/112

⊠ IV63 6UW – ☎ 01456 450991 – www.staylochness.co.uk

LINLITHGOW

West Lothian – Pop. 13 462 – Regional map n° **15**-C1
▶ Edinburgh 19 mi – Glasgow 35 mi – Perth 45 mi

🏠 Arden House

⬩ ⬩ ⬩ **P**

LUXURY · MODERN Purpose built guesthouse bordering a 105 acre sheep farm. Tea and cake on arrival. Spacious, tastefully styled bedrooms boast modern, slate-floored bathrooms and plenty of extras like fresh flowers and magazines. Tasty, wide-ranging breakfasts are a highlight. Welcoming owner pays great attention to detail.

3 rooms ⌕ – ♦£ 88/115 ♦♦£ 98/120

Belsyde ⊠ EH49 6QE – Southwest : 2.25 mi on A 706 – ☎ 01506 670172
– www.ardencountryhouse.com – Closed 25-26 December and restricted opening in winter

✗✗✗ Champany Inn

⬩ ⬩ **P**

MEATS AND GRILLS · INTIMATE Set in a collection of whitewashed cottages – the traditional restaurant was once a flour mill, hence its unusual shape. The focus is on meat and wine, with 21-day aged Aberdeen Angus beef a speciality. There's also a well-stocked wine shop, a more laid-back 'Chop and Ale House' and 16 tartan-themed bedrooms.

Menu £ 26/43 – Carte £ 48/77

16 rooms ⌕ – ♦£ 99/125 ♦♦£ 99/135

Champany ⊠ EH49 7LU – ☎ 01506 834532 – www.champany.com – Closed 25-26 December, 1-2 January, Saturday lunch and Sunday

✗✗ Livingston's

⬩ ⬩

TRADITIONAL BRITISH · INTIMATE This long-standing family-owned restaurant is run by a friendly, efficient team. Two conservatory-style dining rooms overlook a garden filled with wildlife. Cooking is traditional but there's a modern edge to the presentation.

Menu £ 20 (lunch and early dinner) – Carte dinner £ 28/44

52 High St ⊠ EH49 7AE – ☎ 01506 846565 – www.livingstons-restaurant.co.uk
– Closed 2 weeks January, 1 week June, 1 week October, Sunday and Monday

LOCHALINE
Highland – Regional map n° **17**-B3
▶ Edinburgh 162 mi – Craignure 6 mi – Oban 7 mi

✗ Whitehouse
TRADITIONAL CUISINE · FAMILY Understated wood-panelled restaurant in a remote headland village, run by keen, hands-on owners. The constantly evolving blackboard menu showcases local seafood, game and garden produce. Cooking is pleasingly unfussy and flavoursome.

Menu £ 23 (weekdays) – Carte £ 28/54

✉ PA80 5XT – ✆ 01967 421777 – www.thewhitehouserestaurant.co.uk – Closed November-Easter, Sunday and Monday

LOCHINVER
Highland – ✉ Lairg – Pop. 470 – Regional map n° **17**-C1
▶ Edinburgh 251 mi – Inverness 95 mi – Wick 105 mi

🏨 Inver Lodge
TRADITIONAL · PERSONALISED Superbly located on a hillside, overlooking a quiet fishing village. Smart bedrooms have good mod cons and great bay and island views. Relax in the open-fired lounge or billiard room – or try one of their whiskies in the elegant bar.

21 rooms ☐ – ♦£ 165/195 ♦♦£ 250/530

Iolaire Rd ✉ IV27 4LU – ✆ 01571 844496 – www.inverlodge.com – Closed November-April

Chez Roux – See restaurant listing

🏠 Ruddyglow Park Country House
TRADITIONAL · CLASSIC Creamwashed house in a superb location, boasting fantastic loch and mountain views. Spacious guest areas are filled with antiques, paintings and silverware. A high level of facilities and extras feature in classically styled bedrooms; the room in the modern log cabin offers extra privacy.

3 rooms ☐ – ♦£ 120/150 ♦♦£ 130/200

Loch Assynt ✉ IV27 4HB – Northeast : 6.75 mi on A 837 – ✆ 01571 822216 – www.ruddyglowpark.com – Closed December-March

✗✗ Albannach (Colin Craig and Lesley Crosfield)
🕸 TRADITIONAL CUISINE · COSY Substantial 19C Scottish house in a remote location, boasting exceptional bay and mountain views from the conservatory, terrace and garden. Traditional 5 course dinners rely on top quality local produce, with Scottish beef and seafood from the harbour below the specialities. Contemporary bedrooms are spread about the building; one boasts a private terrace and a hot tub.

→ Honey-baked wolf fish with wild asparagus. Roast Highland beef fillet, garden roots and charred onion mash. Vanilla parfait, almond tuile and muscat-poached gooseberries.

Menu £ 75 – tasting menu only

5 rooms (dinner included) ☐ – ♦£ 190/230 ♦♦£ 265/390

Baddidarroch ✉ IV27 4LP – West : 1 mi by Baddidarroch rd – ✆ 01571 844407 (bookings essential for non-residents) – www.thealbannach.co.uk – dinner only – Closed 3 January-10 February Tuesday-Wednesday November-December except for festive fortnight and Monday

✗✗ Chez Roux
FRENCH · INTIMATE Romantic restaurant hung with photos of the eponymous brothers, where well-spaced tables take in fantastic bay and mountain views. Regularly changing, classical French menus make use of the wealth of produce on their doorstep.

Menu £ 43 – bar lunch Monday-Saturday

Inver Lodge Hotel, Iolaire Rd ✉ IV27 4LU – ✆ 01571 844496 (bookings essential for non-residents) – www.inverlodge.com – Closed November-April

🍴 Caberfeidh   ⇐ 🏠 📖

SEAFOOD · COSY An informal lochside sister to the Albannach restaurant, which follows the same ethos of championing fresh local produce. Constantly evolving menus have a seafood slant. The majority of dishes are generously proportioned 'small plates'.

Carte £ 25/35

Main St ⊠ IV27 4JY – ℰ 01571 844321 – www.caberfeidhlochinver.co.uk – Closed 25 December, 1 January and in winter Monday and lunch Tuesday-Wednesday

LOCHRANZA – North Ayrshire ➔ See Arran (Isle of)

LUSS
Argyll and Bute – Pop. 402 – Regional map n° **16**-B2
▶ Edinburgh 89 mi – Glasgow 26 mi – Oban 65 mi

🏨 Loch Lomond Arms   ⚗ 🍽 🏠 ⚐ 🐾 ⚒ 🅿

INN · COSY Retaining the warmth and character of an old inn, this hotel offers individual, contemporary bedrooms. 'Lomond' and 'Colquhoun' are the most luxurious: the former has a four-poster bed; the latter, superb views. Wide-ranging menu: dine in the open-fired bar, the relaxed dining room or the more formal library.

15 rooms 🖙 – 🛏£ 110/150 🛏🛏£ 130/200

Main Rd ⊠ G83 8NY – ℰ 01436 860420 – www.lochlomondarmshotel.com

MELFORT
Argyll and Bute – Regional map n° **27**-B2
▶ Edinburgh 140 mi – Glasgow 112 mi – Oban 18 mi

🏨 Melfort House 🆕   ⚗ 🦢 ⇐ 🍽 🅿 🚭

COUNTRY HOUSE · PERSONALISED Enjoy homemade cake in the splendid sitting room or out on the lovely terrace looking over the loch. Bedrooms are furnished with antiques and rich fabrics and one has wonderful water views. The impressive Victorian gardens include two 150yr old monkey puzzle trees. Communal dinners are served by arrangement.

3 rooms 🖙 – 🛏£ 70 🛏🛏£ 100/130

⊠ PA34 4XD – ℰ 01852 200326 – www.melforthouse.co.uk – Closed Christmas and New Year

MELROSE
The Scottish Borders – Pop. 2 307 – Regional map n° **15**-D2
▶ Edinburgh 38 mi – London 347 mi – Glasgow 84 mi – Aberdeen 170 mi

🏨 Burts   ⚗ 🍽 🏠 🅿

INN · TRADITIONAL Characterful coaching inn on the main square; run by the same family for two generations. Appealing bedrooms blend contemporary furnishings with original features. Cosy bar serves old classics; formal dining room offers a mix of modern and traditional dishes.

20 rooms 🖙 – 🛏£ 75/85 🛏🛏£ 140/150

Market Sq. ⊠ TD6 9PL – ℰ 01896 822285 – www.burtshotel.co.uk – Closed 4-10 January, 25-26 December

at Gattonside North: 2 mi by B6374 on B6360 ⊠ Melrose

🏨 Fauhope House   🦢 ⇐ 🍽 🅿

HISTORIC · PERSONALISED Charming 19C house by the Tweed, overlooking Melrose – its delightful gardens stretching for 15 acres. Quirky interior displays an eclectic mix of art and antiques. Bedrooms are all very different; some boast stylish bold colour schemes.

3 rooms 🖙 – 🛏£ 98 🛏🛏£ 130/145

⊠ TD6 9LU – East : 0.25 mi by B 6360 taking unmarked lane to the right of Monkswood Rd at edge of village – ℰ 01896 823184 – www.fauhopehouse.com

X **Seasons** Ⓝ

TRADITIONAL CUISINE · NEIGHBOURHOOD Friendly restaurant run by an experienced couple. The 'Staples' menu arrives in a cookbook and lists favourites such as chargrilled steak; the daily blackboard is more adventurous. Meats are from Melrose and fish is from Eyemouth.

Menu £ 15 (lunch and early dinner) – Carte £ 19/44

Main St ⊠ TD6 9NP – ☎ 01896 823217 – www.seasonsborders.co.uk – dinner only and lunch Friday-Sunday – Closed 3 weeks January, Monday and Tuesday

MEMUS

Angus – Regional map n° **16**-D2

▶ Edinburgh 76 mi – London 478 mi – Dundee 21 mi

🍴 **Drovers Inn**   ⬅ 🏠 🅿

CLASSIC CUISINE · COSY Attractive Highland inn in an extremely remote spot, with a delightful beamed interior and an open-fired bar. The wide-ranging menu is good value for money and showcases local, seasonal produce; game and vegetables come from the estate.

Carte £ 26/39

⊠ DD8 3TY – ☎ 01307 860322 – www.the-drovers.com – Closed 25-26 December

MOFFAT

Dumfries and Galloway – Pop. 2 582 – Regional map n° **15**-C2

▶ Edinburgh 61 mi – Carlisle 43 mi – Dumfries 22 mi – Glasgow 60 mi

🏠 **Hartfell House**   ⬅ 🍽 🅿

TOWNHOUSE · CLASSIC Keenly run house built in 1866 and located in a peaceful crescent. Original features include parquet floors and ornate cornicing. Bedrooms are spacious and traditional and the comfy first floor drawing room has a southerly aspect.

7 rooms ⊡ – †£ 40/45 ††£ 70/75

Hartfell Cres. ⊠ DG10 9AL – ☎ 01683 220153 – www.hartfellhouse.co.uk – Closed 1 week autumn, 1 week January and Christmas

Lime Tree – See restaurant listing

🏨 **Bridge House**   ⬅ 🍽 🅿

TRADITIONAL · CLASSIC Large Victorian house on a quiet residential road, run by experienced owners and affording beautiful valley views. Relax in deep sofas in the comfortable lounge. Bedrooms are individually decorated; those to the front are the biggest.

7 rooms ⊡ – †£ 60 ††£ 70/100

Well Rd ⊠ DG10 9JT – East : 0.75 mi by Selkirk rd (A 708) taking left hand turn before bridge – ☎ 01683 220558 – www.bridgehousemoffat.co.uk – Closed 25 December-February

XX **Brodies**   🅰🅲 🅸 🕙

REGIONAL CUISINE · TRADITIONAL DÉCOR Large, laid-back, modern eatery that caters for all appetites – serving snacks, light lunches, afternoon tea, more substantial dinners and all-day brunch on Sundays. Cooking has a traditional base and features fresh, local ingredients.

Menu £ 15 (early dinner) – Carte £ 19/35

1-2 Altrive Pl, Holm St ⊠ DG10 9EB – ☎ 01683 222870 – www.brodiesofmoffat.co.uk – Closed 25-27 December

XX **Lime Tree**   🅿

TRADITIONAL CUISINE · COSY Small hotel restaurant with a feature fireplace, attractive marquetry and a large bay window looking down the valley. Good value, weekly changing menus feature well-judged, attractively presented classics that are full of flavour.

Menu £ 29

Hartfell House Hotel, Hartfell Cres. ⊠ DG10 9AL – ☎ 01683 220153 (booking essential) – www.hartfellhouse.co.uk – dinner only – Closed 1 week January, 1 week October, Christmas, Sunday and Monday

MUIR OF ORD

Highland – Pop. 2 555 – Regional map n° **17**-C2

▶ Edinburgh 173 mi – Inverness 10 mi – Wick 121 mi

🏠 Dower House

☆ 🐾 👜 🕦 🅿

TRADITIONAL · CLASSIC Personally run, part-17C house with charming mature gardens. Characterful guest areas include an antique-furnished dining room and a small, open-fired lounge with fresh flowers and shelves crammed with books. Comfy bedrooms; one with a bay window overlooking the garden. Traditional, daily set menu.

4 rooms � – ♦£ 120/135 ♦♦£ 145/165

*Highfield ⊠ IV6 7XN – North : 1 mi on A 862 – 𝒞 01463 870090
– www.thedowerhouse.co.uk – Closed November-March*

MULL (Isle of)

Argyll and Bute – Pop. 2 800 – Regional map n° **16**-A2

▶ Edinburgh 150 mi – Glasgow 125 mi – Fort William 55 mi

Dervaig

Regional map n° **27**-A2

🍴 The Bellachroy

⇐ 🏡 🅿

BRITISH TRADITIONAL · INN The 17C Bellachroy sits in a pretty village at the head of Loch Cuin and is the oldest inn on the island. It might look a little shabby from the outside but it's cosy and characterful inside. Go for the ultra-fresh local seafood – maybe scallops from Tobermory or lobster from Croig. Bedrooms are simple.

Carte £ 20/49

7 rooms ☐ – ♦£ 40/80 ♦♦£ 80/120

⊠ PA75 6QW – 𝒞 01688 400314 – www.thebellachroy.co.uk – Closed Sunday dinner and Monday November-Easter

Fionnphort

✕✕ Ninth Wave

ᕙ 🕦 🅿

SEAFOOD · CONTEMPORARY DÉCOR This remotely set modern restaurant started life as a crofter's bothy and both the décor and the cooking reflect the owners' travels. Seafood plays a key role, with crab, lobster and other shellfish caught by Mr Lamont himself.

Menu £ 44/64

Bruach Mhor ⊠ PA66 6BL – East : 0.75 mi by A 849 – 𝒞 01681 700757 (booking essential) – www.ninthwaverestaurant.co.uk – dinner only – Closed November-April, Monday and Tuesday

Tiroran

🏠 Tiroran House

☆ 🐾 ⇐ 👜 🅿

LUXURY · PERSONALISED The beautiful drive over to this remotely set, romantic Victorian house is all part of the charm. Stylish, antique-furnished bedrooms come with plenty of extras and two lovely lounges look out over 56 acres of grounds which lead down to a loch. Dine from a concise à la carte in the conservatory or cosy dining room. The welcoming owner encourages a house party atmosphere.

11 rooms ☐ – ♦£ 120/160 ♦♦£ 175/230

⊠ PA69 6ES – 𝒞 01681 705232 – www.tiroran.com – Closed November-mid March

Tobermory

✕✕ Highland Cottage

⇐ 🅿

TRADITIONAL CUISINE · FAMILY Long-standing, personally run restaurant in an intimate cottage, where family antiques and knick-knacks abound. Classical linen-laid dining room and a homely lounge. Traditional daily menu with a seafood base features plenty of local produce. Bedrooms are snug and individually styled.

Menu £ 43

6 rooms ☐ – ♦£ 115/175 ♦♦£ 145/175

Breadalbane St ⊠ PA75 6PD – via B 8073 – 𝒞 01688 302030 (bookings essential for non-residents) – www.highlandcottage.co.uk – dinner only – Closed 15 October-1 April

MUTHILL – Perth and Kinross → See Crieff

NAIRN

Highland – Pop. 9 773 – Regional map n° **17**-D2
▶ Edinburgh 172 mi – Aberdeen 91 mi – Inverness 16 mi

🏠 Boath House ⪦ 🛏 & 🅿

HISTORIC · PERSONALISED An elegant 1825 neo-classical mansion framed by Corinthian columns. Inside it cleverly blends contemporary furnishings and original features; most of the modern art is for sale. Bedrooms are elegant and intimate – one has 'his and hers' roll-top baths and some have views over the 20 acre grounds and the lake.

8 rooms ☖ – †£190/260 ††£295/365

Auldearn ✉ *IV12 5TE – East : 2 mi on A 96 – ℰ01667 454896 – www.boath-house.com*
❀ **Boath House** – See restaurant listing

🏠 Cawdor House 🛏 ⅀

TOWNHOUSE · PERSONALISED 19C former manse run by friendly, knowledgeable owners. The cosy lounge has a marble fireplace and bedrooms are clean and uncluttered; original features blend with contemporary styling. Enjoy local bacon and sausages at breakfast.

8 rooms ☖ – †£55/75 ††£80/100

7 Cawdor St ✉ *IV12 4QD – ℰ01667 455855 – www.cawdorhousenairn.co.uk*

XX Boath House ⪦ 🛏 ⟷ 🅿
❀

MODERN CUISINE · INTIMATE An elegant oval dining room in an early 19C mansion. Well-balanced modern menus showcase the chef's skill and understanding. Cooking is accomplished, with vivid presentation and interesting flavours – and much of the produce is from their garden or orchard. Sit at bespoke oak tables and take in the lake view.

→ Langoustine, amaranth, hazelnut and sorrel. Red deer with artichoke, salsify and truffle. Yeast, vanilla, celeriac and honey.

Menu £30/70 **s**

Boath House Hotel, Auldearn ✉ *IV12 5TE – East : 2 mi on A 96 – ℰ01667 454896 (booking essential) – www.boath-house.com*

NEWPORT-ON-TAY

Fife – Pop. 4 250 – Regional map n° **28**-C2
▶ Edinburgh 53 mi – Glasgow 74 mi – Dundee 3 mi

✗ The Newport 🅽 ⟷ ⪦ 🏠 📖 🅿

MODERN BRITISH · COSY The Newport is the place to come for cheery, upbeat service in a great waterside location. It serves colourful, imaginative small plates themed around 'land, sea, garden and ground' and a tasting menu on Friday and Saturday nights.

Menu £45/65 – Carte £24/31

4 rooms – †£100 ††£100 – ☖ £13

1 High St. ✉ *DD6 8AB – ℰ01382 541449 (booking essential at dinner)*
– www.thenewportrestaurant.co.uk – Closed Monday, Sunday dinner and Tuesday lunch

NIGG → See Tain

NORTH BAY – Western Isles → See Barra (Isle of)

NORTH BERWICK

East Lothian – Pop. 6 605 – Regional map n° **15**-D1
▶ Edinburgh 141 mi – London 512 mi – Belfast 163 mi – Dundee 136 mi

SCOTLAND

🏠 Glebe House   ⊗ 🛏 💯 🅿 🚭

FAMILY · PERSONALISED Spacious, welcoming Georgian house with attractive walled gardens and views over the town and sea. It's beautifully furnished inside, with good quality fabrics and antiques. Classically styled bedrooms have lots of extra touches.

3 rooms ⊊ – ♦£ 85/90 ♦♦£ 130

Law Rd ⊠ *EH39 4PL* – *℘ 01620 892608* – *www.glebehouse-nb.co.uk*
– Closed Christmas-New Year and restricted opening in winter

NORTH QUEENSFERRY

Fife – Pop. 1 076 – Regional map n° **16**-C3
▶ Edinburgh 13 mi – London 416 mi – Glasgow 47 mi – Aberdeen 116 mi

🍴 Wee Restaurant

TRADITIONAL CUISINE · BISTRO Simple, quarry-floored restaurant in the shadow of the Forth Rail Bridge. Fresh Scottish ingredients are served in neatly presented, classical combinations. Lunch represents the best value.

Menu £ 18/36 **s**

17 Main St ⊠ *KY11 1JT* – *℘ 01383 616263* – *www.theweerestaurant.co.uk*
– Closed 25-26 December, 1-2 January and Monday

NORTH UIST – Western Isles ➔ See Uist (Isles of)

OBAN

Argyll and Bute – Pop. 8 574 – Regional map n° **16**-B2
▶ Edinburgh 123 mi – Dundee 116 mi – Glasgow 93 mi – Inverness 118 mi

🏠 Manor House   ⚘ ≤ 🛏 🅿

TRADITIONAL · CLASSIC 18C dower house; formerly part of the Argyll Estate. The country house style interior offers traditional comforts, and the spacious lounge and rustic bar boast delightful bay and harbour views. Individually styled bedrooms. Concise daily menu served in the formal dining room.

11 rooms ⊊ – ♦£ 110/185 ♦♦£ 120/250

Gallanach Rd. ⊠ *PA34 4LS* – *℘ 01631 562087* – *www.manorhouseoban.com*
– Closed 25-26 December

🏠 Glenburnie House   ≤ 💯 🅿

TOWNHOUSE · PERSONALISED A bay-windowed house on the main esplanade, affording great bay and island views. Period features include a delightful staircase and etched glass windows, and antiques abound. Good-sized bedrooms have a subtle contemporary style.

12 rooms ⊊ – ♦£ 65/110 ♦♦£ 90/140

Corran Esplanade ⊠ *PA34 5AQ* – *℘ 01631 562089* – *www.glenburnie.co.uk*
– Closed December-February

🍴🍴 Coast

MODERN BRITISH · BRASSERIE Busy high street restaurant in a former bank, with a high ceiling, a stripped wooden floor and khaki fabric panels on the walls. Unfussy, modern cooking is well-seasoned and local produce is key. The 'Light Bites' menus are a steal.

Menu £ 18 (lunch and early dinner) – Carte £ 21/42

104 George St ⊠ *PA34 5NT* – *℘ 01631 569900* – *www.coastoban.co.uk*
– Closed 25-26 December, January, Sunday-Monday October-March and Sunday lunch

ONICH

Highland – ⊠ Fort William – Regional map n° **17**-B3
▶ Edinburgh 123 mi – Glasgow 93 mi – Inverness 79 mi – Oban 39 mi

✗ Lochleven Seafood Café   ⋖ 🏠 ᕚ 🆔 **P**

SEAFOOD · SIMPLE Simple little restaurant in a stunning lochside spot, looking towards the Glencoe Mountains. The seafood platter is a speciality and the fresh fish and shellfish come from the west coast of Scotland. Take some home from the adjoining shop!

Carte £ 23/57 **s**

Lochleven ✉ PH33 6SA – Southeast : 6.5 mi by A 82 on B 863 – ✆ 01855 821048 (bookings advisable at dinner) – www.lochlevenseafoodcafe.co.uk – Closed November-March   •

ORKNEY ISLANDS

Orkney Islands – Pop. 21 349

ISLE OF WESTRAY

Orkney Islands – Regional map n° **18**-A2
▶ Edinburgh 289 mi – London 690 mi – Dundee 270 mi

Pierowall

🏠 No 1 Broughton   🐚 ⪕ 🏠 🛇 🅿

FAMILY · COSY 19C pink-washed house on the waterside, with views over Pierowall Bay and out to Papa Westray. Take in the view from the conservatory or relax in the sauna (on request). Bedrooms are homely. They also offer dry stone walling courses!

5 rooms ☑ – ♦£ 50/60 ♦♦£ 70/80
✉ KW17 2DA – ℰ 01857 677726 – www.no1broughton.co.uk – Closed 24-25 December

MAINLAND

Orkney Islands – Regional map n° **18**-A3
▶ Edinburgh 277 mi – London 677 mi – Dundee 258 mi

Burray

🏠 Sands   🍴 ⪕ 🅿

FAMILY · MODERN Converted 19C herring packing store in a small hamlet overlooking the Scapa Flow. Pleasant bedrooms boast smart bathrooms. The bar has a pool table and a dartboard and offers a traditional menu. The dining room serves more refined dishes, featuring island produce and lots of shellfish.

8 rooms ☑ – ♦£ 65/90 ♦♦£ 80/110
✉ KW17 2SS – ℰ 01856 731298 – www.thesandshotel.co.uk – Closed 1-3 January and 25-26 December

Kirkwall

🏠 Lynnfield   ⪕ 🛏 ♿ 🅿

FAMILY · PERSONALISED 18C manse which was extended during the war to become an officers' mess. Bedrooms have period Orcadian furnishings and ultra-modern bathrooms. It's close to the Highland Park Distillery and has a wonderful collection of over 360 whiskies.

10 rooms ☑ – ♦£ 90/120 ♦♦£ 100/165 – 3 suites
Holm Rd ✉ KW15 1SU – South : 1 mi on A 961 – ℰ 01856 872505
– www.lynnfieldhotel.com – Closed 1-7 January and 25-26 December
Lynnfield – See restaurant listing

XX Foveran

TRADITIONAL CUISINE · FRIENDLY Sit by the large floor to ceiling window or out on the terrace to take in superb panoramic views over the Scapa Flow and the south islands. Traditional menus feature North Ronaldsay lamb, Orkney beef and plenty of fresh seafood from local waters. Homely, well-kept bedrooms have a slight New England edge.

Carte £ 21/48

8 rooms ⌂ - ♦£ 75/95 ♦♦£ 110/116

St Ola ⌂ KW15 1SF - Southwest : 3 mi on A 964 - ℰ 01856 872389
- www.thefoveran.com - dinner only - Restricted opening October-April

XX Lynnfield

MODERN CUISINE · TRADITIONAL DÉCOR Traditional hotel dining room decorated with whisky memorabilia. Lunch is fairly classical, while dinner offers more interesting modern dishes which champion the very best Orcadian produce – including some foraged ingredients.

Carte £ 24/46 - bar lunch

Lynnfield Hotel, Holm Rd ⌂ KW15 1SU - South : 1 mi on A 961 - ℰ 01856 872505
(booking advisable) - www.lynnfieldhotel.com - Closed 1-10 January and
25-26 December

Stromness

X Hamnavoe

TRADITIONAL CUISINE · NEIGHBOURHOOD Homely restaurant in a backstreet of a sleepy harbourside town; its name means 'Safe Haven' and it has the feel of an old family parlour. Unfussy home cooking utilises fresh market produce and dishes are hearty and full of flavour.

Carte £ 26/40

35 Graham Pl ⌂ KW16 3BY - off Victoria St - ℰ 01856 850606 (booking essential)
- dinner only - Closed Monday and restricted opening in winter

 Good quality cooking at a great price?
Look out for the Bib Gourmand ⊕.

PEAT INN

Fife – Regional map n° **16**-D2
▸ Edinburgh 44 mi - Dundee 16 mi - Stirling 50 mi

XXX The Peat Inn (Geoffrey Smeddle)

CLASSIC CUISINE · CONTEMPORARY DÉCOR Whitewashed former pub; now a contemporary restaurant run by a charming team. The smart lounge still has its original log fireplace; ask for a table overlooking the floodlit gardens. Accomplished, classical cooking has subtle modern touches and local ingredients are to the fore. Stylish, split-level bedrooms have plenty of extras and breakfast is served in your room.

→ Smoked monkfish with oyster mousse, pickled cucumber and sea herbs. Dry-aged tournedos with crushed peas, horseradish and onions. Chocolate ganache with malt whisky ice cream and chocolate crackling.

Menu £ 19/50 - Carte £ 34/59

8 rooms ⌂ - ♦£ 175/195 ♦♦£ 210/225

⌂ KY15 5LH - ℰ 01334 840206 (booking essential) - www.thepeatinn.co.uk
- Closed 10 days January, 4 days Christmas, Sunday and Monday

PEEBLES

The Scottish Borders – Pop. 8 376 – Regional map n° **15**-C2
▸ Edinburgh 24 mi - London 382 mi - Glasgow 53 mi - Aberdeen 151 mi

⌂ Rowanbrae   🗶 ⊟

TOWNHOUSE · PERSONALISED Snug Victorian villa with a pretty terrace and a surprisingly spacious interior; in a peaceful cul-de-sac close to town. The long-standing owners provide a warm welcome and a homely atmosphere reigns. Bedrooms are cosy and well-kept, and original cornicing and old pine woodwork feature throughout.

3 rooms ⌂ – ♦£ 45 ♦♦£ 70

103 Northgate ⊠ EH45 8BU – ℰ 01721 721630
– www.aboutscotland.com/peebles/rowanbrae.html – Closed December-February

🗶 Osso

😊 **MODERN CUISINE · FRIENDLY** By day, this is a bustling coffee shop serving a bewildering array of light snacks and daily specials; come evening, it transforms into a more sophisticated restaurant offering a great value, regularly changing menu of well-presented, flavoursome dishes. Service is friendly and attentive, whatever the time.

Menu £ 28 (dinner) – Carte £ 24/35

Innerleithen Rd ⊠ EH45 8BA – ℰ 01721 724477 – www.ossorestaurant.com
– Closed 1 January, 25 December, dinner Tuesday and Wednesday in winter except December and dinner Sunday and Monday

at Eddleston North: 4.5 mi on A703

🗶🗶 The Horseshoe   ⇔ ♿ 🅿

MODERN CUISINE · INN Once a roadside inn; now a smart, columned restaurant with elegant tableware and formal service. Sophisticated menus offer ambitious, well-presented dishes which take their influences from across Europe. Chic, modern bedrooms are located in the old village schoolhouse and come with pleasing extras.

Menu £ 19/40

8 rooms ⌂ – ♦£ 110/135 ♦♦£ 140/165

Edinburgh Rd ⊠ EH45 8QP – ℰ 01721 730225 – www.horseshoeinn.co.uk – Closed first 2 weeks January, last week June, first week July, Monday and Tuesday

PERTH

Perth and Kinross – Pop. 46 970 – Regional map n° **16**-C2
🔲 Edinburgh 44 mi – Aberdeen 86 mi – Dundee 22 mi – Dunfermline 29 mi

⌂ Parklands   ✿ 🖨 🅿

BUSINESS · MODERN Located close to the railway station, a personally run, extended Georgian house with a contemporary interior. Spacious modern bedrooms have good facilities and sizeable bathrooms; those to the front have pleasant views over the park. Modern menu in the intimate 63@Parklands; informal dining in No.1 The Bank.

15 rooms ⌂ – ♦£ 93/149 ♦♦£ 110/189

Town plan: A2-n - *2 St Leonard's Bank ⊠ PH2 8EB – ℰ 01738 622451*
– www.theparklandshotel.com – Closed 26 December-5 January
63@Parklands – See restaurant listing

⌂ Taythorpe   🗶 🅿 ⊟

TRADITIONAL · COSY Modern, stone-built house run by a bubbly owner; superbly located close to Scone Palace, the city and the racecourse. Large, cosy sitting room hung with homely pictures and salmon fishing maps; pleasant communal breakfast room where tasty Scottish dishes are served. Appealing, immaculately kept bedrooms.

3 rooms ⌂ – ♦£ 50 ♦♦£ 80

Town plan: B1-a - *Isla Rd ⊠ PH2 7HQ – North : 1 mi on A 93 – ℰ 01738 447994*
– www.taythorpe.co.uk – Closed 13 December-13 January

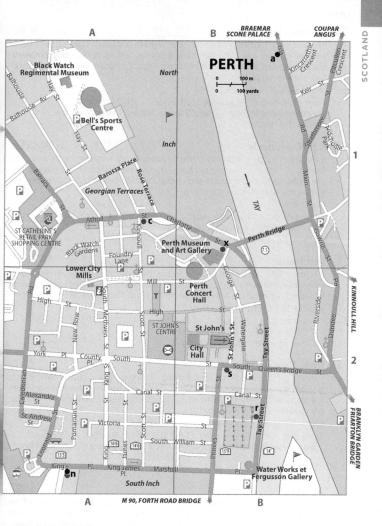

XX **63 Tay Street** 🕸 🍴

MODERN BRITISH · INTIMATE Well-established riverside restaurant run by an attentive team. Ambitious dishes feature an array of flavours and textures; the mid-week pre-theatre menus represent good value and the impressive wine list features over 250 bins.

Menu £ 23/42

Town plan: B2-r – 63 Tay St ✉ PH2 8NN – 𝒸 01738 441451
– www.63taystreet.co.uk – Closed 1-9 January, 4-10 July, 26-31 December, Sunday, Monday and lunch Tuesday-Wednesday

Your discoveries and comments help us improve the guide.
Please let us know about your experiences – good or bad!

✕✕ Deans 🍷 📺

TRADITIONAL CUISINE · FRIENDLY Bottle-green restaurant close to the theatre and the concert hall. All-encompassing menus feature passionately prepared, classically based dishes with an ambitious edge. The smart lounge serves cocktails and sharing platters.

Menu £ 19/20 – Carte £ 26/44

Town plan: A1-c *77-79 Kinnoull St* ⊠ *PH1 5EZ* – ✆ *01738 643377*
*– www.letseatperth.co.uk – Closed 2 weeks January, 1 week November,
Sunday and Monday*

✕✕ 63@Parklands 🛏 🏡 ♿ 🅿

MODERN BRITISH · INTIMATE Intimate conservatory restaurant with a relaxed lounge, set within a privately run hotel. The gourmet-style 5 course menu offers one or two choices per course and changes weekly; cooking is modern and features some interesting combinations.

Menu £ 40

Town plan: A2-n *- Parklands Hotel, 2 St Leonard's Bank* ⊠ *PH2 8EB
– ✆ 01738 622451 – www.63atparklands.com – dinner only – Closed
26 December-5 January, Tuesday and Wednesday*

✕ Pig Halle 📺

FRENCH · SIMPLE Lively bistro; its square, marble-floored room tightly packed with tables and dominated by a mirror stencilled with a Paris Metro map. Menus list Gallic favourites. The adjoining deli serves wood-fired pizzas and tasty pastries.

Menu £ 15 (lunch) – Carte £ 21/38

Town plan: B2-s *- 38 South St* ⊠ *PH2 8PG
– ✆ 01738 248784 – www.pighalle.co.uk
– Closed 26 December and 1 January*

✕ Post Box ♿ 📺

CLASSIC CUISINE · BRASSERIE Striking building with bright red doors, which was the first Post Office in Perth. Classic lunches are followed by an evening menu with a more modern edge. The stone walled cellar bar hosts live jazz and blues on Fridays and Saturdays.

Menu £ 21 (lunch and early dinner) – Carte £ 22/49

Town plan: B1-x *- 80 George St* ⊠ *PH1 5LB* – ✆ *01738 248971
– www.thepostboxperth.co.uk – Closed first 2 weeks January, Sunday and Monday*

at Kintillo Southeast: 4.5 mi off A912

✕ Roost ♿ 🅿

MODERN BRITISH · INTIMATE A converted brick hen house in the heart of the village, with a smart modern interior and poultry references in its décor. Service is engaging and eager to please. The experienced chef prepares refined, classical dishes with some restrained modern touches; meats are local and veg is from the garden.

Menu £ 20 (weekday lunch) – Carte £ 27/45

Forgandenny Rd ⊠ *PH2 9AZ
– ✆ 01738 812111 – www.theroostrestaurant.co.uk
– Closed 1-16 January, 25-26 December, Monday and dinner Sunday, Tuesday and
Wednesday*

PIEROWALL → See Orkney Islands (Isle of Westray)

PITLOCHRY

Perth and Kinross – Pop. 2 776 – Regional map n° **16**-C2
▶ Edinburgh 71 mi – Inverness 85 mi – Perth 27 mi

Fonab Castle

HISTORIC · CONTEMPORARY This 19C baronial-style castle offers superb views over the loch to the hills beyond. Bedrooms have a subtle traditional feel and smart bathrooms; the 'Woodland' rooms are more modern and have terraces or balconies. Dine from a tasting menu in intimate Sandemans or on modern classics in the Brasserie.

34 rooms ☑ – †£ 155/550 ††£ 155/550 – 4 suites

Foss Rd ✉ PH16 5ND – ℰ 01796 470140 – www.fonabcastlehotel.com

Brasserie · Sandemans on the Loch – See restaurant listing

Green Park

TRADITIONAL · CLASSIC Long-standing, family-run hotel on the shore of Loch Faskally; many of its guests return year after year. Well-appointed lounges offer stunning loch and countryside views. Bedrooms vary in style; the largest and most modern are in the newer wing. A traditional dinner is included in the price of the room.

51 rooms (dinner included) ☑ – †£ 80/91 ††£ 160/182

Clunie Bridge Rd ✉ PH16 5JY – ℰ 01796 473248 – www.thegreenpark.co.uk
– Closed 17-27 December

East Haugh House

TRADITIONAL · PERSONALISED 17C turreted stone house in two acres of gardens; originally part of the Atholl Estate. Cosy, traditionally appointed bedrooms are named after fishing flies and are split between the house, a former bothy and the old gatehouse.

13 rooms ☑ – †£ 50/90 ††£ 90/190

✉ PH16 5TE – Southeast : 1.75 mi off A 924 (Perth Rd) – ℰ 01796 473121
– www.easthaugh.co.uk – Closed 1 week Christmas

Two Sisters – See restaurant listing

Craigmhor Lodge and Courtyard

COUNTRY HOUSE · MODERN Spacious, cosy house just out of town, with an airy breakfast room where local fruits, bacon and sausages are served. Well-kept modern bedrooms are set in the courtyard – some have balconies. Supper hampers can be delivered to your room.

12 rooms ☑ – †£ 64/135 ††£ 89/170

27 West Moulin Rd ✉ PH16 5EF – ℰ 01796 472123 – www.craigmhorlodge.co.uk
– Closed Christmas

Craigatin House and Courtyard

TOWNHOUSE · MODERN Built in 1822 as a doctor's house; now a stylish boutique hotel. The stunning open-plan lounge and breakfast room centres around a wood burning stove and overlooks the garden. Contemporary, minimalist bedrooms – some in the old stables.

14 rooms ☑ – †£ 90/118 ††£ 101/128

165 Atholl Rd ✉ PH16 5QL – ℰ 01796 472478 – www.craigatinhouse.co.uk
– Closed Christmas

Dunmurray Lodge

TOWNHOUSE · PERSONALISED Imposing 19C former doctor's surgery, set close to the town and boasting views across to the mountains. Cosy, open-fired lounge and snug, well-equipped bedrooms with co-ordinating décor; the best outlooks are from the front. Bright breakfast room – choose from a huge array of very locally sourced produce.

4 rooms ☑ – †£ 60/70 ††£ 79/89

72 Bonnethill Rd ✉ PH16 5ED – ℰ 01796 473624 – www.dunmurray.co.uk – Closed mid November-mid March

XXX Sandemans on the Loch

MODERN CUISINE · INTIMATE Despite its name, this intimate hotel restaurant – of just 8 tables – does not overlook the loch. Choose between two well-balanced set menus; cooking is clean and precise and showcases top Scottish ingredients, from mountain to coast.

Menu £ 65 – tasting menu only

Fonab Castle Hotel, Foss Rd ⊠ PH16 5ND – ℰ 01796 470140
– www.fonabcastlehotel.com – dinner only – Closed Sunday and Monday

XX Two Sisters

REGIONAL CUISINE · INTIMATE Charming fishermen's bar and a bright, laid-back restaurant, located in a lovely 17C stone house. The seasonal Scottish menu is served in both areas; cooking is clean and exact, with fish and game to the fore and tasty home-baked breads.

Carte £ 25/38

East Haugh House Hotel, ⊠ PH16 5TE – Southeast : 1.75 mi off A 924 (Perth Rd)
– ℰ 01796 473121 – www.easthaugh.co.uk – Closed 1 week Christmas and lunch in winter

XX Brasserie

MODERN CUISINE · BRASSERIE Start with a cocktail in the 'Bar in the Air', then head back down to the fashionable hotel restaurant and terrace with their panoramic loch views. The concise menu offers modern classics and grills. Service is warm and friendly.

Carte £ 26/68

Fonab Castle Hotel, Foss Rd ⊠ PH16 5ND – ℰ 01796 470140
– www.fonabcastlehotel.com

⑩ Auld Smiddy Inn

TRADITIONAL CUISINE · PUB Old blacksmith's forge with a small, colourful garden and a large terrace and courtyard. It has a likeable simplicity, with polished slate floors and wood burning stoves. Summer menus feature fish and salads; winter menus, hearty classics.

Carte £ 20/43

154 Atholl Rd ⊠ PH16 5AG – ℰ 01796 472356 – www.auldsmiddyinn.co.uk
– Closed last week January-first week February, last week in November and 25-26 December

at Killiecrankie Northwest: 4 mi by A924 and B8019 on B8079 ⊠ Pitlochry

⑪ Killiecrankie

TRADITIONAL · CLASSIC A whitewashed former vicarage built in 1840 and set in 4.5 acres of mature, rhododendron-filled grounds, with a small kitchen garden to the rear. There's a charming open-fired lounge, a snug bar and well-appointed bedrooms which offer everything you might want, including a hot water bottle. Choose between light suppers and traditional dinners. Service is excellent.

10 rooms ⌂ – ♦£ 100 ♦♦£ 200
⊠ PH16 5LG – ℰ 01796 473220 – www.killiecrankiehotel.co.uk – Closed 3 January-17 March

PLOCKTON

Highland – Regional map n° **17**-B2
▶ Edinburgh 210 mi – Inverness 88 mi – Fort William 77 mi

⑩ Plockton Hotel

TRADITIONAL CUISINE · INN A one-time ships' chandlery with a distinctive black exterior and stunning views over Loch Carron to the mountains beyond. Cooking is honest and hearty with a strong Scottish influence, so expect haggis and whisky or herring in oatmeal – and don't miss the Plockton prawns. Simple, comfortable bedrooms.

Carte £ 18/40

15 rooms ⌂ – ♦£ 45/95 ♦♦£ 90/140
41 Harbour St ⊠ IV52 8TN – ℰ 01599 544274 – www.plocktonhotel.co.uk

POOLEWE

Highland – Regional map n° **17**-B2

▶ Edinburgh 230 mi – London 635 mi – Inverness 76 mi – Elgin 112 mi

🏠 Pool House

FAMILY · PERSONALISED A unique, family-run Victorian house by the water's edge, with a quirky whisky bar in the old billiard room. Bedrooms are all large suites – each individually themed with incredible attention to detail; the Ashanti room features a 19C marriage bed. The formal restaurant offers a classic seasonal menu.

5 rooms 🖙 – †£ 160/180 ††£ 225/375

✉ IV22 2LD – ☎ 01445 781272 – www.pool-house.co.uk – *Closed mid November-mid March*

PORT APPIN

Argyll and Bute – ✉ Appin – Regional map n° **16**-B2

▶ Edinburgh 136 mi – Ballachulish 20 mi – Oban 24 mi

🏠 Airds

LUXURY · PERSONALISED A characterful former ferryman's cottage fronted by colourful planters and offering lovely loch and mountain views. Two sumptuous, antique-furnished sitting rooms; bedrooms offer understated luxury; ask for one with a waterside view.

11 rooms 🖙 – †£ 195/410 ††£ 195/410

✉ PA38 4DF – ☎ 01631 730236 – www.airds-hotel.com – *Closed 1-12 December and Monday-Tuesday November-January*

Airds – See restaurant listing

🟏🟏 Airds 🅝

MODERN BRITISH · ELEGANT An intimate, candlelit restaurant with superb loch and mountain views. Classic dishes are presented with a modern edge and much use is made of west coast seafood and local meats, with game a highlight in season. Don't miss the Mallaig crab or the scallops – and ensure you ask for a table in the window!

Menu £ 20/55 – Carte £ 19/39

Airds Hotel, ✉ PA38 4DF – ☎ 01631 730236 (bookings essential for non-residents) – www.airds-hotel.com – *Closed 1-12 December and Monday-Tuesday November-January*

PORT CHARLOTTE – Argyll and Bute → See Islay (Isle of)

PORT ELLEN – Argyll and Bute → See Islay (Isle of)

PORTMAHOMACK

Highland – Regional map n° **17**-D2

▶ Edinburgh 194 mi – Dornoch 21 mi – Tain 12 mi

🟏🟏 Oystercatcher

SEAFOOD · BISTRO Set in a lovely spot in a tiny fishing village, with lobster pots hanging outside. One formal and one rustic room, with walls crammed with memorabilia. Menus offer fresh seafood in some unusual combinations; the boats that land the fish can be seen by the jetty. Modest bedrooms; nearly 20 choices at breakfast.

Menu £ 37 **s**

3 rooms 🖙 – †£ 54/82 ††£ 85/115

Main St ✉ IV20 1YB – ☎ 01862 871560 (booking essential) – www.the-oystercatcher.co.uk – *dinner only and Sunday lunch – Closed November-March and Sunday dinner-Wednesday lunch*

PORTPATRICK

Dumfries and Galloway – ✉ Stranraer – Pop. 534 – Regional map n° **15**-A3

▶ Edinburgh 141 mi – Ayr 60 mi – Dumfries 80 mi – Stranraer 9 mi

🏠 Knockinaam Lodge

TRADITIONAL · PERSONALISED Charming country house, superbly set in its own private cove, with the sea at the bottom of the garden. Classical guest areas include a wood-panelled bar and open-fired sitting rooms; a relaxed atmosphere pervades. Traditional, antique-furnished bedrooms; 'Churchill' boasts its original 100 year old bath.

10 rooms (dinner included) ☲ – †£ 140/290 ††£ 220/380

✉ DG9 9AD – Southeast : 5 mi by A 77 off B 7042 – ✆ 01776 810471
– www.knockinaamlodge.com

Knockinaam Lodge – See restaurant listing

✕✕ Knockinaam Lodge

CLASSIC CUISINE · INTIMATE A traditionally furnished, smartly dressed dining room with delightful sea views, in a charming country house, idyllically set in its own private cove. The set four course menu evolves with the seasons and offers good quality produce – often from their own gardens – cooked in classic combinations.

Menu £ 40/68 – tasting menu only

Knockinaam Lodge Hotel, ✉ DG9 9AD – Southeast : 5 mi by A 77 off B 7042
– ✆ 01776 810471 (booking essential) – www.knockinaamlodge.com

PORTAVADIE

Argyll and Bute – Regional map n° **16**-B3
▶ Edinburgh 107 mi – Dunoon 28 mi – Oban 55 mi

🏠 Portavadie

HOLIDAY HOTEL · DESIGN This peaceful lochside complex consists of a marina, self-catering apartments, a small hotel and an impressive spa. Good-sized bedrooms have a modern Scandic style and pleasant views; some have kitchenettes but there's also the choice of a brasserie and an informal dining room with a leather-furnished lounge.

16 rooms ☲ – †£ 65/135 ††£ 65/135

Portavadie Marina ✉ PA21 2DA – ✆ 01700 811075 – www.portavadie.com

PORTREE – Highland ➜ See Skye (Isle of)

RANNOCH STATION

Perth and Kinross – Regional map n° **16**-B2
▶ Edinburgh 108 mi – Kinloch Rannoch 17 mi – Pitlochry 36 mi

🏠 Moor of Rannoch

FAMILY · COSY This 19C hotel is perched high on the moor and is the ultimate in hiking getaways. The views are delightful, the whole place has a serene feel and wildlife is in abundance. Bedrooms are cosy and the open-fired guest areas come with jigsaws instead of TVs. Rustic home cooking utilises Scottish ingredients.

5 rooms ☲ – †£ 115 ††£ 140

✉ PH17 2QA – ✆ 01882 633238 – www.moorofrannoch.co.uk – Closed
November-mid February

RATHO

City of Edinburgh – Pop. 1 634 – Regional map n° **15**-C1
▶ Edinburgh 10 mi – Glasgow 40 mi – Dunfermline 15 mi

🍽 Bridge Inn

MODERN CUISINE · PUB Friendly pub on the tow path between Edinburgh and the Falkirk Wheel. Fruit and veg come from their walled garden, pork comes from their saddleback pigs and the eggs, from their chickens and ducks. All of the cosy bedrooms have water views. For a treat, book a cruise on their restaurant barge.

Carte £ 21/39

4 rooms ☲ – †£ 70/100 ††£ 80/120

27 Baird Rd ✉ EH28 8RU – ✆ 0131 333 1320 – www.bridgeinn.com – Closed
25 December

RESIPOLE

Highland – Regional map n° **29**-B3
▶ Edinburgh 148 mi – Fort William 31 mi – Oban 58 mi

🏠 **Rockpool House**   ✤ 🐾 ≤ 🛶 🅿

FAMILY · MODERN Be at one with nature in this comfy guesthouse on the Ardnamurchan Peninsula. Take in the views of the loch and the mountains from both the upstairs lounge and the modern, well-equipped bedrooms. Local meats and fish feature on the menu and you can buy local and homemade gifts from their craft shop.

3 rooms ☑ – †£ 80/105 ††£ 99/130

✉ PH36 4HX – On A 861 – ✆ 01967 431335 – www.rockpoolhouse.co.uk – Closed 10 days Christmas

ST ANDREWS

Fife – Pop. 16 870 – Regional map n° **16**-D2
▶ Edinburgh 51 mi – Dundee 14 mi – Stirling 51 mi

🏨 **Old Course H. Golf Resort & Spa**   ≤ 🖼 🗻 🏊 🐾 🛁 ⬆ 🖑 🖹 🚫

LUXURY · CLASSIC Vast resort hotel with an impressive spa, set on a   ⛳ 🅿
world-famous golf course overlooking the bay. Luxurious guest areas have a subtle Scottish theme and bedrooms are chic, sumptuous and well-equipped; those in the wing are the most modern.

144 rooms ☑ – †£ 190/400 ††£ 220/450 – 15 suites

Old Station Rd ✉ KY16 9SP – West : 0.75 mi off A 91 – ✆ 01334 474371
– www.oldcoursehotel.co.uk

Road Hole · Sands Grill – See restaurant listing

🏨 **Rusacks**   ✤ ≤ ⬆ 🖑 ⛳

LUXURY · PERSONALISED The oldest hotel in St Andrews sits in a commanding position overlooking the 18th green of the Old Course. Original 1846 columns feature in the lobby and a huge array of paintings pay homage to golfing greats. Bedrooms are stylish; choose one with a view. Dine in the pub or the formal restaurant.

70 rooms ☑ – †£ 235/300 ††£ 250/315 – 4 suites

Town plan: A1-s – Pilmour Links ✉ KY16 9JQ – ✆ 0344 879 9136
– www.macdonaldhotels.co.uk

Rocca – See restaurant listing

🏠 **Rufflets Country House**   ✤ 🐾 🛶 ⛳ 🅿

COUNTRY HOUSE · PERSONALISED This country house hotel is surrounded by well-tended gardens and has been owned by the same family since 1952. Inside it's a mix of the old and the new, with original Arts and Crafts features sitting alongside stylish, contemporary bedrooms. Menus offer modern interpretations of classic dishes.

24 rooms ☑ – †£ 120/205 ††£ 175/315 – 2 suites

Strathkinness Low Rd ✉ KY16 9TX – West : 1.5 mi on B 939 – ✆ 01334 472594
– www.rufflets.co.uk – Closed 3-21 January

🏠 **Five Pilmour Place**   🚫

TOWNHOUSE · CONTEMPORARY Victorian terraced house with a surprisingly stylish interior. There's a bright, clubby lounge and a locker room with underfloor heating. Bedrooms have bold feature walls and smart walk-in showers; Room 3 also has a claw-foot bath.

7 rooms ☑ – †£ 70/105 ††£ 90/170

Town plan: A1-x - 5 Pilmour Pl. ✉ KY16 9HZ – ✆ 01334 478665
– www.5pilmourplace.com – Closed 12 December-1 March

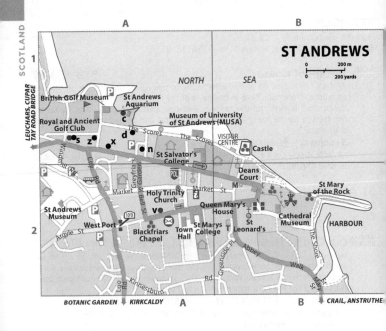

ST ANDREWS

0   200 m
0   200 yards

NORTH   SEA

British Golf Museum
St Andrews Aquarium
Royal and Ancient Golf Club
Museum of University of St Andrews (MUSA)
VISITOR CENTRE
c
The Scores   The Scores
Castle
s z x d
n
St Salvator's College
Deans Court
M
St Mary of the Rock
Market Market St
Holy Trinity Church
Queen Mary's House
St Andrews Museum
v
Cathedral Museum
HARBOUR
West Port
Blackfriars Chapel
Town Hall
St Marys College
St Leonard's
Argyle St
Kinnessburn   Rd   Greenside Pl   Abbey   Walk

BOTANIC GARDEN ↓ KIRKCALDY   A   B   ↓ CRAIL, ANSTRUTHE

Fairways

TOWNHOUSE · CONTEMPORARY This tall Victorian building is the closest guest-house to the Old Course – ask for Room 3 and sit on the balcony overlooking the 18th hole. Bedrooms are contemporary and of a good size. Nothing is too much trouble for the owners.

3 rooms ⌂ – †£ 65/100 ††£ 80/130

Town plan: A1-z - *8a Golf Pl.* ⊠ *KY16 9JA* – ℰ *01334 479513*
– *www.fairwaysofstandrews.co.uk*

Road Hole

MODERN CUISINE · CLASSIC DÉCOR Formal wood-panelled restaurant on the top floor of a smart golf resort, with stunning views of the 18th hole and the beach. Modern versions of classic dishes use local produce; watch the chefs in the open kitchen while you eat.

Menu £ 20 (lunch) – Carte £ 34/64

Old Course Hotel Golf Resort & Spa, Old Station Rd ⊠ *KY16 9SP – West : 0.75 mi off A 91 –* ℰ *01334 474371 – www.oldcoursehotel.co.uk – Closed January, February, Monday, Tuesday and Wednesday lunch*

Rocca

MODERN CUISINE · DESIGN A formal hotel restaurant with designer wallpapers, richly coloured fabrics and great Old Course views. Interesting modern menus feature Scottish dishes with Italian twists and use artisan produce both from the region and from Tuscany.

Carte £ 36/55

Town plan: A1-s *Rusacks Hotel, Pilmour Links* ⊠ *KY16 9JQ –* ℰ *01334 472549 (booking essential) – www.roccarestaurant.com – dinner only – Closed Sunday December-March*

XX Sands Grill

MEATS AND GRILLS · BRASSERIE An informal grill restaurant with smart wood panelling and a clubby feel – part of a stylish golf resort and spa. Classically based menus comprise mainly of seafood and steaks, with all meats cooked on the Josper grill.

Menu £ 20 **s** – Carte £ 24/51

Old Course Hotel Golf Resort & Spa, Old Station Rd ⊠ KY16 9SP – West : 0.75 mi off A 91 – ℰ 01334 474371 – www.oldcoursehotel.co.uk – dinner only – Closed Wednesday October-March

XX Adamson

MEATS AND GRILLS · BRASSERIE A stylish brasserie and cocktail bar set within a house once owned by eminent photographer John Adamson (it was also later the town's Post Office). The wide-ranging menu of tasty dishes includes steaks from the Josper grill.

Menu £ 15 (lunch and early dinner) – Carte £ 21/50

Town plan: A2-v - *127 South St ⊠ KY16 9UH – ℰ 01334 479191 – www.theadamson.com – Closed 25-26 December and 1 January*

XX Seafood

SEAFOOD · DESIGN This striking glass cube juts out over the sea and offers commanding bay views. The immaculate modern interior comes complete with an open kitchen where you can watch Fife coast seafood being prepared in elaborate combinations.

Menu £ 50 (dinner) – Carte £ 28/63

Town plan: A1-c - *Bruce Embankment, The Scores ⊠ KY16 9AB – ℰ 01334 479475 – www.theseafoodrestaurant.com – Closed 25-26 December and 1 January*

X Grange Inn

TRADITIONAL CUISINE · COSY A former pub, atop a hill, with great views over the bay. Have an aperitif beside the fire, then head for the stone-walled restaurant with its huge stag's head. The experienced chef serves a menu of tasty, well-prepared classics.

Menu £ 16 (weekday lunch)/40

Grange Rd ⊠ KY16 8LJ – Southeast : 1.75 mi by A 917 – ℰ 01334 472670 (booking essential) – www.thegrangeinn.com – Closed 3 weeks January, Sunday dinner and Monday

ST BOSWELLS

The Scottish Borders – ⊠ Melrose – Pop. 1 279 – Regional map n° **15**-D2
▶ Edinburgh 39 mi – Glasgow 79 mi – Hawick 17 mi – Newcastle upon Tyne 66 mi

🏠 Buccleuch Arms

INN · COSY A smart, long-standing coaching inn which offers popular golfing, fishing and shooting breaks. Cosy bedrooms have co-ordinated headboards and soft furnishings. After dinner, sink into a squashy sofa in the semi-panelled, fire-lit bar.

19 rooms ⚏ – ♗£ 79/105 ♗♗£ 99/130

The Green ⊠ TD6 0EW – ℰ 01835 822243 – www.buccleucharms.com – Closed 24-25 December

Blue Coo Bistrot – See restaurant listing

🏠 Whitehouse

TRADITIONAL · PERSONALISED Former dower house built in 1872 by the Duke of Sutherland, with a cosy, country house feel. Traditionally furnished bedrooms boast excellent views across the estate. Many people come for the on-site shooting and fishing; wild salmon and local game – including venison – feature at dinner.

3 rooms ⚏ – ♗£ 90/95 ♗♗£ 130/150

⊠ TD6 0ED – Northeast : 3 mi on B 6404 – ℰ 01573 460343 – www.whitehousecountryhouse.com

🏠 Clint Lodge

TRADITIONAL · PERSONALISED Former shooting lodge with superb river and hill views. Characterful interior boasts antiques and fishing memorabilia. Traditionally decorated bedrooms; luxurious No. 4 and the south facing rooms are the best. Daily changing 5 course dinner served at a beautiful table.

5 rooms ☲ – †£ 70/110 ††£ 100/140

✉ TD6 0DZ – North : 2.25 mi by B 6404 on B 6356 – ✆ 01835 822027
– www.clintlodge.co.uk

✗ Blue Coo Bistrot

MEATS AND GRILLS · RUSTIC The heart of the Buccleuch Arms is this relaxed, shabby chic bistrot comprising three different rooms. Accessible menus offer classics and grills, alongside afternoon tea and daily blackboard specials. Local fish and game feature.

Carte £ 18/43

Buccleuch Arms Hotel, The Green ✉ TD6 0EW – ✆ 01835 822243
– www.buccleucharms.com – Closed 25 December

ST FILLANS

Perth and Kinross – Regional map n° **16**-C2
▶ Edinburgh 65 mi – Lochearnhead 8 mi – Perth 29 mi

🏠 Achray House

TRADITIONAL · COSY Superbly located Edwardian villa offering stunning views over Loch Earn. Bright breakfast room and an inviting lounge with open fires and a polished Douglas Fir floor. Modern bedrooms have bespoke pine furnishings and contemporary bathrooms. Simple restaurant offers global dishes crafted from local produce.

8 rooms ☲ – †£ 120/140 ††£ 130/215

✉ PH6 2NF – ✆ 01764 685320 – www.achrayhouse.com – Closed 4-31 January, 1-22 December and Monday

ST MONANS

Fife – Pop. 1 265 – Regional map n° **16**-D2
▶ Edinburgh 47 mi – Dundee 26 mi – Perth 40 mi

✗✗ Craig Millar @ 16 West End

MODERN CUISINE · FRIENDLY An unassuming former pub with an attractive interior, run by a charming team. There's a characterful lounge and a smart restaurant with a small terrace and great harbour views. The experienced chef offers refined, flavoursome dishes.

Menu £ 26 (weekday lunch)/60 – Carte £ 28/45

16 West End ✉ KY10 2BX – ✆ 01333 730327 (booking essential)
– www.16westend.com – Closed Monday-Tuesday and restricted opening October-March

SANQUHAR

Dumfries and Galloway – Pop. 2 021 – Regional map n° **15**-B2
▶ Edinburgh 57 mi – London 362 mi – Dundee 113 mi – Paisley 56 mi

✗✗ Blackaddie House

TRADITIONAL BRITISH · TRADITIONAL DÉCOR A stone-built former manse with 16C origins, set by the river. Lunch offers good value classics, while dinner is more elaborate and features original modern cooking; ingredients are luxurious and dishes are well-presented. Bedrooms are named after game birds – ask for 'Grouse', which has a four-poster bed.

Menu £ 36/58

7 rooms ☲ – †£ 95/175 ††£ 105/195

Blackaddie Rd ✉ DG4 6JJ – ✆ 01659 50270 (booking essential at lunch)
– www.blackaddiehotel.co.uk

SCALPAY – Western Isles ➜ See Lewis and Harris (Isle of)

SCARISTA – Western Isles ➜ See Lewis and Harris (Isle of)

SCRABSTER – Highland ➜ See Thurso

SHETLAND ISLANDS
Shetland Islands – Pop. 21 800 – Regional map n° **18**-B2

MAINLAND
Shetland Islands – Regional map n° **18**-B2
▶ Edinburgh 360 mi – London 543 mi – Dundee 86 mi

Lerwick

🏨 Kveldsro House ✿ ⌀ 🅿

BUSINESS · PERSONALISED Spacious Georgian house hidden in the town centre; its name means 'evening peace'. There's a cosy sitting room with original ceiling mouldings and a comfy bar with views of the islands; bedrooms are traditionally styled. Menus offer mainly island produce; portions are hearty.

17 rooms ☷ – ♦£ 95/115 ♦♦£ 125/145

Greenfield Pl ✉ ZE1 0AQ – ℰ 01595 692195 – www.shetlandhotels.com – Closed 25-26 December and 1-2 January

Veensgarth

🏨 Herrislea House ✿ 🅿

TRADITIONAL · CLASSIC Large, family-run hotel set just out of town. Unusual African hunting theme with mounted antlers, animal heads and skins on display. Cosy, individually designed bedrooms; some with valley views. Fresh cooking uses local produce and meats from the family crofts.

9 rooms ☷ – ♦£ 90/120 ♦♦£ 120/150

✉ ZE2 9SB – ℰ 01595 840208 – www.herrisleahouse.co.uk – Closed 10 December-10 January

SKYE (Isle of)
Highland – Pop. 10 008 – Regional map n° **17**-B2

Broadford

🏨 Tigh an Dochais ✿ ⪡ 🛏 ⌀ 🅿

LUXURY · MODERN Striking house with award-winning architecture, overlooking Broadford Bay and the Applecross Peninsula. Comfy lounge has well-stocked bookshelves. Modern, minimalist bedrooms boast superb views and good facilities, including underfloor heating and plenty of extras. Communal, home-cooked meals by arrangement.

3 rooms ☷ – ♦£ 80/90 ♦♦£ 95/105

13 Harrapool ✉ IV49 9AQ – on A 87 – ℰ 01471 820022 – www.skyebedbreakfast.co.uk – Closed November-February

Colbost

🏨 Hillstone Lodge ✿ ⛷ ⪡ 🛏 ⌀ 🅿

LUXURY · DESIGN With its superb outlook over Loch Dunvegan and plenty of stone, slate and wood on display, this striking modern house is at one with nature. Vibrant Scottish art covers the walls and stylish bedrooms have a minimalist feel. Local ingredients feature at breakfast and dinner (in winter only), often showcases island seafood. The owner is also qualified in 'sound massage'.

3 rooms ☷ – ♦£ 75/103 ♦♦£ 110/138

✉ IV55 8ZT – ℰ 01470 511434 – www.hillstonelodge.com – Closed Christmas-New Year

XX Three Chimneys & The House Over-By ⇔ ⊗ ≤ ⛵ & 🅿

MODERN CUISINE · RUSTIC Immaculately kept crofter's cottage in a stunning lochside setting. Contemporary art hangs on exposed stone walls in the characterful low-beamed dining rooms. Modern Scottish menus showcase good regional ingredients and seafood from local waters is a highlight. Spacious, split-level bedrooms are stylishly understated and the residents' lounge has a great outlook.

Menu £ 38/90

6 rooms � – ♦£ 250/345 ♦♦£ 250/345

✉ IV55 8ZT – ☎ 01470 511258 (booking essential)
– www.threechimneys.co.uk – dinner only and lunch April-November
– Closed 12 December-13 January

Duisdalemore

🏨 Duisdale House ⇔ ⊗ ≤ ⛵ ⟿ 🅿

TRADITIONAL · PERSONALISED Stylish, up-to-date hotel with lawned gardens, a hot tub and coastal views. Comfortable bedrooms boast bold décor, excellent bathrooms and a pleasing blend of contemporary and antique furniture. Modern cooking makes good use of local produce. Smart uniformed staff.

19 rooms ⊃ – ♦£ 149/210 ♦♦£ 188/318 – 1 suite

Sleat ✉ IV43 8QW – on A 851 – ☎ 01471 833202 – www.duisdale.com

Dunvegan

🏨 Roskhill House ⛵ ⟿ 🅿

COUNTRY HOUSE · CONTEMPORARY Welcoming 19C croft house, in a peaceful location close to the water. Formerly the old post office, the lounge boasts exposed stone, wooden beams and an open fire. Fresh, bright bedrooms have a contemporary edge and smart bathrooms.

5 rooms ⊃ – ♦£ 65/78 ♦♦£ 82/100

Roskhill ✉ IV55 8ZD – Southeast : 2.5 mi by A 863 – ☎ 01470 521317
– www.roskhillhouse.co.uk – Closed 15 December-20 February

Edinbane

🍴 Edinbane Inn ⇔ 🅿

TRADITIONAL CUISINE · COSY This traditional-looking former farmhouse is the perfect place to cosy up by the fire on a misty night. Choose a pub favourite or one of the appealing specials. Come on a Wednesday, Friday or Sunday for the popular music sessions, then stay the night in one of the comfy, cosy bedrooms.

Carte £ 25/38

6 rooms ⊃ – ♦£ 90/110 ♦♦£ 100/130

✉ IV51 9PW – ☎ 01470 582414 – www.edinbaneinn.co.uk
– Closed 2 January-2 February

Elgol

Regional map n° **17**-B2

X Coruisk House ⇔ ≤ 🅿

TRADITIONAL CUISINE · SIMPLE This traditional croft house is very remotely set on the west of the island and offers superb views over the hills to the mountains. It's very personally run and seats just 16. Skye produce features in fresh, flavoursome daily dishes. Two simply furnished bedrooms share the stunning outlook.

Carte £ 36/45

2 rooms ⊃ – ♦£ 140/160 ♦♦£ 140/160

✉ IV49 9BL – ☎ 01471 866330 (booking essential) – www.coruiskhouse.com
– Closed November-February except 1 week New Year

Flodigarry

🏠 Flodigarry ✿ ⅗ ≤ 🛋 🅿

COUNTRY HOUSE · PERSONALISED This Victorian house was once Jacobite hero-
ine Flora MacDonald's home. Lawned gardens lead down to the coast and it has excellent panoramic views; stylish designer décor features throughout. The bar is in the old
billiard room and has its original ceiling windows. Cooking is modern and Scottish.

17 rooms ⚏ - 🛏£160/315 🛏🛏£160/315

✉ IV51 9HZ - ☎ 01470 552203 - www.flodigarry.co.uk - Restricted opening in winter

Portree

🏠 Cuillin Hills ✿ ⅗ ≤ 🛋 ⅙ ⅗ 🅿

TRADITIONAL · CLASSIC Set in 15 acres of grounds, a 19C hunting lodge offering
stunning views over Portree Bay towards the Cuillin Mountains; enjoy top Scottish
produce in the restaurant, which shares the outlook. Bedrooms have good facilities
– the best are to the front. The stylish open-plan bar serves over 100 malt whiskies.

28 rooms ⚏ - 🛏£80/220 🛏🛏£100/320

✉ IV51 9QU - Northeast : 0.75 mi by A 855 - ☎ 01478 612003
- www.cuillinhills-hotel-skye.co.uk

🏠 Bosville ✿ ≤ ⅗

INN · CONTEMPORARY The Bosville sits in an elevated spot overlooking the harbour and the Cuillin Mountains; choose a bedroom at the front to best appreciate
the view. Enjoy a dram by the fire in the lively red and black bar then head for
the bistro-style dining room, which showcases the best of Skye's natural larder.

20 rooms ⚏ - 🛏£85/170 🛏🛏£85/180

Bosville Terr ✉ IV51 9DG - ☎ 01478 612846 - www.bosvillehotel.co.uk - Closed
Christmas

X Scorrybreac

MODERN CUISINE · BISTRO Simply furnished restaurant with distant mountain
views and just 8 tables; named after the chef's parents' house, where he ran his
first pop-up. Creative modern cooking uses meats from the hills and seafood
from the harbour below.

Menu £33 (dinner)/38

7 Bosville Terr ✉ IV51 9DG - ☎ 01478 612069 (booking essential at dinner)
- www.scorrybreac.com - Closed Monday

Sleat

🏠 Kinloch Lodge ⅗ ≤ 🛋 ⅗ 🅿

COUNTRY HOUSE · CLASSIC With a loch in front and heather-strewn moorland
behind, this 17C hunting lodge affords fantastic panoramic views. Inside, it has a
traditional country house feel; comfy antique-filled lounges are hung with photos
of the Macdonald clan and each of the contemporary bedrooms is themed
around a different tartan.

19 rooms (dinner included) ⚏ - 🛏£139/300 🛏🛏£220/420 - 3 suites
✉ IV43 8QY - ☎ 01471 833214 - www.kinloch-lodge.co.uk
⊛ Kinloch Lodge - See restaurant listing

XXX Kinloch Lodge ⅙ ≤ 🛋 ⇔ 🅿
⊛ **MODERN CUISINE · CLASSIC DÉCOR** Elegant dining room in a 17C hunting
lodge, offering stunning views across a loch. Dine beneath portraits of the Macdonald clan or watch the kitchen action from the chef's table. Cooking is classically based but has clever modern touches. Good service and a well-written
wine list complete the picture.

→ Home-cured salmon wrapped seafood mousse with dill dressing. Black Isle
lamb with cashew nut & black olive crust, apples and pears. Apple crumble parfait with blackcurrant and cinnamon doughnut.

Menu £33/80 **s**

Kinloch Lodge Hotel, ✉ IV43 8QY - ☎ 01471 833214 (booking essential)
- www.kinloch-lodge.co.uk

Struan

🏠 Ullinish Country Lodge   🕭 ⪅ 🛏 🕉 **P**

TRADITIONAL · CLASSIC Personally run, 18C former hunting lodge in a wind-swept location, affording lovely loch and mountain views. The lounge is filled with ornaments and books about the area. Warmly decorated bedrooms boast good facilities and extras.

6 rooms ⌑ – ♦£ 125/160 ♦♦£ 190/260

✉ IV56 8FD – West : 1.5 mi by A 863 – ☎ 01470 572214 – www.theisleofskye.co.uk – Closed January, Christmas and New Year

Ullinish Country Lodge – See restaurant listing

XX Ullinish Country Lodge   ⪅ 🛏 **P**

MODERN CUISINE · CLASSIC DÉCOR Formal hotel dining room with a traditional masculine style and a house party atmosphere. The daily changing, 2-choice set menu uses good quality local ingredients; dishes are modern and inventive and combinations are well-judged.

Menu £ 55

Ullinish Country Lodge Hotel, ✉ IV56 8FD – West : 1.5 mi by A 863 – ☎ 01470 572214 (bookings essential for non-residents) – www.theisleofskye.co.uk – dinner only – Closed January, Christmas and New Year

Teangue

🏠 Toravaig House   🏹 ⪅ 🛏 🕉 🕪 **P**

COUNTRY HOUSE · CONTEMPORARY Stylish whitewashed house with neat gardens, set on the road to the Mallaig ferry. Cosy, open-fired lounge with a baby grand piano and heavy fabrics. Individually designed bedrooms boast quality materials and furnishings. The two-roomed restaurant offers a concise, classical menu of island produce.

9 rooms ⌑ – ♦£ 85/185 ♦♦£ 85/280

Knock Bay ✉ IV44 8RE – on A 851 – ☎ 01471 820200 – www.skyehotel.co.uk

Waternish

X Loch Bay ⓝ   **P**

MODERN CUISINE · SIMPLE A pretty little crofter's cottage in an idyllic hamlet. It's a simple place, with blue and white walls and a quarry-tiled floor. The experienced chef offers bold, interesting dishes with traditional French and Scottish foundations.

Menu £ 28/38

1 Macleods Terr, Stein ✉ IV55 8GA – ☎ 01470 592235 (booking essential) – www.lochbay-restaurant.co.uk – Closed January, Christmas, Tuesday lunch, Sunday dinner and Monday

SLEAT – Highland ➜ See Skye (Isle of)

SORN

East Ayrshire – Regional map n° **15**-B2

▶ Edinburgh 67 mi – Ayr 15 mi – Glasgow 35 mi

🏠 Sorn Inn   ⇆ 🔥 **P**

TRADITIONAL BRITISH · PUB It's very much a family affair at this unassuming inn – the father checks you in and the son does the cooking. Sit in either the smart bar or larger dining room. The extensive menu includes a variety of British dishes plus some more elaborate international offerings. The neat, simple bedrooms are good value.

Menu £ 14 (weekday lunch)/17 – Carte £ 19/35

4 rooms ⌑ – ♦£ 50/55 ♦♦£ 60/90

35 Main St ✉ KA5 6HU – ☎ 01290 551305 – www.sorninn.com – Closed 10 days January and Monday

SPEAN BRIDGE

Highland – Regional map n° **17**-C3

▶ Edinburgh 143 mi – Fort William 10 mi – Glasgow 94 mi – Inverness 58 mi

⌂ Corriegour Lodge   ⚡ ⟨ 🛏 ✦ 🅿

TRADITIONAL · COSY A traditional 19C hunting lodge with pretty gardens, set in a great lochside location – they even have their own private beach. Inside there's a homely curio-filled lounge and comfy bedrooms featuring top quality beds, linens and fabrics. Classical dinners comprise 4 courses; every table has a loch view.

11 rooms ⌂ – ♦£ 90/179 ♦♦£ 179/204

Loch Lochy ✉ PH34 4EA – North : 8.75 mi on A 82 – ℰ 01397 712685
– www.corriegour-lodge-hotel.com – Closed November-22 March

⌂ Old Pines   ⚡ ॐ ⟨ 🛏 ⑆ 🅿

TRADITIONAL · COSY A friendly couple run this log cabin style property, which blends well with the Highland scenery. Guest areas are comfy and homely. Feature walls add a splash of colour to the pine-furnished bedrooms and the slate-tiled bathrooms come with underfloor heating. Dining has a classic dinner party feel.

7 rooms ⌂ – ♦£ 60/80 ♦♦£ 90/120

✉ PH34 4EG – Northwest : 1.5 mi by A 82 on B 8004 – ℰ 01397 712324
– www.oldpines.co.uk – Closed November-Easter

✕✕ Russell's at Smiddy House   ⟨ ⑆ 🅿

TRADITIONAL BRITISH · INTIMATE Friendly, passionately run restaurant in an appealing Highland village, with a smart ornament-filled lounge and two intimate dining rooms. Tasty dishes use locally sourced ingredients and old Scottish recipes take on a modern style. Cosy, well-equipped bedrooms come with comfy beds and fine linens.

Menu £ 35

5 rooms ⌂ – ♦£ 85/125 ♦♦£ 95/160

Roybridge Rd ✉ PH34 4EU – ℰ 01397 712335 (booking essential)
– www.smiddyhouse.com – dinner only – Closed Monday to non-residents and restricted opening in winter

SPITTAL OF GLENSHEE

Perth and Kinross – ✉ Blairgowrie – Regional map n° **16**-C2

▶ Edinburgh 79 mi – London 489 mi – Glasgow 98 mi – Livingston 81 mi

⌂⌂ Dalmunzie Castle   ⚡ ॐ ⟨ 🛏 🖾 ✕ 🔁 🅿

HISTORIC · CLASSIC A traditional baronial style castle and Edwardian hunting lodge, on a stunning 6,500 acre estate encircled by mountains; the open hall has a large window looking towards the snow-capped peaks. Bedrooms are classical, the cosy bar stocks over 100 whiskies and the dining room offers pretty valley views.

17 rooms ⌂ – ♦£ 185/250 ♦♦£ 185/250

✉ PH10 7QG – ℰ 01250 885224 – www.dalmunzie.com – Closed 3 January-4 February and 1-23 December

STIRLING

Stirling – Pop. 36 142 – Regional map n° **16**-C2

▶ Edinburgh 37 mi – Glasgow 28 mi – Perth 34 mi

⌂⌂ Park Lodge   ⚡ 🛏 ✦ 🜁 🅿

TOWNHOUSE · CLASSIC Lovely part-Georgian, part-Victorian, creeper-clad house, with a mature garden and fruit trees to the rear. Warm, intimate bar and sitting room. Traditional, individually designed bedrooms; the four-poster room is particularly popular. Formal dining room has a beautiful ornate ceiling and traditional menu.

9 rooms ⌂ – ♦£ 75 ♦♦£ 95/110

32 Park Terr ✉ FK8 2JS – ℰ 01786 474862 – www.parklodge.net – Closed 25-26 December and 1-2 January

🏠 Victoria Square   ℀ P

TOWNHOUSE · ELEGANT Many original features remain in this detached 1880s house overlooking Victoria Square – from the stained glass on the staircase to the impressive ornate cornicing in the sitting room. Spacious bedrooms; some with four-posters.

7 rooms ☑ – †£ 70/88 ††£ 85/140

12 Victoria Sq. ✉ *FK8 2QZ* – ☎ *01786 473920*
– www.victoriasquareguesthouse.com
– Closed 1-15 January and 22-28 December

🏠 West Plean House   🐾 🛏 ℀ P

TRADITIONAL · PERSONALISED An attractive house with a long history and a hospitable owner; next to a working farm. Beautiful tiled hall, classic country house lounge and warm, traditionally styled bedrooms. Eggs come from their hens and jams, from the kitchen garden.

4 rooms ☑ – †£ 65/70 ††£ 100

✉ *FK7 8HA* – *South : 3.5 mi on A 872 (Denny rd)* – ☎ *01786 812208*
– www.westpleanhouse.com – Closed 15 December-15 January

STONEHAVEN

Aberdeenshire – Pop. 11 431 – Regional map n° **16**-D2
▶ Edinburgh 111 mi – Glasgow 130 mi – Dundee 50 mi – Aberdeen 15 mi

🏠 Beachgate House   ⪡ ℀ P ⇥

LUXURY · PERSONALISED Well-run guesthouse looking out over Stonehaven Bay. Super views from well-appointed, first floor lounge. Bedrooms are furnished in a luxurious, modern style. Breakfast includes fresh poached fish or a full Scottish with hen or duck eggs.

5 rooms ☑ – †£ 75/95 ††£ 85/95

Beachgate Ln ✉ *AB39 2BD* – ☎ *01569 763155 – www.beachgate.co.uk*

✕✕ Tolbooth

SEAFOOD · RUSTIC Stonehaven's oldest building, located on the harbourside: formerly a store, sheriff's courthouse and prison. Classic dishes have modern touches; the emphasis being on local seafood, with langoustines and crab the highlights. Choose table 3.

Menu £ 20 (weekday lunch)/28 – Carte £ 32/51

Old Pier, Harbour ✉ *AB39 2JU* – ☎ *01569 762287*
– www.tolbooth-restaurant.co.uk – Closed 3 weeks January, 1 week October,
25-26 December and Monday. Sunday dinner and Tuesday October-April

STORNOWAY – Western Isles ➜ See Lewis and Harris (Isle of)

STRACHUR

Argyll and Bute – Pop. 628 – Regional map n° **16**-B2
▶ Edinburgh 112 mi – Glasgow 66 mi – Inverness 162 mi – Perth 101 mi

🏠 Creggans Inn   ⚲ ⪡ 🛏 P

INN · CLASSIC A well-established inn on the shores of Loch Fyne; the conservatory is a popular spot for taking in the enviable view. Spacious, well-kept bedrooms have traditional décor in keeping with the building's age. Dine in the cosy bar-bistro or the classical restaurant – both serve the same wide-ranging menu.

14 rooms ☑ – †£ 80/105 ††£ 100/190 – 1 suite

✉ *PA27 8BX* – ☎ *01369 860279 – www.creggans-inn.co.uk – Closed 2 weeks*
January and Christmas

X Inver ⟨ 🏠 P

BRITISH MODERN · VINTAGE A former crofter's cottage and boat store in a beautifully isolated spot on the loch shore. Enjoy afternoon tea sitting in sheepskin covered armchairs in the lounge-bar or take in the view from the vintagestyle restaurant, where concise modern menus are led by the finest local and foraged ingredients.

Menu £ 42 (dinner) – Carte £ 22/42

Strathlaclan ⊠ PA27 8BU – Southwest : 6.5 mi by A 886 on B 8000
– 𝒞 01369 860537 – www.inverrestaurant.co.uk – Closed Wednesday dinner,
Sunday and Tuesday September-June, Wednesday lunch and Thursday
November-December, Christmas, January- mid March and Monday except bank
holidays

STRATHPEFFER
Highland – Pop. 1 109 – Regional map n° **17**-C2
▶ Edinburgh 173 mi – Dundee 155 mi – Inverness 20 mi

Craigvar ⟨🛏 ⅍ P

TRADITIONAL · CLASSIC Proudly run by a charming owner, an attractive Georgian house overlooking the main square of a delightful spa village. Traditional guest areas include a comfy lounge and an antique-furnished breakfast room. Spacious bedrooms have a modern edge and plenty of personal touches. Good breakfast selection.

3 rooms ⌑ – ♦£ 65 ♦♦£ 98

The Square ⊠ IV14 9DL – 𝒞 01997 421622 – www.craigvar.com
– Closed 18 December-14 January

STRATHY
Highland – Regional map n° **17**-D1
▶ Edinburgh 264 mi – Inverness 110 mi – Thurso 20 mi

Sharvedda 📶 ⟨ 🛏 ⅍ P ↦

FAMILY · PERSONALISED You won't find a warmer welcome than at this remotely located guesthouse on a working croft. Homemade fudge and cake are served on arrival and breakfast is taken in the sunny conservatory, with its wild views over the Pentland Firth.

3 rooms ⌑ – ♦£ 55/60 ♦♦£ 80

Strathy Point ⊠ KW14 7RY – North : 1.5 mi on Strathy Point rd – 𝒞 01641 541311
– www.sharvedda.co.uk – Closed 25-26 December

STRATHYRE
Stirling – ⊠ Callander – Regional map n° **16**-B2
▶ Edinburgh 62 mi – Glasgow 53 mi – Perth 42 mi

XX Creagan House ↤ 🛏 P

TRADITIONAL CUISINE · COSY Long-standing, personally run restaurant in a 17C farmhouse. Snug sitting rooms lead to a baronial-style dining room with a vast fireplace and handmade local china. Traditional cooking uses Perthshire's natural larder; the 'Smokie in a Pokie' is a speciality. Watch red squirrels from the comfy, cosy bedrooms.

Menu £ 38

5 rooms ⌑ – ♦£ 90/100 ♦♦£ 135/155

⊠ FK18 8ND – On A 84 – 𝒞 01877 384638 (booking essential)
– www.creaganhouse.co.uk – dinner only – Closed 26 October-7 April, Wednesday
and Thursday

STROMNESS → See Orkney Islands (Mainland)

STRONTIAN
Highland – Regional map n° **17**-B3
▶ Edinburgh 139 mi – Fort William 23 mi – Oban 66 mi

STRONTIAN

SCOTLAND

🏨 Kilcamb Lodge

COUNTRY HOUSE · TRADITIONAL A charming lochside hunting lodge in an idyllic location, where 22 acres of meadows and woodland run down to a private shore. The traditional interior boasts rich fabrics and log fires yet has a modern edge. Bedrooms 5 and 8 have terrific loch and mountain views. Dine in the brasserie or the formal restaurant.

11 rooms (dinner included) ♨ – ∳£ 110/145 ∳∳£ 170/225

*On A 861 ⊠ PH36 4HY – ℰ 01967 402257 – www.kilcamblodge.co.uk
– Closed January, 1-14 December and restricted opening in winter*

Driftwood Brasserie – See restaurant listing

✗ Driftwood Brasserie 🔘

MODERN CUISINE · BRASSERIE An intimate cream wood panelled brasserie in a lochside hunting lodge. The menu covers all bases, from traditional British dishes to Asian fare. Don't miss the West Coast seafood specials or the Ardnamurchan Peninsula venison.

Menu £ 22 – Carte £ 33/46

Kilcamb Lodge Hotel, On A 861 ⊠ PH36 4HY – ℰ 01967 402257 (booking essential at dinner) – www.kilcamblodge.co.uk – Closed January, 1-14 December and restricted opening in winter

STRUAN – Highland ➜ See Skye (Isle of)

TAIN

Highland – Pop. 3 655 – Regional map n° **17**-D2
▶ Edinburgh 191 mi – Inverness 35 mi – Wick 91 mi

at Nigg Southeast: 7 mi by A9, B9175 and Pitcalnie Rd

🏨 Wemyss House

FAMILY · PERSONALISED Remotely set guesthouse run by charming owners; sit in the conservatory extension or on the terrace to enjoy views across the Cromarty Firth to the mountains. The bright Scandic-style interior features bespoke furniture from Stuart's on-site workshop and Christine often plays the grand piano in the cosy lounge.

3 rooms ♨ – ∳£ 115/120 ∳∳£ 115/120

*Bayfield ⊠ IV19 1QW – South : 1 mi past church – ℰ 01862 851212
– www.wemysshouse.com – Closed October-Easter*

at Cadboll Southeast: 8.5 mi by A9 and B9165 (Portmahomack rd) off Hilton rd ⊠ Tain

🏨 Glenmorangie House

TRADITIONAL · CLASSIC Charming 17C house owned by the famous distillery. Antiques, hand-crafted local furnishings and open peat fires feature; there's even a small whisky tasting room. Luxuriously appointed bedrooms show good attention to detail; those in the courtyard cottages are suites. Communal dining from a classical Scottish menu.

9 rooms (dinner included) ♨ – ∳£ 195/325 ∳∳£ 260/390

Fearn ⊠ IV20 1XP – ℰ 01862 871671 – www.theglenmorangiehouse.com – Closed January

TARBERT – Western Isles ➜ See Lewis and Harris (Isle of)

TAYNUILT

Argyll and Bute – Regional map n° **16**-B2
▶ Edinburgh 114 mi – Oban 12 mi – Fort William 46 mi

740

🏠 **Taynuilt** ⇔ 🛋 **P**

BRITISH MODERN · INN Coleridge and Wordsworth enjoyed this inn's hospitality back in 1803 and today it's run with pride and enthusiasm by the McNulty family. Food is their passion and the beautifully presented, assured modern cooking displays many intricate components. Well-kept bedrooms are named after lochs.
Carte £ 25/55

9 rooms ⌷ – ♦£ 95/165 ♦♦£ 115/195

✉ PA35 1JN – ℰ 01866 822437 – www.taynuilthotel.co.uk – Closed Sunday, Monday and restricted opening in January

TEANGUE – Highland → See Skye (Isle of)

THORNHILL

Dumfries and Galloway – Pop. 1 674 – Regional map n° **15**-B2
▶ Edinburgh 64 mi – Ayr 44 mi – Dumfries 15 mi – Glasgow 63 mi

🏠 **Buccleuch & Queensberry Arms** 🏠 🛋 க் 🏠

TOWNHOUSE · CONTEMPORARY Smartly refurbished coaching inn, designed by the owner, who also runs an interiors shop. Boldly coloured bedrooms are named after various estates owned by the Duke of Buccleuch and come with eclectic artwork and superb bathrooms. Informal dining options range from bar snacks to a more adventurous à la carte

14 rooms ⌷ – ♦£ 55/90 ♦♦£ 65/175

112 Drumlanrig St ✉ DG3 5LU – ℰ 01848 323101 – www.bqahotel.com

🏠 **Holmhill Country House** 🏠 🐾 ⇐ 🏠 🕸 **P**

COUNTRY HOUSE · PERSONALISED 18C country house, peacefully set beside the river, in 8 acres of woodland. It was given to Charles Douglas by the Duke of Buccleuch and the elegant sitting room is filled with his family photos. Spacious bedrooms feature Egyptian cotton linen and have great country views. Communal dinners must be pre-booked.

3 rooms ⌷ – ♦£ 70/85 ♦♦£ 100/115

Holmhill ✉ DG3 4AB – West 0.5mi on A702 – ℰ 01848 332239
– www.holmhill.co.uk – Closed Christmas to New Year

🏠 **Gillbank House** 🏠 🕸 **P**

TOWNHOUSE · PERSONALISED Red stone house built in 1895; originally the holiday home of the Jenner family of department store fame. A lovely stained glass front door leads to a spacious light-filled interior. The breakfast room has distant hill views and two of the large, simply furnished bedrooms have feature beds; all have wet rooms.

6 rooms ⌷ – ♦£ 70 ♦♦£ 90

8 East Morton St ✉ DG3 5LZ – ℰ 01848 330597 – www.gillbank.co.uk

THURSO

Highland – Pop. 7 933 – Regional map n° **17**-D1
▶ Edinburgh 289 mi – Inverness 133 mi – Wick 21 mi

🏠 **Forss House** 🏠 🐾 🏠 🕸 **P**

TRADITIONAL · COSY Traditional Scottish hotel geared towards fishing; they have a 'rod room' and mounted fish sit beside deer heads on the walls. Bedrooms are of a good size – those in 'River House' are the most private with great views. The elegant dining room serves a classic Scottish menu – Scrabster seafood is a speciality.

14 rooms ⌷ – ♦£ 102/125 ♦♦£ 135/175

Forss ✉ KW14 7XY – West : 5.5 mi on A 836 – ℰ 01847 861201
– www.forsshousehotel.co.uk – Closed 24 December-4 January

🏠 Pennyland House ⟨ 🛖 P

FAMILY · PERSONALISED Old farmhouse built in 1780; where the founder of the Boys' Brigade was born. Simple, stylishly furnished bedrooms with quality oak furnishings, golf course pictures and modern bathrooms. Open-plan lounge-cum-dining room with harbour views.

6 rooms 🖙 – ♦£ 70 ♦♦£ 80/90

✉ KW14 7JU – Northwest : 0.75 mi on A 9 – ☎ 01847 891194
– www.pennylandhouse.co.uk – Closed Christmas and New Year

at Scrabster Northwest: 2.25 mi on A9

🍴 Captain's Galley

SEAFOOD · RUSTIC Classic seafood restaurant on the pier, with a vaulted stone dining room and an old chimney from its former ice house days. The owner was once a fisherman so has excellent local contacts – he keeps some produce in creels in the harbour.

Menu £ 54

The Harbour ✉ KW14 7UJ – ☎ 01847 894999 *(booking essential)*
– www.captainsgalley.co.uk – dinner only – Closed 25-26 December, 1-2 January, Sunday and Monday

TIGHNABRUAICH

Argyll and Bute – Regional map n° **16**-B3
▶ Edinburgh 113 mi – Glasgow 63 mi – Oban 66 mi

🏠 Royal An Lochan ☆ ⟨ 🐾 P

FAMILY · PERSONALISED Spacious 19C hotel located in a peaceful village, overlooking the Kyles of Bute. Comfortable bedrooms; some with excellent outlooks. The characterful bar with its nautical theme serves a snack menu, while the formal conservatory restaurant offers water views and seasonal seafood dishes.

11 rooms 🖙 – ♦£ 85/135 ♦♦£ 100/150

Shore Rd ✉ PA21 2BE – ☎ 01700 811239 – www.theroyalanlochan.co.uk

TIRORAN – Argyll and Bute → See Mull (Isle of)

TOBERMORY – Argyll and Bute → See Mull (Isle of)

TORRIDON

Highland – ✉ Achnasheen – Regional map n° **17**-B2
▶ Edinburgh 234 mi – Inverness 62 mi – Kyle of Lochalsh 44 mi

🏠 Torridon ☆ 🐾 ⟨ 🛖 🖵 & P

TRADITIONAL · CLASSIC A former hunting lodge built in 1887 by Lord Lovelace; set in 40 acres and offering superb loch and mountain views. The delightful interior features wood-panelling, ornate ceilings and a peat fire. Bedrooms are spacious and luxurious, with top quality furnishings and feature baths. The whisky bar has over 350 malts and the smart dining room offers a modern daily menu.

18 rooms 🖙 – ♦£ 210/245 ♦♦£ 210/450 – 2 suites

✉ IV22 2EY – South : 1.5 mi on A 896 – ☎ 01445 791242 – www.thetorridon.com
– Closed January and Monday-Tuesday November-March

🏠 Torridon Inn ⟨ 🐾 🛖 🍴 & P

TRADITIONAL CUISINE · INN Tranquil inn geared towards those who enjoy outdoor pursuits. The timbered bar features stags' antlers and an ice axe; the restaurant overlooks the gardens and loch. Satisfying walkers' favourites mix with more elaborate dishes. Simply furnished, modern bedrooms; the larger ones are ideal for families.

Carte £ 18/36 **s**

12 rooms 🖙 – ♦£ 120 ♦♦£ 120

✉ IV22 2EY – South : 1.5 mi on A 896 – ☎ 01445 791242 – www.thetorridon.com
– Closed mid-December-January and Monday-Thursday November, February and March

TROON

South Ayrshire – Pop. 14 752 – Regional map n° **15**-A2

▶ Edinburgh 77 mi – Ayr 7 mi – Glasgow 31 mi

🏠 Lochgreen House

COUNTRY HOUSE · CONTEMPORARY Edwardian country house in a pleasant coastal spot, with sumptuous lounges and a Whisky Room stocked with an extensive range of malts. Bedrooms in the main house are cosy and traditional; those in the extension are more luxurious.

32 rooms ☲ – ♦£ 115/165 ♦♦£ 175/195 – 1 suite

Monktonhill Rd, Southwood ✉ KA10 7EN – Southeast : 2 mi on B 749
– ℰ 01292 313343 – www.costley-hotels.co.uk

Tapestry – See restaurant listing

XXX Tapestry

MODERN BRITISH · ELEGANT A cavernous country house dining room with exposed rafters, huge mirrors and chandeliers – but no tapestries! Interesting set menus feature refined, flavoursome modern dishes that use the best of Scottish produce. Service is formal.

Menu £ 17 (weekday lunch)/43 – Carte £ 33/56

Lochgreen House Hotel, Monktonhill Rd, Southwood ✉ KA10 7EN – Southeast :
2 mi on B 749 – ℰ 01292 313343 – www.costley-hotels.co.uk

TURNBERRY

South Ayrshire – ✉ Girvan – Regional map n° **15**-A2

▶ Edinburgh 97 mi – London 416 mi – Glasgow 51 mi – Carlisle 108 mi

🏨 Trump Turnberry

GRAND LUXURY · DESIGN A resort-style Edwardian railway hotel boasting a smart spa and 3 golf courses – one a championship course. Bedrooms are luxurious and the suites have stunning coast and course views. 1906 offers Italian-influenced dishes and Duel in the Sun (in the clubhouse) serves dishes from the charcoal grill.

203 rooms ☲ – ♦£ 250/280 ♦♦£ 425/455 – 5 suites

✉ KA26 9LT – On A 719 – ℰ 01655 331000 – www.trumpturnberry.com

1906 – See restaurant listing

XXX 1906

ITALIAN · ELEGANT This grand hotel restaurant is named after the year that the Turnberry opened and it boasts lovely views out across the sea. Sit beneath ornate plaster ceilings and enjoy Scottish ingredients in dishes with modern Italian overtones.

Carte £ 35/88

Trump Turnberry Hotel, ✉ KA26 9LT – On A 719 – ℰ 01655 334088
– www.trumpturnberry.com – dinner only

UDNY GREEN

Aberdeenshire – Regional map n° **16**-D1

▶ Edinburgh 140 mi – London 543 mi – Dundee 80 mi

XX Eat on the Green

MODERN BRITISH · ELEGANT An attractive former inn overlooking the village green, with a cosy lounge and two traditionally furnished dining rooms. Well-presented modern dishes change with the seasons and feature vegetables and herbs from their smallholding.

Menu £ 24 (weekday lunch) – Carte £ 34/50

✉ AB41 7RS – ℰ 01651 842337 (booking essential) – www.eatonthegreen.co.uk
– Closed Monday, Tuesday and Saturday lunch

UIG – Western Isles ➔ See Lewis and Harris (Isle of)

UIST (Isles of)
Western Isles – Pop. 3 510 – Regional map n° **17**-A2

NORTH UIST
Western Isles

Carinish
Western Isles

🏠 Temple View
☆ ⋖ 🛏 **P**

TRADITIONAL · FUNCTIONAL Victorian house with an uncluttered interior and a homely style. Small bar, sitting room and sun lounge. Simple, comfortable bedrooms: those to the rear have moor views; those at the front overlook the sea or the 13C ruins of Trinity Temple. Cosy dining room offers popular seafood specials.

10 rooms ⌖ – 🛏£ 75/90 🛏🛏£ 110/120

✉ HS6 5EJ – ☎ 01876 580676 – www.templeviewhotel.co.uk – Closed Christmas

Langass
Western Isles

🏠 Langass Lodge
☆ ⅍ ⋖ 🛏 ♿ **P**

HISTORIC · CLASSIC Victorian former shooting lodge nestled in heather-strewn hills and boasting distant loch views. Characterful bedrooms in the main house; more modern, spacious rooms with good views in the wing. Eat in the comfy bar or linen-clad dining room from simple, seafood based menus.

11 rooms ⌖ – 🛏£ 80/95 🛏🛏£ 95/170

✉ HS6 5HA – ☎ 01876 580285 – www.langasslodge.co.uk – Closed November-April

Lochmaddy
Western Isles

🏠 Hamersay House
☆ 🛖 ⅍ 🛋 ♿ **P**

TRADITIONAL · CONTEMPORARY Stylish hotel with a sleek, boutique style, a well-equipped gym, a sauna, a steam room and bikes for hire. Chic, modern bedrooms offer good facilities. The forward-thinking owner continually reinvests. Smart bar and dining room; menus display plenty of seafood.

8 rooms ⌖ – 🛏£ 90/95 🛏🛏£ 110/135

✉ HS6 5AE – ☎ 01876 500700 – www.hamersayhouse.co.uk

ULLAPOOL
Highland – Pop. 1 541 – Regional map n° **17**-C2
▶ Edinburgh 215 mi – London 616 mi – Inverness 58 mi – Elgin 94 mi

🏠 Westlea House
P

FAMILY · CONTEMPORARY It might look like an ordinary house but inside, Westlea has been transformed into a stylish, boutique-style B&B. Individually decorated bedrooms feature bold modern artwork and have a funky feel; two have roll-top baths in the room.

5 rooms ⌖ – 🛏£ 40/50 🛏🛏£ 80/100

2 Market St ✉ IV26 2XE – ☎ 01854 612594 – www.westlea-ullapool.co.uk

VEENSGARTH ➔ See Shetland Islands (Mainland)

WALKERBURN
The Scottish Borders – Pop. 700 – Regional map n° **15**-C2
▶ Edinburgh 30 mi – London 362 mi – Aberdeen 161 mi – Hartlepool 120 mi

⌂ Windlestraw

LUXURY · ELEGANT Attractive Arts and Crafts property built in 1906, boasting original fireplaces, old plaster ceilings and great valley views. Stylish, tastefully modernised bedrooms. Comfy bar, plush lounge and an attractive, wood-panelled dining room offering a daily changing menu.

6 rooms ⌑ – †£135/195 ††£185/245

✉ EH43 6AA – On A 72 – ☏ 01896 870636 – www.windlestraw.co.uk – Closed 24-26 December and 31 December- 14 February

WATERNISH – Highland → See Skye (Isle of)

WESTRAY (Isle of) → See Orkney Islands

WICK
Highland – Pop. 7 155 – Regional map n° **17**-D1
▶ Edinburgh 282 mi – Inverness 126 mi

⌂ Clachan

FAMILY · PERSONALISED Smart detached house on the edge of town, a short drive from the Queen Mother's former holiday residence, the Castle of Mey. Stylish, well-kept bedrooms blend oak furnishings with tartan fabrics. Black and white photos of the town's herring fishing days decorate the cosy dining room. Extensive breakfasts.

3 rooms ⌑ – †£70/75 ††£82/85

13 Randolph Pl, South Rd ✉ KW1 5NJ – South : 0.75 mi on A 99
– ☏ 01955 605384 – www.theclachan.co.uk – Closed 2 weeks Christmas-New Year

✗ Bord De L'Eau

CLASSIC FRENCH · BISTRO Long-standing riverside bistro run by keen, hands-on owners. Sit in the small conservatory or in the bright dining room, surrounded by French posters and Eiffel Tower prints. Classic Gallic dishes feature plenty of local seafood.

Carte £26/40

2 Market St (Riverside) ✉ KW1 4AR – ☏ 01955 604400 – Closed 25-26 December, 1-2 January, Sunday lunch and Monday

WORMIT
Fife – Regional map n° **16**-C2
▶ Edinburgh 53 mi – Aberdeen 70 mi – Dundee 5 mi

✗ View

TRADITIONAL CUISINE · FRIENDLY Unassuming former pub run by a husband and wife team, set in a small village and boasting superb views over the Tay Bridge to Dundee. Unfussy, classically based dishes include their ever-popular haggis fritters; lunch is good value.

Menu £13 (lunch) – Carte £28/46

Naughton Rd ✉ DD6 8NE – ☏ 01382 542287 – www.view-restaurant.co.uk
– Closed 25-26 December, 1-2 January and Monday

WALES

It may only be 170 miles from north to south, but Wales contains great swathes of beauty, such as the dark and craggy heights of Snowdonia's ninety mountain peaks, the rolling sandstone bluffs of the Brecon Beacons, and Pembrokeshire's tantalising golden beaches. Bottle-nosed dolphins love it here too, arriving each summer at New Quay in Cardigan Bay. Highlights abound: formidable Harlech Castle dominates its coast, Bala Lake has a railway that steams along its gentle shores, and a metropolitan vibe can be found in the capital, Cardiff, home to the Principality Stadium and the National Assembly.

Wales is a country which teems with great raw ingredients and modern-day chefs are employing these to their utmost potential; from succulent slices of Spring lamb farmed on the lush mountains and valleys, through to the humblest of cockles; from satisfying native Welsh Black cattle through to abundant Anglesey oysters, delicious Welsh cheeses and the edible seaweed found on the shores of the Gower and known as laverbread.

- Michelin Road maps
  n° 503 and 713
- Michelin Green Guide:
  Great Britain

Wales

Place with at least:

- • a hotel or a restaurant
- ✸ a starred establishment
- 🏵 a "Bib Gourmand" restaurant
- ✗ a particularly pleasant restaurant
- 🏠 a particularly pleasant accommodation

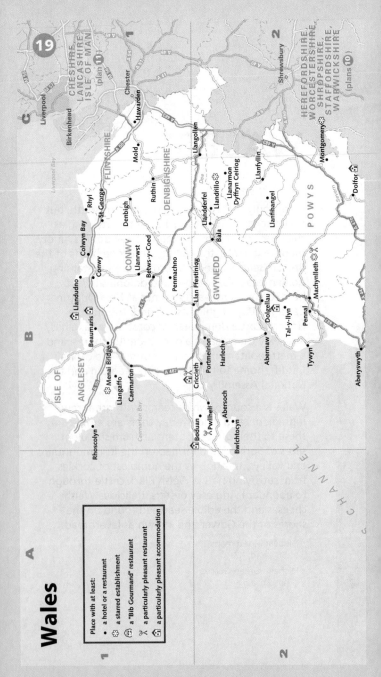

748

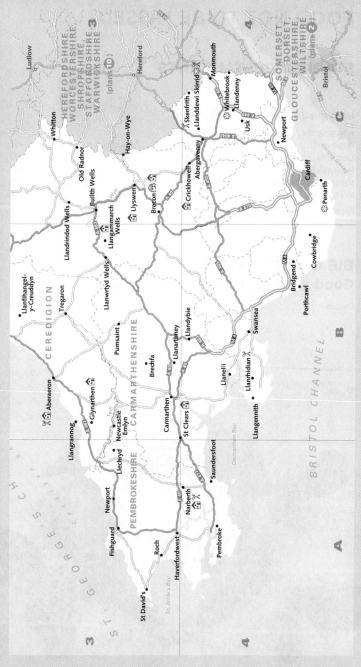

FOOD NOT TO BE MISSED

STARRED RESTAURANTS

❀
High quality cooking, worth a stop!

Abergavenny / Llanddewi Skirrid....Walnut Tree	....	755
Anglesey (Isle of) / Menai Bridge...Sosban and The Old Butchers **N**	....	757
Llandrillo........................Tyddyn Llan	....	772
Machynlleth.....................Ynyshir	....	777
Monmouth / Whitebrook..........The Whitebrook	....	778
Montgomery.....................The Checkers	....	778
Penarth ....James Sommerin **N**	....	780

BIB GOURMANDS ❀
Good quality, good value cooking

Brecon ....Felin Fach Griffin	....	759

Michelin

OUR TOP PICKS

Gloriously remote

3 Pen Cei 🏠 . . . . .Aberaeron. 754
Cleifiog 🏠 . . . . .Anglesey (Isle of)/Beaumaris 756
Old Vicarage 🏠. . . . . .Dolfor 768
Penbontbren 🏠 . . . . .Glynarthen 769
Old Rectory 🏠 . . . . .Pwllheli/Boduan 782
Coedllys Country House 🏠. . . . . . . .St Clears 784

Good value home from home

Outbuildings 🏠. . . . . .Anglesey (Isle of)/Llangaffo 757
Rhedyn 🏠 . . . . .Builth Wells 760
Firgrove 🏠. . . . . .Rhuthun 783
Pilleth Oaks 🏠 . . . . .Whitton. 787

It's all about the food

The Hardwick ✗ . . . . .Abergavenny 755
Loft ✗✗ . . . . .Angelsey (Isle of)/Beaumaris 757
Carlton Riverside ✗✗ . . . . .Llanwrtyd Wells. 776
Stonemill ✗ . . . . .Monmouth 777
Barratt's at Ty'n Rhyl ✗✗ . . . . .Rhyl 783
Coast ✗. . . . . .Saundersfoot 785
Slice ✗. . . . . .Swansea 786
Salt Marsh Kitchen ✗ . . . . .Tywyn 786

Made their mark

Harbourmaster 🍴	Aberaeron	754
Walnut Tree ✗☸	Abergavenny/Llanddewi Skirrid	755
Felin Fach Griffin 🍴☺	Brecon	759
Plas Bodegroes ✗✗	Pwllheli	782
Bell at Skenfrith 🍴	Skenfrith	785

More than just the village pub

Y Polyn 🍴	Carmarthen/Nantgaredig	766
Bear 🍴	Crickhowell	768
Hand at Llanarmon 🍴	Llanarmon Dyffryn Ceiriog	771
Harp Inn 🍴	Old Radnor	780
Dolaucothi Arms 🍴	Pumsaint	782
Kinmel Arms 🍴	St George	784
Y Talbot 🍴	Tregaron	786

Michelin

Michelin

Quintessential country houses

Ffynnon 🏠........................Dolgellau..................................769
Bodysgallen Hall 🏰🏰..............Llandudno 772
Lake Country House and Spa 🏰🏰....Llangammarch Wells 775
Grove 🏰🏰 ....Narberth..................................778

Special Occasion

Fairyhill XxX......................Llanrhidian 776
Llangoed Hall 🏰🏰🏰.................Llyswen...................................777
Ynyshir XX🕸 ....Machynlleth 777

ABERAERON ABER AERON

WALES

Ceredigion – Pop. 1 422 – Regional map n° **19**-B3

▶ London 231 mi – Cardiff 104 mi – Birmingham 138 mi – Liverpool 124 mi

🏠 3 Pen Cei   ⇐ 🍸

TOWNHOUSE · PERSONALISED Vibrant blue house on the harbourfront; formerly the Packet Steam Company HQ. Stylish modern bedrooms are named after local rivers: those to the front overlook the water; Aeron has a free-standing bath and large walk-in shower. Good choice at breakfast, from fruit salad to smoked salmon and scrambled eggs.

5 rooms ☲ – †£ 95/120 ††£ 105/165

3 Quay Par ⊠ SA46 0BT – ℰ 01545 571147 – www.pencei.co.uk – Closed 25-26 December

🏠 Llys Aeron   🛏 🍸

FAMILY · PERSONALISED Well-run Georgian house with a conservatory lounge and a breakfast room overlooking the walled garden; choose from extensive Aga-cooked options and homemade granola and preserves. Bedrooms come in neutral hues, with modern bathrooms.

3 rooms ☲ – †£ 50/75 ††£ 75/120

Lampeter Rd ⊠ SA46 0ED – on A 482 – ℰ 01545 570276 – www.llysaeron.co.uk – Closed 15 December-31 January

🍴 Harbourmaster   ⇔ ⇐ ♿

TRADITIONAL BRITISH · INN Vibrant blue inn with a New England style bar-lounge, a modern dining room and lovely harbour views. Choose between the bar menu, a more substantial evening à la carte and daily specials. Smart bedrooms, split between the house and a nearby cottage, are brightly decorated and well-equipped; some have terraces.

Menu £ 28 (dinner) – Carte £ 22/38

13 rooms ☲ – †£ 75/110 ††£ 120/250

Quay Par ⊠ SA46 0BA – ℰ 01545 570755 – www.harbour-master.com – Closed dinner 24 December-26 December

ABERGAVENNY Y-FENNI

Monmouthshire – Pop. 13 423 – Regional map n° **19**-C4

▶ London 163 mi – Cardiff 31 mi – Gloucester 43 mi – Newport 19 mi

🏠 Llansantffraed Court   🐾 ⇐ 🛏 📶

HISTORIC · CLASSIC Attractive William and Mary country house, with an ornamental lake and a chapel in its 20 acre grounds. Have afternoon tea in the traditional lounge. Bedrooms come in dark-hues – the corner rooms have both mountain and valley views.

20 rooms ☲ – †£ 95/135 ††£ 135/195

Llanvihangel Gobion ⊠ NP7 9BA – Southeast : 6.5 mi by A 40 and B 4598 off old Raglan rd – ℰ 01873 840678 – www.llch.co.uk

The Court – See restaurant listing

🏠 Angel   🍽 📶 ♿ 📶

HISTORIC · PERSONALISED A family-run Georgian coaching inn and outbuildings. Characterful guest areas have a modern, shabby-chic feel and bedrooms are a mix of the traditional and the more contemporary. Have afternoon tea in the Wedgewood Room or dine from a classic menu with global influences in the oak-furnished brasserie.

33 rooms ☲ – †£ 99/188 ††£ 99/188 – 2 suites

15 Cross St ⊠ NP7 5EN – ℰ 01873 857121 – www.angelabergavenny.com – Closed 25 December

XX The Court 🛏 🛋 🅿

MODERN BRITISH · CLASSIC DÉCOR Contemporary country house restaurant hung with large photos of local scenes. Dishes have a classical British base but are given a modern twist; fruit, veg and herbs are from the walled garden. The wines provide plenty of interest.

Menu £ 15 (weekday lunch)/33 – Carte £ 34/54

Llansantffraed Court Hotel, Llanvihangel Gobion ⌖ *NP7 9BA – Southeast : 6.5 mi by A 40 and B 4598 off old Raglan rd –* ☎ *01873 840678 (booking essential) – www.llch.co.uk*

X The Hardwick ⇦ ♿ 🅿

REGIONAL CUISINE · RURAL Smart modern pub conversion with a large bar, great mountain views and a trio of interconnecting dining rooms. Well thought-through dishes combine modern and classic elements and seasonal Welsh produce forms the backbone of the menu. Stylish modern bedrooms are set around a courtyard and have superb comforts.

Menu £ 26 (weekdays) – Carte £ 28/44

8 rooms – 🛏£ 125/155 🛏🛏£ 155/170

Old Raglan Rd ⌖ *NP7 9AA – Southeast : 2 mi by A 40 on B 4598 –* ☎ *01873 854220 – www.thehardwick.co.uk*

at Llanddewi Skirrid *Northeast: 3.25 mi on B4521*⌖ *Abergavenny*

X Walnut Tree (Shaun Hill) 🎖 🛋 🆎 🅿
😋

MODERN BRITISH · COSY A long-standing Welsh institution, set in a wooded valley and always bustling with regulars; start with drinks in the flag-floored lounge-bar. Classic, seasonal dishes are well-priced and refreshingly simple, eschewing adornment and letting the natural flavours of the ingredients speak for themselves.

➔ Red mullet and scallop bourride. Rack of lamb with sweetbread and morel pie. Orange and almond cake.

Menu £ 30 (weekday lunch) – Carte £ 34/55

⌖ *NP7 8AW –* ☎ *01873 852797 (booking essential) – www.thewalnuttreeinn.com – Closed 1 week Christmas, Sunday and Monday*

at Cross Ash *Northeast: 8.25 mi on B4521*

XX 1861 🅿

TRADITIONAL BRITISH · COSY Part-timbered Victorian pub named after the year it was built; now a cosy restaurant and lounge with contemporary furnishings. Classically based cooking has modern twists – much of the fruit and veg is grown by the owner's father.

Menu £ 22/35 – Carte £ 36/49

⌖ *NP7 8PB – West : 0.5 mi on B 4521 –* ☎ *01873 821297 – www.18-61.co.uk – Closed first 2 weeks January, Sunday dinner and Monday*

ABERSOCH

Gwynedd – ⌖ Pwllheli – Pop. 783 – Regional map n° **19**-B2
▶ London 265 mi – Caernarfon 28 mi – Shrewsbury 101 mi

XX Venetia ⇦ ♿ 🅿

ITALIAN · BRASSERIE Double-fronted house once owned by a sea captain, with a minimalist bar-lounge and a contemporary dining room with lime and aubergine seating. Classic Italian dishes are presented in a distinctly modern style. Friendly, efficient service. Chic, well-equipped bedrooms; one has a jacuzzi with a waterproof TV.

Carte £ 19/43

5 rooms ⌑ – 🛏£ 65/133 🛏🛏£ 80/148

Lon Sarn Bach ⌖ *LL53 7EB –* ☎ *01758 713354 – www.venetiawales.com – dinner only and Sunday lunch – Restricted opening in winter*

at Bwlchtocyn South: 2 mi ⊠ Pwllheli

🏠 Porth Tocyn ☆ ⑤ ≤ 🛏 ⏉ ✕ ⩗ P

FAMILY · PERSONALISED High on the headland overlooking Cardigan Bay, a traditional hotel that's been in the family for three generations. Relax in the cosy lounges or explore the many leisure and children's facilities. Homely, modernised bedrooms; some with balconies or sea views. Menus offer interesting, soundly executed dishes.

17 rooms ⌸ – ♦£80/90 ♦♦£110/190

⊠ LL53 7BU – 𝒞 01758 713303 – www.porthtocynhotel.co.uk – Closed early November-mid March

ABERYSTWYTH ABERESTUUTH

Ceredigion – Pop. 18 093 – Regional map n° **19**-B2

▶ London 238 mi – Chester 98 mi – Fishguard 58 mi – Shrewsbury 74 mi

🏠 Gwesty Cymru ☆ ≤ 🛏 ⑨ ⑩

TOWNHOUSE · MODERN Grade II listed Georgian townhouse on the seafront, with a brightly painted exterior and a terrace overlooking the bay. Thoughtfully designed modern bedrooms vary in size and décor – all are colour themed, with smart bathrooms. Small, stylish basement bar and dining room; ambitious, adventurous dishes.

8 rooms ⌸ – ♦£70/80 ♦♦£90/165

19 Marine Terr ⊠ SY23 2AZ – 𝒞 01970 612252 – www.gwestycymru.com – Closed 1-2 January and 23-31 December

ANGLESEY (Isle of) SIR YNYS MÔN

Isle of Anglesey – Pop. 68 900 – Regional map n° **19**-B1

▶ London 270 mi – Cardiff 205 mi – Liverpool 92 mi – Birkenhead 86 mi

Beaumaris

🏠 The Bull ⊡ ♿

INN · PERSONALISED Characterful 1670s coaching inn – look out for the old water clock and ducking stool in the bar. Bedrooms in the main house are named after Dickens characters and are traditional; those in the townhouse are more modern and colourful.

25 rooms ⌸ – ♦£103/158 ♦♦£115/170

Castle St ⊠ LL58 8AP – 𝒞 01248 810329 – www.bullsheadinn.co.uk – Closed 25-26 December and 1 January

Brasserie · Loft – See restaurant listing

🏠 Cleifiog ≤ 🛏

TOWNHOUSE · PERSONALISED Delightful seafront guesthouse overlooking the mountains and the Menai Strait; run by a welcoming owner. Watercolours hang on wood-panelled walls in the cosy, antique-furnished lounge. Comfortable bedrooms have fine linens and large bathrooms. Excellent communal breakfasts feature tasty fresh juices.

3 rooms ⌸ – ♦£60/90 ♦♦£90/120

Townsend ⊠ LL58 8BH – 𝒞 01248 811507 – www.cleifiogbandb.co.uk – Closed Christmas-early January

🏠 Churchbank 🛏 ⑨ P

TOWNHOUSE · PERSONALISED Georgian guesthouse with a homely, antique-furnished interior and modern day comforts. Cosy bedrooms look out over the large walled garden and the church opposite; one has a private bathroom. Helpful, amiable owner and hearty breakfasts.

3 rooms ⌸ – ♦£70/80 ♦♦£85/100

28 Church St ⊠ LL58 8AB – 𝒞 01248 810353 – www.bedandbreakfastanglesey.co.uk

XX Loft

MODERN BRITISH · ELEGANT Formal restaurant under the eaves of an old coaching inn, with a plush, open-fired lounge and an elegant candlelit dining room with exposed beams and immaculately laid tables. Creative modern cooking champions top Anglesey produce.

Menu £ 50

The Bull Hotel, Castle St ⊠ LL58 8AP – ℰ 01248 810329 – www.bullsheadinn.co.uk
– dinner only – Closed 25-26 December, 1 January and Sunday-Tuesday

X Brasserie &

MODERN BRITISH · FASHIONABLE Set overlooking a courtyard, a large brasserie in the old stables of a 17C coaching inn, with a Welsh slate floor, oak tables, a fireplace built from local stone and a relaxed feel. Wide-ranging modern menus feature lots of specials.

Carte £ 24/36

The Bull Hotel, Castle St ⊠ LL58 8AP – ℰ 01248 810329 (bookings not accepted)
– www.bullsheadinn.co.uk – Closed 25-26 December and 1 January

Llangaffo

Outbuildings ⌂ ⅏ ⋖ ⌕ ⅍ P

TRADITIONAL · PERSONALISED A tastefully converted former granary set close to a prehistoric burial ground and offering fantastic views over Snowdonia. Stylish modern bedrooms come with local artwork and smart bathrooms; for a romantic hideaway, choose the 'Pink Hut' in the garden. Afternoon tea is served in the cosy open-fired lounge and a concise, seasonally led menu in the spacious dining room.

5 rooms ⊃ – ♦£ 75/90 ♦♦£ 75/90

Bodowyr Farmhouse ⊠ LL60 6NH – Southeast : 1.5 mi by B 4419 turning left at crossroads and left again by post box – ℰ 01248 430132
– www.theoutbuildings.co.uk

Menai Bridge

X Sosban & The Old Butchers (Stephen Stevens)

❀ MODERN CUISINE · INTIMATE A brightly painted restaurant displaying Welsh slate and hand-painted tiles from its butcher's shop days. A well-balanced 6-7 course surprise menu offers boldly flavoured modern dishes with original, personal touches, which demonstrate an innate understanding of cooking techniques and flavour combinations.

→ Celeriac 'risotto' with apple and coffee. Lightly smoked cod with dried ox heart and cauliflower. Lemon posset with fresh mint and liquorice.

Menu £ 50 – surprise menu only

Trinity House, 1a High St ⊠ LL59 5EE – ℰ 01248 208131 (booking essential)
– www.sosbanandtheoldbutchers.com – dinner only and Saturday lunch – Closed January-mid February, Christmas-New Year and Sunday-Wednesday

X Dylan's ⋖ ⌕ &

MODERN CUISINE · FAMILY An old boat yard timber store; now a smart, busy, two-storey eatery by the water's edge, overlooking Bangor. Extensive menus offer everything from homemade cakes and weekend brunch to sourdough pizzas. Find a spot on the terrace if you can.

Carte £ 18/58

St George's Rd ⊠ LL59 5DE – ℰ 01248 716714 (booking advisable)
– www.dylansrestaurant.co.uk – Closed 25-26 December

Rhoscolyn

White Eagle ⋖ ⌕ ⌕ & P

TRADITIONAL BRITISH · PUB Set in a small coastal hamlet on the peninsula, this large pub boasts stunning sea views from its dining room and spacious decked terrace. The menu offers something for one and all, including tasty nibbles and various sharing boards.

Carte £ 21/37

⊠ LL65 2NJ – ℰ 01407 860267 – www.white-eagle.co.uk – Closed 25 December

BALA

Gwynedd – ⊠ Gwynedd – Pop. 1 974 – Regional map n° **19**-B2

▶ London 213 mi – Cardiff 160 mi – Chester 48 mi

🏠 Bryniau Golau   ⌂ 🐾 ⟨ 🛏 🍽 **P**

COUNTRY HOUSE · PERSONALISED Victorian tiling, plasterwork and fireplaces are all proudly displayed in this elegant house. Bedrooms overlook the lake and mountains: one has a four-poster bed; another, a bath which affords lake views. Their own honey features at breakfast, while dinner – served Fri and Sun – showcases local produce.

3 rooms ⊊ – ♦£ 90/100 ♦♦£ 110/120

Llangower ⊠ LL23 7BT – South : 2 mi by A 494 and B 4931 off B 4403 – ℰ 01678 521782 – www.bryniau-golau.co.uk – Closed December-February

BARMOUTH ABERMAW

Gwynedd – Pop. 2 315 – Regional map n° **19**-B2

▶ London 231 mi – Chester 74 mi – Dolgellau 10 mi – Shrewsbury 67 mi

🍴 Bistro Bermo

TRADITIONAL CUISINE · BISTRO An intimate, personally run bistro with a lively atmosphere. The concise menu follows the seasons and tasty dishes are neatly presented; go for the dry-aged Welsh Black rib-eye, or one of the local fish specials listed on the blackboard.

Carte £ 26/40

6 Church St ⊠ LL42 1EW – ℰ 01341 281284 (booking essential) – www.bistrobarmouth.co.uk – dinner only – Closed Sunday, Monday and restricted opening in winter

BEAUMARIS → See Anglesey (Isle of)

BETWS-Y-COED

Conwy – Pop. 255 – Regional map n° **19**-B1

▶ London 226 mi – Holyhead 44 mi – Shrewsbury 62 mi

🏠 Tan-y-Foel Country House   🐾 ⟨ 🛏 🍽 **P**

FAMILY · PERSONALISED Personally run, part-16C country house in 4 acres of grounds, which affords stunning views over the Vale of Conwy and Snowdonia. The snug lounge and breakfast room display traditional features. Modern, individually styled bedrooms have smart bathrooms; the spacious loft room has a vaulted ceiling.

6 rooms ⊊ – ♦£ 100/185 ♦♦£ 100/185

⊠ LL26 0RE – East : 2.5 mi by A 5, A 470 and Capel Garmon rd on Llanwrst rd – ℰ 01690 710507 – www.tyfhotel.co.uk – Closed December and January

🏠 Pengwern   ⟨ 🛏 🍽 **P**

TRADITIONAL · PERSONALISED Cosy Victorian house with stunning mountain and valley views. Warm, well-proportioned bedrooms retain charming original features like the old fireplaces and are named after famous artists who stayed at the house during the 1800s.

3 rooms ⊊ – ♦£ 57/69 ♦♦£ 72/84

Allt Dinas ⊠ LL24 0HF – Southeast : 1.5 mi on A 5 – ℰ 01690 710480 – www.snowdoniaaccommodation.co.uk – Closed 22 December-3 January

at Penmachno Southwest: 4.75 mi by A5 on B4406⊠ Betws-Y-Coed

🏠 Penmachno Hall   🐾 ⟨ 🛏 🍽 **P**

TRADITIONAL · PERSONALISED A former rectory in a pleasant valley location, with delightful views. Cosy lounge, eclectic art collection and lovely mature gardens. Boldly coloured bedrooms contain a host of thoughtful extras. Light supper by arrangement.

3 rooms ⊊ – ♦£ 75/100 ♦♦£ 90/100

⊠ LL24 0PU – On Ty Mawr rd – ℰ 01690 760410 – www.penmachnohall.co.uk – Closed Christmas-New Year

BODUAN – Gwynedd → See Pwllheli

BRECHFA
Carmarthenshire – Regional map n° **19**-B3
▶ London 216 mi – Cardiff 71 mi – Birmingham 183 mi – Liverpool 164 mi

Ty Mawr 🗻 ⛲ 🏠 🅿

TRADITIONAL · TRADITIONAL 16C stone farmhouse, set in the centre of the village next to the river. It's personally run and boasts charm and character aplenty, with exposed bricks, wooden beams and open fires. It has a comfy lounge and pine-furnished bedrooms. The modern menu has Welsh twists and produce is homemade or from the valley.

6 rooms ⌷ – ♦£ 80 ♦♦£ 115/130

✉ SA32 7RA – ✆ 01267 202332 – www.wales-country-hotel.co.uk

BRECON
Powys – Pop. 8 250 – Regional map n° **19**-C3
▶ London 171 mi – Cardiff 40 mi – Carmarthen 31 mi – Gloucester 65 mi

🏠 Felin Glais 🗻 ⛲ 🏠 🅿 ⚡

TRADITIONAL · COSY 17C stone barn and mill, set in a tranquil hamlet and run with pride. Spacious interior has a pleasant 'lived in' feel; cosy, homely bedrooms have toiletries and linen from Harrods. Large beamed lounge; dine here, at the communal table, or in the conservatory in summer. Lengthy menu – order two days ahead.

4 rooms ⌷ – ♦£ 90/100 ♦♦£ 90/100

Aberyscir ✉ LD3 9NP – West : 4 mi by Cradoc rd turning right immediately after bridge – ✆ 01874 623107 – www.felinglais.co.uk – Closed 25 December

🍴 Felin Fach Griffin

😊 **MODERN BRITISH · INN** Located in picturesque countryside; a rather unique pub with bright paintwork, colourful artwork and an extremely laid-back atmosphere. The young serving team are friendly and have good knowledge of what they're serving. Following the motto 'simple things, done well', dishes are straightforward, tasty and refined. Pleasant bedrooms come with comfy beds but no TVs.

Menu £ 22/29 – Carte £ 30/37

7 rooms ⌷ – ♦£ 110/140 ♦♦£ 130/170

Felin Fach ✉ LD3 0UB – Northeast : 4.75 mi by B 4602 off A 470 – ✆ 01874 620111 – www.felinfachgriffin.co.uk – Closed 25 December and early January

BRIDGEND PEN-Y-BONT
Bridgend – Pop. 46 757 – Regional map n° **19**-B4
▶ London 177 mi – Cardiff 20 mi – Swansea 23 mi

🏠 Great House 🏠 🏯 ⛲ 🅿

HISTORIC · CLASSIC A welcoming 15C listed property; reputedly a gift from Elizabeth I to the Earl of Leicester and once home to the Lord of the Manor. The guest areas have character and bedrooms are comfy – those in the coach house are the most modern.

13 rooms ⌷ – ♦£ 75/90 ♦♦£ 99/135

High St, Laleston ✉ CF32 0HP – West : 2 mi on A 473 – ✆ 01656 657644 – www.great-house-laleston.co.uk – Closed 24-27 December

Leicester's – See restaurant listing

XX Leicester's ⓝ

MODERN CUISINE · INTIMATE A friendly team welcome you to this smart hotel restaurant, where striking sculptures are dotted about. Lunch sees a good value, flexible menu, while at dinner you'll find more interesting combinations and eye-catching presentation.

Menu £ 20/30 – Carte £ 24/48

Great House Hotel, High St, Laleston ✉ CF32 0HP – ✆ 01656 657644 – www.great-house-laleston.co.uk – Closed 24-27 December, Sunday dinner and bank holidays

BUILTH WELLS LLANFAIR-YM-MUALLT

Powys – Pop. 2 829 – Regional map n° **19**-C3

▶ London 191 mi – Cardiff 63 mi – Brecon 20 mi – Swansea 58 mi

🏠 Rhedyn   ✿ ⌂ ⟨ 🛏 🅿

FAMILY · PERSONALISED Former forester's cottage with a small garden and pleasant country views, run by very welcoming owners. Tiny lounge with a bookcase full of local info and DVDs; cosy communal dining room where home-cooked, local market produce is served. Good-sized, modern bedrooms feature heavy wood furnishings, good facilities and quirky touches. Tea and cake are served on arrival.

3 rooms 🖙 – 🛉£ 85 🛉🛉£ 95

Cilmery ✉ LD2 3LH – West : 4 mi on A 483 – ☏ 01982 551944
– www.rhedynguesthouse.co.uk

BWLCHTOCYN – Gwynedd ➜ See Abersoch

CAERNARFON

Gwynedd – Pop. 9 493 – Regional map n° **19**-B1

▶ London 249 mi – Birkenhead 76 mi – Chester 68 mi – Holyhead 30 mi

🏠 Plas Dinas   ✿ ⌂ 🛏 🅿

TRADITIONAL · CLASSIC The former family home of Lord Snowdon, set in large gardens and filled with antiques, historical documents and family portraits. The spacious drawing room has an open fire and a piano; smart bedrooms boast designer touches and immaculate bathrooms. Traditional 4 course dinners are served on request.

10 rooms 🖙 – 🛉£ 109/249 🛉🛉£ 109/249

✉ LL54 7YF – South : 2.5 mi on A 487 – ☏ 01286 830214 – www.plasdinas.co.uk
– Closed Christmas

🍴 Blas   🏠

MODERN CUISINE · SIMPLE Relaxed, friendly restaurant set into the old city walls – which you can see in the upstairs room. It's open all day but menus are the most ambitious and creative at dinner. Framed recipes and striking modern art hang on the walls.

Menu £ 45 (dinner) – Carte £ 27/40

23-25 Hole in the Wall St ✉ LL55 1RF – ☏ 01286 677707
– www.blascaernarfon.co.uk – Closed 2 weeks January, 25-26 December,
1 January, Sunday dinner and Monday

at Seion Northeast: 5.5 mi by A4086 and B4366 on Seion rd ✉ Gwynedd

🏠 Ty'n Rhos Country House   ✿ ⟨ 🛏 🏠 ⌗ 🅿

FAMILY · PERSONALISED Personally run former farmhouse with a large conservatory and a cosy lounge with an inglenook fireplace. Comfortable, modern bedrooms; some have balconies or terraces and others, their own garden. The formal restaurant offers pleasant views over Anglesey; classically based dishes are presented in modern ways.

19 rooms 🖙 – 🛉£ 72/85 🛉🛉£ 95/139

✉ LL55 3AE – Southwest : 0.75 mi – ☏ 01248 670489 – www.tynrhos.co.uk

GOOD TIPS!

Wales' capital combines a rich history with top-class sporting venues, big name shops and a lively cultural scene. This is reflected in our selection, with restaurants like **Park House** – set in a late 19C property built by the founder of modern Cardiff, the 2nd Marquess of Bute – and the ultra-modern, glass-fronted **St. David's Hotel & Spa**.

CARDIFF

Cardiff – Pop. 346 090 – Regional map n° **19**-C4
London 155 mi – Birmingham 110 mi – Bristol 46 mi – Coventry 124 mi

Hotels

St David's H. & Spa

BUSINESS · MINIMALIST Modern, purpose-built hotel on the waterfront, affording lovely 360° views. Good-sized, minimalist bedrooms have a slightly funky feel; all boast balconies and bay outlooks. Smart spa features seawater pools and a dry floatation tank. Stylish restaurant with superb terrace views serves modern British dishes.

142 rooms – †£ 109/299 ††£ 109/299 – 12 suites

Town plan: D3-a - *Havannah St, Cardiff Bay ✉ CF10 5SD – ☎ 029 2045 4045 – www.principal-hayley.com/thestdavids*

Park Plaza

BUSINESS · MINIMALIST Formerly municipal offices, now a light, airy hotel with a stylish lounge, extensive conference facilities and a vast leisure centre boasting a smart, stainless steel pool and 8 treatment rooms. Stark, modern bedrooms have laptop safes and slate bathrooms. Informal brasserie serves international dishes.

129 rooms – †£ 89/320 ††£ 89/320 – ☕ £ 13

Town plan: C1-s - *Greyfriars Rd ✉ CF10 3AL – ☎ 029 2011 1111*
– www.parkplazacardiff.com
– Closed 25-26 December

Cathedral 73

TOWNHOUSE · CONTEMPORARY Delightful Victorian terraced house on the edge of the city, with boutique furnishings, designer bedrooms and a chauffeur-driven Rolls Royce. Afternoon tea is served in the spacious sitting room and breakfast, in the orangery.

10 rooms ☕ – †£ 150/350 ††£ 150/350

Town plan: B1-c - *73 Cathedral Rd ✉ CF11 9HE – ☎ 029 2023 5005*
– www.cathedral73.com

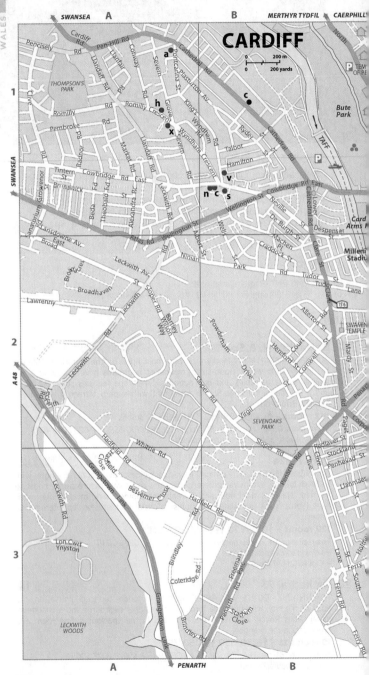

CATHAYS · Miskin St
Park Dr
CATHAYS · UNIVERSITY
PARK   COLLEGE
Salisbury Rd
ALEXANDRA
GARDENS
NATIONAL MUSEUM
OF WALES
City
Hall   Gorsedd
Gardens
Law
Courts
Cardiff
Castle
Military
Museums
Queen
St David's
SHOPPING
CENTRE
St John's
Church
Castle
St
Central
Market
TABERNACL
Wood
CARDIFF
CENTRAL
CALLAGHAN
SQUARE

Partridge
Elm · St · Lane
Elm
Broadway
Four
Elms Rd
Diamond
St
Pearl
CARDIFF
NEW SYNAGOGUE
Moira Terrace
Moira
Janer St
Ordell
St
Adamsdown
Lane
Sanquahar
St
Tyndall
St
Lewis
Rd

Bute East Dock

Keen Rd
East Moors Rd
Ocean Way
Nettle
Rd
East Moors Rd
Galleon
Way
ROATH
DOCK

CARDIFF
BAY   THE RED DRAGON
CENTRE
BUTETOWN
Coal
Exchange
Wales Milennium
Centre
Pierhead
Building   Y Senedd
Techniquest
MERMAID
QUAY
Norwegian
Church
CARDIFF BAY
HAMADRYAD
PARK
TAFF
CARDIFF BAY
WETLANDS RESERVE
CARDIFF BAY
YACHT CLUB
Windsor Esplanade

1

2

3

WALES

Restaurants

XXX Park House

MODERN CUISINE · ELEGANT Striking building designed by William Burgess in the late 1800s, overlooking Gorsedd Gardens. The oak-panelled dining room has a formal air. Menus are modern – each dish is matched with a wine from the impressive New World list.

Menu £ 25 (lunch) – Carte £ 40/66

Town plan: C1-p - *20 Park Pl.* ⊠ *CF10 3DQ –* ✆ *029 2022 4343*
– www.parkhouserestaurant.co.uk – Closed 24-25 December, 1-11 January and Monday

XX Purple Poppadom

INDIAN · DESIGN Smart Indian restaurant with bold purple décor. Classic combinations are cooked in a refined modern style and given a personal twist. The tasting menus provide plenty of interest and the seafood dishes are particularly popular.

Menu £ 11 (weekday lunch)/45 – Carte £ 20/37

Town plan: B1-n - *185a Cowbridge Rd East* ⊠ *CF11 9AJ –* ✆ *029 2022 0026*
– www.purplepoppadom.com – Closed 25-26 December, 1 January and Monday

X 'Bully's

FRENCH · NEIGHBOURHOOD A hands-on owner runs this established neighbourhood bistro, which displays a fascinating array of memorabilia. Classic French dishes feature on a wide choice of menus – some with wines to match. They also hold regular themed evenings.

Menu £ 20 (weekday dinner) – Carte £ 27/45

Town plan: A1-x - *5 Romilly Cres.* ⊠ *CF11 9NP –* ✆ *029 2022 1905*
– www.bullysrestaurant.co.uk – Closed Christmas and Sunday dinner

X Arbennig

REGIONAL CUISINE · SIMPLE Homely neighbourhood bistro with a buzzy feel. Daily baked bread is made to match the dishes on the weekly changing menu. Cooking covers all bases, from soup to steak, and there's a great value set selection available at lunch.

Menu £ 16 (lunch) – Carte £ 19/42

Town plan: A1-h - *6-10 Romilly Cres.* ⊠ *CF11 9NR –* ✆ *029 2034 1264*
– www.arbennig.co.uk – Closed Sunday dinner and Monday

X Potted Pig

TRADITIONAL BRITISH · RUSTIC Atmospheric restaurant in a stripped back former bank vault, with brick walls, barrel ceilings and a utilitarian feel. Lesser-known products and cuts of meat are used in robust, tasty dishes. The gin cocktails are a speciality.

Menu £ 12 (weekday lunch) – Carte £ 28/44

Town plan: C1-s - *27 High St* ⊠ *CF10 1PU –* ✆ *029 2022 4817*
– www.thepottedpig.com – Closed 23 December-3 January, Monday and dinner Sunday

X Mint & Mustard

INDIAN · NEIGHBOURHOOD Well-run, welcoming neighbourhood restaurant with a modern, laid-back feel; ask for a table in the front room. The chef's training in Kerala is reflected in the extensive menu of original, authentic Indian dishes and well-balanced spicing.

Menu £ 33/53 – Carte £ 17/32

134 Whitchurch Rd ⊠ *CF14 3LZ – Northwest : 1.75 mi on A 469*
– ✆ *029 2062 0333 (booking essential at dinner) – www.mintandmustard.com*
– Closed 25-26 December and 1 January

✕ La Cuina   AC 🍽

SPANISH · BISTRO A smart, well-stocked deli sells top quality imported Spanish produce and the rustic restaurant serves authentic Spanish dishes with strong Catalonian influences. Tapas is served at lunch and on Wednesday evenings.

Carte £ 26/46

Town plan: B1-v - *11 Kings Rd* ⊠ *CF11 9BZ* – ℰ *029 2019 0265*
– www.lacuina.co.uk – Closed 3-24 August, 23-27 December and Sunday-Tuesday

✕ Ffresh   🛖 � & AC 🍷

TRADITIONAL BRITISH · BRASSERIE Located within the striking, modern 'Wales Millennium Centre', overlooking the piazza and frequented by theatregoers. Large, airy interior with a relaxed atmosphere. Simple, classical cooking is founded on fresh Welsh ingredients.

Menu £ 17/24 – Carte £ 23/38

Town plan: D3-x - *Wales Millennium Centre, Bute Plas, Cardiff Bay* ⊠ *CF10 5AL*
– ℰ 029 2063 6465 – www.ffresh.org.uk – Closed 25 December, Monday in winter and Sunday dinner

✕ Fish at 85

SEAFOOD · SIMPLE Simplicity is key at this unpretentious, pared-down restaurant, where a large fish counter displays the latest catch from the day boats. Choose your fish, your cooking method and your accompaniments, and let the chef do the rest.

Menu £ 20 (weekday lunch) – Carte £ 26/45

Town plan: A1-a - *85 Pontcanna St* ⊠ *CF11 9HS* – ℰ *029 2023 5666 (booking essential at dinner) – www.fishat85.co.uk – Closed Sunday dinner, Monday and Tuesday*

✕ Chez Francis   AC

FRENCH · SIMPLE Intimate eatery run by an experienced French owner. Dine at tightly packed tables in the narrow bistro or at barrels which act as the bar. All the classics are here from Bayonne ham to coq au vin, roast duck to tarte au citron.

Menu £ 15 (lunch) – Carte £ 22/34

Town plan: B1-c - *185 Cowbridge Rd East* ⊠ *CF11 9AJ* – ℰ *029 2022 4959*
– www.chez-francis.co.uk – Closed 2 weeks August, Sunday and Monday

✕ Casanova

ITALIAN · SIMPLE Long-standing restaurant near the stadium. Flavoursome country dishes are a perfect match for the rustic, osteria-style interior, and range from carpaccio of beef to homemade pasta with a rich ragu or roast mallard with polenta.

Menu £ 15/30

Town plan: C1-c - *13 Quay St* ⊠ *CF10 1EA* – ℰ *029 2034 4044*
– www.casanovacardiff.co.uk – Closed Sunday and bank holidays

✕ Chai St   AC

INDIAN · EXOTIC DÉCOR Vibrantly decorated Indian restaurant with a mix of wooden seating; some tables you share. Simple menus focus on thalis, which come with meat, rice, vegetables, naan, poppadoms and raita. Dishes are well-spiced and good value.

Carte £ 11/18

Town plan: B1-s - *153 Cowbridge Rd East* ⊠ *CF11 9AH* – ℰ *029 2022 8888 (bookings not accepted) – www.chaistreet.com – Closed 25-26 December*

CARMARTHEN

Carmarthenshire – Pop. 15 854 – Regional map n° **19**-B3

▶ London 219 mi – Fishguard 47 mi – Haverfordwest 32 mi – Swansea 27 mi

WALES

at Felingwm Uchaf Northeast: 8 mi by A40 on B4310 ⊠ Carmarthen

🏠 Allt y Golau Uchaf   🛋 ⅛ 🅿 🚬

TRADITIONAL · COSY Converted farmhouse dating from 1812, set up a steep slope on a two acre smallholding. Well-kept, rustic interior; neat, pine-furnished bedrooms have a homely feel. Extensive breakfasts feature local meats and eggs from their own hens.

3 rooms ⊴ – †£ 45 ††£ 70

⊠ SA32 7BB – North : 0.5 mi on B 4310 – 𝒞 01267 290455 – www.alltygolau.com – Closed 20 December-2 January

at Llanllawddog Northeast: 8 mi by A485

🏠 Glangwili Mansion   🛁 🛋 ⅛ 🅿

FAMILY · MODERN Part-17C mansion rebuilt in a Georgian style, set in a great location on the edge of the forest. The spacious interior features sleek tiled floors, contemporary artwork and bright, bold bedrooms with modern oak furnishings.

3 rooms ⊴ – †£ 89/95 ††£ 105/145

⊠ SA32 7JE – 𝒞 01267 253735 – www.glangwilimansion.co.uk – Closed 24-25, 31 December and 1 January

at Nantgaredig East: 5 mi by A4300 on A4310 ⊠ Carmarthen

🍴 Y Polyn   🛋 🅿

TRADITIONAL BRITISH · PUB Small, rustic pub on a busy country road, set close to a stream and boasting pleasant views. Cooking is stout, filling and British at heart, offering satisfying soups, fresh salads, slow-cooked meats and classical puddings.

Menu £ 17 (weekday lunch)/35

⊠ SA32 7LH – South : 1 mi on B 4310 – 𝒞 01267 290000 (booking advisable) – www.ypolyn.co.uk – Closed Sunday dinner and Monday

COLWYN BAY BAE COLWYN

Conwy – Pop. 29 405 – Regional map n° **19**-B1

▶ London 237 mi – Birkenhead 50 mi – Chester 42 mi – Holyhead 41 mi

🍴 Bryn Williams at Porth Eirias 🆕   ≤ & 🆎 🍽

MODERN BRITISH · DESIGN If you're looking for a relaxed, friendly environment, this striking beachside brasserie with faux industrial styling and blue leather banquettes is the place to come. Cooking is pleasingly unfussy and local seafood is to the fore.

Carte £ 18/34

The Promenade ⊠ LL29 8HH – 𝒞 01492 577525 – www.portheirias.com – Closed 25 December

🍴 Pen-y-Bryn   🛋 🛋 & ⇔ 🅿

TRADITIONAL CUISINE · PUB Unassuming pub with a spacious, open-plan interior, a laid-back feel and impressive panoramic views over Colwyn Bay, especially from the garden and terrace. The extensive all-day menu ranges from pub classics to more adventurous fare.

Carte £ 20/37

Pen-y-Bryn Rd, Upper Colwyn Bay ⊠ LL29 6DD – Southwest : 1 mi by B 5113 – 𝒞 01492 533360 – www.penybryn-colwynbay.co.uk

at Rhos-on-Sea Northwest: 1 mi ⊠ Colwyn Bay

🏠 Plas Rhos House   ≤ ⅛ 🅿

TRADITIONAL · PERSONALISED Smartly refurbished 19C house with a pleasant terrace, on a small street overlooking the sea. Cosy lounge and bright, cheery breakfast room. Bedrooms have modern bathrooms and thoughtful extras such as chocolates and a decanter of sherry.

5 rooms ⊴ – †£ 65/85 ††£ 85/110

53 Cayley Promenade ⊠ LL28 4EP – 𝒞 01492 543698 – www.plasrhos.co.uk – Closed November-Mid March

CONWY

Conwy – Pop. 3 873 – Regional map n° **19**-B1

▶ London 241 mi – Caernarfon 22 mi – Chester 46 mi – Holyhead 37 mi

XX Signatures 　　　　　　　　　　　　🛋 ⅗ AC P

MODERN CUISINE · DESIGN Stylish restaurant with elegantly laid tables and a well-versed team – set in a holiday park close to the sea. Brasserie classics and snacks at lunch; more inventive, modern choices at dinner including the chef's 'Signature' dishes.

Menu £ 22 (weekday dinner) – Carte £ 33/52

Aberconwy Resort and Spa ⊠ LL32 8GA – Northwest 1.5 mi by A 547 – ☏ 01492 583513 (booking advisable) – www.signaturesrestaurant.co.uk – Closed Monday and Tuesday

🍴 Groes Inn 　　　　　　　　　　　　🖙 ⇐ 🍴 🛋 P

TRADITIONAL CUISINE · INN The first licensed house in Wales, dating from 1573, in a great location in the foothills of Snowdonia. An appealing menu offers traditional dishes with the occasional international flavour. Spacious, comfy bedrooms – some with a balcony or terrace; ask for one at the rear with far-reaching rural views.

Carte £ 21/41

14 rooms ⌧ – ♦£ 100/175 ♦♦£ 125/200

⊠ LL32 8TN – South : 3 mi on B 5106 – ☏ 01492 650545 – www.groesinn.com – Closed Sunday dinner and Monday November-mid March

at Rowen South: 3.5 mi by B5106

🏠 Tir Y Coed 　　　　　　　　　　　　🌲 🐾 🍴 P

COUNTRY HOUSE · PERSONALISED Late 19C house in a secluded valley at the foothills of Snowdonia. With mature gardens which are a haven for wildlife, this is an ideal spot for those who have come away to unwind. Cosy bedrooms feature smart, modern bathrooms. The intimate dining room offers a daily menu of tried-and-tested classics.

7 rooms (dinner included) ⌧ – ♦£ 120/170 ♦♦£ 135/185

⊠ LL32 8TP – ☏ 01492 650219 – www.tirycoed.com

COWBRIDGE Y BONT FAEN

The Vale of Glamorgan – Pop. 3 616 – Regional map n° **19**-B4

▶ London 170 mi – Cardiff 15 mi – Swansea 30 mi

X Arboreal 　　　　　　　　　　　　　　　　🖳

MEDITERRANEAN CUISINE · RUSTIC There's a lively Antipodean vibe at this all-day bar and café, where the chef uses local produce in dishes with a Mediterranean, Asian and North African edge. Bespoke, wood-fired pizzas feature highly and folk music accompanies.

Carte £ 20/33

68 Eastgate ⊠ CF71 7AB – ☏ 01446 775093 – www.arboreal.uk.com – Closed first 2 weeks January and Monday

CRICCIETH

Gwynedd – Pop. 1 753 – Regional map n° **19**-B2

▶ London 249 mi – Caernarfon 17 mi – Shrewsbury 85 mi

🏠 Bron Eifion 　　　　　　　　　　🌲 🐾 🍴 🍽 ⚒ P

COUNTRY HOUSE · CONTEMPORARY Characterful country house built in 1883 for a wealthy slate merchant; the feature staircase is constructed from Oregon pitch pine, which he brought back from the USA. Spacious modern bedrooms; some with carved wooden beds from the Middle East. Lovely garden views and an extensive menu in the restaurant.

18 rooms ⌧ – ♦£ 95/135 ♦♦£ 145/215

⊠ LL52 0SA – West : 1 mi on A 497 – ☏ 01766 522385 – www.broneifion.co.uk

✗ **Dylan's** Ⓝ   🍸 ⌕ 🏠 ♿ 🅰️Ⓒ

MODERN BRITISH · FAMILY A striking art deco inspired seafront building designed by Sir Clough Williams-Ellis in the 1950s. Extensive all-day menus offer everything from coffee and cake to seafood specials. Sit in one of two wings or out on the terrace.

Carte £18/57

Esplanade ✉ LL52 0HU – ☎ 01766 522773 – www.dylansrestaurant.co.uk – Closed 25-26 December

CRICKHOWELL CRUCYWEL

Powys – Pop. 2 063 – Regional map n° **19**-C4

▶ London 169 mi – Abergavenny 6 mi – Brecon 14 mi – Cardiff 40 mi

🏨 **Bear**   🛏️ 🏋️ 🅿️

TRADITIONAL · COSY Well-known, family-run coaching inn filled with various charming rooms and dating from the 15C. Bedrooms are modern; the most characterful are in the main house and feature beams, four-posters and fireplaces; some have jacuzzis.

36 rooms ☲ – ♛£ 84/141 ♛♛£ 104/177 – 1 suite

High St ✉ NP8 1BW – ☎ 01873 810408 – www.bearhotel.co.uk – Closed 25 December

Bear – See restaurant listing

🍽️ **Bear**   🛏️ 🅿️

TRADITIONAL BRITISH · INN Well-maintained 15C coaching inn adorned with hanging baskets and full of nooks and crannies. The menu offers honest pub classics alongside more elaborate specials. Sit in the hugely characterful lounge-bar or more formal restaurant.

Carte £23/47

High St ✉ NP8 1BW – ☎ 01873 810408 (bookings not accepted) – www.bearhotel.co.uk – Closed 25 December

CROSS ASH – Monmouthshire → See Abergavenny

CROSSGATES – Powys → See Llandrindod Wells

DENBIGH

Denbighshire – Pop. 8 514 – Regional map n° **19**-C1

▶ London 215 mi – Cardiff 162 mi – Swansea 151 mi – Telford 70 mi

🏨 **Castle House**   ⌕ 🛏️ 🅿️

COUNTRY HOUSE · PERSONALISED Set by the ruins of the 16C cathedral, overlooking the Vale of Clwyd; its gardens incorporate the old town walls. Bedrooms retain their period character and the décor blends the old and new. Have afternoon tea by the fire or in the garden.

4 rooms ☲ – ♛£ 85/170 ♛♛£ 145/180

Bull Ln ✉ LL16 3LY – ☎ 01745 816860 – www.castlehousebandb.co.uk – Closed Christmas

DINAS CROSS – Pembrokeshire → See Newport

DOLFOR

Powys – Regional map n° **19**-C2

▶ London 199 mi – Cardiff 93 mi – Oswestry 34 mi – Ludlow 39 mi

🏨 **Old Vicarage**   🌿 ⌕ 🛏️ 🍽️ 🅿️

TRADITIONAL · PERSONALISED Extended 19C red-brick house – formerly a vicarage – with large gardens where they grow the produce used in their home-cooked meals. Classical, country house style lounge and dining room. Cosy bedrooms – named after local rivers – mix period furnishings with bright modern colours. Chutney, preserves and soaps are for sale and afternoon tea is served on arrival.

4 rooms ☲ – ♛£ 70/150 ♛♛£ 95/150

✉ SY16 4BN – North : 1.5 mi by A 483 – ☎ 01686 629051 – www.theoldvicaragedolfor.co.uk – Closed Christmas-New Year

DOLGELLAU

Gwynedd – Pop. 2 688 – Regional map n° **19**-B2

▶ London 221 mi – Birkenhead 72 mi – Chester 64 mi – Shrewsbury 57 mi

Penmaenuchaf Hall

COUNTRY HOUSE · PERSONALISED Personally run Victorian house with wood panelling, ornate ceilings and stained glass windows. Bedrooms blend the traditional and the modern; some have balconies overlooking the beautiful grounds, mountains and estuary. Classic dishes and a well-chosen wine list in the formal conservatory dining room.

14 rooms 🖭 – †£ 130/195 ††£ 180/290

Penmaenpool ✉ LL40 1YB – West : 1.75 mi on A 493 (Tywyn Rd) – ℰ 01341 422129 – www.penhall.co.uk – Closed 12-22 December and 4-17 January

Ffynnon

TOWNHOUSE · PERSONALISED A spacious Victorian house which once operated as a cottage hospital. Original features and period furnishings abound, offset by stylish modern designs which pay great attention to detail. Keep your wine and snacks in the pantry and enjoy homemade crumpets or pancakes for breakfast. Outdoor hot tub.

6 rooms 🖭 – †£ 100/210 ††£ 150/210

Love Ln, off Cader Rd ✉ LL40 1RR – ℰ 01341 421774 – www.ffynnontownhouse.com – Closed Christmas

at Llanelltyd Northwest: 2.25 mi by A470 on A496

✕✕ Mawddach

MODERN CUISINE · RUSTIC Stylish barn conversion run by two brothers and set on the family farm. The terrace and dining room offer superb views of the mountains and estuary. Unfussy Italian-influenced cooking features lamb from the farm and veg from the garden.

Carte £ 26/41

✉ LL40 2TA – ℰ 01341 421752 – www.mawddach.com – Closed 2 weeks November, 1 week January, 1 week spring and Sunday dinner-Wednesday

FELINGWM UCHAF – Carmarthenshire ➡ See Carmarthen

FISHGUARD

Pembrokeshire – Pop. 3 419 – Regional map n° **19**-A3

▶ London 265 mi – Cardiff 110 mi – Haverfordwest 16 mi

Manor Town House

TOWNHOUSE · PERSONALISED Well-run, listed Georgian townhouse, boasting fabulous harbour views. Stylish, elegant lounges and individually designed, antique-furnished bedrooms; some in art deco and some in Victorian styles. Tasty breakfasts; charming owners.

6 rooms 🖭 – †£ 75/95 ††£ 85/120

11 Main St ✉ SA65 9HG – ℰ 01348 873260 – www.manortownhouse.com – Closed 24-27 December

GLYNARTHEN

Ceredigion – Regional map n° **19**-B3

▶ London 237 mi – Swansea 53 mi – Carmarthen 25 mi

Penbontbren

COUNTRY HOUSE · CONTEMPORARY Converted farm buildings surrounded by an attractive landscaped garden and 35 acres of rolling countryside. Spacious, stylish bedrooms; each has a sitting room, a mini bar, a coffee machine and a patio. The smart breakfast room features exposed stone, bold wallpaper, Portmeirion china and an extensive menu.

5 rooms 🖭 – †£ 80/95 ††£ 99/125

Glynarthen ✉ SA44 6PE – North : 1 mi taking first left at crossroads then next left onto unmarked lane – ℰ 01239 810248 – www.penbontbren.com – Closed Christmas

WALES

HARLECH
Gwynedd – Pop. 1 762 – Regional map n° **19**-B2
▶ London 241 mi – Chester 72 mi – Dolgellau 21 mi

XX **Castle Cottage**
CLASSIC CUISINE · COSY Sweet little cottage behind Harlech Castle, with a cosy yet surprisingly contemporary interior. Start with canapés and an aperitif in the lounge; the table is yours for the evening. Classical menus feature local produce and modern touches. Spacious bedrooms have smart bathrooms and stunning mountain views.

Menu £ 40

7 rooms ⌷ – ♦£ 85/125 ♦♦£ 130/175

Pen Llech ✉ LL46 2YL – By B 4573 – ☏ 01766 780479 (booking essential) – www.castlecottageharlech.co.uk – dinner only – Closed 3 weeks October-November and Sunday-Wednesday November-February

HAVERFORDWEST HWLFFORDD
Pembrokeshire – Pop. 14 596 – Regional map n° **19**-A3
▶ London 250 mi – Fishguard 15 mi – Swansea 57 mi

🏠 **Lower Haythog Farm**
TRADITIONAL · COSY Welcoming guesthouse with mature gardens, part-dating from the 14C and set on a working dairy farm. Cosy bedrooms feature bespoke cherry wood furniture and organic toiletries. Pleasant lounge and conservatory. Aga-cooked breakfasts.

4 rooms ⌷ – ♦£ 55/65 ♦♦£ 75/85

Spittal ✉ SA62 5QL – Northeast : 5 mi on B 4329 – ☏ 01437 731279 – www.lowerhaythogfarm.co.uk

🏠 **Paddock**
FAMILY · MODERN Contemporary guesthouse on a working dairy farm. Comfy lounge with books, board games and a wood-burning stove. Modern bedrooms feature chunky wood furniture and sleigh beds made up with Egyptian cotton linen. Home-cooked meals rely on local and market produce; eggs are from their own hens.

3 rooms ⌷ – ♦£ 60/65 ♦♦£ 80/85

Lower Haythog, Spittal ✉ SA62 5QL – Northeast : 5 mi on B 4329 – ☏ 01437 731531 – www.thepaddockwales.co.uk

HAWARDEN PENARLÂG
Flintshire – Pop. 1 858 – Regional map n° **19**-C1
▶ London 205 mi – Chester 9 mi – Liverpool 17 mi – Shrewsbury 45 mi

🍴 **Glynne Arms**
MODERN CUISINE · PUB 200 year old coaching inn opposite Hawarden Castle; owned by the descendants of PM William Gladstone. Choose between bar snacks, steaks from the estate or classically inspired dishes with modern twists. Desserts are a highlight.

Carte £ 22/34

3 Glynne Way ✉ CH3 3NS – ☏ 01244 569988 – www.theglynnearms.co.uk – Closed 25 December

HAY-ON-WYE Y GELLI
Powys – Pop. 1 846 – Regional map n° **33**-C3
▶ Cardiff 59 mi – Brecon 16 mi – Hereford 21 mi

🏠 **Bear** ❿
TOWNHOUSE · PERSONALISED A listed 16C building which blends the old and the new; it has, over the years, been a private house, a pub and even an antiques shop. The walled garden is something of a hidden gem – relax with a book from their extensive collection.

3 rooms ⌷ – ♦£ 55/80 ♦♦£ 80/100

2 Bear St ✉ HR3 5AN – ☏ 01497 821302 – www.thebearhay.com – Closed Christmas and New Year

HOWEY – Powys → See Llandrindod Wells

LLANARMON DYFFRYN CEIRIOG
Wrexham – Regional map n° **19**-C2
▶ London 196 mi – Chester 33 mi – Shrewsbury 32 mi

🛏 Hand at Llanarmon

TRADITIONAL CUISINE · INN Rustic, personally run inn with stone walls, open fires and ancient beams, which provides a warm welcome and wholesome meals to those travelling through the lush Ceiriog Valley. Generous portions of fresh, flavoursome cooking. Cosy bedrooms offer hill views and modern bathrooms; most have a roll-top bath.

Carte £ 16/37

13 rooms ⌂ – ♦£ 55/95 ♦♦£ 95/150
✉ LL20 7LD – ☎ 01691 600666 – www.thehandhotel.co.uk

LLANARTHNEY
Carmarthenshire – Regional map n° **33**-B3
▶ London 207 mi – Cardiff 62 mi – Fishguard 52 mi

🏠 Llwyn Helyg Ⓝ

FAMILY · PERSONALISED A striking modern house with marble floors and stylish furnishings. A grand oak staircase leads to luxurious bedrooms with jacuzzi baths and rain showers. Music lovers will appreciate the comfy, well-equipped 'Listening Room'.

3 rooms ⌂ – ♦£ 105/125 ♦♦£ 135/155
✉ SA32 8HJ – South : 0.25 mi by the side road across from Wright's
– ☎ 01558 668778 – www.llwynhelygcountryhouse.co.uk

LLANDDERFEL
Gwynedd – Pop. 4 500 – Regional map n° **19**-C2
▶ London 210 mi – Cardiff 157 mi – Birmingham 97 mi – Liverpool 72 mi

🏰 Palé Hall

HISTORIC · PERSONALISED An impressive Victorian house with a beautiful wood-panelled hall and some lovely marquetry on display; it's coming to the end of an extensive refurbishment as we go to print. Smartly refurbished bedrooms retain a classic feel; one has a half-tester bed thought to have been slept in by Queen Victoria. The elegant dining room features Zoffany wallpaper and custom-made chandeliers.

18 rooms ⌂ – ♦£ 165 ♦♦£ 190/400 – 2 suites
Palé Estate ✉ LL23 7PS – ☎ 01678 530285 – www.palehall.co.uk

LLANDDEWI SKIRRID – Monmouthshire → See Abergavenny

LLANDENNY
Monmouthshire – Regional map n° **33**-C4
▶ London 136 mi – Cardiff 30 mi – Brecon 33 mi

🛏 Raglan Arms Ⓝ

MODERN CUISINE · PUB Dine by the open fire in the bar or in the bright conservatory which overlooks the spacious terrace. Menus feature a few pub favourites but cooking is very much in the modern vein; dishes take on an extra degree of refinement in the evening.

Menu £ 18 (weekday lunch) – Carte £ 25/43
✉ NP15 1DL – ☎ 01291 690800 – www.raglanarms.co.uk – Closed
24-25 December, Sunday dinner and Monday

LLANDRILLO
Denbighshire – ✉ Corwen – Pop. 1 048 – Regional map n° **19**-C2
▶ London 210 mi – Chester 40 mi – Dolgellau 26 mi – Shrewsbury 46 mi

WALES

✖✖ Tyddyn Llan (Bryan Webb) 🍴 🔄 🧺 🛏 🅿

🐝 **CLASSIC CUISINE · ELEGANT** Attractive former shooting lodge in a pleasant valley location, surrounded by lovely gardens and run by a husband and wife team. Spacious country house lounges and a blue-hued, two-roomed restaurant. Hearty, satisfying cooking is based around the classics; tasting menus show the kitchen's talent to the full. Smart, elegant bedrooms offer a good level of facilities.
→ Griddled scallops with cauliflower purée, pancetta, caper and raisin dressing. Loin of venison with goat's cheese gnocchi, port and elderberry sauce. Chocolate and lime cheesecake.
Menu £ 34/60

13 rooms � – †£ 155/200 ††£ 190/320

✉ LL21 0ST – ☎ 01490 440264 (booking essential) – www.tyddynllan.co.uk – dinner only and lunch Friday-Sunday – Closed last 3 weeks January, Monday and Tuesday

LLANDRINDOD WELLS

Powys – Pop. 5 309 – Regional map n° **19**-C3
▶ London 204 mi – Brecon 29 mi – Carmarthen 60 mi – Shrewsbury 58 mi

at Crossgates Northeast: 3.5 mi on A483 ✉ Llandrindod Wells

🏠 Guidfa House 🛏 ⚭ 🅿

TRADITIONAL · COSY A Georgian gentleman's residence with a pleasant garden, a smart breakfast room and a period lounge featuring an original cast iron ceiling rose. Bright, airy bedrooms; the best is in the coach house. Friendly owners serve tea on arrival.

6 rooms ⊐ – †£ 85/120 ††£ 105/140

Crossgates ✉ LD1 6RF – ☎ 01597 851241 – www.guidfahouse.co.uk

at Howey South: 1.5 mi by A483 ✉ Llandrindod Wells

🏠 Acorn Court 🔄 ≤ 🛏 ⚭ 🅿 ⇥

FAMILY · PERSONALISED Chalet-style house set in 40 acres, with views over rolling countryside towards a river and lake. Welcoming owner and a real family feel. Spacious, well-kept bedrooms come with good extras. Try the Welsh whisky porridge for breakfast.

3 rooms ⊐ – †£ 55/80 ††£ 78/90

Chapel Rd ✉ LD1 5PB – Northeast : 0.5 mi – ☎ 01597 823543
– www.acorncourt.co.uk – Closed 23-31 December

LLANDUDNO

Conwy – Pop. 15 371 – Regional map n° **19**-B1
▶ London 243 mi – Birkenhead 55 mi – Chester 47 mi – Holyhead 43 mi

🏠 Bodysgallen Hall ☂ 🔄 ≤ 🛏 🖥 ⬚ 🐎 🏋 🖤 ⚭ 🎣 🅿

LUXURY · HISTORIC A stunning National Trust owned country house in 200 acres of delightful parkland, with a 13C tower and a superb outlook to the mountains beyond. It has a welcoming open-fired hall, a characterful wood-panelled lounge and antique-furnished bedrooms – some in cottages and some affording splendid Snowdon views. The grand dining room serves modern versions of classic dishes.

31 rooms ⊐ – †£ 130/385 ††£ 180/435 – 21 suites

Royal Welsh Way ✉ LL30 1RS – Southeast : 2 mi on A 470 – ☎ 01492 584466
– www.bodysgallen.com

🏠 Osborne House ☂ ≤ 🆎 ⚭ 🅿

LUXURY · PERSONALISED Victoriana reigns in this smart townhouse overlooking the bay. Bedrooms are spacious, open-plan suites with canopied beds and lounges; chandeliers cast a romantic glow and marble bathrooms come with double-ended roll-top baths. Breakfast is served in your room. The opulent restaurant offers a wide-ranging menu.

7 rooms ⊐ – †£ 135/200 ††£ 135/200

Town plan: A1-c - 17 North Par ✉ LL30 2LP – ☎ 01492 860330
– www.osbornehouse.co.uk – Closed 18-31December

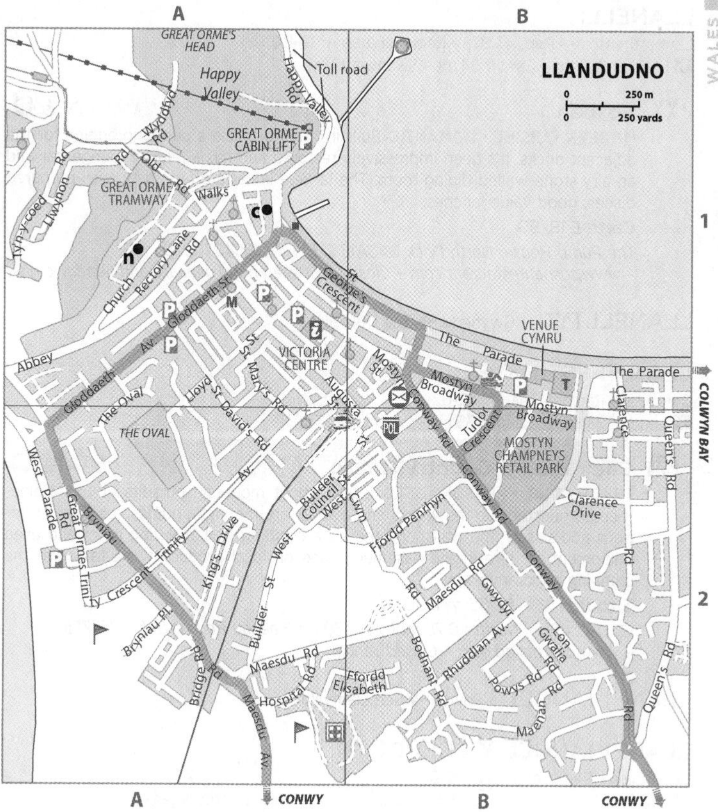

Escape Boutique B&B

TOWNHOUSE · DESIGN Attractive Arts and Crafts house with stained glass windows, parquet floors and a chic, modern interior that sets it apart. Stylish lounge and spacious, contemporary bedrooms; those on the top floor have a stunning view of the bay.

9 rooms – £ 80/134 £ 95/149

Town plan: A1-n - *48 Church Walks* ✉ *LL30 2HL* – ✆ *01492 877776* *– www.escapebandb.co.uk – Closed 18-26 December*

LLANDYBIE

Carmarthenshire – Pop. 2 813 – Regional map n° **19**-B4

London 204 mi – Birmingham 122 mi – Bristol 97 mi – Leicester 192 mi

Valans

INTERNATIONAL · FRIENDLY Simple little restaurant run by a local and his wife, with a bright red, white and black colour scheme. Fresh, unfussy dishes rely on local produce and offer classical flavour combinations. Good value light lunches; more elaborate dinners.

Menu £ 13 (lunch and early dinner) – Carte £ 28/39

Primrose House, 29 High St ✉ *SA18 3HX* – ✆ *01269 851288 (booking advisable)* *– www.valans.co.uk – Closed 25 December-2 January, Sunday dinner and Monday*

LLANELLI
Carmarthenshire – Pop. 43 878 – Regional map n° **19**-B4
▶ London 202 mi – Cardiff 54 mi – Swansea 12 mi

✗✗ Sosban ⚿ 🛆 **P**
MODERN CUISINE · ROMANTIC Built in 1872 to house a pumping engine for the adjacent docks. It's been impressively restored and has a relaxed lounge-bar and an airy stone-walled dining room. The large à la carte offers tasty, well-prepared dishes; good value lunches.
Carte £ 18/50
The Pump House, North Dock ✉ *SA15 2LF* – ✆ *01554 270020*
– www.sosbanrestaurant.com – Closed 25 December, 1 January and Sunday dinner

LLANELLTYD – Gwynedd ➜ See Dolgellau

LLAN FFESTINIOG
Gwynedd – Regional map n° **19**-B2
▶ London 234 mi – Bangor 35 mi – Wrexham 52 mi

🏠 Cae'r Blaidd Country House ⚐ 🌤 ≼ 🛏 🕸 **P**
TRADITIONAL · PERSONALISED It's all about mountain pursuits at this alpine-themed guesthouse: the welcoming owners are mountain guides; ice axes, crampons and skis fill the walls; and there's a climbing wall, a drying room and even equipment for hire in the basement. Dine on local produce while taking in the stunning panoramic view.
3 rooms ☲ – 🛉£ 55 🛉🛉£ 90
✉ *LL41 4PH – North : 0.75 mi by A 470 on Blaenau Rd* – ✆ *01766 762765*
– www.caerblaidd.com – Closed January

LLANFIHANGEL – Powys ➜ See Llanfyllin

LLANFIHANGEL-Y-CREUDDYN
Ceredigion – Regional map n° **19**-B3
▶ London 235 mi – Cardiff 109 mi – Birmingham 121 mi – Liverpool 123 mi

🏠 Y Ffarmers 🛏
REGIONAL CUISINE · RUSTIC Life in this remote, picturesque valley revolves around the passionately run village pub. Sit in the locals bar or the homely restaurant which opens onto the garden. Regional and valley produce features in satisfying, original dishes.
Carte £ 21/33
✉ *SY23 4LA* – ✆ *01974 261275 – www.yffarmers.co.uk – Closed first week January and Sunday dinner-Tuesday lunch*

LLANFYLLIN
Powys – Pop. 1 105 – Regional map n° **19**-C2
▶ London 188 mi – Chester 42 mi – Shrewsbury 24 mi – Welshpool 11 mi

✗ Seeds
REGIONAL CUISINE · RUSTIC Converted 16C red-brick cottages in a sleepy village; run with pride by a friendly husband and wife team. Cosy, pine-furnished room with an old range and a country kitchen feel. Unfussy, classical dishes and comforting homemade desserts.
Menu £ 25 (dinner) – Carte lunch £ 20/35
5 Penybryn Cottages, High St ✉ *SY22 5AP* – ✆ *01691 648604 – Closed Wednesday in winter and Sunday-Tuesday*

at Llanfihangel Southwest: 5 mi by A490 and B4393 on B4382⊠ Llanfyllin

⌂ Cyfie Farm   ♨ ⩽ 🛏 🐾 🕸 P

TRADITIONAL · PERSONALISED A 17C longhouse and several barn conversions which boast far-reaching views across the valley – take it all in from the 6-person hot tub. There's a mix of bedrooms and self-catering cottages; some with beams and wood-burning stoves.

3 rooms ⊑ – 🛉£ 85/110 🛉🛉£ 120/140

⊠ SY22 5JE – South : 1.5 mi by B 4382 – 𝒞 01691 648451 – www.cyfiefarm.co.uk – Closed November-February

LLANGAFFO → See Anglesey (Isle of)

LLANGAMMARCH WELLS

Powys – Regional map n° **19**-B3

▶ London 200 mi – Brecon 17 mi – Builth Wells 8 mi – Cardiff 58 mi

⌂ Lake Country House and Spa   ⛲ ♨ ⩽ 🛏 🖼 🖥 🕘 🐾 🎿 ✂ ⅄

TRADITIONAL · PERSONALISED Extended, part-timbered 19C country ⅄ P house in 50 acres of mature gardens and parkland, with a pond, a lake and a river. Comfortable lounges and well-appointed bedrooms with antiques and extras; some are set in a lodge. The impressive spa overlooks the river. Breakfast is in the orangery; the elegant restaurant is perfect for a classical, candlelit dinner.

32 rooms ⊑ – 🛉£ 100/145 🛉🛉£ 150/195 – 8 suites

⊠ LD4 4BS – East : 0.75 mi – 𝒞 01591 620202 – www.lakecountryhouse.co.uk

LLANGENNITH

Swansea – Regional map n° **19**-B4

▶ London 207 mi – Cardiff 61 mi – Swansea 17 mi – Newport 71 mi

⌂ Blas Gŵyr   🕸 P

FAMILY · PERSONALISED Converted farm buildings on the Gower Peninsula. Smart, well-equipped bedrooms are set around a courtyard and feature local fabrics and slate bathrooms with underfloor heating. Breakfast is taken in the small, stone-walled coffee shop.

4 rooms ⊑ – 🛉£ 105/115 🛉🛉£ 115/130

⊠ SA3 1HU – 𝒞 01792 386472 – www.blasgwyr.co.ok

LLANGOLLEN

Denbighshire – Pop. 3 466 – Regional map n° **32**-C2

▶ London 194 mi – Chester 23 mi – Holyhead 76 mi – Shrewsbury 30 mi

⌂ Geufron Hall   ♨ ⩽ 🛏 🕸 P

FAMILY · STYLISH A homely, welcoming house in a great location, with impressive views of the Vale of Llangollen. Bedrooms feature retro furnishings; Eglwseg with its private terrace is the best. Enjoy local produce at breakfast.

4 rooms ⊑ – 🛉£ 60/75 🛉🛉£ 90/120

⊠ LL20 8DY – North : 1 mi by A 539 and Wharf Hill off Dinbren Rd – 𝒞 01978 860676 – www.geufronhall.co.uk – Closed 24-25 December

LLANGRANNOG

Ceredigion – Regional map n° **19**-B3

▶ London 241 mi – Cardiff 96 mi – Aberyswyth 30 mi – Carmarthen 28 mi

⌂ Grange   ♨ 🛏 P ⇥

COUNTRY HOUSE · PERSONALISED Traditional Georgian manor house with a pretty breakfast room and individually decorated bedrooms which feature brass beds and cast iron slipper baths. On arrival, the hospitable owner welcomes you with a pot of tea beside the fire.

4 rooms ⊑ – 🛉£ 60/90 🛉🛉£ 60/90

Pentregat ⊠ SA44 6HW – Southeast : 3 mi by B 4321 on A 487 – 𝒞 01239 654121 – www.grangecountryhouse.co.uk – Restricted opening in winter

LLANLLAWDDOG – Carmarthenshire ➜ See Carmarthen

LLANRHIDIAN
Swansea – Pop. 512 – Regional map n° **19**-B4
▶ London 198 mi – Cardiff 56 mi – Aberystwyth 83 mi

XXX Fairyhill

MODERN BRITISH · ELEGANT Attractive Georgian country house with a lake and well-manicured gardens; take it all in from the terrace or the red and gold dining room. Modern menus rely on seasonal Gower produce. Spacious bedrooms blend the traditional and the contemporary and come with good facilities. Charming guest areas include a cosy bar and a modern lounge with a piano.

Menu £ 20 (weekday lunch)/50

8 rooms ☐ – †£ 180/310 ††£ 200/330

Reynoldston ✉ SA3 1BS – West : 2.5 mi by Llangennith Rd – ✆ 01792 390139 – www.fairyhill.net – Closed 3 weeks January, 25-26 December, Monday and Tuesday in winter

LLANRWST
Conwy – Pop. 3 323 – Regional map n° **19**-B1
▶ London 229 mi – Holyhead 51 mi – Chester 54 mi

Ffin y Parc Country House & Gallery

HISTORIC · PERSONALISED This Victorian slate house is an impressive art gallery, a comfy café and a likeable guesthouse all in one. The elegant, well-proportioned interior mixes the classic and the contemporary and has a slightly bohemian feel; bedrooms are bold and bathrooms are modern. Dinner is served on Fridays and Saturdays.

4 rooms ☐ – †£ 165/215 ††£ 165/215

Betwys Rd ✉ LL26 0PT – South : 1.75 mi on A 470 – ✆ 01492 642070 – www.ffinyparc.com – Closed January

LLANWRTYD WELLS
Powys – Pop. 630 – Regional map n° **19**-B3
▶ London 214 mi – Brecon 32 mi – Cardiff 68 mi – Carmarthen 39 mi

XX Carlton Riverside

TRADITIONAL BRITISH · COSY Traditional stone building in the centre of the village, with two comfy lounges and a small bar filled with books and modern art. Well-spaced tables in the dining room, which overlooks the River Irfon. Concise menu utilises local produce; classic dishes have a modern touch. Neat, tidy, well-priced bedrooms.

Carte £ 28/45

4 rooms ☐ – †£ 50 ††£ 65/100

Irfon Cres ✉ LD5 4SP – ✆ 01591 610248 – www.carltonriverside.com – dinner only – Closed 23-30 December, Sunday and Monday

LLECHRYD
Ceredigion – Pop. 875 – Regional map n° **19**-A3
▶ London 238 mi – Cardiff 93 mi – Swansea 53 mi – Newport 102 mi

Hammet House

COUNTRY HOUSE · DESIGN Attractive Georgian house built for a former Sheriff of London, Sir Benjamin Hammet. It has contemporary monochrome styling, quirky furnishings and a relaxed, bohemian feel. Bedrooms boast locally hand-made beds, good facilities and views over the grounds. The smart restaurant offers appealing modern dishes.

15 rooms ☐ – †£ 95/200 ††£ 120/220

✉ SA43 2QA – ✆ 01239 682382 – www.hammethouse.co.uk

LLYSWEN

Powys – ✉ Brecon – Regional map n° **19**-C3

▶ London 188 mi – Brecon 8 mi – Cardiff 48 mi – Worcester 53 mi

Llangoed Hall

HISTORIC · PERSONALISED Homely country house beside the River Wye, redesigned by Sir Clough Williams-Ellis in 1910 and restored by the late Sir Bernard Ashley. Delightful sitting rooms and sumptuous bedrooms feature rich fabrics, mullioned windows and antiques; the impressive art collection includes pieces by Whistler. Ambitious modern cooking is led by what's fresh in the kitchen garden.

23 rooms ☑ – †£150/500 ††£150/500

✉ LD3 0YP – Northwest : 1.25 mi on A 470 – ✆ 01874 754525
– www.llangoedhall.com

MACHYNLLETH

Powys – Pop. 2 235 – Regional map n° **19**-B2

▶ London 220 mi – Shrewsbury 56 mi – Welshpool 37 mi

ХХ Ynyshir

🕸

CREATIVE · INTIMATE Set within a beautiful part-Georgian building, an opulent restaurant with azure blue walls, striking artwork and a summery vibe. The talented chef uses superb local and foraged ingredients to create original dishes with wonderfully balanced flavours and some are finished at the table which adds a sense of theatre. Bedrooms have a chic, contemporary country house style.
→ Mackerel sweet and sour. Deer with black bean and bitter chocolate. Miso treacle tart with sour cream and sake.

Menu £40/55 – tasting menu only

10 rooms ☑ – †£250/495 ††£250/495 – 3 suites

Eglwysfach ✉ SY20 8TA – Southwest: 6 mi on A 487 – ✆ 01654 781209 (booking essential) – www.ynyshirhall.co.uk – Closed first 3 weeks January, Sunday and Monday

MENAI BRIDGE → See Anglesey (Isle of)

MOLD YR WYDDGRUG

Flintshire – Pop. 10 058 – Regional map n° **19**-C1

▶ London 211 mi – Chester 12 mi – Liverpool 22 mi – Shrewsbury 45 mi

🍴 Tavern

CLASSIC CUISINE · PUB Modern-looking pub with leather chairs and a formal feel; in contrast, the cooking is hearty and comforting. Blackboard specials, particularly the market fish, prove popular. Regular themed gourmet dinners best show the chef's talent.

Carte £20/39

Mold Rd, Alltami ✉ CH7 6LG – Northeast : 2.5 mi by A 5119 on A 494
– ✆ 01244 550485 – www.tavernrestaurant.co.uk – Closed 26 December and Monday

MONMOUTH TREFYNWY

Monmouthshire – Pop. 10 110 – Regional map n° **19**-C4

▶ London 135 mi – Abergavenny 19 mi – Cardiff 40 mi

Х Stonemill

REGIONAL CUISINE · RUSTIC Attractive 16C cider mill with exposed timbers and an old millstone at the centre of the characterful, rustic restaurant. Good value set menus are supplemented by a more ambitious evening à la carte. Dishes are hearty and classically based.

Menu £19/22 – Carte £30/41

Rockfield ✉ NP25 5SW – Northwest : 3.5 mi on B 4233 – ✆ 01600 716273
– www.thestonemill.co.uk – Closed 2 weeks January, 25-26 December, Sunday dinner and Monday

WALES

at Whitebrook South: 8.25 mi by A466 ✉ Monmouth

⭑⭑ The Whitebrook ⬅ 🛋 🏠 🎡 Ⓟ

🏵 **MODERN BRITISH · INTIMATE** You'll find this relaxed, intimate, whitewashed property off the beaten track, in a wooded valley. Cooking is modern and understated and menus showcase top quality local and foraged ingredients; descriptions are concise and the elegantly presented dishes are more complex than they first appear. Bedrooms come in muted tones and follow the theme of bringing nature inside.

→ Wye Valley asparagus with hogweed, pine and Tintern mead. Huntsham Farm suckling pig with caramelised celeriac, pear and sorrel. Black cherry with meadowsweet, cherry stone ice cream and hazelnut.

Menu £ 29/54

8 rooms 🗔 – 🛏£ 105/165 🛏🛏£ 130/190

✉ NP25 4TX – 𝒞 01600 860254 (booking essential) – www.thewhitebrook.co.uk – Closed first 2 weeks January, Tuesday lunch and Monday

MONTGOMERY TREFALDWYN

Powys – Pop. **986** – Regional map n° **19**-C2

▶ London 194 mi – Birmingham 71 mi – Chester 53 mi – Shrewsbury 30 mi

⭑⭑ The Checkers (Stéphane Borie) ⬅ 🏠

🏵 **FRENCH · FRIENDLY** Charming 18C coaching inn on the main square of a hilltop town, run by an enthusiastic Frenchman and his family. It has a characterful beamed lounge and a stylish two-roomed restaurant. Seasonal menus offer a mix of modern and classical French dishes that are executed with a deft touch, and flavours are sharply defined. Elegant bedrooms are furnished with antiques.

→ Scottish scallop with crab cannelloni, fennel, ginger and sauce vierge. Assiette of pork with pommes mousseline, caramelised pear and madeira jus. Hot raspberry soufflé with vanilla ice cream.

Menu £ 55/75 – tasting menu only

5 rooms 🗔 – 🛏£ 135/170 🛏🛏£ 150/190

Broad St ✉ SY15 6PN – 𝒞 01686 669822 – www.checkerswales.co.uk – dinner only – Closed 3 weeks January, 1 week late summer, 25-26 December, Sunday and Monday

NANTGAREDIG – Carmarthenshire → See Carmarthen

NARBERTH

Pembrokeshire – Pop. 2 265 – Regional map n° **19**-A4

▶ London 234 mi – Cardiff 88 mi – Swansea 51 mi – Rhondda 79 mi

🏠 Grove ⬰ ⬅ 🛋 Ⓟ

HISTORIC · PERSONALISED Set in 35 acres, in a charming rural location, the Grove comprises a 15C longhouse and a whitewashed property with Stuart and Victorian additions. Bedrooms blend boldly coloured walls and bright fabrics with more traditional furnishings, while the bathrooms boast underfloor heating and deep cast iron baths.

28 rooms 🗔 – 🛏£ 195/535 🛏🛏£ 210/550 – 8 suites

Molleston ✉ SA67 8BX – South : 2 mi by A 478 on Herons Brook rd – 𝒞 01834 860915 – www.thegrove-narberth.co.uk

Grove – See restaurant listing

⭑⭑ Grove ⓝ ⬅ 🛋 🎡 Ⓟ

MODERN CUISINE · ELEGANT A meal here is thought of as an event: start with a drink in the bar or in one of the lounges, then move on to either the cosy dining room or the orangery overlooking the sheltered courtyard. Refined cooking carefully balances ingredients to create some interesting combinations with original touches.

Menu £ 32/59 **s**

Grove Hotel, Molleston ✉ SA67 8BX – South : 2 mi by A 478 on Herons Brook rd – 𝒞 01834 860915 – www.thegrove-narberth.co.uk

NEWCASTLE EMLYN

Carmarthenshire – Pop. 1 883 – Regional map n° **19**-B3
▶ London 232 mi – Cardiff 88 mi – Carmarthen 21 mi

Gwesty'r Emlyn

INN · CONTEMPORARY A 300 year old coaching inn set in the centre of town and concealing a surprisingly modern interior. Guest areas include a stylish lounge, a snug bar, a small fitness room and a sauna; bedrooms are contemporary and well-equipped. The smart restaurant offers a classic menu centred around local produce.

29 rooms ⌹ – ♦£ 59/85 ♦♦£ 70/120 – 4 suites

Bridge St ⌗ SA38 9DU – ℰ 01239 710317 – www.gwestyremlynhotel.co.uk

NEWPORT

Newport – Pop. 128 060 – Regional map n° **19**-C4
▶ London 145 mi – Bristol 31 mi – Cardiff 12 mi – Gloucester 48 mi

Celtic Manor Resort

RESORT · PERSONALISED A vast resort hotel set in 1,400 acres, boasting two floors of function rooms, a shopping arcade, 3 golf courses and an impressive swimming pool and spa. Bedrooms range from Standards to Presidential Suites and from classical to modern in style. The many restaurants offer everything from grills, buffets and carveries to French bistro dishes and modern fine dining menus.

332 rooms ⌹ – ♦£ 126/271 ♦♦£ 149/308 – 14 suites

*Coldra Woods ⌗ NP18 1HQ – East : 3 mi on A 48 – ℰ 01633 413000
– www.celtic-manor.com*

Epicure by Richard Davies – See restaurant listing

XXX Epicure by Richard Davies ℕ

MODERN BRITISH · INTIMATE Start with drinks on the hotel terrace then head through to this intimate, eye-catching restaurant. Accomplished modern cooking focuses on one main ingredient per dish, with accompaniments matched to enhance its flavour.

Menu £ 33/65

*Celtic Manor Resort Hotel, ⌗ NP18 1HQ – ℰ 01633 413000 (booking essential)
– www.celtic-manor.com/epicure – dinner only and lunch Friday-Saturday
– Closed 2 weeks January, 2 weeks June-July, Sunday and Monday*

NEWPORT TREFDRAETH

Pembrokeshire – Pop. 1 162 – Regional map n° **19**-A3
▶ London 258 mi – Cardiff 118 mi – Fishguard 7 mi

Cnapan

TOWNHOUSE · PERSONALISED Keenly run, part-Georgian house in a busy coastal village. The bar and lounge have a homely feel. Well-maintained, compact bedrooms have a clean, modern style and smart shower rooms; a shared bath is available. The candlelit restaurant opens onto a large garden and offers an extensive menu of home cooking.

5 rooms ⌹ – ♦£ 65 ♦♦£ 95

East St ⌗ SA42 0SY – on A 487 – ℰ 01239 820575 – www.cnapan.co.uk – Closed January-mid-March and 25-26 December

XX Llys Meddyg

MODERN CUISINE · RUSTIC Centrally located restaurant with a kitchen garden and a slightly bohemian style. Eat in the formal dining room or the characterful, laid-back cellar bar; the owner's father's art is displayed throughout. Cooking showcases local produce in ambitious, complex dishes. Modern bedrooms have a Scandinavian style.

Carte £ 23/46

8 rooms ⌹ – ♦£ 70/140 ♦♦£ 90/160

*East St ⌗ SA42 0SY – ℰ 01239 820008 – www.llysmeddyg.com – dinner only
– Closed Monday and Tuesday November-Easter*

at Dinas Cross West: 3.25 mi on A487

🏠 Y Garth ✗ P

FAMILY · PERSONALISED Welcoming pink-washed guesthouse in a small village. Comfy lounge with a conservatory extension where homemade cakes are served on arrival. Stylish bedrooms have bright, bold décor; 'Strumble Head' has views to the peninsula.

3 rooms ☑ – †£ 70/105 ††£ 90/105

Cae Tabor ✉ SA42 0XR – Via un-named road opposite bus stop – ☎ 01348 811777 – www.bedandbreakfast-pembrokeshire.co.uk – Closed 1 week Christmas

OLD RADNOR PENCRAIG

Powys – Pop. 400 – Regional map n° **19**-C3

▶ London 180 mi – Cardiff 81 mi – Birmingham 86 mi – Liverpool 121 mi

🍺 Harp Inn ⇔ ≤ 🏠 P

TRADITIONAL CUISINE · INN This 15C stone inn welcomes drinkers and diners alike. The charming flag-floored rooms boast open fires and beams hung with hop bines and the terrace offers glorious views. 'Seasonality' and 'sustainability' are key, and menus are concise but original. Simple bedrooms come with wonderful views.

Carte £ 20/40

5 rooms ☑ – †£ 65/80 ††£ 95/110

✉ LD8 2RH – ☎ 01544 350655 – www.harpinnradnor.co.uk – Closed Monday except bank holidays, Tuesday and lunch Wednesday-Thursday

PEMBROKE PENFRO

Pembrokeshire – Pop. 7 552 – Regional map n° **19**-A4

▶ London 252 mi – Carmarthen 32 mi – Fishguard 26 mi

🏰 Lamphey Court ⇗ 🐾 ⇛ 🔲 🌐 🜨 ♨ ℔ ✗ ✗ ♿ P

HISTORIC · CLASSIC Impressive Georgian mansion, fronted by columns and surrounded by mature parkland. There's a typical country house feel throughout, from the classical lounge to the well-kept mahogany-furnished bedrooms. Smart modern spa and leisure facilities. Dine in the informal orangery or traditional dining room.

39 rooms ☑ – †£ 99/129 ††£ 109/179

✉ SA71 5NT – East : 1.75 mi by A 4139 – ☎ 01646 672273 – www.lampheycourt.co.uk

PENARTH

The Vale of Glamorgan – Pop. 27 226 – Regional map n° **19**-C4

▶ London 152 mi – Birmingham 111 mi – Bristol 47 mi – Leicester 149 mi

🏨 Holm House 🆕 ⇗ ≤ ⇛ ℔ P

BOUTIQUE HOTEL · PERSONALISED Built in 1926, this characterful Arts and Crafts house sits on the clifftop in a smart residential neighbourhood and looks over the Bristol Channel to the tiny island after which it is named. The restaurant faces the gardens and some of the bedrooms have baths by the window to make the most of the view.

12 rooms – †£ 110/130 ††£ 120/290

Marine Par ✉ CF64 3BG – ☎ 029 2070 6029 – www.holmhousehotel.com

XX James Sommerin ⇔ ≤ 🔲 ♿ ⇔
❀

MODERN CUISINE · CONTEMPORARY DÉCOR A smart yet laid-back restaurant on the esplanade, which affords panoramic views over the Severn Estuary; five of the sophisticated modern bedrooms share the wonderful outlook. Choose from the à la carte or a customisable 6 or 10 course tasting menu. Confidently executed dishes are hearty and boldly flavoured, with more playful elements appearing in the desserts.

→ Slow-cooked pork belly with octopus, peanut and soy sauce. Wild sea bass with butternut squash, fennel and spiced butter. Kalamansi with sesame and orange blossom.

Carte £ 34/52

9 rooms ☑ – †£ 140/180 ††£ 150/190

The Esplanade ✉ CF64 3AU – ☎ 029 2070 6559 – www.jamessommerinrestaurant.co.uk – Closed 26 December and Monday

XX Pier 64

MODERN CUISINE · FASHIONABLE Modern, wood-clad, all-day restaurant, set on stilts in an enviable harbour location. Light, airy interior with a smart bar and huge windows giving every table a view. Accessible menu features plenty of seafood and 28 day dry-aged steaks.

Menu £16 (weekday lunch) – Carte £24/80

Penarth Marina ⊠ CF64 1TT – ℰ 029 2000 0064 – www.pier64.co.uk
– Closed Sunday dinner

X Mint and Mustard

INDIAN · NEIGHBOURHOOD Fashionable high street restaurant with bare brick walls and exposed ducting. The menu features an extensive selection of vibrantly flavoured curries, tandoor dishes and Keralan-inspired recipes. Ingredients are locally sourced.

Carte £34/46

33-34 Windsor Ter ⊠ CF64 1AB – ℰ 029 2070 0500 (booking essential)
– www.mintandmustard.com – dinner only – Closed 25 December

The Pilot

TRADITIONAL BRITISH · PUB A neat dining pub that's part of the local community. Regulars gather in the front room; diners head to the rear. A good-sized blackboard menu mixes hearty, honest pub dishes with more adventurous offerings. Ingredients are laudably local.

Carte £21/33

67 Queens Rd ⊠ CF64 1DJ – ℰ 029 2071 0615 – www.knifeandforkfood.co.uk/pilot

PENMACHNO – Conwy → See Betws-y-Coed

PENNAL

Gwynedd – Regional map n° **19**-B2
▶ Cardiff 118 mi – Caernarfon 59 mi – Machynlleth 4 mi

Riverside

TRADITIONAL CUISINE · PUB Enter under the 'Glan Yr Afron' (Riverside) sign, then make for the 'Cwtch' with its wood-burning stove. Despite its Grade II listing, it has a bright modern feel. Hearty, no-nonsense pub classics are full of flavour and keenly priced.

Carte £19/37

⊠ SY20 9DW – ℰ 01654 791285 – www.riversidehotel-pennal.co.uk – Closed
2 weeks January and Monday October-May

PORTHCAWL

Bridgend – Pop. 15 672 – Regional map n° **19**-B4
▶ London 183 mi – Cardiff 28 mi – Swansea 18 mi

Foam Edge

TOWNHOUSE · PERSONALISED A smart, modern, semi-detached house – a family home – set next to the promenade, with great views over the Bristol Channel. Spacious, stylish bedrooms offer good facilities. Comfortable lounge and communal breakfasts.

3 rooms ⊡ – ♦£70/90 ♦♦£95/110

9 West Dr ⊠ CF36 3LS – ℰ 01656 782866 – www.foam-edge.co.uk – Closed
25 December

PORTMEIRION

Gwynedd – Regional map n° **19**-B2
▶ London 245 mi – Caernarfon 23 mi – Colwyn Bay 40 mi – Dolgellau 24 mi

WALES

🏛 Portmeirion

HISTORIC · ART DÉCO A unique, Italianate village built on a private peninsula and boasting wonderful estuary views – the life work of Sir Clough Williams-Ellis. There's an appealing 1930s hotel and snug, well-appointed bedrooms which are spread about the village. The dining room has an art deco feel and a lovely parquet floor.

46 rooms ⊡ – †£ 99/199 ††£ 119/259 – 22 suites

✉ LL48 6ER – ✆ 01766 770000 – www.portmerion-village.com – Closed 31 August-4 September

PUMSAINT
Carmarthenshire – Regional map n° **19**-B3
▶ London 227 mi – Cardiff 81 mi – Llandovery 12 mi

🍴 Dolaucothi Arms

TRADITIONAL BRITISH · RUSTIC ⋀ 300 year old drovers' inn in the picturesque Cothi Valley; it's a cosy, rustic place with a garden looking out over a river where they have 4 miles of fishing rights. One menu lists pub classics while the second is more adventurous. Bedrooms are comfy and cosy – ask if you want a TV.

Carte £ 17/29

3 rooms ⊡ – †£ 60 ††£ 75/85

✉ SA19 8UW – ✆ 01558 650237 – www.thedolaucothiarms.co.uk – Closed 16-29 January, 25-26 December, Tuesday lunch, Monday except bank holidays and midweek lunch November-February

PWLLHELI
Gwynedd – Pop. 4 076 – Regional map n° **19**-B2
▶ London 261 mi – Aberystwyth 73 mi – Caernarfon 21 mi

XX Plas Bodegroes

MODERN CUISINE · INTIMATE A charming, Grade II listed Georgian house set in peaceful grounds; inside it's beautifully decorated and features an eclectic collection of modern Welsh art. There's a well-chosen wine list and the kitchen uses the best of the local larder to create classic dishes with a contemporary edge. Understated bedrooms are named after trees and have sleek, modern bathrooms.

Menu £ 49

10 rooms ⊡ – †£ 110/160 ††£ 140/190

✉ LL53 5TH – Northwest : 1.75 ml on A 497 – ✆ 01758 612363 (bookings essential for non-residents) – www.bodegroes.co.uk – dinner only and Sunday lunch – Closed December-February, Sunday dinner except bank holidays and Monday

at Boduan Northwest: 3.75 mi on A497✉ Pwllheli

🏛 Old Rectory

HISTORIC · PERSONALISED Lovely part-Georgian family home with well-tended gardens and a paddock. Comfy lounge features a carved wood fireplace; communal breakfasts at a large table include plenty of fresh fruits. Tastefully decorated, homely bedrooms overlook the garden and come with complimentary chocolates and sherry or sloe gin.

3 rooms ⊡ – †£ 80/95 ††£ 95/115

✉ LL53 6DT – ✆ 01758 721519 – www.theoldrectory.net – Closed Christmas

RHOSCOLYN → See Anglesey (Isle of)

RHOS-ON-SEA – Conwy → See Colwyn Bay

RHYL
Denbighshire – Pop. 25 149 – Regional map n° **19**-C1
▶ London 228 mi – Cardiff 181 mi – Birmingham 114 mi – Wolverhampton 108 mi

✗✗ Barratt's at Ty'n Rhyl

TRADITIONAL CUISINE · COSY Built in 1672 and retaining many original features, including a carved wooden fireplace reputed to have been the top of a bed owned by Catherine of Aragon! The characterful drawing rooms have a cosy, lived-in feel; the dining room, by contrast, is light and airy. Classically based menu. Traditional bedrooms.

Menu £ 45

3 rooms ☲ – ♦£ 80 ♦♦£ 98

167 Vale Rd. ⊠ LL18 2PH – South : 0.5 mi on A 525 – ☏ 01745 344138 (booking essential) – www.barrattsattynrhyl.co.uk – dinner only and Sunday lunch – Closed Sunday and Monday

ROCH

Pembrokeshire – Pop. 463 – Regional map n° **19**-A3

▶ London 258 mi – Swansea 64 mi – Haverfordwest 8 mi

🏠 Roch Castle

HISTORIC · DESIGN An intimate 12C castle set over 7 storeys, which has been fully refurbished by its architect owner. It's modern and stylish throughout, from the bedrooms with their quality linens to the fantastic 'Sun Room' with its far-reaching views.

6 rooms ☲ – ♦£ 200/230 ♦♦£ 210/240

⊠ SA62 6AQ – ☏ 01437 725566 – www.rochcastle.com

ROWEN – Conwy → See Conwy

RUTHIN RHUTHUN

Denbighshire – Pop. 5 461 – Regional map n° **19**-C1

▶ London 210 mi – Birkenhead 31 mi – Chester 23 mi – Liverpool 34 mi

🏠 Firgrove

FAMILY · COSY Attractive stone-built cottage set in stunning gardens. Sit in the snug by the cosy inglenook fireplace in winter or in the delightful plant-filled glasshouse in summer. Two comfortable four-poster bedrooms and a self-contained cottage offer pleasant valley views. The owners join guests for hearty, home-cooked dinners which showcase locally sourced farm produce.

3 rooms ☲ – ♦£ 60/80 ♦♦£ 80/110

Llanfwrog ⊠ LL15 2LL – West : 1.25 mi by A 494 on B 5105 – ☏ 01824 702677 – www.firgrovecountryhouse.co.uk – Closed November-February

✗✗ Manorhaus Ruthin

MODERN CUISINE · DESIGN A lovely Georgian townhouse which retains its period character whilst also boasting a stylish, 'of-the-moment' feel. The formally laid conservatory serves classically based seasonal dishes, presented in a modern style. A cocktail bar, a basement cinema and cosy, cleverly designed bedrooms also feature.

Menu £ 30

8 rooms ☲ – ♦£ 72/80 ♦♦£ 80/95

10 Well St ⊠ LL15 1AH – ☏ 01824 704830 (booking advisable) – www.manorhaus.com – dinner only and lunch Saturday-Sunday by arrangement

✗ On the Hill

TRADITIONAL CUISINE · RUSTIC Immensely charming 16C house in a busy market town; a real family-run business. It has characterful sloping floors, exposed beams and a buzzy, bistro atmosphere. The accessible menu offers keenly priced, internationally-influenced classics.

Carte £ 25/39

1 Upper Clwyd St ⊠ LL15 1HY – ☏ 01824 707736 (booking essential) – www.onthehillrestaurant.co.uk – Closed 25-27 December, 1 January and Sunday lunch

ST CLEARS

Carmarthenshire – Pop. 1 989 – Regional map n° **19**-B3

▶ London 221 mi – Cardiff 76 mi – Swansea 37 mi – Llanelli 33 mi

⌂ Coedllys Country House   ⏃ ⪪ ⇛ ⋒ **P**

TRADITIONAL · PERSONALISED Lovely country house in a peaceful hillside location, complete with a sanctuary where they keep rescued animals – the hens provide the eggs at breakfast. Comfy, traditional guest areas and charming, antique-furnished bedrooms with good mod cons and binoculars for bird watchers. Welsh cakes served on arrival.

4 rooms ⌑ – ♦£ 80/85 ♦♦£ 90/110

Llangynin ⊠ SA33 4JY – Northwest : 3.5 mi by A 40 turning first left after 30 mph sign on entering village – ℰ 01994 231455
– www.coedllyscountryhouse.co.uk – Closed 22-28 December

ST DAVIDS TYDDEWI

Pembrokeshire – ⊠ Haverfordwest – Pop. 1 959 – Regional map n° **19**-A3

▶ London 266 mi – Carmarthen 46 mi – Fishguard 16 mi

⌂ Penrhiw   ⇛ ⅌ **P**

COUNTRY HOUSE · ELEGANT A fine house built from local red stone, set in 12 acres of gardens which offer great country views. The original stained glass door is delightful and the guest areas are impressive. Spacious, stylish bedrooms come in muted tones.

8 rooms ⌑ – ♦£ 180/230 ♦♦£ 180/230

⊠ SA62 6PG – Northwest : 0.5 mi by A 487 and Quickwell Hill Rd
– ℰ 01437 725588 – www.penrhiwhotel.com

⌂ Ramsey House   ⪪ ⇛ ⅌ **P**

TRADITIONAL · PERSONALISED An unassuming looking house located on the edge of the UK's smallest city. Stylish modern bedrooms have a bold boutique style and either coast or country views. The smart Italian-tiled shower rooms feature aromatherapy toiletries.

6 rooms ⌑ – ♦£ 70/130 ♦♦£ 100/130

Lower Moor ⊠ SA62 6RP – Southwest : 0.5 mi on Porth Clais rd – ℰ 01437 720321
– www.ramseyhouse.co.uk – Closed January, December and restricted opening November and February

✗ Cwtch

TRADITIONAL BRITISH · RUSTIC Popular, laid-back restaurant; its name meaning 'hug'. The three rustic dining rooms boast stone walls, crammed bookshelves and log-filled alcoves. Classic British dishes arrive in generous portions and service is polite and friendly.

Menu £ 26/32

22 High St ⊠ SA62 6SD – ℰ 01437 720491 (booking advisable)
– www.cwtchrestaurant.co.uk – dinner only – Closed 1 January-8 February and Monday-Tuesday November-March

ST GEORGE LLAN SAIN SIÔR

Conwy – Regional map n° **19**-C1

▶ London 227 mi – Cardiff 180 mi – Dublin 62 mi – Birmingham 113 mi

⌂ Kinmel Arms   ⬦ ⌸ **P**

TRADITIONAL CUISINE · INN Early 17C stone inn hidden away in a hamlet by the entrance to Kinmel Hall, with a delightful open-fired bar and two spacious dining areas. Lunch offers pub favourites, while dinner is more complex; home-reared beef is a feature. Stylish, contemporary bedrooms boast large kitchenettes designed for breakfast.

Menu £ 15 (weekday dinner) – Carte £ 27/45

4 rooms ⌑ – ♦£ 115/155 ♦♦£ 135/175

The Village ⊠ LL22 9BP – ℰ 01745 832207 – www.thekinmelarms.co.uk
– Closed 25 December, 1 January, Sunday and Monday

WALES

SAUNDERSFOOT

Pembrokeshire – Pop. 2 767 – Regional map n° **19**-A4
▪ Cardiff 90 mi – Haverfordwest 18 mi – Swansea 51 mi

🏠 St Brides Spa   ≤ 🕸 🏵 ⅃ₒ 🖃 ₕ ℘ ₕ 🅿

LUXURY · PERSONALISED Nautically styled hotel overlooking the harbour and
bay, featuring wood panelling and contemporary Welsh art. The stylish spa boasts
an outdoor infinity pool. Well-appointed bedrooms come in cream and blue hues
and have smart bathrooms.

46 rooms ⌧ – ♦£135/210 ♦♦£170/320 – 6 suites
St Brides Hill ✉ *SA69 9NH* – *ℰ 01834 812304* – *www.stbridesspahotel.com*
Cliff – See restaurant listing

XX Cliff   ≤ 🍴 ₕ 🆎 🅿

MODERN CUISINE · BRASSERIE Smart yet casual restaurant in a New England
style hotel, boasting beautiful decked terraces and stunning views over the bay.
Extensive lunch menu; dinner is more refined, offering modern British dishes with
local produce to the fore.

Carte £30/46

St Brides Spa Hotel, St Brides Hill ✉ *SA69 9NH* – *ℰ 01834 812304*
– www.stbridesspahotel.com

X Coast   ≤ 🍴 🅿

MODERN CUISINE · MINIMALIST Striking modern restaurant; when the weather's
right, head for the terrace with its stunning coastal views. Seafood dominates the
menu, which ranges from nibbles to a tasting selection. Local produce features in
creative dishes.

Menu £30 (weekdays) – Carte £36/57

Coppet Hall Beach ✉ *SA69 9AJ* – *ℰ 01834 810800*
*– www.coastsaundersfoot.co.uk – Closed 25-26 December and Monday-Tuesday in
winter*

SEION – Gwynedd → See Caernarfon

SKENFRITH

Monmouthshire – Regional map n° **19**-C4
▪ London 135 mi – Hereford 16 mi – Ross-on-Wye 11 mi

🏨 Bell at Skenfrith   ୫୫ ⇦ 📧 🍴 ⇔ 🅿

CLASSIC CUISINE · PUB Well-run pub in a verdant valley, offering hearty, classical cooking with the occasional ambitious twist and using ingredients from the
organic kitchen garden. There's an excellent choice of champagnes and cognacs,
and service is warm and unobtrusive. Super-comfy bedrooms have an understated elegance.

Carte £28/38

11 rooms ⌧ – ♦£90/130 ♦♦£130/230
✉ *NP7 8UH* – *ℰ 01600 750235 (booking essential) – www.skenfrith.co.uk*

SWANSEA

Swansea – Pop. 179 485 – Regional map n° **19**-B4
▪ London 191 mi – Birmingham 136 mi – Bristol 82 mi – Cardiff 40 mi

🏠 Morgans   ⌖ 🖃 ₕ 🆎 ℘ ₕ 🅿

BUSINESS · PERSONALISED Impressive Edwardian building by the docks; once
the harbour offices. Beautiful façade and charming interior with original plasterwork, stained glass and a soaring cupola. Modern bedrooms – those in the main
house are the most spacious. The restaurant boasts an original hand-painted mural and a modern menu.

42 rooms ⌧ – ♦£90/250 ♦♦£90/250
Somerset Pl ✉ *SA1 1RR* – *ℰ 01792 484848 – www.morganshotel.co.uk*

XX Hanson at The Chelsea

TRADITIONAL BRITISH · FRIENDLY This rustic pub conversion is found in the city's heart, close to St Mary's Church. A blackboard announces the specials – which are formed around the latest produce available from the nearby market – and dishes are tasty and filling.

Menu £ 19 (lunch)/35 – Carte £ 25/42

17 St Mary's St ⊠ SA1 3LH – 𝒞 01792 464068 – www.hansonatthechelsea.co.uk – Closed Sunday and bank holiday Mondays

X Slice

MODERN BRITISH · INTIMATE Sweet former haberdashery in a residential area; the name reflecting its tapered shape. It's run by two friends who alternate weekly between cooking and serving. Precisely prepared, appealing modern dishes are packed with flavour.

Menu £ 30/39

73-75 Eversley Rd, Sketty ⊠ SA2 9DE – West : 2 mi by A 4118 – 𝒞 01792 290929 (booking essential) – www.sliceswansea.co.uk – dinner only and Friday-Sunday lunch – Closed 1 week autumn, 1 week Christmas, Monday and Tuesday

TAL-Y-LLYN

Gwynedd – ⊠ Tywyn – Regional map n° **19**-B2

▶ London 224 mi – Dolgellau 9 mi – Shrewsbury 60 mi

Dolffanog Fawr ☆ ≤ ⇔ P

FAMILY · PERSONALISED This homely 18C farmhouse stands in the shadow of Cadair Idris, just up from a lake; kick-back in the hot tub to make the most of the terrific valley views. Modern bedrooms are furnished in solid oak. Breakfast could include Welsh cakes and dinner might feature local lamb or sea trout caught by the owner.

4 rooms ⊊ – ♥£ 90/120 ♥♥£ 110/120

⊠ LL36 9AJ – On B 4405 – 𝒞 01654 761247 – www.dolffanogfawr.co.uk – Closed November-March

TREDUNNOCK – Newport → See Usk

TREGARON

Ceredigion – Regional map n° **19**-B3

▶ London 245 mi – Cardiff 100 mi – Aberystwyth 18 mi

Y Talbot ⇔ ⇔ 斦 ゟ ☐ ⇔

TRADITIONAL CUISINE · CLASSIC DÉCOR Originally a drover's inn dating back to the 17C; the bar rooms are where the action is, and the best place to sit. Seasonal menus offer full-flavoured traditional dishes made with Welsh produce. Bedrooms are bright and modern: ask for one of the newest. Oh, and there's an elephant buried in the garden!

Carte £ 22/38

13 rooms ⊊ – ♥£ 65/110 ♥♥£ 110/140

⊠ SY25 6JL – 𝒞 01974 298208 – www.ytalbot.com – Closed 25 December

TYWYN

Gwynedd – Regional map n° **19**-B2

▶ London 230 mi – Chester 85 mi – Aberystwyth 34 mi

X Salt Marsh Kitchen

TRADITIONAL BRITISH · SIMPLE Sweet little café-cum-bistro run by a proud, hardworking owner. Scrubbed wooden tables and a blue floor give it a New England feel. Cooking is honest and generous; the owner is a keen fisherman and will advise you of what's best.

Menu £ 13 (weekdays) – Carte £ 24/43

9 College Green ⊠ LL36 9BS – 𝒞 01654 711949 – www.saltmarshkitchen.co.uk – dinner only – Closed January and Monday-Wednesday November-March

USK

Monmouthshire – Pop. 2 834 – Regional map n° **19**-C4

▶ London 144 mi – Bristol 30 mi – Cardiff 26 mi – Gloucester 39 mi

WALES

🏠 Glen-Yr-Afon House   ☆ 🛏 🔁 ♿ 🏋 🅿

TRADITIONAL · PERSONALISED Olive-green, extended Victorian villa just across the bridge from town. Comfortable, traditionally styled guest areas overlook well-tended gardens. Mix of country house and more modern bedrooms; one is a four-poster. The wood-panelled, two-roomed restaurant serves traditional dishes made with Welsh produce.

28 rooms � – ♟£ 120/140 ♟♟£ 140/160

Pontypool Rd ✉ NP15 1SY – ℰ 01291 672302 – www.glen-yr-afon.co.uk – Closed 24-28 December

at Tredunnock South: 4.75 mi by Llangybi rd✉ Newport

🍴 Newbridge on Usk   ⇔ ≼ 🛏 ♿ ♤ 🅿

TRADITIONAL BRITISH · BISTRO 200 year old inn by a bridge over the River Usk; choose from several dining areas set over two levels or sit on the terrace to have the snack menu. Classic British cooking has a modern twist; sharing plates are popular and include a crumble dessert. The smart, comfortable bedrooms are in a separate block.

Menu £ 16 (weekday lunch) – Carte £ 30/49

6 rooms ⊆ – ♟£ 80/130 ♟♟£ 80/130

✉ NP15 1LY – East : 0.5 mi – ℰ 01633 451000 – www.celtic-manor.com

WHITEBROOK – Monmouthshire ➜ See Monmouth

WHITTON

Powys – Pop. 300 – Regional map n° **19**-C3

▶ London 185 mi – Cardiff 84 mi – Birmingham 84 mi – Liverpool 108 mi

🏠 Pilleth Oaks   ⚓ ≼ 🛏 ⚙ 🅿

FAMILY · CLASSIC Double-gabled country house set in 100 acres, overlooking two lakes and the surrounding hills. The traditional, antique-filled interior features an elegant lounge and comfortable bedrooms; one has a balcony and great views. The welcoming owner offers tea on arrival and communal breakfasts at a smart oak table.

3 rooms ⊆ – ♟£ 50/75 ♟♟£ 75/85

✉ LD7 1NP – Northwest : 1.25 mi on B 4356 – ℰ 01547 560272
– www.pillethoaks.co.uk – Closed 25-26 December

IRELAND

NORTHERN IRELAND

Think of Northern Ireland and you think of buzzing Belfast, with its impressive City Hall and Queen's University. But the rest of the Six Counties demand attention too. Forty thousand stone columns of the Giants Causeway step out into the Irish Sea, while inland, Antrim boasts nine scenic glens. County Down's rolling hills culminate in the alluring slopes of Slieve Donard in the magical Mourne Mountains, while Armagh's Orchard County is a riot of pink in springtime. Fermanagh's glassy, silent lakelands are a tranquil attraction, rivalled for their serenity by the heather-clad Sperrin Mountains, towering over Tyrone and Derry.

Rich, fertile land, vast waterways and a pride in traditional crafts like butchery and baking mean that Northern Ireland yields a wealth of high quality produce: tender, full-flavoured beef and lamb, and fish and shellfish from the lakes, rivers and sea, including salmon, oysters, mussels and crabs. You can't beat an eel from Lough Neagh – and the seaweed called Dulse is a local delicacy not to be missed.

- Michelin Road maps n° 712, 713 and 501
- Michelin Green Guide: Ireland

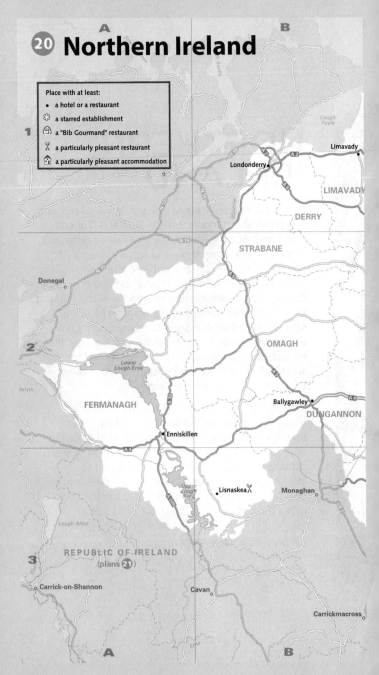

⓴ Northern Ireland

Place with at least:
- • a hotel or a restaurant
- ❀ a starred establishment
- 🅑 a "Bib Gourmand" restaurant
- ✕ a particularly pleasant restaurant
- 🏠 a particularly pleasant accommodation

Limavady

Londonderry

LIMAVADY

Lough Foyle

DERRY

STRABANE

Donegal

OMAGH

Lower Lough Erne

FERMANAGH

Ballygawley

DUNGANNON

Enniskillen

Lisnaskea ✕

Monaghan

Upper Lough Erne

Lough Allen

REPUBLIC OF IRELAND
(plans ㉑)

Carrick-on-Shannon

Cavan

Carrickmacross

Erne

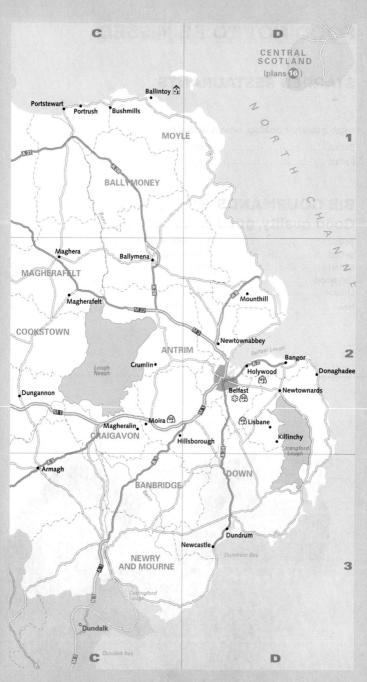

FOOD NOT TO BE MISSED

STARRED RESTAURANTS

❀

High quality cooking, worth a stop!

| Belfast | Eipic | 800 |
| Belfast | OX | 801 |

BIB GOURMANDS 😄
Good quality, good value cooking

Belfast	Bar + Grill at James Street South	801
Belfast	Deanes at Queens	801
Belfast	Home	802
Holywood	Fontana	807
Lisbane	Old Schoolhouse Inn	807
Moira	Wine and Brine **N**	809

Michelin

OUR TOP PICKS

A warm welcome awaits

Whitepark House ⌂ . . . . .Ballintoy 796
Cairn Bay Lodge ⌂ . . . . .Bangor 797
Causeway Lodge ⌂ . . . . .Bushmills 803
Caldhame Lodge ⌂ . . . . .Crumlin 804
Newforge House ⌂ . . . . .Magheralin 809
Edenvale House ⌂ . . . . .Newtownards. 810
Shola Coach House ⌂ . . . . .Portrush 811

City hotspots

Moody Boar X .Armagh. 796
James Street South XX . . . . .Belfast. 801
Saphyre XX . . . . .Belfast. 800
Shu XX . . . . .Belfast. 801
Browns In Town X. . . . . .Londonderry 808

Likeable locals

Deanes Deli X .Belfast. 802
Il Pirata X . . . . .Belfast. 802
Molly's Yard X . . . . .Belfast. 803
Watermill Lodge XX. . . . . .Lisnaskea 808
Church Street XX . . . . .Magherafelt 809
Sleepy Hollow X . . . . .Newtownabbey 810

Spa retreats

Galgorm Resort and Spa 🏨 . . . . . . .Ballymena/Galgorm 796
Lough Erne Resort 🏨 . . . . .Enniskillen. 805
Culloden 🏨 . . . . .Holywood. 806

ANNAHILT EANACH EILTE – Lisburn ➜ See Hillsborough

ARMAGH ARD MHACHA
Armagh – Pop. 15 020 – Regional map n° **20**-C3
▶ Belfast 39 mi – Dungannon 13 mi – Portadown 11 mi

X **Moody Boar**　　　　　　　　　　　　　🛋 ⛵ 🖥 **P**

TRADITIONAL CUISINE · BISTRO Set in the stables of the former Primate of All Ireland's house and run by a young team. Characterful, rustic interior with a vaulted ceiling, a stone floor and booths in the old stalls. Wide choice of classic dishes with personal touches.
Menu £ 13/23 – Carte £ 24/36
Palace Stables, Palace Demense ✉ BT60 4EL – South : 0.5 mi off A 3 – ☎ 028 3752 9678 – www.themoodyboar.com – Closed 25-26 December and Monday

BALLINTOY
Moyle – Regional map n° **20**-C1
▶ Belfast 59 mi – Ballycastle 8 mi – Londonderry 48 mi – Lisburn 67 mi

🏠 **Whitepark House**　　　　　　　　　　　🛏 🕸 **P**

TRADITIONAL · CLASSIC Charming 18C house near the Giant's Causeway, decorated with lovely wall hangings, framed silks and other artefacts from the personable owner's travels. Large, open-fired lounge where cakes are served on arrival. Bright, antique-furnished bedrooms have four-posters or half-testers, and smart modern bathrooms.
4 rooms ☕ – ♦£ 80 ♦♦£ 120
150 Whitepark Rd ✉ BT54 6NH – West : 1.5 mi on A 2 – ☎ 028 2073 1482 – www.whiteparkhouse.com – Closed December and January

BALLYGAWLEY
Dungannon – Pop. 642 – Regional map n° **20**-B2
▶ Belfast 53 mi – Dungannon 14 mi – Londonderry 51 mi

X **Black Cat**　　　　　　　　　　　　　　 ≼ 🛋 🆎 **P**

CLASSIC CUISINE · SIMPLE Friendly, rustic restaurant with a small lounge and a light-filled dining room which looks out across fields and a lake. Well-proportioned, classically based dishes keep the focus on their main ingredient; desserts are a strength.
Menu £ 15 (weekdays) – Carte £ 23/35
32 Dungannon Rd ✉ BT70 2JU – Northwest : 1 mi on A 4 – ☎ 028 8556 7040 – www.theblackcatrestaurant.com

BALLYMENA AN BAILE MEÁNACH
Ballymena – Pop. 29 782 – Regional map n° **20**-C2
▶ Belfast 27 mi – Dundalk 78 mi – Larne 21 mi – Londonderry 51 mi

at Galgorm West: 3 mi on A42

🏰 **Galgorm Resort and Spa**　　🕊 🐾 🛏 📺 🌀 💈 🍴 ⛵ 🕸 🏋 **P**

LUXURY · CONTEMPORARY Victorian manor house with newer extensions, set in large grounds. Stylish interior with plenty of lounge space, a huge function capacity and an excellent leisure club with a superb outdoor spa pool. Modern bedrooms boast state-of-the-art technology; some have balconies. Extensive all-day menus served in characterful Gillies; informal Fratelli offers Italian fare.
122 rooms ☕ – ♦£ 145/195 ♦♦£ 145/285 – 1 suite
136 Fenaghy Rd ✉ BT42 1EA – West : 1.5 mi on Cullybacky rd – ☎ 028 2588 1001 – www.galgorm.com
River Room – See restaurant listing

XXX **River Room** ≼ 🍴 ⚹ 🆔 🕮 🅿

MODERN BRITISH · INTIMATE Formal, warmly decorated dining room set on the ground floor of a stylishly furnished, whitewashed Victorian manor house, with good views across the River Maine. Refined, classically based cooking and attentive service.

Carte £ 38/43

Galgorm Resort and Spa Hotel, 136 Fenaghy Rd ⊠ BT42 1EA – West : 1.5 mi on Cullybacky rd – ℰ 028 2588 1001 – www.galgorm.com – dinner only and Sunday lunch – Closed Monday and Tuesday

BANGOR BEANNCHAR
North Down – Pop. 60 260 – Regional map n° **20**-D2
▶ Belfast 15 mi – Newtownards 5 mi – Hillsborough 24 mi

🏠 **Cairn Bay Lodge** ≼ 🍴 ⚹ 🅿

FAMILY · COSY Large, whitewashed Edwardian house just out of the town centre, overlooking the bay. Comfy guest areas feature unusual objets d'art and ornaments; spacious, individually styled bedrooms boast plenty of extras. The friendly owners leave homemade cake on the landing. Small beauty and therapy facility.

8 rooms � – ♦£ 50/55 ♦♦£ 80/99

278 Seacliffe Rd ⊠ BT20 5HS – East : 1.25 mi by Quay St – ℰ 028 9146 7636 – www.cairnbaylodge.com

🏠 **Salty Dog** ⚹ 🛏

INN · PERSONALISED Welcoming hotel in a pair of bay-windowed, red-brick Victorian townhouses overlooking Bangor Marina and Belfast Lough. Contemporary bedrooms vary greatly in shape and size; go for one of the larger front rooms with a view. The bistro, with its terrace, serves a mix of classics and more ambitious dishes.

15 rooms ⊠ – ♦£ 70/90 ♦♦£ 85/120

10-12 Seacliff Rd ⊠ BT20 5EY – ℰ 028 9127 0696 – www.saltydogbangor.com

XX **Boat House** 🛏 🆔

MODERN CUISINE · FRIENDLY This former lifeboat station is home to an intimate dining room with a harbourside terrace and is run by two experienced brothers. Ambitious modern dishes have the occasional Dutch twist. Be sure to try one of the specialist gins.

Menu £ 33 (lunch and early dinner) – Carte £ 19/30

Seacliff Rd ⊠ BT20 5HA – ℰ 028 9146 9253 – www.theboathouseni.co.uk – Closed 1 January, 12-13 July, Monday and Tuesday

X **Wheathill** 🆕 ⚹ 🆔

MODERN CUISINE · NEIGHBOURHOOD Gray's Hill was once known as Wheathill, as it was the route used to transport wheat to the harbour. Choose from hearty, wholesome classics and dishes with an Italian twist. Service is bubbly and the wine list is keenly priced.

Menu £ 18 (early dinner) – Carte £ 22/40

7 Gray's Hill ⊠ BT20 3BB – ℰ 028 9147 7405 – www.thewheathill.com – Closed 2nd week July, Sunday dinner, Monday and Tuesday

GOOD TIPS!

Optimism abounds in this city, with industry, commerce, arts and tourism all playing a role. With it has come a vibrant and ever-expanding restaurant scene that offers something for everyone, from delis and fish bars to bistros and brasseries. The Cathedral Quarter is the new dining hub attracting the foodies, while **Eipic** and **OX** have brought Michelin Stars.

BELFAST BÉAL FEIRSTE

Belfast – Pop. 267 742 – Regional map n° **20**-D2

▶ Dublin 103 mi – Londonderry 70 mi – Enniskillen 83 mi

Hotels

🏨 Merchant

LUXURY · ELEGANT Former Ulster Bank HQ with an impressive Victorian façade. Plush, intimately styled bedrooms; those in the annexe have an art deco theme. Rooftop gym with an outdoor hot tub and a skyline view; relax afterwards in the swish cocktail bar. British dishes with a Mediterranean edge in the opulent former banking hall. Classic French brasserie dishes and live jazz in Berts.

62 rooms – 🛏£ 150/270 🛏£ 160/280 – 🍽£ 14 – 2 suites

Town plan: B1-x - *16 Skipper St* ✉ BT1 2DZ – ☎ 028 9023 4888

– www.themerchanthotel.com

🏨 Fitzwilliam

LUXURY · CONTEMPORARY Stylish hotel by the Grand Opera House. Smart modern bedrooms have striking colour schemes, contemporary furnishings and good facilities; the higher up you go, the better the grade. Informal dining in the bar and afternoon tea in the lobby.

130 rooms 🍽 – 🛏£ 210/270 🛏£ 220/280 – 1 suite

Town plan: A2-e - *Great Victoria St* ✉ BT2 7BQ – ☎ 028 9044 2080

– www.fitzwilliamhotelbelfast.com

Fitzwilliam – See restaurant listing

🏨 Ten Square

BUSINESS · MODERN Sizeable Victorian property in the city centre, hidden behind the City Hall. Stylish, modern bedrooms display bold feature walls and offer a good level of facilities. The vibrant bar has a pavement terrace and entertainment at weekends. The Grill Room offers something for everyone on its extensive menu.

22 rooms 🍽 – 🛏£ 105/125 🛏£ 115/125

Town plan: B2-x - *10 Donegall Sq South* ✉ BT1 5JD – ☎ 028 9024 1001

– www.tensquare.co.uk – Closed 24-25 December

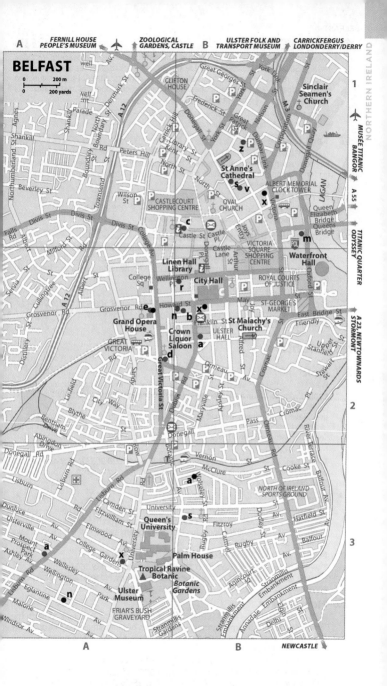

BELFAST

0   200 m
0   200 yards

CLIFTON HOUSE

St Anne's Cathedral

ALBERT MEMORIAL CLOCK TOWER

CASTLECOURT SHOPPING CENTRE

OVAL CHURCH

VICTORIA SQUARE SHOPPING CENTRE

Waterfront Hall

Linen Hall Library

City Hall

ROYAL COURTS OF JUSTICE

Queen Elizabeth Bridge
Queens Bridge

ST-GEORGE'S MARKET

Grand Opera House

Crown Liquor Saloon

St Malachy's Church

ULSTER HALL

NORTH OF IRELAND SPORTS GROUND

Queen's University

Palm House

Tropical Ravine ▲
Botanic Gardens

Ulster Museum

FRIAR'S BUSH GRAVEYARD

Malone Lodge ⇧ ⊟ & ⅍ 🏋 🅿

BUSINESS · MODERN Well-run, privately owned townhouse, in a peaceful Victorian terrace. Smart, spacious bedrooms are spread over various annexes and range from corporate rooms to presidential suites and apartments. State-of-the-art function rooms include a large ballroom. Characterful bar and next door grill restaurant.

100 rooms ☲ – ♦£ 89/139 ♦♦£ 99/149 – 3 suites
Town plan: A3-n - 60 Eglantine Ave ⊠ BT9 6DY – 𝒞 028 9038 8000
– www.malonelodgehotelbelfast.com

Tara Lodge ⊟ & ⅍ 🅿

TOWNHOUSE · CONTEMPORARY Small hotel close to the Botanic Gardens, not far from town. Smart contemporary bedrooms are split between two buildings; go for a 'Signature' room, which comes with bluetooth speakers, hair straighteners and a coffee machine.

34 rooms ☲ – ♦£ 78/103 ♦♦£ 83/133
Town plan: B3-a - 36 Cromwell Rd ⊠ BT7 1JW – 𝒞 028 9059 9099
– www.taralodge.com – Closed 24-27 December

Ravenhill House ⅍ 🅿

TRADITIONAL · CLASSIC Red-brick Victorian house set in the city suburbs. Bright, homely lounge and wood-furnished breakfast room; colourful bedrooms boast good facilities. Organic breakfasts feature homemade muesli and the wheat for the bread is home-milled.

5 rooms ☲ – ♦£ 60/85 ♦♦£ 85/110
690 Ravenhill Rd ⊠ BT6 0BZ – Southeast : 1.75 mi on B 506 – 𝒞 028 9020 7444
– www.ravenhillhouse.com – Closed January, first 2 weeks July,
27 August-2 September and 20-31 December

Restaurants

✗✗✗ Eipic & 🆎 ⑩ ⇆
✿
MODERN CUISINE · ELEGANT An elegant, intimate restaurant featuring a glass-fronted wine room and adjoined by a smart champagne bar. Top quality local ingredients feature on modern, seasonal menus and combinations are original and creative. Flavours are clearly defined and the occasional playful element features too.
→ Grilled langoustines with kohlrabi and coastal greens. Mourne Mountain lamb, Jerusalem artichoke and black garlic. Chocolate, candied celeriac and hazelnuts.
Menu £ 40/60
Town plan: B2-n - 28-40 Howard St ⊠ BT1 6PF – 𝒞 028 9033 1134 (booking essential) – www.deaneseipic.com – dinner only and Friday lunch – Closed 5-31 July, 25-26 December, 1 January and Sunday-Tuesday

✗✗ Saphyre 🏠 & ⑩
MODERN CUISINE · ELEGANT A former church houses this intimate, opulently styled restaurant, as well as an interior design showroom and boutique. Time-honoured flavour combinations are given a modern twist; make sure you save room for dessert.
Menu £ 20 (lunch and early dinner) – Carte £ 40/48
Town plan: A3-a - 135 Lisburn Rd ⊠ BT9 7AG – 𝒞 028 9068 8606
– www.saphyrerestaurant.com – Closed Sunday, dinner Monday and Tuesday and bank holidays

✗✗ Meat Locker & 🆎 🍴 ⇆
MEATS AND GRILLS · BRASSERIE Sit on smart banquettes and look through the large window into the meat fridge, where cubes of pink Himalayan salt gradually dry age the beef. Try the Carlingford rock oysters, followed by a prime Irish cut, cooked on the Asador grill.
Menu £ 18 (lunch and early dinner) – Carte £ 26/53
Town plan: B2-n - 28-40 Howard St ⊠ BT1 6PF – 𝒞 028 9033 1134
– www.michaeldeane.co.uk – Closed 12-14 July, 25-26 December, Easter Sunday-Monday, 1 January and Sunday

XX James Street South

MODERN CUISINE · DESIGN A light and airy restaurant with a vibrant colour scheme, funky light pendants and a large bar for pre-dinner cocktails. Classic dishes use good quality seasonal produce and the cooking is hearty and masculine with bold flavours.

Menu £19 (weekdays) – Carte £30/45

Town plan: B2-b - 21 James St South ⊠ BT2 7GA – ✆ 028 9043 4310 – www.jamesstreetsouth.co.uk – Closed 12-17 July, 25-26 December, 1 January, Easter Monday and Sunday

XX Shu

MODERN BRITISH · DESIGN A well-established neighbourhood restaurant with a modern look and a lively, vibrant atmosphere. Menus are guided by seasonality and the ambitious, modern British dishes have international influences. Good value set price menu.

Menu £14/31 – Carte £26/41

253 Lisburn Rd ⊠ BT9 7EN – Southwest : 1.75 mi on A1 – ✆ 028 9038 1655 – www.shu-restaurant.com – Closed 1 January, 11-13 July, 24-26 December and Sunday

XX Fitzwilliam

MODERN CUISINE · FASHIONABLE Bright, three-roomed restaurant on the first floor of a stylish hotel. If you're in a group choose one of the large communal tables; if you're a couple, opt for one of the intimate booths. Concise menus feature modern Irish dishes.

Menu £16 – Carte £25/42

Town plan: A2-e - Fitzwilliam Hotel, Great Victoria St ⊠ BT2 7BQ – ✆ 028 9044 2080 (booking essential) – www.fitzwilliamhotelbelfast.com – dinner only

X OX (Stephen Toman)

☆

MODERN BRITISH · BISTRO Top quality seasonal produce guides the menus at this buzzy, rustic restaurant, where the cooking is flavoursome and precise with Scandic influences. The minstrel's gallery is now a bar and the large windows offer river views; arrive early for an aperitif in the Wine Cave. Tasting menus only on Fri and Sat.

→ Cured halibut with oyster, buttermilk, fennel pollen and sea aster. Mourne Mountain lamb, wild garlic, smoked potato and endive. 70% chocolate with miso, blood orange, coconut and pecans.

Menu £25 (lunch) – Carte £34/42

Town plan: B1-m - 1 Oxford St ⊠ BT1 3LA – ✆ 028 9031 4121 – www.oxbelfast.com – Closed Christmas-early January, 2 weeks July, 1 week Easter, Sunday and Monday

X Bar + Grill at James Street South

MODERN BRITISH · BRASSERIE A vibrant modern bistro that's popular with one and all. It's a simple place with red brick walls, a high ceiling and warehouse-style windows. Menus are classic brasserie style. The grill dishes are a hit and the succulent steaks are cooked on the Josper, served on boards and come with a choice of sauces.

Carte £19/42

Town plan: B2-b - 21 James St South ⊠ BT2 7GA – ✆ 028 9560 0700 (booking advisable) – www.belfastbargrill.co.uk – Closed 1 January, 12 July and 25-26 December

X Deanes at Queens

MODERN BRITISH · BRASSERIE This bustling brasserie is part of Queen's University and is just a short walk from the city centre. Those after coffee and cake – or a cocktail – should make for the bar, while the terrace is a great spot on a sunny day. Refined modern dishes are full of flavour; the Mibrasa charcoal grill is a feature.

Menu £20 (weekdays) – Carte £26/38

Town plan: A3-x - 1 College Gdns ⊠ BT9 6BQ – ✆ 028 9038 2111 – www.michaeldeane.co.uk – Closed 5-6 April, 12-13 July, 25-26 December, 1 January and Sunday dinner

✗ Home   🕭 AC

😵 TRADITIONAL BRITISH · RUSTIC A popular restaurant with a deli and café to the front offering sandwiches and cakes, and a simple, rustic dining room to the rear. As its name suggests, cooking is straightforward, focusing on tasty, refined versions of dishes that are often prepared at home. Service is attentive and has personality.

Menu £16 (weekday dinner) – Carte £22/37

Town plan: B2-r - *22 Wellington Pl* ⊠ *BT1 6GE* – ℰ *028 9023 4946* – *www.homebelfast.co.uk* – *Closed 12 July and 24-26 December*

✗ Ginger Bistro   🏮

TRADITIONAL CUISINE · BISTRO Rustic neighbourhood bistro close to the Grand Opera House. The two rooms feature bright modern artwork and bespoke fish-themed paintings. Good-sized menus feature simply cooked Irish ingredients and display some Asian influences.

Carte £21/45

Town plan: A2-d - *7-8 Hope St* ⊠ *BT2 5EE* – ℰ *028 9024 4421* – *www.gingerbistro.com* – *Closed Christmas, New Year, Easter, 5 days mid-July, Sunday and lunch Monday-Wednesday*

✗ Deanes Deli   🍷 AC 🛋 🐝

MODERN BRITISH · BISTRO Glass-fronted city centre eatery. One side is a smart restaurant offering an appealing menu of classical dishes with some Asian and Mediterranean influences; the other side acts as a coffee shop by day and a buzzy tapas bar by night.

Menu £19 (early dinner) – Carte £22/43

Town plan: B2-a - *42-44 Bedford St* ⊠ *BT2 7FF* – ℰ *028 9024 8800* – *www.michaeldeane.co.uk* – *Closed 25-26 December, 12-13 July, 1 January, Easter Monday and Sunday*

✗ Muddlers Club 🆕   🍷 🕭 AC

MODERN CUISINE · DESIGN Tucked away in a labyrinth of passageways is this modern, industrial-style restaurant named after a 200 year old secret society. Cooking shows off local ingredients: starters and mains are rustic, while desserts are more refined.

Carte £20/34

Town plan: B1-v - *1 Warehouse Ln* ⊠ *BT1 2DX* – *(off Waring St)* – ℰ *028 9031 3199 (booking advisable)* – *www.themuddlersclubbelfast.com* – *Closed 2 weeks July, 1 week Easter, 24-27 December, Sunday and Monday*

✗ Deanes Love Fish   🕭 AC 🍽 ⇔

SEAFOOD · ELEGANT If it comes from the sea, they'll serve it here! A glass ceiling makes it light and airy and the décor has a maritime feel. The à la carte offers three sizes of platter and everything from cod croquettes to lobster. Lunch is good value.

Carte £17/35

Town plan: B2-n - *28-40 Howard St* ⊠ *BT1 6PF* – ℰ *028 9033 1134* – *www.michaeldeane.co.uk* – *Closed 12-14 July, 25-26 December, Easter Sunday-Monday, 1 January and Sunday dinner*

✗ Il Pirata   🕭 AC 🍽 🏮

MEDITERRANEAN CUISINE · RUSTIC Rustic restaurant with scrubbed wooden floors and an open kitchen. Mediterranean-influenced menus offer an extensive range of mainly Italian small plates; 3 or 4 dishes per person (plus dessert) should suffice. Bright, friendly service.

Carte £17/31

279-281 Upper Newtownards Rd ⊠ *BT4 3JF* – *East : 3 mi by A 2 on A 20* – ℰ *028 9067 3421* – *www.ilpiratabelfast.com*

X **Hadskis**   🛋 AC 🍴 ⇔

CLASSIC CUISINE · RUSTIC This modern conversion is in the up-and-coming Cathedral Quarter. The long, narrow room has an open kitchen, where you can watch the chefs use the latest market produce to prepare globally-influenced dishes and tasty small plates.

Carte £ 21/40

Town plan: B1-s - *33 Donegall St* ✉ *BT1 2NB* - ℰ *028 9032 5444*
- www.hadskis.co.uk - Closed 25-26 December, 1 January and 12 July

X **Coppi**   🛋 & AC 🍴 ⬚

MEDITERRANEAN CUISINE · BISTRO Set on the ground floor of a purpose built property in the Cathedral Quarter. It's big and buzzy, with rustic furnishings and leather booths, and staff are bright and friendly. Good value Italian dishes; start with a selection of cicchetti.

Menu £ 13 (weekday lunch)/23 - Carte £ 17/36

Town plan: B1-z - *St Annes Sq* ✉ *BT1 2LD* - ℰ *028 9031 1959* - *www.coppi.co.uk*
- Closed 25-26 December and 12 July

X **Mourne Seafood Bar**   AC ⇔

SEAFOOD · BISTRO This popular seafood restaurant comes complete with a small shop and a cookery school. Blackboard menus offer a huge array of freshly prepared dishes; go for the classics, such as the Carlingford oysters, accompanied by a pint of stout.

Carte £ 20/33

Town plan: B1-c - *34-36 Bank St* ✉ *BT1 1HL* - ℰ *028 9024 8544 (booking essential at dinner)* - *www.mourneseafood.com - Closed 24-26 December, 1 January, 17 March, Easter Sunday, 12 July and dinner Sunday*

X **Molly's Yard**   🛋 & 🕪 ⬚

TRADITIONAL BRITISH · BISTRO Split-level bistro in a former coach house and stables, with exposed brickwork and a pleasant courtyard. Simple lunches and more ambitious dinners with classical combinations given a personal twist. Fine selection of ales and stouts.

Menu £ 20 - Carte £ 20/44

Town plan: B3-s - *1 College Green Mews, Botanic Ave* ✉ *BT7 1LW*
- ℰ 028 9032 2600 (booking essential) - www.mollysyard.co.uk
- Closed 11-12 July, 24-26 December, 1 January and Sunday

BRYANSFORD - Down → See Newcastle

BUSHMILLS MUILEANN NA BUAISE

Moyle - ✉ Bushmills - Pop. 1 343 - Regional map n° **20**-C1
▶ Belfast 57 mi - Ballycastle 12 mi - Coleraine 10 mi

🏨 **Bushmills Inn**   🍴 🛋 ⊡ 🕪 🅿

TRADITIONAL · CLASSIC Proudly run, part-17C whitewashed inn that successfully blends the old with the new. The conference room features a state-of-the-art cinema. Up-to-date bedrooms are split between the original house and an extension. Have a drink beside the peat fire in the old whiskey bar before dining on classic dishes.

41 rooms ⌓ - ♦£ 110/320 ♦♦£ 120/420

9 Dunluce Rd ✉ *BT57 8QG* - ℰ *028 2073 3000* - *www.bushmillsinn.com - Closed 24-25 December*

🏨 **Causeway Lodge**   ⅏ ≤ 🛋 & 🕪 🅿

FAMILY · CONTEMPORARY Set inland from the Giant's Causeway, in a peaceful location. Guest areas come with polished wood floors, leather furnishings and artwork of local scenes. Spacious, boutique bedrooms have bold feature walls and a high level of facilities.

5 rooms ⌓ - ♦£ 90/140 ♦♦£ 100/140

52 Moycraig Rd, Dunseverick ✉ *BT57 8TB - East : 5 mi by A 2 and Drumnagee Rd*
- ℰ 028 2073 0333 - www.causewaylodge.com

CRUMLIN CROMGHLINN

Antrim – Pop. 5 117 – Regional map n° **20**-C2
▶ Belfast 14 mi – Ballymena 20 mi

🏠 Caldhame Lodge
🚗 ♿ ⚙ 🅿

FAMILY · PERSONALISED Purpose-built guesthouse near the airport, with a pleasant mix of lawns and paved terracing. Comfy guest areas include a conservatory breakfast room and a lounge filled with family photos. Good-sized, individually decorated bedrooms are immaculately kept and feature warm fabrics and iPod docking stations.

8 rooms ☑ – ∤£ 40/50 ∤∤£ 60/100

*102 Moira Rd, Nutts Corner ✉ BT29 4HG – Southeast : 2 mi on A 26
– ℰ 028 9442 3099 – www.caldhamelodge.co.uk*

DERRY/LONDONDERRY → See Londonderry

DONAGHADEE DOMHNACH DAOI

Ards – Pop. 6 856 – Regional map n° **20**-D2
▶ Belfast 18 mi – Ballymena 44 mi

🍽 Pier 36
⇔ 🏠 AC ⇕

TRADITIONAL CUISINE · PUB Spacious family-run pub set on the quayside, opposite a lighthouse, overlooking the picturesque harbour. Extensive menus feature a mix of classic, modern and international influences, with good weekday deals and plenty of fresh, local seafood. Bright, modern bedrooms; some with great sea and harbour views.

Carte £ 20/48

6 rooms ☑ – ∤£ 50/99 ∤∤£ 70/120

36 The Parade ✉ BT21 0HE – ℰ 028 9188 4466 – www.pier36.co.uk – Closed 25 December

DUNDRUM DÚN DROMA

Down – Pop. 1 522 – Regional map n° **20**-D3
▶ Belfast 29 mi – Downpatrick 9 mi – Newcastle 4 mi

🏠 Carriage House
🚗 ⚙ 🅿

TRADITIONAL · CLASSIC Sweet, lilac-washed terraced house with colourful window boxes. Homely lounge with books and local info. Simple, antique-furnished bedrooms; some affording pleasant bay views. Breakfast in the conservatory, overlooking the pretty garden.

3 rooms ☑ – ∤£ 80/90 ∤∤£ 110/120

71 Main St ✉ BT33 0LU – ℰ 028 4375 1635 – www.carriagehousedundrum.com

✗ Buck's Head Inn
🚗 🏠 ♿

SEAFOOD · NEIGHBOURHOOD Converted village pub. Have drinks in the lounge then head for the front room with its cosy booths and open fire, or the rear room which overlooks the garden. Unfussy, traditional lunches and more ambitious dinners; seafood is a strength.

Menu £ 30 (dinner) – Carte lunch £ 22/35

77-79 Main St ✉ BT33 0LU – ℰ 028 4375 1868 – Closed 24-25 December and Monday October-March

✗ Mourne Seafood Bar

SEAFOOD · RUSTIC Friendly, rustic restaurant on the main street of a busy coastal town. Simple, wood-furnished dining room with nautically themed artwork. Classic menus centre around seafood, with oysters and mussels from the owners' beds the specialities.

Carte £ 18/31

*10 Main St ✉ BT33 0LU – ℰ 028 4375 1377 (booking essential)
– www.mourneseafood.com – Closed dinner 24 December, 25 December and Monday-Wednesday in winter*

DUNGANNON DÚN GEANAINN

Dungannon – Pop. 14 380 – Regional map n° **20**-C2

▶ Belfast 42 mi – Ballymena 37 mi – Dundalk 47 mi – Londonderry 60 mi

🏠 Grange Lodge   ⊗ 🖨 ⬚ 🅿

TRADITIONAL · CLASSIC An attractive Georgian country house with well-kept gardens (an ideal spot for afternoon tea!) Antique-furnished guest areas display fine sketches and lithographs. Snug, well-appointed bedrooms are immaculately kept with good extras.

5 rooms ⌂ – ♦£ 79/89 ♦♦£ 99/109

7 Grange Rd, Moy ⊠ BT71 7EJ – Southeast : 3.5 mi by A 29 – ℰ 028 8778 4212
– www.grangelodgecountryhouse.com – Closed 20 December-1 February

ENNISKILLEN INIS CEITHLEANN

Fermanagh – Pop. 13 757 – Regional map n° **20**-A2

▶ Belfast 84 mi – Londonderry 60 mi – Craigavon 62 mi – Portadown 59 mi

🏨 Lough Erne Resort   ⋔ ⟨ 🖨 🖥 🖵 ☺ 🏠 ᐧᔆ ⬚ ᴴ 🍽 🏊 🅿

LUXURY · MODERN Vast, luxurious golf and leisure resort on a peninsula between two loughs. Bedrooms have a classical style and are extremely well-appointed; the suites and lodges are dotted about the grounds. Relax in the beautiful Thai spa or the huge pool with its stunning mosaic wall. Ambitious, contemporary dining and lough views in Catalina; steaks and grills in the clubhouse.

120 rooms ⌂ – ♦£ 129/249 ♦♦£ 149/269 – 6 suites

Belleek Rd ⊠ BT93 7ED – Northwest : 4 mi by A 4 on A 46 – ℰ 028 6632 3230
– www.lougherneresort.com

🏨 Manor House   ⋔ ⊗ ⟨ 🖨 🖥 🖵 🏠 ᐧᔆ 🍽 ⬚ ᴴ 🍽 🏊 🅿

TRADITIONAL · MODERN Impressive yellow-washed manor house overlooking Lough Erne and surrounded by mature grounds. Comfy, stylish guest areas mix the traditional and the contemporary. Bedrooms range from characterful in the main house to smart and modern in the extensions. The formal dining room offers classical cooking and there's a more casual all-day menu served in the old vaults.

79 rooms ⌂ – ♦£ 80/130 ♦♦£ 90/325 – 2 suites

Killadeas ⊠ BT94 1NY – North : 7.5 mi by A 32 on B 82 – ℰ 028 6862 2200
– www.manorhousecountryhotel.com

Belleek – See restaurant listing

XX Belleek   ⟨ 🖨 ᴴ 🅿

CLASSIC CUISINE · ELEGANT Formal hotel dining room comprising three rooms – two with high ceilings and ornate plasterwork and the third in a glass-fronted cube which offers unrivalled views across the marina. Classic dishes are presented in a modern manner.

Menu £ 35 – Carte £ 30/47

Manor House Hotel, Killadeas ⊠ BT94 1NY – North : 7.5 mi by A 32 on B 82
– ℰ 028 6862 2200 – www.manorhousecountryhotel.com – dinner only

GALGORM → See Ballymena

HILLSBOROUGH CROMGHLINN

Lisburn – Pop. 3 738 – Regional map n° **20**-C2

▶ Belfast 12 mi – Lisburn 4 mi – Craigavon 21 mi

🏠 Lisnacurran Country House   🖨 ⬚ 🅿

FAMILY · PERSONALISED Homely Edwardian house, where spacious rooms are furnished with antiques. Choose a bedroom in the main house, the former milking parlour or the old barn. Breakfasts are hearty – the homemade soda and potato bread is a must.

9 rooms ⌂ – ♦£ 55 ♦♦£ 80

6 Listullycurran Rd, Dromore ⊠ BT25 1RB – Southwest : 3 mi on A 1
– ℰ 028 9269 8710 – www.lisnacurrancountryhouse.co.uk

🍴 Parson's Nose

TRADITIONAL BRITISH · PUB Characterful Georgian property built by the first Marquis of Downshire. The restaurant sits above the rustic bar and overlooks a lake in the castle grounds. Unashamedly traditional menus and generous portions; the daily fish specials are a hit.

Menu £ 17 (weekdays) – Carte £ 21/39

48 Lisburn St ⊠ BT26 6AB – ℰ 028 9268 3009 (booking advisable)
– www.theparsonsnose.co.uk – Closed 25 December

🍴 Plough Inn

TRADITIONAL CUISINE · PUB Family-run, 18C coaching inn that's three establishments in one: a bar with an adjoining dining room; a café-cum-bistro; and a seafood restaurant. Dishes range from light snacks and pub classics to more modern, international offerings.

Menu £ 15 – Carte £ 21/39

3 The Square ⊠ BT26 6AG – ℰ 028 9268 2985 – www.theploughhillsbrough.co.uk
– Closed 25-26 December

at Annahilt Southeast: 4 mi on B177⊠ Hillsborough

🏠 Fortwilliam

TRADITIONAL · CLASSIC Attractive bay-windowed farmhouse with neat gardens, surrounded by 80 acres of land. Homely lounge and a country kitchen with an Aga. Traditional bedrooms have flowery fabrics, antiques and country views; two have private bathrooms.

3 rooms ⊡ – ♦£ 50 ♦♦£ 75

210 Ballynahinch Rd ⊠ BT26 6BH – Northwest : 0.25 mi on B 177
– ℰ 028 9268 2255 – www.fortwilliamcountryhouse.com – Closed 24-27 December

🍴 Pheasant

TRADITIONAL CUISINE · PUB Sizeable creamwashed pub with Gothic styling, Guinness-themed artwork and a typically Irish feel. Internationally influenced menus showcase local, seasonal produce, with seafood a speciality in summer and game featuring highly in winter.

Menu £ 13 (lunch and early dinner) – Carte £ 20/38

410 Upper Ballynahinch Rd ⊠ BT26 6NR – North : 1 mi on Lisburn rd
– ℰ 028 9263 8056 – www.thepheasantrestaurant.co.uk – Closed 12 July and 25 December

HOLYWOOD ARD MHIC NASCA
North Down – Pop. 12 131 – Regional map n° **20**-D2
▶ Belfast 7 mi – Bangor 6 mi

🏨 Culloden

BUSINESS · CLASSIC An extended Gothic mansion overlooking Belfast Lough, with well-maintained gardens full of modern sculptures, and a smart spa. Charming, traditional, antique-furnished guest areas have open fires and fine ceiling frescoes. Characterful bedrooms offer good facilities. Classical menus and good views in formal Mitre; wide range of traditional dishes in Cultra Inn.

102 rooms ⊡ – ♦£ 140/220 ♦♦£ 230/300 – 3 suites

142 Bangor Rd ⊠ BT18 0EX – East : 1.5 mi on A 2 – ℰ 028 9042 1066
– www.hastingshotels.com

🏠 Rayanne House

TRADITIONAL · CLASSIC Keenly run, part-Victorian house in a residential area. Homely, antique-filled guest areas. Smart, country house bedrooms with a modern edge; those to the front offer the best views. Ambitious, seasonal dishes in formal dining room; try the Titanic tasting menu – a version of the last meal served on the ship.

10 rooms ⊡ – ♦£ 80/90 ♦♦£ 120/140

60 Demesne Rd ⊠ BT18 9EX – By My Lady's Mile Rd – ℰ 028 9042 5859
– www.rayannehouse.com

XX Fontana

😊 **MODERN CUISINE · NEIGHBOURHOOD** A favourite with the locals is this smart, modern, first floor restaurant; accessed down a narrow town centre passageway and decorated with contemporary art. Menus offer British, Mediterranean and some Asian dishes, with local seafood a speciality. Good value set menus are available at both lunch and dinner.

Menu £ 23 – Carte £ 28/47

61A High St ⊠ BT18 9AE – ☏ 028 9080 9908 – www.restaurantfontana.com
– Closed 25-26 December, 1-2 January, Saturday lunch, Sunday dinner and Monday

KILLINCHY

Ards – Regional map n° **20**-D2

▶ Belfast 16 mi – Newtownards 11 mi – Lisburn 17 mi – Bangor 16 mi

▤ Balloo House

CLASSIC CUISINE · PUB Characterful former farmhouse with a smart dining pub feel. Lengthy menus offer a mix of hearty pub classics and dishes with more international leanings. Pies are popular, as is High Tea, which is served every day except Saturday.

Menu £ 15 (weekday lunch)/35 – Carte £ 30/43

1 Comber Rd ⊠ BT23 6PA – West : 0.75 mi on A 22 – ☏ 028 9754 1210 (bookings advisable at dinner) – www.balloohouse.com – Closed 25 December

LIMAVADY LÉIM AN MHADAIDH

Limavady – Pop. 12 669 – Regional map n° **20**-B1

▶ Belfast 62 mi – Ballymena 39 mi – Coleraine 13 mi – Londonderry 17 mi

XX Lime Tree

TRADITIONAL CUISINE · NEIGHBOURHOOD Keenly run neighbourhood restaurant; its traditional exterior concealing a modern room with purple velvet banquettes and colourful artwork. Unfussy, classical cooking features meats and veg from the village; try the homemade wheaten bread.

Menu £ 25 – Carte £ 25/36

60 Catherine St ⊠ BT49 9DB – ☏ 028 7776 4300 – www.limetreerest.com
– dinner only and lunch Thursday-Friday – Closed 25-26 December, Sunday and Monday

LISBANE AN LIOS BÁN

Ards – ⊠ Comber – Regional map n° **20**-D2

▶ Belfast 14 mi – Newtownards 9 mi – Saintfield 7 mi

X Old Schoolhouse Inn

😊 **MODERN BRITISH · FAMILY** Just a stone's throw from Strangford Lough is this stylish, sumptuous restaurant, which has been passed down from parents to son. Modern dishes are skilfully prepared, full of flavour and use top notch ingredients – including plenty of local seafood and game. Satisfyingly, the chef isn't afraid to prepare some simpler dishes too. Homely bedrooms complete the picture.

Menu £ 19/25 – Carte £ 26/36

8 rooms � – ♦£ 50/60 ♦♦£ 75/90

100 Ballydrain Rd ⊠ BT23 6EA – Northeast : 1.5 mi by Quarry Rd on Ballydrain Rd – ☏ 028 9754 1182 (booking essential) – www.theoldschoolhouseinn.com – Closed Monday

▤ Poacher's Pocket

TRADITIONAL BRITISH · PUB Modern-looking building in the centre of a small village; the best seats are in the two-tiered extension overlooking the internal courtyard. Wide-ranging menus offer rustic, hearty dishes; come at the weekend for a laid-back brunch.

Menu £ 15 (weekdays) – Carte £ 20/39

181 Killinchy Rd ⊠ BT23 5NE – ☏ 028 9754 1589
– www.poacherspocketlisbane.com – Closed 25 December

LISNASKEA

Fermanagh – Pop. 2 880 – Regional map n° **20**-B3

▶ Belfast 82 mi – Dublin 91 mi – Londonderry 67 mi – Omagh 33 mi

XX Watermill Lodge ⇦ ≤ 🛏 🎍 ⅋ AC P

CLASSIC FRENCH · CLASSIC DÉCOR Charming red-brick cottage with a thatched roof, a delightful terrace and superb water gardens flowing down to Lough Erne – where you can hire one of their fishing boats. Characterful, rustic interior with smartly laid tables and a 25,000 litre aquarium; classical Gallic menu. Comfy, airy bedrooms have stone floors and heavy wood furnishings; some look over the water.

Menu £ 18/20 – Carte £ 22/44

7 rooms ⌚ – ♦£ 59 ♦♦£ 89/95

Kilmore Quay ⊠ BT92 0DT – Southwest: 3 mi by B 127 – ℰ 028 6772 4369 (booking advisable) – www.watermillrestaurantfermanagh.com – dinner only and Sunday lunch – Closed January and Monday-Tuesday

LONDONDERRY/DERRY

Derry – Pop. 85 016 – Regional map n° **20**-B1

▶ Belfast 70 mi – Dublin 146 mi – Omagh 34 mi

🏠 Beech Hill Country House ⅋ ⅍ 🛏 🗗 ⅊ 🛄 P

TRADITIONAL · CLASSIC Once a US Marine HQ, this 18C house is now a welcoming hotel and wedding venue. Characterful guest areas feature ornate coving and antiques, and most of the bedrooms have a country house style. Dine overlooking the lake and water wheel – traditional menus use produce from the walled garden.

31 rooms ⌚ – ♦£ 75/110 ♦♦£ 95/140 – 2 suites

32 Ardmore Rd ⊠ BT47 3QP – Southeast : 3.5 mi by A 6 – ℰ 028 7134 9279 – www.beech-hill.com – Closed 24-25 December

🏠 Ramada Da Vinci's ⅋ 🗗 ⅊ ⅍ 🛄 P

BUSINESS · MODERN The hub of this hotel is its extremely characterful bar, which was established as a pub in 1986 and once owned by a local artist. Bedrooms are spacious and modern, the events rooms are stylish and the atmospheric brasserie offers something for everyone. Photos of stars who have stayed here fill the corridors.

65 rooms – ♦£ 59/120 ♦♦£ 59/120

15 Culmore Rd ⊠ BT48 8JB – North : 1 mi on A 2 (Foyle Bridge rd) – ℰ 028 7127 9111 – www.davincishotel.com – Closed 24-25 December

XX Browns ⅊ AC ⅋

MODERN BRITISH · NEIGHBOURHOOD The original Browns sits across from the railway station and comes with a plush lounge and an intimate, understated dining room. Dishes are eye-catching and showcase top Northern Irish produce in some interesting combinations.

Menu £ 15/22 – Carte £ 31/43

1 Bonds Hill, Waterside ⊠ BT47 6DW – East : 1 mi by A 2 – ℰ 028 7134 5180 (booking advisable) – www.brownsrestaurant.com – Closed Monday, Saturday lunch and Sunday dinner

X Browns In Town ⅋ ⅊ AC ⅋

MODERN BRITISH · BRASSERIE Across the river from the first Browns, is its laid-back bigger sister. A bewildering array of menus offer everything you could want, from light snacks to hearty Irish meats and veg. Cooking is modern and comprises many elements.

Menu £ 20 (dinner) – Carte £ 24/40

Strand Rd ⊠ BT48 7DJ – ℰ 028 7136 2889 – www.brownsrestaurant.com – Closed 25-26 December and Sunday lunch

MAGHERA MACHAIRE RÁTHA

Magherafelt – Pop. 3 886 – Regional map n° **20**-C2

▶ Belfast 40 mi – Ballymena 19 mi – Coleraine 21 mi – Londonderry 32 mi

🏠 Ardtara Country House   🏡 🐾 🛖 🍽 **P**

COUNTRY HOUSE · CLASSIC Spacious, elegant 19C country house, originally built for a local linen manufacturer. It's set in 8 acres of mature grounds and has a calming, restful air; many period features remain. The intimate wood-panelled restaurant offers a menu of modern classics which feature ingredients foraged for by the chef.

9 rooms ♒ – ♦£ 79/99 ♦♦£ 89/149

8 Gorteade Rd, Upperlands ✉ BT46 5SA – ℰ 028 7964 4490 – www.ardtara.com – Closed Monday and Tuesday in winter

MAGHERAFELT

Magherafelt – Pop. 8 881 – Regional map n° **20**-C2
▶ Belfast 76 mi – Dublin 117 mi – Londonderry 5 mi – Craigavon 75 mi

✗✗ Church Street   & 🅰🅲 ⇔

TRADITIONAL BRITISH · NEIGHBOURHOOD Bustling eatery on the main street of a busy country town. The long, narrow room has a mix of bistro, pew and high-backed seating, and there's a second smart room above. Unfussy, classical dishes rely on good quality local produce.

Menu £ 14 (early dinner) – Carte £ 23/34

23 Church St ✉ BT45 6AP – ℰ 028 7932 8083 (booking advisable) – www.churchstreetrestaurant.co.uk – dinner only and Sunday lunch – Closed 4-14 January, 1 week mid-July, Monday and Tuesday

MAGHERALIN

Craigavon – Pop. 1 403 – Regional map n° **20**-C2
▶ Belfast 20 mi – Downpatrick 32 mi – Londonderry 77 mi

🏠 Newforge House   🏡 🐾 🛖 🍽 **P**

COUNTRY HOUSE · PERSONALISED A traditional Georgian building with an old linen mill behind and colourful gardens and a meadow in front. Bedrooms are named after former inhabitants of the house and are tastefully furnished with period pieces. Three course dinners are replaced by simpler suppers on Sundays and Mondays.

6 rooms ♒ – ♦£ 85/125 ♦♦£ 125/190

58 Newforge Rd ✉ BT67 0QL – ℰ 028 9261 1255 – www.newforgehouse.com – Closed 20 December-1 February

MOIRA

Lisburn – Pop. 4 221 – Regional map n° **35**-C2
▶ Belfast 18 mi – Enniskillen 67 mi – Larne 40 mi

✗ Wine & Brine   & 🅰🅲
😊 MODERN CUISINE · BISTRO Local chef Chris McGowan has transformed this fine Georgian house into a bright modern restaurant displaying local art. Top regional ingredients feature in appealing dishes with a comforting feel. As its name suggests, some of the meats and fish are gently brined, using whey from the nearby cheese factory.

Carte £ 20/32

59 Main St ✉ BT67 0LQ – ℰ 028 9261 0500 – www.wineandbrine.co.uk – Closed 2 weeks January, 2 weeks August, Sunday dinner and Monday

MOUNTHILL

Antrim – Pop. 69 – Regional map n° **20**-D2
▶ Belfast 15 mi – Templepatrick 7 mi – Larne 5 mi

🍴 Billy Andy's ⬅ 🅿

TRADITIONAL BRITISH · RUSTIC It used to be the village store as well as a pub, and although the groceries are gone, this place still seems to be all things to all people. Cooking is filling, with a strong Irish accent. They offer a fine selection of whiskies, there are four modern bedrooms and Saturday music sessions pack the place out.

Menu £ 17/20 – Carte £ 23/38

4 rooms 🖙 – †£ 40/60 ††£ 45/85

✉ BT40 3DX – ☎ 028 2827 0648 – www.billyandys.com – Closed 25-26 December

NEWCASTLE AN CAISLEÁN NUA

Down – Pop. 7 723 – Regional map n° **20**-D3

▶ Belfast 32 mi – Londonderry 101 mi

XX Vanilla 🅰 🔠

INTERNATIONAL · NEIGHBOURHOOD Contemporary restaurant; its black canopy standing out amongst the town centre shops. The long, narrow room is flanked by brushed velvet banquettes and polished tables. Attractively presented, internationally influenced modern dishes.

Menu £ 21 (lunch and early dinner) – Carte £ 29/46

67 Main St ✉ BT33 0AE – ☎ 028 4372 2268 – www.vanillarestaurant.co.uk
– Closed 25-27 December, 1 January and Wednesday dinner in winter

at Bryansford Northwest: 2.75 mi on B180

🏠 Tollyrose Country House ⬅ 🛏 🍸 🅿

FAMILY · PERSONALISED Purpose-built guesthouse beside the Tollymore Forest Park, at the foot of the Mourne Mountains. Simple, modern bedrooms come in neutral hues; those on the top floor have the best views. Lots of local info in the lounge. Friendly owners.

6 rooms 🖙 – †£ 45/55 ††£ 75/85

15 Hilltown Rd ✉ BT33 0PX – Southwest : 0.5 mi on B 180 – ☎ 028 4372 6077
– www.tollyrose.com

NEWTOWNABBEY

Newtownabbey – Pop. 61 713 – Regional map n° **20**-D2

▶ Belfast 7 mi – Templepatrick 12 mi – Carrickfurgus 13 mi

X Sleepy Hollow 🅰 🅿

MODERN CUISINE · RURAL This remote, passionately run restaurant is a real find, with its rustic rooms, large terrace, cosy hayloft bar and farm shop! Cooking is contrastingly modern, and the chef prides himself on using seasonal ingredients with a story.

Menu £ 20 (lunch) – Carte £ 23/38

15 Klin Rd ✉ BT36 4SU – Northwest : 1 mi by Ballyclare Rd and Ballycraig Rd
– ☎ 028 9083 8672 – www.sleepyhollowrestaurant.com – Closed 25-26 December

NEWTOWNARDS BAILE NUA NA HARDA

Ards – Pop. 28 437 – Regional map n° **20**-D2

▶ Belfast 10 mi – Bangor 5 mi – Downpatrick 22 mi

🏠 Edenvale House 🐾 ⬅ 🛏 🍸 🅿

TRADITIONAL · CLASSIC Attractive Georgian farmhouse with a charming owner and pleasant lough and mountain views. It's traditionally decorated, with a comfy drawing room and a wicker-furnished sun room. Spacious, homely bedrooms boast good facilities.

3 rooms 🖙 – †£ 65 ††£ 110

130 Portaferry Rd ✉ BT22 2AH – Southeast : 2.75 mi on A 20 – ☎ 028 9181 4881
– www.edenvalehouse.com – Closed Christmas-New Year

NORTHERN IRELAND

PORTRUSH PORT ROIS

Coleraine – Pop. 6 640 – Regional map n° **20**-C1
▶ Belfast 58 mi – Coleraine 4 mi – Londonderry 35 mi

🏠 Shola Coach House   🕹 ⌘ **P**

TOWNHOUSE This attractive stone coach house once belonged to the Victorian manor house next door. Inside it's light and airy, with a tasteful contemporary style and modern facilities. Bedrooms are spacious; one is in the colourful garden.

4 rooms ⊑ – †£ 80/120 ††£ 100/120

110A Gateside Rd ⊠ BT56 8NP – East : 1.5 mi by Ballywillan Road
– ℰ 028 7082 5925 – www.sholabandb.com – Closed December and January

PORTSTEWART PORT STIÓBHAIRD

Coleraine – Pop. 7 368 – Regional map n° **20**-C1
▶ Belfast 60 mi – Ballymena 32 mi – Coleraine 6 mi

🏠 Strandeen   ≤ ⌘ **P**

FAMILY · CONTEMPORARY A great place to escape everyday life: the rooms are light and airy, the atmosphere is serene and the open-plan lounge takes in beach and mountain views. Organic breakfasts feature smoothies, chai porridge and bircher muesli.

5 rooms ⊑ – †£ 85/110 ††£ 110/125

63 Strand Rd ⊠ BT55 7LU – ℰ 028 7083 3872 – www.strandeen.com

✗ Harry's Shack   ≤ 🏡 ♿

TRADITIONAL CUISINE · RUSTIC The location is superb: on a sandy National Trust beach, with views across to Inishowen. It's an appealingly simple place with wooden tables and classroom-style chairs. Concise menus wisely let local ingredients speak for themselves.

Carte £ 21/35

118 Strand Rd ⊠ BT55 7PG – West : 1 mi by Strand Rd – ℰ 028 7083 1783 – Closed Sunday dinner and Monday

811

REPUBLIC
OF IRELAND

They say that Ireland offers forty luminous shades of green, but it's not all wondrous hills and down-home pubs: witness the limestone-layered Burren, cut-through by meandering streams, lakes and labyrinthine caves; or the fabulous Cliffs of Moher, looming for mile after mile over the wild Atlantic waves. The cities burst with life: Dublin is one of Europe's coolest capitals, and free-spirited Cork enjoys a rich cultural heritage. Kilkenny mixes a medieval flavour with a strong artistic tradition, while the 'festival' city of Galway is enhanced by an easy, international vibe.

This is a country known for the quality and freshness of its produce, and farmers' markets and food halls yield an array of artisanal cheeses and freshly baked breads. Being an agricultural country, Ireland produces excellent home-reared meat and dairy products and a new breed of chefs are giving traditional dishes a clever modern twist. Seafood, particularly shellfish, is popular – nothing beats sitting on the quayside with a bowl of steaming mussels and the distinctive taste of a micro-brewery beer.

- Michelin Road maps n° 712 and 713

- Michelin Green Guide: Ireland

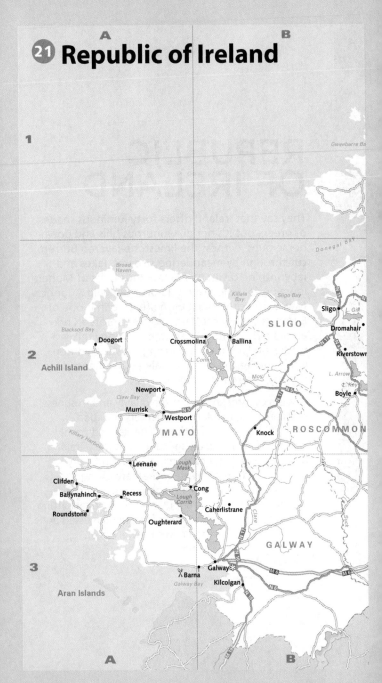

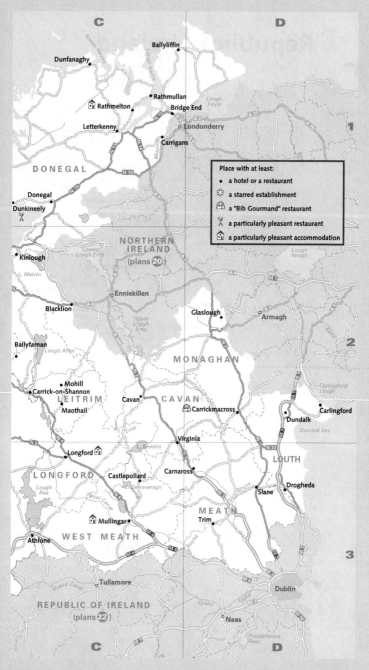

Dunfanaghy

Ballyliffin

Rathmullan

Rathmelton

Bridge End

Letterkenny

Londonderry

Carrigans

DONEGAL

Lough Foyle

1

Donegal

Dunkineely

Place with at least:
- • a hotel or a restaurant
- ❀ a starred establishment
- 🕲 a "Bib Gourmand" restaurant
- 🍴 a particularly pleasant restaurant
- 🏠 a particularly pleasant accommodation

NORTHERN IRELAND
(plans 20)

Kinlough

Enniskillen

Glaslough

Armagh

Lough Neagh

Blacklion

2

Ballyfarnan

MONAGHAN

Mohill

Carrick-on-Shannon

LEITRIM

Cavan

CAVAN

Carrickmacross

Carlingford Lough

Maothail

Dundalk

Carlingford

Dundalk bay

Longford

Virginia

LONGFORD

Castlepollard

Carnaross

LOUTH

Longford

Mullingar

MEATH

Trim

Slane

Drogheda

WEST MEATH

Athlone

3

Tullamore

Dublin

REPUBLIC OF IRELAND
(plans 22)

Naas

Poulaphouca Resr.

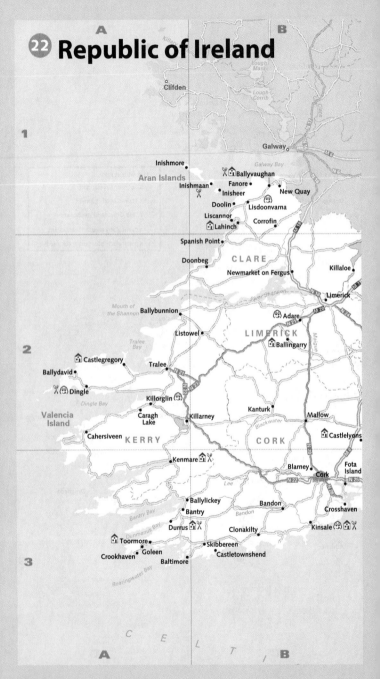

A   B

1

Clifden

Galway

Inishmore
Aran Islands   Ballyvaughan
        Inishmaan   Fanore
                Inisheer   New Quay
            Doolin
                Lisdoonvarna
            Liscannor   Corrofin
            Lahinch

Spanish Point   CLARE

Doonbeg

Newmarket on Fergus   Killaloe

                    Limerick
    Mouth of
    the Shannon   Ballybunnion   River Shannon

            Listowel   Adare
                    LIMERICK
2   Ballingarry
        Castlegregory
Ballydavid   Tralee
    Dingle   Killorglin
    Dingle Bay   Killarney   Kanturk
                Caragh   Mallow
                Lake
Valencia   Castlelyons
Island   Cahersiveen   KERRY   CORK

                Kenmare   Blarney   Fota
                            Cork   Island
                    Ballylickey   Bandon
                    Bantry   Crosshaven
                Durrus   Clonakilty   Kinsale
        Toormore   Skibbereen
    Crookhaven   Goleen   Castletownshend
3   Baltimore

Place with at least:

- • a hotel or a restaurant
- ❀ a starred establishment
- ⓐ a "Bib Gourmand" restaurant
- ✕ a particularly pleasant restaurant
- ⌂ a particularly pleasant accommodation

FOOD NO TO BE MISSED

STARRED RESTAURANTS

❀ ❀
Excellent cooking, worth a detour!

Dublin............................Patrick Guilbaud 856

❀
High quality cooking, worth a stop!

Ardmore	House	824
Dublin	Chapter One	856
Dublin	L'Ecrivain	856
Dublin	Greenhouse	857
Dublin / Blackrock	Heron & Grey **N**	864
Galway	Aniar	872
Galway	Loam	872
Kilkenny	Campagne	878
Thomastown	Lady Helen	897

BIB GOURMANDS ⊛
Good quality, good value cooking

Adare	1826	822
Carrickmacross	Courthouse	837
Cashel	Cafe Hans	839
Clonegall	Sha-Roe Bistro	842
Dingle	Chart House	848
Dublin	Delahunt	859
Dublin	Etto	860
Dublin	Pichet	858
Dublin	Pig's Ear	860
Dublin / Clontarf	Pigeon House	864
Duncannon	Aldridge Lodge	865
Fennor	Copper Hen	868
Killorglin	Giovannelli	882
Kinsale	Bastion	884
Kinsale	Fishy Fishy	884
Lisdoonvarna	Wild Honey Inn	887

OUR TOP PICKS

Impressive for golf

Radisson Blu Farnham Estate 🏨 . . .Cavan. 840
Inchydoney Island
   Lodge and Spa 🏨 . . . . .Clonakilty 842
Trump International Golf Links
   and H. Doonbeg 🏨 . . . . .Doonbeg. 849
Powerscourt 🏨 . . . . .Enniskerry. 868
Fota Island 🏨 . . . . .Fota Island 869
Waterford Castle H.
   and Golf Resort 🏨 . . . . .Waterford. 899

Little gems

Kilgraney Country House 🏠. . . . . . . .Bagenalstown 826
Shores Country House 🏠 . . . . .Castlegregory 839
Ballyvolane House 🏠 . . . . .Castlelyons. 839
Gallán Mór 🏠. . . . . .Durrus 867
Sallyport House 🏠 . . . . .Kenmare 876
Moy House 🏠 . . . . .Lahinch 885
Viewmount House 🏠. . . . . .Longford. 888
Moorfield Lodge 🏠 . . . . .Ramelton 892
Fortview House 🏠 . . . . .Toormore 898

Michelin

Notably neighbourhood

Wild Geese XX	Adare	822
Left Bank Bistro X	Athlone	825
Cafe Paradiso X	Cork	845
Cavistons X	Dun Laoghaire	867
Packie's X	Kenmare	877
Zuni XX	Kilkenny	878
Courthouse X⊛	Kinlough	882

Serious about food

Inis Meáin Restaurant & Suites XX	Aran Islands/Inishmaan	823
O'Grady's on the Pier X	Barna	832
Olde Post Inn XX	Cavan/Cloverhill	841
Old Convent XX	Clogheen	842
Eastern Seaboard Bar & Grill X	Drogheda	850
Tannery XX	Dúngargvan	866
Castle Murray House XX	Dunkineely	866
Blairscove House XX	Durrus	867
Moran's Oyster Cottage ⓘ	Kilcolgan	877
Toddies at The Bulman ⓘ	Kinsale	884
Brabazon XX	Slane	895
Aherne's XX	Youghall	902

Michelin

Patrick Guilbaud

Some grandeur

Ballyfin 🏰🏰🏰🏰	Ballyfin	829
Hayfield Manor 🏰🏰🏰🏰	Cork	843
Solis Lough Eske Castle 🏰🏰🏰	Donegal	848
Merrion 🏰🏰🏰	Dublin	851
Shelbourne 🏰🏰🏰🏰	Dublin	851
Sheen Falls Lodge 🏰🏰🏰	Kenmare	876
K Club 🏰🏰🏰🏰	Straffan	897

The classics

Mustard Seed at Echo Lodge 🏰	Ballingarry	827
Gregans Castle 🏰🏰	Ballyvaughan	830
Ashford Castle 🏰🏰🏰	Cong	843
Castle Leslie 🏰🏰	Glaslough	874
Marlfield House 🏰🏰	Gorey	874
Park 🏰🏰🏰	Kenmare	876
Delphi Lodge 🏰	Leenane	885
Longueville House 🏰🏰	Mallow	888
Ballymaloe House 🏰🏰	Shanagarry	895

ACHILL ISLAND ACAILL

Mayo – Regional map n° **21**-A2

▶ Dublin 288 km – Castlebar 54 km – Galway 144 km

Doogort Dumha Goirt

 Gray's 🎍 🛎 **P**

FAMILY · CLASSIC Two adjoining whitewashed houses; one displaying an old clock face from its former life as a mission. Well-kept, modest bedrooms have small shower rooms and colourful throws and cushions. Striking artwork of local island scenes adorns the dining room walls. Simple dinners often feature the catch of the day.

14 rooms ⊡ – 🛉 € 40/56 🛉🛉 € 80/100

– ☎ 098 43244 – www.grays-guesthouse.ie – Closed October-March

ADARE ÁTH DARA

Limerick – Pop. 1 106 – Regional map n° **22**-B2

▶ Dublin 210 km – Killarney 95 km – Limerick 16 km

Dunraven Arms 🛎 🖾 🕸 🗓 🖂 🏋 **P**

TRADITIONAL · CLASSIC A charming extended former coaching inn dating from 1792 and very personally run by the Murphy brothers. Classically furnished lounges and a wood-panelled bar. Smart, spacious bedrooms; some with four-poster beds and garden views.

86 rooms ⊡ – 🛉 € 100/150 🛉🛉 € 150/195

Main St – ☎ 061 605 900 – www.dunravenhotel.com

Maigue – See restaurant listing

XX **1826** 🛖

😊 MODERN CUISINE · RUSTIC This pretty little thatched cottage was built in 1826; inside it's cosy and characterful, with a wood burning stove and a rustic feel. Interesting, attractively presented dishes use well-sourced ingredients and have subtle modern touches. It's owned by an experienced young couple: he cooks and she serves.

Menu € 34 (early dinner) – Carte € 30/46

Main St – ☎ 061 396 004 (booking essential) – www.1826adare.ie – dinner only
– Closed last 3 weeks January and Monday-Tuesday

XX **Wild Geese**

TRADITIONAL CUISINE · COSY Long-standing restaurant located in a delightful terrace of thatched cottages, on the main street of a pretty village. The atmosphere is intimate and cosy, and the service, friendly. Traditional menus make good use of local produce.

Menu € 27/37

Rose Cottage – ☎ 061 396 451 (booking essential) – www.wild-geese.com
– Closed 24-26 December, Sunday dinner and Monday

XX **Maigue** 🛎 ⅃ 🖾 **P**

TRADITIONAL CUISINE · CHIC Named after the nearby river, this is a traditional hotel dining room with a formal feel and professional service. Menus focus on Irish produce and are firmly rooted in tradition; a trolley features, offering prime roast rib of beef.

Carte € 26/43 – bar lunch Monday-Saturday

Dunraven Arms Hotel, Main St – ☎ 061 605 900 – www.dunravenhotel.com

ARAN ISLANDS OILEÁIN ÁRANN

Galway – Pop. 1 280 – Regional map n° **22**-B1

▶ Dublin 260 km – Galway 43 km – Limerick 145 km – Ennis 111 km

Inishmore

🏚 Óstán Árann   ☆ ← 🛏 🏠 📺 & 🐾 🅿

TRADITIONAL · CLASSIC Comfortable, family-owned hotel with a great view of the harbour. Bustling bar with live music most nights in high season. Spacious, up-to-date bedrooms are decorated in bright colours. Traditional dishes in the wood-floored restaurant.

22 rooms ☖ – ♦ € 64/84 ♦♦ € 78/118

*Kilronan – ☏ 099 61104 – www.aranislandshotel.com
– Closed November-February*

🏠 Ard Einne Guesthouse   🐾 ← 🛏 🅿

TRADITIONAL · COSY Close to the airport, an attractive chalet-style guesthouse set back on a hill and boasting superb views of Killeany Bay; take it all in from the comfy lounge. Uniformly decorated bedrooms have pine furnishings and great outlooks.

6 rooms ☖ – ♦ € 60/80 ♦♦ € 80/100

Killeany – ☏ 099 61126 – www.ardeinne.com – Closed November-February

Inishmaan

✕✕ Inis Meáin Restaurant & Suites   ⟷ 🐾 ← 🛏 🅿

REGIONAL CUISINE · FRIENDLY Set on a beautiful island, this futuristic stone building is inspired by the surrounding landscapes and features limed walls, sage banquettes and panoramic views. Cooking is modern, tasty and satisfyingly straightforward, showcasing island ingredients including seafood caught in currachs and hand-gathered urchins. Minimalist bedrooms feature natural furnishings.

Menu € 75

5 rooms ☖ – ♦ € 300/450 ♦♦ € 300/450

*– ☏ 086 826 6026 (booking essential) – www.inismeain.com – dinner only
– Closed October-March and Sunday, 2 night minimum stay*

Inisheer

🏠 South Aran House   ☆ 🐾 ← 🐾

FAMILY · FUNCTIONAL Simple guesthouse on the smallest of the Aran Islands, where traditional living still reigns. With its whitewashed walls and tiled floors, it has a slight Mediterranean feel; bedrooms are homely, with wrought iron beds and modern amenities. Their next door restaurant serves breakfast, snacks and hearty meals.

4 rooms ☖ – ♦ € 49 ♦♦ € 80

– ☏ 087 340 5687 – www.southaran.com – Restricted opening in winter

ARDMORE AIRD MHÓR

Waterford – Pop. 435 – Regional map n° **22**-C3
▶ Dublin 240 km – Waterford 71 km – Cork 60 km – Kilkenny 123 km

🏚 Cliff House   ☆ ← 🖵 🌐 🐷 ⅃♨ 📺 🅰🅲 🐾 🖙 🅿

LUXURY · MODERN Stylish cliffside hotel with a superb bay outlook and a lovely spa. Slate walls, Irish fabrics and bold colours feature throughout. Modern bedrooms have backlit glass artwork and smart bathrooms; some have balconies and all share the wonderful view. Choose from an extensive menu in the delightful bar and on the terrace; the restaurant serves more creative dishes.

39 rooms ☖ – ♦ € 150/170 ♦♦ € 225/310 – 3 suites

*Middle Rd – ☏ 024 87800 – www.thecliffhousehotel.com – Closed
24-26 December*

❀ **House** – See restaurant listing

✗✗✗ House   ← 🅰🅲 🅿

CREATIVE · DESIGN Full length windows give every table an impressive coastal view at this smart hotel restaurant. Concise menus showcase local and garden produce and cooking is complex – a host of ingredients are used for each course. Creative dishes combine a good range of flavours and textures and presentation is unique.

→ Bantry Bay organic salmon with pickled vegetables and horseradish. Roast Irish veal with garlic fudge, romanesco and mushroom. Organic chocolate 65% with white coffee ice cream, olive oil and sea salt.

Menu € 75/95

Cliff House Hotel, Middle Rd – ℰ 024 87800 – www.thecliffhousehotel.com
– dinner only – Closed 24-26 December, Tuesday November-February and Sunday-Monday

ARTHURSTOWN COLMÁN

Wexford – Pop. 135 – Regional map n° **22**-D2
▶ Dublin 166 km – Cork 159 km – Limerick 162 km – Waterford 42 km

🏚 Dunbrody Country House   🐾 ⇌ 🛗 ⅍ 🅿

COUNTRY HOUSE · ELEGANT Part-Georgian former hunting lodge; once owned by the Marquis of Donegal and now by celebrity chef, Kevin Dundon, who runs his cookery school here. Comfy lounge-bar with a marble-topped counter. Spacious bedrooms furnished in a period style.

16 rooms 🖙 – 🛉 € 125/165 🛉🛉 € 180/320 – 6 suites

– ℰ 051 389 600 – www.dunbrodyhouse.com – Closed 9 January-12 February and 16-26 December
Harvest Room – See restaurant listing

✗✗✗ Harvest Room   ⇌ 🛖 🅿

MODERN BRITISH · ELEGANT Light, spacious, classically styled restaurant in keeping with the Georgian country house hotel in which it is sited; bright rugs and vividly coloured seats add a modern touch. Classic dishes feature produce from their own kitchen garden.

Menu € 65

Dunbrody Country House Hotel, – ℰ 051 389 600 (booking essential)
– www.dunbrodyhouse.com – dinner only and Sunday lunch
– Closed 9 January-12 February, 16-26 December and Monday-Tuesday except July-September

ASHFORD ÁTH NA FUINSEOG

Wicklow – Pop. 1 449 – Regional map n° **22**-D2
▶ Dublin 43 km – Rathdrum 17 km – Wicklow 6 km

🏠 Ballyknocken House   🏡 🐾 ⇌ ⅍ 🅿

TRADITIONAL · PERSONALISED Part-Victorian house with neat gardens and an adjoining cookery school, located next to the family farm. Classical lounge and good-sized bedrooms with antique furnishings, modern feature walls and bright fabrics; some have claw-foot baths. Dine on traditional dishes of local produce at gingham-clothed tables.

7 rooms 🖙 – 🛉 € 79/119 🛉🛉 € 105/129

Glenealy – South : 4.75 km on L 1096 – ℰ 0404 44627 – www.ballyknocken.com
– Closed December-February

ATHLONE BAILE ÁTHA LUAIN

Westmeath – Pop. 15 558 – Regional map n° **21**-C3
▶ Dublin 120 km – Galway 92 km – Limerick 120 km – Roscommon 32 km

🏠 Shelmalier House　　　　　　　　🛏 ⌂ ℀ 🅿

TRADITIONAL · PERSONALISED Well-run guesthouse with neat gardens, homely décor and strong green credentials. Relax in the sauna then head for one of the comfy bedrooms – Room 1 is the best. Extensive breakfasts often include a daily special such as pancakes.

7 rooms 🖵 – ♦ € 50 ♦♦ € 80/85

Retreat Rd., Cartrontroy – East : 2.5 km by Dublin rd (N 6, junction 9)
– 𝒞 090 647 2245 – www.shelmalierhouse.com – Closed December-February

✗ Thyme　　　　　　　　　　　　　　　🅰🅲

REGIONAL CUISINE · FRIENDLY Welcoming corner restaurant with candles in the windows; set next to the river and run by a chatty, personable team. Hearty, flavoursome dishes are a mix of the traditional and the modern. Local suppliers are listed on the menu.

Menu € 30 – Carte € 28/50

Custume Pl., Strand St – 𝒞 090 647 8850 – www.thymerestaurant.ie – dinner only and Sunday lunch – Closed 24-26 December, 1 January and Good Friday

✗ Left Bank Bistro　　　　　　　　　　🅰🅲

INTERNATIONAL · FRIENDLY Keenly run, airy bistro with rough floorboards, brick walls and an open-plan kitchen. Extensive menus offer an eclectic mix of dishes, from light lunches and local fish specials to tasty Irish beef and even Asian-inspired fare.

Menu € 25 (dinner) – Carte € 25/39

Fry Pl – 𝒞 090 649 4446 – www.leftbankbistro.com – Closed 1 week Christmas, Sunday and Monday

✗ Kin Khao　　　　　　　　　　　　　　🅰🅲

THAI · FRIENDLY Vivid yellow building with red window frames, hidden down a side street near the castle. The upstairs restaurant is decorated with tapestries and there's a good selection of authentic Thai dishes – try the owner's recommendations.

Menu € 10 (weekday lunch)/20 – Carte € 26/38

Abbey Ln. – 𝒞 090 649 8805 – www.kinkhaothai.ie – dinner only and lunch Wednesday-Friday and Sunday – Closed 25 and 31 December

at Glasson Northeast: 8 km on N55 ⊠ Athlone

🏨 Wineport Lodge　　　🔆 🦢 ≪ 🛏 🛋 ⊡ ⅙ 🅰🅲 ℀ 🧖 🅿

LUXURY · DESIGN A superbly located hotel where the bedroom wing follows the line of the lough shore and each luxurious room boasts a balcony or a waterside terrace (it's worth paying the extra for the Champagne Suite). The outdoor hot tubs make a great place to take in the view. Extensive menus utilise seasonal produce.

30 rooms 🖵 – ♦ € 105/235 ♦♦ € 150/300

Southwest : 1.5 km – 𝒞 090 643 9010 – www.wineport.ie – Closed 23-26 December

🏠 Glasson Stone Lodge　　　　　　　　🛏 ℀ 🅿

FAMILY · PERSONALISED Smart guesthouse built from local Irish limestone. Pine features strongly throughout; bedrooms boast thoughtful extras and locally made furniture – Room 4 is the best. Breakfast includes homemade bread and fruit from the garden.

6 rooms – ♦ € 50 ♦♦ € 70

– 𝒞 090 648 5004 – www.glassonstonelodge.com – Closed November-April

AUGHRIM EACHROIM

Wicklow – Pop. 1 364 – Regional map n° **22**-D2
▶ Dublin 74 km – Waterford 124 km – Wexford 96 km

🏨 Brooklodge H & Wells Spa   ⓢ 🛋 📶 📺 🌐 🏊 ⓕ ✗ 🔲 ⚹ ⚹ **P**

SPA AND WELLNESS · CLASSIC Sprawling hotel in 180 peaceful acres in the Wicklow Valley. Flag-floored reception, comfy lounge, informal café and pub. Smart, modern bedrooms with large bathrooms; some in an annexe, along with the conference rooms. State-of-the-art spa.

86 rooms 🖵 – 🛉 € 100/140 🛉🛉 € 120/200 – 18 suites

Macreddin Village – North : 3.25 km – ℰ 0402 36444 – www.brooklodge.com
– Closed 24-25 December

Strawberry Tree • Armento – See restaurant listing

✗✗✗ Strawberry Tree   ⓕ 🔲 **P**

ORGANIC · ELEGANT Ireland's only certified organic restaurant. It's formal, with an intimate, atmospheric feel, and is set on a village-style hotel estate. Menus feature wild and organic ingredients sourced from local artisan suppliers.

Menu € 65 – Carte approx. € 59

Brooklodge Hotel, Macreddin Village – North : 3.25 km – ℰ 0402 36444
– www.brooklodge.com – dinner only – Closed 24-25 December

✗ Armento   ⓕ 🔲 **P**

ITALIAN · BISTRO Informal Italian restaurant set in a smart hotel on a secluded 180 acre estate. Southern Italian menus feature artisan produce imported from Armento and pizzas cooked in the wood-fired oven.

Menu € 35/40 – Carte approx. € 37

Brooklodge Hotel, Macreddin Village – North : 3.25 km – ℰ 0402 36444
– www.brooklodge.com – dinner only – Closed 24-25 December

Good quality cooking at a great price?
Look out for the Bib Gourmand ⊛.

BAGENALSTOWN MUINE BHEAG

Carlow – Pop. 2 775 – Regional map n° **22**-D2

▶ Dublin 101 km – Carlow 16 km – Kilkenny 21 km – Wexford 59 km

🏠 Kilgraney Country House   ⓢ ⭩ ⓕ 🏊 ⚹ **P**

COUNTRY HOUSE · PERSONALISED Georgian country house which adopts a truly holistic approach. Period features blend with modern, minimalist furnishings and the mood is calm and peaceful. It boasts a small tea room, a craft gallery and a spa with a relaxation room, along with pleasant herb, vegetable, zodiac and monastic gardens.

7 rooms 🖵 – 🛉 € 120/135 🛉🛉 € 170/240

South : 6.5 km by R 705 (Borris Rd) – ℰ 059 977 5283 – www.kilgraneyhouse.com
– Closed November-February and Monday-Wednesday

BALLINA BÉAL AN ÁTHA

Mayo – Pop. 10 490 – Regional map n° **21**-B2

▶ Dublin 241 km – Galway 117 km – Roscommon 103 km – Sligo 59 km

🏨 Mount Falcon   ⓢ ⭩ ⓕ 📺 🏊 🕭 ⓕ ⚹ ⚹ ⚹ **P**

HISTORIC · PERSONALISED Classic country house built in 1872, with golf, cycling, fishing and archery available in its 100 acre grounds. Characterful bedrooms in the main house; spacious, contemporary rooms in the extension. The Boathole Bar has a clubby feel.

32 rooms 🖵 – 🛉 € 140/180 🛉🛉 € 160/200 – 1 suite

Foxford Rd – South : 6.25 km on N 26 – ℰ 096 74472 – www.mountfalcon.com
– Closed 24-26 December

Kitchen – See restaurant listing

🏠 Belleek Castle 🕭 🖛 🎗 🛁 🅿

HISTORIC · ELEGANT An imposing house built on the site of an old medieval abbey and surrounded by 1,000 acres of mature park and woodland. An amazing array of characterful rooms come complete with open fires, ornate panelling, antiques and old armour.

10 rooms ⌂ – ♦ € 50/180 ♦♦ € 90/220

Northeast : 2.5 km by Castle Rd – ℰ 096 22400 – www.belleekcastle.com – Closed 1 January-13 February

Belleek Castle – See restaurant listing

XX Belleek Castle 🖛 🕪 ♻ 🅿

MODERN CUISINE · ELEGANT Start with a drink in the bar, which is fitted out with original pieces from a 16C Spanish galleon, then head through to the dramatic candlelit dining room. Seasonal modern dishes include fillet of beef flambéed on a sword at the table!

Menu € 35 (weekdays) – Carte € 34/71

Belleek Castle Hotel, Northeast : 2.5 km by Castle Rd – ℰ 096 22400
– www.belleekcastle.com – dinner only – Closed 1 January-13 February

XX Kitchen ← 🖛 🅿

MODERN CUISINE · INTIMATE Set in the high-ceilinged former kitchens of the Mount Falcon hotel, with woodland views from the windows. Classic dishes have been brought up-to-date and use seasonal ingredients including veg, herbs and fruits from the kitchen garden.

Menu € 59

Mount Falcon Hotel, Foxford Rd – South : 6.25 km on N 26 – ℰ 096 74472
– www.mountfalcon.com – dinner only – Closed 24-26 December

BALLINGARRY BAILE AN GHARRAÍ
Limerick – Pop. 527 – Regional map n° **22**-B2
▶ Dublin 227 km – Killarney 90 km – Limerick 29 km

🏠 Mustard Seed at Echo Lodge 🏠 🕭 🖛 🕭 🅿

TRADITIONAL · CLASSIC This cosy former convent is surrounded by well-kept gardens and filled with antique furniture, paintings, books and fresh flowers. Bedrooms in the main house have period styling, while those in the former school house are brighter and more modern. Dinner is an occasion – the two grand rooms are candlelit and have gilt mirrors; cooking is elaborate and boldly flavoured.

16 rooms ⌂ – ♦ € 100/200 ♦♦ € 130/330

– ℰ 069 68508 – www.mustardseed.ie – Closed mid-January-early February and 24-26 December

BALLSBRIDGE DROICHEAD NA DOTHRA – Dublin → See Dublin

BALLYBUNION BAILE AN BHUINNEÁNAIGH
Kerry – Pop. 1 354 – Regional map n° **22**-A2
▶ Dublin 283 km – Limerick 90 km – Tralee 42 km

🏠 Teach de Broc Country House 🏠 🖭 🕭 🎗 🅿

TRADITIONAL · MODERN A purpose-built house by the Ballybunion golf course, with a spacious, open-plan lounge and bar and eye-catching modern Irish art. Comfortable, good-sized bedrooms with smart bathrooms; ask for one at the front, which looks to the links. The simple bistro dining room serves a wide-ranging menu.

14 rooms ⌂ – ♦ € 90/120 ♦♦ € 130/150

Link Rd – South : 2.5 km by Golf Club rd – ℰ 068 27581
– www.ballybuniongolf.com – Closed November-February

🏠 19th Lodge 🛏 ⟨ AC ⟩ 🛜 P

TOWNHOUSE · PERSONALISED Run by a welcoming couple, this guesthouse overlooks the fairways of the famed course and is filled with golfing memorabilia. Spacious bedrooms are named after golfers or courses; the best have whirlpool baths. Substantial breakfasts.

14 rooms ⌂ – ♦ € 80/150 ♦♦ € 100/200

Links Rd – South : 2.75 km by Golf Club rd – ℰ 068 27592
– www.ballybuniongolflodge.com – Closed Christmas and restricted opening in winter

🏠 Tides ≤ ⟨ 🛜 P

FAMILY · PERSONALISED Generously sized bedrooms, superb views and welcoming hosts are the draw at this purpose built guesthouse. Quiz David about the local area in the comfy lounge and, at breakfast, enjoy Doreen's pancakes amongst a host of other delights.

6 rooms ⌂ – ♦ € 120/160 ♦♦ € 120/160

East : 1.75 km. by R 551 on R 553 – ℰ 086 600 0665 – www.ballybunionbandb.ie
– Closed December-January

BALLYCOTTON BAILE CHOITÍN
Cork – Pop. 476 – Regional map n° **22**-C3
▶ Dublin 265 km – Cork 43 km – Waterford 106 km

🏨 Bayview 🛏 ≤ ⟨ 🛗 🛜 P

FAMILY · PERSONALISED This hotel is set in an elevated position, with superb views over the bay, the harbour and the island opposite. Two cosy lounges; one on each floor. Spacious bedrooms with floral fabrics and sea views – many have Juliet balconies. Ambitious modern menus; ask for a seat in one of the bay windows.

35 rooms – ♦ € 89/149 ♦♦ € 89/149 – ⌂ €15 – 2 suites

– ℰ 021 464 6746 – www.thebayviewhotel.com – Closed November-March

BALLYDAVID BAILE NA NGALL
Kerry – ✉ Dingle – Regional map n° **22**-A2
▶ Dublin 362 km – Dingle 11 km – Tralee 58 km

🏠 Gorman's Clifftop House 🛏 ≤ ⟨ 🛜 P

FAMILY · CLASSIC Purpose-built house in a wonderfully rural location, offering great views out across Ballydavid Head and the Three Sisters. It's family run and has a lovely homely feel. Bright, spacious bedrooms have good facilities; those to the front share the view. The small menu features home-cooked local produce.

8 rooms ⌂ – ♦ € 95/125 ♦♦ € 120/150

Slea Head Dr, Glashabeg – North : 2 km on Feomanagh rd. – ℰ 066 915 5162
– www.gormans-clifftophouse.com – Closed mid October-mid March

BALLYFARNAN BÉAL ÁTHA FEARNÁIN
Roscommon – Pop. 205 – Regional map n° **21**-C2
▶ Dublin 111 km – Roscommon 42 km – Sligo 21 km – Longford 38 km

🏰 Kilronan Castle 🛏 🛏 ≤ ⟨ 🖥 🌐 🦅 🛗 ⟩ AC 🛜 🛁 P

HISTORIC BUILDING · CLASSIC Impressively restored castle with characterful sitting rooms, a library and a palm court; wood panelling, antiques and oil paintings feature throughout. Smart leisure club and hydrotherapy centre. Opulent red and gold bedrooms offer a high level of comfort. The formal dining room serves a classical menu.

84 rooms ⌂ – ♦ € 99/179 ♦♦ € 109/250

Southeast : 3.5 km on Keadew rd – ℰ 071 961 8000 – www.kilronancastle.ie

BALLYFIN AN BAILE FIONN
Laois – Pop. 633 – Regional map n° **22**-C1
▶ Dublin 69 km – Portlaoise 11 km – Cork 114 km – Limerick 67 km

🏨 Ballyfin   🏇 🐴 ← 🛏 🍽 🖼 🛁 🍴 🔲 🚿 🏊 🅿️

GRAND LUXURY · HISTORIC An immaculate Regency mansion built in 1820 and set in 600 acres. The interior is stunning, with its cantilevered staircase, breathtaking ceilings and restored antiques. The library features 7,000 books, the drawing room is decorated in gold leaf and the bedrooms are luxurious. Produce grown in the kitchen garden informs the dishes served in the State dining room.

20 rooms (dinner included) ⌂ – ♦ € 360/595 ♦♦ € 560/850 – 3 suites
– ✆ 057 875 5866 – www.ballyfin.com – Closed January

BALLYGARRETT BAILE GHEARÓID
Regional map n° **39**-D2
▶ Dublin 101 km – Wexford 35 km – Cork 213 km

🏨 Clonganny House 🆕   🏇 🐴 🛏 🚿 🅿️

COUNTRY HOUSE · ELEGANT Close to the coast you'll find this Georgian manor house, which has been stylishly and comfortably refurbished. Bedrooms are located in the old coach house and have a wonderfully classical style: all feature handmade and antique furnishings and open onto private terraces overlooking the garden. The formal linen-laid dining room offers a traditional set priced menu.

4 rooms ⌂ – ♦ € 180 ♦♦ € 180
Southwest : 4.5 km. by R 472 – ✆ 053 948 2111 – www.clonganny.com

BALLYLICKEY BÉAL ÁTHA LEICE
Cork – ✉ Bantry – Regional map n° **22**-A3
▶ Dublin 347 km – Cork 88 km – Killarney 72 km

🏨 Seaview House   🏇 🛏 🚿 🅿️

TRADITIONAL · CLASSIC Well-run Victorian house that upholds tradition in both its décor and its service. Pleasant drawing room, cosy bar and antique-furnished bedrooms; some with sea views. The attractive gardens lead down to the shore of the bay. A classical menu is served at elegant polished tables laid with silver tableware.

25 rooms ⌂ – ♦ € 85/105 ♦♦ € 140/165
– ✆ 027 50073 – www.seaviewhousehotel.com – Closed mid November-mid March

BALLYLIFFIN BAILE LIFÍN
Donegal – Pop. 461 – Regional map n° **21**-C1
▶ Dublin 174 km – Lifford 46 km – Letterkenny 39 km

🏨 Ballyliffin Lodge   🏇 ← 🛏 🖼 💆 🧖 🛁 🔲 🚿 🏊 🅿️

BUSINESS · MODERN Remote hotel with well-kept gardens, affording a superb outlook over the countryside to the beach. Bedrooms offer good facilities; ask for one facing the front. Relax in the lovely spa and pool, or enjoy afternoon tea with a view in the lounge. Informal, bistro-style dining, with international menus.

40 rooms ⌂ – ♦ € 60/85 ♦♦ € 118/200
Shore Rd – ✆ 074 937 8200 – www.ballyliffinlodge.com – Closed 24-26 December and 10-11 January

BALLYMACARBRY BAILE MHAC CAIRBRE
Waterford – ✉ Clonmel – Pop. 132 – Regional map n° **22**-C2
▶ Dublin 190 km – Cork 79 km – Waterford 63 km

🏠 Glasha Farmhouse 🏠 🐾 ⟨ 🛏 🌿 🅿

TRADITIONAL · CLASSIC Large farmhouse between the Knockmealdown and Comeragh Mountains. Guest areas include a cosy lounge, an airy conservatory and a pleasant patio. Bedrooms are comfortable and immaculately kept; some have jacuzzis. The welcoming owner has good local knowledge. Home-cooked meals, with picnic lunches available.

6 rooms 😑 – 🛉 € 70 🛉🛉 € 100

Northwest : 4 km by R 671 – 𝒞 052 613 6108 – www.glashafarmhouse.com
– Closed December

BALLYMORE EUSTACE AN BAILE MÓR
Kildare – Pop. 872 – Regional map n° **22**-D1
▶ Dublin 48 km – Naas 12 km – Drogheda 99 km

🍴 Ballymore Inn 🏠 ⟨ 🔊 🎜 🅿

TRADITIONAL CUISINE · PUB Remote village pub with a small deli selling home-made breads, pickles, oils and the like. The owner promotes small artisan producers, so expect organic veg, meat from quality assured farms and farmhouse cheeses. Portions are generous.

Menu € 24 (weekday lunch)/38 – Carte € 26/51
– 𝒞 045 864 585 – www.ballymoreinn.com

BALLYNAHINCH BAILE NA HINSE
Galway – ✉ Recess – Regional map n° **21**-A3
▶ Dublin 225 km – Galway 66 km – Westport 79 km

🏰 Ballynahinch Castle 🐾 ⟨ 🛏 🎜 🛠 🌿 🅿

TRADITIONAL · CLASSIC Dramatically located on the Wild Atlantic Way, amongst 450 acres of woodland, with a salmon fishing river in front and the mountains behind. Relax by a peat fire in one of the cosy sitting rooms. Bedrooms have a country house style.

45 rooms 😑 – 🛉 € 140/330 🛉🛉 € 160/450 – 3 suites
– 𝒞 095 31006 – www.ballynahinch-castle.com
Owenmore – See restaurant listing

✕✕ Owenmore 🆕 ⟨ 🛏 🅿

MODERN CUISINE · INTIMATE Within a 17C country house you'll find this bright, elegant restaurant which looks out over the river and the estate. Modern dishes are delicate and subtly flavoured. In winter, end the evening with a drink beside the marble fireplace.

Menu € 65 **s**
Ballynahinch Castle Hotel, – 𝒞 095 31006 (booking essential)
– www.ballynahinchcastle.com – dinner only

BALLYVAUGHAN BAILE UÍ BHEACHÁIN
Clare – Pop. 258 – Regional map n° **22**-B1
▶ Dublin 240 km – Ennis 55 km – Galway 46 km

🏰 Gregans Castle 🐾 ⟨ 🛏 🌿 🅿

FAMILY · PERSONALISED Well-run, part-18C country house with superb views of The Burren and Galway Bay. The open-fired hall leads to a cosy, rustic bar-lounge and an elegant sitting room. Bedrooms are furnished with antiques: two open onto the garden; one is in the old kitchen and features a panelled ceiling and a four-poster bed.

21 rooms 😑 – 🛉 € 160/200 🛉🛉 € 235/265 – 4 suites
Southwest : 6 km on N 67 – 𝒞 065 707 7005 – www.gregans.ie – Closed 6 November-16 February
Gregans Castle – See restaurant listing

🏠 Ballyvaughan Lodge   🅿

TRADITIONAL · PERSONALISED Welcoming guesthouse with a colourful flower display and a decked terrace. The vaulted, light-filled lounge features a locally made flower chandelier; bedrooms boast co-ordinating fabrics. Breakfast uses quality, farmers' market produce.

11 rooms ☲ – ♦ € 45/60 ♦♦ € 75/100

– ☏ 065 707 7292 – www.ballyvaughanlodge.com – Closed 23-28 December

XX Gregans Castle   ⇐ 🛎 🅿

MODERN CUISINE · ELEGANT Have an aperitif in the drawing room of this country house hotel before heading through to the restaurant (ask for a table close to the window, to take in views stretching as far as Galway Bay). Interesting modern dishes have clean, clear flavours and showcase the latest local produce. Service is attentive.

Menu € 72 **s**

Gregans Castle Hotel, Southwest : 6 km on N 67 – ☏ 065 707 7005 (booking advisable) – www.gregans.ie – dinner only – Closed 6 November-16 February

BALTIMORE DÚN NA SÉAD

Cork – Pop. 347 – Regional map n° **22**-A3

▶ Dublin 344 km – Cork 95 km – Killarney 124 km

🏠 Casey's of Baltimore   🏖 ⇐ 🕉 🐟 🅿

FAMILY · CLASSIC Extended 19C pub with a terracotta façade, well located near the seashore. Comfy lounge and simple pine-furnished bedrooms with good facilities. You're guaranteed a warm welcome from the family owners. The restaurant and beer garden overlook the bay; classical menus, and traditional music at the weekend.

14 rooms ☲ – ♦ € 107 ♦♦ € 158/175

East : 0.75 km on R 595 – ☏ 028 20197 – www.caseysofbaltimore.com – Closed 20-26 December

🏠 Slipway   ⇐ 🛎 🕉 🅿 🚭

TRADITIONAL · COSY Laid-back guesthouse in a lovely spot. The open-fired lounge is hung with tapestries made by the charming owner and the breakfast room leads onto a veranda with stunning views over the bay. Modest, well-kept bedrooms feature fresh flowers.

4 rooms ☲ – ♦ € 58/70 ♦♦ € 72/80

The Cove – Southwest : 0.75 km – ☏ 028 20134 – www.theslipway.com – Closed 15 September-1 May

BANDON DROICHEAD NA BANDAN

Cork – Pop. 1 917 – Regional map n° **22**-B3

▶ Dublin 181 km – Cork 20 km – Carrigaline 28 km – Cobh 33 km

🍴 Poachers   🅿

REGIONAL CUISINE · PUB Cosy neighbourhood pub that's popular with the locals. There's a snug, a wood-panelled bar, and an upstairs restaurant which opens later in the week. West Cork seafood takes centre stage and you can buy home-made bread to take home.

Menu € 22 (weekday dinner)/32 – Carte € 24/42

Clonakilty Rd – Southwest : 1.5 km on N 71 – ☏ 023 884 1159 – www.poachers.ie – Closed 25 December

BANTRY BEANNTRAÍ **Cork**

Cork – Regional map n° **22**-A3

▶ Dublin 215 km – Cork 53 km – Killarney 49 km – Macroom 34 km

✗ O'Connors   AC

SEAFOOD · BISTRO Well-run harbourside restaurant, with a compact, bistro-style interior featuring model ships in the windows and modern art on the walls. The menu focuses on local seafood, mostly from the small fishing boats in the harbour.

Menu € 25 (dinner) – Carte € 25/49

Wolf Tone Sq – ☏ 027 55664 (booking essential) – www.oconnorsbantry.com
– Closed Tuesday and Wednesday November-April

BARNA BEARNA
Galway - Pop. 1 878 – Regional map n° **21**-B3
▶ Dublin 227 km – Galway 9 km

🏠 Twelve   ❄ ⊟ ६ AC ⚔ P

BUSINESS · MODERN An unassuming exterior hides a keenly run boutique hotel complete with a bakery, a pizza kitchen and a deli. Stylish, modern bedrooms have large gilt mirrors, mood lighting and designer 'seaweed' toiletries; some even boast cocktail bars! Innovative menus in Upstairs @ West; modern European dishes in The Pins.

48 rooms ☑ – ♥ € 100/160 ♥♥ € 100/170 – 10 suites
Barna Crossroads – ☏ 091 597 000 – www.thetwelvehotel.ie
Upstairs @ West – See restaurant listing

✗✗ Upstairs @ West   🍸 ६ AC P

MODERN CUISINE · INTIMATE Stylish first floor restaurant in a smart boutique hotel, with a chic champagne bar, booth seating and a moody, intimate feel. Seasonal menus offer ambitious, innovative dishes, showcasing meats and seafood from the 'West' of Ireland.

Menu € 30 (weekdays) **s** – Carte € 34/57 **s**

Twelve Hotel, Barna Crossroads – ☏ 091 597 000 – www.westrestaurant.ie
– dinner only and Sunday lunch – Closed Monday and Tuesday

✗ O'Grady's on the Pier   ⩽ AC

SEAFOOD · RUSTIC Smartly painted white and powder blue building on the water's edge, with views across Co. Clare and a charming interior with real fires and fresh flowers. Fish is from Galway or Kinsale; go for the daily catch, which could be classically presented or may have a modern twist. Cheerful, attentive service.

Carte € 29/58

– ☏ 091 592 223 (booking essential) – www.ogradysonthepier.com – Closed 24-26 December

BARRELLS CROSS - Cork → See Kinsale

BIRR BIORRA
Offaly - Pop. 4 428 – Regional map n° **22**-C1
▶ Dublin 140 km – Athlone 45 km – Kilkenny 79 km – Limerick 79 km

🏠 Maltings   ⅍ P

TOWNHOUSE · TRADITIONAL Characterful stone house, once used to store malt in the production of Guinness. Enjoy homemade soda bread, scones and jams in the breakfast-room-cum-lounge, which overhangs the river and looks out towards the castle grounds.

6 rooms ☑ – ♥ € 50/55 ♥♥ € 80
Castle St – ☏ 057 912 1345 – www.themaltingsbirr.com

BLACKLION AN BLAIC
Cavan - Pop. 229 – Regional map n° **20**-A3
▶ Dublin 194 km – Drogheda 170 km – Enniskillen 19 km

XxX MacNean House   ⇦ AC 🕪

CREATIVE · ELEGANT Stylish restaurant in a smart townhouse, with a chic lounge, a plush dining room and a cookery school. Choose between a 4 course set selection or a 9 course tasting menu – cooking is ambitious and uses complex techniques, and dishes are attractively presented. Bedrooms are a mix of modern and country styles.

Menu € 85

19 rooms ⌂ – ♦ € 96 ♦♦ € 134/192

Main St – ℰ 071 985 3022 (booking essential) – www.macneanrestaurant.com
– dinner only and Sunday lunch – Closed January, Sunday dinner, Monday and Tuesday

BLACKROCK Dublin → See Dublin

BLARNEY AN BHLARNA
Cork – ✉ Cork – Pop. 2 437 – Regional map n° **22**-B3
▶ Dublin 268 km – Cork 9 km

🏠 Killarney House   ⇦ ⅏ P

FAMILY · PERSONALISED Well-kept, friendly guesthouse on the edge of town, with immaculate gardens, simple, spacious bedrooms, comfortable lounges and a wood-furnished breakfast room. The extensive breakfast menu includes a 'full Irish'.

6 rooms ⌂ – ♦ € 50/60 ♦♦ € 75/85

Station Rd – Northeast : 1.5 km on Carrignavar rd. – ℰ 021 438 1841
– www.killarneyhouseblarney.com – Closed November-December

XX Square Table

FRENCH · COSY Sweet restaurant with a warm, welcoming, neighbourhood feel. Menus offer French-influenced dishes crafted from Irish produce; the early evening menu is good value. It's proudly and enthusiastically run by twins Tricia and Martina.

Menu € 24 (dinner) – Carte € 29/45

5 The Square – ℰ 021 438 2825 (booking essential) – www.thesquaretable.ie
– dinner only and Sunday lunch – Closed last 2 weeks January, first week February, Sunday dinner, Monday and Tuesday

at Tower West: 3.25 km on R617 ✉ Cork

🏠 Ashlee Lodge   ⅏ & AC ⅏ P

FAMILY · PERSONALISED Smart hotel with a cosy lounge featuring a wood-burning stove, board games and an honesty bar. Comfortable bedrooms offer all you could want; some have whirlpool baths. Outdoor hot tub, sauna and in-room treatments. Extensive breakfasts.

10 rooms ⌂ – ♦ € 89/200 ♦♦ € 89/220

Tower – ℰ 021 438 5346 – www.ashleelodge.com – Closed November-mid March

BORRIS AN BHUIRÍOS
Carlow – Pop. 646 – Regional map n° **22**-D2
▶ Dublin 121 km – Carlow 36 km – Waterford 66 km

🏠 Step House   🖄 ⇦ ⅏ 🖥 & ⅏ 🏋 P

TOWNHOUSE · PERSONALISED A welcoming, family-run Georgian townhouse in a small heritage village. An impressive staircase leads up to spacious modern bedrooms – most have lovely mountain views and the penthouse boasts a large terrace. The comfortable brasserie, 1808, is named after the year the original hotel was built.

20 rooms ⌂ – ♦ € 79/119 ♦♦ € 99/170 – 1 suite

Main St – ℰ 059 977 3209 – www.stephousehotel.ie – Closed 15 August and 25 December

XX Clashganny House ⬟ P

CLASSIC CUISINE · INTIMATE Hidden away in a lovely valley, this early Victorian house is the setting for the realisation of one couple's dream. The modern restaurant is split over three rooms; appealing menus balance light options with more gutsy dishes.

Menu € 35

Clashganny – South : 5 km by R 702 and R 729 – ℰ 059 977 1003
– www.clashgannyhouse.com – dinner only and Sunday lunch
– Closed 24-27 December, Sunday dinner, Monday and Tuesday

BOYLE MAINISTIR NA BÚILLE

Roscommon – Pop. 1 459 – Regional map n° **21**-B2
▶ Dublin 168 km – Roscommon 43 km – Galway 103 km

🏠 Rosdarrig House ⬟ ⬟ P

FAMILY · PERSONALISED Neat house on the edge of town, close to the abbey; the friendly owners offer genuine Irish hospitality. Guest areas include two homely lounges and a linen-laid breakfast room. Simply furnished bedrooms overlook the colourful garden.

5 rooms 🍽 – ♦ € 45/50 ♦♦ € 70/75

Carrick Rd – East : 1.5 km on R 294 – ℰ 071 966 2040 – www.rosdarrig.com
– Closed November-March

🏠 Lough Key House ⬟ P

HISTORIC · CLASSIC Welcoming Georgian house with a neat garden and mature grounds, located next to Lough Key Forest Park. Homely guest areas are filled with antiques and ornaments; bedrooms in the original house are the best, with their antique four-posters and warm fabrics. You're guaranteed a warm Irish welcome.

6 rooms 🍽 – ♦ € 49/59 ♦♦ € 90/98

Southeast : 3.75 km by R 294 on N 4 – ℰ 071 966 2161 – www.loughkeyhouse.com
– Closed 2 January-16 March

BRIDGE END CEANN AN DROICHID

Donegal – Pop. 497 – Regional map n° **21**-C1
▶ Dublin 158 km – Lifford 25 km – Belfast 78 km – Londonderry 5 km

XX Harrys P

REGIONAL CUISINE · BISTRO Long-standing, passionately run restaurant with an open-plan interior and a modern bistro feel. Menus evolve with the seasons, offering flavoursome, classical dishes. Traceability is key, with much produce coming from their walled garden.

Carte € 25/50

– ℰ 074 936 8544 – www.harrys.ie – Closed 24-26 December

CAHERLISTRANE CATHAIR LOISTREÁIN

Galway – Regional map n° **21**-B3
▶ Dublin 256 km – Ballina 74 km – Galway 42 km

🏠 Lisdonagh House ⬟ ⬟ ⬟ ⬟ ⬟ P

TRADITIONAL · CLASSIC Ivy-clad Georgian house with pleasant lough views. The traditional country house interior boasts eye-catching murals and open-fired lounges. Antique-furnished bedrooms have marble bathrooms; the first floor rooms are larger and brighter. The grand dining room offers 5 course dinners and simpler suppers.

9 rooms 🍽 – ♦ € 98/120 ♦♦ € 140/180

Northwest : 4 km by R 333 off Shrule rd – ℰ 093 31163 – www.lisdonagh.com
– Closed November-April

CAHERSIVEEN CATHAIR SAIDHBHÍN

Kerry – Pop. 1 168 – Regional map n° **22**-A2

▶ Dublin 355 km – Killarney 64 km – Tralee 67 km

X QC's ⇔ 🚗 🅿

SEAFOOD · PUB A cosy, atmospheric restaurant with a nautical theme. Seafood-orientated menus offer fresh, unfussy classics and more unusual daily specials; the family also own a local fish wholesalers. Stylish, well-equipped bedrooms are located just around the corner; continental breakfasts are brought to your room.

Menu € 45 (dinner) – Carte € 21/47

11 rooms 🖵 – ♦ € 75/105 ♦♦ € 99/145

3 Main St – ℰ 066 947 2244 (booking advisable) – www.qcbar.com
– Closed Monday-Wednesday in winter and Sunday lunch

⒟ O'Neill's (The Point) Seafood Bar ⇐ 🚗 🆊 🅿

TRADITIONAL CUISINE · PUB Traditional pub in a great location by the ferry slipway; run by the O'Neill family for over 150 yrs. Locally landed seafood arrives in generous portions and includes salmon smoked nearby. Unusually, they don't serve chips or desserts.

Carte € 27/35

Renard Point – Southwest : 4.5 km by N 70 – ℰ 066 947 2165 (bookings not accepted) – Closed November-March and lunch March-May,October-November and Sunday

CAPPOQUIN CEAPACH CHOINN

Waterford – Pop. 759 – Regional map n° **22**-C2

▶ Dublin 219 km – Cork 56 km – Waterford 64 km

XX Richmond House ⇔ 🖨 🕼 🅿

TRADITIONAL CUISINE · CHIC Imposing Georgian house built in 1704 for the Earl of Cork and Burlington, and filled with family curios. Have a drink in the cosy lounge before heading to the cove-ceilinged dining room. Cooking is classically based; be sure to try the delicious local lamb. Cosy bedrooms are decorated in period styles.

Menu € 33/55

9 rooms 🖵 – ♦ € 60/80 ♦♦ € 110/140

Southeast : 0.75 km on N 72 – ℰ 058 54278 – www.richmondhouse.net – dinner only – Closed Christmas-New Year and Monday-Thursday January-February

CARAGH LAKE LOCH CÁRTHAÍ

Kerry – Regional map n° **22**-A2

▶ Dublin 341 km – Killarney 35 km – Tralee 40 km

🏡 Ard-Na-Sidhe 🕏 🛥 ⇐ 🖨 🕭 🕫 🅿

COUNTRY HOUSE · CLASSIC 1913 Arts and Crafts house set on the shores of Lough Caragh and surrounded by mountains. A subtle yet stylish modernisation has emphasised many original features such as oak-panelled walls and leaded windows. Bedrooms are smart and contemporary. The restaurant offers classic dishes with subtle modern twists.

18 rooms 🖵 – ♦ € 200/310 ♦♦ € 220/330

– ℰ 066 976 9105 – www.ardnasidhe.com – Closed October-April

🏡 Carrig Country House 🕏 🛥 ⇐ 🖨 🕫 🅿

TRADITIONAL · CLASSIC Victorian former hunting lodge set down a wooded drive, located on the lough shore and surrounded by mountains. Cosy, country house interior with traditionally furnished guest areas. Individually decorated bedrooms boast antique furnishings. Beautiful views from the dining room; fresh, country house cooking.

17 rooms 🖵 – ♦ € 125/180 ♦♦ € 150/380 – 1 suite

– ℰ 066 976 9100 – www.carrighouse.com – Closed November-February

CARLINGFORD CAIRLINN

Louth – Pop. 1 045 – Regional map n° **21**-D2

▶ Dublin 106 km – Dundalk 21 km

⛪ Beaufort House   ♨ ⪡ 🛏 🕸 **P**

FAMILY · PERSONALISED Modern house in a lovely spot on the lough shore. The welcoming owners used to run a sailing school and the spacious lounge is filled with old maritime charts and memorabilia. Large, bright bedrooms have water or mountain views.

6 rooms ⍁ – 🛉 € 65/90 🛉🛉 € 90

– ℰ 042 937 3879 – www.beauforthouse.net

⛪ Carlingford House   🛏 🕸 **P**

TRADITIONAL · PERSONALISED Early Victorian house close to the old ruined abbey; the owner has lived here all her life. Smart, understated bedrooms have good mod cons and are immaculately kept. Pleasant breakfast room; tasty locally smoked salmon and bacon.

5 rooms ⍁ – 🛉 € 65/100 🛉🛉 € 90/100

– ℰ 042 937 3118 – www.carlingfordhouse.com – Closed 3 January-6 February and Christmas

✕✕ Bay Tree   ⬌ ⬗

MODERN CUISINE · FRIENDLY Keenly run neighbourhood restaurant fronted by bay trees and decorated with branches and hessian. Attractively presented, well-balanced modern dishes feature herbs and salad from the garden and seafood from nearby Carlingford Lough. Service is polite and organised, and the bedrooms are warm and cosy.

Menu € 24 (weekday dinner)/35 – Carte € 32/45

7 rooms ⍁ – 🛉 € 65/75 🛉🛉 € 89/99

Newry St – ℰ 042 938 3848 (booking essential) – www.belvederehouse.ie – dinner only and Sunday lunch – Closed 24-26 December and Monday-Tuesday October-May

CARLOW CEATHARLACH

Carlow – Pop. 13 698 – Regional map n° **22**-D2

▶ Dublin 80 km – Kilkenny 37 km – Wexford 75 km

⛪ Barrowville Town House   🛏 🕸 **P**

TOWNHOUSE · ELEGANT Attractive Georgian house on the main road into town. Comfortable, characterful drawing room with heavy fabrics, period ornaments and a grand piano. Breakfast is in the conservatory, overlooking the pretty garden. Spacious, brightly decorated bedrooms offer a good level of comfort and modern facilities.

7 rooms ⍁ – 🛉 € 40/65 🛉🛉 € 70/99

Kilkenny Rd – South : 0.75 km on N 9 – ℰ 059 914 3324 – www.barrowville.com – Closed 24-26 December

CARNAROSS CARN NA ROS

Meath – ✉ Kells – Regional map n° **21**-D3

▶ Dublin 69 km – Cavan 43 km – Drogheda 48 km

✕✕ Forge   🛏 ⬗ **P**

TRADITIONAL CUISINE · RUSTIC Stone-built former forge in rural Meath; its atmospheric interior features flagged floors and warm red décor. Two fairly priced menus offer hearty dishes made from local produce, with some of the veg and herbs taken from the garden.

Menu € 25/45

Pottlereagh – Northwest : 7 km by R 147 and N 3 on L 7112 – ℰ 046 924 5003 – www.theforgerestaurant.ie – dinner only and Sunday lunch – Closed 1 week February, 1 week July, 24-26 December, 1 January, Sunday dinner, Monday and Tuesday

CARNE

Wexford – Regional map n° **22**-D3
▶ Dublin 169 km – Waterford 82 km – Wexford 21 km

🏠 Lobster Pot   🛖 AC P

SEAFOOD · PUB Popular pub filled with a characterful array of memorabilia.
Large menus feature tasty, home-style cooking. Fresh seafood dishes are a
must-try, with oysters and lobster cooked to order being the specialities. No children after 7pm.

Carte € 27/58

Ballyfane – 𝒞 053 913 1110 – www.lobsterpotwexford.ie – Closed
1 January-10 February, 24-26 December, Good Friday and Monday except bank
holidays

CARRICKMACROSS CARRAIG MHACHAIRE ROIS

Monaghan – Pop. 1 978 – Regional map n° **21**-D2
▶ Dublin 92 km – Dundalk 22 km

🏯 Nuremore   🏊 ≼ 🛖 🖼 🖼 🛖 ⅃♨ ✕ 🖻 & ⅋ ⅏ P

COUNTRY HOUSE · PERSONALISED Long-standing Victorian house with extensive gardens and a golf course. Classical interior with a formal bar and a comfy
lounge serving three-tiered afternoon tea. Good leisure facilities. Peaceful bedrooms; many have rural views.

72 rooms ⬚ – 🕴 € 80/120 🕴🕴 € 100/160

South : 2.25 km by R 178 on old N 2 – 𝒞 042 966 1438 – www.nuremore.com
Nuremore – See restaurant listing

🏠 Shirley Arms   ✿ 🖻 & ⅋ ⅏ P

INN · MODERN An early 19C coaching inn, which forms part of the Shirley Estate
and sits beside the Courthouse Square. Bedrooms are surprisingly modern; those
in the original house are slightly more characterful. There's a welcoming bar, an
informal bistro and, for private parties, a stylish bar-cum-nightclub.

25 rooms ⬚ – 🕴 € 85/95 🕴🕴 € 120/130

Main St. – 𝒞 042 967 3100 – www.shirleyarmshotel.ie – Closed 25-26 December
and Good Friday

✕✕✕ Nuremore   🛖 & AC P

MODERN CUISINE · ELEGANT Traditional split-level dining room within a well-
established Victorian hotel. Formally set, linen-laid tables are well-spaced and
service is attentive. Menus showcase luxurious seasonal ingredients and dishes
are stylishly presented.

Menu € 30 – Carte € 29/48

Nuremore Hotel, South : 2.25 km by R 178 on old N 2 – 𝒞 042 966 1438
– www.nuremore.com – dinner only and Sunday lunch

✕ Courthouse   AC 🕼

🌝 REGIONAL CUISINE · RUSTIC Relaxed, rustic restaurant featuring wooden floors,
exposed ceiling rafters and bare brick; ask for table 20, by the window. Great value
menus offer carefully prepared, flavourful dishes which are a lesson in self-restraint
– their simplicity being a key part of their appeal. Friendly, efficient service.

Menu € 26 (weekdays) – Carte € 28/42 **s**

1 Monaghan St – 𝒞 042 969 2848 (pre-book at weekends)
– www.courthouserestaurant.ie – dinner only and Sunday lunch – Closed 1 week
January, 25-26 December, Good Friday, Monday except bank holidays and
Tuesday

CARRICK-ON-SHANNON CORA DROMA RÚISC

Leitrim – Pop. 3 980 – Regional map n° **21**-C2
▶ Dublin 156 km – Ballina 80 km – Galway 119 km – Roscommon 42 km

🍽️ Oarsman

TRADITIONAL CUISINE · PUB Traditional family-run pub set close to the river and filled with pottery, bygone artefacts and fishing tackle; it's a real hit with the locals. Flavoursome cooking uses local produce. The upstairs restaurant opens later in the week.

Menu € 22 (weekdays)/35 – Carte € 23/46

Bridge St – ☏ 071 962 1733 – www.theoarsman.com – Closed
25-27 December, Good Friday and Sunday-Monday October-April

CARRIGANS AN CARRAIGAIN

Donegal – Pop. 336 – Regional map n° **21**-C1
▶ Dublin 225 km – Donegal 66 km – Letterkenny 230 km – Sligo 124 km

🏠 Mount Royd

TRADITIONAL · PERSONALISED Traditional, creeper-clad house in a quiet village. It's immaculately kept throughout, from the snug lounge and pleasant breakfast room to the four cosy bedrooms – one of which opens onto a terrace overlooking the well-tended gardens and fountain. Tasty, locally smoked salmon features at breakfast.

4 rooms ⌂ – ♦ € 40/45 ♦♦ € 70/75

– ☏ 074 914 0163 – www.mountroyd.com – Closed 1 week Christmas and restricted opening in winter

CASHEL CAISEAL

South Tipperary – Pop. 2 275 – Regional map n° **22**-C2
▶ Dublin 162 km – Cork 96 km – Kilkenny 55 km – Limerick 58 km

🏠 Baileys of Cashel

TOWNHOUSE · MODERN Extended Georgian townhouse, used as a grain store during the Irish famine. Small lounge with a library and spacious, contemporary bedrooms, furnished to a high standard. Popular cellar bar offers live music and traditional dishes. More contemporary restaurant serves modern European cooking.

20 rooms ⌂ – ♦ € 75/85 ♦♦ € 90/120

42 Main St – ☏ 062 61937 – www.baileyshotelcashel.com – Closed
23-28 December

🏠 Aulber House

FAMILY · PERSONALISED Within walking distance of the Rock of Cashel and the 13C Cistercian abbey ruins. Well-kept gardens with a wooden gazebo. Comfy, open-fired lounge. Bespoke mahogany staircase leads to an open-plan landing; many rooms have king-sized beds.

11 rooms ⌂ – ♦ € 60/80 ♦♦ € 80/85

Deerpark, Golden Rd – West : 0.75 km on N 74 – ☏ 062 63713
– www.aulberhouse.com
– Closed November-February

✗✗ Chez Hans

TRADITIONAL CUISINE · TRADITIONAL DÉCOR Longstanding family-owned restaurant in an imposing former Synod Hall built in 1861. Good value set price midweek menu and a more interesting à la carte of classic dishes at the weekend. Quality local ingredients are prepared with care.

Menu € 28 (weekdays) – Carte € 40/65

Rockside, Moor Ln. – ☏ 062 61177 (booking essential)
– www.chezhans.net – dinner only
– Closed last week January, 1 week Easter, 24-26 December, Sunday and Monday

✗ Cafe Hans   AC P ⌖

☺ **TRADITIONAL CUISINE · FRIENDLY** Located just down the road from the Rock of Cashel; a vibrant, popular eatery set next to big sister 'Chez Hans' and run by the same family. Sit at closely set tables amongst an interesting collection of art. Tasty, unfussy lunchtime dishes are crafted from local ingredients. Arrive early as you can't book.

Menu € 20 – Carte € 24/38

Rockside, Moore Lane St – ℰ 062 63660 (bookings not accepted) – lunch only – Closed 2 weeks late January, 1 week October, 25 December, Sunday and Monday

---

 If you are looking for particularly charming accommodation, book a hotel shown in red: 🏨, 🏠… 🏛️.

CASTLEGREGORY CAISLEÁN GHRIAIRE

Kerry – Pop. 243 – Regional map n° **22**-A2

▶ Dublin 330 km – Dingle 24 km – Killarney 54 km

🏠 Shores Country House   ≤ 🛏 ⌦ P

LUXURY · ELEGANT Modern guesthouse, beautifully set in an elevated position between Stradbally Mountain and a spectacular beach. The friendly owner has added a touch of fun to the place. Stylish bedrooms, some with antique beds; all with good attention to detail. Room 3 has a balcony. Plush breakfast room.

6 rooms ⌷ – 🛉 € 55/140 🛉🛉 € 70/150

Conor Pass Rd, Cappateige – Southwest : 6 km on R 560 – ℰ 066 713 9195 – www.shorescountryhouse.com – Closed 2 December-10 January

CASTLELYONS CAISLEÁN Ó LIATHÁIN

Cork – Pop. 292 – Regional map n° **22**-B2

▶ Dublin 219 km – Cork 30 km – Killarney 104 km – Limerick 64 km

🏠 Ballyvolane House   ⌂ ⌘ ≤ 🛏 ⌦ P

FAMILY · PERSONALISED Stately 18C Italianate mansion surrounded by lovely gardens, lakes and woodland; children can help feed the hens, collect the eggs, pet the donkeys or go on a tractor tour. Comfy guest areas and bedrooms match the period style of the house, and family antiques and memorabilia feature throughout. The walled garden and latest farm produce guide what's on the menu.

6 rooms ⌷ – 🛉 € 135 🛉🛉 € 198/240

Southeast : 5.5 km by Midleton rd on Britway rd – ℰ 025 36349 – www.ballyvolanehouse.ie – Closed 24 December-4 January and restricted opening in winter

CASTLEMARTYR BAILE NA MARTRA **Cork**

Cork – Pop. 1 277 – Regional map n° **22**-C3

▶ Dublin 174 km – Cork 20 km – Waterford 58 km

🏨 Castlemartyr   ⌂ ⌘ ≤ 🛏 ⌱ ⌻ ⊕ ⌂ L₃ ⊟ ⌖ AC ⌔ P

GRAND LUXURY · MODERN Impressive 17C manor house in 220 acres of grounds, complete with castle ruins, lakes, a golf course and a stunning spa. Luxurious bedrooms have superb marble bathrooms. Look out for the superb original ceiling in the Knight's Bar. Franchini's offers an extensive Italian menu; the Bell Tower is more formal.

103 rooms ⌷ – 🛉 € 175/205 🛉🛉 € 190/275 – 28 suites

– *ℰ 021 421 9000 – www.castlemartyrresort.ie*

Bell Tower – See restaurant listing

XxX Bell Tower   🛋 ♿ AC P

CLASSIC CUISINE · LUXURY A bright, formally laid restaurant set on the ground floor of a 17C manor house, with traditional décor and plenty of windows overlooking the attractive gardens. Classic dishes with a modern twist from an experienced team.

Carte € 40/60 **s**

Castlemartyr Hotel, – ☎ 021 421 9000 (bookings essential for non-residents) – www.castlemartyrresort.ie – dinner only – Closed Monday and Tuesday October-March

CASTLEPOLLARD BAILE NA GCROS
Westmeath – Pop. 1 042 – Regional map n° **21**-C3
▶ Dublin 63 km – Mullingar 13 km – Tullamore 37 km

🏠 Lough Bishop House   🏡 🐾 🛋 ⚘ P

TRADITIONAL · PERSONALISED Charming 18C farmhouse on a tranquil, south-facing hillside. The hospitable owners and their dogs greet you, and tea and cake are served on arrival in the cosy lounge. Simple bedrooms have neat shower rooms and no TVs. Communal dining – home-cooked dishes include meats and eggs from their own farm.

3 rooms ☲ – ♦ € 60 ♦♦ € 120

Derrynagarra, Collinstown – South : 6 km by R 394 taking L 5738 opposite church and school after 4 km – ☎ 044 966 1313 – www.loughbishophouse.com – Closed Christmas-New Year

CASTLETOWNSHEND BAILE AN CHAISLEÁIN
Cork – Pop. 187 – Regional map n° **22**-B3
▶ Dublin 346 km – Cork 95 km – Killarney 116 km

🗗 Mary Ann's   🏡

TRADITIONAL CUISINE · PUB Bold red pub set up a steep, narrow street in a sleepy village. Dine in the rustic bar, the linen-laid restaurant or the lovely garden; be sure to visit the art gallery. All-encompassing menus often feature seafood and several Asian dishes.

Carte € 26/51

Main St – ☎ 028 36146 – www.maryannesbarandrestaurantcork.com – dinner only – Closed 10 January-3 February, 24-26 December and Monday-Tuesday November-March

CAVAN AN CABHÁN
Cavan – Pop. 3 649 – Regional map n° **21**-C2
▶ Dublin 114 km – Drogheda 93 km – Enniskillen 64 km

🏨 Radisson Blu Farnham Estate   🏡 🍴 ♿ 🎾 🏊 ⚘ ⚘ 👘 ⅃ₐ 🔺 ⚘ 🏋 P

LUXURY · DESIGN Set in extensive parkland and boasting every conceivable outdoor activity and an impressive spa. Original Georgian features are combined with contemporary furnishings and the luxurious bedrooms offer superb views. Traditional menus feature local, seasonal ingredients and afternoon teas are a speciality.

158 rooms ☲ – ♦ € 160/250 ♦♦ € 160/300 – 4 suites

Farnham Estate – Northwest : 3.75 km on R 198 – ☎ 049 437 7700 – www.farnhamestate.com

🏨 Cavan Crystal   🎾 🔺 👘 ⅃ₐ 🔺 ♿ ⚘ 🏋 P

BUSINESS · MODERN Modern hotel next to the Cavan Crystal factory, with an impressive atrium, a stylish lounge-bar and red and black bedrooms in a uniform design. It comes with good meeting and leisure facilities and is popular for spa breaks. The contemporary first floor restaurant serves attractively presented modern dishes.

85 rooms ☲ – ♦ € 55/125 ♦♦ € 75/190

Dublin Rd – ☎ 049 436 0600 – www.cavancrystalhotel.com

at Cloverhill North: 12 km by N3 on N54 ⊠ Belturbet

✗✗ Olde Post Inn   ⟸ 🖕 ⚹ 🅰 🕦 ⟺ 🅿

TRADITIONAL CUISINE · RUSTIC Enjoy a fireside aperitif in the characterful, flag-floored bar or the wood-framed conservatory of this red-brick former post office. The well-established restaurant serves traditional dishes made with Irish produce, wherein classic flavour combinations are given a modern twist. Contemporary bedrooms.

Menu € 63

6 rooms ☲ – 🛏 € 55/65 🛏🛏 € 110/120

– ☎ 047 55555 – www.theoldepostinn.com – dinner only and Sunday lunch
– Closed 24-27 December, Monday and Tuesday

CLIFDEN AN CLOCHÁN

Galway – Pop. 2 056 – Regional map n° **21**-A3
▶ Dublin 291 km – Ballina 124 km – Galway 79 km

🏨 Clifden Station House   🍴 🖼 🕥 🀄 🛌 ⊟ ⚹ ⚓ ✗ 🎿 🅿

BUSINESS · MODERN Purpose-built hotel beside the old Galway-Clifden railway line, in a modern residential and leisure complex, with a residents-only kids' club, gym and wellness centre. Spacious, uniform bedrooms have good facilities. Local seafood-orientated menus in the restaurant. Classic pub dishes in the Signal Bar.

78 rooms ☲ – 🛏 € 55/140 🛏🛏 € 60/200

– ☎ 095 21699 – www.clifdenstationhouse.com – Closed 25-26 December

🏠 Quay House   ⟸ 🎿

FAMILY · PERSONALISED A former harbourmaster's house and monastery overlooking the bay. The relaxed bohemian-style interior is filled with antiques and wild animal memorabilia. Bedrooms are comfortable and spacious; those in the wing have kitchenettes.

14 rooms ☲ – 🛏 € 85/110 🛏🛏 € 135/160

Beach Rd – ☎ 095 21369 – www.thequayhouse.com – Closed November-March

🏠 Sea Mist House   🖕 🎿 🅿

TRADITIONAL · COSY Centrally located, stone-built house with pleasant gardens, a homely lounge and a bright conservatory breakfast area. Spacious, modern bedrooms boast colourful co-ordinating fabrics and fresh flowers; no TVs. Eclectic Irish art collection.

4 rooms ☲ – 🛏 € 75/95 🛏🛏 € 85/110

– ☎ 095 21441 – www.seamisthouse.com – Closed November-March

🏠 Buttermilk Lodge   ⟸ 🖕 🎿 🅿

TRADITIONAL · COSY Immaculate guesthouse filled with bovine memorabilia. Homely, colour co-ordinated bedrooms; games, hot drinks and a real turf fire in the lounge. Friendly owners offer local info, packed lunches and walking tours. Extensive breakfasts.

11 rooms ☲ – 🛏 € 50/75 🛏🛏 € 80/100

Westport Rd – ☎ 095 21951 – www.buttermilklodge.com – Closed
November-February

✗ Mitchells

SEAFOOD · FAMILY Long-standing, family-run restaurant which specialises in seafood. It's set over two floors and decorated with regional prints and seascapes. They offer a huge array of traditional dishes; local prawns, mussels and oysters feature.

Menu € 29 (dinner) – Carte € 29/47

Market St – ☎ 095 21867 – www.mithcellsofclifden.com – Closed November-mid
March

CLOGHEEN AN CHLOICHÍN

South Tipperary – Pop. 491 – Regional map n° **22**-C2
▶ Dublin 122 km – Tipperary 23 km – Clonmel 21 km – Dungarvan 28 km

REPUBLIC OF IRELAND

XX Old Convent ⇦ ⪕ 🛏️ 🛎️ ⇦ 🅿️

MODERN CUISINE · CHIC A very personally run restaurant in a former convent set on the edge of the village. The candlelit former chapel with its delightful original stained glass windows is where dinner is served. The set 8 course daily changing menu features original, modern dishes. Smart, comfortable bedrooms have good quality linens; help yourself to goodies from the pantry.

Menu € 65 – tasting menu only

7 rooms ☑ – 👤 € 150/175 👥 € 175/225

Mount Anglesby – Southeast : 0.5 km on R 668 (Lismore rd) – ℰ 052 746 5565 (booking essential) – www.theoldconvent.ie – dinner only
– Closed 4 January-4 February, 10-28 July, 18-27 December, Sunday except before bank holiday and Monday-Thursday

CLONAKILTY CLOICH NA COILLTE

Cork – Pop. 4 000 – Regional map n° **22**-B3
▶ Dublin 310 km – Cork 51 km

🏨 Inchydoney Island Lodge and Spa ✿ ⪕ 🔲 🌐 🏊 ♨️ 🔲 ♿ 🍽️ 🛗 🅿️

FAMILY · MODERN Superbly located on a remote headland and boasting stunning views over the beach and out to sea; all of the contemporary bedrooms have a balcony or terrace. The impressive spa boasts a seawater pool and 27 treatment rooms. Dine in the modern restaurant or in the nautically styled bistro-bar.

67 rooms ☑ – 👤 € 158/250 👥 € 158/250 – 4 suites
South : 5.25 km by N 71 following signs for Inchydoney Beach – ℰ 023 883 3143
– www.inchydoneyisland.com – Closed 24-25 December

Gulfstream – See restaurant listing

XX Gulfstream ⪕ ♿ 🅰️🅲 🅿️

MODERN CUISINE · CHIC Contemporary New England style restaurant set on the first floor of a vast hotel and offering superb views over the beach and out to sea. Modern menus highlight produce from West Cork and feature plenty of fresh local seafood.

Carte € 46/64

Inchydoney Island Lodge and Spa Hotel, South : 5.25 km by N 71 following signs for Inchydoney Beach – ℰ 023 883 3143 – www.inchydoneyisland.com – dinner only and Sunday lunch – Closed 24-25 December

🍴 Deasy's 🍴 🅿️

TRADITIONAL CUISINE · COSY An appealing pub in a picturesque hamlet, offering lovely views out across the bay. Its gloriously dated interior is decorated with maritime memorabilia. Menus are dictated by the seasons and the latest catch from the local boats.

Menu € 32 (early dinner) – Carte € 30/48

Ring – Southeast : 3 km – ℰ 023 883 5741 – Closed 24-26 December, Good Friday, Sunday dinner, Monday, Tuesday and restricted opening in winter

CLONEGALL CLUAIN NA NGALL

Carlow – Pop. 245 – Regional map n° **22**-D2
▶ Dublin 73 km – Carlow 20 km – Kilkenny 39 km – Wexford 30 km

X Sha-Roe Bistro

😊 **TRADITIONAL BRITISH · FRIENDLY** Rurally located restaurant with a good reputation, set in a pretty little cottage and run by an keen, friendly couple. Rustic lounge and a small dining room with an enormous inglenook and a kitchen table. Flavoursome, classical cooking of local produce; the cheese comes from the weekly farmers' market.

Carte € 32/44

Main St – ℰ 053 937 5636 (booking essential) – dinner only and Sunday lunch – Closed January, 1 week April, 1 week October, Sunday dinner, Monday and Tuesday

CLONTARF CLUAIN TARBH – Dublin ➡ See Dublin

CLOVERHILL DROIM CAISIDE – Cavan ➡ See Cavan

CONG CONGA
Mayo – Pop. 178 – Regional map n° **21**-A3
▶ Dublin 257 km – Ballina 79 km – Galway 45 km

🏰 Ashford Castle
HISTORIC BUILDING · ROMANTIC Hugely impressive lochside castle surrounded by a moat and formal gardens; try your hand at archery, falconry and clay pigeon shooting in the large grounds. Handsome guest areas feature antiques and bedrooms are sumptuously appointed. Dine casually in Cullen's; elegant George V requires a jacket and tie.

83 rooms ☲ – ♥ € 245/2980 ♥♥ € 265/3000 – 6 suites
– ☎ 094 954 6003 – www.ashfordcastle.com
Cullen's at the Cottage – See restaurant listing

🏰 The Lodge at Ashford Castle
COUNTRY HOUSE · MODERN This extended Georgian house is younger sister to Ashford Castle and offers lovely views down to Lough Corrib. Most of the stylish modern bedrooms overlook a courtyard and some are duplex. Unwind in the hot tub while the children are busy in the 'Wii' room. Modern menus feature in the four-roomed restaurant.

50 rooms ☲ – ♥ € 140/435 ♥♥ € 140/435 – 12 suites
The Quay – Southeast : 2.25 km by R 345 off R 346 – ☎ 094 954 5400
– www.thelodgeac.com – Closed 24-25 December and midweek in winter

🏠 Michaeleen's Manor
FAMILY · COSY 'The Quiet Man' was filmed in the village over 60 years ago and this house pays homage – with black and white stills on the walls and rooms named after various characters. Homely lounges and brightly decorated bedrooms. Friendly owners.

10 rooms ☲ – ♥ € 50 ♥♥ € 70
Quay Rd – Southeast : 1.5 km by R 346 – ☎ 094 954 6089
– www.quietman-cong.com

XX Cullen's at the Cottage
INTERNATIONAL · BRASSERIE A thatched cottage with a terrace and lovely views, located within the grounds of an imposing castle and named in honour of a former maître'd, who was here for 25 years. The relaxed, all-day restaurant serves a modern bistro menu.

Carte € 32/56
Ashford Castle Hotel, – ☎ 094 954 5332 – www.ashfordcastle.com – Closed November-March

CORK CORCAIGH
Cork – Pop. 119 230 – Regional map n° **22**-B3
▶ Dublin 253 km – Limerick 99 km – Waterford 123 km

🏰 Hayfield Manor
LUXURY · CLASSIC Luxurious country house with wood-panelled hall, impressive staircase and antique-furnished drawing rooms; the perfect spot for afternoon tea. Plush bedrooms have plenty of extras, including putting machines. Well-equipped residents' spa.

88 rooms ☲ – ♥ € 235/340 ♥♥ € 235/340 – 4 suites
Perrott Ave, College Rd – Southwest : 2 km by R 608 – ☎ 021 484 5900
– www.hayfieldmanor.ie
Orchids · Perrotts – See restaurant listing

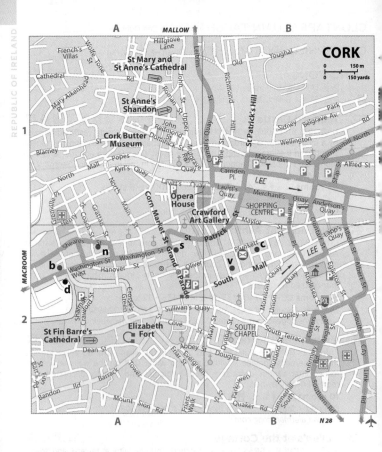

🏠 The Kingsley   ⚑ ◨ 🕒 🏊 🛋 🗐 ♿ 🗚 💱 🛅 🅿

BUSINESS · MODERN Set just outside the city centre, on the banks of the River Lee, with a smart spa and leisure club and state-of-the-art conference rooms with a traditional feel. Stylish bedrooms have a high level of modern facilities. The appealing restaurant has a small terrace, a river outlook and a brasserie-style menu.

131 rooms – 🛉 € 99/195 🛉🛉 € 109/215 – 🖙 €13 – 2 suites

Victoria Cross – West : 3 km on N 22
– ☎ 021 480 0500 – www.thekingsley.ie
– Closed 25 December

🏠 Lancaster Lodge   🗐 ♿ 💱 🗚 🅿

BUSINESS · FUNCTIONAL Purpose-built hotel next to the River Lee and within easy walking distance of the town centre. Spacious, bright bedrooms with bold fabrics and modern artwork; the executive suites have whirlpool baths. A good choice for the business traveller.

48 rooms – 🛉 € 86/156 🛉🛉 € 86/166 – 🖙 €13

Town plan: A2-d - - *Lancaster Quay, Western Rd* – ☎ 021 425 1125
– www.lancasterlodge.com
– Closed 23-26 December

XXX Orchids 🛋 ⚹ ＡＣ Ｐ

MODERN CUISINE · LUXURY Sophisticated formal dining room in a well-appointed country house. Pillars dominate the room, which is laid with crisp white tablecloths. Menus offer refined dishes with some modern twists.

Menu € 69

Hayfield Manor Hotel, Perrott Ave, College Rd – Southwest : 2 km by R 608 – ☏ 021 484 5900 (booking essential) – www.hayfieldmanor.ie – dinner only – Closed Sunday and Monday

XX Perrotts 🛋 🛋 ⚹ ＡＣ ⇔ Ｐ

MODERN CUISINE · BRASSERIE A conservatory restaurant overlooking the gardens of a luxurious country house. It's smart but comfortably furnished, with an adjoining wood-panelled bar. The menu offers a modern take on brasserie classics.

Carte € 34/59

Hayfield Manor Hotel, Perrott Ave, College Rd – Southwest : 2 km by R 608 – ☏ 021 484 5900 – www.hayfieldmanor.ie – Closed 25 December

XX Les Gourmandises

CLASSIC FRENCH · ELEGANT Smart, contemporary restaurant which is proudly run by experienced owners – he cooks and she looks after the service. Accomplished dishes have a classic French heart and original Irish twists. The set menus represent good value.

Menu € 33/48

Town plan: B2-v - - *17 Cook St – ☏ 021 425 1959 (booking essential) – www.lesgourmandises.ie – dinner only – Closed Sunday and Monday*

XX Jacques ＡＣ

REGIONAL CUISINE · INTIMATE Personally run restaurant with an intimate feel and friendly, helpful service. Honest regional cooking uses good quality local ingredients and has clearly defined flavours. In the evening, they also serve small plates in the wine bar.

Menu € 24 (weekday dinner) – Carte € 32/48

Town plan: B2-c - - *23 Oliver Plunket St – ☏ 021 427 7387 – www.jacquesrestaurant.ie – Closed 25 December-3 January, Sunday, Monday dinner and bank holidays*

X Cafe Paradiso ⇐ ＡＣ 🍷

VEGETARIAN · INTIMATE They have been serving creative, satisfying vegetarian dishes at this stylish restaurant for over 20 years now – and it's as busy and as popular as ever. Service is bright and friendly and the atmosphere, intimate yet lively. The spacious, modern bedrooms upstairs come in bright, bold colours.

Menu € 29/40

2 rooms ☡ – 🛉 € 180 🛉🛉 € 220

Town plan: A2-b - - *16 Lancaster Quay, Western Rd – ☏ 021 427 7939 (booking essential) – www.cafeparadiso.ie – dinner only and Saturday lunch – Closed 25-28 December, Sunday and bank holidays*

X Fenn's Quay ＡＣ 🖥

TRADITIONAL CUISINE · BISTRO Modest little bistro with whitewashed brick walls, closely set tables and a loyal local following. Simple, flavoursome cooking, with light lunches and more substantial dishes at dinner; pop in for morning coffee or afternoon tea.

Menu € 25 (early dinner) – Carte € 29/47

Town plan: A2-n - - *5 Sheares St – ☏ 021 427 9527 – www.fennsquay.net – Closed 24-27 December, 1 January, Sunday and bank holidays*

✗ Farmgate Café

REGIONAL CUISINE · BISTRO Popular, long-standing eatery above a bustling 200 year old market; turn right for self-service or left for the bistro. Daily menus use produce from the stalls below and are supplemented by the latest catch. Dishes are hearty and homemade.

Carte € 20/40

Town plan: A2-s - - *English Market (1st floor), Princes St* – ℰ *021 427 8134 – www.farmgate.ie – lunch only – Closed 25-27 December, Sunday and bank holidays*

CORROFIN CORA FINNE

Clare – Pop. 689 – Regional map n° **22**-B1
▶ Dublin 228 km – Gort 24 km – Limerick 51 km

🏠 Fergus View

FAMILY · PERSONALISED Charming bay-windowed house – in the family for four generations; the delightful owners offer superb hospitality. Open-fired lounge, cosy breakfast room and country views. Bright, superbly kept bedrooms: smart but tiny bathrooms; no TVs.

5 rooms 🖙 – 🛉 € 53/55 🛉🛉 € 78

Kilnaboy – North : 3.25 km on R 476 – ℰ 065 683 7606 – www.fergusview.com – Closed November-February

CROOKHAVEN AN CRUACHÁN

Cork – Pop. 1 669 – Regional map n° **22**-A3
▶ Dublin 373 km – Bantry 40 km – Cork 120 km

🏠 Galley Cove House

FAMILY · RURAL Detached house just outside the town, affording superb southerly views over the sea towards Fastnet Rock. Conservatory breakfast room and simple, pine-furnished bedrooms with bright colour schemes; all have a sea outlook. Hospitable owners.

4 rooms 🖙 – 🛉 € 40/55 🛉🛉 € 70/90

West : 0.75 km on R 591 – ℰ 028 35137 – www.galleycovehouse.com – Closed November-March

CROSSHAVEN BUN AN TÁBHAIRNE

Cork – Pop. 2 093 – Regional map n° **22**-B3
▶ Dublin 170 km – Cork 15 km – Limerick 78 km – Galway 140 km

🍴 Cronin's

SEAFOOD · PUB In the family since 1970, a classic Irish pub now run by the 3rd generation. Interesting artefacts and boxing memorabilia. Unfussy seafood dishes feature local produce. Limited opening in the restaurant, which offers more ambitious fare.

Carte € 25/38

– ℰ 021 483 1829 – www.croninspub.com – Closed 25 December and Good Friday

CROSSMOLINA CROIS MHAOILÍONA

Mayo – Pop. 1 061 – Regional map n° **21**-B2
▶ Dublin 252 km – Ballina 10 km

🏠 Enniscoe House

HISTORIC · PERSONALISED Classic Georgian manor, part-dating from 1740 and overlooking Lough Conn; the formal walled garden, heritage museum and tea shop are open to the public. Generously proportioned rooms are filled with antiques and family portraits. Traditional set menu of home-grown ingredients served in the formal dining room.

6 rooms 🖙 – 🛉 € 100/140 🛉🛉 € 200/240

Castlehill – South : 3.25 km on R 315 – ℰ 096 31112 – www.enniscoe.com – Closed November-March except 28 December-2 January

DELGANY DEILGNE

Wicklow – ✉ Bray – Pop. 6 682 – Regional map n° **22**-D2

▶ Dublin 30 km – Wicklow 21 km – Naas 58 km

✗ Pigeon House Cafe

MODERN BRITISH · BISTRO This former pub now houses a bakery, a deli and a large restaurant complete with a counter of homemade cakes. Breakfast morphs into coffee, then into lunch and dinner; you can have anything from a bacon sarnie to duck liver parfait.

Menu € 25 (dinner) – Carte € 28/42

– ☎ 01 287 7103 – www.pigeonhouse.ie – Closed 25-26 December and dinner Sunday-Wednesday

DINGLE AN DAINGEAN

Kerry – Pop. 1 965 – Regional map n° **22**-A2

▶ Dublin 347 km – Killarney 82 km – Limerick 153 km

⌂ Castlewood House

COUNTRY HOUSE · CLASSIC Spacious house overlooking the bay. Modern bedrooms come with whirlpool baths and extras like robes and chocolates. There's an extensive breakfast buffet and a wide range of cooked options; don't miss the bread and butter pudding.

12 rooms ⌂ – ♦ € 90/150 ♦♦ € 100/220

The Wood – Northwest : 1 km on R 559 – ☎ 066 915 2788
– www.castlewooddingle.com – Closed 6-27 December and 6 January-13 February

⌂ Greenmount House

FAMILY · CLASSIC Well-run hotel in an elevated position above the town, with views of the hills and harbour. Comfy lounges and spacious, modern bedrooms; some have balconies and others, small terraces. Excellent breakfasts with a view.

14 rooms ⌂ – ♦ € 65/135 ♦♦ € 80/155

Gortonora – by John St. – ☎ 066 915 1414 – www.greenmounthouse.ie – Closed 20-28 December

⌂ Heatons

FAMILY · MODERN Large, family-run house, a short walk from town; a warm welcome guaranteed. Modern bedrooms; most have sea views and Room 8 has a balcony. Comprehensive breakfasts include homemade scones, pancakes, omelettes and Drambuie porridge.

16 rooms ⌂ – ♦ € 59/92 ♦♦ € 86/128

The Wood – Northwest : 1 km. on R 559 – ☎ 066 915 2288
– www.heatonsdingle.com – Closed 2 January-1 February

⌂ Coastline

TOWNHOUSE · PERSONALISED This large, peach-painted house overlooks the harbour. Bedrooms are spacious and well-kept and the cosy front lounge is filled with local info. At breakfast, enjoy home-made bread; choose a window seat to make the most of the view.

7 rooms ⌂ – ♦ € 50/65 ♦♦ € 70/90

The Wood – Northwest : 1 km. on R 559 – ☎ 066 915 2494
– www.coastlinedingle.com – Closed January

✗✗ Global Village

TRADITIONAL CUISINE · FRIENDLY Homely restaurant with local artwork and a relaxed vibe. Wide-ranging menu makes good use of seasonal, organic and home-grown produce; fantastic fresh fish dishes feature. The well-travelled owner has visited 42 different countries!

Menu € 28/60 **s** – Carte € 33/69 **s**

Upper Main St – ☎ 066 915 2325 (booking essential)
– www.globalvillagedingle.com – dinner only – Closed January-February and restricted opening in winter

XX Idás

MODERN CUISINE · NEIGHBOURHOOD This rustic, slate-faced restaurant is found right in the heart of town. Creative modern cooking uses produce from the Dingle Peninsula. The chef-owner, Kevin, went to art school and it shows in the presentation of his dishes.

Menu € 45 – Carte € 45/60

John St – ℰ 066 915 0885 (booking essential) – www.idasdingle.com – dinner only – Closed January, Tuesday in winter and Monday

X Chart House

REGIONAL CUISINE · RUSTIC This characterful former boathouse sits in a pleasant spot on the quayside. The charming open-plan interior features exposed stone and stained glass, and oil lamps give off an intimate glow. Seasonal, local ingredients feature in rustic, flavoursome dishes and service is friendly and efficient.

Menu € 32 – Carte € 32/48

The Mall – ℰ 066 915 2255 (booking essential) – www.thecharthousedingle.com – dinner only – Closed 2 January-12 February, 22-27 December and Monday

X Out of the Blue

SEAFOOD · RUSTIC Simple blue building with a small terrace and views out to the harbour. Rustic interior with nautical artwork. Daily changing menu offers generous portions of the freshest seafood from the day boats. Buzzy atmosphere. Efficient service.

Carte € 37/56

Waterside – ℰ 066 915 0811 (booking essential) – www.outoftheblue.ie – dinner only and Sunday lunch – Closed December-February

DONEGAL DÚN NA NGALL

Donegal – Pop. 2 607 – Regional map n° **21**-C1
▶ Dublin 264 km – Londonderry 77 km – Sligo 64 km

Solis Lough Eske Castle

LUXURY · CLASSIC Beautifully restored 17C castle, surrounded by 43 acres of sculpture-filled grounds. There's a fantastic spa and a swimming pool overlooking an enclosed garden. Bedrooms are a mix of contemporary and antique-furnished; go for a Garden Suite.

96 rooms ⊊ – ♦ € 195/395 ♦♦ € 195/395 – 1 suite

Northeast : 6.5 km by N15 – ℰ 074 972 5100 – www.solisloughleskecastle.ie – Closed Monday and Tuesday November-March

Cedars – See restaurant listing

Harvey's Point

FAMILY · CLASSIC A sprawling, family-run hotel in a peaceful loughside setting, with traditional guest areas and huge, very comfortable, country house style bedrooms – all offer a high level of facilities and most have lovely countryside outlooks.

64 rooms ⊊ – ♦ € 179/225 ♦♦ € 238/300

Lough Eske – Northeast : 7.25 km. by N 15 – ℰ 074 972 2208 – www.harveyspoint.com – Restricted opening in winter

Harvey's Point – See restaurant listing

Ardeevin

FAMILY · COSY Friendly, brightly painted house set in peaceful gardens and boasting beautiful views over Lough Eske; personally run by the friendly owner. Warm, pleasantly cluttered guest areas are filled with ornaments and curios. Individually designed bedrooms display quality furnishings and thoughtful extras.

4 rooms ⊊ – ♦ € 52 ♦♦ € 85

Lough Eske, Barnesmore – Northeast : 9 km by N 15 following signs for Lough Eske Drive – ℰ 074 972 1790 – www.ardeevinguesthouse.co.uk – Closed November-19 March

XXX Harvey's Point
MODERN CUISINE · CHIC A formal, traditional restaurant set within a family-owned country house hotel; its semi-circular windows afford delightful views of the lough. Classic dishes make use of local Donegal produce and are presented in a modern manner.

Menu € 59

Harvey's Point Hotel, Lough Eske – Northeast : 7.25 km. by N 15 – ℰ 074 972 2208 – www.harveyspoint.com – dinner only – Closed Monday-Tuesday November-March

XX Cedars
TRADITIONAL CUISINE · INTIMATE Stylish, modern restaurant in a 17C castle close to the lough, with romantic booths to the rear and a slate terrace boasting views over the lawns and woodland. Small menu with international influences, but Donegal produce to the fore.

Menu € 55 – Carte € 41/64

Solis Lough Eske Castle Hotel, Northeast : 6.5 km by N15 – ℰ 074 972 5100 – www.solislougheskecastle.com – dinner only and Sunday lunch – Closed Monday and Tuesday November-March

DONNYBROOK DOMHNACH BROC – Dublin → See Dublin

DOOGORT DUMHA GOIRT – Mayo → See Achill Island

DOOLIN DÚLAINM
Clare – Regional map n° **22**-B1

▶ Dublin 275 km – Galway 69 km – Limerick 80 km

XX Cullinan's
CLASSIC CUISINE · FAMILY Run by a keen husband and wife team; an orange building in the middle of the Burren, with two walls of full length windows making the most of the view. Classical, comforting cooking uses Irish produce and portions are generous. Comfy, pine-furnished bedrooms; some overlook the River Aille.

Menu € 33 (early dinner) – Carte € 36/47

10 rooms ☲ – ∮ € 60/100 ∮∮ € 80/120

– ℰ 065 707 4183 (booking essential) – www.cullinansdoolin.com – dinner only – Closed 30 October-14 April, Sunday dinner and Wednesday

DOONBEG AN DÚN BEAG
Clare – Pop. 272 – Regional map n° **22**-B2

▶ Dublin 286 km – Inis 45 km – Galway 115 km – Limerick 91 km

🏨 Trump International Golf Links and H. Doonbeg
LUXURY · DESIGN Smart resort complex now owned by Donald Trump. Stylish, sumptuous bedrooms and suites are spread about the grounds: some are duplex and feature fully fitted kitchens; all have spacious marble bathrooms and are extremely comfortable. Ocean View offers fine dining with a pleasant outlook over the sea; Trump's brasserie, in the golf clubhouse, serves a traditional menu.

75 rooms ☲ – ∮ € 190/300 ∮∮ € 215/395

Northeast : 9 km on N 67 – ℰ 065 905 5600 – www.trumphotelcollection.com

🍺 Morrissey's
SEAFOOD · PUB Smartly refurbished pub in a small coastal village; its terrace overlooking the river and the castle ruins. The menu may be simple but cooking is careful and shows respect for ingredients – locally caught fish and shellfish feature heavily. Bedrooms are modern and they have bikes and even a kayak for hire.

Carte € 26/45

5 rooms ☲ – ∮ € 50/60 ∮∮ € 80/100

– ℰ 065 905 5304 – www.morrisseysdoonbeg.com – dinner only – Closed January, February and Monday

DROGHEDA DROICHEAD ÁTHA

Louth – Pop. 30 393 – Regional map n° **21**-D3
▶ Dublin 46 km – Dundalk 35 km

🏠 Scholars Townhouse   🏠 ⛲ 🖨 ♿ 🚭 **P**

TOWNHOUSE · CLASSIC 19C former priest's house: now a well-run, privately owned hotel with smart wood panelling and ornate coving featuring throughout. Appealing bar and cosy lounge; comfortable, well-kept bedrooms. Dine on classically based dishes under an impressive mural of the Battle of Boyne.

16 rooms ☲ – ♦ € 75/100 ♦♦ € 89/139

King St – by West St and Lawrence St turning left at Lawrence's Gate – ℰ 041 983 5410 – www.scholarshotel.com – Closed 25-26 December

✗ Eastern Seaboard Bar & Grill   🍷 ♿ 🅰 🔲 📓 **P**

INTERNATIONAL · BISTRO A lively industrial style bistro; its name a reference to its location within Ireland and also a nod to the USA, which influences the menus. Share several small plates or customise a hearty main course with your choice of sides.

Carte € 18/46

1 Bryanstown Centre, Dublin Rd – Southeast : 2.5 km by N 1 taking first right after railway bridge – ℰ 041 980 2570 – www.easternseaboard.ie – Closed Good Friday and 25-26 December

✗ The Kitchen   ♿ 🅰

WORLD CUISINE · BISTRO Glass-fronted riverside eatery. By day, a café serving homemade cakes, pastries, salads and sandwiches; by night, a more interesting, mainly Eastern Mediterranean menu is served, with influences from North Africa and the Middle East.

Menu € 30/50 – Carte € 30/41

2 South Quay – ℰ 041 983 4630 – www.kitchenrestaurant.ie – Closed 1 January, 25-27 December and Monday-Tuesday

DROMAHAIR

Leitrim – Pop. 748 – Regional map n° **21**-B2
▶ Dublin 196 km – Leitrim 23 km – Sligo 12 km

✗ Luna   ♿

INTERNATIONAL · FRIENDLY A delightful little cottage on the main road of a sleepy village; the loughside drive over from Sligo is beautiful. It might have a neighbourhood feel but the food has global overtones, from the South of France and Tuscany to Asia.

Carte € 29/45

Main St – ℰ 071 916 4728 – dinner only – Closed January-February, Sunday and Monday

GOOD TIPS!

The Celtic Tiger is back, with a purr if not yet a roar, and the capital's food scene is most definitely showing signs of hotting up. A resurgence in informal dining has seen restaurants like the loft-style **Drury Buildings** and grocer's shop conversion **Delahunt** become popular – and these sit happily alongside the city's collection of Michelin Stars.

DUBLIN BAILE ÁTHA CLIATH

Dublin – Pop. 527 612 – Regional map n° **22**-D1

▶ Belfast 166 km – Cork 248 km – Londonderry 235 km

Hotels

🏨 Shelbourne 🖻 🛞 🕉 ⅃ᵬ 🖭 ᶑ 🄰🄲 ॐ 🛴 🚗

GRAND LUXURY · CLASSIC Famed hotel dating from 1824, overlooking an attractive green; this is where the 1922 Irish Constitution was signed. Elegant guest areas and classical architecture; it even has a tiny museum. The bar and lounge are THE places to go for drinks and afternoon tea. Chic spa and characterful, luxurious bedrooms.

265 rooms – 🛉 € 229/750 🛉🛉 € 229/750 – ☑ €29 – 12 suites

Town plan: G3-c - *27 St Stephen's Grn.* ⊠ *D2* – *€ 01 663 4500*
– *www.theshelbourne.ie*

Saddle Room – See restaurant listing

🏨 Merrion 🌴 🛬 🖻 ⅃ᵬ 🖭 ᶑ 🄰🄲 ॐ 🛴 🚗

TOWNHOUSE · CLASSIC A Georgian façade conceals a luxury hotel and a compact spa with an impressive pool. Opulent drawing rooms are filled with antique furniture and fine artwork – enjoy 'art afternoon tea' with a view of the formal parterre garden. Stylish bedrooms have a classic, understated feel and smart marble bathrooms. Dine from an accessible menu in the barrel-ceilinged bar.

142 rooms – 🛉 € 495/635 🛉🛉 € 515/656 – ☑ €29 – 10 suites

Town plan: G3-e - *Upper Merrion St* ⊠ *D2* – *€ 01 603 0600*
– *www.merrionhotel.com*

🏨 Fitzwilliam 🌴 ⅃ᵬ 🖭 🄰🄲 ॐ 🛴 🚗

BUSINESS · MODERN Stylish, modern hotel set around an impressive roof garden. Contemporary bedrooms display striking bold colours and good facilities; most overlook the roof garden and the best have views over St Stephen's Green. The bright first floor brasserie offers original Mediterranean-influenced menus.

139 rooms – 🛉 € 219/500 🛉🛉 € 219/500 – ☑ €22 – 2 suites

Town plan: F3-d - *St Stephen's Grn* ⊠ *D2* – *€ 01 478 7000*
– *www.fitzwilliamhotel.com*

Thornton's – See restaurant listing

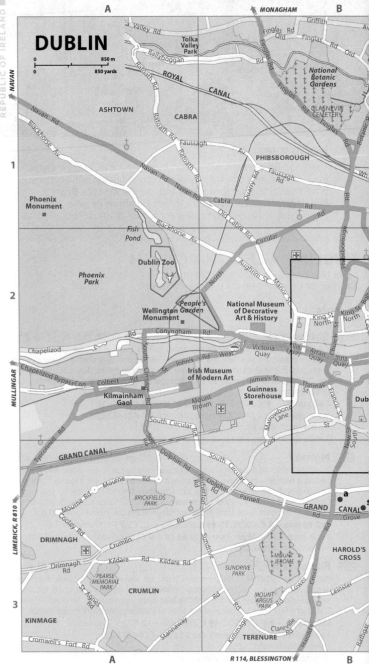

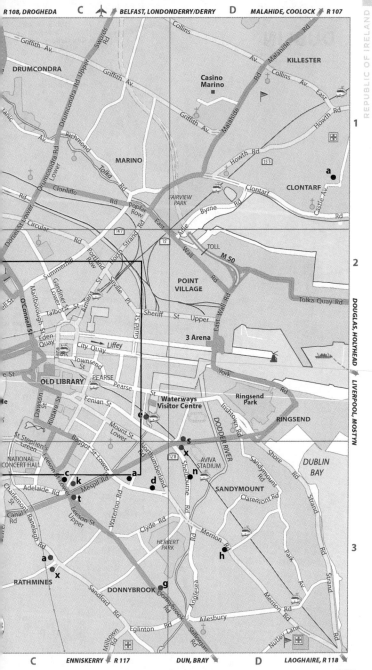

Collins

Griffith Av.

DRUMCONDRA

Griffith Av.

Griffith Av.

KILLESTER

Casino Marino

Collins Av. East

Howth Rd

1

Drumcondra Rd Upper

Swords

Malahide Rd

Richmond

Tolka

MARINO

Howth Rd

153

Clonliffe

Rd

Poplar Row

FAIRVIEW PARK

Clontarf

CLONTARF

a

Castle Av.

Dorset St Lower

North Circular Rd

Clonliffe Rd

East Wall Rd

Byrne Rd

Alfie

Wall Rd

TOLL

M 50

2

Summerhill

Gardiner St Lower

Portland Row

Amiens St

Neville Pl

North Strand Rd

POINT VILLAGE

Tolka Quay Rd

Marlborough St

Talbot St

Sheriff St Upper

East Wall Rd

O'Connell St

Eden Quay

City Quay

Liffey

3 Arena

Townsend St

York Rd

OLD LIBRARY

PEARSE

Pearse

Pearse St

Waterways Visitor Centre

e

Ringsend Park

RINGSEND

Dawson St

Kildare St

Fenian St

Mount St Lower

Inishown Rd

Dodder River

Shore Rd

DUBLIN BAY

St Stephen's Green

Leeson St Lower

Baggot St Lower

Northumberland Rd

s

x

AVIVA STADIUM

Sandymount Rd

NATIONAL CONCERT HALL

c

k

a

Mespil Rd

Waterloo Rd

d

128

Shelbourne Rd

n

SANDYMOUNT

Claremont Rd

Adelaide Rd

t

Charlemont St

Leeson St Upper

Clyde Rd

Merrion Rd

Strand Rd

Canal Rd

Ranelagh Rd

HERBERT PARK

Merrion Rd

Park Av.

3

a

x

RATHMINES

Sandford Rd

DONNYBROOK

g

Donnybrook Rd

Anglesea Rd

h

Ailesbury Rd

Merrion Rd

Milltown Rd

Eglinton Rd

Stillorgan Rd

Nutley Lane

Strand Rd

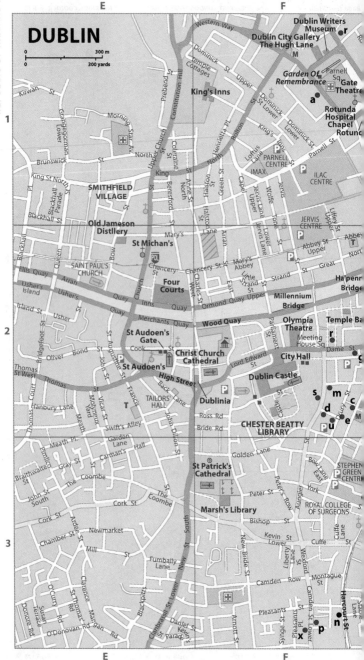

DUBLIN

0   300 m
0   300 yards

E

F

Western Way

Dublin Writers Museum **r**

Dominick St Upper

Temple Cottages

Dublin City Gallery The Hugh Lane **M**

Prebend St

Constitution Hill

Garden Of Remembrance

Parnell Sq

Kirwan St

King's Inns

Dominick St Lower

Gate Theatre

Grangegorman Lower

Morning Star Av

Henrietta Pl

King's Inn St Lower

a

Rotunda Hospital Chapel

1

Upper Church St

King St North

North King St

Coleraine St

King St

Anne St North

Halston St

Green St

Wolfe Tone St

Loftus Lane

Capel St

PARNELL CENTRE
IMAX

Parnell St

Brunswick St

Beresford St

P

Jervis Lane Upper

Jervis St

ILAC CENTRE

Blackhall Parade

SMITHFIELD VILLAGE

Blackhall Pl

Blackhall St

Bow St

Old Jameson Distillery

Mary's Lane

Jervis Lane Lower

Arran St North

JERVIS CENTRE

Abbey St Upper

Jervis St Upper

Ellis Quay

Arran Quay

St Michan's

SAINT PAUL'S CHURCH

POL

Chancery Pl

Chancery St

Mary's Abbey

Charles St West

Little Strand St

Strand St Great

P

Abbey St

P

Ha'penny Bridge

Usher's Island

Usher's Quay

Church St

Four Courts

Inns Quay

Ormond Quay Upper

Millennium Bridge

2

Island St

Usher's Quay

Bridgefoot St

Bond St

Oliver Bond St

Merchants Quay

Wood Quay

Parliament St

Meeting House Sq

Olympia Theatre

Temple Ba

r

Thomas St West

Thomas St

St Augustine St

John St

Cook St

St Audoen's Gate

St Audoen's

Lord Edward St

Dame St

City Hall

P

c

Hanbury Lane

Vicar St

Francis St

Christ Church Cathedral

High Street

Dublin Castle

s

m

c

Back Lane

TAILORS' HALL

T

John Dillon St

Dublinia

Ross Rd

Bride Rd

d

e

Swift's Alley

Moynmuy Yard

Meath St

Garden Lane

Carman's Hall

CHESTER BEATTY LIBRARY

u

P

M

Braithwaite St

Gray St

The Coombe

Golden Lane

St Patrick's Cathedral

Peter's Row

STEPHEN GREEN CENTRE

P

John St South

Cork St

The Coombe

Cork St

Peter St

York St

Aungier St

ROYAL COLLEGE OF SURGEONS

Ardee St

Newmarket

Marsh's Library

Bishop St

New Bride St

Kevin St Lower

Cuffe St

Bow Lane East

3

Chamber St

Mill St

Fumbally Lane

New Row South

Camden Row

Liberty Lane

Wexford St

Montague St

Camden St Lower

Harcourt St

O'Curry Rd

St Thomas Rd

Clarence Mangan Rd

Blackpitts

Clanbrassil St Lower

Daniel St

Kevin St

Pleasants St

Pleasants Pl

p

n

Donore Rd

O'Donovan Rd

Susan Terrace

Synge St

x

E

F

854

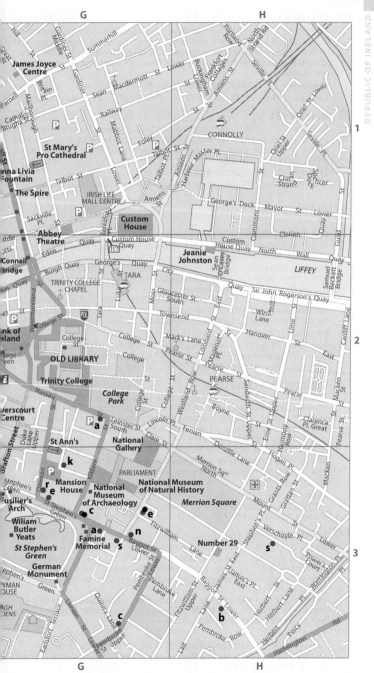

🏠 The Dean 　　　　　　　　　　🏠 🖃 ⚡ AC 🍴 🏋

TOWNHOUSE · DESIGN A cool, informal, urban boutique. Stylish bedrooms include compact rooms named 'Mod Pods'; suites with record players, amps and guitars; and a penthouse with table football, a poker table and a bar! The moody lobby serves an all-day menu and loft-style Sophie's offers Mediterranean dishes and rooftop views.

51 rooms – 👤 € 109/450 👥👥 € 109/450 – 🍽 €15 – 3 suites

Town plan: F3-n - *33 Harcourt St ⊠ D2 – ℰ 01 607 8110 – www.deandublin.ie*

🏠 Number 31 　　　　　　　　　　　　　　　🚐 🍴

TOWNHOUSE · DESIGN Unusual and very individual property – once home to architect Sam Stephenson. It's classically styled around the 1960s, with a striking sunken lounge; the most modern bedrooms are found in the Georgian house across the terraced garden.

21 rooms 🍽 – 👤 € 150/240 👥👥 € 190/280

Town plan: C3-c - *31 Leeson Cl. ⊠ D2 – ℰ 01 676 5011 – www.number31.ie*

Restaurants

XXXX Patrick Guilbaud (Guillaume Lebrun) 　　　　　🦀 AC ⇔
🟢🟢 MODERN FRENCH · ELEGANT
A truly sumptuous restaurant in an elegant Georgian house; the eponymous owner has run it for over 35 years. Accomplished, original cooking uses luxurious ingredients and mixes classical French cooking with modern techniques. Dishes are well-crafted and visually stunning with a superb balance of textures and flavours.

→ Blue lobster ravioli with coconut-scented lobster cream, toasted almonds and curry dressing. Spiced Wicklow lamb with Basque pepper stew, bergamot and olive jus. Chocolate and peanut parfait with salted caramel and popcorn ice cream.

Menu € 45/105

Town plan: G3-e - *21 Upper Merrion St ⊠ D2 – ℰ 01 676 4192 (booking essential) – www.restaurantpatrickguilbaud.ie – Closed 2-3 months from mid August, 25-31 December, 17 March, 14 April, Sunday, Monday and bank holidays*

XXX Chapter One (Ross Lewis) 　　　　　　　　　　　AC 🐾 ⇔
🟢 MODERN CUISINE · INTIMATE
Good old-fashioned Irish hospitality meets with modern Irish cooking in this stylish basement restaurant beneath the Writers Museum. The series of interconnecting rooms have an understated elegance and striking bespoke art hangs on the walls. Boldly flavoured dishes showcase produce from local artisan producers.

→ Pig's tail stuffed with Fingal Ferguson's bacon and Dublin Bay prawn. Turbot with fermented horseradish, cauliflower and pickled red dulse. Salted butter ice cream with caramelised soda bread and soda bread mousse.

Menu € 40/70 **s**

Town plan: F1-r - *The Dublin Writers Museum, 18-19 Parnell Sq ⊠ D1 – ℰ 01 873 2266 (booking essential) – www.chapteronerestaurant.com – Closed 2 weeks August, 2 weeks Christmas, Sunday, Monday and bank holidays*

XXX L'Ecrivain (Derry Clarke) 　　　　　　　　　　🌿 AC 🍷 ⇔
🟢 MODERN CUISINE · FASHIONABLE
A well-regarded restaurant with an attractive terrace, a glitzy bar and a private dining room which screens live kitchen action. The refined, balanced menu has a classical foundation whilst also displaying touches of modernity; the ingredients used are superlative. Service is structured yet has personality.

→ Lambay scallop with cabbage, onion, apple and oyster cream. Aged beef with chanterelles, foie gras, crisp potato and oxtail jus. 'Irish Coffee' mousse with vanilla ice cream and whiskey foam.

Menu € 45/75

Town plan: H3-b - *109a Lower Baggot St ⊠ D2 – ℰ 01 661 1919 (booking essential) – www.lecrivain.com – dinner only and lunch Thursday-Friday – Closed Sunday and bank holidays*

XXX Greenhouse (Mickael Viljanen) ⒶⒸ
⭐

MODERN CUISINE · ELEGANT Stylish restaurant with turquoise banquettes and smooth service. Menus include a good value set lunch, midweek set and tasting menus and a 5 course 'Surprise' on Friday and Saturday evening. Accomplished, classically based cooking has stimulating flavour combinations and creative modern overtones.

→ Foie gras, apple, walnut and smoked eel. Kerry lamb with wild garlic, artichoke and turnip. Milk chocolate and yuzu bar, banana and lime.

Menu € 36 (weekday lunch)/89

Town plan: G3-r - *Dawson St* ✉ *D2* - ℰ *01 676 7015*
– www.thegreenhouserestaurant.ie – Closed 2 weeks July, 2 weeks Christmas, Sunday and Monday

XXX Thornton's ⒶⒸ

MODERN CUISINE · INTIMATE Elegant first floor restaurant overlooking St Stephen's Green. Eye-catching photo montages taken by the chef hang on the walls. Choose from a concise à la carte or a 5 course tasting menu; modern cooking uses classic combinations.

Menu € 45/75

Town plan: F3-d - *Fitzwilliam Hotel, 128 St Stephen's Grn.* ✉ *D2* - ℰ *01 478 7008*
– www.thorntonsrestaurant.com – dinner only and lunch Friday-Saturday
– Closed 24 December-2 January, Sunday and Monday

XXX Forty One ◇

MODERN CUISINE · ELEGANT Intimate, richly furnished restaurant on the first floor of an attractive, creeper-clad townhouse, in a corner of St Stephen's Green. Accomplished, classical cooking features luxurious Irish ingredients and personal, modern touches.

Menu € 35 (weekday lunch)/75 – Carte € 63/79

Town plan: G3-a - *41 St. Stephen's Grn.* ✉ *D2* - ℰ *01 662 0000 (booking advisable) – www.restaurantfortyone.ie – Closed first 2 weeks August, 25-26 December, 17 March, Good Friday, Sunday and Monday*

XXX One Pico ⒶⒸ

CLASSIC FRENCH · ELEGANT Stylish modern restaurant tucked away on a side street; a well-regarded place that's a regular haunt for MPs. Sit on comfy banquettes or velour chairs, surrounded by a muted colours. Classic French cooking offers plenty of flavour.

Menu € 27/49

Town plan: G3-k - *5-6 Molesworth Pl* ✉ *D2* - ℰ *01 676 0300 – www.onepico.com*
– Closed bank holidays

XX Pearl Brasserie ⒶⒸ

CLASSIC FRENCH · BRASSERIE Formal basement restaurant with a small bar-lounge and two surprisingly airy dining rooms; sit in a stylish booth in one of the old coal bunkers. Intriguing modern dishes have a classical base and Mediterranean and Asian influences.

Menu € 25 (lunch) – Carte € 39/66

Town plan: G3-n - *20 Merrion St Upper* ✉ *D2* - ℰ *01 661 3572*
– www.pearl-brasserie.com – Closed 25 December and Sunday

XX Amuse ⒶⒸ

MODERN CUISINE · FRIENDLY Modern, understated décor provides the perfect backdrop for the intricate, innovative cooking. Dishes showcase Asian ingredients – including kombu and yuzu; which are artfully arranged according to their flavours and textures.

Menu € 29 (weekday lunch)/65

Town plan: G3-r - *22 Dawson St* ✉ *D2* - ℰ *01 639 4889 (booking advisable) – www.amuse.ie – Closed 2 weeks Christmas-New Year, last week July, first week August, Sunday and Monday*

XX Pichet 🍸 🖭 🖳 🐨

CLASSIC FRENCH · FASHIONABLE You can't miss the bright red signs and blue and white striped canopies of this buzzy brasserie – and its checkerboard flooring makes it equally striking inside. Have breakfast or snacks at the bar or classic French dishes in the main room. A good selection of wines are available by the glass or pichet.

Menu € 25 (lunch and early dinner) – Carte € 34/50

Town plan: F2-g - 14-15 Trinity St ⊠ D2 – 𝒞 01 677 1060 (booking essential)
– www.pichetrestaurant.ie
– Closed 25 December and 1 January

XX Avenue by Nick Munier ⓝ 🍸 🖭 🕦 ⟷

FRENCH · BRASSERIE A surprisingly large establishment set over 4 levels – the basement houses a private dining room, the top floor a jazz venue and the other two floors a smart brasserie with blue leather chairs. Menus offer unfussy bistro favourites.

Menu € 25 (early dinner) – Carte € 39/42

Town plan: F2-r - 1 Crow St ⊠ D2 – 𝒞 01 645 5102 – www.avenue.ie – dinner only and lunch Friday-Saturday
– Closed 1 week January

XX Hot Stove 🛋 🐨

INTERNATIONAL · ELEGANT A popular pre-theatre spot, in the basement of a Georgian house; it takes its name from the range in one of the immaculate, elegant dining rooms. Flavoursome cooking showcases seasonal Irish produce in carefully prepared dishes.

Menu € 24 (weekday lunch)/34 – Carte dinner € 32/56

Town plan: F1-a - 38 Parnell Sq West ⊠ D1 – 𝒞 01 874 7778 – www.thehotstove.ie
– Closed 25 December- 9 January, Sunday and Monday

XX Saddle Room ৬ 🖭 ⟷

MEATS AND GRILLS · ELEGANT Renowned restaurant with a history as long as that of the hotel in which it stands. The warm, inviting room features intimate gold booths and a crustacea counter. The menu offers classic dishes and grills; West Cork beef is a speciality.

Menu € 23/45 – Carte € 39/109

Town plan: G3-c - Shelbourne Hotel, 27 St Stephen's Grn. ⊠ D2 – 𝒞 01 663 4500
– www.shelbournedining.ie

XX Bang 🖭 🐨 ⟷

MODERN CUISINE · BISTRO Stylish restaurant with an intimate powder blue basement, a bright mezzanine level and a small, elegant room above. There are good value pre-theatre menus, a more elaborate à la carte and tasting menus showcasing top Irish produce.

Menu € 25 (early dinner)/50 – Carte € 41/74

Town plan: G3-a - 11 Merrion Row ⊠ D2 – 𝒞 01 400 4229
– www.bangrestaurant.com – dinner only

XX Fade St. Social - Restaurant 🍸 ৬ 🕦 🐨 ⟷

MODERN CUISINE · BRASSERIE Have cocktails on the terrace then head for the big, modern brasserie with its raised open kitchen. Dishes use Irish ingredients but have a Mediterranean feel; they specialise in sharing dishes and large cuts of meat such as chateaubriand.

Menu € 35 (lunch and early dinner) – Carte € 31/83

Town plan: F2-u - 4-6 Fade St ⊠ D2 – 𝒞 01 604 0066 – www.fadestsocial.com
– dinner only and lunch Thursday-Saturday
– Closed 25-26 December

XX Suesey Street ⓃN 🍷 🎐 AC ⇔

MODERN CUISINE · INTIMATE An intimate restaurant with sumptuous, eye-catching décor in the basement of a Georgian townhouse; sit on the superb courtyard terrace with its retractable awning. Refined, modern cooking brings out the best in home-grown Irish ingredients.

Menu €25/48 – Carte €34/60

Town plan: C3-k - *26 Fitzwilliam Pl* ✉ *D2* – ☏ *01 669 4600* – *www.sueseystreet.ie* – *Closed 25-30 December, Saturday lunch, Sunday and Monday*

XX Dax AC

FRENCH · BISTRO Smart, masculine restaurant in the cellar of a Georgian townhouse near Fitzwilliam Square. Tried-and-tested French dishes use top Irish produce and flavours are clearly defined. The Surprise Menu best showcases the kitchen's talent.

Menu €30 (weekday lunch) – Carte €44/66

Town plan: G3-d - *23 Pembroke St Upper* ✉ *D2* – ☏ *01 676 1494 (booking essential)* – *www.dax.ie* – *Closed 10 days Christmas, Saturday lunch, Sunday and Monday*

XX Dobbin's 🎐 & AC ⇔

TRADITIONAL CUISINE · BRASSERIE Hidden away in a back alley. A small bar leads through to a long, narrow room with cosy leather booths, which opens into a spacious conservatory with a terrace. Good value lunch and early evening menus; cooking is in the classical vein.

Menu €27 (weekday lunch) – Carte €29/52

Town plan: H3-s - *15 Stephen's Ln* ✉ *D2* – *(via Stephen's Pl off Lower Mount St)* – ☏ *01 661 9536 (booking essential)* – *www.dobbins.ie* – *Closed 24 December-2 January, Saturday lunch, Sunday dinner, Mondays except December and bank holidays*

XX Peploe's & AC 🍸

MEDITERRANEAN CUISINE · COSY Atmospheric cellar restaurant – formerly a bank vault – named after the artist. Comfy room with a warm, clubby feel and a large mural depicting the owner. The well-drilled team present Mediterranean dishes and an Old World wine list.

Menu €29 (lunch and early dinner) – Carte €39/59

Town plan: G3-e - *16 St Stephen's Grn.* ✉ *D2* – ☏ *01 676 3144 (booking essential)* – *www.peploes.com* – *Closed 25-26 December, Good Friday and lunch bank holidays*

X Delahunt 🍷 & ⇔

😊 MODERN CUISINE · BISTRO An old Victorian grocer's shop mentioned in James Joyce's 'Ulysses'; the clerk's snug is now a glass-enclosed private dining room. Precisely executed, flavoursome dishes are modern takes on time-honoured recipes. Lunch offers two choices per course and dinner, four; they also serve snacks in the upstairs bar.

Menu €27 (lunch) – Carte €34/44

Town plan: F3-p - *39 Camden Street Lower* ✉ *D2* – ☏ *01 598 4880 (booking essential)* – *www.delahunt.ie* – *dinner only and lunch Thursday-Saturday* – *Closed 15 August-1 September, Sunday and Monday*

X Locks ⓃN ⇔

MODERN CUISINE · BISTRO Locals love this corner restaurant overlooking the canal – the downstairs is buzzy, while upstairs it's more intimate, and the personable team only add to the feel. Natural flavours are to the fore and dishes are given subtle modern touches; come at the start of the week or before 7pm for the best value menus.

Menu €22/45 – Carte €35/56

Town plan: B3-s - *1 Windsor Terr* ✉ *D8* – ☏ *01 416 3655 (booking essential)* – *www.locksrestaurant.ie* – *Closed Sunday dinner, Monday, Tuesday Lunch and Wednesday*

Pig's Ear

MODERN CUISINE · BISTRO Well-established restaurant in a Georgian town-house overlooking Trinity College. Floors one and two are bustling bistro-style areas filled with mirrors and porcine-themed memorabilia; floor three is a private room with a Scandinavian feel. Good value menus list hearty dishes with a modern edge.

Menu € 22 (lunch and early dinner) – Carte € 33/49

Town plan: G2-a - *4 Nassau St* ✉ *D2* – ✆ *01 670 3865 (booking essential)*
– www.thepigsear.ie – Closed first week January, Sunday and bank holidays

Etto

MEDITERRANEAN CUISINE · RUSTIC The name of this rustic restaurant means 'little' and it is totally apt! Blackboards announce the daily wines and the lunchtime 'soup and sandwich' special. Flavoursome dishes rely on good ingredients and have Italian influences; the chef understands natural flavours and follows the 'less is more' approach.

Menu € 25/28 (weekdays) – Carte € 29/44

Town plan: G3-s - *18 Merrion Row* ✉ *D2* – ✆ *01 678 8872 (booking essential)*
– www.etto.ie – Closed Sunday and bank holidays

Taste at Rustic by Dylan McGrath 🅽

ASIAN · RUSTIC Dylan McGrath's love of Japanese cuisine inspires dishes which explore the five tastes; sweet, salt, bitter, umami and sour. Ingredients are top-notch and flavours, bold and masculine. Personable staff are happy to recommend dishes.

Menu € 45 – Carte € 33/100

Town plan: F2-m - *17 South Great George's St* ✉ *D2* – *(2nd Floor)*
– ✆ 01 707 9596 (booking advisable) – www.tasteatrustic.com – dinner only
– Closed Sunday and Monday

Bastible 🅽

MODERN CUISINE · SIMPLE The name refers to the cast iron pot which once sat on the hearth of every family home; they still use it here to make the bread. Modern cooking showcases one main ingredient with minimal accompaniments; menus offer 3 choices per course.

Menu € 36/38

Town plan: B3-a - *111 South Circular Rd* ✉ *D8* – ✆ *01 473 7409 (booking essential)*
– www.bastible.com – dinner only and lunch Saturday-Sunday – Closed Sunday dinner, Monday and Tuesday

Osteria Lucio

ITALIAN · INTIMATE Smart restaurant under the railway arches, run by two experienced chefs. Robust, rustic dishes showcase local produce, alongside ingredients imported from Italy; sit by the bar to watch pizzas being cooked in the oak-burning stove.

Menu € 23 (early dinner) – Carte € 24/44

Town plan: C2-e - *The Malting Tower, Clanwilliam Terr* ✉ *D2* – ✆ *01 662 4198*
– www.osterialucio.com – Closed 25-29 December and bank holiday Mondays

Drury Buildings

ITALIAN · TRENDY A hip, laid-back 'New York loft': its impressive terrace has a retractable roof and reclaimed furniture features in the stylish cocktail bar, which offers cicchetti and sharing boards. The airy restaurant serves rustic Italian dishes.

Carte € 32/54

Town plan: F2-e - *52-55 Drury St* ✉ *D2* – ✆ *01 960 2095*
– www.drurybuildings.com – Closed 25-26 December, dinner 24 December and Good Friday

✗ Fade St. Social - Gastro Bar 🍷 🏠 ♿ 🍴

INTERNATIONAL · FASHIONABLE Buzzy restaurant with an almost frenzied feel. It's all about a diverse range of original, interesting small plates, from a bacon and cabbage burger to a lobster hot dog. Eat at the kitchen counter or on leather-cushioned 'saddle' benches.

Menu € 35 (early dinner) – Carte € 23/39

Town plan: F2-u - *4-6 Fade St* ✉ *D2* – ✆ *01 604 0066 (booking essential)*
– www.fadestreetsocial.com – Closed 25-26 December and lunch Monday-Tuesday

✗ La Maison 🏠 AK

CLASSIC FRENCH · BISTRO Sweet little French bistro with tables on the pavement and original posters advertising French products. The experienced, Breton-born chef-owner offers carefully prepared, seasonal Gallic classics, brought to the table by a personable team.

Menu € 22 (weekday dinner) – Carte € 24/56

Town plan: F2-c - *15 Castlemarket* ✉ *D2* – ✆ *01 672 7258*
– www.lamaisonrestaurant.ie – Closed 25-27 December and 1-2 January

✗ SÖDER+KO 🍷 AC 🍴

ASIAN · FASHIONABLE A vast, vibrant bar-cum-bistro in a former nightclub, with numerous rooms and even a chill-out lounge. Skilfully prepared Asian small plates are a mix of the modern and the classic; they are appealing, satisfying and good value.

Carte € 22/42

Town plan: F2-s - *64 South Great George's St* ✉ *D2* – ✆ *01 478 1590 (booking essential) – www.soderandko.ie – Closed bank holidays*

✗ Rustic Stone 🏠 ♿ AC 🍴

MODERN CUISINE · FASHIONABLE Split-level restaurant offering something a little different. Good quality ingredients are cooked simply to retain their natural flavours and menus focus on healthy and special dietary options; some meats and fish arrive on a sizzling stone.

Menu € 30/55 – Carte € 28/59

Town plan: F2-m - *17 South Great George's St* ✉ *D2* – ✆ *01 707 9596*
– www.rusticstone.ie – Closed 25-26 December and 1 January

✗ l'Gueuleton 🏠 ♿

CLASSIC FRENCH · BISTRO Rustic restaurant with beamed ceilings, Gallic furnishings, a shabby-chic bistro feel and a large pavement terrace. Flavoursome cooking features good value, French country classics which rely on local, seasonal produce. Service is friendly.

Menu € 25/37 – Carte € 37/50

Town plan: F2-d - *1 Fade St* ✉ *D2* – ✆ *01 675 3708 – www.lgueuleton.com*
– Closed 25-26 December

✗ Camden Kitchen

CLASSIC CUISINE · BISTRO Simple, modern, neighbourhood bistro set over two floors; watch the owner cooking in the open kitchen. Tasty dishes use good quality Irish ingredients prepared in classic combinations. Relaxed, friendly service from a young team.

Menu € 19/25 – Carte € 30/50

Town plan: F3-x - *3a Camden Mkt, Grantham St* ✉ *D8* – ✆ *01 476 0125*
– www.camdenkitchen.ie – Closed 24-26 December, Sunday and Monday

✗ Saba 🍷 ♿ AC

THAI · FASHIONABLE Trendy, buzzy Thai restaurant and cocktail bar. Simple, stylish rooms with refectory tables, banquettes and amusing photos. Fresh, visual, authentic cooking from an all-Thai team, with a few Vietnamese dishes and some fusion cooking too.

Menu € 14 (weekday lunch)/35 – Carte € 23/46

Town plan: F2-k - *26-28 Clarendon St* ✉ *D2* – ✆ *01 679 2000*
– www.sabadublin.com – Closed Good Friday and 25-26 December

REPUBLIC OF IRELAND

at Ballsbridge

🏨 InterContinental Dublin

LUXURY · CLASSIC Imposing hotel bordering the RDS Arena. Elegant guest areas, state-of-the-art meeting rooms and impressive ballrooms boast ornate décor, antique furnishings and Irish artwork. Spacious, classical bedrooms have marble bathrooms and plenty of extras. A wide-ranging menu is served in the bright, airy restaurant.

197 rooms – 👤 € 245/390 👥 € 245/390 – 🍴 €28 – 58 suites

Town plan: D3-h – *Simmonscourt Rd.* ✉ D4 – ☎ 01 665 4000
– *www.intercontinental.com/dublin*

🏨 Dylan

TOWNHOUSE · DESIGN Red-brick Victorian nurses' home with a sympathetically styled extension and a funky, boutique interior. Tasteful, individually decorated bedrooms offer a host of extras; those in the original building are the most spacious. The stylish restaurant offers a menu of modern Mediterranean dishes and comes complete with a zinc-topped bar and a smartly furnished terrace.

44 rooms – 👤 € 304/455 👥 € 304/455 – 🍴 €25

Town plan: C3-a – *Eastmoreland Pl* ✉ D4 – ☎ 01 660 3000 – *www.dylan.ie*
– *Closed 24-26 December*

🏠 Ariel House

TOWNHOUSE · CLASSIC Close to the Aviva Stadium and a DART station; a personally run Victorian townhouse with comfy, traditional guest areas and antique furnishings. Warmly decorated bedrooms have modern facilities and smart bathrooms; some feature four-posters.

37 rooms 🍴 – 👤 € 130/290 👥 € 130/290

Town plan: D3-n – *50-54 Lansdowne Rd* ✉ D4 – ☎ 01 668 5512
– *www.ariel-house.net* – *Closed 22 December-4 January*

🏠 Pembroke Townhouse

TOWNHOUSE · CLASSIC Friendly, traditionally styled hotel set in 3 Georgian houses. Small lounge with honesty bar and pantry. Sunny breakfast room offering homemade bread, cakes and biscuits. Variously sized, neutrally hued bedrooms; go for a duplex room.

48 rooms – 👤 € 70/350 👥 € 70/350 – 🍴 €15

Town plan: C3-d – *88 Pembroke Rd* ✉ D4 – ☎ 01 660 0277
– *www.pembroketownhouse.ie* – *Closed 2 weeks Christmas-New Year*

🍽 Old Spot

TRADITIONAL CUISINE · PUB The appealing bar has a stencilled maple-wood floor and a great selection of snacks and bottled craft beers. There's also a relaxed, characterful restaurant filled with vintage posters, which serves pub classics with a modern edge.

Carte € 31/51

Town plan: D2-s – *14 Bath Ave* ✉ D4 – ☎ 01 660 5599 – *www.theoldspot.ie*
– *Closed 25-26 December and 1 January*

🍽 Chop House

MEATS AND GRILLS · PUB Imposing pub close to the stadium, with a small side terrace, a dark bar and a bright, airy conservatory. The relaxed lunchtime menu is followed by more ambitious dishes in the evening, when the kitchen really comes into its own.

Menu € 32 – Carte € 30/55

Town plan: D3-x – *2 Shelbourne Rd* ✉ D4 – ☎ 01 660 2390
– *www.thechophouse.ie* – *Closed Saturday lunch*

at Donnybrook

XX Mulberry Garden 🎁

MODERN CUISINE · COSY Delightful restaurant hidden away in the city suburbs; its interesting L-shaped dining room set around a small courtyard terrace. Choice of two dishes per course on the weekly menu; original modern cooking relies on tasty local produce.

Menu € 49/70

Town plan: C3-g - *Mulberry Ln* ⊠ *D4* - *off Donnybrook Rd* - *ℰ 01 269 3300 (booking essential)* - *www.mulberrygarden.ie* - *dinner only* - *Closed Sunday-Wednesday*

at Ranelagh

XX Kinara Kitchen 🍸 & 🅰️🄲 🎁

PAKISTANI · EXOTIC DÉCOR This smart restaurant has become a destination not just for its cooking but for its cocktails too. The friendly, professional team serve a menu of homely, well-spiced Pakistani classics, including a selection from the tandoor oven.

Menu € 22 (lunch and early dinner) – Carte € 29/50

Town plan: C3-a - *17 Ranelagh Village* ⊠ *D6* - *ℰ 01 406 0066* *- www.kinarakitchen.ie - Closed 25-26 December and Good Friday*

X Brioche & 🎁

MODERN CUISINE · CHIC It's all about France at this lovely bistro in the buzzy village-like Ranelagh district. Attractive, modern French-inspired plates use top Irish ingredients and many have playful touches. Brioche is served at the start of every meal.

Menu € 25/35

Town plan: C3-x - *51 Elmwood Ave Lower* ⊠ *D6* - *ℰ 01 497 9163* *- www.brioche.ie - Closed 25-27 December, 1 January, Sunday, Monday and lunch Tuesday-Wednesday*

X Forest Avenue &

MODERN CUISINE · NEIGHBOURHOOD This rustic neighbourhood restaurant is named after a street in Queens and has a fitting 'NY' vibe, with its jam jar and antler light fittings and stags' heads lining the walls. Top ingredients feature in well-crafted modern dishes.

Menu € 30 (weekday lunch)/52

Town plan: C3-t - *8 Sussex Terr.* ⊠ *D4* - *ℰ 01 667 8337 (booking essential)* *- www.forestavenuerestaurant.ie - Closed last 2 weeks August, 25 December-10 January, 11-16 April, Sunday-Tuesday and lunch Wednesday*

at Rathmines

XX Zen & 🅰️🄲

CHINESE · ELEGANT Long-standing family-run restaurant, unusually set in an old church hall. At the centre of the elegant interior is a huge sun embellished with gold leaf. Imaginative Chinese cooking centres around Cantonese and spicy Sichuan cuisine.

Menu € 31 – Carte € 23/35

Town plan: C3-z - *89 Upper Rathmines Rd* ⊠ *D6* - *ℰ 01 497 9428* *- www.zenrestaurant.ie - dinner only and Friday lunch - Closed 25-27 December*

at Clontarf Northeast: 5.5 km by R 105⊠ Dublin

🏛️ Clontarf Castle 🎿 👭 🛗 & 🅰️🄲 🌂 🧖 🅿️

BUSINESS · HISTORIC A historic castle dating back to 1172, with sympathetic Victorian extensions; well-located in a quiet residential area close to the city. Contemporary bedrooms are decorated with bold, warm colours and many have four-poster beds. The restaurant offers local meats and seafood in a medieval ambience.

111 rooms ☑ – ♦ € 199/469 ♦♦ € 219/489

Town plan: D1-a - *Castle Ave.* ⊠ *D3* - *ℰ 01 833 2321* - *www.clontarfcastle.ie*

X **Pigeon House** 🛋 🖵

😳 MODERN CUISINE · NEIGHBOURHOOD Slickly run neighbourhood bistro that's open for breakfast, lunch and dinner. It's just off the coast road in an up-and-coming area and has a lovely front terrace and a lively feel. Cooking is modern and assured. The bar counter is laden with freshly baked goodies and dishes are full of flavour.

Menu € 27 (dinner) – Carte € 30/48

11b Vernon Ave ⊠ D3 – East : 1 km by Clontarf Rd on Vernon Ave (R808)
– ✆ 01 805 7567 – www.pigeonhouse.ie – Closed 25-26 December

at Blackrock Southeast : 7.5 km by R 118

X **Heron & Grey** Ⓝ (Damien Grey)

🕸 MODERN CUISINE · FRIENDLY A homely, candlelit restaurant in a bohemian sub-urban market; it's personally run by Heron – who leads the service – and Grey, who heads the kitchen. Irish ingredients feature in intensely flavoured dishes which are full of contrasting textures and tastes. The set 5 course dinner menu changes every 2 weeks.

→ Asparagus with dried trompettes and duck egg. Langoustine, fennel and dulse. Pineapple with rum and clove.

Menu £ 26/48 – tasting menu only

Blackrock Market, 19a Main St – ✆ 01 212 3676 (booking essential)
– www.heronandgrey.com – Closed 2 weeks late August, 2 weeks Christmas-New Year, Sunday-Wednesday and Thursday lunch

at Foxrock Southeast : 13 km by N 11 ⊠ Dublin

XX **Bistro One**

TRADITIONAL CUISINE · NEIGHBOURHOOD Long-standing neighbourhood bis-tro above a parade of shops; run by a father-daughter team and a real hit with the locals. Good value daily menus list a range of Irish and Italian dishes. They produce their own Tuscan olive oil.

Menu € 29 (weekdays) – Carte € 29/55

3 Brighton Rd ⊠ D18 – ✆ 01 289 7711 (booking essential) – www.bistro-one.ie
– Closed 25 December-3 January, 18 April, Sunday and Monday

at Rathgar South : 3.75 km by N 81

X **Bijou** 🛋 ☕ 🅰🅺 ⇔

MODERN BRITISH · BRASSERIE Friendly restaurant with dining spread over two levels and a clubby heated terrace complete with a gas fire. Local ingredients feature in classically based dishes with modern touches. The experienced owners also run the nearby deli.

Menu € 20/29 – Carte € 30/48

46 Highfield Rd ⊠ D6 – ✆ 01 496 1518 – www.bijourathgar.ie – Closed
25-26 December

at Dundrum South : 7.5 km by R 117 ⊠ Dublin

XX **Ananda** 🍸 ☕ 🅰🅺 🕃

INDIAN · EXOTIC DÉCOR Its name means 'bliss' and it's a welcome escape from the bustle of the shopping centre. The stylish interior encompasses a smart cock-tail bar, attractive fretwork and vibrant art. Accomplished Indian cooking is mod-ern and original.

Menu € 20/50 – Carte € 31/60

Sandyford Rd, Dundrum Town Centre ⊠ D14 – ✆ 01 296 0099
– www.anandarestaurant.ie – dinner only and lunch Friday-Sunday – Closed
25-26 December

at Sandyford South : 10 km by R 117 off R 825 ✉ Dublin

✗✗ China Sichuan

CHINESE · FASHIONABLE A smart modern interior is well-matched by creative menus, where Irish produce features in tasty Cantonese classics and some Sichuan specialities. It was established in 1979 and is now run by the third generation of the family.

Menu € 15 (weekday lunch)/35 – Carte € 27/57

The Forum, Ballymoss Rd. ✉ D18 – 𝒞 01 293 5100 – www.china-sichuan.ie
– Closed 25-31 December, Good Friday, lunch Saturday and bank holidays

---

DUNCANNON DÚN CANANN

Wexford – Pop. 328 – Regional map n° **22**-D2
▶ Dublin 167 km – New Ross 26 km – Waterford 48 km

✗✗ Aldridge Lodge

(۞) MODERN BRITISH · FRIENDLY This attractive house is set in a great rural location and run by cheery owners. The constantly evolving menu offers tasty homemade bread and veg from the kitchen garden. The focus is on good value fish and shellfish (the owner's father is a local fisherman), with some Asian and fusion influences. Homely bedrooms come with hot water bottles and home-baked cookies.

Menu € 35/40 **s**

3 rooms ⌷ – ♦ € 45/55 ♦♦ € 90/110

South : 2 km on Hook Head rd – 𝒞 051 389 116 (booking essential)
– www.aldridgelodge.com – dinner only and Sunday lunch – Closed 3 weeks
January, 24-25 December, Monday and Tuesday

DUNDALK DÚN DEALGAN

Louth – Pop. 31 149 – Regional map n° **21**-D2
▶ Dublin 82 km – Drogheda 35 km

🏠 Rosemount

FAMILY · COSY An attractive dormer bungalow fronted by a delightful flower-filled garden. The welcoming owners serve tea and cake on arrival and a freshly cooked breakfast the next morning. The lounge is warmly decorated and the individually styled, spotlessly kept bedrooms feature fine fabrics and modern facilities.

12 rooms ⌷ – ♦ € 50 ♦♦ € 70

Dublin Rd – South : 2.5 km on R 132 – 𝒞 042 933 5878
– www.rosemountireland.com – Closed 22-27 December

at Jenkinstown Northeast: 9 km by N52 on R173

▯🍴 Fitzpatricks

TRADITIONAL CUISINE · PUB A hugely characterful pub on the coast road, at the foot of the mountains, featuring beautiful flower displays and a wealth of memorabilia. Extensive menus list hearty, flavoursome dishes; specialities include local steaks and seafood.

Menu € 11 (weekday lunch)/35 – Carte € 30/52

Rockmarshall – Southeast : 1 km – 𝒞 042 937 6193
– www.fitzpatricks-restaurant.com – Closed 24-26 December and Good Friday

---

DUNDRUM DÚN DROMA – Dún Laoghaire-Rathdown → See Dublin

DUNFANAGHY DÚN FIONNACHAIDH

Donegal – ✉ Letterkenny – Pop. 312 – Regional map n° **21**-C1
▶ Dublin 277 km – Donegal 87 km – Londonderry 69 km

XX Mill ⟵ ⟨ ⟨ AC P

TRADITIONAL CUISINE · FRIENDLY Converted flax mill on the waterside, with lovely garden edged by reeds and great view of Mount Muckish. Homely inner with conservatory lounge and knick-knacks on display throughout. Antique-furnished dining room has a classical Georgian feel. Traditional menus showcase seasonal ingredients and fish features highly. Cosy, welcoming bedrooms come in individual designs.

Menu € 45

7 rooms ⌧ – ♦ € 70 ♦♦ € 100/150

Southwest : 0.75 km on N 56 – 𝒞 074 913 6985 – www.themillrestaurant.com – dinner only – Closed Monday and Tuesday except July and August, restricted opening October-May

DUNGARVAN DÚN GARBHÁN
Waterford – Pop. 7 991 – Regional map n° **22**-C3
▶ Dublin 190 km – Cork 71 km – Waterford 48 km

XX Tannery ⟵ AC ⟷

MODERN CUISINE · FRIENDLY Characterful 19C stone-built tannery, close to the harbour; they also run the renowned cookery school here. Have small plates at the counter or head upstairs to the bright restaurant. Attractively presented, classically based dishes use good seasonal ingredients. Stylish bedrooms come with DIY breakfasts.

Menu € 33 – Carte € 41/51

14 rooms ⌧ – ♦ € 60/75 ♦♦ € 95/115

10 Quay St – via Parnell St – 𝒞 058 45420 – www.tannery.ie – dinner only and lunch Friday and Sunday – Closed last 2 weeks January, 25-26 December, Sunday dinner except July-August, Monday and Good Friday

DUNKINEELY DÚN CIONNAOLA
Donegal – Pop. 375 – Regional map n° **21**-C1
▶ Dublin 156 km – Lifford 42 km – Sligo 53 km – Ballybofey 28 km

XX Castle Murray House ⟵ ⟨ ⟨ AC ⟷ P

SEAFOOD · FRIENDLY Established restaurant in a delightful coastal location, offering great castle, sea and sunset views. Start in the snug bar with its seafaring memorabilia then move to the spacious dining room, large conservatory or flag-stoned terrace. The classical menu features mussels and oysters from the bay. Stylish bedrooms have gilt mirrors, plush fabrics and very comfy beds.

Menu € 51

10 rooms ⌧ – ♦ € 90/105 ♦♦ € 120/150

St John's Point – Southwest : 1.5 km by N 56 on St John's Point rd – 𝒞 074 973 7022 – www.castlemurray.com – dinner only and Sunday lunch - light lunch in summer – Closed January-mid February, 24-26 December, Monday-Tuesday except July-August and restricted opening in winter

DUN LAOGHAIRE DÚN LAOGHAIRE
Dún Laoghaire-Rathdown – Pop. 23 857 – Regional map n° **22**-D1
▶ Dublin 12 km – Wicklow 40 km – Cork 265 km

XX Rasam

INDIAN · EXOTIC DÉCOR The scent of rose petals greets you as you head up to the plush lounge and contemporary restaurant. Fresh, authentic Indian dishes come in original combinations and are cooked from scratch; they even dry roast and blend their own spices.

Menu € 24 (weekdays) – Carte € 30/53

18-19 Glasthule Rd, 1st Floor (above Eagle House pub) – 𝒞 01 230 0600 – www.rasam.ie – dinner only – Closed 25-26 December and Good Friday

X **Fallon & Byrne**

MODERN CUISINE · BRASSERIE A former Victorian shelter in the People's Park, offering views over a floodlit fountain towards the sea. Original cast iron pillars lead through to a contemporary room. All-day menus offer cakes and Mediterranean-style bistro dishes.

Carte € 26/44

People's Park – ℰ 01 230 3300 – www.fallonandbyrne.com – Closed 25-26 December and 1 January

X **Cavistons**

SEAFOOD · BISTRO A landmark restaurant in the town. Guests come here for the fresh, carefully cooked fish and shellfish – go for the scallops or lobster when they're in season. In 2017 they are moving to larger premises two doors down (number 56).

Menu € 19 – Carte € 30/51

58-59 Glasthule Rd – ℰ 01 280 9245 (booking essential) – www.cavistons.com – lunch only and dinner Thursday-Saturday – Closed Sunday and Monday

DURRUS DÚRAS
Cork – Pop. 334 – Regional map n° **22**-A3
▶ Dublin 338 km – Cork 90 km – Killarney 85 km

Gallán Mór

COUNTRY HOUSE · HOMELY Proudly run guesthouse named after the 3,500 year old standing stone in its garden; set in a lovely rural location overlooking Dunmanus Bay and Mizen Head. Bedrooms have warm fabrics, good facilities and handmade wooden beds. The delightful owners welcome you with home-made cake beside the wood-burning stove.

4 rooms ☑ – ♦ € 75/90 ♦♦ € 110/130

Kealties – West : 5.5 km. on Ahakista rd – ℰ 027 62732 – www.gallanmor.com – Closed November-February. Minimum 2 nights stay.

XX **Blairscove House**

MODERN CUISINE · ELEGANT Charming 18C barn and hayloft, just a stone's throw from the sea, with fantastic panoramic views, pretty gardens, a courtyard and a lily pond. Stylish bar and stone-walled, candlelit dining room. Starters and desserts are in buffet format, while the seasonal main courses are cooked on a wood-fired chargrill. Luxurious, modern bedrooms are dotted about the place.

Menu € 60 **s**

4 rooms ☑ – ♦ € 105/160 ♦♦ € 150/260

Southwest : 1.5 km on R 591 – ℰ 027 61127 (booking essential) – www.blairscove.ie – dinner only – Closed November-17 March, Sunday and Monday

ENNISCORTHY INIS CÓRTHAIDH
Wexford – Pop. 2 842 – Regional map n° **22**-D2
▶ Dublin 122 km – Kilkenny 74 km – Waterford 54 km – Wexford 24 km

Monart

SPA AND WELLNESS · GRAND LUXURY Comprehensively equipped destination spa in 100 acres of beautifully landscaped grounds; a haven of peace and tranquility. The Georgian house with its contemporary glass extension houses spacious, stylish bedrooms with a terrace or balcony. The Restaurant serves light, modern dishes; the minimalistic Garden Lounge offers global dishes in a more informal environment.

70 rooms ☑ – ♦ € 139/599 ♦♦ € 198/599 – 2 suites

The Still – Northwest : 3 km by N 11 (Dublin rd) – ℰ 053 923 8999 – www.monart.ie – Closed 18-27 December

🏠 Ballinkeele House ⚜ 🐾 ⩽ 🛏 🕭 P

HISTORIC · CLASSIC Impressive Georgian house in 300 acres; family-run with traditional Irish hospitality. Grand, antique-filled sitting rooms. Bedrooms vary from cosy twins to luxurious doubles with four-posters. Four course, communal dinners feature produce from the garden. Homemade breads and fruit compotes for breakfast.

6 rooms ⌖ – 🕴 € 105/150 🕴🕴 € 120/170

Ballymurn – Southeast : 10 km by R 744 and Vinegar Hill rd on Curracloe rd – ℰ 053 913 8105 – www.ballinkeele.ie – Closed December-January and restricted opening February-June and September-November

ENNISKERRY ÁTH AN SCEIRE
Wicklow – Pop. 1 811 – Regional map n° **22**-D1
▶ Dublin 24 km – Belfast 204 km – Cork 273 km – Lisburn 192 km

🏨 Powerscourt ⚜ 🐾 ⩽ 🛏 🖪 🖵 🕸 ⽾ 🛗 🖵 ⴵ ⁂ AC 🧖 P

GRAND LUXURY · CLASSIC Impressive curved building overlooking Sugar Loaf Mountain, featuring stylish guest areas, luxurious bedrooms, state-of-the-art conference facilities and a superb spa; outdoor activities include archery and falconry. Sika offers modern, formal dining, while the plush lounge-bar serves a concise menu of classics. McGills is a traditional Irish pub with a menu to match.

200 rooms – 🕴 € 155/230 🕴🕴 € 170/245 – 93 suites

Powerscourt Estate – West : 1.5 km by Powerscourt rd – ℰ 01 274 8888 – www.powerscourthotel.com

🏠 Ferndale 🛏 🕭 P

FAMILY · RURAL Homely guesthouse filled with family artefacts; located in the centre of the village, close to Powerscourt House and Gardens. The simple bedrooms are fairly priced. The splendid 1 acre garden has lots of seating and a large water feature.

4 rooms ⌖ – 🕴 € 50/70 🕴🕴 € 80/90

– ℰ 01 286 3518 – www.ferndalehouse.com – Closed 24-25, 31 December and 1 January

FANORE
Clare – Regional map n° **22**-B1
▶ Dublin 253 km – Ennis 51 km – Galway 65 km – Limerick 92 km

🍴 Vasco 🗺 P

MODERN CUISINE · SIMPLE Remotely set restaurant opposite the seashore, with a minimalist interior and a glass-screened terrace. The keen owners collect the latest produce on their drive in; the daily menu ranges from sandwiches and cake to soup and light dishes.

Carte € 24/42

Craggagh – West : 1 km on R 477 – ℰ 065 707 6020 – www.vasco.ie – Closed October-mid March, Monday and dinner Tuesday-Wednesday and Sunday

FENNOR FIONNÚIR
Waterford – Regional map n° **22**-C2
▶ Dublin 115 km – Waterford 12 km – Cork 75 km – Limerick 89 km

🍴 Copper Hen P
🐝

TRADITIONAL CUISINE · RUSTIC A simple, likeable little restaurant located above a pub, with rustic décor and a brightly coloured fireplace; set on the coast road from Tramore to Dungarvan. Keenly priced menus offer fresh, hearty, unfussy classics and service is enthusiastic and efficient. The owners raise their own pigs.

Menu € 25

Mother McHugh's Pub – ℰ 051 330 300 – www.thecopperhen.ie – dinner only and Sunday lunch – Closed 2 weeks September, 1 week January, 25-26 December, Sunday dinner, Monday and Tuesday

FOTA ISLAND OILEÁN FHÓTA

Cork – Regional map n° **22**-B3

▶ Dublin 263 km – Cork 17 km – Limerick 118 km – Waterford 110 km

🏨 Fota Island   🎿 🛶 🛗 🖼 ▢ 🕙 ♨ ⬆ 🚿 ♿ ⛹ AC 🏊 ✨ P

LUXURY · DESIGN A resort hotel set within Ireland's only wildlife park. Extensive business and leisure facilities include a golf course and a state-of-the-art spa. Bedrooms are spacious and well-appointed, and most have island views. The stylish restaurant offers modern takes on classical dishes.

131 rooms 🛏 – 🛉 € 160/256 🛉🛉 € 175/271

– ☎ *021 488 3700 – www.fotaisland.ie – Closed 25 December*

FOXROCK CARRAIG AN TSIONNAIGH – Dún Laoghaire-

Rathdown ➜ See Dublin

GOOD TIPS!

When you think Galway, you think music – an effervescent spirit and a non-conformist attitude helped to put it at the heart of the city. A need to do their own thing is also adopted by the city's restaurants, which are an eclectic bunch, from the ground-breaking **Loam** to the rustic tapas bar **Cava Bodega**, and the vibrant Thai restaurant, **Lime**.

GALWAY GAILLIMH

Galway – Pop. 75 529 – Regional map n° **21**-B3
Dublin 217 km – Limerick 103 km – Sligo 145 km

Hotels

Radisson Blu H. & Spa

BUSINESS • MODERN Corporate hotel overlooking a lough, with a striking atrium, vast meeting facilities and a spa with a thermal suite and salt cave. Spacious, modern bedrooms; 5th floor rooms have balconies and share a business lounge. Marina's offers international dishes, with a 'Food Market Buffet' at lunch; Raw serves sushi and raw meats.

261 rooms – € 220/440 € 240/450 – 2 suites

Lough Atalia Rd – 4 mins walk east of train station – 091 538 300 – www.radissonhotelgalway.com

Raw – See restaurant listing

G

LUXURY • GRAND LUXURY Boutique hotel featuring boldly coloured walls hung with flamboyant mirrors designed by Irish milliner Philip Treacy. Bright, spacious bedrooms have a more calming feel. The spa has a thermal suite and a relaxation room overlooking a walled bamboo garden. The colourful restaurant serves modern Irish dishes.

101 rooms – € 150/380 € 150/380 – 2 suites

Wellpark, Dublin Rd – Northeast : 3 km by R 336 and R 338 – 091 865 200 – www.theghotel.ie – Closed 23-26 December

House

TOWNHOUSE • DESIGN Unassuming hotel with a surprisingly luxurious interior. Smart bedrooms are decorated with eye-catching Italian fabrics and feature quality linens. Service is professional yet friendly. Spacious guest areas include a laid-back lounge, and a bar and dining room serving modern day classics, coffee and cocktails.

40 rooms – € 89/360 € 99/380 – 1 suite

Town plan: B2-e – *Lower Merchants Rd – 091 538 900 – www.thehousehotel.ie – Closed 25-26 December*

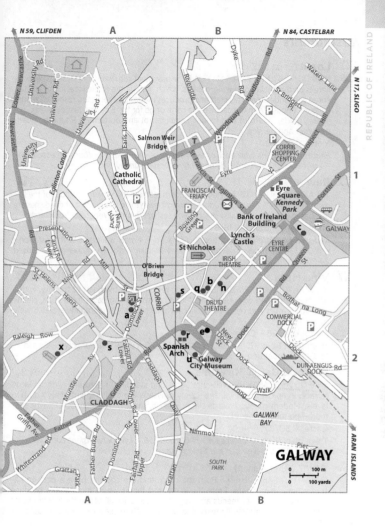

GALWAY

ARAN ISLANDS

0   100 m
0   100 yards

Ardawn House   ⚄ P

TRADITIONAL · COSY Located next to the stadium and the greyhound track, with the city just a stroll away. Good-sized bedrooms are clean and fresh, with modern fabrics. A small lounge leads to a breakfast room laid with silver-plated cutlery. Friendly owners.

8 rooms ⌿ – ♦ € 55/180 ♦♦ € 85/180

College Rd. – Northeast : 2.25 km by R 336 on R 339
– ☎ 091 568 833 – www.ardawnhouse.com
– Closed 15-27 December

Restaurants

XX Loam (Enda McEvoy)   🛦 AC ⑩ ✿

MODERN CUISINE · MINIMALIST A large basement with industrial styling; the focus here is on the quality of the ingredients, which grow in the fertile local loam. The talented chef understands his craft and produces modern, understated dishes with pure flavours. Choose from the concise à la carte or go for the 6 course tasting menu.
→ Eel, golden beetroot and fennel. Lamb, carrot and buttermilk. Rhubarb, meadowsweet and parsley.

Menu € 50/70

Fairgreen – 2 mins walk east of train station – 𝒞 091 569 727 (booking essential) – www.loamgalway.com – dinner only – Closed Sunday and Monday

XX Raw   🛦 AC ▣

JAPANESE · INTIMATE An elegant, modern restaurant on the fourth floor of the Radisson Blu Hotel. As its name suggests, almost everything is raw; most of the dishes are fish-based and they specialise in sushi and sashimi to order. Very tasty 'tuna tataki'.

Menu € 40 – Carte € 18/31

Radisson Blu Hotel and Spa, Lough Atalia Rd – 4 mins walk east of train station – 𝒞 091 538 212 (booking essential) – www.sushiinthesky.ie – dinner only – Closed 24-26 December, Sunday and Monday

XX Vina Mara   AC ⑩

MODERN CUISINE · BISTRO Bistro-style restaurant in the heart of the city, with a rich Mediterranean colour scheme. Modern Irish cooking has a fresh style, clearly defined flavours and relies on quality local ingredients; vegetarians are also well-catered for.

Menu € 10/28 – Carte € 28/38

Town plan: B2-n - 19 Middle St – 𝒞 091 561 610 – www.vinamara.com – Closed 25-27 December and Sunday

XX Seafood Bar @ Kirwan's   🌂 AC

SEAFOOD · BRASSERIE Well-regarded, long-standing restaurant with a large terrace, in an old medieval lane. Lively brasserie atmosphere, with dining on two levels. Modern menus have a classical base; most dishes consist of tasty seafood – go for the specials.

Carte € 30/67

Town plan: B2-s - Kirwan's Ln – 𝒞 091 568 266 – www.kirwanslane.com – Closed 25-26 December and Sunday lunch

X Aniar (JP McMahon)   AC ✿

CREATIVE · FASHIONABLE Both the room and the cooking have a back-to-nature ethos. Aniar means 'From the West' and this is where most of the produce comes from: the 3 set menus are only confirmed once all of the day's ingredients have arrived. Contrasts in texture and temperature play their part in delicate, Scandic-style dishes.
→ Beef, hay and gooseberry. Cod, celeriac and monk's beard. Fennel, barley and honey.

Menu € 90/120

Town plan: A2-a - 53 Lower Dominick St – 𝒞 091 535 947 (booking essential) – www.aniarrestaurant.ie – dinner only – Closed 25-26 December, Sunday and Monday

X Oscar's Seafood Bistro   AC

SEAFOOD · INTIMATE A very welcoming bistro in a bohemian part of the city. The intimate candlelit interior is a striking red with richly upholstered banquettes. Choose something from the daily blackboard menu, which lists the catch of the day.

Menu € 19 (weekday dinner) – Carte € 27/54

Town plan: A2-s - Dominick St – 𝒞 091 582 180 – www.oscarsbistro.ie – dinner only – Closed 1-16 January and Sunday except bank holidays

☓ Le Petit Pois ⓝ

FRENCH · FAMILY Whitewashed walls are offset by colourful lights and a dresser bursting with produce. Dishes are packed with flavour: lunch keeps things light – try the French hams and cheeses; at dinner have the tasting menu with matching wines.

Menu €13 (lunch)/52 – Carte €33/45

Town plan: B1-c - *Victoria Pl* – ℰ *091 330 880* – *www.lepetitpois.ie* – *Closed Sunday and Monday*

☓ Latin Quarter

REGIONAL CUISINE · WINE BAR The menu at this bright, two-floored restaurant alters as the day goes on. Lunch centres around one course – including a soup, a salad and maybe a pie of the day; while dinner is more substantial. Cooking is honest and flavoursome.

Menu €19 (weekday dinner) – Carte €26/42

Town plan: B2-q - *1 High St* – ℰ *091 530 000* – *www.bistro.ie* – *Closed 24-25 December*

☓ Cava Bodega   AC 🎐

SPANISH · TAPAS BAR This split-level tapas bar – with its reclaimed wood tables – has a rustic, neighbourhood feel; sit downstairs to watch the chefs in the open kitchen. It's all about sharing: choose around 3 dishes each and a Spanish beer or wine.

Carte €20/36

Town plan: B2-b - *1 Middle St* – ℰ *091 539 884* – *www.cavarestaurant.ie* – *dinner only and lunch Saturday-Sunday* – *Closed 25-26 December*

☓ Kai   ✿

CLASSIC CUISINE · NEIGHBOURHOOD Lovely, laid-back restaurant with a gloriously cluttered interior and old scrubbed floorboards on the walls. Morning cakes morph into fresh, simple lunches, then afternoon tea and tasty dinners. Produce is organic, free range and traceable.

Carte €34/47

Town plan: A2-x - *22 Sea Rd* – ℰ *091 526 003* – *www.kaicaferestaurant.com* – *Closed Sunday-Monday in winter and bank holidays*

☓ Ard Bia at Nimmos

MEDITERRANEAN CUISINE · COSY Buzzy, bohemian restaurant where tables occupy every nook and cranny. They sell homemade cakes, bread and artisan products. Menus blend Irish, Mediterranean and Middle Eastern influences; the provenance of the ingredients takes precedence.

Carte €31/44

Town plan: B2-u - *Spanish Arch* – ℰ *091 561 114 (booking essential at dinner)* – *www.ardbia.com* – *Closed 25-26 December*

☓ Lime   🎐

THAI · EXOTIC DÉCOR A large, lively eatery run by a well-known local restaurateur. Bright, bold colours feature alongside Asian prints; the lovely terrace overlooks the quayside. Authentic Thai and Malaysian dishes are colourful and full of flavour.

Menu €30 (dinner) – Carte €28/40

Town plan: B2-r - *Spanish Arch* – ℰ *091 534 935* – *www.limegalway.com* – *Closed Christmas*

GARRYKENNEDY

North Tipperary – Regional map n° **22**-C2
▶ Dublin 176 km – Killaloe 14 km – Youghal 2 km

🍴 Larkins 🚗 🛋 P

TRADITIONAL CUISINE · PUB Thatched pub in a charming loughside location. The traditional interior boasts original fireplaces and old flag and timber floors – and plays host to folk music and Irish dancers. Unfussy dishes feature plenty of fresh seafood.

Menu € 20/38 – Carte € 25/42

– *℘ 067 23232 – www.larkins.ie – Closed 25 December, Good Friday, Monday-Tuesday and Wednesday-Friday lunch November-April*

GLASLOUGH GLASLOCH

Monaghan – ✉ Monaghan – Regional map n° **37**-D2
▶ Dublin 133 km – Monaghan 11 km – Sligo 136 km

🏰 Castle Leslie 🏊 ≼ 🚗 🖃 ♿ 🌾 P

HISTORIC BUILDING · HISTORIC Impressive castle set in 1,000 acres of parkland: home to the 4th generation of the Leslie family. Ornate, comfortable, antique-furnished guest areas and traditional, country house style bedrooms. Dine in Snaffles restaurant in the grounds.

20 rooms ☺ – 🛉 € 190/370 🛉🛉 € 210/390

Castle Leslie Estate – ℘ 047 88100 – www.castleleslie.com – Closed 22-27 December

🏰 Lodge at Castle Leslie Estate 🏠 🏊 🚗 📶 🖃 ♿ 🌾 🛶 P

HISTORIC · CONTEMPORARY An extended hunting lodge to the main castle, with contrastingly stylish bedrooms. Unwind in the Victorian treatment room or charming open-fired bar – or hire an estate horse from the excellent equestrian centre and explore the 1,000 acre grounds. The mezzanine restaurant offers modern Mediterranean fare.

29 rooms ☺ – 🛉 € 170/260 🛉🛉 € 190/280 – 1 suite

– *℘ 047 88100 – www.castleleslie.com*

GLASSON – Westmeath → See Athlone

GOLEEN AN GÓILÍN

Cork – Regional map n° **22**-A3
▶ Dublin 230 km – Cork 74 km – Killarney 67 km

🏠 Heron's Cove 🏠 🏊 ≼ 🌾 P

TRADITIONAL · PERSONALISED Long-standing guesthouse hidden away in a pretty location, with views over a tiny harbour. Bedrooms are tidy and pleasantly furnished: all overlook the waterfront and most have a balcony – if you're lucky you might see herons at the water's edge. The busy restaurant offers seasonal menus of local produce.

5 rooms ☺ – 🛉 € 50/80 🛉🛉 € 80/100

The Harbour – ℘ 028 35225 – www.heronscove.com – Closed Christmas

GOREY GUAIRE

Wexford – Pop. 3 463 – Regional map n° **22**-D2
▶ Dublin 93 km – Waterford 88 km – Wexford 61 km

🏰 Marlfield House 🏠 🚗 🛋 🍴 P

COUNTRY HOUSE · ELEGANT Well-appointed, period-style bedrooms look out over the large grounds of this attractive Regency house. Various sitting and drawing rooms have a homely, classical feel and all are packed with antiques, oil paintings and curios. Have afternoon tea in the garden while watching the peacocks wander by, then dine in the conservatory restaurant or the terrace café and bar.

19 rooms ☺ – 🛉 € 100/120 🛉🛉 € 230/670

Courtown Rd – Southeast : 1.5 km on R 742 – ℘ 053 942 1124
– www.marlfieldhouse.com – Closed 3-16 January, Wednesday and Sunday October-April and Monday-Tuesday

The Duck – See restaurant listing

X **The Duck** 🅽   🏮 ♻ 🅿

REGIONAL CUISINE · FRIENDLY The Duck is a smart, rustic bistro which sits within the grounds of a grand country house, next to a superb kitchen garden which informs its menu. Sit on the wonderful terrace with a glass of wine and dine on unfussy, global cuisine.

Carte € 30/52

Marlfield House Hotel, Courtown Rd – Southeast : 1.5 km on R 742
– ☏ 053 942 1124 – www.marlfiledhouse.ie – Closed October-April except
1-2 January

GREYSTONES NA CLOCHA LIATHA
Wicklow – Pop. 10 173 – Regional map n° **22**-D1
▶ Dublin 32 km – Wicklow 22 km – Dundalk 128 km

XX **Chakra by Jaipur**   占 🆎 🍸

INDIAN · EXOTIC DÉCOR Smart, spacious Indian restaurant with warm exotic hues and carved wooden statues, unusually set in a suburban shopping centre. Three themed set menus and an à la carte: accomplished, modern dishes feature original spicing and flavours.

Menu € 24/31 – Carte € 29/58

Meridian Point Centre (1st floor), Church Rd – ☏ 01 201 7222 – www.jaipur.ie
– dinner only and Sunday lunch – Closed 25 December

HOWTH BINN ÉADAIR
Fingal – ✉ Dublin – Pop. 8 186 – Regional map n° **22**-D1
▶ Dublin 22 km – Swords 17 km – Cork 276 km

XX **King Sitric**   🔄 ≼ 🆎

SEAFOOD · CLASSIC DÉCOR A long-standing eatery in a former harbourmaster's house, overlooking the water. Dine in the laid-back ground floor café or the formal first floor restaurant. Seafood is the order of the day, with lobster a speciality. Bedrooms are named after lighthouses; those on the first floor have the best views.

Menu € 32 – Carte € 35/70

8 rooms ☲ – 🛏 € 110/150 🛏🛏 € 150/205

East Pier – ☏ 01 832 5235 – www.kingsitric.ie – dinner only and Sunday lunch
– Closed 25-26 December, last 2 weeks January, Sunday dinner, Monday, Tuesday
and bank holidays

INISHMAAN INIS MEÁIN – Galway → See Aran Islands

INISHMORE ÁRAINN – Galway → See Aran Islands

JENKINSTOWN BAILE SHEINICÍN – Louth → See Dundalk

KANTURK CEANN TOIRC
Cork – Pop. 2 263 – Regional map n° **22**-B2
▶ Dublin 259 km – Cork 53 km – Killarney 50 km – Limerick 71 km

🏠 **Glenlohane**   🌳 🐾 ≼ 🚗 🌿 🅿

HISTORIC · CLASSIC A Georgian country house set in 260 acres – it has been in the family for over 250 years. Traditional interior hung with portraits and paintings. Colour-themed bedrooms; 'Blue' has an antique four-poster and bathtub. Cosy library and drawing room. Open-fired dining room for home-cooked communal dinners.

3 rooms ☲ – 🛏 € 120 🛏🛏 € 220

Southeast : 4 km. by R 576 (Mallow rd) and R 580 on L1043 – ☏ 029 50014
– www.glenlohane.com

KENMARE NEIDÍN
Kerry – Pop. 2 175 – Regional map n° **22**-A3
▶ Dublin 338 km – Cork 93 km – Killarney 32 km

Park

GRAND LUXURY · CLASSIC Grand country house dating from 1897, with superb views over the bay and hills. Elegant interior with a cosy cocktail lounge and a charming drawing room. Tastefully furnished bedrooms have smart marble bathrooms. The spa adds a modern touch. Informal meals in Terrace. Candlelit dining in the restaurant.

46 rooms 🖙 – ♦ € 95/405 ♦♦ € 95/405

– 𝒞 064 664 1200 – www.parkkenmare.com – Closed 6 January-5 March and 27 November-23 December

Park – See restaurant listing

Sheen Falls Lodge

LUXURY · CLASSIC A modern hotel in an idyllic spot, where the waterfalls drop away into the bay. Welcoming, wood-fired lobby; spacious, comfortable guest areas and a lovely indoor pool; the well-appointed, good-sized bedrooms overlook the falls. The split-level, formal restaurant serves classic dishes with a modern touch.

66 rooms 🖙 – ♦ € 180/975 ♦♦ € 180/975 – 9 suites

Southeast : 2 km. by N 71 – 𝒞 064 664 1600 – www.sheenfallslodge.ie – Closed January

Brook Lane

BUSINESS · MODERN Stylish, personally run hotel close to the town centre. Contemporary bedrooms offer a good level of comfort and range from 'Superior' to 'Luxury'; the latter boasting impressive fabric headboards and designer touches. Informal bar and restaurant offer classic Irish and seafood dishes; regular live music.

21 rooms 🖙 – ♦ € 75/130 ♦♦ € 99/170

Gortamullen – North : 1.5 km. by N 71 on N 70 – 𝒞 064 664 2077 – www.brooklanehotel.com – Closed 23-27 December

Sallyport House

FAMILY · CLASSIC Unassuming 1930s house; its charming interior packed with antiques and Irish art. Pleasant lounge with local information. Breakfast is served from the characteristic sideboard and features pancakes, stewed fruits and smoked salmon. Traditionally furnished bedrooms are immaculately kept and boast water views.

5 rooms 🖙 – ♦ € 85/95 ♦♦ € 120/150

South : 0.5 km. on N 71 – 𝒞 064 664 2066 – www.sallyporthouse.com – Closed November-March

XXX Park

CLASSIC CUISINE · ELEGANT Elegant, candlelit dining room in a luxurious hotel, with good views over the grounds and a comforting style. Silver candelabras, cloches and gueridon trolleys feature; start with canapés in the lounge. Classically based dishes have a modern touch, with local ingredients to the fore. Highly professional team.

Menu € 70 – Carte € 32/63

Park Hotel, – 𝒞 064 664 1200 (booking advisable) – www.parkkenmare.com – dinner only – Closed 6 January-5 March and 27 November-23 December

XX Mulcahys

MODERN CUISINE · INTIMATE Come for cocktails and snacks in the bar or settle in for the evening in the intimate restaurant. Unfussy dishes utilise Irish ingredients, including local fish, which is used in the sushi. For dessert, try the tarte Tatin for two.

Carte € 30/47

Main St – 𝒞 064 664 2383 – dinner only – Closed 24-26 December, Tuesday, and Monday and Wednesday October-April

XX Lime Tree   AC P

CLASSIC CUISINE · RUSTIC A 19C property that's taken on many guises over the years. The characterful, rustic interior features exposed stone walls, an open fire and even its own art gallery. Flavoursome, classically based dishes utilise quality local ingredients.

Menu € 45 – Carte € 34/52

Shelbourne St. – 𝒞 064 664 1225 – www.limetreerestaurant.com – dinner only – Closed January-March

X Boathouse Bistro   ≤ ⇔ ⇑ P

SEAFOOD · BRASSERIE Converted boathouse in the grounds of Dromquinna Manor; set on the waterside and overlooking the peninsula and the mountains. It has a nautical, New England style and a laid-back vibe. Menus are simple, appealing and focus on seafood.

Carte € 31/51

Dromquinna – West : 4.75 km by N 71 on N 70 – 𝒞 064 664 2889 (booking advisable) – www.dromquinnamanor.com – Closed December- February, midweek March & November and Monday-Wednesday in April & October

X Packie's

TRADITIONAL CUISINE · RUSTIC Popular little restaurant in the town centre, with two rustic, bistro-style rooms, exposed stone walls, tiled floors and an interesting collection of modern Irish art. Cooking is honest, fresh and seasonal; the seafood specials are a hit.

Carte € 26/55

Henry St – 𝒞 064 664 1508 (booking essential) – dinner only – Closed first 2 weeks February, Monday September-May and Sunday

KILCOLGAN CILL CHOLGÁIN

Galway – ✉ Oranmore – Regional map n° **21**-B3
▶ Dublin 208 km – Galway 19 km – Cork 179 km

🍴 Moran's Oyster Cottage   ⇑

SEAFOOD · COSY Attractive whitewashed pub with a thatched roof, hidden away in a tiny hamlet – a very popular place in summer. It's all about straightforward cooking and good hospitality. Dishes are largely seafood based and oysters are the speciality.

Carte € 26/50

The Weir – Northwest : 2 km. by N 18 – 𝒞 091 796 113 – www.moransoystercottage.com – Closed 24-26 December and Good Friday

KILCULLEN

Kildare – Pop. 3 473 – Regional map n° **22**-D1
▶ Dublin 48 km – Naas 12 km – Navan 88 km

🍴 Fallon's   ⇑ AC P

TRADITIONAL BRITISH · FASHIONABLE A 'proper' bar with a long wooden counter and a flagged floor; albeit one with a boutique colour scheme! The experienced chef offers a wide range of dishes, from pie of the day to grilled salmon, followed by tasty homemade puddings.

Carte € 31/55

Main St – 𝒞 045 481 260 – www.fallonb.ie – Closed 25 December, Good Friday and Monday

KILDARE CILL DARA

Kildare – Pop. 8 142 – Regional map n° **22**-D1
▶ Dublin 54 km – Portlaoise 37 km – Naas 21 km

🍴 Harte's

CLASSIC CUISINE · RUSTIC Have a local artisan beer in the snug open-fired bar or kick things off with a gin tasting board; then move on to tasty, well-prepared dishes with modern twists in the small restaurant with its large mirrors and exposed brick walls.

Menu € 26 (weekdays)/35 – Carte € 29/40

Market Sq – ☎ 045 533 557 – www.harteskildare.ie – Closed Monday except bank holidays

KILKENNY CILL CHAINNIGH

Kilkenny – Pop. 24 423 – Regional map n° **22**-C2
▶ Dublin 114 km – Cork 138 km – Killarney 185 km – Limerick 111 km

🏠 Butler House

TOWNHOUSE · ELEGANT Beautifully restored Georgian house with some fine original features, a delightful formal garden and views of Kilkenny castle. Large, comfortable, up-to-date bedrooms. Breakfast is served in the adjacent Design Museum.

13 rooms 🍴 – ♦ € 80/250 ♦♦ € 99/300

15-16 Patrick St. – ☎ 056 776 5707 – www.butler.ie – Closed 23-29 December

🏠 Rosquil House

FAMILY · PERSONALISED Modern, purpose-built guesthouse on the main road out of the city. Leather-furnished lounge filled with books and local information; spacious, comfortable bedrooms and a smart, linen-laid breakfast room. Extensive buffet breakfasts with a cooked daily special; omelettes feature. Experienced, welcoming owners.

7 rooms 🍴 – ♦ € 65/90 ♦♦ € 80/120

Castlecomer Rd – Northwest : 1 km – ☎ 056 772 1419 – www.rosquilhouse.com – Closed 3-27 January and 24-27 December

🍴🍴🍴 Ristorante Rinuccini

ITALIAN · CLASSIC DÉCOR Set in the basement of a townhouse and named after the 17C papal nuncio, this family-owned restaurant is well-known locally. Classic Italian cuisine with homemade ravioli a speciality. Some tables have views through to the wine cellar.

Menu € 29 – Carte € 30/50

1 The Parade – ☎ 056 776 1575 – www.rinuccini.com – Closed 26-27 December

🍴🍴 Campagne (Garrett Byrne)

🌿 **MODERN BRITISH · FASHIONABLE** Stylish, relaxed restaurant with vibrant, contemporary art and smart booths, hidden close to the railway arches, away from the city centre. Modern cooking has a classic base, and familiar combinations are delivered with an assured touch. Popular early bird menu. Well-run, with friendly, efficient service.

→ Terrine of foie gras with greengage and toasted walnut bread. Aylesbury duck 'en croûte', braised red cabbage and parsnip purée. Orange and chocolate parfait with orange jelly and chocolate ganache.

Menu € 33 (lunch and early dinner) **s** – Carte € 37/58 **s**

5 The Arches, Gashouse Ln. – ☎ 056 777 2858 (booking advisable) – www.campagne.ie – dinner only and lunch Friday-Sunday – Closed 2 weeks January, 1 week July, Sunday dinner and Monday

🍴🍴 Zuni

MODERN BRITISH · BRASSERIE Small wood-furnished café-bar opening out into a chic, light, modern restaurant with mirrored walls, leather panels and a heated terrace. Eclectic modern menus of Irish produce; desserts are a high point. Comfortable black and white bedrooms continue the smart, contemporary theme.

Menu € 30 – Carte € 30/46

13 rooms 🍴 – ♦ € 65/95 ♦♦ € 75/140

26 Patrick St – ☎ 056 772 3999 – www.zuni.ie – Closed 25-26 December

✗ **Foodworks**   🚫 AK

TRADITIONAL CUISINE · FRIENDLY A former bank in the town centre: a high-ceilinged, airy space with a bright, fresh look which matches the style of the cooking. Unfussy dishes use quality local produce, including pork and vegetables from the experienced chef-owner's farm.

Carte € 24/48

7 Parliament St – ☎ 056 777 7696 – www.foodworks.ie – Closed 25-26 December and Sunday

KILLALOE CILL DALUA

Clare – Pop. 1 292 – Regional map n° **22**-B2
▶ Dublin 175 km – Ennis 51 km – Limerick 21 km – Tullamore 93 km

✗✗ **Cherry Tree**   ← 🕿 🚫 ⇔ P

CLASSIC CUISINE · INTIMATE Modern restaurant with interesting local art hung on brightly coloured walls, and views across Lough Derg. Choose from an array of classical menus; dishes are well-balanced, seasonal and nicely presented. Service is cheery and welcoming.

Menu € 26 (early dinner) – Carte € 30/45

Lakeside, Ballina – follow signs for Lakeside Hotel – ☎ 061 375 688 – www.cherrytreerestaurant.ie – dinner only – Closed first week January, 25-26 December, Good Friday, Sunday and Monday

KILLARNEY CILL AIRNE

Kerry – Pop. 12 740 – Regional map n° **22**-A2
▶ Dublin 304 km – Cork 87 km – Limerick 111 km – Waterford 180 km

🏨 **Europe**   🌊 ← 🛎 🏊 🖹 🛜 🛋 £ō ✗ ⊡ & ⅍ 🛄 P

GRAND LUXURY · MODERN A vast hotel in a superb location, boasting views over Lough Leane and Macgillycuddy's Reeks. Opulent guest areas, impressive events facilities and a sublime three-level spa. Bedrooms are lavishly appointed; some overlook the water.

187 rooms ⊆ – 🛉 € 220/350 🛉🛉 € 240/370 – 6 suites

Fossa – West : 4.75 km. by Port Rd on N 72 – ☎ 064 667 1300 – www.theeurope.com – Closed 9 December-2 February

Panorama · Brasserie – See restaurant listing

🏨 **Aghadoe Heights H. and Spa**   🌊 ← 🛎 🖹 🛜 🛋 £ō ✗ ⊡ 🛄 ⅍

LUXURY · DESIGN Striking, glass-fronted hotel looking out over lakes,   P
mountains and countryside. Modern interior with an impressive spa and a stylish cocktail bar complete with an evening pianist. Bedrooms are spacious; many have balconies or terraces.

74 rooms ⊆ – 🛉 € 260/370 🛉🛉 € 310/370 – 2 suites

Northwest : 4.5 km. by N 22 off L 2109 – ☎ 064 663 1766 – www.aghadoeheights.com – Closed 24-26 December and weekdays November-April

Lake Room – See restaurant listing

🏨 **Killarney Park**   🛎 🖹 🛜 🛋 £ō ✗ ⊡ & 🛄 ⅍ 🛄 P

LUXURY · CLASSIC A smart, comfortable hotel run by a well-versed team. Bedrooms range in style, mixing modern furnishings with original features. Plush library and lavish drawing room; light lunches are served in the clubby, wood-panelled bar.

69 rooms ⊆ – 🛉 € 200/485 🛉🛉 € 215/485 – 6 suites

Town plan: B1-k - – ☎ 064 663 5555 – www.killarneyparkhotel.ie – Closed 24-27 December

Park – See restaurant listing

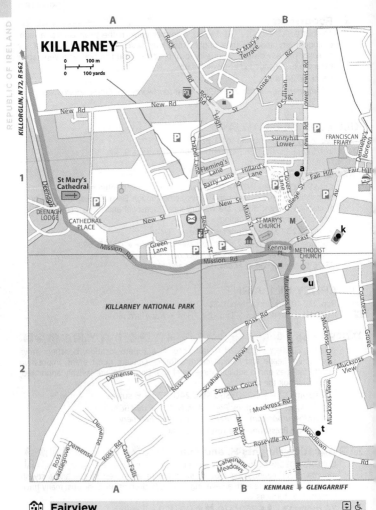

🏨 Fairview

TOWNHOUSE · GRAND LUXURY Stylish house in the centre of town, with a cosy, leather-furnished lounge and spacious, contemporary bedrooms with marble-tiled bathrooms. The Penthouse has a 4-poster, a whirlpool bath for two and mountain views from the balcony.

29 rooms ☑ – 🛉 € 60/199 🛉🛉 € 79/249

Town plan: B1-a - *College St.* - 𝒞 064 663 4164 – www.killarneyfairview.com – *Closed 24-25 December*

🏨 Earls Court House

FAMILY · CLASSIC A well-run hotel close to the town centre. Afternoon tea is served on arrival in the antique-furnished lounges. Spacious bedrooms boast good facilities: some feature half-tester or four-poster beds; some have balconies and mountain views.

30 rooms ☑ – 🛉 € 95/130 🛉🛉 € 110/150

Town plan: B2-t - *Woodlawn Rd.* - 𝒞 064 663 4009 – www.killarney-earlscourt.ie – *Closed November-February*

🏠 Kathleens Country House   🍴 ⌖ **P**

TRADITIONAL · CLASSIC Personally run by a charming hostess: this is Irish hospitality at its best! Comfortable, well-kept and good value hotel, with spacious, pine-furnished bedrooms, an open-fired lounge and a cosy first floor library.

17 rooms ⌂ – ♦ € 70/115 ♦♦ € 100/150

Madams Height, Tralee Rd. – North : 3.75 km on N 22 – 𝒞 064 663 2810
– www.kathleens.net – Closed October-April

🏨 Killarney Lodge   🍴 AC ⌖ **P**

FAMILY · PERSONALISED Well-located on the edge of the town centre. Spacious, immaculately kept, well-furnished bedrooms; No. 12 boasts lovely mountain views. Bright and airy breakfast room where homemade bread and scones feature. Afternoon tea on arrival.

16 rooms ⌂ – ♦ € 70/100 ♦♦ € 100/140

Town plan: B2-u - *Countess Rd. – 𝒞 064 663 6499 – www.killarneylodge.ie*
– Closed November-10 March

𝕏𝕏𝕏𝕏 Panorama   ≼ 🍴 ♿ AC **P**

MODERN CUISINE · LUXURY Large, formal restaurant with a contemporary style, set in a luxurious hotel. Panoramic windows afford superb views across the lough towards the mountains. Creative modern menus follow the seasons and use the very best of Irish produce.

Carte € 34/64

Europe Hotel, Fossa – West : 4.75 km. by Port Rd on N 72 – 𝒞 064 667 1300
– www.theeurope.com – Closed 9 December-2 February

𝕏𝕏𝕏 Lake Room   ≼ 🍴 ♿ AC 🕐 **P**

REGIONAL CUISINE · DESIGN Smart restaurant in a contemporary hotel; its two different levels making the most of the panoramic water and mountain view. Classical dishes showcase local produce and are executed with a modern touch; there's the odd French influence too.

Menu € 55 – Carte € 35/77

Aghadoe Heights H and Spa, Aghadoe – Northwest : 4.5 km. by N 22 off L 2109
– 𝒞 064 663 1766 – www.aghadoeheights.com – dinner only – Closed
24-26 December and weekdays November-April

𝕏𝕏𝕏 Park   🍴 ♿ AC **P**

TRADITIONAL CUISINE · CLASSIC DÉCOR An elegant hotel restaurant boasting chandeliers, ornate cornicing and smartly laid tables. Classic menus with some modern combinations; Irish meats are a feature and the tasting menu a highlight. Nightly pianist in summer.

Carte € 52/68 – bar lunch

Town plan: B1-k - *Killarney Park Hotel, – 𝒞 064 663 5555*
– www.killarneyparkhotel.ie – Closed 23-27 December

𝕏𝕏 Brasserie   ≼ 🍴 🏠 ♿ AC **P**

INTERNATIONAL · BRASSERIE Set in a sumptuous lakeside hotel; a modern take on a classical brasserie, with lough and mountain views – head for the terrace in warmer weather. The accessible all-day menu ranges from soup and salads to steaks cooked on the open grill.

Carte € 34/57 **s**

Europe Hotel, Fossa – West : 4.75 km. by Port Rd on N 72 – 𝒞 064 667 1300
(bookings not accepted) – www.theeurope.com – Closed 9 December-2 February

KILLORGLIN CILL ORGLAN

Kerry - Pop. 2 082 – Regional map n° **22**-A2
▶ Dublin 333 km – Killarney 19 km – Tralee 26 km

REPUBLIC OF IRELAND

✗ Giovannelli

ITALIAN · RUSTIC A sweet little restaurant, hidden away in the town centre, with a traditional osteria-style interior and an on-view kitchen. The concise, daily changing blackboard menu offers authentic Italian dishes which are unfussy, fresh and full of flavour, with homemade pasta and herbs from the owners' garden.

Carte € 33/55

Lower Bridge St – ℰ 087 123 1353 (booking essential)
– www.giovannellirestaurant.com – dinner only – Closed Monday

✗ Sol y Sombra   🍴 ⭫ 🍱 ⟳

SPANISH · TAPAS BAR Spanish restaurant in an imposing 19C former church, with a cavernous interior, stained glass windows and church pews. Fresh, vibrant cooking: go for the raciones, designed for sharing – 3 per person will suffice. Live music is a feature.

Menu € 16/35 – Carte € 22/39

Old Church of Ireland, Lower Bridge St – ℰ 066 976 2347 – www.solysombra.ie
– dinner only and Sunday lunch – Closed 9 January-2 February and
Monday-Tuesday in winter

KINLOUGH CIONN LOCHA

Leitrim – Pop. 1 018 – Regional map n° **21**-C2
▶ Dublin 220 km – Ballyshannon 11 km – Sligo 34 km

✗ Courthouse   ⇦

ITALIAN · BISTRO Boldly painted former courthouse with a pretty stained glass entrance. The Sardinian chef-owner creates extensive seasonal menus of honest, authentic Italian dishes; local seafood and some imported produce feature. The atmosphere is informal and the service, friendly. Simply styled bedrooms offer good value.

Menu € 29 – Carte € 30/46

4 rooms ⌁ – ♦ € 40/50 ♦♦ € 80

Main St – ℰ 071 984 2391 (booking essential) – www.thecourthouserest.com
– dinner only and Sunday lunch – Closed Monday and Wednesday in winter and
Tuesday

KINSALE CIONNE TSÁILE

Cork – Pop. 2 198 – Regional map n° **22**-B3
▶ Dublin 276 km – Waterford 92 km – Cork 25 km

🏠 Perryville House   🍃 🅿

TOWNHOUSE · CLASSIC Luxuriously appointed house in the heart of town, over-looking the harbour and named after the family that built it in 1820. Bedrooms are tastefully styled – the top rooms have feature beds, chic bathrooms and har-bour views. It also boasts two antique-furnished drawing rooms, a smart bou-tique and a tea shop.

23 rooms ⌁ – ♦ € 170 ♦♦ € 170/320

Town plan: B1-f *- Long Quay – ℰ 021 477 2731 – www.perryvillehouse.com*
– Closed November-15 April

🏠 Blue Haven   🍴 🍃

TOWNHOUSE · PERSONALISED A small but well-established hotel right in the heart of town; its cosy, vibrant interior features some interesting artwork. Com-fortable bedrooms are named after vineyards and have a subtle contemporary edge. The modern wine bar serves tapas dishes, while the all-day bistro offers a global menu; the latter, set in the old fish market, resembles an upturned boat hull.

17 rooms ⌁ – ♦ € 59/110 ♦♦ € 80/200

Town plan: A1-c *- 3-4 Pearse St – ℰ 021 477 2209 – www.bluehavenkinsale.com*
– Closed 25 December

⌂ Old Presbytery   🕸 🅿

TOWNHOUSE · CLASSIC 18C building which once housed priests from the nearby church – a few ecclesiastical pieces remain. Bedrooms feature Irish pine furniture and either brass or cast iron beds; Room 6 has a roof terrace. Breakfasts are comprehensive.

9 rooms 🖙 – 🛉 € 70/120 🛉🛉 € 95/180

Town plan: A1-a - *43 Cork St. - 𝒞 021 477 2027 - www.oldpres.com - Closed mid November-mid February*

✗✗ Finns' Table   🄰🄲

REGIONAL CUISINE · FRIENDLY Behind the bright orange woodwork lie two attractive rooms – one with colourful banquettes, the other in powder blue with wine box panelling. Meat is from the chef's family farm and everything from bread to ice cream is homemade.

Menu € 35 (early dinner) – Carte € 35/64

Town plan: A1-b - *6 Main St - 𝒞 021 470 9636 - www.finnstable.com - dinner only - Closed November, Christmas, Sunday-Thursday January-mid March and Tuesday-Wednesday*

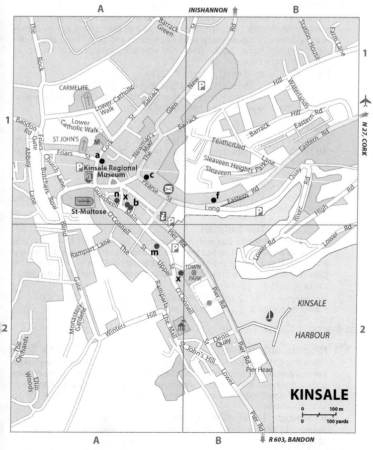

REPUBLIC OF IRELAND

XX Max's   🅰🄲

SEAFOOD · INTIMATE An efficiently run, two-roomed restaurant on a quaint main street, with a simple yet smart rustic style – a spot well-known by the locals! The unfussy, classical seafood menu offers plenty of choice; try the tasty 'Fresh Catches'.

Menu € 25 – Carte € 33/49

Town plan: A2-m - - *𝒸 021 477 2443 (booking advisable) – www.maxs.ie*
– dinner only – Closed Christmas, Sunday, Monday and Thursday September-May and bank holidays

X Fishy Fishy   🍴 ♿ 🅰🄲
😋

SEAFOOD · DESIGN Friendly, informal restaurant that's something of a local institution: dine in the spacious restaurant amongst 'fishy' memorabilia or alfresco on the small terrace. Concise, all-day menus offer well-prepared seafood dishes and interesting specials. The owner often collects the fish himself.

Carte € 30/53 **s**

Town plan: A2-x - Pier Rd – 𝒸 021 470 0415 – www.fishyfishy.ie
– Closed 24-26 December

X Bastion
😋

MEDITERRANEAN CUISINE · FRIENDLY Simple little wine-bar-cum-bistro run by a keen young couple. Modern cooking relies on Irish produce but has Mediterranean influences. Dishes are tasty, carefully prepared and often have a playful element; start with some 'Bastion Bites'. The wine bar serves prosecco on tap, as well as prosecco cocktails.

Menu € 35 (early dinner) – Carte € 32/58

Town plan: A1-n - Market St – 𝒸 021 470 9696 (booking advisable)
– www.bastionkinsale.com – dinner only and Sunday lunch – Closed last 2 weeks January, first 2 weeks February, Monday and Tuesday

X Twisted 🄽   🅰🄲 📖

SPANISH · SIMPLE With French and Fijian owners and Spanish and Italian chefs, this arty tapas bar adds an international twist to proceedings. Have a cocktail and some Iberico ham at the bar or choose from a mix of modern and classic small plates.

Carte € 30/45

Town plan: A1-x - 5 Main St – 𝒸 086 810 0157 – dinner only – Closed Monday and Tuesday in winter

🍴 Toddies at The Bulman   ≤ 🍴

SEAFOOD · PUB Rustic pub with maritime décor and excellent bay views; look out for the Moby Dick mural and the carved Bulman Buoy. Lunch is in the bar and offers simple pub classics and more ambitious blackboard specials; dinner is in the more formal restaurant and presents carefully prepared, globally influenced dishes.

Carte € 32/50

Summercove – East : 2 km by R 600 and Charles Fort rd. – 𝒸 021 477 2131
– www.thebulman.ie – Closed 25 December and Good Friday

at Barrells Cross Southwest: 5.75 km on R600 ✉ Kinsale

🏠 Rivermount House   🐾 ≤ 🛏 🕸 🅿

FAMILY · PERSONALISED Spacious, purpose-built dormer bungalow overlooking the countryside and the river, yet not far from town. It has a distinctive modern style throughout, with attractive embossed wallpapers and quality furnishings. Bold, well-appointed bedrooms display high attention to detail and have immaculate bathrooms.

6 rooms 🍽 – 👤 € 60/85 👥 € 85/100

North : 0.75 km on L 7302 – 𝒸 021 477 8033 – www.rivermount.com – Closed 14 November-9 March

KNOCK AN CNOC

Mayo – Pop. 811 – Regional map n° **21**-B2

▶ Dublin 212 – Galway 74 – Westport 51

*Hotels see : **Cong** SW : 58 km by N 17, R 331 R 334 and R 345*

LAHINCH AN LEACHT

Clare – Pop. 642 – Regional map n° **22**-B1

▶ Dublin 260 km – Galway 79 km – Limerick 66 km

⌂ Moy House
⇪ ⅏ ⪪ 🛏 ⅍ 🅿

TRADITIONAL • ELEGANT 18C Italianate clifftop villa, overlooking the bay and run by a friendly, attentive team. Homely guest areas include a small library and an open-fired drawing room with an honesty bar; antiques, oil paintings and heavy fabrics feature throughout. Individually designed, classical bedrooms boast good extras and most have views. Formal dining is from a 5 course set menu.

9 rooms ☑ – ♦ € 145/200 ♦♦ € 165/380

Southwest : 3 km on N 67 – ℰ 065 708 2800 – www.moyhouse.com – Closed November-March

LEENANE AN LÍONÁN

Galway – ✉ Clifden – Regional map n° **21**-A3

▶ Dublin 278 km – Ballina 90 km – Galway 66 km

⌂ Delphi Lodge
⇪ ⅏ ⪪ 🛏 ⅍ 🅿

COUNTRY HOUSE • PERSONALISED A former shooting lodge of the Marquis of Sligo, in a lovely loughside spot on a 1,000 acre estate. Bright, simple bedrooms with smart bathrooms. 'Special Experience' days, free bike hire and a large walkers' drying room. Communal dining from a set menu; guests are encouraged to mingle in the drawing room.

13 rooms ☑ – ♦ € 140/195 ♦♦ € 230/320

Northwest : 13.25 km by N 59 on Louisburgh rd – ℰ 095 42222 – www.delphilodge.ie – Closed November-February

LETTERKENNY LEITIR CEANAINN

Donegal – Pop. 15 387 – Regional map n° **21**-C1

▶ Dublin 241 km – Londonderry 34 km – Sligo 116 km

✗✗ Browns on the Green
⪪ 🄰🄲 🅿

MODERN CUISINE • FRIENDLY Situated on the first floor of a golf club but with views of the mountains rather than the course. A cosy lounge leads into the intimate modern dining room. Refined dishes are modern interpretations of tried-and-tested classics.

Menu € 12 (lunch) – Carte € 28/46

Letterkenny Golf Club, Barnhill – Northeast : 5.75 km by R 245 – ℰ 074 912 4771 (booking advisable) – www.brownsrestaurant.com – Closed 25-26 December, Good Friday, Monday and Tuesday

LIMERICK LUIMNEACH

Limerick – Pop. 57 106 – Regional map n° **22**-B2

▶ Dublin 195 km – Cork 99 km – Galway 102 km – Waterford 127 km

⌂ No 1. Pery Square
🕸 🛗 ⅍ 🄰🄲 ⅍ 🅿

TOWNHOUSE • CONTEMPORARY A charming hotel in the Georgian Quarter, with a stylish reception and a classically proportioned drawing room overlooking the gardens. Luxurious, classically styled 'Period' bedrooms and more contemporary 'Club' rooms. Superb spa.

20 rooms ☑ – ♦ € 135/165 ♦♦ € 165/195 – 1 suite

Town plan: A2-a - Pery Sq – ℰ 061 402 402 – www.oneperysquare.com – Closed 25-26 December

Sash – See restaurant listing

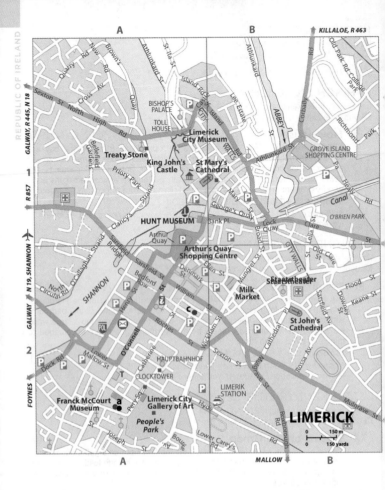

X Cornstore

🍷 🍴 ♿ AC ⇔

TRADITIONAL CUISINE · WINE BAR Head past the bar and up to the larger, more comfortable first floor restaurant to enjoy carefully prepared, traditional cooking. Dry-aged Irish steaks form the core of the menu; seafood also plays a part – and a cocktail is a must!

Menu € 28 (weekday dinner) – Carte € 27/50

Town plan: A2-c - *19 Thomas St* – *☏ 061 609 000* – *www.cornstore.com*

X Sash

♿ AC

TRADITIONAL CUISINE · BISTRO A relaxed modern bistro on the first floor of a hotel in the Georgian quarter; its name comes from the type of window often found in houses of this era. Contemporary styling, with a feature wall of pictures and mirrors. Wide-ranging menus.

Menu € 25 (lunch and early dinner) – Carte € 28/55

Town plan: A2-a - *No.1 Pery Square Hotel, Pery Sq* – *☏ 061 402 402*
– www.oneperysquare.com
– Closed Monday

LISCANNOR LIOS CEANNÚIR

Clare – Pop. 129 – Regional map n° **22**-B1
▶ Dublin 272 km – Ennistimmon 9 km – Limerick 72 km

🛏 Vaughan's Anchor Inn   ⇔ 🏠 AC P

SEAFOOD · PUB Family-run pub in a picturesque fishing village; the pleasantly cluttered bar comes complete with a small grocery shop. Dishes are a step above your normal pub fare and local seafood plays a big role; the seafood platter is a real hit. Smart bedrooms feature bright local art and colourful throws.

Carte € 24/50

7 rooms ⌒ – ♦ € 60 ♦♦ € 90/100

Main St – ℰ 065 708 1548 – www.vaughans.ie – Closed 25 December

LISDOONVARNA LIOS DÚIN BHEARNA

Clare – Pop. 739 – Regional map n° **22**-B1
▶ Dublin 268 km – Galway 63 km – Limerick 75 km

🏠 Sheedy's Country House   🏠 ⛳ ḋ 🕸 P

FAMILY · CLASSIC Mustard-yellow house in the village centre, with a kitchen garden in front. Relax in the comfy library, the Lloyd Loom furnished sun lounge or the traditional bar. Spacious, well-kept bedrooms feature flowery fabrics and have good facilities. A classical menu is offered in the dining room; service is exacting.

11 rooms ⌒ – ♦ € 85/120 ♦♦ € 110/170

– ℰ 065 707 4026 – www.sheedys.com – Closed October-Easter

🛏 Wild Honey Inn   ⇔ ⛳
😊

CLASSIC CUISINE · INN Three-storey building at the end of a short terrace, located close to the limestone landscape of The Burren and the Cliffs of Moher. Menus stick with the classics and champion local produce, particularly seafood. Flavours are bold and presentation is modern. Bedrooms are simply furnished; two open onto the walled courtyard. Have breakfast overlooking the garden.

Menu € 35 (weekday dinner) – Carte € 33/48

14 rooms ⌒ – ♦ € 65 ♦♦ € 100

South : 0.5 km on Ennistimon rd – ℰ 065 707 4300 (bookings not accepted) – www.wildhoneyinn.com – Closed November-February and weekdays March-April

LISTOWEL LIOS TUATHAIL

Kerry – Pop. 4 205 – Regional map n° **22**-B2
▶ Dublin 270 km – Killarney 54 km – Limerick 75 km – Tralee 27 km

🍴 Allo's Bistro   ⇔ ⛬

TRADITIONAL CUISINE · COSY Former pub dating back to 1873; now a simple, well-run and characterful restaurant. Series of homely rooms and friendly, efficient service. Wide-ranging menus rely on regional produce, with theme nights on Thursdays and an adventurous gourmet menu Fri and Sat evenings. Individual, antique-furnished bedrooms.

Menu € 20/40 – Carte € 25/42

3 rooms – ♦ € 70/100 ♦♦ € 70/100

41-43 Church St – ℰ 068 22880 (booking essential) – www.allosbarbistro-townhouse.com – Closed Sunday and Monday except bank holidays

LONGFORD AN LONGFORT

Longford – Pop. 8 002 – Regional map n° **21**-C3
▶ Dublin 124 km – Drogheda 120 km – Galway 112 km – Limerick 175 km

⌂ Viewmount House   🐾 � 👜 ♿ 🛋 **P**

COUNTRY HOUSE · CLASSIC Set in 4 acres of mature grounds, a welcoming Georgian house with a charming period feel – original features include an ornate vaulted ceiling in the breakfast room. Bedrooms are traditionally styled, furnished with antiques and have good modern facilities; opt for a duplex room. The breakfasts are delicious.

12 rooms 🖙 – 🛏 € 75/85 🛏🛏 € 140/150

Dublin Rd – Southeast : 1.5 km by R 393 – 𝒞 043 334 1919
– www.viewmounthouse.com – Closed 29 October-8 November

VM – See restaurant listing

✗✗✗ VM   🚪 ♿ **P**

MODERN CUISINE · TRADITIONAL DÉCOR Formal hotel restaurant in the old stables of a Georgian house. The smart, rustic dining room has stone-faced walls and overlooks a Japanese garden. Cooking is interesting, modern and original, and orchard and garden produce features.

Menu € 60

Viewmount House Hotel, Dublin Rd – Southeast : 1.5 km by R 393
– 𝒞 043 334 1919 – www.viewmounthouse.com – dinner only and Sunday lunch
– Closed 29 October-8 November, Sunday dinner, Monday and Tuesday

MALAHIDE MULLACH ÍDE

Fingal – Pop. 15 846 – Regional map n° **22**-D1
▶ Dublin 19 km – Cork 274 km – Galway 224 km – Waterford 185 km

✗✗ Jaipur   AC

INDIAN · ELEGANT Friendly basement restaurant in a Georgian terrace. The origins of the tasty, contemporary Indian dishes are noted on the menu. The fish curry – sea bass with nigella seeds, lemon leaf, onion and coconut sauce – is a speciality.

Menu € 20 (early dinner) – Carte € 32/49

5 St James's Terr – 𝒞 01 845 5455 – www.jaipur.ie – dinner only and Sunday lunch
– Closed 25 December

✗✗ Bon Appetit   🍷 AC 🍽 ⇔

MODERN CUISINE · BRASSERIE Smart Georgian terraced house near the harbour. The intimate, dimly lit bar offers cocktails and tapas; below is a modern brasserie with a lively atmosphere. Modern dishes have a classical French base; the steaks are a highlight.

Menu € 23/29 – Carte € 36/49

9 St. James's Terr. – 𝒞 01 845 0314 – www.bonappetit.ie – dinner only and lunch
Friday-Sunday – Closed 25-26 December and Monday

MALLOW MALA

Cork – Pop. 8 578 – Regional map n° **22**-B2
▶ Dublin 240 km – Cork 34 km – Killarney 64 km – Limerick 66 km

🏰 Longueville House   ✿ 🐾 ← 🚪 ⅌ 🛁 **P**

HISTORIC · CLASSIC Part-Georgian manor house built in William and Mary style, with pleasant views over Dromaneen Castle. Lovely stone-tiled hall, superb flying staircase and stunning drawing room. Well-appointed bedrooms boast antique furniture. Grand restaurant; traditional menus use produce from the kitchen garden and estate.

20 rooms 🖙 – 🛏 € 95/250 🛏🛏 € 199/299

West : 5.5 km by N 72 – 𝒞 022 47156 – www.longuevillehouse.ie – Closed
24-27 December, Monday-Tuesday and restricted opening in winter

MIDLETON MAINISTIR NA CORANN

Cork – Pop. 3 733 – Regional map n° **22**-C3
▶ Dublin 259 km – Cork 19 km – Waterford 98 km

X **Farmgate Restaurant & Country Store**

REGIONAL CUISINE · SIMPLE A friendly food store with a bakery, a rustic two-roomed restaurant and a courtyard terrace. Lunch might mean soup, a sandwich or a tart; dinner features regional fish and meats – the chargrilled steaks are popular. Cakes served all day.

Carte € 28/53

Coolbawn – ℰ 021 463 2771 (bookings advisable at dinner) – www.farmgate.ie
– Closed 24 December-3 January, Sunday and Monday

X **Sage**

REGIONAL CUISINE · BISTRO Local produce is the focus at this homely restaurant, with most ingredients coming from within 12 miles. Cooking has a classical base and showcases prime seafood and top quality meats. The courtyard is perfect for a summer's day.

Menu € 20/45

The Courtyard, 8 Main St – ℰ 021 463 9682 – www.sagerestaurant.ie – Closed 25-27 December, Good Friday and Monday

MOHILL MAOTHAIL

Leitrim – Pop. 928 – Regional map n° **21**-C2
▶ Dublin 98 km – Carrick-on-Shannon 11 km – Cavan 41 km – Castlerea 44 km

Lough Rynn Castle

LUXURY · HISTORIC 18C country house with superb gardens and peaceful grounds; popular for weddings. Numerous lounges and a baronial hall with original parquet flooring and an impressive fireplace. Large, well-appointed bedrooms – those in the main house are the most characterful. Formal dining room; ambitious French cuisine.

44 rooms ⌑ – † € 89/189 †† € 99/245
Southeast : 4 km by R 201 off Drumlish rd – ℰ 071 963 2700 – www.loughrynn.ie

Lough Rynn Country House

FAMILY · PERSONALISED Purpose-built stone house in a peaceful country setting, boasting lovely views over Lough Rynn – three of the homely bedrooms share the view and one has a small balcony. There's a comfy lounge and a cottagey breakfast room, and the delightful owner welcomes guests with home-baked scones or muffins.

4 rooms ⌑ – † € 50 †† € 100
Southeast : 3.5 km. by R 201 off Drumlish rd – ℰ 087 922 8236
– www.loughrynnbandb.ie

MULLINGAR AN MUILEANN GCEARR

Westmeath – Pop. 9 414 – Regional map n° **21**-C3
▶ Dublin 79 km – Cork 242 km – Galway 146 km – Waterford 177 km

Marlinstown Court

TRADITIONAL · COSY Clean, tidy guesthouse close to the N4; a very homely, personal option for staying away. The light, airy lounge opens into a pleasant pine-furnished breakfast room overlooking the garden. Bedrooms are simply and brightly decorated.

5 rooms ⌑ – † € 45/55 †† € 75/80
Dublin Rd – East : 2.5 km on Dublin Rd off N 4 (junction 15) – ℰ 044 934 0053
– www.marlinstowncourt.com – Closed 23-27 December

MURRISK MURAISC

Mayo – Pop. 235 – Regional map n° **21**-A2
▶ Dublin 260 km – Castlebar 25 km – Galway 95 km

REPUBLIC OF IRELAND

🍴 Tavern   A/C P

TRADITIONAL CUISINE · PUB Vibrant pink pub with designer colours, leather banquettes and quirky basket lampshades. Wide-ranging dishes display a touch of refinement; the meats and seafood are local and the daily cheesecake is a must. Staff are smart and attentive.

Carte € 23/49

– 𝒞 098 64060 – www.tavernmurrisk.com – Closed 25 December and Good Friday

NAAS AN NÁS
Kildare – Pop. 20 713 – Regional map n° **22**-D1
▶ Dublin 30 km – Kilkenny 83 km – Tullamore 85 km

✗ Vie de Châteaux 🛜 も A/C P

CLASSIC FRENCH · BISTRO A smart modern bistro with a great terrace overlooking the old harbour. The keenly priced menu of carefully cooked, fully flavoured Gallic dishes will evoke memories of holidays in France; save room for 'Les Mini Desserts'.

Menu € 25/35

The Harbour – 𝒞 045 888 478 (booking essential) – www.viedechateaux.ie
– Closed 24 December-2 January, lunch Monday, Tuesday, Saturday and bank holidays

at Two Mile House Southwest: 6.5 km by R448

✗✗ Brown Bear 🛜 も A/C P

MODERN BRITISH · BRASSERIE Smart restaurant in a small village, boasting a pubby locals bar and leather-furnished dining room with a subtle brasserie feel. Decide between two menus: a two-choice set selection or a complex, ambitious à la carte with a Gallic twist.

Menu € 23/29 – Carte € 32/52

– 𝒞 045 883 561 – www.thebrownbear.ie – dinner only and lunch Saturday-Sunday
– Closed Monday, Tuesday and 24-27 December

NEW QUAY BEALACLUGGA
Clare – Regional map n° **22**-B1
▶ Dublin 240 km – Ennis 55 km – Galway 46 km

🏠 Mount Vernon ⇧ 🐾 ≤ 🚗 P

COUNTRY HOUSE · PERSONALISED Charming whitewashed house with a pretty walled garden, set close to the beach and affording lovely views. Antiques and eclectic curios fill the guest areas; spacious bedrooms have their own personalities – two open onto a terrace. Simply cooked dinners rely on fresh, local produce. Warm, welcoming owners.

5 rooms ⨀ – 🛏 € 95/145 🛏🛏 € 180/230

Flaggy Shore – North : 0.75 km on coast rd – 𝒞 065 707 8126
– www.mountvernon.ie – Closed November-March

🍴 Linnane's Lobster Bar   ≤ 🛜 も A/C P

SEAFOOD · PUB Simple but likeable place, with peat fires and full-length windows which open onto a terrace. They specialise in fresh, tasty fish and shellfish; watch the local boats unload their catch – some of which is brought straight to the kitchen.

Carte € 23/57

New Quay Pier – 𝒞 065 707 8120 – www.linnanesbar.com – Closed 25 December, Good Friday and Monday-Thursday October-Easter

NEWMARKET-ON-FERGUS CORA CHAITLÍN
Clare – Pop. 1 773 – Regional map n° **22**-B2
▶ Dublin 219 km – Ennis 13 km – Limerick 24 km

Inn at Dromoland

FAMILY · MODERN Spacious modern sister to Dromoland Castle, featuring plenty of meeting rooms and stylish bedrooms. When it comes to leisure, there's a children's games room, a smart pool and gym, tennis courts and a large pitch and putt course. The formal restaurant offers a traditional menu of local ingredients while the pub offers old favourites and bottled artisan beers.

155 rooms ☑ – † € 90/200 †† € 90/220

Northwest : 3 km on R 458 – ℰ 061 368 161 – www.theinnatdromoland.ie – Closed 23-27 December

NEWPORT BAILE UÍ FHIACHÁIN

Mayo – Pop. 616 – Regional map n° **21**-A2
▶ Dublin 264 km – Ballina 59 km – Galway 96 km

Newport House

HISTORIC · CLASSIC Delightful creeper-clad mansion with lovely gardens and river views; they also own Lough Beltra, nearby. Large drawing room with family portraits; traditional, antique-filled bedrooms. The grand staircase is topped by a domed cupola. Dinner is a highlight, with salmon a speciality and a notable wine list.

14 rooms ☑ – † € 130/175 †† € 220/290

– ℰ 098 41222 – www.newporthouse.ie – Closed November-18 March

NEWTOWNMOUNTKENNEDY BAILE AN CHINNÉIDIEH

Wicklow – Pop. 2 548 – Regional map n° **39**-D2
▶ Dublin 35 km – Wicklow 16 km – Glendalough 16 km

Druids Glen H. & Golf Resort ①

RESORT · CLASSIC Hidden away in the countryside but just 30mins from Dublin, you'll find this smart resort hotel and its two championship golf courses – along with a great spa and a vast array of other leisure facilities. The delightful bar overlooks the 13th hole and the appealing restaurant has a lovely terrace too.

145 rooms – † € 135/500 †† € 145/500 – 11 suites

– ℰ 01 287 0800 – www.druidsglenresort.com

OUGHTERARD UACHTAR ARD

Galway – Pop. 1 333 – Regional map n° **21**-A3
▶ Dublin 232 km – Cork 223 km – Galway 25 km – Waterford 253 km

Currarevagh House

TRADITIONAL · CLASSIC Classically furnished Victorian manor house set in 180 loughside acres and run by the same family for over 100 years. It has a pleasingly 'lived-in' feel and offers a real country house experience. Have afternoon tea by the fire or take a picnic out on their boat; set dinners offer unfussy, flavoursome dishes.

12 rooms ☑ – † € 75/95 †† € 140/180

Northwest : 6.5 km on Glann rd – ℰ 091 552 312 – www.currarevagh.com – Closed November-February

Railway Lodge

FAMILY · ELEGANT Stylish house in a remote farm setting, with views across the countryside and a beautifully kept, elegantly furnished interior. Bedrooms come with stripped pine furnishings and a keen eye for detail. The charming owner offers good local recommendations. Homemade bread and scones; tea served on arrival.

4 rooms ☑ – † € 50/60 †† € 100/110

West : 0.75 km by Costello rd taking first right onto unmarked road – ℰ 091 552 945 – www.railwaylodge.net

⛺ Waterfall Lodge   🚗 ✦ 🅿 ⊟

TRADITIONAL · CLASSIC Heavily restored Victorian house run by an infectiously enthusiastic owner. A fishing river runs through the garden – look out for jumping salmon! Sympathetically styled bedrooms with rug-covered floors and modern bathrooms; some have four-posters. Pancakes, French toast and smoked salmon at breakfast.

6 rooms 🖵 – 🛉 € 50 🛉🛉 € 80

West : 0.75 km on N 59 – ☏ 091 552 168 – www.waterfalllodge.net

PORTLAOISE PORT LAOISE
Laois – Pop. 20 145 – Regional map n° **22**-C2
▶ Dublin 88 km – Carlow 40 km – Waterford 101 km

⛺ Ivyleigh House   🚗 ✦ 🅿

TOWNHOUSE · CLASSIC Traditional listed Georgian property in the city centre, run by a welcoming owner. Comfy lounge and communal dining area, with antiques and ornaments displayed throughout. Good-sized bedrooms are decorated in a period style. Homemade breads, preserves, muesli and a Cashel blue cheesecake special at breakfast.

6 rooms 🖵 – 🛉 € 80/85 🛉🛉 € 110/160

Bank Pl, Church St – ☏ 057 862 2081 – www.ivyleigh.com – Closed 26-November-1 February except Christmas and New Year

RAMELTON RÁTH MEALTAIN
Donegal – Pop. 1 212 – Regional map n° **21**-C1
▶ Dublin 248 km – Donegal 59 km – Londonderry 43 km – Sligo 122 km

⛺ Moorfield Lodge   ← 🚗 ✦ 🅿

FAMILY · CONTEMPORARY Striking, modern house run by a welcoming owner. Bright, stylish bedrooms with underfloor heating, floor to ceiling windows and Egyptian cotton sheets. Room 1 has its own terrace, a double jacuzzi bath and a TV built into the bathroom tiles. Communal breakfasts are served around an antique table.

3 rooms 🖵 – 🛉 € 115/165 🛉🛉 € 130/180

– ☏ 074 989 4043 – www.moorfieldlodge.com

⛺ Ardeen   🐾 🚗 ✦ ✦ 🅿

TRADITIONAL · CLASSIC A Victorian house on the edge of the village, with peaceful gardens and a river nearby. Welcoming owner and homely, personally styled interior. Open-fired lounge with local info; communal breakfasts. Simple, well-kept bedrooms without TVs.

5 rooms 🖵 – 🛉 € 45/55 🛉🛉 € 90

bear left at the fork in the village centre and left at T-junction – ☏ 074 915 1243 – www.ardeenhouse.com – Closed October-Easter

RANELAGH – Dublin → See Dublin

RATHGAR – Dublin → See Dublin

RATHMINES RÁTH MAONAIS – Dublin → See Dublin

RATHMULLAN RÁTH MAOLÁIN
Donegal – ✉ Letterkenny – Pop. 518 – Regional map n° **21**-C1
▶ Dublin 265 km – Londonderry 58 km – Sligo 140 km

⛺ Rathmullan House   🐾 ← 🚗 📺 ✦ & 🛁 🅿

TRADITIONAL · CLASSIC Family-run, part-19C house set next to Lough Swilly. Bedrooms in the original house have a fitting country house style; those in the extension are more modern and come with balconies or private terraces overlooking the gardens.

34 rooms 🖵 – 🛉 € 90/150 🛉🛉 € 180/280

North : 0.5 mi on R 247 – ☏ 074 915 8188 – www.rathmullanhouse.com – Closed 8 January-2 February and restricted opening in winter

Cook & Gardener – See restaurant listing

✕✕ Cook & Gardener ≤ ⇧ 🅿

CLASSIC CUISINE · FORMAL Formal hotel restaurant comprising several inter-connecting rooms. Daily menus list the best of what's in season, including pro-duce from the house's original walled kitchen garden. Classic cooking is pre-sented in a modern manner.

Carte € 36/53

Rathmullan House Hotel, North : 0.5 mi on R 247 – ℰ 074 915 8188
– www.rathmullanhouse.com – Closed 8 January-2 February and restricted opening in winter

RATHNEW RÁTH NAOI

Wicklow – ⊠ Wicklow – Pop. 2 964 – Regional map n° **22**-D2
▶ Dublin 45 km – Gorey 44 km – Wexford 97 km

🏚 Tinakilly House ⌂ ≤ ⇧ 🗘 ₺ 🛇 🕍 🅿

HISTORIC · CLASSIC A substantial Victorian house in extensive grounds which stretch to the seashore: built for Captain Robert Halpin. Original features include an impressive staircase. Spacious, classically furnished bedrooms; some have four-posters.

52 rooms ⮂ – ♦ € 89/140 ♦♦ € 90/170 – 1 suite
On R 750 – ℰ 0404 69274 – www.tinakilly.ie – Closed 24-26 December
Brunel – See restaurant listing

✕✕ Brunel ⇧ 🅿

IRISH · ELEGANT Spacious, elegant restaurant in a hotel extension, overlooking the gardens: named after the builder of the Great Eastern ship on which Captain Halpin sailed. Flavoursome, traditional dishes use the best Wicklow ingredients.

Menu € 26/37 – Carte € 40/55

Tinakilly House Hotel, On R 750 – ℰ 0404 69274 – www.tinakilly.ie – Closed 24-26 December

RIVERSTOWN BAILE IDIR DHÁ ABHAINN

Sligo – Pop. 374 – Regional map n° **21**-B2
▶ Dublin 189 km – Cork 309 km – Lisburn 193 km – Craigavon 170 km

Coopershill ⇧ ⌂ ≤ ⇧ 🛇 🅿

TRADITIONAL · CLASSIC Magnificent Georgian house run by the 7th generation of the same family; set on a working farm within a 500 acre estate. Spacious guest areas showcase original furnishings – now antiques – and family portraits adorn the walls. Warm, country house style bedrooms. Formal dining amongst polished silverware.

8 rooms ⮂ – ♦ € 149/172 ♦♦ € 198/244
– ℰ 071 916 5108 – www.coopershill.com – Closed November-March

ROSSLARE ROS LÁIR

Wexford – Pop. 1 547 – Regional map n° **22**-D2
▶ Dublin 167 km – Waterford 80 km – Wexford 19 km

🏚 Kelly's Resort ⇧ ≤ ⇧ 🗔 🕸 🛇 ₷ 🛇 🗘 ₺ 🏌 🛇 🅿

FAMILY · PERSONALISED It started life in 1895 as a beachfront 'refreshment house'; now it's a sprawling leisure-orientated hotel run by the 4th generation of the Kelly family. Various lounges, large bar and sizeable spa. Well-appointed bedrooms; the newer rooms being the largest. Formal Beaches offers an exceptional wine list.

118 rooms ⮂ – ♦ € 88/116 ♦♦ € 176/232
– ℰ 053 913 2114 – www.kellys.ie – Closed December-mid February
La Marine – See restaurant listing

REPUBLIC OF IRELAND

✗ La Marine   🛏 ♿ 🅰🅲 🅿

TRADITIONAL CUISINE · BISTRO A bistro-style restaurant within a beachfront hotel, with an open-kitchen and a glass-fronted wine cellar. A zinc-topped bar from France takes centre stage, while the menu offers tasty brasserie classics, including plenty of fish dishes.

Carte € 31/45

Kelly's Resort Hotel, – 𝒞 053 913 2114 – www.kellys.ie – Closed December-mid February

ROSSLARE HARBOUR CALAFORT ROS LÁIR
Wexford – Pop. 1 123 – Regional map n° **22**-D2
▶ Dublin 169 km – Waterford 82 km – Wexford 21 km

🏠 Archways   ⚘ 🛏 ♿ 🅿

FAMILY · TRADITIONAL Spanish villa style bungalow, conveniently located for Rosslare Harbour. Contemporary bedrooms feature coffee machines and smart bathrooms, with colour schemes themed around a single piece of art from a local artist. Daily changing set three course dinners use the best of seasonal, local produce.

5 rooms 🖙 – ♦ € 55/70 ♦♦ € 75/90

Rosslare Rd, Tagoat – West : 6.25 km on N 25 – 𝒞 053 915 8111 – www.thearchways.ie – Closed February and Christmas-New Year

ROUNDSTONE CLOCH NA RÓN
Galway – Pop. 245 – Regional map n° **21**-A3
▶ Dublin 293 km – Galway 76 km – Ennis 144 km

🍴 O'Dowds   ⇜

SEAFOOD · COSY Busy pub in pretty harbourside town; popular with tourists and locals alike. Owned by the O'Dowd family for over 100 years, it specialises in fresh, simply cooked fish and shellfish. Sit in the cosy, fire-lit bar or wood-panelled restaurant.

Menu € 20 (dinner) – Carte € 17/53

– 𝒞 095 35809 (booking advisable) – www.odowdsseafoodbar.com – Closed 25 December

ROUNDWOOD AN TÓCHAR
Wicklow – Pop. 833 – Regional map n° **22**-D2
▶ Dublin 25 km – Wicklow 12 km – Limerick 144 km

🍴 Byrne & Woods   ⚘ ♿ 🅿

TRADITIONAL BRITISH · COSY Arguably the second highest pub in Ireland, set up in the Wicklow Mountains. 'Byrne' is a cosy bar with a wood-burning stove; dimly lit 'Woods' has leather and dark wood furnishings and a clubby feel. Cooking is fresh and straightforward.

Menu € 14/35 – Carte € 24/42

Main St – 𝒞 01 281 7078 – www.byrneandwoods.com – Closed 25-26 December

SALLINS
Pop. 5 283 – Regional map n° **39**-D1
▶ Dublin 24 km – Kildare 23 km – Maynooth 11 km

✗ Two Cooks 🆕   🅰🅲

IRISH · NEIGHBOURHOOD This delightful restaurant on the first floor of a residential parade is run by – you've guessed it – two chefs. The menu is divided into 'Small', 'Big' and 'Sweet' and offers 3 choices per course. Cooking is honest and well-judged.

Menu € 36

Canal View – 𝒞 045 853 768 – www.twocooks.ie – dinner only and Sunday lunch – Closed 25-26 December, Monday, Tuesday and Sunday dinner

SANDYFORD ÁTH AN GHAINIMH – Dún Laoghaire-Rathdown ➜ See Dublin

SHANAGARRY AN SEANGHARRAÍ
Cork – ✉ Midleton – Pop. 414 – Regional map n° **22**-C3
▶ Dublin 262 km – Cork 40 km – Waterford 103 km

🏠 Ballymaloe House

FAMILY · CLASSIC With its pre-18C origins, this is the very essence of a country manor house. Family-run for 3 generations, it boasts numerous traditionally styled guest areas, comfortable, classical bedrooms and a famed cookery school. The 5 course daily menu offers local, seasonal produce.

29 rooms ⌑ – 🛉 € 200 🛉🛉 € 250/310

Northwest : 3 km on R 629 – ☏ 021 465 2531 – www.ballymaloe.ie – Closed January and 24-26 December

SKIBBEREEN AN SCIOBAIRÍN
Cork – Pop. 2 568 – Regional map n° **22**-B3
▶ Dublin 338 km – Cork 85 km – Killarney 104 km

🏠 Liss Ard

HISTORIC · PERSONALISED With 150 acres of grounds – including a lake – this 200 year old manor house, stables and lodge create an idyllic rural retreat. Inside they're surprisingly modern with sleek furnishings and a minimalist Swiss/German style. Staff are friendly and daily menus are led by the availability of local produce.

25 rooms ⌑ – 🛉 € 145/295 🛉🛉 € 145/295

Liss Ard Estate, Castletownsend Rd – Southeast : 2.5 km on R 596 – ☏ 028 40000 – www.lissardestate.com – Restricted opening October-April

SLANE BAILE SHÁINE
Meath – Pop. 1 349 – Regional map n° **21**-B3
▶ Dublin 34 km – Navan 8 km – Craigavon 69 km

🏠 Tankardstown

COUNTRY HOUSE · CONTEMPORARY A fine Georgian manor house with a lavish interior, set up a sweeping tree-lined drive. Bedrooms in the main house are furnished with antiques; those in the courtyard are more modern and come with kitchens. Have afternoon tea in the cottage, wood-fired pizzas in Cellar or contemporary dishes in Brabazon.

13 rooms ⌑ – 🛉 € 100/300 🛉🛉 € 200/350 – 6 suites

Northwest : 6 km by N 51 off R 163 – ☏ 041 982 4621 – www.tankardstown.ie – Closed 10-30 January and 25-27 December

Brabazon – See restaurant listing

🏠 Conyngham Arms

FAMILY · PERSONALISED 17C coaching inn on the main street of a small but busy town. It has a laid-back feel, an appealing shabby-chic style and a lovely hidden garden. Some of the bedrooms have feature beds and all come with coffee machines and freshly baked biscuits from their nearby bakery. Dine in the bar, with its open kitchen.

15 rooms ⌑ – 🛉 € 65/99 🛉🛉 € 89/160

– ☏ 041 988 4444 – www.conynghamarms.ie – Closed 25-26 December

XX Brabazon

MODERN CUISINE · RUSTIC Relaxed, rustic restaurant in the former piggery of a delightful manor house. Sit at a painted wooden table by the fire or out on the terrace overlooking the landscaped courtyard. Contemporary cooking uses top quality ingredients.

Carte € 50/66

Tankardstown Hotel, Northwest : 6 km by N 51 off R 163 – ☏ 041 982 4621 – www.tankardstown.ie – dinner only and Sunday lunch – Closed 10-30 January, 25-27 December and Monday-Tuesday

SLIGO SLIGEACH

Sligo – Pop. 17 568 – Regional map n° **21**-B2

▶ Dublin 214 km – Belfast 203 km – Dundalk 170 km – Londonderry 138 km

Tree Tops

TRADITIONAL · PERSONALISED An unassuming whitewashed house in a residential area, with immaculately kept bedrooms, a cosy lounge and a smart buffet breakfast room overlooking the garden. The chatty, welcoming owners have an interesting Irish art collection.

3 rooms ⊡ – 🛉 € 48/50 🛉🛉 € 72/74

Cleveragh Rd – South : 1.25 km by Dublin rd – ℰ 071 916 2301
– www.sligobandb.com – Closed 15 December-7 January

XX Montmartre

CLASSIC FRENCH · BISTRO Smart, modern restaurant in the shadow of the cathedral, with a tiled exterior and wooden blinds. The French chefs prepare classic Gallic menus which follow the seasons. The all-French wine list features interesting, lesser-known wines.

Menu € 27/37 – Carte € 26/52

Market Yard – ℰ 071 916 9901 – www.montmartrerestaurant.ie – dinner only
– Closed 8 January-1 February, Sunday and Monday

🏠 Hargadons

TRADITIONAL CUISINE · RUSTIC Hugely characterful pub with sloping floors, narrow passageways, dimly lit anterooms and a lovely "Ladies' Room" complete with its own serving hatch. Cooking is warming and satisfying, offering the likes of Irish stew or bacon and cabbage.

Carte € 18/36

4-5 O'Connell St – ℰ 071 915 3709 (bookings not accepted) – www.hargadons.com
– Closed Sunday

SPANISH POINT RINN NA SPÁINNEACH

Clare – ✉ Milltown Malbay – Regional map n° **22**-B2

▶ Dublin 275 km – Galway 104 km – Limerick 83 km

XX Red Cliff Lodge

MODERN CUISINE · INTIMATE Thatched cottage in a superb spot on the headland; later extensions have created a U-shaped arrangement around a cobbled courtyard. The décor is bright and eye-catching, the tables are elegantly set and modern classics are served with flair. Smart, spacious bedrooms have kitchenettes and coffee machines.

Menu € 35 (weekday dinner)/45 – Carte € 33/49

6 rooms ⊡ – 🛉 € 90/120 🛉🛉 € 120/150

– ℰ 065 708 5756 – www.redclifflodge.ie – dinner only and Sunday lunch – Closed
October-Easter, midweek April- May and Monday

STEPASIDE

Dún Laoghaire-Rathdown – Regional map n° **22**-D1

▶ Dublin 10 km – Dún Laoghaire 7 km – Cork 164 km

XX Box Tree

TRADITIONAL CUISINE · BISTRO Modern eatery beneath a small new-build apartment block. The attractive restaurant serves unfussy, good value classical dishes; to the other side of the bar is the Wild Boar pub, which offers a similar but slightly lighter menu.

Menu € 25 (weekday lunch) – Carte € 38/53

Enniskerry Rd ✉ D18 – ℰ 01 205 2025 – www.theboxtree.ie
– Closed 25-26 December and Good Friday

STRAFFAN TEACH SRAFÁIN

Kildare – Pop. 635 – Regional map n° **22**-D1

▶ Dublin 29 km – Naas 12 km – Cork 238 km

🏠 K Club ✧ ⌂ ⌷ ⎍ ☰ 🔲 ⑨ 🎐 🛁 ✖ ⊡ ⅄ ✥ 🛄 🅿

GRAND LUXURY · CLASSIC A golf resort with two championship courses, an extensive spa and beautiful formal gardens stretching down to the Liffey. The fine 19C house has elegant antique-filled guestrooms and luxurious bedrooms. Elegant Byerley Turk serves a 6 course tasting menu; grand River Room offers refined classics; Legends has a brasserie menu; and K Thai serves Thai and Malaysian fare.

134 rooms – 🛏 € 215/399 🛏🛏 € 215/399 – ⚏ €29 – 9 suites
– 𝄢 01 601 7200 – www.kclub.ie

🏠 Barberstown Castle ✧ ⌂ ⌷ ⊡ ⅄ ✥ 🛄 🅿

COUNTRY HOUSE · HISTORIC Set within 20 acres of grounds; a 13C castle with whitewashed Georgian and Victorian extensions – a popular venue for weddings. Large, luxurious country house bedrooms feature good facilities; many have four-poster beds and garden outlooks. Dine on traditional dishes in the informal, conservatory style bistro or from French menus in the Georgian house and stone keep.

55 rooms ⚏ – 🛏 € 110/219 🛏🛏 € 180/259

North : 0.75 km – 𝄢 01 628 8157 – www.barberstowncastle.ie – Closed January-February and 24-26 December

THOMASTOWN BAILE MHIC ANDÁIN
Kilkenny – Pop. 2 273 – Regional map n° **22**-C2
▶ Dublin 124 km – Kilkenny 17 km – Waterford 48 km – Wexford 61 km

🏠 Mount Juliet ✧ ⌂ ⌷ ⎍ ☰ 🔲 ⑨ 🎐 🛁 ✖ ⊡ ⅄ 🏇 ✥ 🛄 🅿

HISTORIC · CLASSIC Georgian gem situated in 1,500 acres, with a Jack Nicklaus designed golf course, a spa, an equestrian centre and even a stud farm. Bedrooms range from traditional in the main house to two-roomed garden lodges and smaller but equally comfy rooms in the former hunting stables. Grand restaurant; simple French dishes in the brasserie and light lunches in the clubhouse bar.

58 rooms ⚏ – 🛏 € 99/349 🛏🛏 € 99/349 – 13 suites
Southwest : 5.5 km by N 9 on R 4286 – 𝄢 056 777 3000 – www.mountjuliet.ie
🏵 **Lady Helen** – See restaurant listing

🏠 Abbey House ⌷ 🅿

TRADITIONAL · COSY Attractive whitewashed Victorian house with a neat, lawned garden and a friendly, hospitable owner; set opposite the ruins of Jerpoint Abbey. Traditionally styled lounge with plenty of local info. Simple bedrooms with antique furniture.

6 rooms ⚏ – 🛏 € 60/100 🛏🛏 € 85/100

Jerpoint Abbey – Southwest : 2 km on N 9 – 𝄢 056 772 4166 – www.abbeyhousejerpoint.com – Closed 20-30 December

🍴 Lady Helen ⌂ ⌷ ⅄ 🅿
🏵

MODERN CUISINE · ROMANTIC Classical hotel restaurant consisting of two grand rooms with beautiful stuccowork, overlooking the River Nore. Accomplished cooking uses ingredients from the estate, the county and the nearest coast. Original, modern dishes are well-prepared, attractively presented and feature some stimulating combinations.

→ Foie gras with Granny Smith, almond milk and Pedro Ximénez jus. Black sole with fennel pollen, gnocchi and caper emulsion. Tonka bean and caramel soufflé with banana ice cream.

Menu € 75/99

Mount Juliet Hotel, Southwest : 5.5 km by N 9 on R 4286 – 𝄢 056 777 3000 (booking essential) – www.mountjuliet.ie – dinner only – Closed Sunday and Tuesday

TOORMORE AN TUAR MÓR
Cork – ✉ Goleen – Pop. 207 – Regional map n° **22**-A3
▶ Dublin 355 km – Cork 109 km – Killarney 104 km

🏠 Fortview House   🖨 🛇 **P** 🚭

FAMILY · PERSONALISED Well-kept guesthouse on a 120 acre dairy farm, run by a very bubbly owner. It has a rustic, country feel courtesy of its stone walls, timbered ceilings, coir carpets and aged pine furniture. Breakfast is an event, with home-baked scones and bread, eggs from their hens and other local products all featuring.

3 rooms 🍽 – 🛇 € 50 🛇 € 100

Gurtyowen – Northeast : 2.5 km on R 591 (Durrus rd) – 𝒞 028 35324
– www.fortviewhousegoleen.com – Closed October-April

TOWER – Cork ➜ See Blarney

TRALEE TRÁ LÍ

Kerry – Pop. 20 814 – Regional map n° **22**-A2
▶ Dublin 297 km – Killarney 32 km – Limerick 103 km

🏠 Grand   🎿 🛇 ⛷

TOWNHOUSE · CLASSIC Opened in 1928 and located right in the heart of this bustling town. It has a small first floor lounge and contemporary bedrooms. The traditional bar – once the post office – is a popular spot and offers hearty all-day dishes. The classical dining room offers a mix of Irish specialities and more global fare.

49 rooms 🍽 – 🛇 € 55/120 🛇 € 70/210

Denny St – 𝒞 066 712 1499 – www.grandhoteltralee.com – Closed 25 December

🏠 Brook Manor Lodge   🖨 🛇 **P**

COUNTRY HOUSE · PERSONALISED Spacious detached house with views to the Slieve Mish Mountains; good for those who like golf, hiking or fishing. Traditionally styled lounge and airy conservatory breakfast room. Immaculately kept bedrooms; those at the back have the view.

8 rooms 🍽 – 🛇 € 85/99 🛇 € 90/150

Fenit Rd, Spa – Northwest : 3.5 km by R 551 on R 558 – 𝒞 066 712 0406
– www.brookmanorlodge.com – Closed November-March

TRAMORE TRÁ MHÓR

Waterford – Pop. 9 722 – Regional map n° **22**-C2
▶ Dublin 177 km – Waterford 13 km – Cork 123 km

🏠 Glenorney   ≤ 🖨 🛇 **P**

TRADITIONAL · CLASSIC Smart cream house with pretty gardens, set on the hillside, overlooking the bay. A homely lounge leads through to a dark wood furnished breakfast room where they serve pancakes, French toast and homemade preserves. Simply furnished bedrooms are well-kept; the book-filled sun lounge is a good place to relax.

6 rooms 🍽 – 🛇 € 50/80 🛇 € 80/90

Newtown – Southwest : 1.5 km by R 675 – 𝒞 051 381 056 – www.glenorney.com
– Closed December-February

TRIM BAILE ÁTHA TROIM

Meath – Pop. 1 441 – Regional map n° **21**-D3
▶ Dublin 43 km – Drogheda 42 km – Tullamore 69 km

🏠 Trim Castle   🎿 ▣ ⛷ 🛇 ⛷ **P**

BUSINESS · MODERN Modern family-run hotel opposite the castle, complete with a café, a homeware shop and a delightful roof terrace with a great outlook. Good-sized bedrooms come in contemporary hues – those to the front share the view. Dine in the bar or opt for classic European dishes in the stylish first floor restaurant.

68 rooms 🍽 – 🛇 € 65/155 🛇 € 65/170

Castle St – 𝒞 046 948 3000 – www.trimcastlehotel.com – Closed 25 December

🏠 Highfield House   ⇦ 🅿

TOWNHOUSE · PERSONALISED Substantial 18C stone house close to the river and the oldest Norman castle in Europe. Well-appointed lounge and breakfast room, boldly coloured bedrooms and a delightful terraced courtyard. Comprehensive breakfasts; scones on arrival.

10 rooms � – 🛉 € 55/65 🛉🛉 € 86/88

Maudlins Rd. – 𝒞 046 943 6386 – www.highfieldguesthouse.com – Closed 21 December-2 January

TULLAMORE TULACH MHÓR
Offaly – Pop. 11 346 – Regional map n° **22**-C1
▶ Dublin 104 km – Kilkenny 83 km – Limerick 129 km

✗ Blue Apron   AC ⑩

CLASSIC CUISINE · BISTRO Friendly, engaging service sets the tone at this intimate restaurant, which is run by an enthusiastic husband and wife team. All-encompassing menus offer generous, flavoursome dishes that are prepared with care and understanding.

Menu € 27 – Carte € 26/56

Harbour St – 𝒞 057 936 0106 – www.theblueapronrestaurant.ie – dinner only and Sunday lunch – Closed 2 weeks August, 24 January-7 February, 24-27 December, Monday and Tuesday

TWO MILE HOUSE → See Naas

VIRGINIA ACHADH AN IÚIR
Cavan – Pop. 2 282 – Regional map n° **21**-C3
▶ Dublin 89 km – Monaghan 76 km – Belfast 153 km – Craigavon 99 km

✗✗ St Kyrans   ⇦ ≤ ⇦ 🏠 🅿

CLASSIC CUISINE · DESIGN This rurally set restaurant may look plain from the outside but it's a different story on the inside. The smart linen-laid restaurant offers breathtaking views over Lough Ramor and the menu lists classic dishes with an Irish heart and hints of modernity. Five of the modern bedrooms have water views.

Menu € 25 (weekdays) – Carte € 31/48

8 rooms ⍱ – 🛉 € 70/100 🛉🛉 € 100/120

Dublin Rd – South : 2.25 km. on N 3
– 𝒞 049 854 7087 – www.stkyrans.com
– Closed 23-28 January, Christmas, Good Friday, Monday and Tuesday.

WATERFORD PORT LÁIRGE
Waterford – Pop. 46 732 – Regional map n° **22**-C2
▶ Dublin 154 km – Cork 117 km – Limerick 124 km

🏯 Waterford Castle H. and Golf Resort   ⌂ ≤ ⇦ 🖼 ✗ 🖵 ⑨ 🏌

HISTORIC BUILDING · CLASSIC An attractive part-15C castle, set on a 🅿 charming 320 acre private island in the river. The carved stone and wood-panelled hall displays old tapestries and antiques. Elegant, classical bedrooms have characterful period bathrooms.

19 rooms ⍱ – 🛉 € 99/179 🛉🛉 € 159/359 – 5 suites

The Island, Ballinakill – East : 4 km by R 683, Ballinakill Rd and private ferry
– 𝒞 051 878 203 – www.waterfordcastleresort.com – Closed 24-26 December and weekdays 1 January-12 February
The Munster Room – See restaurant listing

Foxmount Country House   🐾 🕭 🍴 ⅌ Ⓟ

TRADITIONAL · CLASSIC Striking Georgian mansion in a delightful 150 acre farm setting; it's immaculately kept, with classical styling and charming hosts. Bedrooms are named after flowers: Honeysuckle and Bluebell are two of the best. Good communal breakfasts.

4 rooms 🖵 – ♦ € 55 ♦♦ € 110

Passage East Rd – Southeast : 7.25 km by R 683, off Cheekpoint rd
– ℰ 051 874 308 – www.foxmountcountryhouse.com – Closed mid October-mid March

XXX The Munster Room   🕭 Ⓟ

CLASSIC CUISINE · INTIMATE Beautiful oak wood panelled dining room in a castle hotel, boasting an ornate ceiling and a delightful hand-carved fireplace. Dine on boldly flavoured classic dishes to live piano accompaniment. The menu name-checks local producers.

Menu € 55 – bar lunch Monday-Saturday

Waterford Castle Hotel and Golf Resort, The Island, Ballinakill – East : 4 km by R 683, Ballinakill Rd and private ferry – ℰ 051 878 203 (bookings essential for non-residents) – www.waterfordcastleresort.com – Closed 24-26 December and weekdays 1 January-12 February

XX La Bohème   🕭 ⇔

CLASSIC FRENCH · INTIMATE Characterful candlelit restaurant in the vaulted cellar of a Georgian house. The French chefs offer an array of classic Gallic dishes and daily market specials. For something lighter, try a sharing platter in the stone-floored bar.

Menu € 25 (early dinner)/36 – Carte € 33/55

2 George's St – ℰ 051 875 645 (booking essential) – www.labohemerestaurant.ie
– dinner only – Closed 25-27 December, Sunday except bank holidays and Monday

X Loko 🆕   🕭 🅰🅲

IRISH · BISTRO Loko means 'place' in the international language of Esperanto and the owners hope it reflects their 'global yet local' cuisine. It's an unusual place, with two casino-style tables, vivid art and large industrial spool tables outside.

Carte € 25/40

Ardmore Shopping Centre, Dunmore Rd – East : 2.5km by R 683 – ℰ 051 841 040
– www.loko.ie – Closed 25-26 December, 1 January, Good Friday and Monday dinner

WESTPORT CATHAIR NA MART

Mayo – Pop. 5 543 – Regional map n° **21**-A2
▶ Dublin 262 km – Galway 80 km – Sligo 104 km

Knockranny House H. & Spa   ≤ 🕭 🖵 ⓦ 🛖 🖺 🖭 ⅌ ❄ 🏊 Ⓟ

FAMILY · PERSONALISED Modern hotel in an elevated position overlooking the town, mountains and bay, and furnished in a contemporary yet classical style. Large, smart bedrooms offer excellent comforts; some have marble bathrooms or four-poster beds. Superb spa.

97 rooms 🖵 – ♦ € 90/180 ♦♦ € 110/220 – 10 suites

Castlebar Rd, Knockranny – East : 1.25 km on N 5 – ℰ 098 28600
– www.knockrannyhousehotel.ie – Closed 24-26 December
La Fougère – See restaurant listing

Augusta Lodge   🕭 ⅌ Ⓟ

TRADITIONAL · COSY Family-run guesthouse with a small pitch and putt course on the front lawn and golfing memorabilia covering every surface inside. Simple, brightly coloured bedrooms have a homely feel. The welcoming owner has good local knowledge.

9 rooms 🖵 – ♦ € 55/95 ♦♦ € 65/105

Golf Links Rd – North : 0.75 km by N 59 – ℰ 098 28900 – www.augustalodge.ie
– Closed 23-27 December

XxX La Fougère

CLASSIC CUISINE · ROMANTIC Spacious hotel restaurant with a large bar, several different seating areas and huge windows offering views to Croagh Patrick Mountain. The three menus feature fresh, local produce, including langoustines from the bay below. Formal service.

Menu € 52

Knockranny House Hotel & Spa, Castlebar Rd, Knockranny – East : 1.25 km on N 5 – ℰ 098 28600 (booking advisable) – www.knockrannyhousehotel.ie – dinner only – Closed 24-26 December

X Idle Wall 🔘

REGIONAL CUISINE · COSY The sun dial by the front door marks the old 'idle wall', where local dockworkers used to sit and wait for employment at the harbour below. Menus continually evolve as the experienced chef sources the latest artisan produce. It's a sweet place, with wonky timbers and charming country and boating memorabilia.

Carte € 29/49

The Quay – ℰ 098 50692 – www.theidlewall.ie – dinner only – Closed January, February, Sunday and Monday

X An Port Mór

CLASSIC CUISINE · COSY Tucked away down a small alleyway and named after the chef's home village. The compact interior has a shabby-chic, Mediterranean-style. Local produce is showcased in elaborate dishes and seafood specials are chalked on the blackboard.

Menu € 24 (early dinner) – Carte € 26/48

Brewery Pl, Bridge St – ℰ 098 26730 – www.anportmor.com – dinner only – Closed 24-26 December, Sunday in winter and Monday

🏠 Sheebeen

TRADITIONAL CUISINE · PUB Pretty pub with lovely bay and Croagh Patrick views. Hearty, unfussy dishes feature shellfish and lobsters from the bay, and lamb and beef from the fields nearby. Sit outside, in the rustic bar or in the first floor dining room.

Carte € 24/43

Rosbeg – West : 3 km on R 335 – ℰ 098 26528 – www.croninssheebeen.com – Closed 25 December, Good Friday and lunch weekdays November-mid March

WEXFORD LOCH GARMAN

Wexford – Pop. 19 913 – Regional map n° **22**-D2
▶ Dublin 141 km – Kilkenny 79 km – Waterford 61 km

🏨 Whites

BUSINESS · MODERN Striking angular hotel built around a paved central courtyard; its spacious lobby decorated with local art. Tranquility spa, coffee shop and library bar. Modern, minimalistic bedrooms; executives are larger with water views. Internationally influenced menu of traditional dishes in the contemporary restaurant.

157 rooms ⌂ – ♦ € 79/109 ♦♦ € 85/170 – 5 suites
Abbey St – ℰ 053 912 2311 – www.claytonwhiteshotel.com – Closed 24-27 December

🏠 Killiane Castle

COUNTRY HOUSE · ELEGANT A 17C house and 12C castle on a family-owned dairy farm. Individually decorated, antique-furnished bedrooms look out over the surrounding farmland. Breakfast includes pork from their own pigs, home-laid eggs and homemade bread and yoghurt.

8 rooms ⌂ – ♦ € 75/85 ♦♦ € 115/140
Drinagh – South : 5.5 km by R 730 off N 25 – ℰ 053 915 8885 – www.killianecastle.com – Closed mid December-mid February

⊗ Greenacres

BRITISH TRADITIONAL · BISTRO Set over 3 floors, with a bistro, deli, wine store, bakery and art gallery. Wide-ranging menu of classic dishes, with daily fish specials. Amazing choice of wine from around the world, with some sensational vintages in the private salon.

Menu € 35 (dinner) – Carte € 36/53

Selskar – ℰ 053 912 2975 – www.greenacres.ie – Closed 25-26 December and Good Friday

⊗ La Côte 🆕

SEAFOOD · NEIGHBOURHOOD On the main promenade of a historic town, you'll find this welcoming, personally run restaurant comprising two homely rooms. Local seafood is at the heart of the good value menu – check the blackboard for the day's recommendations.

Menu € 27/32

Custom House Quay – ℰ 053 912 2122 – www.lacote.ie – dinner only – Closed 2 weeks January and Sunday

YOUGHAL EOCHAILL

Cork – Pop. 6 990 – Regional map n° **22**-C3
▶ Dublin 235 km – Cork 48 km – Waterford 75 km

🏠 Walter Raleigh 🆕

FAMILY · PERSONALISED It might not look it but this immaculately kept inn is over 300 years old. It's named after the one-time mayor of Youghal, who would have approved of the charming way it's run. Have breakfast in the lovely first floor room or on the balcony overlooking Blackwater and dine in the traditional bar or restaurant.

39 rooms – ⍾ € 85/115 ⍾⍾ € 110/220

– ℰ 024 92011 – www.walterraleighhotel.com – Closed 25-26 December

⊗⊗ Aherne's

FISH AND SEAFOOD · FRIENDLY Traditional seafood restaurant dating from 1910, keenly run by the 2nd and 3rd generations of the same family. Have lunch in one of the bars or dinner in the restaurant. Seafood is from the local boats and hot buttered lobster is a speciality. Bedrooms are furnished with antiques and some have balconies.

Menu € 27 (dinner) – Carte € 35/69 – bar lunch

12 rooms ⍁ – ⍾ € 75/110 ⍾⍾ € 100/200

163 North Main St – ℰ 024 92424 – www.ahernes.com – Closed 23-27 December

MICHELIN IS CONTINUALLY INNOVATING FOR SAFER, CLEANER, MORE ECONOMICAL, MORE CONNECTED... BETTER ALL-ROUND MOBILITY.

Tyres wear more quickly on short urban journeys.

? TRUE!

You tend to accelerate and brake more often when driving around town so your tyres work harder!
If you are stuck in traffic, keep calm and drive slowly.

Tyre pressure only affects your car's safety.

? FALSE!

Driving with underinflated tyres (0.5 bar below recommended pressure) doesn't just impact handling and fuel consumption, it will shave 8,000 km off tyre lifespan.
Make sure you check tyre pressure about once a month and before you go on holiday or a long journey.

If you only encounter **winter weather from time to time** - sudden showers, snowfall or black ice - **one type of tyre** will do the job.
?
TRUE!
The revolutionary **MICHELIN CrossClimate** - the very first summer tyre with winter certification - is a practical solution to keep you on the road whatever the weather.

Fitting **2 winter tyres** on my car guarantees maximum safety.

?

FALSE!

In the winter, especially when temperatures drop below 7°C, to ensure better road holding, all four tyres should be identical and fitted at the same time.

2 WINTER TYRES ONLY =
risk of compromised road holding.

4 WINTER TYRES =
safer handling when cornering, driving downhill and braking.

If you regularly encounter rain, snow or black ice, choose a **MICHELIN Alpin tyre**. This range offers you sharp handling plus a comfortable ride to safely face the challenge of winter driving.

MICHELIN

MICHELIN IS COMMITTED

▶ MICHELIN IS **GLOBAL LEADER IN FUEL-EFFICIENT TYRES** FOR LIGHT VEHICLES.

▶ *EDUCATING OF YOUNGSTERS IN ROAD SAFETY,* NOT FORGETTING TWO-WHEELERS LOCAL ROAD SAFETY CAMPAIGNS WERE RUN IN **16 COUNTRIES** IN 2015.

QUIZ

1 ## TYRES ARE BLACK SO WHY IS THE MICHELIN MAN WHITE?

Back in 1898 when the Michelin Man was first created from a stack of tyres, they were made of natural rubber, cotton and sulphur and were therefore light-coloured. The composition of tyres did not change until after the First World War when carbon black was introduced. But the Michelin Man kept his colour!

2 ## FOR HOW LONG HAS MICHELIN BEEN GUIDING TRAVELLERS?

Since 1900. When the MICHELIN guide was published at the turn of the century, it was claimed that it would last for a hundred years. It's still around today and remains a reference with new editions and online restaurant listings in a number of countries.

3 ## WHEN WAS THE "BIB GOURMAND" INTRODUCED IN THE MICHELIN GUIDE?

The symbol was created in 1997 but as early as 1954 the MICHELIN guide was recommending "exceptional good food at moderate prices". Today, it features on the MICHELIN Restaurants website and app.

If you want to enjoy a fun day out and find out more about Michelin, why not visit the l'Aventure Michelin museum and shop in Clermont-Ferrand, France:

www.laventuremichelin.com

MICHELIN
A better way forward

INDEX OF TOWNS

A
	Page
Abbey Dore	248
Abbotsbury	248
Abbots Ripton	433
Aberaeron	754
Aberdeen	656
Abergavenny	754
Abersoch	755
Aberystwyth	756
Abingdon	248
Abinger Common	248
Aboyne	658
Abriachan	658
Achill Island	822
Acton Green	66
Adare	822
Aldeburgh	248
Alderley Edge	249
Alderney	330
Alfriston	250
Alkham	250
Allanton	658
Alnwick	250
Alstonefield	251
Alyth	659
Amberley	251
Ambleside	251
Amersham	253
Ampleforth	419
Ancrum	659
Anglesey (Isle of)	756
Annahilt	806
Anstruther	659
Appleby	253
Applecross	659
Aran Islands	822
Archway	81
Ardchattan	660
Ardhasaig	711
Ardmore	823
Ardshealach	660
Arisaig	660
Arkendale	253
Arlingham	253
Armagh	796

Armscote	254
Arnside	254
Arran (Isle of)	660
Arthurstown	824
Arundel	254
Ascot	255
Ashbourne	255
Ashburton	256
Ashendon	256
Ashford (Kent)	256
Ashford (Wicklow)	824
Ashford-in-the-Water	256
Ashwater	257
Askham	526
Askrigg	257
Aston Cantlow	258
Athlone	824
Attleborough	258
Auchterarder	661
Aughrim	825
Austwick	258
Aviemore	662
Axminster	258
Aylesbury	259
Aylesford	259
Aylsham	259
Ayot Green	611
Ayr	662
Aysgarth	259

B
	Page
Babbacombe	599
Back	710
Bagenalstown	826
Bagshot	260
Bala	758
Balham	120
Ballantrae	662
Ballasalla	478
Ballater	663
Ballina	826
Ballingarry	827
Ballintoy	796
Balloch	663
Ballsbridge	862

Ballybunnion	827	Belchford	272
Ballycotton	828	Belfast	798
Ballydavid	828	Belford	273
Ballyfarnan	828	Belgravia	124
Ballyfin	828	Belper	273
Ballygarrett	829	Belsize Park	54
Ballygawley	796	Benderloch	666
Ballygrant	704	Benenden	273
Ballylickey	829	Bepton	492
Ballyliffin	829	Berkhamsted	273
Ballymacarbry	829	Bermondsey	110
Ballymena	796	Berrick Salome	274
Ballymore Eustace	830	Berwick-upon-Tweed	274
Ballynahinch	830	Bethnal Green	116
Ballyvaughan	830	Bettyhill	666
Balmedie	664	Betws-y-Coed	758
Balquhidder	664	Beverley	274
Baltimore	831	Bewdley	275
Bamburgh Castle	260	Bibury	275
Bampton	261	Bidborough	276
Banchory	665	Biddenden	276
Bandon	831	Bideford	276
Bangor	797	Bigbury	277
Bantry	831	Bigbury-on-Sea	277
Barcaldine	665	Biggleswade	277
Barmouth	758	Bildeston	277
Barna	832	Birkenhead	278
Barnard Castle	261	Birmingham	279
Barnes	106	Birr	832
Barnsley	358	Bishop's Stortford	285
Barra (Isle of)	665	Bispham Green	285
Barrasford	262	Blackburn	285
Barrells Cross	884	Blackheath	103
Barton-on-Sea	262	Blacklion	832
Barwick	636	Blackpool	286
Baslow	262	Blackrock	864
Bassenthwaite	263	Blagdon	287
Bath	264	Blairgowrie	666
Battersea	120	Blakeney	287
Baughurst	270	Blanchland	288
Bayswater and Maida Vale	123	Blandford Forum	289
Beaconsfield	270	Blarney	833
Beaminster	271	Bledington	583
Bearsted	271	Bloomsbury	55
Beaulieu	271	Bodiam	289
Beaumaris	756	Bodmin	289
Beaumont	334	Boduan	782
Beeley	272	Bollington	290
Belbroughton	272	Bolnhurst	290

Bolton Abbey	290
Bordon	291
Boroughbridge	291
Borris	833
Borve	711
Boscastle	292
Boston Spa	292
Boughton Monchelsea	292
Bourn	293
Bournemouth	293
Bourton on the Hill	495
Bourton-on-the-Water	295
Bowland Bridge	296
Bowmore	704
Bowness-on-Windermere	626
Boyle	834
Boylestone	296
Bradford-on-Avon	297
Bradwell	298
Braemar	667
Braithwaite	440
Brampford Speke	389
Brampton	298
Brancaster Staithe	298
Braughing	298
Bray	299
Braye	330
Brechfa	759
Brecon	759
Brent	52
Bridge End	834
Bridgend	759
Bridport	300
Brighton and Hove	302
Brill	306
Bristol	307
Brixton	101
Broadford	733
Broadstairs	311
Broadway	312
Brockenhurst	313
Brodick	661
Bromeswell	632
Bromley	52
Broughton	314
Broughton Gifford	314
Broughty Ferry	675
Bruichladdich	705
Bruntingthorpe	314

Bruton	315
Bryansford	810
Bryher	563
Buckden	315
Bude	315
Budleigh Salterton	316
Builth Wells	760
Bunbury	316
Bunchrew	704
Bungay	316
Buntingford	317
Burchett's Green	317
Burford	317
Burnham Market	318
Burpham	255
Burray	720
Burton Bradstock	301
Burton-upon-Trent	318
Bury	318
Bury St Edmunds	319
Bushmills	803
Butlers Cross	320
Buttermere	320
Bwlchtocyn	756

C
Page

Cadboll	740
Caernarfon	760
Caherlistrane	834
Cahersiveen	835
Callander	668
Callington	320
Calne	321
Camber	553
Camberwell	113
Cambridge	322
Camden	54
Camden Town	58
Camelford	325
Canary Wharf	117
Canonbury	81
Canterbury	325
Cappoquin	835
Caragh Lake	835
Carbis Bay	557
Cardiff	761
Carinish	744
Carlingford	836
Carlow	836

Carlyon Bay	554	Cholmondeley	356
Carmarthen	765	Christchurch	356
Carnaross	836	Church End	52
Carne	837	Church Enstone	357
Carrickmacross	837	Churchill	357
Carrick-on-Shannon	837	Cirencester	358
Carrigans	838	City of London	61
Carthorpe	326	City of Westminster	123
Cartmel	402	Clanfield	359
Cashel	838	Clapham Common	101
Catel	330	Clavering	359
Castle Combe	326	Clearwell	360
Castle Douglas	668	Cleestanton	472
Castle Eden	327	Clerkenwell	82
Castlebay	666	Cley-next-the-Sea	288
Castlegregory	839	Clifden	841
Castlelyons	839	Clifton	526
Castlemartyr	839	Clipsham	360
Castlepollard	840	Clogheen	841
Castletownshend	840	Clonakilty	842
Cavan	840	Clonegall	842
Caxton	327	Clontarf	863
Cerne Abbas	327	Clovelly	360
Chaddesley Corbett	327	Cloverhill	841
Chagford	328	Clyst Hydon	360
Charlton	339	Coggeshall	361
Charmouth	340	Colbost	733
Charwelton	371	Colchester	361
Chatton	340	Colerne	269
Chelmondiston	436	Colston Bassett	362
Chelsea	88	Colwyn Bay	766
Cheltenham	341	Colyford	362
Chester	347	Combe Hay	270
Chesterfield	350	Compton Bassett	321
Chew Magna	350	Comrie	669
Chichester	351	Condover	570
Chiddingfold	352	Cong	843
Chieveley	352	Conwy	767
Chilcompton	352	Cookham	362
Chillaton	592	Corbridge	362
Chillington	353	Corfe Castle	363
Chinnor	353	Cork	843
Chipping Campden	353	Cornhill-on-Tweed	363
Chipping Norton	355	Corrofin	846
Chipping Ongar	355	Corse Lawn	593
Chipstead	355	Corsham	363
Chirnside	669	Corton Denham	363
Chiswick	79	Cotebrook	363
Chobham	355	Coverack	364

Cowan Bridge	364
Cowbridge	767
Cowley	364
Craighouse	705
Cranbrook	364
Crawley	365
Crayke	365
Crewe	365
Criccieth	767
Crickhowell	768
Cricklade	365
Crieff	669
Crinan	670
Crockerton	607
Cromarty	670
Cromer	366
Crookhaven	846
Cropston	366
Cross Ash	755
Crossgates	772
Crosshaven	846
Crossmolina	846
Crosthwaite	438
Crouch End	78
Croydon	66
Crudwell	477
Crumlin	804
Crundale	366
Cuckfield	366
Cumnock	670
Cundall	367
Cupar	671

D   Page

Dalkeith	671
Dalry	671
Dalston	69
Dalton-in-Furness	367
Darley Abbey	373
Darlington	367
Darsham	369
Dartmouth	369
Dartmouth Park	58
Datchworth	370
Daventry	370
Daylesford	583
Deal	371
Dedham	371
Delgany	847

Delph	372
Denbigh	768
Denham	372
Derby	373
Dervaig	716
Devizes	373
Didsbury	484
Dinas Cross	780
Dingle	847
Dingwall	672
Dinnet	672
Ditchling	374
Doddington	374
Dogmersfield	374
Dolfor	768
Dolgellau	769
Dolton	374
Donaghadee	804
Doncaster	375
Donegal	848
Donhead St Andrew	375
Donnybrook	863
Doogort	822
Doolin	849
Doonbeg	849
Dorchester	375
Dorking	376
Dornoch	672
Dorridge	376
Douglas	478
Dover	377
Drewsteignton	377
Drighlington	377
Drogheda	850
Dromahair	850
Droxford	377
Drumbeg	673
Dublin	851
Duisdalemore	734
Dulverton	377
Dumfries	673
Dummer	378
Dunbar	673
Dunblane	673
Duncannon	865
Dundalk	865
Dundee	674
Dundrum (Dublin)	864
Dundrum (Down)	804

Dunfanaghy **865**
Dungannon **805**
Dungarvan.....................**866**
Dunkeld **676**
Dunkineely **866**
Dun Laoghaire **866**
Dunsford **378**
Dunster.......................**378**
Dunvegan **734**
Durham........................**379**
Durness.......................**676**
Duror.........................**676**
Durrus........................**867**
Dyke..........................**676**

E   Page

Ealing (Borough of)............**66**
Ealing **67**
Earl's Court **93**
Earl Stonham **380**
East Chiltington................**456**
East Chisenbury **380**
East Dulwich...................**113**
East End.......................**380**
East Grinstead **381**
East Haddon **381**
East Hendred **381**
East Hoathly **381**
East Sheen.....................**107**
East Wittering **382**
East Witton **382**
Eastbourne **382**
Eastgate......................**383**
Ebrington.....................**354**
Eckington (Derbs) **383**
Eckington (Worcs).............**529**
Eddleston.....................**722**
Edinbane **734**
Edinburgh **677**
Edington **383**
Ednam........................**706**
Egham........................**383**
Egton.........................**384**
Eldersfield **384**
Elgin..........................**689**
Elgol..........................**734**
Elie **689**
Ellastone......................**384**
Ellel **385**

Elmton **385**
Elstree........................**385**
Elterwater **385**
Elton **386**
Elton-On-The-Hill **386**
Ely **386**
Emsworth **387**
Enniscorthy **867**
Enniskerry **868**
Enniskillen **805**
Epping **387**
Epsom........................**387**
Eriska (Isle of) **689**
Ermington **387**
Eshott **496**
Ettington **388**
Evanton **690**
Evershot......................**388**
Ewen **388**
Exeter **389**
Exmouth......................**390**
Eydon **390**

F   Page

Fairlie.........................**690**
Falmouth **391**
Fanore........................**868**
Faringdon **393**
Farnborough (Hants)...........**393**
Farnborough (London).........**53**
Farnham (Dorset).............**289**
Faversham **393**
Felingwm Uchaf **766**
Felixkirk **394**
Fence.........................**394**
Fennor........................**868**
Fermain Bay **330**
Ferrensby.....................**446**
Filey **394**
Filkins **394**
Finsbury **83**
Fionnphort **716**
Fishguard.....................**769**
Fivehead **395**
Flaunden **395**
Fletching **395**
Flodigarry **735**
Fochabers **690**
Folkestone....................**395**

921

Fonthill Bishop	**396**
Fontmell Magna	**396**
Fordingbridge	**396**
Forest Green	**397**
Forest Hill	**103**
Fort Augustus	**691**
Fort William	**691**
Fortingall	**692**
Fortrose	**692**
Fota Island	**869**
Fotheringhay	**397**
Fowey	**397**
Foxham	**398**
Foxrock	**864**
Freathy	**398**
Frilsham	**636**
Frithsden	**398**
Froggatt	**399**
Frome	**399**
Fulham	**75**
Fuller Street	**399**
Fulmer	**399**
Funtington	**352**
Fyfield (Essex)	**399**
Fyfield (Oxford)	**522**

Gorey (Wexford)	**874**
Goring	**401**
Grandtully	**700**
Grange-over-Sands	**401**
Grantham	**402**
Grantown-on-Spey	**700**
Grasmere	**403**
Grassington	**404**
Great Bircham	**404**
Great Dunmow	**404**
Great Limber	**404**
Great Malvern	**405**
Great Milton	**521**
Great Missenden	**405**
Great Tew	**406**
Great Yeldham	**406**
Green Island	**335**
Greenwich	**68**
Greetham	**406**
Greta Bridge	**261**
Gretton	**621**
Greystones	**875**
Grimston	**443**
Grinshill	**570**
Grouville	**335**
Guernsey	**330**
Guildford	**406**
Gullane	**701**
Gulworthy	**591**
Gunthorpe	**407**
Gurnard	**618**

G	Page
Galgorm	**796**
Galson	**710**
Galway	**870**
Garrykennedy	**873**
Gatehead	**693**
Gattonside	**714**
Gedney Dyke	**400**
Gerrards Cross	**400**
Gestingthorpe	**400**
Giffnock	**693**
Gigha (Isle of)	**693**
Gillingham	**400**
Gisburn	**401**
Glasgow	**694**
Glaslough	**874**
Glasson	**825**
Glinton	**529**
Glynarthen	**769**
Godshill	**618**
Golant	**398**
Goleen	**874**
Gorey (Channel Islands)	**334**

H	Page
Hackney (Borough of)	**69**
Hackney	**70**
Haddington	**701**
Hadleigh	**407**
Halford	**407**
Halifax	**408**
Halsetown	**557**
Haltwhistle	**408**
Hamble-le-Rice	**408**
Hambleton	**513**
Hammersmith	**76**
Hammersmith and Fulham	**75**
Hampton in Arden	**409**
Hampton Poyle	**409**
Haringey	**78**
Harlech	**770**

Harome...........................418
Harris (Isle of)..................711
Harrogate........................409
Harrow...........................78
Hartington.......................411
Harwich..........................412
Haselbury Plucknett..............412
Hastings and St. Leonards........412
Hatfield Broad Oak...............414
Hatfield Peverel.................414
Hathersage.......................415
Hatton Garden....................59
Haughton Moss....................415
La Haule.........................335
Haverfordwest....................770
Hawarden.........................770
Hawes............................415
Hawkshead........................415
Hawnby...........................416
Haworth..........................416
Haydon Bridge....................423
Hay-on-Wye.......................770
Haywards Heath...................416
Headlam..........................369
Heathrow Airport.................78
Hedley on the Hill...............416
Helmsley.........................417
Helperby.........................419
Helston..........................419
Hemingford Grey..................433
Henfield.........................419
Henley...........................491
Henley-in-Arden..................420
Henley-on-Thames.................420
Hereford.........................421
Herm.............................333
Herne Bay........................422
Herstmonceux.....................422
Heswall..........................422
Hethe............................422
Hetton...........................423
Hexham...........................423
High Blantyre....................701
Highbury.........................85
Highclere........................423
Highcliffe.......................424
Higher Burwardsley...............424
Hillsborough.....................805
Hinckley.........................424

Hintlesham.......................436
Hinton St George.................424
Hitchin..........................425
Holborn..........................59
Holcombe.........................425
Holkham..........................425
Hollingbourne....................425
Holmfirth........................426
Holt (Norfolk)...................426
Holt (Wilts).....................426
Holyport.........................426
Holywood.........................806
Honiton..........................427
Hook.............................427
Hope.............................427
Hoptonheath......................428
Horley...........................428
Horncastle.......................428
Horndon on the Hill..............429
Horning..........................429
Horningsea.......................324
Horn's Cross.....................429
Horringer........................320
Horsham..........................429
Horsted Keynes...................430
Hough-on-the-Hill................402
Hounslow.........................79
Howey............................772
Howth............................875
Hoxton...........................70
Huccombe.........................430
Huddersfield.....................430
Hullbridge.......................430
Humshaugh........................431
Hunsdon..........................431
Hunstanton.......................431
Hunstrete........................432
Huntingdon.......................432
Hurstpierpoint...................433
Hurworth-on-Tees.................368
Hutton Magna.....................261
Hyde Park and Knightsbridge....127

I

                              Page

Ickham...........................433
Ilfracombe.......................433
Ilkley...........................434
Ingham...........................435
Inisheer.........................823

Inishmaan	823
Inishmore	823
Innerleithen	702
Invergarry	702
Inverkeilor	702
Inverness	702
Ipswich	435
Irby	436
Iron Bridge	436
Irthington	436
Islay (Isle of)	704
Isleham	437
Islington (Borough of)	81
Islington	86
Itteringham	437
Ixworth	320

J	Page
Jedburgh	705
Jenkinstown	865
Jersey	334
Jura (Isle of)	705

K	Page
Kanturk	875
Kelmscott	437
Kelso	706
Kelvedon	437
Kendal	438
Kenilworth	438
Kenmare	875
Kennington	102
Kensal Green	52
Kensington	93
Kensington and Chelsea	88
Kentisbury	439
Kentish Town	59
Kenton	439
Kerne Bridge	548
Kerridge	439
Keston	52
Keswick	439
Kettering	440
Kettlesing	411
Kew	107
Keyston	441
Kibworth Beauchamp	441
Kibworth Harcourt	441
Kilberry	707

Kilchrenan	706
Kilcolgan	877
Kilcullen	877
Kildare	877
Kildrummy	706
Kilkenny	878
Killaloe	879
Killarney	879
Killiecrankie	726
Killinchy	807
Killorglin	881
Kilndown	442
Kilpeck	442
Kinclaven	707
Kingham	442
Kings Cross St Pancras	99
King's Lynn	443
Kings Mills	331
King's Sutton	444
Kingsbridge	444
Kingston upon Hull	444
Kingston upon Thames (Borough of)	100
Kingswear	370
Kingussie	707
Kinlough	882
Kinsale	882
Kintillo	724
Kintyre (Peninsula)	707
Kippen	708
Kirkbean	708
Kirkby Lonsdale	444
Kirkby Stephen	445
Kirkby Thore	445
Kirkbymoorside	445
Kirkcudbright	708
Kirkmichael	709
Kirkwall	720
Kirkwhelpington	446
Kirtlington	446
Knaresborough	446
Knock	885
Knowstone	446
Kylesku	709

L	Page
Lahinch	885
Lambeth	101
Lamlash	661

924

Lancaster 447
Langar..........................447
Langass 744
Langho 286
Langthwaite 543
Lapworth 447
Lavenham 448
Ledbury 448
Leebotwood 449
Leeds (Kent)....................449
Leeds (West Yorkshire) 450
Leenane 885
Leicester.......................453
Leigh-on-Sea 454
Leintwardine....................455
Leith 688
Lerwick 733
Letterkenny.....................885
Levisham 531
Lewannick 455
Lewdown 455
Lewes 456
Lewis (Isle of) 710
Lewisham........................103
Lewiston........................712
Leyburn 456
Lichfield 456
Lickfold........................531
Lifton..........................457
Limavady........................807
Limerick 885
Lincoln 458
Linlithgow 712
Lisbane.........................807
Liscannor.......................887
Lisdoonvarna....................887
Liskeard 459
Lisnaskea.......................808
Liss............................459
Listowel 887
Little Bedwyn...................486
Little Coxwell 460
Little Dunmow...................460
Little Eccleston 460
Little Marlow...................488
Little Thetford.................386
Little Wilbraham................325
Littleton 624
Littlehampton 460

Liverpool 461
Llanarmon Dyffryn Ceiriog 771
Llanarthney.....................771
Llandderfel 771
Llanddewi Skirrid 755
Llandenny 771
Llandrillo 771
Llandrindod Wells...............772
Llandudno.......................772
Llandybie.......................773
Llanelli........................774
Llanelltyd......................769
Llan Ffestiniog 774
Llanfihangel 775
Llanfihangel-y-Creuddyn.........774
Llanfyllin......................774
Llangaffo.......................757
Llangammarch Wells..............775
Llangennith.....................775
Llangollen 775
Llangrannog.....................775
Llanllawddog 766
Llanrhidian 776
Llanrwst 776
Llanwrtyd Wells.................776
Llechryd........................776
Llyswen.........................777
Lochaline 713
Lochinver.......................713
Lochmaddy.......................744
Lochranza 661
Londonderry.....................808
London Fields 71
Long Ashton.....................311
Long Compton....................464
Long Crendon 465
Long Melford 465
Long Sutton 465
Long Whatton 466
Longford 887
Longhorsley 496
Longrock 466
Longstock 466
Looe............................466
Lorton 466
Lostwithiel.....................467
Loughborough....................467
Louth...........................467
Lovington.......................468

Low Fell	468	Marlow	486
Low Row	543	Martinhoe	475
Lower Beeding	468	Marton cum Grafton	488
Lower Dunsforth	292	Marton (Cheshire)	488
Lower Oddington	583	Marton (Shropshire)	488
Lower Peover	469	Masham	488
Lower Slaughter	295	Matfield	489
Ludlow	469	Matlock	489
Lund	472	Mawgan Porth	504
Lupton	445	Mayfair	128
Lurgashall	472	Melfort	714
Luss	714	Mellor (Gtr Manchester)	489
Luton	472	Mellor	286
Lyddington	604	Mells	490
Lydford	473	Melrose	714
Lyme Regis	473	Melton Mowbray	490
Lymington	473	Memus	715
Lymm	474	Menai Bridge	757
Lyndhurst	474	Merton	104
Lynmouth	475	Mevagissey	490
Lynton	474	Mid Lavant	351
		Middlesbrough	490

M	Page		
Machynlleth	777	Middleton Tyas	491
Madingley	324	Midhurst	491
Maenporth	391	Midleton	888
Maghera	808	Milfield	492
Magherafelt	809	Milford-on-Sea	492
Magheralin	809	Milstead	492
Maidencombe	599	Milton Abbot	591
Maidenhead	475	Milton Keynes	492
Maiden Newton	476	Minehead	493
Maidensgrove	476	Minster	493
Mainland (Orkney Islands)	720	Minster Lovell	493
Mainland (Shetland Islands)	733	Mistley	494
Malahide	888	Mitton	615
Maldon	476	Mobberley	494
Mallow	888	Moffat	715
Malmesbury	476	Mohill	889
Maltby	477	Moira	809
Malton	477	Mold	777
Man (Isle of)	478	Monkton Combe	269
Manchester	480	Monkton Farleigh	494
Mansfield	484	Monmouth	777
Marazion	484	Montgomery	778
Margate	485	Moretonhampstead	494
Market Rasen	486	Moreton-in-Marsh	495
Marlborough	486	Morpeth	495
Marldon	486	Morston	288
		Moulton	496

Mounthill **809**
Mousehole....................... **496**
Muir of Ord **716**
Mull (Isle of) **716**
Mullingar **889**
Mullion **497**
Murcott.......................... **497**
Murrisk **889**
Muthill.......................... **670**

N   Page

Naas............................. **890**
Nailsworth...................... **497**
Nairn **717**
Nantgaredig **766**
Narberth........................ **778**
National Exhibition Centre **285**
Nether Burrow.................. **497**
Nether Westcote............... **584**
Netley Marsh................... **574**
New Milton **498**
New Quay **890**
New Romney **498**
Newark-on-Trent............... **498**
Newbottle....................... **499**
Newbury **499**
Newby Bridge **500**
Newcastle **810**
Newcastle Emlyn............... **779**
Newcastle upon Tyne **500**
Newhaven **503**
Newlyn **503**
Newmarket on Fergus.......... **890**
Newport......................... **618**
Newport Pagnell................ **503**
Newport (Mayo) **891**
Newport (Newport)............. **779**
Newport (Pembrokeshire)...... **779**
Newport-on-Tay **717**
Newquay **504**
Newton Longville **505**
Newton-on-Ouse **505**
Newtownabbey.................. **810**
Newtownards.................... **810**
Newtown Mount Kennedy...... **891**
Nigg............................. **740**
Nomansland **505**
North Bay **666**
North Berwick **717**

North Bovey **506**
North Kensington **96**
North Lopham **506**
North Queensferry **718**
North Shields **506**
North Walsham **507**
Northaw........................ **507**
Northleach...................... **507**
Northmoor **507**
North Uist **744**
Norton Disney **508**
Norwell......................... **499**
Norwich **508**
Noss Mayo...................... **510**
Nottingham..................... **510**
Nun Monkton **513**

O   Page

Oakham **513**
Oare............................ **394**
Oban **718**
Old Alresford **514**
Old Burghclere................. **514**
Old Radnor **780**
Oldham......................... **514**
Oldstead....................... **514**
Ombersley...................... **515**
Onich.......................... **718**
Orford **515**
Orpington **53**
Osmotherley.................... **515**
Oswestry **516**
Oughterard **891**
Ouston **516**
Overton **516**
Oxford.......................... **517**

P   Page

Padstow **522**
Painswick....................... **524**
Pateley Bridge **525**
Patrick Brompton............... **525**
Pattiswick **361**
Peat Inn **721**
Peckham **113**
Peebles......................... **721**
Pembroke **780**
Penarth......................... **780**
Penmachno...................... **758**

Penn	**525**
Pennal	**781**
Penrith	**525**
Penshurst	**527**
Penzance	**527**
Perranuthnoe	**485**
Pershore	**528**
Perth	**722**
Peterborough	**529**
Petersfield	**529**
Pett Bottom	**530**
Petts Wood	**53**
Petworth	**530**
Pickering	**531**
Pickhill	**532**
Pierowall	**720**
Piff's Elm	**346**
Pilsley	**532**
Pinner	**78**
Pitlochry	**724**
Plockton	**726**
Plumtree	**512**
Plymouth	**532**
Plympton St Maurice	**534**
Polperro	**534**
Ponteland	**503**
Poole	**535**
Poolewe	**727**
Pooley Bridge	**536**
Porlock	**536**
Port Appin	**727**
Port Charlotte	**705**
Port Ellen	**705**
Port Isaac	**537**
Portmahomack	**727**
Portpatrick	**727**
Portavadie	**728**
Porthcawl	**781**
Porthleven	**537**
Portlaoise	**892**
Portloe	**538**
Portmeirion	**781**
Portree	**735**
Portrush	**811**
Portscatho	**538**
Portsmouth	**539**
Portstewart	**811**
Postbridge	**539**
Preston Saint Mary	**448**

Primrose Hill	**60**
La Pulente	**335**
Pulham Market	**539**
Pumsaint	**782**
Putney	**121**
Pwllheli	**782**

Q	Page
Queen's Park	**52**

R	Page
Rainham	**540**
Rathmelton	**892**
Ramsbottom	**540**
Ramsbury	**540**
Ramsey	**479**
Ramsholt	**540**
Ranelagh	**863**
Rannoch Station	**728**
Rathgar	**864**
Rathmines	**863**
Rathmullan	**892**
Rathnew	**893**
Ratho	**728**
Reading	**540**
Redbridge	**105**
Redditch	**542**
Redhill	**542**
Reepham	**542**
Reeth	**542**
Regent's Park and Marylebone	**140**
Reigate	**543**
Resipole	**729**
Retford	**543**
Rhoscolyn	**757**
Rhos-on-Sea	**766**
Rhydycroesau	**516**
Rhyl	**782**
Ribchester	**544**
Richmond (London)	**107**
Richmond (N. Yorks)	**544**
Richmond-upon-Thames	**106**
Rimpton	**544**
Ripley (N. Yorks)	**545**
Ripley (Surrey)	**545**
Ripon	**545**
Riverstown	**893**
Roch	**783**
Rochdale	**546**

Rock....................................546
Roecliffe.............................291
Romaldkirk.........................261
Romsey...............................547
Rosslare 893
Rosslare Harbour 894
Ross-on-Wye 547
Roundstone.........................894
Roundwood 894
Rowde..................................374
Rowen..................................767
Rowhook 430
Rowsley 548
Royal Leamington Spa 549
Royal Tunbridge Wells 550
Rozel Bay.............................335
Ruddington...........................512
Rugby 551
Rushlake Green 551
Rushton 441
Ruthin 783
Rye......................................552
Ryhall 553

S   Page

St Albans 553
St Andrews 729
St Aubin 336
St Austell 554
St Boswells 731
St Brelades Bay....................336
St Clears..............................784
St Davids 784
St Ewe.................................554
St Fillans.............................732
St George.............................784
St Helens 618
St Helier 337
St Ives.................................555
St James's 148
St Keverne 557
St Kew.................................558
St Martin..............................331
St Martin's 564
St Mary's 564
St Mawes 558
St Mellion 559
St Monans 732
St Osyth 559

St Peter Port........................331
St Saviour (Guernsey)...........333
St Saviour (Jersey)...............339
St Tudy 559
Salcombe.............................560
Salford Quays.......................484
Salisbury 560
Sallins 894
Saltwood 561
Sancton 561
Sandiacre.............................561
Sandsend.............................615
Sandyford 865
Sandypark............................328
Sanquhar 732
Sapperton 359
Sark 339
Saundersfoot 785
Sawdon................................563
Sawley.................................561
Saxilby 562
Scalpay 711
Scarborough.........................562
Scarista...............................711
Scawton 419
Scilly (Isles of) 563
Scrabster 742
Seaham................................565
Seahouses 565
Seasalter 617
Seaview 618
Sedgeford 566
Seer Green...........................271
Seion 760
Sennen Cove........................566
Settle...................................566
Shaftesbury.........................566
Shaldon 567
Shanagarry 895
Shanklin 619
Sheffield..............................567
Shelley 568
Shepherd's Bush...................77
Sherborne 569
Shere...................................407
Sheringham..........................569
Sherwood Business Park 513
Shetland Islands 733
Shilton (Oxon) 318

929

Shinfield	541
Shiplake	421
Shirley	256
Shoreditch	72
Shottle	569
Shrewsbury	569
Shrewton	570
Shurdington	345
Sibford Gower	571
Sidford	572
Sidlesham	571
Sidmouth	571
Sinnington	532
Sissinghurst	572
Skenfrith	785
Skibbereen	895
Skye (Isle of)	733
Slane	895
Sleat	735
Sligo	896
Snape	572
Snettisham	572
Soar Mill Cove	560
Soho	152
Somerton	573
Sonning-on-Thames	541
Sorn	736
South Brent	573
South Croydon	66
South Dalton	275
South Ealing	67
South Ferriby	573
South Hackney	74
South Kensington	97
South Molton	573
South Pool	574
South Rauceby	574
South Woodford	105
Southampton	574
Southbank	103
Southborough	551
Southbourne	295
Southfields	121
Southport	575
Southrop	575
Southwark (Borough of)	110
Southwark	113
Southwold	575
Sowerby Bridge	576
Spanish Point	896
Sparkwell	576
Sparsholt (Hants)	624
Sparsholt (Oxon)	576
Spean Bridge	737
Speldhurst	551
Spitalfields	118
Spittal of Glenshee	737
Sprigg's Alley	353
Staddle Bridge	577
Stadhampton	577
Stafford	577
Stalisfield	578
Stamford	578
Stanford Dingley	579
Stanhoe	579
Stannington	579
Stansted Mountfitchet	580
Stanton	580
Stapleford	512
Staverton	371
Stepaside	896
Stilton	580
Stirling	737
Stockbridge	581
Stockport	581
Stockwell	103
Stoke-by-Nayland	581
Stoke Holy Cross	510
Stoke Poges	582
Stoke Newington	74
Ston Easton	582
Stonehaven	738
Stornoway	710
Stow-on-the-Wold	582
Strachur	738
Straffan	896
Strand and Covent Garden	161
Stratford Saint Mary	584
Stratford-upon-Avon	584
Strathpeffer	739
Strathy	739
Strathyre	739
Strete	370
Stretton	586
Stromness	721
Strontian	739
Stroud	586
Struan	736

Studland.........................587
Summerhouse 368
Sunbury 587
Sundridge 53
Sunningdale 587
Sunniside........................588
Surbiton.........................100
Sutton (Borough of) 116
Sutton (Bedfordshire)..........588
Sutton...........................116
Sutton Coldfield 588
Sutton Courtenay 588
Sutton Gault 386
Swaffham........................589
Swansea.........................785
Sway 589
Swinbrook.......................318
Swiss Cottage 60

T   Page

Tain 740
Talaton 589
Tal-y-llyn 786
Tangmere........................351
Taplow 589
Tarbert (Isle of Lewis)..........712
Tarrant Launceston.............289
Tarr Steps.......................590
Taunton..........................590
Tavistock........................591
Taynuilt.........................740
Teangue 736
Teddington 108
Teffont Evias....................561
Temple Sowerby 526
Tenterden........................592
Tetbury..........................592
Tewkesbury......................593
Thetford.........................593
Thomastown......................897
Thornbury 593
Thornhill........................741
Thornton 287
Thornton Hough 594
Thorpe Market 594
Thunder Bridge 594
Thursford Green 594
Thursley 595
Thurso..........................741

Ticehurst 595
Tickton..........................275
Tighnabruaich 742
Tillington 531
Tiroran..........................716
Tisbury 595
Titchwell........................595
Titley 596
Tobermory.......................716
Tollard Royal....................596
Toormore........................897
Toot Baldon.....................521
Topsham.........................596
Torquay..........................597
Torridon 742
Totnes...........................599
Towcester...................... 600
Tower...........................833
Tower Hamlets.................116
Tralee..........................898
Tramore 898
Treburley 600
Tredunnock......................787
Tregaron........................786
Tregony 600
Trelowarren 419
Trent 600
Tresco..........................564
Trim 898
Triscombe 601
Troon...........................743
Truro 601
Tuddenham......................601
Tullamore.......................899
Turnberry.......................743
Turners Hill 602
Twickenham 109
Two Bridges 602
Two Mile House 890
Tynemouth 602
Tywyn 786

U   Page

Uckfield 603
Udny Green......................743
Ufford..........................603
Uig 711
Isles of Uist 744
Ullapool 744

931

Upper Slaughter	296
Upper South Wraxall	603
Uppingham	603
Upton Bishop	548
Upton Grey	604
Upton Magna	570
Usk	787

V   Page

Vauxhall	103
Veensgarth	733
Ventnor	619
Veryan	604
Victoria	165
Virginia	899
Virginstow	604

W   Page

Waddesdon	605
Waddington	605
Wadebridge	605
Walberswick	606
Walford	548
Walkerburn	744
Wall	457
Wandsworth (Borough of)	120
Wandsworth	122
Wanstead	105
Wareham	606
Waren Mill	260
Warkworth	606
Warmingham	606
Warminster	607
Wartling	422
Warwick	607
Watchet	607
Waterford	899
Watergate Bay	504
Waternish	736
Watford	608
Watlington	608
Watton	608
Wedmore	609
Welburn	609
Welland	405
Wellingham	609
Wells	609
Wells-next-the-Sea	610
Welwyn	610

Wentbridge	611
West Ashling	352
West Bridgford	512
West Byfleet	611
West Didsbury	483
West End	611
West Hampstead	60
West Hatch	611
West Hoathly	612
West Malling	612
West Meon	612
West Overton	486
West Tanfield	612
West Wittering	613
West Witton	613
Westonbirt	613
Weston-sub-Edge	355
Westport	900
Westray (Isle of)	720
Westfield	613
Westleton	614
Weston-super-Mare	614
Wexford	901
Whalley	614
Whashton	544
Whimple	615
Whitby	615
White Waltham	616
Whitebrook	778
Whitechapel	120
Whitehaven	616
Whitewell	616
Whitstable	616
Whittlesford	617
Whitton	787
Wick	745
Wight (Isle of)	618
Wighton	610
Willian	620
Wilmington	620
Wimbledon	104
Wimborne Minster	620
Winchcombe	621
Winchester	622
Windermere	624
Windsor	628
Winsford	629
Winster (Cumbria)	628
Winster (Derbs)	629

Winston 630
Winterbourne Steepleton 376
Winteringham 630
Wiswell 630
Witham on The Hill........... 630
Wiveton 288
Woburn....................... 631
Wold Newton 631
Wolverhampton............... 631
Wombleton 418
Woodbridge 631
Woodstock 632
Woolacombe 633
Wooler 633
Woolhope 633
Wootton...................... 633
Worcester 634
Worksop...................... 634

Wormit 745
Worth 371
Wrington 634
Wrotham 634
Wymeswold 635
Wymondham 635
Wynyard..................... 635

Y   Page

Yarm 635
Yarmouth..................... 620
Yattendon 636
Yeovil....................... 636
York......................... 637
Youghal...................... 902

Z   Page

Zennor 640

INDEX OF MAPS

Great Britain & Ireland (map) 22

● **Greater London**

Greater London North West (1-2) 170
Greater London North East (3-4) 172
Greater London South West (5-6) 174
Greater London South East (7-8) 176

Central London
Key to Central London maps 179
Central London maps 180

● **England**

Bedfordshire, Hertfordshire, Essex (7) 228
Channel Islands (3) 221
Cheshire, Lancashire, Isle of Man (11) 236
Cornwall, Devon, Isles of Scilly (1) 216
Cumbria (12) 237
Derbyshire, Leicestershire, Nothamptonshire, Rutland,
Lincolnshire, Nottinghamshire (9) 232
East Sussex, Kent (5) 224
Hampshire, Isle of Wight, Surrey, West Sussex (4) 222
Herefordshire, Worcestershire, Shropshire, Staffordshire,
Warwickshire (10) 234
Norfolk, Suffolk, Cambridgeshire (8) 230
Northumberland, Durham (14) 241
Oxfordshire, Buckinghamshire (6) 226
Somerset, Dorset, Gloucestershire, Wiltshire (2) 218
Yorkshire (13) 238

● **Scotland**

Borders, Edinburgh & Glasgow (15) 644
Central Scotland (16) 646
Highlands & The Islands (17) 648
Shetland & Orkney (18) 651

Wales

Wales (19) 748

● **Ireland**

Northern Ireland (20) 792
Republic of Ireland (21 and 22) 814

TOWN PLAN KEY

Sights

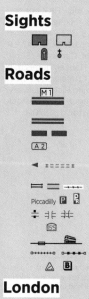

Place of interest
Interesting place of worship

● Hotels
● Restaurants

Roads

Motorway
Numbered junctions: complete, limited

Dual carriageway with motorway characteristics
Main traffic artery

Primary route (GB) and National route (IRL)

One-way street • Unsuitable for traffic or street subject to restrictions

Pedestrian street • Tramway

Piccadilly Shopping street • Car park • Park and Ride

Gateway • Street passing under arch • Tunnel

Low headroom (16'6" max.) on major through routes

Station and railway

Funicular • Cable-car

Lever bridge • Car ferry

London

BRENT WEMBLEY Borough • Area

Borough boundary

Congestion Zone • Charge applies
Monday-Friday 07.00-18.00

Nearest Underground station to the hotel or restaurant

Various signs

Tourist Information Centre

Church/Place of worship • Mosque • Synagogue

Communications tower or mast • Ruins

Garden, park, wood • Cemetery

Stadium • Racecourse • Golf course

Golf course (with restrictions for visitors) • Skating rink

Outdoor or indoor swimming pool

View • Panorama

Monument • Fountain • Hospital • Covered market

Pleasure boat harbour • Lighthouse

Airport • Underground station • Coach station

Ferry services: passengers and cars

Main post office

Public buildings located by letter:

C H J   County Council Offices • Town Hall • Law Courts

M T U   Museum • Theatre • University, College

POL.   Police (in large towns police headquarters)

935

Credits

Céleste, p. 54 – Michelin, p. 61 – HKK London, p. 69 – Michelin, p. 75 – Michelin, p. 81 – Marcus Wareing Restaurants, p. 88 – Five Fields, p. 106 – HKK London, p. 110 – Benares, p. 123 – I. Dagnall/age fotostock, p. 246 – Michelin, p. 279 – Michelin, p. 302 – Michelin, p. 307 – Midsummer House, p. 322 – Michelin, p. 330 – Le Champignon Sauvage, p. 341 – B. Kadic/age fotostock, p. 347 – R. Harding/hemis.fr, p. 450 – P. Frilet/hemis.fr, p. 480 – M. Carassale/Sime/Photononstop, p. 517 – J. Arnold/hemis.fr, p. 637 – P. Hauser/hemis.fr, p. 677 – Michelin, p. 694 – image source/hemis.fr, p. 710 – C. Meier/doc-stock GmbH RM/age fotostock, p. 720 – E. Davis/Robert Harding Picture Library/age fotostock, p. 761 – R. Mattes/hemis.fr, p. 798 – Z. Steger/age fotostock, p. 851 – The Irish Image Colle /Design Pics RM/age fotostock, p. 870.

"Plans de ville : © MICHELIN et © 2006-2015 TomTom. All rights reserved. This material is proprietary and the subject of copyright protection, database right protection and other intellectual property rights owned by TomTom or its suppliers. The use of this material is subject to the terms of a license agreement. Any unauthorized copying or disclosure of this material will lead to criminal and civil liabilities."
For United Kingdom (excluding Northern Ireland):
"Contains Ordnance Survey data © Crown copyright and database right 2015."
Code-Point® Open data:
"Contains Royal Mail data © Royal Mail copyright and database right 2015."

POPULATION - Source:
ONS/Office for National Statistics (www.statistics.gov.uk) [census 2011]
CSO/Central Statistics Office (www.cso.ie) [census 2011]

Michelin Travel Partner
Société par actions simplifiées au capital de 11 288 880 €
27 cours de l'Ile Seguin - 92100 Boulogne-Billancourt (France)
R.C.S. Nanterre 433 677 721
© **Michelin, Propriétaires-Éditeurs**
Dépôt légal September 2016
Printed in Italy - August 2016
Printed on paper from sustainably managed forests
**No part of of this publication may be reproduced in any form
without the prior permission of the publisher.**

Typesetting: JOUVE, Saran (France)
Printing - Binding: Lego Print (Lavis)